THE HEALTH SERVICES SINCE THE WAR

Volume II

GOVERNMENT AND HEALTH CARE THE NATIONAL HEALTH SERVICE 1958-1979

BY

CHARLES WEBSTER

London: The Stationery Office

ISBN 0 11 630963 6

Stationery
Office

Published by The Stationery Office and available from:

The Publications Centre
(mail, telephone and fax orders only)
PO Box 276, London SW8 5DT
General enquiries 0171 873 0011
Telephone orders 0171 873 9090
Fax orders 0171 873 8200

The Stationery Office Bookshops
49 High Holborn, London WC1V 6HB
(counter service only and fax orders only)
Fax 0171 831 1326
68–69 Bull Street, Birmingham B4 6AD
0121 236 9696   Fax 0121 236 9699
33 Wine Street, Bristol BS1 2BQ
01179 264 306   Fax 01179 294 515
9–21 Princess Street, Manchester M60 8AS
0161 834 7201   Fax 0161 833 0634
16 Arthur Street, Belfast BT1 4GD
01232 238 451   Fax 01232 235 401
The Stationery Office Oriel Bookshop
The Friary, Cardiff CF1 4AA
01222 395 548   Fax 01222 384 347
71 Lothian Road, Edinburgh EH3 9AZ
(counter service only)

Customers in Scotland may
mail, telephone or fax their orders to:
Scottish Publications Sales
South Gyle Crescent, Edinburgh EH12 9EB
0131 479 3141   Fax 0131 479 3142

Accredited Agents
(see Yellow Pages)

and through good booksellers

Printed in the UK for the Stationery Office by Hobbs the Printers Ltd
Dd303299 12/96 C9 G3397

CONTENTS

TABLES IN TEXT

CHAPTER VI

CHAPTER VII

MAPS
Facing page

APPENDICES

APPENDIX 1

APPENDIX 2

APPENDIX 3

CONTENTS

The promotion of health and the treatment of illness and injury are among the major concerns of all societies, and in advanced countries a complex technology is joined with a wealth of human and material resources for these purposes. The proper aims of the administrative structure of the National Health Service are to make the most efficient use of resources, allow advances in knowledge to be applied without unnecessary constraints, and give effect as far as possible to the rational priorities of the community as a whole.

Reorganisation of the Scottish Health Services,
Cmnd.4734 (1971) para 55

PREFACE

The present volume completes the commission I received to write an account of the British health service from the inception of planning for a comprehensive health service to 1979. The first volume of this study was published in 1988. Although the second volume picks up themes developed in the first, sufficient explanatory information is provided to render this book reasonably self-contained. The reader will notice some small shifts in interpretation relating to events before 1958, which are largely explained by the fuller body of information available during the second stage of the project. After careful reflection, 1958 has been adopted as the natural starting point for the purposes of the title. Notwithstanding the terminal date stated in the title of volume I, which was adopted at an early stage in the project, in practice, some of the topics discussed were taken up to 1958; others were not considered beyond the beginning of 1957. The starting date adopted in the present volume is dictated by the subject-matter. It will be noticed that the detailed consideration of such issues as health service finance and community care begin in 1957. The Report of the Royal Commission on the Law relating to Mental Illness and Mental Deficiency, which reported in 1957, is also considered in this volume. The agreed termination date for the second volume is 1979, which is a natural point of conclusion. It is of course unrealistic to make absolutely no mention of events after the end of the Labour administration. Sufficient information has been provided to give some indication of the general future course of events relating to the various topics under consideration, without of course drawing on sources in the government archives.

Since much of the documentation used in volume I was open to public scrutiny, it was possible to provide full information about the authorship of items contained in departmental files. Since, inevitably, most of the archives used in the present volume fall within the Thirty Year rule, the guide-lines applying to this project preclude more than a generalised indication of attribution with respect to civil servants. On the same grounds, it is only possible to make generalised reference to ministerial interventions in Cabinet meetings. Some additional insight into ministerial discussions has been obtained from the notebooks of the Cabinet Secretaries, which became available to the author during the second stage of this project.

On account of limitations of space and the complexity of the issues under discussion, this survey does not pretend to offer a comprehensive review of health care in Britain during the period under consideration. Following the precedent of volume I, this study concentrates on central issues of policy. It therefore deals in most detail with those issues attracting ministerial attention and the greatest political controversy, which inevitably were not always dominant elements in health care. Also on grounds of limitation of space, it is not possible to give more than the briefest indication of the course of deliberations of the many committees and commissions mentioned in the text. Generally, the narrative concentrates on the circumstances of the appointment of committees, the main features of reports, and reception of the findings.

A further exclusion relates to Northern Ireland. The specific remit of this study relates to England, Scotland and Wales. Especially where significant differences are evident, as in the case of reorganisation, separate consideration is given to the three parts of Great Britain. Northern Ireland is mentioned only incidentally, although in the appendices, it is included by virtue of utilisation of data relating to the United Kingdom. It is hoped that the present study will pave the way for further specific investigations into the history of health care and health policy in the four parts of the United Kingdom, as well as the English regions.

Adoption of computerised methods has enabled late alterations to be made in the text, permitting reference to some recently published sources, but these tend to be limited to items relevant to the documentary sources utilised. As in the case of volume I, and in line with the documentary bias of the peacetime Official History series, no attempt has been made to evaluate the interpretative literature relating to the British health service.

It will be noted that the chapters relating to each administration follow an approximately similar course of organisation, with reorganisation being assigned to two separate chapters. In order to prevent duplication and provide a less disjointed narrative, the case-studies contained in a particular chapter are not likely to observe strictly the chronological boundaries of a particular administration.

Most of the stylistic conventions in the present volume follow the principles stated in the Preface to volume I. It will be noted both in the text and appendices that statistical and financial data from different sources is not entirely consistent. Except where absolutely essential for the subject under discussion, no interpretation or reconciliation of these differences is offered. On account of the large size of this volume, some simplification of the index has been made; in particular, no attempt has been made to index secondary sources cited in the footnotes or appendices.

First by way of acknowledgment, I would like to thank the Warden and Fellows of All Souls College, Oxford, who provided the opportunity for my participation in this investigation. The College has supported my work in various ways. I am particularly grateful to Deborah McGovern for her assistance with many aspects of this work, and to Joanne Winstone for her help with the appendices and index, as well as general background assistance.

Inevitably, a large investigation of this kind has drawn upon advice from many individuals. I am especially grateful to Departmental Record Officers, their equivalents, and their staffs at the Cabinet Office, the Department of Health, the Treasury, the Welsh Office Records Centre, the Scottish Office, and 10 Downing Street, also relevant staff at the House of Commons Library Research Division, the NHS Executive, the Public Record Office and especially the Scottish Record Office, and the Population Statistics Branch of the General Register Office for Scotland. These departments in particular, but also various other government departments, have given prompt and most courteous assistance throughout my project. Only the Office of Manpower Economics proved unresponsive to the usual channels of communication and therefore could not be induced to supply relevant files by the final deadline for the project. Information on doctors' and dentists' remuneration from 1971 until 1979 is therefore supplied from other sources.

As indicated in volume I, I am grateful to many former Ministers and officials connected with the health departments for their constructive comments and useful guidance on many aspects of my work. I am particularly indebted to Sir George Godber for his inspiring exchanges on health service issues over many years. I should also like again to express my gratitude to Professor Margaret Gowing, my former colleague and fellow official historian, for her assistance and support from the earliest stages of the project. I must also thank my medical colleagues for dealing with my numerous and tiresome queries relating to their work, in particular Dr J K Aronson, Dr N Black, Dr M S Dunnill, Dr H W S Francis, Dr A Gatherer, Dr J Horder, Dr I S L Loudon, Dr J N Morris, and Dr J M Potter. Among my social science colleagues, I am particularly indebted to Professor Margot Jefferys, Dr Alison Macfarlane, Dr Alistair Gray, Dr Signild Vallgårda, and to colleagues who participated with me in the Open University course *Health and Disease* directed by Dr Basiro Davey.

I would like to express my special gratitude to those most closely associated with my project. Pat Andrews of the Cabinet Office has supervised volume II from its outset. Although this has been merely one of her many responsibilities, she been untiringly supportive and given every assistance to ensure the smooth-running of the project.

Richard Ponman, also of the Cabinet Office, has shown inexhaustible energy in assisting with negotiations with relevant departments; I am grateful for the constructive contribution he has made in the course of dealing with innumerable queries relating to my research. Mrs Edith Smith (Revesz) of the Department of Health Record Office in Nelson has displayed a remarkable general commitment to this project; in particular her searches for documentation have involved much ingenuity and expertise, but also a level of pertinacity that the author had no right to expect. Without the support of Pat Andrews, Richard Ponman and Edith Revesz, the present volume would look considerably more threadbare than it now seems. Finally, I would like to thank my family for their support during this lengthy and time-consuming labour, especially Carol for her great understanding. The entire Official History is dedicated respectfully to her.

CHAPTER I

The National Health Service in 1958

The National Health Service started its life on 5 July 1948, which was the 'Appointed Day' for implementation of the comprehensive programme of reforms in the social services foreshadowed in the Beveridge Report of 1942 and carried into effect by the postwar Labour Government. The NHS was one of the most ambitious and certainly the most controversial of these reforms; it also entailed the greatest amount of alteration in existing institutions. In the first decade of the NHS it was necessary to convert a defective and ramshackle collection of inherited medical services into a modern health service appropriate to the needs and expectations of the second part of the twentieth century. The planners attempted this awesome task without anything like the material and human resources needed for this purpose. The scale of this operation was becoming ever greater owing to scientific advance, the rising capacities of medicine, changing demographic and epidemiological circumstances, and not least on account of rising aspirations; it was no longer reasonable to expect the less affluent classes to bear indignities associated with charity, the means test, poor relief, or inappropriate incarceration.

The population was expanding and changing in its geographical distribution; the postwar birth rate was high and this generated a large population of young children; the elderly were steadily expanding in numbers. The young and the elderly were of course the heaviest users of the new health care facilities. It was necessary for the NHS and other new social services to provide a wide range of assistance for mothers, infants and schoolchildren, while also undertaking remedial tasks such as supplying spectacles, dentures and hearing aids on a massive scale, mainly for the benefit of the elderly. The state also undertook to provide for the first time on a universal basis the whole range of family practitioner services. Even more costly was the task of establishing a comprehensive range of consultant and specialist services of a quality and effectiveness that had never previously been available even to the prosperous minority. The accelerating pace of therapeutic innovation and high technology medicine revealed that the entire hospital stock was in urgent need of modernisation.

1

The new health service was an awesome creation, involving some 500,000 personnel at its inception and a slightly higher figure in 1958. During these early years, public expenditure on the NHS amounted to about 4 per cent of the nation's productive resources. By 1979 this labour force had expanded to about one million and the public expenditure on the NHS accounted for about 5.5 per cent of these resources.[1] In the period covered by this volume the NHS evolved to become one of the nation's most prestigious institutions and also an important piece in the jigsaw of the economy.

(i) TENTH ANNIVERSARY

After the troubled inception described in the previous volume of this study, the multiplicity of controversies surrounding the NHS gradually subsided. Although, at its tenth anniversary, the health service was still afflicted by some serious problems, there was little inclination to regard these difficulties as insurmountable. There was broad agreement by this date that the new health service had been amazingly successful in meeting its basic objectives. Opinion polls showed that the NHS had achieved a settled position of esteem among the public. Among the doctors, their original noisy antagonism subsided when they discovered that the NHS conferred many tangible benefits and no significant incursions into their jealously guarded professional freedoms.[2] Although not satisfied that they had secured optimal financial advantages from the NHS, the doctors were sufficiently confident about their prospects, not to allow their lingering grievances over pay to intrude into the general celebratory atmosphere of 1958.

The tenth anniversary therefore concentrated on the achievements rather than the limitations of the NHS. The debate in the House of Commons on 30 July 1958 conveyed a mood of quiet satisfaction.[3] All sections of the press contributed to the positive impression, headed by the *Times*, which produced a substantial supplement recording some of the main achievements of the new service.[4] The *Observer* encapsulated the eulogistic tone of the serious newspapers: 'Skill has been spread evenly; diagnostic facilities without which the doctor is often mute and helpless, have been provided within every hospital, and treatment of the most complex kind is available in every area close to anyone that needs it'.[5] In the medical journals, even old adversaries from the BMA such as Guy Dain came forward to convey their congratulations.[6] More predictably, sympathisers of the NHS among the doctors praised the health service from the perspective of their particular specialties.[7] The sense of satisfaction with the NHS was not merely based on subjective impression or unrepresentative instances of success. Ample evidence to support a favourable construction was provided in

2

the voluminous official reports of the Ministry of Health and the Department of Health for Scotland. A generally positive impression was also conveyed in reports of such independent bodies as the Acton Society Trust, the King's Fund and the Nuffield Provincial Hospitals Trust. Capable reviews of the NHS by overseas experts such as Eckstein, Lindsey, and Peterson also conveyed a favourable impression.[8] Above all, the independent investigation by the Guillebaud Committee, together with the supporting economic analysis conducted by Abel-Smith and Titmuss, reinforced confidence in the new service and authoritatively refuted claims that it was running away with the nation's resources.[9]

The generally-held positive sentiment towards the new health service was therefore supported by objective sources. This initial achievement, accomplished in difficult circumstances and in the face of much initial scepticism and outright opposition, contributed to the idea that the NHS was some kind of inspired creation. Indeed, this view had been cultivated by Bevan in order to gain public confidence and boost morale among health service personnel. Bevan described his health service as 'the biggest single experiment in social service that the world has ever seen undertaken'.[10] A similar note of hyperbole found its way into later evaluations of the NHS, even those stemming from more analytical sources. Every feature of the new health service was likely to be designated as having undergone a renaissance, or even as the very best in the world. Two American commentators, Almont Lindsey, a senior academic at the University of Virginia, and Don Cook, a well-known journalist, echoed the rhetoric of Bevan. The former urged that the NHS 'cannot very well be excluded from any list of notable achievements of the twentieth century', while Cook concluded that 'what has been done here by democratic processes in a free society is a great step forward and an object lesson for democracy throughout the world'.[11]

Even reports concerned with shortcomings of the NHS were forced to acknowledge the immense achievements of the new service. For instance, the experienced economist, Sir Noel Hall, although advocating reconstruction of the administrative career structure, admitted that he knew of 'no case in the democratic world where a service which needs small-scale contacts with its public at all of its points of action, and yet has to maintain a reasonable degree of uniformity throughout the nation, has been so successfully brought into being'.[12] The most extensive review of criticisms of the performance of the early NHS was contained in the report of the Select Committee on Estimates published in 1957. Even here the MPs acknowledged that they were impressed by the high level of devotion and enthusiasm of those engaged in the service and they failed to locate 'evidence of declining efficiency...indeed all the evidence suggests quite the contrary'.[13]

3

In view of the formidable body of sentiment in its favour, it is scarcely surprising that by the tenth anniversary, the NHS had already achieved the status of a national institution; it seemed like the unshakable pillar of the welfare state; it was elevated into a principle commanding almost universal assent.[14] Its receding band of detractors such as the Fellowship for Freedom in Medicine seemed out of phase with the mood of the times, and were, like private medicine itself, appealing to a vanishing clientele.

(ii) CONSTRAINTS ON SUCCESS

The vast and complex machinery comprising the NHS in England and Wales relied for its effectiveness on the power of the Ministry of Health. At first, the engine and machine were appropriately matched. The Ministry of Health was one of the largest departments of government, while Aneurin Bevan, Minister of Health for all except the last few months of the postwar Attlee administration, was one of the most dynamic members of the Cabinet. All of this changed in January 1951, when Bevan became Minister of Labour. The Ministry of Health was sliced in half; both the housing and local government functions of the department were transferred elsewhere.[15] This disruption and break in continuity adversely affected morale within the department and reduced its capacity for creative leadership, at a time when the new health service was facing enormous problems in meeting the level of demand and when decisive guidance was urgently needed in order to create some kind of unity of purpose between the disparate parts of the service.

The rump Ministry of Health, left with few responsibilities apart from the NHS, was a small entity by Whitehall standards, relatively unattractive as a proposition for a civil service career, therefore avoided by the high fliers needed for turning the novel and untried administrative structure into a fully efficient working system, or for negotiating with powerful interests groups from a position of strength.[16]

On account of the reduced status of the health department, the Minister of Health was a departmental head of only moderate importance and not meriting Cabinet rank. The reduced political weight of the health department was further exacerbated by the rapid rotation of Ministers of Health. After the departure of Bevan, six individuals held this office between 1951 and 1958. As Bevan caustically remarked: 'they have followed one after the other, not only to their mutual embarrassment, but to the dismay of the nation as a whole', as well as occasioning 'great mischief to this Service'. He pointed out that this instability had prevented the Ministers from gaining even elementary competence in their complex assignments, but more important they were unable 'to stand up against the importunities of the Treasury' with the result that the health service fared badly in each expenditure round, and was likely to be subject to constant 'nibbling by the Treasury'. Such adverse experience could only be arrested by the appointment of a 'senior, experienced, long-standing minister...able to get their own way'. As Bevan appreciated, absence of Cabinet rank added to the likelihood that important decisions affecting the health service would be made either in Cabinet discussions not attended by the Minister of Health, or by ad hoc meetings of senior Ministers, sometimes intentionally designed to exclude the Minister of Health. The previous volume of this study, and the following two chapters provide many examples of this process in action. It will be seen below that even the pertinacious Enoch Powell proved unable to overcome this position of disadvantage during the period when he was outside the Cabinet.[17]

The health services administration in Scotland escaped the erosion of influence which blighted the prospects of the Ministry of Health. As one of four sections of the Scottish Office, the Department of Health for Scotland retained its broad responsibilities. The Secretary of State for Scotland maintained a seat in the Cabinet, and there was considerable stability in this office, with only two incumbents in more than a decade of Conservative Government following the 1951 General Election victory. There was greater rotation among junior Ministers with responsibilities in the Department of Health, but not to a greater degree than was usual in government departments. The seniority, stability and high morale in the Scottish Office proved beneficial for the NHS in Scotland.[18]

Abundant evidence concerning goodwill towards the new health service and the accumulated rhetoric about the NHS as the flagship of the welfare state have resulted too readily in the assumption that the NHS enjoyed a position of special favour in government circles. The argument presented in the previous volume of this study shows that this was not the case. A new health service was an important asset to the public image of postwar administrations, but they were unprepared to meet the realistic costs of such a venture. At the inception of the NHS, Bevan strove to secure adequate resources, but his efforts were not entirely successful. The NHS struggled along in an atmosphere of suspicion in government quarters, the main objective foundations for which were the unrealistically low speculative estimates for the cost of the new service made before its inception, and the above-mentioned limitations in the performance of the Ministry of Health.

The Treasury in particular cultivated the view that the health service was a wasteful and extravagant experiment, and that it possessed the potential to run away with resources, and therefore undermine the balance of spending on the welfare state. Although both Labour and Conservative administrations behaved as if the NHS was treated with special indulgence, in reality after the first eighteen months, it was subjected to rigid control. During the first decade of the new service there was very little substance in widely circulated idea of the 'escalating cost of the NHS', but this construction assumed the status of an ineradicable myth.

Given the weak position of the Ministry of Health, a parsimonious regime was imposed without difficulty. Although expenditure on the NHS increased, at 1970 prices, the rise between 1950 and 1958 was only 3.6 per cent in cost terms, or 13.3 per cent in volume terms, which represented an average annual rise of 0.5 and 1.7 per cent respectively. Similar trends are evident in the cost or volume estimates applied to current expenditure. These amounts represented a quite inadequate rate of increase for a service faced with growing demand arising from demographic change, and also urgently in need of modernisation, including the complete rebuilding of the hospital system.[19] In the light of these extremely small increases it is scarcely surprising that the share of national resources absorbed by the NHS actually fell between 1949/50 and 1957/58 from 4.15 to 3.58 per cent of GDP, a low point of 3.46 per cent being reached in 1954/55. Since the NHS derived part of its finances from direct charges on patients and insurance contributions, the figures for gross expenditure on the NHS give an inflated impression of its burden on the Consolidated Fund and local taxation. The cost of the NHS to public funds declined from 3.75 per cent of GDP in 1949/50 to 3.01 per cent in 1957/58.[20] At the latter date, defence spending stood at about 9 per cent of GDP.

Dependence of the NHS on direct taxation was reduced by the greater exploitation of other sources than was originally intended by Bevan. In 1949/50, direct charges paid by patients, together with the NHS Contribution paid in association with National Insurance, accounted for only 8.7 per cent of the cost of the NHS. Thereafter, as a repercussion of Gaitskell's campaign to limit Exchequer liability to £400m a year, there was a sustained attempt to increase the share of the cost of the NHS met by charges. As noted in the previous volume, direct charges were increased to only a limited extent owing to political contentiousness, but the increased NHS Contribution proved less problematical, with the result that the proportion of the cost of the NHS met by the NHS Contribution and direct charges increased to 18.5 per cent in 1958/59.[21] This was not a big slice of the cost of the health service, but it was disproportionately borne by the sick and the poorer sections of the community. If allowance is made for such factors as local taxation, the NHS Contribution, direct charges, and correction is made to take account of inflation, the

6

Treasury came remarkably close to maintaining the element of NHS expenditure derived form the Consolidated Fund at a constant level. The Exchequer commitment in constant price terms increased by only about 1 per cent a year during the first decade of the new health service.[22]

The health departments emerge with an indifferent record in the competition for resources between the departments involved in the expanding welfare sector. All departments were responding to pressing needs, but decisions concerning the disposition of resources were determined by political factors rather than reference to any objectively determined scale of priorities. Competition among the social service departments was always acute by virtue of overall constraints on resources, the uncertain state of the economy, and the high priority accorded to defence for such purposes as the Korean War, the Cold War, nuclear armaments, and residual colonialist adventures. It was not until 1958 that the first major cuts in defence spending were implemented. The social services were therefore victims of regular economy campaigns.

Within the social services, in the first half of the decade 1948/58, housing made the most obvious advance, but then it steadily slipped back. Throughout the decade, social security recorded a slow increase, but the most conspicuous gains were made by education, which increased its share of social services resources from 17.4 per cent in 1949/50 to 23.8 per cent in 1957/58. This expansion in rival social services departments was made largely at the expense of services for which the Ministry of Health was responsible. Expenditure on the NHS and local welfare services slipped from 29.5 per cent of the social services budget in 1949/50 to 25.8 per cent in 1957/58.[23] As suggested in the first volume of this study, the failure of the Ministry of Health to secure a front-line position in the expansion of the social services budget necessitated almost complete inaction on some essential policy fronts, such as relocation and replacement of obsolete hospital stock, the building of health centres and the expansion of community care. Consequently, although such groups as the elderly and other priority groups such as the disabled derived immediate benefits from the new health service, they were deprived of the more advanced and humane standards obtainable through community care, and therefore they were exposed to the risk of premature disability and unnecessary institutionalisation, which itself represented a waste of the limited resources available to the health and welfare services.[24]

(iii) UNEQUAL PARTNERS
The above problem was exacerbated by structural features of the NHS, which precluded comprehensive planning and impeded

redistribution of resources in favour of primary and community care. Although formally the 'tripartite' system adopted by the NHS comprised a partnership of equals, the three branches of the NHS were unequal in size and influence. By far the most dominant entity was the new regional hospital administration, whereas the primary care services administered by the Executive Councils and the community care services administered by the local authorities suffered from an inferiority of status, which was reflected in their uncertain pace of improvement. The primary and community care services were recognised as potentially important instruments for bringing about much-needed improvements in health care among the less-favoured sections of the community, but in the first decade of the health service this potentiality was only imperfectly realised.

Understandably the powerful hospital authorities proved more capable than their partners in commanding resources. The dominance of the hospital sector also reflects the priority accorded under the early NHS to hospital improvement and to the creation of a comprehensive consultant and specialist service. Given the great scale of this operation and the severe limitations in resources, it is remarkable that it was achieved with such rapidity and smoothness. Given overall resource limitations, it was inevitable that this development was incurred at the expense of other branches of the health service.

In the first decade of the new health service the share of resources absorbed by the hospital service increased by about 5 per cent, largely at the cost of primary care.[25] By the end of the first decade of the NHS the hospital sector was accounting for nearly 60 per cent of current expenditure, the primary care services for about 27 per cent, and community services for only 9 per cent. Naturally, hospital services were intrinsically more expensive, but virtually all capital investment, as well as the small surplus available for development were concentrated into the hospitals, whereas the other sectors were given little opportunity for modernisation or capital investment.

The above observation is confirmed by evidence relating to the workforces employed in the three sectors of the NHS. Whereas all classes of staff employed by hospital authorities increased considerably between 1949 and 1958, the staff employed by the local health authorities and the Executive Councils remained relatively static in numbers; with limited exceptions such as ambulance staff and home helps, only minor increases were experienced outside the hospital sector. This point is strikingly illustrated by reference to the distribution of medical personnel. Between 1949 and 1958, hospital medical and dental staffs increased by about 32 per cent; local health authority medical and dental staff increased by 10 per cent; Executive Council medical and dental staff increased by 12 per cent.[26] As a result of this changing balance within the medical profession, general practitioners lost the clear numerical superiority that they had enjoyed up to the foundation of the NHS.

The rapid expansion of the medical staff in hospitals was the main factor explaining a rapid improvement in the doctor:population ratio. During the earlier part of the century there was only one doctor for every 1,500 of the population; this ratio improved under the NHS until in the mid-50s there was an average of one doctor for every 1,000 persons.[27] In 1955 the ratio in Scotland stood at 1:950, whereas in England and Wales it was 1:1,165.[28] This ratio placed Scotland ahead of most north European countries, whereas England and Wales were middle-ranking. However, with respect to the rate of change, the medical workforce was expanding more rapidly in most of north-west Europe. For instance Denmark, which in many respects is comparable with Britain, had a ratio of 1:961 in 1950 and 1:758 in 1963.[29]

The above expansion and shift in balance of influence between the main sectors of the medical profession had important implications for career opportunities, status, political standing and capacity to influence the distribution of resources. General medical practice and especially public health medicine lost in attractiveness and prestige. All of the opportunities for a challenging career and a dominant part in health care seemed to be concentrated in the hospital service. Reflecting this uneven balance of forces within the tripartite structure, primary and community care took on the character of a stagnant backwater. The less-favoured branches of the NHS were adversely affected by low morale, recruitment problems and a low level of initiative. There was thus a risk of spiralling decline in the very services which had been singled out as priority areas, and which represented humane and economical alternatives to expensive hospital care.

(iv) COMMUNITY SERVICES

The prestige of local health authorities depended on the promise of developing health centres. The latter were originally envisaged as a key feature of the new health service; they were especially important for linking the three branches of the health service. As explained in the previous volume of this study, this policy was not implemented, undoubtedly to the detriment of primary and community care services, especially for the large section of the population relocated in new towns and housing developments which sprang up during the 1950s. As indicated in below in chapter III, the obstacles against health centre development were not finally removed until 1966.

Abandonment of the health centre experiment deprived local health authorities of their most attractive new function under the

NHS, and it reduced still further the morale of the already dispirited Medical Officers of Health. Although some MOHs maximised their opportunities to develop services for the elderly and other disadvantaged client groups, the majority pursued their responsibilities in the pedantic and restrictive spirit inherited from the harsh regime imposed during the Depression. Because of the reduced status of public health departments of local authorities under the NHS, their services became one of the less attractive branches of local government responsibility, and were therefore not accorded special favour in the competition for rate revenues. Local health authorities were therefore impeded by both Treasury and town hall parsimony.

In view of the limitations of resources and motivation, it is not surprising that local health authority services failed to break away from their traditional limitations, and maximise opportunities for expansion and modernisation. Although the philosophy of community care evolved during the first decade of the NHS, local health authorities failed to develop a coherent programme to meet this objective, and thereby contributed to the continuing disadvantage of the most disadvantaged social classes, or already severely disadvantaged client groups such as the elderly, the disabled, or those affected by mental problems.

Local health authorities were successful in expanding some of their services, for instance, home helps, maternity and child welfare clinics or ambulance services. In other areas the record was uneven. Comparing 1949 and 1958 there was a substantial increase in the home help service, a small increase in the staff of district nurses and health visitors, but a decrease of dentists and domiciliary midwives.[30]

Before the NHS, local authorities had varied enormously in their enthusiasm and capacity to promote health services. By 1948, the more energetic authorities, almost all of which were in affluent South-East, were providing an impressive range of services not greatly inferior in scope and character to the NHS. At the other extreme, a much larger number of small local authorities, especially those located in areas of heavy industry, were not much in advance of the Victorians in their parsimonious and inept provision for public health. The NHS therefore faced a formidable task in bringing laggard authorities up to the standard of the best.

This was not one of the more conspicuous areas of success for the Ministry of Health, which followed its traditional course of permitting maximum local discretion. Little attempt was made to evolve objective standards, or to bring about more uniform levels of provision. Accordingly, especially in traditionally backward areas, the development of services fell seriously behind what was reasonably required.

10

Health visiting, an essential element in the community c⟋ programme, typified the lethargic pace of progress and ι... idiosyncratic character of regional variations. Health visitors were the only group of local authority health and welfare workers for whom guide-lines were evolved during the first decade of the NHS, albeit by an independent working party rather than the health department itself.[31] The Jameson Report recommended 0.23 health visitors per 1,000 population, which was a relatively modest standard, as was the 0.33 norm formally adopted in the 1970s. Very few authorities reached the Jameson target. Even in 1962 the average for England and Wales was only 0.11 per 1,000 population. At this date Newcastle-upon-Tyne, with a level of 0.21, was one of the few large authorities to approximate to the Jameson standard; most large authorities were nearer to the national average.

Even greater diversity existed in the provision of home helps, a relatively new service, where local authorities were allowed a wide degree of discretion. Rotherham and Nottingham employed about 1.3 home helps per 1,000 population, and Newcastle-upon-Tyne 1.1. At the other end of the scale, Derbyshire and Devon had only about 0.25, and Tynemouth 0.06. Wolverhampton, which was represented in Parliament by Enoch Powell, the Minister of Health responsible for the new community care plan, employed only one-third the level of home helps found in Newcastle-upon-Tyne.[32] The examples of health visitors and home helps are illustrative of a situation existing more generally in the local authority health and welfare services. For reasons of local apathy and central departmental reticence, the NHS inspired only minimal concessions towards the principles of rationality and equality. In quantitative terms, home nurses, health visitors and home helps were of course only insignificant groups within the NHS workforce, but limitations imposed on expansion in this area precluded the development of effective domiciliary services, thereby preventing the creation of support services which might have prevented vulnerable groups such as the elderly, the mental handicapped and mentally disordered from drifting into expensive residential accommodation, or even more expensive hospital beds.

(v) PRIMARY CARE

Like the old Insurance Committees upon which they were modelled, the Executive Councils were primarily instruments of regulation. The independent contractors who dominated the Executive Councils gave no encouragement for these bodies to develop wider aspirations. Changes in general medical practice during the 1950s therefore tended to occur at a slow and uncertain pace, dictated more than anything by minor financial inducements, emerging as by-products of pay negotiations, and which gave encouragement to a more even distribution of general practitioners and also induced a slow drift towards group practice.[33] In 1948 the average list size for doctors in England and Wales was about 2,500, and in Scotland 2,200. In 1953 the list size was about 2,300 in England, just below 2,000 in Scotland, and in Wales just above this figure.[34]

In 1952 51 per cent of the population in England and Wales were in 'designated' areas containing too few doctors on the basis of the definitions adopted by the Medical Practices Committee; in 1958 only 19 per cent of the population were located in designated areas.[35] Nevertheless, in 1958, 38 per cent of the population in the English county boroughs were still on lists of over 3,000. In seven county boroughs more than 60 per cent of the population were on lists of over 3,000. Discouragement of large lists proceeded extremely slowly. In 1952 it was agreed to reduce the permitted maximum for a single-handed practitioners from 4,000 to 3,500. Progressive opinion favoured rapid moves towards maximum lists of 2,000, but this objective was not accepted in medico-political circles.

As in the case of the distribution of doctors in general, the distribution of general medical practitioners reflected long-standing regional disparities. This characteristic persisted under the NHS. In 1952, in the North of England, the East and West Midlands, list sizes averaged at about 2,700, while in the South-West of England, Wales and Scotland, list sizes were just above 2,200. The gradual reduction of list sizes during the 1950s brought benefits to the less well-provided regions, but in 1963 the pecking order remained broadly unchanged.[36]

After 1952 terms of remuneration favoured movement towards group practice. Between 1952 and 1958 the percentage of principals in single-handed practice declined from 44 to 32 per cent in England and Wales.[37] Group practice was increasingly accepted as a tolerable substitute for the health centre programme, even though group practice represented only one dimension of the health centre concept.

Despite some positive trends, there was much concern about the state of general practice, especially in the industrial regions and inner cities, which tended to be served by older, single-handed practitioners, often working from lock-up surgeries. The Collings survey, discussed in volume I, led the way in drawing attention to the failure of the NHS to generate a fundamental transformation in general medical practice. General practice was adversely affected by lethargic recruitment, too many elderly practitioners and too few women. In Scotland there were only about 11 per cent women principals in general practice, and slightly above this figure in England and Wales.[38] A further undesirable hangover from the National Insurance system was undue reliance on general

12

practitioners above the age of retirement. In England and Wales, about 10 per cent of principals were aged above 65. In Scotland there were slightly fewer general practitioners over 65, but even in Scotland there was a handful of veterans who had been practising since before the turn of the century.[39]

A more positive role for general practice was not assisted by the prescription charge, introduced in 1951 and increased at the end of 1956. This exerted a measurable deterrent effect, with the result that there was a sharp fall in the number of prescriptions dispensed.[40] There was widespread complaint that the prescription charge acted as a deterrent, preventing the elderly, the chronically sick and the low paid from making advantageous use of the health service.[41] By 1958 the medical and pharmaceutical professions were campaigning actively for removal of the prescription charge, and this view was broadly supported by the Guillebaud and Hinchliffe Reports.[42]

In its attempt to control expenditure on drugs by prescription charges, or by trying to persuade doctors to prescribe smaller quantities, the Government was being unrealistic. As the Hinchliffe Committee concluded, 'the discovery and large scale production of valuable but expensive drugs has been the main factor contributing to the rise in the cost of prescriptions'.[43] The postwar period coincided with an explosion in the production of new, effective and often expensive vaccines, or drugs such as antibiotics, corticosteroids, antihypertensives, diuretics, anticoagulants, analgesics, antiepileptics, and psychotropic agents. The therapeutic revolution started in earnest in the decade before the NHS, with the introduction of sulphonamides, synthetic antibacterials, and antibiotics such as penicillin and streptomycin. Chloramphenicol, the first of the broad-spectrum antibiotics, was first released for general use in 1951; other broad-spectrum antibiotics followed on quickly, chlortetracycline hydrochloride and oxytetracycline in 1954, and tetracycline in 1955. The corticosteroids, prednisone and prednisolone were released in February 1957. Chlorothiazide and hydrochlorothiazide, the first successful oral diuretics were introduced in 1958. Before the end of the first decade of the NHS, the antiepileptic, beclamide, and psychotropic drugs such as amphetamines, barbiturates, chlorpromazine hydrochloride, promazine hydrochloride, imipramine hydrochloride, iproniazid, and meprobamate were being taken up with avidity. The word 'tranquillizer' entered the English language in 1953 in the context of the use of the alkaloid, reserpine, later mainly used an antihypertensive agent.[44] By 1958 antibiotics and hormones accounted for 20 per cent and 8 per cent respectively of the drug bill, whereas they had been negligible factors in 1948.

Such innovations were responsible for increase in the average net ingredient cost per prescription from 16.4d in 1948 to 48.7d in 1958. These trends suggested that any concerns about the rising drug bill needed to be addressed by reference to the profit margins of the drug companies. The pharmacological revolution also ran ahead of the education of general practitioners, with the result that wide discrepancies opened up in prescribing habits between doctors, which were not explicable by reference to rational and objective criteria such as the pattern of ill-health among their patients.

The Hinchliffe and Douglas Committees heard much evidence concerning dangerous and irresponsible use of modern drugs. Recriminations were vented in all directions to explain such potentially frightening lapses. Patients were criticised for demanding the latest drugs; specialists were attacked for encouraging the drug habit; the teaching in medical schools was clearly failing to address itself sufficiently to the principles of economical and safe prescribing; unscrupulous general practitioners were accused of using lavish prescription to build up their lists; the drug companies were censured for unprincipled sales tactics; while the health departments seemed culpable for displaying lack of leadership. In a fairly typical example, a senior and respected Edinburgh general practitioner admitted to average monthly drug costs per patient of only 10d, whereas the area average was 2s 6d. An equally respected, but more innovative colleague was spending about 3s 6d a month. At this date, the prescriptions of some Edinburgh doctors were costing as much as 5s a month. In a more bizarre, but not unique example, a comparison of two similar urban practices in Galloway, one practitioner was obtaining satisfactory results with monthly drug costs of 6d, while another was spending 6s 8d, which was reduced to 2s 9d after disciplinary proceedings. The highest monthly total recorded for Glasgow at this date was more than 10s.[45]

Transformation in the effectiveness of drug therapy greatly increased the capacities and responsibilities of the general practitioner. Paradoxically, morale remained low within general practice, which was attributable to a variety of limitations, especially the lack of financial incentives to undertake improvements in practice premises and organisation, but also absence of proper professional training, and failure to establish a balanced partnership with hospitals and local health authorities. Such factors diminished the confidence of general practitioners, increased their sense of isolation, and contributed to a collective fear that they were trapped in a professional backwater.

A mood of dissatisfaction affected all parts of the political spectrum among general practitioners. The progressive General Practice Reform Association complained that the general practitioner was 'rapidly degenerating into a sorter of patients into those to be sent to one or other of the hospital or local authority clinics, and those who can be satisfied with a prescription'. Representing establishment opinion, the Scottish Association of Executive Councils complained that this state of affairs was the fault of 'nationalisation', which had caused the state to supply a 'completely comfortable and sheltered living to all who qualify and that the continued importance of experience, ability and energy is not fully recognized'.[46] Neither the health departments nor the BMA succeeded in inspiring greater confidence among general practitioners, although more enlightened leadership emerged from such groups as the General Practice Reform Association, the Medical Practitioners' Union and especially the College of General Practitioners, founded in November 1952.[47] These organisations provided a forum for more idealistic, often younger, practitioners, the group which tended to favour health centre practice and the ideas of Michael Balint, whose celebrated *The Doctor, his Patient and the Illness* was published in 1957.[48]

The first volume of this study described the spectacular success of the new health service in dealing with the deluge of demand for dentures and in gradually establishing the dominance of conservative dentistry. Nevertheless, from the start, the NHS dentistry was beset with problems. After the brief heyday of high fees and huge quantities of work, fees were reduced, and incomes fell. Morale declined and recruitment into dental schools, never high, slumped further. In 1958 16 per cent of dentists in England and Wales were over 65, and many of these were unqualified '1921 dentists'.[49] By contrast with the situation in Scandinavia, British dentistry failed to attract women recruits. It was estimated that only 10 per cent of active dentists were women, about the same level as the intake of women into dental schools. It was pointed out that in Scandinavian and Baltic countries, between 40 and 80 per cent of dentists were women. In Finland, 75 per cent of dental students were women. This crisis within the dental profession was addressed by the McNair Committee, which reported in 1956, but the position of dentistry was not radically improved until after the Royal Commission on Doctors' and Dentists' Remuneration.[50]

Even more than in the case of the 'Supplementary Ophthalmic Service', the commitment of the Government to the NHS general dental service was continually in doubt, and periodically the complete abolition of this service was considered. The eye service was less vulnerable because charges accounted in 1958 for 37 per cent of the cost of the service, which was the highest proportion collected for any branch of the NHS.[51] This substantial charge protected the existence of the supplementary ophthalmic service, but its introduction had served as a substantial deterrent.[52]

15

Dentistry benefited less than general practice from improvements in the distribution of personnel. In 1958 areas such as London and the South-East enjoyed twice the concentration of dentists found in areas such as the Midlands. Indeed, in Wales, the Midlands and the North of England, the concentration of dentists declined during the first decade of the NHS.[53] In general, the industrial areas possessed fewer, older and less well-qualified dentists. This difference showed up in the type of work undertaken. In London and the South-East in 1958, for every tooth extracted, more than three were filled, but in Wales and the North of England less than one tooth was filled for every one extracted.[54]

The dental services maintained by local authorities for priority groups were also in a state of crisis, largely owing to adverse remuneration, which resulted in erosion of staff. The expectation that dental fitness would become a high priority of the NHS was disappointed. In this important test case, the NHS conspicuously failed to correct inequalities in dental health. The middle classes were primary beneficiaries of the more enlightened services, while the working classes remained apathetic and ignorant about the benefits of preventive and conservative treatment. This inequality was reinforced by the impact of dental charges introduced in 1951, and increased in 1952. Because of the flat-rate fee of £1 for treatment there existed an incentive to defer visits to the dentist until a substantial amount of work was needed.

(vi) HOSPITAL AND SPECIALIST SERVICES

During the first decade of the NHS, the hospital services were responsible for most of the large-scale innovations and the main planning initiatives. With remarkable smoothness, speed and efficiency, NHS hospital authorities converted the ramshackle and obsolete institutions inherited from their predecessors into a first-class, modern and integrated hospital network. All of this was achieved without the advantage of a major hospital building programme. The hospitals of the NHS were therefore usually grotesque conglomerates, comprising buildings and hutments, some dating from the eighteenth century and even earlier. Great ingenuity was exercised in adapting these antique facilities for housing the most advanced systems of diagnosis and treatment.

An impression of the scale and character of this achievement, as well as a brief insight into some limitations, was provided in the retrospective account by Sir George Godber, a Deputy Chief Medical Officer at the time, and one of the main architects of the new system:

> The result...was an immediate and large increase in the amount of specialist time available, especially in hospital centres outside the

large cities...General medicine and general surgery were the largest medical specialties in 1948 but increased little after the first two years while other specialties were established and grew rapidly. Neurosurgery, thoracic surgery, and plastic surgery which had been established in a few centres were quickly provided by the Health Service in every region. Regional radio-therapy services separate from diagnostic radiology were established. The deficiencies in pathology and diagnostic radiology had been exposed by wartime needs and partially remedied, but needed expansion and re-equipment. Anaesthesiology developed rapidly into the largest specialty followed by pathology and psychiatry. The increase in consultants was thus not only in numbers, but much more importantly in range of expertise. Geriatrics and child psychiatry developed from almost nothing; urological and cardiological units were established at least in main centres; pathology became sub-divided; orthopaedic surgery became predominantly concerned with repair of trauma and defects at birth or of ageing. But rheumatology and rehabilitation were often neglected.[55]

With respect to England and Wales, according to one source, 5,316 consultants were employed in 1949; this rose to 7,109 in 1958, an increase of 34 per cent.[56] An alternative source providing data in terms of whole-time equivalents for consultants and related senior grades, records a rise from 4,711 to 7,215 over the same period, which is an increase of 53 per cent.[57] A further whole-time equivalent estimate for the entire hospital medical and dental staff suggests a rise from 11,900 to 16,000 for this period, which is 34 per cent.[58] On the basis of these estimates, it seems safe to conclude that between 1949 and 1958 the medical labour force increased by at least 30 per cent in England, and by about 50 per cent in Scotland.

As Godber observed, the greatest percentage increases were recorded in new surgical specialties, or in areas like anaesthetics and pathology, which were poorly developed before the NHS and which were in great demand owing to advances in surgery and diagnostic techniques. In 1949, a total of 300 consultants was exceeded in 6 specialties; in 1958 this figure was surpassed in 11 specialties. Of the larger specialties, the greatest increase was recorded by anaesthesiology, which rose by 72 per cent in the number of consultants employed.[59]

The build-up of regional consultant and specialist services, together with proliferation of specialties and associated scientific advances greatly increased the importance of support services, and therefore demanded transformation of facilities for radiography, pathology and blood transfusion. The latter provides a representative

17

indicator of the expansion in high-technology medicine. Blood, blood plasma, and an growing range of blood products such as gamma globulin and anti-haemophiliac fibrinogen were in increasing demand. Blood transfusion was used for such diverse purposes as the prevention of surgical shock following major operations, for the treatment of post-partum haemorrhage, which was a major cause of death in childbirth, for cardiac surgery, for newly evolved heart-lung machines, and even for treating gastro-intestinal haemorrhage. Between 1948 and 1958 the number of bottles of blood issued more than doubled in England and Wales, and more than trebled in Scotland; this represented the contribution of a panel of nearly a million voluntary donors.[60] A further indicator of this technological trend is provided by the numbers of professional and technical staff employed by the NHS, which, despite difficulties in recruitment, expanded by 42 per cent between 1949 and 1958, which is the largest increase experienced within the NHS workforce.[61] Even this degree of expansion was insufficient to meet the demand, but low pay was a barrier to further recruitment.[62]

Women continued to occupy a disadvantaged place in the medical labour force. Those women recruited into medicine tended to gravitate into primary and community care, or less senior posts in the hospital service. In 1958 women constituted about 25 per cent of the medical school population and about 16 per cent of the medical workforce.[63] They tended to work part-time, have limited career prospects and occupy less prestigious posts. In Scotland, only about 5 per cent of consultants were women, and slightly above this figure in England and Wales. Male dominance within the medical profession was evidently not reduced by the transition to the NHS. The position of women doctors was considerably worse than in the comparable health services of Scandinavia.

Perhaps the most obvious change in the character of the medical workforce under the NHS was the increasing reliance on overseas doctors in the training grades of the hospital service, especially in shortage specialties, and in the northern regional boards. By the mid-fifties it was evident that many parts of the hospital service would face breakdown without recruitment to the training and junior grades of overseas doctors, especially from India and Pakistan. In 1958 it was estimated that some 2,500 overseas doctors were working in hospitals in England and Wales and this proved to be an accelerating trend.[64]

Advances in medicine since the beginning of the century entailed a steady increase in the labour intensity of hospital activity. The success of this enterprise was particularly dependent on the rise in numbers and increase in professional competence of nurses. Maintaining buoyant recruitment and steadily increasing the level of training and specialisation of the large nursing workforce constituted one of the greatest problems for the early NHS. This task was rendered more difficult by virtue of the diversification in career opportunities for women, archaic professional structures, a continuing position of subjugation with respect to medical colleagues, the demanding nature of nursing work, and the persistence of an unattractive level of remuneration.[65] The seriousness of this problem was luridly expressed by a London journalist: 'a new Shaftesbury will be needed to do justice to the national - indeed international - scandal of the hours worked by, and the wages paid to, nurses of an almost incredibly high standard of efficiency and gentleness'.[66] Despite the above concatenation of disincentives, between 1949 and 1958 the nursing and midwifery workforce increased by 26 per cent in Scotland, England and Wales.[67] This level of expansion was increasingly dependent on the recruitment of nurses from abroad, especially Ireland and the Commonwealth, but also from various parts of Europe. Areas of the hospital service experiencing the greatest difficulties in recruitment, such as the mental and mental handicap sector, were particularly dependent on nurses from overseas. In some instances, special and sometimes ingenious schemes were devised for the recruitment of overseas nurses and nursing auxiliaries, for instance by the NW Metropolitan RHB for obtaining young women from Germany and Italy for its mental and mental handicap hospitals.[68] Europe was gradually supplanted by the West Indies as a favoured source for recruitment of overseas nurses.

This process of expansion resulted in the most numerous groups within the NHS labour force attaining a high place in the ranking order of occupations in the British labour market. By 1958 the total for nurses and midwives, as well as works, maintenance and ancillary staff had reached about 200,000.[69]

During the first decade of the health service there was very little increase in the number of available beds and only a moderate increase in administrative and clerical staff.[70] Lay administrative staff carried great responsibilities, but their position under the administrative arrangements adopted for the NHS compared unfavourably to their counterparts in local government. Partly out of an intentional aim to preserve flexibility, and partly because it had proved impossible to work out an agreed management structure, relationships between officers at different points in the administrative hierarchy were ill-defined and apt to generate disharmony and inefficiency. In situations where effective management structures were in place for lay administrative staff, confusion persisted owing to lack of clear lines of authority with respect to their medical and nursing colleagues. Career arrangements for administrative staff improved after the Noel Hall report published in 1957, but compared with other organisations of similar scale, the NHS was still deficient with respect to common structures for recruitment, training, and centralised arrangements for promotion and interchange of staff. There was also complaint that administrators in the NHS possessed the disadvantages of both civil servants and local government officials, without possessing enough of their advantages. In particular, it was urged that for the sake of greater efficiency, the powers of officers needed to be strengthened with respect to the regional and group health authorities who were their employers.[71]

Despite its many limitations the hospital service during its first decade recorded a remarkable increase in the volume of work undertaken during the first decade. Taking all departments there was an increase of courses of in-patient treatment from 2.9 million to 3.9 million, which represented a rise of 34 per cent. The increase was not uniform; some of the highest increases were recorded in obstetrics (79 per cent), mental health (50 per cent), and in medical departments (32 per cent). The volume of out-patient care also displayed similar increases. The growth in out-patient care on any scale in mental health was a relatively new phenomenon. It indicated a modest but important shift in attitudes towards therapy, and was the beginning of a concerted attempt to arrest the seeming inexorable rise in the population of long-stay patients in mental hospitals, a trend which seemed likely to continue on account of the growth in numbers of psycho-geriatric patients. As a result of advances in drug therapy, the increased use of out-patient facilities, a rapid rise in short-term treatment for new admissions, and experiments with rehabilitation, the mental hospital population reached its peak in the mid-fifties and by the tenth anniversary of the NHS was displaying signs of a distinct decline.[72] This shift enabled regional authorities to abort most of their ambitious schemes for building new mental hospitals, but they were much slower to abandon their plans for expanding institutional treatment of the mentally handicapped. In 1958 plans for major capital projects still included new mental hospitals and mental handicap institutions as a major priority.[73]

The leading sphere of innovation was the acute sector. It was this area which attracted the greatest concentration of resources and planning. The service began with an average of about 3.5 beds per thousand population, which was fewer than acute services in comparable health services abroad. By 1958 bed provision and occupancy levels had not changed, but the length of stay was reduced by 18 per cent, while the cases treated per thousand population and per bed had both increased by about 30 per cent. The performance of the NHS by comparison with similar health services elsewhere was

20

moderately good. In the acute services the NHS provided rather fewer beds, recorded a similar occupation rate and length of stay for in-patients, but it was somewhat in arrears with respect to the number of cases treated, especially with respect to population, a situation explained largely by the higher level of acute beds provided elsewhere.[74]

Although total bed numbers remained static, the balance of beds between specialties was constantly shifting. Surgical beds increased, beds in medical departments contracted. Obstetrics was a major growth area, spurred on by pressure from the Royal College of Obstetricians and Gynaecologists for the concentration of confinements in hospital under consultant control. Women were converted to this point of view; childbirth in hospital was no longer regarded as the province of poor women referred to institutional confinement for social as well as medical reasons. By 1958 women in Britain had come to regard hospital as the right environment for ensuring maximum safety in childbirth. Consequently maternity wards and new maternity hospitals were assuming a high priority in regional development plans. In Great Britain, between 1949 and 1963 there occurred a 20 per cent increase in the number of maternity beds, mostly in obstetric departments of hospitals rather than general practitioner facilities. During this period there occurred a 42 per cent increase in births per bed. Therefore, although the number of beds scarcely kept up with the increasing birthrate, the more concentrated use of beds allowed a steady increase in the percentage of confinements occurring in NHS hospitals. The latter rose from 45 to 64 per cent in England, 48 to 73 per cent in Wales, and 56 to 79 per cent in Scotland during the first decade of the new health service.[75]

In the first decade of the NHS pressure on hospital facilities was intense. Any saving in resources or space was quickly absorbed owing to fresh demands or capacities. Demand for isolation facilities and infectious diseases beds sharply declined owing to such factors as more extensive exploitation of immunization and vaccination, but this brought little benefit to other specialties because many isolation hospitals were primitive and unsuitable for adaptation for other purposes. This was not the case with tuberculosis; substantial resources had been lavished in building new sanatoria during the interwar period, many of which contained advanced facilities for surgery. This development was a reflection of the seriousness of tuberculosis, which had for a long period been a great scourge as a cause of debility, as well as the major cause of death among adults. Owing to spontaneous remission, the improving general state of health of the community, earlier detection through mass X-radiography, belated implementation of BCG vaccination, and more

21

active pursuit of drug therapy developed during World War II, tuberculosis went into rapid decline.[76] Between 1948 and 1958, deaths in Great Britain from tuberculosis declined from 25,000 to 5,000 a year. However, the bonus available to the NHS from the decline of tuberculosis in the short term was less than might have been expected. Indeed, in the first few years of the NHS tuberculosis hospital facilities were considerably expanded to reach a peak of about 41,000 beds. Thereafter resources devoted to tuberculosis slowly diminished; by 1958 some 10,000 tuberculosis beds had been released for other purposes. They were mainly applied for chronic cases, but the rapid increase in lung cancer, mainly attributable to smoking, ordained that there was an immediate demand for the transfer of pulmonary tuberculosis beds to specialists concerned with other chest diseases.[77] Consequently in the first decade of the health service, the reduction in pressure on facilities in such fields as infectious diseases brought only modest benefits to the rest of the hospital service, which remained burgeoning with demands for additional resources.

The overall shortage of resources in the hospital sector was made worse by virtue of their uneven distribution. The existence of this problem was slow to come to public attention. Social scientists such as Titmuss, or epidemiologists like Morris, whose reputation was based on exposing geographical inequalities in health, were not active in identifying this as one of the main sources of weakness of the NHS. The first effective probing on this issue came from the Select Committee on Estimates in 1957, but this failed to extract the relevant factual information from the Ministry of Health. Hints provided by the Select Committee were followed up by the Acton Society Trust, which in 1958 published the first tabulations indicating the full scale of this problem.[78] A leading finance officer pointed out that this issue had been raised with senior officers in the Ministry of Health as early as 1950, and again periodically since that date, but no systematic investigation had been conducted into the extent of persisting inequalities in resource allocation. With respect to prospective revenue allocations as far forward as 1963/64, it was pointed out that long-standing disparities were persisting. It was concluded that the system of allocations operated to ensure that 'whichever Authority had a relatively fat snowball at the start will tend to maintain that relativity'.[79]

The health departments were not oblivious to this problem. A conscious attempt was made to achieve more equal distribution of hospital and specialist services, but the disparities in provision at the beginning of the NHS were substantial, and by 1958 the extent of the initial disadvantage had been diminished only to a limited extent. As indicated in the previous volume, the efforts of the planners to equalise consultant services were to some extent frustrated owing to the concentration of teaching hospitals in London, as well as the conservative nature of the merit awards system, both of which tended to reinforce inherited inequalities. Twenty-six out of the thirty-six of the teaching hospitals, with some 15,000 beds, were concentrated in London. Consequently, if the teaching hospitals are taken into account in regional comparisons, the advantage of the metropolitan regions is even more pronounced.

According to almost any criterion, the four metropolitan regions emerge favourably, while among the other large regions, the worst-provided regions are located in the industrial Midlands and the North. At the beginning of the NHS the four metropolitan regions employed nearly twice as many consultants per 100,000 population than the four worst-provided regions. In 1949 the average for the metropolitan regions was 16, while for Newcastle, Leeds, Sheffield and Manchester it was less than 9. In attempting to narrow this gulf, the planners were faced with a difficult equation: on the one hand it was necessary to foster improvements in consultant and specialist services in all regions; on the other hand it was necessary to introduce an element of positive discrimination to bring much-needed relief to the less well-provided regions. This balancing process inevitably imposed a limit on the speed of equalisation. Similar difficulties were to be experienced with the introduction of the more ambitious Resource Allocation Working Party exercise two decades later.

By 1958 the metropolitan regions had experienced an average of 18 per cent increase in their consultant establishments, whereas the above four northern regions recorded an average increase of 42 per cent. This still left the metropolitan regions with an almost 50 per cent advantage. Also the catching-up exercise took effect in the various northern regions at very different rates, which reflected striking differences in their levels of initiative and capacity to introduce forward planning. Whereas Newcastle recorded an increase of consultant establishments of more than 60 per cent between 1948 and 1958, the increase in all other Midland and Northern regions was approximately 30 per cent.[80]

Inequalities in the distribution of consultants was merely one aspect of the wider problem of resource distribution. The equalisation of allocations was more easily achieved in the field of capital investment, where the health departments exerted a great measure of direct influence. Although this was a potentially important sphere of activity, in practice it was of only marginal significance, on account of already-mentioned limitations imposed on capital development in the new health service.

During the first decade of the NHS, for Great Britain as a whole, only about £13m a year was available for capital investment. In the mid-fifties it was calculated that in constant price terms, capital expenditure on hospitals was only one-fifth the prewar level of capital spending by local authorities.[81] An alternative calculation by Abel-Smith and Titmuss suggested that capital spending of the NHS was one-third the amount spent by all hospital authorities in 1938/39.[82] Even for the years 1954-59, when more funds were made available for hospital building, the average annual spending was only about £20m, compared with about £100m available for school building. By the tenth anniversary of the NHS no new hospital had been completed in England and Wales, and only one small hospital in Scotland, and this was provided on grounds of civil defence.[83] The absence of hospitals and other buildings needed for health purposes in new towns and other major areas of rehousing underlined the degree to which health had fallen behind education in providing the local physical infrastructure of the welfare state.

Capital investment was an especially urgent priority on account of the advanced age of the hospital stock. The Guillebaud Report warned about the 'advanced degree of obsolescence' of hospitals, while the Minister of Health pointed out that 'more than 300 hospitals are more than 100 years old, nearly 1,200 more than 50 years old, many of them quite unsuited to modern forms of treatment. They include, particularly among the mental hospitals, many buildings which, despite such modernisation as has been possible within our small capital programme, are really a scandal in the modern world'.[84] Another summary pointed out that '45 per cent of the hospitals were originally erected before 1891 and 21 per cent before 1861'; the wartime hospital surveys showed that most hospitals 'ought to be radically reconstructed', while even recent hospitals 'do not conform to modern principles of hospital construction'.[85]

The limited resources available for capital development were distributed with reasonable attention to regional priorities, but there were nevertheless some anomalies and persisting inequalities. On the basis of population, Wales received marginally more than its share, whereas Scotland fared much better, obtaining about 17 per cent of resources, for about 11 per cent of population.[86] Wales therefore ranked with the average English regions, but on the basis of population Scotland received a much larger share of resources than any of the English regions, even those receiving the maximum advantage from capital resources devoted to teaching hospitals.

The negligible funds available during the early years of the new service for major capital projects were directed according to the perceived urgencies of need. Although in retrospect, the regions

24

could be faulted for their judgement on medical priorities, and the health departments might have exercised more far-sighted guidance, the limited funds available were at least distributed with regard to perceived local shortcomings, which brought some advantage to the poorer regions. However, as in the case of current expenditure and for the same reasons, the opportunities for redistribution were limited. The already well-provided metropolitan regions required generous treatment, particularly because of the need to provide hospital facilities in the extensive areas of housing development on the outskirts of London and in new towns in the home counties. Taking the first decade as a whole, the English metropolitan regions received capital allocations roughly in line with their populations, but the Leeds, Birmingham and Manchester regions received noticeably smaller allocations than would have been merited on grounds of their populations.[87] If the above calculation had taken account of the substantial share (approximately 25 per cent) of capital investment directed to the teaching hospitals, the metropolitan regions would have emerged with a substantial advantage, while the disadvantage of the poorer regions would have seemed more pronounced.[88]

At the beginning of the NHS, the distribution of resources was largely dictated by the inherited pattern of spending on hospitals. Consequently, it is not surprising to find that the metropolitan regions received a share of the hospital current allocation larger than would be expected from their populations, while regions containing a high level of heavy industry, such as Newcastle, Sheffield, Birmingham, and Manchester, all received a smaller share of the current allocation in 1950/51 than might have been expected. With respect to these four regions, on the basis of population, this deficit ranged between 15 per cent and 26 per cent. The concentration of resources in the metropolitan regions is to some extent related to the distribution of hospital beds, but this is only part of the explanation. The above four disadvantaged regions collectively contained about 3 per cent fewer general and special hospital beds than might have been expected from their population, while the four metropolitan regions, which were collectively comparable in population size, contained about 3 per cent more general hospital beds than was expected from their populations.[89] The higher share of resources attracted by the metropolitan hospitals therefore largely reflects the more expensive character of the London hospital system. The above estimates take no account of the 13 per cent of current allocation devoted during the first decade of the service to the teaching hospitals, more than half of which went to London, thus further enhancing the advantage of the metropolitan regions.

By the tenth anniversary of the NHS the position of the worst-provided regions had marginally improved. With respect to current allocation the four poorer regions showed deficits between 9 per cent and 20 per cent, with an average of 16 per cent. Only the Newcastle region had experienced spectacular improvement, and even here there remained a 9 per cent deficit. This change was largely brought about by redistribution of resources from the metropolitan regions, although after ten years of the NHS, they retained a substantial advantage.[90]

Naturally, regional comparisons based on crude population are at the best approximate, but if account is taken of demographic and epidemiological weighting of the kind invoked in recent resource distribution exercises, the disadvantage of the deficit regions is likely to appear even greater. The first attempt at estimating the extent of inequality in resource distribution on a weighted basis seems to derive from 1962. This generally confirmed the pattern of inequality in resource distribution described above. According to the weighted estimates, the most disadvantaged regions were Liverpool, Leeds, East Anglia, Manchester and Wales. For non-teaching beds, this estimate suggested that the Liverpool region was nearly 20 per cent in deficit.[91]

(vii) FLAWS IN THE SYSTEM

The National Health Service was of course not a perfect vehicle for the delivery of health care and the optimisation of health. Nevertheless, the new health service succeeded remarkably well in its basic objectives; it did much to alleviate anxieties concerning ill-health, brought about a great deal of relief from pain and disability, and made available the benefits of the latest advances in modern medicine. Popular support for the new service was based on this firm record of achievement.

As in all previous ages of medicine, the judgement of planners and the medical profession was by no means infallible. Resources were not always used to the maximum advantage of the sick. The disposition of resources reflected the self-interest of vested interests and prevailing fashions in therapy, not all of which were supportable, even on the basis of available knowledge of the time. It is for instance perhaps fortunate that the regional boards were denied resources for capital development at the beginning of the service, because their initial plans for new hospitals would have given high priority to the building of new tuberculosis sanatoria, mental hospitals and mental handicap institutions, all of which would soon have become redundant. Judging by the example of Woodberry Down, the grandiose schemes of the local authorities for health centres would have constituted a bizarre extravagance.[92] In the welfare sector, the meagre resources available for the elderly were largely deflected, not into domiciliary services, but into expensive Part III accommodation that perpetuated many of the deficiencies of the geriatric wards of the old poor law institutions.[93]

Bombardments from the feminist, anti-psychiatry, and social science lobbies may have been overdrawn, but they identified genuine weaknesses in the manner in which medical science was conducted and translated into practice.[94] In many cases, critics at a more recent date were often anticipated by experts in the field at a much earlier date, when they were voices crying in the wilderness, or unaccountably exercised less influence than was merited by the quality of their analysis. The field of tuberculosis had long been handicapped by surgical interventions of questionable value; the tenth anniversary review of psychiatric services placed its confidence in such treatments as electro-convulsive therapy, insulin coma therapy and leucotomy.[95] Among children tonsillectomy was still at the height of its fashion.[96] On the other hand, the British health service was slow to promote BCG vaccination; it equivocated over taking up the Salk vaccine for poliomyelitis; and it was slow to recognise the value of immunization against rubella. Although one of the regional boards pointed out that 'cancer of the lung continues to increase year by year at a most alarming rate and is now one of the gravest menaces to life of this generation', the relevant advisory committees were slow even to acknowledge that the rise of lung cancer was associated with smoking, hence providing an excuse for inaction by a Government predisposed to avoid this issue to the maximum extent.[97]

As already noted the new health service was also slow to press forward with new approaches to mental disorder, such as the therapeutic community, or with the exploitation of rehabilitation, especially of the elderly, or more generally with services associated with community care. Accordingly, with respect to a wide range of client groups, greater benefits to those in need could have been achieved by alternative means, and often at much less cost.

It is therefore evident that not all the shortcomings of the early NHS were connected with shortage of resources. Many of the limitations itemised above were connected with failings within the system. Although the NHS was remarkably successful in extending the scope of its services, many opportunities for urgently-needed improvement and more radical change were not exploited.

Given the precipitous and haphazard manner in which the NHS was put together, there was no opportunity to incorporate arrangements for comprehensive and integrated planning, or even to guarantee the efficient use of resources. The best that could be achieved in the circumstances was to apply mechanisms of basic financial control, largely taken over from pre-NHS bodies. The NHS was therefore unable to escape completely from the limitations of the previous system. Many of the notorious inequalities which had contributed towards discrediting the prewar health services were therefore imported unchanged into the NHS. The new health service therefore ossified many of the inherited inequalities in health care, and there was no mechanism for preventing the perpetuation of such evils. Communities in inner cities or former depressed areas, inheriting impoverished services, were likely to witness only limited improvement under the NHS and they were further handicapped by the failure to break away from low expectations.

It has already been pointed out that the Ministry of Health lacked many of the qualities required for the kind of creative leadership needed in a new and innovative service. Since the health departments were under continuous pressure for retrenchment from the Treasury, they were disinclined to take initiatives tending to stimulate demand. Lack of uniformity in standards in part reflected the administrative complexity of the new health service, but it was also partly the consequence of the devolved approach to administration intentionally adopted in order to reassure pre-NHS interest groups that the new service would not entail a shift towards centralised administration. A wide element of local discretion and diversity of practice were regarded as essential features in a service needing to dispel fears among doctors about incursions into clinical freedom, or to attract the supply of capable volunteers needed for health authorities. The new service tried to preserve a humane and intimate ethos and retain the capacity to relate to local circumstances. The devolved system of administration was often invoked by the Ministry of Health in its defence to explain its policy of non-intervention, and as an excuse for adoption of a passive and reactive approach to policy-making.

Given this model of devolved responsibility and absence of central planning control, it was almost impossible to achieve cohesiveness in a system comprising some 800 administrative entities. Although notionally unified, the NHS comprised three separate and entirely different administrative structures.[98] As indicated in the first volume of this study, this 'tripartite system' was adopted reluctantly, in response to the failure to devise a plan for unifying the health services acceptable to the diverse interests participating in health care. The tripartite health service was indeed designed to keep rival interests apart. There were obstacles to planning within each sector of the service and no mechanism to facilitate co-ordination between the three systems at the local level. Local health authorities and Executive Councils at least had the advantage of common boundaries, but medico-political rivalries stood in the way of their collaboration. Although the nationalised hospital service was nominally unified and subjected to integrated planning on a regional basis, in England and Wales the teaching hospitals remained outside this system, while there were damaging ambiguities about the respective authority of the regional and local tiers of administration. Even where hospital services were integrated harmoniously, they tended to act in an imperious manner with respect to their lesser partners in the two other branches of the health service.

It is therefore scarcely surprising that the NHS was unamenable to comprehensive planning initiatives of the kind which were urgently needed by deprived communities of the inner cities, housing estates and new towns. Also without an effective mechanism for involving all three parts of the health service in co-ordinated action, it was difficult to evolve effective policies for care in services relating to tuberculosis, the maternity services, child health, or for other important priority groups such as the elderly, the disabled, the mentally handicapped, or those afflicted by mental disorder, groups which collectively represented a substantial section of the population.

By the tenth anniversary of the NHS, the most widely publicised criticisms related to lack of co-operation between the various arms of the health service. The 800 autonomous units of health service administration were in danger of replicating the omissions, duplications and inefficiencies which characterised the prewar health services, and which the NHS was designed to correct. Although this problem was addressed in various reports, most notably those emanating from the central advisory apparatus, nothing of consequence was done to correct divergent tendencies of health service administration.[99] The notable results achieved in some conspicuous examples of local co-operation, such as in the mental health services in Nottingham and Oldham, merely served to underline the absence of co-ordination elsewhere.[100]

The status of the NHS as a national institution guaranteed a tolerant approach to shortcomings and a degree of immunity from criticism. However, by the date of the tenth anniversary it was apparent to informed observers that all was not well with the new health service. As indicated in chapter IV, some observers were already convinced that the performance of the service could not be radically improved without substantial departure from the organisation established in 1948. As early as 1959 the Treasury concluded that an adequate level of efficiency could not be achieved without reorganisation. It was accepted that it had been a fundamental mistake to entrust £600m of hospital expenditure to some 500 voluntary committees. Such a system could only work by an 'administrative miracle'; the experience of ten years had demonstrated that a multiplicity of authorities had proved themselves to be inefficient and incapable of creating a truly unified health service.[101] The obvious alternatives were either return of the health services to administration by local government, or achieve unification by some other form of reorganisation. Both alternatives had their advocates, but neither was accepted in the main body of the Guillebaud Report, to the evident relief of the Ministry of Health, which cited the authority of this report to defer further consideration of reorganisation; this thorny albeit ultimately inescapable issue was thereby evaded for a further decade.

CHAPTER II

Conservatives and Consolidation

(i) MINISTERS AND DEPARTMENTS

The Conservatives enjoyed thirteen years of continuous responsibility for the National Health Service, extending from October 1951 to October 1964. The previous volume of this study dealt with the administrations of Churchill and Eden. The latter resigned in January 1957 for reasons of ill-health, stress and loss of confidence associated with the Suez affair. The two rivals for the succession were Butler and Macmillan, both of whom had served as Chancellor of the Exchequer. Each was strongly supported within the Conservative Party, but Macmillan was selected.[1]

Under Macmillan, Peter Thorneycroft moved from the Board of Trade to become Chancellor of the Exchequer. Henry Brooke was promoted from the post of Financial Secretary to become Minister of Housing and Local Government. His position as Financial Secretary was taken by Enoch Powell. Two other Ministers who were protagonists in health discussions, Macleod (Minister of Labour) and Boyd-Carpenter (Minister of Pensions and National Insurance), retained under Macmillan the posts they had held under Eden. As described below in greater detail, a major upset occurred in January 1958, when Thorneycroft and Powell resigned, their places being taken by Derick Heathcoat Amory and J E S Simon. When the latter was appointed Solicitor-General in 1959, his place as Financial Secretary to the Treasury was assumed by Sir Edward Boyle.

Supervision of policy discussions in the field of home affairs at this time was the responsibility of the Home Secretary, a post which Macmillan allocated to his rival R A Butler.[2] A further figure in the Macmillan Cabinet contributing to health policy discussions was Charles Hill, who figured prominently in volume I of this study as Secretary of the BMA. In 1957 he entered the Cabinet as Chancellor of the Duchy of Lancaster.

The Conservative administration experienced difficulty in establishing continuity among its Ministers of Health.[3] As noted in volume I, Crookshank was quickly removed from the Ministry of Health to make way for Macleod, who proved his political ability and was promoted to the Ministry of Labour. Eden replaced him with Turton, but Macmillan removed Turton and appointed Vosper. Turton was pro-Eden; he distrusted Macmillan and had no wish to serve in his administration. Turton continued to taunt Macmillan in

31

his capacity as a leader of the anti-European group in Parliament. Macmillan counted Turton among the 'small group of people who really hate me'.[4]

Vosper began his career in the family ships store and exports company in Liverpool. After war service he became a Conservative agent and then MP for Runcorn. In the course of an unenthusiastic review of the Macmillan team in the *Economist*, it was complained that new Ministers like Vosper 'will not stir one corpuscle of blood in the party'; the *Economist* mentioned Walker-Smith and Powell as examples of the few successful new recruits to the senior ranks of the Government.[5]

Vosper soon became ill and required an abdominal operation, which took place in June 1957; as a result of his continuing ill-health, he resigned in September, necessitating a fourth appointment in as many years. Vosper's illness placed additional pressures on John Vaughan-Morgan, his Parliamentary Secretary and the only junior Minister in the Ministry of Health. During the summer months of 1957, Vaughan-Morgan effectively served as Minister of Health. He was rewarded by appointment to Walker-Smith's post at the Board of Trade, when the latter was promoted to the Ministry of Health.[6]

Derek Walker-Smith was a barrister by profession, and son of Sir Jonah Walker-Smith, an engineer, and the first person to be appointed director of housing at the newly-established Ministry of Health from 1919 to 1925; he also served as a Unionist MP from 1931 to 1945. After war service, Derek Walker-Smith entered Parliament as Conservative MP for Hertford. He specialised in building and planning law. He was chairman of the 1922 Committee from 1951-55, and chairman of the Conservative National Advisory Committee on Local Government, 1954-55. He served as Parliamentary Secretary to the Board of Trade, 1955-56, and Economic Secretary to the Treasury, 1956-57. In the Macmillan administration Walker-Smith was appointed Minister of State at the Board of Trade. This brought some acquaintance with the NHS, as for instance over the question of regulation of prices and profits of proprietary medicines available on prescription.[7] With the resignation of Vosper, on 17 September 1957 he was promoted to become Minister of Health. He brought much-needed stability to his office, in which he served unostentatiously for almost three years. His legal background proved particularly helpful with the mental health legislation; it was also useful with the regulation of the pharmaceutical industry, control of dangerous drugs, and legislation relating to various professions engaged in the health service. Walker-Smith later became a Vice-President of Mencap.

Macmillan appointed John Maclay as Secretary of State for Scotland.[8] Maclay, like Vosper, came from a shipping background, but was very much more prosperous. His father was a pious philanthropist and temperance advocate. The younger Maclay was National Liberal MP for Renfrewshire West. Churchill appointed him Minister of Transport and Civil Aviation in 1951, but in 1952 he resigned for reasons of ill-health. Maclay returned to public life in 1956 and was briefly Minister of State at the Colonial Office under Eden, before serving as Secretary of State for Scotland from 1957 to 1962. During Maclay's tenure, responsibility for health was devolved to the junior Ministers, J Nixon Browne until October 1959, and then T G D Galbraith until November 1962.

The General Election in October 1959 was a landslide victory for Macmillan. The Conservative majority increased from 58 to 100; it was Labour's worst result for quarter of a century. This was Macmillan's first electoral test as Prime Minister and it counted as a great personal success.[9] In less than three years, Macmillan and his team dealt with the crisis of confidence associated with the Suez disaster, the lesser storm after the resignation of the Treasury team, continuing instability in the Middle East and Africa, a big rise in unemployment, industrial unrest, and intermittent economic difficulties. The administration was able to take advantage of a general downward trend in Government expenditure and rise in personal savings relative to GNP, enough to allow a margin for tax reductions in the 1959 budget, which helped to generate a sufficient mood of well-being to earn a comfortable victory.[10]

Few major Cabinet changes were made at this point. Macleod, moved out of domestic affairs to become Secretary of State for the Colonies. To his relief, Macmillan found Heathcoat Amory more pliable and congenial than his predecessor. However, Amory was weighed down by his duties and wanted to retire from the Treasury; he was persuaded to stay on until July 1960, when he was replaced by Selwyn Lloyd, another Macmillan loyalist.[11] Boyle stayed on as Financial Secretary. In October 1961, a new senior post of Chief Secretary and Paymaster General was established in the Treasury with a seat in the Cabinet; the first appointee was the former Financial Secretary, Henry Brooke. For a brief time from October 1961 to July 1962, Hill served as Minister of Housing and Local Government, making way for the appointment of Macleod as Chancellor of the Duchy of Lancaster, a post which he held in conjunction with the joint chairmanship of the Conservative Party.

Considering the limitations of his background and interests, Walker-Smith had been a reasonable success as Minister of Health. As indicated below, at certain times he had stubbornly defended the interests of his department, although without being a match for his rival in education, the wily Eccles. However, he was not politically sympathetic to Macmillan, and by 1960 his implacable opposition to

Britain's association with the European Common Market was an additional disadvantage.[12]

Macmillan needed to provide a substitute for Walker-Smith capable of providing dynamic leadership, without enhancing the appetite of the NHS for resources, or losing sight of the need for efficiency. This was a difficult assignment; the public and NHS personnel were restless for more expansionist policies and modernisation, while the Government wanted to avoid adding the NHS to its list of unavoidable commitments to the escalation of public expenditure.

The task of meeting these incompatible objectives fell to John Enoch Powell, whom Macmillan appointed Minister of Health in July 1960. After war service in India, Powell took up a political career. Like Macleod, who came from similar middle-class origins, Powell began his political career by working for the Conservative Party. Powell joined the Parliamentary Secretariat and acted as Joint Director of the Home Affairs Department. He was elected MP for Wolverhampton South West in 1950.[13]

Macleod and Powell attracted attention with their pamphlet, *The Social Services: Needs and Means*, published in 1952.[14] Although Powell played the leading part in drafting this document, Macleod was arguably more actively committed to domestic and social services issues. He also came from a medical family and was chairman of the back-bench committee on health and social security. Consequently it was not unreasonable to appoint Macleod rather than Powell as Minister of Health in 1952. Powell obtained his first Government appointment in 1955, when he became Parliamentary Secretary at the Ministry of Housing and Local Government. As noted above, in 1957 Macmillan gave him the much more elevated post of Financial Secretary to the Treasury. In January 1958 he entered the headlines for the first time when he joined Thorneycroft and Nigel Birch, his colleagues in the Treasury front-bench team, in resigning over the Government's attitude to the control of public expenditure. This led to Powell's temporary exile from Government, but it added to his credentials as a potential successor to Walker-Smith for the health portfolio. Macmillan removed Walker-Smith from his administration and appointed Powell as Minister of Health on 27 July 1960.[15]

There was neither liking nor trusting between Macmillan and Powell, but each served the other's purposes. Macmillan recognised the magnitude of the problems facing Powell: 'to deal with certain immediate difficulties, an immense task lies before you, both psychological and practical. There is really the future of the service and which way it will go'. In an arguably double-edged compliment to the politician he called 'Aristides',[16] Macmillan identified the NHS as an ideal problem for application of the 'energy and integrity of mind which are your characteristics'.[17] Burdening Powell with the health portfolio perhaps appealed to Macmillan's sardonic humour; the new Minister would either make himself unpopular by following his convictions and starving the NHS of resources, or he would suffer the ignominy of inconsistency by demanding a better financial deal for his department. In either case, the Ministry of Health held the potentiality to become the graveyard for Powell's political career.

Macmillan's big and controversial Cabinet shake-up took place in July 1962.[18] This purge, undertaken in a state of panic, was excused on grounds of efficiency and the need to recruit younger talent. Macmillan was censured for the callous handling of his loyal Ministers, and for not promoting some of his most able, albeit less obedient, Ministers, such as Macleod or Eccles.[19]

After a disappointing performance in this office, the 58 year-old Selwyn Lloyd was dismissed from the Government and replaced as Chancellor of the Exchequer by the 45 year-old Reginald Maudling, which was a blow to Macleod who was the more obvious candidate for this appointment.[20] Boyd-Carpenter, the long-standing and effective Minister of Pensions and National Insurance, replaced Brooke as Chief Secretary to the Treasury and Paymaster General. Upon Boyle's promotion to the Ministry of Education, Anthony Barber, Macmillan's former Parliamentary Private Secretary, became Financial Secretary to the Treasury. Eccles expected promotion to the Treasury, but was offered the Board of Trade and refused; he left the Government, but was compensated by elevation to the peerage. Eccles had been Minister of Education for most of the period from 1954 to 1962, a period during which there had been five different Ministers of Health. This continuity, as well as Eccles' not inconsiderable political abilities, had resulted in the success of his department in the competition for resources against the Ministers of Health.

In the 1962 purge, Butler, Macmillan's arch rival, survived and was appointed First Secretary of State. His place as Home Secretary was taken by Brooke. The dismissal of Charles Hill allowed Sir Keith Joseph to enter the Cabinet as Minister of Housing and Local Government. Powell also survived the purge and was indeed promoted to the Cabinet. This was effectively the first time the Minister of Health had achieved Cabinet rank since the time of Bevan.[21] This promotion was no reflection of increased political affinity between Macmillan and Powell; rather, it was a piece of political expediency, since Powell was seen as a reasonably successful Minister, largely on account of his association with the highly-publicised Hospital Plan. His promotion was one of the few pieces of evidence that Macmillan's unpopular Cabinet reshuffle paid some regard to the promotion of talent. Furthermore, higher status entailed little political risk, since Powell was attempting to square the circle by combining modernisation of the NHS with rigorous application of economy. Finally, promotion to the Cabinet was Macmillan's way of denying Powell access to one of the more senior ministerial appointments to which he aspired.[22]

Maclay was one of the notable Macmillan loyalists removed in 1962. His place was taken by Michael Noble, MP for Argyllshire, and Scottish Whip from 1960 to 1962.[23] Noble was relatively inexperienced for such a difficult and senior ministerial appointment, which he took up at the time of a major reorganisation within the Scottish Office. During Noble's brief term of office, the main responsibility for health rested with the junior Ministers, R C Brooman-White, and then J A Stodart. Noble's career prospects were not enhanced by this promotion; he served briefly under Heath as a departmental Minister, but finally left the Government in 1972.

By 1963, the Conservative administration was showing signs of fatigue. The Conservatives were beset by internal divisions over Europe, colonial policy and economic affairs. Unemployment was approaching one million. Following a run of security lapses, the Profumo scandal created adverse publicity for various senior Ministers. Powell's name was the most actively mentioned in the rumours about Ministers considering resignation owing to unhappiness over the handling of the Profumo affair.[24]

A last wave of political turbulence struck the Conservative administration in the autumn of 1963, when illness contributed to Macmillan's decision to resign. The Party conference of October 1963 became the occasion for an intense round of intrigue concerning the succession. Even from his hospital bed, Macmillan showed a capacity to influence events.[25] He and his henchmen determined that the selection went to the 14th Earl of Home, an outside candidate, who had been Foreign Secretary since July 1960. Home was the first peer to become Prime Minister since the 3rd Marquess of Salisbury in 1895. This conclusion was welcome to Macmillan, who was passing through one of his bouts of pessimism; he was depressed about the values of contemporary Britain, where material success and affluence had in his view produced a society in a state of listlessness, introspection and spiritual crisis. Home, he believed, as a representative of the 'old governing class at its best' would inspire instinctive respect for his 'underlying rigidity in matters of principle'.[26] Macmillan originally preferred Hailsham, but realism forced him to change his mind. Douglas-Home may have seemed like a more aristocratic but less clever version of himself, enviable because of his class, but trusted not to outshine.

Home was a compromise candidate, but some of his colleagues were ferociously opposed to the choice of an aristocrat, which they believed represented a piece of recidivism, deeply damaging to the image of the modern Conservative Party. Macleod initially supported Maudling; Powell favoured Butler.[27] Both Macleod and Powell became implicated in a last ditch attempt to block Home, and then became the only two senior Ministers to refuse to serve under him.[28] Home was fatally damaged by adverse publicity, including the jibe emanating from Macleod that his selection was engineered by the 'magic circle' of Etonians controlled by Macmillan.

Only minor changes occurred in the administration as a consequence of Home's leadership.[29] The Ministry of Health was the only major spending department affected. Powell was succeeded by Anthony Barber, who like Powell, had served in the Treasury ministerial team, and had joined the Government as Financial Secretary in July 1962. As noted above, Barber had also served as Macmillan's Parliamentary Private Secretary. Barber had been in office for only a year when Home's administration came to an end.

Health Departments

Permanent Secretaries at the Ministry of Health provided a degree of continuity that compensated for the rapid rotation of Ministers. Between 1919 and 1964 there were 24 ministerial changes during the tenure of only 7 Permanent Secretaries.[30] As noted in the previous volume, Sir John Hawton served as Permanent Secretary from 1951 until 1960. Hawton was a young appointee and he retired at the age of only 56. His period of office was plagued by chronic ill-health, which impaired his qualities of leadership, which was unfortunate, since Hawton possessed unparalleled insight into the NHS, of which he was one of the main architects. Sir Bruce Fraser, his successor was recruited from the Treasury, which was a normal Whitehall pattern in the 1960s. Of the entire cohort of Permanent Secretaries in post in 1966, half had at least some Treasury experience. Most had spent a good part of their careers in the Treasury. Whereas Hawton spent his whole career in the Ministry of Health, Fraser had worked almost exclusively in the Treasury. The change from Hawton to Fraser therefore represented a major shift of culture within the health department, and it was an important preparatory step towards bringing the Ministry of Health into the Whitehall mainstream. The improvement in relations brought about by this change is well-demonstrated below in the account of the background to the hospital plan. From this period also, a small number of senior officials within the Ministry of Health were recruited from the Treasury.[31] This was an additional factor stimulating a more harmonious relationship between the Treasury and the Ministry of Health.

Continuity among the Chief Medical Officers at the Ministry of Health was even greater than among its Permanent Secretaries.[32] Sir John Charles, who served from 1950 to 1960, was a former Medical Officer of Health for Newcastle-upon-Tyne. His successor was Sir George Godber, who was previously a Deputy-CMO. He provided proof that a career within the Ministry of Health need not lead to narrowness of vision or mediocrity. Godber's massive accumulated knowledge was turned to positive effect; the leadership he provided was inspired by a broad vision of health care, informed by latest thinking in the fields of medical science and health care research, on both the national and international fronts.[33]

As noted in the previous chapter, the Ministry of Health experienced a major reorganisation in 1951, after which its staff was halved and its status much reduced.[34] The divisional structure of the Ministry of Health reflected the tripartite character of the NHS. The divisions relating to the regional hospital, family practitioner and local authority services were different in size and character, and only indifferent arrangements existed for their co-ordination. Senior officers within the health department were concentrated in the hospital and family practitioner divisions. The entire hospital service came under a single Under Secretary, while another was responsible for both the Executive Council and local authority services.

The Ministry of Health was dominated by staff whose attitudes were formed in the period before the NHS. They were accustomed to dealing with local government and the National Insurance Committees, where the predominant administrative skills demanded related to regulation, rather than policy and development. The large extent of devolution of responsibility intentionally introduced by the NHS legislation tended to foster this reactive approach to administration. The tendency to treat hospital authorities as if they were local authorities was regarded by a senior Treasury official recruited to the Ministry of Health as 'at the root of the NHS problem'.[35]

It became increasingly evident that the Ministry of Health needed to play a more interventionist role and to some extent the release of more resources for the NHS was conditional on the emergence of such creative leadership. In assuming greater authority over the NHS, the Ministry of Health needed to overcome many disadvantages, some of them associated with the breakup of the department in 1951. For instance, the hospitals division was disadvantaged by its separation from the architectural branch, which along with the Chief Architect had been located in the Ministry of Housing and Local Government as a consequence of the 1951 departmental reorganisation. The hospital work of this branch was neglected and there was indifferent leadership. The Treasury believed that 'with the right man as Chief Architect in the Ministry of Health, millions could be saved in the constructing of hospitals'. [36] The NHS authorities themselves wanted more decisive leadership, and were indeed prepared to accept major changes, but these were precluded 'by the inertia of established ideas in the rest of the Ministry'.[37] In response to criticisms of this kind, the Ministry of Health undertook various leadership initiatives. In 1959 an Advisory Council on Management Efficiency was set up; in 1963 this was reconstructed and strengthened as an Advisory Committee. Other developments included: establishment of a Research and Statistics Unit under a Chief Statistician, the appointment of a Chief Architect, formation of a Design Unit bringing together medical and technical staff concerned with hospital design, and a Hospital O and M Work Study Unit which was a joint Treasury-Ministry of Health venture, intended to supplement the work of the Treasury O and M Unit. In 1958 the Ministry of Health O and M Unit was established on a permanent basis under an Assistant Secretary.[38] In 1959 this unit employed 29 staff; by 1965 it had grown to 202.[39]

The above developments are indicative of change and it is generally conceded that the 1960s marked a distinct alteration in the culture of the Ministry of Health. As described by contemporary observers:

> In the early 1960s the confluence of three remarkable men did a great deal to energise the department and to make its presence felt at all levels of the health service. The minister mainly responsible was Enoch Powell. He was most ably assisted by the then permanent secretary, Sir Bruce Fraser, and by the present chief medical officer, Sir George Godber. All three took up their posts in 1960 and most of the important changes in the ministry can be traced to the next years.[40]

It was widely recognised that the Ministry of Health would not be able to achieve its objectives unless it attained higher status in Whitehall and was headed by a Minister of Cabinet rank. This problem was confronted by Macleod in 1957 in the course of his review of policy in preparation for the next General Election. Macleod recommended assimilation of the Ministry of Labour and National Service with the Ministry of Pensions and National Insurance to form a comprehensive Ministry of Social Security. But he also realised that rationalisation on this front would expose the lack of integration of responsibility for health. He observed that the Ministry of Health was 'a Ministry not for health but for the National Health Service'.[41] It was therefore recommended that the Ministry of Health should assimilate health and environmental control functions

39

from other departments. Macleod claimed support for this idea from Enoch Powell. Macmillan made tentative soundings about these proposals, but they were not pursued in view of strenuous opposition of Boyd-Carpenter, the Minister of Pensions and National Insurance, who argued that his department had still not effectively recovered from the merger of Pensions with National Insurance, and that the imminent recasting of the National Insurance scheme required the undiluted energies of his officials.[42] This brief episode is scarcely worth mentioning, except for the fact that it clearly left a mark on the collective political memory. Paradoxically, the same proposal was reintroduced in 1962, this time by Boyd-Carpenter himself, who tried to persuade Macmillan to establish a giant department of social welfare and pensions, including all functions associated with social security and health. On this occasion the scheme was vetoed by Powell, who claimed that it was unsound to combine into a single department two incompatible services, one concerned with payment of benefits, and the other with provision of caring services.[43] Nevertheless, Boyd-Carpenter's idea fell on fertile ground and was even embodied in the 1964 General Election manifesto. Indeed, by this stage, the principle of amalgamation was embraced by both parties.[44]

Sir Bruce Fraser was exceptional in transferring from health to a parallel civil service appointment. All of his predecessors as Permanent Secretaries at the Ministry of Health were occupying their last career posts. By contrast, during our period, the headship of the Department of Health for Scotland/Scottish Home and Health Department was usually a staging post in a career within the Scottish Office.[45] John Anderson, was recruited from the Scottish Home Department; he served as Secretary of the Department of Health from 1956 to 1959; he then became Secretary of the Scottish Home Department, in 1962 retaining oversight for the amalgamation of his department with the Department of Health for Scotland, which took place on 1 June 1962, before in 1963 moving on briefly to become Chairman of the Board of Customs and Excise.[46] When in 1959 Anderson left the Scottish Department of Health, he was succeeded by Douglas Haddow, who had risen through the ranks in the Health Department, where he had gained intimate experience of the workings of the NHS. Upon the SHHD amalgamation in 1962, Haddow transferred briefly to the Scottish Development Department before in 1965 succeeding Sir William Murrie as Permanent Under-Secretary of State at the Scottish Office. In 1963 Ronald Johnson was appointed Secretary of the reorganised Scottish Home and Health Department; Johnson's previous career had been in the Scottish Home Department.[47] During the period 1956 to 1972 (with the exception of the Haddow tenure from 1959 to 1962), the senior appointees responsible for the health service in Scotland were recruited from a Scottish Home Department background.

As in the case of their counterparts in London, especially after 1940, the Chief Medical Officers in Scotland tended to occupy their posts for a substantial period.[48] Dr H K Cowan, who served from 1954 to 1964, was previously MOH for Kent. He was arguably a less formidable presence than either his predecessor or successor.

Prior to 1962, the Department of Health was similar to the Ministry of Health before its break-up in 1951, combining health, local government, planning and housing functions.[49] The combined Scottish Home and Health Department was something like a hybrid between the post-1951 Ministry of Health and the Home Office. The health services and professional sides of the department were little changed; they resembled the professional and health divisional organisation of the Ministry of Health.[50] Such functions as establishments and finance were shared between the home and health sides of the department, anticipating the sharing arrangements eventually introduced between the health and social security sides of DHSS after 1968. In the 1950s, about 200 out of about 1,000 administrative staff within the Department of Health were specifically engaged in health service work. In addition about 60 professional and technical staff were involved with the health service. Although the health departments in London and Edinburgh were broadly similar in their organisation, there were many differences in detail, some of them connected with differences in the health service legislation. For instance, the Scottish department was directly responsible for providing health centres; also, whereas the Ministry of Health had direct administrative links with the teaching hospitals, this was not the case in Scotland, since teaching hospitals were absorbed into the regional hospital board structure in 1948.

SHHD was an odd amalgamation, with one half of its staff being concerned with prisons. However, the health side of the department was well-integrated and its organisation permitted greater co-ordination of activity at senior levels than was possible within the Ministry of Health. This organisation, together with the more centralised structure of the NHS in Scotland, encouraged a more interventionist approach to health service policy than was found within the Ministry of Health.[51]

As noted in the previous volume, Wales exercised only a limited amount of freedom of action in the field of health. The Welsh Board of Health performed some minor administrative functions; Wales also constituted a single hospital region. Otherwise few concessions were made to a separate Welsh identity. From 1951 a Cabinet Minister exercised oversight for Welsh affairs. From 1957 this function was performed by the Minister of Housing and Local

Government, a post that was occupied by Sir Keith Joseph from July 1962 onwards. This incremental advance made little difference to the administration of the health services in Wales. Committees of investigation habitually included a single Welsh member, but Wales was fortunate if it received special consideration in reports, statistical documents or White Papers. One small cosmetic change occurred in 1961, when the Government gave support to a private member's Bill which had the effect of changing the title of the Welsh Regional Hospital Board to Welsh Hospital Board, to remove the offensive suggestion that Wales occupied no greater status than the fourteen English hospital regions.[52] Despite this change, the important Hospital Plan 1962 and the associated plan for Community Care 1963 observed custom by treating Wales as last in order of the fifteen regions.

(ii) OPPORTUNITY STATE

As noted in the previous chapter, by the tenth anniversary of the NHS, the Conservatives had come to tolerate the NHS; indeed they saw no problem in adopting a state health service as one of the institutions in what they increasing called their 'opportunity state'. However, the Conservative administration inherited its Labour predecessor's obsession that the health service represented a potentially dangerous drain on national resources. Containing this perceived threat dominated the Conservative administration's thinking about the health service. The health services therefore tended to be selected as a first target in campaigns to contain public expenditure. The miscellaneous assortment of direct charges, as well as the insurance contribution associated with the health service, proved to be a fertile source of revenue. Under the Conservatives, the consistent application of a stern regime of containment exercised an efficient break on expenditure on health care, while the opportunistic exploitation of charges and the NHS Contribution reduced the extent of its dependence on the Exchequer. Consequently, while anxieties about excessive spending on the health service were justified with respect to specific instances such as the rising cost of pharmaceuticals, in reality, on the basis of the impact of a succession of retrenchment campaigns, by 1964 it was no longer realistic to regard the NHS as the indulged child of the welfare state.

Increasing resources were required to maintain a constant level of service, owing to such factors as the increasing population of the elderly, a high birth rate, medical innovation, and the need to replace obsolete hospital stock. A brief examination of the period from 1957/58 to 1963/64 indicates that the NHS improved to a modest extent upon the resources record described in the previous chapter, but hardly to the extent required to meet the accumulating backlog of its obligations.

Over this period, the share of national resources devoted to the NHS rose slowly from 3.58 to 4.10 per cent of GDP.[53] The share of NHS costs derived from the Consolidated Fund fell from 81.9 to 76.5 per cent, while the share from local taxation and direct charges remained constant at about 4 and 5 per cent respectively; the main increase therefore emanated from the NHS Contribution.[54]

At 1970 prices, over the period from 1958 to 1964, expenditure on the NHS increased by 34.1 per cent in cost terms, but this reduced to 20.0 per cent in volume terms. This represents an average annual rise of 5.7 per cent in cost terms, and 3.3 per cent in volume terms. Similar conclusions derive from cost or volume estimates relating specifically to current expenditure. However, the pattern was not entirely uniform. Thus, the important volume estimate applied to current expenditure shows a 15.8 per cent increase over this period, but after a rise to a peak of about 3.5 per cent under Walker-Smith, there was a reversal of this trend, and much lower rates of growth under Powell, with a recovery to the former level of growth in 1964.[55] Over the last six years of the Conservative administration, the increase in expenditure on the NHS was about one-third less than education, while the rise for health and welfare combined was also lower than the increases in housing, roads, or social security.[56] During this period education increased its share of social services expenditure from 23.8 to 25.7 per cent, whereas the NHS fell from 21.6 to 20.0 per cent.[57]

Each annual round of the regime of rigid containment of NHS spending added to the embarrassment of health Ministers, owing to their failure to capture the resources needed to meet the demands of modernisation. It was self-evident that the health service, especially the hospitals, were not benefiting from the ambitious programmes adopted for defence, nuclear power, roads, air transport, housing, and education. Each Minister in turn attempted to set an agenda for modernisation, but, as seen below, with indifferent results. As in the earlier part of the decade, increments in NHS spending were sufficient to keep up with essential wage and price increases, but with little else.

Even though modernisation of the health service remained an elusive goal, Ministers were ever hopeful that a greater volume of resources would be forthcoming to meet their most urgent priorities. For instance, in 1957 the Minister of Health outlined main priorities for the future development of the health service. He particularly called for a 'new drive' in hospital development, which he justified on the basis of: redistribution of population due to rehousing, the need to provide advanced diagnostic and treatment facilities, more extensive outpatient, accident and emergency departments, more decent facilities for the chronic sick and those affected by mental illness or mental handicap, and finally the urgent requirement for new dental hospitals. Even in 1957 it was stressed that high priority needed to be given to maximisation of primary and community care in order to reduce pressure on expensive hospital facilities. Although the Minister commended development of domiciliary services, and introduction of such facilities as chiropody, he attached greater importance to the building residential facilities for the elderly.[58] The Minister's priorities seem innocuous and self-evidently justifiable, but there is little evidence that his department and NHS authorities were in a position to launch a comprehensive programme of hospital development. Also many of their ideas about capital development, especially the building of new mental, mental handicap and other long-term accommodation were doubtfully appropriate. There was little evidence of ability to undertake planned initiative in the fields of primary and community care. By this date, health centres had dropped off the agenda as a focus for thinking on co-ordination of services, and no obvious alternative had emerged. In practice, the strengths and weaknesses of planning initiatives of the late-fifties were largely irrelevant. In view of the continuing inability of the health departments to escape from the strait-jacket of resource restraint, any planning exercises were likely to be little more than an exercise in fiction.

(iii) FINANCING THE HEALTH SERVICE

As the previous section indicates, the Government was largely successful in preventing the new health service from making greater incursions into the Consolidated Fund. This was the preoccupying feature of Conservative management of the health service and its success in meeting this objective is recorded in the following pages.[59] It was already noted in the previous volume of this study that the retrenchment regime was well in place by 1958. These efforts were not invariably successful. For instance, apart from a reduction in capital expenditure on hospitals, the economy exercise conducted by the Swinton Committee in 1954 achieved no savings in the health sector. The 'Five Year Survey' exercise begun in the following year was a more determined affair. Social Services Ministers were urged to introduce major changes in policy. It was proposed to adopt a ceiling for social services expenditure for each year within the five-year review period; the Ministers concerned would then be required to devise their priorities and agree on a distribution within the confines of the allocated total. This proposal can be seen as one of the germs of the PESC arrangements introduced at the instigation of the same individuals more than five years later. Although at the time this was regarded as a 'brilliant idea', and as an important method of educating social services Ministers, in the short term it came to nothing.[60] In the absence of a taste for long-term thinking, Ministers were pressed to offer an immediate package of cuts amounting to £146m. These ambitious goals were abandoned, but minor economies were made, such as an increase in the school meals charge from 9d to 10d, which maintained the charge at the level of the price of the food ingredients. This increased charge was introduced in September 1956. The five-year review left one significant legacy with respect to the health services in the form of the increased prescription charge, introduced on 1 December 1956.[61] It is doubtful whether this economy would have been agreed without the unforeseen economic emergency precipitated by the Suez campaign.

Looking back on the unproductive labours of the ministerial Social Services Committee, the Treasury expressed frustration that nearly all of its proposals for economies were immediately rejected, while most others were pigeon-holed for consideration at a later date. The device of a ministerial committee was therefore judged to be counterproductive, while in view of the failure of the Guillebaud Committee to recommend economies in the NHS, the same conclusion was reached about enquires conducted by an independent committee.[62]

Macmillan and the NHS Economy

The year 1956 ended on a note of frustration for the Treasury. The original target for social services savings was revised downwards. As on previous occasions, little progress was made with proposals to eliminate the general dental service and supplementary ophthalmic service, with introduction of a hotel charge for hospital patients, or with removal of subsidies for school meals, school milk, welfare milk and other welfare foods. Even the increased prescription charge was less than was originally wanted, with the result that the annual yield was £5m rather than the £25m originally anticipated.

The Treasury was looking for a much more substantial reduction in the 1957/58 estimates than £5m. The social services review having exhausted all the obvious sources of economy, the Treasury reluctantly fell back on considering an increase in the NHS Contribution. This 'health stamp' had remained unaltered since the outset of the NHS, at a level of 10d (8½d employee, 1½ d employer). There was some ground for arguing that the NHS Contribution was originally expected to provide about 20 per cent of the cost of the NHS, but the actual yield was only about 10 per cent at the beginning of the NHS; since then it had fallen to about 6 per cent.[63] During the deliberations of the Social Services Committee, the Minister of Health had expressed a preference for increasing the health stamp, which seemed altogether less problematical than most of the rival proposals for economy under consideration. After the disappointing outcome of the prescription charge exercise, Macmillan, as Chancellor of the Exchequer, was attracted by the prospect that the health stamp might constitute a substantial source of additional revenue for the NHS, perhaps as much as £100m, which would establish a 20 per cent norm for the contribution from the National Insurance Fund.

Despite its obvious attractions, the Treasury was unenthusiastic about pursuing this alternative; the Scottish Office was also unsympathetic, while the Ministry of Pensions and National Insurance was vehemently opposed. These departments argued that designation of the insurance system as an ear-marked source of additional funds for the NHS would encourage uncontrolled expansion in health service expenditure and fatally undermine efforts to impose a more economical regime. The Ministry of Pensions and National Insurance also pointed out that increasing the NHS Contribution would exacerbate the problems associated with the mounting deficit in the National Insurance Fund. Any rise in the deductions for the health stamp was likely to spark off pressures for a general increase in insurance benefits and add to demands for wage increases. Finally, it was pointed out that the health stamp, since it involved flat-rate deductions, was an inequitable form of taxation, unreasonably transferring the cost of the NHS to the least well-paid. On the basis of such formidable arguments against an increase in the health stamp, the Treasury recommended that on this occasion, as in previous reviews, the objections should be regarded as decisive.[64]

This verdict was confirmed without demur at senior levels within the Treasury and it was sanctioned by Henry Brooke, the Financial Secretary, who recommended that the Minister of Health should be told to find cuts by legislation for a hotel charge or an increased charge for dentures.[65] On this occasion the officials received a petulant reaction from Macmillan: 'I do not agree. But we must argue it out. Remember that Britain is on the verge of bankruptcy'.[66]

In further discussion, Macmillan seemed to revert to the Treasury line. It was recorded that he would delay any increase in the health stamp until such date that there was a general review of National Insurance charges and benefits, with the expectation that this might be deferred until 1958.[67] However, Macmillan was not entirely persuaded to abandon the idea of increasing the NHS Contribution. At the Cabinet meeting on 8 January 1957, the last occasion on which Eden presided over business discussions, Macmillan announced that he wanted to reduce the 1957/58 estimates by £300m and make tax cuts amounting to £50m.[68] His main target was defence, but also he wanted £80-£100m savings on the social services, especially the NHS.

He proposed a reduction of £15-£20m on the NHS estimates, to be achieved through increased charges, but also he raised the possibility that £50m could be generated by increasing the NHS Contribution by 1s. He appreciated that the cuts proposed would require changes in policy, but he urged that drastic changes were necessary. Boyd-Carpenter and Turton expressed reservations about Macmillan's approach, but Eden summed up in favour of his Chancellor.

Enter Thorneycroft
At this stage, further discussions of economies in the NHS were interrupted by the resignation of Eden. The debate was continued by many of the same individuals, but some of them occupying different offices. Vosper, the Minister of Health, was new to the scene. The notable change was the more aggressive nature of the Treasury team, which exhibited determination to achieve reductions in estimates for the social services for the financial year 1957/58. Already, on 14 January 1957, Thorneycroft drew up an extensive list of possible economies in defence and civil spending. With respect to the health service, he favoured a big reduction in capital expenditure and an increase in the NHS Contribution, and he asked for further briefing on the 'drug racket'.[69] A few days later, the new Chancellor of the Exchequer developed his ideas more fully; his goal to 'produce more, to spend less, to tax lower' would entail a 'harsh but rewarding struggle'. Having attained an adequate level of social security, it was now necessary to create 'real opportunity as well', a goal which would entail giving the first priority to education and technical training: 'we should feature it in a big way'. In order to afford this degree of educational expansion, it would be necessary to limit other social services obligations, 'either new services must be postponed or where the cost of old ones is rising, the increase must be paid by those who in the main draw benefit from them'.[70] In preparation for his first discussion with Cabinet colleagues on the state of the economy, Thorneycroft accepted that they should 'edge forwards' in education, while the health service should be cut or financed by a higher yield from the health stamp.[71] Powell suggested that £15m might be shaved off the estimates without making policy changes. He also wanted as a guide for subsequent years to evolve a ceiling for Exchequer liability to the NHS. The mood of Thorneycroft and Powell was quickly transmitted to their officials. It was agreed that, with respect to public expenditure, they would take 'a very tough line this year and that the general doctrine should be no expansion'.[72]

Like his predecessor, Vosper continued to drag his feet over economies. Vosper insisted that he needed £325m for maintaining the service, which entailed cutting back on development commitments from the agreed minimum needed of 3 per cent to less than 2 per cent. Turton had made a similar concession the previous year. Vosper also agreed to consider cutting £3m off the agreed levels of the new hospital capital programme. In his capacity as Chancellor of the Exchequer, Macmillan had already pressed for this reduction, but Turton had refused. In order to increase the rate of hospital modernisation, Vosper reluctantly offered to consider abolishing the dental service or increasing charges, but he preferred Turton's previous suggestion that the NHS Contribution should be increased.[73]

Thorneycroft reviewed the papers concerning the NHS Contribution, rejected the advice of the officials, and followed Macmillan in favouring an increase. Thorneycroft and Macmillan were also united in sympathy for the hospital boarding charge. To confirm his radical credentials, the new Chancellor also suggested that his colleagues should consider abolishing the general dental service for those over the age of 15, that an economic cost should be charged for school meals and milk, and for all welfare foods for mothers and infants, and finally that family allowances should be removed from the second child. It was calculated that the entire package would generate savings of about £90m.[74]

At an informal meeting of Ministers, Thorneycroft adopted the more moderate target of £30m for social services economies. The Chancellor's aggressive stance yielded some signs of compromise. The Ministers agreed that a package of cuts was unavoidable, but they were entirely at odds over the choice of economies. Vosper rehearsed the objections to all proposals for cuts or charges; by a process of elimination he was left with the rise in the health stamp; he was supported by Macleod and Maclay. The latter was also willing to consider the hotel charge and reduction of family allowances. Charles Hill's favoured option was elimination of the dental service and increasing the cost of welfare foods. Boyd-Carpenter maintained his opposition to increasing the NHS Contribution; he was the Minister most unsympathetic with the approach of Thorneycroft, but reluctantly agreed to consider the hotel charge or abolition of the dental service.[75]

Because the Conservative administration called the Social Services Committee of Ministers into existence for only for specific purposes, and because the Home Affairs Committee was not a particularly appropriate forum, the debate over economies in the social services was taken directly to the Cabinet. As already indicated, this placed the Minister of Health and other Ministers outside the Cabinet, such as the Minister of Pensions and National Insurance, at a disadvantage, because they were only present for discussions specifically relating to their departments, but absent at wider discussion of the state of the economy.

Thorneycroft's preliminary skirmish with Cabinet colleagues on the question of social services economies occurred on 21 January 1957. At this stage he announced a target of £50m reduction in public expenditure, warning that the NHS 'must bear a large proportion' of this burden. He was unwilling to accept minor reductions or the health stamp increase as a contribution towards this target; instead he wanted elimination of 'some less essential service' such as the general dental service. Vosper asked for time to consider the implications of abolishing the dental service, and he repeated his preference for a rise in the NHS Contribution. Boyd-Carpenter pointed out some of the dangers of increasing the NHS Contribution. Macmillan gave no decisive guidance to his colleagues.[76]

Preparatory discussions between senior Ministers (not including Vosper or Boyd-Carpenter) exposed continuing antipathy to specific cuts, but the Prime Minister was surprised by the enthusiasm displayed by Heathcoat Amory and Macleod for placing the NHS on a contributory basis. They appreciated the objections to increasing the NHS Contribution. As an alternative, they evolved the notion that the NHS Contribution should be abolished, and replaced by an entirely new NHS deduction from income, which could then be expanded at will, without risk of implications for the National Insurance Fund. Both Prime Minister and Chancellor were excited by this 'quite new policy for the Health Service - not a policy to dismantle it but to put it on to a contributory basis'. Initially it was suggested that the 10d NHS Contribution should be replaced by the new Health Stamp at 1s 6d, but Macmillan favoured 'springing' the new stamp at 2s. Unlike the NHS Contribution, which involved both employee and employer elements, it was proposed that the Health Stamp should be entirely paid by the employee with no arrangements for opting out.[77]

In his memorandum prepared for the Cabinet, Thorneycroft gave prominence to the proposal to increase the NHS Contribution, which was attractive by virtue of its high potential yield, but he was now more circumspect about the merits of this tax, which he admitted was 'a regressive tax applied to wage earners, a poll tax which would be applied to a limited class of people in a service available to all'. He therefore placed the emphasis on other alternatives for cuts and charges. He attacked predecessors for having shrunken 'from measures necessary to cut expenditure decisively'. In view of the need for political prudence, he proposed that Ministers should commit themselves to a long-term programme for restructuring their social services commitments.[78] Vosper objected to abolition of dental charges, but was willing to sacrifice welfare foods. On the other hand Hailsham, as Minister of Education, was vigorously opposed to reducing subsidies on nutritional supplements for mothers, infants and schoolchildren, or to abolition of family allowance on the second child. He calculated that the Chancellor of the Exchequer's proposals could add as much as 19s a week to the liabilities of a poor family with two children. On the basis of such prospects, he 'wished to vigorously contest the proposition that a sound economy can be assisted by penalising parenthood'. Boyd-Carpenter also attacked the idea of abolishing family allowances which, he pointed out, went against their recent General Election pledges, and was contrary to their general policy of increasing the family allowance to compensate for reductions in food subsidies.[79]

The social services cuts were discussed briefly at the Cabinet meeting on 31 January and then more fully on 5 February.[80] The meeting was confused because it was dealing both with specific and often trivial economies, but also with the wider issue of financing the welfare state. Thorneycroft insisted on pursuing some of the smaller cuts, but his attention focused on big changes of policy. He concluded that the welfare state was a heavier liability than the economy could sustain. It was therefore necessary to introduce major changes of policy, and in particular he favoured taking steps to place the NHS on a contributory basis.

Macmillan was unhappy about the proposal to eliminate the family allowance on the second child, but he detected sufficient support for the other cuts to merit further discussion. His own preferences were for increasing the price of welfare milk and school meals, but he was enthusiastic about neither. Even if selective economies of this kind were introduced, the Prime Minister suggested that they should be accompanied by steps to place the NHS on a contributory basis and he proposed 1s 6d as the starting level for the new Health Stamp. He believed that the 'Insurance principle has got hold on the public mind - cf. friendlies etc. before State insurance came in. NHS is government boon to middle classes (clerks etc.) - should keep it universal, but make contributions a bigger feature. Beveridge assumed 1/3rd cost from contribution: now only 1/12th. Flexible instrument for future. Better than once-for-all measures'.[81]

Discussion naturally concentrated on the new proposals for the Health Stamp, the supporters of which hoped would provide an escape from other problematical economies. Boyd-Carpenter outlined some of the likely objections, but Heathcoat Amory, Maclay, Macleod, Salisbury and Vosper were supportive. It was recorded that there was 'general agreement that the NHS should now be established on a compulsory contributory basis'; the administrative details and starting level for the new stamp were left for future determination.

Officials within the Treasury were less than euphoric about the suggestion to extend the contributory principle; a senior figure asked

Thorneycroft to consider whether 'the British working man can be prepared to carry water on both shoulders?', while a colleague warned that 'trade unions and the working class generally are revolting against the contributory principle'. The new charge would draw attention to the fact that compulsory deductions from income were being extended, while benefit rates were steadily declining in value.[82]

The Prime Minister held a dinner party on 3 February 1957 to consider further progress; it was agreed to investigate further the possibility of a separate Health Stamp, and also proposals for savings on welfare foods. A minimum yield of £35m for 1957/58 was expected from the two exercises.[83] To the disappointment of the enthusiasts for the contributory principle, investigations by the Ministry of Pensions and National Insurance soon established that it was not feasible to introduce a separate health contribution. All of the alternatives were found to be impracticable. Ministers therefore retreated to the proposal for increasing the existing NHS stamp.[84] Although this also was objectionable, it was the only means to rescue the contributory principle.[85] The Cabinet faced Boyd-Carpenter's assertion that the rise in the health stamp should be deferred until there was a general review of deductions and benefits. This was rejected, and it was agreed to double the NHS Contribution to 1s 8d. It was also agreed to increase the school meals charge from 10d to 1s, and welfare milk from 1 1/2 d to 4d a pint, both with effect from 1 April 1957.[86]

Discussion of the NHS Contribution Bill at the Home Affairs Committee revealed an unanticipated degree of hostility to the underlying principle, but it was too late to delay or modify the Bill. Many points of detail remained to be settled, in the course of which Boyd-Carpenter attempted to modify the increase from 10d to 9d, in order to produce a total National Insurance deduction of a round figure, 13s 6d, but this was not accepted. It was agreed to split the 10d increase with 8d paid by the employee and 2d by the employer, in order to avoid a half-penny appearing in the employee's total insurance deductions. Under the agreed increase to the NHS Contribution, the employee paid 1s 4 1/2d and the employer 3 1/2d. The rise in the contribution rate was announced by Thorneycroft on 19 February and by Vosper on 4 March 1957.[87] To the Government's relief, the NHS Contributions Bill attracted an unexpectedly small amount of opposition when it was discussed in the House of Commons. The two full days allocated for debating the Bill were not fully taken up, and the Third Reading lasted for only 45 minutes.[88] The increased contributions under the National Health Service and National Insurance (Contributions) Act 1957 took effect from 1 September 1957. The increased stamp restored the NHS

Contribution to 9 per cent of the cost of the NHS, the level operative at the outset of the service; the joint share from the contribution and direct charges stood at 14 per cent.

The results of this retrenchment exercise were presented in Thorneycroft's budget statement on 9 April 1957. For the year 1957/58 he reported that defence estimates would be less than 1956/57 by £95m, while civil estimates would be limited to an increase of £189m. On the basis of this success in holding down supply expenditure, he was able to offer a variety of tax reductions amounting to about £130m.

Exit Thorneycroft

With respect to NHS expenditure, the Treasury accepted the increased charges agreed in February 1957 as defeat. Welfare foods were a peripheral item, whereas the increased NHS Contribution was merely a tax increase to fund additional expenditure. The Treasury continued its traditional policy of keeping 'grinding away on any parts of this large expenditure which we consider may be open to compression'.[89] In preparing for the autumn campaign over the 1958/59 estimates, the Treasury considered in a desultory manner such options as charges for visits to out-patient departments or general practitioners, increased dental and eye service charges, abolition of these services, or introduction of a limited list of drugs. Powell asked for a review of health and welfare charges with a view to reducing the 'haphazard system to better order'.[90]

In July 1957 the Home Affairs Committee agreed to place limitations on the supply of orange juice, but they were not in favour of complete removal of this nutritional subsidy.[91] This trivial economy had been under consideration for some time. Defenders of orange juice insisted on taking guidance from experts, and in 1956 a committee under Lord Cohen was set up to consider this issue. Its report was published in July 1957, but the experts were not unanimous in their recommendations. The Treasury regarded the orange juice supplement as an anachronism, preserved for purposes of 'waving the flag of empire'.[92] In the face of opposition from the Colonial Office, the Home Affairs Committee accepted that it would be safe to terminate the supply of subsidised orange juice to 2-5 year olds, while retaining the provision for pregnant women and those under 2. A saving of less than £1m in a full year was anticipated, and it was likely that the saving would be less owing to the need to compensate West Indian producers, whose entry into orange production had been induced by the Colonial Office entirely for the sake of this service. Powell, Thorneycroft and Macmillan were annoyed at this limp response from the Home Affairs Committee.[93] The matter was therefore referred to the Cabinet, which agreed to the partial removal of the subsidy from September 1957, and it asked for investigation of the possibility of complete elimination of this subsidy in 1958.[94]

The orange juice affair indicated the extreme sense of agitation in the Treasury team of Ministers concerning what they perceived as wild excesses in public expenditure. Although in the spring of 1957 Thorneycroft was receiving optimistic messages from his Budget Committee, he wrote to the Prime Minister about the dangers of public expenditure, predicting that there was 'still a good chance, that we will have an economic crash'. The Chancellor's immediate instinct was to call for rigid containment of public expenditure. It was a 'prerequisite to any solution...that we should not spend more than were are spending already'. He felt besieged by pressures for additional public expenditure commitments. In demanding Macmillan's support, Thorneycroft told the Prime Minister that their most pressing problem was not emanating from foreign policy or defence, nor from spending too little on the social services, but from 'progressive decline - even ultimately the collapse - of the currency and the dramatic and world consequences which must follow'.[95] This apocalyptic forecast evoked a relaxed response from Macmillan, who only gave backing for selective public expenditure savings and for continuation of the credit squeeze.[96]

In July 1957 Thorneycroft called on his colleagues to hold down spending in 1958/59 to the level of the current year, and he proposed to undertake a review of public investment. Following an unsympathetic response among Cabinet colleagues, the Chancellor appealed to the Prime Minister to support his call for keeping down civil estimates to the level of the current year.[97] The Prime Minister complied somewhat grudgingly, dispatching a minute to Ministers along the lines of a draft provided by the Chancellor.[98]

Thorneycroft's categorical line on public expenditure was taken in the face of advice from his officials; it signified an increasing tendency to swim against the tide of thinking within the Treasury. Given his aim to reduce taxation, control of public expenditure assumed primary importance among the fiscal measures designed to control the money supply, reduce inflation and suppress the level of wage demands. Thorneycroft appreciated that his deflationary measures were likely to increase unemployment, but this was regarded as an acceptable and necessary consequence of the achievement of currency stabilisation. He was the first Chancellor of the Exchequer to depart from the doctrine of full-employment which had held sway since 1944 White Paper on Employment Policy. Although his policies were primarily dictated by the domestic agenda, he invoked the spectre of devaluation to goad along his recalcitrant colleagues, and devaluation of the French franc added to the strength of his determination.

The Cabinet went along with Thorneycroft, but they were uneasy about the hardship and bitterness likely to stem from their policies. The Prime Minister reassured his colleagues that 'the total value of bank advances will affect many people, of course, but not in the same way as cutting down their teeth, or spectacles, or wages or welfare milk, or other forms of economy'. The people were unlikely to notice when school building or other capital investment was being rephased. Also, by past standards 2-3 per cent unemployment was 'still negligible'. He was therefore confident that 'we shall lose no votes and injure nobody'.[99]

In the autumn of 1957 Britain therefore embarked on Thorneycroft's brief experiment with proto-monetarism, but with little understanding or sympathy from within the Cabinet. On 19 September Thorneycroft presented his deflationary package, involving a rise in the Bank Rate to 7 per cent, ceilings on capital expenditure by nationalised industries and local authorities, and a limit on the volume of bank advances.[100] As a subsidiary feature of his announcement, Thorneycroft mentioned that 'steps have been taken and are being taken to limit current civil and defence expenditure'.[101] It was therefore by no means evident that teeth, spectacles, welfare milk would be exempt from the retrenchment package.

The Chancellor persisted with his objective of limiting total estimates for 1958/59 to the level of the current year. Powell was committed to the same objective. He warned the Chancellor that the provisional estimates submitted by departments would amount to the biggest increase ever recorded in peace time. It was conceded that these increases were primarily the result of the Government's own policies rather than the effects of wage and price increases. He warned that 'we cannot go blundering on as we are at present', and proposed that they should stand up to the farmers, cut out civil defence, impose new health service charges, drastically cut colonial, commonwealth and foreign aid, and halt public building at home and abroad.[102] With respect to the health service, Powell suggested that hospital authorities should be told to absorb all minor increases in costs, including wage agreements, within their existing allocations, and he reintroduced proposals for the hospital boarding charge, cuts in nutritional subsidies, and the limited list for drugs.[103]

In view of the resignation of Vosper on grounds of ill-health and the recent appointment of a new and untried Minister, the NHS perhaps looked like a soft target. However, Treasury officials were visibly disconcerted and annoyed by the implied rebuke from Powell. They denied that the problem was as serious as claimed by Powell; they refuted any suggestion that past policy could be construed as blundering on. Ministers were warned that decisions had been 'conditioned by political and economic forces which are real and compelling: they cannot be disregarded, and violent action will make matters worse'.[104]

Thorneycroft was more in tune with Powell than with his officials. He described the concession of supplementary estimates as a 'swollen outturn', or a 'swingeing increase', which he regarded as a 'major defeat'. He believed that despite his September announcement they were witnessing the beginning of a wage-price spiral which would lead to uncontrolled inflation. These circumstances required a quick exercise to cut provisional estimates for 1958/59 by £200m.[105] Thorneycroft advised the Prime Minister that the proposed increase in estimates 'is clearly not a position which I could defend'.[106] Macmillan met a group of senior Ministers to discuss this ultimatum; it was agreed to give general support to Thorneycroft, but they insisted that where changes in policy were involved, these must be consistent with the Government's long-term programme.[107]

In the course of Christmas holiday season, the unacceptable excess was revised down from £200m to £175m, and then to £153m.[108] Treasury Ministers aimed to reach this target by three roughly equal packages of cuts, the first by pruning the existing estimates, the second by reductions in defence expenditure, and the third by reductions in civil expenditure.

This diversification enabled the shopping list of civil expenditure cuts to be reduced from seven to four items.[109] Thorneycroft's final proposals adopted the £153m target for savings, to be achieved by pruning estimates, abolition of family allowance on the second child or other health and welfare economies, and by reductions in defence expenditure. He appreciated that these savings could not be effected without major policy decisions, and that 'economies of this nature would be difficult to achieve and politically unpopular. But they were unavoidable if the Government were to succeed in imposing an effective check on inflation and averting the threat to the stability of sterling'.[110]

With encouragement from Powell, Thorneycroft threw down the gauntlet before his Ministerial colleagues, in full knowledge of their likely adverse reaction.[111] Even before issue of the Chancellor's ultimatum, Macmillan realised that his Chancellor was making unrealistic demands; Thorneycroft wanted 'some swingeing cuts in the Welfare State expenditure - more, I fear, than is feasible politically'. A meeting of senior Ministers on 23 December 1957 exposed bitter opposition to Thorneycroft's proposals, while Thorneycroft was intransigent, even to the extent of implying that he was considering resignation. Ministers were especially opposed to Thorneycroft's favourite idea of abolishing the family allowance on the second child, but they were also unsympathetic to his second favourite, the abolition of the ophthalmic service. Although Macmillan called for full support for the Chancellor, he urged that a selective approach to the cuts was necessary, advising that it was 'essential to bear in mind the possible impact of any significant changes in the structure of the social services on the attitude of organised labour to the prosecution of further wage claims'. Macmillan thereby broadly implied that the Chancellor's proposals risked being in conflict with the Government's objective of wage stability.[112]

At the Cabinet meeting on 31 December 1957, not attended by departmental Ministers, Thorneycroft plainly stated his position: his deflationary measures in September had narrowly averted devaluation, but they needed reinforcing by further controls on public expenditure, especially in view of the bad impression made by recent supplementary estimates. The Government needed to hold down wages by limiting the amount of money available and also by control of public expenditure. He insisted that the greatest danger was not war but the collapse of sterling. Further increase in taxation was not an option. On this basis he refused to approve provisional estimates for 1958/59 at their current level. If decisive action was not taken immediately along the lines proposed in his memorandum, the same problem would recur the following year, when remedial measures would be more difficult owing to the proximity of the General Election.

On this occasion the response of Thorneycroft's colleagues was not entirely adverse. Most Ministers appreciated the argument for economies, but they differed sharply in their preferences. The case was made for greater cuts in the colonial, defence and civil spheres. Hailsham pointed out that all of the proposed avenues held the potential for political disaster. In his lengthy summing up, Macmillan tried to reconcile the parties, suggesting general support for the objectives of the Chancellor, but appealing for no rigid adherence to the £153m target. He also believed that major savings could be made in fields like defence if a longer time-scale were adopted; it was therefore unrealistic to make sudden policy changes on such issues as nuclear disarmament in the context of a minor economy exercise. The Prime Minister's main concern was to avoid actions provocative to the trade unions, and liable to strengthen their case for higher wage claims. That priority suggested that cuts in the social services were particularly imprudent. The Prime Minister asked his colleagues to evolve a formula which should 'not be such as to prejudice the paramount objective of securing wage stability or involve the Government in a politically indefensible position'.[113]

History had determined to repeat itself. As in the spring of 1951, when Gaitskell's plan for a small package of NHS economies threatened the Labour Government with disintegration and precipitated the resignation of Bevan and two other Ministers, Macmillan discovered that a small disagreement over reductions in estimates had turned into a major conflagration. As in 1951, a trivial difference of opinion laid bare the tensions within the Cabinet over the entire philosophy of the administration.

The problem was particularly acute because Macmillan was due to leave on a five-week commonwealth tour on Tuesday 7 January 1958. Given the absence of consensus, Macmillan wrote to the Ministers concerned and asked for their cooperation in reaching a compromise.[114] Meetings between the Prime Minister and relevant Ministers on 1 and 2 January secured provisional agreement on abolition of the supplementary ophthalmic service, reduction of the subsidy on welfare milk, and an increase in the NHS Contribution. The full package of cuts was assessed at £126m, which was tolerably close to the £153m target. It was agreed to hold the hospital boarding charge in reserve, but not to pursue increased charges on school milk and school meals. Macmillan was far from supportive of Thorneycroft. He appreciated that the Government needed to demonstrate that it was subjecting its own activities to firm disciple, but warned that the Chancellor was pursuing a reckless course, risking undermining prospects for wage restraint, exacerbating grievances among workers, tempting them to engage in strikes, thereby incurring economic losses. He also spoke to colleagues about the duty of government in modern society, reminding them of their inescapable obligations to the community, the evasion of which would be inequitable and unacceptable to public opinion. He warned Thorneycroft that their ultimate decisions must be based on political as well as economic judgement.[115]

Two long Cabinet meetings on Friday 3 January, involving participation by departmental Ministers, revealed that Ministers were unable to settle their differences. The first meeting started favourably; Thorneycroft thanked colleagues for their co-operation; the meeting ended with encouraging comments from Macmillan about good progress having been made. Thorneycroft was not categorical about the £153m target for savings. However, he pressed for further savings and listed various possibilities, including defence economies, removal of the family allowance on the second child, and a larger than previously envisaged increase in the NHS Contribution. Duncan Sandys on behalf of the service Ministers explained why it was not possible to add further to their already extensive share in the economy package. Walker-Smith insisted that abolition of the eye service and further increase in the price of welfare milk were unacceptable. He was concerned to avoid adding to the feeling that 'the Tories always go for the NHS'. Accordingly, he urged attention to other welfare economies, such as family allowances or the NHS Contribution. In discussion, the hospital boarding charge was introduced as a further possible economy, but this was opposed by Walker-Smith. Macleod favoured placing the burden on the NHS Contribution. The most cogent contribution to this part of the debate was made by Boyd-Carpenter, who argued that reduction in family allowances would be disastrous, that abolishing the eye service and further reduction in the welfare milk subsidy would produce minimal returns and be deeply damaging politically. By a process of elimination, he concluded that a big increase in the NHS Contribution was the only practicable alternative within the social services. Maclay said little, but he was not favourable to increasing the NHS Contribution, since this was likely to add to pressure for wage claims; he urged adoption of a lower target for economies. Butler also was unenthusiastic about increasing the health stamp, or indeed any of the other social services economies. He urged that the cuts exercise was not the right occasion for introducing major changes in social policy. On this basis he recommended adoption of a modest target for cuts, followed by a thorough review of contributions and benefits.[116]

At the second Cabinet meeting on 3 January, Thorneycroft was pressed to accept a limit of £50m, including £30m savings on civil expenditure, to be achieved largely by substantial rise in the NHS Contribution. Butler tried to tempt Thorneycroft into accepting this by offering to support an increase in the price of welfare milk to guarantee that the target was met. Thorneycroft reluctantly accepted £30m, providing that it was met according to his satisfaction, but Walker-Smith entered a late objection. He vigorously protested that his colleagues were volunteering the NHS for all cuts in the social services; he pointed out that the addition to the NHS Contribution being proposed would take the combined yield from the contribution and charges to the 'Beveridge limit' of 20 per cent, which he was unwilling to contemplate; he regarded £20m as the reasonable limit for savings from NHS sources, of which no more than £14m ought to come from the NHS Contribution. At this point Boyd-Carpenter, Maclay and Harold Watkinson (Minister of Transport) pressed Thorneycroft to accept a lower target for savings. It was pointed out that a rise in Government expenditure was unavoidable owing to such factors as an increase in the numbers of schoolchildren or the elderly, circumstances that forced an increase in agricultural subsides, and wage increases granted before introduction of deflationary measures. It was argued that Thorneycroft's package would undermine confidence in Britain's position as an ally and cause 'social and industrial discontent on a damaging scale'.[117]

Appreciating that Ministers were drifting into further disagreement, Macmillan referred outstanding issues to a group comprising Thorneycroft, Macleod, Butler and Sandys. In fact, this meeting evolved into a full meeting of the Cabinet. Prior to this meeting, scheduled for 10.30am on Sunday 5 January, Macmillan met Thorneycroft and asked for his co-operation, but received no indication concerning compromise; the Prime Minister believed that the Chancellor was 'obviously being pushed on by the Treasury Ministers'.[118] Macleod insisted that none of Thorneycroft's economies was a practicable proposition.[119]

At the Cabinet meeting, Thorneycroft reiterated that his overriding objective had been to support sterling. Integral to this aim was holding down the level of wages and public expenditure. Therefore 'he conceived it to be his duty not to accept Departmental Estimates foreshadowing an increase of Government expenditure in 1958/59 on the level of 1957/58'. Seven Ministers pointed to the pitfalls of adopting a rigid target and appealed to Thorneycroft to adopt a lower short-term target for savings. On account of his Chancellor's rejection of this proposition, Macmillan agreed to review all the specific options to discover whether the £153m target could be achieved. Discussions opened with the social services field; Macleod, rehearsed the objections to the hospital boarding charge, abolition of the eye service, and reduction of the subsidy on welfare milk. Even the NHS stamp was not immune from difficulties. However, by way of compromise, Macleod suggested that a social services package of £30m might be obtained by raising £20m from an increase in the NHS Contribution, and £10m from a reduction in the welfare milk subsidy. Other Ministers suggested adopting a programme for regular increases in the NHS Contribution, and declaring a ceiling for the Exchequer share of health service costs. Maclay was willing to offer small reductions on capital expenditure, but felt that the National Insurance deductions were already too high. Sandys refused to make a higher contribution from defence cuts. The Prime Minister warned that the benefits of Thorneycroft's disinflation measures would be cancelled out if they now provoked economic stagnation or industrial unrest. It was therefore unwise to embark on further cuts; even the £30m for welfare was not expedient in the short term. He urged that total reductions of between £76m and £110m were adequate to affirm the Government's commitment to Thorneycroft's policies. This would limit the increase in estimates to no more than 1 per cent. Thorneycroft was unpersuaded by these arguments; he was unconvinced that the £100m target would be met, and insisted on £153m as his minimum demand.[120]

Macmillan was despondent about the failure to reach a compromise on the estimates. He feared that his administration was about to break up and that Labour would return to office. The Cabinet was clearly united against Thorneycroft, who resigned with evident ill feeling. Resignations immediately followed from Powell and Nigel Birch, Thorneycroft's Treasury colleagues. At its meeting on Monday 6 January, the Cabinet expressed solid backing for Macmillan.[121] Although the resignation of the Treasury team might have constituted an adverse factor on the financial markets, it provided to have no more than marginal impact. Although inconvenient, the Thorneycroft crisis was politically beneficial to Macmillan. Without any effort on his part, three abrasive and dissonant influences were removed from his ministerial team. His position within the Cabinet was strengthened by this opportunity to restructure the Cabinet, which was used to appoint Treasury Ministers more suitably attuned to the political exigencies of the run-up to a General Election.

Amory at the Treasury

Departure of Thorneycroft was not followed by a more relaxed approach to public expenditure. Thorneycroft and his allies made political capital out of the alleged '£50m' gap in economies; indeed, they were also sceptical about the prospects for realisation of the agreed package of £100m cuts. In order to controvert the dissidents, Macmillan insisted on proving that a handsome package of savings could be generated in the course of pursuit of the Government's settled policies. Accordingly, Derick Heathcoat Amory, the new Chancellor of the Exchequer, and his team, came under immediate pressure to realise economies on the scale proposed by Thorneycroft, but without causing a political storm, or introducing offending policies, which was of course an almost impossible objective. Also, for a mixture of prudential and practical reasons, it was not possible for Macmillan to disentangle his administration very rapidly from the fiscal and monetary policy associated with Thorneycroft.

With respect to public expenditure, the new Treasury team pursued the old objectives, but with less determination. Jocelyn Simon, the Financial Secretary, produced a blueprint for future action, but this made no lasting impact.[122] Simon wanted to dispel the idea that the Treasury was a 'bottomless purse'; as noticed by his predecessors, the Cabinet Committee structure generated demands for additional expenditure on all fronts. In order to contain this tendency, he reverted to the old idea of adopting ceilings for each class of expenditure, and leaving the Ministers in each group to work out distribution of resources according to their agreed priorities. The Cabinet would adjudicate on demands for additional expenditure from the ministerial groups. He suggested that co-ordination might be improved if all the social service ministries were united into a single Ministry of Social Service. In the short term Simon sought Cabinet agreement to reduce public expenditure in order to permit lower taxation. Officials were unimpressed by Simon's contribution; they detected no possibility for proceeding with any of his suggestions.[123]

In practice, expenditure on the NHS was under effective control. Not allowing for the projected increase in the NHS Contribution, the agreed estimates for 1958/59 were only £15m above the anticipated outturn for 1957/58. Even a modest increase in the NHS Contribution would therefore eliminate the projected marginal increase in expenditure on the health service. Since the NHS had carried the entire burden of the current round of social services economies, it was scarcely reasonable to consider adding to economies from this quarter. Nevertheless, the 1958/59 health estimates were further reduced by cuts in hospital current and capital expenditure amounting to £6.5m and £1m respectively, as well as some other small savings. Although the Treasury reviewed the possibility of also increasing the various charges on family practitioner services, these were not actively pursued.

1958 NHS Contribution Increase

During the opening months of 1958, the primary task was implementation of the increase in the NHS Contribution agreed in general terms by the Cabinet. As noted above, the NHS Contribution had emerged as the only social service economy upon which Ministers could agree. A much larger increase than originally envisaged was therefore implied. At first a 4d increase had been proposed, but the Cabinet provisionally decided on 10d.

In connection with the 1957 increase in the NHS Contribution, some Ministers had argued that it was reasonable to adopt 20 per cent as the correct limit for the insurance contribution to NHS expenditure, which was assumed to be the level anticipated by Beveridge. However, the Financial Memorandum to the NHS Bill 1946 adopted 9 per cent as the yield from the NHS Contribution. In debate, Powell had conceded that the 20 per cent ceiling ought to apply to the combined yield from direct charges and the NHS Contribution.[124] This uncharacteristic expression of leniency on the part of Powell, induced at the insistence of Walker-Smith, was regretted by his officials, because it tied their hands for the future. On this basis, the maximum permissible increase in the NHS Contribution was 8d, which would take the combined yield from charges and the health stamp to 20 per cent of the cost of the NHS.[125] Even within this limitation, the additional yield from the NHS Contribution would still amount to £32m in a full year.[126] Having agreed on the size of the increase, its division between employee and employer needed to be settled. As in 1957, this occasioned a row between the Treasury and the Ministry of Pensions and National Insurance; the former wanted the entire increase to be borne by the employee; the later argued for an equal split. A compromise was reached whereby the employee paid 6d and the employer 2d.[127] This took that total for the NHS Contribution to 2s 4d (employee 1s 10½d, employer 5½d). This proposal was accepted by the Cabinet and the legislation proceeded according to plan, as in the case of the 1957 changes, meeting with only moderate opposition protest.[128] The increased charges under the NHS Contribution Act 1958 took effect on 1 July 1958.

Grinding Away

The estimates for 1959/60 provided the next opportunity for general reassessment of NHS expenditure. Simon suggested economies in the pharmaceutical services and removing the guarantee to compensate hospital authorities for increases in wages and prices, but he was told that neither was worth pursuing. Already various attempts were on foot to control drug cost, while the 'guarantee' relating to hospital costs could not be removed unless this was adopted as a general policy in the public services. The question of removing the guarantee had been pursued by Powell, but the Treasury had accepted the arguments from the Ministry of Health concerning its retention.[129]

A preliminary meeting of Ministers to discuss economies in civil expenditure was convened by the Prime Minister on 29 August 1958. With respect to the NHS, it was agreed to investigate the possibility of abolishing the supplementary ophthalmic service, introducing hospital boarding charges, and increasing dental charges by 50 per cent. Notwithstanding pessimism among officials within the Treasury concerning the potential for further cuts in the health sector, as well as confidence that health service expenditure was under satisfactory control, Treasury Ministers pressed on with their search for significant economies. At a further meeting of Ministers in September 1958, Amory reported that he and the Prime Minister were particularly concerned with the cost of the NHS. In order to facilitate tax reductions, Amory called for reductions in the NHS estimates of £21m.[130] Walker-Smith refused, arguing that a further increase in the NHS Contribution was impracticable in view of recent rises in two successive years. The Minister of Health also pointed out that further increase in direct charges would be difficult to defend, while other economies would entail cutting back services, which would have adverse political consequences. Walker-Smith pointed out that cuts in the eye service, dental service and the hospital boarding charge had only recently been considered and rejected by the Cabinet. The favoured candidate for excision was the supplementary ophthalmic service, but this would produce negligible savings, bankrupt opticians, and it ran against pledges given by the Conservative administration.[131] Increased charges in the family practitioner services were objectionable because they were politically disadvantageous, hard on the elderly population, and low in their yield. Walker-Smith offered to consider continuation of recent reductions in hospital expenditure, but warned about the impact on development and maintenance. The only prospect for future economy offered by the Minister of Health was further increase in the NHS Contribution, but he warned that this would lead to demand for compensating reductions in other health service charges. In desperation, the Treasury offered to drop its demand for further reduction in the subsidy on welfare milk in return for agreement to remove the subsidy on orange juice and vitamin supplements. Walker-Smith replied indignantly that such cuts would bring 'trifling financial gains with the maximum of political odium and embarrassment'. He warned that the Government risked obtaining a reputation for victimising mothers and children, the very persons who 'ought to be the last people at whose expense the Government should economise. Your proposals would make them the victims once more'.[132]

The Chancellor reported to the Prime Minister on his discussions with Walker-Smith. The latter had demanded a 'fallow year' and refused to consider any of the specific proposals for economies, apart from the reduction in hospital expenditure, which the Minister regarded as a false economy. The Chancellor conceded that NHS expenditure was not 'really out of control'. The provisional estimates allowed for only a £20m increase for the following year, mostly accounted for by increased costs, allowing only £4m for new development. Amory advised in the short term continuing with the policy of steady grind, albeit with likelihood that this would not produce spectacular results.[133]

Long-Term Solution
Following this negative result, officials explored means for limiting Exchequer commitment to the NHS in the longer term. This resulted in the aptly-named 'Ways Out' memorandum of 9 September 1958, which evolved into a memorandum for presentation by the Chancellor to the Prime Minister, boldly entitled 'N.H.S.- New Financial Basis' (11 September 1958). The Chancellor responded positively: 'I like this paper, with its interesting proposals'.[134]

For the longer term, Amory considered the arguments for remitting the problem to a Royal Commission, but concluded that this was likely to reproduce the unsatisfactory Guillebaud exercise.

He suggested that the Government was best advised to concentrate on longer-term policies for financing the health service. Building on ideas discussed within the Treasury since the time of Macmillan, he proposed that an opportunity existed to transfer a greater burden of the costs of the NHS to compulsory insurance. The Chancellor and his advisers were no doubt influenced by the relaxed approach of Parliament to the 1957 and 1958 increases in the NHS Contribution. Amory proposed abandoning the idea that 20 per cent was a 'sacrosanct' ceiling for an insurance contribution; he advised an increase to 33 per cent: 'indeed, I would not mind seeing most of the service financed by something like a co-operative insurance scheme, with the contribution varying either according to earnings or according to the number of the contributor's family'. In line with this thinking, it was suggested that the health stamp might be increased at the rate of 7d each year, or 9d if health service charges were abolished. Adoption of a ceiling of £540m for the Exchequer contribution to the health service could be imposed in connection with the change to insurance. To illustrate the application of these principles, Amory took the various components of health service expenditure and suggested how each might be financed from combinations of Exchequer sources, insurance contribution and direct charges.[135] A compensating feature of this long-term reconstruction of NHS finance would be the adoption of a programme for hospital building equivalent to that agreed for schools or roads.

The response to Amory's memorandum by the Prime Minister's advisers was extremely hostile. They judged it 'a rather extraordinary document' on account of its evasion of the immediate problem of short-term economies. Whatever the merits of the long-term objectives as a basis for discussion, the Prime Minister urgently needed advice on the merits of proposals for economy applicable in the next financial year.[136] Macmillan pressed Amory for a more positive response on short-term economies, and for a more precise indication of his plans for reaching a decision on longer-term policy. He complained that the Chancellor was too much preoccupied with apportionment of costs, while paying insufficient attention to the continuing escalation in expenditure on the NHS.[137]

Discussions among Treasury officials confirm that Amory had concentrated on questions of long-term finance on account of his pessimism about locating opportunities for immediate economies. His officials reinvestigated their files, but could only discover insignificant possibilities. The most positive hope was elimination of the subsidy on orange juice, but even this provoked protest from the Colonial Office. Without much enthusiasm, Amory agreed to write to Ministers asking for reductions in welfare foods subsidies, and he instigated discussions about reducing the cost of pharmaceutical services.[138] His officials saw no alternative to their habitual 'long grind'.

Amory's response to the Prime Minister's rebuke confirms that he had given up any expectation of achieving short-term economies on the NHS. He temporarily acted as apologist for the NHS, pointing out that its costs had risen to a minimal extent, that its share of GNP was declining, that none of the proposed economies were practicable or productive of significant savings. It was therefore more realistic to concentrate on evolving a policy for cost-containment over the next five years. He therefore proposed that the Government should immediately establish their new policy, publish a White Paper and then introduce necessary legislation.[139]

Macmillan appreciated that the relentless pressure for NHS economies was becoming counterproductive. He consulted Butler, and they agreed that parallel committees of Ministers and officials might profitably examine the longer-term problem of NHS finance.[140] As in the case of the establishment of the Guillebaud Committee, Amory's device offered the NHS a brief but welcome respite from the ceaseless pressure for additional charges and excision in services. However, Macmillan was not content to allow the NHS to escape without consideration of a change of direction. He wanted evidence of steady improvement in mechanisms of control, but also believed that after ten years experience of the service the Government should consider 'large and dramatic changes of a policy nature', such as reorganising hospital administration, or cutting back such functions as the hospital service, the general dental service, and restricting drugs available on prescription.[141] Macmillan, Amory, Butler and Walker-Smith met to discuss the NHS on 20 January 1959.[142] Walker-Smith defended the record of the NHS, rehearsed the objections to cuts and charges on the various fronts, and indeed went on to the offensive, suggesting that steps should be undertaken to remove direct charges completely, and he pressed for introduction of a chiropody service, consistent with promises already made by the Government. It was agreed that following the precedent set by recent reviews of pensions and defence policy, it was appropriate to establish an ad hoc committee of Ministers, served by a committee of officials, to review NHS finance. A parallel interdepartmental meeting of senior officials outlined the scope for such an enquiry. It was agreed to concentrate on placing the NHS on a contributory basis. Even from preliminary discussions, it was evident that there were strong objections to departure from existing arrangements.[143] The imminence of this exercise forced officials, perhaps for the first time, to take notice of the growth of private health care.

Ministerial Committee on NHS Finance

Establishment of the Ministerial Committee on NHS Finance infused new life into the Treasury's efforts to alter the basis of funding of the health service. The enthusiasm evidently emanated from certain senior officials rather than Ministers. It was argued that something more radical than abolishing charges and substituting an increase in the health stamp was needed. The only way forward was adoption of a contributory basis for funding. Since the idea of a separate health service deduction had run into difficulties, the most practicable approach was increasing the share of NHS expenditure met by the NHS Contribution: 'Illogical as the NHS Contribution is in some respects, I am in favour of putting as much on to it as the traffic will bear'. It was argued that increasing the contributory element in funding the health service was much preferable to eroding its coverage or increasing direct charges. The result of this change would be an injection of resources, which would enable much-needed improvements to be introduced.[144] The proposal to increase the burden of NHS costs carried by the health stamp, together with the objective of evolving a calculus to determine the apportionment to each part of the health service of resources emanating from insurance, direct charges and general taxation, provided a precise set of objectives for the ministerial committee. However, it was realised that the new committee, like other reviews of health services, such as the Guillebaud Committee and the Royal Commission on Mental Illness, also carried the danger of exposing the Government to pressures for additional spending on the NHS. Already, it had been necessary to sanction spending on the chiropody service; it was also clear that the committee would add to pressure for elimination of health service charges, for additional resources for hospital building, for spending on other new services such as community care, and even for removing charges on drugs prescribed for private patients.[145]

Memoranda prepared for the Ministerial Committee on NHS Finance indicate lack of unanimity of purpose. Amory conceded that the cost of the health service would inevitably increase. He expressed no sympathy for elimination of individual services. Apart from small economies to be achieved by efficiency gains, and possibly slight reduction in the scope of the pharmaceutical service, his main hope rested upon the scheme for determining what part the three main sources of finance should play in financing particular services. He also wanted to evolve means of facilitating greater recourse to private treatment.[146] The Ministry of Health emphasised the low level of health service expenditure with respect to its share of national resources and its place in the league-table of social services expenditure. Even with increases in efficiency, it was not possible to offer realistic prospects of lower expenditure. With respect to future financing, the alternatives of making no changes, excision of parts of the health service, and adoption of a different pattern of finance were briefly reviewed, but it was evident that the Ministry of Health wanted the elimination of direct charges, and it was by no means enthusiastic about increasing reliance on the NHS Contribution.[147] Walker-Smith was particularly attracted to the idea of abolishing NHS charges, and he personally drafted a memorandum reinforcing the case against direct charges.[148] He produced a further memorandum warning that it would not be easy to design a scheme to ensure savings by voluntary limitation on quantities of drugs supplied by general practitioners.[149]

The Ministerial Committee on NHS Finance suffered death through inanition. The Treasury quickly lost confidence in controlling the outcome. It even proved difficult to convene a meeting of the committee; after postponements of meetings arranged for March, April, June, and early July, the Committee eventually met on 14 July 1959; this was its first and last meeting.[150] The meeting was unavoidable owing to the need to agree about a ministerial statement following the Hinchliffe Report, which was required for a debate in the House of Commons on the NHS scheduled for the following day. By this stage it was appreciated that the approach of the General Election precluded Ministers from making progress on the complex issues raised by their remit. The meeting on 14 July therefore possessed little more than ritual significance. It was agreed that in the circumstances it was impracticable to consider radical alteration of financing the health service. The main practical outcome was agreement to support the Hinchliffe recommendation for a trial of voluntary methods for limiting the costs of prescribing. The Committee also backed the Home Affairs Committee in opposing the access of private patients to drugs on the same terms as NHS patients. It was agreed postpone further consideration of other aspects of NHS finance such as the abolition of prescription charges.

What an official called the 'end' of the Ministerial Committee was reported to the Cabinet in Butler's first account of its work, from which it was evident that Ministers 'baulked at anything fundamental just now'.[151] At the Cabinet discussion, financial restructuring and economies were hardly mentioned, while Walker-Smith and Maclay used the meeting as an opportunity to re-emphasise their demands for greater resources, especially for investment in hospitals.[152]

Not only was the Ministerial Committee on NHS Finance a failure in promoting the objectives of the Treasury, it was counterproductive in other respects. In particular, it drew attention to the manner in which the NHS was falling behind in the competition for social services resources. This encouraged the Ministry of Health to attempt to break out of the spiral of containment successfully imposed since the departure of Bevan. From this point the health department began to adopt a more aggressive approach to funding. The Treasury's five-year programme for containing NHS expenditure, prompted the Ministry of Health to produce a counter-proposal for a five-year programme of expansion. As noted below in the discussion of the hospital capital programme, the Minister of Health used the Treasury's economy drive as a springboard to mount a more determined campaign for a long-term programme for hospital investment.

Medicine for Private Patients
A vociferous new claimant for additional expenditure on health care emerged from the unusual direction of private medicine. This was a hardly unexpected guest, but its appearance was not particularly welcome to the Conservative administration. Walker-Smith found it increasingly difficult to resist supplying drugs to private patients on the same terms as NHS patients. An obligation to pay the full cost of their drugs had virtually extinguished access of general medical practitioners to private patients. This 'discrimination' against private patients was a constant source of grievance among organisations such as the Fellowship for Freedom in Medicine. The Conservative Party was vulnerable to criticism on account of its general support for private medicine. Free drugs for private patients were specifically promised in the 1950 General Election manifesto, but this was dropped from the 1951 manifesto. Reporting in 1954, the Cohen Committee on General Practice advised against providing drugs for private patients on NHS terms, but the committee was not entirely unanimous on this issue. The BMA had no such reservations. In 1954, when receiving a BMA deputation on this question, Macleod accepted that this idea was not repugnant to Conservative thinking, but was not practicable at the time on account of economic difficulties. In April 1956, in receiving a further BMA deputation, Turton listed further objections, but promised to continue discussions with the BMA. Campaigners on behalf of private patients kept up the pressure through questions in Parliament. Naturally, the BMA persisted and drove the Ministry of Health forward until by the beginning of 1959 a detailed scheme had been prepared, which was duly presented to the Home Affairs Committee by Walker-Smith, but without enthusiasm on his part.[153] He merely offered legislation at some unspecified future date. The approach of a General Election added to the temptation to introduce this small concession, possibly costing only £2m a year and attractive to Conservative voters, but Ministers were not convinced that supporters of this idea were

particularly numerous. They also feared that this measure would add to pressure for assistance with private school fees. They were also sensitive to the political capital likely to be made by the opposition out of this evidence of the Government's bias against NHS patients. Ministers were unable to agree a response, but the general reaction was unsympathetic. The Royal Commission on Doctors' and Dentists' Remuneration and the Hinchliffe Committee were cited as an excuse for further deferment. In the short term it was agreed to remit this question to the Ministerial Committee reviewing NHS finances.[154] As noted above, this committee turned out to be less active than was originally anticipated. However, Ministers attending its only meeting agreed with the reservations expressed by the Home Affairs Committee, although Ministers avoided ruling out this concession at some future date.[155]

Further action was delayed until after the 1959 General Election. Backbenchers were increasingly restive about Walker-Smith's diffidence. Representations to Macmillan were made by the 1922 Committee, while 170 Conservative MPs signed a Supply Day motion supporting drugs on prescription for private patients. Macmillan hoped to stifle this rebellion by speaking confidentially to the MPs' leaders without Walker-Smith being present, but he was advised not to encourage the dissidents. It was explained that this concession to private medicine would set a dangerous precedent, possibly even undermining the unification of the health service and starting the drift towards a two-class service.[156]

This storm forced the subject on to the Cabinet agenda. Walker-Smith urged that this was primarily a political issue, and recommended that it should be decided without reference to the usual health service criteria. He was now inclined to make a vague promise of legislation in order to appease the protesters, but without making countervailing sacrifices in the NHS budget. Amory was opposed to concession on account of the seemingly inexorable rise of the pharmaceutical bill; he was therefore unwilling to consider a further gratuitous increase. He was advised that the proposed concession would constitute a licence for general practitioners to engage in lavish supply of drugs as an inducement to their private patients, therefore relegating their NHS patients to a second class.[157]

Ministers who supported the concession cited the strength of feeling on this issue among backbenchers, but the Cabinet was generally unsympathetic, indeed some members were completely opposed. Butler was the sole member of the Cabinet favouring keeping open the possibility of introducing the concession. Macmillan favoured further procrastination, and remitted to a group of Ministers the delicate responsibility of framing a statement that would not alienate the Parliamentary Party.[158]

The Chief Whip complained that Walker-Smith handled a demonstration at the Conservative Party Central Council on private medicine tactlessly, which inflamed opinion still further and added to case for a conciliatory public statement.[159] Even this expectation was not fulfilled. In view of slower than anticipated progress of discussions with the medical profession on the implementation of the recommendations of the Pilkington Report, Walker-Smith argued that it was preferable to defer a public statement, and Government supporters were persuaded to accept this further delay.[160] Drafts of the statement on private medicine passed regularly between the Ministry of Health and the Treasury between March and April 1960, without an agreed conclusion being reached.[161] Discussions were interrupted by the change of health Minister in July 1960. This question was one of the first sensitive issues to engage Powell's attention. He calculated that embarrassment would be caused unless some reasonable compromise was reached by the date of the October Party Conference.

In his first recorded communication with the Prime Minister on health policy, Powell called for an end to vacillation on the question of medicine for private patients: 'the concession should be made, and made now'. Powell tried to enlist the support of Macmillan in advance of any communication with the Treasury. He pointed out that failure to act on this matter had bedevilled relations between the Conservative Party and the Minister of Health.[162] Without commitment on the part of the Prime Minister, Powell was referred to the usual channel, the Home Affairs Committee, to which he appealed without support from Maclay. The cost of this concession was now given as £2.5-£3m. On behalf of the Treasury, Boyle was totally opposed, pointing out that resolution of delicate negotiations over implementation of the Pilkington Report would be undermined if this concession were adopted, because it would necessitate reopening of old arguments concerning the level of private earnings, which would inevitably stir up ill-feeling among the doctors. Opinion in the Home Affairs Committee was divided, but Butler reported a balance of opinion in favour of legislation in the next session of Parliament.[163]

The private medicine recommendation was now remitted to the Cabinet. The Prime Minister was once again warned not to support this proposal, which was seen as objectionable on political, social and financial grounds; it was particularly unrealistic to consider this concession at a time when the Government was considering a further increase in the NHS Contribution. This would seem like imposing increased charges on the poor to finance handouts to the rich. The only permissible compromise would be to agree to reconsider introducing the drugs concession for private patients at such time that the prescription charge was abolished.[164]

70

Defence of the concession to private patients provided the occasion for Powell's first attendance at a Cabinet meeting on 6 October 1960. Opposition to Powell's proposal was led by Selwyn Lloyd, the new Chancellor of the Exchequer, while Butler was now unenthusiastic. Even those providing mild support, such as Charles Hill, appreciated that linking this concession with a rise in the NHS Contribution would lead to embarrassing political repercussions. Notwithstanding the appeal of Powell's plea for making an announcement of this concession to party faithful at the annual Party conference, it was decided that no decision could be made until the question of the increased NHS Contribution was resolved. Macmillan implied that the decision about granting this concession would depend on the extent to which the Minister of Health was able to produce an acceptable package of countervailing economies. There was a general feeling that this issue should be resolved once and for all; otherwise it was likely to become a serious irritant to morale within the Conservative Party. Also, a later date for the concession was impossible because it would be evident that the new wave of economies conceived by Powell was being implemented to offset the concession to private patients.[165] Discussions resumed on 18 October, when it was clear that strong opinions were held on both sides, but again no decision could be reached because of continuing disagreement over the NHS Contribution. The decision was again deferred.[166]

Lloyd offered to make the concession to private patients, but only if the rise in the NHS Contribution yielded £50m. Other Cabinet members insisted that any rise in the NHS Contribution would preclude the concession to private patients. Of those unable to attend the Cabinet meeting, Henry Brooke expressed support for Powell, but Eccles, Macleod and Maudling were strongly against.[167] Finally, the Cabinet meeting on 27 October 1960 decisively ruled out concessions to private patients.[168] Powell and the Chief Whip were instructed to present this decision to the Government's supporters. Careful preparations were required in order to prevent a further eruption of discontent. It was agreed that the door should not be completely closed to the revival of this idea at some future date, but the Government was unwilling to make a public statement to this effect.[169]

Stalling of the Stamp

The problem of medicine for private patients was to the Treasury an irritating digression, albeit ending satisfactorily without this potentially explosive addition to NHS expenditure being conceded. Private medicine deflected attention away from the main preoccupations of the Treasury, elaboration of alternative long-term

71

arrangements for financing the health service, and the perennial search for immediate economies. The estimates for 1959/60 and the previous year, even though offset by compensatory rises in the NHS Contribution, were held down to a minimum. Deliberations on the estimates for 1960/61 gave every impression of repeating the experience of the two previous two years. The Prime Minister was warned that civil expenditure was rising dangerously; he was advised that the post-General Election period was the time for 'draconian decisions', and that economies in the NHS should be adopted as the 'major target in the social services field for the present Parliament'.[170] Questions of immediate economies and the more radical overhaul of the mechanism for financing the NHS became inextricably bound together in the deliberations of the new team of Ministers. Immediately the reconstructed administration had settled down, plans were made for resuscitation of the Ministerial Committee on NHS Finance. However, given the unresponsiveness and lack of impetus demonstrated by this committee, there was no instinct on the part of the Treasury to continue its life without substantial modification.

Not without reservation, it was decided to revive the Social Services Committee, which had been dissolved in the summer of 1956 after its inconclusive deliberations on economies in the NHS. The Treasury trusted that a ministerial committee, advised by a parallel committee of officials, might be steered towards a more decisive conclusion. Any improvements in the committee arrangements were more than counterbalanced by the appointment of the elderly Viscount Kilmuir as chairman. As Lord Chancellor, Kilmuir was unfamiliar with the social services, inexperienced in chairing such committees, and although trusted by Macmillan, was much less competent than Butler or Macleod to handle delicate political social affairs questions. The terms of reference of the Social Services Committee were not agreed until December 1959. The Committee was commissioned to keep under review the Government's policy on National Insurance and National Assistance, and also to consider possible modifications of the financial structure of the NHS. As in the case of the earlier 'Social Services' committee established under Attlee, control of NHS expenditure was the primary objective of the new committee. Treasury officials still believed that control of NHS spending offered one of the most hopeful prospects for long term economy in public expenditure.[171]

The initial deliberations of the Social Services Committee were guided by amended versions of the memoranda considered by the Ministerial Committee six months earlier, but these were edged to one side on account of the need to determine policy with respect to the next financial year. On account of the General Election, the scrutiny of estimates had been delayed. It was not until November 1959 that the Treasury drew up lists of possible economies in the NHS. All the usual candidates for excision and charges were listed. The Financial Secretary was offered assessment of the various possibilities, but warned that the experience of previous years suggested that all proposals would be rejected. Indeed, suggestion of an increase in the prescription charge was likely to prompt renewed calls from Walker-Smith for complete abolition, now strengthened by support from the recently-published Hinchliffe Report. Boyle, the new Financial Secretary, declined to follow up proposals for specific economies, while Amory 'thought about holding his own, but has not deemed it expedient to go forward on the bigger proposals for limiting the Exchequer cost of the NHS in general' as set out in GEN 677/2.[172]

Compared with the NHS Contribution, all alternative economies and charges were complicated and disadvantageous. Consequently, the known objections to this form of taxation were discreetly forgotten. The temptation of easy returns once again proved to be an irresistible attraction. The yield from the NHS Contribution had increased from £63m in 1957/58 to £110m in the following year, taking the level from 10 to 15 per cent of the gross cost of the NHS, while the combined yield from the health stamp and direct charges rose from 14 per cent to above 18 per cent.[173]

Treasury thinking was now inclined to regard the Beveridge notional limit of 20 per cent as 'nothing sacrosanct', or merely a 'historical hang-over'. Continuing adoption of a limit of 20 per cent for the joint yield of the health stamp and charges was inconvenient because it suggested a limit on any further increase of 4d, which was scarcely worth pursuing. Officials favoured an increase of 1s 3d, to bring the yield from the NHS Contribution alone to 20 per cent, but it was realised that this might be politically objectionable.[174] Treasury officials appreciated that the NHS Contribution was a tax rather than insurance premium, possessing the disadvantage of being regressive in its effect. This was not necessarily regarded as a disqualification if it was accepted that the welfare state should derive as much revenue as possible from those able to pay. In this case the level depended on 'what the traffic will bear'; experience demonstrated that this form of taxation had been absorbed with surprisingly little protest.[175] It was speculated that this unexpected acquiescence to increased taxation was explained by the endemic misconception among wage earners that the entire cost of the NHS was borne by their health stamp.[176]

The Treasury campaign for an increase in the NHS Contribution was not motivated by concern over health service costs, which it was accepted were under reasonable control, but with the totality of other demands for increased public spending. The Prime Minister was advised that the Chancellor of the Exchequer was less concerned about the cost of the NHS than the general problem of containing the estimates.[177] Amory complained that the estimates for 1960/61 were set to rise by an 'astonishing' 8 per cent, even in circumstances where there was little wage or cost inflation. This reflected new demands connected diverse commitments such as with civil service and forces pay, roads, aviation, the BBC, local employment policy, Jordan and Cyprus. In order to accommodate these demands, it was inevitable that the Chancellor should fix on such apparently unproblematical sources of additional revenue as the NHS Contribution. For the year 1959/60, Walker-Smith had 'successfully pleaded for a holiday from unpopular measures', but this was now over and further health service economies were essential.[178]

Amory opted for a moderate course, proposing an increase in the NHS Contribution of 1s. The Treasury completely underestimated the extent of opposition to this measure. Having succeeded with increases in 1957 and 1958 almost painlessly, it was tempting to believe that a precedent had been set, and that future increases would be accepted as a matter of routine, if necessarily on an annual basis. This attempt at a third increase broke the tolerance of the critics of this form of taxation. The Minister of Pensions and National Insurance had never been enthusiastic for such changes on account of general implications for the National Insurance scheme; the proposed increase in the stamp looked set to undermine the credibility of the new system of contributions currently being introduced. The Minister of Health was unsupportive because it breached the 20 per cent limit for charges and contributions hitherto accepted by the Government. Both Boyd-Carpenter and Walker-Smith also objected to the proposed increase on grounds of principle and political calculation.

The first obstacle for Amory was the Social Services Committee.[179] Amory argued that there was nothing sacrosanct about the Beveridge 20 per cent limit; he advocated regular health stamp increases until this source accounted for 33 per cent of the cost of the NHS. In the first place he needed some increase in taxation to offset the £52m proposed increase in expenditure on the NHS for 1960/61. If implemented in July 1960, the extra 1s would produce a yield of £36m in the year 1960/61. This increase would only take the combined level of charges and the health stamp to 21.7 per cent of the gross cost of the NHS. This was likely to fall back to 20 per cent when supplementary estimates were taken into account.

Boyd-Carpenter advised that the National Insurance Act 1959 precluded the proposed rise in the NHS Contribution. It had been agreed that the current 18s 2d deduction represented a reasonable upper limit for the total insurance contribution in the period before the introduction of graduated deductions. Amory's proposal would breach this limit without giving any compensatory increase in benefits; it would undermine the Government's stated intention of reducing the burden on the low-paid; and it was inconsistent with election pledges promising national insurance contributors that they would share in the nation's rising prosperity.

For the first time since the start of high-level discussions on the NHS Contribution at the beginning of 1957, the Government's vulnerability to criticism on questions of principle was fully exposed. Boyd-Carpenter described the Chancellor's proposals as a political disaster. The opposition would be justified in claiming that the Government's insurance scheme was being used as a massive transfer operation, increasing taxes on the poor to fund tax cuts for the better-off. The proposed increase in the NHS Contribution was a 'hypothecated poll-tax' or 'poll tax which, unlike income tax disregards alike the means and family circumstances of the tax payer'; it fell equally on the rich bachelor and the low wage-earning family man. Low income groups would rightly be hostile to the prospects held out by the Chancellor that they would be subjected to regular increases in their contributions without any reference to the level of benefits.

Walker-Smith was equally hostile to Amory's proposal. He pointed out that his estimates for the NHS in 1960/61 were only £24m above the revised estimates for 1959/60. Accordingly, the Chancellor was using the NHS as an excuse for exploiting a regressive tax striking at the low-paid, apprentices, widows, and working people over the age of retirement. Such a measure was just palatable in the exceptional circumstances of 1957 and 1958, when everyone was braced to expect harsh expedients, but such excuses were no longer available in the alleged prosperity of the 1960s. Walker-Smith therefore decisively distanced himself from the line previously adopted by his department, which had sheltered behind the NHS Contribution as a painless alternative to other forms of economy. In a new spirit of confidence, the Minister defended the spending record of his department, contending that there was no need for economies or cuts, and he attacked the Chancellor's proposal on grounds of principle. He believed that it would be 'impossible to satisfy Government supporters that such an increase was financially necessary, politically appropriate, or equitable in its incidence'. Given the political dangers involved, Walker-Smith was determined to extricate himself from the firing line.

Two long discussions at the Social Services Committee revealed little enthusiasm for Amory's proposal. It was agreed that the only prospects for launching a further increase in the NHS Contribution was dependent on the outcome of any restructuring of financial arrangements for the NHS. Macmillan was in South Africa when the Chancellor took his proposal to the Cabinet. Butler reported that since only half the Cabinet was likely to support Amory, he was trying to carry the Chancellor along, and ensure that if the increased NHS Contribution failed, other ways would be found to cut the health service estimates by £80m.[180]

At this stage Amory made only token efforts to secure the health stamp increase. The only paper before the Cabinet was an impartial summary by Kilmuir, which gave little encouragement to the Amory's supporters.[181] At the Cabinet meeting, Amory presented the health stamp rise as a necessary response to an adverse economic situation.[182] He indicated that the prospective growth in public expenditure necessitated economies in the NHS. It was admitted that the stamp was one form of taxation among many, but Amory justified this choice on account of the need to preserve balance between the different sources of revenue for the NHS. He claimed that it was not unreasonable to levy 20 per cent of the cost of the NHS from this source. Since the health stamp needed upward adjustment at least once during the next few years, the current date seemed the least politically inopportune of the alternatives. His percentage target was of course considerably lower than proposed to the Social Services Committee, and his comments about future intentions were now more guarded.

The more temperate tone made no difference to the basic proposition, which evoked implacable opposition from the Minister of Health and the Minister of Pensions and National Insurance. Walker-Smith concentrated on the question of principle; he stated his opposition to this regressive poll tax and declared that general taxation was the only equitable basis for financing the health service. Boyd-Carpenter concentrated on the implications for benefits, arguing that the increase in the health stamp would provoke demands for increases in pensions that would be impossible to resist. He suggested that any rise in the stamp should be postponed until the amount and timing of pensions rises were determined.

Detecting little support for Amory, Butler postponed discussion of the health stamp proposal until after deliberations by the Economic Policy Committee the following day. Reporting to Macmillan, Butler was initially optimistic that the increase could be pushed through, but after the Economic Policy Committee he noted that Amory had abandoned his plan, but the Home Secretary claimed that the meetings had been profitable because they demonstrated that other Ministers appreciated the Chancellor's difficulties.[183] Despite these brave sentiments, it was clear that the NHS had proved an unprofitable avenue for extracting reductions in the 1960/61 estimates. Amory tersely told the Cabinet that he had decided not to press for an immediate rise in the NHS Contribution, but he reserved the right to reintroduce the proposal at a future date, perhaps even before the budget.[184]

Overhaul of NHS Finance

Reclamation of a more active role for the NHS Contribution in the fiscal system now rested on the success of the fundamental review of long-term arrangements for financing the NHS, which was the primary aspect of the remit of the resuscitated Social Services Committee. This gave Amory an opportunity to try for a second time to win support for proposals originally contained in GEN 677/2 of March 1959. Amory now accepted that the share of the nation's resources devoted to health care would inevitably increase. Even with the most effective restraint of expenditure, future administrations would face unavoidable additional commitments in such fields as remuneration and hospital building. Recent experience had demonstrated that it was unrealistic to propose reducing the scope of the service by lopping off such functions as dentistry or the eye service, or limit resort by forcing sections of the population into private medicine. It was therefore necessary to devise a formula for allowing expansion in the cost of the NHS within the scope of resources at the Government's disposal. Amory also wanted to escape from the 'haphazard method of proceeding, depending on what the Government of the day considered politically feasible at any particular moment'. Of the alternative sources of revenue, he favoured the NHS Contribution and recommended 'putting as much on the stamp as the traffic will bear'.[185]

In initial discussion, Amory faced considerable scepticism about his proposals. He argued that the health stamp was a preferable alternative because it did not affect cost of living index, it was not levied on non-wage earners, and it was relatively uncontroversial. He had arrived at no firm commitment to a proportion, but this should not be less than 20 per cent of the gross cost of the health service. Walker-Smith reiterated the arguments against greater reliance on the NHS Contribution, but he accepted the case for further investigation and proposed remitting this problem to a working party of officials, which received the agreement of the committee.

On 8 February 1960, the Social Services Committee approved the establishment of the Working Party on NHS Finance under the chairmanship of F E Figgures of the Treasury Home Finance Division.[186] The remit of this working party was to review the current method of financing the NHS, excluding the local health services, and in particular to consider: (a) whether it was feasible to devise a formula for the automatic determination of shares of total cost of services to be borne by general taxation, 'special imposts' and direct charges, (b) whether the NHS Contribution was the best form of special impost and, (c) whether legislation for the impost should derive from the Finance Act or specific legislation, and where ministerial responsibility should lie.[187] The working party was asked to report by 1 July 1960.

Ministers and officials tied themselves in knots trying to decide whether to announce the existence of a review of NHS finance, and whether to divulge details concerning the committees involved and the options under investigation.[188] It was hoped that an announcement would confirm the seriousness of the Government's determination to control public spending, although in view of their controversial and unpopular character, it was essential not to divulge the nature of the proposals under review. In order to demonstrate that the Government was determined to take decisive action, the Treasury favoured announcing the existence of a 'radical review of the methods by which the necessary resources are raised' to support the NHS, but no such announcement was forthcoming.[189]

While the question of NHS finance was under consideration among the experts, the Social Services Committee continued to meet to consider issues relating to National Insurance, National Assistance and social security. Eleven meetings were held, the last being on 21 October 1960. The Prime Minister dissolved the Social Services Committee on 24 October 1960, without any further discussions having been held on the question of long-term finance of the NHS.

Absence of progress was not attributable to indolence on the part of officials. Representatives of half-a-dozen departments met occasionally to exchange ideas, and they produced many technical reports. Guidance on prospective changes in health service expenditure were available from the Treasury's Long-Term Resources Review, which ran in parallel with the Working Party on NHS Finance. The Treasury entered discussions with enthusiasm and optimism. It was reported that Amory was 'running hard' and that he was likely to be able to carry along his colleagues. The two main aims of the Treasury were establishing the NHS Contribution as a separate hypothecated tax, and evolving a sharing calculus, so that rises in any sector of health service expenditure would automatically trigger off increases in relevant charges and contributions.[190] On the other hand, although Walker-Smith was the instigator of the working party, the Ministry of Health representatives proved unhelpful to the Treasury, and refused to consider alternatives implying changes in current policy.[191] Both health departments were opposed to suggestions from other departments for substantial increases in direct charges, which were likely to appear 'pusillanimous', even though the adverse effects would be reduced by the introduction of some kind of national medical care insurance scheme.[192]

Production of an agreed report was held up because of disagreements over the practicability of some main alternatives. For instance the Treasury favoured introduction of a flat-rate hypothecated tax, whereas the Inland Revenue and the Ministry of Pensions and National Insurance favoured a flat-rate charge per head.[193] The Treasury appreciated that hypothecation was 'inherently undesirable and dangerous', but it existed already in the NHS field, and no other alternative was less objectionable. This was the only way in which the yield from a specific tax was likely to rise in line with expenditure on the health service.[194]

An interim report was ready in July 1960, but officials were prevented from reaching definitive conclusions by absence of guidance from Ministers over policy changes needed to introduce a special hypothecated health tax, or a new system of boarding charges for hospital patients. The Lord Chancellor was asked to consult Ministers on these questions.[195] Further progress was held up by Treasury doubts about to ratifying the report. Continuity of discussions was not helped when Figgures was promoted to become Secretary General of EFTA in Geneva. Also in the summer of 1960 some of the most important ministerial players were replaced by very different personalities: Amory was replaced by Selwyn Lloyd as Chancellor of the Exchequer, while Powell replaced Walker-Smith as Minister of Health.

At higher levels within the Treasury there was little support for the idea of a separate hypothecated health service tax. It was noted that the Inland Revenue and the Ministry of Health were opposed, while at the most senior level within the Treasury it was felt that the arguments against this tax were 'compelling and conclusive'.[196] Accordingly, on its merits, the idea was not worth pursuing. It was already rumoured that Amory was about to leave his post, but in view of his special interest in this problem, he was asked to look at the relevant papers. Initially he had been favourable to the hypothecated tax, but became convinced that this proposal was undesirable, and he expressed satisfaction that the Figgures Committee had reached the same conclusion.[197]

After Amory's departure, Lloyd examined the papers relating to the Figgures working party, but discovered nothing to indicate that there was a basis for recommending any change in current arrangements for financing the NHS. All of the alternatives had been examined but were found to be problematical, at least in the short-term. Kilmuir and Lloyd agreed that the draft report was of little relevance to present policy.[198] Enquiries emanating from

Ministers prompted exchanges about completion of the interim report, which resulted in circulation of the report in its provisional state. Those Ministers consulted agreed that it offered no basis for further action.[199]

Bad Taxes on Poor Families

New to his office, and without experience of the long-running arguments concerning the NHS Contribution, Lloyd revived the proposal abandoned by his predecessor to increase the health stamp by 1s. This proposal was now even more disadvantageous to the low-paid because they would also face an increase in their National Insurance deduction. The Government's original intention that their new scheme for graduated deductions would lead to lower contributions by the low-paid would be frustrated. Lloyd hoped to disguise this anomaly by introducing two separate Bills for the increases, with the hope of emphasising the separation of the payments. Lloyd was heartened by a meeting with Powell in which the latter gave assurances that he was committed to introducing economies in the health service regardless of any increase in the NHS Contribution. Powell asked for the stamp increase to be introduced as a Treasury measure, which might suitably be presented as late implementation of a change deferred from the previous year.[200] Powell's reaction was seen as confirmation of the Treasury expectation that the new Minister of Health might be more radical over retrenchment than his predecessor.[201]

Lloyd took his proposal for an increase the NHS Contribution by 1s to the Cabinet in October 1960. Like his predecessor, Lloyd accepted that the costs of the health service were under reasonable control, but the NHS was the service most suited to bear economies needed to contain the rise in public expenditure. Lloyd described the health contribution as an 'easy way of raising money outside the normal fiscal channels' which would helpfully 'show our determination to keep the burden on the general tax-payer under control, and at the same time keep inflation in check'. Despite the known disadvantages of the NHS Contribution, Lloyd argued that a combined yield from direct charges and the health stamp of 22 or 23 per cent was tolerably close to the Beveridge ceiling. He felt that low wage earners would regard a deduction of 2s 8½d as a 'small price to pay towards a National Health Service free to themselves and their families'. Even though the burden on the low-paid would be increased, the new National Insurance scheme remained moderately beneficial to this class of contributor. Total deductions after the 1958 rise in contributions amounted to 3.9 per cent of average weekly earnings; with the fresh health stamp increase, deductions would amount to only 3.6 per cent of average earnings.[202]

Powell completely reversed the attitude of his department to the proposal to increase the NHS Contribution, and towards the general level of NHS expenditure. He accepted the increase in the health stamp as a useful fiscal device, but insisted that although it was a form of taxation, it failed to address the essential question of controlling health service expenditure. Indeed, he warned that the increase might be detrimental to the search for economies in the NHS. Therefore it was essential that the stamp increase should be accompanied by positive measures to reduce NHS expenditure. Although the forecast estimate for 1961/62 was only marginally above the revised estimate for the previous year, he aimed to make economies totalling £45-£50m.[203]

Contrary to advice from his officials, Boyd-Carpenter kept up his hostility to this form of taxation, and he also cautioned that the timing of proposed increase in April 1961 was politically inopportune. This was the date of the introduction of the new graduated system of contributions under the National Insurance Act 1959, which would introduce heavy increases in contributions from many workers. It was evident that Crossman would aim to make political capital on this point on behalf of the Labour Party. The health stamp was regarded by workers as integral to their general contribution; therefore raising this deduction would exacerbate the Government's embarrassment. He contradicted the statistic given by Lloyd, pointing out that low wage earners would face deductions of 5.3 per cent under the new system. Boyd-Carpenter repeated his objections in principle to the exploitation of the NHS Contribution as a form of taxation, and argued that it would be counterproductive because it would inflame industrial relations and increase calls for wage increases. As a measure relating to health service finance it was also unsound; the increase in health service expenditure was negligible; if anything resort to the health stamp encouraged laxity rather than economy within the health sector. Finally, the Minister of Pensions explained that including the stamp increase in the forthcoming National Insurance Bill was open to objections on both procedural and political grounds.[204]

Macleod, who was unable to attend the Cabinet meeting on account of illness, wrote to the Prime Minister in support of Boyd-Carpenter. He believed that this attempt to raise £50m in taxes was objectionable: it was a 'bad tax because it hurts the poorer families only. The figures for the NHS increase clearly do not justify it'. The Cabinet Secretary advised Macmillan that the Cabinet would not find it easy to support Lloyd's proposal.[205]

At the Cabinet meeting, Lloyd conceded that the NHS Contribution was a 'bad tax', but its continuing use was unavoidable. His memorandum reiterated the usual justification that the health stamp offered a means to hold down public expenditure, whereas in Cabinet Lloyd stressed the need to bring the public's attention to the rising cost of the health service. Contrary to Boyd-Carpenter, he believed that the low-paid would not make a connection between the rise in the health stamp and the level of other National Insurance deductions. Supporters of Lloyd argued that the stamp must continue to bear its share of health service costs, and they pointed out that the Government's commitment to reduce general taxation would not be fulfilled unless regressive taxes were substituted. Opponents of the health stamp increase pointed out the graduated insurance system would be a disappointment to workers, since its contributions would be higher and its benefits lower than the Government had promised. The rise in the health stamp would compound this problem. The stamp rise would also make it more difficult to gain acceptance for the package of economies in the health service evolved by Powell. It was scarcely possible to increase payments for a service and at the same time reduce its scope. If Powell reduced NHS estimates in the manner intended, then the Government's embarrassment would be increased because the Beveridge limit would be exceeded to an even greater extent. It was also suggested that it was unwise to make changes of the kind suggested in advance of the expert study on health service finance, which had not been discussed by Ministers. It was also necessary to take account of the argument for reducing direct charges in compensation for an increase in contributions. Other critics of Lloyd pointed out that his proposal would aggravate demands for concessions to private patients. Ministers particularly emphasised their vulnerability to criticism on account of contradicting recent assurances about observing the 20 per cent combined ceiling for charges and contributions, as well as the promised limit on the level of the absolute contribution for the low-paid.

Discussion exposed little enthusiasm for Lloyd's proposal. Almost all Ministers expressed reservations. Even those giving some degree of support, suggested significant compromises; for instance Thorneycroft, now politically reinstated as Minister of Aviation, proposed a higher increase on the stamp, combined with abolition of the prescription charge and the drug concession to private patients. The few Ministers sympathetic to a hard line urged that if unpalatable measures were adopted, then they were best introduced at the earliest opportunity, and as a single package. Despite the substantial volume of reservation, Macmillan concluded that the Cabinet was generally favourable to an increase in the NHS Contribution, but he agreed that the timing and method of its introduction required further discussion. Ministers also wanted further information on the economies in the health service envisaged by Powell. Despite the latter's instinct for retrenchment, he found it difficult to locate significant economies.[206]

Boyd-Carpenter showed no sign of capitulating. He pointed out that, as the Minister most exposed to criticism stemming from any failings of the state insurance system, he would be accused of a breach of faith, especially in the light of the 1959 General Election manifesto undertaking that the Government's 'new pension scheme will put national insurance on a sound financial footing, concentrate Exchequer help on those with the lowest earnings', none of which suggested that additional benefits would be wiped out by increased contributions to subsidise the NHS. The Minister of Pensions also pointed out that the opposition was already making political capital over disadvantageous features of the new insurance scheme. He was particularly concerned that increased revenue from contributions would produce a handsome surplus in the Insurance Fund; adding further to insurance deductions would inevitably draw further attention to this anomaly.[207] The strength of Boyd-Carpenter's case was not lost on the Treasury, where is was accepted that there was a danger of *argument à l'outrance*: 'if we overdo it, if we overload the graduated part of the scheme, we may smash it; it is a creaking vehicle, a bad bargain which people may accept as a tax, but not with too much overloading'.[208]

Powell's department was unenthusiastic about conceding further economies. Having looked into the question of charges, the Minister ruled out increases in direct charges; indeed he met with suggestions for abolishing these charges completely. Powell favoured delaying review of the prescription charge until after the end of the voluntary scheme on limiting prescriptions, with the result that abolition of dental and ophthalmic charges would come up first for consideration.[209] Indicating the state of uncertainty within the Treasury, Lloyd suggested three alternative methods of introducing an increase in the NHS Contribution, without precisely indicating his own preference. The first and second involved alternative dates for introducing the increase, either January or July 1961; the latter had the disadvantage of loss of revenue, but it disentangled the higher contribution from the forthcoming National Insurance Bill. The third alternative included balancing the increase with two compensatory concessions, medicines on NHS terms to private patients, and abolition of the prescription charge. Neither Lloyd nor Powell was favourable to the third package.[210] Boyd-Carpenter fired two more salvos, the first containing statistical information about the levels of contributions implied by the National Insurance Act 1959, and with the addition of the 1s on the health stamp, and the second containing the text of his recent letter to the Prime Minister and a long extract from the speech by Crossman.[211]

The Prime Minister was reminded that the package of increased contributions and charges would be represented by the opposition as a concerted attack on the NHS. On the other hand, the idea of a direct NHS tax was accepted by the 'great mass of the people', and acquiescence to this principle suggested great extension of this source of financing for the health service in the future, even though this possibility was not worth considering currently.[212] Discussion of the Chancellor's alternatives stretched over a further two Cabinet meetings. Lloyd recognised the presentational advantages of separate legislation and delayed implementation of the stamp increase. He warned that abolition of the prescription charge would need to be followed by drastic economy measures in the health service. The Cabinet was divided over two alternative courses of action: first, announcement in February 1961 of an increase in the health stamp to take effect in July, secondly, abandonment of the health stamp increase, but offsetting prospective rises in health service expenditure by other economies. Although politically the more disadvantageous, the former was attractive because of its higher yield, its immediate relief to the national economy and its sufficiency to meet anticipated increases in NHS expenditure over the next two years. Cabinet members were finally persuaded to take the risk and introduce the 1s rise in the stamp without compensation either to NHS or private patients; for presentational purposes it was decided to proceed by separate legislation to be published in February at the same time as the publication of the civil estimates, with a view to the NHS Contribution increase taking effect in July 1961.[213]

Ministers agreed to a 10d-2d split between employee and employer, taking the total NHS Contribution to 3s 4d; this measure was predicted to yield £50m in a full year. It remained only to decide the method for introducing the increase. The departments briefly discussed the introduction of two separate cards and two stamps on one card, alternatives which had been considered in detail in 1957, but it was agreed that if the Government was not willing to adopt an hypothecated tax collected through the Inland Revenue, it was impracticable to depart from the current single stamp.[214]

At first, Powell was accused by the Treasury of being 'coy' or evasive about direct health service economies, but he vindicated his reputation for parsimony, offering a package of economies amounting to £27m in a full year. The combined yield from the stamp increase and health service economies for 1961/62 was expected to be about £60m, which was sufficient to keep health service expenditure at the level of the original estimates for 1960/61 (i.e. the estimates submitted in the autumn of 1959, not taking into account the cost of the Pilkington settlement). Powell therefore began his tenure by exercising a degree of control more stringent than any of his predecessors. He also showed a willingness to advance on many fronts simultaneously, which had also been resisted by earlier Ministers, who tried to narrow the field for criticism by the opposition, and also because they were genuinely opposed to making inroads into the relevant services. Powell recoiled from the sentimentalism of his predecessors and took the scalpel to the services highest on the Treasury list of candidates for cuts, acting very much as if he was still Financial Secretary operating under the Thorneycroft regime.

The new Minister of Health initially offered economies valued at about £40m, sufficient in themselves to eliminate the prospective rise in the health estimates. These reductions were offered 'not only in the general interest of economy, but in order to facilitate the developments and shifts of emphasis for which modern trends in medicine will call'.[215] This was perhaps a gnomic assurance that a regime of rigid economy would be imposed as a condition for attracting additional resources for hospital development. Regardless of this hint at higher longer-term spending, Lloyd was naturally pleased with this spontaneous offer of co-operation; he responded that the Minister's letter opened up 'really substantial possibilities'.[216]

Powell initially proposed to abolish the 50 per cent subsidy on welfare milk, remove completely the subsidy on all other welfare foods, increase the charges for dentures, increase the price of spectacle lenses, raise the cost of amenity beds in hospitals, make minor economies in hospital running costs intended as an earnest of more substantial economies to come, and finally to increase the cost of prescriptions from 1s to 2s per item.

The Treasury was naturally appreciative of Powell's efforts, but they were taken by surprise and were doubtful whether other Ministers would be supportive because of the evident political risks involved, especially because the level of NHS expenditure would fall as a result of the combined effects of the increased charges and contributions. The Treasury was particularly sceptical about prospects for doubling the prescription charge, anticipating that the arguments evoked in the past would be again cited against all of these proposals. The increase in the prescription charge was likely to create the greatest difficulties. The Guillebaud and Hinchliffe committees were unsympathetic to this charge, and the Government had pledged itself to consider its abolition. Powell's proposal seemed against the tide of events and therefore was particularly incautious politically. Furthermore, the largest increase justifiable on grounds of rising costs was 6d; the Financial Secretary was advised that this lower target would be advisable in the current circumstances.[217]

While the Treasury was attracted by the prospect of more substantial NHS economies than ever previously achieved, there was suspicion that the entire package might be lost unless a more prudential approach was adopted. The anomalous character of Powell's proposals would be evident from the resistance of the education department to introducing parallel economies in school milk and school meals.

Lloyd and Boyle were briefed about potential difficulties raised by Powell's suggestions, and they were prepared to sacrifice them all, providing the full increase in the health stamp was implemented. However, in the first instance, they agreed to support the full package.[218] A preparatory meeting was held to introduce Maclay to Powell's ideas. Although Maclay was unenthusiastic, he agreed not to oppose Powell, providing the welfare milk subsidy was reduced rather than abolished.[219]

The economies presented to the Home Affairs Committee by Powell followed the above outline, except for reducing the subsidy on welfare foods to 25 per cent instead of complete abolition and omitting the small economies in hospital expenditure. The revised target for savings had shrunk to £25m. Butler, as chairman of the committee, emphasised that Powell's sacrifice and parallel economies in housing expenditure would be politically unpopular. Other Ministers raised difficulties about specific proposals, and pointed to trouble likely at the time of legislation, but the committee was swayed by the need to counteract the rise in public expenditure; it concluded that 'the political effect of doing nothing to meet this would be more damaging than that of going forward with the proposals'.[220] The Treasury was displeased that a minority of members of the Home Affairs Committee regarded the Powell package as unreasonably 'stiff' on the NHS, but their lack of opposition to doubling the prescription charge was greeted with relief.[221]

Advisers of both Macmillan and Lloyd were apprehensive about the Cabinet's reception of the Home Affairs Committee's recommendations.[222] However, when Butler established that Macleod had decided not to speak actively against Powell's proposals, it was clear that there would be no consolidated opposition.[223] The Cabinet meeting was therefore an anti-climax. Powell discovered broad support for his economies. Indeed, he was congratulated and encouraged in his investigations of economies in hospital expenditure. Allies of Lloyd and Powell were attracted by the prospects for tax reductions made possible by savings on the NHS. Other Ministers were more struck by the likely political difficulties. They pointed to the cumulative adverse effect of the measures, particularly on poor families with large numbers of children. The only completely unsympathetic voices were Eccles and Macleod, who continued the attack on the stamp increase on account of its regressive character, and they contended that the economies made tax reductions politically more difficult, since it would be apparent that the poor were being penalised to permit tax relief for the rich. Butler warned that dependence on measures requiring legislation or changes in regulations would lead to difficulties in Parliament and enhance the unpopularity of the Government.

Macmillan expressed some sympathy with the liberals, but pointed out that the Government's philosophy required measures of this kind; otherwise taxation would continue to increase. He appreciated that adding to the burdens on the least affluent gave rise to some apprehension, but on balance he felt that the Cabinet favoured Powell's full package of economies, subject to further consideration of minor variations calculated to reduce adverse criticism.[224]

Macmillan was nevertheless uneasy about the trend of events. As in the case of the Thorneycroft-Powell economies, he instinctively detected political dangers in the Lloyd-Powell package. His response in December 1961 was similar to that in December 1957. He asked Lloyd to be satisfied with one main economy, preferably the rise in the NHS Contribution. If some further concession was needed to satisfy Powell, then he should be allowed to introduce legislation to increase dental and ophthalmic charges, primarily because this could allow for future increases to be introduced by regulation. Lloyd stoutly rejected this advice.[225]

The Cabinet fell into disarray. Some Ministers, led by the Treasury team, favoured stiffening the economies on the grounds that more was needed in order to facilitate tax cuts; others insisted that cuts should be considerably reduced to remove the most obvious sources of grievance. The economies were reviewed by Lloyd, Maclay, Soames (Minister of Agriculture) and Powell, who presented their agreed conclusions to the Cabinet. The only variation proposed was to enable families with four or more children to obtain their welfare milk at an unchanged price. This ministerial group also considered but rejected introducing a smaller increase in the prescription charge, since this would reduce the yield of the health service economies by £2.5m.[226] This conclusion was contested by Boyd-Carpenter. Displaying his habitual pertinacity, he argued that the current subsidy should be preserved for families with three or more children, as well as the families of widowed mothers.[227] This concession was rejected by Lloyd, who argued primarily on the basis of the impact of the charge on general milk consumption and the effect on subsidies to farmers.[228] Advice to the Prime Minister showed sympathy for Boyd-Carpenter; Macmillan was reminded of his own words: 'If we have to produce milk (and pay the farmers to do it) and then turn it into buttons and paperknives, we may as well give it to the children'. Since it was not feasible to withdraw the milk subsidies, then the Government should be careful not to court adverse publicity by drawing boundaries based on family size.[229] The Cabinet discussion of welfare milk stretched over two meetings; it demonstrated much antipathy to any reduction in the welfare milk subsidy. It was agreed that the subsidy should be retained, thereby preventing the opposition from claiming that the Government was directing a blow at children and their health, but it was agreed that there was a case for a comprehensive review of subsidies affecting children. Powell was authorised to announce the increase in the NHS Contribution and his package of economies on 1 February, shortly before publication of the Civil Vote on Account.[230] Ministers were not entirely finished with health service cuts; Powell used his ingenuity to compensate for the reduction in the saving on welfare milk by proposing a greater increase in the charges for spectacle lenses and amenity beds. Both of these changes were approved without dissension by the Cabinet.[231]

The 1s NHS Contribution increase, the doubling of the prescription charge, the reduction in subsidy on welfare milk, the removal of the subsidy on other welfare foods, the increased dental and ophthalmic charges, and other increased charges were announced by Powell on 1 February 1961.[232] Powell thereby succeeded in introducing economies analogous to those rejected by his colleagues in 1958, the cause of his resignation as Financial Secretary. Any glow of satisfaction over this belated vindication of the Thorneycroft philosophy must have been diminished by the political storm which engulfed the Government during the implementation of the economies. Opposition to these economies even extended to Government supporters, whose protest motion Powell dismissed as no more than 'scribbling on the lavatory wall'.[233] His calculation proved to be correct; backbenchers complained bitterly, but the Government comfortably retained its majority. However, this affair was undoubtedly damaging to the Government. Powell handed to Labour a much-needed opportunity to improve its performance as an opposition and regain its credibility as a Party of government.[234] For an entire month taken to process the required legislation and amended regulations, Labour extracted every opportunity for political advantage, and its efforts were widely covered in the press.[235] Particularly damaging to the Government was the censure motion debated on 8 February 1961.[236] Labour made a credible bid to persuade the public that it was engaged in a crusade to save the welfare state. This effort was regarded with cynicism by Government supporters, one of whom called it the 'Hiroshima of the British

National Health Service'.[237] This MP was referring to the raucous antics of the opposition, but this image was more appropriate than he realised at the time, since Labour was striking one of its first nails into the coffin of the Macmillan administration. This political advantage for Labour was not the last of the benefits stemming from Powell's zealous pursuit of principle.

Arresting the Thaw

Painful experiences associated with the economies announced in February 1961 brought the retrenchment policies pursued since 1949 to a conclusion. Nutritional subsidies were reduced to such an extent that there was virtually no opportunity for further savings; additions to the NHS Contribution or direct charges to patients were ruled out politically. It was already conceded that excision of services was not feasible. In the absence of evidence that significant efficiency savings were possible, it was inevitable that increases in spending on the health service would fall primarily on the Exchequer.

Although the Treasury looked back on a record of successful containment of health service spending during the 1950s, it was evident that in future the forces of expansion would be much more difficult to resist. This problem therefore gave no grounds for complacency. It was appreciated that Powell, having committed himself to a policy of rigorous control, would find it difficult not to co-operate with further measures of austerity. In July 1961 Lloyd suggested a limit of 2.5 per cent annual increase in NHS expenditure, which was estimated to be approximately half the average increase in cash terms over the previous four years. If Powell envisaged financing this by final elimination of the subsidy on welfare milk, Lloyd proposed to allow only half this saving to be retained by the health departments. It was recognised that this rate of growth would necessitate a slow-down in capital investment, both in hospitals and welfare services. Powell rose to this challenge and approved the Treasury formula, providing that he was allowed discretion to seek additional resources for expansion of community care services.[238]

This agreement immediately caused difficulties for the Ministry of Health, which pointed out that projected increases for 1962/63 were already higher than 2.5 per cent. However, the Treasury pointed out that the new PESC exercise had adopted a 2.5 per cent limit for the NHS; any increase above this level would therefore need to be offset by such measures as economies in hospital expenditure, cuts in the drug bill, or elimination of welfare foods subsidies. The Treasury warned that it was no longer possible for the NHS to be awarded a 'huge ration' of public resources to use unconditionally.[239] The Ministry of Health came up with an increase in the 1962/63 estimates of 2.36 per cent; about half of this was attributable directly to pay and price increases. Once the 2.5 per cent norm was introduced, even if it was derived arbitrarily, and was practicable only under limited circumstances unlikely to be realised in practice, it immediately attained the status of an iron law, enshrined in PESC forecasts for years to come, and thereby imposed a ceiling on NHS estimates for these years. The 2.5 per cent norm was announced by Lloyd in Parliament as an agreed basis of NHS funding for about four years.[240] This became known as Powell's 'contract' with the Treasury.

PESC introduced a new level of precision, stability and certainty, but it also imposed limitations on any department starting from a low threshold and accepting artificially stringent targets at the outset. However, despite this known disadvantage, the health departments attempted to keep within the PESC guide-lines by adopting a target growth rate of 2.5 per cent for local health and welfare services, and only 2 per cent for hospitals. This pattern of spending was never effectively imposed on the health service. It rested on various assumptions that were quickly falsified. For instance it was assumed that local authorities would be lethargic over their plans for community care. Their spending was only under central control to a limited extent; in pursuance of the new community care plan, local authorities generated demand for an expansion rate of 3.8 per cent to be reached by 1964/65. This implied that the increase in hospital expenditure should be reduced below 2 per cent, but it became clear that hospital modernisation was rapidly making this limit unsustainable. The Ministry of Health resorted to tackling the many anomalies created by the PESC system by a process of 'arbitrary beastliness', but this was not regarded as satisfactory or viable in the long-term.[241]

Powell was therefore forced to seek relaxation of the restrictions applying under his contract with the Treasury. Although the 2.5 per cent limit on expansion of current expenditure was a condition for allowing growth of the hospital investment programme, the Treasury acknowledged that Powell had been 'more austere than anyone else' among his colleagues.[242] The Minister had even been willing to refuse to offset price increases in his allocations, thereby forcing limitations of service, ward closures and reductions in staff in his effort to restrain expenditure. The health service in the hands of Powell had therefore turned into a 'shining example of this policy of control', an exemplary justification of the utility of the PESC mechanism. It was already apparent that a relaxation of the agreed limit would be necessary from 1965/66 onwards, the last year of the 2.5 per cent contract. SHHD was equally unhappy about the 2.5 per cent limit. Even in 1962/63, the first year of the restriction, serious cuts had been made, which had produced crisis of morale, especially among nursing staff, where essential vacancies were left unfilled; also building maintenance and repairs of equipment were being neglected, and other false economies were being forced on hospital authorities. The 2.5 per cent limit had effectively prevented improvements which were essential for the more economical use of resources. SHHD therefore asked for an urgent reconsideration of the 2.5 per cent norm.[243]

The Treasury was determined to prevent a general thaw in its restrictions, and its reservations were strengthened by the onset of new worries about the expansion of public expenditure.[244] In order to accommodate the higher costs of running new hospital facilities, the Ministry of Health pleaded for an adjustment from 2 to 3 per cent in the annual increment allowed for hospital current spending. Powell made only a token attempt to break out of the Treasury restriction; he agreed to retain the 2.5 per cent norm, entailing limiting hospitals to 2 per cent, but he asked for a special dispensation, an ad hoc contingency allowance of £3-4m, for use in case of emergencies experienced in hospital authorities facing the greatest difficulties. Powell now discovered that the tables were turned; he was faced with Boyd-Carpenter as Chief Secretary, who insisted on rigid adherence to the 2.5 per cent norm, insisting that the Government would be placed in an impossible position if it were to abandon its spending limits half-way through the agreed four-year cycle.[245] At first Boyd-Carpenter was disinclined to sanction an ad hoc grant of £4m above the 2 per cent allowance for hospitals for 1964/65, but after negotiations, it was permitted, on the understanding that limitations would be imposed on community care expenditure and the capital investment programme, which were expected to introduce a saving of about £4m.[246] A small concession was made to Scotland on a similar basis.

Powell left office in October 1963, leaving Anthony Barber to wrestle with the increasing crisis in hospital finance. In May 1964 a high-level meeting of officials was held to discuss the difficulties in staying within the agreed limits. This problem was exacerbated by the costs of hospitals coming on stream under the expanded programme of hospital building. The hospital plan also exercised a further indirect effect by creating a demand for modernisation of older hospitals. It was already evident that new hospitals were going to be a great deal more expensive to maintain than was originally anticipated. The £4m 'crock of gold' for 1964/65 was already over-subscribed; hardship and disappointment were therefore anticipated if this increment was not repeated the following year. This prospect added to the pressure for upward revision of the 2.5 per cent norm. Initially, the Treasury responded positively, agreeing that the four year contract had been unrealistic, but blaming the idea on Powell.

Officials agreed to work out a new contract on a more realistic basis, including a firm figure for hospital running costs projected for three years ahead. This was a matter of urgency because the Treasury aimed to confront the new administration with a settled policy that would be difficult to reverse; the new Minister of Health would be told: 'this is the way it is done; and this is what the Health Service understands'.[247] With good reason, officials were beginning to detect the wind of political change, and were taking the necessary prudential measures to prevent interference by politicians with the policies to which they were attached.

It was accepted that the 2 per cent norm for hospital current expenditure was unsustainable. Not only would it preclude the efficient use of new assets made available under the hospital plan, but was also preventing application of established policies and much-needed improvements in staffing and facilities. The health departments pressed for a second ad hoc grant for 1965/66 to augment their funds available for hospitals, followed by a new long-term agreement incorporating an annual increase of 3.5 per cent in hospital current expenditure.

As noted below, Treasury Ministers proposed to deal with this problem rather differently, by slowing down the capital spending programme on hospitals and community care to enable the health departments to keep within their current 2.5 per cent limit. Officials continued their negotiations, attempting to derive a new formula for calculating on an objective basis the increment required for hospital current spending. The Treasury remained convinced that the health departments were running an inefficient system, whereas the health departments insisted that the system was being crippled by the existing limits. Despite intensive discussions lasting from May to October 1964, the various parties gradually abandoned hope of agreement before the General Election, even on the level of expenditure to be adopted for 1965/66.[248]

(iv) GENESIS OF THE HOSPITAL PLAN

The Macmillan administration's best-known claim to initiative in the field of health care was the Hospital Plan unveiled by Enoch Powell in 1962. The Hospital Plan is also remembered as an indication of the constructive abilities of the new Minister of Health. However, as the following paragraphs indicate, like most other things connected with the health service, the story of the Hospital Plan is more drawn out and less dramatic than might appear on the surface. Indeed, the ancestry of Ten Year Hospital Plan reaches back at least to the tenth anniversary of the NHS.[249]

The new health service was unable to achieve its basic objectives without complete modernisation of its hospitals. This was the most expensive task facing the NHS, but as already indicated in chapter I and in the earlier part of this chapter, serious assault on this problem was frequently deferred owing to resource constraints. By the tenth anniversary of the NHS, there was a growing public outcry over the neglected state of hospitals. It was clear that other western states were much ahead of Britain in modernising their hospital systems; big programmes of capital spending in such areas as housing, education, roads, and even atomic energy enhanced grievances concerning Britain's antiquated hospitals. The failure to mount an effective hospital modernisation programme even evoked an expression of concern from the Queen.[250] The Treasury conceded that 'education is this Government's favoured child'; it was allowed an over-generous share of capital investment, adding to the embarrassment over persistently low capital spending on hospitals.[251]

Within the health departments the hospital problem was not unappreciated, but in the struggle to maintain levels of service, capital development was the first candidate for sacrifice. As noted in volume I of this study, Macleod was the first Minister to obtain resources for major capital projects. In 1955 he announced a list of major capital schemes for the years 1956/57 and 1957/58 costing £17.5m.[252] In December 1956 Turton announced major projects valued at £20m for 1958/59 and 1959/60. This commitment was confirmed by Vosper in March 1957. Vosper hoped to improve on the levels announced by his predecessor. Hospital modernisation was high on the list of priorities of Vosper. He called for a 'new drive' for hospital building, aiming to reach the prewar level of capital spending by 1959/60, and he adopted a target one-third higher than this for the following five years. Although this represented a modest expectation, not commensurate with the scale of the problem, it was at least the embryo of a long-term hospital plan.[253] Inaction was not an option for Vosper on account of demands for higher spending on hospitals emanating from the Guillebaud Committee. Indeed, this was the most widely publicised recommendation of the Guillebaud Committee. Vosper also faced demand for modernisation and expansion of dental schools from the McNair Report, and insistence on improvement in the entire field of mental health stemming from the Royal Commission on Mental Illness. In addition, the Royal Colleges and their allies exerted pressure for improved facilities for the specialties they represented, in order that patients should not be deprived of the most advantageous forms of treatment. Their claims implied major expenditure in such fields as maternity units, out-patient departments, accident and emergency departments, operating theatres, radiology departments, and pathology laboratories. Ministers of Health were therefore ground between the millstones of the expansionary dynamic of high technology medicine and the retrenchment mentality of the Treasury.

In the short term, the health Ministers were primarily concerned with hanging on to the slender gains achieved by Macleod. Naturally, hospital investment was one of the targets for cuts in the social services advanced by Thorneycroft and Powell. For 1958/59 and 1959/60 the Ministry of Health proposed a total capital budget of £20m and £25m; Powell responded with a proposal for £18m and £21m; with some reluctance Walker-Smith suggested a compromise of £19m and £22m, warning that any less would result in 'bitterness and ill will' within the health service.[254] A meeting between Thorneycroft and Walker-Smith was inconclusive. The Minister of Health claimed that the proposed reductions were inconsistent with the public commitments of the Government; Thorneycroft insisted that such reductions were essential since they would demonstrate the Government's determination to check inflation.[255] Walker-Smith volunteered a further £1m cut in the total for 1959/60, which was accepted by the Treasury. No reductions were made in the small capital programme for Scotland. The Treasury was satisfied with this outcome; hospital development was limited to a small scale, while in the absence of long-term guarantees for hospital spending, opportunities for planning were limited, which resulted in consistent underspending by about 10 per cent. Accordingly, in practice the capital budget was consistently below the agreed limits. Although this system was a source of inefficiency in spending, it generated savings to the Exchequer.

In view of the large scale and complexity of any hospital planning operation, the efficient use of capital resources for hospitals was dependent on ability to commit funds over a number of years, certainly longer than allowed for under the one or two year cycle implicit in negotiations between the health departments and the Treasury. For its success, the hospital drive proposed by Vosper necessitated adoption of a long-term programme. At this stage, little attention was paid to assessment of the cost, scope and general planning outlines for reconstruction of the nation's hospital system. Speculations about the scale of this problem were at best crude approximations. In the absence of more reliable estimates, they were granted greater authority than was justifiable. Particular reliance was placed on estimates derived from the Guillebaud Committee, especially on the conclusion of the Guillebaud Report that '£30m annually would be a desirable rate of capital expenditure for the National Health Service at which to aim over the seven years succeeding the year 1957-58'.[256] The £30m figure was only one of the estimates under discussion at that time, but it was a nice round figure, not wildly unrealistic politically. It thus assumed a degree of canonical authority which was neither intended nor deserved.

During 1958, further opportunities to reintroduce the idea of a long-term hospital plan presented themselves. First, in response to a request from Butler, who was conducting a review of social services policy, Walker-Smith briefly sketched out his main objectives for development in the health services. His short paper included proposals for the prevention of illness, a shift towards community care, and 'the improvement of hospitals and institutions'.[257]

Looking ahead to a period of less tight money and less severe inhibitions on capital investment, further actions required, - and would be both socially and economically rewarding - to remove the handicap of inadequate and outworn hospital premises. Investment in the hospital field should take the form of:

(a) Strategically situated new general hospitals to replace the small scattered, obsolete and uneconomic units, particularly in big towns.
(b) New psychiatric units appropriate for modern treatment.
(c) Out-patient clinics and day hospitals.
(d) Acute treatment units at general hospitals.
(e) Special annexes for long-stay patients.

The above proposals are not capable of early implementation - at any rate to any significant extent - as are my earlier proposals. I have however included them as they conform to my general pattern i.e. they will yield a dividend expressed in both social and economic terms when sufficient capital is forthcoming to finance them.

Walker-Smith therefore attached importance to a comprehensive plan for hospital development, which would be integrally related to planning for prevention and community care. However, in the retrenchment atmosphere of the early months of 1958, he acknowledged that it was unrealistic to identify expensive proposals for capital investment as his first priority.

A second and more precise exercise in long-term planning occurred when the Treasury undertook a Long Term Investment Review. The primary motivation for this initiative was balancing competing claims on capital resources, and economising on individual programmes. At least the investment review gave the health departments the opportunity to offer approximate projections for hospital development reaching as far as 1962/63, for which date £34m was adopted for England and Wales, and £4.5m for Scotland.[258] In the course of discussions on the investment review, officials agreed that a ten-year programme was desirable, but they realised that it would be 'unreal to attempt to get one' on the grounds that this would necessitate adoption of the current low levels of capital expenditure, which would expose the Government to criticism and was accordingly politically unacceptable. Such an arrangement 'would be interpreted that they would give inadequate sums in perpetuity'.[259] The Long Term Investment Review culminated with submissions from the spending departments to the Cabinet. Ministers were faced with claims from the social services departments far in excess of current resource limits. Rather than attempt to resolve these sensitive issues in Cabinet, they were referred to relevant Ministers meeting in committee.[260] At a preliminary discussion between Ministers, Walker-Smith advanced the case for expansion, indicating that hospitals were his first priority, but also urging the importance of building old people's homes and capital developments relating to mental health. Ministers concluded that the Treasury had adopted an unrealistically low limit for capital investment in the social services; the Cabinet was recommended to give higher priority to schools, hospitals and prisons.[261] The Treasury refused to increase the ceiling of social services capital expenditure; indeed, social services Ministers were presented with a cut of £30m. Both the education and health departments claimed that reductions in their programmes would prejudice their opportunity to launch a long-term spending programme.[262]

When social investment was discussed by the Cabinet, Ministers were presented with Treasury proposals for a £26.5m reduction in the public investment programme for 1960/61, with cuts shared between education, hospitals and housing.[263] Opposition to these cuts was led Geoffrey Lloyd, who contended that it was essential to respond to opposition policy initiatives, which led him to propose a 'forward drive' in education. He sketched out a five-year programme of new schools and training colleges, which he wanted to announce in a White Paper. The level of spending on new schools would be increased from the current level of £50m to reach a peak of £75m per annum. Parallel proposals for Scotland were made by Maclay.[264] The scale of Lloyd's ambitions prompted Walker-Smith to issue a competing claim. He pointed out that adoption of a new programme for schools would draw even greater attention to the neglect of hospitals, and underline the extent to which the Government had failed to implement the recommendations of the Guillebaud and McNair Reports. He reminded colleagues of the seriousness of the problem of antiquated hospitals, and absence of hospitals in new towns. The tenth anniversary of the NHS had led to 'strong and unanimous' criticism concerning the lack of capital provision for hospitals. Accordingly, as a supplement to his investment submission up to 1961/62, which contained the totals cited above, Walker-Smith declared that in the light of the education forward drive he would be making more ambitious proposals for a 'programme for the longest possible period ahead'.[265]

Cabinet discussions featured resistance to cuts by the Ministers of Education, Health, and Housing. The £8.5m and £3m reductions proposed for schools and hospitals were particularly vigorously contested; it was agreed that cuts of a much smaller order should be negotiated with the relevant departments.[266] The result was promising enough for Lloyd to be able to announce his five-year forward drive for schools at the Conservative Party conference.[267] This also indicated that education was becoming established as the leading social services priority of the Conservatives. The health service and its hospitals were yet again relegated to the sidelines. Walker-Smith had failed to gain firm acceptance of his own five-year plan, and furthermore he was left fending off pressures for reduction in his projected spending for hospitals. In October 1958 he agreed to a small reduction from £27m to £25.5m for 1960/61.[268] In addition to warding off cuts in their investment programme, Walker-Smith's officials also made tentative plans for a five-year hospital programme, which reached a maximum figure of £36m for 1964/65.[269]

Although the Investment Review and the associated breakthrough by the Ministry of Education, which was granted a £300m schools programme, brought no immediate relief to hospital development, these events caused the health departments to draft their first five-year plans, and they rendered it increasingly perverse to resist their implementation. The Treasury candidly acknowledged that 'since hospitals have been held back since the war (and indeed since Florence Nightingale) much more than Education', opposition to a long-term programme was no longer realistic.[270]

Although privately Amory confided to Macmillan that they should expect a long-term hospital programme, the health departments received little immediate encouragement to join education in a forward drive.[271] Amory regarded the decision concerning schools as a specific policy initiative taken for reasons of political advantage. In education, Ministers were merely honouring their long-term commitment to provide secondary education for all. Having adopted education as a priority, it was inevitable that other social services, including health, should be subjected to offsetting economies. In any case the Chancellor objected to any general move to increase long-term commitments in public expenditure.[272] The Ministry of Health retorted that it was a 'great disappointment to the Minister that it has not been possible to let us have a long term hospital capital programme'.[273]

Beginning in 1959, the health departments presented their capital investment plans on a five-year basis, although without the expectation of commitment from the Treasury for this longer time-span. The investment plan from the Ministry of Health envisaged that hospital spending would reach £40m in 1963/64. Before 1960, hospital capital spending had been dominated by plant replacement and normal works; after that date the balance was pushed in the opposite direction. Accordingly, in 1958/59 major schemes accounted for only £6m out of a £20m total, whereas for 1963/64 major projects were expected to absorb £22m out of the £40m total. Scottish spending plans envisaged a similar switch in priorities.[274]

Negotiations over immediate expenditure plans were overtaken by preparations for the General Election. This provided Walker-Smith with an opportunity to revive his proposal for a long-term hospital plan. In response to a request from the Prime Minister for departmental policy plans, Walker-Smith revived his statement of three objectives originally produced in February 1958; this was slightly recast as a 'Conservative Five Year Plan for the Health Services', imitative of the recent plan for education. The only additional comments about improvement in hospital services involved emphasis on the five-year commitment, but also a hint for the first time that an additional five years would be necessary: 'to secure the economies of rationalisation, we shall need to develop a capital expenditure of about £50m a year, and maintain it for perhaps ten years thereafter. By the end of the 5-year plan we should be on the threshold of the £50m level'.[275] Previous representations on capital investment in hospitals had not been specific about the need for a ten-year plan, because refinements of this kind were otiose in a situation where the Treasury was resisting commitments extending beyond two years. However, in making the case for a five-year plan, the health departments pointed out that major projects took seven years or longer to plan and execute. It was therefore self-evident that whereas schools could be accommodated by a five-year plan, a meaningful hospital plan would range over ten years or longer. By this stage the Treasury was becoming attuned to such longer term planning, largely on account of its increasing preoccupation with large investment schemes in the nationalised industries, road-building, or universities.

The hospital plan was accordingly merely one five-year programme among many. The Treasury was not disconcerted by the level of expenditure involved, although it favoured reducing the maximum annual figure to £40m. In general it was felt that hospitals were faring badly when compared with schools.[276] However, the Cabinet discussion of long-term public investment resulted in no commitment to a hospital plan.[277]

98

The General Election added to the momentum towards a long-term hospital plan. For some time Labour had been complaining about low capital investment in hospitals and its manifesto called for spending at the level of £50m per annum. The Conservatives responded with the promise of a big programme of hospital building: 'We have already have sixteen new general or mental hospitals and some fifty major extension schemes under way'. The Conservatives adopted a target to double the capital programme over the next five years.[278]

It is surprising that medical organisations were not more vocal in voicing their concern about the obsolescent state of hospitals. As indicated in the first volume of this study, some leading doctors issued public statements, but these were sporadic events and exercised little direct influence. By 1959, the signs of change were sufficient for medical authorities to devote more active attention to the future shape of the hospital system. A report commissioned by the BMA was published in April 1959, and this was followed up by a conference on hospital planning. A House of Lords Debate on the hospital service on 19 November 1959 introduced by the opposition peer, Lord Stonham, also added to the clamour for greater capital investment in hospitals.[279]

With the rise in the capital budget and the emergence of more realistic prospects for a long-term programme, the Ministry of Health gradually adapted itself to deal more effectively with hospital development. In 1958 the Treasury was still complaining about lack of information, skills and unsuitable departmental organisation, lamenting about 'lack of knowledge, lack of people, particularly on the technical side, of adequate quality'.[280] Departmental organisation was not modified to the extent desired by the Treasury, but a permanent Organisation and Management Service for hospitals was established; a Chief Architect was appointed, and the Ministry established its own separate architectural branch and design unit. On the model of the much-publicised work of the Ministry of Education, the Ministry of Health sponsored the preparation of hospital building bulletins and building notes for the guidance of health authorities; the first of these was issued in 1958 and eight had been produced by the end of 1960. As a sign of growing confidence in the capacity of the health departments to handle a large capital programme, in 1959 the Scottish Department of Health was allowed greater freedom in allocating capital funds, and in 1960 a general relaxation was agreed, which took effect in February 1961.[281]

It is therefore evident that by the autumn of 1959 most of the necessary conditions were in place for the hospital plan. However, it was some time before agreement could be reached on public commitment concerning the size and duration of this exercise. Without this fundamental advance, it was not possible for the regional boards to plan on a realistic basis or invest in the skills requisite for a long-term hospital programme. In the mean time agreement was secured without difficulty on capital expenditure for 1961/62, which raised the ceiling to £31m, although no concession was made on the much-disputed year 1960/61, where the reduction to £25.5m remained in force. About half the allocation for 1960/61 was assigned to major schemes.

This more favourable climate was undoubtedly prompted by the Conservative manifesto promise, which necessitated some immediate moves towards expansion. Probing questions in the House of Commons ensured that there was no retreat from the Government's promise. The Ministry of Health lost no time in renewing its pressure on the Treasury to extract a public commitment to spending for five years ahead. Without such an undertaking, it would not be possible to break away from the inefficient patch and mend philosophy which had been prevalent since the beginning of the NHS.[282] Establishment of the important Committee on Control of Public Expenditure under Lord Plowden, which was especially concerned with the evolution of long-term expenditure controls, provided an additional avenue for the promotion of the hospital plan, and this matter was raised without delay in Subcommittee 3: Health Services of the Plowden Committee.[283]

The Treasury was more easily reconciled to the idea of a long-term programme in principle than to public announcement of such intentions. Already in 1959, the Treasury agreed with the Scottish Department of Health that the capital investment programme would rise to £6m by 1965 and to £8m by 1970, but this was on a confidential basis, subject to review from year to year.[284] The Ministry of Health argued that the larger scale of the building operations south of the border required regional boards to be allotted a five-year allocation, with lesser commitment to a ten-year figure.[285]

In continuing its resistance to the ten-year plan wanted by the Ministry of Health, the Treasury resorted to its usual arguments, such as lack of confidence in the Ministry's ability to use resources efficiently, or impossibility of progress in the absence of a master plan for hospital development. However, the Ministry kept up its demands, and new dynamism was infused into its campaign by the change of Permanent Secretary. In his Treasury capacity Fraser was intimate with the argument concerning hospital investment, including recent deliberations of the Plowden Health Services Sub-committee. Upon taking up his office, he quickly committed himself to establishing a 'really long-term and communicable programme' for hospitals. He was optimistic that this idea would be welcome to all parties, including the Treasury. The hospital plan presented a test-case for application of the Plowden philosophy; it therefore merited enthusiastic support within the Treasury: 'I know that the Treasury are hoping at last to get Ministerial acceptance for the view that constant 'stop and go' in long-term public sector investment is thoroughly unsound. So the tide is with us'. Fraser accepted that the plan would need to be flexible, especially with respect to its later years, but he was satisfied that anything less than ten years was unrealistic. A hard-core of projects ought to be adopted as 'firm', short of an economic cataclysm. On this basis he planned to approach the regional boards to discover what projects should be introduced before the end of the decade. The exercise would be in two stages, first a short and firm forward programme for the next four to five years, supplemented by a realistic plan for the rest of the decade. Already in June 1960, Fraser outlined a practical scheme, which contained all the essential elements of the plan published in 1962.[286] The small amount of available evidence suggests that Fraser was not unrealistic in his expectations about the receptivity of Treasury officials. Even before their meeting with the Ministry of Health, their habitual scepticism seems to have suddenly evaporated. The long-term plan for hospitals was now viewed as a trivial concession, similar in scale to university building, and amounting to only 3 per cent of the public investment programme.[287] In considering cuts in public investment for 1961/62, it was agreed that hospitals should be excluded because 'this programme is just getting going after being held down for a long time'; this expenditure needed to be protected in order to enable a 'sound and coherent programme' to be worked out.[288]

It seems that Fraser held a brief informal discussion with Sir Thomas Padmore about his plan on 30 June 1959.[289] This was followed by a more formal meeting a month later, which was described as amicable and constructive; it was accepted uncontroversially that a long-term, publicly announced plan was a desirable objective; and it was agreed to evolve a 'New Deal', 'forward look' or 'new look' hospital plan, for which a provisional total of £50m was adopted for the annual rate when the programme was in full swing.[290]

This small incident is indicative of a remarkable transformation in relations between the Treasury and the Ministry of Health brought about by the change in Permanent Secretary. For more than two years before the summer of 1960, the Ministry fought an uphill struggle to establish its long-term hospital programme; it slowly eroded the objections emanating from the Treasury, but even after the Conservative manifesto pledge, concessions were only grudgingly achieved. With the appointment of Fraser, the Treasury abandoned its obstructionism, and adopted the long-term plan as a self-evidently desirable objective. Accordingly, the hospital plan was set in firmly place by the civil servants before the change in Minister and the entry of Powell.

Reflecting the change of mood within the Treasury, rapid strides were made to finalise the hospital plan. Already by October 1960 the text of the important circular entitled 'Hospital Building' was ready for ratification by the Treasury.[291] It was confidently announced that 'the Minister's main object is to tackle the immense task of hospital capital development and reprovision as quickly and as efficiently as possible'. The regional boards were informed that they would be beneficiaries of an expanded hospital plan extending over ten years. While only provisional totals would be available for the second five-year period, firm figures would be indicated for the first five years. Under this new system it was intended to transfer to a method of control by allocation of starts for major projects. Once projects were adopted, the boards would be allowed to oversee these until their completion. The draft contained provisional allocations for the next five years. It was expected that expenditure would amount to £227m over the six years ending in 1965/66, for which a ceiling of £50m was adopted. Regional boards were asked to provide information about their capital investment priorities within the context of these guide-lines.[292]

The equanimity of the Treasury was strained by the figures proposed by the Ministry of Health. The Treasury argued that the election pledge and Guillebaud recommendation justified a ceiling of no more than £40m, but the Ministry of Health retorted that Guillebaud, other sources from that date, and the election pledge implied a rise to at least £45m. Once the plan was accepted, the Ministry insisted that the older guide-lines were redundant and that the expansion of the programme should be determined by what was needed and what the economy could afford. The Ministry therefore stood firm on its figures for the hospital programme; these were meekly accepted by the Treasury and ratified without query by the Chancellor of the Exchequer.[293]

It seems that Powell was not introduced to the hospital plan until 6 December 1960, when he was presented with the draft circular and provided with information necessary for introducing the plan to RHB Chairmen.[294] Powell discussed the hospital plan with officials on 9 December. His comments focused on two issues: first, he asked the department to evolve standards for bed provision extending for the next fifteen years; secondly, he insisted that the plan should make special reference to the value of voluntary effort, which he regarded as important for preventing the whole burden of the development of community care from falling on local authorities.[295]

The idea of a long-term hospital plan was unveiled by Powell to RHB Chairmen on 20 December 1960. This was in fact Powell's first full discussion of policy issues with the Chairmen, and he announced that this was the prelude to much fuller consultations with them - an intention that was not unfulfilled.[296] Immediately after his positive reception by the Chairmen, Powell informed Butler about the hospital plan, which he described as a 'durable asset politically', as well as a boost for morale within the NHS. Powell envisaged that the plan would include details of starts up to 1970/71, and therefore would outline building schemes covering a period of approximately 15 years. The only new element in his letter was the suggestion that the collective ideas of the regions should be issued in the form of a White Paper, which he anticipated could be ready by December 1961.[297] Observing the enthusiasm with which Powell had taken up the hospital plan, Treasury officials satisfied themselves that the plan originated with Fraser, before Powell became Minister, and was first unveiled to the Treasury on 30 June 1960, one month before Powell's appointment. By the end of the year, this origin risked becoming obscured: 'I don't know who claims authorship nowadays, but it looks as though Mr Powell is making the running'.[298]

Although the idea of a White Paper was imitative of the education forward drive, the Treasury was less than enthusiastic about the proposal for a hospital White Paper. It was felt that this public undertaking would introduce pressures for enhanced levels of expenditure and would tie the hands of the Treasury and health departments to a greater degree than was desirable.[299] The Treasury was even more adamantly opposed to Powell's subsequent suggestion for a White Paper published every six months to give a running commentary on progress with the hospital plan, a proposal which ran against Government policy to halt the proliferation of White Papers.[300]

The circular informing regional boards about the hospital plan was distributed on 17 January 1961.[301] In something of an understatement, the Permanent Secretary described the framing of the plan as a 'novel and complex job'. Building Note No.1 was available to give general advice on procedure, but also each region would be visited by a team of officers, who would provide more specific guidance and ensure that the plans for the various regions were produced according to a common pattern and were maintained in reasonable harmony. These visits would be completed by the end of March, and submissions from the regions were requested by 31 May.

To launch the new planning initiative a Press Conference was held on 17 January 1961, amplified by a written answer on 25 January.[302] Powell described his initiative as the 'beginning of a new phase in the history of the hospital service and therefore the National Health Service as a whole'. The Ministry of Health was cautious about committing itself to an overall total for the ten-year plan, but on the basis of a limit of £50m for 1965/66, Powell hinted that the ten-year plan might cost in the region of £500m, and the same figure was given by the Prime Minister in a speech delivered in Brighton.[303] Powell's public addresses were an important source of publicity concerning the hospital plan. Especially notable was his speech to the annual conference of the National Association of Mental Health, which announced bold targets for the closure of beds in the mental sector, together with the compensating expansion of community care.[304] This topic will be further considered in the next section of this chapter.

The outlines for a parallel long-term hospital building programme from Scotland were not discussed until March 1961. Because of the small scale of the Scottish capital programme, inclusion of a modest number of major schemes could not be achieved without increasing the relative share of capital investment allocated to Scotland. The urgent need to modernise Scotland's medical schools also argued for a generous share of resources. This minor weighting in favour of Scotland was not contested by London; an agreed budget of about £70m was adopted as a realistic basis for the Scottish plan for the ten years ending in 1971, which entailed expenditure of £7.8m in 1965/66, and adoption of £10m as provisional level for 1970/71. Since Scotland possessed a settled list of priorities, it was relatively straightforward to arrive at a programme of expenditure for a ten-year period.[305]

The unanticipated and sudden adoption of expanded opportunities for hospital building, although not in objective terms a dramatic advance on the existing trend, threw the health departments and NHS authorities into turmoil. The previous regime of uncertainty and retrenchment had provided an excuse for avoiding comprehensive and scientific planning exercises. Although the new plan could be assembled on the basis of the existing ad hoc framework, it was hardly possible to avoid some of the questions raised by integrated planning. In the few months available for drawing up regional returns and drafting a White Paper, it was hardly possible to address difficult and controversial problems that had been shelved since the beginning of the health service.

Given that even the best-provided regions possessed lists of urgent priorities for hospital development far in excess of the sums available for distribution under HM(61)4, their preparation of returns for the new hospital plan represented an unenviable exercise of selection. Typically, visiting teams found that northern regions were 'in process of retreating from the terrifying totals that objective needs suggested'. On the other hand, the visitors discovered that these boards were not 'optimistic of achieving even their more modest targets because, mainly, of shortage of architects and engineers but in the North East shortage of labour also'. The visitors appealed to the boards to face their new responsibility in less of a spirit of defeatism.[306] Regions cited the restrictive timetable as an excuse for not establishing the recommended planning teams, by-passing consultation with Hospital Management Committees, Boards of Governors and local authorities; their ten-year plan was therefore not a deliberate and considered planning statement, but a hastily-contrived rendition of their currently-available lists of building schemes. The regional plans inevitably reflected the shortcomings of the current decision-making process, constituting an awkward compromise between the forces of inertia and modernisation. Inevitably, a substantial part of the envisaged expenditure was directed towards investment in old hospitals which arguably should have been closed and relocated rather than modernised.

In view of the haste with which the hospital plan was concocted, the documentation presented by the regional boards commanded little confidence as an objective statement of priorities likely to be durable in the long term. There was also little consistency in the boards' methodology; most presented plans which were grossly inflated, and even worse contained many elements of miscalculation, mostly suggesting that they had under-appreciated levels of prospective expenditure. The hospital authorities also possessed little idea of the revenue implications of their capital schemes.

The worst problem related to absence of fixed expectations; neither the health departments nor the NHS authorities had reached settled conclusions about the scope and character of the modern hospital system to which they were aspiring. Without any particular coherent justification, the district general hospital had emerged by consensus as the guiding feature of planning arrangements, but this proposal was not particularly well-worked out. The planning exercise revealed that the regional boards possessed very incomplete information about demographic and epidemiological criteria relevant to planning. Their data on the existing system was also inadequate, but it revealed wild and irrational differences between the regions, and the plans for the future relating to the main specialties also revealed big differences of intentions. There was in particular a lack of consensus over plans for mental health, mental handicap and services for the elderly and the disabled.[307] The above difficulties were not unappreciated in the health departments, but political exigencies dictated that they were not allowed to interfere with the timetable adopted for the hospital plan. Also, for fear of derailing the much-welcomed opportunity to build new hospitals, outside experts were reticent about criticising the planning arrangements. Consequently, those involved placed the most optimistic gloss on the evidence reaching them and invested their expectations in the future learning process. However, the commitments made precipitously in the course of a few months in 1961 constituted a strait-jacket from which there was only the most limited opportunity for escape.

Powell was briefed sufficiently to be alerted to many of the above problems, but his keen wit seems not to have been exercised by the potential hazards contained within the hospital plan. In the autumn of 1961, Powell returned to the suggestion of a White Paper, emphasising that this would maximise the political benefit to the Government. He also requested prominent attention to the hospital plan at the Party Conference and in the Queen's Speech.[308] The Treasury remained steadfast in its opposition to a White Paper, primarily on the grounds that it would render more difficult the containment of expenditure on the hospital programme.[309] In presenting his proposal for a White Paper to the Treasury, Powell outlined a programme increasing from the agreed limit of £50m for 1965/66 to £75m in 1970/71. The total for the ten-year programme ending in 1971 was £525m, which Powell claimed was parsimonious, considering that the regional boards had submitted schemes amounting to about £850m. Powell also pointed out that the creation of a modern hospital system would enable the department to keep within its 2 per cent increment for spending on hospital running costs.[310] In fact, as already indicated, neither the capital nor current expenditure ceilings proved sustainable, but in the short term Powell's projections were not contested.[311] RHB Chairmen expressed general satisfaction with the draft White Paper.[312] During the final stages of preparation of the White Paper, the Treasury raised only minor drafting points. If the underlying weaknesses of the enterprise were recognised at all, they were passed over in silence. The only flurry of ministerial correspondence related to the total for the entire scheme. Powell recommended a total of £525m, while the Treasury favoured £500m. Powell eventually conceded to the Treasury limit. No doubt the health department was relieved by this concentration on such a trivial point of presentation.[313]

The Hospital Plan for England and Wales was published on 23 January 1962.[314] Powell proclaimed that his plan 'marked one of the most important days of the health service, because it gave the opportunity to plan the hospital service on a scale not possible anywhere else certainly on this side of the Iron Curtain'.[315] The Hospital Plan itself was a formidable document of nearly three hundred pages, but the general introductory sections comprised only 14 pages, and they contained only the most rudimentary information.

Three short appendices contained some summary financial and statistical information. The bulk of the document was taken up by synopses of the plans for each region. Wales received no greater prominence than other regions. Although the brief preface contained exhortations characteristic of Ministers, somewhat unusually for a White Paper, it was unsigned.

Within the limits of the spending indicated above, the English and Welsh plan included a commitment to 90 new hospitals, 134 substantially modernised hospitals, and 356 other big schemes. This ten-year plan contained details of schemes which would have the effect of replacing 750 of the existing 2,000 hospitals in England and Wales.

The Scottish Hospital Plan was also published on 23 January 1962.[316] The Scottish Plan was naturally shorter than its English equivalent, comprising only 43 pages, but it was a more discursive document, the text being dominated by ordered discussion of the rationale for the plan, with synopses of regional plans constituting only one out of six chapters. Beside the rebuilding of most of the teaching hospitals, the main feature of the Scottish plan was the proposal for ten district general hospitals in centres of larger population and smaller hospitals able to provide acute services for remote areas.

The hospital plans were given a warm welcome, and Powell himself was accorded much credit for the successful launch.[317] In the House of Commons, the English plan was praised, but Robinson argued that it was an over-hasty concoction, based on guess work and that its costs were seriously underestimated.[318] The notes of reservation sounded by Robinson came increasingly to the fore as the initial euphoria surrounding the hospital plans rapidly ebbed away. In fact, the funds set aside for major schemes during the first years of the hospital plan were extremely modest, only slightly above the already established trend in spending, and below the level of such medium-sized undertakings as the capital programme of the Atomic Energy Authority.[319]

Naturally, some of the most prominent complaints came from hospitals and areas not scheduled to benefit from the great rebuilding.[320] Even hospitals with a greater chance of benefiting from the new programme were dismayed by the prospect of many years of delay before their conditions could be improved.[321] Also, when it was appreciated that new district general hospitals would be developed at the cost of closing cottage hospitals, much anger was ventilated from the Tory shires, which won a favourable response from the Prime Minister, who was by no means convinced by Powell's explanations.[322] No sooner was the Hospital Plan launched than its basic premises were questioned. For instance, on account of the rising birthrate and demands for providing facilities to permit all confinements to take place in hospitals, the health Ministers appealed unsuccessfully to their colleagues for additional funds dedicated to expansion of maternity units.[323]

In England and Wales, regular progress reports were issued on the hospital plan. In 1963 a short document indicating revisions to the plan was published. This comprised mainly a list of new schemes to be added in the period up to April 1973. Nothing was said about the revision of the programme caused by escalating costs which, despite upward revision of the totals in the light of inflation, were necessitating deferment of starting dates for major schemes.[324] A longer revision was issued in May 1964, taking the starting dates to April 1974.[325] It was now estimated that projects hitherto scheduled for the ten-year programme were unlikely to be completed within a fifteen-year period, even if expenditure was maintained at the peak level beyond 1971.

The spring of 1964 marked a turning point in hospital building in England and Wales. For the first time since the beginning of the health service, NHS authorities had succeeded in spending up to the limits of their estimates. This was a welcome indication of greater capacity of the planning mechanism of the regions, but it meant that assurances given to the Treasury concerning likely underspending were falsified.[326]

In 1964 SHHD revised its hospital plan, the main new element being the proposal for another district general hospital in Glasgow. As in England, expanding costs of the scheme were already causing starting dates for major hospitals to be deferred.[327] The estimated cost of the hospital plan for England and Wales increased to £750m for the decade 1964 to 1974. The revised total for the Scottish plan for the same period was £105m. These increases were partly explained by inflation and partly by continuation of expenditure at the peak rate after 1970.[328] The struggling hospital programme increasingly attracted comment in the press.[329] On behalf of the opposition, Robinson questioned Ministers about the Government's reticent concerning revaluation of the cost of the hospital plan. He castigated the Government's recent White Paper as 'misleading to the point of dishonesty', claiming that the hospital programme would cost twice as much as the Government had admitted.[330] In his long defence of the Government's record, Barber made no attempt to contradict Robinson's assertion.[331] The health departments were alert to the accusation of miscalculation. It was accepted that the original programme might take as long as 26 years, and cost as much as £2,000m. In the mean time it was admitted that delays in the programme had caused disappointment and discontent; indeed some authorities were engaging in 'silly spending' on obsolete accommodation on account of the prospect of major delays affecting plans for efficient replacements.[332] Even more ominously, the *Lancet* claimed that a realistic hospital plan might cost as much as £100m a year for the next forty years.[333] A further study, virtually complete by the summer of 1964, estimated that for the period 1960 to 1975, capital investment in the health sector would cost £1,700m for the United Kingdom as a whole. Such calculations introduced a note of realism about the spending implications of the hospital plans.[334]

By the summer of 1964, the spirit of triumphalism which was associated with the launch of the hospital plans had largely been dissipated. Estimates of the likely scale of building attainable under the ten or fifteen-year plan were being radically revised downwards. Sanguine critics appreciated that the hospital plans were unlikely to erase Britain's dismal recent record in hospital building. As the Secretary of State for Scotland was reminded:

> In 1938 expenditure on hospitals amounted to 1.67 per cent of the total capital investment in Great Britain. By 1965, when the expenditure is supposed to rise to £56m, that figure is likely to be no more than 1.25 per cent of the total capital expenditure. In 1938/39, the hospital capital expenditure in England and Wales seems to have been about 20 per cent of the current expenditure. There are post-war American figures which support this ratio of about 1:5. On the other hand, so far as we can foresee, the Great Britain ratio of capital to current hospital expenditure in 1965/66 will be less than 10 per cent. In other words although, in industry generally, increasing emphasis is put on the importance of maintaining a high rate of capital investment, in this particular 'industry', the rate planned is only about half of what seems to be desirable.[335]

(v) INVENTING COMMUNITY CARE

It is only a minor exaggeration to claim that 'community care' has been at least notionally a main priority since the inception of the health service. Indeed, the idea of community care was inherited from the prewar era as an objective in the services for vulnerable groups.[336] Because each new administration has adopted the idea as if it was its own discovery, introducing changes of meaning to suit the prevailing ideology, the extent of the longer term preoccupation with community care tends to be obscured.

As evident from the previous section, from the outset, plans for hospital modernisation assumed that costs could only be kept within manageable proportions if unnecessary resort to hospital was prevented through the maximisation of preventive and community care. The latter was not clearly defined; sometimes it was regarded

109

as all alternatives to hospital care, perhaps with an emphasis on Part III residential accommodation and other forms of residential and institutional care provided by local health and welfare authorities. Alternatively, community care was used in the more modern sense to suggest that the sick should be supported in their homes, by expanding domiciliary services, provided by such professional groups as health visitors, district nurses and home helps. In either definition, the local authority was the main agency for supplying services. At least before 1979, community care as a concept implied that health authorities and local authorities rather than families themselves, should play the lead in providing care, and therefore in devising services and committing resources to this objective.

In the period before health service reorganisation, services administered by local health and welfare authorities were fundamental to the development of community care. However, as noted in the previous chapter, these parts of the new health service risked becoming a neglected corner of local government activity. However, after a period of disorientation, Medical Officers of Health gradually became alerted to their responsibilities in the field of community care, and expansion of their services became a real possibility. The growing population of the elderly, the high cost and shortage of acute care facilities, as well as increasing dissatisfaction with most forms of long-term institutional care, all suggested an important strategic role for alternative services administered by local government.

Already in its 1955 General Election manifesto, the Conservative Party pledged support for development of local health authority services, especially home helps and half-way houses. The Treasury recognised that pressure was building up for greater expenditure on services for the elderly, and that some concession in this field was unavoidable.[337]

In January 1957, in advocating a 'new drive' for hospitals, Vosper also emphasised that demand for in-patient treatment needed to be restrained to a minimum by developing local authority and general practitioner services; he specifically called for expansion of home support services, and reminded colleagues of the Government's promise to introduce a chiropody service. Significantly, Vosper also attached high priority to increasing the amount of residential accommodation provided by local authorities. He envisaged that residential homes for the elderly would be provided at a rate of at least 6,000 places per annum. Vosper's thinking on care in the mental sector was still dominated by modernisation of hospital facilities, albeit with diversification into out-patient departments, day hospitals and acute treatment units in general hospitals.[338]

110

One year later, in February 1958, Vosper's successor produced a similar list of priorities, on this occasion categorising them under three headings:

1. Prevention of illness.

2. A shift of emphasis away from hospital and institutional treatment towards community care.

3. The improvement of hospital and institutional buildings and administration with a view to increased efficiency.[339]

Without exaggerating the significance of these particular ministerial pronouncements, arguably they indicate a crystallisation of priorities, entailing appreciation of the potential importance of community services. Also it is evident that in the 1958 document, 'community care' has become established in the terminology, whereas this term was absent from Vosper's memorandum. Community care not only possessed advantages as a forward-looking form of health care, but it could be presented as an economical alternative, helpful to the image of the health departments since it offered a potential means to arresting the seemingly inexorable rise in expenditure on hospitals. In considering the future of the hospital service, George Godber insisted that 'hospitals must be organised primarily for the support of home care'.[340]

It is therefore not surprising that community care also occupied a key place in the list of priorities drawn up by Walker-Smith in preparation for the 1959 General Election. On this occasion Walker-Smith advocated:

(a) A progressive 5-year increase in the amount taken into account in the General Grant calculations for the local authority health and welfare services;

(b) a progressive five year increase in the capital allocation for these services;

(c) a progressive expansion of staff to man the local authority services and in particular the mental health services.[341]

By this stage Walker-Smith's thinking had advanced to the point of envisaging developments in the health service in terms of a five-year plan. Not only was community care integral to this plan, it was accorded just as much importance as hospital modernisation. Walker-Smith's ambitious plan for community care was not incorporated in the Conservative 1959 General Election manifesto, but it received tacit recognition in the pledge to establish a National Council for Social Work Training, which was promised as a prelude to further development of local authority health and welfare services, including better provision for the meals on wheels service.[342]

Ministerial proposals for the future development of the health service suggest that by the beginning of 1959 community care had become established as a significant priority. Direct influences accounting for the rising importance of community care are not difficult to find. The slow and intangible changes in practice and thinking among those responsible for serving and representing the various client groups, found expression in a plethora of official reports.[343] Especially important was the Report of the Royal Commission on Mental Illness, the influence of which was reinforced by the two Dunlop Reports concerned with mental health reform in Scotland, the Guillebaud, and Piercy Reports, other committees such as the CHSC, the SHSC and their Standing Advisory Committees, as well as the Jameson and Younghusband investigations dealing respectively with recruitment and training of health visitors and social workers.

The Royal Commission on the Law Relating to Mental Illness and Mental Deficiency was established in 1954 under the chairmanship of Eustace Sutherland Campbell Percy, Baron Percy of Newcastle (1887-1958). The latter was a younger son of the seventh Duke of Northumberland; as Lord Eustace Percy, he was one of the two MPs appointed to the 1924 Royal Commission on Lunacy and Mental Disorder, but had resigned in the same year upon his appointment as President of the Board of Education.[344]

The Commission reported in May 1957.[345] It fulfilled a long-desired aim to modernise and harmonise the complex and often antiquated body of law concerning the certification and detention of patients classified as being affected by mental illness or mental handicap. This task was the main piece of business left unfinished by the founders of the National Health Service. The wide-ranging recommendations of the Royal Commission suggested the virtual abandonment of compulsion with respect to admission to hospitals or institutions concerned with mental health. It was envisaged that hospital care would be provided informally with no greater restriction on the patient's freedom than would be the case in other forms of illness. The Commission recommended that 'the law should be altered so that wherever possible suitable care may be provided for mentally disordered patients with no more restriction of liberty or legal formality than is applied to people who need care because of other types of illness, disability or social difficulty'.[346] Compulsory detention, hitherto the dominant form of treatment, would be reduced to a residual category, determined on strict criteria, and containing greater safeguards for the patient than under the previous regime. The Royal Commission proposed to establish Mental Health Review Tribunals comprising legal, medical and lay elements, designed to give an increased level of protection for patients compulsorily admitted to hospital.

Given the normalisation of treatment, it was proposed to abolish the distinction between designated and other hospitals, and allow treatment to be provided at any location where appropriate facilities were provided. The Royal Commission proposed a new classification for the groups involved, under the general terminology of 'mental disorder'; this new terminology may not have possessed long-term durability, but was an improvement on the traditional rebarbative language applied in the fields of mental illness and handicap. With the normalisation of mental treatment, the Royal Commission suggested that it was no longer necessary to preserve the Board of Control, which under the NHS had been maintained, but in a much-reduced form within the Ministry of Health.

Suggestions for the development of community care appear in chapter 10 of the Royal Commission Report, which was concerned with the division of functions between hospital and local authorities, and with the development of services provided by local authorities.[347] The Commission recommended that local authorities as well as hospitals should provide residential care for patients not in need of medical or nursing services, and that local authorities should develop their occupational and training centres, as well as other support. It was argued that these community services would facilitate early discharge or even treatment without admission to hospital. To speed up the provision of non-hospital accommodation, it was suggested that small hospital units might be transferred to local authority control. More important but problematical, it was recommended that a special Exchequer contribution should apply to all local authority capital expenditure on mental health services for a limited period. Given the huge size of the mental sector hospital population, creation of local authority institutional services clearly entailed a formidable capital commitment, as well as a big shift in the responsibilities of local health and welfare authorities. In order to encourage local authorities to give greater priority to mental health provision, the Royal Commission made the radical suggestion that the grant in aid for developments in the mental health services might be as high as 75 per cent rather than the usual 50 per cent.[348]

The recommendations of the Royal Commission closely reflected advanced thinking of the period; they received an enthusiastic reception and were embodied in the Mental Health Act 1959. This complex piece of legislation relating to freedom of the individual as well as health was well-calculated to bring out the strengths of a

113

Minister of Health who was a lawyer by professional experience. The 'Mental Care and Treatment Bill' occasioned little difficulty when it was presented to Ministers in February 1958. Walker-Smith explained that the Bill departed from the recommendations of the Royal Commission in two important respects. First, in response to criticisms of the threefold categorisation of mental disorder (mentally ill, severely subnormal, psychopath), it was proposed to define 'psychopath' more narrowly and add a fourth category of 'subnormal'. Secondly, whereas the Royal Commission proposed to leave the residual power to discharge from compulsory detention in the hands of the Minister, it was suggested that this responsibility should rest with the new Mental Health Review Tribunals. By coincidence, Jocelyn Simon, who had served briefly on the Commission, was present at the Home Affairs Committee, having replaced Powell as Financial Secretary in January 1958. Simon argued the case for the Commission's recommendations, but it was agreed that final decision should be left to Parliament.[349] The Bill, now called 'Mental Health Bill', was published in December 1958; this received its Second Reading in the House of Commons in January 1959. Large numbers of amendments were introduced in both the House of Commons and House of Lords, without affecting the main provisions of the Bill. The parliamentary response to the Bill has been described as 'consensual acclamation'.[350] The Mental Health Act received the Royal Assent on 20 July 1959.

Before introducing its scheme for reforming the law on mental health, the Department of Health in Scotland took the advice of the Dunlop Committee.[351] The Scottish recommendations generally followed the English, but were different in significant respects. It was proposed to divide mental disorder into only two categories, mental illness and mental deficiency; the 21 age limit for compulsory admission of psychopaths and subnormal patients in England was not to be adopted; in addition to medical opinions, the Scottish proposed to maintain a role for the sheriff in compulsory admissions; and it was proposed to preserve the General Board of Control for Scotland (renamed Scottish Mental Welfare Commission) rather than set up mental health review tribunals. Despite the precedents for independence on law relating to mental illness, Ministers were unenthusiastic about all the proposed departures from the English Bill. It was argued that inconsistencies between the two systems would cause embarrassment and possibly disrupt the later stages of the English Bill. It was also suggested that the Scottish approach was in some respects less protective of the freedom of the individual. Maclay, whose brother served on the Royal Commission, refused to accept the quadripartite division of mental disorder, which he described as 'repugnant to Scottish opinion'. Maclay also pointed out that the sheriff in Scotland was a professional lawyer, who occupied a different role from the magistrate in England and Wales. Since the sheriff 'occupied a special position of a paternal nature, any attempt to displace him from the field of mental health would meet with determined opposition'. Maclay's only concession was to accept the 21 age limit for compulsory admission for certain classes of patient.[352] The separate Scottish approach was reluctantly accepted by Ministers and the differences outlined above were incorporated in the Mental Health (Scotland) Act 1960.

Although community care was only an indirect consequence of the English and Welsh Bill, it was one of the most actively discussed issues throughout the parliamentary debates. There was distinct suspicion that the Government would be unwilling to invest the resources necessary to enable the reform to have its full impact. Also, the general view that the Mental Health Bill represented a definitive measure of enlightenment was not universally shared. In both Houses, but especially in the House of Lords, and best expressed by the social scientist, Barbara Wootton (Baroness Wootton), there was strong dissent on libertarian grounds about the danger that any form of alleged deviant behaviour was likely to be labelled as mental disease, thereby exposing these individuals to arbitrary detention as psychopaths on the testimony of medical experts.[353] The dangers were particularly pronounced with respect to the mentally handicapped, who suffered the indignity of being appropriated as a branch of mental disorder. It took a further twenty years for this germ of criticism to mature into a full anti-authoritarian critique of the 1959 mental health legislation.

The Mental Health Act had widespread ramifications. For instance, representations made at the Committee Stage of the Mental Health Bill prompted the Ministry of Health to undertake an enquiry into State Institutions.[354] The Act was also only indirectly concerned with community care. However, the reorientation of policy brought about by the Report of the Royal Commission and the Mental Health Act 1959 drew attention to the full potentialities of community care. The new perspective inevitably threatened the monopoly on treatment by big and remote mental hospitals, and facilitated the entry into mental treatment of specialist units in general hospitals and related out-patient departments. It also paved the way to increasing the part played by preventive work, after-care, day, occupational and training centres, and residential hostels located outside hospitals. Such changes inevitably offered an extended role for the services administered by local authorities, not only health and welfare authorities, but also education authorities, who wished to take on responsibility for occupation and training centres, and thereby increase the links of educational facilities for the mental handicapped with other schools and colleges.

The Royal Commission Report created the preconditions for pluralism in treatment which was scarcely possible under the previous legislation. At an early stage in its deliberations the Royal Commission appreciated the importance of community care. Even for patients who were subjected to compulsion, it was argued that 'after-care by the medical staff or social workers of the hospitals or through the community care services of the local health authority should be given as long as necessary irrespective of the legal power to recall the patient to the hospital'. The Royal Commission realised that existing administrative divisions stood in the way of continuity of treatment, and they found it difficult to designate precise roles for workers employed by health and local authorities. They felt that these difficulties might be resolved if personnel were employed jointly by health and local authorities.[355] This emphasis on integrated planning and continuity of treatment was expounded by such organisations as the Royal Medico-Psychological Association and the Society of Medical Officers of Health. Their advocacy of integration was influenced by experience of a handful of experimental schemes in co-ordination which, although not of long-duration, were already yielding promising results.

Only a small part of the evidence received by the Royal Commission related to community care. While this objective was generally approved, informed sources were concerned about the disparity in provision among local authorities, and it was suggested that there was much neglect of statutory duties, and indeed little sympathy for the problems of mental health.[356] On account of such disparities in attitude and performance, such organisations as the Society of Mental Welfare Officers and the Society of Medical Officers of Health recommended that community care should be designated as a duty of the local authority. NHS and medical organisations also recognised that local authorities would not perform their duties efficiently unless they were given more resources.[357]

Given general support for the recommendations of the Royal Commission and the prominence of the recommendations concerning residential accommodation, the Ministry of Health had little option but to try to realise this objective. However, the timing was inconvenient because the structure of local government finance was under review, and more important, the health service was passing through one of its bouts of imposed retrenchment. The Ministry estimated that adequate provision of all forms of residential and training accommodation amounted to a programme costing £40m. This would allow for residential accommodation for 24,000 persons, and training and occupational centres for 33,000 persons, half of which would be residential. The Ministry acted upon the Commission's proposal for an Exchequer grant at the level of 75 per cent. It was proposed that a programme extending over ten years should be adopted. Some long-term savings were anticipated, but in the short term the Ministry admitted that increased expenditure on mental hospitals and mental handicap institutions was unavoidable owing to the extent of dilapidation and overcrowding.[358]

The Treasury reacted negatively to the community care proposals emanating from the health departments; particular objection was taken to expenditure-related propositions stemming from the Royal Commission. The proposal for a 75 per cent grant was objectionable in itself, but it was also viewed as a dangerous precedent, capable of upsetting the complex negotiations with local government concerning transition to a general grant. An earmarked grant for mental health was regarded as contrary to the drift of thinking about future local government finance. The Treasury was also annoyed that the health departments were pressing forward with many proposals for additional expenditure in the field of community care at a time of retrenchment and without any attempt at indicating priorities, either between the community care proposals, or with respect to the wider health programme. It was pointed out that the health departments were expecting simultaneous expansion in community care and modernisation of hospitals and dental schools, without any real guarantee that community care would lead to offsetting savings in the hospital sector.[359]

In preparing for activation of their community care programme, the health departments ran up against Thorneycroft's campaign for reduction in public capital investment undertaken in connection with his defence of sterling. The first steps to obtain support of Ministers for an extension in community care were made in July 1957, during the awkward intermission caused by the illness of Vosper. The Ministry of Health outlined a package of proposals deriving from the Percy, Piercy, and Guillebaud Reports. To allow for a programme of residential homes, hostels, training and occupational centres in the field of mental health, the Ministry proposed a programme of £40m capital expenditure, over a period of ten years, rising to a level of £10m by the end of the period. The Royal Commission's proposal for a 75 per cent grant was regarded as reasonable in the light of the 100 per cent Exchequer commitment to hospitals. The Guillebaud Committee had proposed that the Exchequer aid for old people's homes should be converted into the standard 50 per cent grant.[360] However, the new general grant being negotiated with local government entailed phasing out arrangements for percentage grants. Accordingly, the Ministry of Health proposed that old people's homes should be treated in the same way as other local health authority services in the assessment of the general grant. It was proposed to begin with an expenditure of £0.5m, rising substantially in subsequent years. The least expensive part of the Ministry's proposals related to disablement, where the Piercy Committee had argued the case for an expansion of services for rehabilitation, training and resettlement.[361] The additional annual cost of expanded services not connected with employment was estimated at a maximum of £2m. The Government had already given a general welcome to the Piercy Report. The Ministry of Health conceded that it was unrealistic to introduce a percentage grant in advance of the reorganisation of local government finance, but it insisted that an allowance for these services should be made in the new general grant to local authorities. Ministers prevaricated about these proposals. It was agreed that they should be reconsidered in the light of final decision reached about local government finance and the Government's decision concerning the Royal Commission on Mental Illness.[362]

Further consideration of additional resources for community care was delayed until after the change of Minister. Walker-Smith restated the case for the development of community care, but this was hotly contested by the Treasury. With respect to mental health, the Treasury insisted that any additional expenditure on residential accommodation should financed by reduction in the hospital capital budget. On subsidies for local authority accommodation for the elderly, the Treasury resisted any change in current arrangements; on the Piercy recommendations, no objection was raised on the principle, but on grounds of economy, it was proposed that action should be deferred. Powell argued that it was 'unjustifiable, at the very inception of the block grant system and in the present economic climate, to admit three new items of expenditure'. Walker-Smith reminded Ministers of the great humanitarian benefits of community care. The proposed changes 'would enable patients who at present spend many years of their lives in hospital to live a more natural and useful life in the general community, many of them in employment'. If the Government failed to act they would lay themselves 'open to the charge that we are preventing the proper handling of one of the outstanding social problems of the present time, of which Parliament and the general public are becoming increasingly conscious'. He therefore argued that in the light of the recommendations of three independent committees, whose findings had been widely supported, it was 'neither socially nor politically expedient to adopt an entirely negative attitude'. The most Walker-Smith was willing to concede was limitation of additional expenditure to a minimum during the current economic emergency.

The Home Affairs Committee agreed that some concession in the field of community care was unavoidable. Ministers appreciated that the current proposals related to some of the most neglected social services. The amounts of expenditure involved were trivial, and therefore not likely to add to the Government's economic problems. It was recommended that further minimum provision should be made as an 'earnest of the sincerity of the Government's intentions in the matter'.[363]

Fearing that Walker-Smith would be able to derive further support from Ministers if community care policy was referred to the Cabinet, Thorneycroft offered a compromise. On condition that Walker-Smith was prepared to absorb any capital expenditure on mental health within the currently agreed level for local authority loan sanctions for the following two years, Thorneycroft hinted that he would not require further cuts in these loan sanctions, and he promised that the planned expenditure with respect to the Percy and Piercy Reports would be included within the general grant for the period after April 1960. Walker-Smith reluctantly agreed to abandon proposals for implementation of the Guillebaud Committee's recommendation relating to the change in the basis for the subsidy on old people's homes. He also accepted under protest Thorneycroft's suggestion, on condition that the level of loan sanctions to local authorities was discussed on the merits of the case. He protested that he was already offering to maintain capital expenditure in the local authority field at the depressed level of £4.4m for three years from 1957 to 1960; local authorities would therefore complain that nothing was being done to reduce the large backlog of capital schemes in the local health and welfare area, and that no real incentive was being given to the immediate implementation of the Percy and Piercy proposals. With the resignation of Thorneycroft, a reply was received from Amory, which conceded that Walker-Smith should be given an extra £1/2m for the next financial year to make a start with the mental health reforms.[364]

The supplementary proposal of the Royal Commission to transfer surplus NHS property to local authorities for community care purposes initially seemed capable of yielding promising results. NHS authorities inherited much accommodation unsuitable for hospital purposes, some of which was capable of adaptation for residential care. Local authorities were enthusiastic to avail themselves of this opportunity; indeed, in many cases they would be repossessing facilities sacrificed to the health authorities in 1948. However, this proposal ran up against opposition from the Treasury, which had for long been campaigning for NHS authorities to completely dispose of their surplus property. The health departments and Treasury negotiated over this scheme for some years, but in 1965 it was abandoned after 'immense trouble throughout with very little result'.[365]

Given the failure to obtain more than minimal resources for expansion of community care, the Ministry of Health fell back on exhortation. This entailed giving publicity to hopeful initiatives which were already underway. It was especially relevant to circulate advice on co-ordination between hospitals and local authorities. This was already the subject of a report by the Mental Health Standing Advisory Committee, produced in 1956, which collated the latest available information on joint ventures. It was therefore a relatively simple matter to update this report and issue it in edited form for guidance of relevant authorities on best practice.[366] The new circular was distributed in 1959, accompanied by a press release headed 'Minister Calls for Expansion of Local Health Services'.[367] This was part of a general public relations exercise designed to demonstrate that the community care proposals of the Royal Commission were not being allowed to lapse by default, and that the 1959 changes were a general turning point in mental health care.[368] This was convincing with respect to the legal changes, but less so in the case of resources. The upward trend in capital investment in hospitals was presented as a hopeful sign, but with respect to integration of treatment, comprehensive schemes remained limited to pioneering locations such as Cardiff, Nottingham, Oldham, Woking and York. With respect to the local authorities, it was regarded as a major step forward that under the new legislation ambiguities concerning their powers were cleared up, while certain powers were converted into a duties to provide services. Local authorities were directed to prepare schemes for the development of their services. However, there was no compulsion to act on these plans until resources were provided. Consequently, extension of services in the field of community care continued in a slow incremental manner, with very little acceleration. The attempt to accompany the major change in law associated with the Mental Health Act 1959 with the launch of a sizeable community care programme was therefore an abject failure. The health departments fell back on their customary piecemeal approach, making minor advances when the opportunity presented itself.

Failure to implement the promise made in 1956 to offset the impact of the increased prescription charge on the elderly by allowing development of a chiropody service was an increasing source of embarrassment. Questions were regularly tabled by MPs on this issue.[369] The shortfall was to a limited extent compensated for by the National Corporation for the Care of Old People, which contributed substantial grants for this purpose during a three-year period ending in 1959. When this subsidy ended, embarrassment concerning government inaction was unavoidable. In 1958 Labour incorporated the chiropody service in its policy for the health service. The Treasury successfully resisted pressure for introduction of the chiropody service each year until consideration of the estimates for 1959/60, when it was argued somewhat incongruously that the health departments should not be given the resources for chiropody on the grounds that they were also requesting funds for BCG vaccination. At this stage Walker-Smith's patience ran out; he warned his senior colleagues that the chiropody service was no longer avoidable.[370] The Treasury agreed to an announcement concerning chiropody, providing it was made clear to the health departments that the introduction of the service would be delayed until the year 1961/62.[371] It was explained that this length of time was needed to evaluate proposals from local authorities. The very modest sum of £1m was allowed for development of the chiropody service in the course of the first five years.[372] In pursuance of this decision, in 1959 local health authorities were invited to submit proposals for development of their chiropody services.[373]

In the light of the Conservative General Election manifesto promise, it was also necessary to extend provision for meals on wheels. The importance of this service had not been completely appreciated at the beginning of the health service. Under the National Assistance Act 1948 local authorities were allowed to make a grant to voluntary organisations for this purpose, but were not themselves allowed to provide meals. In 1957 Ministers considered whether to support a private member's Bill to remove this restriction, but in view of Treasury objections, government backing was withheld.[374] A recommendation for direct local authority provision of meals on wheels emanated from the Conservative Policy Committee on the Care of the Old, which was the source of the manifesto pledge. The Home Affairs Committee had little alternative but to support this proposal, but it discovered an unanticipated complication over imposition of charges on National Assistance recipients, which raised the problem of interference with the rights of local authorities to determine the level of charges. This issue was only settled after acrimonious and protracted debate between departments.[375] Local authorities were not allocated their power to provide meals until this provision was included in the National Assistance Act 1948 (Amendment) Act 1962, which received the Royal Assent on 24 May 1962.[376]

A further example of delay in acting on a general election pledge related to recommendations of the Younghusband Report concerning the expansion of social work and the reorganisation of social work training. As noted above, the Conservatives promised to establish a National Council for Social Work Training to supervise training arrangements for the more numerous and more highly-qualified non-graduate social workers required for new developments in community care. The Younghusband Committee, which had been established in 1955, reported in May 1959. Discussions between the Treasury and health departments on implementation of the Younghusband Report began in April 1960, but no statement concerning the Government's intentions had been made by the first anniversary of the report. This naturally provoked probing questions in Parliament, as well as adverse comment in the press.[377] This reaction prompted the Government to issue a statement that it would introduce legislation to set up councils for the training of social workers and also for health visitors.[378] Further squabbling between the Treasury and the health departments concerning the composition of the new training bodies further delayed the introduction of legislation until 1962.[379] Under the Health Visiting and Social Work (Training) Act 1962, the National Council for Training in Social Work and the Council for the Education and Training of Health Visitors were established in October 1962, with Sir John Wolfenden as the chairman of both councils. Sir Charles Morris replaced Wolfenden in August 1963, when the latter became Chairman of the University Grants Committee. The first report of the National Council for Training in Social Work was not published until September 1965. It was only at this point that it became possible to mount a concerted effort to increase the recruitment of nongraduate social workers.

Failure to act decisively on community care evoked some stinging remarks from leading experts in the field. Richard Titmuss pointed out that in real terms there had been a decline in resources available to community care since the beginning of the NHS. Peter Townsend observed that failure to act on the principle of caring for the elderly in their own homes would be selected by social historians of the future 'as the most striking failure of social policy in the last decade'.[380] The insignificant level of expenditure on community care is indicated by such comparisons as the £7m a year dispensed on compensation to chicken farmers for fowl pest, or the £10m set aside for providing the infrastructure for five bases for intercontinental ballistic missiles.[381]

Despite the restrictions imposed by the Treasury, local authority health and welfare capital spending inched forwards, to reach the level of £7.25m in 1960/61. On the basis of the newly-imposed duties of local authorities with respect to the Mental Health Act, the health departments made a determined attempt to obtain resources for local government on a more realistic level. Walker-Smith supported a PESC bid for £16m for 1961/62 on the basis that it was necessary 'to start making good the effects of successive years of restrictions' and to take the first significant stride forwards with respect to mental health services obligations. Officials within the Treasury were divided over this issue. Since the Chancellor of the Exchequer instructed his officials not to concede 'anything not really needed in the furtherance of current plans and policies', there was an inclination to prevent any increase in expenditure for the next three years. However, others felt that 'when there is a long history of relative starvation in local health authority investment, it seems a great pity that we cannot launch out a bit now'. In view of interest by the Prime Minister in this issue, it was agreed to follow a moderate course and offer £10m.[382] This decision was contested by the Ministry of Health with more than its usual resolve, and it was not until December 1960 that the level of capital expenditure for 1961/62 was agreed. The Treasury was accused of attempting 'to stop a separate and independent authority from doing, with its own funds, urgent works which the local people want and need'.[383] Walker-Smith appealed for a more generous settlement on account of pressing need to implement community care policies on a more realistic basis, but the Treasury refused to raise their limit beyond £11.25m for 1961/62. Walker-Smith ended his term of office complaining about the threat to community care services offered by cuts in capital expenditure.[384]

At the same time as their bid to increase capital spending, negotiations over the level of the general grant to local authorities for its second period, 1961-1963, gave the health departments their first real opportunity to press for an increase in expenditure on domiciliary services, which were recognised as the foundation for the community care policy, but had until this date attracted less attention than capital projects.[385] In this area of current expenditure, the health departments adopted the modest target of doubling expenditure between 1960 and 1964. In the key field of mental health, this entailed an increase from about £5m to £10m.

The hospital plan infused new life into the campaign for additional expenditure on care within the community, since this was the most obvious way of guarding against excessive cost of hospital expansion. Immediately the idea of a long-term programme for hospitals was accepted, the Ministry of Health argued that local authorities should be allowed to plan their capital development on the same basis.[386] It was realised that on account of the small scale of capital projects in the local authority field, it was not necessary to secure commitments concerning capital expenditure for more than two years in advance, but for efficient use of resources, long-term planning was essential. The health departments appreciated that conceding planning on a long-term basis would make it difficult for the Treasury to resist expansion of community care on at least the time-scale adopted for the hospital plan. With this goal in mind, in the spring of 1961 the health departments presented proposals for local authority expenditure up to April 1966.[387]

Powell was fully aware of the need for integrated planning of community care and hospital services. Indeed, maximisation of community care was a fundamental prerequisite for preventing escalation of the costs of the hospital service. In his speech to the National Association of Mental Health, Powell called for a 50 per cent or greater reduction in beds in mental hospitals. In arguably his own most important statement on health policy, and one of the most acute comments ever made by a Minister of Health, Powell insisted that:

> We have to strive to alter our whole mentality about hospitals, and about mental hospitals especially. Hospital building is not like pyramid building, the erection of memorials to endure to a remote posterity...The old Roman virtue of pietas becomes a vice when it is directed towards a hospital building...I am certain of this, that it is the duty of a Minister of Health and the duty of a National Association for Mental Health...to favour wherever they have the choice, the course of more drastic and fundamental change: for we may be pretty sure that even so the progress of medical thought and method will still be well on ahead of our practice.

Powell ended with a plea for expansion of community care. The hospital plan:

> makes no sense therefore unless the medical profession outside the hospital service can be supported in this task by a whole new development of the local authority services for the old, for the sick and for the mentally ill and mentally subnormal...That is why, at the earliest moment possible, I intend to call on local health and welfare authorities...to take a hand in mapping the joint future of the hospital and the local authority services.[388]

There was no diminution in Powell's formal commitment to community care. In presenting the draft of the hospital plan to the Prime Minister, with respect to the undertaking to develop community care, Powell remarked that 'I personally regard this as one of the best things about the plan'.[389] Such sentiments became a commonplace in ministerial and indeed prime ministerial statements. Macmillan promised that the ten-year plan for hospitals would be associated with a parallel programme for community care: 'it is now recognised that care within the community is often the most effective, especially, of course, for the mentally ill and for old people'. He promised a big effort to provide old people's housing and domiciliary services.[390]

Initially, Powell was confident that he could maintain a healthy rate of growth in community care expenditure within the 2.5 per cent ceiling which he voluntarily adopted for the rate of expansion of NHS expenditure. He envisaged that increasing resources for community care would be available from economies in hospital running costs, family practitioner services and welfare milk subsidies.[391] In practice, the health departments developed no precise estimate of the resources required to develop community care. Early expectations that the ten-year plan would embrace both hospitals and community care were quickly abandoned. The tight timetable for the hospital plan also precluded meaningful discussions between hospital authorities and local authorities about the integration of their services. The Ministry of Health also feared that the local authorities were so inured to hand-to-mouth funding of community care that they would find it difficult to accommodate themselves to forward planning.[392] It was decided to use the hospital White Paper to signal the importance of community care, and warn both the local authorities and Executive Councils that they would be required to prepare long-term plans for their services.[393] With respect to community services, the hospital White Paper was described as a 'signpost rather than a map'.[394] It was not practicable to defer the community care planning exercise until after publication of the hospital White Paper. Powell met local authority representatives on 30 May 1961 and warned them that guidance on preparation of a long-term plan would be circulated within a few weeks. This exercise was delayed mainly owing to the difficulty in arriving at quantitative guide-lines for the many services involved. Indeed in areas such as mental illness and mental handicap it was altogether unclear what levels of service were needed on account of lack of clarity concerning the rate of run-down of institutional services. It was also difficult to arrive at targets consistent with likely resource limitations. The circular soliciting information from local authorities about their long -term plans for community care was eventually dispatched in January 1962.[395] In view of the magnitude of the task of collating information from the large number of local health and welfare authorities, the community care White Paper was not published until April 1963.[396] For the same reasons, the community care White Paper was a large document, dominated by tabulations providing a synopsis of the plans of individual authorities with respect to all services under their control. The opening sections provided more expansive treatment of the guide-lines included in the hospital plan. The wide and inexplicable variations exposed by these tabulations were excused on the basis that 'each authority has an independent responsibility in its own area, and no attempt was made either to indicate common standards to which the plans should conform or to suggest

125

modifications before publication'.[397] The community care White Paper was therefore a planning exercise only in the most rudimentary sense, and unlike the hospital plan it contained no prospective costings on an annual basis, indeed not costings at all except quinquennial estimates for capital expenditure. Another obvious difference from the hospital plan was the insertion of a set of photographs indicating relevant services in action, but no explanation for their inclusion was given. These limitations, together with the wide interval between publication dates of the hospital and community care White Papers, and the appearance of the latter towards the end of the life of the administration, help to explain the obscurity into which the community care White Paper sank.

A further limitation of community care planning was abandonment of the earlier intention to produce a long-term plan for the family practitioner services. Although these services were essential to the community care concept, and although they were recognised as the 'Cinderella of the NHS', the difficulties involved in negotiating with all the interest groups involved, suggested that improvement in these services should be treated as a separate exercise.[398]

Although in the political rhetoric, community care was a high priority, in practice it was treated as an expendable luxury. Given the high cost of the hospital programme, it was difficult in practice for Powell to insist on equal treatment for community care. Given his instinct for parsimony, community care tended to be left among the areas where sacrifice was offered in the interests of the national economy. Even at an early stage of planning, Powell indicated that 'I should feel it right to make almost any sacrifice rather than agree to any scaling down of the announced hospital building programme'.[399] This principle was immediately put to the test when in 1962, Lloyd embarked on a fresh round of economies in public capital investment. Powell offered to leave local authority health and welfare capital spending for 1963/64 at the 1962/63 level of £21.5m, which introduced a saving of £3.5m.[400] This compared with the assumption under the community care White Paper that capital spending would average £31m during the first five years of the programme.

Treasury officials attached importance to this outcome because they regarded this area of spending as the 'rogue item in health service expenditure. Left unchecked, it will burst the PESC quinquennial frame for the health services'.[401] To the relief of the Treasury, in discussions about expenditure implications of the hospital plan, the Permanent Secretary at the Ministry of Health agreed to 'keep down the growth of the local health and welfare programme to maintain the hospital programme'.[402]

During the final phase of the Conservative administration, current expenditure on local authority services increased at the annual rate of about 4 per cent, which was about half the level assumed in the local authority long-term forecasts. The local authorities also claimed that the operation of the general grant placed them in a disadvantageous position, especially with respect to the welfare services.[403] Local authority capital investment was also maintained well below the notional level of £31m assumed in the long-term plan. The economy in this field was even greater than appears at first sight because loan sanctions each year tended to be considerably less than the amount allocated. For 1964/65, it was expected that no more than £16.5m of loan sanctions would be incurred, leaving capital expenditure on community care only just over half the level assumed in the community care plan.[404] In the event local authority capital spending gradually gained momentum, for the first time breaking through the £20m barrier in 1964/65, but it was still far in arrears of the White Paper target. During its last months, the Conservative administration was again seeking cuts in this field. In ministerial discussions on capital expenditure for 1965/66, the Chief Secretary proposed a 3 per cent reduction for the health services. Ministers decided to exempt hospitals from the cuts.[405] Given this concession, the Ministry of Health decided not to resist a 3 per cent cut in community care expenditure. Barber complained that the NHS was being asked to bear more than its share of economies because its services were more 'cuttable', protesting that the Government was opening itself to damaging public criticism on account of its failure to honour its obligations in the field of community care.[406]

(vi) PREVENTION AND PROMOTION

Vaccination against poliomyelitis, fluoridation of water supplies, and action against smoking to combat lung cancer and other diseases, constitute three major issues in preventive medicine which came into prominence during the 1950s. Technical solutions were available in each of these fields, but in every case major obstacles stood in the path of prompt and effective response. These three instances illustrate various channels by which preventive and promotive medicine were shaped by wider political considerations. Given this situation, it was extremely difficult for the new health service to establish a central body to promote health education, which was effective, independent, and yet not a source of irritation to the health departments and an embarrassment to the Government. This dilemma will be illustrated by brief reference to the Central Council for Health Education.

Control of the quality of water supply and protection of the public against infectious disease constituted two of the long-standing and

127

most important responsibilities of Medical Officers of Health. Vaccination and immunization were central to this function. Under section 26 of the National Health Service Act 1946, local health authorities were given the duty to provide vaccination against smallpox and immunization against diphtheria. By 1958, the Minister had exercised his public health responsibilities by also advising local health authorities to provide vaccination against tuberculosis, and immunization against whooping cough and tetanus.

Poliomyelitis

The entire history of vaccination and immunization was surrounded by contentiousness, and the sensitivity of this form of medical intervention showed no signs of abating. Britain experienced a sharp polarisation of attitudes; at one extreme, the anti-vaccination movement was opposed to all varieties of this invasive treatment; at the other polarity, others were concerned that Britain was slower than its western neighbours to exploit these prophylactic measures. From the point of view of the latter camp, there was criticism concerning Britain's late adoption of protection against at diphtheria, rubella, and tuberculosis. BCG vaccination gradually became accepted practice during the 1950s and BCG was important in big anti-TB campaigns such as those mounted in such towns as Glasgow and Liverpool. In 1958 freeze-dried BCG vaccine was introduced and this quickly supplanted the Danish liquid vaccine used until that date. As tuberculosis receded as a public health hazard, its place was taken by poliomyelitis.[407]

Although poliomyelitis had been on the horizon for many years, the first major epidemic dated only from 1947; a second epidemic occurred in 1950; the problem was intermittent, but it showed no signs of remission. The next major outbreak occurred in 1957. The Salk inactivated vaccine against poliomyelitis was introduced in 1955, but the British authorities announced that they were pursuing tests on their own vaccine, which was confidently expected to possess a higher degree of safety. Initially the Government supported the local vaccine, among other reasons because an American vaccine would have increased the level of dollar imports. The committee advising the Government on this aspect of vaccination suggested that first priority should be given to vaccination of children below the age of 11 and hospital staff exposed to the risk of the disease. By the summer of 1957 only 1m out of 7.5m children below the age of 11 had been vaccinated. The two British manufactures of the vaccine ran into difficulties, causing delay in production, which in turn resulted in an outcry in the press, complaints from the TUC, demands in Parliament for purchase of the Salk vaccine from America, and even complaints from medical experts.

On 15 May 1957 Vosper attempted to assuage criticisms by promising an improvement in home production of the vaccine. He also suggested that the UK vaccine would be safer than the Salk vaccine.[408] However, production on any scale was not a realistic prospect until the end of the year. By this stage Macmillan was expressing concern, and asked to be fully briefed about the problems being experienced by the British manufacturers.[409]

Owing to Vosper's illness, his Parliamentary Secretary went to the Home Affairs Committee to ask for purchase of American vaccine to permit continuation of the vaccination programme. There was need for sufficient vaccine to provide for two vaccinations for all children below the age of 16, a total child population of 11 million. The Home Affairs Committee agreed to import vaccine, but also asked for assurances to be given to the British firms in order that their vaccine should be substituted at the first opportunity. There were other problems concerning the use of the Salk vaccine. First, since the Salk vaccine was not officially sanctioned, its import was illegal under the Therapeutic Substances Act. It was in fact being imported illegally on a small scale without sanctions, but it was not possible to accept importation on a larger scale without scientific acceptance. Repeatedly since 1955, the MRC Advisory Committee on Safety Tests for Polio Vaccine had warned against import of the Salk vaccine. Only on 19 July 1957 had the Secretary of MRC modified this advice to accept that the medical dangers were outweighed by the risk of leaving the population unvaccinated against the epidemic. On the basis of this modified advice, the Government conceded that the Salk vaccine after all was no less safe than its largely hypothetical UK rival.[410]

The expenditure aspect of this proposal necessitated consideration of this issue by the Cabinet, where it was agreed to sanction purchase of 5,000 litres of Salk vaccine from USA and Canada. The Government announced that it would begin a vaccination programme against polio targeted at all those aged under 15, expectant mothers and some other groups exposed to particular risk.[411] The target population amounted to some 15m persons. The aim was to attain 50 per cent coverage by the end of June 1958. The American supplies were soon exhausted. In the continuing absence of supplementary supplies from Britain, in January 1958 the Cabinet reluctantly agreed to the purchase of a further 2,500 litres of North American vaccine. With the prospect of greater UK supplies becoming available in the summer of 1958, the Government was under pressure to increase the scope of the vaccination campaign to reach the 15-19 age group, and also to aim at higher acceptance rates. In the absence of firm prospect of supplies of UK vaccine, the Government was reticent to publicly accept more comprehensive targets, but in the face of public pressure, this was reluctantly agreed.[412] Demand for vaccination was higher than expected, while teething problems with the home vaccine supply continued. Consequently it was clear by the spring of 1958 that the 50 per cent target would not be met by the end of June. The Government was therefore obliged to order a further 4,000 litres of vaccine from North America, a decision which caused further embarrassment owing to the fact that MRC had not validated the vaccine, which therefore remained without licence under the Therapeutic Substances Act. Since it was impossible to carry out MRC tests without falling further behind with the vaccination programme, the Home Affairs Committee recommended, and the Cabinet agreed to proceed without these tests.[413] The Government learning process was not quite over; further difficulties were occasioned by the continuing high uptake rate, the need for three rather than two injections, and the further failure of the British pharmaceutical industry to fulfil its commitments. As before, the Government sanctioned further purchases of North American supplies, abandonment of testing, and it was agreed that supplementary supplies from abroad should be obtained for as long as necessary to complete the polio vaccination programme.[414] Thereafter, extensions of the Salk vaccination programme became a routine affair.[415]

By the end of 1958 60 per cent of those under 15 had received at least two injections against poliomyelitis. Despite this improving performance, Britain was in arrears of its western neighbours in promoting the Salk vaccine; the record was particularly bad with respect to expectant mothers and adolescents; but it was not until November 1958 that a start was made with a national publicity campaign.[416] By 1960, 75 per cent of children under 16 had been vaccinated at least twice with the Salk vaccine. In February 1960, supplies of the vaccine were sufficiently plentiful to allow the vaccination programme to be extended to those under 40, and a year later to all age groups. The number of reported cases of polio declined from above 3,000 in 1957 to 250 in 1960.

This successful outcome was not quite conclusive. 1961 witnessed a recrudescence of the disease in certain localities. The question now arose whether the Sabin vaccine, a live attenuated vaccine, administered orally, should be substituted for the Salk vaccine. Ministers insisted on independent trials in Britain.[417] After successful trials by MRC, in 1961 Ministers sanctioned general use of the Sabin vaccine.[418] On the advice of the expert committee, the Government decided to continue with the Salk vaccine for routine purposes, preserving Sabin for emergencies. Owing to renewed public concern, demand for vaccination again increased. An embarrassment immediately occurred with the failure of supplies of Salk vaccine, necessitating once again imports from North America. Sabin proved its worth, especially in an exemplary campaign of mass vaccination at Hull.[419] By this stage it was unrealistic to hold back the general use of Sabin vaccine; in October 1961, the month of the Hull campaign, Powell announced that Sabin would be substituted for Salk. One further logical step towards protecting the population from polio, considered at this time, was a 'blanketing' campaign of vaccination for all children. This was recommended by experts as a means to secure the virtual elimination of the disease. The Ministry of Health supported this proposal and funds were set aside for this purpose, but the idea was abandoned when unexpectedly it was not ratified by the Joint Committee on Poliomyelitis Vaccine.[420]

Fluoridation
Public health intervention with respect to purity of water supplies was relatively uncontentious. However, fluoridation of water provoked opposition from a small but vocal lobby, motivated by ethical and technical considerations. Legal complexities, together with divisions of administrative responsibility for water supply and its safety, meant that the protesters had little difficulty in holding up plans to introduce fluoridation. The health departments took up fluoridation with enthusiasm because it was one of the few instances where a simple and cheap prophylactic measure offered the prospect of major savings in the £40m bill for dental treatment.

The possibility that fluoridation might reduce dental decay had been known before World War II. On the basis of tried experience in the USA, it seemed as if dental decay might be cut by as much as 60 per cent by the introduction of fluoridation. An expert mission was sent to America in 1952; it reported at length and extremely favourably on American experience of fluoridation.[421] Fluoridation trials were undertaken at two locations in England, one in Scotland and one in Wales. This experiment attracted the interest of Churchill.[422] In 1956 the Ministry of Health established a Research Committee to investigate the safety of fluoridation.[423] The legal situation concerning the rights of water authorities to add fluoride to water supplies was not free from ambiguity. It was desirable to attain clarification by means of fresh legislation, but departments vacillated concerning the merits of a private member's Bill or Government-sponsored legislation.[424]

The prospect of fluoridation provoked a strong protest movement, involving such organisations as the British Housewives League, the London Anti-Fluoridation Campaign, and especially the National Pure Water Association. The antis concentrated their first attack on the small local authority in Andover, where they enjoyed success in local elections held in May 1958.[425] Court actions instigated by the protesters against the water authorities of Andover and Watford were sufficient to deter other interested water authorities from embarking on trials. Furthermore, the Attorney General advised that addition of fluoride to water was ultra vires. This issue was considered by the relevant government departments, by the Home Affairs Committee and the Future Legislation Committee of the Cabinet, and finally in April 1958 by the Cabinet itself. Given additional support for fluoridation from the World Health Organisation, it was agreed that the Government should sponsor a short Bill to permit water authorities to introduce fluoride, and without controversy, arrangements were agreed concerning the funding of this scheme.[426]

After this promising start the Government's enthusiasm was quickly extinguished. Ministers were alarmed when they discovered that their Bill would be highly controversial, and that opposition would be particularly strong in areas of Conservative support. Consequently it was agreed to defer action until the results of the Andover and Watford cases were known.[427] The Andover water authority agreed to desist with fluoridation. Most other water authorities were unwilling to proceed with fluoridation without clarification of the legal situation. Once again the Government deferred action, this time on the grounds that a campaign of public education was necessary before the introduction of a Bill.[428] The Government made a minor start with its campaign by inclusion of a reference to fluoridation in the Minister of Health's speech during the debate to mark the tenth anniversary of the NHS. The Government was pleased by support from a dental expert in the debate, and by favourable notice in the press. On this basis and because of continuing pressure from certain big local authorities, including Birmingham, Ministers agreed to give further attention to the presentation of a Bill, but while they appreciated the strength of the argument for fluoridation, each time the matter was considered they found reasons for prevarication owing to fear of adverse publicity from protesters.[429]

One of the more plausible excuses for inaction was removed in 1962, when a report on the three surviving pilot studies was published.[430] This suggested that dental decay among children had been reduced by fluoridation without any sign of harm. This finding was supported by other investigations, which collectively disposed of most of the health scares ventilated by protesters. Nevertheless, Ministers decided to defer further action until responsible public opinion had generated a more favourable climate for legislation.[431] This criterion safely excused delay for the rest of the life of the Conservative administration. Macmillan's advisers complained about the prevarication of the Ministry of Health in handling the fluoridation issue.[432] A further set-back to the fluoridation cause occurred in October 1962, when Kilmarnock, the Scottish area associated with the trials, opted to withdraw from the scheme. Nevertheless, some action was called for in response to accumulating scientific support for fluoridation. In December 1962, the Minister of Health invited applications for fluoridation schemes under section 28 of the National Health Service Act 1946.[433] In the light of the limited response to this invitation, the Ministry of Health issued a further circular notifying local authorities that they were invited to undertake fluoridation under section 28 of the National Health Service Act 1946 without the need to make application to the Minister. Local health authorities and water undertakings were asked 'not to deny the benefits of fluoridation to the community they serve'.[434] However, uncertainties associated with the continuing Watford court action were sufficient to nullify the effects of these pious circulars.

Smoking and Health

As noted in volume I of this study, lung cancer associated with smoking was increasingly recognised in the course of the 1950s as one of the most serious of the new public health hazards.[435] From 1950 onwards, the Annual Reports of the Chief Medical Officer soberly presented a digest of the state of knowledge on this important problem. Ministers were slow to respond. The first Ministerial statement expressing guarded recognition of the link between tobacco smoking and lung cancer was not made until June 1957, and only then on account of the need to keep in line with more active responses emanating from MRC. Lengthy deliberations were conducted, and some obligation to give a positive lead to combat tobacco smoking was recognised, but the temporising lobby won the day. The Cabinet agreed that 'the Government should not admit a "duty" to warn the public of the connection between smoking and lung cancer. This disease could be differentiated from those, such as tuberculosis and poliomyelitis which were infectious or contagious'.[436] It was not until August 1958 that local health and education authorities were circularised and asked to report on their initiatives on smoking and lung cancer.[437]

The issue was not discussed again by Ministers until March 1959, when it was pointed out that despite increasing public awareness of the problem, cigarette smoking was continuing to increase. Since resources available to the Central Council for Health Education had been cut, Ministers considered but rejected making a special grant to assist publicity on smoking and lung cancer. As the only new action approved, Ministers narrowly agreed that further information should be sought through the Social Survey.[438] Official and unofficial surveys soon indicated that there was a high degree of awareness concerning the dangers of smoking. Ministers therefore decided that further surveys were unnecessary. Despite continuing escalation of the lung cancer problem, Ministers confirmed their decision not to release additional funds for campaigns by the Central Council for Health Education.[439]

Given the inertia within the government machinery, the advocates of action against smoking turned for support from outside bodies. They were successful in co-opting a powerful ally in the form of the Royal College of Physicians. The latter was not conspicuous for taking up controversial issues, but its Report, *Smoking and Health* (1962) constituted a candid and effective summary of the case against smoking, and it alerted the public to the dangers of smoking extending far beyond lung cancer. The Royal College of Physicians Report forced the Government to reconsider its position. The line taken by the Report was strongly backed by MRC, the Secretary of which advised Lord Hailsham that the evidence on the harmful effects of smoking was 'massive in quantity and consistent in its implications'.[440]

Events followed the same course as in 1957. The Cabinet was divided over its response. Immediate reaction to the report was therefore confined to a brief statement in reply to a parliamentary question.[441] Once again a committee of Ministers was formed, and they were briefed at length by a parallel committee of officials. Ministers were again unable to reach a consensus. The Treasury kept up its opposition to imposing higher taxes on cigarettes. Citing libertarian arguments, the Treasury called for minimum intervention, whereas the Ministry of Health insisted that the Government should at least sanction modest health education campaigns and impose some limitations on the advertisement of cigarettes.[442] Given the lack of agreement among Ministers, it was decided once again to make a temporising statement, on this occasion announcing a stepping up of the health education effort. In July 1962 Ministers changed their minds, deciding to embark on a small publicity campaign without an announcement, in order to evade parliamentary demands for more concerted action.[443]

The next external stimulus to government action came in 1964, with the report on smoking and health by an advisory committee to the US Surgeon General. This reinforced the findings of the Royal College of Physicians. Ministers were under pressure to introduce some of the measures being tried in the USA, such as restriction of smoking in public places, a ban on cigarette advertisements on television, or more general restriction of tobacco advertising. Ministers debated these possibilities, but they were not pursued on account of raising too many difficulties. It was also decided to block a private member's Bill emanating from the Labour MP, Laurie Pavitt, which aimed to introduce a health warning on cigarette packets. However, it was agreed to reconsider this issue after the General Election. In the period before the General Election it was agreed that nothing further should be attempted other than giving mild encouragement for display of warning posters in those government offices open to the public.[444] The anti-smoking lobby was scarcely helped by the supposedly authoritative Cohen report on health education, which came down squarely against limitations on the advertising of tobacco or other products which it was lawful to retail.[445]

Health Education

Failure of the Government to sanction more than token gestures to deter tobacco smoking was an increasing source of informed concern, which was acutely embarrassing to the health departments' senior medical personnel, whose position was compromised by their political superiors. Their unhappiness with this situation was self-evident. Sir Kenneth Cowan on his retirement as Chief Medical Officer at the Scottish Home and Health Department frankly admitted that his pleasure concerning successes in the field of preventive medicine such as the 1957 mass radiography campaign to detect pulmonary tuberculosis, or the introduction of Salk vaccine to combat poliomyelitis, was tempered by embarrassment over the failure of the health service to combat the increase in lung cancer associated with smoking. This sense of frustration concerning inactivity on the part of the Government in this crucial area of preventive medicine was shared by Sir George Godber in London.[446]

The three instances discussed above indicate only a minor role for the Central Council for Health Education. When any issue in the field of promotive or preventive medicine assumed major public importance and urgent action was required, the health departments tended to take the necessary action and closely supervise the relevant operations. The main co-ordinating bodies for health education tended to be left on the sidelines; they were trusted with only minor, routine responsibilities. The two agencies concerned, the Central Council for Health Education and the Scottish Council for Health Education, were established in 1927 and 1943 respectively, primarily for the modest purpose of advising and assisting with co-ordination between local authorities. The Councils fulfilled a similar function under the NHS, but they were even less important owing to the decline in importance of local government involvement in health and reduction in status of the Medical Officer of Health. Health education risked falling between the stools; neither the health departments nor the central councils displayed the aptitudes or mobilised the resources needed to convert health education into an effective function of the National Health Service.

There was need for a more effective central presence in the field of health education, and this became ever more evident in the course of the 1950s, not only with respect to the problems discussed in the preceding paragraphs, but also for contributing to the development of community care, and for dealing with other topical issues such as sex education and family planning. It was widely recognised that the central councils were starved of resources and that their inept performance was becoming a source of embarrassment to the Government.

By 1959 the argument for some kind of enquiry was recognised within the Ministry of Health, but the Chief Medical Officer advised caution on account of the risk of demands for additional expenditure. The argument tilted in favour of an enquiry by the perverse factor that the Central Health Services Council was aggrieved about being excluded from important policy questions; an investigation into health education seemed the most convenient way for the health departments to demonstrate their good faith towards the central advisory machinery. The dangers of the committee exhibiting wild enthusiasms was precluded by the choice of the ubiquitous Lord Cohen of Birkenhead as Chairman, and in the selection of a team of members not likely to express unconventional ideas. The Scottish Department of Health chose to participate in the investigation, with the consequence that the committee became a joint CHSC-SHSC venture. The terms of reference were agreed in January 1960. There was however some further delay, partly because of exchanges concerning the membership. The new Chief Medical Officer in London was in favour of a more innovative membership, but the final list included none of his suggestions. The health departments were anxious to avoid the committee becoming 'too high-powered'.[447]

The Joint Committee on Health Education was given the restricted remit to 'consider whether, having regard to recent developments in medicine, there are any fresh fields where health education might be expected to be of benefit to the public; how far it is possible to assess the results of health education in the past; and in the light of these considerations what methods are likely to be most effective in future'. The committee began work in July 1960. Officials quickly became perturbed 'by the impressions which the Committee collectively and individually continue to give of failure to grasp the scope of their terms of reference and to get to grips with the problems involved'. This was no doubt one of the adverse effects stemming from avoidance of high-power among the membership.[448] Given this problem, it is not surprising to find that the enquiries of the committee dragged along in a desultory manner; one-third of the original members of the committee resigned or died, while the remaining members terminated their labours only under protest in early 1964. Their report was published on 8 May 1964.[449]

Assessment of health education is notoriously difficult, and the Cohen Report well-illustrates the pitfalls. The report was well-meaning, but diffuse and lacking in insight. It reflected the limitations of health education at the time rather than indicating any way forward. Most attention was attracted by the recommendations of the committee relating to the reorganisation of central arrangements for health education, and by its proposal to establish a new profession of 'Health Educators'. Neither of these questions was central to the remit of the committee and neither was convincingly handled in the report.

With respect to central organisation, the committee was mobilised by the Ministry of Health to achieve its own objectives. Indeed, the committee fully consulted the Ministry of Health, and it allowed the decision on this important question to be decided by the health departments. However, the officials were themselves divided over this issue; one party argued that the health departments should take over all the essential responsibilities for health education, and that this was an essential prerequisite for effectiveness. In that case, the CCHE would be preserved, but with limited functions in such fields as in-service training. The opposite view prevailed. It was decided that a strengthened 'semi-independent Board' conferred certain advantages for carrying out health education campaigns. It was envisaged that the department would continue to dictate policy and priorities, and intervene directly when necessary. This added degree of central control could not be achieved without changing the balance of finance from the local authorities to the Exchequer. The sceptics predicted that the new independent body would be insufficiently dissimilar from its predecessor to avoid replicating its faults. The optimists argued that better organisation, more determined central direction, and an improved staff would inject new life into the central body responsible for health education.[450]

Final decision to establish a new independent health education body was delayed by lengthy negotiations with the Treasury, which was firmly on the side of the sceptics. Treasury officials were not convinced either by the Cohen Report, or by arguments adduced by the Ministry of Health. The Treasury inclined to agree with dissenting comment in the Cohen Report by Dr H D Chalke, one of the leading authorities on health education among the Medical Officers of Health, which recommended strengthening the existing CCHE.[451]

137

The Ministry of Health's case was not helped by a change of mind in Scotland, where it was decided to retain the Scottish Council for Health Education in an attenuated form for training purposes, while transferring all essential health education functions to the central department. Increasingly bad-tempered exchanges between the Treasury and the Ministry of Health began in April 1964 and lasted until December 1965.[452] The impasse was finally broken under the new administration by the intervention of the Minister.[453] This prepared the way for a statement announcing the establishment of a new 'health education council'.[454] In 1968 the CCHE was wound up and the new Health Education Council established as a Company registered as a charity. Also in 1968, SHHD set up a Health Education Unit within the department to undertake essential work in this field.

(vii) CONTROLLING PHARMACEUTICAL COSTS
Despite the imposition of prescription charges and the introduction of other deterrents, between 1957/58 and 1963/64 the cost of the pharmaceutical service increased from £61.7m to £114.0m.[455] This seemingly inexorable rise in the drug bill was fixed upon by the Treasury and other critics as one of the features of the new health service most vulnerable to criticism. Even with adjustment for rising prices, the increase was alarming. There was an approximate doubling since the beginning of the health service, while at 1958 prices, there was an increase of 36 per cent between 1958 and 1964, a rise of approximately 6 per cent a year.[456] The pharmaceutical service was also absorbing a steadily increasing proportion of the resources of the family practitioner services, again approximately doubling its share since the beginning of the NHS, reaching almost 40 per cent in 1963/64. At the beginning of the health service, expenditure on general medical practice had been approximately twice that on the pharmaceutical service; in 1963/64, for the first time, the pharmaceutical service cost more than the general medical service; already more than a 20 per cent lead had opened up, and the differential continued to increase.[457] Despite these apparently worrying trends, the cost of the pharmaceutical service as a proportion of the gross cost of the NHS remained fairly constant at about 10 per cent.

For reasons already mentioned in chapter I, the escalating cost of the pharmaceutical service seemed like a problem capable of solution by investigation of the underlying causes and then attacking abuse and laxity on various specific fronts. This problem was high on the agenda of the Conservative administration. This section deals with efforts by the Conservatives to improve prescribing habits of doctors, and further reduce the profits of the drug companies. However, these methods were subsidiary to the prescription charge. As already noted, control of demand by the prescription charge, introduced in 1952, increased in 1956, and again in 1961, was the favoured option. On political grounds, the prescription charge was the most unpopular of all health service levies, undoubtedly unhelpful to the Conservative Party, while the promise of abolition was advantageous to Labour. It was also a failure as a source of revenue because its effects were to a large extent evaded by changes in prescribing habits of general practitioners. When the 1952 flat-rate charge of 1s per form was introduced, the GP increased the number of items on the form. When the basis of the charge was altered to the item on the form, the GP prescribed larger amounts more infrequently. After the 1956 prescription charge increase, the Treasury complained that doctors had 'robbed', or 'cheated us' out of 80 per cent of the anticipated yield from the increased charge.[458] The prescription charge was therefore counterproductive since it encouraged wasteful prescribing habits and generated only minor yields as a form of taxation.

In the light of frustration over the limited success of the prescription charge, the Treasury occasionally suggested complementary reinforcing measures such as introducing a limited list of drugs, charging on the basis of a percentage of the costs of drugs, introduction of a consultation fee, forcing doctors to undertake their own dispensing, establishing Government-owned cheap-rate dispensaries, reducing fees to chemists, and even transfer of primary care to an insurance basis.[459] None of these options was pursued to any extent by Ministers; instead, officials fell back on their traditional nostrums, attempting to close loopholes and improve methods of regulation.

The prescription charge alone was no better than a leaking sieve. It was a pointless exercise unless simultaneous action was taken to influence the prescribing habits of general practitioners. It was particularly important to limit quantities prescribed, but also in view of the rise in the availability of expensive drugs, it was necessary to induce GPs to opt for the cheapest alternative among the most efficacious medicines.

Persuading GPs to co-operate was even more problematical than gaining acceptance for the imposition of increased charges on patients. Ever since the idea of the NHS was announced, doctors were fearful that the new service would interfere with their traditional freedoms, and one of the most cherished of these was the right to prescribe without limitation. In general terms this had been conceded under National Health Insurance since 1911; even though drug therapy had become infinitely more expensive, there was no realistic expectation that doctors would voluntarily agree to limitation of their rights in prescribing. Any chance of co-operation was also reduced by the traditionally indifferent relations between the BMA and the Government, mainly because of perennial disputes over pay and conditions. Finally, doctors had a financial interest in generosity with prescribing, since this was thought to satisfy their patients, and therefore assist in the building up of their capitation lists, the size of which determined their payments from the NHS.

Inducing economy in prescribing was therefore an operation bristling with difficulties, and not likely to yield rapid results. However, improvement of standards in this aspect of general practice was defensible on grounds of principle and it was indeed a matter of urgency in view of the damage to health likely to ensue from incompetent prescribing. Thus, although the Treasury initiative on this question was inspired by the mundane quest for economies in spending, it also deserved high priority on grounds of objective merit.

The Ministry of Health calculated that the only way to secure more economical prescribing was to remit the problem to the BMA and GMSC, with the hope that responsible elements in the leadership of the profession would act on the merits of the case by instituting an investigation into the reasons for increasing drug costs and take steps to improve professional standards. Informal contacts with the BMA were made in the autumn of 1955, which suggested that the prospects of intervention by the Ministry seemed likely to induce the GMSC to take up an initiative.[460]

Long experience had taught health officials that non-confrontational and oblique methods offered the best prospects of prodding the temperamental machinery of the BMA into frictionless motion. This plan was quickly upset by Turton, who insisted in revising the letter to the BMA to indicate his concern about rising costs, and threatening sanctions such as placing a ceiling on spending on the pharmaceutical service. The GMSC reacted angrily and accused the Minister of incorrectly blaming GPs for the rise in the drug bill. However, representatives met officials and agreed to participate in a joint working party to investigate the reasons for increasing prescribing costs. This offer of co-operation was politically important to the health departments because it enabled them to reassure the Public Accounts Committee that the problem of the rising pharmaceutical bill was not going unattended.

Douglas and Hinchliffe Committees
After a promising start, progress on establishing a working party soon slowed down. Turton vetoed the idea of a working party including officials on the grounds that they might be led into an embarrassing position with respect to Government policy. The choice was then between a separate investigation by the profession, which

was refused by the BMA, or an independent committee, which was acceptable to the doctors, on the understanding that they would be fully consulted and well-represented. At first it was intended to have a single enquiry to cover England, Wales and Scotland, but this was rejected by the Scottish GMSC, with the result that a separate Scottish enquiry was instituted. All parties in Scotland were also inclined to adopt a wider remit for the investigation, embracing both general medical and hospital services, whereas in England and Wales the enquiry was limited to general medical services. This produced a difference in the perspective of the two committees. The Scottish committee was specifically concerned with investigating prescribing practice among general practitioners and in hospitals, whereas the English and Welsh investigation dealt with all factors contributing to the rising drug bill.[461] The Treasury was by no means confident that independent committees containing a preponderance of medical members would reach conclusions helpful to the Government. The plan for two committees was also not welcomed by the Treasury on the grounds that it was likely that they would reach different conclusions and thereby dilute expression of important findings relating to economy. The proposal for a committee to investigate prescribing costs was also attacked from the direction of the Guillebaud Committee, which had recently investigated pharmaceutical costs in the context of its general review of spending on the health service. The proposal for a new committee was understandably seen as an attempt by the Government to overturn recommendations of the Guillebaud Committee.[462] There was also difficulty in assembling two committees possessing the same weight of expertise. English planners originally intended to include leading Scottish medical academics on its committee, but these candidates were ruled out when the idea of a separate Scottish committee was adopted.

It was not until October 1956 that the terms for the enquiries were agreed with the Treasury, and the decision ratified to embark on two enquiries.[463] At the beginning of 1957 the chairmen of the two committees were appointed. The London committee was chaired by Sir Henry Hinchliffe, an industrialist, who had served on government committees relating to the Department of Scientific and Industrial Research and the Independent Television Authority. The Scottish Committee was chaired by James Boyd Douglas (knighted 1958), a farmer and land valuer, who was Chairman of the Scottish Milk Board.

The Douglas and Hinchliffe Committees were further delayed owing to the arguments over doctors' and dentists' remuneration, which reached a new level of crisis in the early months of 1957. At first the GMSC refused to nominate its five members for the

Hinchliffe Committee, while the Scottish GMSC nominees for the Douglas Committee were unable to take up their places. The impasse was broken when the Government offered an interim pay increase; the general practitioner members were nominated in May and the membership of the two committees was announced in June 1957.[464]

The terms of reference required the Hinchliffe Committee, 'having regard to the increase in the cost of prescriptions issued under the National Health Service, to investigate the factors contributing to this cost'. The Douglas Committee was asked to enquire into 'prescribing practice in the General Medical Service and in the Hospital and Specialist Services in Scotland, with particular reference to the factors governing cost'.

Apart from the chairman, the Hinchliffe Committee comprised five general practitioners, two general physicians, a dean of a medical school, a pharmacologist, a pharmacist, and a statistician. The Douglas Committee included one general physician, two pharmacologists, a pharmacist, three general practitioners, the head of a student health service, a retired SAMO, an academic lawyer, and an accountant. The two committees were conscientious and open-minded; both pursued their investigations in depth, and in considerably greater detail than had been possible for the Guillebaud Committee. Both took longer than anticipated to produce their interim report and their final report. The Hinchliffe Committee submitted its interim report in May 1958, and its final report in March 1959. The Hinchliffe Report was published in May 1959.[465] The Douglas Committee produced its interim report in February 1958, and it submitted its final report on 7 March 1959. The Douglas Report was also published in May 1959.[466]

At the opening meeting of the Hinchliffe Committee, Vosper admitted that 'no problem was more worrying to the Minister or had been to his predecessors than the increasing size of the national drug bill'. In view of the seriousness of this problem he invited the committee to make interim recommendations to guide doctors on 'principles of economical prescribing', which Vosper regarded as the most serious question facing the investigators.[467] This request for interim reports was largely in response to hectoring from the Treasury, which demanded an earnest of the committees' capacity to make a direct contribution to the economy campaign and proof that they were adopting a realistic approach to their remit, rather than embarking on sterile academic exercises.

The unwillingness of the committees to fit in with the cost-cutting priorities of the Government was quickly revealed in their attitude to interim reports. The Douglas Committee issued a few sentences, containing a list of suggestions for improving the provision of intelligence about prescribing patterns and costs in the hospital service. Much to the embarrassment of health department officials, the Hinchliffe Committee took a whole year to produce its interim report. This extended to 51 paragraphs, but it was an innocuous document, its main proposal being for production of a new, loose-leaf prescribing handbook for general practitioners. Its most radical passage comprised positive remarks about restrictions imposed in New Zealand on amounts prescribed by doctors, but no specific recommendation on this point was offered.[468]

Background notes indicate that already by the date of the interim reports, the two committees were pulling in different directions. The Hinchliffe Committee was very attached to its idea of a new prescribing handbook, whereas the Douglas Committee believed that this would add further to the confusion created by too many sources of information. Accordingly the Scottish Committee favoured reliance on existing sources of information, and it went on to suggest improvements to the *British National Formulary* and *Prescribers' Notes*.

Both interim reports confirmed the anxieties of the sceptics; it was clear that these investigations possessed no brilliant new insight about containing costs, which suggested that the committees were likely to be an irrelevance from the point of view of Treasury preoccupations. In the light of such limitations, the *Times* accorded the interim Hinchliffe Report a scathing reception.[469]

The two committees conducted a competent survey of prescribing practice and their final reports contained a variety of sensible and constructive proposals for improvements in medical education, postgraduate training, supply of reliable intelligence to doctors, prescribing practice, investigation into excessive prescribing, the education of the public, the testing and approval of new products, regulation of advertising, and control of the pharmaceutical industry. The committees decisively rejected coercion and statutory regulation, which they regarded as impracticable and possibly counterproductive. Instead they outlined proposals relying on exhortation, peer pressure, and education. Such approaches were likely to be slow-acting, but the committees believed that they would eventually exercise a substantial summative effect, and were desirable on the grounds of cultivating improved standards of professional practice, regardless of their cost-saving aspect. Indeed, the question of economy, although accepted as a significant consideration, occupied a secondary place in the thinking of the committees. They were primarily concerned with laying down guide-lines for the improvement of professional standards.

The committees heard a great deal of evidence about the incompetence of general practitioners and wasteful prescribing in hospitals. They came up with credible explanations for the wild divergences in prescribing costs mentioned above in chapter I. There was no complacency about this problem. It was recognised that irresponsible prescribing needed to be stamped out in order to ensure the safety of patients. It was also appreciated that wasteful prescribing was endemic, but this was more difficult to define and required more subtle methods of control. The dilemma of the committees was aptly summarised by the eminent pharmacologist, Professor D M Dunlop, who urged the Douglas Committee not to lose its sense of perspective. He argued that the 3 per cent of the cost of the health service devoted to the pharmaceutical service represented one of the most effective uses of health service resources, bringing direct improvements to health, and yielding considerable hidden economies by limiting resort to in-patient facilities and by reducing the number of lost working days. He frankly acknowledged that 'overworked practitioners who have more patients than they can adequately cope with, find in the writing of a prescription an easy way of clearing their surgeries and getting to their dinners'. This bottle of medicine habit was a fault common to patient and practitioner; Dunlop speculated that at the most generous estimate, one-third of the prescription costs were wasted in this way. However, there was no immediate way of addressing this problem. Effective coercive and bureaucratic measures would be impossible to devise and would merely antagonise doctors. The loss to the Exchequer was only £15m per annum, even according to the most generous estimate, which amounted to the cost of an aircraft carrier. Dunlop advised adopting exclusively educative methods, beginning with improvements in medical education, which he was confident would bring about a steady elevation of professional standards.[470] The two reports expressed their conclusions in more measured terms, but they were broadly in line with the thinking of Professor Dunlop.

The Douglas Committee was more forthright in its conclusions:

> Our investigations have satisfied us that there is, in fact, unnecessary and excessive expenditure on drugs and dressings under the National Health Service attributable to prescribing practice. We do not consider, however, that the solution lies in excessive interference by the State in prescribing practice of individual doctors. Such interference would be costly and cumbersome to enforce and might well defeat the main purpose of the Health Service.

The unhelpful nature of this conclusion resulted in pressure from Scottish officials for some stronger admonition against laxity, with the result that an addition was included at a late stage in drafting, warning doctors that the NHS did not constitute 'an unqualified licence to prescribe' and that shortcomings were not only bad professional practice but also unlawful.[471]

The Douglas Committee was not in favour of a limited list of drugs, or the introduction of a blacklist of drugs available only if the patient paid privately, and it was only moderately in favour of introducing a limit on the quantity of drugs that could be prescribed on any one occasion. If such a scheme were to be introduced, it favoured trials in restricted districts and adoption of 10 or 15 days as the maximum period covered by a single prescription.[472] The Douglas Committee was opposed to increasing the prescription charge, but it was not in favour of its abolition.[473]

The Hinchliffe Committee came near to implicit contradiction of the Douglas Committee in concluding that there was only a minor problem of waste in the existing system :

> while there is no evidence of widespread and irresponsible extravagance in General Practitioners' prescribing, there is scope for economy; some waste is involved in the present tendency to order larger quantities on each prescription. The aim should be to keep the Service as economical as possible, compatible with the best available modern treatment, to ensure good value for money and to check waste.[474]

Like its Scottish counterpart, the Hinchliffe Report rejected the limited list, or the blacklist, but it was more forthcoming on the question of the limitation of amounts prescribed, and it proposed a two-year voluntary trial period of limiting quantities to one week's supply or less, except in chronic cases.[475] Whereas the Douglas Report, partly because of the nature of the Committee's remit, made only passing mention of the prescription charge, this issue was considered at length by the Hinchliffe Report.[476] Already, in advance of the report, Hinchliffe advised Douglas that his committee was unfavourable to an increase in the prescription charge, while he himself expressed opposition to the charge as a matter of principle.[477] These reservations were amplified in the report, which attacked the prescription charge as a 'tax which stimulates avoiding action and is resented by patients and doctors as a tax on illness'.[478] In a politically shrewd conclusion which had not occurred to the Douglas Committee, the prescription charge was identified as the main cause for wasteful prescribing, and it was seen as an obstacle to securing the compliance of doctors and patients with schemes for restraint in prescribing. Accordingly, the committee concluded on grounds of economy that the 1956 increase in the prescription charge should be rescinded, and at the first opportunity the Government was recommended to abolish the prescription charge completely.[479]

The Treasury was dismayed by the Douglas and Hinchliffe Reports. The damning evidence presented to the committees contrasted with their anodyne conclusions. The Hinchliffe report was attacked for its turgidity and for spurious impressions conveyed concerning the innocence of doctors. Both reports were regarded as a political nuisance. Not only had the committees failed to offer constructive advice on economies, they had effectively made it impossible to proceed with many options for economy favoured by the Treasury Ministers and their advisers.[480] The only Treasury satisfaction with the Hinchliffe Report related to the strictures aimed at the Ministry of Health for its lack of judgement and positive leadership with respect to the control of prescribing costs.[481]

Walker-Smith was ambivalent about the findings of the Hinchliffe Report. On the one hand he was unfavourable to the prescription charge, with the result that Hinchliffe was helpful in resisting attempts to increase the charge, and it assisted in his efforts to persuade colleagues to contemplate eventual abolition. On the other hand, the Douglas and Hinchliffe recommendations more than confirmed the prophecies of the sceptics; not only were they unhelpful in the immediate economy exercise, but also they assessed and ruled out many of the controls that the Government might like to consider at some later stage. Finally, by arguing that the pharmaceutical service had established itself as one of the most effective aspects of the health service, the reports had undermined the justification for identification of this service as a primary target for cuts.

From the Treasury perspective, the only tangible benefit of the Hinchliffe exercise was the possibility of a trial period of voluntary restraint on prescribing. Even this minor gain was problematical because the Douglas Committee made no parallel recommendation, and informal soundings with the medical profession in Scotland also produced a negative response. It was also impossible to introduce the voluntary prescribing limitation without also conceding Hinchliffe's associated recommendation that consideration should be given to abolition of the prescription charge. With the support of the Ministerial Committee on NHS Finance, Walker-Smith announced that the Government would investigate the feasibility of the voluntary regulation scheme, and 'if such a scheme proves successful in controlling expenditure on drugs we would, naturally, consider whether the saving justified the abolition of the prescription charge at the end of the two-year period'.[482] After consultation with the GMSC, an agreed letter to doctors was produced, asking with effect from 1 February 1960 for quantities to be limited to one week's supply except in chronic illnesses or other cases where there was special justification. Treasury officials thought that they had fallen

146

into a trap by exchanging the prescription charge for the voluntary prescribing limit. It was predicted that the Exchequer stood 'to lose several millions if and when this quasi-commitment comes home to roost'.[483]

The Government failed to take up the Hinchliffe Committee's suggestion that the whole question of the costs of the pharmaceutical service should be kept under continuous review by an Economic Advisory Committee, which would advise the Ministers and publish annual reports. The Treasury suspected that such a mechanism would be dominated by the medical profession, and would therefore tend, in the same way as the Douglas and Hinchliffe Committees, to tie the hands of Governments with respect to controversial policy initiatives. There was less objection to a cognate initiative from the CHSC, which set up a standing committee under Lord Cohen to consider operational research relating to the pharmaceutical services. This was established in May 1960, but it functioned only sporadically, had collapsed by 1963, and was formally wound up in 1964.

This conclusion was most unsatisfactory from the point of view of the Treasury. In return for very uncertain gains from voluntary restraint, the Government had committed itself to contemplate reversal of policy on the prescription charge. Although this concession was offered in the most guarded terms, it was bound to energise Labour and the BMA into more active demand for abolition. Furthermore, as soon happened in January 1961, the statement on the Hinchliffe Report added to Conservative discomfort when Powell reversed Walker-Smith's policy, and doubled the prescription charge. The rise in the prescription charge effectively killed the voluntary agreement to restrain quantities prescribed. As on previous occasions, doctors responded to the rise in the prescription charge by increasing quantities prescribed. This trend provided Powell with an excuse to reject further discussion of abolition of the prescription charge.[484]

With respect to the Government's original intentions concerning retrenchment, it is tempting to conclude that the Douglas and Hinchliffe Reports yielded no positive savings, and were in other respects counterproductive. However, the Government's action had the unintended effect of permitting the entire question of prescribing practices to be investigated. Even if their immediate results were limited, the Douglas and Hinchliffe Committees undertook an intelligent review of this important problem, and their reports comprised a repository of wise advice concerning the improvement of professional standards. Partly in response to the Douglas and Hinchliffe recommendations, in April 1961 the Standing Joint Committee on Classification of Proprietary

147

Preparations produced one of its series of technical reports, on this occasion on equivalence between unbranded and proprietary drugs, which eventually percolated down to general practitioners as practical guidance; then in 1960 the Ministry of Health produced its loose-leaf *Handbook on Prescribing*; finally in 1961, *Prescribers' Notes* was replaced by the more authoritative *Prescribers' Journal*.

Voluntary Price Regulation Scheme

Given failure to cut the drug bill decisively by resort to the prescription charge or controls on prescribing by doctors, the only other alternative was stepping up pressure on the pharmaceutical industry. This had always been recognised as the option potentially capable of yielding the greatest savings. However, as described in the previous volume of this study, the pharmaceutical industry proved adept at defending its position, with the result that the Voluntary Price Regulation Scheme, introduced in April 1957 for a three year trial period, was calculated to yield extremely small returns, and in the event even these predictions proved to be over-optimistic.[485] Savings of £750,000 a year were predicted, but the savings amounted to only £250,000 in the first year, and £400,000 in the second.[486] This failure to extract significant savings from the VPRS was viewed seriously because expensive proprietary medicines were the single largest factor explaining the increasing drug bill. The impact of this pharmaceutical revolution has already been mentioned above in chapter I. The trends described there continued without interruption until the end of the Conservative administration. The average net ingredient cost per prescription increased from 48.7d in 1958 to 82.2d in 1964. At 1958 prices this represented an increase to 73.7d, which was an real increase of 51 per cent. This trend towards higher ingredient costs largely reflected the increasing dominance of proprietary products. Between 1949 and 1958, the proportion of the net ingredient cost in the drug bill accounted for by proprietary products increased from about 40 per cent to about 75 per cent. This trend continued; proprietaries reached 88 per cent of the net ingredient cost in 1964. Since the VPRS covered nearly 90 per cent of proprietary drugs, improving the yield from this source was the obvious target for any attempt to achieve major economies on the drug bill.

The Ministry of Health was disappointed by the VPRS, but it represented a hard-won compromise after three years of negotiations with the Association of the British Pharmaceutical Industry. The health departments feared that nothing better would be forthcoming from further protracted negotiations. The Ministry of Health made a spirited defence of its expenditure on drugs, arguing that the problem was not as serious as asserted by the critics; if inflation was taken into account, and it was accepted that increased costs were needed to sustain the rapid increases in the efficacy of drug therapy, there was no basis for regarding the drug bill as a matter of special concern.[487] The Ministry took comfort from support given to the VPRS by the Hinchliffe Committee, and from the continuing view within the profession that costs of pharmaceutical products were not a serious cause for concern. The experts generally supported the view of Professor Henry Miller that the current level of costs represented the 'inevitable price of the present scientific revolution in medicine'; there was therefore a degree of irresponsibility in the 'quite disproportionate surprise and alarmism' surrounding this facet of health service expenditure.[488]

As the initial trial period for the VPRS neared its end, the combined forces of the Comptroller and Auditor General, the Public Accounts Committee, and the Treasury pressed an unwilling Ministry of Health into establishing a working party to review the scheme. The Treasury even suspected that the Ministry was in collusion with the manufacturers to prevent further investigation of profits made at the expense of the NHS.[489] The Treasury was also concerned that this problem would become worse because imminent trade liberalisation would open the way to the unrestricted flow of dollar imports into Britain; this would further benefit American pharmaceutical firms, whose products were already regarded as prime suspects for excessive profits. This view was reinforced by evidence from the USA that pharmaceutical companies were making exorbitant profits on drugs featuring prominently in the NHS drug bill.

The Working Party on Drug Price Regulation reported in October 1959.[490] Having gone over all the alternatives, it was agreed that the VPRS offered the only basis for proceeding with the full co-operation of the pharmaceutical industry. In order to improve the credibility of the scheme, some minor alterations in its regulations were proposed. However, no major concessions to the critics were offered. The Public Accounts Committee wanted termination of the 'three years freedom' granted to manufacturers to enable them to recoup research and development costs, but since the proportion of the cost of proprietaries covered by this side of the agreement had fallen from 30 to 20 per cent, it was agreed not to interfere with this arrangement for the next phase of the scheme. The VPRS also was not addressed to the questions of patents, sales promotion costs, or the general level of profits, all of which had been criticised by the Comptroller and Auditor General and by the Public Accounts Committee.

Almost half the cost of proprietaries was covered by the Export Price Criterion of the VPRS. The Public Accounts Committee

149

suspected that this was the main avenue for excessive profits. In the revised scheme, it was proposed that prices for products covered by the Export Price Criterion should be assessed on the basis of comparison with prices in the six most important export markets for the relevant drug, whereas the Public Accounts Committee favoured price assessment with reference to the lowest export price. The criterion of eligibility for consideration under the Export Price Criterion was slightly tightened up, while some of the main drugs were excluded altogether by virtue of an agreement to introduce direct negotiation over the price of products accounting for about 20 per cent of the drug bill. The further important group of drugs was covered by the Trade Price Formula, assessed on the basis of prices charged by main reputable firms. It was agreed to reduce the profit margin permitted under this section of the VPRS. The agreement with the ABPI also allowed for the health departments to obtain detailed information concerning the accounts of a groups of major pharmaceutical companies in order to establish more adequate data on levels of profit, and further information would also be sought on spending on advertising.[491]

Although it was entirely uncertain whether the revised scheme would yield significantly more economies than the original VPRS, there was little appetite either in the health departments or the Treasury for questioning the code produced by the Working Party on Drug Price Regulation. The Treasury was ambivalent about applying further restrictions for fear of aligning themselves with the 'Socialist view that high profits are incompatible with fair prices'.[492] None of the officials wanted to risk unscrambling the delicate agreement by prematurely bringing it to the attention of Ministers. Having won the confidence of the leadership of the ABPI, the officials preferred to tie up details of the agreement at permanent secretary level, which was the course followed in the latter half of 1960.[493] There is no evidence that Walker-Smith was briefed about negotiations between his department and the ABPI. Powell was introduced to the agreement in December 1960; apart from insisting that the next phase of the scheme should run for three rather than five years, he accepted the compromise. It was announced on 15 December 1960 that the second phase of the VPRS would run from 1 January 1961 to 30 June 1964.[494]

With the *entente* between civil servants and moderates within the industry, the scene was set for the question of the costs of pharmaceutical products to slide off the political agenda. The VPRS had emerged as the basis for a common understanding. Even if the VPRS yielded only modest savings, it at least guaranteed that prices would not escalate upwards at an embarrassing pace. The VPRS was founded on two major shared assumptions between the ABPI and the health departments; first, that the pricing policies of the major firms were broadly reasonable; and secondly, that intensive competition existed in the drug market, providing assured continuation of reasonable pricing.

By 1960, the image of an overwhelmingly responsible pharmaceutical industry was being actively questioned, even before the ink was dry on the new VPRS agreement. Any complacency concerning the profits of drugs companies was shattered by the publicity associated with the hearings of the Senate Sub-Committee on Antitrust and Monopoly, chaired by Senator Estes Kefauver, which produced its final, vast report in 1961.[495] The greatest concern related to profits on broad-spectrum antibiotics, where there was suspicion of both excessive profits and conspiracy to monopolise on the part of major companies in the field. After the Kefauver hearings, the US government began proceedings against three major drugs companies. The suggestion that companies were recording profit margins of more than 90 per cent became widely-publicised and sent shock-waves through the British press.[496] In response to adverse publicity, Cyanamid, one of the companies under Kefauver scrutiny, took out big advertisements in the British press headed 'What Does it Cost to Go Sick'.[497] This was not sufficient to save Cyanamid from investigation by the Board of Trade, which suspected profits in the range asserted in America. This enquiry proved helpful to the health departments, which immediately began negotiations with four major companies to attain reduction in prices on their broad-spectrum antibiotics.[498] Lower prices for tetracycline and related products were negotiated in 1963 and 1964, but even after the latter reduction it was estimated that Cyanamid was making a 41 per cent return on its capital.[499]

It was immediately evident that the drugs pricing structure was less rational and competitive than assumed by the VPRS. This was confirmed in a practical way when a foreign importer offered to supply tetracycline to the NHS for one tenth the price of Pfizer, the company which held the patent. The Minister's decision to accept the lower-price import was successfully defended in the courts on the basis of section 46 of the Patents Act 1949.[500]

The growing American disquiet about the drug industry was reflected by the Public Accounts Committee, which in 1960 pressed Ministry of Health representatives for its reaction to the American investigations, and it hinted that the Ministry was being too casual about its own investigations. Harold Wilson was the main accuser of the health departments.[501] Once its suspicious were aroused, the Public Accounts Committee continued to make searching criticism about the profits of pharmaceutical companies and this issue continued to cause disquiet in Parliament.[502] With difficulty the

151

Conservative administration staved off pressure for drastic action on the costs of pharmaceutical products, with the result that this intractable problem was handed down to the Wilson administration.

(viii) PAY CONTESTS

As indicated in the first volume of this study, the new health service inherited a serious pay problem. A large part of the non-medical workforce was underpaid, while doctors, dentists and other independent contractors were dissatisfied about their levels of remuneration and also suspicions about many aspects of their contracts. The Whitley Council system imported order into the pay system and it slowly corrected the worst defects of low-pay, but its slow, bureaucratic operations were not calculated to bring about improvements sufficiently quickly to give health service staff the assurance that they were keeping pace with comparable groups of workers elsewhere.[503] The Whitley system came under increasing strain; as noted below, mainly because of Ministerial interference, various groups of health workers resorted to outside arbitration to secure more satisfactory pay settlements. However, this stretched out negotiations and was only partly successful in eliminating pay disadvantages. The NHS therefore continued to be plagued by the problem of low pay. This affected recruitment in general, but especially in such fields as nursing and radiography, where increased numbers were required, but which were also adversely influenced by the expansion of general employment opportunities for women. Doctors and dentists largely operated outside the Whitley structure. These professions adopted a more confrontational approach to their pay questions. Only limited success was experienced in reducing controversy over pay for doctors and dentists by the establishment of a review body.

Opticians and Chemists

Of these two categories, opticians proved much the less problematical. They were reimbursed for the cost of supplying lenses, frames and cases, and also remunerated through fees for sight-testing and dispensing. The latter had been adjusted sharply downwards at the beginning of the NHS, but were then gradually increased to reach their original level by 1958. The earnings of opticians had long been a matter of dispute. An enquiry conducted between 1953 and 1955 was worthless on account of the low response rate from opticians.[504] In the light of a further, more scientific enquiry into the income of the various classes of opticians, it was agreed that there was a case for increasing the sight-testing fee by an average of 2s 1d. The Government was not convinced that all opticians merited this increase, and at first it insisted that the

Management Side of the Optical Whitley Council should limit the increase to 1s. Ministers proposed a larger increase, but at Treasury insistence it was agreed to introduce a compensatory saving by insisting on a 20 per cent reduction in the 'hybrid' dispensing fee (the fee paid for dispensing NHS lenses in private frames). Increased sight-testing fees were introduced in December 1958. Since hybrid dispensing was a lucrative and expanding source of income for opticians, they were not enthusiastic to accept this cut, but it was introduced in January 1960.[505]

Like opticians, chemists were reimbursed for their costs, and also they received remuneration, mostly in the form of a dispensing fee and an on-cost allowance. The dispensing fee was a payment for professional services at an agreed level depending on the cost of the prescription, but averaging about 15d; the on-cost allowance was set at 25 per cent of the ingredient cost derived from the Drug Tariff. With the escalation in the cost of individual prescriptions, the income derived from the on-cost allowance proved to be buoyant.

Neither side was content with this system of remuneration. The chemists felt underpaid and underrated, whereas the Government suspected that they were exploiting their contractual terms to make excessive profits. In February 1956, the chemists claimed an increase of 25 per cent in the combined yield from the dispensing fee and the on-cost allowance. In 1956 the chemists reluctantly agreed to a temporary settlement giving a target income based on about 4 per cent profit on turnover. It was also agreed to undertake a more detailed enquiry into chemists' earnings. After some delay, this was begun in 1958. The enquiry was undertaken under the auspices of the Pharmaceutical Whitley Council, and it was conducted jointly by accountants from a London firm and the Board of Trade. The findings were unreliable owing to the low response rate, especially from independent chemists. On the basis of this inadequate data, department statisticians attempted to arrive at levels of earnings for 1959 and 1960, but these projections were obviously open to dispute. The Ministry of Health believed that the 1956 settlement had yielded acceptable levels of earnings; it favoured adopting 5 or 6 per cent profit on turnover as the target level; 5 per cent was the maximum acceptable to the Treasury; the chemists argued for 7.5 per cent, which the Treasury was unwilling to countenance.

By 1961, failure to establish an agreed basis for chemists' remuneration was becoming an embarrassment. Not only were the chemists restive at failure to settle their claim originally made in 1956, but also the Public Accounts Committee was showing signs of impatience at failure to address this aspect of the drug problem. The Treasury favoured a complete change in the basis of chemists' remuneration, but this was ruled out by the health departments, which pointed out that chemists had entered into negotiations on the understanding that the current remuneration arrangements would be preserved.[506] Failing radical change, the Treasury insisted on a drastic reduction in the on-cost allowance, envisaging 12.5 per cent as the target level. The Ministry of Health countered with a proposal for a variable on-cost allowance, ranging from 12.5 to 25 per cent, and averaging at 18 per cent. In order to assist small firms, the largest allowance would be paid to chemists with the smallest amount of business. This proposal was suggested to the chemists in February 1961, but it was rejected, and protracted negotiations failed to achieve a settlement. The impasse was broken in November 1961, when the Government imposed the above sliding scale of on-cost allowances, with some compensation through a small upward adjustment in the dispensing fee to an average of 17.1d, but this compared with the 24d demanded by chemists. This imperious line against the chemists was approved by Powell, who promised his colleagues that the profits of chemists would be reduced from £5.6m to £4m.[507]

The Central Contractors Committee, representing the chemists, was taken by surprise by this rough treatment, and much speculation arose concerning the likelihood that they would withdraw from their NHS contracts.[508] However, their response was unexpectedly conciliatory. They asked to enter into further negotiations with a view to arriving at a fair professional fee. It was agreed to hold a fresh enquiry into earnings, on this occasion with a much smaller sample, but with more intensive investigation. The Government agreed to the investigation being undertaken by Associated Industrial Consultants Ltd., who were nominated by the chemists.[509]

The AIC activity sampling exercise temporarily defused the crisis. The results were not available until after Powell's departure. In further negotiations, the Government adopted 5 per cent profit on turnover and a £1,450 target income for chemists. Settlement at this level would have cost about £1m. However, the AIC report adopted 7.5 per cent as the reasonable profit level, and this generated a target income of £1,700. Including retrospection, the chemists claim amounted to £10m. The departments were taken by surprise and they reacted with indignation when investigators nominated by the chemists came to conclusions favourable to their sponsors.[510] The chemists made the most of their advantage by publicising the findings of the AIC enquiry. It was impracticable for the Government to openly contest the findings of the independent investigators. Consequently, final negotiations proceeded with the Government operating from a position of disadvantage. Ministers tried, but failed to lure the chemists into accepting a notional salary of £1,520.[511] The agreement concluded in June 1964 essentially granted the chemists what they requested. Their new terms introduced a notional salary of £1,750; the cost was £11m including retrospection. It is therefore clear that Powell's attempt at an imposed settlement was entirely counterproductive.[512]

Doctors and Dentists

Although the long-running disagreement over doctors' and dentists' pay looked likely to become one of the most irritating controversies facing the Macmillan administration, this prospect turned out to be a false alarm. The extended investigations of the remuneration problem by the Pilkington Royal Commission exercised a calming effect; afterwards, setting in place the new review body extended still further the tranquil intermission. The habitual pessimism of the medical profession concerning pay only resurfaced when it was discovered that the review body procedures had failed to resolve their underlying grievances.

It will be recalled from the first volume of this study that in April 1956, doctors and dentists entered a claim for an increase in remuneration not less than 24 per cent. The estimated cost of this increase would have been about £20m. On 17 June 1958, the BMA increased its claim to 29 per cent. Anxiety among doctors and dentists was eased by interim increases granted in May 1957 and January 1959; the former increased salaries by 5 per cent (10 per cent for junior hospital doctors), and the latter by 4 per cent.[513] After a shaky start, the doctors and dentists agreed to cooperate with the Royal Commission on Doctors' and Dentists' Remuneration established at the suggestion of the Government, under the chairmanship of the industrialist, Sir Harry Pilkington.[514] The Pilkington Commission provided the Government with a valuable breathing space. Although the Commission was asked to treat its work as a matter of urgency, the Government was not dissatisfied when the investigators became submerged by their intractable subject-matter. Originally it was hoped to complete the task by Easter 1958, but the report was not completed until November 1959, and it was not published until 18 February 1960.[515] With the exception of a long dissenting memorandum by Professor John Jewkes, the report was supported by the whole Commission.

Since consideration of the pay of NHS doctors and dentists entailed examination of recruitment, training, and career structures, the Commission was unavoidably plunged into a major investigative exercise touching on many aspects of the workings of the NHS. Beside conducting its impressive investigation into professional earnings, entailing questioning 15,000 doctors and dentists, as well as 27,000 individuals from nine other professions, the Pilkington Report also made publicly available for the first time detailed information concerning Distinction Awards. More important, it contained an invaluable body of data on many aspects of medical and dental manpower. In addition, the published minutes of evidence provide a comprehensive insight into the experience and outlook of the two professions, their professional organisations, and employing authorities.

All sides watched progress of the Pilkington enquiry with apprehension. Mindful of the disastrous performance of the Ministry of Health at the time of the Danckwerts award, and the unabating power of the BMA public relations machine, the Treasury urged the Ministry to adopt an aggressive approach to the enquiry, in response to which Vosper promised to 'fight their case with the utmost vigour'. The Treasury was also pleased and surprised when it emerged that the Commission was 'keeping in close touch with the Ministry of Health and supplying them with all the papers'; from the Government point of view, this 'approach to the matter could not be better'.[516] When Vosper retired on account of ill-health, the effort of the Ministry of Health flagged. Invitations from the Commission for supply of documentation failed to produce a prompt response, while the Permanent Secretary failed to take up the opportunity to present his views informally to the Commission. The Treasury was concerned that the Ministry of Health was showing signs of complacency, and it even seemed disinclined to enter into debate with the BMA on many issues which the Treasury regarded as fundamental, such as methods or levels of remuneration.[517] The draft evidence of the Ministry was attacked as 'abdication with a vengeance'.[518]

In order to ensure that the contentions of the BMA were answered in full, the Treasury intervened to play a greater role in representations to the Commission than was originally intended.[519] A joint working party formed of officials from the two departments took the lead in settling policy on points requiring clarification during the final stage of the Pilkington enquiry.[520] Transfer of D A V Allen from the Treasury to the Ministry of Health also increased confidence between the two departments on this issue.[521]

The professional side based their case on continuity with Spens and Danckwerts, arguing that the principles applying in these settlements should continue to be upheld. As the Central Statistical Office observed, 'in effect they regard the Spens Reports and Danckwerts Award as sacrosanct and rest their case on what they consider necessary to take account of the changes that have taken place since April 1951'.[522]

The Government side invested its energies into achieving a decisive break with the earlier settlements, favouring determination of pay on the basis of comparabilities with other professional groups and in the light of the economic situation. The Willink Report came to the assistance of the Government by suggesting that there was an over-supply of doctors. On the other hand, the widespread lack of confidence in the Willink findings assisted the profession. Also, since the Treasury was attaching paramount importance to outside comparisons, the demand and supply argument was not crucially significant.[523] A further objective agreed by the Government departments at an early stage was to press for establishment of an independent review body comparable to the recently-established Coleraine Committee, which dealt with higher civil service pay. It was hoped that a review body would provide an escape from the haphazard and semi-legal system of negotiation and arbitration applying in the past. This had proved advantageous to the BMA, which had become skilled at playing the role of the indignant plaintiff.[524] Since its inception in 1956, it was envisaged that the Coleraine Committee might extend its remit to included higher-paid health service personnel.[525] During the final stages of his Commission, Pilkington engaged in detailed discussions with the Government departments on the practicalities of extending Coleraine procedures to the health service.[526]

With respect to hospital medical staff, the Treasury argued strongly for creation of a new cadre of sub-consultants. It was envisaged that these would undertake routine work, thereby restricting numbers entering the expensive consultant grades. This proposal had already been introduced in 1955, and had been subject to some unsuccessful negotiations, but the Royal Commission gave a new opportunity to revive this proposal. There was less certainty about handling the notorious Distinction Award. It was accepted that 'by all the canons of public finance, Distinction Awards represent a blot on the landscape, and in particular, we in the Treasury ought to favour their abolition'. The Ministry of Health was reported to be ambivalent on this issue. Despite objections to these awards, it was recognised that the profession was determined to retain and indeed extend their application. The departments realised that alternative systems of remuneration for consultants were potentially extremely expensive. Such factors caused them to soften their objections to this system.[527]

The government departments were allowed to see page proofs of the Pilkington Report about ten days in advance of publication. With respect to the primary purpose of the exercise, levels of remuneration, the Royal Commission recommended an increase of 22 per cent above 1957 levels for doctors, and 21 per cent for dentists. This increase was to be paid from 1 January 1960. The Pilkington Report recommended £2,425 as the average net income for general medical practitioners from official sources, compared with £1,975 in 1956. An average net income of £2,500 was recommended for dentists. The recommended scale for full-time consultants was £2,550 to £3,900, compared with £2,100 to £3,100 in 1956. The Report suggested augmenting the value of existing Distinction Awards and also creation of one hundred new 'A-Plus' awards; it also suggested that the awards should be a fixed number rather than a percentage of consultants in employment. These modifications took the maximum salary attainable by consultants to £7,900. The Royal Commission gave no verdict on the grading structure for hospital doctors, but it expressed support for the decision of the health departments and the profession to establish a joint working party to consider this issue.[528]

In order to extend merit payments to general medical practitioners, the Commission requested that £0.5m should be set aside from the Central Pool to reward family doctors of outstanding ability. The Commission approved of the £100,000 set aside annually to encourage group practice, but suggested that in future it should come from the Exchequer, not from the pool. The perpetuation and increase in the value of 'loadings' paid for moderate numbers of patients on doctors' lists was intended as a further slight inducement to group practice. In reaching its conclusions about salaries the Commission had difficulty in establishing the level of private practice earnings of general practitioners. It concluded that private practice earnings and Exchequer superannuation payments should be excluded from calculations of the pool, which should therefore be confined to payments to doctors for the various types of work undertaken for official bodies.

Doctors had already received 9 per cent of their increase in the two interim awards. The estimated cost of the residual increase for doctors was £11.5m a year, with £20m for retrospective payments, and a further sum of £8m to clear accumulated balances in the pool. There was no additional cost for dentists because their estimated receipts from fees had increased sufficiently to cover the award. The estimated cost of the package to the Exchequer for the financial year 1960/61 was £41.5m. It was recommended that the new rates of pay should stand for at least three years, provided there was no change in current trends and economic circumstances, and that subsequent settlements should apply for a similar period.[529]

The main recommendation of long-term importance was for establishment of an independent 'Standing Review Body of eminent persons of experience in various fields of national life to keep medical and dental remuneration under review'.[530] Such a body would act as a 'better judge than either the Government or the representatives of the professions as to what the levels and spread of medical and dental remuneration should be'.[531] It was recommended that the seven members of the Review Body should be appointed after consultation with the professions.[532] The Royal Commission recommended that the Review Body should be supplied with reliable statistical information by the Government, especially the Inland Revenue. Also, this mechanism was expected to give prompt consideration to claims, thereby preventing the build up of animosity created by the past tendency of the Government to protract salary negotiations. The Review Body was normally expected to take the initiative in conducting reviews, but it was accepted that the professions might ask for a review.[533] The Royal Commission hoped that the Review Body would provide a mechanism for settling salaries without the destructive public wrangles which had been such a prominent feature of the past.[534]

The memorandum of dissent by Professor John Jewkes advocated a higher settlement, but no retrospective payments. He was not in favour of introducing the 'A-Plus' Distinction Award, but wanted the values of existing awards increased. Instead of the Review Body, he advocated an Advisory Council, possessing somewhat wider functions and more accessible to representations from the professions. He also differed from his colleagues over various other minor issues.[535]

The recommended award represented a success for the professions. The Treasury frankly accepted that the Government might have conceded less if it had negotiated on the basis of the profession's original claim.[536] The Government side had perhaps been naive in believing that a Royal Commission would be immune to the superior forces always available to the medical profession on such occasions. There were few causes for rejoicing in government circles, but some comfort was taken from the rejection of the Spens-Dankwerts 'principles', and indeed any suggestion that salaries should increase according to a specific formula.[537] There was also relief that no additional cost was incurred with respect to the dentists.

The health departments pressed for endorsement of the Pilkington recommendations as a whole on the grounds that partial or staged implementation was likely to stir up further confrontation, which might well result in an even worse financial settlement.[538] They feared that the profession might revert to reactivating a claim on the Spens-Dankwerts basis, in which case the profession was likely to demand an increase of 39 per cent above the 1956 levels of remuneration. It was pointed out that the Pilkington Report was not entirely welcomed by doctors, and that dentists were actively disappointed. Accordingly, it was necessary to give prompt approval to the Report in order to strengthen the position of moderate elements within the professional leaderships. The Treasury was soon converted to this conclusion. On this occasion the Treasury and health departments were united in belief that there was no

159

alternative to accepting the Royal Commission Report in its entirety. This view was ratified without discord by the Wages Policy Committee and the Cabinet.[539]

On 11 April 1960 Walker Smith announced the Government's complete acceptance of the Pilkington Report, on condition that the professions would do likewise.[540] The health Ministers held preliminary discussions with the medical profession on 29 March and this was followed up by a formal offer. After consideration by the relevant professional bodies, the BMA and the Joint Consultants Committee accepted this offer in September 1960.[541] A positive response from the dental profession followed in March 1961.

Agreement reached on the principles of the award cleared the way for detailed discussions between the Government and the medical profession over setting up the Review Body and the distribution of the extra sums included in the central pool. A joint working party between the health departments and the profession agreed to increase the capitation fee from 18s to 19s 6d, and it worked out other increases in other fees. It proved impossible to evolve a form of merit award acceptable to general medical practitioners, but it was agreed to set aside £1m annually for encouraging good general practice. The majority of this fund was allocated to increasing the loading fee further than was required under the Pilkington recommendations. The working party also agreed, for the purpose of encouraging group practice, to contribute an amount from the pool equal to that paid by the Exchequer .

The Pilkington implementation exercise gave an opportunity for further consideration of issues that had been considered by the Commission, but which were remitted for further discussion by the negotiating parties. Particularly important was the modest suggestion stemming from the Working Party on Doctors' and Dentists' Remuneration that the maximum list should be reduced from 3,500 to 3,250. This change needed to be made in the context of a general pay increase; otherwise doctors whose lists were reduced were likely to suffer actual financial loss. In the event, it proved impossible to reach agreement on a method of reducing the maximum list other than by the incentive created by loading.[542]

A second important issue affecting the pool was the level set for maternity fees. The inadequacy of the maternity fee was raised by the Cranbrook and Montgomery reviews of the maternity services. The maternity fee had remained at the level of 7gn since the beginning of the NHS. The Ministry of Health favoured an increase to 15gn, hoping that the higher fee would be restricted to specially-qualified practitioners. The Treasury resolutely rejected this proposal, especially when it became clear that there was no way in which agreement could be secured to restrict the higher fee to a limited group of highly-qualified practitioners. A compromise of 10gn was adopted. In principle, this prospect made no difference to the cost of the settlement, since the maternity fee was a deduction from the pool.[543] Although increase of the maternity fee was handled as a technicality, it had profound implications, since it was the largest of the fees which took precedence as deductions from the pool. Increase of the maternity fee, together with expansion of sums earned by work for hospitals, local authorities, government departments, dispensing etc. was advantageous to those doctors engaged in this kind of work, but it eroded the value of the residue left for distribution in connection with the main professional work of general practitioners. Unless there was a healthy surplus in the pool from the previous year, as was the case during implementation of the Pilkington award, those doctors undertaking less additional work were likely to receive only small increases in their remuneration and thereby feel cheated.

Discussions with the profession over setting up the Review Body proceeded slowly. Indeed, the BMA leadership faced complaints on this score at its Annual Representative Meeting held in July 1961. In March 1962, after the relevant consultations with the professions, the Review Body was appointed by the Prime Minister. The Royal Commission had recommended that the Review Body should comprise 'seven independent persons of eminence and experience'.[544] Lord Kindersley, the Chairman of Lazard Bros., with many other financial interests, who was also an Honorary Fellow of the Royal College of Surgeons, was recruited as the Chairman; there were six other members drawn from academic, professional and commercial backgrounds. J H Gunlake, a past-President of the Institute of Actuaries, provided a link with the Pilkington Commission. None of the members of the Review Body were doctors. The Review Body was asked to 'advise the Prime Minister on the remuneration of doctors and dentists taking any part in the National Health Service'. This remit was wide and intentionally ill-defined, which resulted in much misunderstanding, since the Review Body aspired to wider functions than the health departments and the professions were willing to concede. This caused uneasy relations between the Review Body and the Government, and created an impression within the Review Body that it was being marginalised. Accordingly, there was some dissatisfaction within the Review Body and this may have increased the rate of turn-over of members. Only three of the original members survived on the Review Body until 1966.

At the time of the Pilkington settlement and the establishment of the Review Body, it was not entirely clear when the first reassessment of remuneration would take place. However it was reasonable to believe that the Review Body would conduct its first evaluation three years after the Pilkington Report. The medical profession prepared its claim on the basis of this timetable; this was sanctioned by the Review Body and not contested by the health departments. The professions applied for an increase of 20 per cent; the Government suggested 8 or 9 per cent. The Review Body began discussions of the doctors' and dentists' claim in June 1962. One of its most difficult decisions related to the question of periodicity of its pay reviews. The Review Body was not entirely satisfied with the suggestion of the Royal Commission for triennial reviews, or for the reviews to entail both retrospective and prospective elements. However, since the Royal Commission, the profession, and especially the health departments favoured the triennial arrangement, it was decided to adopt this formula. The Review Body hoped that by adopting a method calculated to put the professions 'ahead of the game', long-running grievances concerning pay would finally subside; this would allow the parties to concentrate their energies on improvement of professional standards and the quality of service.[545] The vaguely defined triennial system complicated the task of the Review Body in reaching conclusions about a fair recommendation. There was initially support for a generous gesture in order to gain the confidence of the professions. It was agreed that the award would assume that the professions were adequately remunerated in January 1960, as a consequence of the Royal Commission settlement. At first the Review Body considered an increase in the region of 20 per cent, but this was whittled down until agreement was reached on 15 per cent. Then, last minute doubts emerged, and it was argued that at a time of pay restraint, there was risk of the Review Body appearing to be unreasonably generous, with the result that the recommendation was reduced to 14 per cent, which was still regarded as possibly over-generous.[546] After a great deal of eleventh-hour revision, the report was completed and dispatched to the Prime Minster on 18 February 1963.[547] The short Review Body Report side-stepped all the delicate questions of differentials between consultants and general practitioners by recommending a general rise of 14 per cent, effective from April 1963. Before dentists were awarded their increase, the Review Body suggested that there should be an investigation into levels of earnings from fees.

The estimated cost of this proposal was £16m. The Ministry of Health argued for prompt acceptance of the Review Body's recommendations on the basis that it had operated as anticipated, and had reached reasonable conclusions, especially if the new rates applied for at least three years. At the Economic Steering (Incomes) Committee, the Treasury argued that the proposed award was at least twice what was consistent with incomes policy. Some thoughts were given to rejection, referral back to the Review Body for downward revision, or part application of the award. However, at the Wages Policy Committee, Powell argued for ratification of the Review Body recommendations, primarily on the grounds that the Government was tied into the Review Body procedure, which could not be varied without accusation of bad faith on the part of the professions. He suggested that the new system for determining remuneration had produced better relations between the Government and the professions than at any time since the beginning of the NHS. He acknowledged that the Government was paying a high price for this new spirit of accord, but urged that this was worthwhile. The Treasury reluctantly concurred that there was no choice but to apply the award in full. The Wages Policy Committee deliberated at length on presentational difficulties. They agreed that by stressing that the award included a retrospective element and that it was intended to cover a further three years, it could be presented as a 3.5 per cent a year increase, which was tolerably near to the 2.5 per cent 'guiding light'. The Cabinet discussed Treasury reservations, but Ministers feared the consequences of rejection of the Kindersley system at its first test. It was agreed that the findings were a tolerable first step towards controlling medical and dental salaries, especially if the award lasted for three years or more. The decision to accept the Kindersley Report was announced on 25 March 1963.[548]

Negative reactions to the first report of the Review Body were at first limited to the dentists, who intimated that they favoured an entirely new system for determining their pay. With respect to doctors, the Review Body procedure revealed a new state of harmony between the departments and the leadership, and they worked together to achieve smooth application of the award.[549] However, initial satisfaction concerning the efficiency of the new pay machinery soon turned to disappointment. By virtue of the pool system for distribution, translation of the 14 per cent award into an incomes increase entailed a complex calculation. Owing to the absence of pool surpluses from 1961/62 onwards, there was no cushion to protect general practitioners from the realities of the pool calculation. After deductions had been made from the pool to account for special funds, or payments to doctors for specified services, and because expenses were reimbursed at an only slightly amended rate, the 14 per cent increase on net income converted itself into an average 5 per cent increase in gross income.[550] This truth came home to general practitioners when they received their amended pay in October 1963.

General practitioners disadvantaged by the pool system were inclined to blame the new mechanism for determining their salary, which they thought was being manipulated by the Government to their disadvantage. The irritation of these doctors was increased by the apparently more favourable treatment accorded to consultants. The anger of general practitioners was evident at the Annual Representative Meeting of the BMA held in July 1963, where attacks were mounted on the BMA leadership as well as the Government. This meeting also indicated the difficulty of preventing fratricide between general practitioners and consultants. Discontent within the BMA caused activists to establish a new organisation, the General Practitioners' Association, specifically to represent the interests of general medical practitioners. Other discontents transferred their loyalties to the Medical Practitioners' Union, which was then at the height of its influence.

In order to retain its credibility, the BMA was forced to adopt a more militant line. The GMSC and JCC worked hard to achieve accord and prevent the erosion of confidence among general practitioners. A greater spirit of unity was generated by the decision of the professional bodies to press for a substantial increase in remuneration for general practitioners, and also for a change in distribution arrangements, with the pool being reserved for payments in respect of main Executive Council services; all other payments would then be covered by other means. The other main demand was for additional payments to reward maturity and experience.[551] The total cost of this claim was £20m, representing a 32 per cent increase in net income; the likely cost of retrospective payments was estimated at an additional £30m.[552] Separate from the claim, the professional bodies opened up negotiations with the health departments on other grievances, especially with a view to achieving a more equitable way of reimbursing practice expenses. In his first public speech since taking office, Barber conceded that the method of reimbursing practice expenses was a 'very odd System' and he looked forward to discussing its improvement with representatives of the profession.[553] The resultant Fraser Working Party and associated committees not directly relating to the level of remuneration will be considered in the next chapter.

After an informal meeting with the Review Body in January 1964, the Joint Evidence Committee of the medical profession submitted its claim in June 1964.[554] Between these dates, the professional negotiating committees were thrown into turmoil. A strong move was made by militants among the general practitioners to bring about much greater equality between the remuneration of general practitioners and consultants. In the course of this contest, in March 1964, Dr A B Davies resigned as chairman of the GMSC and he was replaced by Dr J C Cameron. Further agonising exchanges took place between general practitioners and consultants before their agreed memorandum of evidence was forwarded to the

Ministry of Health on 1 June 1964 for submission to the Review Body.

The Government naturally recoiled with horror at this new huge claim made only one year after the previous settlement. The Kindersley Committee itself was not so discomforted. Kindersley stated that his committee was never in favour of a three-year settlement, which he claimed had only been adopted reluctantly in the face of demands from the Government.[555] The Review Body argued that its remit could only be efficiently executed if it was free to take up problems as they arose, which was likely to entail an almost continuous process of review.[556] The Review Body was also annoyed that the health departments were establishing working parties to investigate issues which Kindersley and his colleagues clearly believed lay within their province. Thus, in 1964 a confused situation developed, with the territory of doctors' pay being contested by the Review Body, the Fraser Working Party, and a variety of other formal and informal working groups. As noted in the next chapter, this duplication was not finally disadvantageous, although in the short term it undoubtedly generated anxieties.

At the Wages Policy Committee, Minsters agonised angrily over the doctors' claim. They felt that the medical profession was guilty of a fundamental breach of faith. They were advised that the claim was without foundation; general practitioners may have had grievances about their professional status, but they had no grounds for complaining about incomes. The Government side was united in indignation, but divided over its response. Characteristically, the Ministry of Health favoured a low-key approach, placing its expectations on complete rejection by the Review Body on the merits of the case. The Treasury called for public denunciation of the doctors on the grounds that other groups would be tempted to emulate their example, thereby contributing to the spiral of inflationary wage claims. The Government finally accepted the view of the Ministry of Health, primarily on the grounds that publicity would inflame the anger of the doctors and undermine the already shaky position of the moderate leadership within the BMA.[557] The campaign of covert opposition to the doctors' claim was still being prosecuted at the time of the change of government.

Administrative and Clerical Pay

As noted in the previous volume, the Whitley Councils operated under strain, but they effectively prevented the outbreak of industrial unrest. As the tenth anniversary of the NHS approached, the system came under severe test. As noted above, Thorneycroft attached high priority to contesting wage demands, and he was not averse to a rise in unemployment if this would restrain pressure on wages. Thorneycroft persuaded his Cabinet colleagues to make a stand against railwaymen; in what he saw as the national interest, the Government rejected the railwaymen's claim for a wage rise beyond the level recommended by the Railway Arbitration Tribunal.

At the very moment of the controversial decision concerning the railwaymen, in October 1957, the Chancellor of the Exchequer was confronted with a proposal from the Whitley Administrative and Clerical Staffs Council for an increase of 3 per cent for clerical and lower or 'general' administrative grades, and 5 per cent for higher or 'designated' administrative grades. This settlement came after a general increase of 3 per cent in January 1957 paid as a result of arbitration in the Industrial Court.[558] The Staff Side regarded these two awards as interim settlements, pending action on its request dating from January 1956 for a complete salary and grading revaluation. There was no response to this request until March 1957, when Sir Noel Hall was appointed to review the grading structure. The October 1957 agreement, which was regarded by the Staff Side as a further interim settlement, coincided with the completion of the Noel Hall Report into grading. In view of the general economic situation and the need for consideration of the Noel Hall Report, the Minister of Health advised the Management Side to reject this interim award. However, this advice was not followed, partly because the Government was open to criticism for delaying consideration of a general revaluation.[559]

Thorneycroft was preoccupied with what he perceived as a major crisis over public sector pay. The Government accepted the 5 per cent award for the small group of designated staff, but Thorneycroft insisted on rejection of the 3 per cent award to the much larger numbers of clerical and general administrative staffs. Thorneycroft appreciated the seriousness of rejection of a Whitley recommendation, which would constitute the first such interference by the Minister in free collective negotiation, but the Chancellor recommended that the Government should set the precedent for rejection of the results of agreed arbitration procedures, urging that 'the Minister who has to find the money is entitled to say that he is neither going to provide additional finance for the Health Service nor curtail its benefits to foot this bill'.[560]

The Cabinet was unenthusiastic about the Chancellor's call for confrontation. Ministers urged that rejection would constitute a serious precedent, not merited by the current situation. Walker-Smith was unhappy about being used as a Trojan Horse for tough policies against workers; and he pointed out that the Government was in the case of the NHS proposing to reject a recommendation reached by agreed negotiating machinery, whereas in the case of railwaymen, the problem arose from rejection of an arbitration

166

award. Macleod urged that the award to clerical and general administrative workers would be justifiable if a short delay was introduced before its implementation. The Cabinet agreed that a more conciliatory approach was desirable, and it also suggested that the Government should draw up general guide-lines for dealing with wage claims in the public sector.[561]

This decision might have moved the health service out of Thorneycroft's firing line, but this proved not to be the case. The health Ministers recommended that approval of the increase to clerical and general administrative grades should be delayed for six months, while granting that some further improvements might in due course be contemplated.[562] Thorneycroft, with half-hearted support from Macleod, fell back in demanding that the costs of all recommendations arrived at by collective bargaining and arbitration should be borne by public bodies through efficiency savings or cuts in their services. This recommendation was not contested by Watkinson, but he predicted many difficulties in its application in the field of transport. With respect to the health service, Thorneycroft proposed that the Whitley award should be rejected, therefore forcing the staff to seek arbitration. Walker-Smith objected, and again proposed that delay in applying the existing award was preferable. He also argued that there was no room for significant economies, while reduction in the scope of the services by closing hospital beds was wholly unacceptable. With little dissent, the Cabinet approved the line advocated by Walker-Smith.[563]

The administrative and clerical staff reacted adversely to the Minister's 'veto' on their award, and as a matter of principle insisted that the Whitley award should be honoured without delay. They stepped up the pressure by introducing a ban on overtime from 18 November 1957. They were supported by the TUC and the Staff Side of the General Whitley Council, both of which wrote to the Prime Minister, pointing out that repeated Ministerial promises had been made about Whitley recommendations constituting 'effective decisions'; departure from this principle was destructive to the goodwill built up in the NHS as a consequence of the Whitley system.[564] The Staff Side of the General Council asked to meet the Prime Minister, but the Cabinet referred them to the health Ministers. Ministers were divided about action; Walker-Smith favoured allowing the matter to reach arbitration, while Macleod wanted to tempt the Staff Side into a general revaluation in the context of the Noel Hall Report. Macleod's view prevailed.[565] The meeting with the health Ministers was unproductive; it merely led to reiteration of the demand for an interview with the Prime Minister.[566] Macmillan met the delegation representing the Staff Side of the General Council and the Staff Sides of the two relevant sectional Councils on 23 December 1957. The delegation explained its grievance at length, almost exclusively concentrating on questions of principle concerning the standing of Whitley awards, but they failed to extract a compromise from the Government. The attitudes of the delegation were further inflamed by the Government's recent acceptance of Whitley awards to other groups of health workers.[567] For instance, because of a shortage of radiographers estimated at about 15 per cent in England and Wales, health Ministers recommended acceptance of a Whitley award ranging from 5 to 10 per cent; this was agreed by Ministers, who overruled objections from the Treasury.[568] Such concessions rendered it unrealistic to hold down wages of the clerical and general administrative grades. In discussions with colleagues, Walker-Smith pointed out that the NHS had not brought unmitigated financial benefits to its staff. His staffs had not been 'in the van of inflation; on the contrary they are panting distinctly, if doggedly, in the rear. It would be wrong that the need for disinflationary policies should fix them at a permanent disadvantage'.[569]

In response to continuing prevarication on the part of the Government, in January 1958, the Administrative and Clerical Staff Side withdrew its 3 per cent claim and substituted a new 5 per cent claim. Following the lines advised by Macleod, Walker-Smith persuaded the staff to defer this claim on the grounds that complete revaluation of their pay structure in the context of the Noel Hall Report was likely to yield more substantial benefits. This offer was accepted with some reluctance and suspicion by the Staff Side. Ministers also agreed to this course of action, but only on the understanding that the total package would be limited initially to a 3 per cent increase.[570] The effect of this manoeuvre seemed likely to delay the 3 per cent Whitley award of 1957 for about a year, and therefore render it innocuous. This prospect was of course unknown to the bodies negotiating on behalf of the clerical and general administrative grades. The Staff Side was soon again affected by delays, on this occaison over the Noel Hall Report. They accused the Minister of dictating the course of negotiations. It was therefore 'difficult to avoid the conclusion that the Administrative and Clerical Staffs Council had ceased to be a Whitley council'. The Staff Side therefore threatened to by-pass the Whitley Council and take its future claims directly to the Minister.[571] This threat produced immediate results; specific proposals were presented for discussion on 14 April 1958.

In order to bring NHS clerical and general administrative staffs in line with local government, the Noel Hall proposals involved reducing the number of scales from nine to five, and an increase in salaries ranging from 10 to 20 per cent. Walker-Smith evolved proposals for phasing in these increases, entailing an initial increase averaging at 3.7 per cent. With some opposition from the Treasury, this was accepted by the ministerial Committee on Wage Claims, and by the Cabinet.[572] The Staff Side agreed to the new career structure, but wanted an earlier date of implementation and more rapid movement towards the target rates of pay, especially for lower-paid clerical workers. Furthermore they threatened an application to the Industrial Court if agreement was not reached without delay. Ministers found it impossible to obstruct reference to the Industrial Court, but it was able to secure consideration of the entire problem, rather than specific issues, as wanted by the Staff Side.[573]

An appreciation of the Government's case concerning general economic policy was shown by the Industrial Court, which proposed to spread the award over three years ending in July 1961. Any satisfaction derived by Ministers from this outcome was quickly dispelled because awards of similar size to comparable groups of workers outside the NHS were agreed without transitional periods, and indeed included elements of retrospection. In these circumstances, the Administrative and Clerical Staff Side appealed to have their award applied in full from 1 July 1958. The Minister of Health expressed sympathy for the Staff Side, suggesting that this group of workers could understandably claim that it was being singled out for stringent application of the Government's pay policy. He was anxious to avoid a recrudescence of the bitterness associated with the Government's earlier interventions. Walker-Smith suggested a compromise, by which the transitional period would end in July 1959. The Chancellor of the Exchequer favoured keeping to the original transitional plan, but if this was not tenable, he argued that the matter should be referred again to the Industrial Court, and that the Government should ensure that the Management Side contested the assertions of the Staff Side.[574] The arbitration by the Industrial Court found in favour of the Staff Side, and the transitional period was ended in July 1959.[575]

The Industrial Court settlements for clerical and general administrative staffs highlighted the unresolved problem of the pay of designated administrative staff. In the light of their 5 per cent interim increase in the autumn of 1957, Ministers agreed that no further interim increase should be granted. Instead they were offered an investigation into comparabilities, with guarantee of retrospection. This was accepted by the Staff Side, who were confident that the investigation would confirm that the salaries of top administrators in the hospital system were in arrears of comparable groups within the public service and private enterprise. This was a serious problem since the NHS was under constant criticism for the quality of its senior management. In 1959 this investigation by a three-person team headed by Sir Noel Hall called for substantial increases, in certain cases as high as 60 per cent. The Noel Hall committee was satisfied that these recommendations were not out of line with levels of remuneration in comparable outside employment. After some hesitation this argument was accepted by the Treasury, which cleared the way for ratification by the Whitley Council. It was hoped that this would contribute towards improving standards of recruitment into NHS management.[576]

Nurses and Midwives

Nurses' and midwives' pay represented the most serious test of the Whitley Council machinery. The conflict over clerical and general administrative grades proved to be a rehearsal for a more dramatic confrontation over nurses' pay. As reported in the first volume of this study, nurses ran into trouble with the Whitley system in 1954, at which juncture their case was referred to the Industrial Court. During the first decade of the health service, nurses and midwives received periodic economic increases, generally in the region of 5 per cent, without much interference with the relativities within the profession established in 1949. It was increasingly clear that the pay system was beset by anomalies; separate consideration of each issue was inefficient and likely to add to injustice and confusion. Accordingly, following the example of administrative and clerical staff, in April 1957 the nurses applied for a complete revaluation. This was rejected and they settled for their usual 5 per cent economic increase. Following the Noel Hall revaluation for administrative and clerical staff, and other similar reviews with respect to other hospital staff groups, nurses and midwives were expected to reapply for a complete revision of their salary structure. This was also necessary by virtue of worsening comparabilities with respect to outside groups such as teachers. However, to the surprise of the Government, the Staff Side applied for a further 5 per cent economic increase, warning that at some future stage they intended to return to the issue of revaluation.[577]

Given the instability of the situation, especially with respect to nurses in the mental sector, somewhat exceptionally, the Ministry of Health took up the case for revaluation and on this occasion the proposal was not contested by the Treasury.[578] Because the revaluation initiative derived from the Ministry of Health, its officials largely determined the framework of expectations. The Treasury was impressed by the modest scale of the Ministry's proposals, which seemed much less than would have emanated from the nurses' organisations or any process of arbitration. The Ministry also intended to claw back as much as one-third of the proposed award in higher deductions for such items as accommodation and meals. Also, the concertina approach, which granted the greatest increases to senior grades, represented the most economical formula for revaluation.[579] To the surprise of the Treasury, the Staff Side accepted the health departments' proposals with few cavils. The Government departments regarded themselves as fortunate to have escaped so lightly with this economical settlement.[580]

Despite its limitations, this award, paid in March 1959, constituted the biggest increase since the beginning of the NHS. It amounted to about 12 per cent for staff nurses, with higher increases for more senior grades. Staff nurses were established on a scale from £500 to £625 (replacing £446-£557), which gave approximate parity with non-graduate schoolteachers.[581]

Among negotiators, gratitude was not universal. There was particular annoyance that the Management Side, at the behest of the health departments, had adopted an inflexible attitude to the proposed pay package. However, feeling was insufficiently strong within the Staff Side to merit confrontation. Adverse feeling among nurses themselves was even stronger, and it was further inflamed by renewed disadvantage with respect to teachers, brought about by increases amounting to about 10 per cent made in two stages during 1959.

In August 1960 the Staff Side entered a claim for increases averaging 10 per cent; it also reintroduced proposals for changes in relativities resisted by the Management Side in 1959. The latter entered the suspect defence that the 1959 settlement was the definitive occasion for revaluation, both with respect to other occupations and in arriving at balanced relativities within nursing; further modifications were therefore not acceptable at such an early date. The Management Side favoured offering 5 per cent all-round increase, but Ministers initially insisted on 4 per cent. This was rejected by the Staff Side, but notwithstanding the vulnerability of the Management Side's argument, the Staff Side agreed to the compromise of a general increase of 5 per cent, on the understanding that further investigations would be undertaken into anomalies within the salary and grading structure.[582] The Staff Side warned that they were likely to submit proposals for revaluation at some future date. The 5 per cent increase took effect from December 1960.[583]

This agreement was taken badly within nursing organisations, which were subjected to spontaneous and widespread protests from members. This reflected a mood of general discontent, confirming that the 1959 revaluation was not the palliative supposed by the Government departments. Nurses felt disadvantaged not only with respect to teachers, but also local authority social workers, who acquired rather effortlessly a favourable regrading following the

Younghusband Report. The introduction of minimum educational standards for entry into nursing further strengthened the nurses' claim to be treated in parity with teachers. Dissatisfaction among nurses increased in April 1961, when after four abortive meetings, it was agreed to dissolve the joint sub-committee concerned with revision of grading structures. There were many signs of adverse changes within nursing. Greater numbers of nurses were required because of the increase in the amount of skilled work in hospitals, yet the number of nurses in March 1961 had fallen to the same level as March 1958. This necessitated the closure of some 10,000 beds. The character of the nursing workforce was also changing, with greater reliance on immigrant nurses, part-time nurses and unqualified nursing staff. Numbers of new entrants into nurse training steadily declined from March 1959 to March 1961, the greatest decrease occurring in the mental and mental handicap fields, which were already the worst shortage areas. The wastage rate continued to be alarmingly high, with one-third of student nurses withdrawing before the end of training. Wastage was blamed on increased competition of remunerative and attractive careers in commerce and industry, inconvenience and stress of nursing work, demands for higher educational standards, and such general social factors as earlier marriage. The effect of the shortage was increased by the gradual implementation of an agreement to reduce hours worked in a fortnight from 96 to 88 hours, and by some small increases in leave allowances.

The above factors prompted the Staff Side to reactivate its claim for full revaluation of salaries, but it quickly discovered that nurses were destined to become the first victims of the Government's new effort to constrain public sector pay. On 25 July 1961, the Chancellor of the Exchequer announced introduction of a 'pay pause'. Perhaps coincidentally, the Staff Side also made its decision on 25 July, and its claim was submitted on 11 August.[584] The Permanent Secretary of the Ministry of Health wrote to the chairman of the Management Side of the Nurses and Midwives Whitley Council on 10 August, passing on information about the implications of the Chancellor's announcement.[585] In fact the pay pause was not intended to interfere with the negotiating process, only with the implementation of awards. The new claim from nurses was substantial, envisaging an average increase of 33 per cent, with the greatest increases being directed to senior staff. The health departments calculated that the full increase would cost about £45m.

As the basis for its claim, the Staff Side cited comparisons with clerical and general administrative staff, teachers, local authority social workers, and other occupations open to women with similar educational qualifications, and also unrest concerning the December

1960 increase. The Staff Side urged that they were reacting to a revolt of their constituents concerning low pay. Some officials were sceptical, believing that the crisis was being artificially generated by the trade union COHSE. Although the Management Side asked for more information, and was unattracted by some aspects of the claim, the initial response was by no means unsympathetic.[586] In framing their advice to Powell, officials were also supportive of some of the main objectives of the nurses; they were not inclined to stand in the way of revaluation, and it was conceded that the staff nurse should be granted parity with a three-year trained, non-graduate teacher, which suggested a new minimum salary of £600. Officials believed that the Management Side would neither support outright rejection of the claim, nor merely a further economic increase. If revaluation was not accepted, it was pointed out that the merits of the case suggested that a more expensive outcome would result from arbitration, or an independent enquiry. Support for the latter was being spearheaded by COHSE on the model of the Pilkington review of doctors' and dentists' pay, which had produced a favourable outcome from the point of view of these professions.[587] As noted below, a Royal Commission was also favoured as a last resort by Walker-Smith, the recent Minister of Health.

The new Permanent Secretary believed that his colleagues had been too easily persuaded by the Staff Side, and he questioned the desirability of admitting a link between of nurses' and teachers' remuneration.[588] The new Minister supported this 'astringent approach' and was not even willing to discuss a package with the Treasury, or allow the Management Side of express views on the claim until he had been fully convinced about decline in recruitment and increase in wastage. The claim gave the department an opportunity to 'declare public war on the myth of "shortage" of nurses'.[589] Officials generated arguments for rejection of the nurses, claim, albeit without enthusiasm.[590] The papers relating to this problem must have acquainted Powell with the extent of reliance on immigrant nurses. There is no evidence of his response to this phenomenon, but at this stage he perhaps was relaxed about immigration because in nursing it provided a plentiful supply of cheap labour, reduced wastage, and undermined the shortage argument. Immigration therefore strengthened his hand in pressing for a strong line against the nurses' pay claim, which itself was his chief weapon in his wider campaign to induce colleagues to adopt a more aggressive approach to the control of public sector pay.

Powell initially agreed to present a paper to his colleagues adopting the line favoured within the department, proposing either a revaluation, estimated to introduce a rise of 11 per cent, or an economic increase at the usual rate of 5 per cent. Informally the

Treasury agreed that it would not resist 8 per cent. At the last moment Powell advocated a much lower increase of 2.5 per cent. This represented the most severe reading of the Government's pay pause; not only was it intended to defer the date of the pay increase, but also to limit the amount according to the most rigid interpretation of the Government's pay policy. The decision to apply the rod to the backs of the nurses was scarcely consistent with the compliant attitude taken shortly afterwards by Powell with respect to the pay of doctors and dentists. Nurses were evidently judged to be more suitable for exemplary treatment. His Permanent Secretary pointed out that if Ministers followed Powell's advice with respect to nurses, they would scarcely be in a position to adopt a more relaxed policy with other groups of public sector employees. This would expose the Government to the charge of inconsistency and victimisation of nurses. Powell wanted it to be known that unless the pay policy was pursued with complete consistency, he would face further deterioration in morale in the health service.[591] In discussion Powell admitted that the comparison with two-year trained non-graduate teachers would justify an increase of 11 per cent for qualified nurses, but he argued that anything more than 2.5 per cent would be irreconcileable with pay policy. He believed that nothing in the nurses' case suggested that they deserved specially favourable treatment over pay. Ministers resisted Powell's invitation to elevate the nurses' pay claim into a test case. They insisted that all claims should be decided on their merits; if Powell felt that 2.5 per cent was the correct level for the increase, they agreed to allow him to proceed on this basis. Powell also announced that he would be 'playing long' in negotiations, in order to further reduce the inflationary impact of the claim.[592]

The 2.5 per cent offer was made by the Management Side on 13 February 1962. It was presented with little enthusiasm and promptly rejected by the Staff Side on 13 March.[593] The nurses thereupon embarked on a public campaign, attacking Powell for breach of faith and accusing him of undermining the workings of the agreed negotiation procedures. The Royal College of Nursing and the Royal College of Midwives convened a large public meeting on 12 March 1962, on the eve of the Whitley Council meeting. The nurses effectively enlisted support in Parliament and much unflattering publicity about Powell appeared in the press.[594] The Prime Minster expressed concern, only to be told by Powell that 'we must clearly stand firm if the whole of the Government's pay policy is not to be imperiled'.[595] He also accused the trade unions of deliberately preferring 'agitation to arbitration'. Powell was confident that the wave of demonstrations was a passing phenomenon, and that nurses would eventually settle for his 2.5 per cent offer.[596]

Powell's calculation proved to be erroneous. Instead of accepting the Government's offer, the Staff Side stepped up its campaign and planned a big rally, to be held in the Albert Hall on 19 May 1962. Labour capitalised on this opportunity and put down a motion for debate on 14 May. Powell's colleagues recognised that the Government's position was untenable and they pressed him to devise some means for retreat from the inflexible policy into which he had led them. The first sign of compromise was a statement made by Lord Hailsham, Lord President of the Council and Minister for Science, to the Westminster Conservative Association, where he acknowledged that the nurses 'had been persistently undervalued and would be better valued in the future'; he announced that the 2.5 per cent 'guiding light' was never intended as a rigid or permanent instrument of wage control.[597] At the first full ministerial discussion of this problem, Powell was relaxed and he suggested that a minor concession was likely to end the dispute. This proved to be a further miscalculation. Ministers agreed to Powell's suggestion that the nurses should be offered an immediate interim increase of 2.5 per cent costing £3m, with a promise of a joint 'study' into their grading structure, to be followed by a further staged increase, if this proved necessary. Powell calculated that a further £3m paid in 1963 might satisfy the nurses.[598] Powell was satisfied that his 'démarche' would carry the day. His test came at the debate on 14 May. This proved to be yet a further Powell miscalculation. The debate opened with an effective and uncharacteristically passionate speech by Kenneth Robinson.[599] Powell's reply was lack-lustre, perfunctory and unpersuasive. He allowed that the final settlement would be permitted to exceed 2.5 per cent, but the concession was announced in such guarded terms that it failed to satisfy critics.[600] Powell was subsequently attacked from all sides. Perhaps the most important intervention came from his predecessor, Derek Walker-Smith, who was making his first intervention on health questions since his demotion from the Government. The former Minster presented a cogent analysis of the problem of nurses pay, making evident his lack of support for Powell, and urging establishment of a Royal Commission, a solution which he claimed to have favoured during his period in office.[601]

The House of Commons debate was a further public relations set-back for the Government. Even the Conservative press was indignant about Powell. The *Daily Telegraph* complained that the Government was 'making the whole burden of its pay policy fall on its own relatively underpaid employees'.[602] The negative publicity was reinforced by the rally on 29 May, which was addressed by Dame Irene Ward, who had tried, but failed to obtain more concrete promises of concessions from her Conservative ministerial colleagues.[603] Ministers again met in crisis session; Powell advised them that the prospect of a total settlement amounting to £10m would satisfy the nurses.[604]

Powell once again miscalculated. By this stage the Staff Side had been whipped into a state of fury by Powell's prevarications, which they had come to regard as disingenuous delaying tactics. The Management Side formally went along with Powell, but their sympathies were with the nurses. On 7 June 1962 the Management Side offered a 2.5 per cent increase, with the possibility of further staged increases up to a ceiling of £10m, to be determined by negotiations over grading structures. The Staff Side insisted on an immediate increase above 2.5 per cent, and unfettered negotiation over the rest of their revaluation claim.[605] Their resolve was increased by experience of various recent settlements at 4 per cent in the public sector.

At this stage arbitration offered the obvious means for the Staff Side to secure its objectives. However, because this was likely to result in a relatively uniform wage increase, this course was favoured more by the trade unions than by the professional associations. The continuing impasse rendered arbitration an increasingly unavoidable option, an outcome especially unwelcome within the Ministry of Health on account of the likelihood of a large award.[606]

From the perspective of the Staff Side, the Government's proposals were completely unacceptable. By the summer of 1962, most nursing groups had lost most of the advantages secured in 1959, and they had fallen behind the groups with whom they claimed comparison. Staff nurses, for instance, under the Government's proposals would have received a minimum of £550, whereas two-year trained, non-graduate teachers started at £570. The Staff Side therefore finally elected to appeal to the Industrial Court.[607] This was the first occasion on which the nurses had taken their general claim to the Industrial Court, which was in pointed contrast with other major groups of NHS staff, and this reticence had arguably been to the cost of the nurses.

Terms were quickly agreed and the application was made on 16 July 1962.[608] The Industrial Court expressed displeasure that its arbitration was being sought without prior negotiation between the two sides. On the case for higher pay, the Court sided with the nurses, recommending an immediate general increase of 7.5 per cent with effect from April 1962, but also insisting introduction of a revised grading structure.[609] This award gave staff nurses a scale extending from £564 to £705, which was still in arrears of three-year trained, non-graduate teachers, who were also expecting further increase consequent upon a pay claim made in the summer of 1962.

The Government was heavily criticised for its part in the nurses pay affair, and the award was called by the *Times* a 'Justified Exception'.[610]

The controversy over nursing pay was far from over. The two sides met to discuss further revisions of salary and grading structure. Powell calculated that the new pay adjustments could be held down to a further 3 per cent, but in December 1962 it was acknowledged that the two sides were unlikely to reach agreement. Powell would not allow the Management Side to offer more than an additional 3.5 per cent, while the Staff Side demanded 7.5 per cent. The Management Side broke off negotiations and there was no choice but a return to arbitration.[611]

This further appeal to the Industrial Court resulted in an increase of 6.5 per cent effective from July 1963.[612] This established staff nurses on the scale £600 to £750. During the final stages of the Conservative administration the nurses gained one further small concession relating to their hours of work. Other groups of NHS staff had successfully negotiated reductions in their working week. Nurses were in arrears of other groups. In 1958 the health departments agreed to adopt a phased reduction of working hours to reach a 88-hour fortnight by February 1962. This target was largely but not completely achieved. In October 1963 the nurses appealed for a further reduction in their working time to 78 hours. In January 1964 it was agreed to adopt a 84-hour fortnight as the target, to be implemented by January 1966.[613]

The concessions gained by nurses were helpful to other groups of workers within the health service whose industrial strength was even weaker. For instance, the disparate, but important groups of paramedical workers, followed nurses by appealing to the Industrial Court, which recommended that their pay should be linked to nurses. The Government quickly conceded without further appeal to the Industrial Court, by granting paramedical staffs a 7.5 per cent increase to maintain their parity with nurses.[614]

CHAPTER III

Labour Restored

Thirteen years of Conservative government ended with the General Election on 15 October 1964. The optimism and self-confidence of the Macmillan era irretrievably slipped away; in the short time before the election was forced on Douglas-Home, although there was some recovery from the weariness of the old regime, it was insufficient to save the Conservatives from the effects of the winds of change. Harold Wilson, who became the Labour leader after the death of Gaitskell in 1963, superintended over a remarkable transformation in his Party's fortunes. Although Labour was returned with an effective majority of only 5, this involved an increase of Labour seats from 258 to 317, substantially reversing the sweeping election victory of the Conservatives in 1959. Given the small size of the Labour majority, a further General Election was unavoidable. This was held on 31 March 1966, securing for Wilson a comfortable majority; Labour gained 364 seats, only about 30 seats less than the landslide success of 1945. Although this election confirmed the political craftsmanship of Wilson, it also increased doubts about the quality of his political thinking.

In 1964, Harold Wilson, at 48, was the youngest Prime Minister of the century and his administration looked forward to consolidating the fortunes of Labour in a new spirit of innovation and youthful optimism. Despite Labour's traditional attachment to the NHS, health policies were not given special prominence in its policy reviews. From the vantage point of 1964, the most recent substantial policy statement dated from 1959.[1] Although a nicely designed brochure, the latter contained no challenging ideas, and was in the main a call for acceleration of the drive to meet elementary objectives which commanded universal assent. The section on health in the 1964 General Election manifesto included a general pledge to expand services and correct shortages of personnel. A general undertaking was given to revise and augment the 1962 hospital plan, especially with respect to provision of maternity accommodation and beds for geriatric care and mental illness, proposals which in some respects ran contrary to Labour's pledge to expand community care. On the sensitive political issue of health service charges, the 1964 manifesto was less categorical than its 1959 predecessor. A slightly ambiguous undertaking was given to abolish the prescription charge, but with respect to other charges, it was merely indicated that Labour would 'restore as rapidly as possible a completely free health service'.[2] The section on health care in the 1966 manifesto was largely a defence of the Government's handling of the main parts of the health service during its first two years in office, with suitably vague promises of continuing commitment to improvement. It is notable that neither the Labour nor the Conservative manifestos contained reference to the possibility of administrative reorganisation of the health services.

As evident below, Labour was not particularly well-prepared to deal with the many important policy issues which demanded urgent attention. Even on the crucial issue of the organisational weaknesses of the NHS, the well-informed Laurie Pavitt complained that there was no evidence of 'any great pressure building up within the wider Labour Movement for radical changes when the next Labour Government is elected'.[3] The low priority of health policy in Labour circles was underlined by the negligible influence of the Socialist Medical Association and the Medical Practitioners' Union. In the thousand pages of Crossman's *Diaries* concerned with his period as Secretary of State for Social Services, the SMA and MPU are each mentioned once. There is an additional reference to David Stark Murray, the SMA secretary, who was a tireless health campaigner, well-known even before World War II. Nevertheless, Crossman recorded Stark Murray's name erroneously.[4]

(i) MINISTERS AND DEPARTMENTS

Since the Ministry of Health was not regarded as a particularly prestigious assignment, the appointment of the new Minister of Health was treated as a routine matter. Wilson broke with recent practice by leaving the Minister of Health outside the Cabinet. For all of Labour's attachment to principle of the NHS, few of its MPs were active and well-informed in this field of social policy. In 1964, the most worthy health activist among the MPs was Laurie Pavitt, a former organiser of the MPU, but he had only entered Parliament in 1959; other useful new recruits like the medically-qualified Shirley Summerskill (daughter of the formidable Dr Edith Summerskill, who became a life peer in 1961), had only just entered Parliament. Most of the veterans of 1948 had departed from the scene. Of the junior Ministers in place before the election defeat of 1951, only Arthur Blenkinsop was a feasible candidate. He was a figure of some seniority and was elected Chairman of the Parliamentary Labour Party in November 1964; he had served as chairman of the parliamentary health services group during the 1950s, and was chairman of the UK Committee of WHO, a member of the Medical Research Council, and served on committees dealing with the

179

problem of drug abuse. However, his primary interests lay in the fields of pensions and town and country planning.

Compared with the above names, Kenneth Robinson, although not a well-known public figure, was a more suitable candidate for the health portfolio; it was therefore no surprise when Wilson appointed him Minister of Health.[5] Like Macleod, Robinson was the son of a general practitioner, who worked in the north of England. His father's premature death at the age of 42, with overwork as a contributory factor, left a lasting impression on his politically-minded son.[6] Formerly a company secretary, Robinson served as MP for St.Pancras North from March 1949. From the outset of his parliamentary career Robinson specialised on health affairs; he was a member of the North West Metropolitan RHB from 1951 and soon was appointed chairman of its Mental Health Committee. In 1958 he became a Vice-President of the National Association for Mental Health. Robinson was also one of the most active members of the Select Committee on Estimates, when in 1957 it examined the running costs of hospitals.[7] From 1961 onwards Robinson proved himself to be a conscientious and resourceful front-bench spokesman on health. Powell's blunders respecting the hospital plan and nurses' pay gave Robinson an opportunity to shine.

Robinson noticed his exclusion from the Cabinet, and the disadvantage of his position was appreciated by others.[8] The weakness of this position perhaps accounts for his tendency to fall back on the threat of resignation. From the outset, Robinson must also have been apprehensive about possibility of his department being swallowed up in some larger conglomerate. As already noted, since 1962 at least amalgamation of health and social security had been under consideration. Robinson's tenure was blighted by this prospect.

Merger of departments was very much the fashion during the Wilson administration. Indeed, it has already been noted that the Conservatives considered various schemes for amalgamating departments concerned with social security. In 1963 Labour advocated the formation of a ministry of social security in its pamphlet, *New Frontiers for Social Security*. By the mid-sixties amalgamation of social security departments was favoured by both main political parties and it was warmly supported in the press. Early in 1966 Wilson considered four major amalgamations, including the establishment of a large social security group, including health, but he decided against this alternative and opted for a narrower Ministry of Social Security, bringing together the Ministry of Pensions and National Insurance and the National Assistance Board.[9]

Robinson may have recognised the formation of the Ministry of Social Security in 1966 as a step towards the loss of identity of his own department. Perhaps as a defensive measure, he proposed to retitle his department as the 'Ministry of Health and Welfare'.[10] This proposal was decisively rejected by other social services Ministers, and by their co-ordinator, Douglas Houghton, the Chancellor of the Duchy of Lancaster and Chairman of the Ministerial Committee on Social Services. The idea of amalgamating the Ministries of Health and Social Security remained under discussion. For instance, in November 1967, when Robinson announced his intention to review the reorganisation of the NHS, Lord Balniel, the opposition spokesman, insisted that the review should also consider amalgamation of the two departments, a possibility clearly not relished by Robinson.[11] In the event, Robinson was granted a short stay of execution. Robinson relied on Douglas Houghton for general representation of the health interest in the Cabinet.[12] However, Houghton was not effective and he was dropped from the Cabinet in 1967. As Chairman of the Social Services Committee he was replaced for a short time by Patrick Gordon Walker, and then Michael Stewart, two other senior politicians in decline. The Social Services Committee finally came under more dynamic management in April 1968 as a consequence of a Cabinet reshuffle, when the chair passed to Richard Crossman. This was not welcome news to Robinson, because Crossman was also given direct control of the Ministeries of Health and Social Security and was set the task of amalgamating these departments. The amalgamation was achieved by creating a new Secretary of State under the prerogative, and by transferring to this office, by Order, the powers of the Ministers of Health and Social Security, and abolishing their separate departments.[13] Although Wilson liked the idea of making Crossman 'overlord' of an amalgamated department, it was far from clear how this would be accomplished, and what timetable was feasible. Crossman admitted that the only virtue of this scheme was 'to create a Ministry for me!'.[14] As Crossman's diaries richly testify, this policy was not without its disadvantages and it was not welcomed by the departments involved. Discussions about amalgamation were conducted without enthusiasm and there was a tendency to prevarication.

Even Crossman, who forced the pace, realised that the different ethos of the two departments would be difficult to reconcile.[15] There were also practical problems connected with relating two departments, which in Whitehall terms were geographically widely-separated and one of which had moved south of the Thames to the notorious Elephant and Castle site. The demoralising environment created for the Ministry of Health was immediately appreciated by Crossman, whose reaction efficiently communicates the nature of the problem:

181

I made my first visit to the collection of huge modern glass blocks that was custom-built for the Ministry of Health at the Elephant and Castle. It is on a ghastly site and Kenneth Robinson told me they chose it for its cheapness. It cost only half as much as normal sites for government buildings but a great deal of the money they saved is now being spent on air-conditioning and double-glazing...It was hoped that one effect of plonking the building down there would be to improve the area and attract other government buildings. It hasn't happened and the Ministry stands isolated and terrible.[16]

Crossman assumed the title of Secretary of State for Social Services on 1 November 1968, and the two departments were amalgamated from this date. It was unrealistic to expect Robinson to continue with his former responsibilities, but as a junior Minister to Crossman. Accordingly, in November 1968, Robinson accepted transfer to a junior ministerial post in the Ministry of Housing and Local Government, although after a year he became the victim of a reshuffle and left the Government. Crossman's *Diaries* were not altogether flattering about Robinson when he was Minister of Health, but his final judgement was considerably more positive. He praised Robinson as an efficient and hard-working departmental Minister, who was especially successful in gaining the confidence of the medical profession at a particularly perilous time for relations between doctors and the state.[17] This echoed the general praise for Robinson over his dealings with the medical profession. At the height of the controversy with doctors, Wilson congratulated him for the 'dignity and restraint with which he had dealt with a difficult and potentially dangerous situation'.[18] Lord Kindersley, Chairman of the doctors' and dentists' Review Body, praised the 'great skill and patience' displayed by Robinson in his negotiations with the medical profession.[19] Certainly patience could not be regarded as one of the prime assets of Crossman. The latter described Wilson's dismissal of Robinson as an 'outrage', and a telling symptom of the Prime Minister's mishandling of ministerial appointments.[20]

With the establishment of Crossman's direct responsibility for the health service, the NHS was again represented in the Cabinet, and Crossman's position as a Minister in charge of a super-department gave him a position of seniority, which granted the health services more powerful representation in the Cabinet than at any time since Bevan. In November 1968 Crossman also joined the recently-established Parliamentary Committee of the Cabinet (later called Management Committee), which considered 'the management of the Government's business in terms of Parliamentary and political tactics and presentation to public opinion'.[21] While Crossman was not always satisfied with the interventions of this committee, it provided a useful further instrument for exercising his influence.

Crossman experienced a steady growth in his influence in the course of the Wilson administration, being first Minister of Housing and Local Government, then Lord President and Leader of the House, and finally Secretary of State for Social Services.[22] Although with no particular expertise in the field of health policy, Crossman freely intervened in Ministerial exchanges on health issues from the outset of the Wilson administration. As early as February 1968, Crossman advised Wilson that Robinson needed 'effective supervision'.[23] Only a month later Wilson asked Crossman to take on general ministerial responsibility for the social services, promising that 'you could be as memorable as Beveridge if you...make a go of the two years of reorganisation there'. Crossman realised that he was being given a 'really big chance to be right at the top with a key job and a genuine promotion'.[24] Robinson's quiet, unassertive approach was exchanged for Crossman's abrasive interventionism. The contrast of their styles is well-exhibited in their handling of the difficult reorganisation issue, discussed in Chapter IV. Crossman congratulated himself on his attentiveness and relaxed social manner, but officials and others found him authoritarian, impatient and erratic.[25]

Because of his wide-ranging responsibilities and activism within the Cabinet, Crossman was dependent on his junior Ministers. With the amalgamation of the two departments, David Ennals was recruited from the Home Office and Stephen Swingler from the Ministry of Transport, to become Ministers of State, with responsibility for Health and Social Security respectively. This arrangement worked well, but Swingler died in February 1969, after which Ennals was moved to Social Security and his place in Health was taken by Beatrice Serota, the former Chairman of the Children's Committee of the LCC, who was made a Life Peer in 1967.[26] Serota's commitment and hard work were praised by Crossman,[27] but it was disadvantageous for this key post to be located in the House of Lords, and this caused resentment among Labour MPs.[28] Serota's appointment was initially welcomed by officials, but later they complained about her indecisiveness. This criticism was to some extent shared by Crossman, but on the whole he found Serota a more congenial and reliable colleague than Ennals.[29]

In Scotland formal responsibility for health affairs resided with the Secretary of State, William Ross, but he delegated main duties for health to this subordinates.[30] Until the 1966 General Election, the resourceful Judith Hart was the Joint Parliamentary Under-Secretary of State with main responsibilities for health, after which she was promoted to the Commonwealth Office, where she was

Minister of State. Then in 1967 she was appointed Minister of Social Security. Hart's place at the Scottish Office was taken by the more conventional Bruce Millan.

As noted in the previous chapter, the Secretary of the Scottish Department of Health until 1962 was the experienced T D Haddow, who in 1965 became Permanent Under-Secretary of State at the Scottish Office. R E C Johnson was Secretary of the amalgamated SHHD from 1963 until 1972.[31] The Chief Medical Officer in Scotland until 1964 was Sir Kenneth Cowan, who was replaced by J H F Brotherston, who had served as Professor of Public Health and Social Medicine at Edinburgh and had also been Dean of the Faculty of Medicine. Brotherston held office until 1977. During this period of major change in the health service, Brotherston proved to be a worthy counterpart to Godber in London.[32]

In Wales, since 1919, the Minister of Health had exercised certain health functions through the Welsh Board of Health. In recognition of its General Election promises made in 1959 and 1964, the Labour administration established the Welsh Office and appointed a Secretary of State for Wales.[33] Although the Labour Party document, *Signposts to the New Wales* (1962) listed health services among the administrative areas suitable for supervision by the new Welsh Office, owing to resistance from the Minister of Health this was not acted upon. The first stage of Welsh devolution therefore made no immediate difference to health service administration. Wales thus remained disadvantaged in many minor ways, for instance in consultation and representation on some important committees of investigation established during this period, as indicated below in the discussion of the Royal Commission on Medical Education.

In response to the growth in nationalist and devolutionist pressures, Labour returned to the issue of devolution for both Scotland and Wales. In 1966, James Griffiths and then Cledwyn Hughes repeated the demand to extend the functions of the Welsh Office. Both listed health as the primary candidate for assimilation by the Welsh Office. Wilson and Crossman were sympathetic, and examination of this issue was remitted to Patrick Gordon Walker. However, with strong backing from the Treasury and the Ministry of Health, Gordon Walker's report reached completely negative conclusions about extension of the functions of the Welsh Office.[34] Effectively by-passing the Gordon Walker Report, with the encouragement of Wilson, Crossman convened a committee of Ministers which investigated the case for devolution in both Scotland and Wales. In the face of further representations by Robinson, this committee recommended transferring authority for the health service to the Welsh Office.[35] This view was supported by Ministers. Accordingly, from April 1969, the Welsh Board of Health was abolished and its functions were absorbed into a new health department within the Welsh Office.[36] The Secretary of State for Wales, George Thomas, also took over most of the statutory functions for the health service previously exercised by the Secretary of State for Social Services. The effects of this change will be observed in the following narrative. For instance, whereas the first Green Paper on NHS reorganisation in 1968 related to England and Wales, and made only peremptory reference to Wales; in 1970 separate Green Papers were issued, and there was even consideration of separate legislation for Welsh reorganisation.

Health Departments
After a brief and successful spell as Permanent Secretary at the Ministry of Health, in 1964 Sir Bruce Fraser moved to become the Second Permanent Secretary at the Department of Education and Science.[37] Fraser was replaced by Sir Arnold France, who, like his predecessor, had risen to a senior position in the Treasury. When France transferred to the Inland Revenue in 1968, there arose the sensitive issue of appointing the first incumbent as head of the merged health and social security departments. At the Ministry of Housing and Local Government, Crossman had intervened actively over the successor to Dame Evelyn Sharp.[38] At the DHSS, after a little hesitation, he was guided by official advice. After making a few independent enquiries, Crossman agreed that the merged DHSS should be headed by Sir Clifford Jarrett, formerly the Permanent Secretary at Social Security, and that the Second Permanent Secretary should be Alan Marre, who had served most of his career in the Ministry of Health, but was at the Ministry of Labour from 1966-1968.[39] Jarrett retired in 1970 and Marre became Parliamentary Commissioner for Administration in 1971.

Jarrett was personally domineering and very much the senior partner, and his bias was naturally towards social security. In general, the heterogeneous health side of the department felt at a disadvantage to the more hierarchical, coherently-organised and numerically much larger Social Security part of the department. Crossman was never enthusiastic about Jarrett, but at the end of 1969 their relations seriously deteriorated when the Secretary of State took exception to Jarrett's retirement plans.[40] There is some suggestion that Jarrett's difficulties with Crossman stemmed from disapproval of the DHSS merger. Perhaps more important was the temperamental incompatibility between two determined personalities. Also, Jarrett failed to warm to ethos of social services departments after the alleged glamour of a previous career in the Admiralty.[41]

The formidable Chief Medical Officer, Sir George Godber, outlasted Fraser, France and Jarrett and did not retire until 1973.[42]

185

The eminence of Godber was appreciated as an asset by Crossman and they retained good personal relations, cemented in part by their common association with New College, Oxford. Crossman fluctuated in his attitude towards the health side of his department. For much of the time he found their methodical procedures slow and tiresome, and the officials themselves uncongenial and unresponsive. In better moods he was more condescending and expressed sneaking regard for some of the personnel. At his most expansive state, he characterised the Permanent Secretary and the Ministry of Health as 'highly intelligent' and 'wonderfully old-style', something like the old Colonial Office or the India Office.[43] Harder heads tended to be more judgmental. Despite improvements in performance during the 1960s, the Treasury was not satisfied that the Ministry of Health was exercising sufficient central direction and control over the health services.[44] It was felt that the highly-devolved pattern of administration adopted out of necessity at the beginning of the health service was no longer acceptable. As noted in the previous chapter, the Ministry of Health recognised the need for a more interventionist approach, but the Treasury was not satisfied that the health department was fully-converted to this new philosophy. Senior officials were too wedded to the tradition whereby their interventions were limited to minimum, regulatory functions; they seemed too much in awe of medical authority to assume a more positive role. The Treasury was doubtful whether senior appointees within the health department possessed the calibre to achieve a fundamental shift towards a more aggressive style of management.[45] The Ministry of Health was accused of being almost totally lacking in numeracy and 'fliers'.[46]

It seemed that too much responsibility for economic and financial management rested on the Permanent Secretary himself. There was, in the Treasury view, too much fragmentation of responsibility at senior levels within the department, with the result that initiatives connected with efficiency were difficult to promote or sustain. The Treasury tried to remedy this situation by suggesting establishment of a high-level 'Health Policy Committee' with representation for the Treasury and Department of Economic Affairs, but this was at first resisted. When established as the Health Programmes Committee, this committee functioned reasonably smoothly in dealing with the first problem in its remit, but it proved incapable of adaptation to deal with further business and gradually lapsed into abeyance. It is doubtful whether constant hectoring from the Treasury improved the situation, because this provoked obstructionism and a sense of grievance within the Ministry of Health. The Treasury thought that Sir Arnold France was particularly over-defensive and irritable about their attempts at helpful intervention. Treasury estimates of the

Ministry of Health were of course not infallible. Neither was the line taken by the Treasury entirely consistent. Criticisms made in the heat of the moment were not always reflected in more sober assessments. For instance, 'Operation Vigilant', which looked at the administration of various departments between 1964 and 1966 made no serious criticisms of either the Ministry of Health or the Scottish Home and Health Department. With respect to the Ministry, it concluded that there existed 'as yet just below the surface, the right systems and most of the right resources of expertise to develop a policy which would bring better value for money from the outlay on the health services', which was as near to satisfaction that the Treasury was ever likely to express.[47]

Ministers increasingly expanded their sources of advice. In addition to their civil servants and the statutory advisory machinery, they obtained assistance through a variety of more informal channels of advice. For instance, in July 1965 Robinson established an Advisory Committee on Long Term Development, which contained both senior officials and academics, many of them not particularly closely associated with Labour.[48] This Committee continued to meet until 1968, but it exercised very little influence.

Crossman was more at home than Robinson in the company of academics, and he adopted a more selective approach, forming particularly close links with a small group of experts known to be in sympathy with the welfare aims of Labour. On the health side of his department, Crossman particularly depended on the advice of Professor Brian Abel-Smith of the London School of Economics, who joined the Secretary of State's staff in 1968 upon the recommendation of Richard Titmuss, Abel-Smith's head of department and collaborator.[49] On both health and social security questions Titmuss and Abel-Smith played a prominent advisory role, and on health they also often involved the long-standing associate of Titmuss, Professor J N Morris of the London School of Hygiene and Tropical Medicine. These three also found their way on to some of the most important committees dealing with health and social services issues during this period. Officials and outside advisers came together at various regular meetings, for instance the weekly sessions on future policy, initiated in July 1969, which acted as a useful forum for handling the growing crop of troublesome issues which surfaced during the final months of the Wilson administration. As noted below with respect to the Post-Ely Policy Working Party, Crossman's taste for intruding NHS personnel and academics into the work of his department was not altogether welcomed by his officials.

(ii) GOALS OF LABOUR

The Labour Government established in 1964 aroused the

expectation that the welfare state as a whole would be modernised and supported with a new level of commitment. A Ministerial Committee on Social Services was established without delay. Therefore, for the first time in the postwar period, a high-level committee of Ministers concerned entirely with the development of the social services maintained a permanent presence, rather than being called into existence for the sake of some emergency. The initial remit for this committee was to 'keep under review and to co-ordinate the Government's policies for social services'.[50] It has already been mentioned that until the appointment of Crossman in 1968, this committee passed through the hands of three ineffective chairmen, of whom the longest serving was Douglas Houghton. By virtue of his interest in the social services and well-known association with the radio programme 'Can I Help You?', Houghton was a credible chairman, but he displayed limited powers of leadership and his interventions tended to be unproductive. Furthermore, the health service was among the least of his interests, and did not figure in the list of six major objectives which he announced at the inception of the committee.[51]

As soon as December 1964 Robinson complained that the programme of the committee was dominated by education and social security, resulting in the neglect of other important questions of social welfare.[52] The immediate result of this complaint was a proposal by Robinson to give prominence to the problems of the elderly, the chronic sick and the handicapped. A report on this rather diffuse subject area was duly commissioned, but it was too generalised to ignite interest within the Committee. Although some health-related topics were discussed, Robinson's expectation that community care would become a main priority was not fulfilled. It also became clear that progress in this field was dependent on the outcome of a review of the organisation of the personal social services, which was a lengthy process, undertaken by the Seebohm Committee. Consequently, many practical problems associated with community care were deferred until the last months of the Wilson administration. The Social Services Committee was largely preoccupied with social security issues. On the health services front, apart from NHS reorganisation, the committee was mainly concerned with a trickle of specific and largely uncontroversial items of business.

High on the agenda of the health Ministers was attention to the manifesto commitments made in 1964 and 1966. As described below, much energy was absorbed by the promise to abolish prescription charges and restore a completely free health service. A further expensive undertaking was the promise to revise the 1962 hospital plan and double the amount spent by the Conservatives on new hospital building. In 1964 the manifesto also gave a pledge to greatly

188

increase the number of doctors in all parts of the NHS, for which purpose it would be necessary to expand existing medical schools and establish new medical schools. As with the personal social services, this objective could not be pursued without meticulous preparation, in this case provided by the Royal Commission on Medical Education. The manifestos also contained some vague promises concerning general improvement in primary care and community services, with hints about increased attention to preventive medicine. Nothing was said about reorganisation of the personal social services and the health services, renegotiation of the contract for family doctors, the restructuring of nursing services, correcting abuses in the long-stay hospitals, abortion and family planning, all of which forced their way on to the political agenda during the term of the Wilson administration.

Labour's goals were not attainable without an increase in the resources available to the National Health Service. The Wilson administration sustained a modest increase in health service expenditure, but on aggregate the record was only marginally better than the final years of the previous Conservative administration. Between the 1963/64 and 1969/70 the share of national resources devoted to the NHS rose slowly from 4.10 to 4.50 as a percentage of GDP.[53] Because of the decline in the share of NHS costs borne by the NHS Contribution and direct charges, the share from the Consolidated Fund rose from 76.5 to 83.8 per cent.[54] The highly-publicised policy of removing direct charges produced a decline in the yield from this source from 4.3 to about 2 per cent, but the reimposition of the prescription charge and an increase in other charges took the yield from this source back to 3.2 per cent of the gross cost of the NHS by the end of our period.

At 1970 prices, over the period 1964 to 1970, expenditure on the NHS increased by 39.0 per cent in cost terms, but this reduced to 23.3 per cent in volume terms. Very similar rises apply for cost or volume estimates relating specifically to current expenditure. At first sight this appears like an improvement on Macmillan-Home record. The important volume estimate applied to current expenditure shows a 21.3 per cent increase, giving an average of 3.5 per cent a year, but this disguises some sharp irregularities. After maintaining an increase averaging about 4.5 per cent for the first three years, imposition of the post-devaluation economies caused a steep decline, ending with a 1.0 per cent deficit in 1969, after which there was a small recovery in 1970. 1969 was the first year of actual deficit since 1952.[55] This perturbation proved to be the foretaste of greater instability and even more serious checks to growth in the 1970s.

As under the Conservatives, the NHS was less successful than education in attracting additional resources. Over the period under consideration, education increased its share of GDP from 4.9 to 5.9. With respect to the share of social services expenditure, education increased from 24.8 per cent to 25.4 per cent, whereas the NHS fell from 20.0 per cent to 19.1 per cent.[56] The political struggle to maintain the competitive position of the NHS in the league-table of public expenditure will be considered in the following section.

(iii) FINANCING THE HEALTH SERVICE
As indicated in chapter III, during the thirteen years of Conservative administration, the NHS was a main target for successive rounds of economies in spending on the social services. Although a gradual rise in the cost of the NHS was unavoidable, this increase was held down to a minimum. Periodic exploitation of opportunities to increase charges and the NHS Contribution prevented a steep rise in the Exchequer commitment to the health service.[57]

Abolition of the Prescription Charge
Superficially at least, the ethos of the NHS changed under Labour, although this alteration was not sustained. The Labour Party had vigorously contested rises in health service charges. In its 1959 General Election manifesto, Labour had promised to abolish all charges, starting with the prescription charge. The 1964 manifesto was more circumspect. It promised to deal with the 'burden of prescription charges in the Health Service'. A pledge was made to abolish the prescription charge, and also to 'restore as rapidly as possible a completely free Health Service'.[58] Statements by Labour in opposition implied that the NHS Contribution was not a favoured source for health service funding. It was therefore inevitable that the burden on the Exchequer would be proportionately increased; this was the only source able to meet the substantial commitments made concerning the development of services after the long period of alleged resource starvation under the Conservatives.[59]

An immediate objective for Labour was elimination of health service charges. The Treasury appreciated that it was unrealistic to block this action; instead it opted for a policy of maximum containment, hoping to limit concessions to the prescription charge, delaying its reduction for as long as possible, and offsetting the loss incurred through such expedients as an increase in the NHS Contribution, or reduction in the subsidy on welfare milk or school meals.[60]

Abolition of charges was a major expectation of the public. Indeed, it was perhaps the single best-known policy objective associated with Labour. Naturally, it figured in the Queen's Speech.[61] Robinson immediately took up the pledge to abolish health services charges, but his proposals were noticeably restrained. He suggested that the

Queen's Speech should contain a promise to abolish the prescription charge, but he avoided requesting an immediate reduction in other charges.[62]

An initial package for expansion in the social services was considered at a meeting of relevant Ministers, and then by the Cabinet on 28 October 1964. Callaghan was opposed to abolishing the prescription charge during the first session of the administration, and he proposed to limit the increase in the old age pension to 10s. As recompense, he offered to provide a small sum to transfer the cost of old people's homes from local authorities to the Exchequer. In the euphoria of the moment Ministers were unwilling to listen to this call for restraint. They insisted on immediate abolition of the prescription charge and an increase in the pension by 12s 6d. The Prime Minister made only a token attempt to urge caution.[63]

George Brown complained that it had been a mistake not to mention abolition of the prescription charge in the November budget statement; he appealed for prompt announcement in order that Labour should obtain full credit for its initiative. Wilson supported Brown. Callaghan argued that there was no point in an early announcement if abolition was not due until 1 April, but his colleagues insisted on abolition at an earlier date. Robinson aimed to relieve the sick of paying the charges over a full winter. He therefore proposed abolition on 1 February 1965. This date was agreed by the Social Services Committee and it was announced on 17 December. [64] Removal of the prescription charge was widely welcomed, although opposition came from an unexpected direction. After many years of antagonism to prescription charges, in July 1964 the Annual Representative Meeting of the BMA reversed its policy on grounds that elimination of the prescription charge would increase frivolous calls on doctors' time. Removal of the charge therefore marginally exacerbated already troubled relations with the doctors, and it assisted this group's pay demands on the grounds that their workload was increased.[65]

This was by no means the end of the adverse fall-out from the Government's best-intentioned gesture over prescription charges. The anticipated cost of abolition of the prescription charge was £22m in a full year, but it soon became clear that this was a serious underestimate.[66] The final cost was about £50m, which Callaghan found disturbing.[67] Within a few months Ministers regretted that they had taken precipitate action on the prescription charge, and subsequently they engaged in mutual recriminations concerning the source for this decision.[68] It soon became evident that the National Health Service would be penalised for abolition of the prescription charge. Robinson assumed that this policy change would be a political obligation, and accordingly that it would be treated as a free bonus for the NHS. In practice, the Treasury counted the additional expenditure incurred as a result of loss of prescription charge against the health departments, thereby allowing less for other areas of development when assessing long-term limits in public expenditure.

Long-Term Spending Limits

As under the Conservatives, the Treasury was vigilant to prevent escalation in NHS spending. Immediate steps were taken to ensure continuing containment. At the end of the Conservative period in office, the NHS was still absorbing just less than 4 per cent of GDP. The PESC estimates allowed for growth at about 3 per cent. As noted in chapter II, it had proved unrealistic to hold down the increase in hospital current and capital expenditure to the levels agreed by Powell. There was pressure to amend the annual rate of increase in hospital current expenditure from 2 per cent to at least 3 per cent. On the capital front there had been a £5m overspend in 1964/65; the health departments appealed for this rise to be continued into the following year.[69] Despite appreciation of problems likely to arise from perpetuating unrealistic expenditure constraints, Treasury estimates relating to the NHS for the period up to April 1970 were scarcely relaxed. Originally an expansion of 20 per cent over the five-year period was contemplated; this was modified to 22.5 per cent, but with an understanding that at least 27 per cent would have been required for Labour to meet its election promises. Treasury officials acknowledged that the Ministry of Health was being 'pretty roughly treated'.[70] The rough treatment extended to procedural conduct. The Treasury postponed its meeting with the Permanent Secretary of the Ministry of Health until after the decisive Cabinet discussion, to which Robinson was not invited. Inevitably, both the Permanent Secretary and Robinson complained about this unsophisticated attempt to prevent the Ministry of Health from stating its case.[71]

The Cabinet decision of 28 January 1965 was important because it effectively determined the pattern and level of expenditure on the health service for the rest of the Wilson administration.[72] Allowance was made for abolition of the prescription charge, but not for elimination of other charges. No increase was allowed in the capital programme agreed under the Conservatives, even though it was evident that the targets were unrealistic. The recently-agreed rise from 2 to 2.5 per cent in the annual increase in hospital current expenditure was adopted as a limit, although it was already being argued that something like 3.5 per cent would be needed.[73] An increase in local health and welfare spending of £10m a year was anticipated to meet local authority spending plans, which were not directly controlled by the Treasury. A further £10m increment was allowed to include anticipated increases in the pharmaceutical bill and also the cost of the new scheme to reimburse general practitioners for ancillary staff.[74] The Ministry of Health demanded higher spending limits to allow for a 25 per cent increase over the quinquennium, but this was resisted by the Treasury, which retaliated by calling for efficiency savings, such as greater economy in hospital building, and redoubled efforts to control the pharmaceutical industry.[75] Callaghan told Robinson to apply to the 'kitty' for any extra resources. Robinson complained that the Labour Government was holding expenditure on the NHS to the level existing under the Tories, which they had attacked as inadequate when in opposition. He agreed not to contest the PESC limits, although warning that he would be making 'considerable demands on the kitty'.[76]

Robinson frequently expressed resentment concerning the continuing harsh regime to which the NHS was subjected. When pressed by the Prime Minister for a report on progress with expansion in the health service, Robinson gave a report on advances, but complained that 'we have much evidence of the tremendous squeeze that the National Health Service has been subjected to in recent years; an acceptable level of expansion and development, quite apart from the fulfilment of our pledge to abolish the remaining charges, must depend upon our getting a generous share of the resources available'. He warned that the current level of allocations would not allow for anything like the degree of expansion to which Labour was committed.[77]

Hospital Plan

Having argued in opposition that the Conservative administration had drastically miscalculated the cost of their hospital plan, Labour could scarcely hide behind obfuscations of the kind used in the past to defend low capital spending. During their period in office, the Conservatives could plausibly claim that regional authorities were not capable of spending up to the limits of available resources. This excuse had ceased to possess credibility even by the time of the Conservative defeat. Labour either needed to devote considerably more resources to the hospital plan, or conclude on the basis of the volume of expenditure originally envisaged, that only a small fraction of the schemes listed in the original ten-year plan could be executed within the stated period. The cost of the original plan was steadily escalating, not only on account of inflation, but also because modern hospitals were more expensive than originally anticipated. Plans were also disrupted by unforeseen circumstances, such as the discovery of major structural defects in major children's hospitals at Edinburgh and Glasgow, which necessitated redirecting resources from other high-priority projects.

Robinson began his campaign for additional resources with an appeal to the Cabinet for an increase in hospital capital expenditure for the year 1965/66 by £5m in order to prevent overspending on the hospital plan for a second year running. Treasury Ministers had rejected this request.[78] Given the high priority attached to hospital modernisation by Labour, Robinson appealed for support from other Ministers. He promised that this request for additional resources would not be repeated in later years, but pointed out the damage to the reputation of the Government if this small concession was rejected. In the course of discussion Robinson was heavily criticised and given virtually no support; even Ross remained silent. The matter was referred back for further negotiations between the Minister of Health and the Treasury, with a view to finding countervailing savings if overspending was unavoidable.[79] Subsequent to the Cabinet discussion Callaghan agreed to grant an additional £5m for hospital building, but on the understanding that there was subsequently a reversion to previously agreed levels of spending for the rest of the period covered by the first phase of the hospital plan, and also an attempt to find offsetting savings.[80] Treasury officials were depressed about this capitulation, which they regarded as a dangerous precedent, likely to presage a 'rocketing' in health service expenditure.[81] Their attempts to obtain economies by reducing the subsidy on welfare milk or cutting local authority capital spending came to nothing.

In view of the refusal of the Treasury to expand the scale of the hospital plan, the Labour health Ministers were unable to turn their revision of the hospital plan into a further publicity boost of the kind achieved with the abolition of the prescription charge. Indeed, they realised that the latter had absorbed the resources which might have been used to even greater benefit in hospital building. Although the revisions of the hospital plan were presented as a major step forwards, they were in fact a face-saving device, to disguise the slowing down of the hospital programme. The revised plans evaded detailed statements on annual allocations, either for the nation as a whole, or for the regions. The most they were able to offer was the assurance that a substantial level of spending would extend into the 1970s. The England and Wales plan contained an assurance that 'roughly £1,000m will be spent over the next ten years', which was only one-third the level thought realistic by the Ministry of Health in August 1964.[82] This was £80m greater than the last revision undertaken under the Conservative administration, which covered the same period, 1966-1976. Under Labour, it was agreed to add about £10m each year to the programme, but only from 1969 onwards. Robinson aimed to complete about 90 new hospitals, about the same number as envisaged by the Conservatives, but he drastically scaled-down the plans for major reconstructions from 134 to 59, and other large schemes were reduced from 356 to 318.[83] On account of limitation of the hospital budget, the pressure intensified for adoption of more economical systems of hospital building. At precisely this time, the methods of the entrepreneur and architect, John Poulson, were attracting much publicity. NHS authorities found it difficult to resist the temptation of methods that promised the building of 20 new 600-bed hospitals within four years for a total cost not exceeding £50m.[84]

The Scottish health department lamented that on the basis of the current rates of building, even the modest target of replacing all pre-1939 beds would only be achieved by the year 2015. Pessimism concerning prospects for hospital renewal caused the SHHD to reconsider its plans, place more emphasis on health centres and primary care, and also general integration of services, which inevitably increased the argument for reorganising the health service. The failure to resource the hospital plan at a realistic level is therefore one of the factors which led Scotland to take a lead in discussions on NHS reorganisation, a conclusion which will be amplified in the next chapter. Given escalation of costs and unavoidable changes in priorities, SHHD reduced the scope of its plans, and provided firm details only for the next quinquennium. In the detailed plans there was a tendency to defer plans for district general hospitals in favour of providing more facilities for maternity and geriatric care.[85]

Given restrictions on the hospital programme, the NHS authorities concentrated on improving their planning system, with particular emphasis on preventing overspending.[86] As noted below, in the final years of Wilson administration, one of the main preoccupations of the health departments was preventing erosion in the hospital programme. This was successfully achieved, but at the cost of economies elsewhere, including the parallel capital programmes relating to community care.

As indicated below with reference to the mental health services, Labour failed to convert into reality the promised run-down of mental hospitals or mental handicap institutions and the associated transfer to community care. The anticipated liberation of capital resources for use in the acute sector was therefore not available. Indeed, the growing scandal of conditions in the long-stay hospitals increased pressure for resources to be diverted into modernising these hospitals. Somewhat late in the day the planners attempted to provide a rational framework for the modern hospital system. In particular they worked out more fully the consequences of developing a comprehensive system of district general hospitals, with the hope that such a scheme would prepare the way for closure of small and uneconomical units, and thereby provide an alternative avenue for freeing resources for use in the acute sector. The district general hospital philosophy was more dominant within the Ministry of Health than in SHHD, partly because geographical factors in much of Scotland precluded the centralisation of hospital facilities.

The Hospital Plan and its associated Building Note No.3 (1961), as well as the 1966 revision of the plan, assumed that hospital planning would be based on the premise of the district general hospital, although without providing justification for this concept.[87] The Ministry of Health studiously avoided producing an argued defence of the district general hospital. In the absence of initiative from the Ministry of Health, this difficult task was taken on by the Central Health Services Council. This body was not noted for its effectiveness, and it stumbled into a review of the district general hospital without any concentrated preparation. The topic arose at one of a series of talks in which experts briefed the CHSC on recent developments in the health service. This discussion on hospital planning revealed disquiet about current hospital planning, and suggested that the district general hospital required fuller justification.[88] This subject was referred to a large subcommittee chaired by Sir Desmond Bonham-Carter, a Director of Unilever, and Chairman of the South West Metropolitan RHB, who had the distinction of being related to Florence Nightingale, herself a pioneer of hospital planning.[89] The report of this committee was finally sanctioned by the CHSC on 15 April 1969 and it was published later that year.[90] The Bonham-Carter Report was brief, schematic and poorly focussed. Many of its proposals were uncontroversial and universally acceptable, but with respect to more problematical topics, it was unconvincing. The draft report was not widely criticised within the Standing Advisory Committees, or by the CHSC, but it attracted much adverse comment elsewhere. In receiving the CHSC report, Ministers warned of the need for its flexible application.[91]

Those outside the acute hospital sector attacked the document for its assumption that all other services were secondary in their importance to the district general hospital. Doctors working in the mental sector were particularly incensed by the recommendation that 'all hospital psychiatric (including mental sub-normality) and geriatric treatment to be based on district general hospitals; existing hospitals in these specialties to be run down and closed'.[92] Ministers discussed their response to the Bonham-Carter Report at the Post-Ely Policy Working Party, where the response was unenthusiastic. It was claimed that the district general hospital plan was 'more orientated to the needs of the hospital consultant than of his patients'. It was therefore agreed that the published report should be accompanied by reservations from Ministers.[93] Lack of documented argument and its contentious features perhaps explain the inclusion of a page of disclaimers in the foreword by the CHSC, and the prefatory note by the Secretaries of State for Social Services and for Wales, suggesting that the main function of the report was to stimulate discussion, that the recommendations would have to be considered in the light of the reorganisation of health and social services, that it was necessary to take account of the need to vary the pattern of services according to population, and that it would be necessary to give further thought to the future pattern of long-term care and the functions of smaller hospitals supplementary to the district general hospital.[94] Although the district general hospital model continued to be the prevailing orthodoxy within DHSS, its reputation was not much assisted by the Bonham-Carter report.

Continuing Containment
The Ministry of Health tried various means of breaking free of PESC constraints. In January 1966, the Chief Medical Officer produced a memorandum making the case for additional resources, especially for the hospital service. He compared Britain's expenditure on health care unfavourably with the record of its Western counterparts, emphasising that the benefits of high technology medicine would inevitably involve additional expenditure. He instanced the high cost of introducing such services as renal dialysis, a recent innovation, which was attracting considerable press publicity, which contributed to the demand for a prompt response on the part of the NHS.[95] In view of the need for the NHS to respond rapidly and appropriately to such medical advances, the Chief Medical Officer suggested it needed to be freed from some of the controls applying to other social services. The Treasury was not persuaded. It recognised no case for exonerating the health service from PESC discipline, and no prospect was held out that the health service would be allocated a larger share of resources. It was recognised that competing services were likely to be more successful in this contest on account of commanding stronger political support.[96] Robinson was too late in mounting his campaign for additional resources. Already economic realism was gaining the ascendancy. Operating from April 1966 onwards, the ministerial Steering Committee on Economic Policy exercised stern control over public expenditure. Having made no progress in his search for additional funds, Robinson soon found himself in an embattled position, resisting implications for his department of the first round of public expenditure cuts under the Wilson administration, imposed in July 1966.

As part of its tightening-up exercise, the Treasury and DEA proposed establishment of a joint committee with the health departments to analyse development and control of expenditure in the health services. This initiative was modelled on similar committees established for education services and roads. It was anticipated that this 'Health Programmes Committee' would enable the Ministry of Health to raise the standard of bids for additional resources. The Treasury believed that the Ministry of Health fared 'relatively badly in the rat race for a share of available resources amongst other things because they have completely failed to sort out their priorities in a convincing fashion'.[97] The Ministry of Health was unable to resist the Health Programmes Committee, but it was not entirely welcoming. From the health department's perspective, this committee was a further avenue of incursion into its affairs by the Treasury and DEA. The energies of the Health Programmes Committee were deflected into relatively abstract questions and no real momentum was achieved in its affairs. The committee persisted for most of the lifetime of the Wilson administration, but it never exercised real influence; periodic attempts at resuscitation were unsuccessful.[98]

Immediately after the 1966 General Election Robinson approached Callaghan directly, complaining that in its first term of office Labour had done no better than the Conservatives in directing the necessary resources into services and modernising 'much that is quite disgracefully inadequate'. He appreciated that resources were constrained by adverse economic factors, but he insisted that the health and welfare services merited a larger share of national resources. He accepted that his demands were more extensive than appropriate for consideration in the normal PESC mechanism. He therefore asked if his proposals could be examined by a small group of Ministers.[99] Robinson's papers were rambling and unspecific; their essential argument repeated points made previously by the Chief Medical Officer. This rather diffuse initiative on the part of Robinson was considered on two occasions by Ministers in the inhospitable environment of the ministerial Committee on Public Expenditure. Robinson returned to his demands for additional resources, and refused to offer countervailing economies, explaining that it was unrealistic to reintroduce the prescription charge, increase other charges, or reduce subsidies such as that on welfare milk. In discussion Robinson came under pressure to introduce a consultation fee for general medical practitioner services, an idea which, as seen below, briefly flourished in BMA circles at the time of the Family Doctors' Charter. Robinson refused to consider this proposal, which he regarded as contrary to Labour's entire philosophy, but the idea was noted down, and periodically reintroduced by the Treasury.[100]

From the beginning of 1967, in the context of its efforts to improve the balance of payments situation, SEP pressed for reductions in public expenditure.[101] In response to continuing complaints from the health departments, the Treasury returned to considering alternative methods for raising revenue for the NHS, in the course of which it unearthed some of its old panaceas. All forms of the direct charges discussed regularly under the Conservatives were again reconsidered. Much the most favoured option was an increase in the NHS Contribution. Attack by the Labour opposition on the increase in the NHS Contribution introduced in 1961, as well as the intrinsic vulnerability of this tax to criticism on account of its regressive nature, effectively rendered this subject heretical under the Wilson administration. However, even Labour Ministers were known to speculate that the NHS should be financed on an insurance basis.[102] It was recognised that the 1967/68 uprating would rule out increasing this levy in the short term, but a 1s increase was held up as a practical possibility for the future.[103] A further obstacle to action on this front was the Government's commitment in the 1966 General Election manifesto to introduce an earnings-related pension and social security plan, which would leave no place for the flat-rate NHS Contribution. Decision on the role, if any, of the NHS Contribution under the new social security arrangements was clearly unamenable to speedy resolution.

Until the autumn of 1967, financing the health service under the Wilson administration may be characterised as an uneasy equilibrium; the health departments pleaded for a larger share of national resources, but they were resisted without much discomfort by the Treasury, which nevertheless offered minor concessions when these were unavoidable. This situation changed dramatically with the devaluation crisis of November 1967.

Devaluation Crisis
After a long period of resistance, at the beginning of November 1967, Callaghan was persuaded that there was no alternative to devaluation. He announced his decision to the Cabinet on 16 November. Even then it was not intended to devalue immediately, but acceleration of speculation against sterling necessitated immediate action. Devaluation of the pound by 14.3 per cent (reducing the parity from $2.80 to $2.40) was announced by Callaghan on 18 November.[104] This was associated with steps to reduce domestic consumption, limit imports, and shift the use of resources into exports. The bank rate was increased to 8 per cent; lending ceilings, which had only been relaxed in the previous year, were reimposed.[105] At the end of November 1967, Callaghan, the Chancellor of the Exchequer, and Jenkins, the Home Secretary, exchanged seats in the Cabinet.

Jenkins was expected to consent to strong measures to restore confidence in sterling. He came under pressure from overseas creditors, the Bank of England and other financial advisers to introduce immediate reductions in public expenditure.[106] The economies package applied to the years 1968/69 and 1969/70, for which reductions of £330m and £360m respectively were eventually agreed. The aim was to restrain growth in public expenditure to 4.75 per cent in the first year and 1 per cent in the second.

Defence was the prime target for cuts, but the health service was high among the candidates for economies in the civil sector. During the hectic preparations for public expenditure reductions during December 1967, with respect to the health service, Treasury deliberations recapitulated much of the ground covered during similar exercises supervised by Thorneycroft and Powell in December 1957, or Lloyd and Powell in December 1960. The Treasury conceded that the Ministry of Health under Robinson had been among the best-disciplined departments, by contrast with transport and housing, which had continued to extend the boundaries of their empires. Given the seriousness of the crisis, even the NHS needed to make sacrifices.

On this occasion the Treasury pressed for cuts in the hospital capital programme. It was irritated that this expanding and arguably extravagant project had been immune from economies; 'if this escapes again, but local health and welfare is done for once more, the pattern of the NHS will become increasingly distorted'. In addition, a cut in spending on hospitals would be a powerful symbol of the Government's determination to tackle its economic problems realistically.[107] However, reversal of the hospital plan was against Labour policy; also the hospitals had been intentionally spared at the time of the July 1966 cuts, while in November 1967 the Prime Minister had given a personal undertaking to safeguard this area of spending.[108] It was therefore futile to pursue cuts in the hospital plan, except for later years of the programme, which was irrelevant to the current economy exercise. Somewhat incongruously in the light of its strictures cited above, the Treasury reverted to its customary practice, imposing a big cut in the modest local health and welfare capital programme.[109]

As noted above, the Treasury had prepared for an increase in the NHS Contribution. A 1s increase would yield the attractive total of £47m in savings. However, this alternative also failed to withstand critical scrutiny. As a notoriously unsound tax, it was concluded that 'the NHS stamp is an anachronism and will almost certainly disappear when we move over to earnings-related benefits and contributions in the National Insurance field'.[110] Although an increase in the NHS Contribution was the most favoured of Robinson's options, further consideration of this possibility was initially rejected by Jenkins.[111] The Treasury also was favourable to the hitherto little-considered general practitioner service consultation fee, or an annual registration fee, but these were mentioned only as outside possibilities.[112]

From the Treasury perspective, the least problematical area for economy was reintroduction of the prescription charge, although this was accepted as one of the politically most contentious of all the retrenchment proposals. Jenkins agreed to accord high priority to the prescription charge, but he doubted whether his colleagues would sanction a charge of more than 2s, and then only if exemptions applying before 1965 were reintroduced. The Treasury also speculated about prospects for increasing other health service charges, especially raising the standard charge for dental treatment from 20s to 40s. Jenkins thought that 30s might be tolerated by Ministers.[113] The health charges package was scarcely consistent with Callaghan's announcement that the Government would 'protect the most vulnerable sections of the community from hardships resulting from the change in the exchange rate'.[114]

At the preliminary meeting of the Cabinet on 20 December 1967 and two meetings of senior Ministers to discuss economies in public expenditure, at which Robinson was not present, it was accepted that the Government would need to 'slaughter sacred cows', especially postponement of raising the school leaving age to 16, and restoration of the prescription charge. Jenkins is reported as commenting that a £40m saving with respect to the prescription charge was disproportionately valuable on account of the 'impression it makes on bankers'.[115] It was anticipated that the Cabinet would only sanction reintroduction of the prescription charge if the scope of exemptions was extended. If the prescription charge was adopted, Ministers agreed to forego cuts in hospital current and capital expenditure.

At the meetings of the Cabinet to confirm the package of economies, the health departments were asked to accept a reduction in local authority health and welfare capital expenditure of £20m over two years, a prescription charge of 2s 6d, and increase from 20s to 30s in the maximum charge for dental treatment.[116] Even before the Cabinet discussions, Robinson warned of his opposition to cuts in the health service. He pointed out that the NHS had struggled forward to achieve a rate of growth of about 3 per cent a year, which was less than other departments. He was therefore unwilling to countenance economies on any of the fronts proposed by the Treasury; his energies were particularly directed against reintroduction of the prescription charge. He stated that charges were a 'gratuitous breach of the basic concept of the National Health Service, and one of the issues genuinely dividing the two parties'.[117]

At the Cabinet meetings Robinson displayed dogged resistance to the prescription charge and suggested substituting a 1s increase in the NHS Contribution. Jenkins reluctantly conceded an increase of 6d in the employee's share of the NHS Contribution in order to cover the cost of a broader range of exemptions than had originally been contemplated.[118] Introduction of exemptions for those above 65 and under 15, expectant and nursing mothers, and the chronic sick, rendered the scheme acceptable to the majority of the Cabinet, despite Robinson's complaints that exemptions would be costly and administratively cumbersome. The Cabinet also agreed to the proposed rise in the dental treatment charge, and the cut in the local authority health and welfare capital programme to achieve an average reduction of £5m a year between 1968 and 1971. Also, confirming an earlier decision by the Cabinet connected with an increase in the family allowance, it was confirmed that the price of welfare milk would rise from 4d to 6d a pint.[119] In the field of education, in addition to postponement of the higher school leaving age, it was agreed to cease the supply of school milk to secondary school pupils. In connection with the family allowance increase, the price of the school meal was adjusted from 1s to 1s 6d.

The above economies in public expenditure were ratified at the Cabinet meeting on 15 January with little discord. Crosland made a mild attempt to reverse the decision over the school leaving age, but this was rejected. Within the Cabinet, the economies exercise was less controversial than had been anticipated. The Prime Minister announced the agreed package of cuts on 16 January 1967.[120]

The social services economies were not welcomed in Labour circles, but they were not as severe as anticipated, or indeed as much as demanded by the financial press.[121] Also they were more palatable because the main cuts fell in the area of defence. Lord Longford was the only Minister to resign, in his case as a protest against deferment of the rise in the school leaving age. Jennie Lee was rumoured to be considering resignation on account of the prescription charge, but she remained in office. Many other Ministers were unhappy with the outcome; Robinson was among the most sour. Although reintroduction of the prescription charge was unpopular with Labour MPs, it was not vigorously contested.[122] The items requiring legislation were consolidated into a multi-purpose Bill, the Public Expenditure and Receipts Bill 1968, which passed though Parliament during February and March, and which received the Royal Assent on 20 March 1968. The smooth passage of this Bill contrasts with the lengthy contests surrounding equivalent legislation in 1961.

The main difficulty about prescription charges resided in the elaboration of a mechanism for dealing with exemptions, for which purpose the co-operation of general practitioners and chemists was essential. Much energy was dissipated in evolving a scheme relying on embossed cards, or 'season tickets' suitable for use by the exempt classes, but this was deferred in favour an interim arrangement relying on signed declarations by the patients themselves, which the Public Accounts Committee regarded as unsound because it was more susceptible to fraud.[123] Changes of plan with respect to the exemption scheme caused delay in the introduction of the prescription charge until 10 June. After further dilatory activity on the part of the Ministry of Health, then DHSS, the interim exemption scheme was further extended. Finally in 1969, after refusal of the professions to co-operate, the embossed card idea was abandoned.[124] The embossed card fiasco convinced Crossman that the prescription charge was 'an albatross round our necks'.[125] Adoption of widespread exemptions reduced the anticipated yield of the prescription charge from £50m to £25m. In practice, exemptions applied to 40 per cent of the population and 50 per cent of prescriptions; the yield from charges never reached the Treasury target and was below £20m in the first full year.

Further Economies for 1968/69
In the context of the new determination of the Government to achieve a 'massive shift of resources to exports and for raising productive investment to a level which would enable Britain to gain and keep the required competitiveness in world markets', SEP subjected public expenditure to fresh critical scrutiny. The new economic strategy called for strict observance of planned levels of public expenditure. Hence, when it emerged in the spring of 1968 that revised estimates for 1968/69 and 1969/70 were higher than anticipated, it was decided to call for a supplementary package of cuts.

For the financial year 1968/69 a target of £81m was adopted for further economies, out of which only a small contribution was expected from the Ministry of Health in view of its earlier substantial share. It was proposed to introduce a 25 per cent increase in charges for lenses supplied under the ophthalmic service, but in view of the prescription charge and the higher dental charges currently being introduced, it was considered inopportune to proceed with ophthalmic charges. The Cabinet decided to defer these charges until 1970/71.[126]

With respect to the civil sector, the Treasury was increasingly concerned about escalation of spending on the social services. The Treasury criticised the 'obstinate tendency to act as if more room could always be found for more expenditure on the public services'.[127] SEP complained that its sister Social Services Committee had been entirely reactive, and that it had given no positive guidance on priorities and selectivity in the distribution of resources. The main objective was to keep social services spending on a plateau, with planned increases in expenditure due to inescapable developments in one area being matched by economies elsewhere. SEP also wanted the Social Services Committee to handle the distribution of cuts within its sector, which would preclude any suggestion that these economies should be shouldered by other spending departments.[128] With prompting from the Prime Minister and the Treasury, Stewart, who assumed the chair of the Social Services Committee in October 1967, took up the challenge to 'sort out social priorities in the context of our economic difficulties'.[129] In particular, Stewart aimed to obtain agreement on a 'new concept of selectivity' before the Seebohm Report was completed.[130] Stewart was over-optimistic in his expectations about bringing about a culture shift in the social services departments. Characteristically, Robinson insisted that the new enquiry was unlikely to cause significant changes in the National Health Service. He concluded:

> The situation I have sketched above explains why, when we have addressed our minds, as we have done repeatedly in recent years, to the question as to what activities in the health and welfare services might be abandoned or reduced in favour of more urgent needs, we have always come to the conclusion that there is nothing of significance to offer. The squeeze to which we are continually subject automatically pushes out the less essential activities and some of the more essential too. We have always been forced to say that net public expenditure in our field can only be further reduced by charging for services. I take it that extension of charging is not one of the matters to be considered in your exercise. I for my part would still think that abolition of the charges we have should be our aim at rate in the long term.

Consistent with this analysis Robinson made yet another appeal for additional resources for the hospital building programme, hospital current expenditure, local health and welfare building, especially health centres, and for maintaining local authority services (especially for the elderly and family planning). He also appealed for resources to improve the amenity of disabled groups, for instance to assist the physically-disabled by replacing their tricycles by cars, or introducing head-worn hearing aids for the deaf.[131] This unconciliatory response to demands for restraint was by no means confined to the Ministry of Health. The Treasury complained that Stewart's review had generated 'practically every conceivable idea for progress in the social services' on the understanding that financial constraints would be short-lived.[132] The Stewart initiative was further undermined when he was replaced by Crossman as chairman of the Social Services Committee on 30 March 1968. The latter was less retrenchment-minded, and unenthusiastic about pursuing the priorities exercise, which was finally deflected into a complicated technical investigation conducted by officials, which involved reviewing the system of charges and contributions.[133] The main result of this enquiry was a proposal to establish charges on a fixed percentage basis, but this was rejected by Ministers on the grounds that decisions about charges needed to be made on the merits of the case in each instance, with the decision being determined by political as well as economic factors.[134]

Post-Devaluation Cuts for 1969/70
The target eventually accepted for phase II of the devaluation package of cuts in public expenditure was reduced from £360m to £300m. Some voices within the Treasury insisted that the health departments were being expected to shoulder an unreasonable proportion of the burden, risking an end to the high level of co-operation hitherto displayed by the health Ministers.[135] However, the NHS was not allowed to escape from further substantial economies without long-drawn-out and acrimonious debate. The main and long-sought-after target for the Treasury in the health and welfare area was the complete abolition of the subsidy on welfare milk. In the event, both the higher cost of welfare milk and the increase in schools meals charges were rejected on the grounds that they would be seen as a tax on children. Other controversial ideas which were costed and discussed by SEP and the Social Services Committee, but abandoned, were doubling the prescription charge and introducing a hospital boarding charge. In view of assurances by the Prime Minister that the hospital capital programme would be protected, it was difficult to make direct incursions into the agreed totals for the hospital plan. Nevertheless, Jenkins tried for a reduction of £10m in hospital capital spending, but this was rejected. Instead, it was agreed to introduce a minor restriction in the growth of hospital current spending.[136]

The Treasury was pleasantly surprised with the positive efforts made by Crossman to hold down expenditure for 1969/70 and the following year, both in DHSS and other departments falling under his co-ordinating responsibility.[137] The economies finally required from the health and welfare sector for 1969/70 were extremely small, amounting to less than £5m, mainly achieved by a small reduction in spending on minor capital projects, and a slight saving in hospital current expenditure. Ominously, Crossman intimated that he intended to 'explore ways to find extra resources for health in 1970/71'.[138]

205

Public Expenditure Controls 1970/71 Onwards

On the advice of the Medium Term Assessment Committee and other new bodies concerned with long term control of public expenditure, especially the Public Expenditure Review Committee, together with the associated committee of senior officials, the Steering Committee on Public Expenditure, control of public expenditure was elevated into a high priority.[139] Therefore, although the immediate post-devaluation economies applied only to the years 1968/69 and 1969/70, it was urged that a similar level of vigilance was required for the following years to prevent public expenditure further outstripping the capacities of the national economy. For 1970/71, the Treasury and SEP agreed to limit the growth in public expenditure to 3 per cent, which implied adopting £250m as a target for cuts in civil expenditure.[140] Furthermore, it was assumed that a similar exercise would be required in the following financial year, which of course lay outside the term of the current administration.

Given the institutionalisation of the regime of retrenchment and Crossman's conclusion that a major injection of additional resources for the NHS was required, it was inevitable that his accord with the Treasury would soon evaporate. Crossman was keen to demonstrate that he was no less solicitous concerning the interests of the NHS than the late Robinson, and politically he was the biggest force among Ministers to enter the fray on behalf of the health service since the tenure of Bevan, whose example he sought to emulate. Not only was the health service continuing to inch forwards in its demands for resources, but also pay revaluations, or major policy decisions connected with Todd, Salmon, Seebohm, the Ely enquiry, and especially forthcoming NHS reorganisation, collectively entailed formidable resource implications.

The Treasury was primary engaged on resource containment rather than with supervising plans for development. Consistent with their newly-established regulatory routines, Treasury officials undertook feasibility studies on the familiar charges and contributions, but with noticeably greater determination than before, and with the suggestion that big policy changes might be the eventual outcome. A joint committee with the Ministry of Health was established to investigate hospital boarding charges.[141] It was necessary for this subject to be handled with discretion because the existence of the working party was unknown to Ministers. This initiative was excused on the grounds of election contingency planning, and its possible relevance to future government policy.[142] Also, for the first time since 1960, the Treasury actively discussed funding the NHS on the basis of compulsory insurance.[143] As in 1960, the Treasury was divided in its response to hypothecation, but on the whole the conclusions were as negative as they had been in the

Figgures Report. It was argued that the 'question of the resources to be devoted to the Health Service is one that should be kept firmly in central Government hands, not tied any more than they were at the moment, and that the decisions should be taken against the background of overall resources and overall revenue'.[144]

The first direct clash between Crossman and the Treasury occurred over health service charges. As already noted, Crossman regarded charges for services tiresome and unproductive. Privately he was coming to favour the option currently being considered but rejected by the Treasury - replacement of charges by an increased and restructured NHS Contribution.[145]

A painful reminder of the capacity of health service charges to create political havoc occurred on Monday, 5 May 1969, when Crossman ratified changes in regulations and made an announcement concerning an increase in charges for dentures and spectacles.[146] Crossman was immediately attacked from his own side, especially by Michael Foot and Dr John Dunwoody. The latter described the charges as 'deeply repugnant' to Labour opinion. Crossman's response was entirely lacking in conviction.

This episode immediately captured the headlines of the evening newspapers. Crossman was deeply embarrassed when he realised that the local elections were scheduled for Thursday of the same week. His ignominy was compounded by admission that he had forgotten about the elections. His blunder was exploited by the media and adverse publicity concerning health charges was thought to contribute to Labour's poor election performance.[147] This minor episode incited the Labour Party into renewed protest against health service charges. The Government was accused of incorporating charges as a fixed and expanding element in health service funding. The anger of the many sections of the Party was vented primarily on Crossman.[148]

Crossman was only temporarily deflated. He quickly sought and found a way to regain his reputation with the Party. On 26 June he was due to deliver the Herbert Morrison Lecture to members of the London Labour Party. He used this occasion to mention his disdain for direct charges and speculate about the superiority of contributory insurance for financing the health service. Crossman 'dismissed out of hand' the idea of using charges as a main source of health service revenue. Indeed, given access to slightly more resources, he inclined to accord 'high priority on merits to abandoning prescription charges, even in their improved form'.[149] An opportunity to gain much greater publicity for his ideas occurred on 1 July 1969, in a short opposition-instigated debate in the House of Commons on the financing of the NHS. Crossman congratulated himself on his statesmanlike remarks concerning charges. He had intended to be more forthright, but his text was much amended in response to protest from Jenkins.[150] The main feature of his speech was its measured defence of contributory insurance in the funding of health care. Most attention was captured by a last-moment alteration indicating his negative attitude towards charges. Crossman insisted that charges for domiciliary attendances to general practitioners and hotel charges would give minimum yields; he described them as 'outrageous' suggestions.[151] Further complaints from Jenkins perhaps explain why Crossman avoided criticism of health service charges in the short knock-about concluding speech in a further short debate in which the opposition attempted to embarrass him for his confusion in handling the augmented health service charges.[152] This juvenile performance left Crossman more than usually self-satisfied, convinced that he had 'atoned for the mess about the local elections'.[153]

Others were not so happy about Crossman's interventions, especially because they were unhelpful to ongoing interdepartmental discussions. The stage had been reached when SHHD was appeased by withdrawal of the DHSS proposal for abolishing the dental service, in return for which SHHD was expected to drop its opposition to the hospital boarding charge.[154] Crossman's gratuitous intervention forestalled this plan to extend the charges system, and also introduced the unwelcome suggestion that the NHS Contribution could be regarded as a credible substitute.

Having regained his popularist image, Crossman was in no mood for compromise. On the other hand, as he realised himself, continuing confrontation with Jenkins would further prejudice his chances of securing a favourable outcome in the gathering storm over economies in public expenditure. Despite his good intentions, Crossman squabbled with Jenkins over the appropriate response to be made by the Government to a motion engineered by Pavitt designed to annul the Order for increased charges. Crossman wanted to make an explicit declaration that prescription charges were a temporary expedient. Jenkins argued that nothing should be said to preclude the continuation of these charges.[155] An uneasy compromise was secured when it was discovered that the Prime Minister had written to Pavitt conceding that 'it would be wrong for you to assume that these charges reluctantly introduced to meet a serious economic situation, carry the implication of a permanent change of the Government's policy or of its approach to health service financing'. Crossman was therefore permitted by the Cabinet to indicate that the prescription charge was not a permanent feature of the NHS.[156]

The row over charges was trivial in its outcome, but it illustrated a state of nervousness and disorientation within the Labour Party. Wilson's own lack of firm commitment to retrenchment, as witnessed by his letter to Pavitt and his ambivalence in the Cabinet over health charges, added to the annoyance of the Treasury over what it regarded as recklessness on the part of Crossman. The same disarray was repeated in the more serious context of the debate over cuts in public expenditure for 1970/71. Ministers considered the Treasury proposals for economies at three meetings of the Cabinet in July 1969. Jenkins adopted an overall target of £400m for cuts, including £250m in civil expenditure. In the face of concerted criticism, the overall target was eroded until it finally reached £292m, and the civil contribution was proportionately reduced. Crossman was among the main critics of Jenkins. The Treasury initially required £39m in economies from health and welfare. Among its original suggestions were the hospital boarding charge, eliminating the subsidy on welfare milk, or abolition of the general dental service. The final compromise suggested by the Treasury envisaged delay of spending on new policy commitments, reductions in hospital current expenditure, postponement of starts in the hospital capital programme for three months, an increase in the motor accident levy, and reduction in loan sanctions to local authorities.[157] Crossman made noisy criticisms, but he was not entirely unco-operative. He offered to absorb the cost of new policy developments, and accepted most of the other cuts without much modification. However, he vigorously contested the proposal to save £9m on the hospital programme; first this was reduced to £4m, and then it was abandoned in the concluding discussions. Crossman pointed out that the health departments had conceded prescription charges, then other health service charges in order to protect hospital building. It was therefore a breach of faith to continue demanding cuts in the hospital sector. Furthermore this could not be accomplished without a public announcement, which he warned he would refuse to make; this step would be 'political madness' for the Government. These arguments convinced his colleagues, and gave Crossman grounds for regarding this result as a great victory over Jenkins.[158]

School meals charges constituted a further point of controversy in this round of economies. The Treasury and Education Ministers favoured increasing the charge from 1s 6d to 2s. Education Ministers argued that savings in school meals were required for increasing their programme of minor works in schools. However, this argument was received unsympathetically by other Ministers, who insisted on limiting the school meal charge to 1s 9d, and sacrificing part of the minor works programme.[159]

Crossman's machinations over his share of reductions in public expenditure were not over. During Cabinet discussions he affected dislike for increasing the motor accident levy, which he portrayed as a further tiresome and unproductive manner of raising resources for

209

the health service. Consistent with his preference for shifting the burden towards contributory insurance, he proposed this avenue for replacing the £9m, which he was supposed to derive from the motor accident levy.[160] Officials in the Treasury were divided over the merits of the motor accident levy. In the absence of more viable alternatives, Jenkins was sympathetic, but this idea was rejected out of hand by the Ministry of Transport. Therefore, although the Cabinet had asked for this proposal to be pursued, in view of lukewarm support within the Social Services Committee and SEP, and dangers of upsetting the motoring lobby, the Prime Minister decided that it was politically inopportune to increase the motor accident levy in the run-up to a General Election.[161]

At the outset of preparations for the new earnings-related insurance scheme, the Treasury assumed that the NHS Contribution would be abolished. It was suspected by the Treasury that retention of the NHS Contribution would undermine the concept that benefits under the new scheme would be strictly related to contributions.[162] This proposal was rejected by DHSS, urged on by Crossman, who looked forward to the new percentage contribution becoming a lucrative source of revenue. It was therefore agreed to retain a health service deduction, but instead of being largely an employee contribution, it should be drawn equally from employer and employee. It was proposed to deduct the equivalent of 0.5 per cent of earnings from both the employer and the employee for the purposes of the new NHS deduction.[163] In November 1969, Crossman came forward with an alternative proposal to deduct 1 per cent, to be paid entirely by employers. For the interim, it was proposed to introduce a 2s increase in the flat-rate employer contribution, which Crossman estimated would yield £100m in a full year. This proposal was completely without merit from the perspective of the Treasury, where it was seen as an inflammatory gesture towards industry, which would have the effect of stimulating a rise in prices and wages. Jenkins and Crossman met to argue their cases; they agreed on a compromise entailing shifting the balance of the NHS deductions: the employee would pay 6.75 per cent of earnings, of which 0.3 per cent would pass to the NHS, while the employer would pay 7 per cent of earnings, of which 0.6 per cent would be earmarked for the NHS.[164] In order to move towards the higher deduction from the employer, it was proposed, and the Cabinet accepted that the employer's share of the NHS Contribution should be increased from 8d to 1s. On this basis, Crossman was excused from pursuing the increase in the motor accident levy. This was a minor gain for Crossman, but both sides in the argument appreciated that it represented a rich precedent. Crossman estimated that he had tapped a rich source of additional funding for the NHS; the Treasury was fearful that the

NHS deduction would be used to undermine the authority of the Chancellor of the Exchequer and as a device for avoiding the financial discipline of the kind applied to other spending departments.[165] During the last few months of the Wilson administration, the two sides subsisted in an uneasy truce over the implicit shift towards the contributory insurance principle. The Treasury was left without any realistic scope for imposing cuts in the health programme, but it continued to press forward with unrealistic demands in order to make DHSS 'suffer the consequences of the Secretary of State's rash proposal for a little longer'.[166]

PESC Straitjacket

Tensions between the Treasury and Crossman were most in evidence over the preparation of expenditure plans for the years 1970/71 to 1974/75, conducted in the context of the PESC exercise, but not completed by the date of the General Election. The two sides began to cross swords in February 1970 over the preparation for tables for the 1970 PESC report. The Treasury insisted on giving precedence to tabulations according to Cmnd.4234, which entailed a lower baseline than adopted under the 1969 PESC survey data. DHSS, with Crossman's support, insisted on structuring its bids on the basis of the 1969 PESC figures. Furthermore additional expenditure was required for pharmaceutical services, while Crossman also authorised substantial new bids in connection with services for the mentally handicapped, vehicles for the severely disabled, and family planning.[167]

This disagreement was not greatly different from the jockeying for position taking place at each PESC round, but on this occasion there was the making of a deeper crisis. Sensing that his alternative plans to raise additional resources for the NHS from such sources as the NHS Contribution were running into the ground, Crossman made an apparently unpremeditated decision to mount an audacious attack aimed at finally breaking out of the pocket into which the PESC system had pinned his health and welfare expenditure. He calculated that dramatic action was needed to meet the big challenges facing the health service. Even 'if we are going to have the Health Service running on the same principles as we have now, we shall have to get a larger part of the national product and a larger share of the budget'. Crossman announced his plan for escape from the 'PESC strait-jacket' to astonished Ministers and officials of his department on 19 February 1970. This was the kind of big ministerial gesture which appealed to Crossman: 'It was I who had to do it and that is what a Minister is for'.[168] Crossman's own remarks about this strictly confidential meeting are confirmed and amplified by an account communicated immediately by one of his officials to a Treasury opposite number.[169]

Crossman instructed his officials to prepare forward estimates for the period from 1972/73 onwards on the basis of very substantial increased provision on all fronts, with the aim of achieving a 7 per cent rate of growth by 1973/74. The Treasury was thrown into turmoil by Crossman's initiative. It was evident that he was not only breaking ranks with his Cabinet colleagues by departing from the Cabinet decision to limit the growth in public expenditure to 3.5 per cent, but also challenging 'the whole philosophy of the White Paper and the hard-won system of public expenditure control'.[170]

On 17 March 1970, Crossman sprang his suggestions on a supposedly unsuspecting Chancellor. His brief but revealing letter accompanying a draft Cabinet memorandum is worth quoting in full:

I do not often bother you with 'trial trips'; and if I do so on this occasion it is because I realise that the attached paper could, if wrongly handled, precipitate the kind of conflict in the Cabinet which we want at all costs to avoid this summer. On the other hand the more I think about the way the PESC exercise is likely to go this year the more I realise that I cannot let it pass without doing my best to ensure

(1) that impossible Health and Welfare 1972/73 figures are not inserted into next winter's Public Expenditure White Paper, and

(2) that we do this year during the course of the PESC proceedings undertake the serious discussion of our medium term priorities in Government expenditure which pressure of economic circumstances has denied us ever since we took office.

That is why I took the liberty of instructing my officials to submit to PESC figures from 1972/73 onwards which truly relate to our Departmental needs and which are markedly discordant with your plans for Government expenditure.

Of course I can see the importance you give to getting figures for that year which fit in with Treasury policy. But as the Minister responsible for the development of the Health Service I attach equal importance to pointing out in good time that the kind of expenditure totals which we have been accepting since 1966, and which I can still accept for 1970/71, and even with great difficulty for 1971/72, may well precipitate a breakdown in the Service if they are continued in the following year. This is the argument set out in detail in the attached paper which I am submitting to justify the figures my officials have submitted to PESC.

P.S. I am sending a copy to the P.M. and no-one else. The three of us might talk.[171]

On account of its intelligence sources, the Treasury was forewarned about Crossman's memorandum; indeed, a draft reply from Jenkins was prepared before Crossman's letter was received. On 19 March Jenkins and his officials discussed their response to Crossman. Jenkins favoured slowing down the PESC exercise, fearing that before the General Election Ministers might be less retrenchment-minded than afterwards. He also discussed minor concessions which might be promised to the Prime Minister and other Ministers in order to purchase their support for the Treasury line and ensure the isolation of Crossman.[172] Jenkins accordingly substituted a low-key reply to Crossman, asking for his co-operation in completing the PESC exercise on the agreed basis, leaving open the possibility of introduction of major changes for later years in the light of ministerial discussions. Crossman complied, but on the understanding that discussions on his additional bids should begin without delay.[173] DHSS submitted its forward projections according to the limits observed by other departments, but Crossman refused to adopt the base-point specified in Cmnd.4234 and this impasse continued up to the point of the General Election.[174] Crossman's *putsch* was mounted too late to stand any chance of success, but his efforts were not entirely wasted. As observed in chapter V, Crossman's expansionist gambit might have been distasteful to his successor, Sir Keith Joseph, but it was in fact seized by him, and pursued with some effect.

(iv) PHARMACEUTICAL INDUSTRY
Despite the placatory conclusions of the Hinchliffe Report, the Public Accounts Committee continued to express concern, and the Treasury complained about the rise in the pharmaceutical bill.[175] This expanded from £52m in 1957/58 to £90m in 1963/64.[176] Over the same period the cost per prescription increased by 122 per cent and the ingredient cost by 170 per cent. As noted in the previous chapter, the Voluntary Price Regulation Scheme was due to expire at the end of June 1964. Negotiations concerning a revised agreement were not concluded until July 1964. The Treasury was perturbed that only minor tightening-up had been achieved; it considered insisting on further negotiations, trusting that the approach of a General Election might secure a more favourable outcome. The Ministry of Health held the opposite conviction, believing that the industry would exploit the intermission to increase its prices. Accordingly, an agreement was concluded in July 1964; the second phase of the VPRS was sanctioned to run from July 1964 until the end of 1967.[177] On the

basis of previous experience, it was unrealistic to expect a transformation in savings from this source. The Treasury was particularly alarmed that the health departments had not used this occasion to insist on taking account of advertising costs in the assessment of drug prices.

Given this unsatisfactory outcome, the Chief Secretary demanded that Robinson should attach high priority to obtaining economies in the pharmaceutical bill. Robinson reassured Diamond that 'you can safely assume that my desire to effect all proper economies in the drug bill is no less than yours'.[178] The TUC expressed concern about profits of the drug companies and demanded an enquiry into the pharmaceutical industry, with a view to considering 'whether it would be desirable for the State itself to undertake or participate in the manufacture of drugs'.[179] The President of the ABPI raised no objection, providing the enquiry was independent, objective and comprehensive.[180] In the absence of better alternatives, the Treasury approved the plan for an independent review. Further upward spiralling of the drug bill following abolition of the prescription charge added to the argument for an enquiry. The Treasury was also concerned about evidence suggesting a recent increase in advertising expenditure from 9.7 per cent to 11.2 per cent of the value of NHS sales, and it suspected a 'deplorably low ethical standard' of sales practice.[181] Also, despite efforts by the health departments to drive down the prices of certainly widely-used drugs such as tetracylines, there was no abatement in publicity about excessive profits.[182] The problem of profits in the pharmaceutical industry was also thrown into focus by the wide publicity attracted by the revelations, amply confirmed by the report produced by Sir John Lang in July 1964, concerning unreasonable levels of profits made by Ferranti in contracts for Bloodhound missiles. The Government therefore needed to demonstrate that it was imposing more rigorous limitations on profits in its dealings with suppliers.

Excessive profits were only one of the dimensions of the drug problem. The tragedy of congenital deformities in babies born to women using the sedative thalidomide, which was marketed between 1958 and 1961, alerted public attention to the laxity of controls over the safety of drugs. A further aspect of the dark side of the pharmacological revolution was the increasing awareness of expanding opportunities for drug misuse and addiction. Despite an increase in legal constraints, it was widely recognised that the market was becoming flooded with habit-forming drugs outside the framework of legal prohibitions, and that over-prescribing by doctors, hoarding by patients, and trade in illicit substances were expanding to such an extent that drug abuse was already by 1964 the germ of a serious social problem.[183]

214

Officials within the Ministry of Health were divided over the merits of an enquiry into the pharmaceutical industry. Some believed that a new enquiry, soon after the Hinchliffe Report, was unlikely to be productive; it was also widely appreciated that it was difficult to construct a committee able to reach helpful conclusions. However, some fresh initiative was needed to appease critics, especially the Public Accounts Committee. In December 1964, the membership of the investigative committee was first sketched out, but in view of difficulty and delay experienced in agreeing on the membership, Robinson was obliged to announce the decision to establish the committee without revealing the identity of the chairman or members.[184]

Some preference was expressed for a judicial chair; various alternatives were considered, but early in the discussions Lord Sainsbury was mentioned as a suitable figure to head the enquiry; in March 1965 he was approached and accepted.[185] Alan John Sainsbury was the grandson of the founder of the Grocery and Provision firm of that name, and was chairman of the company. He was a well-known supporter of Labour in the House of Lords, and was much sought-after for government, quasi-government and philanthropic committees. Sainsbury agreed to the membership proposed by the health departments, but four of the nominees declined, with the result that substitutes were needed. In the selection of a general practitioner member, an obvious alternative was ruled out on grounds of suspicion that he held communist convictions.[186] The membership of the Sainsbury Committee was announced by Robinson on 31 May 1965; the ten members comprised academics from the fields of economics, social administration, chemistry, medicine, and pharmacy, a general practitioner, a Scottish industrialist, a barrister specialising in the field of patent law, a retired senior civil service accountant, and a banker.[187] The committee contained one woman, the economist, Edith Penrose. Robinson was under pressure to include a trade unionist, but this was rejected, partly because this would add to the argument for including a representative of the pharmaceutical industry. Sir James Cook, a chemist, and Vice-Chancellor of Exeter University, who provided a link with the Guillebaud Committee, resigned in 1966 upon being appointed Vice-Chancellor of the University of East Africa.

The terms of reference of the Sainsbury Committee were: 'to examine the relationship of the pharmaceutical industry in Great Britain with the National Health Service, having regard to the structure of the industry, to the commercial policies of the firms comprising it, to pricing and sales promotion practices, to the effects of patents and to the relevance and value of research; and to make recommendations'. The Committee began its work on 9 June 1965.[188]

Originally it was anticipated that the enquiry would be completed in one year; this was soon extended to two years. The work of the Committee was assisted by some new standing committees, established in an attempt to improve standards of safety following the thalidomide tragedy. On the advice of the Joint Standing Committee on the Classification of Proprietary Preparations, in June 1963 the Committee on Safety of Drugs was established by the health Ministers. This committee was formed with the co-operation of the industry and the pharmaceutical profession, which was essential for the success of this initiative. The chairman of this committee was Sir Derrick Dunlop (1902-1980), the distinguished Professor of Therapeutics and Clinical Medicine at Edinburgh University. Although his name had been considered, Dunlop had not been selected as a member of either the Hinchliffe or Douglas Committees. The Dunlop Committee began work in 1964; it was concerned with assessment of new drugs for trials, their safety in relation to efficacy before release into the market, and finally evidence about adverse effects of any drug in use. The Dunlop Committee was authorised to recommend that particular drugs should be limited to supply on prescription, or that their availability should be limited according to other restrictions. The Dunlop Committee was not concerned with assessing the efficacy of one drug relative to its competitors. Subcommittees of the Dunlop Committee were established to deal with questions relating to toxicity, clinical trials and therapeutic efficacy, and adverse reactions.[189] The large scale of pharmaceutical innovation was indicated by the volume of submissions handled by the Dunlop Committee, which soon reached about 1,000 a year.[190]

In 1964, the Standing Joint Committee of the Central and Scottish Health Service Councils on the Classification of Proprietary Preparations, which had been in existence almost since the beginning of the NHS, under he chairmanship of Lord Cohen, was reorganised under a new chairman, Professor Alastair G Macgregor. Some of the functions of the Cohen Committee were absorbed by the Dunlop Committee. The Macgregor Committee advised on 'the classification of proprietary pharmaceutical preparations with the object of helping doctors to decide which should be used in the treatment of their patients, and to identify those preparations the prescribing of which appears to call for special justification'. The Macgregor Committee issued its new classification in 1965;[191] recommendations utilising this classification were issued a publication, *Proplist*, first circulated to all doctors in 1967 and intended to be updated regularly thereafter.[192] The Macgregor Committee was faced with a massive problem of evaluating evidence, and it lacked the resources or authority to achieve the desired result.

Consequently, the Macgregor exercise proved no less controversial than its predecessor; it failed to command the confidence of either the profession or the pharmaceutical industry. The Macgregor Committee and its journal were wound up in 1968.

The Sainsbury enquiry was also linked with the deliberations of the health departments on the licensing of pharmaceutical products. Early in the Wilson administration, the health departments decided to introduce a licensing system to be applied initially to new drugs, but ultimately to be extended to all drugs. It was envisaged that licences would relate to the safety, efficacy and quality of drugs, and that it would control labelling, description and advertising. In order to command authority, it was recognised that this licensing mechanism would need to be guided by a body of expert opinion capable of producing objective advice. The health departments discussed this agency with relevant professional organisations in an effort to arrive at an acceptable balance between independent expert advice and Government supervision of the regulatory system. The outcome was a proposal for a Medicines Commission and associated expert committees to provide the authoritative guidance necessary for the issue of licences. The profession accepted assurances that in operating the licensing mechanism, Ministers would not use their powers to interfere with the judgement of the Medicines Commission. Proposals for the Medicines Commission were developed during 1966 and agreed before the Sainsbury Committee reported.

The Sainsbury Committee completed the drafting of its report in August 1967 and publication occurred on 28 September 1967.[193] The Sainsbury Report was timed to follow the White Paper on legislation on the safety of Drugs, which was published on 7 September 1967.[194] The Sainsbury Report presented a somewhat spurious impression of depth. Of the 232 pages, only 98 comprised the text of the report, and this contained a moderate amount of repetition and elementary explanatory material. The longest section of the report was the 85 pages reproducing the Government Social Survey Report on Information for the Prescriber. When compared with other reports into the health service dating from this period, the Sainsbury Report emerges as an eccentric and not entirely adequate product.

This shortcoming is perhaps surprising, considering that the Sainsbury Committee benefited from access to the massive findings of the Senate Sub-committee on Antitrust and Monopoly headed by Senator Estes Kefauver, which exhaustively examined the performance of the pharmaceutical industry in the United States. The Kefauver investigations acted as a pace-setter; in many respects Sainsbury was an echo of Kefauver. Although Sainsbury was bolder in its conclusions than any previous British enquiry, it was not altogether convincing and noticeably less radical than its American counterpart.

Sainsbury was careful to accord credit to the record of the British pharmaceutical industry in the fields of research, innovation, and trade. The recommendations rejected demands for nationalisation of the industry or other forms of direct state regulation. On the whole it was satisfied that the industry possessed the right competitive structure for maintaining its record in research and innovation. Nevertheless, the Sainsbury Committee recommended many refinements in methods of regulation and pricing, which, if fully applied, would have collectively amounted to a substantial increase in the level of state regulation of the industry.

The Report supported the VPRS as a basis for pricing, but recommended improvements in the supply of standardised financial information to the health departments regarding new products. This information was needed in order to permit more accurate evaluation of such items as research and administrative costs, or the transfer prices of pharmaceutical materials. In cases where the two sides failed to agree on prices for particular products, the report recommended establishment of procedures for securing agreement.[195]

The Committee endorsed the use already made of section 46 of the Patents Act 1949, which had been applied in isolated cases under the previous administration to permit disregard of all patents when making crown purchases. Powell had used this power to purchase antibiotics for use in hospitals at low prices from foreign suppliers, and this device had been upheld in the courts. The Sainsbury Committee recommended that consideration should be given to extending the use of this emergency power to general practitioner services.[196]

The Sainsbury Report made elaborate recommendations concerning the establishment of a new independent regulatory body, to be known as the Medicines Commission. This idea constituted an extension of the proposal for body of the same name already featuring in planning documents within the health departments. It was envisaged that ultimately no medicine available on prescription should be retailed without a licence from the Commission.[197] This licence would be awarded only with proof to the Commission that the medicine met the requirements of safety and efficacy claimed for it. The Commission would lay down regulations for the conduct of clinical trials. It was expected to take over the functions performed by the Joint Standing Committee on the Classification of Proprietary Preparations and the Committee on the Safety of Drugs, and the functions of the General Medical Council with respect to publishing the *British Pharmacopoeia*. The Commission would also take over responsibility for the *Classification of Medicines*, as well as the various digests of information produced by the health departments for the benefit of NHS personnel. Other possible functions of the Commission are noted below.

Separate from the Medicines Commission, it was proposed to establish an Economic Development Committee for the pharmaceutical industry, which was expected to link with the Government's advisory structures concerned with economic development in other sectors of the economy.[198]

Given the evidence of increasing domination of proprietary preparations, an important aspect of the Report was its consideration of brand names and the duration of patents. The Committee recommended consideration of these subjects by the recently appointed Banks Committee, which was reporting on the Patents Act. The Sainsbury Report believed that the current patent life of 16 years gave unnecessary long protection for the industry.[199]

The Sainsbury Committee recommended that there should be no brand names for new pharmaceutical products licensed by the Medicines Commission and that the Trade Marks Act should be appropriately amended.[200] All such products, whether the subject of patents or not, should be marketed only under a name approved by the Medicines Commission. The promotion of drugs would be conducted according to a 'control document' prepared by the Commission. This control document was expected to occupy a crucial part in determination of advertising and promotion of pharmaceutical products.[201]

The Sainsbury Committee calculated that promotion expenditure accounted for about 14 per cent of the value of NHS sales, which indicated continuation of an upward trend recorded in the period before the committee was established.[202] On the basis of its analysis of survey information which it had commissioned, the Committee reached sceptical conclusions concerning the reliability and worth of drug-industry promotion.[203] It was suggested that the new Medicines Commission should control information tendered to doctors concerning pharmaceutical products. All doctors would also receive the control document prepared by the Commission.[204]

The Sainsbury Committee adopted an ambivalent attitude towards the level of profits within the pharmaceutical industry. This important problem was addressed somewhat tangentially in one of the least satisfactory chapters of the Report. While accepting that a high level of profitability was a necessary consequence of a successful industry, and essential for sustaining the research base upon which the future of the companies depended, on the basis of the study of return on capital employed over the period covered by the report, it was concluded that the level of profit was sometimes 'outside the limits of reasonableness'.[205] However, such statements were usually hedged around with such qualifications that they generated ambiguity and confusion about the record of the industry as a whole. Also no attempt was made to define what constituted reasonable levels of profit.[206]

Responses to the Sainsbury Report varied widely. Critics of the pharmaceutical industry judged the recommendations too timid, while the industrialists and their allies were scathing in their criticism of the Report's lack of understanding and judgement. The pharmaceutical industry was indignant, less because of the immediate recommendations, but on account of the danger of stimulating potentially damaging interference by the Government, which might irrevocably undermine the performance of what was claimed to be one of the most conspicuously successful British industries. The spectre was raised of the collapse of the industry, adverse effects on the balance of payments, emigration of some of the nation's best scientists; consequently, 'yet another flourishing industry will be forced into the strait-jacket of mediocrity'.[207] The ABPI accused Sainsbury of making recommendations, which 'if rigidly implemented, would effectively amount to State control of the industry and its activities'.[208] On the other hand, the chemicals giant, ICI, which had been quick to market cut-price tetracyclines after the end of the Pfizer patent, was unperturbed about most of the Sainsbury recommendations.[209] Immediate responses in the media were generally positive; the *Times* epithet, 'unexceptionable' characterised the general reaction.[210] Even the more radical *New Society* regarded the report as moderate and recommended its prompt implementation by the Government.

It is doubtful whether the media possessed sufficient technical understanding to judge the real worth of the Sainsbury Report. The Government response indicated that prompt acceptance was not a viable option. Robinson formally thanked the Sainsbury Committee, but merely announced that the report would be further studied, and that the comments about a Medicines Commission would be considered in the context of related proposals included in the recent White Paper on the intended legislation on the safety of medicines.[211]

After an initial positive response, the Government found little of practical assistance in the Sainsbury Report. DHSS was especially disappointed by the 'general wooliness in substantiating the findings about excessive profits'. The Treasury found the Report 'pretty disappointing and inadequate'.[212] The Sainsbury proposal concerning standard cost returns for individual drugs presented the Government with a dilemma. On the one hand this was the method currently in favour with the Treasury and DEA for preventing excessive profits in government contracts. Superficially the standard cost return seemed like the definitive way to establish the level of profits for any product. It was expected, once and for all, to demonstrate the massive level of profitability existing with respect to particular drugs in high demand in the health service. However, in practice, on the basis of past experience, it was clear that the pharmaceutical industry would be able to justify profits higher than those applied for other government contracts. If low profits were imposed, there would be a breakdown of relations with the pharmaceutical industry; if high profits were admitted, other contractors would demand parity of treatment. The Treasury therefore abandoned its initial enthusiasm for standard cost returns. Treasury Ministers were asked to agree that the differences between NHS drug procurement and other procurement were so great and the circumstances of the drug industry so particular, that the Government should not expect the pharmaceutical companies to be subject to the profit formula criteria being evolved for application elsewhere. It was also concluded that standard cost returns were impracticable on account of the high cost of administering such a scheme.[213]

The promised consultations with industry produced further indentations in the credibility of the Sainsbury Report.[214] Technical enquiries questioned some of its findings, while its economic analysis was also soon found to be vulnerable to criticism. The vague conclusions reached about excessive profits were criticised on account of failing to take account of longer-term trends in profits, the levels of risk involved, or profitability of comparable industries. Accordingly, economists reinvestigating this subject were able to conclude that by the standards of other growth industries, the level of profitability of the pharmaceutical industry was not excessive.[215] Even the negative conclusions concerning the reliability and worth of drug-industry promotion were reached on the basis of evidence that was not altogether conclusive or assembled on the basis of investigations that were methodologically sound.[216] The fallibility of the Sainsbury Committee's examination of profit levels was a set-back to the critics. Nevertheless, some informed sources continued to urge that excessive profits were more than an isolated phenomenon based on unrepresentative instances within the pharmaceutical industry.[217]

The industry was reconciled to further tightening up of the VPRS, but it pointed out that minor gains in accuracy would entail greatly increased labour in production of standard cost returns required from the industry. Furthermore there was fear that once this information was produced, it would also be demanded as a condition of trade by lawyers representing overseas markets. The Government was warned that its demand for standard cost returns might be counterproductive because these would uncover evidence relating to drugs upon which losses had been made. It was predicted that standard cost returns would deter companies from exploiting new drugs likely to yield a poor return, which in many cases would be products connected with rare but important life-threatening illnesses. This led to a demand for returns to be confined to groups of products produced by a company, rather than standard cost returns for individual products. The industry therefore appealed for retention of the system involving estimation of returns on capital relating to overall sales.

The companies strongly contested the recommendations of the Sainsbury Committee concerning brand names. It was argued that this prohibition would place British companies at a disadvantage to their competitors and therefore irrevocably damage their export performance. The Sainsbury suggestions for alternative ways of protecting the interests of the industry were dismissed as inadequate and impracticable. The practical results of the Sainsbury approach would be debasement of standards and loss of quality control. In the view of moderate elements within the industry, the other recommendations of the Sainsbury Committee would be sufficient to control abuses, without taking the extreme step of abolishing brand names. The health departments were largely persuaded by these arguments.[218]

A further target for counterattack by the industry was the proposal to extend the application of section 46 of the Patents Act. In particular, it was argued that use of this emergency power would lead to reprisals by foreign countries, who would invoke similar laws to discriminate against British manufacturers. However, the industry was not united; those companies less vulnerable to the suspicion of profiteering were more relaxed; they regarded section 46 as a reasonable safeguard for the Government's use in the last resort against companies guilty of sharp practice.[219]

The pharmaceutical industry was united in its opposition to reducing the length of the patent protection for drugs. It was argued that research was becoming more complex and expensive, and that this trend would continue owing to the activities of the Dunlop Committee or the future Medicines Commission. Rather than reduce the patent life, the industry pressed for its further extension in line with other European countries. The proposal for a Medicines Commission was also criticised by the *British Medical Journal*, which was suspicious that the Commission would reduce the quality of intelligence available to doctors.[220]

It was increasingly evident that the Sainsbury Report would exercise little influence on policy. Initiatives which were undertaken would have occurred regardless of the Sainsbury exercise, while those proposals unique to Sainsbury were either abandoned, or introduced in a diluted form. The Sainsbury tree was therefore destined to bear only scantlings. However, for presentational purposes the Government was able to suggest a more positive outcome, since both the Health Services and Public Health Bill, as well as the Medicines Bill, both introduced in 1968, contained many provisions that could claim some relationship with the Sainsbury Report.

A new clause was added to the Health Services and Public Health Bill to extend the provisions of section 46 of the Patents Act 1949. The new clause allowed the Secretary of State to authorise, for the purpose of the family practitioner services, the purchase of patented drugs from unlicensed sources on payment of the equivalent of a royalty to the patentee. This coincided with a recommendation of the Sainsbury Committee, but it sorted out an anomaly that had long been apparent and which urgently required attention in order to prevent inconsistency between Part II and Part IV NHS services. The Minister gave assurances that this would continue to be treated as a measure of last resort, to be used only in cases where negotiations had failed to produce an agreed price for a drug.[221]

The Medicines Act, which received the Royal Assent on 25 October 1968, consolidated and extended the legislation relating to the safety, quality and efficacy of medicinal products, and also the regulation of their sale and promotion. The provisions for a licensing system, for the establishment of a Medicines Commission with its related technical committees and responsibility for publication of the *British Pharmacopoeia*, coincided with the aims of the Sainsbury Report, but these plans were already formulated before the Sainsbury Committee began its work. The Medicines Act allowed for the preparation of the *Classification of Medicines* and functions performed by the Macgregor Committee to pass to the Medicines Commission, but these possibilities were reserved for discussion with the Commission. The provisions of the Medicines Act confirmed that the Medicines Commission, which was very much the centre-piece of the Sainsbury Report, was not being granted anything like the extended powers envisaged by Sainsbury. Finally, the Medicines Act established Ministers as the Licensing Authority with ultimate responsibility for the safety, quality and efficacy of medicines.

Robinson came under pressure to make a statement on the Government's general response to the Sainsbury Report. This was not forthcoming until 24 June 1968. The statement was agreed between relevant Ministers without consideration by the Cabinet or ministerial committees, which confirmed the minor status of Sainsbury. The main action promised by the Government related to revising the VPRS. Echoing some of the ambiguity displayed in the

Sainsbury Report, Robinson concluded that the VPRS did 'not always ensure that prices and profits are reasonable', which was considerably less categorical than demanded by the Chief Secretary to the Treasury.

The Minister proposed to extend the right of direct negotiation to the whole field of drugs. This represented a logical development of the trend evident at the 1964 revision of the VPRS. Whereas Sainsbury advised fixing the price of drugs on the basis of standard cost returns relating to individual products, the Government agreed to annual financial returns submitted by each firm. A further change in practice in which Sainsbury recommendations coincided with the consensus among critics lay in the insistence that under the revised VPRS promotional expenditure would be taken into account in assessing costs and profits.

Robinson deferred making a final decision on the controversial issue of the abolition of brand names until he had held further discussions with industry on alternative ways of achieving the objectives of the Sainsbury Committee. However, it was apparent from his remarks that it was virtually impossible to depart from the existing system of brand names without placing British firms at a disadvantage in their export markets. In response to opposition from DEA, Robinson decided not the pursue the Sainsbury proposal for a separate Economic Development Committee for the pharmaceutical industry, but instead he proposed to refer questions relating to the industry to the existing Economic Development Committee for the chemical industry.[222] In view of reference to the Banks Committee, Robinson deferred consideration of the length of patent protection. In a finding which came as a big relief to the industry, the Banks Report recommended an extension of the patent life of drugs from 16 to 20 years in order to bring the British system into line with European practice.[223]

Following his statement on the Sainsbury Report, Robinson proceeded to implement relevant sections of the Medicines Act 1968, especially the sections relating to the establishment of a Licensing Authority and the new Medicines Commission. The first chairman of the Commission was Sir Derrick Dunlop. The latter's place as chairman of the Committee on Safety of Drugs was taken by Professor A C Frazer, and then by Sir Eric Scowen; this committee with its strengthened powers was renamed Committee on Safety of Medicines. The Licensing Authority was concerned with issuing licenses for new products, for which purpose it relied on advice from the Committee on Safety of Medicines. Established drugs were granted temporary licences; the formidable task of reviewing these substances was undertaken by a Committee for Review of Medicines and a parallel committee dealing with dental and surgical supplies.

These extensions of statutory control moved Britain somewhat closer to the regulatory model characterised by the Federal Drugs Agency in the USA.

Immediately after Robinson's statement, negotiations began concerning revision of the VPRS, the second phase of which formally ended in 1968. Agreement was reached on the most important issue, the provision of annual financial returns, which supplied the health departments with standardised information relating to the accounts of each company supplying the NHS. Companies also agreed to provide the health departments with additional information, such as details of unanticipated increases in sales. It was also agreed that a small amount of retrospection should apply in negotiated price reductions, and that direct negotiations would no longer be excluded with respect to pricing of new products, but would apply to all products where justified on the basis of the financial situation of the company.

The Government experienced great difficulty in reaching a conclusion on the level of 'reasonable' profit to be adopted in the new VPRS. The Treasury recommended that 20 per cent return on capital invested might be adopted as a threshold for general guidance of health department investigators, but it was conceded that a stated limit was impracticable, and that flexibility was unavoidable. Gradually the Treasury line softened. It was conceded that there were only limited possibilities for improving the performance of VPRS on account of the special factors operating in the field of pharmaceuticals:

> The extent to which pressure can be applied to the industry is very limited. It may be that they are largely dependent on the Health Service but the Health Service is also dependent on them. The Government is not one of the contracting parties; we are dealing with firms, some of whom are providing a product for which there is no substitute; and some of those products are life saving. If any confrontation is fought to the limit, the sick are going to be hurt. This puts a considerable restraint on the amount of pressure which the Department can apply.[224]

In the absence of target profit levels, it was agreed to secure the most favourable outcome possible in the context of the VPRS.

The most contentious issue in the VPRS negotiations, over which the parties quickly became deadlocked, related to proposals to limit sales promotion expenditure on proprietary products. This issue was not addressed by the Sainsbury Committee because it assumed that brand names would be abolished. The Treasury insisted on a target of 5 per cent of home sales, compared with an average of about 14 per cent existing at the time. The ABPI negotiators rejected this limit and eventually proposed a limit of 10 per cent to be reached over a three-year period. This suggestion was regarded as too lenient by the Chief Secretary, but it was disowned by the constituents of ABPI on account of its severity. DHSS urged that negotiations should proceed on the basis of a more modest target for reductions in spending on promotion. This was reluctantly agreed by the Treasury on the understanding that a satisfactory overall settlement was negotiated.[225]

APBI continued its retreat on the control of expenditure on promotion. On 28 February 1969, ABPI revealed its final negotiating position. It merely intended to ask companies to avoid extravagant expenditure, and review the problem again in the light of information from the first annual financial returns.[226] The Chief Secretary reluctantly concurred with his advisers that the Government should abandon for the time being its attempt to control spending on drug promotion. This allowed the completion of negotiations; in April 1969 Crossman reported upon the provisional agreement concerning the revised VPRS. It was then necessary for the negotiators from the industry to consult their constituents. Crossman again met the representatives of ABPI in October 1969 to tie up the agreement. This necessitated one last concession on the part of the Government, which entailed reduction of the element of retrospection in price adjustments. The new VPRS agreement was announced on 22 October 1969.[227]

With respect to the pharmaceutical bill, the Wilson administration ended as it had begun. In the last months of the Labour Government, the Chief Secretary expressed alarm about the continuing escalation in costs. Regardless of all the effort invested in enquiries, new committee structures, and revision of the VPRS, in 1970, the increase was running at 8 per cent a year. The pharmaceutical bill had increased from £157m in 1966/67 to £207m in 1970/71, and was projected to reach £244m in 1974/75.[228]

Although reintroduction of the prescription charge had exercised a minor deterrent effect, it was evident that general practitioners had compensated by increasing the amounts prescribed and by prescribing more expensive drugs to alleviate the effect of charges. The charges exercise had therefore once again proved to be largely counterproductive. Health Ministers refused to consider further and more drastic steps to limit these alleged abuses. The Treasury reviewed various radical courses of action, but ruled out most of the alternatives. The only possibilities worth further investigation were either insistence on offsetting economies, or imposing a ceiling on NHS expenditure, within which the drug bill would be included. It was however predicted that health Ministers would refuse to allow the level of their services dependent on the vagaries of the drug bill. The Treasury therefore opted to propose offsetting economies on a rising scale, enforced through the PESC system from 1970/71 onwards, with a view to at least stabilising the cost of pharmaceutical services.[229] Treasury officials and Ministers concluded that further progress on controlling the drug bill could not be achieved without greater willingness on the part of the health departments to risk a major confrontation with the medical profession. The Chief Secretary appreciated that it was impossible to provoke action by the health departments in advance of the General Election, but he encouraged his officials to compose 'an extreme and provocative statement' of the Treasury position, with a view to precipitating a confrontation with the health departments on this issue immediately after the election.[230] Accusations of excessive profits of the pharmaceutical companies also were never far from the headlines. In 1969, a long-running dispute with Merck, Sharp and Dohme was brought to an end after a threat of referral to the NBPI. The Government immediately entered into a more serious dispute with Swiss pharmaceutical companies who were members of ABPI, but refused to comply with the requirements to supply standardised financial information agreed under the revised VPRS. This dispute ran on into the Heath administration.[231]

(v) PROTECTING THE VULNERABLE

The previous volume of this study drew attention to the unsatisfactory state of mental health services under the NHS. The Royal Commission on Mental Illness, Mental Health Act 1959, Powell's brave words about running down long-stay hospitals and expanding community care, signified a shift in attitudes, but these aspirations were slow to be translated into tangible improvements in care for those who were designated as mentally ill and mentally handicapped. It has already been noted that the regime of continuing resource constraint inhibited the progress of community care. Also, the realities of resource distribution in the hospital service continued to operate to the disadvantage of the long-stay sector. Nothing happened to break with the inertia and low expectations prevalent within long-stay institutions.

During the Wilson administration, the depressing truth about long-stay hospitals became impossible to disguise. It was to the credit of Richard Crossman that he frankly acknowledged the failings of these services, and he made an sincere attempt to set in place systems capable of bringing about genuine improvement. Once the situation in the long-stay hospitals was addressed in realistic terms, it raised important questions relating to the handling of complaints, the inspection of hospitals, and the rights of the many vulnerable client groups whose quality of life was determined by the NHS.[232]

Sans Everything

After a long period of murmurings of dissatisfaction, the Wilson administration was suddenly confronted with accusations of serious malpractice. Mrs Barbara Robb was the spark that ignited an explosion. Aid for the Elderly in Government Institutions, founded in 1965 by Mrs Robb, and supported by well-connected London intellectuals, captured the headlines in the press and threw the Ministry of Health into panic.[233] By 1967 the organisation had built up a formidable dossier of case histories, much of the information deriving from concerned health service personnel. This material found its way into the press, which also launched its own investigations, adding further to the volume of allegations. Beginning with the *Sunday Mirror* on 15 January 1967, a stream of sensational reports appeared in all sections of the press. The most weighty press allies of Mrs Robb were Hugo Young in the *Sunday Times* and Mrs Yvonne Cross editor of the *Nursing Times*; she was also assisted by Mrs Mary Applebey, the Secretary of the National Association for Mental Health. Particularly damaging was Young's article, 'The Old in Hospital. A Public Scandal'.[234] Young concluded that not only was there urgent need to introduce radical improvements in training and services, but also there were compelling reasons for creation of an inspectorate for hospitals and extension of the powers of the ombudsman to investigate complaints about hospitals. The *Nursing Mirror* utilised its links with the nursing profession to gather its own collection of relevant evidence.

The next stage in the campaign occurred on 30 June 1967, with the publication of *Sans Everything*. This book not only contained case histories and evidence from witnesses, but it also included proposals for development of psycho-geriatric services. Among the contributors were the writer, C H Rolph, Professor Brian Abel-Smith, and the well-known psychiatrists, Russell Barton and J Anthony Whitehead.[235] *Sans Everything* attracted sympathetic media coverage, including from newspapers as diverse as the *Daily Telegraph*, the *Daily Mail*, the *News of the World*, and the *Daily Sketch*. Even more important was a full-length BBC television programme devoted to the allegations contained in *Sans Everything*.[236]

As already indicated the Minister of Health was a specialist on mental health. He was therefore well-equipped to respond to the issues raised by AEGIS. His initial reaction was to instigate a general enquiry designed to 'remove any general feeling that ill-treatment was taking place in all mental hospitals'. This course had the advantage of appearing to be a spontaneous gesture not dictated by the complaints of Mrs Robb, but it was not favoured by his senior advisers; Robinson was reminded that the findings would be embarrassing, expose prevalence of bad conditions, indicate widespread location of patients in the wrong kind of institution, and inevitably lead to demands for additional expenditure. The Minister was persuaded to adopt a more limited approach, by instituting series of specific enquiries, concerned only with complaints contained in *Sans Everything*.[237] Well before the date of publication of *Sans Everything*, the Ministry of Health drew up lists of names for six teams of independent investigators, which were activated by the relevant RHBs on the prompting of Robinson immediately after the appearance of *Sans Everything*.[238] These reports were published on 9 July 1968.[239] The investigations went according to plan; the hapless critics were subjected to all the firepower that Robinson's artillery could muster. The reports were promptly published and the Minister announced that his six independent enquiries had demonstrated that the allegations were 'totally unfounded or grossly exaggerated'. [240] Robinson's exhibition of righteous indignation was echoed by a stage army of the Minister's supporters from the back-benches.

Any complacency on the part of the health departments about this outcome was entirely misplaced. Robinson's reports failed to dispel disquiet among the public. Complaints multiplied, and it became clear that the NHS had finally lost credibility in its capacity to handle complaints. The press continued to support Mrs Robb, while television accorded AEGIS further positive publicity.[241] Even more important, the influential and respected Council on Tribunals not only upheld the complaints of Mrs Robb that the enquires had been mishandled, but it also commented on the unsatisfactory state of complaints procedures in the NHS, as well as on the inadequacy of proposals for their improvement in the reorganisation Green Paper.[242] Baroness Burton, on behalf of the Council on Tribunals, made strong representations to Robinson about the failure to establish impartial machinery for handling complaints relating to the health service, and she made no secret of the Council's dissatisfaction with the outcome of the Robb enquiries. Robinson was uncompromising and defensive; he refused to accept that his department needed to alter its practices for dealing with complaints of the kind made by Mrs Robb. After fruitless exchanges, Baroness Burton made similar approaches to Crossman, but on a more personal and friendly basis, in which she denounced the six enquiries established by Robinson, and was particularly scathing about the intemperate manner in which the enquiry most relating to Mrs Robb had been handled.[243] By this stage Crossman was satisfied that the Council on Tribunals was entirely justified in its expressions of concern.

The Ministry of Health was to some extent aware that its exhortations about improvement in services were being ignored, and that the abuses within long-stay hospitals needed to be confronted more actively. Since the beginning of the confrontation with Mrs Robb, the relevant officers had been working conscientiously on a reappraisal of policy for mental handicap and mental illness.[244] This new level of initiative was assisted by changes of personnel on both the administrative and medical sides of the department. Indeed, by the date of establishment of the six enquiries, they had prepared the outline of a new policy initiative, which was presented to RHB Chairmen in July 1968.[245] The paper expressed disappointment with the failure of the regions to follow the guide-lines laid down in the hospital plan, or to introduce improvements advocated in the circulars HM(65)45 and 104. It was acknowledged that the service was afflicted by recidivism: the 1966 review of the hospital plan showed that proposals for closure of mental hospitals had been largely abandoned; unjustifiable discrepancies between regions over estimates of bed requirements for mental health were opening up; little progress had been made in providing day hospitals, or mental illness units in district general hospitals. The department called for renewed concentration on services in the district general hospital, with appropriate support from day hospitals and community services: 'whether we shall also need separate hospitals for medium and long-stay patients is less clear, but experience in the Manchester Region and elsewhere suggests that this may not be necessary'. Such bold statements indicate that behind the scenes, Ministry of Health thinking on the mental health services was neither complacent nor unimaginative. For both mental illness and mental handicap, the department urged regions to make a determined effort to prevent the build-up of populations of long-stay patients. On this basis, regional authorities were asked to revise downwards their targets for beds per 1,000 population in 1975, from the level of 1.8 adopted in 1962, to 0.5. Since the department believed that its alternative scheme of services was more economical than institutional care, it was suggested that NHS authorities possessed little excuse for failing to promote change. There is little direct evidence about the response of RHB Chairmen, but from a related meeting of their Senior Administrative Medical Officers, it is evident that the department's new thinking was not entirely welcomed. The SAMOs reacted with scepticism, pointing out that current plans for district general hospitals could not be easily adapted to the department's thinking, and that it was not practicable to interfere with existing programmes of hospital development.[246] This little test demonstrated that the powerful regional hospital administration was not likely to be an ally in the department's mission to transform mental health services.

Ely and Post-Ely

The next step towards change was dictated by further outside developments. The allies of Mrs Robb recovered the initiative owing to an obscure complaint emanating from an unlikely source. Robinson's teams were concerned with silencing critics of the regime operating in English long-stay hospitals. On 20 August 1967, the *News of the World*, under the heading 'Heartbreak Hospitals', publicised complaints made by Mr Michael Pantiledes, a Greek Cypriot, who had worked for one year as an untrained nursing assistant at Ely Hospital, Cowbridge Road, Cardiff. Ely was an old workhouse, which was designated as a mental hospital and mental deficiency institution under the NHS. The Welsh Board of Health appointed Geoffrey Howe QC to head the enquiry. Howe had been the Conservative MP for Bebington, Merseyside between 1964 and 1966, but he was brought up in South Wales and had contested the Aberavon seat in 1955 and 1959. Howe's team completed its report in August 1968.[247] The 83,000 word text of this one enquiry was almost twice as long as the report on the six hospitals published a month earlier. The unanimous verdict delivered in exhaustive detail in Howe's document was, as admitted by an official in London, a 'devastating indictment not only of the hospital itself, but of pretty well all concerned with it'.[248] The introduction to the report also contained a stinging rebuke concerning procedures for conducting enquiries, which Howe regarded as fundamentally flawed.[249]

First reactions of the Welsh Board of Health and the Welsh Hospital Board were to insist on publication being confined to a summary of the report. Under some protest Howe produced a slightly reduced version of his report, as well as a 20,000 word summary. The health administrations in England and Wales were in no hurry to publish Howe's report, and they allowed their disagreements with Howe to drag on and excuse continuing delay in publication. Equivocation ended when George Thomas insisted that the Ely Report should be published before he was due to take over responsibility for the health services in Wales on 1 April 1969. Thomas was additionally embarrassed because Ely Hospital was located in his constituency.[250] There ensued in March 1969 a hectic rush to issue the report before the end of the month. Of necessity, the Ely Report was brought to the attention of Crossman. Given Robinson's close personal involvement with this issue and the extreme political sensitivity of this matter, it is perhaps surprising that his successor was not alerted to the Ely Report at an earlier stage. Crossman was furious about being kept in the dark for four months.[251] He immediately insisted that there was no alternative to publication of the full report.[252] Furthermore, he concluded:

231

I could only publish and survive politically if in the course of my Statement I announced necessary changes in policy including the adoption by the Ministry and the RHBs of a system of inspectorates, central and regional, such as there are in almost every other Ministry and such as the Health Service has never yet permitted itself.[253]

Even allowing for the high degree of self-regard evident in his diaries, it is clear from this and other evidence that Crossman personally was responsible for introducing a new spirit of candour and self-criticism with respect to conditions in long-stay hospitals, and also for insisting on immediate action to introduce a mechanism for inspection and an overhaul of complaints procedures.[254] It is also evident that his proposals for an inspectorate were forced through in the face of opposition from his officials. However, on 12 March he obtained support from the Prime Minister for an inspectorate.[255] In the course of the next fortnight this evolved into a proposal for a policy or professional 'advisory service', which although less than an inspectorate, would be independent and able to report direct to the Secretary of State. Crossman's proposals for a public statement striking the balance between acknowledgement of responsibility, determination to rectify past errors, and tactful respect for the high quality of service displayed by the majority of personnel employed in long-stay hospitals, met with support and sympathy from the Social Services Committee and the Cabinet. The main reservation of Crossman's colleagues related to the date of publication, which coincided with three by-elections.[256] Crossman's statement made on 27 March 1969, the date of publication of the report, was well-received, and taken as a sign that there was genuine commitment to improve the state of long-stay hospitals.[257] There is no evidence that Ely added to the difficulties of Labour, but the by-election results were bad from the perspective of the Government, the worst being the loss of Walthamstow to the Conservatives with a 16 per cent swing.

In the short term, Crossman conveyed sufficient evidence of good faith for the pressure groups to suspend their public campaign. However, scandals relating to the long-stay hospital continued to erupt with regular frequency. Hard on the heels of Ely came Farleigh, South Ockendon and Whittingham, all of which were subject to full-scale enquiries, and many of the criticisms were discovered to be well-founded. The results of these enquiries were not available until between 1971 and 1974; their immediate impact was therefore limited, but they imported a sense of urgency into Crossman's mission.[258]

Crossman's main chosen instrument to plan improvements in the long-stay sector was a working party containing both officials and outsiders. This Post-Ely Policy Working Party was a somewhat shadowy body, with a shifting remit, and even without a settled title, which persisted for about nine months in the latter part of 1969.[259] The idea of a working party arose during discussions of responses to the Ely Report in March 1969.[260] Crossman saw the working party as a means to overcome opposition among senior officials to his ideas. In his statement on the Ely Report, Crossman promised that a 'new service for the regular visiting and scrutiny of hospitals' would be established, while as an interim measure he intended to set up a 'small working party in my Department to analyse the knowledge already available on these hospitals and to supplement this survey, where necessary, with its own investigations'. It was also anticipated that PEP would advise on other matters arising from the Ely Hospital Report, including consideration of conditions in long-stay hospitals, related policy questions, and procedures for dealing with complaints. In the course of the next few weeks, Crossman established that the working party would draw about half its members from the NHS and outside experts, and that it should perform a wider range of functions than was originally envisaged. Invitations to the outsiders were sent out on 11 April. These comprised two independent experts, Geoffrey Howe QC, and Peter Townsend, Professor of Sociology at Essex University; and from the NHS, Dr Gerald O'Gorman, Physician Superintendent, Borocourt Hospital, Reading, Dr John Revans, SAMO Wessex RHB, and Miss F E Skellern, Superintendent of Nursing, Bethlem and Maudsley Hospital. Various officials also attended the meetings of PEP, as did Crossman's chief adviser, Professor Brian Abel-Smith, and also Pauline Morris, author of *Put Away: A Sociological Study of Institutions for the Mentally Retarded* (1969). PEP was therefore by no means a forum for rubber-stamping departmental thinking. The membership and a fuller details about the aims of PEP were announced on 24 April 1969.[261] Background minutes, as well as the letters of invitation, mentioned that PEP was an interim venture, with an expected life of three months, but the wide remit clearly envisaged an existence of longer duration. Also, at the insistence of the outside members, the remit was further widened to relate to services in the community.

PEP met every two weeks for about nine months, and in this time it considered about sixty memoranda. Apart from giving direct advice on such issues as the establishment of the Health Service Commissioner (initially called Health Commissioner) and the Hospital Advisory Service, PEP also supervised a complex of working parties dealing with complaints procedures, production of guide-lines for minimum standards and immediate improvement in services, and it took on the weighty task of determining definitive long-term policy. Most of this PEP machinery included both departmental and extra-departmental members. Crossman noted that his officials were unenthusiastic about the inclusion of outsiders, and in order to curtail this development, the officials pressed for the winding up PEP once the Hospital Advisory Service had been formed, but it was decided that it would be allowed to continue at least for the limited purpose of considering a draft policy document on the future of mental handicap services.[262] Lack of enthusiasm within the health department for PEP and its satellites perhaps stems from two main causes. First, the officials had been working actively on the formulation of a new policy since 1968; they saw the new Secretary of State's action as an unnecessary complication of their labours, also hardly a vote of confidence in their efforts. Secondly, their initial experience of discussions with NHS authorities and professional interest groups suggested that importing outsiders would lead to controversy and possibly undermine their plans for a radical shake-up of the services. PEP created a forum for debate, but outside influences were exercised according to the vagaries of Crossman's selection process for the various working parties. Since it was unrealistic to evolve the long-term policy document without reference to outside interests, it was inevitable that the department would come under pressure to dilute the policy objectives announced in 1968.

It is striking the extent to which Crossman by-passed the central advisory machinery in the post-Ely exercise. The Mental Health Standing Advisory Committee in particular might have expected to play an active part in these deliberations; it was indeed consulted, but very much consigned to the sidelines, perhaps on account of its known orientation towards a more traditionalist view of the mental health services than held within the department.[263]

Pressure on regional boards to improve standards in the long-stay hospitals began immediately after the Ely Report. Crossman discussed interim action with RHB Chairmen in April, July and December 1969. Agreement was achieved on minor measures such as improving the quality of food, but Crossman wanted Boards to take more dramatic actions reliant on reallocation of resources. His target was a $1\frac{1}{2}$ per cent reallocation, but the Boards offered only negligible transfers. Despite continuing pressure on this front, and ingenuity in finding small sums on the part of DHSS, by the end of the Wilson administration, only a minor increase in resources for the long-stay hospitals had been obtained.[264]

In the light of this not unexpected negative response, Crossman calculated that NHS authorities were unlikely to respond more constructively unless they were subjected to continuous surveillance. The Secretary of State invested his hopes in the proposed NHS Hospital Advisory Service, which he championed in the face of scepticism from his officials, NHS authorities, the Mental Health SAC, and the medical profession.

The proposal to establish 'some system of inspection' of hospitals like Ely, constituted one of the main recommendations of the Ely Report.[265] As already noted, Crossman was fully supportive of this proposal and he quickly obtained the backing of his colleagues. However, his officials were opposed to an inspectorate; they persuaded Ministers that an advisory system was preferable, being more likely to gain acceptance by the medical profession and NHS authorities. It was also decided that 'in principle this system should cover all hospitals but priority should be given to long-stay patients of all kinds and among them to the subnormal and the elderly'.[266] Very quickly, 'National Health Service Hospital Advisory Service' became adopted as the favoured title for this new body.

The HAS was first unveiled to RHB Chairmen on 30 April 1969. Crossman described the HAS as a 'means of keeping himself directly informed of conditions in hospitals, particularly long-stay hospitals' by means of a 'small central staff under a Director who would have direct access to and report to Ministers'. Multidisciplinary teams of visitors undertaking the bulk of work of the HAS would be drawn from the NHS and be appointed on short-term contracts. The Secretary of State hoped that the Chairmen would be inspired to create a parallel advisory structure at regional level. The Chairmen were unenthusiastic and cautious in their response to the HAS proposal, but they agreed that the central service should be given a trial.[267] The JCC was consulted on 29 April. The consultant leadership reacted with suspicion, seeking a guarantee that the HAS would be confined to long-stay hospitals. They insisted on independence from the health department, but wanted it tied in with the professional consultative mechanism.[268] Geoffrey Howe, who was consulted on this suggestion, protested that this would undermine the independence of the inspectorate and destroy the protection of the 'hapless consumers'.[269]

A further idea stemming from Crossman was open competition for the post of Director of the HAS. At the beginning of July the post was widely advertised; applicants were not limited to clinicians. This exercise proved fruitless and delayed the appointment. The next step was a confidential trawl of names, which resulted in the appointment of Dr A A Baker, who was a recent and successful recruit to the medical staff of the department. Baker had served as Medical Administrator and consultant psychiatrist at Banstead Hospital and consultant psychiatrist at St Mary Abbots Hospital, a large mental handicap hospital in Kensington, which contained a forty-bed psychiatric unit and day hospital. Baker's appointment was regarded as a coup for the HAS, but his departure from the department was regretted by the Chief Medical Officer.[270] The NHS Hospital Advisory Service was launched on 15 October 1969. Dr Baker took up his appointment on 1 November 1969.

Dr Baker completed his 'Plan of Operation' for the HAS in January 1970. This was accepted by Crossman, subject to one alteration. Also, before distribution to health authorities, the text was altered to remove the suggestion that the service would eventually extend its work to all NHS hospitals.[271] Under its methodical Director, rapid progress was made in establishing four multidisciplinary teams, each selected for its suitability for specialised work in mental hospitals, mental handicap hospitals, or geriatric hospitals. Priority was given to inspections of mental handicap hospitals, which commenced in February 1970. Naturally these visitations constituted a formidable operation, but all of these institutions had been inspected by the end of 1971, shortly before the publication of the first annual report of the HAS. The initial reports of the HAS on individual hospitals made depressing reading. Even in cases where improvements were recorded, they made only limited impact on the way of life of the inmates. For instance, at the massive institution at Calderstones in Lancashire, a reduction from more than 2,000 to 1,750 patients had been achieved, but there was a severe shortage of nursing staff, no attempts to personalise clothing, create an atmosphere of homeliness, neglect of rehabilitation, and lack of hygiene. Although continuing changes were envisaged, preoccupation with health service, local government, and social service reorganisation were tending to slow down the pace of progress.[272]

Despite limited prospects for change, Crossman was satisfied that the HAS was the right solution. Indeed, with conviction he commented that 'this is possibly one of the most exciting and successful things I have done'. The HAS model was taken up by a few regions, but it was not pursued systematically at the regional level. As indicated in chapter V, relations between NHS authorities and Baker's organisation deteriorated, while after Crossman's departure, the HAS was not protected from its critics by strong friends within DHSS.

Given the importance of Wales in the genesis of the scheme for a hospital inspectorate, the Welsh Office took an active interest in proposals for improving conditions in the long-stay hospitals. Initially, the Welsh Office was affronted by failure of DHSS to consult or offer participation in the Post-Ely Policy Working Party.[273] After this poor start, full information about the working party was supplied to the Welsh Office. Indeed, the Welsh Hospital Board anticipated the visitations of the HAS by setting up its own Survey/Study Team, which undertook an urgent review of all mental handicap hospitals in Wales.[274] However, George Thomas decided that the advantages for the long term rested with an advisory service covering England and Wales. Accordingly, he informed Crossman that Wales would not seek to establish a separate advisory service.[275]

In Scotland, it was decided to establish a separate Scottish Advisory Service. The scheme devised by SHHD was slightly different from its English counterpart. It envisaged a small central team, headed by a medically-qualified Director, which would be part of SHHD. The visitations would be conducted by members of the central team together with nominated officers from the respective regional board.[276] This scheme was retained in a consultative document circulated in August 1969, except that each regional board was expected to assist in a more informal manner.[277] Information about the finally-agreed scheme was circulated to health authorities in March 1970, and the service was established from 1 April 1970. The first director of the Scottish HAS was Dr J K Hunter, a Principal Medical Officer in SHHD.[278] It was envisaged that visitations by the Scottish HAS would involve members of the central team and officers from the regional boards.

PEP became caught up in the discussions over the role of the Parliamentary Commissioner for Administration. Debates on the Parliamentary Commissioner Bill in 1967 exposed widespread demand for extension of the powers of the Parliamentary Commissioner for Administration to cover the actions of hospital authorities. The health service was excluded from the remit of the Parliamentary Commissioner on the grounds that services were ineligible for inclusion when there was an autonomous local statutory authority. Since local health authorities and Executive Councils were automatically excluded from the scope of the Parliamentary Commissioner, then it was felt improper to include the hospital service. In addition, it was argued that the Parliamentary Commissioner was not equipped to deal with the large proportion of cases likely to entail reference to clinical judgement. Finally, it was felt that existing complaints and tribunals arrangements would be impossible to maintain in tandem with the procedures of the Parliamentary Commissioner. Exclusion of hospital services from the remit of the Parliamentary Commissioner was fiercely contested in Parliament. The argument was by no means over. In 1968 the Select Committee on the Parliamentary Commissioner took the view that hospital authorities had been unreasonably excluded, but it was recognised that further review of this issue needed to be made in the light of proposals for health service reorganisation.[279]

As noted below in chapter IV, in order to appease the ombudsman lobby, the first reorganisation Green Paper introduced a tentative proposal for a 'Health Commissioner' to deal with complaints in the NHS, and left open the possibility that this function might be linked with the Parliamentary Commissioner for Administration. This suggestion received a mixed response. However, demand for a Health Commissioner steadily increased, assisted by the Ely affair. PEP considered that there was need for an improved complaints procedure, a Health Advisory Service, and a Health Commissioner. [280] Accordingly, in February 1970, a consultative paper on the Health Commissioner was circulated for comment.[281] While it was accepted that the great majority of complaints in the hospital service were likely to be dealt with at the local level, the Health Commissioner would be an independent person to whom complaints of maladministration could be referred if satisfaction was not obtained from the health authority itself. The consultative paper suggested that there should be a single Health Commissioner for England, but with a staff at offices throughout the regions.

The Government discovered a wide range of responses. The medical profession remained unconvinced that a Health Commissioner was necessary, and it was suspicious that this mechanism would constitute an interference with clinical freedom. Hospital administrators were also unenthusiastic. Nursing groups were divided in their views. Most other interest groups, including the Regional Hospital Boards, were favourable. However, active enthusiasm for the Health Commissioner extended little beyond consumer interest groups.[282] Because discussions over the health ombudsman became tied up with the NHS reorganisation timetable, the Wilson administration came to an end before a final decision had been reached on the establishment of the Health Service Commissioner.

A further important priority of PEP was to revise the inadequate guide-lines for dealing with complaints by patients contained in HM(66)15. As noted in chapter V, this issue was also taken up in Scotland at the suggestion of the Farquharson-Lang Committee. Revision of complaints procedures was discussed during the preparation of Robinson's Green Paper on NHS reorganisation, in the general context of the handling of complaints and representation of consumer interests by the proposed area health boards.

A working group mainly comprised of officials was set up in April 1969 to review this problem. Its report, completed in July, advanced discussions only to a limited extent.[283] In effect the working group admitted that it lacked the competence to produce further guidance; it therefore recommended establishment of a new working group including a membership with greater specialist competence to undertake further investigations. Discussion of the report confirmed this inadequacy. Geoffrey Howe outlined no fewer than ten major reservations about this report. In particular, he concentrated on the difficulties facing junior staff who wished to

238

complain about their seniors, or representation of patients who were unable to make their own complaints. PEP agreed that a new Working Party should be established.[284] Early expectations that the HAS or the Health Service Commissioner would absorb some of the burden of local complaints turned out to be unfulfilled. Accordingly, in April 1970, Crossman's officials were asked to produce proposals for an expert working party to deal with the local complaints mechanism. The scope and membership of this working party were discussed with the Secretary of State on 4 May 1970, but further action was deferred until after the General Election.[285] The next steps will be considered in chapter V.

Better Services for the Mentally Handicapped

Understandably, in the light of the Ely affair, the main priority of the post-Ely exercise was drafting a policy document on 'mental subnormality'. During this exercise, the mental handicap terminology gradually elbowed the subnormality language into the sidelines. The production of the new policy was entrusted to the Working Group on the Future Pattern of Mental Subnormality Services established in May 1969, which comprised about equal numbers of departmental and extra-departmental members. PWG was chaired by Dr R Wilkins, who ensured that this group benefited fully from the work of the department's own Mental Subnormality Subcommittee formed in the spring of 1968. Already in July 1968 this latter subcommittee had produced 'An approach to a comprehensive policy statement on health and welfare services for mentally subnormal persons', which contained many of the main elements of the White Paper published in 1971.[286]

PWG was guided by the principle that the desirable objectives of running down institutions and 'turning off the tap' to prevent entry into them of potential long-stay patients, could not be achieved without development of fully integrated services. The dominant view within PWG insisted that 'the balance will be shifted even more decisively in the direction of helping them to live at home' and that the aim was 'not an integrated service for the mentally subnormal but the integration of the mentally subnormal with the rest of us'.[287]

At first Crossman favoured a low-key approach to the long-term policy document, which he considered might comprise an updating of HM(65)104, but on 20 August he changed his mind and authorised the production of a White Paper, following the lines of the 'Approach to comprehensive policy' document. Given this high level of preparedness, it was possible to telescope the timetable for the White Paper. It was agreed that a working draft version should be completed by PWG in mid-September, followed by discussion at a small conference convened by the Secretary of State in early October, and by a large conference in January 1970, with a view to publication in the early spring of 1970.[288] The small conference exposed the thinking of the department and its allies for the first time to the blast of outside criticism. PWG was not itself entirely united, but the deinstitutionalisation lobby was dominant. At the conference, the dominant voices were the defenders of the larger hospitals, who were quick to point out that the utopian expectations of the planners about the adequacy of the system based on district general hospitals and community care were unlikely to be fulfilled. It was suggested that the more certain way to advance services was to concentrate on improvements within the existing institutional mechanism, supplemented by slow evolutionary changes supported by proven experience. Crossman reassured his critics that the changes envisaged would take thirty years to complete, and therefore need not affect morale within the long-stay hospitals. He also promised to take account of the observations of further conferences before finalising the Government's policy.[289]

In practice, further preparations for the White Paper took little further account of outside opinion.[290] Many sections required amplification of technical detail.[291] Professor Abel-Smith, who had already been co-ordinating collection of information on improvement of services, was brought in to supervise redrafting. In December 1969, the document reappeared in a nine-chapter form, but still following the general structure of the earlier drafts.[292] At this stage, the intentions of the Government were leaked to Ann Shearer, who publicised the forthcoming White Paper in the *Guardian* under the headline 'New Deal planned for Subnormal'. This article stressed the intention to close down subnormality hospitals and replace them by units attached to general hospitals and by community care.[293]

The process of revision went more slowly than anticipated, with the result that the schedule was revised to allow for Cabinet approval by the end of June and publication in July 1970. Given the provisional nature of the draft produced by Abel-Smith, an official from HS2 prepared a further draft. A second more senior official from HS2 was then commissioned by Crossman to produce a more polished version of this draft, with a request to complete this version by the end of February 1970. Crossman was still dissatisfied with the result; he therefore called Professor Abel-Smith back to produce further drafts, ending with what was known as the 'sixth edition'. At this stage, views were taken from outside experts, including members of the PEP working party. Crossman's last discussion with his officials on the White Paper occurred on 5 May.[294] This meeting confirmed the following general principles for long-term policy:

240

(a) that no new all-age hospitals would be built and that the local authorities would be responsible for the mentally handicapped except where hospitalization is necessary on <u>medical</u> grounds (ie there should be no decanting to hospital on economic grounds alone); and

(b) that hospitals should decant into the community as many mentally handicapped people as possible, and should provide hostels for those mentally handicapped people who do not in fact need full hospitalization.

Both Crossman and Serota expressed satisfaction with the final drafts available to them. The final reference to the White Paper made by Crossman indicates his confidence that this document was sufficiently bipartisan to be acceptable for publication by his successors.[295] The accuracy of this supposition will be tested in chapter V.

(vi) PREVENTION AND PROMOTION

The previous chapter described the irresolute behaviour of the Government with respect to various areas of preventive medicine, all of which were the responsibility of local health authorities. Two notable pieces of unfinished business related to the prevention of dental caries through fluoridation of water supplies, and initiatives connected with the health dangers of tobacco smoking. As noted below, Labour found these issues quite as intractable and uncongenial as its Conservative predecessors. This section will also consider the difficulties encountered in the course of the modest attempt to extend provision for family planning.

Fluoridation
After the fierce resistance to fluoridation experienced by the Conservative administration, Labour was circumspect in its approach to this problem. Robinson himself was pro-fluoridation, and from the outset of his term as Minister of Health he made his position clear: 'I am completely convinced of the desirability, on health grounds, of fluoridation, and also of its safety'.[296] The tide suddenly turned in favour of fluoridation. The Watford action in the High Court was withdrawn;[297] a Privy Council ruling about a case in New Zealand strengthened the view that fluoridation was within the powers of water undertakings; also legislation in Ireland and associated court hearings cleared the way for general fluoridation there. Robinson was emboldened to issue a new circular inviting local health authorities and water undertakings to initiate fluoridation, and this was backed up with a popular pamphlet. The CCHE also gave modest support for Robinson's campaign.[298]

Robinson's initiative provoked a backlash from an anti-fluoridation lobby that was becoming ever more vociferous.[299] In 1966, Francis Douglas, Lord Douglas of Barloch, a former Labour MP, and a leading parliamentary opponent of fluoridation, complained to the Prime Minister that Robinson was rumoured to be favourable to making fluoridation compulsory. In response Robinson issued a statement confirming that the Government favoured voluntary adoption of fluoridation.[300] In the face of determined popular opposition, the Government showed little enthusiasm for addressing this issue, but it again became unavoidable with the publication in July 1969 of the Eleven Year Study of Fluoridation. This report was produced by the Government's Committee on Research into Fluoridation chaired by Dr R M Shaw. It produced further evidence of the favourable effects of fluoridation.[301] These findings were backed by the Chief Medical Officer, who concluded that 'alternative measures are no effective substitute; some might contribute to better dental health but none offers such certainty of general improvement in the teeth of children'.[302]

Although support for fluoridation was widespread among local health authorities and water undertakings, since cooperation of a number of authorities was usually necessary, it was possible for a small minority to be effectively obstructive. Crossman considered using his powers under section 12 of the Health Services and Public Health Act 1968 to direct local health authorities to support fluoridation, but he concluded that this was politically impossible. Although a Fluoridation Society had been founded in 1969 to promote fluoridation, Crossman was resigned to the fact that the anti-fluoridation lobby was gaining in influence.[303] The same conclusion was confirmed by Ministers, who were not willing to go further than produce a circular for local health authorities and water undertakings setting out the latest evidence in favour of fluoridation.[304] By 1970 fluoridation was being applied within seventeen local health authorities, covering a population of only 2m. Crossman was increasingly irritated by his critics in Parliament, cautioning them that he was 'being gradually but inevitably driven to the view that we may have to legislate to deal with this problem'. Crossman's mood of petulance and frustration indicates the extent to which the momentum had been lost in this experiment in prophylactic medicine.[305]

Tobacco Smoking
The previous chapter described the irresolute meanderings of the Conservative administration over the control of cigarette promotion. This was a significant issue because reducing the consumption of cigarettes was arguably the single most effective intervention

possible within the field of preventive and promotive health. This conclusion was supported by the cumulative evidence of research. It became clear that the harmful effects of tobacco were not confined to lung cancer, but extended to cardiovascular disease and many other health problems. Britain noticeably lagged behind the USA in its responses concerning limitation of cigarette promotion.

In opposition, Labour MPs were active in anti-smoking agitation. Laurie Pavitt promoted a Cigarettes (Health Hazards) Bill, aiming to introduce warning signs on cigarette packets, and this objective was supported in debate by Robinson.[306] Wilson, although an inveterate pipe-smoker himself, when interviewed on television in January 1964 commented that he was in favour of limitations on cigarette promotion, including a ban on television advertisement and possibly also on newspaper advertisements.[307] Robinson, a heavy smoker of cigarettes,[308] discussed this question with Wilson and obtained the latter's permission to cite the television comments in an address delivered at the Royal Society of Medicine and in the House of Commons. Wilson also agreed to support Robinson's efforts to persuade an unenthusiastic Home Affairs Committee to support a ban on television advertisement of cigarettes.[309] The Ministers directly concerned with this proposal were supportive, and the Home Affairs Committee came into line. The proposal was referred to the Cabinet for further discussion.

Wilson was strongly recommended not to support the proposed restrictions, and they were also opposed by the Chancellor of the Exchequer. There were some other expressions of reservation, but the Cabinet came round to Wilson's view that additional measures were required in order to deter the young from taking up smoking.[310] Owing to keen support for the ban on cigarette advertising on television by Anthony Wedgwood Benn, the Postmaster General, Robinson was able to announce this measure on 8 February 1965 and it was introduced three months later.[311] Robinson immediately pursued the question of wider controls on tobacco advertising. With the support of the Home Affairs Committee, he embarked on discussions with manufacturers, and it was agreed to hold the possibility of legislation in reserve.[312]

A meeting of Ministers on 12 May 1965 agreed that the industry should be asked to offer voluntary limitations on tobacco advertisements and also to end cigarette packet coupon schemes.[313] Robinson met representatives of the industry on 16 September. Further discussions produced only a meagre response. The industry offered to cease advertising cigarettes in cinemas. Robinson wanted more substantial reductions in the tobacco promotion budget. He recommended to his colleagues that there should be a ban on cigarette vending machines in places accessible to children, and also a ban on coupon schemes. The Home Affairs Committee was unco-operative. Labour Ministers fell back on many of the arguments used by their Conservative predecessors. They were not favourable to legislation, or to further restrictions aimed at smokers, but it was agreed that the industry should be asked to reduce the level of its promotion expenditure.[314]

After failure of negotiations with the industry, Robinson returned to the Home Affairs Committee in October 1966, and again in January 1967 with further proposals for limiting smoking. He again called for a ban on coupon schemes, introduction of a warning notice on cigarette packets, and limitations on vending machines. He also advocated further action to restrict smoking in public places, elimination of the tobacco concession for the armed forces, removal of duty-free arrangements for travellers, and increased tax on tobacco. None of these proposals were endorsed by Ministers.[315]

Eruption of a 'coupon war' between tobacco companies, and the prospect of a rise in tobacco smoking prompted Robinson to return to his colleagues with proposals for legislation to ban coupon schemes and for other limited controls on advertising. Some Ministers were completely opposed on grounds of possible discrimination against Imperial Tobacco; others were more sympathetic and believed that it was necessary to make some response to media and public concern; but they were in no hurry to sanction legislation.[316] Robinson was permitted to make a statement threatening legislation to ban cigarette coupon gift schemes, control other promotional schemes, limit certain forms of tobacco advertising, and impose restrictions on expenditure on tobacco advertising.[317] Some months later Robinson obtained further lukewarm support from his colleagues, and reluctant agreement to proceed with legislation.[318] However, partly owing to the intervention of Crossman, who was unsympathetic to prohibition of cigarette coupons, especially in the pre-election period, Robinson's attempts to promote legislation were thwarted. This was one of the issues which contributed to the animosity between Crossman and Robinson during the transitional period leading up to establishment of DHSS in 1968. When Robinson departed from office and Crossman became Secretary of State, further initiatives of this kind were ruled out.[319] Somewhat hypocritically, Crossman maintained the fiction that the Government was committed to introducing legislation to restrict cigarette advertising and promotion.[320]

The health departments were thrown back on initiatives within their own control, especially in the field of health education. Crossman instructed the new Health Education Council to give priority to its anti-smoking campaigns.[321] The Chief Medical Officer in London was particularly vigorous in pursuit of anti-smoking policies, and his annual reports made no effort to conceal an anti-smoking perspective.[322] However, even minor advances proved awkward to achieve. The Chief Medical Officer worked hard to introduce a prohibition on smoking in public areas of the health department, and at committees associated with the health service. This effort was not entirely successful. For instance, Crossman refused to ban smoking in conference rooms in DHSS. In 1967, Robinson had written to colleagues asking them to ban smoking in premises attended by the public, but they were not willing to do more than display notices carrying the wording 'It is better not to smoke'.[323]

With Crossman's blessing, and positive support from Ennals, DHSS agreed that its main energies on the legislative front would be devoted to giving assistance to a further private member's Bill promoted by Dr John Dunwoody, aiming to introduce warning notices on cigarette packets.[324] Crossman confirmed that the Government was still considering supporting introduction of warning notices on cigarette packets.[325] Dunwoody had been one of the persistent opponents of smoking, but in October 1969 he was given a junior ministerial post in Crossman's department, which inevitably curtailed his freedom to pursue this issue.[326] The Wilson administration ran out of time before Dunwoody was able to generate greater influence for the anti-smoking faction within DHSS.

Family Planning
Provision of advice on contraception by local authorities had been permitted since the 1930s, but on the most restricted basis, being confined to Maternity and Child Welfare clinics, only as an *incidental* function, and confined to *married* women requiring the service on *medical* grounds. The NHS left these formal restrictions unchanged. The same kind of family planning assistance could be provided under section 22 of the NHS Act 1946 in connection with the care of expectant and nursing mothers. Section 28 permitted extension of this care to other women, but no schemes were approved by the Minister under this rubric. The main change came in the opportunity given to local health authorities under the NHS Act 1946 and the Local Government Act 1948 to make grants to voluntary bodies, subject to ministerial approval. By 1950 about one-third of local health authorities were providing birth control clinics, one-third were making grants to voluntary agencies, especially the Family Planning Association, while one-third took no action. Limited possibilities also existed for birth control activity on the part of general medical practitioners and regional hospital services, but these were quantitatively unimportant.[327]

During his tenure as Chief Medical Officer, Sir John Charles presided over a restrictive approach to family planning services.[328] This view was not adopted by his successor, Sir George Godber. Ministers also became more overt in their support for family planning activity. Notable in this respect was the agreement of Iain Macleod to visit the Family Planning Association on the occasion of its silver jubilee in 1955. Nevertheless, as late as 1964, the official line of the Ministry of Health on the Family Planning Association was that it was 'controversial and we are careful to avoid any appearance of approving or sponsoring'.[329]

The voluntary agencies extended their work in an important respect in 1964, with the establishment of the Brook Advisory Centres intended to give family planning advice to young people. The availability of oral contraception from 1961 onwards created a further incentive for a change in policy. A further important determinant which came to prominence during the Wilson administration was the groundswell of opinion in favour of abortion law reform. Although initial efforts with Bills sponsored by Private Members were unsuccessful, the prospect of legalisation of abortion inevitably gave rise to the conclusion that it would be illogical for the NHS to provide abortion facilities, while narrowly restricting the provision of services associated with contraception. This message was pressed by the Abortion Law Reform Association and its ally, the Family Planning Association. With the growth of influence of these organisations, the contrary view was represented by various groups who came together in the Society for the Protection of Unborn Children, which was founded in 1967.

Both as an opposition spokesman and as Minister of Health, Robinson called for more active support to be given to the Family Planning Association.[330] When in office Robinson quickly set on foot the first review of family planning policy to be undertaken since 1934.[331] This was completed in July 1965. Robinson discovered that public expenditure on family planning services was only £100,000 a year. In view of existing legal restrictions, Robinson was unable to suggest more than giving 'discreet encouragement to authorities to use what we have hitherto understood to be their powers to subscribe to voluntary bodies, such as the Family Planning Association, and to make premises available to them'.[332] Although Robinson's scheme implied only a trivial increase in expenditure, it roused objections from the Treasury, which saw this scheme as symptomatic of the Ministry of Health's tendency to want to advance on too many fronts simultaneously. The Treasury therefore advised the Ministry of Health to defer its draft circular, and return with proposals indicating the place of family planning in the order of NHS priorities.

Robinson soon reappeared with his circular and the suggestion for an additional modest but distinct change in policy. He sought permission to include clauses in a Miscellaneous Health Services Bill allowing local health authorities to provide family planning advice to all persons, and also to supply appliances and drugs on prescription. This plan was approved by the organisations consulted as an appropriately prudential first step. Leading advocates of family planning among the Medical Officers of Health preferred a more robust approach. Parallel proposals were supported in Scotland by Judith Hart, who was convinced by the argument concerning the right of women to control their fertility as expounded by Professor Sir Dugald Baird in his influential paper, 'The Fifth Freedom?'.[333]

Despite the limited scope of Robinson's scheme, the Treasury was sceptical; it acknowledged that 'free advice on family planning might help with some immigrants and by reducing a hard native core of large "problem families" which create social waste through delinquency etc', but the savings were speculative, while the costs of likely further expansion in services would be considerable.[334]

In January 1966 Robinson's proposals for a circular and legislation on family planning were taken to the Social Services Committee. He met with only moderate support from Ministers; Treasury Ministers objected to giving encouragement for expansion in local authority services at a time when they were being told to economise; other Ministers expressed qualms about possible adverse reaction, especially from the Roman Catholic church.[335] On account of possible political embarrassment, the Prime Minister was consulted by Houghton. Wilson shared his colleagues' anxieties and suggested that a change of policy on family planning should not be announced in the run-up to the General Election.[336]

The family planning circular was issued by Robinson in February 1966, primarily in order to signify his commitment to the issue.[337] The delay over the proposed change in the law created no inconvenience since there was no chance of legislation before the General Election. Afterwards, the possibility soon arose for extension of provision for family planning owing to a Private Member's Bill introduced by Edwin Brooks, the new MP for Bebington, Merseyside, who had just defeated Geoffrey Howe. Like many new MPs elected in 1966, Brooks was liberal in his social views, and personally concerned with family planning issues through his experience as a local councillor in Birkenhead.[338]

The Prime Minister granted that he had been over-anxious and that his fears had 'proved totally unfounded' about the political disadvantages of Government sponsorship of legislation on family planning; he encouraged Robinson to give full backing to the new private member's Bill.[339] The Treasury raised no objection, on the understanding that local authorities would be able to levy charges.[340]

The sensitivity of the family planning issue was still sufficient to cause last-moment complications. The Scottish Ministers, Ross and Millan became fearful of adverse political consequences if Scotland introduced further liberalisation of family planning services without more consultations, particularly if the Bill was inexplicit about the availability of services to younger unmarried women.[341] Ross accordingly informed Robinson that 'we are not quite ready' to make these changes.[342]

The Brooks National Health Service (Family Planning) Bill received its Second Reading on 17 February 1967. To the surprise of its advocates, the Bill sped through its parliamentary stages with remarkably little opposition and no significant amendment. It received the Royal Assent on 28 June 1967. All the emotive energy was channelled into David Steel's Medical Termination of Pregnancy Bill, which aroused unremitting controversy in Parliament from the moment of its inception. The Second Reading took place in July 1966. This Bill survived to become the Abortion Act, reaching the statute book on 27 October 1967.[343] The combatants locked in conflict over abortion had no surplus energy to expend over a trivial liberalisation in the law relating to family planning.

The National Health Service (Family Planning) Act 1967 gave local health authorities in England and Wales the power to provide contraceptive advice and treatment to anyone for whom it was required. Advice was free, but a charge could be levied for prescription and supply in non-medical cases, as in other local health authority services, at the discretion of the authority.[344] In Scotland similar powers were introduced through section 15 of the Health Services and Public Health Act 1968. However, the Home Affairs Committee intervened to prevent implementation of the new powers in Scotland, ostensibly on grounds of manpower economies. Ross complained about discrimination against Scotland. This second deferment was unfortunate for him because it gave rise to the impression that he disfavoured family planning.[345] This set-back was disappointing to the advocates of planned parenthood because local authority family planning services were developed even less in Scotland than in England and Wales. The Home Affairs Committee rescinded its decision, but the circular allowing extension of family planning facilities in Scotland was not issued until August 1970.[346]

Between 1967 and 1970 family planning and abortion became the object of increasing public attention. These services were supported on the grounds of women's rights by liberal opinion, whereas on the right they were advocated by those fearing population growth among social problem groups, especially immigrants in the inner city areas.

248

Notwithstanding the noisy and emotive debate over population questions, and the emergence of dangerous racist overtones, the 1967 legislation made little difference to the family planning services. Services provided by the Family Planning Association continued to predominate. Indeed, with the increasing appreciation that domiciliary services were necessary to reach deprived sections of the community, it was the Family Planning Association which received a government grant to train health visitors for this purpose. By 1969 only 25 per cent of local health authorities were implementing the 1967 Act. As in other services administered by local health authorities, there were big disparities between areas. Authorities like Islington and Camden were active in this field; by the spring of 1970 they were preparing to introduce completely free services. Crossman expressed disappointment that of the 204 local authorities, only 34 had developed an adequate family planning service, 129 possessed a restrictive service, whereas 40 had no service at all. On this account, he was under pressure to make the local authority family planning services mandatory, and he sympathised with this objective, but regretted that this was not possible under the current rate support arrangements.[347]

One obvious omission in the family planning services was absence of activity on the part of hospital authorities. With the support of Crossman and seemingly in the face of opposition from some of his officials, in 1969, for the first time, hospital authorities were encouraged to play their part in co-ordinated local family planning services.[348] A free family planning service was advocated by Crossman, both in his meetings with officials, and in his evidence to the Select Committee on Science and Technology investigation into population growth.[349] As noted below in chapter V, moves towards this objective under the Heath administration presented the Government with unanticipated political difficulties.

(vii) NURSING PAY AND PROFESSION
Salmon and Mayston

As noted in the previous chapter, the Government believed that its perpetual squabbles with the nursing profession over pay might be relieved if senior nurses were better integrated into the NHS management structure and rewarded accordingly.[350] The Ministry of Health hoped that the reorganisation of hospital services consequent upon the hospital plan would stimulate adoption of new patterns of nursing administration. It was expected that general hospitals and nurse training schools would be amalgamated into larger groups, while hospitals in the mental sector were expected to run-down fairly rapidly and their functions be transferred to general hospitals. These factors, together with the changes in nursing ascribable to the advance of medical science, suggested that there was a strong case for review of the changing work pattern of senior nursing staff. Agitation of the Staff Side of the Nurses and Midwives Whitley Council for increases in remuneration to reflect the higher responsibilities of senior nurses created a further imperative for such a review.

Characteristically, Powell agreed to an enquiry, provided that it was 'astringent' in its approach and designed for the objective of 'getting better results with fewer'.[351] Officials agreed that the general aims for the proposed review were:

> to see a clear chain of command established in nursing services from the HMC (or BG) down to the management of the individual ward; a recognition of the importance of management as distinct from skill in nursing techniques; and an economical use of manpower by defining and limiting the various responsibilities of management. In this way there should be streamlining and concentration of talent and effort with a good deal of simplification of the existing grades.[352]

The Scottish Department of Health agreed to participate in this enquiry.[353] The Treasury raised no objection, providing assurances were given that the secretary to the committee would be able to exercise a strong influence.[354] Much difficulty was experienced in reaching agreement on the balance of membership and in identifying a suitable chairperson. Further delays were caused by the disputes concerning pay. The senior nursing staff review was not finally established until July 1963, under the chairmanship of Mr Brian L Salmon, a member of the family associated with the Joseph Lyons bakery and restaurant concern. Salmon was a member of the Board of Governors of Westminster Hospital. With respect to membership, there was little support within the health departments for a committee composed entirely of nurses. The departments favoured placing nurses in minority, or giving them small majority. It was finally agreed to have an equal balance between nurse and non-nurse membership. When an academic from the field of management declined an invitation to serve on the committee at the last moment, nurses and midwives were left with five of the nine members. When Salmon is included, only four out of the ten members were women. Nurses predicted that their influence would be heavily outweighed by the non-nursing membership and secretariat. Disquiet about the composition of the committee particularly emanated from nurse tutors and the mental health sector, both of which felt underrepresented, and this criticism was repeated after the presentation of the report.[355]

The terms of reference of the Salmon committee were 'to advise on the senior nursing staff structure in the hospital service (ward sister and above), the administrative functions of the respective grades, and the methods of preparing staff to occupy them'. The Salmon Committee met for the first time on 18 September 1963. The Committee embarked on an exhaustive programme of visits and evidence gathering. The report was not drafted until after the change of administration. It was completed in March 1965 and published on 12 May 1966.[356] The report itself was an exemplary product, well-organised, fully-argued, and comprehensive, without containing masses of otiose material. The text was 115 pages, and it contained about the same length of tabulations and appendices. In its effort to reflect the latest style of management thinking, it adopted a vocabulary which traditionalists found inaccessible. One senior medical figure complained that the 'new language is very confusing and at times rather ganglionlike'.[357]

The main Salmon recommendations were to introduce a new grading structure based on first line, middle and top management, to organise nursing services on the basis of definite 'spheres of authority', identified as sections, units, areas and divisions, and to introduce management training courses for nurses prior to their promotion. A new grading structure was designed to provide acceptable opportunities for career advancement in either specialised nursing, teaching, or nursing administration, although the latter was where the greatest financial inducements were likely to be found. The new grading structure extended from the Grade 10 Chief Nursing Officer down to Staff Nurses at Grade 5. The Salmon Committee considered completely abandoning the title Matron, but finally agreed that it should be retained for those in Grade 7 and above because 'it has a long and honoured tradition and has profound significance to the general public'.[358] The Salmon report also made recommendations for relief of nurse administrators from duties such as organising catering or cleaning, which it was proposed to delegate to specialist officers in these fields.

The general response to the Salmon Report was positive, even enthusiastic, although the report aroused many different and sometimes conflicting expectations.[359] Salmon was particularly attractive to senior nurses because it promised them power and parity with other leading professional elites within the NHS. For senior nurses, the Salmon structure promised that the 'present rigid and authoritarian system' would become 'merely a hideous memory'.[360] For those lower down the hierarchy, there was a fear that a new authoritarian system was being born. The main reservation related to the effects of the expansion in numbers of nurse managers above the level of ward sister, which was likely to result in loss from the wards of experienced sisters, who would be impossible to replace. It was also suspected that the new structure would erode the influence and responsibility of ward sisters. The new grading structure was criticised for being over-complicated. With respect to the main groups of nurses, the chief reservations emanated from nurse tutors, who saw themselves disadvantaged by the new career structure, compared with nurse administrators and equivalent teaching grades in technical colleges.[361] The report was also rapidly overtaken by events with respect to the administrative structure of the health service, which threatened a complete reconstruction of services and their management. As noted in chapter IV, this possibility was taken into account by many reports dating from this period, but not by the Salmon Report.[362]

The health departments were committed to the Salmon approach to nursing management, but they realised that substantial additional costs would be incurred in implementing the new grading structure, the elaborate training proposals, the new national and regional staff committees, and the staffing of services no longer performed by senior nurses. In March 1967, with the agreement of Ross, Robinson announced proposals for implementing the Salmon reforms in England, Scotland and Wales.[363]

Reacting to Treasury vigilance respecting costs, the health departments worked out a plan for the controlled and phased implementation of the Salmon reforms, calculated to ensure that the new grading structure was not introduced precipitously for the purposes of financial advantage to senior nurses without proportionate increases in efficiency.[364] The plans made by the health departments anticipated incremental progress towards introducing the Salmon structures. A National Nursing Staff Committee with functions connected with management training and supervision over the selection of staff was appointed and began work in 1968. It was intended to proceed by pilot schemes, initially in only some 20 hospital groups in England and Wales. This plan was undermined by the NBPI Report No.60, dated March 1968, which is discussed below, which necessitated speeding up of the Salmon operation. However, by the end of 1971, only about one-quarter of hospital groups had made substantial progress in introducing the Salmon structure; a further third had not even appointed their Chief Nursing Officer.[365] Regardless of the degree of progress, the NBPI report insisted on introduction of Salmon grading structures on 1 January 1969. Therefore, contrary to the intentions of the health departments, the new system of remuneration was introduced before the management structures or training schemes were in place.

The Salmon review was concerned exclusively with hospital nursing. No allowance was made for a parallel review of nursing in the community sector. Immediately the Salmon Report was produced, community nurses expressed alarm that they were being relegated to the sidelines. This was regarded as an unfortunate defect, given the alleged high priority for community care.[366] The prospect of health service reorganisation further exacerbated unease within community nursing. Accordingly in December 1968, the departments established a committee under Mr E L Mayston of DHSS to examine the application of Salmon principles to local authority nursing services. This review was quickly accomplished. The report was completed in the summer of 1969 and it was published without delay.[367] The Mayston Report envisaged that the Salmon principles would be applied to local authority nursing, and it recommended a geographical rather than functional division for management purposes. However, by this stage it was clear that whatever arrangements were adopted would be of a strictly provisional nature, since both the forthcoming Seebohm changes and the scheme for health service reorganisation entailed the elimination of separately administered community nursing services.

Remuneration
Under Labour, the 350,000 nurses and midwives employed by the NHS faced the awkward task of securing pay increases sufficient to keep their earnings in line with other comparable groups in a deteriorating situation with respect to inflation, while also attempting to secure adjustments to eliminate inherited disadvantages, and establish pay scales suitable for a profession that was advancing and changing more rapidly than at any stage in its history. Although this process was by no means painless, the degree of trauma was much less than under the Powell regime.

The first years of the Wilson administration witnessed minor technical adjustments in pay. In 1964 an agreement was reached to reduce the 88 hour fortnight to 84 hours, according to local agreements scheduled to be in place by January 1966.[368] In response to a claim submitted in November 1964, the Nurses and Midwives Whitley Council negotiated an economic increase averaging at 11 per cent, to run from July 1965 until July 1967.[369] The new salary scale for a staff nurse was £690-£880. This award was generally accepted, but nurses noted that teachers had received a marginally higher awards.

In May 1967, the Staff Side submitted a major claim, which related to general economic factors, but also regrading associated with the recommendations of Salmon Report, and also further special claims connected with the long-running attempt to reduce hours of work and obtain an extension of overtime pay and special duty allowances. This claim would have entailed an average increase of 33.4 per cent, at a cost of £72m. Given the size of this claim and problems of relating it to criteria for exceptional pay increases laid down in the White Paper on Prices and Incomes Policy (Cmnd.3235), Robinson advised referring the claim to the National Board for Prices and Incomes for a full review. Ross, who inclined to hold down nursing pay in order to ease his dealings with Scottish teachers, opposed this suggestion on the grounds that the NBPI might respond with embarrassingly generous recommendations, which would be impossible to resist. However, the ministerial Prices and Incomes Committee sided with Robinson, and his suggestion was also endorsed by both sides of the Whitley Council.[370]

The NBPI adopted an ambitious remit for its investigation; it undertook the first full-scale review of nursing pay and recruitment since the beginning of the NHS. Its report was published in March 1968.[371] This contained wide-ranging recommendations, relating to training and management as well as pay. For instance, it included proposals for lowering the age of entry to nurse training, the amalgamation of nurse training schools, increasing the independence of nurse training schools, and for making conditions endured by nurse trainees less punitive. The NBPI also made suggestions for increasing the use of married women as part-time nurses, for improvements in the planning of shift work and off-duty periods, and for pooling staff in order to alleviate staff shortages in the less popular specialisms. The NBPI even suggested establishing a National Nursing Management Council to supervise the introduction of new working methods. Finally, like other committees of enquiry active at this period, the NBPI concluded that the existing organisation of the hospital service was inimical to the progress of nursing.

With respect to central issue of pay, the NBPI recommended a two-stage award, the first being a 14 per cent increase on basic rates with effect from 1 October 1967, and the second from January 1969, involving increases ranging between 5 and 9 per cent in connection with the Salmon grading structure. Slightly higher increases were recommended for nurses in the mental and geriatric fields. The NBPI recommended applying the new grading structure from 1 January 1969, as an inducement for NHS authorities to speed up the introduction of the new management arrangements in nursing. The NBPI was in favour of premium rates of pay for weekends and nights, but it accepted that these would require phased implementation. Whereas the Staff Side claim envisaged for the staff nurse a scale of £800-£1,200 from July 1967, the NBPI recommendations granted the staff nurse (new equivalent Grade 5 nurse) £785-£925 from 1 January 1969.[372]

The NBPI calculated that its recommendations represented the 'equivalent of an annual rate of compound increase of $3\frac{1}{2}$ per cent'.[373] Although the Treasury grumbled about the award, other departments pointed out that there was no basis for rejection or modification. The NBPI recommendations were accordingly ratified by the Government and duly applied by the Nurses and Midwives Whitley Council.[374] Despite its attractive features, this award failed to stem a new tide of dissatisfaction within the nursing profession. As noticed above, the award fell far short of the original claim. Although the proposals were in some respects forward-looking, they caused unease on all sides. Both sides had reservations about early implementation of Salmon gradings. The Management Side feared that this would make staff resistant to the Salmon changes, whereas the Staff Side believed it would prompt management to fix salaries for top posts at artificially low levels. Opening up of prospects for much higher remuneration for a handful of Grade 10 Regional Nursing Officers and Chief Nursing Officers of hospital groups was insufficient to suppress the anxieties of the lower grades. Nurse tutors and staff nurses in particular felt undervalued. However, the main initial indignation related to the new 'pay-as-you-eat' arrangements, which were disadvantageous to the most junior grades. The NBPI proposed that all nurses should in future pay for their meals, which it estimated to add £100 a year to the expenses of resident student nurses.[375] These nurses were in the event compensated by reduction of their boarding charge from £156 to £50 a year, which was insufficient, with the result that resident student nurses and other junior grades discovered that the effects of pay-as-you-eat wiped out any advantage stemming from the NBPI award. [376] The pay-as-you-eat system inspired vocal protest in the early months of 1969 and contributed to a mood of disappointment concerning the NBPI report. The Government was slow to address this obvious anomaly.[377] Officials initially worked out a scheme for compensating low-paid nurses with meal vouchers worth about £50 a year, but this was scrapped in favour of a further £18 reduction in the annual charge for board and lodging, and waiving charges for hot drinks taken outside meals. The Chairman of the Management Side argued against any concession, calculating that protests would soon subside. Both officials and Management Side underestimated the depth of indignation among nurses. The £18 proposal was rejected by the Staff Side, which demanded either a payment of an additional £1 a week, or vouchers of equivalent value.[378] Crossman and Serota sympathised with the nurses and called for a more generous response and also for an early review of student nurse remuneration. Jenkins and Castle rejected the proposal for a general review, but agreed reluctantly to a proposal for vouchers or a meals allowance of equivalent value.[379] This proposal was approved by the Prices and Incomes Committee.[380] The cash meals allowance of £48 for younger resident students, pupils, nursing auxiliaries and nursing assistants was conceded with reluctance on the part of the Chairman of the Management Side.[381]

The NBPI award expired in April 1970. The Staff Side entered a new claim in November 1969. The character of this bid was influenced by the general tide of industrial unrest as well as factors intrinsic to nursing. The annual conference of the Royal College of Nursing held in October 1969 indicated the strength of feeling among nurses; it was even claimed that morale among nurses was lower than at any time in the past.[382] Apart from a general increase in pay, the most expensive item in the claim was for a reduction in the working week from 42 to 40 hours. The new claim, if met in full, would have added about 37 per cent to the salary bill, with the general salary increase accounting for about 28 per cent. Consistent with the Salmon philosophy, the largest awards were advocated for the more senior grades, whereas the proposed increase for first-year students was 18.5 per cent. The claim for staff nurses would have amended their scale to £1,000-£1,325, which represented an increase of 27.5 per cent at the bottom of the scale, and 34.5 per cent at the top.

On the basis of soundings with the Staff Side, DHSS recommended a generous offer on pay, on condition that other aspects of the claim were sacrificed. Discussions among officials edged up the targets until they arrived at totals only marginally lower than the claim. Ministers ratified this approach on 17 November 1969.[383] Ministerial discussions of the nursing pay claim were delayed by the illness of Crossman. The issue was considered by the ministerial Prices and Incomes Committee on 31 December 1969. Crossman proposed to grant the claim for higher pay virtually in full, but defer consideration of reduction in the working week. This increase averaged 24.5 per cent, which would add £70m to the NHS pay bill. He argued against staging the settlement. His justification for this generous award closely followed the case made by the Staff Side: a substantial settlement was required on grounds of low pay, unsocial working conditions, demanding work, rising skill requirements, fall in recruitment, high levels of wastage, undesirable reliance on immigrant nurses, and the state of crisis existing in long-stay hospitals. The collective disadvantages of nursing had given rise to 'demonstrations on a scale and of a type in which nurses have never engaged before'. A generous pay award was expected by the public and demanded by nurses. This would be insufficient to solve the severe problems facing nursing, but it was an essential part of the package of measures to deal with the nursing crisis predicted by the health departments. Crossman admonished his colleagues that they should not repeat the mistake of the Macmillan administration, which had allowed Powell to make nurses the first victims of their incomes policy.[384]

Unconvinced by Crossman's argument, the Treasury contended that there was no serious problem of recruitment, that nurses were keeping in step with non-graduate teachers in their pay, and that high skills were demanded only from a minority. The size of the award was therefore a matter of political calculation. Treasury officials recommended a staged settlement, involving 10 per cent in the first year and 8 per cent in the second.[385]

Crossman's proposals were better received at the Prices and Incomes Committee. Jenkins argued for a lower settlement of 16 per cent over two years, whereas Short was unhappy about the linkage proposed between teaching and nursing salaries, but Crossman carried the debate with a proposal for a two-stage increase, granting 15.3 per cent from April 1970, followed by 7.7 per cent from April 1971.[386] This offer was described within the health departments as the most generous ever made to nurses and midwives.

At the Nurses and Midwives Whitley Council in January 1970, to the surprise of the health departments, and indicative of the high state of militancy among the nurses, Crossman's offer was rejected.[387] A further complication emerged in the form of a generous pay award to the armed forces, the announcement of which was imminent. Crossman urged that settlement with the nurses needed to be made in advance of the forces award. Jenkins advised the Prime Minister that he was prepared to accept generous treatment of teachers and nurses, but he would resist complete surrender.[388] A meeting between Jenkins, Castle and Crossman agreed to a minor improvement of the second stage to 9.2 per cent, to bring the award into line with the forces settlement. Jenkins insisted that no further concession was permissible without collective consideration by Ministers.[389] On 10 February 1970 the Management Side proposed three different permutations of the two-stage offer, but these were rejected by the Staff Side, which asked if a one-year offer might be forthcoming. The Management Side insisted that any one-year settlement would be subject to a 15.3 per cent limit, which was unacceptable to the Staff Side. The latter was adamant that it wanted a one-year offer approximating to its original claim.

In a gathering atmosphere of crisis, nursing pay was referred to the Cabinet. Crossman proposed either offering a one-year settlement of 20 per cent, or bringing forward the second stage to October 1970. Either suggestion was odious to the Treasury, which felt that nurses' pay was getting completely out of hand. The Prime Minister was cautioned by Jenkins that Healey in defence and Crossman in the health service were precipitating a 'wage explosion'. Ministers had demonstrated that they were 'never prepared to stand firm when it came to the crunch in any particular case'. Jenkins insisted that 20 per cent public sector wage increases would make it impossible to run the economy.[390] Naturally, these apocalyptic anxieties took no account of the low base-line from which nurses were negotiating. Even if the current claim had been granted in full, staff nurses would at the top of their scale have earned only the average wage of male manual workers. Also the proposed settlement scarcely maintained their parity with non-graduate teachers.[391] The ministerial Prices and Incomes Committee failed to reach agreement on Crossman's proposals. The Cabinet considered various permutations, but fell short of agreeing to Crossman's favoured option of 20 per cent for one year. Crossman complained that Ross failed to support him at a crucial moment. Crossman also blamed himself for leaving the meeting before the decision was recorded.[392] The question of an amended offer was referred for further discussions between Jenkins, Castle and Crossman, who considered yet further permutations entailing bringing the second stage forwards and marginally reducing its amount; they also agreed to a one-year offer of 20 per cent, but only as a fall-back position.[393] This approach was sanctioned by the Cabinet.

Chairman of the Management Side favoured insisting on a two-stage agreement, believing that minor concessions would be sufficient to secure final agreement from the Staff Side. This prospect was undermined by the appearance in the press of an informed leak of the Cabinet discussions, revealing that Ministers were prepared to concede a single-stage award of 20 per cent.[394] This leak was profoundly embarrassing for the Government; not only did it undermine the Management Side's negotiating position with respect to nurses, it also set the seal on the general escalation of salaries in the public sector. Crossman faced a formal protest and was obliged to apologise to the Whitley Council; his draft letters and diaries show that he was unsure whether the leak originated with Ministers in his own department.[395]

The Management Side felt humiliated by the leak and threatened to reject the health departments' request to give precedence to three alternative proposals for a two-stage award. Only with the intervention of Serota were they prevented from simultaneously presenting all the alternatives, including the one-year 20 per cent offer.[396] The Nurses and Midwives Whitley Council meeting ran a predictable course. The Management Side went through the ritual of presenting its three two-stage packages. These were duly rejected by the Staff Side, which pressed for 22 per cent, but agreed to a settlement 'in the region of 20 per cent' operative from 1 April 1970.[397]

The nurses therefore obtained an offer approximating to their original claim. The public controversy was therefore ended, but difficulties were still experienced behind the scenes in the course of working out the details of the application of the award by the Nurses and Midwives Whitley Council. Although the general terms of the agreement were announced by Crossman on 2 March, the final details were not sorted out until 24 March 1970.[398] The new award placed staff nurses on the scale £930-£1,182, which was just short of the symbolic target £1,000 adopted in the original claim for their starting salary.

As the Treasury predicted, the award to nurses was not without its parallels elsewhere in the NHS. By the spring of 1970, the Government faced claims for increases of 25 per cent from many groups of NHS personnel, including certain administrative and clerical grades, medical laboratory technicians, as well as claims for rises of 20 per cent or above for ancillary workers and professions supplementary to medicine. The health departments assumed that large settlements for other groups would soon prompt nurses into further agitation for higher pay and shorter working hours.

Committee on Nursing

Crossman's statement on the pay settlement also gave the terms of reference for an independent enquiry into nursing, to be headed by Professor Asa Briggs. This initiative was designed to give further reassurance that the Government recognised the case for a fundamental review of the problems facing the nursing profession.

The possibility of an enquiry had been under discussion for nearly two years. Nursing organisations had on previous occasions argued that a comprehensive enquiry into nursing was necessary. This request was usually made in the context of indignation against the Government, especially during crises over remuneration. During the Wilson administration, there developed a much higher level of initiative in the field of nursing policy, but the various enquiries, instigated by a variety of bodies, represented at best an unsatisfactory and piecemeal approach to issues that required more authoritative examination. Not surprisingly, their findings were open to objection, and were often inconsistent with one another. These recommendations were also regularly a source of embarrassment to the Government. The prospect of reorganisation of the NHS, or major changes in care, such as the shift towards community care, also raised important questions about the future of the nursing profession.

Apart from the Salmon, Mayston and NBPI Reports discussed above, the other main initiatives of the Wilson era were the Platt Report into nurse education instigated by the Royal College of Nursing, the curriculum revision undertaken by the General Nursing Council, and a departmental committee chaired by the Chief

Nursing Officer on nurse tutors. The Platt Committee was a controversial venture and involved much dispute. Its findings were seen as radical, indeed revolutionary. It called for complete reorganisation of nursing education, fewer schools of nursing, which would be granted a high level of independence under Regional Councils for Nursing Education. The Platt Report revived the idea that nurses should be firmly established as full-time students, receiving educational grants like other full-time students. The Platt Committee also proposed lowering the age of recruitment, but increasing the level of educational qualification of students. [399] Although the health departments were generally sympathetic with the Platt recommendations, they were regarded as completely unrealistic on account of their manpower and financial implications. Although the Platt Report was approved by neither the health departments nor the General Nursing Council, on account of acclamation at the grass roots, the departments were forced to make some response. Somewhat belatedly, the Ministry of Health drew up proposals for minor improvements in training and for promoting research and more imaginative experiments in nurse education. A lukewarm ministerial statement and the relevant HM circular (usually known as the 'pink' nursing circular, signifying the colour of paper used when the contents were regarded as particularly important) failed to convince nurses that the Government was committed to more than cosmetic changes in nurse education.[400] The circular also raised the suspicion that the Ministry of Health was trespassing into GNC territory. The ideas of the Platt Committee continued to find favour, and many of them were reflected in NBPI Report No.60.

Further improvements were dependent on the GNC, which exercised statutory authority over nurse education. The GNC commanded incomplete confidence, and its recommendations were made without full regard for the manpower considerations of the NHS. Following the Platt Report, the GNC embarked on a revision of the syllabus for nurse training, and this was introduced in 1969. Many of the changes were acceptable to service organisations, but hospital and local authorities were displeased that there had been little consultation over the changes. Local authorities in particular complained that they lacked the capacity to provide teaching for the extended tuition required in the field of community nursing. Hospital authorities were perturbed about increased costs, and they were sceptical about being able to find the additional tutors required for the new syllabus, or replacement staff for nurses under instruction or seconded out.[401]

In response to the anxieties of nurse tutors about their treatment in the Salmon Report and the NBPI Report, in 1968, the Ministry of Health set up a working party jointly with the RCN and the GNC, and chaired by the Chief Nursing Officer, to examine the numbers and kinds of teachers required for nurse training. It was suggested that this working party might extend its activities to consider other relevant problems in nursing. However, it soon became apparent that this working party was not likely to command sufficient authority within the profession.[402] DHSS was concerned that the working party was repeating the mistakes of the Platt Committee by concentrating on long-term and unrealistic objectives, whereas the department needed suggestions on practicable methods for improving tutor:student ratios. The draft report of the Nurse Tutor Working Party was produced at the end of 1969. This concentrated on minor short-term improvements in training, mostly of a kind congenial to DHSS. Since this report encapsulated the likely contents of departmental submissions to any definitive enquiry, DHSS was reluctant to allow its publication, but at the insistence of its partners in the working party, in April 1970 the report was circulated to relevant NHS authorities.[403] The department was anxious to disband the working party to prevent any over-enthusiastic initiatives, but delicate relations with the GNC and the RCN argued for the working party being allowed to fall into abeyance without formal disbandment.

The plethora of competing advice outlined above risked creating a chaotic situation in nursing. This situation was bad for morale and it gave nurses little assurance that their ailing profession would be restored, or that the Government possessed any real command of policy. There was clearly a need for new and decisive leadership on nursing policy. The proposal for a general review of nursing policy was favoured by the RCN, in all probability on the model of the Royal Commission on Medical Education. In 1968, the RCN suggested informally that a Royal Commission would be a suitable vehicle to balance the competing claims of manpower and training, and introduce ordered progress into the nursing profession. Discussions concerning the merits of this proposition began in earnest in the autumn of 1968.

Opinion within the Ministry of Health/DHSS was divided over the merits of a full-scale enquiry. Some officials believed that only an authoritative review would solve the practical problems relating to training and recruitment, and restore confidence within the profession. A review of this kind would fill the vacuum created by deficiencies in leadership from the GNC. Only such an enquiry was likely to finally lay to rest the ghost of Platt, and prevent the working party on nurse tutors from pursuing its unrealistic programme. Another camp believed that an enquiry could be influenced by the health departments to stifle trends in policy which it found embarrassing, while a lengthy enquiry would be especially useful in delaying implementation of the many expensive changes that were in prospect in nursing services. Others appreciated the argument for a review, but doubted whether the time was ripe, suggesting that it would be better to wait until greater experience had been gained with the Salmon reforms. The advocates of delay also applied the curious argument that the nature of nursing was likely to be better defined at some date in the future.[404] There was also vocal opposition to an enquiry on the grounds that it would inevitably make recommendations that were expensive to implement and embarrassing to reject. Such an initiative coming at a time of increasing financial stringency was likely to fuel complaints that policy initiatives in the NHS were taken without any regard for overall priorities.[405] This group believed that 'following all the difficulties there have been over Todd, I think the Treasury will take a lot of convincing that we ought to embark on what might be seen as the nursing counterpart'.[406]

The prevailing view held that the balance of argument favoured a high-level enquiry, providing that suitable terms of reference could be agreed. On the merits of the case, and in light of reservations expressed about the Todd enquiry, it was doubted whether Ministers would agree to a Royal Commission. The health departments also favoured a modest exercise on the grounds that it would be more susceptible to departmental influence. In order to maintain a strong degree of control and limit opportunities for escalation of costs, it was proposed initially to introduce tight limitations in the remit of the committee. It was suggested that the review should address the central dilemma of nurse training, by finding 'an authoritative compromise between modern and effective nurse training and the needs of the service for student and pupil nurses to nurse in the wards'.[407] DHSS suggested limiting the review to the organisation of nurse training, so avoiding possible conflict with the GNC on the question of the content of education. It was also proposed to exclude consideration of post-basic training, management training, midwifery, health visiting, district nursing, or national statutory arrangements. As noted below, most of these restrictions were abandoned as a result of the Prime Minister's insistence that the political situation demanded a wide-ranging enquiry.

The first interdepartmental meeting to discuss the possibility of an enquiry into nursing was held on 20 December 1968. There was general agreement that an enquiry should be established, and September 1969 was adopted as the provisional starting date. SHHD insisted on the inclusion of midwifery as a condition for its participation.[408] Ministers were briefed in the summer of 1969; they confirmed that a committee of enquiry was preferable to a Royal Commission.[409] By this stage, the dissatisfaction over nursing remuneration added to the argument for a definitive investigation.

Discussions with the Treasury and CSD produced an unexpectedly positive response. DHSS naturally argued that an enquiry sponsored by the Government was likely to produce more palatable conclusions than piecemeal changes dictated by outside organisations. The Treasury and CSD were suspicious about cost implications, but allowed the proposed enquiry to go forward on condition that a suitable chairman could be found, that this person should be briefed about the expectations of the Government, that the health departments' evidence should be discussed with the Treasury and other departments, and that the terms of reference should open by indicating the limits of likely availability of human resources.[410]

The growing state of restlessness among nurses persuaded Ministers to speed up their deliberations on the nursing enquiry. The Prime Minister showed close interest in developments. Wilson suggested that a broad-ranging enquiry was needed to satisfy the nurses, but he also insisted on urgency of its operations, hoping at least for an interim report within six months.[411] The Prime Minister also asked Crossman to report on steps being taken to improve morale among nurses. He added as an afterthought: 'On the nursing enquiry I believe that there is no time to be lost. So when you say 'shortly' I hope it will be shortly'. Crossman responded immediately with seven proposals for improving morale, the proposed terms of reference for the enquiry, and he suggested three possible candidates (all male) for the chair.

Wilson displayed keen interest in the choice of the person to head the nursing enquiry.[412] With little delay, Professor Asa Briggs was asked and agreed to accept the chair.[413] It was then necessary to hold informal meetings with the main nursing organisations and engage in the delicate task of selecting members for the committee. The membership had not been finally decided when the terms of reference of the Committee on Nursing and identity of the chairman were announced on 2 March 1970.[414] Indeed, of the provisional list of members of the committee submitted to Professor Briggs on 3 March, only five figured among the fifteen members eventually selected.[415] The tenure of the Labour administration ran out just as the Briggs Committee was commencing its work. This committee will be further considered in chapter V.

One further initiative which ran into the Heath administration was the preparation of the circular 'Action to improve the Nursing Situation', HM(70)35, which was finally issued in June 1970.[416] As noted above, this originated from the Prime Minister's urgent request for Crossman to take steps to improve the morale of nurses. The circular contained many mundane suggestions, but its primary concern was to promote understanding of Salmon principles. In particular it emphasised that senior nurses should be recognised by NHS authorities as important figures in the management structure. The Salmon grading exercise endowed nurses with a level of seniority which placed them on an equal footing with other senior management personnel. The Salmon reforms and the subsequent politically-induced drive to reaffirm the high status of nurses further shifted thinking about management in the NHS in the direction of multidisciplinary and consensus management. As noted in chapter VI, the nursing reforms set a precedent, which soon proved important when the structure of management for the reorganised National Health Service came under consideration during the Heath administration.

(viii) REMUNERATING DOCTORS AND DENTISTS

As noted in the previous chapter, the Review Body on doctors' and dentists' remuneration failed to stem the tide of anxiety among general medical practitioners. Labour inherited a growing crisis. As the Lancet remarked, 'in the history of general medical practice in this country, 1965 is likely to be remembered either as a year of crisis surmounted or as a year of total disaster'.[417] During 1964 tension mounted among general practitioners. Their dissatisfaction with the 14 per cent award effective from April 1963 precipitated their 1964 claim for a 32 per cent increase. As already noted, the 1963 award was made on the understanding that it was intended to be effective for three years. Only changed circumstances would justify modification of the award, and it was far from evident that the circumstances of 1964 were sufficiently changed to merit anything like a 32 per cent award.

In June 1964, the Review Body commenced its discussions on general practitioners' remuneration.[418] The fifth report dealing with this question was prepared during December. Preparation of this report was remitted to officials. By contrast with the anxious deliberations over the first report, the Review Body treated its recommendations as a formality, without expectation that they were likely to arouse a high degree of controversy.[419] The report was presented to the Prime Minister on 25 January 1965, and it was published on 8 February.[420]

The underlying reasoning adopted by the Review Body was aptly summarised by the Chairman:

...we ought to recommend some increase because:
(a) the fall in numbers (of doctors) justifies it;

(b) I think that the consequences of recommending no increase could be extremely serious;

264

(c) some new money would facilitate the introduction of the sensible new schemes for direct reimbursement of some practice expenses.

On the other hand we must avoid an increase so large that the hospital doctors will feel bound to come back with a leap-frogging claim.[421]

Thus, in framing its recommendations, the Review Body was clearly influenced by general medico-political calculations, as well as by economic and professional factors. In the interests of protecting the higher status of consultants, the Review Body favoured limiting the award to general practitioners. Since some concession was necessary for prudential reasons, a small all-round increase was regarded as appropriate. As in 1963, the distribution system had the effect of deflecting much of the award away from the majority of general practitioners. Compared with a claim amounting to a total of about £20m, the award was only £5.5m, and most of this was specified for purposes associated with encouraging good practice. Initially, Ministers were relieved by the response of the Review Body. The award was accepted by the Cabinet on the recommendation of the Sub-committee of Prices and Incomes of the Economic Development Committee, but with some concern that it might not be palatable to the profession.[422]

The Review Body must have been naive if it believed that this echo of the 1963 award would suppress the sense of injustice harboured by general practitioners. As in the previous year, the BMA leadership seems to have misjudged the mood of the rank and file. Initially, the GMSC was disinclined to provoke a crisis which might jeopardise the continuation of the Review Body procedure, which it emphasized was a fundamental and hard-won gain for the profession. Doctors were told that it was unrealistic to expect the Review Body invariably to produce an outcome favourable to the professions.[423] Within a month, in response to a hostile response from militants, encouraged by some members of the GMSC, the conciliatory line was abandoned and general practitioners were asked to place their undated resignations in the hands of the British Medical Guild for use from 1 April onwards.[424] According to a Gallup Poll, the militant stance adopted by the BMA leadership was supported by 74 per cent of general practitioners. It also enjoyed support of 55 per cent of a sample of patients, although this compared unfavourably with the 90 per cent support for the nurses in 1962.[425] With the notable exception of the *Daily Telegraph*, this exercise in confrontation evoked little sympathy in the press. Even the *Lancet* reprimanded the BMA for its inconsistency, rejection of the findings of arbitration, its appearance of obscurantism, and for gratuitously picking a quarrel with a Government that was negotiating constructively on their grievances concerning conditions of employment and on the method of determining their income and reimbursement for practice expenses. The *Lancet* contended that if doctors were dissatisfied with the consequences of the system of remuneration in force since 1948, indeed in many respects since 1911, this was the fault of the profession itself for having rejected all attempts to modify these arrangements.[426]

The negotiators on behalf of the profession avoided questioning the scale of the award, but instead fastened on what they regarded as unacceptable conditions imposed on the distribution of the greater part of the £5.5m award. The GMSC argued that the Review Body award was in breach of assurances given by Barber and Robinson that no scheme for reimbursement of practice expenses would be imposed on general practitioners against their wishes. They therefore insisted that the £5.5m award should be dedicated to net remuneration in the form of capitation fees.[427]

In order to placate the doctors, the BMA was also forced to address wider grievances. These were summarised in a short document drawn up by a drafting committee comprised of six GMSC members. This hastily concocted document was initially called a 'charter for family doctoring in the future'. As noted below, this draft was soon to be elaborated into the ultimately much-heralded 'Charter for the Family Doctor Service' or 'Family Doctors' Charter'. The title for this statement of the income and policy demands of the BMA was perhaps recollected from the *Daily Telegraph*, which had called the Gillie Report a 'Charter for Britain's Family Doctors'.[428]

The BMA charter was first released on 17 February 1965. It demanded:

(1) the opportunity to practice from well-equipped, adequately staffed accommodation, the current and capital costs being subsidised by grants from the state, without interference with the independence of practitioners.

(2) protection of doctors' practice from intrusion by the state, or unreasonable demands from patients, and safeguarded against unjustifiable and punitive litigation.

(3) a guaranteed minimum income not related to the number of doctors employed in the service, with levels of pay related to the work-load and responsibilities of doctors, and remuneration reflecting their status in the community and comparable with other professions.

266

(4) a guarantee of financial security for doctor and their dependants after retirement.[429]

Reporting to the House of Commons, Robinson expressed sympathy with the causes of dissatisfaction among doctors, but he refused to discuss the family charter proposals, or bargain under duress.[430] His restrained but principled stand against the militants won general sympathy in the media. In fact, notwithstanding a spurious air of belligerence, neither side was in a mood for the kind of confrontation recorded on many previous occasions. Already the ground was well-prepared for constructing a viable *rapprochement*. Rapid moves towards reconciliation were instituted. On 18 February, the two sides exchanged letters, preparatory to five hours of talks on 19 February, which ended in agreement to seek clarification of the Review Body's intentions respecting the criteria for distribution of its award.[431]

The Review Body was disconcerted and divided over this request. Some members argued that their offer of an increase in remuneration was conditional on introduction of an agreed reimbursement scheme. The increase was designed as belated compensation for good practice. The profession was guilty of breach of faith by attempting to deflect the increase into the pockets of all doctors regardless of their investment in improved practice arrangements. Notwithstanding the strength of this argument, the Review Body was swayed by the view of Kindersley that allowing the parties to exercise discretion over the distribution of the award would prove of 'critical importance' in breaking the impasse between the Government and the professions. It would therefore allow the parties to embark on negotiations to arrive at a radically altered system of remuneration.[432] The Review Body accordingly stated that its initial proposal to allow the bulk of the £5.5m award to support schemes for direct reimbursement of practice expenses had been made on the assumption that negotiations were almost completed on proposals for direct reimbursement. Since the parties had not reached agreement, the Review Body conceded that the award might be distributed according to terms agreed between the parties. However, Kindersley made clear his team's dissatisfaction with this outcome, emphasising that the Review Body would 'deplore it if the schemes for partial direct reimbursement were not introduced'.[433] Ministers were relieved by the Kindersley response; they agreed to recommend handing over the total amount available without deflecting anything into direct reimbursement schemes.[434] This proposal was endorsed by the Cabinet, but not without reservation; Robinson was told to prevent exploitation of this concession by the BMA to extract further gains.[435]

This outcome was seen by the press as a victory for the doctors. The award was distributed as an augmentation to capitation; it took average net pay to £2,765. This modest concession cleared the way for the more serious objective of securing a further economic gains associated with the new doctors' charter, which became official policy when it was granted formal approval from the BMA Council. The press estimated that the charter would bring gains worth between £30m and £45m, to be achieved mainly by an increase of the capitation fee from 22s 6d to 36s, which was exactly double the level adopted in 1960 as a consequence of the Pilkington settlement.[436]

Some of the main short-term aims of the BMA listed at this stage included: abolition of the pool, one fixed and invariable capitation fee, specified fees for items outside general medical services, sessional fees for hospital work, a contract for a 12-hour day, reform of disciplinary procedure, and a 'purge of the regulations'.[437] The GMSC reappointed its six members to draw up a fuller manifesto expanding the four principles of the original draft into a list of specific demands.[438] The manifesto, given the final title 'A Charter for the Family Doctor Service' was unanimously approved by the GMSC on 4 March, and by the Council of the BMA on 5 March. The published form of the Charter was dated 8 March 1965. Dr J C Cameron, the Chairman of the GMSC, and one of the main authors of the Charter, went into negotiations with a strong mandate, and with an unusual show of unity within the profession.[439] Press reaction to the Doctors' Charter was lukewarm; whereas it was appreciated that the Charter included many reasonable and positive suggestions, it was regarded primarily as a vehicle for securing substantial financial benefits for general practitioners beyond what was attainable through the review body procedures.[440]

The immediate confrontation over pay having temporarily abated, Robinson tried to move the discussions on to a more constructive plane by pointing out the advantages of group practice and team-work; he offered to give encouragement to attachment schemes whereby local authority health visitors, nurses and midwives might be located at group practice premises, or alternatively he offered to 'gladly do everything possible to encourage local authorities to provide more' health centres. This probably constituted the first enthusiastic remark about health centres emanating from a Minister of Health since the beginning of health service.[441] By the use of these examples, Robinson tried to persuade general practitioners that their professional status and satisfaction might be improved by methods not relating directly to their remuneration.

Preparations for negotiations stalled for two reasons; first, because the doctors failed to withdraw their threat of resignation; and secondly, on account of the insistence by the doctors that the cost of the new package should be negotiated with the Government, rather than being subject to reference to the Review Body. The impasse was broken by a letter from Robinson to the profession agreeing to negotiate about a new type of contract of service and new methods of remuneration, but excluding direct discussions about the pay 'quantum'. The Cabinet insisted upon changes rendering Robinson's draft letter less conciliatory, even if this would worsen relations with the doctors.[442] This letter was dispatched to the profession on 16 March; to the relief of Robinson, it was not badly received by the profession. On this basis the doctors' leaders advised postponement of the resignations from 1 April until 30 June. This decision was ratified by representative bodies on 24 March 1965. The doctors' leaders also recommended acceptance of pricing the new contract by the Review Body, subject to some further clarification of the Government's intentions. This also was agreed by the representative bodies, but with greater reluctance.[443]

The Government and negotiators representing the profession agreed to begin negotiations on 7 April 1965. At the Prime Minister's instigation, a subcommittee of the Social Services Committee was formed to keep Ministers in direct contact with the negotiations.[444] The Treasury was unenthusiastic about this subcommittee. Because it was chaired by Houghton and dominated by social services departments, the Treasury suspected that it would not be sufficiently vigilant on questions relating to expenditure. The subcommittee was also an inconvenience to Robinson because its members were insufficiently expert on the highly technical matters under discussion. This group of Ministers was nevertheless likely to be more palatable to Robinson than other alternatives, which would include a stronger Treasury voice. The general practice subcommittee of Ministers met on only three occasions and exercised virtually no influence on the negotiations.

At the only meeting of the ministerial subcommittee to consider the Doctors' Charter in detail, Ministers agreed to Robinson's request for a package of significant inducements, including early legislation to establish an independent corporation to finance improvements to practice premises, additional finance to support the employment of ancillary help, and action to reduce the burden of certification. Ministers also agreed that the pricing of the new contract by the Review Body would involve abolition of the pool, assessment of professional remuneration *ab initio*, consideration of various alternative methods of remuneration, and finally, that the Review Body would not be restricted by criteria laid down by the Royal Commission on Doctors' and Dentists' Remuneration. Robinson pointed out that the proposals made by the general practitioners for alteration of the basis of their remuneration were either in line with the thinking of his department, or otherwise not unreasonable. In some instances, such as the proposal for salaried service, Robinson argued that this would assist his aim to extend provision of health centres.[445]

It was agreed to negotiate on the basis of the Doctors' Charter. Talks proceeded relatively smoothly; provisional agreement was soon reached on many of the points at issue. This sudden transition to productive discussion was assisted by the large amount of preliminary preparation undertaken by joint working parties which deliberated on technical issues and which attracted little public attention.

The main agency for these discussion was the joint working party set up at the invitation of Anthony Barber in February 1964. This working party was chaired by Sir Bruce Fraser. In fact the working party split into two panels, one of which was chaired by Fraser and the other by Godber. Ostensibly the Fraser working party was concerned with issues raised by the Gillie Report, but in reality the health departments hoped that it would work out the details of a new contract which might relieve the state of anxiety within general practice, and thereby reduce the pressure of pay demands. The Fraser working party began its deliberations in April 1964 and was still meeting when it was overtaken by the crisis that erupted over the Fifth Report of the Review Body in February 1965.[446] The working party examined such subjects as terms and conditions of service, the distribution of doctors, list size, refresher courses and other continuing education, practice premises, access to hospital facilities, attachment schemes for local authority staff, appointments systems, and methods of remuneration. Instead of producing a consolidated report, the working party generated technical commentaries on each of the areas of investigation. A further initiative relevant to the Doctors' Charter was the Joint Study Group established in 1963, and which reported in April 1964 on schemes for the reimbursement of practice expenses.[447] The Fraser Working Party and its offshoots constituted a successful exercise in bipartisan co-operation. Away from the glare of publicity over remuneration, pragmatists among the officials and doctors quietly laid the foundations for a new ethos in general practice. The efficiency of this 'apparatus for keeping under informed and continuous review the many problems of general practice in the National Health Service' provided resources for the authors of the Doctors' Charter, and it contributed to bringing the parties sufficiently into consensus to ensure that negotiations on the Charter started from a reasonable basis of common understanding.[448]

During the Doctors' Charter negotiations, the Treasury and the Review Body essentially occupied the sidelines. The Treasury exercised only marginal influence.[449] The Review Body complained that it was being excluded from decisions fundamental to its remit. Both the health departments and the profession assured Kindersley and his colleagues that the negotiators were sensitive to the authority of the Review Body. They promised not to cause embarrassment to the Review Body through forcing it to adjudicate over remuneration proposals which it regarded as unsound and likely to meet an antagonistic response.[450]

The first joint report on the negotiations was completed in mid-May, discussed with the Treasury and Review Body, circulated to the Ministerial subcommittee, and published on 2 June 1965.[451] The main obstacle to agreement at this stage was raised by the Treasury, which attempted unsuccessfully to hold down the level of subsidy for employment of ancillary staff. Robinson held his ground and the Chief Secretary withdrew his objections. Robinson argued that final conclusion to the long-running debate over direct reimbursement for ancillary help and introduction of the new scheme in advance of the new contract, would boost morale among general practitioners, and help to secure their acquiescence to less palatable features of the eventual settlement.[452] The direct reimbursement scheme became the first part of the Doctors' Charter to be implemented. It was introduced in October 1965, financed initially from unspent balances left from the pool. This was an attractive short-term gesture, but it forced the Review Body to be more generous than otherwise it might have been, partly in order to avoid problem of disappointment of the kind experienced by rank and file general practitioners after the 1963 settlement.

The first report outlined specific proposals for legislation to introduce the General Practice Finance Corporation, agreement on a scheme for subsidising ancillary help within the practice, plans for reducing the burden of work connected with National Insurance certification, and reassurances concerning the profession's demands relating to procedures to be adopted by the Review Body in considering the pricing of the new contract.[453] In its exchanges with the Treasury, the Ministry of Health emphasised that the negotiated agreements implied only marginal additional expenditure. Major questions relevant to remuneration were being deferred to the pricing stage. The Ministry was quietly confident that it could persuade the Review Body to resist demands by the profession for a large settlement. Robinson assured the Prime Minster that rumours about the high cost of implementing the Doctors' Charter were totally irresponsible. He assured Wilson that his proposals were fully supported by the Treasury, and that they would lead to only modest additional costs. He believed that the compromises offered would secure the 'maximum amount of goodwill at minimum cost to the

Exchequer'.[454] This optimism was not shared within the Treasury, where it was predicted that the complicated system of remuneration being evolved was a recipe for inflation of costs.[455] This conclusion finds confirmation in the rhetoric of the profession. The doctors' leaders themselves proclaimed their initial agreements as a step towards a large pay increase. The GMSC pointed out to the Council of the BMA that:

Once the new contract is agreed and priced there are quite considerable financial prospects from:

(i) the realistic reassessemnt of the value of the work of the family doctor;

(ii) the direct reimbursement of the greater part of the cost of ancillary help;

(iii) the direct reimbursement of the cost of rents and rates of practice premises;

(iv) special inducements for doctors to work in under-doctored areas.

In addition there are the not inconsiderable economic factors, to be taken into consideration when the remuneration of all doctors in the NHS for the period 1963-66 is examined during the next few months.[456]

On the basis of this optimistic forecast, the GMSC advised the BMA Council that it was safe to destroy the undated resignations held by the British Medical Guild. Although the Council generally supported the GMSC and recommended continuation of negotiations, it refused to relinquish the resignations in case they were needed as a bargaining counter.[457]

Further negotiations received an unwelcome jolt from the Annual Representative Meeting of the BMA held in Swansea in July 1965. Until this point, the profession had negotiated on the understanding that three alternative forms of remuneration would be available: capitation, salary, and fee for service. The meeting generally supported the leadership, but it also passed a resolution calling for a further alternative form of remuneration to be available, in the form of direct payments from patients for services rendered by general practitioners. To their embarrassment, this fourth alternative was imposed on the negotiators as an integral element in the Doctors' Charter. The leaders knew that the Government had gone along unwillingly with discussions on payment by fee for service; they appreciated that direct payment by patients was even more obnoxious to an administration committed by its manifesto to abolition of all direct charges to patients.[458]

The 'Swansea resolution' exercised less influence than was originally feared; indeed it was in some respects politically helpful to Robinson. The professional leaders were out of sympathy with the Swansea proposal, which they deftly relegated to a low priority, allowing it to wither and eventually vanish without trace. Robinson cited the Swansea episode as evidence of latent radicalism among the general practitioners. This helped him more readily to gain backing from his colleagues for compromises worked out in his negotiations. On methods of remuneration, the two sides were in general agreement that capitation should continue as the dominant method, but allowance was made for experiments with salary (an alternative favoured by Robinson), or fee for service (to satisfy the profession). Ministers expressed minor reservations about the proposals, but accepted that they went a long way to offering general practitioners a 'new deal'.[459] Robinson was authorised to continue negotiations on the basis of a system of remuneration embodying the following features:

(a) A distinction between 'normal' hours of work and night and weekend work,.for separate payment, related to list size, and for stand-by duty at nights and weekends supplemented by small payments by item of service for night visits.

(b) Recognition.of the obligation to make deputizing arrangements during holiday and study leave up to 6 weeks in the year.

(c) experiments with item of service as the normal method of payment in a very few areas, under strict control and subject to a limit on the total sum to be paid.

(d) The trying out of salaried service in suitable circumstances as soon as the necessary terms and conditions of service can be worked out.

(e) Continuance of a modified capitation system, with certain additional special allowances and a limited additional number of items of service payments, as the method of payment for the majority of family doctors.[460]

Robinson was given little further supervision from his colleagues. The Treasury complained that negotiations were proceeding too rapidly towards conclusive results, but only limited efforts were made to suggest alternative courses of action.[461] In September 1965, Robinson reported to his colleagues the outline of his provisional agreement with the profession on the new contract. The arrangements for remuneration followed the lines set out in his July memorandum. Most of the modifications related to minor points of detail, such as the addition of weighting to capitation payments in respect of elderly patients, and introduction of an addition to the basic payment for seniority. The main difficulties related to realisation of schemes for alternative methods of payment. Given the complexity of the main capitation-based arrangements, it was difficult to evolve alternatives for payment by fee for service or salary that would generate similar incomes. These alternatives were pursued with decreasing enthusiasm by the negotiators, whose energies and patience had been exhausted on the capitation scheme.

Robinson told his colleagues little about the likely cost of the new contract. He admitted that the new method of assessment of salaries on the basis of an aggregation of different fees might constitute an inducement for the Review Body to recommend higher levels of payment than would have been the case under the pool system. However, he took a relaxed approach to this problem and expressed confidence that the Review Body would 'make a proper assessment of fair remuneration under the new system'.[462] The outline proposed by Robinson was regarded as sufficiently uncontroversial to merit no more than circulation to Ministers for written comment, and only four days were allowed for this intervention. Robinson's proposals were ratified by an ad hoc committee of Ministers comprising Robinson, Diamond and Maurice Foley representing DEA, and they were elaborated in the second report on the joint discussions, which was published on 6 October 1965.[463] The high degree to which the provisional new contract addressed the anxieties of general practitioners was indicated by the positive reception given to the second report, and by the large majority attained in a postal ballot.[464] This exercise also confirmed that the profession as a whole was not particularly concerned to have access to alternative modes of remuneration.

Ratification by the BMA membership cleared the way for submission of evidence to the Review Body. The latter began its deliberations at the end of October 1965. The Review Body was faced with the biggest and most politically sensitive task since its inception. Although general practitioners' pay was the dominant issue, it was also necessary to reach decisions about the remuneration of hospital medical staff and dentists, both of which contained areas of difficulty and contentiousness. There was general agreement that ending of the pool system, and adoption of a new basis for the contract would represent a more equitable method for remunerating general practitioners. The separation of arrangements for reimbursing expenses was a further step in this direction. However, the two sides differed in their expectations concerning the cost of the new contract. The Government insisted that changes in the method of remuneration should not add to the pay bill; indeed, the Review Body was also reminded to avoid recommendations conflicting with the Government's policy on pay restraint. In the rival camp, general practitioners in particular were given by their leaders the clear expectation that the new contract would entail a very large pay increase.

The delicate decision over the pay 'quantum' was remitted to the Review Body. As already noted, from the outset, the Treasury was convinced that the Ministry of Health was misplaced in its confidence about holding down the cost of the settlement. Even before the Review Body began its work, the Treasury and DEA estimated that the award was likely to cost between £27m and £50m.[465] At George Brown's instigation, Niall MacDermot and William Rodgers, Ministers representing the Treasury and DEA respectively, intervened to strengthen the Ministry of Health's evidence to the Review Body. George Brown was indignant that negotiations on the general practitioners' contract had reached an advanced stage without senior Ministers having been consulted.[466] Robinson was co-operative to only a limited extent. He placed preservation of his good relations with the profession above the merits of an aggressive line with the Review Body.[467]

Brown's 'senior Ministers' were given a further brief insight into developments concerning doctors' and dentists' pay, when Robinson intervened to warn them that any failure to implement the findings of the Standing Advisory Committee on the Pay of the Higher Civil Service (Franks Committee), was likely to stir up fears among doctors that the Government was not committed to accepting recommendations made by the Kindersley Review Body.[468] Notwithstanding Robinson's warning, the Cabinet referred the Franks recommendations to the National Board for Prices and Incomes.[469] This decision undoubtedly added to the tension concerning the outcome of the Kindersley review.

Kindersley submitted the seventh report of his Review Body to the Prime Minister on 25 March 1966. Wilson explained that delay would be unavoidable owing to the General Election due on 31 March.[470] The seventh report was published on 4 May, a month after the General Election.[471] This delay, although not unreasonable in the circumstances, caused annoyance within the profession and was subsequently cited by the BMA as evidence of Labour's tendency to acts of bad faith.

As already noted, the seventh report was concerned with all groups within the remit of the Review Body. The report fulfilled the intention of the Fifth Report in 1963 to undertake a further full review after three years. With respect to general medical practitioners, the basis for remuneration was now a flat-rate basic practice allowance of £1,000. This was supplemented by the capitation fee set at 20s (28s for patients aged 65 or over). The Review Body also established fees for out-of-hours responsibilities, and additions to the basic practice allowance. The latter comprised four new incentive payments covering fees for practice in designated areas, for group practice, for seniority, and for 'special experience and service to general practice'. A new post-graduate training allowance limited to a five year period was also introduced. Finally, the Review Body set out revised fees for additional health service work, such as maternity medical services, emergencies, temporary residents, and rural practice. In view of the tentative basis of the above scale of fees, it was agreed to undertake a further complete review after a further two rather than three years. Under the new contract, general practitioners stood to gain about 33 per cent, at an estimated cost of about £24m. Given the new situation in general practice, it was difficult to make comparisons with the previous system of remuneration, but the Treasury estimated that the award to general practitioners exceeded the most that was permissible by about 5 per cent.[472]

The Government hoped that hospital medical and dental staff, for whom no special circumstances applied, might be kept within the official pay norm of 3.5 per cent, which for the 2½ year period under consideration implied an increase of about 9 per cent. The average increase proposed for hospital doctors was 13.5 per cent, and the total cost was estimated at £7.7m. The increase for consultants was about 10 per cent, but in response to angry representations from dissidents among the junior hospital staff, awards to this group were higher, and were a maximum of 35 per cent for pre-registration house officers. Proposals to increase the value and number of distinction awards raised their cost by about 19 per cent.

General dental practitioners were remunerated on the basis of a target average net income. This was set at £2,740 in 1963, and had been adjusted periodically since that date. The Review Body proposed a target figure increasing annually, and averaging at £3,262 over the period to covered by the review. This implied an average increase of 10.6 per cent, at a cost estimated at £3.3m. This increase was justified on general economic grounds, but it was also hoped that it would stimulate a rise in recruitment, which had recently shown signs of flagging.

The total cost of implementing the seventh report of the Review Body was estimated by the Treasury at £38m.[473] Government departments differed in their reaction to the Kindersley report. The Ministry of Health placed emphasis on its positive aspects. It was pointed out that the award to hospital medical staffs and dentists was moderate. The average increase of 15 per cent for these groups was therefore tolerable, and only half the cost of the claim made by the profession. Only the increase to general practitioners could be regarded as generous, but the award needed to be viewed in the context of long-term discontent. The settlement was regarded as an acceptable price for purchasing a new spirit of accord likely to bring about big improvements in general practice. The Treasury was unenthusiastic, but it was unable to find grounds for suggesting rejection of any part of the recommendations. DEA was angry on account of implications for pay policy and likely repercussions in other fields of public service. Brown insisted on full exploration of alternatives to direct implementation.[474]

The Treasury and DEA agreed to press Robinson to propose a two-stage implementation of the part of the Review Body report relating to general practitioners, but Robinson refused; he and Ross made the case for immediate implementation.[475] His critics retaliated with the suggestion for implementation in two stages, half the value of the award from 1 April 1966, and the second half from 1 April 1967.[476] With the support of Ross, Robinson remonstrated that in the light of assurances previously given by the Government, any tampering with the Review Body's recommendations was likely to be regarded by the profession as a breach of faith. This would provoke united indignation and reactivation of the threat of mass resignation, which he pleaded would have disastrous consequences for the NHS as a whole. Callaghan countered that two-stage implementation was essential if trade unionists were to be persuaded of the seriousness of the Government's incomes policy. He believed that doctors would forfeit public support if they threatened resignation. Robinson received a generally unsympathetic and sometimes indignant response from Ministers, who decided in favour of the two-phase implementation of the general practitioners' award.[477] Robinson reacted angrily to this decision; in a personal letter to Wilson, he described the Cabinet decision as a 'bitter blow to me', which would undermine his efforts to build up confidence between his department and the medical profession. He held out the prospect of 'destruction of the service which means so much to me and the people of this country'. Given rejection of his arguments by colleagues, he hinted at resignation.[478] Kindersley responded less vehemently, but also expressed his disappointment.[479] Wilson and Robinson met the representatives of the profession on 4 May. Wilson explained his administration's difficulties over the economy and pay policy, but he assured them that the Government was fully committed to the

Kindersley proposals. The Prime Minister pointed out that the outcome would have been worse if the award had been referred to National Board for Prices and Incomes. The representatives expressed disappointment, but their general tone was conciliatory.[480]

Robinson dutifully presented the proposal for two-stage implementation to the profession. He pleaded for further tolerance in the interests of introducing a 'new era for general practice in Britain'.[481] Robinson was not quite reconciled to defeat; he proposed revival of the one-stage implementation, but delay until 1 July or 1 October 1966, but this was angrily rejected by his colleagues, who insisted on strict compliance with the Cabinet decision.[482] In pursuance of their new and more rigorous incomes policy, Ministers amended the Cabinet decision, but in the opposite direction from that wanted by Robinson. In the light of the standstill on incomes announced on 20 July 1966, the first phase of the award to general practitioners was deferred until 1 October 1966.[483] DEA also wanted the second phase to be deferred, but Wilson refused to contemplate this further delay, which was likely to be taken as an affront by the doctors.

Once again Wilson met the representatives of the medical profession for a 'frank talk' to explain the Government's reasons for deferring the pay increase. The only alternative was submission to the National Board for Prices and Incomes, an outcome likely to have even worse consequences for the doctors. He confirmed that the Government was committed to paying the second instalment of the pay rise due in April 1967. The Prime Minister explained that the undertaking given by Robinson concerning the date for implementation of the first instalment, although carrying the approval of the Government, would need to be revoked. The profession on this occasion complained bitterly, but the Prime Minister said that there was no alternative; otherwise the six month pay standstill and six month period of severe restraint would be breached.[484] Once again the Prime Minister's intervention was successful. The leaders of the profession persuaded their members to comply with the Government's pay policy. Robinson praised them for their skill, 'dignity and a concern for the national good'. Wilson personally thanked the profession for its co-operation.[485]

The recommendations of the seventh report of the Review Body were duly implemented in two stages, with effect from 1 October 1966 and 1 April 1967, although the actual revisions in payments were not made until three months after these dates. The effect of these delays introduced a loss of about £10m to the profession. For a short time, remuneration of doctors and dentists fell into the background and took on the routine character hoped for by believers in the Doctors' Charter. The Ninth Report of the Review Body published on 7 May 1968 proposed no general adjustments in remuneration, but the Review Body reserved the right to propose changes if this was justified by economic circumstances. The 'twin principles of comparability and non-discrimination' were announced as the continuing guiding themes of the review operation.[486] The cost of this award was about £3m, mostly representing a £100 addition to the basic practice allowance of general practitioners. This award was approved by the Government with evident relief. It was reported that the Negotiating Subcommittee of the profession was 'bitterly disappointed', particularly by the rejection of claims made on behalf of hospital medical staff.[487] The *Times* described the doctors' mood as 'seething indignation'.[488] Nevertheless, there was no inclination among the professions to overturn the Review Body decision.

The Tenth Report of the Review Body published on 6 February 1969 recommended increases for all groups, averaging at about 8 per cent, which was expected to cover the period until 1 April 1970.[489] The overall cost was £17.6m.[490] This award was judged by the health departments to be marginally within the 3.5 per cent a year ceiling applying at that date. The apparently uncontroversial nature of this award disguises much underlying tension. Among Ministers there was a feeling that doctors and dentists were being excused the more rigid constraints applied to other professional groups. In particular, it was argued that a double standard was being applied. Teachers and university lecturers were being denied comparability awards by the NBPI, whereas Kindersley was applying this criterion to justify an award to doctors and dentists. Feelings ran high on this issue. Aubrey Jones, the Chairman of the Prices and Incomes Board, campaigned vigorously against the Kindersley award, whereas according to Crossman, Sir George Godber, the Chief Medical Officer, threatened to resign if the Kindersley award was rejected or referred to the NBPI. On this issue the Treasury believed that the NBPI was misguided. On 23 January 1969, after tense discussion in the Cabinet, the Kindersley award was sanctioned, but only on the basis that the teachers were also granted their award. Some Ministers called for the Kindersley Review Body to be wound up on the grounds that it was unduly favourable to the professions. This outcome was profoundly unpopular to the Treasury, which had hoped to at least delay implementation of the Kindersley award, and completely suppress the increase to teachers.[491] The *British Medical Journal* judged the award 'fair though not generous'.[492]

The Labour administration was almost off the hook. The much applauded 'New Deal' for general practitioners seemed to be having its desired effect. The Review Body system appeared to be working smoothly. Any complacency on the part of the Government was dispelled in March 1970, when it was rumoured that the Review Body was about to recommend a substantial increase in excess of 25 per cent.[493] The draft of the twelfth report was ratified by the Review Body on 24 March 1970. Kindersley presented this report to the Prime Minister on 2 April.[494] The Review Body proposed a 30 per cent increase for all groups, with larger increases in some of the special payments for general practitioners. The basic grounds for this increase were maintenance of comparability with other professional groups, improvement of recruitment, and reduction of wastage. Compensation for this latter factor had not been possible earlier because it had been necessary for the Review Body to undertake extensive investigations to update the findings of the Pilkington Commission. The Review Body was also swayed by evidence accumulated by the Royal Commission on Medical Education concerning manpower shortages, high rates of emigration, and low levels of recruitment of medical students from the UK and Ireland.

The Treasury and its allies were determined not to allow repeat of the complacency demonstrated in 1969; from the outset they contested the Kindersley findings vigorously. The Treasury was unimpressed by the arguments used by the Review Body; it favoured remitting the award to the Prices and Incomes Board, with the expectation that a settlement of about 15 per cent would emerge. In that case, the Review Body would be discredited; it was hoped that the Review Body would be replaced by a review process linked more closely to other pay-determination machinery. This view was shared by Barbara Castle, the Secretary of State responsible for incomes policy. Crossman found the Kindersley report 'astonishing'; he reached the conclusion that the Kindersley team were a bunch of reactionaries, who were determined to use their report to cause the maximum embarrassment to the Labour Government.[495] Although the Review Body report received some support within DHSS, it was agreed that at least phased implementation would be necessary.

For the first time in the history of the Review Body, Wilson delayed his acknowledgement of the report. Not until 29 April was Kindersley advised that consideration of the report 'might take a little time'.[496] Ministers were extremely slow to deal with this problem, seemingly unaware that their reticence would compound the Government's political difficulties. The fault for this inaction must lie with Crossman. The Kindersley recommendations were given a first cursory review by Ministers in their Management Committee, with the target of reaching a decision by 30 April, but this objective was abandoned and the issue was referred to an ad hoc committee of Ministers.[497] This transfer of responsibility to a small committee was intended to preserve strict security, presumably attempting to prevent a repeat of the damaging leak that had undermined the Government's negotiating position over nurses' pay in February 1970.

The ad hoc group of Ministers first met on 6 May. Crossman admitted that the Review Body's report was open to criticism and in conflict with the Government's wages policy. He conceded that this presented a 'formidable problem' for the Government. Nevertheless, he warned that the profession was 'in a fractious mood and the militant attitude of the younger doctors threatened the unity of the BMA'. He therefore advocated an immediate award of not less than 20 per cent, together with a promise of negotiations with the Review Body and the profession concerning the outstanding element in the award, which he presumed would take place in the summer after a General Election. Other Ministers were highly critical of both the award and the Review Body, which they favoured replacing by the new Commission for Industry and Manpower. Ministers decided that the award could not be accepted as it stood. The majority were in favour of an award of 15 per cent, with reference to the National Board for Prices and Incomes over the further recommendations of the Review Body.[498]

The Review Body was increasingly disturbed by the delay in publishing its report, and it was given little insight into the Government's intentions. The Report was in final page proof on 17 April; publication was expected by the Review Body on 21 April, 30 April, 12 May, and less certainly on 19 May, and 26 May.[499] By the beginning of May, the profession was restive and suspicious. It complained repeatedly about delay, and insisted on a reply by the date of its national conference arranged for 27 May.[500] Wilson assured the BMA that the Government was making progress with preparations for publishing the report and that the issue was under active consideration by Ministers.[501] However, in the course of reviewing the implications of the Dissolution and the associated public announcement scheduled for 18 May, the Management Committee decided to defer publication of the Review Body report and delay decision about it until after the General Election. This gave the Prime Minister an opportunity to suggest deferring any meeting with representatives of the professions until after the General Election.[502] This deferment was intended to grant the Government much needed-breathing space, among other things because Crossman was tied up on Government business in Malta between 16 and 26 May.

Ministers completely miscalculated about the mood within the BMA, which formed an Action Committee to prepare for an offensive; it attacked the Government's announcement as a 'cynical disregard of its obligations' especially to younger doctors. The Government was accused of creating a 'very grave situation...in every way comparable to the crisis of confidence in 1965'. The BMA advised that it would embark on a campaign of non-co-operation unless the Kindersley Report was published by the end of May.[503]

In the light of the growing crisis, the great amount of publicity attracted by the BMA, and unpredictable electoral consequences of this dispute, the Government realised that some compromise was unavoidable. Ministers decided that they would have to publish the Kindersley report and also reach a decision on the Government's response. Crossman proposed publishing the report, offering full implementation for junior doctors, an immediate increase of 20 per cent to the others, together with a promise of a prompt Prices and Incomes Board report on the balance.[504] The Management Committee ratified Crossman's proposal, but decided to reduce the initial payment to more established doctors and dentists to 15 per cent.[505] At this last meeting ever held by the Management Committee, the Kindersley award was its only business.

Kindersley was informed about the Government's change of mind with respect to a meeting with the professions and publishing of the report, and he was given advance indication of the Government's statement. He expressed relief that his report would be published but complained that the delay in settling doctors' and dentists' pay had harmed the health service.[506] At this stage, neither Kindersley, the professions, nor Parliament possessed any indication of the Government's response to the Kindersley recommendations.[507]

At a meeting between the Prime Minister and a delegation representing the professions on 28 May, the Government representatives announced that they would publish the Kindersley report, together with the Government's decision on 4 June. Wilson refused to give a commitment that the Government would accept the Kindersley recommendations in their entirety. The BMA leadership complained that the Government was undermining their authority and that militants were gaining in strength and might create chaos in the NHS. In his concluding remarks, the leader of the delegation sarcastically thanked 'the Government for uniting the profession as it had never been united before'.[508] The Prime Minister also faced criticism from Kindersley, who accused the Government of failing to abide by undertakings given at the time of the Pilkington Commission, and thereby undermining the credibility of his Review Body.[509]

Notwithstanding agitation from the professions and the Review Body, Ministers endorsed the decision of the Management Committee. The Twelfth Report was published on 4 June.[510] On the same day at 10.00am Crossman communicated the Government's decision to Kindersley. Taken by surprise, Kindersley warned that this was unlikely to be acceptable to the Review Body. The same negative reaction was expressed by representatives of the professions when they met Crossman at 10.30am. Crossman then went ahead and issued his announcement.[511] On two separate occasions on 4

June, Crossman asked Kindersley for a further interview, but this was not taken up. Instead, at the Review Body meeting which was held at 6.30pm, Kindersley and his colleagues decided unanimously to resign and to release their resignation letter to the press that evening, without notifying Crossman.[512]

The British Medical Association reacted with predictable fury. For a few days, the headlines were dominated by the 'threat to the health service', or 'pay freeze' rumoured to be brought about by Ministers' fears of imminent collapse of the economy. However, even at its peak, this issue attracted only marginally more attention than skirmishes over Powell's racist politics. The *Times* sympathised with the doctors over the handling of the Review Body report, but it regarded the Government's eventual response as a reasonable compromise; the doctors were firmly told that militant action was not justified.[513] In the short period before the General Election, Wilson was persuaded by his colleagues to offer no further talks or concessions. The doctors stepped up their campaign. They continued to attract some publicity, but there is no evidence to suggest that they exercised more than marginal influence on the electorate.[514]

(ix) ROYAL COMMISSION ON MEDICAL EDUCATION

As reported in the first volume of this study, the Willink Committee examined the problem of medical manpower and concluded that an excessive number of doctors was being produced.[515] The Willink Committee suggested reducing the pre-clinical intake to 1,760 a year from the level of admissions in the mid-1950s of about 2,000.[516] Willink was broadly supported by the Royal Commission on Doctors' and Dentists' Remuneration, although the dissenting memorandum by Professor Jewkes was less categorical.[517] The Willink conclusions carried little weight and they were increasingly greeted with scepticism. The UGC adopted a lukewarm response, while the medical schools were resistant to more than minor adjustments in their intakes. It was soon evident that Willink had misjudged the situation. There was growing evidence of a shortage of doctors, which was resulting in an undesirable degree of reliance on overseas recruits to junior hospital posts. By 1960, about 40 per cent of these posts were occupied by doctors from overseas. Alarm was also caused by the gathering evidence concerning increased emigration by doctors trained in British medical schools. The credibility of Willink evaporated with the circulation of a paper by Professor J R Squire, Professor of Experimental Pathology, University of Birmingham (soon published in a revised form, in conjunction with his colleague, François Lafitte, Professor of Social Policy and Administration), which pointed out that Willink was the victim of various fallacies, all leading to an underestimation of the future need for medical personnel. This study called for an urgent increase in the medical school intake, and for a 'fresh and searching inquiry...to determine the number of doctors likely to be required in the next decade in all branches of the profession'.[518] Squire's paper not only invalidated the Willink Report; it also initiated a train of events which led to establishment of the Royal Commission on Medical Education.

The Squire episode touched off media publicity concerning an impending crisis in medical staffing and the degree of reliance on immigrant doctors. These fears were exacerbated by the parallel crisis over shortage of nurses and reliance on immigrant nurses discussed in the previous chapter. Representatives of the Ministry of Health warned colleagues that in important specialties such as surgery, overseas registrars outnumbered their British colleagues, while in a representative northern hospital at Bury, out of eight surgical staff, six were from Pakistan, and two from Spain. The officials were sufficiently alarmed to hold preparatory discussions with the Treasury with a view to briefing their new Minister.[519] This submission was presumably Powell's first formal introduction to the human resources issues in the NHS associated with emigration and immigration. It was reported that Powell was exhibiting a 'lively interest (asking for more facts etc.)' on this problem.[520] Powell sanctioned an urgent review of medical school numbers, which concluded that the intake should be immediately increased by 10 per cent above the Willink target, and this was accepted by the Government. This increase was implemented in October 1962; it took the intake to about 2,200, including overseas students.[521] At this stage a more formal review was avoided on account of the existence of the Robbins Committee on higher education, which was at liberty to investigate medical education. However, the Robbins Report (1963), contained only incidental references to this important aspect of higher education, although it included estimates for the expansion of medical schools, which were founded on evidence even more dubious than that utilised by Willink.

The Platt Report (1960) and the Gillie Report (1963) implied a further substantial increase in the medical personnel employed in hospitals and in general practice respectively. A further increase to about 2,150 British students was permitted with effect from October 1963. In July 1964, an addition to the UGC grant was sanctioned to support an intake of 2,300 British students by October 1966.[522] By this stage it was self-evident that expansion could not be accommodated by the existing medical schools.

In 1963 the departments began serious discussions about establishing new medical schools. This was the first such development since establishment of the Welsh National School of Medicine at Cardiff in 1893. An announcement approving in principle at least one new medical school was made in December 1963.[523] Nottingham, the home and headquarters of Boots the Chemist, its University linked with Jesse Boot, and for long a supplicant for a medical school, was the favoured candidate for this development.[524] Barber was determined to gain the credit for a specific commitment to the Nottingham medical school before the General Election, and the announcement was made in July 1964.[525]

The departments were increasingly uncertain whether maximising the intake into existing medical schools and establishing one new school would be sufficient to meet the demand for additional doctors. In November 1963 the Ministry of Health estimated that an entry of 2,400 would be required in 1974; in March 1964 this forecast was revised to 2,700.[526] In July 1964 the Ministry of Health speculated that the 1974 intake would need to be 2,900, while in November 1964 this estimate was revised to 3,000. At this stage, the Ministry speculated that as many as four new medical schools would be required.[527] The Ministry of Health found it difficult to alert its partners in the government mechanism to the urgency of the need for a major programme to expand the medical schools. Unless immediate steps were taken to expand intakes, the Ministry warned that there would be no hope of reaching a level of 3,000 in 1974. Shifting assessments and alterations in targets, outside the system of UGC quinquennial reviews, was disconcerting for the Treasury and added to its sympathy for a comprehensive review of medical education.[528]

In opposition, Labour (largely through the mouthpiece of Robinson) pressed for expansion of medical schools, establishment of at least four new medical schools, and a Royal Commission to investigate medical education.[529] As noted above, these policies were incorporated into the 1964 Labour General Election manifesto.

Rejection of Willink and pressures for a radical increase in the output of doctors was the most urgent aspect of the problem of medical education. Also, rationalisation of the undergraduate and postgraduate medical schools in London was long overdue. It was also necessary to consider the appropriateness of the existing structure of medical education and training. The Treasury was particularly concerned to see justification of the length and costliness of medical education. Training opportunities for intending general practitioners were particularly unsatisfactory, while despite the build-up of the regional hospital system, facilities for training hospital medical staff outside the teaching hospitals were still in a primitive state.

The last and only previous full-scale review of medical education was the Goodenough Report(1944).[530] As already observed, the Robbins Committee on higher education avoided the vast and intractable tangles relating to medical schools. Direct responsibility for medical education was divided between the Department of Education and Science (acting through the University Grants Committee and its Medical Sub-committee) and the General Medical Council (acting through its Education Committee). The Ministry of Health was of course also involved because it determined the demand for medical personnel, and provided the teaching hospital facilities for their training. On account of indifferent co-ordination, medical education was a serious problem at risk of falling between the stools of government agencies.

The suggestion for an enquiry into medical education cropped up in various contexts. Even the proposal to set up the Hinchliffe Committee raised the question of need to improve relevant aspects of the training of doctors, and therefore prompted the idea of a comprehensive enquiry into medical education.[531] The immediate suggestion for a 'Medical Robbins' emanated from the Medical Sub-committee of UGC. In the context of reductions in quinquennial estimates for universities for 1962-67, the Medical Sub-committee complained that cuts in expansion plans for medical schools would have damaging consequences. The Sub-committee discussed the possibility of an enquiry to look into the nature and cost of medical education, with the object of providing better objective justification for big expansion plans emerging from the medical schools.[532] The argument for an enquiry was strengthened by the emergence of competing proposals for new medical schools, and growing concern within the Sub-committee about the wisdom of current plans for medical school rebuilding in London. A group led by Janet Vaughan, the Principal of Somerville College, Oxford, urged that some of the London medical schools should be closed down and replaced by new medical schools in the provinces.[533] The Medical Sub-committee produced a brief memorandum outlining the range of issues requiring urgent attention. The Sub-committee concluded that 'nothing short of a full-scale enquiry into the whole of medical education can possibly suffice'.[534] This suggestion immediately found favour with the UGC. It then passed to the Government departments, who were also satisfied that an investigation into medical education, preferably a Royal Commission, was needed as a matter of urgency.[535] Outside experts were informally consulted and they also were supportive.[536] In April 1964 the enquiry was sanctioned by the ministerial Education and Research Policy Committee. Officials went on to discuss the scope of the review and the membership of the committee. By the summer of 1964 most of the medical members who eventually served on the committee had been shortlisted and agreement had been reached on the choice of chairman. It was decided to select a distinguished non-medical academic scientist, and an agreed candidate was informally approached by Sir Edward Boyle, but after much discussion, declined the assignment.[537] At this stage, an irritating obstacle intervened, in the form of the General Medical Council, and especially its influential chairman, Lord Cohen of Birkenhead, who was suspicious and discouraging about the proposed enquiry. Not unreasonably, Cohen believed that the medical education enquiry was likely to stray into the area which had been the statutory preserve of the GMC since 1858. Cohen proposed limitations to the scope of the enquiry, which were indignantly rejected by Boyle.[538] Intervention by the GMC and failure to secure the preferred chairman frustrated Boyle's attempt to establish the enquiry into medical education before the 1964 General Election.[539]

In the autumn of 1964 the Labour administration resumed preparations for the medical education enquiry. Stewart approached Robinson and suggested a committee along the lines of the Robbins Committee. Robinson agreed with enthusiasm, but he suggested that the enquiry should be upgraded to the status of a Royal Commission. Stewart was informed that Robinson had been taken into its confidence about this undertaking by the previous administration. Robinson urged that in view of the controversiality of the issues involved, especially regarding possible reorganisation of London medical schools, and the need to carry authority with the medical profession, a Royal Commission was preferable to a committee appointed by the Prime Minister.[540] Stewart and his successor Crosland readily agreed to upgrading the status of the enquiry. This suggestion and the terms of reference for the Commission were accepted without difficulty by the Social Services Committee and by the Cabinet. Some Ministers, led by the Prime Minister, were concerned that granting a Royal Commission might add to pressures for the proliferation of Royal Commissions to examine such areas of controversy as general practice or nursing, but Ministers were assured that these demands could be resisted.[541]

The GMC continued its sour attitude towards the Royal Commission; Cohen retaliated by instituting his own enquiry into the medical curriculum. The Ministry of Health feared that this committee would be out of step with the Royal Commission on account of its membership containing a preponderance of elderly doctors.[542]

The departments searched for a substitute eminent non-medical scientist, eventually settling on Alexander Robertus Todd, Lord Todd of Trumpington, a Nobel prize-winner in chemistry, Professor of Biochemistry and Master of Christ's College, Cambridge, who had served as the chairman of the Government's Advisory Council on Scientific Policy from 1952 to 1964. Deciding on the balance of membership of the Royal Commission gave some difficulty. The Goodenough Committee had comprised ten members; only the Chairman and one other were non-clinicians. Eight was regarded as the minimum for the medical constituency, but in the conditions of 1964 it was agreed that it was unrealistic to have such small lay membership. Medical officials dominated early discussions on membership, and they concluded that perhaps four out of twelve members might be laypersons, a suggestion which was rejected by Boyle, who suggested nine medical and seven non-medical members.[543] Discussions under Labour gradually drifted towards the idea of parity of the medical and lay constituencies, the final list comprising nine medical and nine non-medical members. Most of the discussion on membership related to the medical section; the primary difficulty related to attainment of an acceptable balance of specialties, while including three Scottish doctors and one representative of the GMC, and not allowing the average age level to rise above 55. This puzzle entailed many changes of plan; the delicate balance was immediately upset when two medical members died during the first months of the Commission, one of whom was Professor Squire, one of the key members. A further constituency requiring satisfaction was Wales, which at an early stage was allocated one place; by selecting a Welsh general practitioner, two interests perceived as marginal were conveniently covered by a single appointee. This decision was made without discussion with the Welsh Office or the Welsh Board of Health. The Scottish total was increased to four by inclusion of a senior, non-medical Scottish academic. No layperson from Wales was included. Gender representation was taken care of by appointment of a woman obstetrician and the woman Principal of Bedford College, London.[544] The lay membership was settled with little discussion, and with the exception of the scientist members, seems to have been regarded as an artificial concession required for public relations purposes.

On 27 July 1965 the Prime Minister made the long-expected announcement concerning the establishment of the Royal Commission on Medical Education.[545] The Royal Commission was asked to:

> review medical education, undergraduate and postgraduate, in Great Britain, and in the light of national needs and resources, including technical assistance overseas, to advise her Majesty's Government on what principles future development (including its planning and co-ordination) should be based; in particular, in the light of those principles and having regard to the statutory functions of the General Medical Council and the current review by that Council of recent changes in the undergraduate

curriculum, to consider what changes may be needed in the pattern, number, nature or location of the institutions providing medical education or in its general content; and to report.

The insertion of limitations into the remit of the Commission was made to appease the GMC, but in practice the Royal Commission duplicated the work of the GMC committee, and despite disclaimers to the contrary, the two reviews of the curriculum were not entirely consistent with one another.

The Royal Commission commenced its work on 10 September 1965. Shortly afterwards, an interdepartmental liaison group, formed to co-ordinate Government representations to the Commission, also began organising presentation of evidence.[546] The Commission performed most of its work in subcommittees, with remits which roughly approximated to the subject-matter of the chapters of the final report.

The most urgent issue facing the Royal Commission related to the expansion of the medical school intake. Decision was required on targets for the long-term and their implications for current and medium-term policy. As noted above, since 1963, the Ministry of Health had been pressing for more rapid expansion of the medical school intake. The Royal Commission needed to decide whether the problem of the medical workforce should be addressed by expanding the medical school intake, reducing the length of training, or by other means, such as using medical labour more efficiently, disincentives to emigration, or attracting women back into practice on a greater scale. The Ministry of Health urged consistently that the only realistic measure was expansion of the medical school intake; all other approaches to the problem were more uncertain in their effects; if successful, other boosts to the medical workforce would be welcome additions, easily absorbed into the health service owing to a steady increase in demand.

During the first months of the Labour administration the UGC expressed full agreement with the Ministry of Health over the expansion of the medical schools. Accommodation between the Ministry of Health and the Department of Education and Science was undoubtedly assisted by Sir Bruce Fraser, during his brief tenure as Second Permanent Secretary responsible for Higher Education within DES. The Ministry of Health made repeated high-level representations to DES over the need for more rapid build-up of numbers in the medical schools. Robinson observed that on the basis of the current intentions of DES relating to 'short-step' proposals to increase intakes, only 2,600 British students would be admitted by the mid-1970s. It was urged that at least two new medical schools should be established without delay. The health department pressed for the Nottingham medical school to be established immediately, and for urgent consideration to be given to medical schools in such places as Bath, Leicester, Southampton, and Keele. Unless such possibilities were exploited, it was estimated that by the mid-1970s a deficit of at least 7,000 doctors would have opened up.[547] As a staging post towards its longer-term target, the Ministry of Health evolved proposals designed to increase the intake to about 2,500 by 1970.[548] The Treasury suggested that all consideration of expansion should be deferred until after consideration by the Royal Commission. Both the Health and Education Ministers insisted that 'short-step' proposals for modest increases in the intake should be pursued regardless of the Royal Commission. Robinson and Crosland agreed on proposals for some 250 additional places at existing medical schools by 1969.[549] However, this programme was delayed by cuts in the budget for higher education and by pressure on DES to devote more resources to competing areas of higher education. The Ministry of Health once again complained that medical education was not being accorded the priority it deserved.[550]

Failure to achieve unambiguous commitment to expansion of the medical schools prompted the Ministry of Health to solicit support from the Royal Commission, which was naturally appreciative of the argument, and predisposed to use its authority to promote expansion without waiting for detailed consideration of other means of solving the medical human resources problem. Some leading members of the Commission, at the outset of its deliberations, were anxious to seize the initiative with a view to influencing the level of the 1966/67 intake into medical schools. They were reminded by the chairman that their recommendations would exercise greater influence if based on a fuller consideration of the evidence.[551] The Commission therefore waited for a judicious interval to elapse before issuing its advice. In May 1966 the Manpower Sub-committee of the Royal Commission, chaired by Todd himself, drafted a report, containing interim recommendations for accelerating the expansion of the medical schools. This report was ratified by the Commission on 2 June and dispatched to Crosland on 17 June 1966.[552]

The Treasury waited for 'the storm to break' and hoped at least that expansion could be accomplished considerably more cheaply than had been envisaged in current projections.[553] As the Treasury feared, the Royal Commission identified with the arguments emanating from the health departments. The interim report concluded that to 'bring the numbers in general practice and in the hospital service up to the minimal reasonable standard within a moderate period of time' an increased intake of home students of 1,100, or 1,300 if overseas students were included, was required over a ten-year period.[554] The interim report was taken by the government departments as implying adoption of a target of 3,400 for the medical school intake in 1975. This was derived from the Ministry's figure of 3,100 for home students, with the addition of 10 per cent for overseas requirements. However, the interim report could also be interpreted as implying a total intake of 4,000 in 1975.

The Royal Commission insisted that its projections represented the 'minimum reasonable standard within a moderate period of time' or a 'deliberately conservative' estimate. If not adopted, the Commission warned that a deficit of 10,000 doctors was in prospect for 1975. The Commission pointed out that its proposals for expansion would merely prevent continuing deterioration in the doctor:population ratio and by 1975 restore this ratio to the level of 1961.[555]

In February 1968 Todd informed the Prime Minister that his final report was virtually complete. The Commission was alarmed by the recent economic downturn; Todd expressed hope that this would not be allowed to obstruct full implementation of his report. He assumed that the Government would appreciate that 'good medical care is one of the foundations of civilized living and without an adequate system of medical education it cannot be assured'.[556]

The departments waited apprehensively for the full report; the only advanced warning came in the form of a rough summary produced by DES in February; the first comment by the Treasury dates from 19 February.[557] The final Report of the Royal Commission was published on 4 April 1968.[558] It was accompanied by the briefest statement from the Prime Minister in the form of a written answer, announcing that the report would be 'now examined urgently' by the Government.[559] The Report comprised 233 pages of text, and about 150 pages of unlisted appendices. The committee was unanimous in its recommendations. The bulk of the report was uncontroversial. Its recommendations were based on the assumption of continuity; it was understandably predicted that long-term evolutionary trends in medicine and the medical profession were likely to continue. The Commission was at a disadvantage in having been led to believe that the existing tripartite administrative structure of the health service would not be disrupted. The first Green Paper on NHS reorganisation, in draft at the time of publication of the Todd Report, rudely undermined this basic premise. As noted below, the Commission itself concluded that the system of hospital administration was unsustainable, and that at least this part of the health service required reorganisation.

The Royal Commission suggested only minor changes to the undergraduate medical curriculum, but proposed a strengthening in the academic and scientific component. The Commission expressed general support for the specific recommendations on the undergraduate curriculum produced by the GMC in 1967. The most innovative proposal with respect to the undergraduate course was amplification and strengthening of the GMC recommendation concerning the teaching of the behavioural sciences, including sociology. It was argued that the behavioural component should be used to inform each stage of undergraduate medical education.[560]

The proposals for professional training particularly emphasised the need to give more active and suitable training for the large group of doctors likely to enter general practice. The proposals for professional training were based on a one-year intern year, followed by a three-year period of general professional training, designed to be flexible and suitable for all doctors, including opportunities for training appointments in general practice.

For the further professional training stage, major revisions were proposed to the hospital career structure and a new terminology was suggested for its training and career grades. An attempt was made to revive the fortunes of the unpopular Medical Assistant grade, suggesting replacement by the 'Hospital Specialist', which it was hoped would become the standard senior appointment for those not selected to become consultants. Much attention was given to systematisation and elaboration of training for general practice, which it was hoped would develop into a 'satisfying and challenging speciality'.[561] These expressions of optimism were written against a background of crisis within general practice, but also higher expectations born out of the recent Doctors' Charter. These recommendations were largely based on the scheme advocated by the Royal College of General Practitioners.[562] The specialty which the report now called by its new name, 'community medicine', was also recognised as requiring fundamental improvements in its training arrangements.[563]

The later parts of the report included consideration of the likely labour requirements of British medicine, estimates of the extent of expansion of medical schools needed to meet the projected labour needs, and the costs of medical education. An entire chapter was devoted to the reorganisation of undergraduate and postgraduate medical education in London.

In defending and amplifying the conclusions of its interim report, the Commission was obliged to justify its statistical projections. For this part of its work, the Commission had access to the advice of Dr William Brass, a demographer from the London School of Hygiene. The Commission arrived at credible doctor:patient ratios on the basis of comparisons with other Western states, and on the assumption that long-term trends in Britain were likely to continue. The Commission discovered what it believed was a settled trend over the years 1911 to 1961, which was identified as a natural course of development or some kind of law, which should not be interrupted and deserved to be guaranteed by enshrinement in policy.[564]

On the basis of its extrapolation, the Commission estimated that the number of active doctors should roughly double in the period between 1965 and 1995 to reach 119,000. It was recognised that it was not practicable to expand medical schools to meet this demand, but the Commission nevertheless proposed a substantial continuing expansion. It was proposed that the average annual intake into the medical schools should double from 2,430 in 1967/68 to reach 5,000 in the quinquennium 1985/89.[565] A target of 1,150 additional places by 1975 was adopted, which would increase the intake to 3,700, including allowance for overseas students, which was consistent with the estimate adopted in the interim report. The Commission pointed out that even this degree of expansion would leave a substantial shortfall in the number of doctors required.

Specific recommendations were made about meeting the requirement for expansion. In addition to Nottingham and Southampton, where the decision had already been made to establish new medical schools, the Commission proposed establishing a further four new medical schools - Leicester, Swansea, Keele, Warwick and Cambridge were listed as possible candidates. One of the most controversial proposals of the report was the suggestion that the existing 12 undergraduate schools in London should be grouped into 6 pairs, with each pair being associated with one of the multi-faculty colleges of the University of London, with the preclinical school being located on the college site where possible.[566] The Commission appreciated that its proposal for this 'radical reorganisation' would be controversial, costly, and that it was only realisable in the long term. Nevertheless, this scheme was held up as an ideal model to guide future planning. Of the six pairs proposed, only two eventually came to fruition, but the others were ultimately amalgamated in different pairings.

Of the same degree of controversiality were the proposals for reorganisation of postgraduate medical education in London. It had long been recognised that the arrangement hurriedly adopted in 1948 constituted an unsatisfactory compromise. The Goodenough Report had recommended assembling the postgraduate institutes into a single postgraduate hospital centre. Studies undertaken in connection with the hospital plan proposed that most of the postgraduate hospitals and institutes could be amalgamated into two groups, to be located in Holborn and Chelsea. Lord Todd and his colleagues came to different conclusions founded on a rival philosophy. They believed that the senior academic staffing of the undergraduate medical schools was impoverished on account of separation from the postgraduate institutes. They therefore argued that the postgraduate institutes and specialist hospitals should be drawn into close alignment with the proposed six groupings of undergraduate medical schools and general teaching hospitals.[567] The Commission offered tentative proposals for these groupings.[568] It was appreciated that the proposed scheme was an extremely distant prospect.

Commitment to expansion of medical schools inevitably raised the question of making additional hospital resources available for teaching purposes. Since provision of these teaching facilities on the scale envisaged was beyond the capacity of the Boards of Governors, they inevitably depended on access to beds administered by the Regional Hospital Boards. Continuing administration of these beds by the RHBs weakened the authority of the Boards of Governors; formal transfer to the Boards of Governors reduced the capacity of the RHBs to perform their statutory responsibilities. This problem was unique to England and Wales; in Scotland, teaching hospitals were integrated into the regional hospital system. In England, it had already been decided that the new medical school in Nottingham would be administered under the RHB. The Royal Commission decided in favour of the Scottish system, concluding that the 'teaching hospitals in England and Wales should be brought within the framework of administration of the regional hospital service generally'.[569] This recommendation was singled out for special mention in Todd's letter to the Prime Minister.[570] The Commission emphasised that in return for swallowing up the Boards of Governors, the RHBs should be modified to increase the degree of university influence; also, with respect to the metropolitan area, the Commission made the controversial suggestion that the regions should be increased from four to five.[571] The review of medical education therefore added to the mounting argument in favour of an overhaul of the organisation of the NHS.

Most of the recommendations of the Royal Commission required lengthy consideration, and were likely to exert little influence in the short term. As appreciated by the Commission, economic difficulties also stood in the way of active pursuit of its recommendations. As the Treasury lamented: 'the thing that sticks out a mile from the Commission's proposals is the substantial expenditure involved'.[572] This conclusion was impossible to escape.

As noted in the following chapter, the decision to undertake reorganisation of the health service presented the Government with an opportunity to act on some of the Commission's recommendations, although, as indicated by the example of London, the Todd recommendations proved applicable only in the most diluted form. The urgency of the Commission's work related to its findings on the human resources of medicine. The level of expansion advocated by the Commission was fully supported by DHSS. Indeed, in this sphere, it is arguable that the Commission was little more than the mouthpiece for the policies of the department.

The programme for expansion of existing medical schools and building of new schools was a formidable undertaking, not attractive to the Treasury, and rendered particularly unattractive on account of the economic downturn. However, the controversy surrounding this issue was less than might have been anticipated. The case for expansion was largely conceded in the context of the interim report of the Royal Commission. In 1967 DES and the Ministry of Health agreed on a united front based on the estimates given in the interim report.[573] The Treasury conceded that immediate action was needed to boost numbers in the medical schools. In December 1968 Shirley Williams announced that funds would be available for increasing the medical school intake to 2,700 by 1968 and 3,300 by 1975.[574] The Treasury hoped to hold the total to this level, but following the publication of the Commission's Report, DHSS argued the case for adopting 3,700 as the target intake for 1975.

Treasury officials were sceptical about the presuppositions and methodology of the expansionists. It understandably regarded the regularity expounded by the Commission as a specious construct, but little use of this potentially compelling criticism was made in debate with the spending departments. With some insight, it was concluded that 'the vital point is that there is really no such thing as the "need" for doctors; especially in the circumstances of the U.K., the need is a function of and to a considerable degree created by the supply'.[575]

Although the Treasury was unconvinced by the justifications produced by the Ministry of Health, it was not contested that a shortage of doctors was imminent. The Treasury accepted that such factors as medical advance and rising public expectations would generate further demand for medical personnel, which could not be satisfied without increasing the intake into medical schools. In the absence of its own convincing forecasts, the Treasury was disinclined to precipitate a crisis by proposing rejection of the Todd estimates. DHSS predicted that even full implementation of the Todd proposals would leave a deficit of 7,000 doctors. As noted above, decisions announced in 1968 introduced a commitment to an intake of 3,300. It was calculated that full implementation of schemes already sanctioned would result in 3,500 places by 1975. The Treasury hoped to hold down expansion to this level, or delay an increase to 3,700 until a later date.[576] DHSS intimated that the 'Secretary of State (who is taking personal responsibility for Todd matters) has expressed the view that 3,500 places for UK-based students by 1975 represents "an absolute minimum"'.[577] Crossman promptly wrote to the Chief Secretary complaining that he and Crosland were embarrassed over the failure to reach agreement on expansion of medical school places. He urged that a public statement could not be deferred much longer, and he insisted on no further delay concerning commitment to the Todd intake target of 3,700.[578] Treasury officials were not entirely united over their response to Crossman; one party favoured giving in to Crossman, but insisting on reciprocal concessions. In the event, the party advocating resistance to further compromise won the day. With the encouragement of the Chief Secretary, the Treasury bombarded DHSS with searching queries, and they introduced a new delaying tactic, demanding investigations into the imposing of restrictions on the emigration of doctors. In exasperation, Crossman met Jenkins on 4 March 1969 to underline the political advantages of accepting the Todd recommendation.[579] Jenkins referred the matter to Diamond, who retorted with a long exposition of technicalities, and proposed a statement giving general support for the Todd findings, but avoiding commitment to an intake of 3,700.[580] Crossman rejected this suggestion, after which the parties met to debate their disagreement. The Crossman team carried the argument, but the Treasury insisted that the decision to accept 3,700 places in 1975 implied no commitment to further expansion after that date.[581] Crossman recorded contemptuously that this episode 'shows what an appalling waste of time Treasury tactics really are, especially when there is a surrender'.[582] This acrimonious exchange prepared the way for Crossman's announcement accepting the 3,700 target for the medical school intake, which gave him the first opportunity to pronounce positively on the Royal Commission on Medical Education and promise further statements in due course with respect to other policy decisions derived from consideration of the Todd Report.[583]

(x) REORGANISING PERSONAL SOCIAL SERVICES

Reorganisation of social work services, brought about by the Seebohm Report (1968), had profound implications for the health service because it removed an important and expanding function of local health authorities. Thereby, separate local authority health services were no longer viable entities, which effectively sounded the death knell for the Medical Officer of Health. The Seebohm exercise therefore contributed further to the pressure for reorganisation of the NHS. The Seebohm review therefore possessed implications extending way beyond the social services.[584]

Although Labour ultimately claimed the credit for initiating this fundamental review of social work, the extent of these changes far exceeded the expectations of the Labour administration when it assumed office in 1964. The roots of Seebohm can be traced back to the 1950s, especially to growing concern with limitations in the capacities of welfare agencies to deal with the problems of broken marriage, single parent families, maladjustment in education, and juvenile delinquency. The desire to improve care of juvenile delinquents led to the Ingleby enquiry which reported in 1960, and later in Scotland to the more important and innovative Committee on Children and Young Persons, chaired by Lord Kilbrandon, which reported in April 1964.[585] Indicative of concern about these problems within the Labour Party was the report of a committee chaired by Lord Longford published in June 1964, *Crime - A Challenge to us All*. Longford became Lord Privy Seal in the Wilson administration.

Leading pressure groups argued that problem families were given insufficient support owing to fragmentation in responsibility for services and lack of co-ordination between departments. They called for concentration of responsibility into 'Family Departments', which would be able to provide integrated Family Advice Centres dealing with all aspects of family breakdown. Most of the debate was tangential to the health services, except that health visitors and many of the relevant social workers were employed by local health authorities. The reformers were divided over the way forward. The more widespread demand related to the narrower objective of improving services to families with problems. This group was headed by Dame Eileen Younghusband, who called for an expansion of integrated services based on the existing children's departments of local authorities.[586] The rival group argued that family service departments would leave many problems of co-ordination unresolved, and indeed that this change would be subversive to unification of the social work profession, which was regarded as one of the primary objectives of reform. The relevance of this latter philosophy to the health services was explained by Professor Richard Titmuss in a much-publicised address to the Royal Society of Health, where he attacked the 'Balkanised rivalry' between local authority departments, and called for unified departments which would deal with all client groups, including services for the elderly and the mental health sector.[587]

Contrasting with its state of unreadiness with respect to health service reorganisation, Labour was well-prepared to undertake reform of the social services; indeed, not only Longford, but other Cabinet Ministers had been actively implicated in working parties in this field. It is perhaps surprising that the 1964 General Election manifesto contained no hint of moves in the Seebohm direction. 'Modern Social Services' figured prominently among Labour's promises, but the list of specific policy commitments contained no reference to the personal social services. Nevertheless, in October 1964, the Queen's Speech promised 'more effective means of sustaining the family and of preventing and treating delinquency'.[588]

In outlining the tasks of the ministerial Social Services Committee, both Houghton and Robinson called for examination of services for the elderly, the chronic sick and the handicapped.[589] The Social Services Committee risked dissipating its effort in separate investigations relating to many different client groups requiring improved services. In order to avoid this, the Home Office argued that it was also necessary to consider establishment of an integrated family service. This idea was first discussed by Ministers in March 1965.[590] The Home Office called for an independent committee to review local authority services connected with family support. Robinson broadly supported this proposal. However, reflecting the trend of its thinking following the Kilbrandon Report, the Scottish Office warned that it was arbitrary to separate family service from services to other client groups; Ross called for the Government to 'work out the most practicable proposals for reorganisation of social work services not only for children, but over the whole field described in the Minister of State's present paper'. Although appreciating the merits of an independent investigation, it was evident that the Home Office was inclined to the Younghusband camp, whereas the Scottish Office was in agreement with Titmuss.[591] Although the Home Office's favoured approach was likely to involve reductions in the field of control exercised by the Ministry of Health, Robinson was not initially supportive of the Scottish Office, even though this option was intrinsically more favourable to his department.

The proposal to remit this problem to an independent committee was not favoured by Houghton, who argued that there had been sufficient investigations and expert reports. He made the counter-suggestion that a solution to this problem could be worked out by a committee of officials chaired by himself. This course of action was no doubt attractive to the Chancellor of the Duchy of Lancaster, because it gave his little department a tangible mission. This approach was also generally favoured within the departments, because it enabled officials to exercise more firm control over events. Reservations were expressed about this course of action, but the Home Office was generally supportive because it needed to respond promptly to local authorities wanting to establish family service departments. Houghton was known to support this latter objective. Given the likelihood that Houghton would supervise further discussions relating to England and Wales, the Scottish Office declared that it would pursue this issue independently.[592]

Once it was known that a policy initiative on the reorganisation of the personal social services was imminent, social work interest groups made active representations both to Houghton and other Ministers.[593] In further ministerial discussions, Houghton clung on to the idea of heading the social services review. He was supported by

Bacon, but Robinson argued for the advantages of an independent enquiry.[594] Houghton's influence was eroded by Robinson and other Ministers, who pointed out that the new policy was bound to involve major upheavals, and therefore needed to command authority within local government and among all the disparate groups participating in social work. It was also clear that Houghton's team would be incompetent to examine issues such as the recruitment and training of social workers, which required urgent attention, and were best considered in conjunction with service organisation. Finally, it was pointed out that the independent review need not be slower and might indeed be completed within a year.[595]

Support for Houghton's view also faded among the officials, who appreciated that a more comprehensive reform offered the best prospects for efficiency and economy in the use of scarce human and material resources.[596] It was appreciated that this objective could only be attained on the basis of a full-scale and independent review. There remained the problem that an initiative to deal with the problem of juvenile offenders could not be delayed; indeed a White Paper containing the Government's proposals was published in August 1965.[597] It was realised that most of the changes proposed could be introduced in advance of establishment of family service departments, but the White Paper had announced that a small interdepartmental committee was examining the possibility of establishing family service departments. It was therefore necessary to take note of this commitment in setting up an independent enquiry.[598]

Houghton was persuaded to comply with the proposal for an independent committee. The Treasury suggested that he was particularly swayed by the response of the local authority associations.[599] Robinson insisted that the committee should be small, 'above the battle' and 'objective and impartial in its approach'.[600] In the genteel, but sharply competitive bidding between departments over membership, each believed that objectivity was epitomised by partisans of its own position.[601] The agreed committee composition represented a distinct victory for the integrationists.

It was quickly agreed that Frederic Seebohm (1909-1990) was the most appropriate chairman. Seebohm belonged to a notable Quaker family involved in confectionery manufacture. He was the grandson of Frederic Seebohm, the historian, and he was related to Benjamin Seebohm Rowntree, the social analyst and philanthropist. In the course of a long career in banking, Seebohm became Chairman of Barclay's Bank International. Throughout he was active in philanthropic work and was a Trustee and later Chairman of the Joseph Rowntree Memorial Trust.[602] Seebohm was the obvious candidate for this assignment. Although formally impartial, he was

299

chairman designate of the National Institute for Social Work Training, which possessed strong links with the recently-founded Standing Conference of Organisations of Social Workers. Both of these bodies favoured the establishment of comprehensive social work departments.[603] The Seebohm Committee was dominated by members having close links with these two bodies, and with Richard Titmuss. Only one member, Beatrice Serota, obviously represented the family service lobby, but she resigned from the committee upon her appointment as Baroness-in-waiting in April 1968.[604] This resignation reduced the woman representation on the committee to one, Lady James of Rusholme.[605] The membership of the Seebohm Committee arguably represented a balance of the relevant constituencies, but it noticeably underrepresented or entirely omitted certain important groups, especially senior social work professionals, public health doctors, other relevant medical interests such as mental health specialists, and advocates of major client groups, especially in the mental health field. Given the emphasis of Titmuss on links between medical personnel and social workers, and the prospect that unified social service departments would lead to the 'renaissance of the family doctor', it is understandable that doctors should feel excluded from the Seebohm review.[606] The Medical Officers of Health, as the medical specialty with the most direct interest in the social services, had reason to be affronted because the only doctor included on the Seebohm Committee was an academic specialist in epidemiology.

Seebohm accepted the chairmanship of the committee on 22 November 1965; the formal announcement of the appointment of the committee was made one month later.[607] The Committee was jointly appointed by the Home Secretary, the Secretary of State for Education and Science, the Minister of Housing and Local Government, and the Minister of Health, the departments responsible for social work in local authorities. Establishment of this committee had therefore taken more than a year of delicate negotiations.[608]

The terms of reference of the Seebohm Committee were 'to review the organisation and responsibilities of the local authority personal social services in England and Wales, and to consider what changes are desirable to secure an effective family service'. This form of words was compatible with the previous priority of introducing a strengthened family service, but it was sufficiently broadly drawn to allow for consideration of unification of what were now called 'personal social services'.

The first meeting of the Seebohm Committee took place on 7 January 1966.[609] From the outset, the Committee and the relevant Government departments had an uneasy relationship. The departments were eager for the Committee to complete its deliberations and arrive at recommendations; it was therefore asked to pursue its work with the utmost urgency. However, the Committee adopted an ambitious scope for its work, with the result that it was impossible to reach conclusions as quickly as the Government had envisaged. The departments accused Seebohm of trying to embark on lengthy enquiries, and turning his committee into a standing advisory committee, aiming to monitor development in the individual services. They were equally concerned that the Committee was straying into examination of services not provided by local government and also central departmental administration of the social services.[610] Efforts were made to speed up the work of the Committee, with a view to production of a report by the spring of 1967. On his side, Seebohm complained that the Government was taking independent initiatives affecting the social services, which were not always notified to his Committee, and which inevitably set back the timetable.[611] These complicating issues included alterations in departmental responsibilities associated with the formation of the Ministry of Social Security, and establishment of the Royal Commission on Local Government. Nevertheless, Seebohm promised to report by March, then July 1967; after further delays, which occasioned embarrassment to Ministers in Parliament, the report was eventually dispatched to the Home Secretary in April 1968.[612] The 370-page report of the Seebohm Committee was published on 23 July 1968, the same date as the first Green Paper on NHS reorganisation.[613]

Not surprisingly, in view of the homogeneity of the committee, the Seebohm recommendations were unanimous. However, with respect to its main recommendation relating to comprehensive local social service departments, it cannot be claimed that Seebohm reflected unanimity, broad consensus, or even a majority voice within the evidence submitted. Nevertheless, the best organised lobby and most effective presentation of argument emanated from the allies of the dominant nucleus within the Seebohm Committee.[614]

The Seebohm Report adopted an holistic, preventive, and community-orientated philosophy. The Committee was satisfied that the patchwork of separate services provided by disparate administrative bodies were incapable of meeting the requirements of a modern service. These services were not only incomplete and unsatisfactory from the point of view of the user, but also they were wasteful in the use of human and material resources . The Seebohm Committee proposed a radical, new form of organisation at the local level, entailing establishment of unified administration of all local authority personal social services by a single social service department under its own principal officer, who would report to a separate social service committee. This strengthened social service department would not only correct the above shortcomings, it would strengthen the capacity to plan social services effectively and attract the requisite resources.

Notwithstanding the recommendation of the Maud Committee on the Management of Local Government that central government should repeal statutes requiring local authorities to establish specified committees for particular services, appoint certain officers and seek Ministerial approval for some of these appointments, the Seebohm Committee recommended the imposition of all of these statutory requirements with respect to the new social service departments.

Like its contemporary, the Royal Commission on Local Government, the Seebohm Committee recommended that the local authority administering the personal social services should also be the authority responsible for education, housing and local health services. The Seebohm Committee was aware that local health services were liable to be reorganised; in that case it proposed that alternative arrangements for co-ordination should be devised. Unlike the Royal Commission, the Seebohm Committee pointedly avoided consideration of the possibility that the reorganised health service might be administered by local government.

The Seebohm Report proposed that the new social service departments should be responsible for: (a) all the services provided by local authority Children's Departments (Home Office responsibility); (b) almost all services provided by Local Welfare Authorities (Ministry of Health responsibility); (c) many of the services provided by Local Health Authorities, including day nurseries, home helps, mental health services,[615] social workers; also mental health social workers employed by hospital authorities (Ministry of Health responsibility); (d) and finally, the child guidance service and the educational social work service provided by Local Education Authorities (Department of Education and Science responsibility).

Through the above integration of functions, the Seebohm Committee believed that social workers would become united into a single, homogeneous profession, with much improved career prospects. The Committee appreciated that the full advantages of a career structure could only be gained if professional training was reorganised to contain a greater element of common knowledge and skills.

Questions relating to central administration were outside the remit of the Seebohm Committee, but it urged that the unification of local services would be useless without corresponding changes in central government. The Report advocated that there should be one

302

government department responsible for local social service departments, for planning and for co-ordination with other central departments with interests relevant to the social services.

The Seebohm Committee appreciated the argument that its reforms should take place concurrently with the anticipated reorganisation of local government and the health services, but it decided that unification of the personal social services was such an urgent matter that it should be implemented as soon as possible, even if further administrative change was needed at a later date.

As noted in Chapter IV, to the chagrin of Robinson, the Seebohm Report attracted considerably greater publicity than the NHS reorganisation Green Paper, and it was received rather more enthusiastically. Newspapers even compared Seebohm to Beveridge in its importance. The press generally supported the Report's call for early action in advance of decisions concerning local government or health service reorganisation. The *Times* warned that the Seebohm problems would not entirely solve the problem of lack of co-ordination:

> All too often at the moment co-ordination between local health and welfare workers is not so effective as it should be, and unless deliberate efforts are made it is likely to be even less so when both are part of new, larger groups. The danger is particularly evident if the area health authorities are not part of local government structure.[616]

The newspapers recognised that formation of unified social service departments at the local level would precipitate a major redistribution of functions within central departments. The *Guardian* detected signs that 'a battle is shaping up between Mr.Callaghan and Mr.Crossman over the Children's Department's future'.[617] The *Times* was explicit about its preference; it declared that central responsibility for the social services could only reasonably pass to Crossman's 'new Ministry of Social Affairs, or whatever it is to be called - and it is of importance for the future of the social services that this reform should come about'.[618] The two major medical journals reacted differently to Seebohm. Both contained editorials dealing with both the Green Paper and Seebohm. The *Lancet*, devoted most of the space to Seebohm; its fluent exposition reads like something from the pen of Titmuss. Despite the intended 'grievous blow' to Medical Officers of Health, the *Lancet* recognised the 'compelling logic in these proposals. A few years hence we may wonder how anything else seemed defensible'.[619] The *British Medical Journal* had much less to say; predictably, it concentrated on the Green Paper; its remarks about Seebohm were unappreciative and combative, warning that any attempt by social workers to take over 'medical and social functions now carried out by doctors raises questions of principle which are of concern to all doctors, and this issue must be seen as one which goes far beyond simply depriving medical officers [of health] of a function'.[620] Arguably the strongest criticism of Seebohm came from its own camp: in *New Society*, Peter Townsend complained that the Seebohm recommendations were insufficiently radical, and especially they had failed to indicate the high cost of the operation required to give realistic effect to the policy of community care.[621]

Regardless of reservations expressed about the Seebohm Report, its proposals represented a major gain for the social work profession. In one step they had achieved the objectives of decolonisation, independence and imperialism. However, the final realisation of these aspirations was dependent on implementation, which represented a minefield of complexity.

By opting for independent action, Scotland placed itself ahead in the race. The Kilbrandon Report embraced both the public order and social work aspects of the problem of juvenile delinquency. In addition to suggesting that juvenile panels should replace juvenile courts, Kilbrandon also advocated establishment of integrated 'Social Education Departments'.[622] Soundings taken by the Scottish Office demonstrated broad support for both of these proposals, but it was decided to use this opportunity for an even more ambitious reorganisation of social work. The new plan, anticipating the Seebohm recommendations, proposed to amalgamate all local authority social work services into a single department. The paper to Ministers emphasised that 'these proposals have been devised with the assistance and advice of Professor R. M. Titmuss and two other independent professional advisers, all of whom are in general agreement with the terms of the draft White Paper'.[623] Ministers sanctioned publication of the White Paper, but were concerned that it should not appear to pre-empt the outcome of the Seebohm enquiry, which was only just beginning its work.[624] The Scottish White Paper was published in October 1966.[625] Despite opposition to these proposals from medical and probation interests, the only significant concessions related to distribution of responsibilities within the unreconstructed local government system. The legislation was introduced in March 1968 and it received the Royal Assent in July. The Social Work (Scotland) Act 1968 provided for gradual build-up of unified social work departments, the first stage occurring on 17 November 1969, after which there was a long intermission pending local government reorganisation, which was delayed until May 1975, at which point comprehensive social work departments were established in Scotland.[626]

In England and Wales numerous obstacles stood between the Seebohm Report and the statute book. Representations from the interest groups displayed precisely the same divisions of opinion as were evident in Scotland. Most complaint emanated from potential losers, such as the medical and health service interests, or those classes of social work specialists, especially groups having Home Office or Department of Education and Science links, who feared loss of independence and status through absorption into larger social work units.[627] As in the case of the evidence submitted to Seebohm, reactions to the Report demonstrated continuing support for the family service alternative, or for departments formed by integration of local health and welfare departments.

By virtue of unavoidable implications of the Seebohm proposals for the distribution of functions within central government, there was much mutual suspicion between the four main sponsoring departments. It was therefore a complicated balancing act to arrange mutually acceptable procedures for Government examination of the Seebohm Report.[628] Since his department was likely to be the beneficiary of the Seebohm amalgamation, Crossman could afford to take a relaxed attitude to the changes. By contrast, Callaghan at the Home Office was highly defensive; he was determined not to relinquish control of his Children's Department. His relations with Crossman only became more amicable when the latter assured him that he would not seek to take over the Children's Department until after a change of Home Secretary.[629] After preliminary consideration of the case presented by the Home Office and the Ministry of Health, the Cabinet Office referees in this matter concluded that 'in making a transfer in either direction one could cause damage hardly less than the important benefit that could be gained from integrating these services'. It was therefore decided to explore methods of central administration not reliant on major departmental reorganisation.[630] Opinion within the Cabinet Office and Treasury shifted towards granting the Ministry of Health oversight for the social services, partly because it was already the dominant player in this field, and also because the arguments in its favour were increased by the imminent establishment of the DHSS. Any other solution, such as some kind of federal command structure, seemed impossibly complicated, and contrary to the principles enunciated by Seebohm.[631] The Cabinet, sensitive to tensions aroused by the Seebohm recommendations, opted for a non-committal public statement, followed by interdepartmental negotiations in an effort to find an agreed solution consistent with the findings of the Royal Commission on Local Government.[632]

Crossman discussed the Government's response with Seebohm. The latter complained that especially in London, local authorities were reorganising their services in a direction contrary to the recommendations of his committee. Crossman offered to discourage such developments, but regretted that little more could be promised in advance of local government reorganisation. He also confessed that it was not practicable to remove the Children's Department from the Home Office in the near future. Crossman wondered whether the Seebohm Committee would be satisfied if the Government encouraged voluntary experiments in unification of the social services at the local level. Seebohm resoundingly rejected such a suggestion.[633]

At the departmental level, the balance was clearly in favour of Seebohm. The Ministry of Health, supported by the Home Office, urged immediate action to establish the unified local social service departments advocated by Seebohm. It was pointed out that anxiety and confusion within the social services had been generated under the Labour administration. Given uncertainty about the date of local government reorganisation, the Ministry of Health called for prompt action. It was recognised that this would necessitate two separate upheavals for most social service departments, but prompt action was unavoidable because many local authorities were already reorganising their social service departments, often with the intention of thwarting the Seebohm recommendations.[634] This argument was contested by MHLG, which insisted that the authority of the Royal Commission on Local Government would be undermined if the Government embarked on this major reorganisation within the field of local government. MHLG also predicted that a long period of continuous disruption would be the likely result of introducing the new social work departments in two stages. This problem was discussed by officials in their committee on local government reorganisation, when it was agreed to investigate further the possibility of a compromise, whereby steps towards Seebohm would be facilitated within the current framework of legislation.[635] A further cause for delay was introduced by the costing exercises conducted by the Treasury. While the Seebohm reforms were defended on the grounds of rationalisation, efficiency and economy, the Treasury concluded that the strengthened social service departments would be more expensive from the outset and that they would generate demands for 'very fast' expansion, with potential cost implications 'virtually without limit'.[636]

In summarising responses to the Seebohm Report, Crossman frankly recognised the division of opinion among the relevant administrative and professional bodies. All of the conflicts of outlook exposed in the evidence to the Seebohm Committee resurfaced in the discussion of its report. The local authority associations insisted that any outcome should be based on a comprehensive policy embracing the personal social services, the National Health Service and local government reorganisation. The Association of Municipal Corporations in particular, opposed any changes in the personal social services in advance of local government reorganisation. Most other bodies were in favour of incremental change or at least some delay. The Standing Conference of Organisations of Social Workers was in a minority in demanding implementation without delay. Support for rapid implementation was therefore less than implied by the initial media response to the Seebohm Report. With respect to departures of the Seebohm Report from Maud recommendations concerning appointment of committees and chief officers, the Standing Conference was firmly behind Seebohm, but the majority of local authority associations expressed reservations.[637] In view of continuing diversity of opinion on most aspects of the Seebohm Report, Ministers opted for further explorations among officials to discover points upon which agreed policy could be reached.[638]

MHLG became less confident about an early date for local government reorganisation. Since it was possible that changes in local government might be delayed until 1975, the Home Office and the Ministry of Health insisted that prior action on Seebohm was inescapable. Especially in London, where local government reorganisation had already occurred, and in Scotland, where the social work legislation was in place, reorganisation of social work departments was already taking place. This was forcing local authorities elsewhere to rush into decisions, which were being made according to the balance of local forces, rather than agreed Government policy. Urgent action was needed to prevent anarchy in service organisation and demoralisation of staff. The Home Office and Ministry of Health proposed that a Bill embodying the 'essential minimum' of Seebohm recommendations should be introduced at the beginning of the 1969/70 session. Under this essential minimum, local social service departments would comprise the entire children's and welfare departments, together with all health functions recommended by Seebohm. This approach had the virtue of leaving to one side controversial issues such as child guidance. Also, unlike the Scottish social work legislation, which was complex on account of its inclusion of both public order and social work elements, it was envisaged that the essential minimum Seebohm legislation would be short, uncontroversial, and therefore easy to timetable.[639] The above compromise was generally accepted among officials, but MHLG continued to oppose the 'nonsense of legislating on one aspect of local government organisation when decisions had not been taken on a major review'.[640] MHLG and its allies, the major local government associations, continued to press for no action other than announcement that policy would be formulated in the light of

307

decisions on local government reorganisation. As observed in Chapter IV, these bodies were also hoping that their intransigence would bring about acceptance of unification of health services under local government, a possibility which attracted Crossman, but which he regarded as impracticable owing to the veto exercised by the medical profession.

At two peevish meetings of the Social Services Committee, Callaghan and Crossman pressed for immediate legislation to make the essential Seebohm reforms mandatory. The opposition was led by Kenneth Robinson, the Minister for Planning and Land, and George Thomson, the Minister without Portfolio, who was in charge of discussions on local government reform. Robinson and Thomson were supported by the Treasury, which believed that insufficient account had been taken of objections to Seebohm. Given disarray within the Social Services Committee, the issue was referred to the Cabinet, where a similar wrangle ensued among the same participants.

By this stage, the delay was frustrating and embarrassing to Crossman. In reply to persistent Commons' questioning, he had promised to make a statement on Seebohm, either immediately after the publication of the Report of the Royal Commission on Local Government, which occurred in June 1969, or at the latest, before the summer recess. The Cabinet considered authorising a tentative statement indicating that a policy announcement would be made in the autumn after further discussions with outside bodies. However even this was objectionable to Thomson, who argued that this promise of action in advance of a decision on local government reform was not only wrong in principle, but would cause embarrassment to the Government because it would lead to the charge of inconsistency on account of refusal by the Government to express its view on the recommendations of the Boundaries Commission until after a decision had been reached on local government reorganisation.[641] Crossman was limited to making a statement that a decision would be reached in the autumn.[642] Exercise of such evasive tactics on the part of the Government was the cause of outrage among social service groups, mobilised by the Seebohm Implementation Action Group, which had been formed in January 1969.[643]

In October 1969, the Queen's Speech promised legislation on Seebohm.[644] In November and December, Seebohm was again considered at meetings of the Social Services Committee. Each of the parties staked out its territory, without evidence of compromise. The Treasury described Crossman's proposals as 'the worst features of an unsatisfactory compromise'.[645] The Treasury joined forces with Anthony Crosland, the new Secretary of State for Local Government and Regional Planning, who added to the strength of the opposition against Callaghan and Crossman. The Seebohm camp was weakened at the second meeting owing to the absence of Crossman, who was ill. A majority of the Social Services Committee supported the proposals of Callaghan and Crossman, but a minority remained implacably opposed. The Seebohm group insisted that unified social service departments should be established 'across the board', at particular mandatory dates, decided on the merits of the case for Wales, London, and the rest of England, where necessary, ahead of local government reorganisation. By way of compromise, it was agreed to allow individual authorities to apply for exemption from these arrangements. Crosland and his allies argued that imposing an obligation on all county councils and county boroughs to undertake these radical changes in 1971, and then a further reorganisation in 1974, would be an unreasonable imposition on the local authorities and harmful to continuity of services. The arrangements for exemption were criticised as unworkable. Crosland, supported by Treasury Ministers, preferred to bring in the new arrangements at specified dates for types of local authority, the sequence being determined by decisions reached on local government reorganisation. The second area of disagreement related to the Seebohm proposals concerning statutory Social Services Committees and statutory arrangements concerning chief officer appointments. The Seebohm advocates were willing to reduce the scope of statutory controls, but not to the extent required by Crosland and his colleagues.[646]

Crosland and his Treasury allies made a last stand at the Cabinet meeting on 13 January 1970. The arguments were unchanged, but Crossman was perhaps at a psychological advantage, because this was his first Cabinet meeting after his illness. The Seebohm proposals were carried by a majority, without further significant compromise. The Cabinet therefore agreed that implementation of the Seebohm reforms should be mandatary rather than selective, and that the there should be a statutory obligation to appoint a social service committee and a director of social services. The only minor concession on this front was that the Secretary of State's powers with respect to the appointment of the chief officer were limited to a right of veto.[647]

The belated resolution of the impasse between departments over Seebohm allowed just sufficient time for introduction of the legislation in the 1969/70 session. The lateness of the decision led the Government to consent to legislation of the simplest kind, making no attempt to consolidate, modify, or extend the powers and duties of authorities to provide services. The short Local Authority Social Services Bill was published on 12 February 1970; it received its

309

second reading on 26 February, when Crossman proclaimed the Seebohm reform as the foundation stone of the second stage of the welfare state.[648] The Bill was criticised by the Seebohm lobby on account of failing to establish a central government department to oversee the personal social services, and for not including a commitment to promote social welfare as an explicit obligation of the kind included in section 12 of the Social Work (Scotland) Act. The advocates of Seebohm were also disappointed that education welfare and child guidance services, as well as housing welfare services were to be left outside the unified social service departments. The critics of Seebohm were particularly determined to prevent mental health social workers from being transferred from hospitals to the new social service departments and this issue was deferred pending legislation on NHS reorganisation. A final decision concerning the Probation and After Care Service was not made until March 1970, when, by contrast with the position in Scotland, it was agreed to leave this service outside the unified social service departments for the 'foreseeable future'.[649]

The Local Authority Social Services Bill passed through its parliamentary stages without incurring any significant changes; the consensus was sufficient for the final stages to be telescoped in order to complete the parliamentary stages before the dissolution. The Royal Assent was received on 29 May 1970, the date of the dissolution.[650] Under the Local Authority Social Services Act 1970, the county councils and county boroughs, the City of London, and the London boroughs were required to create unified social service departments on 1 April 1971. A second reorganisation on 1 April 1974, coinciding with local government and NHS reorganisation, reduced the number of these departments from 174 to 116. The Act also amended the Health Visitor and Social Work (Training) Act 1962 to allow for the new arrangements for supervision of training standards, as described in further detail in chapter VI. It was necessary to establish the Central Council for Education and Training in Social Work as a matter of urgency, in order to have new training arrangements in place by the date of local government reorganisation.

(xi) PROFESSIONAL POLITICS
Relationships between the dominant professional groups within the health service was constantly shifting. Consequently, in a piecemeal fashion, the traditions inherited from former days were found to be wanting and they were replaced by new arrangements more in keeping with modern services, and with the aspirations of the professional groups concerned. The Salmon reforms, discussed above, provide an example of a particularly concerted effort to

310

transform traditional working relationships in nursing into new hierarchical structure dictated by the expectations of current management theory. The rapid strides forward made by nurses inevitably had repercussions throughout the system. This point was communicated unintentionally, but graphically, by the illustration on the front cover of the first report of the joint working party on the organisation of medical work in hospitals in England and Wales, which showed one central cogwheel engaging with three peripheral cogwheels. The following sections will briefly consider the attempts made to devise an effective and harmonious working structure for hospital medical staff, hospital scientific and technical staff, and public health medical staff.

Organisation of Medical Work in Hospitals

The Cogwheel initiative was an unintended by-product of the crisis existing within the medical profession in the mid-sixties. As noted above, in 1965 general practitioners forced their grievances into the open, dominated events with their Family Doctors' Charter, and secured for themselves a 'New Deal', which was important for consolidation of their financial and professional status. Throughout this process, hospital medical staff went along with the tide, but were uneasy about the impact of the new deal on their own standing within the medical hierarchy. Beside making direct representations through the Kindersley machinery and in negotiation with the health departments on their contracts, the leadership of hospital medical staff looked for other ways of consolidating their position, and preventing an erosion of talent within their ranks through defection of able juniors into general practice.

As noted below in chapter IV, hospital medical staffs, through their Joint Consultants Committee attempted to regain the initiative by promoting the Porritt proposals for health service reorganisation. Through establishment of integrated area health boards, the consultants expected to be able to preserve the dominance of teaching hospitals and district general hospitals, and ensure that any sacrifices forced on the health service would be directed at what they regarded as peripheral services. The Chief Medical Officer criticised this policy as a manifestation of the 'extreme selfishness' of the consultant elite.[651] On the model of the joint committees that supervised implementation of the Family Doctors' Charter, the JCC pressed for a joint working party to keep up the momentum begun by Porritt. The health departments realised that endorsement of this suggestion would provoke adverse repercussions from a wide range of important interest groups excluded from the working party. They therefore considered what alternative, less-controversial function a joint working party might perform.

311

The dilemma facing the health departments was assisted by the departure of Porritt to New Zealand, and subsequently by clashes of personality within the JCC. The health departments decided that the joint working party might be turned to advantage and be usefully employed in examining ways of increasing efficiency in the use of hospital medical personnel. The working party might therefore assist with the twin objectives of easing the human resources shortage, and bringing greater rationality into management operations. There was support within the Ministry of Health for a pattern of the organisation of medical personnel along the lines of American chiefs of service, but this was known to be unacceptable to consultants. The Ministry therefore fell back on seeking further progress with the 'firm' system, which had been endorsed by the Platt Report and introduced in some hospitals subsequently.

Proposals for a joint working party along these lines were communicated by Robinson in July 1965. The JCC pressed for a broader enquiry, but this was rejected by the Minister. In September 1965, the JCC accepted the original remit, not without dissension among the consultant leaders. Arguments concerning the chairmanship delayed the formal establishment of the working party until March 1966. On account of Scottish JCC preference, a separate Scottish working party was formed in December 1965.[652]

The Scottish initiative was also justified by the need for hospital medical staffs to respond to the challenge posed by the Farquharson-Lang Report. The later initiative derived from the Scottish Health Services Council, which in 1962 established a committee chaired by W M Farquharson-Lang to study the administrative practice of hospital boards. Its report, completed in August 1965, outlined many possible improvements; it was particularly concerned with committee structures and the extent of powers exercised by officers. Most relevant to doctors was the proposal, little noticed at the time, that the post of Chief Executive should be established at all levels of administration. It was also envisaged that this post should be occupied by either a lay or professional officer, according to 'his ability and experience as a manager not his professional qualifications'.[653] The Committee appreciated that this system of management by chief executive would 'require careful planning and would take time', but it was presented as a practical possibility. Given this pre-emptive strike from a committee dominated by lay managers, it was clearly necessary for the medical interests to mount their own management initiative.

The terms of reference of the English working party were 'to consider what developments in the hospital service are desirable in order to promote improved efficiency in the organisation of medical work'. The terms of reference of the Scottish working party were

312

similar. The working parties were chaired by the respective Chief
Medical Officer; they co-operated closely and reached similar
conclusions.[654] The Scottish working party was very much the pace-
setter; its 79-page report was published in May 1967, while the more
limited 24-page English report, containing its emblematic cogwheel
title-page, was published in October 1967.[655]

The two reports made tentative and undogmatic suggestions for
the improvement of the management of medical personnel. The
English 'Cogwheel' report admitted that the medical advisory
arrangements established in 1948 were a failure. The absence of
effective management structures had reduced hospitals into
collections of petty jurisdictions presided over by individual
consultants. Advocates of the American model were critical of the
'anarchy' or 'cult of individualism' predominating in British
hospitals. This excessive degree of devolution had conspired against
all forms of aggregative decision-making. As a consequence, 'hospital
medical committees have tended to drift away from the mainstream
of management...It is not too soon to redefine the problem of the
administration of medical care services, and to design a system that
will produce a better solution of the management problems
involved'. [656]

Building on examples of practice in the more innovative hospitals,
the reports suggested that specialties should be grouped on a
divisional basis. Each division would then carry out management and
planning functions. For the purpose of co-ordination between
divisions, the two reports differed in their representative
arrangements, but both suggested that a Medical Executive
Committee, chaired by a senior clinician, was required. It was hoped
that these arrangements would strengthen medical management
within hospitals and create structures capable of relating to other
branches of management within the hospital service and indeed
more generally within the health service for planning purposes.

The Cogwheel message was disseminated by means of conferences
and meetings with major medical bodies. The new scheme was not
universally welcomed. Certain leading hospitals believed that they
already possessed superior management arrangements. Hospital
administrators complained that the Cogwheel left the consultant
vested interests and the notoriously unsuccessful system of bed
allocation virtually untouched.[657] Medical Officers of Health were
assured that the Chairman of the new Medical Executive
Committees would facilitate co-operation with the community
services, but the MOHs argued that if they were destined to become
community physicians, they should assume the chair of these
executives, or whatever health service executives were established
when amalgamation of services took place.[658] If this was not

313

conceded, Medical Officers of Health claimed that there should at least be some formal mechanism for linking them with the chairmen of the Medical Executive Committees; Chief Nursing Officers and group secretaries also wanted a similar link. Although a modest beginning Medical Executive Committees were important because they constituted one of the developments facilitating the establishment of 'general management teams', which were incipient consensus management bodies of the kind soon to be applied universally under the reorganised NHS.

Cogwheel was an entirely voluntary arrangement. Progress was painfully slow. However, by the end of 1970, more than one hundred hospital groups in England and Wales possessed Cogwheel systems of some kind. The Chief Medical Officer acknowledged that 'Cogwheel had to develop against resistance from some quite influential doctors and from many hospital administrators'. It was not a panacea, but if implemented in the intended spirit, it was a 'basis for fixing responsibility on a small and effective group to promote best current practice in the delivery of medical care'. It was recognised that only 'dogged persistence' would bring about the full benefits inherent in the Cogwheel system.[659] Cogwheel certainly captured the imagination of many groups committed to improving management within the hospital service. By 1971 more than a dozen papers had been written in support of this idea. The advocates came together to promote their views at a large conference on 'Harmony in Management' held in November 1970. By the end of 1971 about half of all hospital groups had implemented some kind of Cogwheel mechanism; by this date Cogwheel was established in two-thirds of large acute groups. However, the divisional structure was much more widely applied than the Medical Executive Committee.[660] Only limited further progress had been made before the Cogwheel initiative was submerged by the new management system devised for the reorganised health service.

Hospital Scientific and Technical Services
As pointed out in chapter I, the most rapid percentage expansion of staff within the health service occurred within the scientific and technical sector. This trend continued and indeed escalated. During the second decade of the service, the staff within these categories doubled in numbers. Although the numbers were small by comparison with some other groups of staff, still below 30,000 in 1968, they played a vital role in the development of the high-technology services upon which the service increasingly depended.[661] The largest numbers were employed as radiographers, medical laboratory technicians and pharmacists. Many of the groups comprised fewer than two-hundred individuals, scattered throughout

the hospital service, working as clinical psychologists, dietitians, orthoptists, darkroom technicians, EEG technicians etc. The arrival of new functions such as computer services or intermittent haemodialysis, created conditions for the proliferation of the sub-groupings of scientists and technicians.

The expansion of scientific and technical services occurred in an unco-ordinated manner. The thirty groups of staff classified under this heading were fragmented into almost as many disco-ordinated professional organisations, without uniform arrangements for recruitment, training, or remuneration. Pay tended to be low, recruitment difficult, and shortages of staff were endemic. Not surprisingly, the scientific and technical services were the commonest ground for industrial strife within the NHS. On account of the haphazard growth of these services, there was risk of waste and inefficient use of scarce labour. Training was difficult to organise, with the result that recruitment was adversely affected, while staff lacked transferable skills, or facilities for updating their qualifications. These problems were analogous to those faced in the social service field, which were addressed by the Seebohm Committee, and which, as already noted, produced proposals for unifying the social service profession and its training.

Some hospital regions attempted to introduce greater integration in the planning of scientific and technical services, but this met with resistance from HMCs, which resented regional interference with their planning. By the beginning of 1966 the Ministry of Health concluded that a 'new concept of scientific and technical organisation' was urgently needed. This issue was referred to the new Long Term Study Group in January 1966; it was considered by consultant advisers in August 1966, and by the JCC in the following month.[662]

The health departments were united in favouring an enquiry into the scientific and technical services. They envisaged a two-stage operation: first, advice on broad principles from a group of eminent clinicians and scientists; secondly, a technical working parting consisting of NHS authority experts to evolve ways of applying these principles within the hospital service.[663] This approach was approved by the SAMOs and RHB Chairmen.[664] Intentionally the representatives of scientific and technical groups, and NHS authorities were excluded from the first stage of the enquiry.

The first step was establishment of a small expert committee under Sir Solly Zuckerman, the Chief Scientific Adviser in the Cabinet Office, with a remit to 'consider the future organisation and development of hospital Scientific and Technical services in National Health Service hospitals and the broad pattern of staffing required and to make recommendations'.

This committee raised sensitive issues for the groups concerned and for their professional colleagues, but unlike the Seebohm Committee, its findings were not likely to be politically controversial. The Zuckerman Committee was appointed in August 1967; it reported one year later.[665] As in the case of the Salmon Report, it was decided that the Zuckerman Report was not sufficiently sensitive politically to merit issuing as a Command Paper.[666] The report was published on 4 December 1968.[667] This document was brief, comprising only 28 pages of text; it was intentionally limited to schematic guide-lines. The Zuckerman Report was largely a statement of the objectives of the scientific and technical groups themselves; it entailed importing into the NHS a career structure of the kind already existing in the Scientific Civil Service. It proposed establishment of a Hospital Scientific Service organised hierarchically, and including national, regional, and district officers and committees. Zuckerman suggested appointment of a Chief Scientist at both DHSS and the Scottish Office, a National Hospital Scientific Council for England and Wales, with a parallel Council for Scotland, Regional Scientific Advisory Committees and Regional Scientists, who would act as the principal scientific officer to the regional boards, and within each district general hospital a Division of Scientific Services, organised along the lines of the divisions proposed in the Cogwheel system discussed above. For planning purposes it was clearly impracticable to create a completely unified scientific and technical profession. It was therefore proposed to assimilate the professions into four branches, which represented the maximum degree of grouping feasible among the heterogeneous specialisms. The Zuckerman Report suggested the inclusion of medical and non-medical staff in the new service, with adoption of a new career structure following the lines of the Scientific Civil Service. The Zuckerman Committee hoped that its guide-lines would 'allow the Hospital Scientific Service to develop in a more orderly way than in the past and that the resources made available to it would be used more efficiently in the interests of the patients and the national economy'.[668]

With calculated deference to the sensitivities of the Treasury, the Zuckerman Committee suggested that its proposals represented the application of rigorous principles of rationality, efficiency and economy. In December 1968, Ennals announced the Government's general acceptance of the Zuckerman Report, and the institution of discussions about its implementation.[669]

At first, application of Zuckerman principles seemed unproblematical. It was necessary to undertake the customary consultations, which were more than usually complicated owing to the large number of organisations involved, but no special problems were anticipated. The planners underestimated the difficulties in moving forward. Not only was it difficult to evolve schemes for detailed application acceptable to the scientific and technical grades, but also there was the problem of similar magnitude in reconciling clinicians to these proposals. In addition, delays were caused by incomes policy, the onset of discussions concerning reorganisation and its accompanying management changes.

The Zuckerman planners therefore recapitulated many of the difficulties experienced in microcosm a decade previously in the Cope exercise to unify professional structures relating to eight groups of medical auxiliaries.[670] Responses to the Zuckerman Report were requested by the end of March 1969, but some of the leading organisations were unable to meet this target. In parallel with these consultations, a working party of officials examined prospects for further action. This working party produced a draft report in March 1969, but little further progress was made before the end of the year. It became increasingly evident that influential medical voices were suspicious about the implications of Zuckerman; further negotiations would be needed to satisfy them that the new arrangements constituted no threat to clinical authority.

The appearances of inaction caused anxiety within the General Whitley Council and the two Professional and Technical Whitley Councils, prompting a letter of complaint about the Government's failure to make a commitment to implement the Zuckerman proposals.[671] The Whitley interests were particularly concerned to become directly engaged in the promised second stage of working parties considering detailed implementation. Having regard for the successes enjoyed by nurses as a result of Salmon, scientific and technical workers were determined not to sacrifice this opportunity to improve their professional prospects, with corresponding benefits in improved remuneration and the promise for the first time of an adequate career structure. The Staff Side were increasingly concerned that Zuckerman was being used as an excuse for equivocation over their demands for pay revaluation.

Ministers met the Whitley representatives on 22 December 1969, when the Government representatives reaffirmed their positive attitude towards Zuckerman. It was clearly not practicable to further delay a statement on Zuckerman. In February 1970, Crossman speaking for England and Wales, formally accepted in principle the main recommendations of the Zuckerman Report and promised further consultation with hospital authorities and staff interests on the proposals relating to staffing structures.[672] The Staff Side was still apprehensive about absence of commitment to full consultation on the organisation and staffing recommendations of the Zuckerman Report. During the remaining months of the Wilson administration this impasse remained unresolved. The Staff Side reiterated its demands to Serota, but her advisers stubbornly refused to concede more than an opportunity for the staff interests to comment on a draft HM circular.[673] The further efforts of scientific and technical workers to improve their professional fortunes dragged on slowly and were indeed not even accomplished in the course of the Heath administration.

Community Medicine

The Seebohm initiative represented a big step forwards for the social work profession, largely at the expense of the older public health specialty. Seebohm therefore represented a notable setback in the long march of medicalisation. Public health medicine had scarcely risen to its feet after the erosion of authority occasioned by loss of control of hospital services and other functions in 1948.[674] The biggest expansion of the activities of local health authorities occurred in the area of community care, the staff of which included social workers of various kinds, as well as other non-medical personnel such as home helps. The increasing tendency to amalgamate local health and welfare departments under the Medical Officer of Health, created embryonic social service departments. At the time of the Seebohm Committee, some local authorities were making preparations to establish comprehensive social service departments administered by their Medical Officers of Health. The Government's endorsement of the Seebohm Report swept away for ever the social service ambitions of Medical Officers of Health. Indeed, the Seebohm system was intentionally designed to prevent medical personnel from becoming chief officers of the new social service departments.

Ever since the beginning of the NHS, the hunt had been on for a new role for the Medical Officer of Health. Gradually the term 'community physician' came into prominence and became established as the main life-line for this group. It was widely appreciated that the community physician of the future would not be engaged in administering a particular set of supplementary treatment services, but would exercise an administrative and intelligence function relating to the mainstream of the health service. This prospect was expressed in more tangible terms by the Royal Commission on Medical Education and the Seebohm Report.

The Royal Commission on Medical Education recognised that in the light of the trends in the health service and likely recommendations of the Seebohm Committee, 'the Medical Officer of Health in his traditional form, with both clinical and administrative functions, may well disappear completely'. Nevertheless, it conceded that there was likely to be a sizeable role for medical administrators.[675] The Commission made recommendations for the reconstruction of the public health specialty as 'community medicine'.[676] Consistent with the advice contained in the Todd Report, the various branches of the public health specialty tried to bridge the gulf between academic epidemiology and administrative public health medicine. In 1972, they formed the Faculty of Community Medicine of the Royal College of Physicians of London, which effectively took over leadership within the profession from the Society of Medical Officers of Health.

Published on the heels of the Todd Report, the Seebohm Report also called for Medical Officers of Health to transmute themselves into community medicine specialists or 'community physicians'. It was suggested that these specialists would 'ensure the joint working of the local medical services among themselves' and also relate them to the social services.[677]

In October 1969, the Society of Medical Officers of Health discussed the Seebohm recommendations with the Secretary of State, arguing that most of the services earmarked for transfer to the new unified social service departments should remain within the health service. SMOH also wanted a delay in implementation of Seebohm in order that the social services and health service changes would occur simultaneously. None of this was acceptable to the Government, but Crossman expressed sympathy with the plight of SMOH and promised to take steps to improve their morale and feeling of uncertainty. The Chief Medical Officer suggested that they would be helped by a speedy enquiry into the work of all doctors falling within the scope of the new specialty of community medicine. This gesture was appreciated by SMOH.[678] The promised working party was established in April 1970, under the chairmanship of Dr R B Hunter, Vice-Chancellor of the University of Birmingham, and formerly Dean of the Faculty of Medicine at the University of St Andrews.[679] This large working party, containing fifteen members apart from the chairman, represented all sides of the intended new specialty of community medicine, together with a minority of members drawn from the health departments, other medical specialties, and two lay members, Mr G A Phalp, the Secretary of the King's Fund, and Professor Abel-Smith. Despite greater gender awareness demonstrated with respect to other committees, this committee contained no women members, no social scientists involved in primary care or community medicine, and no representatives of community interests. These omissions perhaps help to explain some of the limitations evident in the Hunter Report.

The Hunter working party was asked to 'define the scope of the work of medical administrators at regional, area, and district levels

319

in a reorganised health service, and to indicate how training and retraining for such doctors could be provided'. DHSS hoped that the working party would quickly reach its conclusions, and at least have interim recommendations available in time for inclusion in the White Paper on National Health Service reorganisation which the Labour administration hoped to issue in the summer of 1970. In the event, the Hunter working party had only met twice by the date of the 1970 General Election. After the change in government, Hunter approached the new Secretary of State for fresh instructions.[680] The Labour Government therefore failed in its objective to provide reassurances to the Medical Officers of Health in order to offset blows to their morale occasioned by uncertainties associated with NHS reorganisation, the Seebohm legislation, and preparations for transfer of a major part of their staff to the new social service departments.

CHAPTER IV

Labour and Reorganisation

The administrative structure of the NHS introduced in 1948 persisted with virtually no change for quarter of a century. Then, after an extensive period of preparation and consultation, a comprehensive reorganisation took place in 1974. While the Wilson administration was committed to strengthening the NHS, reorganisation did not count among its stated policy objectives. However, this issue quickly appeared on the agenda, and soon it became one of the dominant social services policy concerns of the Labour Government. As will be seen below, the opportunity for reorganisation was not initially greeted with enthusiasm by Kenneth Robinson. There was much vacillation before the idea of comprehensive reorganisation was taken seriously. It was nevertheless initially expected that the entire process of reorganisation could be accomplished by 1970. This underestimated the complexity of the problem, and it assumed a greater degree of certainty of purpose than was possessed in practice by the Wilson administration.

Robinson issued the first Green Paper on reorganisation in July 1968. The reorganisation issue assumed even higher profile under Richard Crossman, who was responsible for a second Green Paper in February 1970, and shortly afterwards a draft White Paper, but the latter never materialised owing to the general election defeat in June 1970. As indicated below, Edinburgh was quicker than London to take up the question of reorganisation, but the early lead was soon lost. Thereafter, the separate Scottish Green Papers were produced slightly in arrears of their English counterparts. Initially, little consideration was given to separate planning documents for Wales. The first Green Paper related to both England and Wales, but thereafter, continuing indifference to Welsh sensitivities was no longer an option, with the result that an independent Welsh Green Paper was issued in 1970.

Although public discussion of change began in earnest with the first Green Paper, formally the reorganisation process was initiated in November 1967, when the health Ministers issued a tentative parliamentary statement indicating their intention to examine the administration of the health services. Even this was by no means the start of their deliberations. Although the decision to embark on NHS reorganisation is sometimes presented as a momentous initiative of

321

the Minister of Health, the documentary evidence suggests little support for such a conclusion. Indeed, the Minister of Health and his advisers seem to have been among the last to be persuaded of the need for comprehensive reorganisation of the health services.

(i) CASE FOR CHANGE

During the early years of the NHS, the health departments devoted their energies to optimising the performance of the admittedly imperfect structures established in 1948. Among the parties involved in the protracted disputes of the 1940s there was no enthusiasm for reopening old wounds; their reticence was no doubt fuelled by the suspicion that an even worse compromise might result from a new round of horse-trading. None of the component entities of the labyrinthine NHS administrative structure assumed the initiative for change. Each of the main elements in the tripartite structure recognised its vulnerability to criticism and the likelihood that rationalisation would entail the possibility of extinction. Nevertheless, as indicated in the previous volume, there were always voices arguing that the tripartite system was inherently unsound and favouring substantial organisational change. The most fully-argued discordant view emanated from Sir John Maude, in his lengthy reservation to the Guillebaud Report in 1956, in which he contended that the health services should be unified and returned to local government.

The medical profession was never slow to indulge in hostile criticism of the NHS, and its perpetual grievance over remuneration tended to increase this antagonism. During the 1956/57 dispute over pay, the Council of the BMA found itself under pressure from the membership to institute an inquiry into the entire health service; also from this date derives their more active enthusiasm for insurance-based alternatives to the NHS.[1]

By 1960, the deficiencies of the tripartite structure were abundantly clear. These inherent weaknesses were summarised in the consultation document circulated by the Scottish Home and Health Department in 1968, which aptly reflects the thinking of this period and therefore merits citing in full:

> The basic criticism directed against the existing organisation of the National Health Service is that the tripartite division into hospital services, executive council services and local authority services does not make the most effective use of the total resources available to meet the needs of patients, which do not fall into three corresponding compartments but can often be met only by the joint efforts of different parts of the service. More specifically, it is suggested by critics of the present organisation-

(a) in relation to the day-to-day operation of the service, that while effective co-operation between those who provide the various parts of the service is often achieved, it would be more easily and more generally achieved if the service were not managed by three separate authorities. This leads to the conclusion that administrative integration is desirable to promote fully effective operational (or 'functional') co-ordination.

(b) in relation to the long-term development of the service, that it is not easy at present to ensure that all the health service resources in any area are deployed to the best advantage, since there is no single authority responsible for looking at the total need and the total resources. The statutory framework introduced in 1948 has made it difficult to depart from the pattern then laid down, and does not permit flexibility and change in response to new requirements. Here again, while co-operation between the various authorities does take place, effective planning is likely to be achieved more easily in any particular area if it is the responsibility of one body, not three.

(c) that the present pattern of financial responsibility for the service - the separate system of budgeting and accountability for the different parts of the service, and the division between the partly rate-born expenditure of local authority health services and the Exchequer-financed hospital and executive council services - may have a distorting effect on the allocation of resources and the balance between the services in particular areas.[2]

Porritt Report

Structural shortcomings within the NHS were a source of criticism and mounting frustration. Typically, a review conducted in 1965 into the workings of an elaborate machinery for co-ordination established in Scotland at the start of the NHS, discovered that its impact had been minimal; most of the relevant committees had lapsed into inactivity within a short time of their establishment.[3] It was abundantly clear that neither bureaucratic nor ad hoc methods of stimulating co-ordination and efficiency were exercising sufficient impact. Given mounting frustration concerning problems associated with the fragmentation of health service administration, it is scarcely surprising that there emerged a demand for examining the feasibility of simplifying and integrating the hugely-elaborate structure which, in Britain as a whole, comprised more than 850 separate administrative bodies.

The first significant impulse for change emanated from the medical profession. Although the profession itself was largely responsible for the over-complicated and inefficient structure of the health service, doctors complained when they discovered that their professional work was adversely affected by administrative complexities. It is therefore not surprising that the pressure built up within the profession for a high-level investigation of the case for integration.

As described in volume I, tensions over the 1956/57 remuneration crisis were defused by the establishment of the Pilkington Commission, but this failed to satisfy deeper anxieties concerning shortcomings in the health services. Reflecting the seriousness of this problem, the profession overcame its habitual sectarian disunity and pressed for a high-level enquiry into the health service to complement the Pilkington enquiry. Given the unresponsiveness of the Government to this wider demand, in 1958 the profession instituted its own enquiry. Following the pattern of the Medical Planning Commission in 1942, a large committee representing nine leading medical organisations, under the chairmanship of Sir Arthur Porritt, was formed to investigate the state of the medical services in Britain. The substantial report of this committee was published in November 1962.[4] The value of this report is enhanced by data on health care gathered by outside consultants.

Like the Medical Planning Commission of 1942, the Porritt Committee proved to be more liberal than the medico-political establishment. Like the Guillebaud Report, the Porritt Report pronounced firmly in favour of the NHS, but it came to a contrary conclusion concerning organisation. Whereas Guillebaud placed its confidence in improvements within the existing structure, the Porritt Committee found evidence that the system was incapable of adaptation, and was increasingly unable to meet the requirements of modern medical planning. Accordingly, the Porritt Report pronounced firmly in favour of reorganisation, and it called for the assimilation under a single authority of all health services located in each natural area of administration.[5]

The Porritt committee was in fact faithfully reiterating the conclusions of the Royal Sanitary Commission expressed as far back as 1871, which subsequently guided the thinking of various influential reports, until finally during World War II, the planners of the NHS adopted this idea as their guiding principle. Political circumstances precluded realisation of anything like this degree of unification and rationalisation of health service administration, but the merits of this approach were so obvious that it provided a natural basis for the analysis conducted by the leaders of medical opinion.

The Porritt Report was unspecific about precise administrative arrangements, but it envisaged that the future health service would be administered by a relatively small number of 'area health boards'.

The rationality of the Porritt proposals was not entirely altruistic or free from medico-political considerations.[6] In line with deep-seated antagonism to local councils, it was proposed that the new administrative authorities for the health services should not be linked with local government. Also in line with long-standing aspirations of the profession, it was proposed that the new boards would take over the school health service, many welfare services of local government, as well as all occupational health services. The Porritt Report therefore fully reflected the deep-seated urge for extension of the medical empire.

Somewhat inconsistently with this integrationist philosophy, it was accepted that teaching hospitals in England and Wales should keep their independent administration, although it was conceded that area health boards in Scotland would retain control of these hospitals in line with arrangements that had operated successfully since 1948. Although the Porritt Committee was imprecise about the constitution of area health boards, it was anticipated that the medical profession would be strongly represented, and would exercise an additional powerful influence through separate statutory advisory committees concerned with each major sector of the health service. Although the Porritt Report was ostensibly addressed to the long-term requirements of the health service, in practice its thinking was dominated by the immediate objectives of dominant groups of hospital specialists, whereas such important areas as mental health and community services were accorded little attention.

Despite its ambitious scope and wide-ranging proposals, the Porritt Report seemed to attract only limited interest. Indeed, even the authoritative account of professional affairs during this period by Stevens mentions the Porritt Committee only in passing and refers only incidentally to the reorganisation aspect of the report.[7] On the political front, little of note appeared to happen until the ministerial announcements in November 1967.

In fact, the Porritt Report exercised more influence than was superficially apparent. Although initially not attracting much media attention, support for reorganisation steadily intensified. In the absence of any rival planning exercise, the Porritt Report established itself as the basis for future action, confirming that the medical profession, through its timely intervention had effectively dictated the agenda for change. However, among the nine sponsoring medical organisations, the Porritt Report attained only a moderate degree of acceptance, partly owing to the absence of procedures for securing general assent on policy issues. Even negotiating the labyrinthine committee structures of the BMA was a tortuous operation. In this instance discussions dragged on inconsequentially within the BMA until they were eventually overtaken by the 1968 Green Paper.

The first notable success of the Porritt Committee occurred in Wales. In December 1964, the Welsh Committee of the BMA set up a committee which produced proposals for organising the Welsh health services on Porritt lines.[8] The scheme adopted by the Welsh Committee in May 1966 was remarkably like the plan implemented in 1974. In the short-term, the influence of this Welsh initiative was limited owing to lack of interest in the Welsh health administration, as well as reticence on the part of the BMA in London. Indeed, the Welsh Board of Health even refused to send a representative to meet the Welsh BMA Porritt Committee.[9] Eventually a revised version of the Welsh report was approved in June 1967, but it was not formally adopted by the BMA Council, and it was not published until January 1968, and then only in an abridged version.[10]

The Porritt Report also attracted interest in BMA circles in Scotland, where in 1965 the issue of unification of health services was taken up by the Scottish GMSC. Scottish general practitioners harboured particular grievances about their exclusion from hospital services; negotiations with hospital authorities achieved little and added to the frustrations of general practitioners. Such experiences inclined the BMA in Scotland to favour greater functional integration. In March 1966 the Scottish GMSC passed a resolution calling for the 'closest functional integration of all parts of the Health Service' in Scotland.[11] As noted below, the Scottish GMSC and SHHD discovered a high degree of common purpose.[12] This facilitated joint action in preparing the ground for the first Green Paper and also ensured that this document was accorded a smooth reception.[13]

The first contact between Porritt and Ministers occurred in January 1963, when Powell wrote privately to congratulate Porritt on the work of his committee. This led to a meeting between Powell and Porritt, but detailed discussions were precluded until after ratification of the report by the sponsoring bodies. The next move came from Porritt, who wrote to Robinson in November 1964 requesting an interview between members of his committee and the Ministry of Health.[14] Kenneth Robinson, accompanied by Judith Hart representing SHHD, met the Porritt Committee on 9 February 1965.[15] On behalf of his Committee, Porritt complained that the tripartite structure of the NHS was 'inherently faulty' and that the three parts were drifting further apart. Change was therefore urgently needed. He claimed that their report represented a generally accepted basis for reform. Robinson expressed scepticism about the need for change beyond the encouragement of comprehensive planning among existing authorities. He promised to sponsor pilot studies to improve co-ordination and encourage more widespread secondment of local authority nursing staff to general medical practitioners, but he was unconvinced that further action was needed.[16] On the advice of his officials, Robinson was unconvinced that the Porritt Committee reflected the mood of the medical profession. Robinson was told that 'only Sir Arthur himself is still really enthusiastic about the whole thing'.[17] Porritt pressed the Minister for further discussions, making a bid for his Committee to act as the main channel of communication between the Ministry and the profession over health service reform. Again on the advice of his officials, Robinson firmly refused to be drawn into further discussions.[18]

This rebuff by the Minister might have stifled further action by the Porritt Committee. However, the Committee was not easily discouraged. Its resolve was strengthened by two new factors: first, indications that general practitioners were breaking rank and independently attempting to determine the future of the NHS in the context of their Family Doctors' Charter campaign; and secondly, suspicion that consultants were being outflanked by the Minister's newly-appointed Advisory Committee on Long Term Development. The next avenue of approach was the JCC, upon which Porritt members represented a substantial element. In April 1965 the JCC requested a meeting with Ministers to discuss 'matters affecting the efficiency, development and reorganisation of the NHS'.[19]

The JCC met Robinson and Hart on 28 June 1965.[20] The significance of this event was indicated by full attendance of the JCC. Indeed this was the first occasion on which the full JCC had met the two health Ministers. Robinson was clearly taken by surprise. Evidently, he expected the JCC to concentrate on questions relating to medical manpower. Instead he faced a vitriolic attack, in the course of which the JCC complained that the Government was avoiding facing up to serious defects in the health service, as well as refusing to recognise the right of the JCC to give advice on policy questions relating to organisation. Robinson replied with some consternation, defending the record of the NHS, and he gave no indication of sympathy with the demand for a review of NHS organisation.

On this occasion Robinson was successful in deflecting the JCC away from the general issue of reorganisation by promising them a high level of involvement in an ambitious review of hospital policy, which gradually became narrowed down until it resulted in the Cogwheel exercise, already discussed in chapter III.[21] Porritt himself was removed from the scene in January 1967, when he was appointed Governor-General of New Zealand. The Porritt mission accordingly seemed to have ended in failure, but a leading participant in these events records that notwithstanding initial 'harsh criticism in government quarters, some of it distinctly unfair,...the report was the stimulus for what the Government was to attempt 5 years later'.[22]

One positive response to the growing pressure for change was the establishment by Robinson of his Advisory Committee on Long Term Development, which first met in July 1965. One of the primary objectives of this committee was providing Robinson with a credible programme for co-ordination within the existing framework of the NHS. This was the first issue considered by the Committee, which immediately responded with ideas about experiments with Porritt forms of administration.[23] Robinson assured the Committee that he was sympathetic to experiment, but advised them to avoid proposals outside the existing framework of organisation. This limitation was observed, with the result that the Long Term Development Committee played no further significant part in discussions concerning reorganisation. This anomaly caused Robinson some embarrassment, because he came under pressure in the House of Commons to involve the Long Term Committee in his reflections on integration, in response to which he gave the impression that their advice on this question was being taken, and the same impression was given in the introduction to the 1968 Green Paper.[24] In fact, throughout 1965, 1966 and indeed early 1967, the only concession made by Robinson to the integrationist lobby was his agreement to enter into discussions on the legislative powers needed to permit experiments with new forms of health service administration.[25]

Inherited Deficiencies

Robinson was increasingly swimming against the tide. His negative response towards reorganisation was at odds with the ethos increasingly prevailing in planning circles. The Wilson administration was confronted by a plethora of demands for modernisation of the welfare state. Planners and professionals in the field were disenchanted with the organisational compromises of 1948, and they needed to respond to rising expectations concerning quality of services. Modernisers were convinced that urgently-needed advances in the quality of welfare provision necessitated correction of organisational deficiencies endemic in the system. Reorganisation overtook co-ordination as a dominant theme in social administration. Because of the interrelatedness of services, attention to reorganisation in one field inevitably impinged on related services, while plans for local administration raised questions about the machinery of central government. Consequently, any specific impulse for change was likely to possess implications for the entire system of central and local administration of the social services.

There was nothing very deliberate about the drift into reorganisation instituted in the course of the Wilson administration.

Ministers tended to be inhibited from innovation on account of the inbuilt prejudice in favour of the status quo among officials, reinforced by instinctive Treasury fears that innovation entailed enhanced expenditure. Even the ebullient Crossman, as Minister of Housing and Local Government, was slow to overcome the bias in his department against a general review of local government. However, he soon came to conclusion that the system was becoming unworkable, and in September 1965, without prior consultation with his Cabinet colleagues, he announced his intention to institute a radical review of local government.[26] At the least, such an exercise necessitated a reassessment of local health and welfare authorities, thereby raising the prospect of revival of demands for returning all health services to local government. Indeed, in 1967 this possibility was canvassed by the Mallaby Committee investigating the staffing of local government departments.[27] As indicated below, this conclusion was also supported by the Royal Commission on Local Government.

A further stimulus for change emanated from the Royal Commission on Medical Education established in June 1965. As noted in chapter III, while health service reorganisation was not within the remit of the Royal Commission, its urgent demand for expansion of the medical school intake first made in an interim report of June 1966, presupposed greater integration between teaching hospitals and the rest of the hospital system, having the effect of bringing England and Wales into line with Scotland. The Royal Commission advocated unified administrative entities compatible with the divisions adopted for reorganised local government. If regions were preserved, the Royal Commission recommended an increase from four to five regions in London, and subdivision of some regions outside the capital, especially the Sheffield RHB. Because Labour in opposition had promised to expand existing medical schools and establish at least four new medical schools, the Wilson administration should have appreciated the impact this change was likely to exercise on the hospital system as a whole.[28]

Also decisive for the NHS was the demand for sweeping changes in the organisation of the personal social services. Social workers were distributed among a variety of local government departments, while central government responsibility was similarly widely diffused, mainly between the Department of Education and Science, the Home Office, and the Ministry of Health. One of the largest groups of personnel engaged in social work operated under the Medical Officer of Health. By 1964 there was widespread dissatisfaction with these arrangements within the social work profession. As in the health services, it seemed evident that co-ordination was an

329

imperfect solution. As explained in chapter III, the Government conceded that the case for substantial change deserved investigation, and for this purpose the Seebohm Committee was established in the autumn of 1965.[29] From the outset it was clear that the Seebohm Committee was likely to favour unification of the personal social services. Any such development was likely to remove one of the largest and most rapidly expanding elements in the department of the Medical Officer of Health and thereby threaten the viability of the small rump of services remaining with the local health authority.

The case for reorganisation was increasingly appreciated within the NHS. Reports or planning documents relating to specific services such as the Cranbrook Report into maternity services (1959), the Gillie Report on general practice (1963), the Hospital Plan (1962), or the parallel review of community care services (1963), while not specifically advocating reorganisation, recognised that the goals of co-ordination and efficiency were virtually impossible to achieve under the tripartite system. Even more explicit, the revision of the Scottish Hospital Plan called for closer integration and co-ordination of services and recognised that it would be necessary to address questions of 'health service organisation lying behind these developments'.[30] The two reports on the organisation of medical work in hospitals, which were completed early in 1967, called for a closer degree of integration that 'seems at variance with the continuance of administrative divisions within the National Health Service'.[31] Approaching the problems of the hospital service from the perspective of its labour force, the National Board for Prices and Incomes on the basis of its investigations into the pay of ancillary workers and nurses, came to the conclusion that it was desirable to replace 'the existing RHBs and HMCs with single-tier authorities, or some form of Area Health Board'.[32]

By the autumn of 1965 it was evident that reorganisation was favoured by the local authority associations, some health service trade unions, the TUC, and some Labour MPs.[33] In 1965 the Fabian Society reissued a pamphlet by Laurie Pavitt calling for unification of the health service along Porritt lines.[34] Among the expert voices, particularly influential was the National Institute of Economic and Social Research, which in 1956 had published the important analysis of the spending record of the NHS, *The Costs of the National Health Service*, by Brian Abel-Smith and Richard Titmuss. In 1965 the NIESR issued a study on *The British Economy in 1975*, which was followed by an expanded version of the chapters on health and welfare, *Health and Welfare Services in Britain in 1975*. The authors supported Porritt, and concluded that an inescapable argument existed for 'basic reorganisation and administrative improvement' of the NHS.[35]

The strength of the case for reorganisation was not universally acknowledged. This possibility was not considered in the Salmon Report on nursing published in 1966, or in the Farquharson-Lang Report on administrative practice of hospital boards in Scotland which appeared in 1966. It has already been noted that NHS administrative bodies in general were cautious about change and that the BMA in London was reticent to commit itself to comprehensive reorganisation. Also, despite their concern with forward planning in the health services, neither the King's Fund, nor the Nuffield Provincial Hospitals Trust were quick to adopt the Porritt Report, or indeed to accept that the health service required complete administrative reorganisation.[36] The political parties were also slow to commit themselves to reorganisation, and this issue was not raised in the general election manifestos of the Labour and Conservative Parties in either 1964 or 1966.

Notwithstanding reticence to face the reorganisation issue in some main centres of influence, it was evident that a strong impetus for change was building up. It was clear that health service administration needed to be adapted to match the more general transition taking place within medicine. The growing sentiment in favour of change was aptly expressed by the Royal Commission on Medical Education, which pointed out that the doctor of the future needed to be prepared for a 'world in which everything - the content of medicine, the organisation of medical care, the doctor's relationships with his colleagues and the community, and indeed every feature of his professional life and work - is on the move'.[37]

The demand for change eventually reached Parliament. In August 1966 Robinson came under criticism from both sides of the House of Commons for his insensitivity to the integration issue. Bernard Braine, an opposition health spokesman, drew attention to the arguments of the Porritt Report.[38] David Owen attacked the NHS administration as a 'tripartite monster' and demanded that the time had come for a more imaginative lead on the question of integration.[39] Robinson reiterated his customary defence of the record of the NHS in promoting co-ordination, but for the first time the Minister conceded that he would not for all time exclude the possibility of changing the administrative structure of the service.[40]

(ii) CONCORD IN SCOTLAND

The only significant step towards reorganisation by Robinson during 1965 was to initiate discussions among officials with a view to introducing clauses into a prospective miscellaneous health services Bill, which would permit at the Minister's discretion, introduction of new forms of administration in areas such as new towns, where existing arrangements for co-ordination proved insufficient.

331

Robinson favoured this limited adaptation to facilitate developments like the much-acclaimed 'Livingstone experiment' in Scotland. Success of integrated planning in such areas as new towns was calculated to defuse the campaign for more general reorganisation.

Within SHHD there was less enthusiasm for experiment on account of the disproportionate effort required to sustain such developments as the Livingstone scheme. It was suspected that legislation permitting limited experiments would only reduce administrative complications to a minor extent. Accordingly energies were better spent in examining the case for general reorganisation. This view was supported by Judith Hart, who had also reacted more positively than Robinson to the overtures of the Porritt Committee.[41] The Treasury insisted that the health departments should clarify 'basic policy in your thinking about the future administration of the health services' before embarking on the course of experiment.[42]

In March 1965 SHHD established a working party to consider the case for reorganisation. This examined the Porritt Report in detail; it produced an interim report in May,[43] and a final report in September.[44] Scottish officials took note of frustrations experienced by general practitioners in gaining access to diagnostic facilities in their local hospitals, as well as the difficulties experienced in establishing integrated health services in new towns such as Livingstone. It was concluded that the tripartite system had the effect of 'freezing the pattern of care' into a form appropriate in 1948, but inappropriate for the 1960s. Officials therefore aimed to secure more flexibility within the system, for which purpose they were predisposed to favour administration of all health services by a single local body. The working party report therefore proposed that the health services in Scotland should be divided into 18 units, each administered by an 'area health board'. Scottish plans therefore broadly followed the lines of the Porritt Report. At this stage consideration was given to implementation of this plan in two phases, the first step being amalgamation of the hospital and family practitioner administrations. Local health authorities were excluded from consideration initially on account of likely adverse response from local government. However, it was thought unrealistic to stop with the limited option, since the already adopted plan for integrated personal social services departments undermined the viability of separate local health authorities. The working party was undecided about the need for a regional tier, but opinion within the department at this stage was marginally against dispensing with the region, because this would entail assimilation of many regional functions into the central department and thereby incur the accusation of excessive centralisation.[45]

Scottish officials reached their decision in favour of general reorganisation without controversy. An important ally of reorganisation was John Brotherston, the recently-appointed and influential Chief Medical Officer, whose involvement was crucial with respect to consultation with the medical profession.[46] To the delight of Scottish officials, it transpired that the Scottish GMSC, the leading voice of medical opinion in Scotland, favoured reorganisation, and furthermore - as noted above - was also in favour of the Porritt approach. Under the guidance of Brotherston, SHHD and the Scottish GMSC formed a joint working party to bring their plans into final harmony.[47]

The next step was formal consultation with Ministers with a view to approaching English colleagues about a joint policy initiative. Mrs Hart was already generally conversant with the subject and known to be sympathetic with the conclusions reached by officials. Both Mrs Hart and William Ross had underlined the need for greater integration in their speeches on the health services during 1965. In January 1966, both Hart and Ross agreed enthusiastically to support reorganisation. They preferred joint action with England and Wales, but in the absence of co-operation they were willing to sponsor a separate initiative. This period marked the zenith of the separate Scottish initiative. After only a few months of deliberation, reorganisation, with a multiplicity of attendant benefits, seemed practicable and attainable without delay. This initial euphoria was soon dispelled and the opportunity for immediate action was lost.

(iii) STALEMATE

In London, Robinson, supported by Sir Arnold France, rejected the Scottish proposals and refused to embark on any consideration of general reorganisation until after a substantial phase of experiment.[48] Further discussion was delayed by the General Election held in March 1966. Robinson and Ross remained in office, but at the crucial junior level in Scotland, Judith Hart was replaced by Bruce Millan. It was therefore necessary to allow Millan time to resume his new duties, and then to begin the ministerial consultations afresh.

Scottish officials discovered no convergence of thinking with their London colleagues. Robinson continued to urge the merits of experiment within the existing framework of administration, regarding reorganisation as a possibility for consideration only in the long term.[49] London officials pressed their Scottish counterparts to commit themselves more actively to preparing legislation for experiment, but Scottish officials remained sceptical about the value of this less radical course of action, and they discovered that the Treasury shared their point of view.[50] Faced with the two rival concepts, the Treasury, in its first responses on this policy area, dating from July 1966, preferred complete reorganisation because this alternative promised greater efficiency savings, and therefore could be used to counter demands from the Ministry of Health for a larger share of public resources to be devoted to the health services.[51] This response may partly explain why Robinson was unfavourable to wholesale reorganisation, because this course would fatally undermine his campaign for additional resources, the credibility of which depended on the assumption that substantial efficiency savings were not attainable. If reorganisation held the prospect of major efficiency savings, the Treasury was likely to reject increases in health service spending until the extent of these efficiency savings was established.

Immediately after the 1966 General Election, Scottish officials resumed discussions with Ministers and discovered that Ross was still favourable to comprehensive reorganisation.[52] They held an initial discussion with Millan on 8 July 1966, and over the next year they periodically held further meetings, but failed to enlist his support for reorganisation.[53] Perhaps because of his greater experience of Scottish politics than Hart, Millan was more responsive to Scottish Labour's local government sensitivities. He was therefore unsympathetic to a plan which would remove an important local government function, evolved without consultation with local government bodies, and at a time when a Royal Commission was deliberating over the reform and strengthening of local government. The area health board plan also seemed like a capitulation to medical interests. Millan therefore refused to press on with the reorganisation scheme. He insisted on consultation with local government and agreement with London over joint action. Indeed, he favoured deferring decision over policy and remitting this problem to an independent committee of enquiry. Millan's unsympathetic reaction effectively undermined the separate Scottish initiative; after some hesitation, Ross came to share many of the same reservations, and eventually became even more insistent than Millan that any plan for reorganisation should be fully discussed with local government.[54]

National Health Service Board

Robinson was disinclined to abandon his plan for experiments, while among his officials opinion was divided and uncertain. By contrast, the Treasury was predisposed to favour some kind of radical solution in line with its continuing mission to shake up the errant Ministry of Health and bring efficiency to the NHS. The first serious exchanges between the Ministry of Health and the Treasury on the question of reorganisation took place over preparation of evidence for the Fulton Committee. The latter was established in February 1966 with a remit to 'examine the structure, recruitment and management, including training' of the home civil service. The scope of this committee was drastically limited by the decision to exclude machinery of government from its remit.[55] Although the Treasury realised that the question of reorganisation was beyond the remit of the Fulton Committee, this seemed like a convenient opportunity to draw attention to management deficiencies within the NHS and force the Ministry of Health to address such issues.

Acrimonious and unfruitful exchanges between the Ministry of Health and the Treasury over Fulton evidence began in December 1966 and extended over about six months.[56] This minor digression merits retrospective attention because it constitutes the first detailed discussion between departments of the merits of devolving the management of the NHS to a separate national board or public corporation. This idea was not new. It had been advocated since the earliest discussions of a National Health Service and this idea was particularly associated with the name of Stephen Taylor (since 1958, Lord Taylor) a former medical journalist and writer on primary care. This possibility was also briefly considered and dismissed by the Acton Society Trust, the Guillebaud Committee, and by Enoch Powell. The corporation proposal received wider public attention when it was advocated in the *British Medical Journal* by Jack Wiseman, the York University economist.[57] Also, the proposals of the Welsh BMA for area health boards, mentioned above, contained proposals for a 'National Health Council', which approximated to a national corporation, albeit without managerial associations. Resurrection of this proposal reflects Treasury aspirations to strengthen management within the health service. Devolving the administration of the NHS to a separate board seemed to offer the prospect for a unified management structure, thereby freeing the health departments from irksome, routine management responsibilities. Despite the attractions of such a scheme, it failed to command consensus even within the Treasury, and from the outset it was greeted with suspicion by Sir Arnold France. Indeed, France accused the Treasury of exceeding its rights by evolving far-ranging schemes for reform without consultation with the department concerned. France was reluctant even to mention the corporation idea in his evidence to the Fulton Committee, and he was unwilling to accord it any support from his own department. The idea was abandoned because of the likely parliamentary opposition, where it would be seen as undermining the detailed financial accountability of Parliament for the NHS budget, and limiting the ability of MPs to make representations in the interests of their constituents on health service affairs. Although some Treasury officials urged that these objections were not definitive obstacles, the corporation idea for the moment faded out of the reorganisation debate. Perhaps on account of limitations in its remit, the Fulton Committee itself received little evidence on the question of hiving-off public services to autonomous boards or corporations, and its report gave only passing consideration to this issue. While it was appreciated that many services, including personal services to the local community, could be provided in this manner, it was felt that this proposal raised such difficult constitutional issues that it required a separate review.[58] It is worth noting that the Regional Hospital Boards, despite their expressions of dissatisfaction with the health departments, and their undoubted acquaintance with the idea of an autonomous corporation, failed to examine this concept in their evidence to the Fulton Committee.[59]

Agreed Position

The Fulton digression, although immediately unproductive, at least increased the profile of the debate over reorganisation, reinforcing the Treasury view that radical change was necessary. Having sacrificed the national corporation proposal, Treasury officials explored other alternatives. Unification of the health service under local government was seriously considered, but was eliminated on account of the dependence of the health service on funding from central government. It was therefore likely that there would be insufficient incentive for local government to economise in its management of health services. Accordingly the local government alternative was quickly, although not decisively, eliminated. Given the rejection of a national corporation and local government, the Treasury directed its energies into determining whether other schemes for reorganisation would introduce more effective management and a greater degree of functional integration into the health service.[60]

By this stage the Ministry of Health was exposed to compelling advocacy in favour of reorganisation. Partisans of unification of the social services also tended to work for parallel changes in the health service.[61] Sir George Godber, the Chief Medical Officer, was exposed to the influence of the Porritt camp and his Scottish counterpart, Brotherston, who was a confirmed advocate of reorganisation. It is therefore not surprising that in June 1966 it was reported that within the Ministry of Health, the most conspicuous support for reorganisation emanated from the committee headed by Godber on the organisation of medical work in hospitals. As already noted, this committee was a filial descendant of the Porritt Committee, and it worked closely with its counterpart in Scotland, chaired by Brotherston.[62] As early as September 1966, it was reported that Sir Arnold France had decided that experiment was a waste of time.[63] In December 1966 and January 1967, senior officials from Edinburgh and London held two meetings in the course of which they worked out an agreed view on the 'one bite' approach to reorganisation.[64] However, within the Ministry of Health there was no immediate conversion to the idea of reorganisation. As late as an office meeting on 16 October 1967 a minority recorded spirited opposition to Porritt-style reorganisation favoured by the majority.[65] Whatever their personal reservations, Robinson's senior advisers came into line with their Scottish colleagues. This change of heart was reflected in Ministry of Health dealings with the Royal Commission on Local Government. At a discussion with the Commission in January 1967, France was unwilling to concede that significant change was needed, but in April, France and Godber frankly admitted the strength of the case for reorganisation.[66]

Ministers were not readily persuaded to accept the new orthodoxy. In Scotland, both Ross and Millan refused to consider policies adverse to local government, especially ahead of the report of the Scottish Royal Commission on Local Government. J Dickson Mabon, another junior Minister at the Scottish Office, recorded his general sympathy with integration, but believed that 'an integrated service must have some functional relationship with local government'.[67] The only course of joint action acceptable to the Scottish Ministers was a statement that they would sanction discussions 'concerning means of improving co-ordination between the different parts of the NHS, including in this review of the possibility of changes in the structure of the service'.[68]

At an important meeting 10 April 1967, officials strongly advised their Ministers to adopt a joint statement announcing that they would examine the case for reorganisation. However, none of the Ministers concerned was supportive and Robinson in particular warned that any hint that the departments were considering reorganisation would result in uncertainty within the health service and cause all the interest groups concerned to take up doctrinaire positions. However, it was conceded that some kind of review was unavoidable and that this could not be handled without outside consultations. Accordingly, a public statement was needed, but it was agreed to avoid terms such as 'integration' and place the main emphasis on 'co-ordination'.[69]

Ministers inclined to sponsor a confidential review, followed by an independent enquiry, perhaps in the form of a Royal Commission. This latter course attracted some support within the BMA, where it had been ritually unearthed at times of crisis since the beginning of the NHS. Without enthusiasm, the BMA Secretary conveyed the Royal Commission suggestion to the health department, while privately mentioning that he had no confidence in this approach.[70] The BMA favoured reorganisation, but it was still undecided about the Porritt plan and could not agree on an alternative. Retreat into

337

the idea of an independent enquiry is indicative of this state of indecision, a factor which reduced the impact of the BMA on government thinking in the months during which the joint statement was being discussed.

As already noted, the Scottish plan had been formulated by the autumn of 1965, whereas the first English proposals were circulated for discussion only in July 1967, a few months in advance of the ministerial statement made by Robinson on 6 November 1967. Although the question of reorganisation had been under consideration since the beginning of the Wilson administration, Robinson had arrived at no settled convictions on this crucial issue of policy, and there was no firm guidance available from the Labour Party. The most detailed, accessible advice derived from the Porritt Report and the new Scottish plan, which itself derived from Porritt. Also relevant were the papers prepared for the Royal Commission on Local Government, which focussed thinking on realistic units for administration, an aspect of planning which was beyond the competence of the Porritt Committee.

Although Robinson marginally shifted his position on reorganisation in the spring of 1967, there was little outward sign of a change of heart. For instance, in reply to further interrogation from David Owen enquiring about the Minister's intentions concerning integration, Robinson issued his stock response that he was encouraging improvements within the existing structure of the NHS.[71] In June 1967 the Treasury discovered that Sir Arnold France had 'very secretly put in hand an examination of NHS organisation'.[72] At about this time, the Minister held a preliminary discussion with senior officials, after which a small working party was established to prepare a plan for administrative unification of the health services. This committee was co-ordinated by the newly-formed Long Term Planning Division of the Ministry.

The planning committee first met on 24 July 1967. Also at about this date, the first outline plan for reorganisation, LP (67)9, was circulated within department on a restricted basis.[73] This document was also shown to SHHD, but was not known to the Treasury until late September.[74] LP(67)9 expressed no reservations concerning the need for radical change. It urged that full integration was required to secure 'wise and economical strategic planning and deployment of resources' and the 'efficient and successful day to day management of front-line operational units'. This could be attained through unification within the framework of local government, or through a national corporation, but the preferred alternative was independent, all-purpose, area health boards. Although not specifically stated, this scheme was generally in line with Porritt and Scottish thinking. This memorandum advocated a '60+/-15 solution', a plan for between 45 and 75 area boards. It was also regarded as desirable to relate this plan to the 30 'city regions' thought to be favoured as the basis for local government reform. On this account, a minority within the Ministry favoured between 30 and 40 authorities. If the number of authorities could be restricted within the above limits, it was felt that regional authorities could be eliminated in favour of 'direct drive' from the Ministry of Health. If regions were maintained, there were arguments in favour of increase to 20 regions, or reduction to 9, the latter corresponding with the nine Economic Planning Regions.

The above scheme was not attractive to the local authority, primary care and welfare interests within the department, who regarded it as a dictated exclusively by hospital planning requirements. The areas were criticised for being too remote from local communities, but insufficiently large for major planning purposes. Such a scheme would therefore entail the risk of over-centralisation. There was not much support at this stage for the region, but the Chief Medical Officer strongly urged maintaining the region and basing local services on a relatively large number of districts. There was also much uncertainty over the composition of the area authorities. The medical group urged that substantial professional representation was unavoidable as compensation for loss of autonomy of the Executive Councils; it was thought that the Royal Commission on Medical Education would make a similar demand. Others insisted on domination by local government appointees, as compensation for loss of local health authorities.

The Minister was adamant on some main points of policy: he rejected administration by local government; he was not attracted by the less-seriously considered option of administration of the health services by a separate national corporation; he favoured a single tier, with the consequent abolition of the region; and he insisted that professional representation should not exceed 25 per cent of the membership of health authorities.[75] The scheme reaching the Treasury suggested that there would be 40 per cent local authority representation on the unified health authorities.[76]

In preparing papers for the Social Services Committee, the health departments agreed on the desirability of a brief, unspecific, joint statement. The only major point of disagreement related to procedure following the statement. In the light of criticism concerning lack of consultation over the social work White Paper in Scotland and because of the extensive consultation already held, Ross insisted on further outside discussions, on the basis of which a policy statement would be prepared. By contrast, Robinson feared that outside consultations would cloud the issue. Robinson therefore proposed to prepare his plans with a high degree of confidentiality within the department, and even limited to a narrow circle of

339

officials.[77] The Social Services Committee accepted without controversy the different paths to formulating policy on reorganisation proposed by Robinson and Ross.[78]

The cautious and lukewarm statement made by Robinson betrays its tangled origins. Robinson announced that he had 'begun full and careful examination of the administrative structure that is needed not only for today, but looking ten or twenty years ahead'. His policy intentions would be revealed in some months time, probably in the form of a Green Paper, after which there would be appropriate public discussion and consultation. In marginally more positive terms, Ross announced a 'thorough examination of the administrative structure of the health service in Scotland in order to ensure that it is adequate to ensure the development of these services in future'. By contrast with Robinson, Ross mentioned that he would consult relevant interests and publish proposals based in these discussions. Nothing was said about the precise form of the intended policy statement, therefore leaving open in Scotland the choice of a Green or White Paper.[79]

(iv) GREEN PAPER FOR ENGLAND AND WALES

Consistent with Robinson's late conversion to reorganisation and the known complexities of the issue, he instinctively sought the protection of a Green Paper for the initial launch of his ideas. White Papers were the standard mechanism for announcing legislative intentions. The Green Paper was a new device, introduced earlier in 1967 in connection with the proposal for a regional employment premium. The Green Paper was conceived as a way to test opinion on a financial measure favoured by the Government, but not yet adopted as definitive policy.[80] A tentative approach was also necessary on account of the sensitivities of the two Royal Commissions on Local Government and the Seebohm Committee.

A first sketch of the Green Paper was circulated within the health departments shortly after Robinson's statement.[81] The next six months were occupied in clarifying many outstanding points of difficulty, reaching an agreed position between the health departments, interdepartmental discussions, consultation with Ministers, and finally the issue of the Green Paper in July 1968. The decision to fall back on a Green Paper inevitably stretched out the reorganisation timetable, and it indicated lack of confidence about policy within the Government. Even though the plan adopted largely derived from a medical source, the Labour administration, no doubt with memories of the conflicts of the 1940s in mind, was hesitant to take any steps towards reorganisation without committing itself to full consultation, especially with the medical profession.

The English and Scottish Royal Commissions on Local Government also presented a potential source of hazard. Although Robinson and, with greater reluctance, Ross, were persuaded to drop any consideration of returning the health services to local government control, there was a real possibility that the Royal Commissions would recommend unification of health services under local government. The risk of direct intervention on health service administration was to some extent precluded when then terms of the Royal Commissions were narrowed down to consideration of existing local government services.[82] But it was entirely legitimate for the Commission to review local health and welfare authority services, and informal agreement with the chairman of the English Commission opened the way to broader consideration of any function possessing an integral relationship with local government services. Consequently, the health departments watched the Local Government Commissions with apprehension. The Royal Commissions were faced with demands for unification of the health services under local government, especially from the most influential local authority associations. Earlier reports of the thinking of Redcliffe-Maud suggested that he would be recommending continuing involvement of local authorities in the health services, and perhaps the administration of the health services by some 80 or 90 local government units.[83] However, a meeting with the Royal Commission in April 1968 suggested that they were satisfied to leave the Government to decide whether the area health boards would be associated with local government, while at this date the number of likely local government units was given as 40.[84]

The two Green Papers were therefore prepared against the background of rumours concerning the intentions of the Local Government Commissions. Also relevant to the drafting of the English Green Paper were the recommendations of the Seebohm Committee, which became available in April 1968. Consistent with proposals already evolved in Scotland, the central proposal for unified social service departments threw doubt on the continuing viability of local health authorities. But the detailed implications were unclear. Some social work planners favoured community-orientated health service established on the basis of parallel health and social services departments of multipurpose local authorities. Others wanted assimilation of the remnant of services administered by Medical Officers of Health into unified, but independent health authorities unassociated with local government.

The draft Green Paper relating to England and Wales was circulated for comment by relevant government departments in April 1968. The basic conception of the earlier drafts was maintained. Following the Porritt formula, in England and Wales it

341

was proposed to unify all three parts of the health service under some 40 new authorities, separate from local government, to be known as 'area health boards'. It was intended to include all public health and environmental hygiene functions in this amalgamation, but out of deference to the Seebohm Committee's known preferences, this draft abandoned the suggestion in earlier drafts that all welfare services should also be included within the health service. The areas would correspond with the main tier of local government administration believed likely to emerge from the recommendations of the Royal Commission on Local Government. With the disappearance of local government involvement in the health services, an additional burden would fall on the Exchequer, but it was anticipated that this would be to some extent offset by reductions in the Rate Support Grant. The area health boards would, like the existing Regional Hospital Boards, serve as agents of the Minister. Under the new arrangements it was proposed to dispense with the regional tier. Local authorities would be compensated for their loss of powers by inclusion of a 'democratic element' on the area health boards, amounting to 6 out of 15 members, with the medical profession being represented by 4 members. The doctors and five other members would be appointed by the Minister. Finally, the draft Green Paper recognised the need for improved arrangements for dealing with complaints. Officials considered and discarded proposals for local consumer councils, considering that consumer problems could be handled adequately by a system equivalent to the recently-established Parliamentary Commissioner for Administration.

The main objections against the Ministry of Health proposals emanated from the Treasury and the Ministry of Housing and Local Government. Treasury officials recognised the importance of this issue for both central and local government; they were determined to be 'right in the middle of this one!'.[85] However, they were not in a particularly good position to intervene; the Green Paper was already largely drafted and apart from this, Treasury officials were not agreed on a common line of policy.[86] Consequently, the Treasury exerted little influence on the April draft of the Green Paper. This draft was judged particularly vulnerable to objection because it appeared to sacrifice the objective of improved efficiency of management owing to its preoccupation with lateral integration. With respect to this goal, the Treasury therefore sought to reaffirm the priority of management efficiency. The Treasury attacked the proposals relating to the composition of the area health boards on account of exaggerated sensitivity to local democratic accountability, which had obscured the role of effective management. It was therefore necessary to recast the area boards to give at least a majority to full-time members with managerial qualifications. Ideally the Treasury wanted the area board to consist entirely of full-time managers under close civil service supervision.[87] This difference of outlook between the Ministry of Health and the Treasury on the constitution and function of health boards proved impossible to resolve, and it revealed a fundamental incompatibility of outlook concerning the administration of the health service.

The Ministry of Housing and Local Government also demanded substantial modifications of the draft Green Paper, but in the opposite direction to the Treasury. Sir Matthew Stevenson was sensitive to the interests of his department, but also concerned to avoid criticism from the Royal Commission on Local Government. Stevenson argued that the Ministry of Health had produced a White Paper rather than a Green Paper. The document was insufficiently provisional in tone; it adopted a partisan position on policy issues, rather than reviewing the alternatives. He accused the Minister of Health of using the Green Paper formula as a device for by-passing consultation with colleagues in order to secure his own policy objectives. In particular, Stevenson urged that the local government option should be presented as an equal alternative, and that assurance should be given that health service areas would coincide with the areas to be adopted for the personal social services. He insisted that a less partisan approach was essential at a time when the Royal Commission on Local Government was deliberating. Otherwise the Government would seem to be prejudging an important element in the Commission's remit.[88]

As already noted, Robinson, unlike his Scottish colleagues, avoided consultation with outside bodies until after publication of the Green Paper. However, once the November 1967 announcement was made, inevitably he came under pressure to meet representatives of the main interest groups. As usual, the BMA was most active in demanding immediate consultation, although on this occasion the BMA was in a weak position. As already seen, the BMA had failed to consolidate upon its early policy initiative, and at the time of Robinson's announcement, was in a state of indecision. Yet a further interim statement on the Porritt Report was forthcoming in March 1968, but there was no certainty that this would be supported by conferences of constituent bodies planned for June 1968.[89] Consequently, the BMA negotiators were in a weak position, with the result that their dealings with the Ministry of Health were little more than a formality, and made no impact on the content of the Green Paper.[90] Local government associations also made representations at the drafting stage of the Green Paper, but they also were persuaded to wait for the consultation process. Their views were made clear at a conference held in April 1968 on the future of local government, which demonstrated the strength of feeling in local government circles in favour of returning the health services to local government. [91]

The final stages of preparing the two Green Papers presented few problems for the health departments. Robinson pacified the Lord President's Office and MHLG by agreeing to present the local government option as a realistic alternative.[92] The Treasury maintained scepticism, fearing that the Green Paper scheme would not yield significant economies or efficiency gains. But it was too late to abort the reorganisation process. The Treasury proved unable to come up with compelling objections to the Green Paper; instead it fell back on some impracticable suggestions, such as the proposal to undertake reorganisation in stages. By limiting initial action to amalgamating hospital and family practitioner services, local authorities would retain minimum health functions; thereby the Treasury would ensure continuing input from local rates.[93] Even during the final stages of drafting, Robinson maintained his objection to outside participation and he also rejected the suggestion by officials that the final draft might be shown to trusted departmental advisers.[94]

The draft Green Paper passed through the Social Services Committee and the Cabinet with little discussion and with few objections being raised.[95] However, especially in the Cabinet debate, Robinson was criticised on two counts. The Chancellor of the Exchequer insisted that the Green Paper should be revised to give greater priority to improvement of management. No fewer than five Ministers called for a more open-minded attitude to local government control of the health services. Robinson was supported in a perfunctory way by only two colleagues. However, his position was strengthened by a positive response from the Prime Minister who, after reading the draft Green Paper sent his thanks to the Minister and commented 'how impressed he was by the thoroughness and imagination with which the review was carried out'.[96] It was agreed to sanction publication of the Green Paper, but in the final redrafting Robinson was asked to strengthen references to management and also to leave open the possibilities of either local government administration of the health services, or strong local authority representation on independent health authorities.

Robinson was helped by lack of opposition from the Conservative Party. Indeed, in June 1968, Maurice Macmillan announced Conservative support for a 'clean sweep' approach to reorganisation on the lines recommended in the Porritt Report. Consequently, the Green Paper was arguably more acceptable to the Conservatives than to many of Robinson's Cabinet colleagues. Crossman, who was by this stage Robinson's overlord, was especially scathing about the Green Paper.

Having scored a minor success in steering the Green Paper through the ministerial discussions, Robinson was keen to secure maximum publicity for his policy initiative, for which purposes appropriate publication arrangements were essential. He aimed to publish the Green Paper on 5 July to coincide with the twentieth anniversary of the NHS and a conference convened by the Minister to mark this event. With respect to his relations with the NHS workforce, Robinson urged that publication was essential to indicate that NHS reorganisation was not merely a subsidiary by-product of the Seebohm changes.[97] However, the Social Services Committee, on the advice of Crossman, in his capacity as social services co-ordinator, insisted on publication either simultaneously with, or after the Seebohm Report. With evident dismay, Robinson accepted publication on 23 July 1968, upon the same date as the Seebohm Report. This date came uncomfortably near the summer holiday break, and robbed the Green Paper of special publicity.[98] The impact of the Green Paper was further diminished by other, more sensational news. Even the *Times* relegated the Green Paper to page 4, and on that page devoted considerably more space to the Seebohm Report. The front page was dominated by the crisis over Russian menaces towards Czechoslovakia, while home news was preoccupied by breach of parliamentary privilege accusations against Tam Dalyell, the Parliamentary Private Secretary to Richard Crossman.[99]

The Green Paper, still carrying the uninspiring title of the first draft, *National Health Service. The Administrative Structure of the Medical and Related Services in England and Wales*, comprising twenty-three pages of text, amounting to about ten thousand words, was less than one-fifth the length of the 1944 White Paper, its counterpart in the original planning exercise for the National Health Service. As mentioned above, the document related to both England and Wales, but no separate paragraphs were devoted to Wales. In this respect, London fared rather better, receiving two paragraphs of special mention.

The proposals generally followed the lines of the first draft described above. There were, however, some subtle changes of emphasis. The Green Paper was less precise about the number of area boards, now giving between 40 and 50 as the likely total for England and Wales.[100] In the draft, the statement of responsibilities of board members emphasised overseeing an 'efficient and humane service', whereas the Green Paper, in deference to Treasury demands, placed the emphasis on 'efficient allocation and management of resources'.[101] Also, reflecting Treasury support for the ideas of the Farquharson-Lang Report concerning management by chief executive, the Green Paper hinted that the administrative staff of area boards would be organised hierarchically under a 'directing head', or 'directing posts' appointed on the criterion of management ability.[102]

The precise role of the Minister in the selection of area health boards was left unclear, although it implied that the Minister would make the final nomination. With respect to the much-debated issue of the composition of area boards, the detailed recommendations of the draft were eliminated in favour of general remarks about categories eligible for membership. The lesser emphasis on local authority representation was calculated to appease the medical profession, as was the introduction of a reference to the special importance of professional advisory bodies to the area boards.[103] Consistent with the Green Paper image, the intention to absorb all public health and environmental hygiene functions into the health service was now expressed in more tentative terms.[104] Finally, somewhat reluctantly, the Green Paper mentioned, but gave no prominence to the possibility that the proposed commissioner for complaints might be directly linked with the Parliamentary Commissioner for Administration.[105] Although the Green Paper briefly mentioned that it would be necessary to divide areas into 'operational districts', by contrast with the Scottish proposals there was no mention of special arrangements for community participation at this level.[106]

(v) GREEN PAPER FOR SCOTLAND

Failure of their early initiative on reorganisation caused disappointment in Scotland, but experience gained as far back as 1965 paid dividends when it came to preparation of the Green Paper. Not only had SHHD reviewed the entire subject, but also joint working parties had been functioning since 1966, and consultations with all the major interest groups had begun by the autumn of 1967. Consequently, the drafting of a consultation document in late 1967 was straightforward; this was assured an easy transition into the Green Paper. The latter was well-placed to receive as good a reception as was possible in circumstances where most of the existing health authorities were facing abolition.

After briefly considering and rejecting less radical approaches to reorganisation, the draft Green Paper concentrated on the achievement of full functional integration under area health boards. It was conceded that such bodies might operate under local government, but this was not favoured on the grounds that more than ninety per cent of the resources of the NHS were derived from the Exchequer. As compensation, the draft conceded that social work would come within the province of local government.

On the basis of geographical and local government considerations, it seemed likely that between 15 and 20 area boards would be required to replace about two hundred existing administrative bodies responsible for the health service in Scotland. On the sensitive issue of the membership of the area boards, the document limited itself to reviewing the alternatives and acknowledging the various interests requiring satisfaction. This was scarcely compatible with the stated intention to establish boards which were small, expert, and possibly with paid membership.

Given the intention to grant area boards a high degree of responsibility, and the evident enthusiasm for augmenting power at the centre, although the document was by no means categorical on this delicate issue, it was recognised that there was a case for dispensing with the region. By contrast with its reservations about regions, the document displayed unguarded enthusiasm for some kind of new Scottish 'services board' to control services requiring provision on an all-Scotland basis.[107]

Extensive discussions with outside organisations made little difference to the content of the Green Paper.[108] However, this consultation process resulted in a delay of consideration of the Scottish Green Paper by the Social Services Committee until the autumn of 1968. As in the case of the English Green Paper, the Scottish document was accepted without controversy, clearing the way for its publication on 12 December 1968.[109]

The Scottish Green Paper was similar in length and general character to its English counterpart.[110] Nevertheless, there were some significant differences in style, especially because the Scottish document was presented more as a review of opinion than as a statement of departmental thinking. In practice, the Green Paper differed little from the consultative document previously circulated by the department. By the time the Green Paper was issued, the Scottish social work legislation had become law, confirming social work as the province of local government. This concession to local government paved the way for the categorical view adopted in the Green Paper that health services should be administered outside local government. The objection relating to health service funding emphasised in the discussion paper was strengthened by reference to the overwhelming hostility to the local government option displayed in discussions with outside bodies. Out of deference to objections by the Social Services Committee, this recommendation was slightly qualified, but it was clear that local government administration of the health services was strongly disfavoured in Scotland, especially by organisations representing the medical profession.

The proposal for a single tier of area health boards was confirmed as the basis for unification of the health services. In the light of thinking on local government reform, it was now suggested that 10-15 areas would be sufficient, rather than the 15-20 originally proposed. Although it was acknowledged that the regional tier found its advocates, the Green Paper contained strengthened arguments against the region. It was urged that a strong area and enhanced central common services agency would be more efficient and comprehensible to the community. By contrast with the ambiguity of the English Green Paper on this issue, the Scottish document proposed that the members of area boards should be appointed by the Secretary of State after appropriate consultation. The Green Paper came no nearer than the consultative document to making precise recommendations on the balance in membership of the area boards. It merely stated at greater length the arguments for representation of local communities, the professions, and nominees of the Secretary of State. Upon the suggestion of Millan, the Green Paper, unlike its English counterpart, contained a lengthy homily on the importance of close links of health authorities with their local communities. It was suggested that local committees (eventually called Local Health Councils) should be established in each district 'which could be consulted about the operation of the services in their district, could facilitate links with other relevant services, and could give advice both to the area board and to the board's officers'. Such committees were calculated to provide a further degree of compensation for the loss of direct local authority involvement in the health services.[111]

(vi) RECEPTION OF THE GREEN PAPERS

Despite some lack of conviction displayed at the outset, the Green Papers looked like a bold and coherent programme for unifying health service administration. In England and Wales it was proposed to reduce the number of administrative entities from about 700 to 40, and in Scotland, from 162 to 10-15. Such changes seemed to offer prospects for a transformation in the efficiency and effectiveness of the health services. However, as the authors of the 1944 White Paper found when they devised a similar scheme, there were considerable practical difficulties in converting paper plans into administrative realities. The Chief Medical Officer in London observed that he had from its conception regarded the 1968 plan as an 'office exercise in tidiness and I was unsure of its impact on the real world'.[112] Crossman was similarly sceptical, describing the Green Paper as 'a very simple view of life'; he blamed Robinson for producing 'an abstract document, cooked up in the Ministry without any outside consultation'. As Crossman soon discovered, the path of consultation also entailed its problems.[113]

There was a striking difference between Scotland and England in responses to the 1968 Green Paper. Reflecting the careful attention to consultation at the preparatory stages, in Scotland there was remarkably little opposition to the Green Paper. Consultations involved slight intensification of discussions already in progress. Responses followed the lines already evident in earlier discussions. The argument for change was largely accepted and there was general approval for the area health board proposals. Conferences convened by such bodies as the Scottish Association of Executive Councils and the Scottish Institute of Hospital Administrators were broadly supportive. By contrast with the BMA in London, the Scottish BMA was content to allow general practitioners to enter into contracts with area boards.

The Scottish TUC was one of the few major organisations to oppose change; it was even unsympathetic to local government administration of the health services. Support for the latter position was expressed in The *Scotsman*, but this was not echoed among the local government associations, nor among the Scottish Medical Officers of Health.[114] The Royal Commission on Local Government in Scotland was noticeably more circumspect in its consideration of the local government alternative than its English counterpart. It merely stated the arguments for and against this proposition, without giving an opinion, but the overall tone was discouraging.[115] The main difference of opinion related to the upper administrative tier. Understandably, the Regional Hospital Boards demanded retention of a regional tier, but their position was not actively supported, even among hospital doctors and Boards of Management. With varying degrees of enthusiasm, other organisations favoured elimination of the region. Opinion was evenly divided over the method of appointment to be adopted for area boards and over the desirability and value of local health councils. The balance in favour of local health councils was affected by the Report of the Royal Commission on Local Government in Scotland, which recommended the establishment of community councils in all local government areas. It was therefore difficult to defend the absence of a parallel mechanism in the health service.[116]

As noted below in chapter VI, although differences of opinion concerning points of detail necessitated further discussion, the 1968 Scottish Green Paper formed the substantial basis for the 1974 reorganisation. In the spring of 1970, Scottish Ministers hoped to issue a White Paper before the summer recess, but this plan was undermined by the General Election and the subsequent change of government.

In England, progress towards a settled plan for reorganisation was much slower than in Scotland. There was even uncertainty about procedures for consultation. Robinson and Sir Arnold France favoured remitting the consideration of the Green Paper to a small committee of eminent figures, chaired by the Permanent Secretary.

Although this proposal was open to many objections, in July 1968 it was accepted as the basis for action.[117] Robinson began his consultations with outside bodies in the autumn of 1968. Little progress had been made by the date of his replacement by Crossman. The latter initially proposed to adhere to the Robinson's procedure when he took over responsibility for the health service in November 1968. A similar proposal was advocated by the *Lancet*.[118] However, in the face of adverse comment from officials, Crossman abandoned this idea in favour of utilising working parties constituted from within the department to revise the plan for reorganisation. Outside advisers were called upon according to the discretion of Ministers or working parties.[119] Especially in the later stages of preparation of the second Green Paper, Crossman relied on private discussions, especially with his friend and senior adviser, Professor Brian Abel-Smith.

It was also necessary to take notice of wider expressions of opinion from the relevant interest groups. Comments on the Green Paper were invited by the end of October 1968, but they were received rather more slowly; the BMA was not able to complete its deliberations until the end of January 1969, while the local authority associations were unwilling to give more than tentative comments until after the publication of the Redcliffe-Maude Report.[120] The department was relieved to receive favourable responses from such important bodies as the CHSC, the Royal College of Physicians, and the Royal College of Obstetricians and Gynaecologists. While initial responses were often constructive and supportive, most of the interest groups expressed substantial reservations. Indeed, the Executive Councils Association and the GMSC wanted to preserve the tripartite system. Some of the teaching hospitals associations were also lukewarm about the case for change. The local authority associations favoured change, but in the direction of local government control not favoured in the Green Paper.

The idea of unification was widely supported, but the Green Paper scheme was not accepted. Although the medical profession was author of the area health board, on reflection it was realised that abolition of the region would remove an essential channel of influence for the profession in planning, resource distribution, and control of human resources. It was feared that much of this influence would accrue to the central department, while at the area level, medical influence was likely to be swamped by virtue of the need to give strong representation to local government. Consequently, when taken together with other points of reservation, the medical profession, whose many organisations dominated submissions on the Green Paper, feared that it was being expected to make too many concessions for the benefit of unification.

Almost in unison, hospital administrators and medical organisations complained that the 40 intended area health boards were too small for planning purposes, but too remote for efficient administration and local accountability.[121] Some organisations pressed for an increase in the number of area boards to meet this criticism, but most demanded the retention of the regional tier to superintend a substantially larger number of areas. Rather than abolish regions, it was suggested that they should be strengthened, and possibly reduced in number. It was appreciated that the Hospital Management Committees needed to be radically reduced in number. Consolidation of these into 150-200 areas was commonly suggested.

Professional bodies also feared that their influence would be reduced on the area boards; they disliked handing over medically-related social work functions to local authorities; they feared that general practitioners would suffer loss of independence and erosion of their status with respect to hospital doctors; and they demanded enhanced guarantees of independence for the teaching hospitals. On the evidence of such reservations, the *Times* suspected that the doctors would be unco-operative and might even embark on the kind of confrontation witnessed in the run-up to the Appointed Day in 1948.[122]

(vii) CROSSMAN'S PROGRESS

The feared confrontation failed to materialise. Neither Ministers nor officials were sufficiently attached to the Green Paper proposals to merit more than token defensive gestures. Given the sceptical response to the first Green Paper, DHSS was not averse to beginning its planning exercise afresh. This conciliatory mood was emphasised in Crossman's informal meeting with the BMA Secretary in November 1968.[123] Stevenson insisted that the profession would not contemplate local government administration of the health services. Crossman assured him that there was no demand for this option in Government circles. In the course of the new planning exercise this alternative was scarcely considered within the department, although, as noted below, this was not a faithful reflection of either Crossman's own inclinations, or the attitudes expressed among his colleagues, yet it was undoubtedly helpful for smoothing relations with the medical profession.

In an early and seemingly well-founded rumour concerning the direction of Crossman's thinking, the *Sunday Times* suggested that 'the new NHS will be controlled by area groups consisting of local councillors nominated by town councils and county halls, doctors, representatives of professional organisations and a few people nominated by the Minister'.[124] This approach provided some comfort to both the medical profession and local government, but it raised

351

anxieties in the Treasury, where the Minister's nominees were regarded as of paramount importance.

A meeting with Regional Hospital Board representatives on 17 January 1969 reminded Crossman of the strength of feeling against a single-tier structure and in favour of preserving regions. Given the total absence of support for the single tier at this meeting, Crossman 'ruled out the Green Paper at one stroke'.[125] Although Crossman faced pressure from his officials and the regions to preserve a strong regional tier, he was from the outset unsympathetic to the idea of vesting substantial authority in the hands of remote regional authorities, which he characterised as self-perpetuating oligarchies.[126] He was almost equally averse to concentration of power in the hands of the central department. This was given as another reason for throwing out Robinson's 'highly autocratic, centralised structure'.[127] Distaste for the bureaucrats within the central department and the regions contrasted with his respect for local government. He enjoyed good relations with negotiators from local government and was helped by their advice.[128] When colleagues argued that local government administration of the health services was unacceptable on account of the difficulty in controlling local government expenditure, Crossman argued that local authorities were under more effective control than his own Regional Hospital Boards.[129] Notwithstanding his sympathy for the local government position, and sensitivity to the local government case at all levels within the Labour Party, including the Cabinet, Crossman regarded administration by local government as unacceptable on account of opposition from the medical profession. If this substantial concession was made to the medical interest, Crossman was insistent that local government and other community interests should be a dominant element on statutory authorities administering the unified health service. This aspiration was also widely held within the Cabinet, but Crossman was not convinced that it was sufficiently understood by his officials, or by the Treasury and CSD.

Crossman's officials were open-minded about new plans for health service unification. In the course of 1969 they considered virtually every possible permutation involving one, two or three tiers. The most fully-developed conception originated from the Chief Medical Officer who, from the outset favoured a two-tier system comprising a 'basic tier' constituted from one or a small number of adjacent district general hospitals, with district groups being amalgamated under regional authorities. Godber favoured about 20 regions and 300 districts. In departmental discussions the latter were often called 'Godber bricks'.[130] The district units seemed like a realistic basis for the co-ordination of all services, while the regions would protect broader planning interests. Although this represented a major reversal of the Green Paper proposals, it seemed better related to the realities of the health service. The obvious defect was its incompatibility with the area pattern basic to local government reform, including the Seebohm scheme for the social services. The principle of territorial congruity between health and social service authorities was adopted at the insistence of Ministers in the first Green Paper; it gradually assumed the status of an unquestioned assumption, and indeed was one of the few features of the original plan destined to survive through all the twists and turns of the subsequent labyrinthine planning process.

Crossman held his first office discussion on 17 December 1968; this was followed by two office 'seminars' on 10 and 17 January 1969. Although Crossman entered into discussions about reorganisation with ominous intensity, the evidence of his diaries and related documentation suggests that this problem failed to engage his imagination before August 1969. Although officials were divided among themselves about future action, they were satisfied that most of the criticisms of the first Green Paper were justified. They generally favoured modifying their proposals in accordance with the demands of the most powerful interest groups within the NHS. During the first phase of preparation for the second Green Paper, Crossman also adopted this line, opting for a more cautious approach to unification, relying on 'steady progress rather than a revolution', and possibly without recourse to legislation. This was clearly a reflection of the influence of the Regional Hospital Boards, which at their first discussion of the Green Paper with the Minister of State had urged integration by a 'natural process of evolution'.[131]

At this stage Crossman was prevailed upon to preserve the expertise and positive functions of the regions, although, because of his distaste for large and remote administrative bodies, and his liking for Wessex as a model region, he considered increasing the number of regions to between 20 and 30. His officials recommended between 100 and 200 district authorities.[132] Working parties of officials were commissioned to produce papers outlining a two-tier plan for unification. Before details of this new scheme were settled, on 28 February 1969, in a speech at the venerable Bethel Hospital in Norwich, Crossman announced his provisional thinking.[133] He spoke hopefully about progress and announced that his new plans would soon be revealed. Unification was affirmed as the primary objective of reorganisation. He conceded that the Government had been mistaken in its initial Green Paper. It was not appropriate to administer 'essentially a personal service through quite a small number of appointed boards' which would be 'aloof and remote' from their local communities. Crossman noted that 'consensus now seems to be emerging in favour of a two-tier solution' comprising regions and local services based on district general hospitals.

The Norwich speech was designed to forestall criticism from the organisations representing doctors and hospital authorities, with whom formal negotiations were about to begin. At the first of these meetings, with the BMA on 5 March 1969, Crossman disarmed his critics but frankly admitting that the scheme in the first Green Paper was wrong; he confirmed that he was working on various models, 'but was particularly impressed by the need to have a strong district structure'.[134] These assurances were repeated to the Joint Consultants Committee on 29 April 1969.[135] Crossman's subsequent speeches and meetings with outside bodies repeated assurances that he was convinced by their criticisms of the first Green Paper. This emollient approach undoubtedly helped to stave off confrontation with health administrators and the medical profession. Even the local authorities were pacified by promises that there would be a strong element of democratic representation on the district-level authorities.

The obvious limitation of Crossman's tactic lay in stimulating mutually incompatible expectations among the rival parties. Crossman was himself uneasy about this situation. For instance, in meetings with the doctors on 5 March and 29 April 1969, he complained that it was unrealistic of them to expect local government to be eliminated from involvement in administration of the health services. This point was made even more forcefully to nurses on 24 April 1969.[136] Crossman's insistence on a strong role for local government in the health services was offensive to the medical profession and it also worried his officials, who were concerned about the erosion of central influence, which the health departments and especially the Treasury regarded as essential for guaranteeing that reorganisation would bring about increased efficiency.[137]

Crossman was anxious to make an early parliamentary statement outlining his conclusions on health service reorganisation. An opportunity emerged in the context of the Seebohm Report. It seemed as if the Government was nearing decision on early implementation of the Seebohm proposals. Since this would split up local health authorities and throw doubt on the future of the Medical Officer of Health, Crossman favoured issuing a statement on the future of both the social services and the health service. He calculated that a statement confirming local government administration of unified social service departments would render more palatable to these bodies the rejection of local government administration of the health services. Crossman also wished to give a general indication about the proposed two-tier system in order to satisfy dominant voices in the NHS administration.[138]

A memorandum describing the region-district scheme, together with a draft statement, were prepared for the Social Services

Committee, which was conveniently chaired by Crossman himself.[139] On this and most other occasions when the second Green Paper was considered at the Social Services Committee, the discussion was led by Baroness Serota. Events failed to proceed according to Crossman's wishes. Because of slow progress with discussions on the Seebohm Report, the meeting of the Social Services Committee on 20 May 1969 failed to reach agreement on the implementation of Seebohm, and it was evident that no conclusion was likely to be reached at least until after initial discussions on the imminent report of the Royal Commission on Local Government. In the light of disagreements over the timetable for the Seebohm reforms, the paper on the health service received an unenthusiastic reception. Ministers were even unwilling to reject the local government option, and Crossman's alternative ideas failed to capture their imagination. In advance of the Royal Commission Report, they were unwilling to take steps to antagonise local government or court accusations of bad faith concerning the Commission. Accordingly, discussion of both Seebohm and health service reorganisation was postponed, and Crossman was denied the opportunity to make his important public announcement. Crossman made no complaint about this outcome. Nevertheless, he and Callaghan, his supporter on this occasion, felt 'utterly defeated'.[140]

Crossman returned to the Social Services Committee on 23 June with a very much more limited proposal in which he sought agreement to a more leisurely timetable, envisaging a statement in the autumn and a further health service Green Paper in December. On this occasion, the Social Services Committee agreed without difficulty to a non-committal statement reassuring relevant groups that the Secretary of State would continue with consultations designed to prevent loss of morale, and deflecting local authorities from taking unilateral action in the reorganisation of their social services.[141]

The Treasury played little part in the preparation of the first Green Paper, but this seemed at least to offer a constructive basis for improving the management efficiency of the NHS. The new proposals revealed by Crossman severely detracted from the positive attractions of the original plan. Treasury officials reacted with surprise and consternation, although their responses also revealed a state of indecision on the question of reorganisation. Given a predisposition to query everything about the new thinking within DHSS, the Treasury even found itself mounting a spirited defence of the local government option, despite its former categorical opposition to allowing local government to administer services financed largely by central government.[142] Rather than the two tiers, complicated administrative structures, and hybrid district

355

authorities of the new proposals, which constituted 'phoney local authorities with no financial responsibility', the Treasury believed that more effective financial management was attainable through the normal mechanics of local government.[143] Given the unacceptability of this line of argument with Treasury Ministers, officials were asked to produce alternative destructive criticisms of Crossman's proposals.

The opposing forces finally clashed at the Social Services Committee on 3 July 1969.[144] In his renewed attempt to obtain ministerial acceptance of the reorganisation proposals, Crossman faced an additional obstacle in the form of the report of the Local Government Commission for England published in June 1969, which drew attention to the arguments in favour of administration of the health services by reformed local government.[145] Serota on behalf of DHSS argued vehemently against the local government option, but also offered significant inducements to local authorities. By relinquishing their direct involvement in health service administration, local authorities were to be promised strong representation on health authorities, concurrence of boundaries of health and social services authorities (usually called coterminosity), and generous treatment in arrangements for the dividing up of environmental health and social services. On behalf of the Treasury, Taverne declared that the proposed local participation on the new health authorities represented an unacceptable degree of 'power without responsibility'. He argued for further delay pending further discussion of the Royal Commission findings. The Social Services Committee took little interest in Taverne's strictures; they were more concerned about the political consequences of the proposed changes, and once again refused to allow rejection of local government administration of the health services. Crossman was given no choice but to accept a further period of delay. This outcome left both sides dissatisfied. DHSS was frustrated by further delays, which complicated its problems in maintaining morale within the health service and the confidence of negotiating parties, while the Treasury was convinced that Crossman was insensitive to their point of view, inclined to make endless concessions to local authorities and the medical profession, and that DHSS was drifting out of control towards an outcome worse than either the current administrative system, or the local government option.[146] In July 1969 Treasury attitudes noticeably hardened; without a strong managerial structure in the new system at both region and district levels, they would completely oppose reorganisation.[147]

From the perspective of the Treasury, the situation deteriorated even further. It was reported that DHSS was being thrown into disarray by Crossman's interventions. His endless concessions to local government and the medical profession risked undermining the work of high-level, interdepartmental committees of officials examining policy issues in the field of the social services and local government.[148] Also disconcerting to the Treasury was lack of clarity about the intentions of Crossman, owing to oscillations in his thinking.

Even experienced DHSS officials found difficulty in keeping up with new proposals streaming from Crossman's fertile imagination. Further complications resulted from plans submitted by Crossman's outside advisers. It was frankly admitted that the papers submitted to Ministers had been tentative and sketchy, largely because 'a considerable number of discussion papers had been submitted, without firm decisions having been reached by the Secretary of State'.[149] This trend continued. On 28 July Crossman asked for a paper on the implications of much greater departmental interference in routine business of the NHS, but this never reached formal consideration. Much energy was devoted to the possibility of establishing at regional and district levels 'joint health boards', to be formed by health authorities and local authorities to manage community health services, and possibly family practitioner services. This scheme allocated a new and important role for the Medical Officer of Health, but it was soon abandoned on account of retaining the administrative fragmentation of the health services. When Crossman found it impossible to arrive at a satisfactory arrangement for composition of regional authorities, he proposed abandoning the region altogether, or creating a 'partial two-tier' system, involving two tiers for slightly less than half of the population and a single tier for the rest. This idea also was soon shelved.[150]

Lack of consistency in formulating policy was to some extent explained by the effort to conciliate dominant interest groups. As already indicated, the broad interests of the medical profession and local government were paramount factors during Crossman's term of office. Both of these groups represented a wide federation of interests, and neither was particularly homogeneous. Crossman was accordingly subjected to numerous and diverse pressures. In the months following the first Green Paper, he received some 400 sets of written comments, while Ministers and officials held meetings with representatives of more than 50 organisations.[151]

Plans for health service reorganisation were also vitally affected by the important reports on personal social services and local government. As anticipated, the Seebohm Report recommended transfer of many groups of personnel from the Medical Officer of Health to local authority social service departments. Although the Royal Commission on Local Government in England was discouraged from concerning itself with the NHS, it expressed a

357

discreet, but firm preference for transfer of the health services to local government. The Commission concluded that the local government alternative would achieve unification, while maintaining a higher level of local democratic accountability, and a closer working relationship with the personal social services and other personal and environmental services. The same case was argued with much greater force in the widely-publicised Memorandum of Dissent by Derek Senior.[152]

Difficulties in reaching a settled policy were also increased by the conflicting interests of the Government departments having a stake in health service reorganisation. The Treasury wanted maximum simplicity in administration and optimisation of management structures.[153] CSD stood for sound management, but it was also committed to bringing a new level of rationalisation of local administration. MHLG was protective of the local government interest, but in addition favoured the development of regional administration. It was also necessary for DHSS to bear in mind the need to avoid commitments unacceptable in Scotland and Wales, and of course it was necessary to respond to Ministers such as the Paymaster General, who was responsible for devolution and actively protective of the principle of local participation. Judith Hart, the Paymaster General, was well-equipped to intervene on account of her health service experience at the Scottish Office.[154]

In view of the clash of incompatible interests, both on the outside and within the Government, it is understandable that Crossman found it difficult to reach a settled conclusion on the administrative framework to be adopted in the second Green Paper. His diaries record that he had 'never had a more intractable problem'.[155] Unhappy with the assistance given within his department, he turned to his outside advisers for guidance.[156] Initially, this outside contribution made only marginal difference to his plan, but in December 1969 it became crucial.

Crossman made his next attempt at gaining sanction for his reorganisation proposals at the Social Services Committee on 9 October 1969.[157] The original timetable for issue of a further statement of Government policy in the autumn of 1969 was now completely unrealistic. It was indeed difficult to contemplate issuing a second Green Paper by the end of 1969. Embarrassment was being caused by the delay, and it was especially important to obtain sufficient support from Ministers to permit further discussions with outside bodies. It was now necessary to contend formally with the recommendations of the Royal Commission on Local Government, which rendered it politically impracticable to persist with a region-district scheme. In view of his commitment to pursue the two-tier option, he was now forced to adopt the Redcliffe-Maud local government areas as the lower tier.

Crossman now proposed to establish 18 regions and about 125 local divisions, now called 'unitary health authorities', as far as possible coinciding with the unitary authorities and metropolitan districts proposed by the Royal Commission on Local Government. Much of the exposition of this plan by Serota was devoted to arguing that a satisfactory compromise had been reached concerning the composition of regional and area management bodies. It was hoped to satisfy the Treasury by provision for appointment of the chairman and key members of the regional authority by the Secretary of State, and by the promise of exercise of essential control at the area level by the chairman and a small executive appointed by the Secretary of State and possibly remunerated for their services. However, it was also intended to include a large local government element, as well as significant professional representation at both regional and area levels. This compromise was defended as the only realistic solution capable of reconciling all the disparate interests.

Crossman recorded that the new plan met with a 'tremendous indictment' from Taverne and Shackleton on behalf of the Treasury and CSD respectively. Taverne expressed no satisfaction with the compromise, which seemed not to rectify any of the main defects of the original proposals. He was afraid that professional and local representation would preclude proper attention to financial restraint. The discussion displayed little regard for Taverne's reservations. Ministers were more preoccupied with introducing administrative changes which would improve the quality of services, especially in development areas such as new towns where there were evident failures in planning arrangements. They were not hospitable to the view that local government representation was likely to lead to financial mismanagement, and they were critical of any dominance of health administration by ministerial nominees. Also on political grounds they accepted that substantial concessions to local government were unavoidable.

Crossman acknowledged that he received particularly effective support from Crosland, but agreement was precluded by virtue of unyielding Treasury objection. Consequently, the issue was referred back for further discussion between departments. There was no change of heart within the Treasury. A memorandum, regarded by the Chancellor of the Exchequer as 'powerful' and convincing, argued the case for a single tier and the appointment of all members of authorities by the Minister on the basis of their managerial skills.[158] Notwithstanding its strong antagonism to Crossman's proposals, the Treasury was isolated and it seems that this particular issue failed to attract much attention from the Chancellor of the Exchequer. However, some support for the Treasury position was forthcoming from the Parliamentary Committee, which criticised

Crossman's intention to give one-third shares on the area boards to local government, the medical profession, and the Secretary of State. The Committee also rejected a proposal from Crossman for an interim arrangement whereby regional boards would be reconstituted to give local authorities half the membership. The Committee furthermore insisted that nominees of the Secretary of State should be in a majority on NHS administrative bodies, and that the latter should be small and with a distinct managerial bias.[159]

Despite the uncertain state of policy, DHSS officials were unable to delay further the drafting of the second Green Paper. An outline was prepared in August 1969, which was accepted by Crossman on 21 August and further discussed on 4 September. A full draft was circulated on 17 October and again on 31 October. An abbreviated form was also produced at this stage suitable for examination by the Social Services Committee.[160]

Crossman's next attempt to gain support for his proposals occurred on 3 November 1969, when he presented draft proposals for the second Green Paper to the Social Services Committee. On this occasion it was proposed that the Minister's nominees on health authorities would be in a small majority. Taverne objected to the large size of these authorities and he pointed out that in reality many of the Minister's nominees represented local authority and professional interests. Consequently, although the proposals were generally accepted, they were referred back for further discussion on the size and membership of regional and area health authorities, as well as on a number of less contentious items. Despite the qualified nature of this advance, Crossman recorded this meeting as a minor triumph, noting the effective support received from Shirley Williams, and scorning the 'amazing amateurishness of the Treasury'.[161]

Taverne immediately approached Crossman to discuss further changes in the composition of regional and area health authorities. The Treasury demanded a reduction in size, a genuine majority for ministerial nominees, and also some representation of DHSS officials.[162] Allowing for the usual degree of compromise on both sides, the parties came near to a settlement. At last, the Treasury believed that the regional tier might be advantageous, and that area health authorities could be subjected to a reasonable degree of control.

Any complacency concerning an agreed outcome was dispelled when it became apparent that Crossman had decided to abandon the plan that was on verge of acceptance by the Social Services Committee. He was never fully committed to this scheme: it contained too many concessions to the regional oligarchs, only incomplete compatibility with the unitary authorities of local government, and too much remoteness from local communities. His change of mind was also affected by his first serious discussion on the draft proposals with the main outside interests. In particular, the roots of Crossman's new thinking can be traced to his meeting with the local authority associations on 20 October, when he invited them to evolve a scheme for NHS reorganisation 'neither wholly inside or wholly outside local government'.[163] These discussions continued at a meeting with the BMA in the first week of November, which revealed much criticism of Crossman's scheme, and once again convinced him that he had no choice but to retain the region.[164] Crossman was depressed about prospects for agreement, but soon regained his equanimity, largely as the result of a further meeting with local government representatives on 19 November.[165] Crossman pursued his new approach with enthusiasm and gained the impression that his ideas were acceptable to both local government and the medical profession.[166] Crossman even hoped to convene a meeting between the BMA and local authority associations to work out agreement on outstanding points. However, prospects for such a meeting soon receded, and others failed to capture Crossman's enthusiasm about new policies. Serota doubted whether the second Green Paper would be 'seen to be sufficiently better than the first to justify the time spent on it'.[167]

Crossman perfected his new plan while recovering from an illness at his home in Prescote, near Banbury. On 4 December 1969 it was recorded that the 'Secretary of State intends himself to prepare a draft paper for PI [sic, SS] Committee presenting revised proposals in the light of his meetings with the BMA and the secretaries of the local authority associations'.[168] The final scheme owed much to the intervention of Professor Brian Abel-Smith, who pointed out that the region-area plan, like the first Green Paper, was vulnerable to criticism for its remoteness from the local community. After rejection of various alternative regional arrangements, it was decided to discard the region altogether, and adopt a two-tier plan based on the area and the district. Crossman had of course previously created the expectation that he would be producing a two-tier plan incorporating the region and district, but it was hoped that the area-district scheme would be accepted as a credible alternative. A sketch of this plan was distributed on 10 December; it was discussed with about ten officials at Prescote on 12 December. Crossman records that his officials were 'tremendously excited' and supportive. However, Crossman was forced to compromise in response to strong, although by no means unanimous feeling in favour of the region within the department. In response it was agreed to include a regional council with extremely limited authority. Although Crossman's new plan emerged from this meeting as the basis for the Green Paper, sceptics within the department were far from convinced about its appropriateness.

361

Many officials remained convinced of the superiority of a 20 regions-180 districts plan. Advocates of the region were critical of the shadowy nature of the regional bodies, while others condemned the scheme on account of its complexity, arguing that it would leave all the major objectives of reorganisation unfulfilled.[169] A meeting between Crossman, the BMA and the JCC on 22 December also revealed much scepticism about the new plan, but the medical representatives stopped short of outright opposition.[170]

Notwithstanding these doubts, after a period of hectic preparation, at the end of December 1969 Crossman circulated for comment on a confidential basis a draft of the memorandum for the Social Services Committee embodying his fundamental change of policy. He now proposed to reduce the region to the level of an advisory body, and revert to a single tier of statutory bodies comprising about 90 unitary health authorities coterminous with the unitary local authorities accepted by the Labour Government as the basis for local government reorganisation.[171] It was also proposed to establish local committees responsible for some 150-200 districts equivalent to the 'Godber bricks' of their earliest deliberations on the second Green Paper. Crossman employed this new plan to jettison Treasury ideas on the composition of the new authorities, instead reintroducing his original proposals for allocating one-third of the membership of the unitary health authorities to local government, a further one-third to the medical profession and representatives of health professions, and one-third to nominees of the Secretary of State. It was proposed to administer the districts through subcommittees containing strong representation from local government and the medical profession. On the basis of his compact with the local authorities, Crossman tentatively suggested a new approach to the funding of the NHS, entailing a direct contribution from local authorities in return for their participation in the control of all allocations.

Crossman's generosity to the local authorities was not entirely altruistic. By increasing their stake in the health service, he was hoping that they would agree to deviating from the proposals of the Seebohm Committee by agreeing to leave social services relating to mental health under NHS administration. Equally, by guaranteeing strong medical representation on health authorities, Crossman hoped that the BMA would be more accommodating about the transfer of home help services to local authorities.

Crossman soon discovered that he had miscalculated in believing that his concessions had purchased support from the local authority associations and the BMA. On 31 December the Secretary of the Association of Municipal Corporations complained that it was not possible to give categorical undertakings in a situation in which 'attitudes and approaches should show such variation from one point of time to another'. This negative response was immediately reinforced on 1 January 1970 by a joint statement from the two main local authority associations stating their demand for a high degree of control of the reorganised health service. The following day the BMA bluntly informed Crossman that it was unwilling to give 'any indication that the latest proposals...would be acceptable to the medical profession'.[172]

For Crossman the new plan embodied essential concessions to local government and the medical profession, but from the Treasury point of view it represented a combination of the worst features of all previous schemes. From this perspective it represented a 'massive syndicalist organisation' incapable of even the minimum degree of essential control.[173] The Chancellor of the Exchequer concluded that his department was 'back where we started'.[174] Even within DHSS senior officials expressed their concern about confusion over the role of the region, and the possible adverse consequences stemming from disruption of important regional functions.[175]

Crossman knew that his audacity was courting danger; he was particularly apprehensive about the response from the Social Services Committee. In the event his alarm was unjustified. Taverne and Shackelton repeated their customary objections, but most Ministers were positively supportive.[176] Although Crossman's new proposals were subject to long discussion at meetings of the Social Services Committee on 2 and 12 January 1970, the basic scheme was regarded as an improvement on its predecessor.[177] From a presentational point of view the new plan seemed more consistent with the single-tier scheme of the 1968 Green Paper, with an increase in the number of area authorities to maintain compatibility with the new local government areas. Some members of the Social Services Committee also recommended that the regions should be made coterminous with the provincial authorities proposed for local government, and perhaps even be absorbed into these provincial bodies. Crossman believed that specific assurances on the membership of health authorities were necessary to secure the support of local government and the medical profession. This suggestion met with opposition from the Scottish Office, because Scottish discussions on local government reform were not complete and they were not pointing to conclusions helpful to Crossman. In Scotland there was less demand for local government representation, allowing the Secretary of State to propose that his nominees should constitute a majority on health authorities.[178] Misgivings emanating from Scotland and the Treasury concerning the composition of the new authorities were referred to the Cabinet for final consideration.

Briefs for Treasury Ministers in connection with the two Cabinet meetings held on 15 and 20 January 1970 indicate no softening in reservations concerning the defects of the second Green Paper.[179] The first of these meetings was relatively uncontroversial. It was concerned with confirming that reorganisation would take place outside local government and with the question of conformation boundaries between the health and personal social services. Only one Minister argued for the local government option, and significantly this issue was not pressed by Crosland, the Minister most likely to represent the local government case. This discussion was mainly concerned with minor, technical points. A contributory factor in the success of Crossman at this first meeting was the state of exhaustion of Ministers after a lengthy wrangle over the Industrial Commission Bill. Crossman was also assisted by deferment to a second meeting of the contentious issue of membership of health authorities. This first meeting was therefore not quite the triumph described in Crossman's diaries.[180] At the long discussion of composition of health authorities in the second meeting, Diamond, the Chief Secretary, was the only uncompromising critic and he was not entirely supported by Jenkins, the Chancellor of the Exchequer, while Shackleton on behalf of CSD was moderately supportive of Crossman. Consequently, after a token display of opposition, the case against Crossman was abandoned by the Treasury-CSD prosecution. Crossman correctly recorded that this successful outcome in dealing with the Treasury was assisted by the supportive role of Wilson in directing the Cabinet discussion.[181]

Crossman's diaries suggest that the only significant objections to his scheme for composition of health authorities emanated from Treasury-CSD circles. In fact the most telling opposition came from Crossman's colleagues responsible for the health services in Scotland and Wales. Ross argued that the proposed one-third share was inadequate to give effective ministerial control, enough representation to satisfy local authorities, or sufficient to comply with the demands of the Redcliffe-Maud report. He was opposed granting a specific membership allocation to the medical profession. Finally, Ross contended that remunerating chairmen would be detrimental to the ethos of health authorities. Ross was supported by Thomas, who expressed concern that there was a fundamental incompatibility between the objectives of representation and management. Wilson circumvented these criticisms by proposing that Scotland and Wales should be allowed to adopt their own approach to the constitution of health authorities. The final amendments to the English Green Paper were accepted as a formality by the Social Services Committee without reference back to the Cabinet.[182]

(viii) WELSH GREEN PAPER

As noted above, the BMA in Wales drew up the first proposals for the practical implementation of the Porritt model. Not only was it proposed to unify the administration of health services under 6 or 7 area health boards, but the Welsh plan also contained some other novel and interesting ideas. For instance, at the local level the Welsh BMA suggested 'Public Representative Councils' to keep the area boards informed about community thinking on policy issues. At the national level it was proposed to establish a Welsh Health Council, an autonomous body representing all the areas together with members of the Welsh Board of Health. It was proposed to give sweeping powers to this council, which in reality would constitute an independent planning authority controlling the health service in Wales, and reducing the Welsh Board of Health to a minor executive agency.[183] The revised version of this report included similar recommendations, and it called for bold action consistent with the new mood of devolution: 'Wales can anticipate moving separately in a new direction because her national status is being increasingly recognised by the trend towards administrative devolution in the Welsh Office'.[184]

Despite the replacement of the ineffectual Welsh Board of Health by the Health Department of the Welsh Office, there was no rush towards a separate Welsh initiative on reorganisation. Indeed, the Welsh Office took little part in preparation of the first Green Paper, provoking criticism from Welsh MPs for failure to produce a separate policy document on reform of either the personal social services or health services. Sensitivities concerning separate Welsh policy on reorganisation were heightened by the upsurge in nationalist feeling during the period of the Wilson administration. The Royal Commission on the Constitution was impressed by a 'general sympathy for nationalist ideas', which called for a response in many areas of administration.[185] Demonstration of support for separate planning of reorganisation in Wales was evident at a conference to discuss the first Green Paper, called by the Board of Health in October 1968, at which the Welsh Hospital Board produced a plan for one region and 6 or 7 areas.[186]

Embarrassment over inaction at the time of the first Green Paper necessitated a separate Welsh initiative with respect to the second Green Paper. In June 1969, George Thomas signified to his colleagues that he was considering issuing a separate Welsh Green Paper.[187] The resolution of Thomas was strengthened by the near loss of the Caerphilly parliamentary seat at a by-election in July 1969, when the Labour majority slumped from above 21,000 to under 2,000. Although the Treasury lamented about the proliferation of Green Papers, this trend was accepted with resignation as a consequence of the new fervour for devolution. Because Thomas was more responsive than Crossman to pressures for efficiency and centralisation of management, his Green Paper was treated more sympathetically by the Treasury during its drafting stages, and as a matter of routine by the Social Services Committee.[188]

Preparations for a separate Welsh Green Paper began in the autumn of 1969. George Thomas held a preliminary meeting with officials on 12 September 1969, where it was agreed that their Green Paper would follow the general lines of the second English Green Paper. There was no problem about consistency with the English plan for areas, but the Welsh were less convinced about the need for district committees in many parts of Wales, and they experienced particular difficulties in deciding about organisation at the national level.

At first Thomas was sympathetic to the radical Welsh BMA plan for placing the health services under a central board, although he favoured the existing Welsh Council rather than a separate Welsh Health Council.[189] The idea of mobilising the Welsh Council for this purpose was a logical response in light of the problem of finding wider functions for the new Council. The Welsh Council was formed in 1968, to replace the Welsh Economic Council. Naturally, it tended to remain preoccupied with economic affairs. An opportunity to expand in the health direction occurred in April 1969, when the Welsh Office took responsibility for the health service in Wales and the Welsh Board of Health was disbanded. The Welsh Council responded by establishing a Health Panel.[190] Further extension of this health responsibility therefore seemed desirable from the perspective of the Secretary of State and the imaginative idea of handing over the health service to the Welsh Council seemed likely to satisfy growing nationalist aspirations. This response by Thomas was also calculated to demonstrate the Secretary of State's devolutionist credentials to the Royal Commission on the Constitution. Thomas may also have been reacting to criticism from Crossman, who was annoyed by his Welsh colleague's unresponsiveness on the devolution issue. However, the above proposal was not favoured by officials, partly because the Welsh Council was a nominated body, with only weak medical representation, and only minor experience in the health care field. Furthermore, the future of the Welsh Council was uncertain. It seemed likely that the Council would be radically strengthened as a result of the deliberations of the Royal Commission on the Constitution. Such prospects were regarded with distrust within the Welsh Office.[191]

Welsh officials recognised that the various alternatives for all-Wales organisation were likely to be subject to major criticism. It was impossible to resuscitate the Welsh Board of Health. Conversion of the existing Welsh Hospital Board into a Regional Health Authority was briefly considered, but this idea was quickly abandoned because it was likely to result in confusion of responsibility between this authority and the Health Department of the Welsh Office.[192] At least in the short term, it was decided to dispense with both the regional board and proposed substitutes. This was seen as a means to increase the influence of the central department and improve the quality of management. These ideas seemed sufficiently firm to merit the production of a White Paper, but eventually the Green Paper option was preferred.[193]

The absence of regions in the Scottish plan, and Crossman's late decision to reduce the status of regions, reinforced the case for eliminating the region in Wales. But the Welsh plan was vulnerable to criticism on account of lacking any central consultative body equivalent to the elaborate central planning machinery which featured prominently in the Scottish scheme. To accommodate this criticism, the draft proposals presented to the Social Services Committee suggested establishing a non-statutory advisory body, which would act as a forum for discussion between the main agencies involved in health affairs in Wales.[194] This idea was immediately abandoned, and without enthusiasm the Welsh Office reverted to the original proposal of George Thomas to utilise the Welsh Council for this central consultation.

The Welsh Green Paper, which was published on 17 March 1970, followed the main lines of its English equivalent.[195] The main statutory bodies were seven 'area health boards' coinciding with the four counties and the three unitary authorities proposed for South-East Wales. This administrative structure for local government had been originally suggested by the Local Government Commission for Wales in 1961, modified in a White Paper in 1967, but it was not introduced immediately owing to controversy over arrangements for South-East Wales. The tripartite division of this area was confirmed by a separate report published in March 1970.[196] Suggestions for membership of the area boards followed the lines of the proposals for area health authorities in the English Green Paper. Early drafts of the Welsh Green Paper intended to leave district committees to local discretion, but the final version gave a slightly stronger lead, although without the degree of emphasis shown in Crossman's Green Paper.

It was not intended to interpose a regional body between the areas and the central department. With only seven area health boards, it was argued that a satisfactory direct relationship between the area boards and the Welsh Office could be established, and that the functions assigned to regional health councils in England could be distributed between the Welsh Office and the area boards. For the provision of central services, as in Scotland, it was proposed to establish a central services agency. After all of the twists and turns of policy on the central consultative machinery, no formal all-Wales mechanism was suggested, although it was conceded that the Secretary of State would take advice from a suitably strengthened Welsh Council and convene regular meetings between the chairmen of the health boards and officers of the Welsh Office. Any further action was to be postponed until after the Royal Commission on the Constitution had reported.

The Welsh Green Paper was issued in the closing phase of the Wilson administration. The final date for comment, 30 June 1970, fell after the General Election. Despite preoccupation with the election, the Green Paper proved topical and attracted much immediate comment. The issues attracting most attention, and the range of opinions expressed, closely resembled the pattern already evident in Scotland and England. About half the planned consultative meetings had been held before the dissolution of Parliament.[197] The fruits of this consultation process are more properly discussed in Chapter VI.

(ix) FROM GREEN TO WHITE

Preparation of the second English Green Paper was a hectic rush. Responsibility for converting the new plan agreed on 12 December into a Green Paper was divided between Crossman's outside advisers and the Long Term Planning Division of DHSS. Drafts of the first parts of the Green Paper were available on 29 December 1969, but the full version was not circulated for comment until 7 January 1970. Therefore the full text of the Green Paper was not available for discussion at the Social Services Committee on 2 January; and it had received almost no scrutiny by other departments by the date of the second consideration by the Social Services Committee on 12 January. Preparations for publication were compressed into three weeks following the Cabinet meeting of 15 January. The early drafts circulated carried the title 'The Future of the National Health Service'. On 22 January, this was changed to 'The Future Administration of the National Health Service'. By the end of the month this had become 'The Future Structure of the National Health Service'.[198] Finally, the second Green Paper, clumsily entitled *National Health Service. The Future Structure of the National Health Service*, was published on 11 February 1970.[199] This was one week after publication of the White Paper on local government reorganisation, and a day before publication of the Bill on reorganisation of the personal social services. In appearance, the Green Paper was strikingly similar to its uncharismatic predecessor, and the two documents were about the same length. The stated aims of the Green Paper 'unification, co-ordination, local participation and effective central control' were consistent with the policy objectives of 1968. Formally, the new scheme preserved the elegance of a single tier, and merely increased the number of areas from 40 to 90 in response to the Government's conclusions on local government reform. However, it is also possible to construe Crossman's plan an embryonic three-tier system. Indeed, drafts of this scheme overtly regarded the areas and districts as a two-tier structure. When the proposed 14 regional councils, 90 areas and 200 districts are taken into account, Robinson's 40 administrative bodies for England and Wales are seen to expand into more than 300 for England alone under Crossman's plan. A further complication, representing a concession to the BMA, was the intention to establish separate 'statutory committees' within the proposed area health authorities to take over the responsibilities of Executive Councils. Family practitioners were therefore assured of continuing independence and separate identity. By contrast, the Medical Officer of Health and local authority services not transferred to local government were to be absorbed into the framework of the area authorities. The MOH was given reasonable expectation of promotion to senior administrative medical officer of the new authorities, but the precise status of this officer, as well as the prospects for the medical staffs of the MOH, now called 'community physicians', were left altogether unclear.

Notwithstanding these administrative complications, the Green Paper placed its main emphasis on the 90 unitary health authorities, now called 'area health authorities', which were compatible with the new local government unitary authorities, which were ceasing to be called 'unitary' because many responsibilities were to be devolved to district local government. District committees in the NHS were only briefly mentioned, but it was evident that they would be administered by committees comprising representatives of local government and the professions. There was little clarity about the remit of these district committees. For instance, it was unclear the degree to which they would be responsible for all services within their district. After a great deal of vacillation, the proposed 'regional health councils' were accorded certain executive functions, but considerably less than the existing Regional Hospital Boards. There was ambiguity over their part in employment of senior medical staff, and no reference was made to a role in planning and hospital building.

The second Green Paper displayed a more advanced state of thinking than its predecessor on the problem of complaints. Because of embarrassments associated with scandals in long-stay hospitals, the Hospital Advisory Service was already under way, and because of the decision to introduce an ombudsman for local government, the Prime Minister had announced that a similar system for the NHS would be contemplated. The Green Paper mentioned these intentions, but no reference was made to a further possibility, discussed in a sporadic manner within the department, that there was also a case for establishing local consumer councils for the health service.

The press reception of the second Green Paper ranged from mildly favourable to highly critical. On 12 February 1970, the *Guardian* was generally supportive, but the *Times* editorial attacked the Green Paper, concentrating on two points: first, it suspected that the plan for regional councils represented a plot to strengthen the power of the central department; secondly, it argued that a fundamental opportunity to unify services had been lost by failure to transfer the health services to local government. Accordingly, the *Times* predicted that under Crossman's plan, major problems would arise in co-ordinating the health and social services.

The *Lancet* departed from professional orthodoxy by attacking the Green Paper as a move towards syndicalism, suggesting: 'instead of clamouring for a medical hand at every lever, the profession should insist on a strong advisory role'.[200] The more characteristic medical reaction emanated from the *British Medical Journal*, which denounced the second Green Paper as a 'blunder'. Crossman had promised to correct the deficiencies of the first Green Paper by introducing a region-district structure. Instead, the area had remained paramount, confirming suspicions that the new system would strengthen the control of central government, thereby perhaps paving the way for absorption of the health services into local government. The introduction of regions and districts into the second Green Paper was regarded as a helpful concession, but it was felt that these aspects of the Green Paper were lacking in conviction.[201] The case against the second Green Paper was elaborated at further meetings convened by the BMA, and in discussions of medical organisations with health department officials. However, as the eight hours of discussion on the second Green Paper at a BMA meeting on 6 May indicated, the doctors were still divided over policy on reorganisation.[202] Hospital administrators were even more hostile than the doctors to the Green Paper. Administrators stood by the region-district structure; they attacked the many distortions of this model as disastrous concessions to vested interests on the part of Crossman. It was even claimed that there was 'no proof that the new system would be any better than the old'.[203]

Even within the Labour movement Crossman was not immune from criticism. There was widespread complaint that the Secretary of State had failed to take advantage of a realistic opportunity for integrating the health services under local government. In a Fabian pamphlet, Maurice Kogan, the newly appointed Professor of Government and Social Administration at Brunel University, claimed that the Green Paper should 'not unfairly be characterised as syndicalism run wild'.[204]

It is doubtful whether the second Green Paper was received more favourably than the first. Crossman's elaborate attempt at reconciling hospital administrative, medical, and local government interests seemed at first to succeed, but ultimately it reduced all parties to a state of greater dissatisfaction. Contrasting with this reality, Crossman's own perception of the response to his Green Paper was sanguine, even self-congratulatory. Although his parliamentary statement was an uncharacteristically diffident affair, he was very pleased with its reception.[205] A Labour Party conference also seemed to be generally supportive.[206]

By contrast, once the promised informal discussions on the Green Paper were initiated, there was no escaping from the wrath of opposition. The attack was led by the Regional Hospital Boards, the dominant entities in the existing system, which were now facing virtual extinction under Crossman's plan.[207] As already noted, Crossman was initially unsympathetic to the regions, but he had come to appreciate the need for some kind of regional entity, and had developed a particular admiration for Wessex. A visit to Wessex alerted him to the damaging effects of the Green Paper.[208] In the face of hostility from the regional chairmen, who threatened to publish an attack on the Green Paper, Crossman made hurried moves to elevate the status of the regional councils.[209] His crucial concession involved restoring regional responsibility for all significant hospital planning and building.[210] Less palatable to the RHBs were Crossman's ideas about modifying the number of regions, or his intention to draw half the membership of regional health councils from the area health authorities, with the remaining half being shared equally between universities, the professions, and the Secretary of State's nominees.[211] These concessions to the region were confirmed at the last recorded consultative meeting, held on 2 June with the CHSC, when Crossman also announced an important change in his thinking about the balance between areas and districts. He now described area committees as large representative bodies, which would meet only occasionally to co-ordinate the work of districts, which was radically different from the concept announced in the second Green Paper.[212]

In order to avoid the further extension of an already over-extended timetable, it was decided to prepare the White Paper without taking into account the ongoing consultations. Crossman's

371

advisers were given a lead part in preparing the White Paper.[213] The Secretary of State was still not entirely satisfied with his plan and he continued to adjust his ideas on important aspects of management, for instance, by proposing to reduce supervisory functions of his department, allocation of block budgets to area authorities, and further redistribution of functions between area and region. He was also uncertain about the number of regions: the papers circulated at this time proposed as few as 5 or as many as 25. Some of his advisers even asked Crossman to reconsider abolishing the region. Given this continuing flexibility of thinking, Crossman instructed his officials to avoid communication with other departments, especially the Treasury. Contrary to Crossman's instructions, the draft of the White Paper and its associated explanatory memoranda were circulated to other departments on 19 May 1970. In fact these documents differed little from the Green Paper. Consultations were represented as supporting Crossman's basic concept. They took little account of adverse comment or even Crossman's latest thinking.[214] The response from other departments was predictably hostile. The Treasury and CSD felt that Crossman was further eroding the influence of the central department, creating confusion about the roles of area and region, and generally failing to apply any coherent basis of management principle.[215] The Treasury was particularly critical of the failure of DHSS to indicate 'a more positive and direct role than hitherto in guiding and supervising the administration', which was regarded as a 'vital' omission. In common with previous plans of Crossman, the White Paper also failed as far as the Treasury was concerned to: (i) secure short and clearly defined chains of responsibility and accountability; (ii) distinguish between management and representation in health authorities; and (iii) place management in the hands of small and competent authorities.[216] MHLG was also far from satisfied with the White Paper; it wanted maximum emphasis on area authorities since these were compatible in their boundaries with local government, but the White Paper eroded the power of area authorities by expanding the functions of regional councils and district committees, with the result that Crossman had allowed the NHS to degenerate into a three-tier structure.[217] While the Treasury, CSD and MHLG were hostile, on the basis of past experience, they were pessimistic about their chances of counteracting Crossman. In the event, there was no need for a further confrontation. Wilson called a General Election, and the date was fixed for 18 June.

Crossman hoped to publish his White Paper in the last week of July, but in June he was forced to defer the publication date until the autumn. The General Election prevented him from circulating this document to the Social Services Committee or the Cabinet for approval. Crossman cancelled various consultative meetings, such as the one with the BMA arranged for 9 June, but the White Paper was one of the projects upon which he continued to work. His last interventions occurred on 8 and 10 June, when he held his final meetings with officials to deliberate about the relationship between the tiers, and where Crossman characteristically preached about the need to write 'genuine devolution' into the reorganisation Bill.[218] Given this frame of mind, the defeat of the Labour Party and Crossman's departure from office, brought an element of relief to the embattled Treasury. As described in Chapter VI, the next stage in the lengthy contest over reorganisation became the responsibility of the Conservative administration.

CHAPTER V

Value for Money

Harold Wilson entered the 1970 General Election campaign confident about retaining a working majority. The opinion polls fluctuated, but generally pointed in the direction of a comfortable Labour majority. The Conservatives concentrated on economic targets, insisting on the general vulnerability of the economy. They were helped by adverse trade figures published a few days before the election. After a hesitant start at the beginning of his term as leader of the opposition, Edward Heath had become a serious and effective contender, and he was a good campaigner. Wilson was in possession of all the circus arts, but his performance in the 1970 General Election was facile. The Conservatives won the election with a majority of 30. This was the first occasion since 1945 that an opposition had overturned a Government with a working majority and itself achieved a working majority.

The health service was not a prominent issue in the election campaign. However, as noted in chapter III, to the embarrassment of Labour, the row over doctors' and dentists' pay made the headlines shortly before the vote. For a few days the newspapers were awash with rumours about collapse of the health service owing to mass resignation of doctors. The BMA publicised the story that Crossman, in rejecting full implementation of the pay award, had cited 'extreme economic peril' as the Government's excuse, a version of events which was vigorously denied by Crossman, who accused the BMA Secretary of 'spending more time on Conservative propaganda than he was on the good of the BMA'.[1]

(i) MINISTERS AND DEPARTMENTS
The Heath Cabinet was generally regarded as a skilful blend of experience and youth, as well as representing a judicious political balance. Macleod was potentially an outstanding Chancellor of the Exchequer, but on 20 July he died after an operation for appendicitis. He was replaced by another former Minister of Health, Anthony Barber, who remained in office for the duration of the Heath administration. The Treasury team underwent some changes, but was not outstanding in any of its permutations.

Ministerial appointments caused few surprises, although some relatively untried hands moved into senior ministerial positions.

Slightly above this group in experience was Sir Keith Joseph, who had entered the Cabinet when he served as Minister of Housing and Local Government and Minister for Welsh Affairs between 1962 and 1964. Joseph was appointed Secretary of State for Social Services by Heath. Joseph was an entirely credible candidate for this assignment. His concern with the health and social welfare can be traced back to his earliest days in politics. In the tradition of paternalism of his social class, he engaged in good works among deprived social groups. Absorption with the relief of poverty was also consistent with his personal inclination to moral austerity. After his entry into Parliament in 1956, he became secretary of the Conservative parliamentary Health and Social Services Committee, in which capacity he was recruited into such activities as the Conservative Party policy committee on the care of the old, which issued its well-informed report in 1958. He was at this time chairman of the National Corporation for the Care of Old People's committee looking at the problem of mental confusion among the elderly; he was also involved in the administration of the National Council of Social Service. As early as 1957, the Acton Society Trust identified Joseph as the leader of a small group of MPs who were attaining expertise in the field of hospital administration. On controversial social issues such as hanging, homosexuality, abortion, or family planning, Joseph lined up with the liberals.

In opposition, under Douglas-Home, Joseph was the opposition chief spokesman on social services. In this capacity he was interviewed by the Seebohm Committee at the outset of its deliberations to gain an idea of Conservative thinking on NHS reorganisation.[2] When Heath assumed the leadership of the opposition, Joseph transferred briefly to labour, and then to trade and technology. This provided a congenial platform for his advocacy of competition and private enterprise. It was rumoured that his appointment as Secretary of State for Social Services was designed to curb his opportunities for imaginative intervention in the field of industrial policy.[3]

At this stage he was close to Heath politically, and was trusted with an important role in the overhaul of Conservative policy. His political service and reputation for genuine humanitarianism provided sound credentials for a place in the Cabinet, and the Social Services portfolio seemed like an appropriate assignment. Joseph formally occupied the same rank as Crossman, but he exercised much less power within the Cabinet. Despite preserving the same title as Crossman, Joseph was not given responsibility for co-ordinating social services beyond the Department of Health and Social Security, although this possessed even more extensive departmental functions than applied during Crossman's tenure owing to reorganisation of the personal social services and transfer of the Children's Department of the Home Office to DHSS. The home affairs and social services committees of Ministers were chaired by the Home Secretary.[4]

Others with health experience, and possible alternative candidates for the Social Services portfolio, such as Howe, Balniel and Macmillan, carried less political weight than Joseph.[5] Howe was arguably the nearest rival. He possessed evident intellectual capacity, and like Joseph aspired to became an ideologue of Conservatism. As a lawyer in South Wales, Howe gained a good reputation in the field of personal injuries law, in which field he worked closely with the trade unions. This specialisation provided a good working knowledge of occupational health and he was also alert more generally to the problems of social welfare in South Wales. As already noted, Howe had made his views known on the role of the NHS as early as 1961, when he sided with the critics of the welfare state, and complained that both Joseph and Powell were insufficiently committed to driving back the frontiers of state involvement in health care.[6] Howe was elected to Parliament in 1964, but lost his seat in 1966, and was not returned again until 1970. After entering the House of Commons in 1964, Howe served as secretary of the Conservative parliamentary Committee on Health and Social Security. He was also a shadow health spokesman.

As noted in chapter III, Howe sprang into public prominence through his determined conduct of the Ely enquiry. Crossman also included him on the important Post-Ely Policy Working Party, which provided Howe with an invaluable insight into the problems of long-stay hospitals.[7] Howe participated in the BMA Advisory Panel on the funding of the NHS, and he held strong and original views on reorganisation.[8] Despite Howe's limited parliamentary experience, his ability was recognised; in 1970 he was appointed Solicitor General, and then in 1972, Minister for Trade and Consumer Affairs. As noted below, Howe continued his interest in health and personal social services affairs, and this connection was reinforced by his wife's participation in the important Briggs enquiry into nursing.

Lord Balniel, Maurice Macmillan, and Richard Wood, who had been opposition front bench speakers on health and social security matters prior to the General Election were not appointed as Joseph's junior Ministers, but instead became Minister of State in the Ministry of Defence, Chief Secretary to the Treasury, and Minister for Overseas Development respectively.[9] Crossman had been particularly scathing in his comments about the abilities of Balniel and Macmillan as opposition spokesmen on health and social security; he thought that the Conservatives would have been more effectively represented by Hogg or Joseph.[10]

Joseph's two junior Ministers on the health side of his department were Lord Aberdare, Minister of State (Health), who was also deputy to Lord Jellicoe, Leader of the House of Lords, and Michael Alison, who was Parliamentary Under-Secretary of State. This team remained unchanged until nearly the end of the Heath administration.[11]

The Prime Minister appointed Gordon Campbell as Secretary of State for Scotland. Campbell was a natural choice in view of his earlier experience as a junior Minister in the Scottish Office, and for the period before the General Election he had been the chief opposition spokesman on Scottish affairs.[12] The junior Ministers with main responsibility for health in the Scottish Office were Edward Taylor until July 1971, and then Hector Monro for the rest of the Heath administration. The Secretary of State for Wales was Peter Thomas, who was vulnerable to disparagement on account of having lost his seat in Conway in 1966 and subsequently having returned to Parliament as the member for Hendon South.[13] His Minister of State, David Gibson-Watt, whose duties related to health, was a member for Herefordshire, also an English seat, but in this case only just over the Welsh border.

Health Departments

Sir Clifford Jarrett conveniently came up for retirement at DHSS just after the 1970 General Election. Jarrett's obituaries suggest that Joseph asked him to stay on at DHSS, but there is no independent confirmation of this rumour. Some insight into discussions concerning his replacement can be obtained from Crossman's diaries. Crossman was mildly in favour of a promotion from within his department, and canvassed the names of two of his officials. Sir William Armstrong was not amenable to these suggestions; instead he nominated his own deputy, Philip Rogers, Second Permanent Secretary at CSD. Rogers followed the pattern established in the 1960s, by transferring into a social services department after holding senior appointments in the Treasury, the Cabinet Office or CSD. However, Rogers was a late-comer to these centres of power; his career up to 1964 had been in the spheres of colonial and technical co-operation. Rogers took over from Jarrett in July 1970 and remained at DHSS until his retirement in 1975. Rogers was a less strident character than Jarrett; he brought the strengths of a conciliatory personality to the department at a time of major upheaval, when these attributes were especially helpful.[14] Rogers' appointment created a problem concerning the role of the recently-knighted Alan Marre, who had reached the position of Second Permanent Secretary at DHSS after a career spent almost entirely at the Ministry of Health. Marre was described by Lady Serota as 'by nature a rather shy and cautious man who disliked personal publicity'.[15] Marre was appointed Parliamentary Commissioner for Administration in 1971; in 1973 he also took on additional responsibility as the first Health Service Commissioner for England, Scotland and Wales. Marre's departure from DHSS paved the way for the appointment of Mildred Riddelsdell as Second Permanent Secretary, with responsibility for the social security side of the department, which was the field of her professional experience. She in turn was succeeded by her deputy, Lancelot Errington, who had worked with Rogers at the Cabinet Office for a short time before his promotion to the Ministry of Social Security in 1968.

It is evident from this summary that the retirement of Jarrett marked an important change at the top of the department. Jarrett was the head of department with direct responsibility for social security, with his deputy, Alan Marre being in charge of health. Unlike Jarrett, Rogers possessed no special experience or technical competence in the field of social security. He therefore took over direct responsibility for the HPSS side of his new department, leaving the experienced Mildred Riddelsdell and then Lancelot Errington to handle social security. Although the HPSS sector was smaller than social security with respect to the number of personnel, there were good arguments for locating the Permanent Secretary on this side of the department. The diversity and difficulties of co-ordination of the separate hierarchies within the HPSS divisions of the department, as well as the delicacy of handling relations with largely autonomous NHS authorities and powerful professional interest groups, called for the presence of the Permanent Secretary on this side of the department.

Not the least of the Permanent Secretary's duties was reconciliation of the professional and administrative dimensions of advice to the Secretary of State. The high status of the professionals was symbolised by the presence of Sir George Godber, whose long career as Chief Medical Officer had in 1970 already outlasted three Permanent Secretaries. Godber's long and distinguished tenure ended in 1973. Following the practice in his own case, he was replaced by his deputy, Dr Henry Yellowlees.[16] In 1972, following the Rothschild recommendations and the White Paper, *A Framework for Government Research and Development* (Cmnd.5046), DHSS appointed a Chief Scientist, assisted by a Chief Scientist's Research Committee. After an interim arrangement, the first appointee as Chief Scientist was the eminent physician, Sir Douglas Black, who held the post until his retirement in 1977. The Chief Scientist was responsible for assisting on an advisory basis with research activities for the department as a whole, although most of his attention was directed to the HPSS sector.

378

At the Scottish Home and Health Department, the experienced Sir Ronald Johnson retired in 1972. He was replaced by R P Fraser, who had spent most of his recent career in SHHD, and had risen to the position of Deputy Secretary in 1971.[17] Sir John Brotherston's long tenure as Chief Medical Officer at SHHD included the duration of the Heath administration.[18] In parallel with the arrangements at DHSS, SHHD also appointed a Chief Scientist and established a Chief Scientist's Organisation. The first incumbent as Chief Scientist was Sir Andrew Kay, Regius Professor of Surgery at Glasgow, who held the appointment in a part-time capacity.

As already noted in chapter II, a major reorganisation of the Scottish Office took place in 1962. The SHHD, involving its old-fashioned twin 'policing' functions relating to health and law and order, persisted well into the future.[19] The main changes on the health service side of the department took place as a consequence of general expansion and NHS reorganisation. In the combined SHHD, one Under Secretary was exclusively concerned with the health services, whereas another was responsible for family practitioner services together with some aspects of law and order. By the eve of NHS reorganisation the health responsibilities of this latter Under Secretary had become more extensive, whereas law and order was limited to prisons.

In preparation for reorganisation, the Scottish Office Management Services Unit undertook a study of the central organisation of the Scottish health services. This work began in August 1971 and the report was published in March 1972.[20] This report itemised seven major areas of weakness within SHHD, many of them coinciding with the limitations in DHSS identified by a parallel enquiry in London. The elements of organisation proposed for a restructured SHHD comprised a Planning Group, an Administration Group, and a Resources Group.

In March 1974 the separation of health and law was taken a step further; two Under Secretaries became exclusively concerned with health; one superintended a group concerned with 'Health Care' (approximating to the above Administration Group) i.e. functional aspects of health administration; whereas the other Under Secretary was in charge of the 'Resources' group, i.e. establishments, salaries, operational efficiency, building and supplies. These changes followed the same pattern as the restructuring in the HPSS section of DHSS described below. By contrast with the situation in England where the reorganised social services were placed under DHSS, the Social Work Services Group, which performed the central control and co-ordination function with respect to the social services, was formed in 1967 and attached to the Scottish Education Department. This undoubtedly created a greater problem of integration of health and social work than under the English arrangement, where health and personal social services were integrated into the same central department.[21]

As further described in chapter VI, as a part of NHS reorganisation exercise, a Planning Group, was projected, although never more than incompletely realised, with the purpose of superintending the new planning system and facilitating planning activities generally. The Planning Group included a new Planning Unit, a small but important body, which provided the secretariat and other support services for the new Scottish Health Services Planning Council. Reorganisation also entailed establishment of the Common Services Agency, which will be also be discussed in the following chapter.[22] In order to bring these disparate entities together, the Secretary of SHHD presided over a Health Services Policy Group composed of senior administrative and professional officers.

Within DHSS, new responsibilities were assumed in line with the reorganisation of the personal social services at the local level, which occurred in 1971. As noted in chapter III, out of deference to the feelings of Callaghan, Crossman deferred take-over of the Children's Department of the Home Office. However, after a decent interval, the absorption of Children's Department into DHSS was agreed. On the professional side, the combined Children's Department Inspectorate and Social Work Division of DHSS became known as the Social Work Service. This contained a small headquarters staff and a larger regional organisation, serving primarily to supervise the local authority personal social services.[23] NHS reorganisation in 1974 entailed further expansion of the DHSS domain with take over of the School Health Service from the Department of Education and Science.

Although some ambitious ideas had been entertained about linking the health and social security sides of DHSS, not much effort was made at integration. Even such functions as the Principal Finance Officer, which were amenable to integration, remained largely separate until 1975. The main area of integration was the miscellaneous field of services under the Principal Establishments Officer.

The main changes within DHSS took place within the Health and Personal Social Services groups. Already, major changes had taken place in 1969 with the reorganisation of the hospital divisions. It was acknowledged that a more radical review was required. Jarrett realised that 'the problem of organising top management of anything so large and multifarious as the new NHS is extremely difficult' and that he had 'never experienced an organisational problem anything like so daunting'.[24] Plans for this review were interrupted by the change of Government. The large Steering Committee headed by the

Permanent Secretary, as well as its subordinate and smaller Review Committee, began work in the autumn of 1970. It was decided to conduct this review separately from the review of management of the reorganised NHS, a decision that was not universally applauded. Since McKinsey and Co. Inc. was selected for the departmental review, a link was attained with the NHS management review, but complaint was still occasioned by the selection of an American consultancy firm.[25] The departmental review was completed in June 1972.[26] Its consequence was a major reorganisation of the HPSS side of the department in late 1972.[27] Substantial alterations were introduced with respect to the functions of the Deputy Secretaries. The two main thrusts of these changes were a move towards a more client-group orientated form of management, and strengthening of the organisational links with NHS authorities on a territorial basis.

Since the beginning of the health services, the division of functions among Deputy Secretaries had followed the lines of administrative division of the services themselves. The onus for integration and balance of services fell on the Permanent Secretary. In the new structure it was proposed to give the Deputy Secretaries a more comprehensive and coherent function connected with the client groups served by the health and personal social services, thereby reducing the burden of co-ordination on the Permanent Secretary.

The 1972 reorganisation placed HPSS work under three Deputy Secretaries. The first was responsible for the Services Development Group, which was set up to advise on national objectives, priorities and standards for the health and social services. This group was concerned with general policy, with services to client groups using the acute hospital services, and with the elderly, children and the mentally ill. The second group was the Regional Group, which further extended the links with the regions introduced in 1969. The Regional Group provided guidance to NHS authorities on the implementation of national objectives and priorities, and it assisted the department with intelligence concerning the field authorities. This group was also concerned with the allocation of resources to regions and areas, supply functions, and with health industries and exports. The third group was the Personnel Group, responsible for NHS pay and conditions of service, including Whitley matters, recruitment and training, and for the Medicines Division.[28]

Following long-established tradition, each of the professional groups maintained its own hierarchy separate from the three main administrative groups, and each retained its own lines of communication with the Permanent Secretary. The figure at the head of the professional hierarchies was the Chief Medical Officer. This system of parallel organisation of administrators and professionals necessitated introduction of careful guide-lines to ensure the smooth functioning of multi-disciplinary management. Less clearly worked out were arrangements for co-operation between the three administrative groups and for links between the central department and NHS authorities. These difficulties soon came to the surface after the 1974 reorganisation. A further problem of the headquarters organisation adopted in 1972 was the absence of any formal mechanism for attaining co-ordination of effort at the highest levels within the department. This omission was particularly serious in view of the over-stretched role of the Permanent Secretary. A large Planning Committee was set up in 1973, but this fell into abeyance. Much adverse comment was attracted by lack of a consistent means of formulating new policy and keeping existing policy under review.

(ii) NEW BROOMS

The past record of Sir Keith Joseph gave no indication that he would fundamentally reassess, or reverse the policies of the previous administration. In opposition he displayed little sign of responsiveness to the more radical critics within his own party. As Minister of Housing and Local Government he followed the customary path of policy, involving active state intervention and a high level of public expenditure. As Secretary of State for the Social Services he pursued precisely the same approach.

The General Election pledges of the Conservative Party provide only limited insight into the Heath administration's intentions respecting the NHS. The health service made only a minor appearance in the 1970 Conservative manifesto, *A Better Tomorrow*. The health service was subsumed in the short section headed 'Care for those in Need', which was dominated by social security. The Conservatives promised to implement the Seebohm reforms. It was accepted that 'more emphasis is required on the provision of care for the elderly, the chronic sick and handicapped people, and particularly on the expansion of those services which provide help in the home'. Beside promising an expansion of local authority services, the Conservatives emphasised the continuing role for voluntary effort in the social services. This promise to develop community services was repeated on more than one occasion in the short section relating directly to the health service. The Conservatives complained about the inadequate funds going into the health services, with the result that insufficient resources were being invested in community care, health centres, or new hospitals. By improving the co-ordination of services, the Conservatives promised to achieve 'better value for money and better care for the patient'. The only other specific promise was to improve ways of dealing with suggestions and complaints from both patients and staff in the health service - a clear indication of continuing echoes from Howe's Ely report.[29] It is striking that the manifesto devoted more space to race relations and immigration than to health, and indeed this was granted a separate section. The promise to assist local authorities in addressing 'problems of poverty, decay and squalor in our towns and cities' implied special attention to health problems of the inner cities.[30]

Some insight into the initial response to these election promises is given by a memorandum outlining urgent initiatives planned by Sir Keith Joseph shortly after he assumed office. The list was headed by a vague proposal to review the hospital plan. His main concern was to reassess the fashion for large hospital projects and to improve management. For advice on hospitals, Joseph wanted to import a consultant from a large building construction firm with which he was associated, a prospect which the Prime Minister advised against. The second item on Joseph's list fitted in with the manifesto promise to tackle 'shirkers and the scroungers' who abused social security benefits. The final two priorities relating to abortion and family planning implicitly connected with the manifesto's pledges concerning inner cities and immigrants. Joseph was obviously personally committed to the extension of family planning services, and he attached particular importance to domiciliary services, which he saw as the only means to reach the lowest stratum of his social problem groups. Joseph believed that this proposal would be uncontroversial and he assured the Prime Minister that he was supported by his Roman Catholic colleague, Norman St John-Stevas. Joseph's related idea of legislation to restrict the use of private nursing homes for abortion by foreign women, may perhaps have been a quid pro quo to satisfy the St John-Stevas faction. This proposal was unattractive to the Prime Minister, who was disinclined to reopen the parliamentary debate on abortion for fear of reopening the bitter controversies experienced in 1967.[31] Joseph discussed the above programme with the Prime Minster in December 1970, reassuring Heath that, contrary to some press speculation, 'he had no intention of and no mandate for abolishing the NHS'. Indeed he made an urgent bid for £100m in additional resources for the hospital programme and for development of local authority services.[32] The main priority for Joseph was therefore the search for a greater share of national resources to support the expanding obligations of his department, continuing the effort mounted by Crossman in the final days of the Wilson administration.

The extent of Joseph's success is indicated by the data provided in Appendix 3. Naturally, trends in health and personal social service expenditure must be seen in the context of changes in the national economy. The Heath administration at first adopted a cautious and neutral economic policy, but soon substituted a more expansionary approach in the attempt to arrest rising unemployment and low output. Since the October 1970, and 1971 budgets only marginally reduced unemployment, a series of expansionary measures were applied from the summer of 1971 onwards, reaching a climax with the 1972 budget. This policy led to modest relaxation in the control of public expenditure, with the result that there was an acceleration in the year-on-year increase in 1970, 1971, 1972 and 1973. The climax of this policy was an especially large rise in output in 1973. This 'Heath-Barber Boom', together with adverse external events such as the steady rise in primary commodity prices, and the 400 per cent increase in the price of oil which began in October 1973, plunged the economy into crisis. During the latter stages of its existence, the Heath administration struggled to rein back demand, and it was faced with a plunge into a huge balance of payments deficit. Inflation was high, and was constrained with difficulty by the Government's incomes policy. Following renewed speculation against sterling, in June 1972 the Government allowed the pound to float, as a consequence of which it fell in value by about 9 per cent. From then onwards, there was a gathering air of crisis about the state of the economy.[33]

From 1955/56 onwards, with the exception of only two years, there was year-on-year increase in the share of national resources devoted to the NHS as a percentage of GDP. 1972/73 and 1973/74 were the first two consecutive years in which there was a decline. This was of course explained primarily by the short boom occurring at this time. As indicated in Appendix 3.3, there was a small rise in 1971/72 to 4.83 per cent, followed by the two years of decline, to reach 3.78 per cent, which was the lowest level for more than a decade. By contrast with the later years of the previous Conservative administration, there was no sharp increase in the contribution to the cost of the NHS from direct charges and the NHS Contribution. The proportions from these two sources changed slightly, but the total share remained at about 13 per cent. The share from the Consolidated Fund and local taxation increased from 87.5 to 90.1 per cent between 1969/70 and 1973/74, continuing the trend evident under the Wilson administration.[34]

In constant price terms, with respect to both cost and volume estimates, an annual increase was maintained throughout the Heath administration, in both cases at about the average rate experienced during the previous Wilson administration. Over the period from 1970 to 1974, at 1970 prices, NHS expenditure increased by 26.8 per cent in cost terms and 13.2 per cent in volume terms. The cost estimate was much affected by the pay increases of 1974, occurring mainly during the first months of the new Wilson administration. Owing to the pay factor, 1974 accounts for virtually half of the total cost increase for the 1970-1974 period. The volume estimate irons out the wage inflation element, and suggests a much more steady rate of increase, which averages at 3.3 per cent a year over this period. With respect to current expenditure, of the formidable 26.7 per cent increase in the cost estimate, 14.8 per cent is attributable to 1974 and its associated pay escalation. The volume estimate applying to current expenditure displays a more even pattern, averaging at 3.4 per cent a year over this period. The Heath administration in fact marked the end of a long period of gradual increase in spending in volume terms, which had gone on since about 1953, and which marginally gathered in pace with each new administration.[35]

Education maintained its place in the social services spending league table, absorbing about 26 per cent of resources throughout this period, whereas the share taken by the NHS fell from 19.8 per cent to 18.8 per cent. This was to some extent compensated for by the slight increase in the resources available to community care; the personal social services share increased from 4.5 per cent to 5.1 per cent.[36] Having summarised the level of funding devoted to the health service, the following section will deal with the political context for these trends.

(iii) FINANCING THE HEALTH SERVICE
Under its election pledges, the Heath administration was committed to the proposition that insufficient resources were being directed into the health service. It also promised to encourage private health care, and it was not opposed to the principle of direct charges. The Treasury had already obtained some experience with Crossman's enthusiasms for extending insurance funding of health care. Under the Conservatives this alternative assumed renewed importance.

Working Party on NHS Finance
As noted in chapter III, the Macmillan administration was divided over the virtues of the NHS Contribution and it had taken little notice of the advocates of private health insurance. However, the enthusiasts for alternative methods of funding health care continued their campaigning; by 1970 they had gained wider support for their ideas. The Jewkeses, Lees, Seldon, and the Institute of Economic Affairs were no longer voices in the wilderness. Among the Heath Ministers, Geoffrey Howe in particular was associated with their ideas. Howe and Arthur Seldon, the editorial director of the Institute of Economic Affairs, were the only two lay members on a BMA advisory panel which produced a lengthy report, entitled *Health Service Financing*, a summary of which was issued just before the 1970 General Election.[37] The BMA panel concluded that the NHS would continue to be under-financed unless it broke away from reliance on direct taxation. It concluded that the only way to guarantee adequate

funding for the health service was to expand the role of compulsory and voluntary health insurance. The BMA document was rather more forceful in its advocacy of the insurance option than Conservative Party planning documents, most of which mentioned insurance as a radical option, but conceded that this policy could be politically damaging owing to the general popularity of the NHS and support for its existing form of funding.[38] The insurance option also gained support from Ronald Butt in the *Times*, who was clearly in possession of information about the confidential discussions among Ministers concerning increased health service charges. Butt advised Macleod and Joseph to avoid this course of 'candle-end economies' and instead advised them to take up and extend Crossman's ideas about insurance. The Treasury acknowledged that Butt's contribution was giving 'new zest' to the insurance lobby.[39] The insurance option was also favoured by the Conservative parliamentary Health and Social Security Committee study group reporting on NHS organisation. In the short term this group advised increasing the role of national health insurance. In the longer term, it favoured more radical change: 'the basis of finance should be compulsory health insurance (normally non-state) which would allow patients to buy either NHS or private services as they preferred'.[40]

Despite the seeming compatibility of the BMA document with Conservative policy, and underpinning from some well-known economists, the Treasury was unmoved by the new presentation. It was concluded that the BMA proposals would not reduce reliance on direct taxation, while the additional resources from insurance were likely to be wastefully spent, and unlikely be bring about the intended benefits. The initial Treasury response was to stand by the conclusions reached in the Figgures Report of 1960, and continue to rely on financing the health service from direct taxation. By adoption of a more cohesive administrative structure, allowing more rigid control of regional allocations and budgetary ceilings throughout the unified services, it was anticipated that substantial economies would ensue, allowing much better value for money to be derived from the 4.9 per cent of GNP devoted to the health service. The Treasury was convinced that consistent pursuit of these policies would undermine the case for radical reform and demonstrate that, in value for money terms, competitors abroad would be shown to offer little for the additional resources that they were devoting to health care.[41]

Notwithstanding the disinclination of the Treasury to reopen the question of insurance funding, Joseph instructed his officials to examine the idea of raising substantial sums through the channel of compulsory insurance. Albeit without enthusiasm, DHSS officials worked out a scheme under which hospital patients would pay £20 a week for six weeks, to be covered by private insurance for those able to pay. Treasury officials were equally unsympathetic with this idea. They pointed out that this scheme was open to objection on the grounds that it was a flat-rate poll tax of a regressive type; it ran against the principles of insurance, since payments would relate neither to use nor actuarial risk. It was argued that insurance companies would never take on this function unless they were indemnified against loss by the Government. Since the insurance companies would merely be acting as collecting agents, it would be preferable to use the existing National Insurance scheme to levy such charges. The Treasury believed that all the objections to increasing the NHS Contribution applied with even greater force to the proposal emanating from Joseph; it was also concerned that the hypothecated income derived from this source would be used by DHSS as a vehicle for evading the discipline of current methods of controlling public expenditure. The scheme suggested by Joseph would make it even more difficult for the Government to persuade the public that their compulsory insurance contributions were not paying for the entire health service. The Joseph proposal occasioned a prompt and thorough review of the past history of the discussions concerning hypothecated taxation and the NHS Contribution. As on most previous occasions, an entirely negative conclusion was reached. Indeed, in reviewing the problems facing the National Insurance scheme, officials from the relevant Treasury divisions were favourable to complete abolition of the NHS Contribution.[42]

Oblivious to the conclusions reached by officials, on 28 July 1970 Joseph arranged to see Howe to discuss the new thinking. They were joined by other Ministers from the Treasury and DHSS. The extensive briefing documents provided for this meeting were as pessimistic as was prudent about the BMA report. New approaches to NHS funding were outlined by Macmillan and Howe. The latter gave an exposition of the BMA document. Macmillan favoured a scheme requiring patients to pay for services upon use, with the State contributing either a fixed amount, or a proportion of the cost. Either voluntary or compulsory insurance would be used to cover payments made by patients. The Howe and Macmillan variants were designed to apply to all parts of the health service. Contribution to this discussion by officials from the Treasury and DHSS was mainly confined to outlining the disadvantages of insurance schemes. They stressed the high level of administrative costs compared with the current health service. Joseph also concentrated on the difficulties of the new schemes. He also 'doubted whether the Government had a mandate to switch the NHS fully to an insurance-based system'. The most that could be tolerated was an experiment relating to one part of the service. The only candidate seeming appropriate for such an experiment was the general dental service. The meeting agreed to give further thought to the possibility of an experiment, and officials were asked to review evidence from other countries to discover what practical problems emerged from rivals to the NHS.[43]

Notwithstanding the indifferent response to the insurance option, Joseph adopted this as a working assumption. He was evidently impressed by the analysis conducted by Howe in his recent address to the Fellowship for Freedom in Medicine, which he recommended to DHSS officials as a guide to their thinking on financing the health service. Howe called on a new Conservative Government to 'give people a vested interest in the expansion of private health' to such an extent that it could not be reversed by a future socialist administration.[44] With these aspirations in mind, Joseph proposed a joint Treasury-DHSS working party on NHS Finance, to examine the proposition that over a period of 5 to 6 years most of NHS costs currently borne by direct taxation should be shifted to pay-rolls, with appropriate division between employer and employee. The working party would also be asked to make recommendations for substantial hospital boarding charges. Joseph was optimistic that this change to a contributory basis of funding, together with 'substantial bed charges, specified and inspected minimum standards and growth in private insurance facilities, various benefits of supply and stimulus in the hospital field might follow'.[45] Treasury officials were unconvinced, also alarmed about Joseph's continuing belief that the NHS Contribution constituted some kind of insurance payment and his failure to understand that it was merely a form of taxation.[46]

Macmillan complained that Joseph had misunderstood the insurance proposition; Jenkin urged the Treasury to clarify its position on these issues before agreeing to a working party; Barber avoided commitment and asked for further discussions.[47] Notwithstanding confusion about the objectives of the joint working party, in the course of their negotiations on reductions in public expenditure, Macmillan and Joseph agreed to pursue this idea.[48] The working party was launched in October 1970, and asked to report by April 1971.[49] The working party comprised members of five departments. It was asked to:

examine possible alternative methods of financing health and welfare services in the public and private sectors, having regard, particularly, to probable continuing increase in demand for the services, the inevitable continuing constraint on resources, the planned reorganisation of the structure of the National Health Service and of local government, and the government's general taxation policy.

The working party on NHS Finance was dutiful rather than enthusiastic. The group was told not to attach too much importance to the option of allowing tax relief on health insurance premiums, since the Government was already unable to fulfil its intended programme of tax reductions.[50] The working party investigated the case for tax relief on health insurance, but on the merits of the case confirmed the negative conclusion reached in previous reviews.[51]

The working party discovered that Joseph's expectations shifted rapidly away from the propositions contained in his original proposal to the Chancellor of the Exchequer. By the end of November 1970 he accepted that general taxation should retain its current role in funding the NHS.[52] His revised suggestions were options considered on previous occasions. His list of additional sources of finance for the NHS comprised: higher charges to insurance companies for treatment of road traffic victims, the hospital boarding charge, introduction of a two-class hospital service with charges for the higher class, charges levied on employers for treatment of employees injured at work, and finally an increased NHS Contribution hypothecated to the NHS. The Treasury was irritated by this reversal of position; Joseph was accused of shifting the enquiry in the direction of discovering additional sources of funding for the NHS to support his bids for higher expenditure, which had not been the purpose for which the working party was established.[53]

The arguments against the above additional sources of funding were well-rehearsed. In order to dampen still further any inclination for radical change, the Treasury dispatched the Figgures report to DHSS, confident that 'it should curb any enthusiasms there may be to revive some of the larger nonsenses'.[54] Embarrassment was caused by a leak to the press of accurate information about the alternatives under investigation within the working party.[55] In response to this leak, Joseph issued an assurance that 'as far as I can see, the National Health Service will remain overwhelmingly financed by taxation and contributions, even when these [alternatives] have been brought about'.[56]

The Institute for Economic Affairs also kept up the pressure for a change of policy, and its views evoked some positive response from Treasury Ministers, but its reports were subjected to scathing criticism within the Treasury.[57] The working party explored the ground conscientiously, but eliminated all the radical alternatives. There remained a small residuum of viable suggestions for supplements to general taxation, which merely comprised sources already being exploited, of which the only significant items were direct charges and the NHS Contribution. The working party decided that there was no scope for departing from the existing formula for financing the health service.[58] The only scope for change was in the dental, ophthalmic and pharmaceutical services, where there was the possibility increasing direct charges. The were also some opportunities for introducing charges for general medical practitioner services, but all of these alternatives were objectionable on medical grounds. With respect to the main area of Joseph's proposals, the working party concluded 'that any substantial switch from public to private provision of hospital services, general medical services, and local health and personal social services would increase the cost and would reduce the effectiveness of publicly provided services'.[59] This verdict was communicated to Macmillan on 8 June 1971, when: 'In general, the Chief Secretary accepted the main findings of the Working Party Report - viz, that, short of a major revolution in the whole NHS system, there was very limited scope for any changes whose benefits would outweigh the practical difficulties to which they would give rise'.[60]

1970 PESC Report and Graduated Prescription Charge
Joseph's flirtation with alternatives to the established pattern of NHS funding constituted a brief diversion. As in the case of his predecessors, his main energies were absorbed in prising additional resources out of the PESC system, without conceding more than minimal offsetting savings or increases in charges.

Joseph inherited Crossman's poorly articulated campaign for additional resources for the health service. As in the case of his predecessor, this impulse was in conflict with the Government's targets for reductions in public expenditure, primarily designed to make way for tax reductions. The Cabinet aimed to reduce public expenditure by £1,700m by 1974/75; it adopted £400-£500m as the target for 1971/72, of which more than half was expected to come from the social services.[61] It was agreed that the Chief Secretary should negotiate with the Ministers responsible for spending departments in order to secure offers of economies, leaving any bids for additional resources to be considered in the PESC review.

In their preliminary trawl for candidates suitable for economy or excision, Treasury officials searched in the customary corners. This exercise was not approached with high expectations. At the sight of the first hurdle, it was conceded that although the programme was over £2bn, 'the scope for direct savings is surprisingly small'.[62] Favoured possibilities included abolition of the subsidy on welfare milk, abolition of the ophthalmic service except for priority groups and medical conditions requiring hospital treatment, abolition or a percentage charge for the general dental service, an increase in the prescription charge, the hospital boarding charge, elimination of school milk, and an economic charge for school meals. In effect this package represented reversion to proposals frequently canvassed before 1964. At the head of the list was more serious consideration of the idea of a prescription charge levied as a fixed percentage of the cost of the drugs prescribed, a possibility periodically considered previously, most recently in the final months of the Wilson administration.[63]

Macmillan and Joseph met for an informal discussion on 28 July. The Treasury was more comfortable with Joseph than with Crossman, whose impetuous policy expeditions had been an increasingly source of alarm. The Treasury found that Joseph shared their dissatisfaction with attitudes to the management of expenditure within DHSS, which proceeded 'on the assumption that all demands on the NHS are of equal priority and the remedy for any deficiencies lies in progressively large additional increments of expenditure'. It seemed that Joseph recognised the need for a new approach to management 'based on conscious identification of essential objects of expenditure and choices between relative priorities'.[64]

Building on this propitious start, Macmillan sent his formal requests for concessions to Joseph on 31 July and 4 August. Macmillan wrote optimistically of his hope and expectation that 'as our policies in these respects are more fully developed, we can look for more fundamental reform and relief for the tax-payer'.[65] Less favourable to the Treasury was Joseph's decision to stand by the greater part of the massive bid additional resources made at the behest of Crossman earlier in the year. The Ministers held their preliminary discussion on 19 August. In advance of this meeting Joseph revealed that half of any savings offered with respect to the health services would be reclaimed towards unavoidable additional expenditure in such areas as hospital building and community care. He cited election pledges and existing policy commitments which necessitated immediate increases in expenditure, while economies through improved efficiency or policy changes would be slow in having their effect. Joseph argued that it was unrealistic to wait until 1972/73 before introducing any of the urgently needed improvements in the health personal social services.[66]

At his important meeting with Macmillan, Joseph agreed to abolish the welfare milk subsidy, introduce higher charges for the dental and ophthalmic services levied at 50 per cent and 100 per cent of the cost of treatment respectively, as well as an increased prescription charge, initially levied at 4s(20p), but later to be converted to 25 per cent of the cost of drugs prescribed, with exemptions for hardship only.[67] Ministers also discussed, but decided to defer further consideration of the hospital boarding charge, pending findings from the new working party on NHS finance. Although the hospital boarding charge backed by compulsory insurance was initially favoured by Joseph and Macmillan, Treasury officials believed that it was impracticable and unsound in principle, since it was in effect a 'poll tax of a very regressive type'.[68]

Joseph warned that about £35m of his savings would be absorbed in his higher PESC bid for 1971/72. In order to soften the effect of this increase, he suggested a rise in the levy from insurance companies respecting the treatment of road accident victims, and also investigated whether it would be more economical for private companies to put up the capital for local authority building projects.[69]

The above package of health service economies, together with Thatcher's proposals for withdrawal of milk from primary and special schools, and introduction by stages of an economic cost for school meals, were discussed by Ministers on 15 September 1970. The health savings were valued at about £60m, and the economies on school meals and milk at about £33m. Both Joseph and Thatcher indicated that they expected to claw back about half of their savings through expansion of services. In discussion, concern was expressed about the effect of these proposals on families supported by low-paid workers, with the greatest reservations being expressed about school meals charges. However, the proposals were broadly endorsed.[70]

Joseph was not able to offer savings in health and welfare on an ascending scale. Consequently, while his prospective savings in 1971/72 amounted to an impressive £60m, he had no concrete plans for additional savings after that date. His bid for additional resources for 1971/72 was a modest £34m, but it was £77m, £135m, and £202m for the following years. This represented about two-thirds of the increases demanded by Crossman, and Joseph reiterated the latter's justification. As Joseph explained:

> What we said in our Manifesto was not an exaggeration. Too little has been spent on these services for too long. As a result, almost all the community services (nursing, social work, day centres, hostels and homes) are under-provided and under-staffed and in many areas some are almost non-existent. Hospital buildings are not only outdated but under-equipped and inadequately maintained. Standards of service in different parts of the country are still markedly unequal. Nurse recruitment is dropping. The doctors are restive because they lack the resources to give their patients the most modern treatment. Standards in psychiatric and geriatric hospitals are scandalously low.

Within his additional bid for 1971/72, Joseph proposed to devote £10m to local authority services, £22m to the hospital service (of which about half was intended for replacement of services associated with the long-stay hospitals), and £2m to family planning.[71]

On the basis of Joseph's agreement to adopt a graduated basis for prescription charges, albeit with retention of existing exemptions and a limit on the charge for each prescription, Barber accepted the extra bids in part, allowing for increases in health and welfare of £20m for 1971/72, and £30m for each of the following three years. Joseph's share was considerably less than requested, but allowed for further increases at a later date. This agreement was endorsed by Ministers, and a public announcement was authorised, the press release for which was headed: '£110m More for NHS: Improved Services for Old People, Mentally Handicapped and Mentally Ill'.[72] The annual growth rate for public expenditure assumed in the PESC Report for 1971 was about 3.6 per cent, which was marginally in advance of the levels approved under the Wilson administration.

Less positive publicity was attracted by the announcement of the increased charges and cuts in subsidies in the health services made by Barber on 27 October 1970 and amplified in the White Paper, *New Policies on Public Spending* (Cmnd.4515).[73] The main item with short-term impact was the increase in the prescription charge from 2s 6d(12½p) to 4s(20p) from April 1971.[74] Just as significant was the intention to introduce further increases as a consequence of transfer of the prescription charge to a graduated basis, which was expected to yield a further £15m in savings. The school meals charge was converted from 1s 9d to 9p, which was a trivial increase, but it was to be followed by a further increase to 12p in April 1971, with the 'aim...that the charge should eventually cover the running costs(c.20p)'.

Barber's statement did little for the image of the Heath administration. An internal review frankly admitted that the whole affair had been mishandled by Ministers and officials. It concluded:

The critics had a fair measure of success in presenting the Government's public expenditure policies as harsh and unfair, while the Government's presentation seems to have lacked a convincingly co-ordinated presentation of the purpose of both the expenditure measures and the tax measures as being to enable all families to grow richer more rapidly.[75]

Bad publicity shook the resolve of Ministers and coloured their reaction to the next round of economies.

The prompt introduction of this second instalment of savings on pharmaceutical costs was one of the offsets agreed as a condition for increases in expenditure. The Treasury watched with suspicion as the health departments laboured to evolve a viable plan for the graduated prescription charge. The outline for legislation to introduce the graduated prescription charge and reduce the age of

393

exemption from dental charges from 21 to 18, as well as other minor variations in arrangements for health service charges, was not presented to Ministers until April 1971. Joseph envisaged a prescription charge rising from a minimum of 20p to a maximum of 50p. His proposals were welcomed, but Ministers realised that legislation could not be introduced during the current session.[76] The Cabinet also authorised the health Ministers to hold further discussions with the professions about the new charges structure, but the Prime Minister was also concerned that the graduated charge would be represented as a callous attempt to undermine the foundations upon which the NHS was built.[77]

This delay was not regarded by DHSS as detrimental, since Joseph decided that it would not be possible to introduce a further increase in prescription charges before January 1972 on account of the outcry over the increase introduced in April 1971. DHSS also warned that it was experiencing difficulty in obtaining the co-operation of doctors and pharmacists over implementation of the graduated system. Accordingly, DHSS suggested a further flat-rate increase with a promise of annual reviews in place of the graduated charge. This reversal of policy announced in Cmnd.4515 was disappointing to the Treasury, but substitution of the flat-rate increase to 30p was regarded as tolerable, on condition that it was introduced in April 1972.[78]

In July 1971, health Ministers took their retreat from the graduated prescription charge to the Cabinet. Given the refusal of doctors, dentists and pharmacists to co-operate, the Ministers proposed investigations into the Swedish system of preparing medicines in standardised packs, but this was likely to delay the graduated charge for a further three to four years. In the short term they proposed reverting to an increase in the flat-rate charge, perhaps from the existing level of 20p to 30p. In discussion, their colleagues regretted abandoning the graduated charge, but were now opposed to any new increase in the prescription charge on account of combating inflationary wage claims and in order to avoid further adverse publicity over alleged indifference to groups with special needs. The Prime Minister agreed that no major increase in the prescription charge was feasible for a further twelve months, but health Ministers were asked to continue their investigations into transfer to a cost-related system of health service charges.[79]

Wrestling with PESC

Failure to arrive at a method for increasing the yield from the prescription charge coloured the Treasury's reception of Joseph's additional bids in connection with the 1971 PESC exercise.[80] Joseph applied for £30m in additional resources for 1972/73, and larger amounts for succeeding years, making a total of £267m over four years. This would have taken the NHS growth rate to about 4.6 per cent. The Treasury was unconvinced that the health service required greater resources than allowed in the 1970 PESC Report. The new bids seemed merely to be requests for additional resources to meet needs already covered in existing allocations. The Treasury was also opposed to Joseph's proposals for offsetting his higher expenditure by increases in the NHS Contribution. Joseph suggested that this proposal might be more palatable to the public if the Government gave guarantees that in the lifetime of the current Parliament no additional health service charges would be introduced. Treasury Ministers were advised to resist both of these ideas. Treasury officials were particularly concerned to prevent Joseph from annexing the NHS Contribution to support growth in health and welfare expenditure, in effect by-passing the framework of PESC controls, and pre-empting the Chancellor's options for fiscal policy. In the light of these objections, Joseph spontaneously reduced his bid for additional resources to £100m for the four year period; this compromise was given a surprisingly relaxed provisional acceptance by Macmillan, and ratified by the Cabinet.[81] The £100m increase (together with £18m for Scotland and Wales) was announced by Joseph on 22 November 1971.[82] This increment brought the HPSS growth rate to about 3.9 per cent.

The aftermath of the graduated prescription charge continued to plague the health Ministers. In October 1971 they were asked to produce a credible substitute for the loss occasioned by abandoning the graduated charge.[83] They came forward with a plan for an annual automatic adjustment in the prescription charge, but this required legislation, which would inevitably be controversial. Their colleagues were less than enthusiastic; they pointed out that this legislation would be difficult to timetable in the 1971/72 session; also it might well tie the Government's hands with respect to more radical alternatives. It was therefore agreed to announce the abandonment of the graduated charge without introduction of an alternative, while any question of increasing the prescription charge was deferred until the following year.[84] The *Financial Times* called this a sensible retreat, and the decision was generally well-received by the press.[85] Ministers were perhaps influenced by the adverse media publicity attracted by evidence of big falls in dental and eye treatment, as well as by the 10 per cent fall in prescriptions dispensed since the higher charges introduced in April 1971.[86] Treasury officials attempted in vain to keep up the momentum on health charges, but DHSS was unco-operative. Ministers returned to the question of health service charges on 25 May 1972, when they decided that it would be imprudent to increase the prescription charge, take any steps to place the yield on a graduated basis, or introduce any further upward revision of direct charges.[87]

Ministers were also more reticent in their approach to their plan for an economic charge for school meals. Treasury officials advised that 'since school meals and school milk have proved to be the most provocative and divisive of the public expenditure cuts, I am sure that Ministers will want at any rate to consider the proposed further increase before it takes place'.[88] With little enthusiasm, Ministers agreed in principle to increase the cost of the school meal by 2p, but deferred their decision about the date of implementation. The Heath administration ended without the higher charge being introduced.

Jenkin, the recently-appointed Chief Secretary, and Joseph met on 15 May 1972 to discuss the way forward on HPSS spending. In the light of the Government's economic problems, Joseph was content with only minor additional bids for the 1972 PESC exercise, but he warned that traditionally neglected areas of the health and personal social services required much bigger injections of resources than they had yet received. He proposed that the Treasury and DHSS should mount a joint review of these problems with the objective of arriving at a statement of priorities, which would become the basis for enhanced bids for resources in the 1973 PESC review. As noted above, the Treasury had long complained about the failure of DHSS to prioritise its expenditure commitments, but Jenkin was less than enthusiastic about the proposed review, primarily because his first objective was reducing public expenditure to make way for cuts in taxation. He was not happy to engage in planning expansion in major expenditure programmes, which in the case of the NHS had already enjoyed two years of favourable treatment.[89]

The Treasury failed to persuade Joseph to divert his proposed enquiry to the Programme Analysis and Review mechanism. The Treasury suspected that Joseph had calculated that he would secure a better deal in bilateral discussions with the Treasury, away from the gaze of collective ministerial discussion.[90] After inconsequential exchanges, in July 1972, to the relief of the Treasury, the idea of a joint review of health and personal social services priorities was called off by Joseph.[91] The Treasury also scored a further victory when its allies in DHSS persuaded Joseph to abandon his idea to give HPSS a 'wholly new priority', with the result that plans for big increases in expenditure were shelved, at least temporarily.[92]

After the gains secured in 1970 and 1971, only small and routine changes in NHS expenditure were introduced in the course of the PESC exercises for 1972 and 1973. Adverse economic indicators implied that from the summer of 1972, further expansion in the HPSS sector was out of the question. By virtue of the worsening economic situation and in an effort to restructure the contingency reserve, from the beginning of 1973, the Treasury searched hard for cuts in public expenditure. With respect to HPSS spending, there was virtual prohibition of consideration of increased direct charges on account of counter-inflationary policy. The only possibilities were minor the adjustment of dental and ophthalmic charges in line with maintenance of the agreed percentage yield. There was virtually no scope for other savings. With difficulty, economies amounting to £25m were devised for 1973/74, the biggest part from hospital running costs, but also with small reductions in the capital programme for both hospitals and local authorities.[93] A larger package of cuts amounting to £60m was suggested for 1974/75. However, in the course of bilateral discussions, these economies were whittled down to vanishing point. In his area of responsibility, Joseph was primarily subjected to pressure on his social security budget, where major restructuring was taking place. With respect to health and the personal social services, Joseph side-stepped threats to review levels of spending on hospitals, and effectively negotiated maintenance of the status quo, with economies being deferred until it was politically feasible to increase direct charges.

The situation concerning funding the NHS in the last months of the Heath administration is well encapsulated in Joseph's letter to Barber, in effect declaring a moratorium over requests for additional funding, providing that the health and personal social services were not targeted for further economies.[94]

May I first deal with health and the personal social services? Conditions in many of our long-stay hospitals - which account for 60 per cent of our beds - are still deplorable and are likely to remain so until additional funds can be injected on a substantial scale. Throughout the service we must press on with our programmes for replacing hospitals no longer acceptable by today's standards and for bringing conditions for both patients and staff up to tolerable levels. Demographic changes, rising public expectations and the requirements placed on local authorities by legislation call for sustained expansion of the Personal Social Services, particularly for the elderly, the mentally ill, the mentally and physically handicapped and for children in residential care. Despite the needs, I have not pressed for increased provision for the Health and Personal Social Services in the period up to 1977/78, although I shall clearly need to look for an addition if Lady Sharp's recommendations for the invalid vehicle service prove expensive. On the other hand, any cut in the programme must be a serious set-back. We received considerable kudos for virtually excluding the social services from the 1974/75 cuts announced in May and, as I said in Cabinet, it is certainly realistic to assume that we can provide say £25m a year for the contingency reserve by raising charges in 2 years time.

The Treasury was unhappy with Joseph's 'pre-emptive strike'. Barber warned that 'an adequate solution to the general problem of excessive claims for public expenditure - which is vital to our whole economic strategy - can hardly be found without a substantial contribution from your programmes', but no further attempts were made at incursions into the HPSS budget.[95] In the bilateral discussion convened by Jenkin on 25 September 1973, Joseph succeeded in deferring any immediate proposals for HPSS economies. It was accepted that no reductions would be imposed for 1974/75, and only £14m in 1975/76.[96]

In the final year of the Heath administration, the main point of contention with respect to HPSS expenditure related to the new family planning service, which turned out to be considerably more expensive than predicted. The other main problems related to the containment of wages. Both of these issues are considered below. The pressures associated with wage inflation were symptomatic of the gathering strains on the economy. The instability of the situation was already evident in the summer of 1972, when the Government was finally forced to abandon the fixed exchange rate for sterling. From then onward virtually all the indicators showed alarming trends; finally a desperate situation was made worse by the quadrupling of oil prices in the final months of 1973. The first direct effect on the NHS followed a statement by the Prime Minister on 8 October 1973, which introduced minor curtailment of demand in order to conserve oil stocks. The main element affecting the health service was the introduction of a moratorium on new building contracts in the public sector for the final quarter of 1973, or appropriate adjustments in the first quarter of 1974 if this target could not be met. This was a small perturbation, but it soon became apparent that more drastic action was needed, especially because the oil crisis was compounded by a worsening balance of payments deficit, as well as a continuing overtime ban by miners. On 17 December 1973 Barber announced a fuller package of measures designed to reduce demand without curtailing exports and productive investment. By a process of elimination, in his effort to reduce demand, Barber fell back on the imposition of public expenditure reductions amounting to £1,200m. The effect was to convert an anticipated increase of public expenditure of 3 per cent for 1974/75 into a reduction of 2 per cent.[97] The HPSS share of the cuts was substantial, but not out of proportion with reductions in other areas of public expenditure. The NHS was subjected to a £69m reduction in capital expenditure and £42m reduction in procurement spending, which represented cuts of 20 per cent and 10 per cent respectively.[98] These measures gave the opposition an opportunity to criticise the record of the Conservatives on the NHS, but the attack was not handled particularly competently and failed to cause embarrassment to the Government.[99]

(iv) PROTECTING THE VULNERABLE

As described in chapter III, the Ely scandal provoked a range of policy initiatives designed to give better care and protection to patients in long-stay hospitals, and also to generally improve arrangements for dealing with complaints about incompetence and injustice, especially within the hospital system. Few of these improvements had come to fruition before the departure of Crossman.

Hospital Advisory Service
As already noted, the Hospital Advisory Service for England and Wales was established in November 1969; its counterpart for Scotland was formed in April 1970. For its success, the HAS needed to achieve a delicate balance between inspecting and consultative functions. Undue weight on inspection was likely to alienate hospital personnel, while a weak admonitory role was likely to permit continuation of abuses and provide too little incentive for improvement of services. The steady tide of fresh revelations about scandals in long-stay hospitals suggested that the Ely Report was not far wrong in demanding an effective inspectorate for the hospital service. As already noted, the Scottish HAS was integrated into the central health department, and its inspectoral and advisory functions were conducted in close harmony with the regional boards. This arrangement was perhaps too closely identified with the NHS establishment, but it ensured that the HAS in Scotland operated more smoothly than its counterpart south of the border. The major critic of the Scottish HAS was the Mental Health Commission, which had opposed the formation of the HAS on the grounds that its essential functions were already being performed by the Commission.[100]

In England and Wales, the first of Dr Baker's teams began work in February 1970; two more teams were established in May, and the final team in August. In mid-May a meeting was held with a delegation from the South East Metropolitan region to discuss the state of its mental handicap hospitals, which was the first of many such regional reviews. The work of Dr Baker and his teams was not universally appreciated. Health authorities tended to be protective of their staffs, and they were apt to complain about misrepresentation by the inspecting teams, even in cases where subsequent formal enquiries essentially supported the findings of the HAS. In order to secure the independence of the HAS, Crossman had made it administratively separate from both NHS authorities and the central department. This formula produced agreeable results when Dr Baker's teams commanded the support of the Secretary of State, but without this backing they were likely to be lacking in friends.

At the second of his monthly meetings with Dr Baker, Joseph complained that the HAS was creating too much work for the department. Baker pointed out that this was the result of the 'cracking pace' needed to fulfil the urgent task of visiting all the mental handicap institutions.[101] Thereafter Baker failed to secure from Joseph anything like the level of backing received from Crossman. Joseph was supportive of an inspectorate, but he preferred a locally organised system dealing with all aspects of care relating to particular client groups such as the elderly. He wanted Baker to concentrate on establishing regional centres to propagate good practice in the mental health sector.[102]

Already by the end of 1970 officials were expressing reservations to the Secretary of State about the HAS. The department admitted that the 'possibility of conflict between the views of the HAS and the Department is inherent in the administrative structure under which the HAS was set up as an isolated organisation not integrated into the main body of the Department'.[103] Given this tension, the department resisted suggestions from Dr Baker concerning extension of the remit of the HAS.

Tensions over the HAS failed to subside. The reports on individual hospitals provoked defensive responses from the hospital authorities, and hence contributed to an atmosphere of confrontation. Further annoyance was caused when the first annual report of HAS, published on 12 May 1971, was distributed to the regions only upon its publication. RHB Chairmen complained that the report was unnecessarily alarmist, and that it paid scant regard to the efforts of hospital authorities to improve services. Hospital interests felt that their efforts were undermined by the report: 'this is not the first time that bad news has driven out good'. The press predictably concentrated on the sensationalist aspects of the report. The Chairmen blamed both the HAS and DHSS for permitting this further blow to morale within the mental health service.[104] This rebuke from the regions prompted DHSS to conduct a full review of the advisory service, and in the mean time suspend action on its reports. Instead the regional boards were invited to keep the department informed about the state of their long-stay hospitals and also continue to encourage good practice.[105] The department's confidential report on the work of the HAS extended to 21 pages.[106] The verdict was predominantly negative. The department insisted that HAS should desist from making suggestions about the replanning of services within a region, that the reports should be shorter and more precise, and that only DHSS should identify and pursue points requiring further action. This report implied that problems were best handled between the department and the regions, and that the HAS was contributing unhelpfully to an already delicate situation. No doubt some of the criticisms in the report were merited, but there was obviously on the part of the department and NHS authorities an instinct to draw negative conclusions about Crossman's brain-child. Reports produced by the HAS provided a frequent and unwelcome reminder of the 'post-Ely' mood of self-examination. For officials and NHS authorities immersed in the problems of reorganisation and doing their best to give higher priority to the mental health service, the irritant grains contributed by the HAS seemed like an excessive additional imposition.

The main objective of the criticisms was to preclude further extension of the field of activity of the HAS, which aspired to cover the entire hospital service and all services relating to long-stay patients. The department urged that this would undermine the department's efforts to cultivate an ethos of self-improvement within the health care professions. Officials were evidently undecided whether to dispense completely with the HAS. In the event it was given a reprieve for a further year, pending assessment of alternative system of monitoring operated jointly by the department and the regional authorities.[107] Attitudes to the HAS were not improved when its second annual report, also critical of the state of the mental health services, was published in August 1972, at the same moment as publication of the White Paper on NHS reorganisation.

Notwithstanding the force of its critics, the HAS was not without its supporters. Some regions saw merit in an independent inspectorate; also it was urged that fresh leadership and reconstructed teams might produce a less controversial outcome.[108] Having achieved a stay of execution, the HAS was permitted to continue on a probationary basis, during which the calls for its dissolution gradually subsided. Nevertheless, RHB Chairmen and the Regional Consultants and Specialists Association demanded alteration of the way in which the HAS operated.[109]

Dr Baker's initial period of appointment ended in October 1972. He remained in office until August 1973, when he returned to clinical work in Gloucestershire. By this stage his teams had undertaken a substantial investigative exercise. All mental handicap hospitals in England had been visited by September 1971. By the end of 1973 all mental hospitals had been visited in eleven regions, and all geriatric hospitals in eight regions. It was difficult to keep up the pace of this activity and build up stable teams of visitors on account of the instability of the situation, compounded by inherent uncertainties over employment at the time of reorganisation.

401

Owing to the pressure of work occasioned by NHS reorganisation, the scale of the HAS was reduced from four to two teams. During 1973, there was much doubt within DHSS whether a place would be found for the HAS in the reorganised health service.[110] However, it was decided to continue the service for at least two further years. The second Director of HAS was Dr Eluned Woodford-Williams, consultant physician in charge of geriatric services in the Sunderland area, who had served for two years on the HAS geriatric team.[111] DHSS made suggestions for improving the performance of HAS, and these were largely accepted by the Director.[112] Modifications within HAS and influx of different personnel improved the prospects for its survival to become a permanent feature of the NHS. Indeed, both public opinion and outside expert advice exerted influence in favour of an expanding role for the HAS.[113]

Better Services for the Mentally Handicapped

By the date of the 1970 General Election, the draft White Paper on services for the mentally handicapped had reached its 'sixth edition', and was regarded by Crossman as suitable for publication with little further emendation. Initial soundings taken by Conservative Ministers revealed distinct lack of consensus over this document; indeed there was distinct polarisation of opinion. Some critics complained that the sixth draft White Paper was insufficiently decisive in its commitment to community care, whereas the rival camp believed that the draft envisaged the run-down of hospital services to an unrealistically low level. The latter urged that the existing policy of retaining comprehensive subnormality hospitals for up to 500 patients should be retained as one of the essential foundations of future policy.

Joseph attached just as much importance as Crossman to improving services for the mentally ill and the mentally handicapped. Michael Alison recalls Joseph's 'unrelenting concentration of thought, effort, and cash resources, on raising standards in the dreadfully neglected long stay mental illness and mental handicap hospitals'. This effort 'persisted unremittingly throughout the whole of his period of office'.[114] Joseph was perplexed by differences of opinion among the experts. His first discussions with specialists in this field inclined him to favour increasing the community care emphasis of the White Paper. Aberdare regarded the draft White Paper as a realistic compromise. In view of the lack of unanimity about policy, as well as uncertainty about resources, Ministers decided on further consultations, but without relaxing efforts to achieve continuing short-term improvements in services.[115] Joseph studied the problem of mental handicap with even more than his habitual diligence. At an early stage, he concluded:

Subject to what the Minister of State and PUSS(H) think, my view is that we should not jeopardise this great initiative. The WP is impressive in range and vigour - though on first reading a shade repetitive and diffuse, as well as being more than obscure. Certainly I would like to go forward. But with what equally urgent NHS objective will this compete for funds. Subject to this I would like to bid for enough resources to embark on the LA as well as the NHS components of the programme and the training and upgrading ingredients.[116]

At first the Secretary of State favoured calling a seminar to adjudicate between the rival parties. He then abandoned this idea in favour of private meetings with the protagonists.[117] Commitment to issue the White Paper was finally made on 29 September 1970.[118] The main instruction for alteration of the text was for inclusion of a costed timetable for introducing the desired improvements, embodying a degree of formal expenditure commitment intentionally avoided in the drafts supervised by Crossman. It was also decided that no useful purpose was served by the extensive account of deficiencies of the existing services contained in the existing draft.

Within DHSS there was also much doubt whether the final drafting stages supervised by Professor Abel-Smith had resulted in improvements. Officials complained that the sixth draft was 'too euphoric, idealistic and vague'.[119] Officials were now free to undertake improvements without the interference of Crossman's advisers, but they were bound by the same constraints. In particular they were faced with the difficult task of producing a document acceptable to rival interest groups, and taking account of the likely limitations on the pace of change within the reorganised health and personal social services. Consequently, although the officials castigated Abel-Smith's drafts for their lack of radicalism and specific policy objectives, the revisions under Joseph tended to further dilute the main policy objectives adopted at the earlier stage. For instance, the redrafting considerably reduced the emphasis on the concentration of services in district general hospitals, thereby offering the possibility of a new lease of life for the traditional mental handicap hospital, or the smaller 500-bed type of hospital widely advocated by consultant specialists in mental handicap. Advocacy of the rapid run-down of hospital facilities was inhibited by realisation that local authorities, for reasons of lack of resources, inexperience, absence of definitive policy guide-lines, and limitations of attitude, were likely to be slow to provide replacement community care facilities.

Preparation of the final version went slowly, prompting expressions of alarm within the media, and accusations that the

Government was avoiding commitment to a long-term policy on mental handicap.[120] However, this was not a case of inaction. Government departments and about six outside organisations were asked to comment on the text. The comments received indicated general satisfaction with the plan, although naturally, the Treasury insisted on avoiding guarantees about funding. In response to Treasury qualms, Joseph agreed to extend the programme over twenty years, so that 'absolutely first class provision for every single person' would have been achieved. He nevertheless hoped to make substantial progress within ten years.[121]

Drafts continued to multiply. At the end of March 1971, Joseph produced no less than 30 pages of comments on the latest version.[122] The long period of drafting had produced no settled general title for the White Paper; in May 1971 the shortlist of possibilities was narrowed down to 'Services for the Mentally Handicapped' and 'A Better Life for the Mentally Handicapped'.[123] The White Paper was published on 23 June 1971 under the title, *Better Services for the Mentally Handicapped*.[124] It was issued by the Secretaries of State for Social Services and for Wales.

A separate and more modest policy document was prepared by SHHD for application to Scotland. This memorandum comprised only 22 pages of text, and it was limited to the barest essentials, and although published in April 1972, contains no reference to its English counterpart, or even any indication that a parallel document was under consideration for England and Wales.[125]

Better Services was the first major policy document issued by DHSS to be illuminated by a striking vermilion front cover. Despite the refreshing image of the cover, the 67 pages of *Better Services for the Mentally Handicapped* were not entirely a statement of new policy; the policy document was in many respects a rather belated attempt to inspire more determined progress towards the objectives outlined by the Royal Commission on Mental Illness in 1957.

It was hoped that the White Paper would at last lead to hospitals divesting themselves of responsibility for those requiring care on social grounds, in order that in future they would concentrate exclusively on the treatment and nursing care of those with the most severe handicaps. All others would leave hospital, or not arrive there in the first place, but would be assured of appropriate support within the community. With respect to the means of arriving at these objectives, like the final Crossman drafts, *Better Services* was of necessity a compromise package, taking account of the realities of inertia within the system, inter-professional disagreements, economic constraints, and limitations imposed by the disposition of responsibilities within the health and personal social services. *Better Services* steered an intermediate course, taking account of the likely limitations in the will and capacity of local authorities to rapidly develop their community care programme, while also recognising the argument that modernised hospital services would continue to be indispensable. The White Paper proposed increased financial allocations to existing hospitals to enable them to perform their functions to an optimum standard. This would enable these hospitals to be compared with the new comprehensive mental handicap units associated with district general hospitals, which it was proposed to develop as resources became available. As their counterpart in the community, local authorities were provided with guide-lines for the development of the services for which they were responsible.

Better Services was generally well-received in both professional and lay circles, but among some experts it was greeted with scepticism. Professor Peter Townsend, who had been an inveterate critic of the drafts produced under Crossman, described *Better Services for the Mentally Handicapped* as 'tragically disappointing in nature and scale', and warned that it might 'result in a pattern of services little better than they are now'.[126.] The success of *Better Services* also was heavily dependent on the rapid build-up of local authority services, about which authorities such as Mary Applebey, the General Secretary of the National Association for Mental Health were deeply pessimistic.[127]

Such reservations were subsequently confirmed by shortcomings of joint planning exercises undertaken by NHS and local authorities. In its first review of progress after publication of *Better Services*, DHSS was disappointed with the response. A minority of regions had produced effective and realistic plans for the development of their mental handicap services, but rarely were local authorities fully consulted, although they were expected to bear an increasing burden of responsibility for services. DHSS called upon other regions to approach their joint planning duties in the spirit exhibited in Wessex, where an unusual combination of circumstances - concentration of expertise, enthusiasm for innovation, and relatively small number of NHS and local authorities - created optimal conditions for success.[128]

Better Services for the Mentally Ill
Given the inevitable delay in arriving at a definitive statement of long-term policy for the mental sector, Crossman urged the RHB Chairmen to concentrate on programmes for interim improvements to raise minimum standards in existing hospitals with relation to such problems as diet, relief from overcrowding, privacy, amenities, and staffing. This request was followed up with a survey of progress in preparation of five-year interim programmes. This information was collected in the summer of 1970. Also, following the first HAS

405

reports, all hospitals in the mental sector were pressed to improve their management arrangements, and in particular to take steps to introduce multi-disciplinary management.

Schemes for short-term improvements in mental handicap hospitals were discussed with RHB Chairmen in the later half of 1971. DHSS tried to persuade regional Chairmen that the opportunity existed to 'turn off the tap' on further admissions to mental handicap hospitals. NHS authorities were not entirely co-operative. Partly owing to the resistance of Hospital Management Committees, virtually no progress was made with the introduction of multi-disciplinary management. The regional authorities also complained that nothing could be done to reduce the size of mental handicap hospitals until local authorities showed more inclination to develop their services. In frustration over this situation, the North West Metropolitan RHB proposed to expand its already large hospitals by adding 30-bed units, intended as substitutes for hostels supposed to be provided by local authorities.[129]

From the outset of the post-Ely policy exercise, it was recognised that psychiatric hospitals were subject to many of the defects found in hospitals for the mentally handicapped and the elderly. The production of guide-lines for improvements in the entire mental sector was pursued as a matter of urgency. As noted above, in view of the possibly greater extent of neglect and stronger media attention, the long-term policy document for mental handicap took precedence.

As the activities of AEGIS suggested, one of the most serious problems facing psychiatric hospitals related to the growing tide of psychogeriatric patients. This trend was already causing concern at the outset of the NHS, and it stimulated pioneers of the new specialty of geriatrics to experiment with day hospitals and other rehabilitative regimes. However, systematic policy initiatives were slow to materialise. The first full review emanated from a sub-committee appointed by the Scottish Standing Medical Advisory Committee, which began work in 1968, and which published its report in 1970.[130] Although this Report advocated giving high priority to community services, day hospitals and other rehabilitation methods, it emphasised that 'mental hospitals will continue to carry a heavy responsibility for these patients'. Accordingly, it envisaged that existing mental hospitals would require considerable resources for their upgrading and rebuilding.[131]

In December 1971 DHSS issued a short document updating HM(64)45, and outlining in schematic terms a comprehensive, integrated, hospital and community service based on the psychiatric service of district general hospitals, and suggesting ways in which the transition to this form of service should be organised.[132] It was suggested that 'mult-disciplinary therapeutic teams' should be established, which would gradually shift the base of their work from existing mental hospitals to psychiatric departments of district general hospitals:

> As the work in the department in the general hospital develops, the work of the mental hospital will increasingly be able to concentrate on rehabilitating the hospital's existing longer-stay patients and the number of wards in use should steadily be reduced. When finally all the new general hospital departments to serve the area are in operation and only a comparatively small number of patients remain in the mental hospital, it should become possible to close the mental hospital by transferring these remaining patients to other appropriate hospitals.

It was expected that the run-down of mental hospitals would be a lengthy process, in any one case being expected to extend over 'several years'.[133] Despite emphasis on this extended time-scale, it nevertheless seemed that the aspirations expressed by Enoch Powell in 1961 were nearer to realisation. However, behind the simple formulation of this model lay increasing self-doubt and confusion of objectives among the planners as they came to terms with the kind of confederations of interests which persuaded the Millar Committee to be less confident about prospects for dispensing with the mental hospitals. The National Association for Mental Health attacked the new circular as 'dangerously superficial', while a psychiatrist labelled the document as 'patronising' and oblivious to contribution of mental hospitals.[134] Also, in view of the disruption in community mental health services brought about by the Seebohm changes, and the state of flux within the NHS during the preparations for reorganisation, the circular was charged with being 'singularly inept' in its timing.[135]

It was evident that a more comprehensive policy review was required. Once *Better Services for the Mentally Handicapped* was completed, Joseph came under pressure to produce a counterpart dealing with psychiatric services. The Secretary of State took advantage of the platforms offered by conferences on mental health to express his commitment to development of these services promising a mental health White Paper by the end of 1974.[136]

This delay in producing the mental health policy document had profound consequences. *Better Services for the Mentally Handicapped* was produced when the Government able to contemplate additional resources to support new developments. The commitment of additional funding for the mentally handicapped was accorded much prominence in the White Paper. By the beginning of work on the mental health White Paper, the economic situation had deteriorated. Indeed, the Treasury appealed for the exercise to be scrapped.

However, in view of Joseph's public commitment there was no choice but to continue. In this adverse climate, the Treasury warned that public expenditure would 'have to be reduced drastically over the next few years and are firmly opposed to departments taking on new commitments which would make that process more difficult'.[137] It was therefore necessary to eliminate any suggestion of additional resources for mental health, and therefore avoid adoption of the kind of targets and specific objectives that had featured in *Better Services for the Mentally Handicapped*. Joseph accordingly instructed his officials that the mental health White Paper should be more provisional or 'Green' than its mental handicap counterpart.

The White Paper on mental health was produced in a much more routine manner than its mental handicap equivalent. It was produced by officials, allowing for much less intervention from outside experts. By June 1973, the officials had produced an outline sketch which contained the main elements of the plan adopted in the final version. Very little further progress was made with the promised White Paper during the final months of the Heath administration. NHS reorganisation and the economic crisis made it unrealistic to continue work on a massive and potentially highly expensive plan for reform of the mental health services. However, from the draft materials preserved, as in the case of *Better Services for the Mentally Handicapped*, it is evident that there was rapid retreat away from any scheme for drastic and rapid change within the service.[138]

Health Service Commissioner
The Crossman tenure came to an end before the consultation process concerning the health service commissioner was complete. However, from reactions to the consultation documents sent out from London and Edinburgh, it was evident that the medical profession in particular was opposed to this development, while the idea had few active supporters within the NHS. Nevertheless, outside pressure groups pursued this idea with determination, and they were assisted by the Council on Tribunals, and within the Heath administration, by Sir Geoffrey Howe. The Conservatives were not committed to the health service commissioner, but their 1970 Campaign Guide had declared in favour. The continuing trickle of embarrassing long-stay hospital scandals made it ever more difficult to indulge in back-sliding on this issue.[139]

The argument in favour of the health service commissioner was marginally less strong in Scotland, where section 2 of the Mental Health (Scotland) Act 1960 provided for a Mental Welfare Commission to replace the General Board of Control and exercise a 'protective function' respecting patients. This allowed for investigation of complaints relating to any patient's conditions. In

England and Wales, the Mental Health Act 1959 abolished the Board of Control, but made no allowance for a replacement.

Immediately after his appointment, Sir Keith Joseph was inquisitive about this subject, and included it among the themes for his first briefing exercises.[140] On 29 July 1970 Joseph rejected the idea of extending the remit of the Parliamentary Commissioner for Administration to include the health service, and indicated his support in principle for appointment of a separate health service commissioner. Joseph asked his officials to ensure that their proposals would provide adequate linkage with the parallel proposal for a local government ombudsman, which was under discussion in the Ministry of Housing and Local Government.[141]

The first public hint at Joseph's thinking concerning the health service commissioner occurred on 31 October 1970, at a conference of the Association of Hospital Matrons, when the Secretary of State frankly admitted that the long-stay hospital scandals and the 'bullying in the back-wards...worried him more than anything else'. He hoped that the Hospital Advisory Service and Ombudsman arrangements would constitute a 'protective mechanism' against such abuses.[142]

In the autumn of 1970 the plan for a health service commissioner was slightly modified. Originally it had been intended to devolve the health service commissioner function to regional offices. This idea was abandoned in favour of a centralised department for England, possibly with separate offices for Scotland and Wales.[143] Some difficulty was experienced in defining the type of problem falling within the remit of the health service commissioner. It was decided that it was unsafe to depart from the 'injustice caused by maladministration' provision, which was the formula adopted in the Parliamentary Commissioner legislation.

Further progress was held up by uncertainties concerning the timetable for implementation of the ombudsman principle. Joseph initially preferred no interim solution, but to wait until legislation was introduced to bring in the health service commissioner at the time of NHS reorganisation. Scottish Ministers differed among themselves, but marginally preferred immediate extension of the powers of the Parliamentary Commissioner for Administration to deal with the hospital service.[144]

Adverse publicity resulting from the Farleigh and Whittingham enquiries convinced Joseph that establishment of the health service commissioner could not be delayed until 1974.[145] The announcement that Sir Alan Marre would take over as Parliamentary Commissioner for Administration from the summer of 1971 added weight to the demand for his office to assimilate functions relating to the health service; this view was strongly advocated from the Office of the

Parliamentary Commissioner, where it was claimed that this work could readily be absorbed, offering the maximum economy of scale.[146] DHSS was strongly against this alternative since it would involve bringing MPs and the Secretary of State further into the process of handling complaints, whereas a statutory health service commissioner might receive complaints and deal directly with health authorities without involving the central department. However, DHSS had no objection to the office of Parliamentary Commissioner for Administration and health service commissioner being exercised by the same person.

Notwithstanding this concession, the Parliamentary Commissioner for Administration still aspired to interim responsibility for handling complaints regarding the hospital service.[147] He also contended that the health service commissioner should have limited powers to examine complaints relating to the exercise of professional judgement. This proposal was vigorously contested by the BMA and the JCC. The medical interests complained that there were already a 'battery of procedures for investigating the actions of doctors' and that further interference would adversely affect medical standards. They therefore opposed extension of the remit of the health service commissioner beyond questions relating to management.[148]

In the absence of agreement, this issue was referred for further discussions between representatives of the medical profession and DHSS, which had the effect of undermining the Prime Minister's wish for an announcement of policy before the summer recess. It was also subversive to the Ministers' target to introduce a health service commissioner legislation early in the 1971/72 session and have the health service commissioner established by the beginning of 1972. Notwithstanding this embarrassment, the health departments believed that substantial concession to the demands of the doctors was unavoidable, since it was not feasible to introduce the health service commissioner in the face of their opposition. The need for conciliation was also important to the Secretary of State on account of the need to secure co-operation of the profession at the time of NHS reorganisation.[149]

Failure to reach a decision by the summer of 1971, as well as absence of reference to the health service commissioner in the Consultative Document on NHS reorganisation issued in May 1971, exposed the Government to further adverse publicity from advocates of the health service ombudsman.[150] The health departments reluctantly conceded to the demands of the medical profession by agreeing that any health service commissioner legislation would introduce statutory exclusion of actions taken in exercise of professional judgement.[151] This inspired protest from the Office of

410

the Parliamentary Commissioner for Administration that such limitation would be seriously detrimental to the functioning of the health service commissioner. The health departments made some concession to the Parliamentary Commissioner's point of view, but the latter was still concerned that a range of legitimate complaints would be excluded from the health service commissioner's remit.[152]

The health Ministers finally went ahead with their compromise proposals without commanding full support from either the medical profession or the Parliamentary Commissioner. The former favoured deferring discussions about the health service commissioner until after NHS reorganisation. The Parliamentary Commissioner continued to advocate immediate extension of his remit to the hospital service, without exclusions concerning clinical judgement.

On account of this impasse, it was no longer practicable to introduce legislation on a Great Britain basis in the 1971/72 session, introducing the prospect that the commissioner would not be established much before NHS reorganisation. In the autumn of 1971 the health service commissioner proposals were being overtaken by the NHS reorganisation. The delay meant that it was not longer practicable to advance on an all-Great Britain basis. Imminence of the NHS Reorganisation (Scotland) Bill, scheduled for introduction in the House of Lords in January 1972, raised the question of its inclusion of provision for the health service commissioner. Scottish Ministers argued in favour on account of the risk that the opposition or even Government supporters might force the issue at the committee stage. DHSS and the Welsh Office were unhappy about the decision of Scotland to break ranks, but they had no way of guaranteeing that a place would be found for separate Great Britain legislation during the 1971/72 session. Exchanges between Ministers failed to come up with a mutually acceptable alternative.[153]

Agreement by Ministers to include health service commissioner clauses brought relief to Scottish Ministers, but debates in the House of Lords on the Scottish reorganisation Bill exposed the anomaly that no public statement had been forthcoming about the application of this principle in England and Wales. Despite the long period of gestation of the health service commissioner proposals, Ministers were still not in a position to make a public statement on account of differences of opinion between departments concerning the stage at which it would be revealed that a connection would be made between the health service commissioner and the Parliamentary Commissioner for Administration. The intention to establish 'Health Service Commissioners' for England and for Wales, in line with the arrangements for Scotland was finally revealed in Parliament on 22 February 1972, a few days after publication of the report of the Whittingham Hospital enquiry. This announcement indicated that the post of Health Service Commissioner might be held jointly with that of Parliamentary Commissioner for Administration.[154] Naturally, this innovation was welcomed by the media, but the Government was rebuked for its equivocation.[155] The announcement that the Parliamentary Commissioner for Administration would assume the duties of the Health Service Commissioners for England, Scotland and Wales was made in November 1972. As indicated in chapter VI, provision for the Health Service Commissioners for England and Wales was included in the NHS Reorganisation Bill, which completed its passage through Parliament in the summer of 1973. The way was then clear for Sir Alan Marre to extend his work and serve as Health Service Commissioner from 1 October 1973. As finally established, the Health Service Commissioner possessed more modest powers than had been envisaged by the proponents of the health service ombudsman during the Crossman era. In response to demands from the vested interests, the functions of the Health Service Commissioner were constricted to a minimum. The Health Service Commissioner was therefore dispatched to the position of long stop on a very large playing field.

Complaints Procedures

Although collectively an asset, the Hospital Advisory Service, the Health Service Commissioner, and the Community Health Councils provided only indirect protection for patients with grievances. The latter's primary and most urgent prerequisite was an accessible and effective local complaints machinery. Overhaul of health service complaints procedures was a further loose-end of the post-Ely initiative needing attention after the departure of Crossman. In Scotland revision of the hospital complaints procedure was agreed without arousing difficulties. In May 1966, as a consequence of a recommendation of the Farquharson-Lang Report, a working party on complaints procedures in hospitals was established.[156] This committee, chaired by Mr E U E Elliott-Binns, an Under Secretary in SHHD, reported in 1969. Its recommendations were accepted, and in February 1970 hospital authorities were instructed to introduce the new complaints procedures.[157]

As reported in chapter III, the internal working party established by Crossman failed to command support of the Post-Ely Policy Working Party. Preparations for a new working party, containing a greater representation of non-departmental and expert members was at an advanced stage when Joseph took up his duties as Secretary of State.[158]

Awareness of the seriousness of this issue was indicated by reference in the Conservative General Election manifesto to the need to 'improve ways of dealing with suggestions and complaints from patients and staff'. On 29 July 1970 Joseph sanctioned a new Working Party on hospital complaints procedure. With respect to membership, Joseph insisted that there should be less NHS presence and greater consumer representation, but in most respects he followed the lines for the constitution of this committee adopted under Crossman.

Preparations for the complaints investigation were momentarily held up by an edict from the Prime Minister against the proliferation of committees, but Joseph convinced him that in this case a committee was unavoidable.[159] Various legal names were considered for the chair of this committee. Michael Davies QC was included in the shortlist from the outset. He was a member of the Midland Circuit, and was regarded as an outstanding success as Chairman of the Birmingham Mental Health Review Tribunal, which constituted directly relevant professional experience.[160] The announcement concerning Michael Davies' appointment as chairman of the committee to investigate hospital complaints procedure was made in February 1971. By contrast with the departmental committee that produced the earlier report, the Davies Committee was superabundant in size and expertise. In addition to the Chairman, the committee contained no fewer than sixteen members. Not the least of the peculiarities of the Davies Committee, was its large representation of women. As already noted, at this time, women noticeably increased their presence on such committees, but mainly in cases where the investigations were concerned with women's issues or health professions in which women were predominant. The Davies Committee contained seven women for a subject that was not specially gender-related. A further striking feature of the membership was the low representation of doctors, of whom there were only two. The other members represented nursing, law, the social sciences, NHS interests, voluntary organisations, and journalism. The four individuals in the last two of these constituencies were presumably intended to honour Joseph's promise to place on the committee 'people who are able to express the point of view of the patients'. None of the members were drawn from the labour movement.[161]

The Davies Committee was asked: 'to provide the hospital service with practical guidance in the form of a code of principles and practice for recording and investigating matters, affecting patients, which go wrong in hospitals, for receiving complaints and suggestions by patients, staff or others, about such matters, and for communicating the results of investigations; and to make recommendations'. The committee embarked on two related tasks; first, specification of a complaints procedure to be administered by the management at all levels of the hospital service; and secondly, it aimed to outline the relationship of these procedures with parallel instruments of public review, audit and participation. The Davies Committee began work on 7 April 1971. Ministers envisaged that its report would be produced within a year. In the event, the first draft of the final report was not produced until March 1973, while the final report, containing a draft code of practice, was not submitted until October 1973.[162] Since the report was not published until 17 December 1973, there was little opportunity for its consideration under Joseph's direction.[163] The Davies Report and its reception are therefore best considered in chapter VII.

With respect to the second part of its remit, the Davies Committee took the unusual step of intervening over the role and method of appointment of the Community Health Councils planned for the reorganised health service. In February 1972 Davies submitted to the Secretary of State recommendations of his committee concerning the part that CHCs might play in the complaints procedure. It was assumed that CHCs would become one of the major avenues for introducing complaints on behalf of patients, and also for monitoring the adequacy of local complaints procedures. In order to guarantee the independence and strengthen to position of the CHCs, the Davies Committee advocated their appointment by the Secretary of State.[164] The intervention of the Davies Committee on CHCs was received politely but coolly by Joseph. The method of appointment of CHCs was directly contrary to the thinking of the department, while the complaints procedure was regarded as a weighty matter, beyond the competence of the Councils.[165] The fate of the Davies recommendations concerning CHCs will be further considered in chapters VI and VII.

(v) PLANNED PARENTHOOD

The uneasy compromises inherent in the legislation of 1967 concerning abortion and family planning were not accepted as a permanent settlement. An ill-sorted alliance of demographers, racists, social liberals and feminists demanded that the NHS should provide a comprehensive and free family planning service, including facilities for abortion on demand. On the right, increasing anxiety over inner-city social problems, recurrence of the scare about over-population, and new eugenicist fears about excessive fecundity of the alleged unfit, added to pressures on the Heath administration to adopt a more vigorous policy over birth limitation.[166]

In 1971 the Birth Control Campaign was established to promote planned parenthood, with Lord Gardiner, Lord Chancellor under Wilson, as its President.[167] The Select Committee on Science and Technology continued its investigations into the population question first commenced under Wilson, and it complained that the

414

Government was failing to take the population issue sufficiently seriously. In response, the Heath administration in 1971 appointed a small committee of experts, chaired by Professor C R Ross, to consider whether the Government should adopt a population policy.

Soon after his appointment, the new Secretary of State was confronted with representations about abortion. The contest between the Abortion Law Reform Association and the Society for the Protection of Unborn Children had smouldered on without remission since 1967. Shortly after the General Election, Joseph received an all-Party delegation pressing for an enquiry into the working of the Abortion Act. The delegation was led by Norman St John-Stevas, who was the author of an Early Day Motion on the same subject supported by more than 250 MPs.[168] The delegation believed that the Abortion Act had run into difficulties because it originated in an unsatisfactory manner, and should have been preceded by an enquiry. This lapse having taken place, it was now essential to institute such an enquiry to consider all aspects of the abortion problem.[169] Joseph was besieged by delegations representing the rival points of view. The pace was set by groups pressing for an independent enquiry with the expectation that this was likely to recommend a more restrictive abortion law.[170] Liberals were therefore suspicious of proposals for an enquiry, arguing that the Abortion Act commanded widespread public support and should be given more time to operate before any change in the law was contemplated.[171]

Joseph vacillated over the demand for an enquiry. In discussion, he tended to adopt the opposite point of view to any delegation he was receiving. Nevertheless, at an office meeting in October 1970, Joseph sanctioned a paper for the Home Affairs Committee recommending an enquiry, with the expectation of an announcement on 2 November.[172] As noted above, Joseph told the Prime Minister that he favoured prompt legislation to tighten up the Abortion Act. Heath was unsympathetic, and was sceptical about the scale of abuse of the Act, but reluctantly he was willing to concede an enquiry.[173] Joseph therefore reverted to the idea of an enquiry. This was quickly agreed between Ministers most actively involved; by the beginning of December the terms of reference had been approved. Ministers endorsed the view of the Reginald Maudling, the Home Secretary, that the committee should not be allowed to question the Abortion Act, but should be restricted to examining its practical working.[174] The proposal for an enquiry into abortion was sanctioned by the Social Services Committee without controversy in January 1971, and it was agreed that it should be conducted on a Great Britain basis.[175]

Sir Keith Joseph took a keen personal interest in the selection of this committee. At the outset it was agreed to nominate a woman as

415

chairperson. With hindsight, this seems like an entirely appropriate decision, but in fact it is indicative of a new level of awareness about the need to allow women to have a dominant voice in issues of decisive importance to their gender. A glance at the constitution of committees dealing with such issues as maternity services or nursing in the period before 1970, indicates little reflection about allowing women to exercise an appropriate level of influence. In the case of the abortion enquiry, not only was it decided to select a woman as chairperson, but Joseph also requested that the committee should be dominated by women of childbearing age. In the choice of both men and women to serve on the committee, the selection followed more conventional lines.

Summarising the consensus within DHSS, the criterion for selection was 'sound judgement not committed to any particular point of view'; the ideal team should be headed by 'a wise and impartial public figure who is not a doctor as Chairman', together with a lawyer, a general practitioner, a gynaecologist, a psychologist, a social worker, a nurse, a headmistress, perhaps a hospital administrator, together with one or two women of childbearing age outside the health professions.[176] It was also decided that controversy would be reduced if Roman Catholics of either conservative or liberal persuasion on this issue were excluded from the committee. This was not in practice achieved, although this was hardly noticed at the time.

In late January 1971 Joseph requested that the Lord Chancellor should release Mrs Justice Lane to chair the committee. Since 1965, Mrs Lane had been a High Court judge in the Probate, Divorce and Admiralty Division. As was often the case with such requests, the Lord Chancellor was unhappy about releasing Mrs Lane, but under pressure from Joseph, Hailsham consented. Once Mrs Lane was appointed, an announcement was made about the enquiry into the working of the Abortion Act.[177] The terms of reference of the Lane Committee were: 'To review the operation of the Abortion Act 1967 and on the basis that the conditions for legal abortion contained in the paragraphs (a) and (b) of subsection (1) and in subsections (2), (3) and (4) of section 1 of the Act remain unaltered, to make recommendations'.

Discussions about the membership of the Lane Committee dragged on until April 1971. In order to satisfy all the competing constituencies, a large team of fifteen was assembled for the Committee. As finally constituted, the Lane Committee reflected the intentions cited above: the group comprised two lawyers (Mrs Lane and a male Scottish Lawyer), two male general practitioners, two obstetricians and gynaecologists (one of whom was male and from Wales, and the other a woman), a young woman sociologist, a

416

male Scottish psychiatrist, a woman hospital social worker, two women nurses, a headmistress, the only woman RHB Senior Administrative Medical Officer, a senior woman manageress from Marks and Spencer, and a young woman from the Confederation of British Industry. Ten of the members were women. The obvious omission was any woman having links with the labour movement or representing the less-affluent social classes, who comprised the majority of the women whose problems were under consideration by the Lane Committee.

The Lane Committee met for the first time on 15 June 1971. It divided into four subcommittees for its investigations, which were conducted with great thoroughness. Given the narrow remit of the Committee, it is remarkable that its work was not completed until early 1974. Publication of the report was in fact delayed until after the 1974 General Election. The results of the Lane Committee's deliberations are therefore best considered in chapter VII.

The factions fighting over abortion directed their primary energies towards influencing the Lane Committee. However, family planning again assumed the limelight for public campaigning. As events of 1967 demonstrated, there was a much greater degree of agreement over this aspect of planned parenthood, although big differences of underlying motivations continued to be evident. Delegations making representations to the Secretary of State on abortion, whatever their disagreements over this issue, were generally united in urging the case for extension of family planning services in order to reduce the incidence of unwanted pregnancies. There was wide support for the recommendation of the Peel Committee 'that family planning is of such importance that it should be provided free as part of any maternity service'.[178] In his discussion with the Royal College of Obstetricians and Gynaecologists, Joseph declared that his aims were restriction of the use of abortion facilities by foreign women, vigilance to prevent approved nursing homes from abusing the Abortion Act, substantial expansion of family planning services, and assistance to hospital authorities for extension of their gynaecological services.[179]

Joseph's proposals about abortion and family planning were developed in the context of his thinking about social deprivation. The problems of the inner-cities had for long been one of his personal interests and it was a growing policy obsession. Naturally, these issues figured in his first policy discussions, which ranged over the whole field of social deprivation and community care, but planned parenthood was always central to his aspiration to eliminate the 'urban sumps'.[180] The first office meetings devoted exclusively to family planning were held in September and October 1970. The idea of a comprehensive, free service for all-comers was ruled out on account of the assumption that most social groups were willing to avail themselves of family planning facilities without the requirement of public subsidy. Joseph instructed his officials to concentrate on planning a comprehensive domiciliary service for problem groups, with encouragement for sterilisation in the case of 'really bad problem families'. Community development projects sponsored by the Urban Programme provided a convenient additional source of funding for these extended family planning services.[181] As noted above, Joseph listed family planning among his policy priorities to the Prime Minister in October 1970.[182] Joseph outlined his plans for more intensive development of family planning services in centres of urban deprivation at the Social Services Committee in January 1971, and obtained general approval for his approach.[183] Joseph used the occasion of the announcement of the abortion enquiry on 23 February 1971 to indicate that he was making funds available for the expansion of family planning services in areas of social deprivation and also that he was undertaking a review of family planning services.[184] One of the consequences of the urban initiative was expansion of local health authority domiciliary family planning schemes, some of them undertaken jointly with the Family Planning Association.[185] In the summer of 1971 the Government encouraged hospital authorities to develop their family planning activities. Joseph also released funds for an unusual experiment conducted at Coalville in Leicestershire, and Runcorn in Cheshire, in which voluntary agencies and NHS authorities co-ordinated their activities to maximise their family planning services in what was called a 'saturation campaign'.[186]

The departmental review of family planning policy was completed by the beginning of May 1972. It was agreed that 'a free and comprehensive family planning service under the NHS was impracticable for resource reasons alone'. The department therefore fell back on a limited service designed to 'reduce the number of pregnancies likely to result in children at risk in the sense that their lives would be blighted by poor social conditions which might be passed on to future generations'. The free service was to be targeted at a group comprising about 100,000 women. The provisional cost of this scheme was given as £3m a year.[187]

Various obstacles delayed Joseph's announcement of the results his review of family planning services.[188] In the first place, the Treasury was unenthusiastic about embarking on expansion in what it perceived as a low-priority sector at a time when reorganisation in the personal social services and the health services were imposing potentially large and unavoidable demands for additional resources. Despite the reticence of the Treasury, Joseph took a modest package of proposals to the Home and Social Affairs Committee in July 1972, and obtained agreement without evident dissent.[189] Further delay in making the policy announcement resulted from further tangling between the health departments and the Treasury over financing the family planning scheme. To Joseph's increasing embarrassment, further delay was suggested by James Prior, the recently-appointed Lord President, who was in charge of the population panel exercise. Prior proposed that since the newly-completed report of the Ross panel had important bearing on family planning, it should be published in advance of any statement on family planning. This issue was referred to the Home and Social Affairs Committee, where Prior argued that since the Government was unlikely on grounds of cost to accept many of the population panel's recommendations, it was desirable to present the extension of family planning as a positive response to the population report. Joseph lamented about embarrassment caused by delays in announcing family planning policy, and cited the backing of the Prime Minister for an announcement no later than the end of 1972. He also objected to 'wrapping up' the current policy decisions on family planning with population issues. Ministers conceded that it was unrealistic to further delay the statement on family planning.[190]

After enduring a great deal of irritating sniping from MPs on this issue, on 12 December 1972 Joseph announced the results of his review. In the main, his new policy comprised a list of items in the existing family planning programme, with assurances concerning their further continuation. It was assumed that integration and comprehensiveness of services would be facilitated by the administrative unification introduced through health service reorganisation. Joseph's main new idea was to require all NHS authorities to provide free family planning advice, but supplies would be charged at full cost, except for one year after childbirth or abortion, in case of 'special social need', or on medical grounds. It was estimated that the expanded services would involve an increase in expenditure from the current level of £4m to £12m a year.[191]

Joseph's package promised a further incremental expansion in family planning services, but the disappearance of local health authority services at reorganisation represented a notable step backwards, since the discretion enjoyed by local authorities to provide free services would then be terminated. Thereafter, all NHS authorities would be obliged to charge for family planning services, apart from exceptional circumstances outlined above. Joseph's statement was badly received; traditionalists were unhappy about further liberalisation; liberals were annoyed by the failure to introduce a comprehensive and free service at reorganisation. Joseph was particularly liable to criticism on grounds of inconsistency on account of eliminating the successful, comprehensive and free

419

services already existing in some inner city areas, which would clearly undermine his own often-stated primary objective of reducing the level of unwanted pregnancies.

The new arrangements for family planning were defined in clause 4 of the National Health Service Reorganisation Bill, which was introduced in the House of Lords and received its Second Reading on 4 December 1972. As noted in chapter VI, clause 4 was the most hotly contested element in this otherwise relatively uncontentious legislation. The vulnerability of Joseph's position was already apparent at many points during the Second Reading debate; Lady Ruthven of Freeland and Lady Gaitskell produced particularly extended and cogent critiques of Joseph's proposals.[192] After this warning shot, a formidable all-Party array of experts on family planning exhibited their dislike of Joseph's proposals during the Committee stage, with the result that an opposition amendment to provide supplies on the same free basis as advice was carried by 76 votes to 51.[193]

The media overwhelmingly supported the amendment. The *Times* declared that 'Prevention is better than Abortion'. The *Guardian* took the view that a free family planning service was essential for gaining population stability and it accused Joseph of complacency on this score.[194] Joseph's tail was twisted by MPs, who demanded that the House of Commons should come into line with the House of Lords. Joseph refused to declare his hand.[195]

Joseph's difficulties were compounded by the draft Population Panel report, which recommended the establishment of a comprehensive family planning service as an integral part of the NHS as a first step towards a positive population policy. The report was not entirely explicit about charging, but it strongly implied that the service should be free, or at the most available for the standard prescription charge. There was no consensus among Ministers about the Population Panel report. The Secretaries of State for Scotland and Wales were supportive of its family planning proposals. The Home Secretary and the Secretary of State for Social Services favoured delaying publication until after the House of Commons had voted on family planning. The Secretary of State for Education was annoyed that the Panel had exceeded its brief, and she requested further ministerial discussion on policy issues before a decision on publication was reached. The Treasury advised Ministers to refer the report to officials for further consideration. At the Home and Social Affairs Committee, Prior suggested that in view of the high degree of public and parliamentary interest in the population problem, it was unrealistic to delay publication of the Population Panel Report. The Committee agreed, but this left them with awkward decisions concerning recommendations on family planning. It was agreed that the report, which was known to be supported by the Lane Committee, was likely to strengthen the position of the free family planning lobby. It was agreed to reconsider this problem if the Government was again defeated, but the Committee took Joseph's advice that their original policy should not at this stage be modified.[196]

During February and early March 1973 Joseph's position was not assisted by further signs of intransigence from the House of Lords, a widely-supported Early Day Motion in the House of Commons calling for establishment of a free NHS family planning service, and publication of the Population Panel Report. Ministers reconsidered charges for family planning services again on 5 March. Joseph conceded that opinion was divided within the Conservative Party, but he was confident that his policy could be maintained, especially if it was understood that any further expenditure on family planning would need to be financed by a cut in the hospital building programme. Prior argued in favour of a compromise under which the prescription charge should be applied to family planning supplies, which would add £13m to the cost of the service, rather than £16m arising from the House of Lords amendment. Ministers supported this more conciliatory approach. Decisions concerning funding were referred to the Cabinet.[197] The proposal to apply the prescription charge to family planning supplies was endorsed by the Cabinet, which also agreed that the additional cost should be offset by reductions in the health programme, or increases in charges to be confirmed at a later date.[198] Joseph complied with this plan, largely owing to his estimate that the higher cost would be met from an increase in the NHS Contribution. As on previous occasions when this alternative was considered, it was contested by Treasury officials, although on this occasion Joseph secured the support of Jenkin, who concluded that 'despite this strong and unanimous advice from officials, I believe that to raise the NHS stamp is the right solution in this very special case'.[199] Other Ministers inclined to favour offsetting savings in the health programme. Joseph feared that this approach would not appease the Government's critics, who were likely to level the accusation that Ministers were being inconsistent by charging for this service, but not other preventive services such as vaccination, cervical cytology, or venereal disease clinics.[200] The Population Panel Report hardly assisted the Government, and its proposals for comprehensive family planning services under the National Health Service were its most widely-publicised recommendation.[201]

Joseph outlined the Government's compromise during the House of Commons Second Reading debate on the NHS Reorganisation Bill.[202] The depth of feeling over this issue was indicated by the frequency of interruption of Joseph's speech, and his evident discomfort in dealing with his critics. No less than one-third of the entire debate was devoted to the single clause relating to family planning.[203]

The attempt to reverse the House of Lords amendment was considered at the Committee stage in the House of Commons on 17 April, when the Government's counter-proposal to impose the prescription charge was carried by a single vote. This decision was confirmed at the Report Stage on 12 June. On 25 June, the House of Lords rallied to reject the House of Commons amendment, and once again by a substantial majority reinstated the provision for free family planning services. The issue returned once again to the House of Commons, where the Government obtained a majority of 27 for its proposal to impose the prescription charge for family planning supplies. At the House of Lords on 5 July, on the basis of minor concessions offered by Joseph, and also in the interests of avoiding a constitutional clash, a further amendment to reinstate a free service was withdrawn. Clause 4 passed into law as part of the reorganisation legislation on 5 July 1973, temporarily concluding the protracted political controversies over the extension of family planning services.[204]

One important element in the proposals outlined by Joseph in December 1972 remained to be implemented. Joseph attached importance to general medical practitioners being drawn into family planning services. Since it was accepted that this work was not part of the regular contractual responsibilities of the general practitioner, it was necessary to negotiate a suitable fee for family planning. Negotiations with the GMSC began in the spring of 1973; as was the wont with the GMSC, there was some hard-bargaining; agreement was not reached until February 1975, under the new administration. An announcement was made in May, and the scheme began in July 1975. Initially, the health departments aimed for the fee of £1.72 recommended by the Doctors' and Dentists' Review Body, but this was rejected by the profession, and the fee finally agreed was £3.50. The fees for general practitioners and hospital medical staff working separately from the established clinics added about £8m to the cost of the family planning service. Advocates of the family planning clinics complained about these additional costs, which they claimed represented disguised pay increases for doctors, paid at the expense of cutbacks in the more economical family planning services provided by the clinics.[205]

(vi) PREVENTION AND PROMOTION

Previous chapters have reported the limited progress made with fluoridation of water supplies and in combating tobacco smoking, two areas in which preventive services were capable of yielding major improvements in health. Interventions in these fields under the Heath administration will now be assessed.

Fluoridation

Fluoridation attracted Joseph's attention soon after his appointment. He believed that his colleagues would need convincing about the importance of taking action on this front, but he agreed to sponsor ministerial discussions. From the outset, he believed that the chances of legislation would be improved this was preceded by an enquiry, preferably headed by a senior legal figure.[206]

Joseph was sufficiently committed to fluoridation to suggest it as a priority in the course of his policy discussions with the Prime Minister held at Chequers on new year's eve 1970.[207] Despite the Prime Minister's evident lack of enthusiasm, Joseph returned to the subject and insisted that fluoridation represented one of the few fields of health policy where a major improvement in health could be effected, and an economy in the dental service could be obtained at negligible cost. He reiterated his proposal for an independent enquiry under an eminent public figure to finally convert public opinion to fluoridation and smooth the path to legislation. The Prime Minister was unmoved and retorted that he had enough political problems already without wanting to stir up a hornet's nest over fluoridation. Joseph conducted a graceful retreat.[208]

For the rest of the Heath administration, fluoridation was left at the foot of the political agenda. Birmingham and Newcastle-upon-Tyne were the only large cities to undertake fluoridation. Few authorities were willing to stir up controversy by attempting to enter the ranks of the fluoridators. There was some excuse for inaction on account of the imminence of major administrative changes in local government, the health service, and water undertakings. The optimists speculated that fluoridation would be easier to introduce under the reorganised health service. In the mean time the rival camps sharpened up their publicity campaigns. A steady stream of reputable research publications strengthened the claims of the advocates of fluoridation. These findings were publicised by the Fluoridation Society and the Health Education Council, both of which were supported by Government grants. They were opposed by anti-fluoridation organisations, whose own researches successfully kept alive fears about the adverse effects of fluoridation among certain sections of the public. Scientific officialdom proved inadequate to the task of combating the sensationalist claims of its fanatical and vociferous opponents.[209] The continuing frustration over inability to make advances with fluoridation will be further considered in chapter VII.

Smoking and Health

Joseph was initially more committed than his predecessor to an assault on the tobacco hazard. Michael Alison has commented upon his Secretary of State's not entirely successful campaign to reduce smoking in his department.[210] Soon after his appointment Joseph asked for a submission on an anti-smoking Bill, comprising the following minimum elements: warning notices on cigarette packets and advertisements, a requirement to publish details of chemical constituents of cigarettes on their packets, prohibition of the sale of loose cigarettes, restriction of vending machines in public places, and power to restrict or ban smoking in specified public places. Joseph appreciated that it would be difficult to obtain support among Ministers for such legislation, but he calculated that the threat of legislation would constitute a spur to voluntary co-operation by the tobacco interests.[211]

Joseph took his ideas to Ministers, armed with even greater accumulated evidence concerning deaths associated with cigarette smoking than was available to his predecessors. He was able to draw on the as yet unpublished second report of the Royal College of Physicians on smoking and health. It was estimated that the annual death toll from smoking exceeded 90,000, and that smoking-related disease was a major cause of lost production. Joseph called the smoking problem 'without exaggeration, a holocaust of human life'. He was not satisfied that support for a private member's Bill carried sufficient chance of success. It was therefore necessary for the Government to frame legislation. Joseph's memorandum amplified the above possibilities for inclusion in a draft Bill; it also suggested the energetic pursuit of health education and an interdepartmental study of the economic, fiscal, social and health aspects of the tobacco smoking problem. Joseph urged that legislation should be introduced during the current session if voluntary agreement with the tobacco industry was not reached within three months. Despite positive aspects of Joseph's proposals, he noticeably avoided suggesting that reduction in smoking should be effected by increasing the price of cigarettes. Indeed this item was intentionally omitted in order to appease the Treasury.[212]

Joseph's memorandum nevertheless constituted an advance in the analysis of the smoking problem, and it seemed possible that for the first time the tobacco barons might be seriously discomforted. The new appeal for action by Ministers was given greater force by signs that the anti-smoking lobby in Parliament was gaining in influence. All of Joseph's proposals had been canvassed by MPs for a decade, but with little impact on the Government. The effectiveness of the anti-smoking movement was greatly increased by the formation in 1971 of Action on Smoking and Health. The widespread attention attracted by Sir Gerald Nabarro's Tobacco and Snuff (Health Hazards) Bill, was a sign of the greater buoyancy of the anti-smoking campaign.

In discussion with his colleagues Joseph argued that success in turning the young away from cigarette smoking would save more lives than any other measure. He warned that the second report of the Royal College of Physicians, due to be published in January 1971, would contain embarrassing criticisms concerning Government inaction. It was therefore imperative that the administration should be seen to display a new level of responsiveness to this issue. Nevertheless, Ministers were unworried by private members' Bills, lukewarm about a commitment to Government legislation, and the Home Secretary warned that no place in the legislative timetable was possible in the foreseeable future. In view of the higher political profile of the smoking issue, Ministers expressed confidence that the industry would be co-operative in fresh negotiations. They also supported Joseph's proposal for an in-depth interdepartmental study of the tobacco problem.[213]

In view of only moderate backing from his colleagues, Joseph scaled down his demands. He called in the Tobacco Advisory Committee and asked for, (a) agreement of the industry to warning notices on cigarette packets, with size and text being subject to agreement of the health departments; (b) printing the details of ingredients on cigarette packets; and (c) that the latter information should to be established by a neutral source.[214] After two months of haggling with the industry over the size and character of the tobacco packet warnings, agreement was reported to Ministers, and a statement to this effect was made in Parliament. This agreement paved the way for inclusion on cigarette packets, posters and advertisements of the message: 'WARNING by H.M. Government. SMOKING CAN DAMAGE YOUR HEALTH'. In return for this concession, the industry extracted from the Government an undertaking that it would desist from preparations for legislative controls and also grant no aid to private members Bills. This latter aspect of the deal represented a set-back to the anti-smoking lobby in Parliament, which witnessed the collapse of the Nabarro Bill in the face of Government obstruction.[215]

It was consistent with concord with the tobacco industry for Joseph to continue with anti-smoking publicity and education, but more ambitious initiatives on this front were deferred pending the report of officials, which was completed in October and discussed by Ministers in December 1971.[216] Joseph pointed out that deaths attributable to smoking were even higher than he had originally indicated, but he admitted that further measures designed to curtail smoking would be difficult to introduce. Ministers were once again sympathetic, but they refused to contemplate the threat of legislation. It was agreed that renewed discussions with the industry should be held with a view to reaching agreement on further limitations on advertising, elimination of coupon schemes, reducing access to vending machines, extension of 'no smoking' areas, and insertion of information on packets about chemical ingredients. Negotiations with the industry dragged on without reaching any further conclusion. Relations became soured over the work of a new joint scientific committee, comprising equal numbers of independent experts and technicians from industry. The first tasks for this committee were establishing tar and nicotine levels in tobacco; it was then intended to investigate possibilities for tobacco substitutes. Although it was initially hoped that this committee would provide a forum for non-controversial investigations, the two groups of scientists found it impossible to work together, with the result that Joseph was obliged to return to Ministers and propose disbanding the joint committee. In its place, Ministers agreed to establish the Independent Scientific Committee on Smoking and Health to undertake the similar work, and also a separate non-technical committee to deal with matters of common concern to the Government and industry. The first chairman of the Independent Committee was Dr R B Hunter, who had recently chaired the committee on community medicine.[217]

Cancer Eradication
A further minor development tangentially connected with the tobacco smoking problem, originated from the Prime Minister, who was alerted by President Nixon's State of the Union message on 22 January 1971, when the President, in the euphoria after the successful Apollo 14 moon programme, announced his plan for a $100m a year programme to find a cure for cancer. Heath was initially attracted by this idea, and dispatched a telegram expressing his support for Nixon's initiative.[218] Experts were less enthusiastic than the Prime Minister. They pointed out that Nixon had been anticipated by General de Gaulle, who had instigated an international centre for cancer research in Lyons, which was supported by both the United Kingdom and the USA. This was on a considerably smaller scale than originally envisaged by de Gaulle, but advisers were sceptical whether any further institution of this kind was justifiable. It was recommended that resources would be better devoted to realistic goals relating to prevention, especially with respect to smoking and lung cancer. It was furthermore pointed out that a reasonable degree of co-ordination between the main bodies responsible for cancer research was attained by a committee chaired by Lord Rosenheim.

The Prime Minister was disappointed about this lack-lustre response to the Nixon initiative, and he insisted on further examination of prospects for advancing cancer research. It was therefore agreed that Lord Zuckerman should undertake a survey of cancer research, which was accepted by the Ministers concerned. Zuckerman was enthusiastic to undertaken this work; his survey was completed in August 1972. Although the report was not to the satisfaction of all Ministers, its publication was permitted.[219] Zuckerman concluded that 'with certain exceptions, a sudden increase in funds for cancer research could not be effectively used'. Instead, he recommended a gradual increase in the cancer research effort along the lines already envisaged by the existing co-ordinating committee, with priority being given to rebuilding the Institute for Cancer Research. The political importance of the cancer research drive received a set-back when Nixon failed to secure the funding for his project. Having failed to ignite interest in Europe in his scheme, Nixon turned to the Russians.

Although the cancer initiative produced no direct result in Britain, it had some indirect repercussions. In particular it suggested to the Prime Minister that his ideas about extending the scope of policy co-operation within the EEC should take account of medicine and health care. An opportunity for Heath to air his thoughts about harmonising European policy on social issues occurred at the EEC summit in October 1972. In preparation for this event Zuckerman produced a memorandum outlining possible socio-medical issues that might be pursued on a Europe-wide basis.[220] These proposals met with an unenthusiastic response from the departments consulted. It was pointed out that most of Zuckerman's more practicable suggestions were already being investigated on an international basis. Of the remaining examples, European intervention was not likely to be feasible since the national interests of one or other EEC members would be prejudiced. Zuckerman's proposal for a Standing Commission for Medicine and Nutritional Affairs was opposed on account of adding unnecessarily to the bureaucracy of the European Commission. Sir George Godber suggested that regular meetings between Chief Medical Officers would fulfil this function equally well. The only tangible suggestion spared by the critics was the idea of greater European co-operation in assisting with the elimination of diseases in the third world such as leprosy and yaws. On account of lack of tangible reference points possessing a basis of common agreement, medicine and health were omitted from the penultimate draft of Heath's speech. The concluding section of the draft of this speech confined itself to a general call for inspiring the young through adoption of broader social goals, such as attack on the 'problems of pollution and poverty, of waste and want'. The final version of the speech delivered on 19 October 1972 included a call for a 'comprehensive social programme for the Community', with much more specific reference to tasks connected with combating pollution. Heath added that 'there may be more that we can do to combine our knowledge and accumulate skills in medicine, nutrition, and public health'. This anodyne comment was the sole legacy of Zuckerman's grandiose proposals. However, at least it ensured that medicine and health care made a token appearance in Prime Minister's call for Europe to give greater attention to the 'historic task' of harmonising social policies.[221]

(vii) PAY POLICY

Following failure of the Labour Government's pay policies, the Conservatives opted to dispense with a formal incomes policy. Instead they attempted to restrain wages by the use of indirect methods, aimed at limiting the scope of trade unions to undertake militant action. The main element in this armory was the Industrial Relations Act 1971. Such blunt instruments were if anything counterproductive. Behind the façade of non-intervention, the Heath administration was driven to adopt rule of thumb norms which amounted to an unspoken but doubtfully competent incomes policy. Under the Conservatives, wages rose even faster than the alarming average annual rate of about 10 per cent reached under Labour.[222]

Conditions of wage inflation created enormous potential for industrial conflict, and this duly materialised in many sectors of the economy. However, as noted below, with the exception of a major dispute with ancillary workers over a trivial pay issue, the health service was not much affected by industrial disputes during the Heath administration. Even doctors and nurses, who in the past had been in the vanguard of controversy over pay, were among the groups more easily contained under Heath. This surface tranquillity was misleading. Resentment over pay steadily built up, with the result that industrial unrest was set to break out on many fronts by the beginning of 1974.

Doctors and Dentists

The initial omens for accord with such groups as doctors and nurses were far from promising. One of the most pressing problems facing Joseph upon his appointment was the pay dispute with the doctors and dentists, which had boiled over into a bad-tempered confrontation during the 1970 General Election period. After the election Joseph immediately entered into negotiations with the professions in order to secure withdrawal of their sanctions. A meeting of senior Ministers decided to offer three concessions: (a) withdrawal of the reference to the National Board for Prices and Incomes of the outstanding element in the claim, (b) the promise of a new review body to replace the defunct Kindersley Review Body, but without guaranteeing an agency of exactly the same kind, and (c) the offer of negotiation on the balance of the last Kindersley recommendation, with the intention of not conceding the entire award.[223]

Joseph met representatives of the professions on 26 June and obtained their provisional acquiescence for his peace plan. They nevertheless laid down stringent conditions for the new review body and insisted that the Kindersley award should be met in full.[224] On the basis of the concessions already offered, a Special Representative Meeting of the British Medical Association enthusiastically voted to call off their sanctions of non-co-operation and non-certification. This response was blessed as a 'Happy Outcome' by a *British Medical Journal* editorial.[225]

Ministers initially expected Joseph to offer less than 5 per cent of the outstanding 15 per cent of the Kindersley award to established doctors. Joseph balked at this extreme parsimony, and insisting that 5 per cent was the minimum likely to be palatable to the professions. Ministers were content with this formula.[226] Representatives of the profession were clearly taken by surprise when Joseph offered 5 per cent in place of the anticipated 15 per cent. This was described as a 'bombshell' by the negotiators. However, this small concession from the Government was reluctantly recommended to the membership and accepted calmly, albeit with evident disappointment.[227] No doubt the BMA leadership appreciated that the deal offered by the Conservatives was no better, and probably worse than would have emerged from the procedures suggested by Labour. The *British Medical Journal* now complained that the Conservative administration was 'equally inept' as its Labour predecessor, and it gave only 'grudging' endorsement. The deal was only acceptable on account of the Government's contentions about the inflationary crisis, and on the understanding that the new review body would be free to review the entire package and make fresh recommendations applicable from April 1971.[228]

Having suffered some indignity over their pay award, the professional leadership approached plans for their new review body with suspicion. The Government's intentions were stated in general terms on 2 November 1970 by the Secretary of State for Employment. Carr announced that for groups for whom the usual negotiating machinery was not appropriate, three interrelated bodies would be established, which would review the remuneration of 'top' public servants, the armed forces, and doctors and dentists. At the insistence of the leadership of the medical and dental professions, this plan was submitted for their observations in advance of Carr's statement, and it was subsequently subjected to further intense scrutiny. The doctors and dentists contested the Government's proposals for appointment of a single chairman for the three review bodies, for overlapping to the extent of about half of the membership of each review body, and for a common secretariat to be provided by the new Office of Manpower Economics. The profession also pressed the Government hard to define the 'compelling reasons' which might lead to rejection of the review body's findings.[229] In response to pressure from the doctors and dentists, the Government conceded separate chairmen for the three review bodies, a smaller degree of overlapping membership, but insisted that the secretariat should be provided by the Office of Manpower Economics, since this was a commitment included in Carr's announcement.[230]

The tangled negotiations between the health departments and the professions derailed the timetable for establishing the review bodies, and precluded completion of a review of doctors' and dentists' remuneration by the agreed date of 1 April 1971. This prompted a demand for an interim pay increase, which the Treasury insisted should be rejected, so further increasing tension between the Government and the professions.[231] This new crisis had the effect of speeding up discussions over the membership of the DDRB, which had been drifting on since October 1970. In something of a scramble, the name of a possible chairman was located on 25 March 1971, but the first and second choices declined the appointment. The name of the Rt Hon. the Earl of Halsbury FRS emerged as the front runner at the beginning of May.[232] Shortly afterwards, he was invited and agreed to chair the DDRB. Appointment of the five additional members of the new review body raised no particular problems. A sixth member was added after production of the first report. The full complement of members comprised two senior executives from industry, a banker, and three academics (an economist, a lawyer, and a statistician). The DDRB was appointed on 5 July 1971, the terms of reference being 'to advise the Prime Minster on the remuneration of doctors and dentists taking any part in the National Health Service'. In constitution and terms of reference, the DDRB was very like its Kindersley predecessor, the main differences being the links in membership with the other two review bodies and servicing by the Office of Manpower Economics instead of the Cabinet Office.

The DDRB was under pressure to produce its first report without delay in order to settle remuneration for the year beginning April 1971. This first review was completed at the beginning of November and it was published on 1 December 1971. The DDRB proposed an increase of 8 per cent for general medical and general dental practitioners, an average of 6.7 per cent for senior hospital medical and dental staff, and nothing for the training grades.[233] The Treasury regarded the 8 per cent award as marginally over the desired target for the public sector, but in general the report was greeted with relief and approved by Ministers without dissent.[234]

Because of the delay in establishing the DDRB, it was necessary to begin work on its next report immediately. This was completed in May 1972 and published in June.[235] It proposed an average increase of 8 per cent. On this occasion the Government expected an award extending for two years, but as with the first of its reports, the DDRB made a recommendation for one year. Once again the award was judged to be constructive and in accord with the Government's guide-lines concerning pay.[236] The doctors and dentists were disappointed by both the 1971 and 1972 recommendations of the DDRB. Junior hospital doctors were especially annoyed. However, the professions possessed no particular basis for elevating their dissatisfaction into a confrontation. Having demanded restitution of the independent review mechanism and insisting that the Government should be bound by its recommendations, consistency demanded that the professions likewise should abide by DDRB findings.

Nurses and Midwives
Indicative of the prevalent inflationary situation regarding wages, in November 1970, the nurses lodged a claim for a 15 per cent increase on basic rates, together with a proposal for a reduction from 42 to a 40-hour week. Together with other elements in the claim, it was estimated that the full claim would add about 27 per cent to the nurses' pay bill. This claim was of course introduced only a few months after the increase of 20 per cent, which took effect in April 1970.

The Management Side saw no alternative to a substantial concession. Negotiations with NHS ancillary workers and teachers suggested that a settlement of between 15 and 18 per cent would be necessary to retain parity with these groups. In addition it was felt that the 42 hour week could not be sustained much longer. Joseph agreed with the line recommended by the department, but he proposed delaying negotiations, which the Cabinet Official Committee on Pay Negotiations regarded as unrealistic. Discussions between officials revealed that settlements below 11.5 per cent were regarded as tolerable. Above this 'trip-wire' level, public sector settlements were regarded as 'exceptional', thereby liable to incur a demand for offsetting reductions in expenditure within the offending departments. To the satisfaction of DHSS, the Official Committee agreed to an package within a ceiling of 10 per cent, which was approved by Ministers as a formality.[237]

The Management Side initially offered an increase amounting to 9 per cent, which was rejected by the Staff Side. Treasury officials believed that Ministers were in a mood for a generous award to nurses, and they were despondent about achieving a settlement below 15 per cent. Macmillan commented: 'The only comment I have is "we can't win a public battle with the nurses"'.[238] Joseph extracted from colleagues agreement for a higher offer of 12.5 per cent, which Ministers calculated would be sufficient to avoid a public dispute with the nurses.[239] The new offer was discussed at three meetings of the Nurses and Midwives Whitley Council, and agreement was finally reached on 23 February 1971. The award amounted to 12.5 per cent, with reduction of the working week from 42 to 40 hours, to take effect in January 1972, which increased the award to 15.5 per cent.[240]

In January 1972, the nurses returned to their demand for a compete revaluation of their salaries, with a view to establishing a 'sound and realistic foundation' for their remuneration consistent with the demands of NHS reorganisation and the Briggs reforms. The total cost of such revaluation was likely to increase the pay bill by almost 40 per cent. Ministers agreed to offer an interim award pending consideration of revaluation at a later date. The Treasury regarded 7.5 per cent as the limit for settlements, but was willing to allow 8.5 per cent for the package as a whole in view of special circumstances applying to nurses. In the event Joseph was able to secure agreement to an immediate increase of 8 per cent, leaving some outstanding points for later negotiation. These added a further 1.4 per cent to the nurses' pay bill.[241] Further consideration of the revaluation claim was intercepted by the Government's decision to introduce formal pay guide-lines.

General and Designated Grades
Indicative of the strains created by the Government's vacillations over the imposition of a formal pay norm was the brief, but potentially damaging confrontation over the pay of general and designated grades of administrative and clerical staff, a group comprising some 45,000 staff. Determination of wages for this group by the Administrative and Clerical Staffs Whitley Council was relatively straightforward on account of an understanding that their pay should be linked with equivalent grades in the non-industrial Civil Service. This procedure worked smoothly during the Wilson administration. Its application under Heath called for an increase of about 10 per cent from 1 April 1971. However, by the spring of 1971, the Ministerial Committee on Pay Negotiations was inclined to adopt a limit of between 7.5 and 8.5 per cent for such groups. Joseph's refusal to accept this limit caused reference of this issue to the Cabinet, where he pointed out that comparable secretarial grades within the NHS had already received 9.9 per cent, while delay in making an offer to the general and designated grades had been excused on the basis of the expectation that they would be awarded the same increase as non-industrial civil servants. The Cabinet was

divided over this issue; after two lengthy discussions, it was decided that an offer of about 9.9 per cent was unavoidable. These discussions concluded with an agreement that in future pay increases within the public sector would be limited where possible to 5 per cent and that no second increase should be allowed within 12 months. This conclusion took the Government a step nearer towards adoption of a formal pay policy.[242]

Incomes Policy: Stages 1 and 2
In the light of the continuing upward surge of wages and fruitless talks with the Trades Union Congress about voluntary restraint, in November 1972 the Government introduced a 90-day freeze on pay and prices. The second stage of the Conservative incomes policy lasted from April to November 1973. This entailed a ceiling on pay increases of £1 per week plus 4 per cent of the wage paid in the preceding year, with a limit of £250 for any individual. All settlements were monitored by the new-established Pay Board.

By December 1972, outbreaks of industrial action were occurring among groups as diverse as dockers and textile workers. Industrial unrest then continued to increase on many fronts during the first months of 1973. The TUC at first resisted demands for a concerted action against the Government's pay policy, but unions in general became more militant over pay and prices. Contrary to the desired intention, the industrial relations legislation tended to exacerbate industrial militancy.

Ancillary Workers
For a short time the NHS found itself at the forefront of industrial militancy. NHS personnel took a lead in confronting stage 2 of the pay policy, in concert with such familiar groups of militants as coal-miners, railwaymen, and dockers. The main flashpoint within the NHS was among ancillary workers, whose negotiations over a routine pay claim had been suspended as a consequence of the standstill on pay and prices. The 220,000 ancillary workers had been offered an increase that averaged £1.88 a week, which the four main unions rejected as unacceptable. The extent of unrest among their membership was indicated by outbreaks of local strike action. The first half-day strikes took place in hospitals on Merseyside on 15 December 1972. When the Management Side of the Ancillary Staffs Whitley Council failed to improve its offer, in January 1973 the unions organised a ballot which reported in favour of strike action. The new campaign of officially-backed militancy commenced at the end of February. This coincided with threats of disruption from other groups of workers, including train drivers and gas workers. The TUC was drawn into more active mobilisation in support of strikers.

433

The ancillary workers targeted major hospitals throughout Britain in the course of their selective strike action. The effectiveness of the ancillary workers' strike was greater than anticipated by the Government. For the first time since the beginning of the NHS, industrial action rendered likely the reduction in services and closure of hospitals. Ministers were concerned that the ancillary workers would attract sympathy on account of their low pay; Joseph was asked to mount a publicity campaign to convince the public that the ancillary workers were acting irresponsibly.[243] When it emerged that the media were generally sympathetic to the workers, the Government feared that this would induce more general sympathy for the more militant unions.

Anger among the NHS workers intensified as a consequence of a statement by Joseph that he was unwilling to increase the pay offer on account of the risk of setting a precedent, tempting other unions to break the pay code.[244] By mid-April, industrial action directly affected about 275 hospitals, and it reduced services by about 10 per cent. The impact was limited on account of sacrifices made by nursing and administrative staff, and by the exercise of restraint by ancillary staff. In return for this moderation, Joseph desisted from bringing in volunteers to break the strike. The strike nevertheless caused great inconvenience, as well as stress among non-striking health personnel, who themselves exerted pressure on the Government to settle the dispute.[245] Within the Government there was some support for taking action under the Counter-Inflation Act 1973, which would allow the Pay Board to serve notice of an intention to make an Order restricting the remuneration which might be paid to ancillary workers; in that case it would be an offence for the unions to continue their industrial action in support of a higher pay increase. Other Ministers were anxious not to use the NHS ancillary workers as a test case for this provision.[246]

Strike action continued without diminution, but the position of the ancillary workers became more exposed as many unions settled within the terms of stage 2 of pay policy. The health unions hesitated about allowing their costly and debilitating strike to drag on for the sake of trivial gains. On 13 April they agreed to meet DHSS, which was authorised to make minor concessions, especially bringing forward by a few months a small increase for women workers in connection with the move to equal pay, and also the speeding-up of discussions concerning bonus schemes, which offered a prospect of a further increase for some workers. The unions accepted this concession 'under duress and protest'. They were also forced to abandon their resistance to consulting the Pay Board, which they now approached to claim special treatment on account of low pay.[247] This dispute with the NHS ancillary workers was a minor but significant symbolic victory for the Government's anti-inflation policy, and it was to some extent a humiliation for the unions. There was some comfort for the unions, which gained members and increased their prestige within the NHS. They also obtained support for their case among the public. The *Times* expressed concern about the dangers of a situation in which 'our hospitals are run to a dangerous extent on cheap labour' and called for more generous remuneration of all low-paid groups within the NHS; otherwise, the effective team-work required for maintaining a modern health service would no longer be sustained.[248]

Nurses, Midwives and Administrators

Potentially, nurses and midwives presented a graver threat than ancillary workers to the new incomes policy. In January 1973, the nurses and midwives resubmitted their massive revaluation claim, now increased by 15 per cent to take account of the average increase of earnings in 1972. The £1 a week plus 4 per cent formula implied an increase of 7.75 per cent; this amounted to an average of about £1.84 a week, or £96 a year. The Staff Side faced the indignity of a settlement below the level of the offer to ancillary workers. Discussions on the nurses' claim extended over more than two months. The nurses eventually agreed to set aside their revaluation claim and settle within the terms of stage 2 of incomes policy. As in the case of ancillary workers, minor concessions were offered to make the settlement more palatable. According to the agreement reached on 3 April 1973, all nurses aged 21 and above received a minimum of £102, while Joseph with difficulty persuaded his colleagues to waive the imposition of increased charges for laundry and meals.[249]

The 1973 award left the nurses and midwives dissatisfied. Their anxieties were increased by the scales evolved for new senior appointments introduced in connection with NHS reorganisation. Nurses were annoyed that other members of the new consensus management teams were being allocated superior salaries. Administrators similarly protested that their remuneration placed them at a disadvantage to administrative medical officers and with equivalent officers in local authorities. Both nurses and administrators accused the Secretary of State of by-passing the Whitley machinery by imposing salary levels for senior posts in the new health authorities. The grievances of nurses and administrators were sufficiently serious for the Prime Minister to receive their delegations.[250] The administrators protested that prevarications of the Government over their pay carried 'unhappy memories of 1957'. The nurses and midwives contended that salaries for their senior personnel were 'ludicrous' compared with the pay of administrators and doctors. Joseph admitted to the Prime Minister that the

435

administrators and nurses had a legitimate grievance.[251] Minor improvements in the scales for senior nursing and administrative personnel were approved by Ministers on 6 July 1973. These concessions were sufficient to secure co-operation in filling the key senior posts in the new NHS administration, thereby avoiding collapse of the reorganisation timetable.

The nursing Staff Side hoped for further improvements in their pay and progress in eliminating anomalies through the medium of the Pay Board. Nurses appealed to the Pay Board to designate nursing as a special case. The Staff and Management Sides presented their evidence during the latter part of 1973, but it became evident that the Pay Board was unable to undertake the full-scale investigation required to resolve this problem.[252]

Doctors and Dentists
The third review of doctors' and dentists' remuneration conducted by the DDRB related to the year commencing April 1973. It was therefore affected by stage 2 of the incomes policy. Through close liaison at the official level between the secretariat of the DDRB and the Pay Board, the review body was prevented from stepping out of line with pay policy. The third report of the DDRB published in July 1973 fell within the £1 plus 4 per cent formula, and was therefore ratified by the Pay Board and Ministers.[253]

Incomes Policy: Stage 3
Following further unproductive talks with the Trades Union Congress, the Government introduced stage 3 of its incomes policy in November 1973. This allowed for increases of £2.25 a week, or 7 per cent, with an individual limit of £350 a year. Also it introduced a new 'threshold' system, whereby for every 1 per cent rise in retail prices above 7 per cent, pay increased by an additional 40p a week, an arrangement that was a doubtful asset in controlling inflation.

In December 1973, the nurses resubmitted for the third time their revaluation claim, once again updated, as on the previous occasion by 15 per cent. This implied a 40 per cent increase on existing salaries. However, this substantial demand was presented as a formality; it was immediately shelved and the Staff Side consented to a stage 3 award without demur. This manoeuvre was related to the proximity of the General Election. It was calculated that the drive to secure a realistic response to the substantial revaluation claim was best deferred until after the General Election.[254]

The review procedure for doctors and dentists also bore the air of spurious calm. In January 1974 the DDRB began its work on the award due to take effect in April 1974. This review was at an early stage when the administration changed. However, it was evident that senior hospital staff in particular were becoming vocal in their complaints about the operation of the DDRB. Halsbury expressed his disquiet to the Prime Minister concerning the degree to which the pay of groups for whom he was responsible was failing to keep pace with the rising cost of living. He calculated that an increase of 17 per cent was required to redress this situation. His Review Body was frustrated that limitations of the pay code had prevented them from introducing realistic recommendations.[255] He warned Heath about disquiet among doctors. However, this rising storm over the pay of the medical profession was insignificant compared with the confrontation developing in the industrial sphere. NHS pay and all other questions relating to incomes policy were dwarfed by the growing confrontation over pay between the Government and the miners. In January 1974, the miners voted for strike action, which was scheduled to begin just after the February 1974 General Election.

(viii) BRIGGS COMMITTEE

Membership of the nursing enquiry presented the usual problems of reconciling competing interests. On this occasion, given the size and diversity of the profession, and the wide scope of the enquiry, this task was especially difficult. There were, for instance, five statutory organisations responsible for training: the General Nursing Council for England and Wales, the General Nursing Council for Scotland, the Central Midwives Board, the Central Midwives Board for Scotland, and the Council for the Education and Training of Health Visitors. Naturally, each of these bodies laid claim to representation on the nursing enquiry. It was clear that the committee would become impossibly unwieldy if all the powerful interest groups were represented. Accordingly it was decided to aim for a committee of twelve members, with only four nurse members, which would rule out a representational character. At first DHSS hoped for only one representative from Scotland and one from Wales, but as a condition for its participation, Scotland insisted on three members. Achieving an appropriate balance between men and women presented a further difficult complication.

In outlining the health departments' proposals on membership for the benefit of Professor Briggs, a total of thirteen, or fourteen including the chairman, was suggested. DHSS suggested five nurses, two doctors, two 'educationalists, an economist and human resources expert, and possibly a sociologist and a representative of the consumer interest'. A trade unionist was also mentioned as a possibility. Of the twenty names specifically suggested to Briggs, six figured in the final membership of his committee.[256] Including the chairman, the committee comprised sixteen members at its inception; with late additions the full complement was eighteen.[257]

Of these, nine were women, and the same number were nurses. The nursing membership was therefore considerably higher than originally anticipated. Women comprised half the committee, which was greater than Salmon , but less than Lane. The interest of the statutory training bodies was satisfied by inclusion of the Chairman of the General Nursing Council; the nursing professional organisations were perhaps less satisfied, but one member of the Council of the Royal College of Nursing was included. Of the non-nurse members, there were three clinicians, one educationalist, an economist-human resources expert, a Whitley Council Staff Side Chairperson, a hospital administrator, and a representative of the consumer interest. The latter was Lady Elspeth Howe, wife of Sir Geoffrey Howe. Of the range of occupational possibilities originally suggested to Briggs, only the sociologist was omitted. In its final form, the committee included three representatives from Scotland and two from Wales. Of some importance was the decision, on the recommendation of DHSS, to attach two expert advisers to the committee; these were Dr Jillian MacGuire, the Director of the General Nursing Council Research Unit and Nicholas Bosanquet, a Lecturer in Economics at the London School of Economics. These appointments further strengthened the links of the Briggs Committee with DHSS and with Crossman's expert advisers from LSE.

The first meeting of the Briggs Committee occurred a few days before the 1970 General Election.[258] The Committee was welcomed by Lady Serota. Professor Briggs outlined the tasks of the Committee and expressed the hope that its report would be produced in eighteen months to two years. It was agreed that the full committee would meet monthly, and that other work would be undertaken by subcommittees, of which two were established immediately.

The Briggs Committee fulfilled its substantial remit efficiently and realistically. Already in November 1970 the chairman circulated a list of chapter headings, which perhaps assumed an over-optimistic pace of progress. Nevertheless, this proved to be one of the few instances among the more important independent committees where the whole mission was accomplished with expedition, allowing the report to be completed in the summer of 1972.[259]

The Briggs Report almost exactly followed the lines of departmental evidence to the nursing enquiry. This Report was therefore broadly welcomed in official circles, and no objections were made to prompt publication. Since the subject was sufficiently weighty to merit publication as a Command Paper, it was necessary to consult Ministers. In view of Joseph's assurances that the report carried few immediate expenditure implications, the subject was not thought to merit discussion by the Home and Social Affairs

Committee, although Ministers were given an opportunity to comment on the text.

The only voice opposing to publication emanated from the Treasury, which argued for delay until after the White Paper on Public Expenditure on the grounds that 'the outlook for public expenditure is bleak and the publication of the Briggs Report might arouse hopes and encourage pressures for increased expenditure on nursing which may not be able to be achieved'. The Treasury therefore urged that it would be better for the report to be published when the grim nature of the economic climate was fully appreciated.[260] The health departments reassured the Treasury that the Briggs Report possessed no immediate expenditure implications; it was therefore pointless to delay the lengthy consultation exercise. Furthermore, expectations arising from the report were already fully aroused by the existence of the committee and leaks concerning its likely findings. It was therefore desirable that reactions to the report should be founded on the report itself. The Treasury withdrew its objections, and since the draft report generated virtually no response from other departments, it was published under the names of the Secretaries of State for Social Services, Scotland and Wales on 17 October 1972.[261]

The Briggs Report in general followed the plan circulated by Briggs in November 1970. The text comprised about 220 pages; there were also about 100 pages devoted to appendices, a glossary, list of references (including three derived from Florence Nightingale), and index. The report was a competent and an unusually scholarly production. The Briggs Report made 75 recommendations, the most important of which were: (a) to lower the age of entry into nursing from 18 to 17, in two stages, occurring in 1973 and 1975. Although it was hoped to attract recruits with high academic qualifications, including graduates aspiring to higher positions in nursing, for the majority it was proposed that entry should not depend specifically on formal educational qualifications, but on a flexible system designed to test motivation and aptitude.

(b) to restructure training, introducing an eighteen-month general training leading to a first statutory qualification, the Certificate in Nursing Practice, which would entitle the holder to undertake basic nursing work in any field of nursing. A further eighteen-month course would lead to full registration. The four specialised parts of the existing Register would be replaced by a single undifferentiated register. Transfer from one field of nursing to another would be facilitated by short courses. Registered nurses would be eligible to take a more elaborate twelve-month course leading to registration as a midwife, or alternatively they could prepare for the award of a Higher Certificate.

(c) to replace the five separate statutory bodies concerned with nurse training by a single Central Nursing and Midwifery Council for Great Britain with responsibility for standards of statutory qualifications and for discipline, supported by three Nursing and Midwifery Education Boards, for England, Scotland and Wales overseeing the detail of education, with a Standing Midwifery Committee of the Central Council to control midwifery practice and to advise the Council and the Boards on midwifery education.

(d) to establish Area Committees for Nursing and Midwifery for the purposes of supervision and finance of local Colleges of Nursing and Midwifery for education of all nurses and midwives, with the possibility of these colleges acting as the nucleus for colleges of health studies, catering for other groups of health service personnel.

(e) to introduce improvements in the career structure in order to attain a clearer designation of nurses and midwives possessing advanced clinical qualifications, and carrying exceptional responsibility in the clinical field. Teachers of nursing and midwifery would take a one-year course leading to the Diploma in Nursing and Midwifery Education. It was proposed that the teaching staff structure should be separated from the service structure.

(f) to take initiatives to improve recruitment and render the profession more attractive and less onerous to new entrants.

(g) to prepare for a gradual transition to a new caring profession with responsibly for the mentally handicapped.

(h) to discontinue the statutory certification of health visitors, thereby eliminating the need for the Council for the Education and Training of Health Visitors. It was also proposed to replace the title 'health visitor' with 'family health sister'.

The health departments, NHS authorities and most professional bodies were enthusiastically supportive of the Briggs recommendations. In general, it was felt that the Report provided acceptable guide-lines for the further natural development of the nursing and midwifery professions, with consequent improvement in attractiveness to potential recruits and all levels within the professions, without introducing such radical restructuring of training that disastrous human resource consequences would ensue. Indeed, reduction of the age of entry into nursing, flexible attitudes towards educational qualifications for entry, and more streamlined training promised positive advantages with respect to size of the effective workforce. Inevitably some additional labour would be required, especially in general hospitals, to compensate for the additional training time allocated, but this was regarded as an acceptable price to pay for improved professional standards.

Many of the recommendations of the Briggs Committee represented changes already taking place, repetition of findings already reached by other committees, or they reflected settled conclusions within the professions and the health departments, reached in the light of experience of such changes as the Salmon reforms. Briggs was therefore absorbed into the culture of nursing as a logical climax of natural evolutionary trends.

Although Briggs quickly became established as the nursing orthodoxy, there were some substantial expressions of unease, providing warning signs that implementation would demand a great deal of delicate negotiation. Health visitors in particular indicated that they would resist loss of their independence and separate statutory identity. They refused to contemplate reduction in the length, or a change in the nature of their training. The health visitors' grievances were echoed to a lesser extent by such groups as community nurses and psychiatric nurses. Midwives had also previously exercised complete autonomy, and were suspicious that their parity with nurses would be lost. There were also fears that Scotland would be disadvantaged by loss of its independent statutory bodies. Educational interests wanted guarantees that the National Education Boards would possess genuine authority and autonomy. There was also resistance to the proposal for segregated nursing and midwifery education, either in colleges for these groups or in colleges of health studies. Instead, it was argued that nursing and midwifery should follow the example of health visiting by locating education in the expanding system of general higher education institutions. The Briggs proposals for relaxation of minimum criteria for entry into training were not entirely easy to understand, but they were treated with suspicion on account of the fear of dilution. Many organisations were opposed to nursing becoming the one major profession not imposing minimum entrance requirements. It was suspected that this would be detrimental to the image of nursing, to recruitment, and to pay levels. The same arguments were advanced against the Briggs Committee's enthusiasm for cadet schemes. There were also strong objections to the proposal for an eighteen-month basic training course, which it was suggested would reduce educational standards and leave younger nurses with unreasonably heavy duties. On account of these fears, it was suggested that the Briggs proposals for an immediate reduction in the minimum age of entry were premature. Taking account of the full range and diversity of reservations, and the influential status of many of the critics, it is evident that the Briggs Report was more vulnerable to criticism than suggested by initial appreciative responses.[262]

Within the health departments, DHSS in particular was not much inclined to allow the critics to undermine confidence in Briggs. The health departments established a Briggs Report Steering Group to oversee the assessment and implementation of the nursing reforms.

This steering group began work in December 1972 and it adopted a demanding timetable. Given the likelihood that the Briggs recommendations would prove generally acceptable, it was hoped to obtain legislation in the 1973/74 session, constitute the new statutory bodies by the end of 1974, and begin implementing the new training structure in September 1975. The steering group believed that 'delay of that order is explicable, but anything beyond that would cause unrest in the profession and hamper integration of the service'. It was therefore regarded as essential for the new nursing structures to be in place as soon after NHS reorganisation as possible.[263]

In determining the timetable for implementation of the Briggs reforms, the steering group was acutely aware that the entire operation might be blighted on account of cost implications. The main concern related to the additional amount of nursing labour required to compensate for the loss in time associated the proposed educational changes. The Briggs Committee estimated that a 5 per cent increase in staff would be required. DHSS calculated that the cost of this expansion in numbers could almost be accommodated within the growth rates for nursing staff allowed under PESC allocations. However, uncertainties about costs and resources caused the steering committee to abandon its initial ideas about comprehensive and immediate implementation of the Briggs reforms. Joseph agreed to a sequential approach, beginning with an announcement, (a) expressing support in principle for the Briggs recommendations, subject to the usual reservations about availability of resources and departmental spending priorities; (b) indicating that future policy would be determined in the light of responses to a consultative document setting out the Government's policy preferences; and (c) stating the Government's intention to introduce legislation to facilitate a unified structure for training and professional matters. This central organisation would then plan the future pattern of nursing education. This course of action would involve negligible cost in the short term and excuse delay over the introduction of changes requiring substantial additional expenditure.[264] The Treasury welcomed these suggestions.[265] However, both James Prior and Gordon Campbell opposed a sequential legislative operation. Both preferred delaying legislation until after full consultation, followed by comprehensive legislation in the 1974/75 session. Joseph acquiesced to this suggestion with only mild protest, perhaps because it was highly unlikely that the Future Legislation Committee would find a place for a Briggs Bill in the 1973/74 session.[266]

This decision left the health department with an awkward public relations problem. Given that the Briggs Committee reported in October 1972, Joseph was anxious to issue some statement of the

Government's intentions before the 1973 summer recess. However, the timetable slipped. A memorandum to Ministers and draft statement were not produced until late August; these were ratified by other departments during September; but then further delay resulted from the need to insert paragraphs concerning Northern Ireland in the memorandum. Ministers finally considered the Briggs Report on 14 December, but they deferred ratification of a draft statement until after the Christmas recess.[267] Joseph modified his draft statement in the light of comments from his colleagues, with the aim of making an announcement before the end of February 1974, but the General Election intervened to preclude this possibility.[268] As 1973 drew towards its conclusion, Joseph was harassed by MPs with embarrassing questions on the Briggs Report, and he was subjected to increasingly unflattering comment in the nursing press. Many of the suspicions voiced in the nursing journals were not wide of the mark, as for instance: 'the fear is that the DHSS will implement the 'easy' recommendations such as the setting up of a single central body responsible for nursing and midwifery in Great Britain and not tackle the more drastic reorganisation of the educational system'.[269] Given the mounting obstacles to implementation of the nursing reforms, Joseph was perhaps not unhappy to hand over the Briggs problem to his successors.

(ix) PROFESSIONS IN FLUX

As the example of nursing demonstrates, advances in health care, difficulties in meeting the economic and career aspirations of the professions, and changes introduced in connection with reorganisation of the health and personal social services, conspired to create an atmosphere of crisis for many professional groups. By the 1960s, intervention by the Government to alleviate these problems became unavoidable. The approach to difficulties affecting hospital scientific and technical staffs, and public health doctors have already been considered. The next stage in these deliberations will now be briefly considered. This is also the appropriate point to raise the related dispute over the professional status of clinical psychologists.

Hospital Scientific and Technical Services

As already noted, the departments made only hesitant moves towards establishment of the National Hospital Scientific Service recommended by the Zuckerman Report. The economic situation itself precluded immediate action on most of the recommendations, since it was appreciated that a unified service would inevitably involve substantial increases in remuneration for the groups concerned. In these circumstances, the first priority was given to the least expensive items in the Zuckerman Report, the appointment of a Chief Scientific Officer in the central departments, the establishment of National Hospital Scientific Councils, the appointment of Regional Scientific Advisory Committees, together with full-time Regional Scientists and small regional staffs. Even the proposals for the regional tier were not universally supported, and there was even wider divergence of opinion on the organisation of scientific and technical services below the regional level.

In Scotland, fewer inhibitions were expressed about implementation of the Zuckerman proposals. A conference of experts held in January 1971 exposed broad agreement between scientists and clinicians over policy, and plans were discussed for establishing a Scottish Hospital Scientific Council as a first priority. A representative of SHHD suggested that in view of the adequacy of existing mechanisms of advice, it was possible to defer consideration of the appointment of a chief scientist and regional scientific officers.[270]

The Zuckerman proposals were implemented in a even more piecemeal fashion than originally envisaged. As already indicated, the Chief Scientist Organisations in London and Edinburgh were established, not especially as a result of Zuckerman, but in the context of general reorganisation of scientific services prompted by the Rothschild Report. It was decided to defer action on the establishment of National Hospital Scientific Councils until experience had been gained of the operation of the Chief Scientist Organisations, which were expected to perform many of the functions envisaged for the National Councils. In the context of NHS reorganisation, DHSS authorised the appointment of Regional Scientific Officers, as well as Regional and Area Scientific Committees. Also general advice was given on arrangements for the organisation of scientific and technical services at the area and unit level in the reorganised service, which for the most part envisaged consolidating existing arrangements.[271]

Much less progress was made on the rationalisation of the staff structure. The Labour administration ended in disagreement between DHSS and the Whitley Staff Sides concerning the degree to which staff groups should be consulted over the general organisation of the new scientific service. On 15 October 1970 Lord Aberdare met Staff Side representatives to discuss the Government's plan for issuing a draft policy document on the organisation of scientific services for comment by the Staff Side and other outside bodies. This meeting was largely a repeat of previous arguments concerning the extent to which the Staff Side should participate in working out proposals for organisation and staffing of the new scientific service.[272]

Further progress with implementation of the Zuckerman recommendations proved to be extremely problematical. With respect to introduction of a unified grading structure, the suggestions of Zuckerman were overtaken by the Fulton Report, which favoured more radical simplification. This latter approach was favoured by various staff interests, led by the Institute of Medical Laboratory Technicians. Some elementary improvements were introduced, but more radical change was precluded by the successive pay policies introduced under the Heath administration. The other avenue of reform related to the reorganisation of services at the local level to allow for greater flexibility of employment and rationalisation of training schemes to allow common training for certain groups of technicians. Discussions with the various interest groups suggested that services might be organised on the basis of four main functional groups, but this scheme was not finally prepared for consultation until 1975. Following further abortive negotiations, a departmental team reviewed the problem again and effectively abandoned the Zuckerman enterprise to establish a unified scientific and technical service. Instead it proposed that scientific and technical staff should be amalgamated into three main groups: medical laboratory services, radiological services, and clinical engineering and physical sciences services. This left a residue of services such as pharmacy, clinical psychology, and dietetics, which could not be fitted into the tripartite scheme. It was proposed to allow these professional groups to develop separately.[273] Regional Scientific Officers complained about delay in moving towards new management arrangements for the scientific and technical services, which they pointed out was 'seriously jeopardising the function of the Regional Advisory Committees'. In the absence of integrated planning, the regional officers pointed out that Area Scientific Committees were assuming a greater degree of importance than originally intended.[274] Thus, even before reorganisation was complete, it was clear that the Zuckerman dream was unlikely to be fulfilled.

Clinical Psychologists
The prospects for advancement of hospital scientific and technical staff offered by the Zuckerman proposals served to remind psychologists employed by hospital authorities of their vulnerable position. The Zuckerman Report made only passing comments about psychologists, but accepted that their professional problems needed consideration. Psychologists were disappointed by this outcome. They had made representations to the Zuckerman Committee, while after the report they appealed to be included under the 'Zuckerman umbrella'.[275] The announcement by DHSS that the problems of psychologists would be considered by a working party appointed by the Mental Health SAC was not welcomed by the British

Psychological Society, partly because not all their members worked in the sphere of mental health, but especially on account of the likelihood that the working party would be dominated by psychiatrists.

This issue was remitted to the Mental Health SAC on 25 June 1969; it was discussed on that occasion, and again on 25 September. Although the Mental Health SAC appreciated that psychologists worked in various fields within the hospital service, as well as in local authorities, it was agreed that the remit of working party should be limited to the 'role of the psychologist in the mental health services'.[276] The working party was chaired by Professor W H Trethowan, Chairman of the Mental Health SAC. In addition, five medical members of the SAC were nominated to the working party (soon known as subcommittee). It was also agreed that the British Psychological Society, the Top Grade Psychologists Advisory Committee, and the Royal Medico-Psychological Association should be invited to propose members.

This degree of medical domination and the limitation of remit were offensive to the psychologists, who had been promised a joint working party. Further irritation was caused by the delay of DHSS in mobilising the working party. During this intermission, the British Psychological Society used its influence to persuade DHSS to propose extending the remit of the working party to include the work of all psychologists employed in the health services, and also to support suggestions for a more balanced membership.[277]

The remit of the subcommittee was extended, but the committee remained dominated by clinicians. Of the eleven members, six were clinicians, three were psychologists, and there were two others, a member of a health authority and a hospital administrator.[278] The Trethowan Committee began work in 1973 and completed its main work at the end of the year with production of a consultation document on the role of psychologists in the health service.[279] Comments on this document were received by the summer of 1974, by which date the Mental Health SAC had been wound up. Trethowan's subcommittee considered responses to its consultation document and completed its report in the autumn of 1974, after which there was a further long delay before the Trethowan Report was published in 1977, virtually ten years after the psychologists had petitioned for urgent consideration of their professional status. The main emphasis of the Trethowan Report was on the role of the multi-disciplinary team, in which the psychologist was recognised as an equal partner. The proposals for granting the psychologist a greater degree of professional autonomy, and freedom to accept referrals were made in the face of opposition from some organisations representing clinicians. Consistent with thinking on the scientific and technical services, it was proposed that psychological services should be planned and administered on the basis of regional and area authorities, with a chief officer and advisory committees being established at both levels. It was also suggested that a full-time clinical psychologist should be appointed in the central department. The Trethowan Report estimated a sharp increase in demand for psychologists working in the health service. Whereas current numbers were given as 600, it was estimated that training would need to be expanded on the basis of an expectation that 2,320 would be required to fulfil all relevant functions under the reorganised health service.

Community Medicine
As noted in chapter III, the reorganisations planned for the health and personal social services entailed the elimination of the Medical Officer of Health, and necessitated urgent consideration of the future role of the large number of doctors engaged in public health. The obvious implication of the changes being introduced was that the public health specialty was redundant. On the other hand, pragmatic considerations suggested that most of the traditional functions of public health doctors would continue to be required. There also seemed a place in the reorganised health and personal social services for a medical specialist performing certain general functions and contributing leadership of a kind hitherto supplied by the elite among the Medical Officers of Health, and which was unlikely to emanate from their clinician colleagues. The Seebohm and Todd Reports, and the two Green Papers on NHS reorganisation, as well as spirited contributions from public health leaders, urged that medicine was about to witness the birth of the new specialty of community medicine, and this was represented an exciting prospect to those concerned.[280] Public health doctors were not entirely convinced. They knew that their existing posts were about to vanish, and it was far from evident that they would find relocations of equal status. The Hunter Committee was formed to give firmer definition to community medicine and to describe in a concrete manner the functions to be performed by community physicians of the future. This enquiry dovetailed into the reorganisation planning process initiated by the Heath administration. Indeed, the outcome of the Hunter deliberations was inevitably affected by the new direction of thinking about NHS reorganisation, especially by the new emphasis on management. The Hunter working party was therefore swept along in the wake of the management review. The characteristics outlined for the new medical specialty were influenced as much by these management considerations, as by the wider social and medical concerns that had dominated earlier discussions over community medicine.

With the change of administration, the Hunter working party sought sanction to continue its work and also it requested a slight change in its remit, which now became 'to review the functions of medical administrators in the health service and to make recommendations regarding the provision required for their training'.[281] It was acutely aware of the demoralisation and collapse of recruitment among public health doctors. The working party therefore produced an interim report recommending the immediate introduction of short training courses in medical administration to prepare public health doctors for their new duties in the reorganised health service. The text of this interim report was ratified on 27 November 1970.[282] The committee hoped to produce its full report by the end of October 1971.

Given the extent of the crisis in public health medicine, it is extraordinary that the interim report was handled in a casual manner. It took six weeks for the interim report to be acknowledged. In January 1971, medical staff expressed alarm about the delay, and the Chief Medical Officer pointed out that he had seen nothing about the interim report.[283] The first public statement briefly mentioning the interim report was made on 6 May 1971.[284]

The working party took longer to complete its deliberations than anticipated, largely because its final recommendations were dependent on Government decisions concerning NHS reorganisation and management arrangements. The working party circulated a consultative document in May 1971, immediately after the appearance of the Consultative Document on NHS reorganisation.[285] Consideration was given to issuing a further interim report in the autumn of 1971, but the working party decided to defer any report until after it had taken account of the Government's provisional thinking on its White Paper and on the management review.[286] The final report was completed in January 1972 and published on 31 May 1972.[287]

The Hunter Report was one of the grey-covered reports produced at the time of reorganisation. Apart from the appendices, the text comprised 50 pages. Although repeatedly stressing the 'key', or 'vital' role of the community physician, or their 'essential' or 'fundamental importance' for the success of reorganisation, the Hunter Report was an uninspiring document. Also, although long-delayed, the report was tentative in character, partly because it was produced without insight into the final management arrangements for the reorganised health service, and even before the decision to assimilate the school medical service into the NHS. The first part of the report therefore considered in generalised terms the functions of medical administrators, or 'specialists in community medicine' under the new terminology, at regional, area and district levels. The report outlined an array of functions both within the health service, and relating to co-ordination with local government. It gave little impression of the balance of these functions likely to emerge in practice. Least information was provided about the district level at which most public health doctors would expect to be employed. In outlook, the Hunter Report represented a hybrid between the cultures of Crossman and Joseph. Some sections reflected the thinking of the second Green Paper, others were in line with the Government's new ideas on management and efficiency. The Hunter Committee accordingly stressed the importance of the role of community medicine specialists in improving efficiency in the use of resources, and therefore the 'key' status envisaged for this specialist tended to rest upon this management role. On the other hand, the new professional structure outlined for community medicine followed the pattern adopted by clinicians, thereby implying the importance of the community physician as a medical specialist. The second part of the Hunter Report outlined the training and career structure for the new specialty. In this latter section, the main innovation was the recommendation that the basic career grade would be regarded as a consultant level appointment. Consistent with this consultant aspiration, the new training structure was modelled on the existing pattern of clinical training. This proposal implied the enhancement of status for the upper echelons of public health doctors and the prospect of healing the rift existing at the time between academic departments of social medicine and public health professionals. This proposal was of little comfort for those designated as lacking the qualifications for consultant status, who were merely promised continuation in some ill-specified established grade, in reality importing into community medicine the 'sub-consultant' grade rejected in the rest of clinical medicine.

The Hunter Report was generally viewed as a modest but constructive step towards the reconsolidation of public health medicine, but the welcome was by no means universal. A minority was suspicious of the absorption of the community physician into the new, collective management structure. The critics were dismayed by the absence of any spirited or visionary message, and they were doubtful whether the non-hierarchical assembly of community medicine specialists would exercise anything like the same force as the Medical Officer of Health hierarchies that were being abolished. Under the new regime it was doubted whether the community physician would continue to perform the traditional 'watch-dog' function. Abandonment of the annual report of the Medical Officer of Health symbolised the decline of this function.[288] The Chief Medical Officer was also unhappy about abandonment of the annual report: 'I do not think they understand how important this has been

449

in helping the Medical Officer of Health to do his job in the past, nor have they appreciated, I believe, the importance of contact with the public in the district'. The changes recommended by the Hunter Report accordingly gave rise to fears that community physicians would evolve into ancillary management functionaries alienated alike from other medical professionals and their local communities.[289]

CHAPTER VI

Conservatives and Reorganisation

When the Conservatives returned to office in 1970 it was not evident what attitude they would take to reorganisation. Their 1964 and 1966 General Election manifestos were silent on this issue. One of the first indications of Conservative thinking was provided in 1967 by Sir Keith Joseph in his evidence to the Royal Commission on Local Government and in discussions with the Seebohm Committee, where he advocated reorganisation along the lines of the Porritt report. At this stage he envisaged establishing between 30 and 40 area health boards, and was open-minded about the retention of the regional tier.[1] In November 1967, Balniel briefly commented on Robinson's announcement about the forthcoming review of NHS organisation, but gave no indication of Conservative thinking, apart from welcoming the 'reconstruction' of the NHS.[2]

In the summer of 1968, before the publication of the first Green Paper, Maurice Macmillan, on behalf of the opposition, expressed support for a 'clean sweep' approach to reorganisation, as characterised by the Porritt scheme.[3] Geoffrey Howe, who was closely in touch with BMA planning activities, also wrote in favour of the Porritt plan, and he sympathised with the profession's fear of a growth of central control, attacking the first Green Paper for making area boards 'no more than the agents of the Minister'. He insisted that these boards 'must be truly independent agencies', representative of their local communities and 'not managerial' in character, although the boards would appoint chief executives, equipped to exert a strong managerial influence.[4]

The first precise and detailed indication of the Conservative attitude to reorganisation was provided by Balniel, the opposition spokesman on the social services, during the Debate on the Address in October 1969. Balniel reiterated the usual reservations about the suitability of areas advocated in the first Green Paper, and expressed preference for a two-tier approach involving regions and districts, which he realised would be incompatible with the Redcliffe-Maude proposals on local government reform. He argued that the upper tier was unavoidable owing to the importance of regional planning, insisting that the reorganised health service must introduce 'massive devolution of responsibility from Whitehall'. This would necessitate severely curtailing the power of the Minister in appointments to health authorities. It was conceded that the Minister might appoint the regional chairmen, but otherwise he insisted on 'firm representation' of local authorities and the medical profession.[5] This statement significantly shifted the Conservatives towards the representative conception of health authorities. This intention was confirmed by a further contribution by Balniel in the debate on the second Green Paper. Once again he concentrated on the principles for determining the membership of health authorities. He again insisted that the bodies administering the health service should be directly representative rather than appointed by the Minister, the preferred plan being to constitute health authorities from 'half of professional people and half people from the new stronger local government which we intend to establish'.[6] In fact Balniel had unwittingly worked round to precisely the conclusion privately favoured by Crossman, but unrealisable owing to antagonism from the Treasury and lukewarm support from DHSS. When Macmillan was sounded out about the Conservative attitude to Crossman's Green Paper, he advised the Second Permanent Secretary that Balniel's views on the need for a regional tier were 'not shared by all' within the opposition, but no similar qualms were mentioned over the local accountability of health authorities.[7]

Despite the advanced state of discussions on reorganisation, the 1970 General Election manifesto was unforthcoming. The Conservatives merely promised to 'improve the administration of the health services so that its three main branches...are better co-ordinated'.[8] The Queen's Speech provided a natural opportunity to clarify the Government's intentions concerning reorganisation. However, this subject was not mentioned, even though the previous administration had reached the stage of draft legislation. On this occasion silence was an indication that the English health Ministers were approaching this issue from a cautious and even sceptical disposition.[9]

The debate on the Queen's Speech gave the opposition a chance to make capital out of the new Government's apparent lack of commitment to reorganisation. However, Barbara Castle, who led the opposition assault, possessed only limited familiarity with health affairs and possessed little direct acquaintance with the Kafkaesque world of reorganisation politics. Her spirited attack on the Government concentrated on easy targets, but made no reference to reorganisation. Joseph was therefore able to dismiss this subject in a few sentences, in which he promised to consider the Green Paper proposals in the context of local government reform.[10] Most other speakers in this debate also by-passed this issue, with the result that the Government was placed under no immediate pressure to declare its position.

The following narrative of policy formulation and legislation will deal principally with England, with appropriate reference to the general political context. This will be followed by consideration of points of essential detail relating to reorganisation in Scotland and Wales, each of which followed a distinctive course on many important areas of policy.

(i) REORIENTATION

During the summer of 1970 Joseph was fully briefed on reorganisation. Additional advice from his own side was available in the form a report from the House of Lords Health Group, but this concentrated on general trends in health care, rather than on practical issues directly pertinent to reorganisation. However, it echoed the common call for regions to be retained and accorded a greater place of prominence.[11] Joseph's first discussion on this issue with officials took place on 8 July, but it was not until a month later that he completed his reading of the second Green Paper, at which point he commented that he had not hitherto appreciated the magnitude of the task facing the department.[12]

The new Secretary of State was wary about accepting a commitment to reorganisation. The department produced a memorandum weighing up the arguments, and as persuasively as possible suggesting that there was little choice but to press forward with reorganisation. Joseph was assured that 'the economic and other gains we want could not be secured without administrative unification of the whole of the National Health Service'.[13] In discussion, Joseph pointed out that the ideal of unification was undermined by the recent decision to place social service departments under local government; this split 'seemed to outweigh any benefits of bringing the other parts of the health services together'.[14] The Secretary of State was also concerned about the absence of a firm management structure in previous plans for reorganisation. In his view, in the second Green Paper 'no provision is made for strong management or indeed for management at all'. Correction of this deficiency seemed to offer the Conservative Government with an opportunity to add a distinctive ingredient to reorganisation. The introduction of sound management principles would improve the quality of service and unlock major efficiency savings, thereby enabling the reorganised health service to achieve a considerably greater volume of output within its restricted budget. Such an approach fitted in with the value for money ethos of the Heath administration. This emphasis was attractive to Joseph, since it enabled him to draw upon his background experience of industry. Reorganisation became a more congenial prospect when it emerged that he could make a distinctive contribution and thereby significantly alter the culture of the National Health Service.

Joseph's preoccupation with efficiency and attachment to managerial solutions was of course not original. Transference of management methods from industry was by no means a novel idea within the NHS. The Oxford Region was particularly active in promoting industrial styles of management. Even before 1958 the Oxford Region in collaboration with Westminster Hospital set up a work study unit with the help of the Work Study Department of ICI. Officials of the RHB were sent on a variety of work-study courses. The management approach was also fostered by such organisations as the Acton Society Trust, the King's Fund, and the Nuffield Provincial Hospitals Trust. The Ministry of Health gingerly trod the same path. In May 1959, at the suggestion of the Royal College of Nursing, the Ministry established the NHS Advisory Council for Management Efficiency under the chairmanship of Sir Ewart Smith.[15] However, neither this committee, nor the O and M Unit within the department were successful in giving dynamic leadership in the field of management.[16] The demand for more systematic attention to management continued to build up. In response, the health departments launched a variety of management initiatives, important examples of which were the Farquharson-Lang enquiry into hospital administration in Scotland, the 'Cogwheel' projects for improving the management of medical work, and the Salmon reorganisation for higher nursing grades. Demand for further action to improve management emanated from the Treasury and this was reinforced by the newly-established CSD. Also, by 1970 the health departments and NHS authorities were co-operating with a wide variety of management studies being undertaken by university departments and independent management consultants. Joseph was more responsive than his predecessor to these diverse management influences.

Initially the Secretary of State favoured establishing a 'NHS Chief Executive' in the central department to head the management structure - this he regarded as a 'titanic job'. Joseph could not envisage the management structure working effectively without the interpolation of a strong regional tier. He appreciated that strong central direction incurred the risk of excessive uniformity and other adverse effects, which were 'brittle and dangerous'; consequently he declared himself by instinct a 'decentraliser'. His officials were commissioned to prepare a variety of papers dealing with the many difficulties raised by the second Green Paper, especially on means of infusing a greater degree of management control, without introducing an unacceptable level of centralisation.[17]

Joseph relapsed into a state of indecision about the merits of reorganisation. Officials urged more rapid progress; otherwise the simultaneous reorganisation of the health and social services would be prejudiced. For the Secretary of State, NHS unification was a new and awesome problem, but his officials were showing palpable signs of fatigue, as they approached the fifth year of deliberations, without arriving at definitive commitments, even on the basic framework of policy.

The indecision of Ministers was mirrored by absence of certainty among officials. In both the Treasury and DHSS there was some residual doubt about the wisdom of the entire reorganisation process, and there was a lack of consensus about crucial points of policy. For instance, certain senior figures within the Treasury continued to be sceptical about the possibility of arriving at an acceptable form of separate health service administration; consequently local government administration of the health services continued to be canvassed as a possibly superior alternative.[18] Within CSD, there was firm support for transferring the service to some kind of national corporation, a proposal previously finding some favour within the Treasury, but always opposed by DHSS. As noted in chapter IV, this possibility had been considered in detail, but it was not pursued further on account of the danger that it would incur an unacceptable erosion of the authority of Parliament and create ambiguities about the responsibilities of the Minister in the spheres of policy and financial accountability. This idea was briefly considered and dismissed at the start of Joseph's policy deliberations, although as noted below, it continued to hold attractions for the CSD.[19]

The Secretary of State displayed evident fascination with the issues raised in the ceaseless flow of memoranda that he had commissioned, often instituting pressing investigations on questions of minor detail. For instance important meetings on 8 and 10 September deliberated about the control of capital programmes in which local authorities and health authorities had a joint interest, and also on incentives for good performance, when Joseph promoted his ideas on the introduction of an equivalent to the Queen's Award to Industry. With respect to unification of the NHS, the Secretary of State 'did not want to appear to commit the Conservative Party to the detailed proposals in the previous Green Paper but, on the other hand, did not wish to publish a further Green Paper'. It was therefore suggested that it would be sufficient to prepare a consultative document, setting out differences of approach from previous proposals, but without giving a formal commitment to a new solution. Joseph would then seek a convenient opportunity to make a statement outlining his latest thinking about unification, underlining the importance of the management theme. It was agreed that a paper along these lines should be prepared for consideration by Ministers.[20]

The draft statement followed the main lines of the previous Government's policy by proposing to unify the health services outside local government; the new stress was 'sound and effective management', the details of which were to be determined in the light of further studies. These principles were accepted as the basis for statements by the three Secretaries of State.[21]

The reorganisation initiative of the Conservative Government was introduced with the minimum of publicity. On 5 November 1970 Joseph issued a brief written statement indicating that the Government intended to unify the administration of the NHS outside local government, and that the changes would come into effect at the same time as local government reform. As noted below a similar statement was made relating to Scotland, but whereas the SHHD was in possession of a settled plan, Joseph declared that Crossman's Green Paper fell short on account of its neglect of the efficiency criterion. He proposed to examine comments on the second Green Paper and undertake consultations with relevant organisations before formulating his own proposals.[22] In fact the views of the Secretary of State were formulated with little further reference to organisations representing the various interest groups within the NHS, but they increasingly took account of ideas emanating from management experts. This new source of wisdom profoundly influenced the character of the proposals adopted by Heath's Ministers.

Notwithstanding this superficial accord, there was doubt about the capacity of the DHSS to introduce an effective management structure into the unified health service. The Treasury was pleased with the new degree of emphasis on efficiency and management. However, the prevailing mood was sceptical. It was admitted that 'we have throughout been seriously concerned that the system previously proposed would result, not in a better service to the public or improved management, but a worse situation than at present'. Contacts with the DHSS over the revised plan failed to dispel this anxiety, but there were insufficient grounds to persuade Treasury Ministers to block the tentative announcement made in November 1970.[23]

Treasury fears about lack of real commitment within DHSS to a rigorous approach to management seemed to be confirmed by reactions to the suggestion that this problem should be remitted to independent management consultants. The Treasury was particularly pleased with the comments of Professor Jacques and his colleagues from Brunel University on the second Green Paper. It was felt that these reinforced Treasury views on the structure of management at area and district level. However, Treasury officials found little evidence that Brunel ideas were being followed up within the DHSS.[24] On the other hand, the Treasury was delighted with the SHHD view that the basic aim of reorganisation was 'liberation of management from the restraints imposed by highly artificial administrative barriers and by well-meaning but ineffectual management committees'.[25]

The Treasury and CSD attached particular importance to insinuating the Government's new Business Team into the reorganisation process. Initial discussions between the businessmen and Aberdare were held in August 1970, but DHSS reported that Richard Meyjes, the head of the Government's Business Team, was doubtful whether the businessmen possessed the capacity to assist with the administrative aspect of reorganisation.[26] The Business Team reported rather differently: they regarded NHS reorganisation as eminently suitable to their talents, but the Secretary of State was unwilling to allow them to conduct an independent appraisal. The Business Team believed that their influence would be lost if their role was limited to participation in an exercise controlled by the department. This impasse called for the lamentation of Cicero 'O tempora, O mores!'[27] Further enquiries confirmed original negative impressions concerning DHSS response to the Business Team; it seemed that the team was being welcomed to examine the internal organisation of the department, but was not being allowed to comment on wider questions of reorganisation. To CSD and the Treasury it looked as if Joseph was pushing the Business Team into a minor niche, and in effect saying 'Hands off my Department'.[28] This initial misunderstanding prevented the Business Team from playing its part during the important formative months of policy reorientation; it complicated relations between CSD, the Treasury and DHSS; and it limited the Ministers' access to an important and congenial source of specialist advice. Not for the first time Joseph faced divided loyalties, and as on other occasions his instinct for radicalism was overcome by the overbearing ascendancy of departmental tradition.

In preparing guide-lines for the new thinking on reorganisation, Joseph was most at home on questions relating to management. For instance, in his first meeting with the RHB Chairmen, the Secretary of State lectured them on the improvement of efficiency, the introduction of objective standards for measuring output, and on the need to establish a new elite cadre of managers. Issues such as the number of tiers, the constitution of authorities, and representation of constituencies such as local government and the medical profession, which had dominated the attention of Crossman, were hardly mentioned.[29]

Old points of controversy could not be evaded for long. Already the General Election and change of Government had introduced a further delay in preparations for reorganisation. The staff of the health service were disconcerted by frequent changes of policy and by equivocation. Public health staff were particularly demoralised owing to uncertainty of their fate after the breakup of their organisation following the Seebohm changes. Initially, DHSS hoped that the change of Government would not add greatly to the delay, but the original timetable, allowing for the production of a new consultative document by the end of 1970, was soon abandoned. In order to arrive at some kind of public statement of policy, the idea of producing a comprehensive plan was rejected in preference for the brief consultative document that was issued in May 1971, with the promise of a fuller White Paper in the summer of 1971.[30] This latter expectation also proved to be over-optimistic. The consultative document was first discussed with the Secretary of State on 12 October 1970; thereafter similar meetings were held at about monthly intervals to consider outstanding issues. Drafting of the consultative document formally began with the circulation of LP(70)1 on 19 October 1970.

Deliberations on the new policy document commanded the attention of the entire ministerial team, not only Joseph, but also Aberdare and Alison were heavily involved in discussions with officials and outside parties. Joseph was a conscientious student; he was meticulous in attending to the minutiae of the many submissions that he commissioned; by this means he built up a good command of the entire field. He was less erratic than Crossman, and less inclined to rely on outside observers, or ideas picked up in the course of discussion with the various pressure groups. Although many of the old causes of contention proved to be no less intractable, at least the Secretary of State seemed to be presiding over discussions that were moving forward towards a workable and widely-accepted conclusion.

Consensus was achieved by taking further steps to accommodate the essential demands of entrenched interests within the NHS, while also superimposing new features in response to the managerial ideology of the new Government. The effect of these changes was to further complicate the already over-complicated system handed down by Crossman. In the light of accumulating concessions to demands for additional layers of administration, Joseph warned that 'we cannot, must not, have 4 tiers', but just like Crossman, he was lured towards this unwelcome conclusion.

Rehabilitation of the Region
The first complication to be sanctioned was the confirmation of the region as an administrative tier. Crossman had already made concessions on this front by agreeing to augment the powers of his regional councils. Having earned a reprieve, the RHB Chairmen

campaigned for further enhancement of regional powers. Indeed, they claimed that, without a strong regional tier, it was pointless to pursue the reorganisation exercise.[31] Essentially the same view was communicated to Joseph by the leaders of the consultants.[32] This conclusion was known to command the support of the medical division of the department.

A final decision in favour of the region was delayed by virtue of opposition from some civil servants; both within the Treasury and DHSS there was a strong objection to the region on the ground that it would interfere with financial control of the areas. This judgement was strengthened when it was confirmed that Scotland and Wales were dispensing with the region.[33] However, by this stage Joseph had been exposed to the full argument in favour of the region and this coincided with his own instincts concerning management. The number of areas envisaged were in his view well beyond the effective span of control of the department; Joseph condemned as 'hubristic madness' any attempt by the department to exercise direct control of 90 area authorities.[34] Direct civil service control would therefore necessitate the radical expansion of regional offices. The Secretary of State was opposed to such a prefectoral form of administration, and he believed that it would trap civil servants into preoccupation with local disputes and prevent their concentration on issues of general principle and wider importance. Accordingly, at an early stage it was agreed that the consultative document would propose the full reinstatement of the region; although this conclusion was not greeted with enthusiasm by all officials, it was not effectively challenged.[35]

Areas, Districts and Consumer Interests
Reflecting the dominant view within the acute hospital sector, the RHB Chairmen made a bid for a reorganisation scheme comprising 18-20 regions and about 200 districts, thereby dispensing with the area, which had been the staple of both the first and second Green Papers. As indicated by the previous history, this suggestion, although justifiable on grounds of hospital planning, was completely unrealistic politically, since it would reopen the wounds of local government and also lead to the charge that co-ordination of health and social services was being jeopardised in the interests of appeasing the powerful hospital lobby. On the basis of the past history, Joseph was not inclined to reopen this question, among other things because he wanted to avoid renewed agitation for local authority take-over of the health services. Consequently, the consultative document preserved the area as the main statutory element of local organisation and also the related principle of identity of boundaries of health service areas and reorganised local

authorities responsible for the new social service departments. Aberdare briefly favoured adopting a region-district arrangement in London, but this idea was not pursued.

Vagueness about arrangements at the district level constituted one of the main weaknesses of the second Green Paper. This reflected discord within the department on this issue. When the question was reintroduced, the nursing interest within the department protested about any erosion of control by the area authority and opposed any move towards 'divisionalisation', whereas the medical lobby regarded the district as the basic operational unit, to be accorded maximum administrative autonomy. When this question was discussed with the Secretary of State, it was agreed, echoing the terminology coined by the Chief Medical Officer, that the district was the 'basic health service brick'.[36] As already noted, this reflected a dominant idea among hospital planners.

Although it was easy to appreciate the virtues of the district as a planning entity, it was notoriously difficult to arrive at tenable administrative structure for this tier of administration. The first Green Paper had been faulted for failing to provide any administration at the district level; the second Green Paper went some way towards meeting this criticism by introducing district committees. Responses to Crossman's scheme exposed considerable demand for representative committees at the district level. Since this was the main operational level for the service, the Chief Medical Officer was satisfied that districts should be managed by committees containing a strong participatory element, and he believed that it was unwise for the Government to frustrate this expectation. However, this view did not prevail. As in the case of Crossman, there was reluctance to formally identify the district as tier of administration, which was easier if it was not accorded the same statutory basis as the region and area. Also, freedom from the obligation to include representatives of the community avoided tangles about the criteria to be adopted for composition of district committees and facilitated imposition of a more rigorous management structure at this level. Consequently, it was agreed that there was 'no need to involve members of the community in the management at this level' and that management was best handled by a small executive of senior officers, although the precise form of this management structure itself proved extremely difficult to resolve.[37]

Given the arousal of expectations concerning community participation at the district level, it was necessary to find some meaningful substitute for district committees. Officials suggested some form of consumer council, possibly the equivalent to parent-teacher associations in schools. The Secretary of State was sceptical whether these would be helpful; either they would be given trivial powers and

460

therefore become ineffective, or they would be granted wider authority, in which case they would interfere with management. It was agreed to explore further this avenue for community participation.[38]

It proved difficult to arrive at a viable role for these community bodies. They were at first employed as a rag-bag for miscellaneous functions that were difficult to locate elsewhere in the administrative apparatus. It was suggested that community health councils could be locations where members of the area authority might meet representatives of the community. Alternatively, they could provide a forum for discussion of matters of mutual interest between health and social services authorities, or provide a convenient outlet for the energies of voluntary agencies and Leagues of Friends. Reflecting this uncertainty, virtually every discussion suggested a different name: 'Patients Services Councils', 'Consumer Services Councils', 'Patients Consultative Councils' were used in the earlier meetings; these names soon gave way to 'District Health Advisory Councils' and 'Community Health Advisory Councils'.[39] The less cumbersome term 'Community Health Council' was adopted in time for the first draft of the consultative document.

At the first full discussion of consumer councils it was recognised, especially by Alison, that insufficient account had been taken of the potential importance of these bodies. He urged that these consumer agencies could be of positive value to the health service, as well as being necessary palliatives to meet public anxieties about the managerial ethos of the reorganised health service.[40]

Chief Executives

Joseph was determined that reorganisation would be used to achieve a radical overhaul in NHS management arrangements. A report by the King's Fund, as well as research undertaken by Professor Jacques of Brunel University on behalf of DHSS, pointed out the complexity and confusion of existing management arrangements and underlined the virtues of general management.[41] As noted in chapter IV, this possibility had been proposed, but not pursued, on previous occasions. The Treasury was surprised and gratified when that these views resurfaced within DHSS. The suggestion of Jacques found some support in the hospital divisions of DHSS.[42]

Although the chief executive idea gained some friends among officials, those with experience of previous negotiations were at the best lukewarm about the prospects of gaining acceptance for such a momentous change within the NHS. The medical profession would be willing to 'support the principle of a general manager, but want to insist that all candidates other than doctors should be automatically disqualified from the post'. The ambiguities of current arrangements were a cause of annoyance to many other professional groups, but

461

they were unlikely to regard general management as a solution to their grievances. Many of them were likely to identify general management as a further threat to their influence and freedom. Advocates of general management were told that decisions on management structures needed to pay heed to political as well as efficiency factors.[43]

Despite warnings about opposition from the doctors and scepticism about the possibility of implementation, Joseph pressed forward enthusiastically with his plan for introducing a chief executive, arguing that this was the only means to attract able administrators and thereby convert management into a driving force within the health service.[44] Advice from officials pointed in the opposite direction. A comprehensive review of this subject pointed out that changes in the health service had tended to promote greater equality between senior professional and administrative staffs. Since non-clinicians were naturally unwilling to concede automatic right of doctors to occupy the top post, they tended to favour some form of collective leadership, each group of course demanding its own presence at the top of such executive structures. The department's review concluded that to appoint a 'single officer in executive command of the whole of the organisation, would be out of place in the new authorities'. It was therefore proposed to fall back on the idea of a 'co-ordinator' for the multidisciplinary team, to be selected by a special panel, which would give impartial consideration to candidates from every group involved in a senior management capacity.[45] A strongly negative reaction to the chief executive idea also emanated from the medical division of DHSS, which advocated the form of dual control traditionally exercised in RHBs. In Scotland, the chief executive idea had long been in favour among planners, but in the face of opposition from medical colleagues, SHHD also fell back on the 'duumvirate' solution.[46]

The Secretary of State continued to urge the advantages of appointing a chief executive. In the absence of support within his department, he turned for help from CSD and the Business Team, with whom relations were being re-established after the shaky start in 1970.[47] Joseph was unrepentant; he displayed none of the loss of self-confidence usual in his dealings with experts. He submitted that 'unless there was one person with ultimate responsibility, there was unlikely to be enough drive and purpose injected into the organisation'. This leadership was also needed to force local authorities to take their proper share of responsibility in developing the social services. Joseph was backed by Meyjes, but the idea of one superior officer was thought to be anathema to most of the senior personnel of health authorities. The most that was acceptable was some kind of loose co-ordination role. In view of the impasse on this fundamental issue, it was agreed to omit reference to the chief executive in the consultative document, and defer the subject for further consideration in the course of detailed examination of management arrangements, possibly involving the use of management consultants.[48] This provided a last tenuous life-line for Joseph's favourite idea.

Ministers and Consultative Documents

Despite many continuing points of uncertainly, conclusions on a sufficiently comprehensive range of items were reached to merit circulating a draft of the consultative document to other departments on 23 December.[49] This target was easier to achieve by virtue of the earlier decision to issue only a short consultative document. The circulated draft indeed achieved this objective; it was extremely brief, in fact only about two thousand words long, approximately one-eighth the length of the second Green Paper.

A slightly revised version of this document was circulated on 15 February 1971; this was essentially the same as the memorandum eventually submitted to Ministers. Officials hoped to issue the consultative document as soon as possible after the White Paper on Local Government Reorganisation, which was published on 16 February 1971.

Joseph was disappointed that the draft consultative document omitted his idea about management by chief executive, but efficient and integrated management was self-evidently elevated into the dominant theme of the document. Also, the way was left open for further management improvements by the promise of two urgent policy reviews, the first dealing with management arrangements within health authorities, and the second with co-operation between health authorities and local authority social service departments.

The problems associated with multiplication of tiers were to some extent concealed by preserving the main emphasis on the area, achieved by confining reference to the district to some passing remarks in the section dealing with the area, and locating the section on the region after that on the area, and finally by expressing proposals for the region in low-key terms.

Commitment to efficiency and sound management now became the most important stated objective of reorganisation. The Treasury was told that 'the overall aim will be to create an efficient structure that promotes good management in the NHS, and this will be the keynote of our proposals'.[50] This basis was evident in the draft, for instance in the sentiment that found its way with very little change into many later documents: 'there should be maximum delegation downwards, matched by accountability upwards; and that a sound management structure should be created at all levels. The line of delegation downwards (with corresponding accountability upwards) would be from the Central Department to regional health authorities, and from the regional health authorities to area health authorities'.[51]

The most evident signal of Joseph's primary commitment to management was his abandonment of the representational conception of health authorities. Completely jettisoning the complicated formulae evolved by Crossman for allocation of places on management bodies, Joseph proposed that the Secretary of State should appoint regional and area chairmen, as well as all members of the regional authority, and that the latter would appoint members of the area authority. An undertaking was given that health authorities would contain local authority and health profession members, but no indication was given concerning their numbers. The statement that appointment would depend on 'ability to contribute to the work of the body concerned' was taken as a sign that management abilities were the primary qualification for membership.[52] Although the criteria for appointing health authority members were taken as a concession to the management ethos, and indeed marked a radical departure from the principles applied by Crossman, Joseph's proposals were not in fact very different from the existing method of appointing the membership of RHBs and HMCs.

Campbell was even more opposed than Joseph to the representative conception of area health authorities. As already noted, Scotland was committed to dispensing with the regional tier. With warm support from the Treasury, SHHD proposed to treat their area authorities as the equivalents to regional authorities in England, thereby justifying the appointment of all members by the Secretary of State. It was realised that this analogy was not altogether easy to sustain and required careful presentation. At this stage, it was agreed between the English and Scottish health departments that introduction of representation in one part of the Great Britain would entail its application in all three health services.[53]

Despite some worries that the management emphasis of the draft consultative document was little more than a veneer, the Treasury was in general relieved with this shift in perspective. A detailed comparison between the second Green Paper and the draft consultative document pronounced the latter a great improvement in all respects.[54] However, the Treasury warned against complacency. It remained to be seen whether the DHSS internal review would result in a reorganised department able to effectively determine national objectives, priorities and standards, and operate more effectively in allocating resources to regional authorities. There was also a risk that management bodies would become too large, and that it would be impossible to retain their strictly non-representational character in the face of complaints from local authorities and the professions. The Treasury was also concerned about lack of definition of the role of the district, which seemed likely to evolve into a third tier, where community health councils might interfere with the efficiency of management. Notwithstanding these reservations, Treasury officials advised their Ministers to give positive support for the draft consultative document.[55]

At this stage an unforeseen hazard materialised. Hitherto, the Treasury and CSD had adopted a common approach to NHS reorganisation, but at this last hurdle their consensus dissolved. Although CSD welcomed the managerial emphasis of the draft consultative document, it came out in favour of the more radical alternative of hiving off the health service to an independent corporation headed by a director general. This idea gained in force because it emanated from the highest level within CSD, and it seemed at least in part to be instigated by the Business Team. CSD insisted that its plan was the only means to bring about completely integrated and unified management within the NHS. Although, as already noted in chapter IV, the Treasury had previously flirted with the idea of a NHS corporation, by 1971 it had completely rejected this alternative, which it regarded as naive and impracticable. The Treasury mounted an aggressive campaign directed at all levels within CSD to abort this unwelcome initiative. CSD was accused of trying to destroy the health department and undermine the emerging consensus concerning Joseph's plan.[56] Indeed, the CSD proposal was presented as a retrograde step, since it 'was wholly counter to the object of securing proper integration at all levels of policy and management which we have throughout been trying to achieve, and which Sir Keith Joseph's proposals would take us a long way towards achieving'. The Treasury also feared that the medical profession would gain control of the management structure and thereby add to the pressure for greater expenditure. The Treasury therefore warned CSD of the dangers of its 'highly mechanistic approach to management'.[57] A blitz of criticism from the Treasury eventually sapped the ardour of CSD for its radical idea of hiving off the NHS to an independent corporation, but it refused to allow this proposal to be entirely laid to rest.

In their exceptional display of harmony over the preparation of the consultative document, the Treasury and DHSS completely miscalculated about the receptivity of Ministers to their programme for imposing a rigorous managerial framework on the NHS. Conservative Ministers turned out to share many of their Labour predecessors' sensitivities on the principle of representation on health authorities. Joseph was therefore not entirely spared from the kind of Ministerial disagreements that had afflicted his Labour predecessors.

Discussion at the Social Services Committee treated most other aspects of the reorganisation plans for England, Scotland and Wales as a formality, but Ministers were not convinced by Joseph's exposition of the management philosophy.[58] Joseph claimed that any system of representative health authority membership was inimical to sound management. Local authority members were likely to be particularly irresponsible; he even suggested that health authority membership would be used as a solatium to compensate failed aspirants for local authority office. Understandably, opposition to Joseph was led by Peter Walker, Secretary of State for the Environment, and Peter Thomas, Secretary of State for Wales, both Ministers responsible for local government. They argued that the abandonment of the representative principle would be unpopular with the public, who would compare this approach unfavourably with Crossman's scheme. Joseph's proposals were also criticised for being inconsistent with the Government's stated policy on devolution of powers to local government, which had been forcefully and repeatedly declared when in opposition. They refuted any suggestion that local government representatives were any less effective than ministerial appointees. It was anticipated that local authorities would be needlessly antagonised by these proposals, which they would take as an aspersion of incompetence.[59]

At the Social Services Committee, Joseph was backed by the Treasury, CSD and Scottish representatives, but no agreement was reached, with the result that the Home Secretary had no choice but to refer the controversy to the Cabinet. The Treasury was dismayed by this result; it was 'no exaggeration to say that the proposal to give the managerial structure a representative basis would wreck' the reorganisation scheme.[60] Walker was accused of wanting power without responsibility and of promoting managerial chaos. Given the possibility that Joseph's plans might collapse into disarray, CSD insisted on keeping open the possibility that the Lord Privy Seal, with support from Meyjes, would reintroduce the proposal to hive off the NHS to an independent corporation. It was added: 'we understand that the Secretary of State [Joseph] may be prepared to accept this', an assertion which alarmed the Treasury, where there was relief when DHSS confirmed that Joseph opposed the CSD suggestion.[61]

Despite forewarning from the Social Services Committee, in Cabinet Joseph seemed taken aback by the hostility of his colleagues. His opening remarks merely reiterated his belief that representation was unacceptable because it was subversive to efficiency. He was supported in a perfunctory manner by the Secretary of State for

Scotland (Campbell), the Chancellor of the Exchequer (Barber), Lord Privy Seal (Earl Jellicoe), and the Secretary of State for Education and Science (Thatcher). As in the Social Services Committee, the opposition to Joseph was led by the Secretary of State for the Environment (Walker) and the Secretary of State for Wales (Thomas). Therefore, of the Ministers directly involved with the health services, Joseph was supported by the Minister responsible for the health service in Scotland, but opposed by his counterpart from Wales.

The Cabinet went over the same ground as the Social Services Committee. It was pointed out that in opposition the Conservatives had called for health authorities comprising equal numbers of local authority and professional members. It was also contended that local authority acquiescence to the loss of their health services and their co-operation over unification of health services had been conditional on being granted a substantial voice in the management of the reorganised health service. Peremptory rejection of the representative principle would therefore look like a breach of faith. These arguments against Joseph were strongly supported by the Chancellor of the Duchy of Lancaster (Rippon). The Secretary of State for Employment (Carr), supported by the Lord President (Whitelaw) and Secretary of State for Defence (Carrington), suggested that it was not worth quarrelling with local authorities over this question because the efficiency of health authorities depended primarily on the management structure adopted for the officers.

Joseph mounted an unconvincing defence of his position. Having prematurely implied that health authorities would be headed by a chief executive, he pleaded that this officer would need the guidance of an effective policy/management board, which he thought could only be constituted from ministerial appointees. By way of compensation for absence of representation at the regional and area levels, Joseph offered to introduce 40 per cent local authority membership on district committees. This represented a further questionable presupposition, since it was unlikely that such district committees would be introduced, since they were completely unacceptable to the Treasury, also inconsistent with Joseph's own strictures against a district tier, and inimical to the idea of management by an executive of senior officers favoured within DHSS. Joseph further undermined the credibility of his position by conceding that he would willingly accept local authority representation, but was chary about making this concession since it would strengthen the demand of the medical profession for similar treatment. Having thrown away the case for his management-orientated reform, Joseph was asked by the Prime Minister to

467

reconsider his proposals with a view to obtaining an acceptable compromise between the management and representation camps.[62]

In the interval before the next deliberations on membership of health authorities by the Social Services Committee, the positions of DHSS and SHHD drifted apart. If concessions were necessary, DHSS preferred granting representation to local authorities but was opposed to any concession to the medical profession, whereas SHHD was confident about resisting local authorities, but was willing to concede representation to the medical profession. SHHD tried out various compromise proposals; first including local authority and medical representatives on health authorities as 'assessors', which was rejected by the Department of the Environment and therefore not tried out on the doctors; secondly, inclusion of 3 local authority and 4 professional members on health authorities, which was rejected by DHSS, and not liked by Treasury and CSD. In the absence of common ground, SHHD suggested that its areas should be treated as the analogues of English regions, justifying the appointment of all members by the Secretary of State. This was an awkward position to maintain, especially because the Welsh Office (which was also abolishing the region), proposed to treat its areas like the English areas.[63] The Treasury recommended its Ministers to support direct appointment of all members of area authorities by the Secretary of State or his agents, failing that, to concede that local authorities should appoint assessors, and as a final fall-back position, they should resist any direct appointment by the health professions on the grounds that this would 'be creating a syndicalist's system in which excessive weight was given to special interests'.[64]

At the Social Services Committee, Joseph proposed a compromise whereby local authorities would be allowed to appoint three out of the fourteen members of area authorities, while the Secretary of State would also undertake to appoint two doctors and one nurse or midwife.[65] This concession gained the support of Thomas, but it was indignantly rejected by other proponents of representation, because it made less concession to community participation than under the Labour proposals, or in previous policy statements by the Conservatives. The package was mocked as a vote of no-confidence in local authorities. Once again the Home Secretary was obliged to refer the disagreement to the full Cabinet for further discussion.[66]

Treasury Ministers were once again advised to concede minimum local authority representation on the understanding that no parallel concession to the medical profession would be offered.[67] The Cabinet discussion in most respects a recapitulated the previous debate, with a similar alignment of forces. On this occasion the Secretary of State for Education made no contribution, but Joseph was supported by the Chief Secretary to the Treasury (Macmillan).

Campbell urged that the Secretary of State should appoint all members of Scottish area boards, whereas Thomas proposed to allow local authority representation on his area authorities; he also warned that public opinion was likely to demand an even greater element of representation. Walker and his allies repeated their argument and the Minister of Agriculture (Prior) added his voice to their criticism. The Home Secretary (who on this occasion was presiding) broke the impasse by pointing out that Joseph was only issuing a consultative document; it was therefore agreed that the consultative document should be amended to make explicit reference to the intention to include representatives of the local authorities. Joseph proposed making allowance for 'three' local authority representatives, but the Lord President suggested 'a few', and the meeting compromised with the Home Secretary's suggestion 'some', with the understanding that Joseph would attempt to keep this number down to three.[68]

The path was now clear for the issue of the new round of planning documents. The English and Welsh consultative documents were published on 17 May and 8 June 1971 respectively.[69] Arrangements for reorganisation were more advanced in Scotland, where in May 1971 the Scottish Office issued a consultative document on the outstanding issue of central management arrangements, preparing the way for the publication in July 1971 of the White Paper, *Reorganisation of the Scottish Health Services* (Cmnd.4734). Further developments in Scotland and Wales will be considered separately in later sections of this chapter.

(ii) ENGLISH CONSULTATIVE DOCUMENT

The English Consultative Document was more than twice the length of the draft circulated in December 1970, but the body of the text was changed very little and expanded to only a modest extent.[70] The main difference between the two versions was the inclusion in Consultative Document of a long introductory foreword by the Secretary of State, amounting to about 1,300 words, longer in fact than its counterparts in the first and second Green Papers.

The Consultative Document was strikingly different in appearance from its predecessors; although the two Green Papers were entirely conventional in design, they were at least efficiently typeset and issued in the standard format of Government publication as Command Papers by HMSO. By contrast, the Consultative Document was an in-house product of DHSS, reproduced in the A4 format usually reserved for less important documents, and in design reflecting the capacities and limitations of the electric typewriter and an operator with only a moderate eye for presentational detail.[71]

469

The Secretary of State excused the brevity of the document on the grounds that it was not necessary to repeat what had been agreed already. However, the Consultative Document was not very forthcoming on matters which constituted innovations of the new Government. Important aspects of reorganisation were passed over with little attention to essential detail, or deferred for later consideration. The entire exercise bore many hallmarks of hasty compilation and indecision. A fuller statement of the Government's intentions was reserved for a future White Paper.[72]

The bulk of the text of the Consultative Document was taken up with the brief sketch of the region:area:district scheme, summarising the provisional conclusions mentioned above. With respect to the geography of the scheme, it was proposed to follow the current regional pattern, except for division of the Sheffield region.[73] The areas outside London were to be determined by the recently-announced plan for local government reorganisation.[74] With respect to the intractable problem of area organisation within London, the second Green Paper introduced a specific plan, but the Consultative Document stepped back from this commitment and the problem was deferred for further consideration.[75]

Family practitioner services were said to 'occupy a central position' in the health service, but primary care was dismissed in a dozen lines, presumably on the understanding that arrangements would be consistent with the second Green Paper, although the Consultative Document was vague on this point.[76] With reference to teaching hospitals, the Consultative Document was more forthcoming than the second Green Paper, which largely ignored this problem. In response to the teaching hospitals' anxieties about integration, some space was devoted to protection of their traditions and endowments.[77]

The Consultative Document if anything further exaggerated the emphasis on efficient management contained in the early drafts. Indeed, the leader of the Business Team had assisted with the redrafting.[78] According to the BMA, the word 'management' was used 30 times in this short document.[79] The key slogan about maximum delegation downwards and accountability upwards already quoted from the draft, was included in its entirety.[80] The bias towards management was also reinforced by elimination of the more idealistic passages about improving services, such as the purpose of reorganisation being 'to secure the greatest possible benefit to the public' or to 'make available good facilities for prevention, diagnosis, treatment and care'.[81]

With respect to the management armory, continuing disagreements meant that it was not possible to make reference to the Secretary of State's ideas about chief executives. The only hint at such thoughts came with the intention to refer management arrangements to 'an expert study', rather than the 'detailed study' promised in the draft.[82] The management bias of the Consultative Document was eroded by the inclusion at Cabinet insistence of a substantial reference to local authority representation at area level. In light of the outcome of the controversy among Ministers over the number of local authority nominees described above, at the eleventh hour the text was emended; 'three' was removed and replaced with 'some'.[83] This vagueness produced an unfortunate inconsistency, because a few lines later a commitment was given to include among the Secretary of State's appointees, a specific number of professional members: 'at least two doctors and a nurse or midwife, appointed after consultation with the professions'.[84] Although intended to be responsive to their demands for participation, this form of presentation was liable to convince both local authorities and the medical profession that they were being treated unfairly. Modest steps were nevertheless offered towards restoring the representational character of area authorities, although still falling short of the second Green Paper. The section of the Consultative Document on community health councils failed to reflect this change, when it explained that the 'creation of a strong managerial structure for the regional and area authorities' necessitated compensating 'representational mechanism by which local attitudes can be known and safeguards built in'.[85] In fact, owing to the concession of representation at the area level, the community health council now constituted an additional participatory element, although the proposal to place the power of appointments to community health councils in the hands of the area health authority largely undermined the credibility of this well-intentioned innovation.

Consistent with the decision to publish the Consultative Document departmentally, it was also decided to limit its distribution. Compared with the 80,000 copies of the second Green Paper produced and largely sold out by HMSO, it was initially decided to restrict the print-run of the Consultative Document to 2,500; this was later revised to 5,000. It was at first intended to limit special distribution of this publication to 14 organisations, later revised to 20, which excluded such important bodies as the Royal College of General Practitioners and National Association of Hospital Management Committees.[86] This decision to adopt a restrictive approach to consultation was dictated by the pressure of the reorganisation timetable, as well as a disinclination to embark on yet another round of full consultation, and perhaps also an instinct to avoid another bruising round of confrontation. In the event this defensiveness proved to be misplaced.

As already indicated, the first Green Paper was widely condemned; many concessions to NHS interests earned the second Green Paper a better reception; further concessions resulted in an even more positive response to the Consultative Document. There was a relaxed response even among the doctors, the group most inclined to pessimism about government planning documents; two-thirds of the respondents to a *General Practitioner* survey thought that the new proposals were practicable.[87]

Joseph also benefited from signs of war-weariness among the combatants, where there was a realisation that compromises were inevitable, given the deadline imposed by imminent local government reorganisation. Thus, despite its hurried production, and evident limitations, Joseph's Consultative Document received a more tolerant treatment than its Labour predecessors. In fact there was relatively little press interest. The *Times* summed up the initial response: it welcomed the full reinstatement of the region, but complained that the document contained too little to satisfy and reassure the public. The *Times* contended that 'efficiency is not the sole criterion' for determination of policy on reorganisation.[88] *New Society* and the *British Medical Journal* were also suspicious about the importation of industrial styles of management into the NHS, but for different reasons; the former was concerned about the 'undemocratic' drift of the changes, whereas the latter was more concerned about erosion of the influence of the medical profession.[89] The leading medical journals were at odds over proposed statutory committees for family practitioners; the *British Medical Journal* demanded fuller guarantees about the independence of these committees, whereas the *Lancet* regarded separate committees as subversive to the objective of unification.[90] The *New Statesman* represented the negative wing of the critics, declaring that the Consultative Document was 'wrecking the health services' and that its proposals were distrusted by managers, doctors and patients.[91] Adverse response to the Consultative Document was not limited to the left. For instance, Dr F A D.Anderson, a leading academic in the field of community medicine, and Geoffrey Smith, a *Times* columnist, acting on hints in a Nuffield Provincial Hospitals Trust publication, both suggested that the new scheme was likely to fail in its essential purpose of unifying the health service. By transferring social services relating to health to local government, and granting of separate statutory committees for family practitioners, the Government would in effect perpetuate the tripartite system, leading to the greater dominance of the hospital sector, and precluding unified planning. Smith concluded that Joseph's plan for reorganisation might well be positively detrimental to the effectiveness of the health service.[92]

Despite the existence of such reservations, response to the Consultative Document within the health service was generally supportive. By contrast with their passionate opposition to the second Green Paper, the RHB Chairmen were enthusiastic about the Joseph proposals principally on account of the reinstatement and strengthening of the regional tier. They were not happy with the establishment of areas on the basis of coterminosity with local authorities since this would create too much diversity in the size of these health authorities. The RHB Chairmen continued to advocate local arrangements based on districts rather than areas. But the provision for district management met their approval, especially if the Secretary of State would permit area authorities to establish district committees for non-teaching as well as teaching districts. In common with most of the NHS administration, the RHB Chairmen's primary reservation related to community health councils, the usefulness of which they doubted.[93] Outside the NHS, the opposite view was prevalent. There was widespread demand for community health councils to be given a stronger voice within the reorganised health service, compensating for the erosion of the participatory element in the proposed management structure. Even the doctors expressed anxiety that the consumer voice would be eliminated under the Consultative Document proposals. The GMSC doubted 'whether bodies dependent upon those whom it may be their duty to criticise can be effective in looking after community interests', while the *Lancet* declared that 'the public will be justified in considering that its opinion is neither wanted nor obtained'.[94] The National Association of HMCs complained that the community health councils would become 'tea party affairs of the Leagues of Friends' unless they were radically strengthened.[95]

Sir Keith Joseph defended his Green Paper in the House of Commons on the occasion of a short debate inspired by the opposition. Joseph confined himself to a low-key descriptive account of the Consultative Document.[96] The opposition attack was lead by Mrs Shirley Williams, who used robust language, but said little of significance, although her strictures about the limited availability of the Consultative Document and the little time available for comment reflected a widespread complaint.[97] The main event in this debate was a revealing speech from Crossman, who lamented about the split between the health and social services, which he believed would stand in the way of true unification of services. He offered no defence of his own Green Paper, instead regretting that the Labour Government had been prevented by the medical veto from coming out in favour of local government administration of the health services. He also attacked his old foes, the regional boards, the members of which he castigated as 'satraps' or 'self-aggrandised oligarchs', or wielders of 'obnoxious power'. The former Secretary of State asserted that local government provided the only legitimate basis for accountability; the solution proposed by Joseph was to isolate the health service further from its community and place it in the hands of an 'imperceptive machine' dominated by regional boards and civil servants.[98] Although this debate was not an important test of the Government, negative responses were sufficiently evident to prevent any sense of elation on the part of the Secretary of State, who was dejected: 'We had a dismal half-day in the Debate on the Consultative Document - not a friend in sight!'[99] Although most of the criticism came from the opposition benches, Joseph could not rely on solid support from his own side. For instance, even upon the question of the region, where consensus seemed to be in sight, he discovered that an influential group of Conservative MPs favoured return to the plan contained in the second Green Paper.[100]

Revision of the Consultative Document
Joseph initially hoped for a quick consultation process, followed by issue of a White Paper in the summer of 1971, and introduction of legislation during the 1971/72 session. However, he pressed the case for a place in the 1971/72 legislative programme only weakly. Whitelaw pointed out that congestion of the legislative timetable, and especially the need to find a place for EEC legislation, effectively ruled out a NHS reorganisation Bill until 1972/3.[101] The new target date adopted for the NHS reorganisation legislation to reach the statute book was Easter 1973, the very latest date practicable if the NHS was to be reorganised in April 1974.

The Secretary of State recognised that deferment of the White Paper would exacerbate anxiety and uncertainty among NHS staff, and would produce an embarrassingly short timetable for the legislation and implementation of reorganisation.[102] However, the new timetable released the department from the almost impossible task of producing the White Paper by the summer of 1971. The new preference was for publication during the first half of 1972, but there was an argument for an even later date, to allow for inclusion of the main findings of the management and local authority collaboration studies.[103] Even this extended timetable was likely to yield a White Paper having some 'green edges'. In the event, delays in completing the management and collaboration studies necessitated a much greater 'green' element in the White Paper, even when publication of the White Paper was delayed until the 1972 summer recess.

A draft 'full summary' was produced in July 1971; this was converted into a definitive summary, which was circulated in September 1971. There was then a delay during which the full draft of the White Paper was drawn up. This was first circulated in May

1972 and in revised form submitted to the Home and Social Affairs Committee in June 1972.[104] In May and June 1971 Joseph discussed the Consultative Document with many health service administrative groups.[105] It was not until November 1971 that he received a delegation from the BMA and JCC, which was in fact his first full-dress discussion of reorganisation with the medical profession since he had assumed office. The medical delegates complained about lack of consultation over the Consultative Document; they demanded and received assurances that they would have more opportunity to participate in the next stage of planning. In particular, it was accepted that their views would be taken into account by the various working parties; the medical profession also demanded substantial representation on these working parties.[106]

Despite the positive reception of the Consultative Document, there were many delicate problems still to be resolved. Hitherto, policy issues concerning reorganisation had been decided within the health department on an informal basis, with varying degrees of consultation with outside parties. The Consultative Document imposed an obligation on the Secretary of State to remit to formal working parties two major outstanding issues, first, management arrangements within the health authorities, and secondly, collaboration between the NHS and local government. It was also necessary to co-ordinate these exercises with the Hunter working party on medical administrators. In addition to these formal enquiries, the department needed to arrive at final decisions on such important issues as the definition of regional boundaries, administrative arrangements for teaching hospitals, adaptations needed in London, the role of community health councils, introduction of a new complaints mechanism and the Health Service Commissioner, and the relationship of the NHS with such services as the school health service, environmental health, and the ambulance service. As in 1948 the Government also came under pressure, especially from the medical profession, to include occupational health within the National Health Service. This represented a formidable agenda of awkward problems, the solution of which had defied the previous Labour government. Given the proximity of reorganisation, final commitment was now unavoidable, and the timetable for the NHS Bill meant that the late summer of 1972 constituted the final deadline for decision.

Regions and Areas
The 1974 reorganisation necessitated a complete review of regional arrangements. As noted in chapter IV, the first Green Paper dispensed with the region completely; this was one of the issues which perplexed Crossman; the region was reinstated in the second

Green Paper, but with reduced powers. The Consultative Document indicated renewed commitment to the region, but left open the possibility of boundary alterations. Boundary changes of local government reorganisation also necessitated modification of regional boundaries since, by contrast with 1948, it was accepted that regional boundaries would not cut across the boundaries of counties and metropolitan districts.

Crossman found difficulty in deciding about the number of regions to adopt. At first Joseph was similarly undecided. The Treasury favoured a reduction to ten regions, but a visit to Wessex convinced Joseph that the small region should be the model. He therefore commissioned a feasibility study to consider establishing some 20 regions.[107] In preparation for a consultative document, many possibilities for creating new regions were considered, but all were found to be objectionable. Consideration of splitting the Birmingham and South Western regions into two were quickly abandoned. The only viable options for new regions were in the North West and East Midlands. There was a case for establishing a new region containing no teaching hospital in the North West; this would be centred on Preston and Lancaster, and would include Cumberland and North Lancashire. Existing sub-regional committees of the Newcastle and Manchester RHBs concerned with these north-western areas provided something of a trial run for a new region of this kind.[108] The second area suitable for recognition as a new region was the East Midlands, where a new medical school at Nottingham was being established, while a new medical school for Leicester was at the planning stage. It was therefore no longer realistic to argue that the East Midlands needed to be maintained within the orbit of the Sheffield medical school. Regardless of the medical school criterion, formation of the Wessex region in 1959 had demonstrated that it was possible to create a viable region without notional dependence on some distant medical school.

After elimination of less suitable candidates, the shortlist for inclusion in the consultative document was narrowed down to two: the North-West Pennines area and the East Midlands.[109] It was decided that a Pennines region would be too small to be viable. It was therefore agreed to extend the Newcastle region to form a new northern region containing a larger segment to the west of the Pennines, constituting the new county of Cumbria, formed the old counties of Cumberland, Westmorland and the part of north Lancashire in the area of Barrow-in-Furness.[110] The Consultative Document cited the East Midlands as the sole candidate suitable for development as a new region.[111] This proposal was warmly welcomed in the East Midlands, where there was long-standing resentment of what was seen as subjugation to Yorkshire. The development of the

476

long-awaited medical school at Nottingham gave focus to the demands of the midlanders, although prospects of a medical school at Leicester produced a complication and suggested that binary fission of the Sheffield region was not the only alternative. Also, it was difficult to arrive at a suitable boundary between Sheffield and East Midland regions without cutting across the boundaries of the counties of Nottingham and Derby, which was not acceptable under the principles governing reorganisation. Many permutations were tried, which involved recombinations including elements from the East Anglia, Birmingham and Oxford regions. In view of these difficulties it was decided to abandon plans for the East Midlands region. This was a useful learning exercise because it demonstrated that the cherished notion in health service circles that the existing regions were 'natural' entities was built upon a myth.[112]

The requirement to avoid cutting across local government boundaries created problems for other regions. For instance, the formation of the county of Humberside from the East Riding of Yorkshire (part of the Leeds RHB), and the Scunthorpe and Grimsby districts of Lindsey adjacent to the River Humber (part of the Sheffield RHB), necessitated one of the two rival Yorkshire regions ceding territory to the other. Since the decision was made in favour of Leeds, it was politically helpful to confirm Sheffield's hold over the East Midlands.

A particularly complicated boundary problem was raised by the old county of Wiltshire, which in 1948 was split between the Oxford and South Western regions, and with the arrival of the Wessex region, Wiltshire was divided between three regions. Under reorganisation it was proposed to include Wiltshire in the Wessex region, which had the effect of isolating Swindon from parts of its hospital catchment area, and more seriously, it threatened links between West Wiltshire (transferred from the South Western Region to Wessex) and the nearby hospital facilities of Bath, which was part of the new county of Avon, thereby located in the South Western Region. This arrangement, although geographically anomalous, was attractive to the administrators because it increased the span of control of this small and compact region from two to three counties and health authority areas.[113] Within the Wessex region, the Isle of Wight represented a further minor complication, indicating the degree to which NHS reorganisation was affected by the politics of local government reorganisation. The health department intended to include the Isle of Wight within the Hampshire area authority, and this was indicated in the 1972 White Paper. However, at the last moment, the Local Government Bill was amended to give the Isle of Wight the status of a separate county, thereby forcing the health department to follow suit and somewhat reluctantly establish the Isle of Wight as the smallest area authority in the English health service.[114]

Reorganisation also raised questions about the viability of boundaries in the London metropolitan area. Already in 1959, with the formation of the Wessex region, the South West Metropolitan region lost its western segment. There had long been dissatisfaction with the lack of unified administration of the hospital system in the capital. In some respects there was greater integration before the NHS was established. The GLC in particular called for a single regional authority; in the hospital world there was some support for two regions, with the Thames as the dividing line. A particular anomaly was created by the concentration of teaching hospitals in the North West Metropolitan region. The Todd Report suggested greater equalisation of the northern sectors by creation of a new north-central region, constituted from parts of the North West Metropolitan and North East Metropolitan regions. Although this proposal had its supporters, it was not adopted, although greater equalisation of teaching hospitals was created by transfer of the Boroughs of Camden and Islington (including two major undergraduate teaching hospitals, University College and the Royal Free) to the North East Metropolitan Region. The effect of these changes was to raise the population of the North East Metropolitan Region by half a million. However, the problem of imbalance was not altogether resolved; Westminster, Chelsea and Kensington (including the Westminster undergraduate teaching hospital) were absorbed into the North West Metropolitan Region, therefore maintaining the comfortable dominance of this region in the teaching hospital field.[115]

London and the Teaching Hospitals
In Scotland teaching hospitals were integrated into the regional system at the outset of the NHS. The Todd Report favoured moving England and Wales in the same direction. Expansion in medical education made the persistence of entirely separate administration of teaching hospitals increasingly untenable. It was no longer possible for teaching hospitals to fulfil their obligations utilising the limited numbers of beds under their direct control. This problem was most acute in London where, in order to fulfil their teaching responsibilities effectively, the undergraduate teaching hospitals required access to virtually all the beds in the inner London area. A positive step towards more effective co-ordination in the utilisation of hospital resources was the establishment in May 1967 of the Joint Working Group of the Thames Joint Consultative Committees.

From the outset of discussions concerning reorganisation it was assumed that teaching hospitals in England and Wales would be assimilated into the general health service administration. Indeed, a first tentative step in this direction was taken in 1965, when it was announced that the new teaching hospital in Nottingham would be administered by a specially constituted Hospital Management Committee of the Sheffield Regional Hospital Board, rather than by a Board of Governors. This represented a notable victory for the Sheffield region, which had enjoyed indifferent relations with the Sheffield Board of Governors. It soon became clear that this move was the precedent to more wide-ranging changes.

The teaching hospitals themselves were unenthusiastic about sacrificing their special status. At first the Teaching Hospitals Association was adverse to change and cited in its favour the Goodenough, Guillebaud and Porritt reports. However, these were superseded by the Todd Report, which was firmly on the other side. Consequently, the Teaching Hospitals Association fell back on laying down conditions for protecting the interests of the teaching hospitals. Especially with respect to the provincial teaching hospitals, the Teaching Hospitals Association and other relevant organisations approached integration with resignation and generally in a constructive manner. However, an influential rump within the teaching hospital leadership, especially in London, vigorously opposed change, and they received some support from within the DHSS. They were unwilling to drift with the tide created by the Todd Report, which they regarded as apostasy.

Needless to say, the twelve undergraduate teaching hospitals and fourteen postgraduate teaching hospitals of London represented a powerful interest group - more strictly, two powerful pressure groups, since their interests only partly coincided.[116] The Green Papers gave the London teaching hospitals little comfort. The first proposed to divide London into five or six areas, including two for the inner London area. These arrangements were calculated to accord with the thinking of the recent Todd Report.[117] The Crossman Green Paper paid little attention to the teaching hospitals, but it included an appendix containing a scheme for London, in which it was proposed to establish in central London five, mainly paired groups of boroughs, containing all the undergraduate teaching hospitals, while the remaining boroughs were to be grouped into eleven areas.[118] These proposals were even less palatable to the teaching hospitals than the Todd recommendations for linking undergraduate teaching hospitals in pairs and assimilating the postgraduate hospitals into the undergraduate structures.

Given the incompatible objectives of the various powerful and articulate organisations involved in health service planning in London, it is not surprising that the Working Party established under the Minister of State during the last months of the Labour administration to consider the application of the second Green Paper principles made virtually no progress. During the drafting of the consultative document the department drew up a plan designed to appease the various interest groups, without stirring up unrest in other parts of the country. It was proposed to establish seven health areas from the thirteen inner London boroughs, six of which would contain teaching districts. At this stage, no attempt was made to keep strict correspondence between health service and borough boundaries. If pairing of teaching hospitals was adopted, then each pair would be within a single district. It was proposed to absorb postgraduate hospitals into the area administration.[119]

Aberdare was initially unsympathetic with the department scheme; instead he advocated the plan favoured by the London undergraduate board secretaries entailing establishment of 13 health districts in inner London, not following borough boundaries, and based on the 12 undergraduate teaching hospitals and the Hammersmith Hospital. He also favoured excluding postgraduate hospitals from the district structure.[120]

The teaching hospital problem threw Joseph into one of his great states of indecision. At first he drifted along with the dominant integrationist line within the department. Then, after exposure to the propaganda of the Teaching Hospitals Association, he was convinced that the teaching hospitals should be preserved as independent entities because they were the only part of the hospital system embodying the form of sound management that the Secretary of State was attempting to propagate. He therefore decided that the teaching hospitals should be preserved for the sake of their 'identity, pride and, in many cases, quality of management'. He appreciated that the interests of integration might involve sacrificing the provincial teaching hospitals, but if this proved necessary, it might be possible to establish something like the Inner London Education Authority to preserve the independence of the London teaching hospitals.[121] This drift of opinion among the Ministers was entirely contrary to thinking within the department. Ministers were tempted by the 'doughnut' offered by the teaching hospitals, thereby spurning the 'starfish' advocated within the department.[122]

The department was already aware of opposition among the postgraduate teaching hospitals to forced marriages with haphazardly selected undergraduate partners. As a protective measure, the postgraduate hospitals proposed a federal form of administration designed to permanently protect their independence. In order to meet the views of the Minister of State, but also prevent the construction of an alternative defensive organisation, the department reluctantly agreed to abandon its proposals for immediate assimilation, and agreed to extend the life of the Board of Governors of the postgraduate hospitals, but it was emphasised that this was a transitional arrangement, creating a period during which the department would promote 'closer association of each hospital with its appropriate undergraduate partner and its local responsibilities'.[123]

Shelving plans for assimilation of the postgraduate hospitals was a convenient way to buy-off half of the teaching hospital lobby opposing the Government's plans for integration. The proposed transitional arrangements were not greatly subversive to integration of services in London, and it was assumed that the postgraduate hospitals would eventually be swept along by the tide created by the Todd reforms. Also, since the postgraduate hospitals were unique to London, there was no risk of adverse repercussions elsewhere. However, any retreat from integration of the undergraduate teaching hospitals would undermine the unified development of health services in the London area, and create demand for retaining the independence of teaching hospitals elsewhere.

The department was disappointed that the Ministers were not satisfied that the proposed teaching district committees would be able to protect the sound management and positive identity of the teaching hospitals. Officials argued that these arrangements should be strengthened rather than integration be abandoned. Joseph's advisers complained that the London undergraduate teaching hospitals were merely trying to preserve their Boards of Governors under a different name. The proposal for an inner London region was described as a disaster, not only for London, but the entire health service; it was also criticised for being extravagant and wasteful. It was pointed out that this idea was opposed on the London Working Party of the previous Government, by the University of London, the University Grants Committee, and even by the London teaching hospital consultants.[124] However, opinion within the department was not unanimous; a minority voice urged the merits of the Boards of Governors and fought for their preservation, even for their establishment as institutions with the same degree of autonomy as universities.[125]

In view of continuing indecision on the part of Ministers, the Consultative Document avoided concrete proposals, although in passing, the continuing 'presence of separate postgraduate teaching hospitals' was assumed.[126] Apart from this isolated statement, the teaching hospitals of London received no more assurances than those granted to teaching hospitals in general regarding special protective clauses applying to the teaching districts that the area authorities would be obliged to establish.[127]

Location of the teaching hospitals at district level of administration added to the alarm of the Boards of Governors. Teaching hospitals seemed destined to become nuclei for minor district authorities, with the result that their district service obligations would become uppermost, while in place of the valued direct links between the Boards of Governors and the central department, they would become the lowest tier in the hierarchy, and thereby be placed at the mercy of both area and region. The London undergraduate teaching hospitals accordingly redoubled their efforts to entice Ministers with their doughnut conception, while the officials clung to their beleaguered starfish.

In the wake of the Consultative Document, the Ministers met the teaching hospital representatives, where they faced demands from Lord Cottesloe on behalf of the postgraduate hospitals, in reply to which the Secretary of State hinted that the Government might be willing to preserve their Boards of Governors. This caused the undergraduate teaching hospitals to redouble their efforts; Lord Cobbold, their main spokesman, made a strong personal plea to Joseph not to throw away the strengths of the teaching hospitals by imposing integration.[128] Although Joseph was not willing to commit himself, at a separate meeting with the London undergraduate teaching hospitals, he was swayed by the department's argument that it was unrealistic to act contrary to the recommendations of the Todd Report. The department was unwilling to consider the hospitals' proposal for an advisory joint planning authority for inner London as an acceptable substitute. Officials were also unwilling to acquiesce to the fragmentation of the health services of central London among a large number of separate authorities, each responsible to central government and unrelated to the boundaries of the London boroughs.[129]

During the autumn of 1971 it seemed that the resolve of the London teaching hospitals was softening; the messages received by the department were not consistent; sometimes they included threats about the trouble that the teaching hospitals were capable of making, possibly to the extent of wrecking the reorganisation legislation by unhelpful interventions in the House of Lords; on other occasions they suggested that further concession would purchase compliance. Two particularly important demands were forthcoming: first, that teaching hospital committees should be established at area rather than district level; secondly, that the teaching districts should have direct protection by the department, particularly of their budgets, at least for a transitional period.[130]

At a meeting with the London teaching hospitals in January 1972, Joseph conceded that teaching authorities would be granted area authority status, that the department would closely monitor financial arrangements, that a strong co-ordinating committee would be established to oversee the transition in London, as well as other minor concessions, but he was unwilling to accept less formal arrangements for integration, and he called for the undergraduate medical schools to play their part in the development of all facets of the regional service. He agreed to establish a working party under the Permanent Secretary to consider these safeguards in detail. The teaching hospitals expressed disappointment at this response and they predicted that their particular spheres of strength would be undermined by the proposed changes.[131] Cobbold complained and continued to press the teaching hospital case.[132] Representing the opposing camp, the RHB Chairmen warned the Secretary of State that any further concessions to the teaching hospitals would be detrimental to the efficiency of regional planning.[133]

Notwithstanding a bleak response from the teaching hospitals, the department issued its proposals for London in the form of a consultation document in March 1972. This was only a minor variant of the scheme favoured at the end of the deliberations of the Labour Government's Working Party; it proposed to establish sixteen area authorities in Greater London, each containing between one and three boroughs; of this number, six would be area teaching authorities, each containing between two and three teaching groups.[134]

By this stage the tide was running in favour of the health department. In May 1972 a meeting between Ministers and the Teaching Hospitals Association wrung out of the latter a reluctant acceptance that they would accept area health authority status and thereby they would be subsumed within the regional framework. The Secretary of State gave assurances that the financial interests of the teaching areas would be protected by the department, but the precise nature of this undertaking was unclear. The London hospitals now changed their ground and concentrated their main energies on determining the boundaries and organisation of the area authorities. Reluctantly, the Secretary of State allowed them to undertake a separate study of this problem, realising that its outcome was likely to be controversial and antagonistic to other negotiating parties.[135] A further effect of this study was to delay a final agreement until after the publication of the White Paper. It was agreed that further consideration of the London problem would be undertaken by a London Working Group headed by the Minister of State and, like its predecessor under the Labour Government, representing all parties in the discussions.

Within the Teaching Hospitals Association difficulty was experienced in holding to the temperate line; the moderates found themselves under attack from such heavyweight politicians as Lord Robens, but such experienced leaders as Lord Reigate were convinced that they had no alternative but to 'bow out sadly but gracefully'.[136]

On the basis of the Scicon study commissioned by them, which was completed in September 1972, the Teaching Hospitals Association proposed to establish eight areas in Greater London, each comprising three to five London boroughs, with Lambeth being split between two areas. Six of the eight areas would be teaching areas, each including two or three teaching groups. As suspected at the outset of the exercise, this study was conducted primarily from the perspective of hospital services and it took little note of primary care or the social services. The teaching hospitals' position was shared by some officials, who argued that at least some multi-borough areas should be adopted for trial purposes.[137] However, the dominant view within DHSS was unsympathetic. The main advantage of the Scicon scheme was that it was intended to reduce the extent to which patients would need to cross area boundaries to secure hospital treatment, but this was not regarded as a decisive argument, since the new area structure involved frequent examples where patients would need to cross boundaries. It was suspected that the large area was being promoted as a further device for preserving the autonomy of teaching hospitals. The large area would operate as a remote umbrella, allowing the teaching hospitals to function with little reference to the area authority. Since each Borough would be limited to one member on the area committee, they would have little capacity to contest teaching hospital domination, or secure a balanced treatment of the health services. For these reasons, it was realised that the London Boroughs, which had always insisted on areas comprising no more than two Boroughs 'will fight the Scicon proposals to the last drop of blood'.[138] By this stage Aberdare was converted to the department point of view; he believed that 'we would be betraying the whole cause of reorganisation to give way to the Teaching Hospitals Association'.[139] Both Aberdare and Joseph now accepted that the serious social and medical problems of the inner city posed an exciting challenge, which would not be recognised under the Teaching Hospitals Association scheme. With no recorded dissent, Ministers and officials decided to reject the Scicon report and they agreed to 'proceed on the basis proposed by the London Boroughs Association with only minor modifications to meet the THA point of view'.[140] It was agreed that this decision would be announced after the next meeting of the London Working Group.

At this final meeting of the London Working Group, Aberdare asked representatives to state their views on regional and area boundaries. This meeting resolved itself into a debate on the respective merits of the proposals made by Scicon and the department in its consultative document. Opinion was evenly divided. The Teaching Hospitals Association defended Scicon; they were supported by London University and the University Grants Committee. The London Boroughs Association led the argument for the department's scheme; this line was adopted by each of the four Regional Hospital Boards, the Inner London Education Authority, and the Greater London Council. The Executive Councils gave a divided response. They favoured the nearest approximation to the existing five Executive Councils within the Greater London area. In an attempt to meet the wishes of the department, they produced a plan for a two-tier structure of family practitioner administration, involving five 'super-FPCs' performing most of the administrative work, with 'second-tier FPCs' being responsible for planning.[141] In promising to report the above discussion to the Secretary of State, Aberdare gave no hints about the decision already effectively made.[142]

In a final discussion within the department, it was agreed that minor inconvenience arose because in a small number of cases the new area boundaries were not consistent with the boundaries of the Inner London Executive Council and the Inner London Education Authority. It was also agreed that other complaints could be met by ensuring that the twinned medical schools recommended by Todd should be located in the same area. Joseph thought of new ways of reconciling the parties, but it was agreed that a final decision was inescapable. An announcement outlining the department's scheme for London was made in both Houses on 16 November 1972.[143]

Districts and Community Health Councils
Crossman's Green Paper solved the problem of participation at the district level by proposing that area health authorities should establish district committees, comprised half from appointees of the area authority and half 'from people living or working in the district'. The Green Paper was criticised for its vagueness about the degree of authority to be exercised by these district committees, but one of their essential functions was acting as a channel for exposing the area authority to 'the full vigour of local opinion'. This 'involvement of people from the local community in the running of their services should help to maintain their quality and the public's understanding and acceptance of them'.[144] Joseph's Consultative Document proposed to administer the health service at district level through some kind of undisclosed management structure; by way of compensation, the area would be required to set up community health councils in each of its constituent districts to 'take full account of the views of the public they serve'.[145] Responses to the Consultative Document exposed widespread feeling that the proposed community health councils were insufficiently robust to effectively represent the concerns of their local community. This

demand for more influential community health councils was consistent with the more general movement for public participation in local affairs. Further incentive to strengthen community health councils arose from the provision for Local Health Councils in the Scottish reorganisation Bill, and by the publication in 1972 of a White Paper on the role of consultative councils in nationalised industries. Professor J N Morris thought that the first Green Paper was rejected because it failed to take account of the strength of demand for local participation. With respect to future developments in health care he insisted that 'local capability to act depends on having the information that creates choice and enables thinking ahead. If central authorities alone have the evidence it is hollow to speak of local devolution'.[146] This sentiment suggests that health planners were beginning to recognise an obligation to take account of the views of the local community.

By virtue of the high priority attached to efficiency and management in the Government's plan for reorganisation, the rising tide of expectation regarding community participation in health service affairs became concentrated on the recommendations relating to CHCs. For this reason, this relatively insignificant innovation assumed disproportionate amount of attention in the final phase of preparation for reorganisation.

Many comments reaching the Secretary of State indicated approval of CHCs, but practical proposals varied greatly. The National Association of Leagues of Hospital Friends complained that unless CHCs were given more authority they would not attract effective members.[147] The National Association for Mental Health advocated an ambitious role for the community health council and its independent secretariat, but NAMH was satisfied for the chairman and a substantial number of members to be appointed by the AHA.[148]

Strong representations on the question of CHCs came from the Association for Neighbourhood Councils, the chairman of which, Michael Young, captured the imagination of the Secretary of State. Indeed, Joseph was initially so enthusiastic about Young's ideas that he proposed to take the lead among Ministers calling for a greater degree of public participation in local affairs. This idea was abandoned when it was pointed out that such a suggestion would strengthen the demands of the Department of the Environment for greater local authority representation on area health authorities.[149]

By the end of 1971, the department accepted that CHCs were an important element in the reorganised health service, but they were undecided about their role. One group within the department supported the Davies Committee in pressing for the CHCs to be established as a part of the formal complaints procedure, but this was rejected on account of creating an adversarial relationship between the community health council and the area authority. The membership envisaged for CHCs would lack the qualifications necessary for an effective part in the complaints procedure.[150]

There was no diminution in the criticism that the proposed CHCs lacked the authority to become effective. Particularly damaging from the point of view of the Government was a project sponsored by the South East Metropolitan RHB into integration of services at the area level. The part of this investigation concerned with the relationship between the consumer and the community health council came to such adverse conclusions that it was issued in advance of the main report. The group from the Centre for Social Research at Sussex University concluded that 'if CHCs are to have neither teeth nor adequate financial support, they were better not to exist at all'. This conclusion was widely-publicised, adding to the Government's difficulties on the question of public participation.[151] Another academic group suggested that CHCs should be directly elected, be provided with their own staff, funded separately on a scale to make them effective, and be involved in planning of health services within their areas.[152]

Complaints about the weakness of the proposed CHCs were not confined to outside bodies. The Department of the Environment was suspicious that area authorities would not consult CHCs unless matters upon which consultation was required were specified in the statute. The health department refused to make this concession, insisting that detailed guidance circulated to area authorities would be sufficient to obtain their co-operation.[153]

By the date of the White Paper, the Secretary of State was facing widespread demands for the independence of CHCs and for statutory guarantees concerning their functions. On the other hand, he was warned by NHS interests that independent CHCs would be difficult to control and at the worst might become irresponsible, even destructive forces, within the health service.[154] As Klein discovered, opinion within the department was divided over the merits of CHCs; some believed that they 'would become "naggers and stirrers up of complaints". Others simply thought the CHCs would be ineffective'.[155] As will be seen below, on the strength of such reservations, the White Paper made only minimum concessions to the lobby demanding strengthened CHCs.

(iii) COLLABORATION WITH LOCAL GOVERNMENT

The decision of the Labour Government to recommend unification of health services outside local government, and its acceptance of the Seebohm proposals to unify social work services within local government, set on foot a large-scale reassortment of responsibilities between health and local authorities. Many of the changes were uncontroversial, but it was clear that no consensus was likely to be achieved on such sensitive questions as movement of hospital social workers to local government employment, transfer of the London ambulance service from the GLC to the health service, the reassortment of personnel concerned with child guidance, or on the care of the severely mentally handicapped.

The biggest problems related to transfer of services from local government to the health service. Although in terms of cost, local government administered health services were not the largest components of the health service, these functions were important, often long-established, and in some cases they extended back to the mid-Victorian period. This was the case with respect to the Medical Officer of Health, under whose aegis, it could fairly be claimed, many of the essential strides towards the National Health Service had been made. Now it was intended to dismember the departments associated with the Medical Officer of Health, abolish the office, and reconstitute the specialty, possibly with a very different end-product in mind. Such proposals entailed not only confrontation with entrenched and honourable traditions of public service, but also the risk that the proposed changes might do more harm than good. In favour of reorganisation was the argument that local government health services had changed considerably over time, and no period had witnessed more alteration than the decades since the beginning of the NHS. The two main candidates for transfer from local government to the National Health Service were the School Health Service and a large part of local health and welfare services.

The School Health Service was an important activity of the local education authority.[156] The annual report, *Health of the Schoolchild*, documented the work of the School Health Service, and attested to its importance in promoting the health and well-being of schoolchildren. The position of the School Health Service had been settled in the Education Act 1944, in advance of the establishment of the NHS, with the result that this service experienced a reasonably settled development since its inception in 1907. Although within the School Health Service there was an appreciation that its activities were less fundamental to the health of schoolchildren than before the NHS, there was still a large body of opinion favouring the continuation of some form of identifiable school health service under education rather than health administration.

In the interests of good relations between the health and education departments centrally, under the early NHS the question of phasing out of the School Health Service was politely shelved. But there was always tension just beneath the surface. The School Health Service was inclined to take initiatives which consolidated its position, whereas the health service encouraged developments that eroded the school service. Doctors working in the School Health

Service aspired to continuing independence, whereas the emerging hospital-based specialty of paediatrics expected to assume comprehensive responsibility for child health.

The relationship between the two sectors was increasingly unstable. The possibility of discontinuing an independent School Health Service was raised even before Robinson's announcement of a review of NHS organisation. As Harris has observed, in 1962, in its report highly critical of the School Health Service, the Select Committee on Estimates favoured takeover by the Ministry of Health.[157] The Report on Child Welfare Centres, dating from June 1967, tentatively suggested unifying all child health services from birth to school-leaving age.[158] Fortuitously, the Sheldon kite-flying occurred at an opportune moment, when the Department of Education and Science was beginning serious preparations for taking over from health authorities responsibility for the training of mentally handicapped children, which provided for integration between ascertainment and training in the hands of education authorities. There was parliamentary support for a change of this kind.[159] The education department was therefore not in a position to argue that the existing boundaries between the health and education services were sacrosanct. Emboldened by this opportunity, officials from the Ministry of Health informed their counterparts at the DES of the possibility that their review of NHS administration might have implications for the future of the School Health Service. It was reported that at the most senior level DES made 'non-committal but not dissenting noises'.[160] Discussions between the departments on this issue proceeded slowly; both sides recognised that the case was by no means clear-cut. The pace of these exchanges increased in November 1968, when the Prime Minister, prompted by a question in Parliament, sought advice on the future of the School Health Service.[161] The two departments took almost five months to agree upon a reply to the Prime Minister, who recognized that it was premature to force a conclusion. Wilson suggested reconsideration of this issue in the light of the recommendations of the Seebohm Committee and the Royal Commission on Local Government.[162]

In view of the delicacy of these discussions, the question of the future administration of the School Health Service was not raised in the first Green Paper. This evasion was noticed at the time and it attracted adverse comment. This tactic could therefore not be repeated on a second occasion. With the agreement of Lady Serota, senior DHSS officials redoubled their efforts to reach agreement, and a critical meeting with the Permanent Secretary of DES was held on 17 June 1969. It was generally agreed that the school health service should be handed over to the NHS. On the difficult boundary question of child guidance, it was agreed to establish a working party of the departments involved. However, there remained one important disagreement; DES was not willing to relinquish all services; it wanted to retain the possibility of employing staff for certain purposes such as providing special hearing aids to schoolchildren, or even providing more extensive services where the NHS failed to make adequate provision.[163] DES also feared that local education authorities would not accept the above proposals unless they were given the right to appoint a Principal School Medical Officer. DHSS urged that all work of this kind in future should be within the province of the NHS community physician.[164]

Progress occurred by slow attrition. In October 1969 a joint paper was submitted to Ministers of the two departments, embodying suggestions which formed the basis for the paragraph on the School Health Service in the second Green Paper, which briefly outlined advantages anticipated from unification and continuity of service.[165] An assurance was given that the service would 'continue to be provided in a manner acceptable to the local education authority and its staff'.[166]

Final confirmation of transfer of the main functions of the school health service to the NHS was slow to materialise. The Consultative Document of May 1971 merely stated that 'Future arrangements for the school health service will require special consideration'.[167] As noted below, inclusion of a firm proposal in the Scottish White Paper of July 1971 to transfer the School Health Service in Scotland to the NHS added to the urgency for a final decision about amalgamation south of the border. The Scottish initiative was welcomed as a precedent by the health department in London, and it was used to apply further pressure on the Secretary of State for Education and Science to follow suit.[168]

The more specific recommendations contained in the Conservative Government's White Paper of August 1972 were made in the light of the provisional advice available from the School Health Service Subcommittee of the Collaboration Working Party. This subcommittee exceeded its remit by undertaking a complete review of alternative policies for the future of the School Health Service. It gave guarded support for unification under the NHS, but only on the basis of elaborate safeguards to protect local education authorities.[169]

The White Paper said less than the second Green Paper on the Government's plans for unifying services for schoolchildren. Following the advice of the subcommittee of the Collaboration Working Party, it was confirmed that local authorities should continue to play a part in the ascertainment of handicapped children, and in the child guidance service; support from NHS authorities was promised for the maintenance of these services.[170] Since it was not possible to establish a unified basis for child guidance, the White

Paper proposed to allow this service to be shared between the child psychiatry specialty of health authorities, the social work services of local authorities, and the educational psychology service of local education authorities.[171]

As in the case of the School Health Service, the main decisions concerning division of the empire controlled by the Medical Officers of Health was made in the interval between the first and second Green Papers. The initial determinant of events was the Seebohm Report, which recommended that the social work services administered by the Medical Officer of Health should be transferred to new local authority social service departments. The latter having spoken for their share of the territory, it was necessary to decide on the fate of the remaining functions. The larger part was earmarked for the reorganised NHS, leaving a smaller public health segment in the hands of local government, where it formed the nucleus of new environmental health departments.

The above bald summary omits reference to much controversy, various shifts in policy, and many difficult boundary problems. For instance, since the institution of public health departments in the mid-Victorian period, public health had been supervised by medical personnel. Now it was intended to remove medical officers entirely and transfer this work to lay environmental health officers, the descendants of the old sanitary inspectors. It was at first thought that some at least of the public health functions would need to reside with the health authority, but in the event it was agreed to allow all of them to remain with local government, and rely on the medical staff of health authorities for specific assistance. The only point of indecision related to health education, which the second Green Paper ordained should be the responsibility of both health authorities and environmental health departments.[172] This division of duties seemed reasonable on paper, but it left awkward doubts about the final responsibility for such areas as prevention of the spread of communicable disease, a function which had been central to public health since its inception, and which was to remain more important than the health planners realised in 1970. The White Paper essentially repeated the recommendations of the second Green Paper.[173] The precise location of environmental health within the local government framework was decided by the local government reorganisation legislation, which itself created complications which were not alluded to in the White Paper; these will be considered briefly below in the context of collaboration arrangements.

The line of division between health services and social work services was particularly difficult to draw. Social services relating to such large groups as the mentally ill, mentally handicapped, and the elderly had developed under the auspices of the Medical Officer of

Health, and the problems affecting these groups contained a large medical element. There was strong opposition, especially from medical interests, to the fragmentation of services for these groups, and it was argued that divorce of medical and social work services would obstruct recognition of medical problems and delay the application of medical and nursing expertise. There was no way of reconciling the conflicting parties, but eventually a criterion was adopted for drawing the dividing-line between the two sets of services. This was embodied in the second Green Paper, where it was ordained that health authorities would be responsible for services where the primary skill was that of the health professions, whereas local authority social service departments would take over those services where the primary skill was social care support.[174] Much to the consternation of the medical profession, this concordat determined that the home help service, adult training centres for the mentally handicapped, and residential care for the mentally handicapped and mentally ill not requiring continuous psychiatric supervision, would pass to the local authorities.[175] The critics of these transfers believed that on the basis of their past record, local authorities had neither the means nor the will to undertake these responsibilities. They predicted that these unfamiliar and specialised services would become neglected backwaters of the social work domain, to the disadvantage of already seriously disadvantaged groups for whom improvement in services was just beginning. This contentious problem was passed over in a few words in the reorganisation White Paper.[176]

The suspicion of neglect was cast in the reverse direction with respect to the ambulance service. Ambulances had been provided by various agencies before the NHS. The 1946 health service legislation placed statutory responsibility for the ambulance service with local health authorities. Although the predominant use of ambulances was in connection with hospitals, hospital authorities were not organised on a geographical basis suitable to take on this service. Also, local authorities were experienced in providing transport services of other kinds, and they possessed the facilities for maintaining such vehicles as ambulances. Ambulance services represented an unspectacular, but successful area of local health authority activity. The growth of social service use of ambulances provided an argument for continuity; the GLC in particular put in a strong bid to administer the London ambulance service. The health department came down decisively in favour of transfer of ambulances to health authorities, but it was unable to devise a uniform plan for administration. The decision was briefly announced in the second Green Paper, while in the White Paper it was indicated that ambulances would be provided by area health authorities in non-metropolitan counties, but by regional health authorities in metropolitan counties.[177] This resulted in the inconsistent arrangement whereby regions undertook general co-ordination for the ambulance service outside the metropolitan counties, but exercised direct control within metropolitan areas. Such a formula was not easily applied to London, where there were four regional health authorities. In this case the White Paper avoided a pronouncement, but promised that the 'Greater London Ambulance Service will not be split up between the RHAs or AHAs but will continue to be administered as a single unit'.[178] Local authorities predicted that the Government's proposal would disrupt continuity in development of the ambulance services, and that the new and more complicated administrative structure would lead to a deterioration in the status and effectiveness of this important function.

Reliance was placed on the Working Party on Collaboration to evolve methods by which health authorities and local authorities could collaborate effectively to optimise services in which they had a joint interest. A long history of failure in collaboration across administrative boundaries in the health service suggested that the collaboration exercise would not be easy to accomplish. The split between social services and health services, which was common to the schemes of both the Labour and Conservative Governments, was criticised as one of the most serious defects of each successive scheme for reorganisation. These criticisms were made about the White Paper, and they were reiterated in Parliament during the debates on the reorganisation Bill.

Unabating concern about the fault-line separating the health and social services led to a special degree of importance being attached to the Working Party on Collaboration between the NHS and Local Government which was established as the twin of the management study under the planning process announced in the Consultative Document.

Unlike the working party on management arrangements, the collaboration working party dealt with both England and Wales. The need to represent many different interest groups and the complexity of the issues necessitated a large membership; the result was a working party comprising 45 members, which met for the first time in August 1971.[179] It was obviously unrealistic to expect this sprawling assembly to function efficiently as a working party. The collaboration working party therefore assumed a function equivalent to the steering committee superintending the management study; detailed enquiries were remitted to three subcommittees, which were concerned with the personal social services, the School Health Service, and the environmental health service. In view of the need to establish harmony between the findings of these subcommittees, it was also necessary to establish a co-ordinating committee. By August

493

1972, the date of the publication of the White Paper, to the embarrassment of the health department, the only complete draft report emanating from the subcommittees related to environmental health, which was available in March 1972. The initial draft reports dealing with main aspects of the personal social services and the school health service were produced between March and July 1972, but they were not published until July 1973, by which date they had been amended slightly in the light of outside consultation, and in this form they were adopted as policy by the Government.[180]

The basic lines of thinking on collaboration were at least available before the detailed drafting of the reorganisation Bill had progressed very far. However, the reports published in 1973 constituted outlines, greatly inferior in detail to the proposals of the management study. Accordingly, the collaboration working party set on foot more elaborate and specific enquires, which greatly extended the life of its activities. After no less than a year of deliberations, a further subcommittee on financial arrangements was added, while a final subcommittee on London was not established until early 1973. Further complication was occasioned by the addition of four specialist groups, established by the co-ordinating committee to investigate supplies, building and engineering, management and statistics, and ancillary services. It was only with difficulty that the supplementary activities of the collaboration working party were completed by the date of reorganisation. The final two working party reports were published in November 1973 and December 1974.[181]

The task of Collaboration Working Party and its satellites was eased by virtue of the tenacity with which both Labour and Conservative administrations, against advice from many medical and NHS interests, had insisted on coterminosity of boundaries between the main statutory units of health and social service administration. This at least removed one complication that had been detrimental to co-ordination since 1948. In practice, this was a limited gain since it was also necessary for health authorities to liaise with local authority departments responsible for education, environmental health, and housing. Since the Conservative Government rejected the Redcliffe-Maude scheme for unitary authorities, NHS authorities related to a multiplicity of local authority agencies, not organised on a uniform geographical basis at important operational district level. Under the Local Government Act 1972, education was administered on approximately the same basis as the social services, but in London it was controlled by the Inner London Education Authority. Outside the metropolitan areas, social services and education were controlled by the counties, but environmental health and housing were managed by districts; within the metropolitan areas all of these functions were administered by metropolitan districts. An additional complication arose from the district organisation adopted by the education and social service departments, which tended to be inconsistent with the district divisions adopted under the NHS. In London, health service arrangements involved transfer of the ambulance service from the GLC to the South West Thames RHA on behalf of the four Thames regions, for which no local government equivalent existed, owing to the Government's decision not to proceed with the Redcliffe-Maude Commission's proposals for provincial local authorities.

Although potentially, collaborative arrangements might have become a leading edge in the development of the health-related services provided by health authorities and local authorities, in practice, they occupied a marginal role. Each authority concentrated on the services over which it exercised complete control; as a goal, co-operation remained an elusive objective, belonging to the realm of pious exhortations and utopian prospectuses.[182]

The difficulty in bringing these interests into harmony reflected long-standing tensions between the health service and local government at all levels of administration. Throughout deliberations on NHS reorganisation, the Ministry of Housing and Local Government (later Department of the Environment) had been a thorn in the side of the Ministry of Health (later DHSS). At Cabinet meetings, Ministers representing health were most likely to find their plans under criticism from the direction of local government. All of these latent animosities were evident in the working party arrangements. The NHS lobby treated local government as a prospective malinger, scheming to avoid its obligations, whereas the latter believed that health authorities were trying to exercise dictatorial influence, thereby further eroding the sphere of activities controlled by democratically elected bodies. With respect to the balance of power, each party remained in a state of discontent; local authorities were recompensed for loss of the local health authority services by modest representation on area health authorities, but not as much as they wanted or had previously been promised. As the party making territorial gains, NHS authorities had to be content with representation at the level of local government liaison bodies; they failed in their objective to obtain any kind of formal representation on parallel local government authorities.

The main recommendations of the collaboration working party were innocuous. It was recommended that health authorities and local authorities should have a duty to collaborate.[183] The proposed mechanism entailed establishing statutory joint consultative committees, which would ascertain needs, devise appropriate plans, and facilitate the execution of these plans by the authorities directly responsible for providing services.[184] Three types of collaboration arrangements were evolved to suit the metropolitan districts, the shire counties, and London. The working party also outlined in some detail the staffing implications of collaboration and recommended terms under which the various authorities would provide each other with appropriate medical, nursing and social work services.[185]

With admirable attention to detail, the collaboration working party had constructed an elaborate, albeit old-fashioned engine, but its joint owners proved unable to locate a line upon which it could run. This exercise was therefore primarily of value as a protective measure, demonstrating to sceptics in the debates on the reorganisation Bill that the Government was taking countervailing measures to prevent health authorities and local authorities from drifting apart in provision of services to the many client groups requiring their joint participation.

(iv) MANAGEMENT STUDY

The 'expert study' of management arrangements, promised in the Consultative Document was the most complex and difficult of the various operations needed for the satisfactory completion of the White Paper. This exercise was especially important because upon it rested any hope of salvaging the Secretary of State's ideas on management by chief executives.

With the adoption of a more relaxed timetable for the preparation of the White Paper, it was anticipated that the management review would be sufficiently complete for its main findings to be included in that document. However the management review turned into an elaborate casuistical exercise, with the result that it took much longer than originally intended.

The management study was supervised by a large Steering Committee dominated by department and NHS representatives, with a senior DHSS official in the chair. This important and delicate responsibility was assumed by the Permanent Secretary. Also included on this committee were R A Meyjes, the senior member of the Business Team, and Professor Elliot Jacques, Director of the Institute of Organisation and Social Studies of Brunel University. Both expected to play an active part in field studies undertaken by the smaller Management Study Group, which was dominated by members of the department, but also contained some representatives of NHS authorities and the professions.

At an early stage it was decided that the Steering Committee and the Management Study Group would also benefit by assistance from professional management consultants. Various alternatives were considered, but the strongest contender was McKinsey & Co. Inc., an organisation which had built up much experience with the health service, not only in England, but also in Ireland, and was also involved in the parallel review of headquarters organisation. With the agreement of CSD, McKinsey & Co. Inc. were appointed as the main management consultant, while workers from Jacques' Institute were also involved in certain specific studies.[186] Meyjes was a full member of the Management Study Group, while Jacques and consultants from McKinsey were involved in an advisory capacity.

The management study began in the summer of 1971, when the Study Group issued its initial 'hypotheses'; these were considered by the Steering Committee at its first meeting on 5 August. At the opening meeting the chairman told the Study Group that its plans should take full account of constraints imposed by political decisions contained in the Consultative Document and other policies which were in process of formulation. Also the management specialists were instructed that although they were addressing questions of efficiency, the fundamental guiding principle of reorganisation was 'satisfactory integration of all three branches of the Service'. Finally, they were also reminded that management structures should take account of the fact that 'universal consent...was the guiding principle behind reorganisation'.[187]

By February 1972 the Study Group had prepared a plan for management arrangements at region, area and district levels, which was then examined by the Steering Committee under the title 'First Tentative Hypotheses'. These preliminary proposals were tested in some sample areas; in May a preliminary report was issued for comment; this was finally modified to take account of the White Paper and published on 15 September 1972.[188] This document became known as the 'Grey Book' on account of the colour of its cover; in fact the whole group of related reorganisation planning documents issued at this time were issued with uniform grey covers. The management study was the longest single publication among this little clutch of reports. It is an indication of the importance attached to the management study, that only this report was known as the Grey Book. The reception of the Grey Book is properly considered below in conjunction with responses to the White Paper. The Government's formal verdict on the Grey Book, accepting its proposals virtually in their entirety, was announced in February 1973.[189] The following paragraphs deal with the manner in which the management study addressed its major problems.

The management study was presented as the encapsulation of the new spirit of business-mindedness which the Heath Government in general, and Ministers such as Joseph in particular, were mobilising to impose a new spirit of enterprise into public service. In practice the impact of the new thinking was less than was suggested by the rhetoric. It would be something of an exaggeration to claim that the management study was evolving from first principles a structure of integrated management for the reorganised health service. The Consultative Document conveyed a somewhat spurious impression that the management structure was an open question. In practice, the Consultative Document itself, and the many already formulated but not entirely agreed policies, largely determined the management framework. Other constraints were imposed by such factors as local government reorganisation and its impact on the boundaries of health authorities, by negotiations of the kind described above relating to the health services in London, by preferences of Ministers and senior officials, and finally by entrenched practices within the health service, all of which severely limited the choices available to the Management Study Group. Acting collectively, and reinforced by the authority of the Steering Group, the above factors largely predetermined the outcome of the management study. The Management Study Group itself and the teams from McKinsey and Brunel University were inferior in status, and able to exercise only a marginal effect. The management experts were in reality employed to make some kind of coherent pattern out of the tangled web of existing policy decisions, and apply a patina of management respectability to the documentation associated with reorganisation. For all of its management jargon and clever heuristic devices, behind its manicured professional façade, the Grey Book embodied a weak and confused system of decision making. It therefore proved to be a frail vehicle for realising the expectations of strong management aroused by the Consultative Document.

With respect to the functions, boundaries, and authority committee membership at the region, area and district levels, the management study was largely concerned to present in a structured form agreements that had already been reached at a political level. In many cases, work undertaken in connection with the two Green Papers could be appropriated with relatively little modification. There remained a residue of intractable issues upon which much energy had been spent over the previous few years, without tangible progress having been made. On such problems, the management steering committee and its expert advisers experienced the same difficulties as the politicians in reaching unanimity. For instance they found it difficult to reach agreement over the functions, size, and membership of the regional authority. There was strong support for a 'slim' executive type of regional authority, with no more than eight members, but with the possibility also for including all the area chairmen on the RHA. After sharp swings of outlook, neither alternative was adopted, and instead the steering committee accepted a variant of the current RHB arrangements, entailing a membership of 15-20, including the traditional representational element, and with exclusion of AHA chairmen.[190]

The officer management structure to be adopted at each level of health administration represented one of the most difficult issues facing the management study. Joseph's insistent enthusiasm for management by chief executive provided the management study with a model for testing, and it also constituted a test of their capacity to confront powerful vested interests within the health service.

There was in reality no chance that Joseph's bird would fly. The health departments had been wrestling with this problem without reaching a generally applicable solution ever since the beginning of the NHS, indeed in some respects since establishment of the Ministry of Health. As indicated in volume I of this study, the issue had been resolved at the regional level by appointment of two senior officers of approximately equal standing, the Senior Administrative Medical Officer and the Secretary to the RHB. This diarchy or duumvirate had sometimes been successful, but it was affected by strain, and was subjected to much criticism. Trends in professionalisation within the health service constituted a strong impetus towards the further fragmentation of management responsibility, and thereby tended to preclude any natural shift towards general management. As already noted, the medical profession was willing to contemplate the prospect of a chief executive, but only under restricted conditions, including limitation of the appointment to medical personnel. By the 1970s it was impracticable to impose such a solution on other professional groups within the health service. Doctors were able to veto elevation of the senior hospital administrator into a chief executive, but the administrator was unwilling to accept a position of inferiority. Also various other professional groups, ranging from finance officers to nurses, asserted their rights to independent command over their respective functions and also equality of access to their employing authority.

Some initial positive gestures towards the Secretary of State's ideas only served to generate false optimism. Even on these occasions, the idea of general management was expressed in only the most guarded terms. For instance, at a meeting of chief officers of regions and areas, Joseph made an important concession that the chief officer would be primarily the co-ordinator of other senior officers. He also offered a confidential assurance that only 10 per cent of appointments would be made from candidates outside the NHS. Given the ambiguity of the role of the chief executive, it was understandably difficult to arrive at a satisfactory title; the initial shortlist included the following possibilities: Secretary, General Secretary, General Manager, Administrator, Comptroller, Co-ordinator, and Commissioner for Health.[191] The Treasury appreciated that the outcome was uncertain, but it seemed at one stage that thinking within the department favoured management by chief executive.[192] In order to keep open this possibility, SHHD was advised by CSD not to issue a consultative document giving prominence to the idea of management by a group executive of principal officers, while Meyjes was called in to brief the Scottish planners on the merits of alternatives including a stronger role for the chief executive. SHHD was told that DHSS had rejected the group executive in favour of the chief executive.[193] However, shortly afterwards, it was reported that DHSS had in fact reintroduced the idea of the executive team 'as a possible model for testing'.[194] This trend was not universally welcomed among DHSS officials, but advocates of the chief executive alternative were increasingly fighting an abortive rearguard action.

In the Steering Committee, the chairman acknowledged that officer arrangements were 'the most difficult single issue', and he was alert to the 'danger of reaching a compromise solution designed to accommodate all interests. What was wanted above all was an effective formulation'.[195] Notwithstanding formal assurances that the management study was open to all suggestions, it was clear from the outset that general management was not regarded as a viable option. Indeed, the Permanent Secretary's insistence that the Management Study Group should be guided by 'universal consent', itself determined that the chief executive idea would be rejected. Also, by beginning their testing procedures at the district level, the investigators became predisposed to favour consensus management, because multidisciplinary co-operation seemed to have the best chances of success at the level of district services.

The 'ground up' approach of the Study Group was supported by the Steering Committee; it was accepted that since 'the prime purpose of reorganisation is to achieve integration of services actually delivering care to communities and these integrated services then become the building blocks on which higher organisation levels are based', then it was necessary to give first priority to the district level of administration.[196]

With the approval of the department, the Study Group quickly evolved the concept of the District Management Team. This represented a laudable attempt to build on the concept of team-work that the department had long been attempting to cultivate within the health service. The District Management Team seemed like a natural evolutionary trend, and it was also the alternative likely to meet with least resistance from the relevant professional groups. However, simplicity was not among its attractions. Among the awkward problems were: determining the core membership of the DMT, the balance between clinician and non-clinician members, and the working relationship within the team, for instance which officer would act as co-ordinator and whether a separate chairman was required. The Study Group was careful to avoid any structure implying that a single officer was superior in status to the rest, even on a temporary basis. Accordingly, not only was the model of general management rejected, but anything associated with general management rigidly avoided. For this reason the Steering Committee abandoned the proposal for additional remuneration of the officer acting as co-ordinator.

In explaining the management team concept, it was emphasised that 'no particular profession should be seen to be in a dominant position on any management team. There should be no chief executive officer, just as there should be no medical superintendent...whatever arrangements were agreed, they should be such as would promote harmony'.[197] Once the DMT was accepted as the foundation stone for the management structure at the district level, it was found impossible to resist its application at the area and regional levels. The management experts asked the Steering Committee to consider excluding the multi-professional style of management the level of area and region, but the committee came down in favour of uniformity at all levels in management.[198]

Consensus management was a line of least resistance with respect to acceptability among the relevant professional groups, but it entailed enormous elaboration in the detail of lateral relationships between management team members, and even more with respect to vertical lines of accountability between officers, at district, area and regional levels of administration. Despite all of its rhetoric about comprehensive co-ordination and monitoring, the Study Group risked undermining the effectiveness of accountability by the complexity of its plans, and the latitude given for individual discretion.

Recognising the dangers inherent in this situation, Professor Jacques pointed out that 'the real problems were how to reconcile hierarchically organised with professionally autonomous services, and how to ensure that from any reconciliation positive action resulted'.[199] Notwithstanding periodic strictures about the dangers inherent in the consensus management approach, the management study had embarked on a voyage from which no return was possible. The labyrinthine management structures of the Grey Book, and its implicit decisive rejection of the ideas of the Secretary of State, were the logical and inevitable conclusion of this exercise.

McKinsey & Co. Inc. were satisfied to operate within the accumulated constraints laid down by their paymasters in the course of the management exercise. However, this same degree of compliance was not forthcoming from Meyjes and Jacques, both of whom were brought into the management investigation with the expectation that they might influence the course of events, even with respect to major policy questions. Both regarded NHS reorganisation as an exciting challenge for the application of their skills and they set about their work with enthusiasm and a keen sense of commitment. Meyjes, as the senior business adviser to the Government, felt that he had built up a good working relationship with Ministers and the Permanent Secretary. From this position of advantage, he felt able to address himself to major policy questions. Meyjes and Jacques evidently struck up a good working relationship; both were dissatisfied about the direction being taken by the management study, which they believed was prejudicial to the Secretary of State's stated aims for reorganisation. Accordingly, while McKinsey and their department associates were building up a management model from district level upwards, Meyjes and Jacques addressed themselves to the question of central management arrangements, and they came to conclusions diametrically opposite to those adopted in the other province of the management study. They concluded that the principles of sound management required comprehensive reconsideration of the plan laid down in the Consultative Document. The bed-rock of their new thinking was a proposal for hiving-off the health service to a separate NHS authority. This was of course a resurrection and more detailed reworking of the scheme recently proposed by the CSD, but never considered in detail on account of objections from the Treasury and DHSS, and because of the impasse created by initial disagreements over terms for Meyjes' participation in the work of the health department. The management study provided an apparently favourable opportunity to reintroduce the CSD proposal. As an outsider, with little experience of the health service, Meyjes alone might have exercised only limited influence, but his effectiveness was strengthened by the co-option of Jacques as an ally. The scheme evolved by Meyjes and Jacques was explained to the Secretary of State and his colleagues on 1 March 1972.[200] The radicalism of their proposals is indicated by the summary included in the minutes of this meeting:

> The essence of their proposals was that there should be a statutory national NHS authority, with a chief officer and NHS staff, located in the DHSS (but with up to 8 regional arms) which would, as an agent of the Secretary of State, be responsible for the management of the NHS through the Area Health Authorities on the basis of policies laid down by the Government. The main advantages over the Consultative Document proposals were first the recognition of the distinction between (a) policy formulation and (b) strategic planning and management, i.e. the matching of

resources to policy needs. The former was the job of the Ministers and civil servants; the latter was the job of a properly organised NHS such as proposed. Secondly, their proposals would, by eliminating a regional management tier, mean more effective accountable management of the NHS as a whole. The NHS authority would also have important central personnel functions which were lacking under existing arrangements. Dialogue and interaction between the authority and senior civil servants would ensure that policy formulation and management were carried out with due regard to the effects of the one on the other.

The management experts realised that their proposals represented a departure from the Consultative Document, but they urged that their plan had been formulated as the result of long and intensive study; they were fully convinced that the Consultative Document proposals were incapable of achieving the aim of an integrated, effectively-managed NHS. They insisted that separation between DHSS and the NHS authority was an essential precondition for effective management of the NHS. In order to make a reality of strategic planning, and avoid the health service fragmenting into fourteen separate parts, both DHSS and the NHS authority needed its own 'top authority'. In order to keep within the reorganisation timetable, the Secretary of State was advised to change course immediately.

Passage of time had not rendered the idea of an independent NHS authority more palatable to DHSS. The proposed change was not welcomed and indeed it was regarded as destructive. In the view of critics, it was essential to maintain unity between policy and management bodies, and for Ministers and civil servants to be involved in both. A separate NHS authority would undermine the constitutional responsibilities of Ministers. The only change required was facilitation of greater interchange between DHSS and NHS staff, but this had been attempted, and had always in practice proved difficult to achieve. The regional authorities and the diversity over which they presided, was presented as a positive advantage to health care.

In the face of an obvious conflict of loyalties, the Secretary of State threw his management experts overboard and aligned himself with his department. Partly on account of the timetable, partly because of the unavoidability of keeping commitments already given, but also on the strength of the argument, Joseph insisted that regional authorities must be retained, and indeed that the fourteen regions represented natural units of administration; he was satisfied that they need not be subversive to sound management. The most he was willing to concede was a further opportunity for the management experts to present their case.[201] A few days later the experts repeated their arguments and presented papers to demonstrate that delegation would operate smoothly under their scheme for regional offices. The fresh presentation made no difference; the alternative management proposals continued to meet with intransigent opposition. The Secretary of State reluctantly allowed presentation of the relevant papers to the Steering Committee, but on the understanding that he had 'come to the conclusion that the proposed NHS authority would not be viable politically or operationally', and that it would be an 'essentially artificial body with no real effectiveness'. The Steering Committee was therefore instructed to continue to operate within the boundaries of the principles embodied in the Consultative Document.[202]

This conclusion represented a serious blow to the credibility of Meyjes and Jacques; in the case of the former it had implications for the relationship between the Business Team and Ministers. As the senior business adviser to Ministers, he was unwilling to allow his name to be associated with a flawed planning exercise, and he wished to spare the Secretary of State the embarrassment of further expressions of disapproval. Meyjes accordingly immediately resigned from the Steering Committee and was not further involved with reorganisation. He expressed resentment about the conduct of the management study, which he regarded as a failure. He also argued that the Secretary of State should have insisted on conducting the reviews of NHS reorganisation and internal organisation of the department as a single exercise. The department, he believed, had committed a fundamental error, and thereby thrown away an opportunity to introduce a decisive improvement into health care management: 'we are moving in the wrong direction towards a bad solution analogous to that in Crossman's Green Paper and thus missing a unique opportunity for positive and much needed reform'.[203] It was not practicable for Jacques to make a similar dramatic exit from the management study, but he may well have shared the conclusion of Meyjes, that rejection of the idea of an NHS authority constituted a bad mistake.

(v) WHITE PAPER AND MANAGEMENT REPORT
In drawing up the White Paper, Joseph must have derived little comfort from echoes of the denunciations of the Government's chief business adviser ringing in his ears. However, Joseph clung to the plan outlined in the Consultative Document and became reconciled to the conceptual approach of the management study. Within this framework, the drafting of the White Paper proceeded smoothly. As noted above, the many residual policy loose ends left over from the Labour administration gradually fell into place in the course of the reasonably relaxed timetable created by postponement of the reorganisation Bill to the 1972/73 session.

Joseph participated in preparation of the White Paper with positive enthusiasm. He commented on drafts at all stages to a much greater extent than had been the case with Robinson or Crossman. Even his initial responses to the first summary ran to seventeen pages. No doubt responding to the widespread complaint that the Consultative Document was too much preoccupied with management and efficiency, he declared: 'I SEE THIS WHITE PAPER AS AN ATTEMPT TO SET OUT THE OBJECTIVES AS WELL AS THE MACHINERY OF THE HEALTH SERVICE'.[204]

Drafts of the White Paper were not distributed to other departments for comment until May 1972, but unofficial soundings showed that the Treasury, although annoyed about lack of consultation, had no serious reservations about the direction taken in the revisions. As far as the Treasury was concerned, the drafts confirmed that DHSS had not recanted from its late conversion to management awareness.[205] The Treasury was apparently unaware about the depth of the reservations held by Meyjes concerning the approach to management within DHSS. Circulation of the final drafts of the White Paper brought no diminution of the mutual confidence between DHSS and the Treasury.[206] Joseph was praised for persisting with his plans through protracted consultations; this achievement was 'much to the credit of the Social Services Secretary'. The draft White Paper seemed to represent a 'positive approach to improved management of the health services at all levels, based on a realistic matching of plans to resources in accordance with a coherent set of priorities, and with clearly defined allocations of responsibility and accountability'. This eulogistic tone was perhaps inspired by the evident difference in spirit between the White Paper and its Green Paper predecessor, which was recalled with distaste for its 'woolly, syndicalist, confusion between management and representation'.[207]

The draft White Paper faced one last hurdle; it required ratification by Ministers. This was the first opportunity for ministerial intervention since their exchanges over the draft consultative document more than a year earlier. As on the previous occasion of their discussion at the Social Services Committee, Ministers listened to Joseph's progress report with equanimity, except for the issue of local government representation on health authorities. This sparked off a further round of recriminations, each side presenting the same arguments as before.

Contrary to the advice of the Treasury, Joseph offered a compromise, suggesting that the local authority share of membership of area authorities should be increased from three to four. The local government lobby, headed by Walker, insisted that this was insufficient, being less than the one-third membership demanded by the Conservative Party when in opposition. Walker pressed the case for increasing the local authority membership to five. He insisted that representatives of the new local authorities would be superior to the nominees of the health Ministers, a group who had in the past proved that they were incompetent to run the NHS. Joseph refused to accept further concession on the grounds that it would stimulate demands for further representation from other health service interests; such increases would also increase the size of area authorities, so undermining their cohesiveness and efficiency. As on the previous occasion, the dispute was referred to the full Cabinet. On the basis of continuing opposition to Joseph from a vociferous minority of the Home and Social Affairs Committee, the Home Secretary advised the Prime Minister about the possible political dangers associated with acceptance of four rather than five local authority members.[208]

The Cabinet reviewed the texts of both the English and Welsh White Papers, again with only minor recorded comment on the bulk of the contents. The debate over local authority representation resumed, with the same arguments as before, and the Prime Minister proposed a similar compromise, entailing reference to the smaller number in the White Paper, but the Government should be prepared for further concessions to both local government and professional interests if necessitated by political circumstances.[209] It was agreed that the English White Paper would be published on 1 August, and the Welsh White Paper on 3 August, allowing time for completion of the Scottish health service reorganisation Bill's passage through Parliament, which was expected by the end of July.

The above timetable was observed; the English White Paper was published on Tuesday, 1 August 1972; the Welsh document followed two days later.[210] The press release associated with the English White Paper was headed 'A Better NHS for the Patient', reflecting suggestions in Cabinet discussion, especially from the new Home Secretary, that in its presentation, the White Paper should be less preoccupied with management and more attentive to the improvement of services to the patient and community.[211]

Comprising a text, excluding appendices, of about 20,000 words, the English White Paper was considerably longer than the Consultative Document, and comparable in length with the two Green Papers. The 208 paragraphs of text were divided up into 25 short sections, not very well organised, and giving a provisional appearance owing to large blank spaces created by starting each section on a fresh page. For some reason the White Paper was provided with an ill-fitting pale blue cover.

Sufficient progress had been made for the legislative intentions of the Government to be described in detail, and for additional information to be included on such issues as relations with the private sector, interim arrangements, and preparations for reorganisation. Obvious limitations of the White Paper were imposed by lack of completion of the working party reports on management and collaboration with local government, as well as absence of agreement on the organisation of services in London. With respect to the management report, at the last moment, a synopsis of its findings was added at the end of the publication.[212] The text of the White Paper contained only one guarded reference to the recommendations of the management study.[213] The management study was finalised more quickly than the White Paper indicated; as noted above, it was published on 15 September. Despite the hints included in the White Paper about possible later modifications, the management study report followed the lines indicated in the appendix to the White Paper. On collaboration, the reader received nothing more than an agenda of items under consideration by the working party.

Both the Secretary of State and the Minister of State played an active part in the drafting, and they contributed particularly to the Foreword and Conclusions. Their interventions modified the White Paper to make it less overtly preoccupied with management, and more humane in its general tone. The Secretary of State apologised for concentration on administration, but assured the public that the 'purpose behind the changes proposed is a better, more sensitive, service to the public'.[214] Similarly, the Conclusions, based on a draft by the Minister of State, contained an assurance that the reorganised service would be focused on the 'needs of the individual citizen of this country. Its purpose is to enable an improved health service for all to be provided'.[215] Equally reassuring, health service personnel were told that the changes were designed to give them greater opportunities to apply their talents. In line with this emphasis, unification rather than management was the leading theme of the opening section of the White Paper, while management questions, although frequently introduced, were not accorded a place of special prominence. Such low-key approach was possible because of the imminence of a separate report on management arrangements.

With respect to some important points of indecision in previous planning documents, mainly relating to services associated with other departments, the White Paper announced a final decision. It was confirmed that the responsibility of local education authorities for school medical and dental services would be transferred to the NHS.[216] On the other hand, environmental health was to remain as a function of local government.[217]

The bulk of the White Paper was taken up with describing the new region, area, and district structure to be adopted in the unified service. The region was discussed briefly and as a subsidiary to the area, but it was evident that the regional tier had been restored to a position comparable to that of the Regional Hospital Boards.[218] Indeed the new Regional Health Authorities would possess enhanced powers, since their remit was extended to the entire health service and teaching hospital groups were subsumed under their control. The idea of changing the number of regions was discreetly dropped.

Most attention was given to the description of area arrangements. The number of areas was determined by the Local Government Bill, which was at the time completing its parliamentary stages. This Bill took almost a year to steer through Parliament, but its recommendations were sufficiently firm to merit inclusion in the White Paper. The Local Government Bill received the Royal Assent on 26 October 1972, without any late changes seriously affecting health service planning arrangements. Although the Conservative plan considerably altered county boundaries, keeping more strictly to historic county boundaries than was suggested by the Royal Commission and Labour, the number of counties and metropolitan districts remained similar to the Labour Government's intentions. The main change affecting health services was abandonment of the unitary authority principle, which was especially inconvenient to health administration in non-metropolitan counties because it was necessary for AHAs to liaise with both county and district local authorities.

The Local Government Bill implied the establishment of 72 Area Health Authorities outside London (38 corresponding with non-metropolitan counties, and 34 with metropolitan districts).[219] The health White Paper was unable to give details of area arrangements to be adopted in London.[220] Although precise arrangements for the subdivision of areas was left to the discretion of the AHAs, it was provisionally indicated that some 154 districts were likely outside London.[221] With respect to teaching hospitals, it was confirmed that teaching groups would be established at the area level as Area Health Authorities (Teaching), while special provisions for these AHA(T)s outlined in the Consultative Document would be strengthened. However, it was also emphasised that the teaching areas were integral parts of the regional system.[222] The full integration of teaching hospitals constituted a distinct gain for the cause of unification, but an opposite trend was evident in the proposal to establish statutory committees to administer the family practitioner services. It will be recalled that the first Green Paper envisaged that family practitioners would enter into contract with area health authorities, but this evoked a storm of opposition from the profession. To rid itself of this incubus, the department quickly promised a statutory committee within the health authority to fulfil the functions of the Executive Council. This concession was embodied in both Crossman's Green Paper and the Consultative Document. In the White Paper, these statutory committees were designated as Family Practitioner Committees, a title which had been under consideration for some time to replace the colourless term Executive Council, which had been selected in an haphazard manner at the beginning of the NHS.[223] Essentially, the Executive Council was being preserved and renamed, but incorporated within the framework of the AHA. Some important responsibilities relating to primary care, such as planning or provision of health centres, which had rested hitherto mainly with local authorities, were directed to the AHA rather than the FPC. Therefore development within the field of primary care depended on the emergence of a constructive working relationship between the AHA and the FPC.[224]

The White Paper confirmed that the chairman and members of regional authorities would be appointed by the Secretary of State, but after consultation with appropriate interest groups, as in the case of appointments to RHBs. With respect to the hotly contested issue of membership of area authorities, the White Paper included provision for four local authority representatives, plus others from the health professions, but it was not specific about the number of doctors, although there was a guarantee of at least one nurse or midwife.[225] In view of the possibility that medical influence might be diminished in the new structure, as in the Labour Government's proposals, the profession was awarded the compensation of a new professional advisory structure. Assurances were also given that the central advisory machinery would be preserved, but it was intended to specify this in subsidiary legislation, rather than in a key part of the primary legislation as was the case in 1946.[226]

The few sentences in the White Paper on professional advisory machinery disguised commitments of mountainous complexity. First, the promise of separate advisory bodies was extended to doctors, dentists, opticians, pharmacists, and nurses and midwives 'at least'.[227] Secondly, the advisory machinery would operate 'at each level of management', which entailed a structure containing the same regional:area:district hierarchy as the reorganised health service. Thirdly, although not indicated in the White Paper, since the district medical committees were destined to contribute clinical members to the DMT, the advisory committees needed to be linked into the management structure and thereby required complex regulations to determine their consistent operation.[228]

Expanding on the proposals of the Consultative Document, compensation for loss of direct local accountability within the health services, especially at the district level, entailed the establishment of Community Health Councils. Instead of the suggestion in the

Consultative Document that all the members would be appointed by the AHA, it was now proposed that half should be appointed in this way, with the rest being nominated by local government district councils. Also, it was made clear that the CHCs would appoint their own chairpersons. It was stated that the secretariat would be provided by the AHA. Some general ideas were given about the functions of CHCs, their basic purpose being to 'represent to the AHA the interests of the public in the health service in its district'.[229]

In the short term, the White Paper and its associated management study were received with resigned acceptance - few signs of overt enthusiasm, but also little effective criticism. The media showed distinct signs of battle-weariness; since the planning documents were dominated by complex and inaccessible technical issues, there was a tendency for the media to abandon the field to the experts. It was perhaps felt that after such a long period of gestation, involving enormous expenditure of energy on the part of planners and professional groups possessing incalculable expertise, the stage must have been reached when reorganisation was road-worthy. Neglect on the part of the press was also due to preoccupation with more newsworthy items such as the European talks over the inflation crisis, violence in Ulster, and with the reopening of the John Poulson bankruptcy proceedings on 1 August, containing new allegations about the financial affairs of Reginald Maudling. It was a sad irony that Poulson had returned to push his former health service partners out of the headlines. On 2 August 1972, the Reorganisation White Paper commanded only three short paragraphs, squeezed into the bottom left-hand corner of the front page of the *Times*; the fuller description of the White Paper was relegated to page 10, while no information was included about Joseph's press conference. The main health service news in the home news pages was the continuing alarm about the state of long-stay hospitals, occasioned by the most recent Annual Report of the Hospital Advisory Service, the publication of which coincided with the issue of the White Paper.

Lack of media attention was a serious set-back to informed discussion on the serious issues raised by reorganisation and this prompted expressions of concern among planners and activists.[230] As noted below, a more alarmist tone within the media was not assumed until after the legislative process was complete, when of course it was too late to turn back.

Responses to the White Paper demonstrated a tendency to cling to well-worn arguments, and a disinclination to adjust to new problems raised by the Government's proposals. On account of the slowness of this learning process, initial responses suggested that the fourth effort at a planning document had reached a viable compromise.

510

However, leading articles in the major broadsheets all expressed serious reservations; of these the *Daily Telegraph* was particularly hostile, predicting that the 'beautiful, streamlined structure' would become an 'instrument of oppression'.[231]

One of the most vitriolic criticisms of the White Paper occurred in Richard Crossman's 'Personal View' column in the *Times*, which the former Secretary of State utilised to mount a further assault on insensitive regional 'satrapies'.[232] The *Guardian* similarly concluded that the 'ruling bodies in the health service would become self-perpetuating oligarchies with no time to listen to the customers'.[233] At an extreme among the critics, Dr David Stark Murray, the veteran Socialist Medical Association leader, called for a campaign to fight this 'antidemocratic legislation'.[234]

A further commonly expressed criticism was represented by the *Economist* and the *New Statesman*, which attacked the autonomy granted to Family Practitioner Committees, which the *New Statesman* predicted would perpetuate the 'cottage industry' mentality in general practice.[235] On the other hand, the *General Practitioner*, representing traditionalist opinion among the doctors, was suspicious of the Area Health Authorities, which it argued were likely to erode the independence of general practitioners.[236] The newspapers were less concerned with reduction of the public participation on health authorities than with the weakness of the new Community Health Councils; these were called 'paper tigers' by the *Observer*, whereas the *Guardian* called them 'very tame watchdogs'.[237]

The *Times* thought that reorganisation would work reasonably well if its management arrangements turned out to be a success, but it was not confident, detecting at the crucial district level, a 'distinct whiff of syndicalism'; the *Guardian* also thought that doctors had increased their control to a point where they could block integration; a pessimistic review in the *Sunday Times* was headed 'Doctors Win Again'.[238] The *Times* made a similar pronouncement on the management report, contending that the 'complex web of tasks and obligations' would introduce contradictory elements into management, and thereby concentrate power into the hands of doctors.[239] The management study at first attracted little notice because it was difficult to understand, but the *Economist* gave a foretaste of later reactions in complaining about its obscurity, opacity, and incomprehensibility. It was pointed out the DHSS was having difficulty in explaining the report to the bewildered staff of the NHS.

One of the few positive welcomes for the management report emanated from RHB Chairmen, who were satisfied that it was a 'well thought out and comprehensive document and we congratulate those

511

concerned with its preparation'. Nevertheless, the Chairmen expressed some reservations. They recommended larger AHAs in large conurbations, insisted that there should be member participation at the district level, complained that key terms like 'responsibility' and 'monitoring' were used in an ambiguous and inconsistent manner, and they were doubtful whether regional authorities would possess the power or resources to exercise the degree of control necessary to secure adequate performance from subordinate authorities. They were also sceptical about the prospects of success for consensus management. The RHB Chairmen were therefore formally enthusiastic, but in practice they were uncertain whether the management arrangements would yield the promised millennium.[240]

(vi) NHS REORGANISATION BILL

Much preparatory work on the reorganisation legislation was undertaken during the Labour administration. The National Health Service Reorganisation Bill itself was accordingly in an advanced state by the time of the publication of the Conservative Government's White Paper in August 1972.[241] This left little time for final modification of the Bill before its publication, which was scheduled to take place at the beginning of the 1972/73 parliamentary session.

The NHS reorganisation legislation was a much less momentous affair than the its predecessor in 1946. As its name suggests, reorganisation was primarily concerned with the recombination of existing elements of the health service; the component services themselves were intended to gain from reorganisation, but in the short term they were unaltered. As the above account demonstrates, many aspects of reorganisation raised delicate issues and continuing controversy. On the general level, there was a widespread scepticism about the Government's proposals; it seemed doubtful whether the new arrangements would be much of an improvement on the old. With respect to specific issues, many groups of health service personnel were dissatisfied, while consumers also had reason to be suspicious about the proposed changes. However, all of the plans for reorganisation generated since the mid-sixties had received the same kind of mixed reception. The Joseph scheme at least had the merit of having attempted to conciliate most of the powerful NHS interests, even to the extent of diluting the original austere managerial purpose of his reform. Therefore the controversy surrounding this Bill was infused with nothing like the passion generated by the controversies of 1946. Joseph's legislation was therefore not exposed to frenzied opposition, but it also inspired little fervent support.

By the date of the White Paper, the Conservative Government had succeeded in dominating the agenda with its own scheme and there was no alternative commanding widespread support. Controversy still waged on, but behind the displays of political rhetoric, practical disagreements were limited to a small number of issues, which the Government thought were of marginal importance. Following the precedent of the recent Scottish reorganisation legislation, which had enjoyed a smooth passage through Parliament, the Government's business managers decided to introduce the NHS Reorganisation Bill in the House of Lords.[242] This had the attraction of reducing congestion of business within the House of Commons, it gave a boost in status to the upper chamber, and possibly it would accelerate the passage of the Bill. On the other hand, persistent reverses in the House of Lords would introduce risk of delay in gaining the Royal Assent. This was not an unrealistic prospect because the House of Lords was inhabited by some of the known critics of the Bill, representing powerful vested interests such as the London teaching hospitals.

This decision has attracted little notice, but it was unusual for a Bill of this importance to be remitted to a subordinate Minister, or to the House of Lords. Subordinates inevitably played a large part in the Committee stages, and in supportive speeches, but it was usual for the Minister with departmental responsibility to play the lead role in strategically important debates. However, in this case, as on other occasions, Joseph was not unhappy to shun the parliamentary limelight, while Aberdare claimed the NHS Reorganisation Bill as a great coup for the House of Lords. Indeed, he suggested that this was the first time a major Bill had started its life in the Lords; it was therefore announced as an important event and a 'unique occasion'.[243]

The National Health Service Reorganisation Bill, giving effect to the White Papers, *National Health Service Reorganisation: England* (Cmnd.5055) and *National Health Service Reorganisation: Wales* (Cmnd.5057), was published on 15 November 1972. The Bill comprised 57 clauses and 5 schedules, exactly the same length as the 1946 Bill. It represented nothing like the burden on the parliamentary timetable as the recent Local Government Bill, which was more than four times the size. Much of the detail of reorganisation such as the setting up of area and regional health authorities, the central advisory bodies, the joint consultative machinery, or guidance on detailed management arrangements, was set aside for coverage by subsidiary legislation.

The Bill was relatively silent about broader aspirations. The Secretary of State continued to be bound by the general framework of obligations stated in previous legislation, undertaking to provide health services considered necessary and appropriate to meet all reasonable requirements. The services specifically mentioned were hospital and other accommodation, medical, dental, nursing and ambulance services.

Client groups specifically mentioned in the opening clauses were expectant and nursing mothers, who were promised appropriate services, and children of school age, for whom arrangements were specified to guarantee continuation of the facilities of the School Health Service. The Bill also promised continuation of the preventive, care and after-care arrangements of the kind previously exercised by local health authorities.[244] An unanticipated point of conflict in this unexceptionable list of aspirations was provided by clause 4, the seeming innocuous provision for taking over family planning services previously provided by local health authorities. As described at length in chapter V, controversy over charging for an extended family planning service was destined to become a major point of turbulence, which risked derailing the timetable for the reorganisation Bill, and it greatly increased the atmosphere of contentiousness associated with the reorganisation legislation.

The structure of the 1946 and 1972 Bills was entirely different. Whereas each main Part of the 1946 Bill was devoted to one of the branches of the tripartite administration adopted for the health service, the 1973 Bill was dominated by its first Part, which covered the organisation of the entire, unified system of administration.

The Reorganisation Bill was divided into four parts: *Part I* was concerned with the administration of the new structure. It required the relevant Secretary of State to reorganise the system of NHS administration established under the NHS Act 1946. As already indicated, the Secretary of State's functions were extended to include those exercised by local health authorities and local education authorities, including family planning services and most aspects of the School Health Service. The relevant Secretary of State was required to establish Regional Health Authorities (in England only), Area Health Authorities and Area Health Authorities (Teaching); while the area authorities were required to establish Family Practitioner Committees. The relevant Secretary of State was empowered to establish Special Health Authorities, which included such bodies as the Welsh Health Technical Services Organisation. The boundaries, constitution and financial responsibilities of the new authorities and committees were to be determined by Order in accordance with Parts I and II of Schedule 1. Part I of the Bill ended with the allocation of functions to various bodies established under the legislation: the statutory recognition of professional advisory committees; the establishment of Community Health Councils in health districts; and finally arrangements for collaboration between health authorities and local authorities, including the establishment of joint consultative committees, and for involvement of voluntary organisations.

514

Part II was occupied with the abolition of existing authorities, the transfer and protection of the rights of staff, property and endowments, and the setting up of the National Staff Commissions for England and for Wales. It also outlined special safeguards for teaching hospitals and provided for the continuation by order of 'preserved' Boards of Governors, an arrangement reflecting the indecision over the future of the London postgraduate hospitals.

Part III provided for the appointment of Health Service Commissioners for England and for Wales to investigate complaints against NHS authorities. Matters excluded from the consideration of the Health Service Commissioner were set out in clause 34 and Schedule 3.

Part IV contained a wide variety of miscellaneous and financial provisions connected with reorganisation. Particularly important were clauses 40, 41 and 44. Clause 40 allowed for the inclusion of special hospitals within the NHS, and gave the Secretary of State authority to transfer their management to a health authority. Clause 41 transferred from local authorities to the Secretary of State responsibility for the supervision and registration of nursing homes. Clause 44 allowed for the provision of technical or other assistance to developing countries.

Finally, five Schedules were concerned with: the membership of health authorities and related provisions; postgraduate teaching hospitals; matters not subject to investigation by the Health Service Commissioners; minor and consequential amendments to previous Acts; and finally, repeals of previous legislation.

The Second Reading of the NHS Reorganisation Bill took place in the House of Lords on 4 December 1972.[245] This proved to be a fairly complete rehearsal for all subsequent discussions; most of the issues of contention were raised at this stage.

By the date of this debate the White Paper had been fully dissected, while the management study had come under increasing criticism. The Government had no reason to believe that its scheme was vulnerable to attack, but it was aware of an undercurrent of distrust, even among its own supporters. The Second Reading confirmed this general lack of zeal or even genuine commitment to Joseph's plan.

DHSS failed to take account of some adverse omens, with the result that Aberdare missed this crucial opportunity to give an inspirational start to proceedings. By contrast with Bevan's eloquent testimony in 1946, Aberdare opened with a short and pedestrian statement, mainly comprising a clause by clause summary of the Bill. He also tried to meet the criticism that reorganisation was primarily a bureaucratic exercise, assuring his colleagues that the Government was not merely establishing a 'more logical administrative set-up', but also that unification would bring about genuine improvements in services and even lead to a new level of concentration on prevention and community care. He described the three pillars of the reforms as sound management, involvement of the professions in the management structure, and full collaboration with local government.[246] Aberdare also wound up the debate, obviously taken aback by the extent of criticism, admitting to some despair and sorrow that he had failed to effectively communicate the imaginativeness and exciting nature of the proposals in the Bill. Shortage of time prevented him from responding fully to criticisms, but he assured members that they had not fully understood the Government's intentions; they had therefore exaggerated the adverse consequences of the proposals.[247]

Baroness Serota opened the attack on Aberdare with the standard opposition arguments. More than twenty peers spoke. None of the speeches were particularly supportive; most were sceptical and they concentrated on specific points of criticism. Contributions from medical peers were particularly diffuse. The most effective and constructive contributions arguably came from Lady Ruthven of Freeland, Lord Grenfell, and Baroness White. The latter, and also Lord Watkins (both former Labour MPs), effectively drew attention to the disadvantages of the Bill with respect to Wales.

There was virtually universal support for unification in principle, but much doubt whether the new arrangements would turn out to be an improvement on the tripartite system. Some peers with special experience in London thought that there was insufficient reason to tamper with the tripartite system. Lords Cobbold and Cottesloe, veterans of negotiations concerning the London teaching hospitals, stoutly defended the record of the Boards of Governors, and argued that their loss would deprive the NHS of exemplars of good practice in the field of management.[248] Lord Milverton, who was accused from the Government side of speaking to a brief provided by the local authority associations, provided a stout defence of the case for local government control of the NHS; failing that, he demanded much stronger local authority representation on NHS bodies, even suggesting that they should provide the secretariat for Community Health Councils.[249]

Serota summed up on the weakness of what she called a 'virtually five tier service' and attacked the 'completely mechanistic and hierarchical system' of administration taken over from industrial and commercial models. This was contrasted unfavourably with the management arrangements in local government advocated in the Baines Report, and with the 'organic, open and more democratic structure' planned by the previous administration. Many speakers fastened on to these criticisms, complaining about the reduction in opportunities for community representation in management, and expressing fears about the excessive growth of bureaucracy, inflexible and unresponsive management, or impossibly complex management arrangements. The management study was called 'ghastly' by Serota; it was frequently criticised in the debate, the main blame was attached to the McKinsey team of consultants, the management structure being castigated as a folly of their creation.[250]

The most concentrated criticism focused on the Government's proposals for family planning and Community Health Councils. As described more fully in chapter V, Lady Gaitskell and Lady Ruthven led the call for universal and free family planning facilities. The majority of speakers complained that the Government had failed to give Community Health Councils sufficient authority or independence.[251] Given the decline in opportunities for community participation in management, about which they also complained, the Community Health Council took on special importance as an avenue for the expression of local aspirations, and for channelling complaints about failures in services. In summing up these expressions of concern, Lady White observed: 'I do not think anyone has supported the proposal that these Community Health Councils should be appointed, staffed or financed by the Area Health Authorities, whose activities it is their job to watch. The gamekeeper has been told to appoint his own poachers, and nobody believes it will work'.[252]

Although there was no sign that the critics would be able to inflict significant damage on the Government's scheme, the cool reception by peers suggested that there was no room for complacency in the handling of their amendments. The Committee stage of the Bill took up parts of five days during December and January, followed by the Report stage on two days in mid-February. This completed the main deliberations of the House of Lords. The formal Third Reading then took place on 27 February 1973.[253] The Bill was then remitted for consideration by the House of Commons. The Committee stage in the House of Lords lasted longer, and the 135 amendments taken were larger in number than was originally anticipated by the Government. Of the five major divisions occurring during the Committee and Report stages in the House of Lords, the Government won the two on accountability and the membership of RHAs, but they lost on three issues. Two of these reverses were important: first, on the administration of the London ambulance service, and secondly on charges for family planning services. The third, payment of attendance allowances for health authority members, was less significant or controversial. In response to amendments stemming from the peers, the Government volunteered a series of amendments designed to strengthen CHCs, and less important amendments on the local advisory machinery, on consultations over transfer of staff, and on the duties of the Health Service Commissioner.

The main difficulties for the Government were posed by clause 4 dealing with family planning, and clause 9 concerning CHCs. As indicated in chapter V, controversy surrounding charges for family planning services was extraneous to the reorganisation process but clumsy handling of this policy intruded family planning into a key position in the reorganisation legislation; it then constituted the main point of discomfort to the Government. Indeed, the Government's mistake imported an unnecessary point of vulnerability into the reorganisation Bill; it also allowed the family planning lobby to blackmail the Government by threatening to derail the reorganisation timetable. Debates on family planning and CHCs were the dominant items at the Committee stage; the former occupied about 60 columns and the latter about 55 columns; these two issues taken together accounted for about one-fifth of the entire Committee stage.

Of the big concessions, the most important and unwelcome was the substantial group of changes greatly increasing the authority of CHCs. As already demonstrated, in demanding greater independence and powers for CHCs, the peers were reflecting a widely-expressed demand. Unsurprisingly, this move was supported by organisations like the Consumers' Association. The Select Committee on Nationalised Industries, which in its Second Report, published in July 1971, advised that consumer bodies in the nationalised industries should be housed in offices of their own, have control of their own staff, and that their chairmen should not in any way be tied up with the boards of the relevant industries. Then in 1972, the Department of Trade and Industry published a White Paper on Consultative Councils in Nationalised Industries, which made similar recommendations. By the time of the introduction of the NHS Reorganisation Bill, the Gas industry had already applied these principles. Despite these awkward precedents, DHSS clung to the view that owing to the uniqueness of the health service, it demanded an entirely different approach. Consequently it was agreed to defend the line announced in the White Paper and resist further concessions.[254] By this stage opinion in the department was divided; some officials favoured responding to outside opinion and treating CHCs as a positive asset to the NHS; others continued to regard the CHC as an unwelcome nuisance. The danger that the CHC might fall under demonic influences evidently preyed on the mind of the Secretary of State: 'I'm more and more worried by the potential it offers for people who will make careers and names out of mischief and distortion'. In view of these risks, he decided to minimise the scope for mischief and even to consider the possibility of scrapping the CHC.[255] By contrast, both Alison and Conservative Central Office called for a more positive approach to the CHC.[256] Clause 9 dealing with CHCs was the main subject for debate in the House of Lords on 23 January 1973. As previously, the attack was effective. The chief protagonists were again Lady Ruthven of Freeland and Baroness White. They were joined by allies who had not spoken in the Second Reading debate, many of them experienced political figures, in general friendly to the Government.

Following exposure to nearly twenty amendments on this clause, it was clear that the Government commanded little support and was facing certain defeat. Aberdare's defensive ammunition was rapidly exhausted. After emergency consultations he was allowed to retreat, trying to avoid complete capitulation, but eventually conceding most of what the critics were demanding.[257] The Government agreed to revise clause 9 to grant greater authority and independence to CHCs. In further discussions, the department exercised its full ingenuity in trying to minimise its concessions, but to little avail. The tide in favour of effective CHCs was running too strongly to be resisted. The critics were supported by Sir Geoffrey Howe, in his capacity as Minister responsible for Consumer Affairs, who cited with praise a *Financial Times* article which described the CHCs as the 'enthralled slaves of the authorities'.[258] The revised clause 9, replete with 11 Government amendments introduced at the Report stage, accepted that it should be a duty imposed on the Secretary of State to establish CHCs covering all areas and their district subdivisions, and that this function would be exercised through RHAs. The latter were to ensure that at least half the members would be drawn from local authorities, and one third selected by voluntary organisations, with the rest being appointed after consultations according to guidelines agreed between RHAs and local authorities. It was furthermore proposed that the CHCs would employ their own staff, occupy separate premises if that was their wish, with funds made available by the RHA. It was finally agreed that the rights of CHCs to consultation should be prescribed in regulations. By means of these guarantees, the CHCs were effectively insulated from AHA control and given a chance to exercise some meaningful influence.[259] The strengthening of CHCs pacified their defenders to some extent, but the intransigence of the health department damaged confidence and if anything exacerbated fears that health service reorganisation was being conducted without regard to acceptable standards of accountability to the consumer.[260]

Beside minor drafting changes instigated by the Government, and more important reverses relating to CHCs and family planning, the

Government experienced a minor defeat on the question of payments to members of health authorities. With respect to Schedule 1 Part III, in the face of some disquiet, the Government was successful in making new arrangements for the payment of part-time salary to the chairmen of RHAs and AHAs. This was contrary to the practice of local government, but was defended by reference to the management responsibilities of the chairmen. Having incurred this expense, the health department wanted to avoid attendance allowances for members of the kind existing in local government, but this was rejected by the peers, and their amendment was not reversed.

Some other lesser amendments were conceded in response to pressure from the peers. For instance, on the basis of representations from professional associations, especially the medical profession, clause 8 was strengthened to transfer ultimate responsibility for establishing local professional advisory committees to the Secretary of State. The Government also agreed to allow staff associations to be consulted over transfers of employment. Finally, as noted in chapter V, an important extension in the powers of the Health Service Commissioner was granted with respect to complaints made by NHS staff on behalf of aggrieved persons who were unable to act for themselves.

The NHS Reorganisation Bill was introduced into the House of Commons on 27 February 1973. The opposition agreed to cooperate in speeding up the Commons' timetable, with a view to completing this phase of proceedings before the Whitsun recess.[261] The reorganisation Bill received its Second Reading on 26 and 27 March, equal time being devoted to England and to Wales. The Committee stage lasted from 5 April to 24 May and absorbed sixteen sittings. The Report stage was taken on 12 June, and the Third Reading on 19 June. As described in chapter V, at this point an embarrassing complication occurred owing to the reluctance of the House of Lords to relinquish its amendments on family planning. With some relief, the Government secured the Royal Assent on 5 July 1973, the exact twenty-fifth anniversary of the introduction of the NHS.

Apart from the continuing row over family planning, the final phase of the parliamentary process proved to be uneventful. In the House of Commons, especially at the Committee stage, Labour used ingenuity in trying to shift the legislation in the direction of its own thinking, but with virtually no success. Labour finally narrowed down its effort to trying to obtain a commitment to introduce an occupational health service in association with the NHS, attempting to establish neighbourhood health councils, seeking more assistance to parents with children in hospital, and finally it advocated an elaborate mechanism for obtaining better distribution of pharmaceutical services.[262] Most of the successful amendments were drafting changes inspired by the Government; in addition a few further minor concessions were made, primarily relating to the amendments already introduced in the House of Lords. In response to Labour amendments in the House of Commons, a small addition was made to clause 2 making it clear that in addition to services specified, the Secretary of State could provide 'other services as are required for the diagnosis and treatment of illness'. Further strengthening of clause 9 was accepted in order make it more explicit that CHCs would elect their own chairmen, and to allow for some members on CHCs representing shire counties and metropolitan counties.

Some other significant issues were finally cleared up without alteration in Government policy. In the House of Lords, at both the Committee and Report stages, a strong move was made to leave the administration of the ambulance service with the Greater London Council, and an amendment to this effect was carried with a substantial majority.[263] Having made the controversial decision to integrate the teaching hospitals of London according to the plan devised by the local authority associations, the Government decided that it would be pernicious to make this further concession to local government, even though in debate, Aberdare accepted that the Greater London Council had made a success of the ambulance service. It was accordingly decided to place the ambulance service in the hands on one of the four London regional health authorities.[264]

A further difficult decision related to the clause affecting hospital social workers. This small group was the only body of staff destined for transfer from hospital authorities to local government employment. The proposal to make this change was consistent with the Seebohm Report, and with the general principles adopted about the division of functions between health authorities and social service departments. However, the hospital authorities complained about the break up of their care teams, and the social workers concerned objected to the transfer. This issue was remitted to the Collaboration Working Party. This backed the Government proposals, but with the dissent of two medical members of the relevant subcommittee.[265] Subsequent consultation about the Working Party recommendation revealed a continuing split between the health and local authority interests. Last minute discussions between the Secretary of State and the relevant parties failed to produce an acceptable compromise. The Government decided to keep to its original policy and it resisted pressures in both Houses to retain hospital social work within the health service, but it agreed to a number of measures to protect the working arrangements of existing staff and prevent neglect of this branch of social work.[266] On

28 March 1973 the Secretary of State announced his intentions in reply to a parliamentary question, underlining various safeguards introduced to protect the position of hospital social work staff.[267] DHSS responded to the anxieties of the hospital social workers by circulating a comprehensive account of the circumstances leading to the Secretary of State's announcement.[268]

One of the curious features of the parliamentary debates on the NHS Reorganisation Bill was the relatively little attention given to the question of local authority representation on Area Health Authorities. At the Legislation Committee it was agreed that in debate on the relevant Schedule 2(1)(d), the Government should if necessary be willing to concede greater representation than the four members provisionally agreed by Ministers.[269] Although amendments on the relevant clause 1(d) were introduced in both Houses, they were not pressed with particular emphasis, and given no more prominence than various other amendments on clause 1 of the second Schedule. The opposition expressed more concern about the level of local authority representation on RHAs than on AHAs. The peers introduced amendments increasing the independence of RHAs and allowing for direct selection of members by local authorities, but these were reversed in the Commons. Local government failed to increase its representation on either regional or area health authorities. Consequently, the passionate debate in the Cabinet on local government representation on AHAs was not ultimately reflected in Parliament.[270]

(vii) LOGISTICS OF REORGANISATION

When the National Health Service Reorganisation Act 1973 entered the Statute Book, scarcely nine months remained for implementation of the new administrative structure. Progress towards reorganisation was charted by an important new series of circulars, the HRC series, about ninety of which were issued between June 1972 and the end of 1974. For the benefit of staff in general, DHSS produced *NHS Reorganisation News*, a brief newsletter, fifteen issues of which were produced between the autumn of 1972 and reorganisation. It was intended to adopt a print-run of 800,000 for this newsletter, and make it suitably attractive through use of colour-printing. However, this newsletter was inferior to its Welsh equivalent; it contained only the most rudimentary information and it was not very systematic. It also deteriorated in quality and informativeness after the first few issues. Fortunately, *NHS Reorganisation News* was not the only means for providing essential information for NHS staff; regions produced progress bulletins, but most of the work of disseminating information was done locally under the auspices of Joint Liaison Committees. By contrast with 1948, virtually nothing was done to inform the public about changes within the health service. Since the services to the individual were not immediately affected by reorganisation, it was not considered that the administrative changes being undertaken needed to be explained to the patient or the community.

Preparations for reorganisation were in fact well-advanced by date of introduction of the reorganisation Bill into Parliament. Vigilance was needed to avoid actions infringing the sensitivities of Parliament. The department would have liked to nominate shadow health authorities, or at least appoint shadow Chairmen of RHAs and AHAs, before the Royal Assent, but it was decided that this was not permissible. It was essential to have these appointees in place in order that they could make an impact on the work of the Joint Liaison Committees.[271] There was not much chance of appointing the first senior officers until the autumn of 1973, with the result that only top appointments would be made by the date of reorganisation. Links between these officers and the liaison committees were likely to be reasonably well-developed, since many of the senior posts in the new authorities were expected to be locally recruited.

Joint Liaison Committees

Outside London, Joint Liaison Committees were established at area level in the summer of 1972. Each of the relevant existing administrative bodies falling within the new areas, including the local authorities, nominated two officers to constitute these committees. These groups selected their own chairmen and secretaries. When area liaison committees were in place, similar groups were established at regional level.[272] Because of delays in deciding the administrative structure in London, the Joint Liaison Committees for this area were not established until January 1973.

Originally the Joint Liaison Committees were devised to perform some minor preparatory surveys. Even in August 1972 it was stressed that they were 'strictly advisory with no executive functions'.[273] However, with the realisation that the reorganisation legislation was not likely to be completed until the summer of 1973, the liaison committees assumed a much greater degree of importance. It was accepted that in practice, the new health authorities would have little choice but to accept the plans and recommendations of the liaison committees.[274]

The Joint Liaison Committees were given an ambitious remit. In practice they performed most of the functions of a shadow authority. They prepared an area profile, made recommendations on planning questions, including the location of the area headquarters and division of the area into districts, and generally made preparations for the changeover. The liaison committees were confronted with a formidable planning exercise, in scale and degree of urgency comparable with the reconstruction initiatives undertaken thirty years previously during the wartime emergency. The magnitude of this undertaking was a reflection of the bizarre administrative complications which had stood in the way of integrated planning under the tripartite system. For instance in the new county of Humberside, which was a compact area, the liaison committee was faced with integrating services administered by six local health authorities, six Executive Councils slightly different in pattern from the local authorities, and finally eight different hospital management committees belonging to two different regions. In many cases Humberside was taking over only part of the area administered by a previous authority. Because of deep-rooted local traditions, even parallel services within each part of the tripartite system were likely to possess idiosyncratic characteristics standing in the way of integration.[275]

The more effective Joint Liaison Committees performed much of their work by the date of the Royal Assent. Consequently, they anticipated Parliament and largely pre-empted the work of the Statutory Committees charged with responsibility for the reorganised service. The degree of initiative shown by Joint Liaison Committees reflected all of the traditional disparities in levels of effectiveness of administrative bodies within the health service. The committees themselves were often very large, sometimes comprising more than forty members. Some of these committees performed a complex and scientific planning exercise, involving setting up expert working groups; others treated reorganisation as a matter of administrative routine. The better liaison committees produced impressive blueprints for the future, and built up a sense of area identity in advance of reorganisation. It was admitted that the Joint Liaison Committees provided members with an entirely new opportunity for interdisciplinary co-operation; and 'many of those concerned were required to consider, for the first time, the total pattern of health care being provided within a district, area or region'.[276] The liaison work therefore became an important vehicle for professional co-operation and enlightenment. The more active committees often produced their own local information bulletins.[277]

This exercise was an important step in integrating the professions into a management structure of the health service. Although the officers remained nominally responsible to their employing authorities, the latter were about to be extinguished and were not in a mood or position to exercise much influence, with the result that the only real control of the joint committees was exercised direct from DHSS.

The task of the Joint Liaison Committees was guided by many HRC circulars, perhaps the most important of which was HRC(73)3

(January 1973), confirming that after brief consultation, the Government had largely accepted the recommendations of the Management Report. In September 1973, further guidance was issued to assist Joint Liaison Committees in their planning of standardised management arrangements for regional and area authorities during the initial phase of the reorganised service.[278] Associated with the management study were proposals for an entirely new planning system, which it was hoped to introduce in 1974. With the help of McKinsey & Co. Inc. the feasibility of the planning system was subjected to field testing in four representative areas, beginning in April 1973. These tests were later extended to a single teaching area in London. The tests took longer than expected, and they were difficult to evaluate, with the result that it was necessary to defer plans to issue guidance to liaison committees and the new area authorities by the end of 1973, or even early in 1974. In the autumn of 1973, the new authorities were told that the new planning system would be introduced shortly after reorganisation; consolidated guide-lines were not in fact produced until 1976.

Among the wide range of activities of the Joint Liaison Committee was the organisation of conferences and training courses for the staff of area and district authorities.[279] The more senior staff had access to residential courses planned by university departments in conjunction with DHSS, while regional authorities made available lecture notes and visual aids for use at the local level. A short film explaining the objectives of reorganisation produced by the NHS Training Aids Unit was distributed to regions in the late autumn of 1973 for use in local training courses.

Although much attention was given to training and publicity, local staff often received little in-service training and were therefore ill-prepared for the changes. Nevertheless, in general the training arrangements were an enormous advance on the situation in 1948, when virtually no formal training was available for the new service.

The peak of the work of the liaison committees occurred between the autumn of 1972 and the summer of 1973. After that date important HRC circulars were still being produced, but many came too late to assist the liaison work. By this stage, the liaison committees began handing over to the new area authorities, and most of them had virtually ceased work by the end of 1973.

NHS Staff Commission and Personnel Arrangements
To the 700,000 health service personnel, reorganisation involved an enormous upheaval and often much anxiety before they could settle down into employment under the new authorities.[280] Virtually all of their existing employing bodies were abolished and new contracts, often for variant appointments, were in the hands of entirely new

administrative authorities. In order to prevent unnecessary insecurity and to provide an independent machinery for overseeing transfer and recruitment of staff, and for dealing with redundancies and grievances, it was decided to follow the example of local government reorganisation, by establishing a National Staff Commission. This proposal was included in the second Green Paper and it was well-received.[281]

The NHS legislation provided for the establishment of two National Staff Commissions, one for England and the other for Wales.[282] In view of the late date of the reorganisation legislation, it was essential for these bodies to begin work well in advance of the Royal Assent. Bearing in mind adverse comment in Parliament when the Parliamentary Commissioner's Office was set up in advance of legislation, careful arrangements were necessary to preclude any impression of irregularity. The local government reformers heeded the same warning. Following the model adopted in 1966 when an informal body was established in advance of the statutory Decimal Currency Board set up in 1967, it was decided to set up a shadow staff board in advance of the NHS Staff Commission. Preparations for the Staff Commissions began in the summer of 1971. The shadow NHS Staff Advisory Committee in England was established at the same time as the Joint Liaison Committees in the summer of 1972. The Chairman of the Staff Advisory Committee and later the Staff Commission was Sir Richard Hayward, a former Deputy-General Secretary of the Union of Post Office Workers, an experienced Whitley Council figure, and Chairman of the Supplementary Benefits Commission 1966-1969.[283] The Commission was not a permanent NHS body; it was wound up on completion of its work in July 1975.[284]

The National Staff Commission built upon the experience of the existing National Staff Committees, as well as more specialised committees, such as the Advisory Committees on Hospital Engineering Training and Ancillary Staff Training. The National Staff Committees had been in existence since 1967; they had gained invaluable experience both at national and local level on manpower, personnel and training questions.

In the spring of 1973, the two existing National Staff Committees, one for Administrative and Clerical Staff, the other for Nurses and Midwives were strengthened.[285] The chair of both committees was assumed by Dame Isabel Graham-Bryce, an influential figure who had chaired the previous committees, and had until recently chaired the Oxford RHB. A J Bennett, an Under Secretary from DHSS, and Secretary to the National Committees, was also appointed as the Secretary of the NHS Staff Commission. These committees continued to give advice on personnel and training problems; to assist the reorganisation process they were expected to evolve improved appraisal systems, but their work was too slow to have an immediate impact, and in the case of the Administrative and Clerical National Committee, the pre-reorganisation appraisal system for middle and senior staff was allowed to lapse.

The small English Staff Advisory Committee and its successor National Staff Commission were powerful influences in determining management appointments in the reorganised service.[286] As expected from the health service experience which predominated on the Commission, it was efficiently protective of current staff; except in the limited case of CHCs, recruitment from outside was only possible in exceptional circumstances. Initially, the main work of the Commission related to the filling of top administrative posts at regional and area levels. In the spring of 1973, the Commission began discussion with the Whitley Councils on the grading of top posts. On 21 May 1973 the Secretary of State announced the salary scales which would be available on a provisional basis for senior appointments. Determination of initial salary scales for the top appointments raised sensitive issues because these top salaries constituted yardsticks which influenced the entire salary structure for the relevant groups. Within the context of its pay restraint policy, the Government wanted to prevent reorganisation from becoming an occasion for the escalation of NHS salaries. Maintaining top salaries at a modest level became central to this effort. The result was an acrimonious row over all of the salary scales for chief officers, which lasted from the summer of 1972 until the summer of 1973. The organisations representing the chief officers argued that their scales compared unfavourably with local government equivalents; nurses in particular were dissatisfied about relativities adopted between the chief officers; all of the groups complained that the Government was attempting to impose salaries in an arbitrary manner, rather than on the basis of agreed procedures of assessment. Community physicians were best protected because they benefited from the relatively favourable terms applying to other doctors, as determined by their pay review body. Nurses were the least well treated, but they took their grievance to the Prime Minister and were given a small concession, allowing the salary of the Chief Nursing Officer to be increased from 70 to 75 per cent of the salary of the chief administrator. Joseph was faced with divided loyalties; he subscribed to a stern wages policy, but conceded that chief officers in the NHS were being paid unrealistically low salaries. He complained about being forced to impose a more parsimonious regime than was being applied in the comparable field of local government.[287] Faced with continuing dissatisfaction, especially over the imposition of salary scales for top nurses, in January 1974 Joseph gave an undertaking to review the top salary structure after a year. As noted in chapter VII, this review was not completed until 1979.

Advertisements for the top posts were made on the basis of provisional salaries. The initial round of appointments was organised on a national basis. The closing date for the first round of applicants was 30 June 1973, a date still in advance of the Royal Assent. With the aid of specialist panels of assessors, shortlists were prepared centrally for consideration by selection committees of the new regional and area authorities which themselves were assisted by assessors selected by the Commission.[288] The final selection was also superintended over by the Commission, taking into account the preferences of both the employing authorities and candidates.

By the end of 1973 the first group of chief officer appointments had been made at both region and area levels. The other senior regional and area appointments involving national competition were made before the appointed day. The last of these posts to be advertised were the Regional Supplies Officers and the Regional Works Officers. Fewer than half of the latter posts had been filled by the date of reorganisation.[289]

The next stage in the work of the Staff Commission, also taking place before reorganisation, was supervising the filling of senior posts at district level, senior support posts at area level, including the administrators of Family Practitioner Committees. In these cases the field of competition was the region. For this purpose each region established a Regional Appointments Unit. AHA committees were assisted by panels of assessors drawn from lists provided by the National Staff Committees, and for community physicians, by the newly founded Faculty of Community Medicine of the Royal College of Physicians. By this stage the task of recruitment was becoming complex and time-consuming. As progress was made in filling each tier in the hierarchy, the appointments procedure became more routine and it was conducted on a more local basis, but it was never simple, and the numbers involved were substantial. By February 1974, about 750 appointments, including 80 per cent of senior regional and area posts, had been filled under the supervision of the National Staff Commission.[290] By mid-May 1974 this total had reached about 2000.[291] Having filled the most of the strategic posts, on the basis of the appointments procedures worked out by the National Staff Commission, the vast majority of other posts were filled by transfer. This group of appointments also included some senior posts, such as Regional Architect, Regional Engineer, Regional Quantity Surveyor and Regional Pharmaceutical Officer. Large groups of transferred staff were alarmed by delays in issuing notices of confirmation of their posts. This problem occasioned a clash between employers and employees. The department and regional personnel officers tended to avoid granting confirmation notices, whereas the staff associations and unions insisted on the issue of these notices in order to relieve anxiety among their members. The department was concerned that premature confirmation would lead to wasteful allocation of staff, and stringent rules were at first in force for the confirmation of posts. However, this machinery proved impossible to implement, with the result that in the autumn of 1974 health authorities were allowed a greater degree of discretion in appointment of their staffs.[292] The demarcation line between posts to be filled by competition and transfer was the cause of controversy. Senior nurses found themselves in the position of being forced to apply on successive occasions for posts little different from the ones they were currently holding: first in connection with the Salmon and Mayston reforms, then with respect to the first round of reorganisation, and finally in connection with the filling of divisional posts. Reflecting the anxieties among those affected, their professional bodies complained to the National Staff Commission, pointing out that their members were being placed in a humiliating position by the appointments procedures.[293]

There was a variable degree of competition for posts. There were on average fewer than three applicants for every area treasurer appointment, but slightly greater competition for the posts of area medical officer and area administrator. There were an average of four applicants for each post of regional treasurer, but much stronger competition for the regional medical and administrator posts.[294] Given the importance of these appointments, it is noticeable that the field of applicants was extremely small. This suggests that the programme of appointments was largely predetermined, an impression that is confirmed by examination of the results of the recruitment exercise. Continuity is the main impression given by the pattern of senior appointments. When it is appreciated that some change was accounted for through the process of natural wastage, the amount of alteration in the top management at the time of reorganisation was particularly small.

The chief officers of the regional authorities, who were the first appointees, are representative of the general pattern. Taking the non-medical appointments as a group (Regional Administrator, Chief Nursing Officer and Treasurer), the superficial impression is one of change.[295] Only two of the smallest regions (Oxford and East Anglia) imported all of their RHB senior officers into the RHA. On the other hand, only N E Thames experienced a complete changeover in these appointments. Continuity was maintained in eight of the appointments of Regional Administrators, six of the Chief Nursing Officers, and ten of the Treasurers.[296] Even where

529

change occurred, the new appointee tended to be recruited either from the same RHB, a nearby HMC, or Board of Governors. Truly outside appointments were rare, and none came from outside the health service. The most adventurous appointment among the Regional Administrators was promotion of the Secretary of Northwick Park HMC to Wessex. The only marginally experimental move among nurses was the promotion of the Chief Nursing Officer from South Teeside HMC to become Chief Nursing Officer of the Yorkshire RHA. Similarly, there was only one unusual change among the Treasurers, where the Treasurer of St Thomas's Hospital moved to Mersey RHA. Appointments at area level tended to be similarly uneventful; in general, where retirement did not intervene, the most senior group administrator, finance officer and nursing officer were confirmed in the senior posts of the new area health authority.

Potentially the promotion situation was more fluid among the administrative medical staff. The Regional Medical Officer appointment opened up the prospects of competition between the medical staffs of the RHBs and the Medical Officers of Health of large local health authorities. As in the case of the 1948 changes, public health doctors were the group of medical staff most disadvantaged by reorganisation. More than 1,250 public health doctors were holding senior appointments in England and Wales, but there were only about 250 assured equivalents under the reorganised health service.[297] Indeed, even this total was uncertain until the summer of 1973, when district arrangements were confirmed. The prospect of wholesale redundancy among public health doctors was an embarrassment to the Secretary of State, who was criticised on this point during the Second Reading debate in the House of Commons. This seemed like evidence of lack of even-handedness with respect to the former local health authorities, and contrary to assurances given about the importance attached to the new specialty of community medicine. In adopting stringent criteria for senior appointments in community medicine, officials were acting in response to instructions from their Ministers, who were told by the Treasury to prevent escalation of administration within the new health authorities. In this instance Joseph encouraged a more flexible approach and personally suggested that the Government should guarantee at least 620 senior appointments.[298] This issue was also taken up aggressively by the BMA, which extracted a promise that at least 850 senior appointments would be forthcoming.[299] Neither this information, nor details about retirement packages were available to the Medical Officers of Health at the time of advertisement of senior regional and area posts in the summer of 1973. It was not until these advertisements appeared that it was made clear that appointments to administrative medical posts would be limited to doctors with previous administrative experience. Hitherto, the impression had been given that an opportunity to enter community medicine would be available to a much wider range of doctors.

In view of the uncertainty and confusion surrounding the new specialty of community medicine, many public health doctors applied for the new administrative posts who might otherwise have preferred early retirement, while other promising candidates drifted out of community medicine because of doubts about prospects for the future. This was the unsatisfactory conclusion to a long period of uncertainty that had extended at least since establishment of the Seebohm Committee.

At the regional level, administrative medical appointments reflected the conservative pattern evident for their colleagues in the regional officer team. Ten of the RMO appointments went to the existing Senior Administrative Medical Officers of the RHBs.[300] In two other cases the SAMO was succeeded by a SAMO from another region or by a Deputy-SAMO. In just two cases, MOHs succeeded in breaking into the regional public health administrative structure at this senior level.

At the area level, some 186 county and county borough MOHs in England and Wales competed for 98 Area Medical Officer appointments. Inevitably this involved some bitter disappointments and even some sense of humiliation. With reorganisation, certain of the most prestigious posts in public health medicine disappeared completely; there was no longer a MOH for greater London, or for the West Riding of Yorkshire. The MOH for the GLC retired, while the MOH for the West Riding went to the much less important post of AMO for the Kirklees area of Yorkshire.

The worst disappointments for MOHs occurred in multi-district areas, where of course, only one person was able to succeed to the AMO post. In regions containing many single-district areas (of which there were 38) the existing MOHs stood a better chance of succeeding to the area appointment. The Yorkshire region had only one single district area whereas there were six in the Northern Region. Thus, in the Northern region, at Newcastle, Gateshead, Sunderland and Hartlepool, the local MOH became installed as the AMO. Consequently, for public health doctors, reorganisation became something of a lottery, in which their chances of professional survival depended on the vagaries of decisions about local government reorganisation in their areas.

Regions, Areas and Districts
The problem of the region had always been central to the reorganisation exercise. After consideration of every alternative from

531

abolition to multiplication, the Joseph proposals were something of an anti-climax, essentially representing a continuation of the existing pattern and reflecting the trend in policy concerning their functions that had been evolving almost since the beginning of the NHS.

The scheme adopted for the Regions followed the lines laid down in the White Paper. At that stage the new regions were given numbers rather than names.[301] In July 1973, as soon as possible after the Royal Assent, the Secretary of State announced the revised list of names for the regions, as well as the identities of their first Chairmen. The orders determining the regions and establishing Regional Health Authorities came into operation on 6 August 1973.[302] The extent of these changes of chairmanship is indicated in Table 6.1, while the area and district composition of the regions is given in Table 6.2. The geography of the 1974 reorganisation for England is indicated on Map 1 (local government) and Map 2 (health service).

The regional pattern of the former Regional Hospital Boards was adopted with minor alterations. The ranking order of populations was only marginally affected. Whereas the population in Wales and Scotland was static, the population in England increased from 41 million to 46 million between 1949 and 1974. Consequently, most of the new RHAs had larger populations than the equivalent RHBs at their formation; the biggest increase had occurred in the Oxford RHA, where the population in 1974 was 57 per cent greater than the Oxford RHB population in 1949, despite transfer to Wessex at reorganisation of the eastern slice of Wiltshire. The populations of the regions ranged from 1.8 million (East Anglia) to 5.2 million (West Midlands).

Changes in regional boundaries have already been discussed. The new names for the regions outside London were more responsive to local sensitivities because they related to geographical and planning areas, rather than being based on the notion that a region was defined as the catchment area for a particular medical school.

As already noted, the East Midlands was a problem area in the definition of regions. In view of disadvantages arising from any split in the Sheffield region, it was decided to retain the link between Sheffield and the East Midlands. Minor compensation was offered by renaming the Sheffield region 'Trent' to emphasise its links with the Midlands, which was inappropriate with respect to Yorkshire, where more than a quarter of the population resided.[303] This failed to resolve the tension between the various parts of the region. A contest took place over the siting of the headquarters for the Trent region, which was not resolved amicably; on this occasion the susceptibilities of the midlanders were sacrificed and the headquarters remained in Fulwood, Sheffield.[304]

Table 6.1
Regional Hospital Boards, Equivalent Regional Health Authorities, and their Chairmen, 1974

Regional Hospital Board	Chairmen	Regional Health Authority	Chairmen
Newcastle	Col W A Lee OBE TD DL	Northern	Col W A Lee OBE TD DL
Leeds	L E Laycock CBE JP	Yorkshire	W Tweddle CBE TD LLM[1]
Sheffield	Ald S P King OBE JP[1]	Trent	Ald S P King CBE JP
East Anglian	Sir Stephen Lycett Green BT CBE DL JP	East Anglia	The Hon Leo Russell CBE TD
N W Metropolitan	Sir Maurice Hackett OBE	N W Thames	Ald Mrs B F R Paterson CBE JP
N E Metropolitan	Sir Graham Rowlandson MBE JP	N E Thames	H R Moore CBE
S E Metropolitan	J C Donne	S E Thames	J C Donne
S W Metropolitan	Sir Desmond Bonham-Carter TD	S W Thames	Mrs Inga-Stina Robson JP[2]
Wessex	Col J W Weld OBE TD[1]	Wessex	Col J W Weld OBE TD
Oxford	D Woodrow MA	Oxford	D Woodrow MA
South Western	Sir John English MBE[3]	South Western	W R Northcott[4]
Birmingham	D A Perris MBE JP	West Midlands	D A Perris MBE JP
Liverpool	D A Solomon MBE LLB BCOM JP[1]	Mersey	E W Driver BSC FICE
Manchester	T Hourigan CBE CA JP	North Western	S C Hamburger CBE JP

Notes: See Maps 1 and 2.

1. At about the time of reorganisation, knighthoods were granted to King, Solomon, Tweddle and Weld.
2. In 1974 Robson was created the Baroness Robson of Kiddington.
3. Owing to the death of English, a temporary appointment preceded Northcott.
4. Northcott was quickly succeeded by B H Bailey JP.

The choice of chairmen for the new regional authorities was made at an early stage. The department produced a list of possible names which was discussed with the Secretary of State on 24 October 1972, and again on 15 February and 16 April 1973. Of the names produced by the department for the first of these meetings, about seven of the first choices were eventually nominated as chairmen. All these candidates were men. At the April meeting, the Secretary of State suggested the two women, who were duly appointed to the chairs of Thames regional authorities. These were the only women among the fourteen regional chairs.[305] As already noted, the list of RHA chairmen was announced by the Secretary of State in July and they formally took up office in August 1973.

The transition from the RHBs to the RHAs was used as an opportunity to increase the rate of turnover of chairmen. Veterans such as Sir Desmond Bonham-Carter, Sir Stephen Lycett Green, Sir Maurice Hackett, T Hourigan, L E Laycock, Sir Graham Rowlandson and D A Solomon were dispatched, mostly willingly, into retirement. Six of the RHB chairmen succeeded to RHA chairs, but three of these were recent appointments; only King, Lee and Perris had been in their post for four years or longer. The changeover was therefore considerable. Of the four labour and trade union RHB chairmen, English died in 1973; the reorganisation phased out Hourigan and Hackett, leaving King and Perris as the two labour survivors to reach the RHA. King was regarded as an outstanding success within his region, while there was no obvious alternative to Perris for a region which possessed a record for disharmony. The labour representation was increased to three by the appointment of Hamburger to succeed Hourigan in Manchester/North Western. The only viable alternative candidate for this chairmanship was also a labour representative. Whether by intent or accident, the labour share of regional chairmanships under reorganisation was precisely the same as in 1948.[306]

It is difficult to generalise about the changes in regional chairmanships which took place during the phase of reorganisation. Crossman was rather scathing about the pre-1970 cohort of chairmen; apart from Bonham-Carter and Rowlandson, he complained that most were 'fairly feeble creatures' ruled by their officials.[307] The political, gender and social class imbalance among the chairmen remained much the same as it had been before 1974. Business executives and solicitors predominated, while representatives of labour, women, and other occupations were little favoured. There was a marginal decline in the average age of the chairmen; in 1948 nine chairmen were aged 65 or over, whereas in 1974 only three were above this age.

One of the few constants in policy-making on reorganisation was the acceptance that the main statutory authorities responsible for health services should coincide with the equivalent areas of local government. In general it was accepted that there would be a one-to-one relationship, but in London, where reorganisation of local government had already occurred, the Labour Government had conceded that most London boroughs would need to be grouped to some extent, its most favoured option entailing pairing in the majority of cases. It has already been seen that this proposal was accepted by the Government at the end of 1972 in the face of strong opposition from the teaching hospitals.

Opinion on the basic units of local government outside London changed considerably in the course of the local government reform process, but the idea of coterminosity persisted, and it was strengthened by the Seebohm reforms; from this point it was taken as an irrevocable maxim in planning for reorganisation that health service and social service areas should be coterminous. The determination of areas in the reorganised health service was in practice remitted to the local government reformers. The local government proposals of the Conservative Government were first announced in a White Paper issued in February 1971, which proposed outside London, 44 non-metropolitan counties, and, as their equivalents, 34 metropolitan districts.[308] The Joseph Consultative Document published in May 1971 briefly mentioned that there would be 'about 70' of these area authorities outside London.[309]

The Local Government Bill was introduced into Parliament in November 1972; its detailed consideration occupied a huge amount of parliamentary time; the Committee stage in the House of Commons had only just been completed by the date of the NHS reorganisation White Paper in August 1972. The latter took account of the current stage of the local government Bill, which implied that outside London, the areas of the reorganised health service would align with the boundaries of 38 non-metropolitan counties and 34 metropolitan districts. These alterations to the original local government White Paper proposals resulted from amalgamation of the some of the 45 existing counties with smaller or more scattered populations, as well as recombination to produce the new non-metropolitan county of Humberside. An eleventh-hour concession led to adoption of the Isle of Wight as a separate county. At the Royal Assent in November 1972, the Local Government Act 1972 allowed for 39 non-metropolitan counties and 36 metropolitan districts, making a total of 75 authorities outside London. The final stage in the local government reform process was the laying orders by the Secretary of State for the Environment setting out the boundaries and names of the metropolitan districts and the much smaller non-metropolitan districts, a process which was completed at the beginning of 1973. The non-metropolitan counties retained their original names, but the Local Government Act permitted alteration on the basis of common agreement. As indicated by Maps 1 and 2, the names adopted in local government reorganisation were taken over without change by the areas of the reorganised health service.

535

The NHS legislation accepted that outside London, the area authorities would coincide with the non-metropolitan counties and the metropolitan districts, the only exception being the combination of the Merseyside metropolitan districts of St Helens and Knowsley into a single area health authority.[310] This produced a total of 74 Area Health Authorities outside the capital. In London, as already observed, it was agreed to combine the London Boroughs into 16 Area Health Authorities, which produced a total of 90 AHAs for England as a whole. Various London boroughs opposed linkage in pairs to form area authorities, but the department resisted attempts at rearrangement, or, as in the case of Newham, an attempted break-away from the three other parts of the City area to form a separate health authority.[311]

Not all of the areas were satisfied with the area organisation adopted. For instance, a deputation from Lancashire complained that the proposed Lancashire AHA was too large; the four largest county boroughs (Burnley, Preston, Blackburn and Blackpool, with a total population of nearly half a million, and their individual populations ranging from 77,000 to 152,000) pointed out that they would have been designated as districts of a metropolitan county. These authorities complained about arbitrary discrimination, contrasting their situation with neighbouring Bury and Rochdale, which gained metropolitan district status, or the Isle of Wight, which was a non-metropolitan county. These four Lancashire petitioners lost control of social services and education as a consequence of local government reorganisation, and were reduced to health districts as a result of changes in the health service. These alterations represented a considerable relegation in status compared with their former position as county boroughs. The mid-Lancashire towns were also concerned that not all local authorities would find a place on the Lancashire AHA. Finally, they pointed out that the proposals for dividing their AHA into six health districts was making their situation even worse because it failed to observe compatibility with the boundaries of the county boroughs, or the administrative divisional arrangements being adopted for the social services and education. The Secretary of State offered to increase the size of the membership of AHAs in such circumstances, and agreed that district boundaries should be reexamined, but he insisted that otherwise, CHCs were sufficient to protect local interests.[312]

The AHAs outside London ranged in population size from the Isle of Wight (110,000) to four (Essex, Hampshire, Kent and Lancashire), each containing between 1.3 million and 1.5 million. The original Redcliffe-Maude proposals were designed to avoid unitary authorities with populations below 250,000, which was regarded as the minimum acceptable for health and social service purposes, but this principle was gradually eroded, with the result that the final arrangements included about 15 AHAs with populations of less than 250,000.

As indicated by the mid-Lancashire example, subdivision of areas into districts offered great scope for controversy. This problem was not handled decisively, with the result that considerable confusion, annoyance and time-wasting ensued. There was confusion about the relative roles to be played by DHSS, the RHAs and the AHAs. The basic preparation was in practice undertaken by the Joint Liaison Committees. District arrangements were of fundamental importance to efficiency and harmony within the areas; accordingly the Joint Liaison Committees adopted this problem as one of their first priorities. The liaison committees were handicapped by vague and inconsistent advice. The 1972 White Paper (para 45), reinforced by HRC(73)4 (February 1973) emphasised that the main goal was identification of 'natural health districts', or 'natural communities for the planning and delivery of comprehensive health care', with populations ranging from 200,000 to 500,000, and not necessarily taking account of local government district boundaries. On this basis, the White Paper suggested that there might be 154 non-metropolitan districts.

The Management Report made somewhat similar recommendations, but it suggested populations of between 200,000 and 300,000 (although elsewhere it recommended between 100,000 and 400,000), but insisted that the boundaries should 'correspond both with local authority district boundaries and with operational divisions of social work departments'.[313] This principle was consistent with the long-standing decision to maintain strict compatibility between health and social service administrations. Sacrificing this criterion in the districts would undermine the justification of its adoption at the area level.

Given difficulties of reconciling the above not entirely consistent guide-lines, tensions resulting from passionate defence of local interests, and the insistence by DHSS that plans should be submitted within two months, it is not surprising that the schemes adopted by Joint Liaison Committees were in many cases hasty compromises. It was assumed that the district proposals would be scrutinised by DHSS and in revised form be submitted to the AHAs for their consideration and ratification in the summer of 1973. However, in view of representations of the kind received from mid-Lancashire, and having observed the difficulties experienced by liaison committees in reaching acceptable conclusions, the Secretary of State intervened and took over the determination of district arrangements. His settlement announced in August 1973, tended to be more attentive to non-metropolitan local government district boundaries, but at the cost of the notion that health districts would be natural units of planning based on patient flows with respect to district general hospitals.

As indicated in Table 6.2, the Secretary of State's intervention increased the number of districts in the English health service to 205, a number which was whittled down to 199 by 1979. This intervention by the Secretary of State may have been politically unavoidable, but it caused much resentment within the liaison committees, who saw a great deal of their most important work peremptorily thrown on the scrap heap.[314] It was also not an auspicious start for the supposedly important Area Health Authorities. However, the AHAs were not in a position to make a decisive contribution; first, the authorities themselves needed some time to recruit their full complement of members; secondly, they needed further time to build up their teams of officers. The formal machinery needed for such operations slowed down the work of the new AHAs, a problem which had not affected the ad hoc Joint Liaison Committees.

In the event, more than one-third of the areas (38) remained undivided; these were often called single-district areas. At the other end of the spectrum, three areas were each divided into six districts. The size of districts ranged from under 100,000 to about 500,000. Many of the large districts therefore exceeded in size the smaller areas. The numbers of areas and districts contained in each region are indicated in Table 6.2. The orders establishing the boundaries and constitution of Area Health Authorities came into operation on 20 and 24 August 1973.[315] The appointments of Chairmen of the Area Health Authorities were announced by the Secretary of State shortly afterwards, and they were then consulted by the RHAs about AHA membership. The AHAs were sufficiently complete to begin their meetings in the autumn of 1973.

Abolition of more than 370 HMCs provided a big reservoir of experienced committee members from which to recruit the smaller numbers required for service on the AHAs. There were more than 6,000 members of HMCs, compared with about 1,500 required by the AHAs. Of the eleven AHAs in the North Western region, the chairs were allocated to seven men from business and commerce, three male solicitors, and one housewife. Of the nine areas in Wessex and the South Western regions, four of the chairs were granted to businessmen, three to retired male colonial civil servants (including the retired Governor General of Malta and the retired Governors of Fiji and Hong Kong), while two went to persons designated as 'housewives'. In these two regions, most of the new chairmen had been members of some kind of health authority, but only half had been chairman of an HMC. Although the area authorities were substantial administrative assignments, introducing for the first

538

Table 6.2
Regional Health Authorities, Areas and Districts, 1979

Region No.	Regional Authority	Population (millions) 1974	No. of Areas	1[1]	2	3	4	5	6	No. of Districts
1.	Northern	3.1	9	6	-	2	1	-	-	16
2.	Yorkshire	3.6	7	1	4	-	2	-	-	17
3.	Trent	4.5	8	3	2	2	1	-	-	17
4.	East Anglia	1.8	3	-	2	1	-	-	-	7
5.	N W Thames	3.5	7	1	3	1	2	-	-	18
6.	N E Thames	3.7	6	-	3	2	-	1	-	17
7.	S E Thames	3.6	5	1	1	1	1	-	1	16
8.	S W Thames	2.9	5	2	-	2	-	-	1	14
9.	Wessex	2.6	4	1	1	1	1	-	-	10
10.	Oxford	2.2	4	1	3	-	-	-	-	7
11.	South Western	3.1	5	3	-	1	1	-	-	10
12.	West Midlands	5.2	11	7	-	2	1	1	-	22
13.	Mersey	2.5	5	3	1	-	-	1	-	10
14.	North Western	4.1	11	9	-	1	-	-	1	18
TOTAL		46.4	90	38	20	16	10	3	3	199

Notes: See Maps 1 and 2.

1. 1-6: Number of Areas with 1 to 6 Districts.

Source: Adapted from N W Chaplin, ed, *Health Care in the UK. Its Organisation and Management* (Kluwer Medical, 1982), Table 1, p 81.

time part-time remuneration for the chairmen, the persons occupying these positions were often relatively untried hands. Of the ninety chairmen, only six were women, and seven labour or trade unionists, compared with thirty-seven business executives and fifteen solicitors and accountants.[316] There were wide differences between the regions in the representation of women on AHAs. The average was about 25 per cent, but in South West Thames, women accounted for 33 per cent of the members, whereas in Yorkshire only 14 per cent were women.

Nineteen area authorities were designated as Area Health Authorities (Teaching). These areas contained the undergraduate teaching hospitals and medical schools. They were the descendants of the prestigious Boards of Governors; they therefore constituted the elite of the area authorities.

As indicated in Table 6.3, six of the new teaching areas were located in London; these contained the twelve undergraduate teaching hospitals. Brent and Harrow applied for teaching status,

Table 6.3
Regional Health Authorities, Teaching Areas and Chairmen, 1974

Region No.	RHA Name	Teaching Areas	Chairmen
1.	Northern	Newcastle-upon-Tyne	M I B Straker CBE JP
2.	Yorkshire	Leeds	J Fattorini MBE TD JP
3.	Trent	Leicestershire	C Adolphe
		Nottinghamshire	D L Evans JP
		Sheffield	J M Carlisle MI MECH. E MI MAR. E MBIM
4.	East Anglia	Cambridgeshire	Mrs P R Burnet CBE JP
5.	N W Thames	Ealing, Hammersmith and Hounslow Kensington, Chelsea and Westminster	T Meyer Mrs C B Bicknell
6.	N E Thames	Camden and Islington City and East London	B L Salmon F M Cumberledge
7.	S E Thames	Lambeth, Southwark and Lewisham	Sir Kenneth Younger PC KBE
8.	S W Thames	Merton, Sutton and Wandsworth	Mrs A Munro CBE MA
9.	Wessex	Hampshire	Ald A Asquith-Leeson CBE JP TD
10.	Oxford	Oxfordshire	W R Gowers MA HON. DCL
11.	South Western	Avon	C W Thomas
12.	West Midlands	Birmingham	J R Bettinson LLB
13.	Mersey	Liverpool	T B Roberts TD LLD
14.	North Western	Manchester Salford	R B Prain R Roberts MBE

Note: See Map 2.

but this was rejected.[317] Most of the provincial regions contained a single teaching area, but owing to establishment of the new medical schools at Leicester and Nottingham, the Trent region contained three medical schools.

As a group, the chairmen of teaching areas were not dissimilar from the chairmen of the non-teaching area authorities. The teaching chairs were dominated by businessmen (9), after which came solicitors (4), finally there was a single farmer, banker, ex-civil servant, an ex-politician turned voluntary sector executive, a headmistress of a London public school, and a single trade union official. Out of the nineteen, three were women. Only two chairmen of the Board of Governors of an undergraduate teaching hospitals (Oxford and St.George's) survived to become the chairman of a new teaching area; in a third case, the chairman of a postgraduate teaching hospital (Moorfields Eye Hospital) was promoted to become chairman of the City and East London teaching area. Many of the other chairmen of teaching areas had been chairmen of HMCs or members of Boards of Governors.[318] Many of these names had been shortlisted as possible chairmen of the regional boards. Consistent with the guiding principles laid down in the Consultative Document, the leadership of the area authorities was selected for its management orientation, rather than with respect to its links with community interests.

Family Practitioner Committees
Establishment of Family Practitioner Committees was in principle a relatively straightforward operation. Owing to the demands of the medical profession, these committees were structured on the model of Executive Councils. The BMA was not entirely satisfied with the outcome. It wanted more safeguards for the independent contractor written into the reorganisation Bill than the Secretary of State was willing to concede. Joseph persuaded the medical profession to accept the current compromise on the grounds that further change would invite a backlash from the large and influential body of opinion opposed in principle to the existence of a statutory committee for independent contractors.[319]

Although FPCs were associated with the Area Health Authorities, the latter delegated all routine functions; links between FPCs and AHAs were therefore somewhat tenuous. However, the AHA appointed eleven of the 30 FPC members, and retained an important role in any matters connected with capital development and planning of integrated work between general practitioners and employees of the AHA. The growth of interest in health centres and the popularity of attachment schemes necessitated communication and some fruitful co-operation, which operated to the advantage of the more progressive practices.

541

Detailed instructions concerning the establishment of FPCs were not available until October 1973.[320] Some delay in establishing FPCs resulted from the many constituencies involved in nominating members. As already noted, the largest block of lay members was drawn from the AHAs, but a small number were nominated by the local authority. The professional side appointed half the members; these were drawn from each of the four groups of independent contractors, all of whom needed to establish their Local Representative Committees. Each of these committees required recognition by the Secretary of State before they could make nominations. The FPCs were fully constituted by the beginning of 1974. They selected their own chairmen; after which their first business was to collaborate with the AHAs in selecting the Administrators FPS. Accordingly there was no chance that they could become fully operational until near the appointed day.[321]

This delay was unsettling for the staff of the local offices, many of whom experienced a period of anxiety and uncertainty. In practice the FPC faced some awkward complications, particularly occasioned by complete changes in the boundaries of the administrative areas. This created difficulties about the location of staff and entailed complicated splitting and merging of records relating to patients. For instance, the Humberside FPC was faced with collating records from five Executive Councils, only two of which were absorbed in their entirety.

Professional Advisory Machinery
Establishment of a comprehensive professional advisory machinery represented a long-standing pledge by Ministers. Owing to the Conservative Government's intention to give NHS authorities a management rather than representative function, advisory committees took on greater importance, because they were needed to satisfy the medical profession that its voice would be heard at each level of administration. Because it was invidious to pay heed exclusively to medical opinion, the Government promised to make arrangements for receiving all relevant professional advice. The Consultative Document promised that 'strong professional advisory machinery should be established at both regional and area level'.[322] The White Paper expanded on this statement, without offering any specific recommendations.[323] Formation of professional advisory bodies was a complex business and the full advisory structure was never fully implemented.[324] Speed in setting up of the local medical advisory bodies was essential, since the area and district Medical Committees contributed directly to the Area Management Team in single-district areas and to the District Management Team in multi-district areas.[325] The extraordinarily elaborate structures required to

balance the representation of general practitioners, hospital staffs, and other medical groups, are indicated in Appendix 2.14.

The reorganisation legislation shifted the balance of emphasis within the professional advisory machinery from the centre to the regions, and especially to the areas and districts. The Government was faced with an awkward policy decision about the structure of the central advisory machinery. In 1969 it was calculated that more than a hundred central committees were in existence, the main statutory elements of which were the Central Health Services Council, its Standing Advisory Committees, and the various subcommittees associated with this structure. As indicated in the first volume of this study, the CHSC-SAC mechanism failed to establish itself as a dynamic force within the NHS, but they provided useful source of advice upon which the department could call, and this resulted in useful reports from a few of the committees. Although servicing the CHSC and its ten surviving SACs was an inconvenience, the health department was disinclined to risk a confrontation with the medical profession by proposing abolition. It was therefore decided to continue the CHSC-SAC structure with little modification. The Consultative Document said nothing on this subject, but the 1972 White Paper contained this undertaking, and the 1946 legislation was suitably amended by the reorganisation legislation.[326] Without controversy the SACs were slimmed down to five. The most important alteration of the SACs occurred in the area of mental health. It was decided to replace the old Mental Health SAC with an entirely new mental health advisory committee structure to take account of the need for coverage of both the social services and the health services. The new committees would be responsible to both the CHSC and the new Personal Social Services Council. It was decided that it was no longer feasible to include all questions relating to mental health under the remit of a single advisory committee. The department decided to establish three committees, dealing with mental health, mental handicap, and alcoholism. The last meeting of the mental health SAC was held in January 1974, but only tentative plans for the replacements had been made by the time of reorganisation and indeed little progress had been made by the end of 1974.[327]

The only major change in the central advisory machinery was the establishment of the Personal Social Services Council. This was a natural development, constituting a central advisory body for the personal social services approximating to the Central Health Services Council for the health services. In practice, the PSSC differed in important respects from the CHSC. The latter was constituted on a statutory basis at the outset of the NHS. The PSSC was not a product of the 1970 personal social services legislation;

indeed a central advisory council for personal social services was not among the recommendations of the Seebohm Committee, which formed the basis for this legislation. The Seebohm Committee advocated a central committee which would be concerned with development and training. The interdepartmental committee of officials considering Seebohm training issues came out in favour of a statutory committee for training, and a separate advisory council. It was intended that the PSSC would serve a more general function than the CHSC; it would advise both Ministers and the local government social service departments; it would act as a forum for exchange of ideas, and as a centre for disseminating information about best practice.[328] This proposal was discussed with outside bodies and accepted by Ministers. The decision to establish the PSSC was announced on 8 December 1971, a few days before the announcement concerning the parallel Central Council for Education and Training in Social Work.[329] It was agreed that the PSSC would be jointly financed by central and local government. After this brisk start, planning for the PSSC slumped to an embarrassingly slow pace, mainly owing to arguments over constitution and membership.[330] Difficulties were experienced in reconciling the different interests: central government, local government associations, the voluntary sector, training organisations, professional associations, local social service departments, the medical profession, and also of course the Central Health Services Council. The announcement confirming the membership of the PSSC was made on 23 July 1973.[331] The first chairman of the PSSC was Lord James of Rusholme. Because of the dominance of interest group considerations, the elimination of nominees known to have connections with the political opposition, and a bias against academic social science and so-called 'pressure groups', it is scarcely surprising that the PSSC experienced difficulty in establishing its authority. The PSSC became more drawn into the centre of social service affairs in 1976, when Lord James was replaced by Lewis E.Waddilove, Chairman of the Joseph Rowntree Trust.[332]

Community Health Councils
By contrast with the FPC, Community Health Councils were a completely new creation. Although the Government was apprehensive about giving greater independence and authority to the CHCs, nobody really believed that they constituted a real threat to the powerful management bodies of the reorganised health service. Sceptics continued to complain that CHCs were nothing more than the 'muzzled watch-dogs of the health service'.[333] In the summer of 1973, draft advice on the establishment of CHCs was circulated for comment. DHSS was still in a suspicious mood and was determined

544

to restrict the activities of CHCs as much as possible, particularly by establishing them at district level and preventing their interference outside the boundaries of the home district. With respect to the contentious issue of staff support for CHCs, the department and the Secretary of State reluctantly accepted the view of the Welsh Office, that if CHCs were not willing to accept NHS staff on secondment, then after discussion with the RHA, the post might be filled by advertisement, including advertisement outside the health service. However, the department was reluctant to accede to the Welsh Office suggestion that CHCs might employ their own staff, utilizing an independent budget. It was thought that this degree of freedom would create a degree of independence that would later be difficult to reverse.[334]

It was not possible to establish CHCs until the division into districts had been settled. Although provisional guidance was available, the main circular relating to CHCs was not issued until January 1974.[335] The number of CHCs established was 207, corresponding with the number of districts, but with two additional CHCs established for the isolated communities in Cumbria and the Isles of Scilly. As already indicated, the operation to establish CHCs was controlled by regional authorities rather than, as was originally intended, the AHAs. The latter played no part and they were not represented on CHCs; half the membership was appointed by local authorities, one-third by voluntary organisations, and the remainder by the RHB after consultation with other appropriate groups representing consumer interests. The size of CHCs was left to local discretion; most of the CHCs contained between 20 and 30 members.

Most CHCs were able to hold their first meetings by the date of reorganisation, usually with the support of staff made temporarily available by the AHA. With the exception of the West Midlands, all the CHCs were fully functioning by the autumn of 1974. Failure to establish CHCs in the West Midlands was blamed on the need to hold elaborate consultations with local authorities in the region.[336] The CHCs were first engaged in selecting their chairpersons, in appointing their secretaries, and in finding accommodation. Many availed themselves of the opportunity to recruit the secretary from outside the NHS, and they located their offices in places convenient to the community rather than in the offices of the local health authority. Some embarrassment was occasioned by the attempt of some RHAs to smuggle retired officers into CHC secretarial appointments; RHBs also tried to persuade adjacent CHCs to share a secretary.[337] CHCs were successfully resisted such efforts to undermine their status.

The precise function of the CHC remained uncertain. The idea of a main part in the complaints procedure had been ruled out. It was also decided that they should not primarily be a forum for local voluntary health organisations. Local authorities dominated the membership, but their members were doubtful about their role in this consultative context, and they found this kind of work trivial and uncongenial compared with their service on council committees. The Regulations gave the CHCs power to solicit information from the health authorities, make representations about the state of services, inspect hospital facilities and play some part in framing local plans. In order to be fully operational, CHCs needed to build up a working relationship with their neighbouring regional, area and district authorities. This was a cumbersome process, which could not be completed within the first year of the new service. Nevertheless, CHCs quickly established themselves as an integral part of the fabric of the NHS, and the consolidation of their work was assisted by a useful practical handbook produced, not by DHSS, but by the Nuffield Provincial Hospitals Trust.[338]

(viii) REORGANISATION IN SCOTLAND

By the date of the 1970 General Election, preparations for the White Paper on reorganisation of the Scottish health services had reached an advanced stage. No special modifications in these plans were rendered necessary by the change of Government. Early in July 1970 Gordon Campbell agreed to the unification of the health services outside local government and to a single tier structure, with the boundaries of area health boards coinciding with the major divisions of reformed local government.[339] However, no public statement was made concerning these intentions. When questioned on this matter Campbell issued a brief reply mentioning that he would issue a statement after the recess.[340]

Major outstanding problems included the distribution of functions between the new area boards and the central department, and devising suitable machinery for handling a variety of disparate functions residing with the central department. In order to be viable, these arrangements needed to command the confidence of area boards and not expose SHHD to the accusation of undue centralisation, at a time when the entire emphasis of policy was on administrative devolution and strengthening of local government.

This problem was approached in an imaginative spirit by SHHD. It was appreciated that local confidence in the central administration required positive measures to provide assurance that SHHD was entering into the reorganisation exercise in a real spirit of partnership. Having won support for unification, SHHD urged the need 'to go further and to achieve the best possible allocation of responsibilities, to meet the circumstances of a country small enough to be a convenient administrative unit for many purposes, yet sufficiently diverse to make an over-rigid structure inefficient as well as undesirable'.[341]

In giving practical expression to these honourable aspirations, SHHD devised a new central apparatus placing emphasis on the theme of partnership. The aim was to reduce the remoteness of the health department by associating it with a strong central structure containing a substantial representation from relevant NHS bodies. SHHD was even willing to consider ceding many of its own functions to this new central agency.

Designing the new central organisation had begun during the Labour administration, immediately it seemed likely that the regional tier would be eliminated. The CMO played a leading part in these deliberations. In May 1969 he suggested that some kind of 'witan' or central council was required to bring area boards and SHHD together.[342] In the following month the CMO produced detailed plans for a 'Central Set-Up', including a description of a 'Central Set-Up Board' similar to the arrangement eventually adopted.[343]

The first detailed progress report was presented to the new Ministers in October 1970, as part of the background guidance for the urgently-required public statement on the Secretary of State's thinking on reorganisation.[344] Given the extensive nature of consultations already undertaken, the settled state of thinking on most major issues, and the advanced level of planning in Scotland, it was proposed to issue early in 1971 a White Paper rather than another Green Paper. This would enable Scotland to regain its earlier lead and begin preparations for reorganisation in advance of England and Wales.

Given the substantial differences in the Scottish and English approaches to reorganisation, and the need to co-ordinate with the proposed reorganisation of Scottish local government, officials advised a separate statement, rather than a paragraph inserted in the draft statement that was being prepared for Sir Keith Joseph. This submission confirmed the preference of Ministers for a single-tier structure outside local government. For the local administrative units, it was proposed to retain the 'area health board' terminology used since the beginning of the planning exercise and originally derived from the Porritt Report. It remained necessary to work out many technicalities, such as the precise division of responsibilities with respect to personal social services between NHS area boards and coterminous local government authorities, and arrangements for absorbing Executive Council functions into the new area boards.

The most intractable problem relating to the area boards was the method to be adopted for appointment of members. In 1968 the Scottish Green Paper had prepared the ground for the appointment of all members by the Secretary of State, and this remained the preferred option. SHHD held a rooted objection to direct appointment of members by local authorities and professional bodies. Officials were particularly concerned that a single local authority might dominate certain of the area boards. They also feared that sectional interests would undermine the sense of collective responsibility, that personal managerial qualities would be at a discount, and that the Secretary of State's rights would be undermined in a service entirely dependent on Exchequer resources. The SHHD approach to the membership of area boards had not been enthusiastically welcomed, but it seemed tenable until at the eleventh hour Crossman produced his plan for substantial direct representation of local authorities and the medical profession. This inevitably generated expectations about a similar pattern in Scotland. With a change of Government, the former policy was reaffirmed; the Treasury was told that all members of area boards would be appointed by the Secretary of State and that no commitments would be made concerning fixed proportions derived from any particular interest group.[345]

Once again, the Scottish Secretary of State gave only a limited insight into his intentions, largely because of the less advanced state of thinking in London. On 5 November 1970 Campbell, like Joseph, issued a brief announcement promising a fuller statement early in 1971 including proposals to unify health administration outside local government.[346]

The intended timetable suggested by Scottish officials proved over-optimistic, but in their submission to Ministers in February 1971, they planned to issue a White Paper in April or May, and submit instructions to parliamentary draughtsmen in August, in preparation for a Bill early in 1972. The first requirement was disclosing Ministers' final thinking on reorganisation to leading NHS interests, especially the RHB Chairmen, in order to allow maximum warning concerning abolition of the regions and the other substantial changes envisaged for the hospital service.[347] Early in 1971, SHHD prepared consultation papers on the main aspects of its plans and was successful in gaining further confirmation of support and in maintaining the general consensus around its proposals.

Under the previous administration it was proposed to establish 10-15 area authorities. In the light of the report of the Wheatley Commission, in May 1970 it seemed appropriate to adopt 12 areas, taking the seven suggested Wheatley local government regions as a basis, but dividing the South East into two and West into five.[348] Modifications of the Wheatley plan incorporated into the Scottish White Paper on local government reorganisation in February 1971, increased the regions to eight by dividing the South East Region into two, bringing the local government and NHS plans into closer alignment.[349] At this date, SHHD thinking on the divisions to be adopted for administration of the health service was not entirely settled; it was recognised that there was a case for 12 or 13 areas, but also perhaps some kind of area status for Orkney and Shetland, which would suggest about 15 areas.[350]

Apart from the RHBs which continued to argue the case for some kind of regional arrangement, most organisations supported the plan for a single tier of area authorities. Unlike their counterparts in England, the general practitioners refrained from demanding a separate statutory committee within the area boards to control their affairs. This enthusiasm for integration was associated with presumption that the medical profession would receive substantial representation on the area boards.[351]

During the early months of 1971 SHHD decided on its plans for the central organisation. Contrary to the Welsh Office, SHHD decided firmly against the 'direct drive' approach, instead favouring a central arrangement embodying 'partnership' with the area health authorities. The new structure involved three elements; first, *SHHD* would determine general policy and exercise financial control on behalf of the Secretary of State; secondly, a newly formed *Scottish Health Service Planning Council* formed of representatives of the department and area boards would fulfil a strategic planning function; and thirdly, a further new central organisation, the *Common Services Agency* would provide the department and the area boards with common services.[352]

SHHD proposals for central arrangements were well-received in Scotland, but the Treasury was more reticent about this experiment in administration. However, after probing discussions concluding in clarification on points of detail, it allowed the plan to proceed. The Treasury required assurances that the role of SHHD would not be eroded by the Planning Council to the point where it could not exercise decisive influence on matters of policy and expenditure. SHHD reassured the Treasury that the Secretary of State would retain ultimate responsibility for the 'efficiency, adequacy and humanity' of the health service, while in the last resort all other bodies engaged in running the service would be regarded as the Minister's agents. SHHD would continue to lay down priorities, retain control over issuing policy directives, maintain surveillance over efficiency and it would monitor performance. The new central arrangement was presented as a positive asset to efficiency because it would ensure that intelligence concerning best practice at the periphery would be readily available at the centre, and then after rigorous assessment it would become effective and universally disseminated through the medium of the central planning structure.[353]

The Treasury was attracted by the prospect that the Common Services Agency would provide an economical way of providing central services without increasing the size of SHHD and therefore not expanding the numbers of civil servants. However there was a danger that the CSA could would take on too much independent authority. The Treasury accepted that the CSA would be suitable umbrella for a variety of miscellaneous functions needing to be provided centrally. The CSA could readily perform functions already provided centrally such as dental estimates work, pharmaceutical pricing, and legal services, also management of the ambulance and blood transfusion services. It could also take over functions performed by SHHD in conjunction with the regional boards, including hospital planning and building, supplies, personnel management, recruitment and training, and health education. The Treasury accepted this ambitious remit for the CSA, but it was unhappy about trusting the CSA with the SHHD Research and Intelligence Unit and statistical functions. The Treasury also insisted that the CSA should be firmly under the control of SHHD. Various arrangements for overseeing the CSA were discussed between the Treasury and SHHD, without a firm preference on either side. The main alternatives were: either appointing a CSA director directly responsible to the Secretary of State, or a chief executive responsible to a committee, which in turn would be accountable to the Secretary of State.[354]

Scottish White Paper
Given the large degree of common understanding in Scotland, by the spring of 1972 SHHD was ready to issue its White Paper on NHS reorganisation. As noted above, at this stage there was an unanticipated delay in the timetable owing to disagreements over the method to be adopted for appointment of members of area authorities. English and Welsh Ministers recognised that direct representation for local government was unavoidable, but they differed over the scale of this representation. They were united in opposition to granting similar representation to the medical profession. The Scottish position was entirely different. SHHD insisted that all appointments should be made by the Secretary of State, but an obligation to include a strong medical element on area health boards was recognised. Local authorities neither demanded nor expected a similar concession. After much agitated discussion between the English and Scottish health departments failed to evolve a common formula for constituting area authorities, the Secretary of State for Scotland decided to propose appointing all members of the area authorities, and present some semblance of compatibility with the English arrangements by suggesting that the Scottish area was equivalent to the English region.[355] However, this rationalisation was

not entirely convincing since Wales offered the most appropriate comparison with Scotland. Wales also was intending to abolish the region and adopt area authorities covering large geographical areas, many of which were not dissimilar in character from Scottish areas. However, as already indicated, the Secretary of State for Wales was even more convinced than his English counterpart of the need for strong local government representation.

The final drafts of the Scottish White Paper were circulated in June 1971.[356] The only minor tension over drafting occurred with respect to interventions of Lady Tweedsmuir, the Minister of State at the Scottish Office. It was reported that she 'had taken a deep personal interest in the drafting, and disliked the reference to Health Boards acting as the Secretary of State's agents'.[357] The agency concept was essential to the thinking of the Treasury; SHHD agreed that it would discreetly press for its retention.

The Scottish White Paper on reorganisation was agreed without dissent by the Home and Social Affairs Committee. Joseph pressed some minor drafting points, the most important one relating to his wish to avoid professional advisory committees gaining a statutory right to consultation.[358] SHHD declined to make this change, and as already noted, this right was eventually conceded in England.

The White Paper was published on 30 July 1971.[359] The Scottish White Paper was strikingly different in character and tone from the English Consultative Document published a couple of months earlier. In particular, there was much less stress on the theme of management. Efficiency was a recurrent theme, but management improvements were presented as a natural consequence of changes brought about in the achievement of unification, rather than as a superimposed principle. The White Paper was therefore presented as the evolutionary consequence of the plans of the Labour administration, rather than as a rival conception. Repeating the original Green Paper, the White Paper accepted that 'the reform of the health service administrative structure is not an end in itself: it is a means of enabling the doctors, nurses and other health care professions to work together with greater ease and effect for the benefit of their patients and the whole community'. The prevailing theme of the White Paper was therefore 'effective partnership', the establishment of which was guaranteed by the introduction of a strong professional consultative machinery, the existence of which would obviate the need for direct representation of the medical profession on health authorities.[360] As noted below, the rhetoric of partnership was slightly at odds with the attitude of SHHD towards local government representation on health boards, or towards community influence exerted through local health councils.

Much of the text of the White Paper was taken up with unveiling the new arrangements for central administration, especially the proposed Scottish Health Service Planning Council and the Common Services Agency.[361] These sections of the White Paper constituted a delicate balancing act; on the one hand it was stressed that there would be no diminution in the authority of SHHD; on the other hand assurances were given that reorganisation would not represent a drift towards centralisation. In fact the description of central arrangements contained some contradictory statements and therefore left a degree of ambiguity over the outcome.[362]

The White Paper outlined proposals for a single-tiered health service, based on 14 area health boards, including both Orkney and Shetland as separate boards. It was stated that the area boards would be 'statutorily responsible to', rather than being 'agents of' the Secretary of State, as stated in the drafts.[363] Since the boundaries of the new local government areas had not been finally determined, it was not possible to give definitive pronouncements on the relationship between local government and the health boards. However, the White Paper on Scottish local government reorganisation, published in February 1971, provided a reasonably firm basis for planning.[364] The map attached to the White Paper possessed only provisional value. It also contained an unfortunate mistake, describing the health service boundaries as 'regional' boundaries, rather than as 'health board' boundaries. The proposed health board boundaries were shown as breaking across existing local authority boundaries at many points.

It was confirmed that the Secretary of State would appoint all members of health boards after appropriate consultations. No indication was given concerning the shares to be allocated to the various interest groups. As in England it was stressed that members would be appointed on the basis of their individual qualities rather than as representative of other organisations. It was proposed to keep the membership of health boards down to 15, which coincided with the preferred figure adopted in England and Wales.[365]

With respect to the scope of the reorganised health service, the White Paper contained the first unambiguous public announcement contained in any of the planning documents relating to Great Britain that the main functions of the school health service would be taken over by the NHS.[366] The White Paper repeated the Green Paper commitment to local health councils, but presented as an alternative the possibility also considered in Wales that the community councils proposed in local government reform could also represent community aspirations with respect to the health services.[367]

By the end of November 1971 most of the main organisations had commented on the Scottish White Paper. At this stage the critics were mainly concerned about lack of detail in the proposals. Given the long period of gestation and large amount of consultation, the response to the White Paper was perhaps less positive than might have been expected. There was still residual support for a regional tier; the substitute central arrangements were subjected to much detailed criticism and there was a suspicion that the Planning Council would not sufficiently represent the views of the area boards.

Plans for area health boards were generally accepted, but there was much criticism over details, especially where it was intended to cut across the regional or district boundaries of the new local authorities. The main attack came from Fife, which demanded recognition as a separate area health board, in opposition to its proposed division between the Tay and North Forth area boards. Similarly, the proposed Ayrshire district objected to the loss of south Ayrshire to the proposed Dumfries and Galloway area health board.

SHHD noted that the proposals for area health boards were 'strongly criticised as being too small and undemocratic'. The larger size was favoured on account of the extensive geographical coverage and diversity of the areas, and range of interests to be represented. A membership of 20-25 rather than 15 was commonly advocated. The local authority associations and committees representing general medical practitioners demanded direct representation on the area boards, while other medical groups wanted at least the rights of co-option of medical representatives to committees of the area boards.

The proposals for local health councils were heavily criticised. As in Wales, opinion was evenly divided about the desirability of linking these with community councils. The main demand was for granting the health councils a greater degree of autonomy and authority. It was also argued that local health councils would only represent community opinion adequately if they were established at district rather than area level.[368]

National Health Service (Scotland) Bill

The Scottish health department was still considering its reactions to the comments on the White Paper while the reorganisation Bill was being drafted during October and November 1972.[369] The reorganisation Bill was discussed by the Legislation Committee, where it was identified as a modest and uncontroversial measure suitable for introduction in the House of Lords. The Committee agreed that the Bill should be introduced at the first opportunity. The only question causing hesitation was the proposal for the Health Service Commissioner for Scotland. There was general preference for the Health Service Commissioner clauses to be deferred until the health service reorganisation Bill relating to England and Wales, in order to secure uniform Great Britain arrangements. However, it was appreciated that it might be difficult to resist amendments requiring provision for the Health Service Commissioner in the Scottish legislation.[370] Despite this risk, it was decided to launch the Scottish Bill without inclusion of provision for the Scottish Health Service Commissioner.

The National Health Service (Scotland) Bill was similar in length to the England and Wales Bill discussed above.[371] The Scottish Bill comprised 56 clauses, which was slender by comparison with the 232 clauses of the Local Government (Scotland) Bill, scheduled for introduction in the House of Commons during 1972. The Scottish Health Service Bill was not very similar to the English Bill in its construction. *Part I* described the duties and powers of the Secretary of State in similar terms to the English Bill, but in rather more detail. *Part II* outlined arrangements for what were now termed 'Health Boards', which were to be required to submit proposals for the establishment of Local Health Councils. The areas administered by Health Boards were to be determined by order of the Secretary of State after consultation with relevant organisations. *Part II* also described provisions for Liaison Committees to protect the interests of teaching hospitals, and local consultative committees to represent five professional groups in each health board area. *Part III* included provision for the new central machinery, the Scottish Health Service Planning Council, the national professional consultative committees, and the Common Services Agency. *Part IV* described arrangements for cooperation between health authorities, local authorities and voluntary agencies. *Parts V to VII* dealt with transfer of property, hospital endowments and miscellaneous provisions, including the establishment of the Commission to oversee arrangements relating to recruitment and transfer of staff. Further consequential details were taken up in six schedules.

The National Health Service (Scotland) Bill was introduced in the House of Lords on 18 January 1972. It received its Second Reading on 8 February; its Committee stage took place on 24 February, its Report stage on 7 March, and its Third Reading on 23 March.[372] The only notable event was a change in plans with respect to the Health Service Commissioner.[373] At this late stage, the Government decided to pre-empt opposition intervention by introducing its own amendments concerning establishment of the Health Service Commissioner in Scotland. Although not a controversial change, this represented an unwelcome complication for the parliamentary draughtsmen, involving introducing at short notice a new substantial Part to the Bill comprising 9 clauses.

These changes were announced at the Committee stage. The only concession during the debates to critics related to the minor point of paying compensation to members of health service bodies who suffered financial loss as a result of their work for the NHS. This rapid transit through the House of Lords was regarded as a good omen by SHHD. The scrutiny of the Bill in the House of Commons was more rigorous; indeed it exceeded the attention given later to the reorganisation Bill for England and Wales. The Debate of the Scottish Grand Committee took place on 2 and 4 May 1972.[374] The Committee stage lasted for nine sittings, between 16 May and 22 June 1972.[375] The final stages of the Bill were concluded in both Houses in July, and the National Health Service (Scotland) Act received the Royal Assent on 9 August 1972.

The final stages of the reorganisation Bill involved exposure to all the criticisms already described with respect to the White Paper. In the House of Commons there was also a vociferous rearguard action, led by John Mackintosh, in favour of local government administration of the health services. However, the Government succeeded in making few concessions in response to the critics. The introduction of a package of amendments relating to Health Service Commissioner for Scotland remained the one substantial change in the Bill. As in the later debates on reorganisation in England and Wales, the fiercest criticism was attracted by the clauses relating to family planning and the local health councils.

The first real embarrassment in the discussion of the Bill was not experienced until 23 May during the discussion of clause 8 relating to family planning. Bruce Millan effectively exploited the weakness of the Government's position by pointing out that some of the most successful family planning services in Britain had been developed by local authorities such as Aberdeen which, under the 1968 legislation had provided a free service. For the first time, the family planning service was reaching the deprived groups, thereby effectively addressing the social problems to which the Government attached high priority. Millan argued that the introduction of charges for the family planning service made possible by the reorganisation Bill would undermine the new and fragile family planning service built up by enlightened local authorities wrestling with serious social problems.[376] The strength of this argument was appreciated by Scottish Ministers, who tried in vain to persuade the Treasury to accede to the continuation of free services where they were already in place. However, the Treasury insisted that any change in policy should await the results of the review of family planing services being undertaken by Joseph. SHHD was unwilling to accept this rigid line; consequently the issue was taken to the Home and Social Affairs Committee, where it was agreed that clause 8 should be amended to allow advice on contraception to be provided without charge, which represented a very modest concession.[377]

The only other point of real turbulence occurred with respect to clause 14, where two significant amendments were conceded; the most important of these removed the power of the Secretary of Sate to dispense with Local Health Councils in cases where he felt that alternative means were available for realising the same objectives. A second significant alteration permitted Local Health Councils to select their own chairmen. Otherwise, the only amendments worthy of comment related to strengthening of clauses relating to payment of expenses to members of Health Boards and Local Health Councils, and removal of the power of the Secretary of State to suppress annual reports of the Scottish Health Service Planning Council.

Logistics of Reorganisation

Preparations for health service reorganisation were announced in the first of a new series of circulars, HRC(72)C1, which was issued on 14 September 1972. This series were popularly known as the 'blue band' circulars, on account of the broad blue band upon which the headings were printed. Sixty-two of these circulars were issued between September 1972 and March 1974. The circulars were derived from discussion papers covering the main aspects of reorganisation, most of which were distributed during March 1973.[378]

More general information was made available in a series of six news bulletins, even more modest in number and appearance than their counterparts in England and Wales. Training of staff for reorganisation approximated to the arrangements already described for England.

The sequence of changes in Scotland paralleled the pattern already described for England, except that the timetable was more relaxed, with the result that there was more opportunity for consultation on many outstanding points of detail, and also it was possible to follow a more rational sequence. For instance, chairmen of Health Boards were appointed sufficiently early to be fully involved in the work of 'area study groups' constituted to fulfil the purposes served by Joint Liaison Committees in England and Wales. However, this lead over England and Wales gradually diminished, with the result that the Area Health Authorities in England and Wales, and the Health Boards in Scotland, were established and their senior officers were appointed at approximately the same time. Consequently, as in the case of the Joint Liaison Committees, the area study groups played a more prominent part than was originally anticipated and they were not disbanded until the autumn of 1973.

Health Boards, Districts, and Councils

The first task of reorganisation was establishing the boundaries of the new Health Boards. A consultation paper on this subject was circulated in October 1972.[379] This exercise largely confirmed previous proposals. It resulted in the establishment of fifteen Health Boards. By this stage, the final plan for local government reform had been devised, but the Local Government (Scotland) Bill was heavily criticised and delayed, with the result that the Local Government (Scotland) Act did not receive the Royal Assent until 25 October 1973.

The final plan for local government reform differed from the White Paper of 1971 in increasing the number of regions from eight to nine, and in designating three instead of two special 'most purpose' Island authorities. The final proposals for Health Boards followed similar lines. The only significant departures from previous schemes involved granting the Western Isles the full Health Board status already envisaged for Orkney and Shetland, and avoidance of splitting of Fife, which was now designated as a separate area. The boundaries of the fifteen Health Boards now avoided breaking across local authority boundaries.

As indicated by Table 6.4 and Maps 3 and 4, the Health Boards followed the local government regional or district boundaries. The largest amount of subdivision of a region occurred in the Strathclyde conurbation, which was divided into four Health Boards.[380] With one exception (Forth Valley), the names of the Health Boards outside Strathclyde followed the names of the local government regions or districts. It will be noticed that Greater Glasgow, the largest Scottish Health Board, compared in population with the largest area authorities in England, while the three Island authorities were less than one-third the size of the smallest area authorities in England and Wales.

In June 1972 nominations were invited for the new health boards; by the beginning of 1973 the chairmen had been appointed by the Secretary of State. Although it was originally intended to have Health Boards and their senior officers in place by the beginning of 1973, this timetable proved to be over-optimistic. Consequently, as noted above, the chairmen assisted by aides nominated by SHHD convened 'area study groups' to perform the functions of the Joint Liaison Committees already described for England. The study groups were responsible for making suggestions for the division of their areas into districts.[381] As seen from Table 6.4, the only single-district areas emerging from this process were the Borders, Dumfries and Galloway, and the three Island areas.

As already noted, the chairmen of the Health Boards were appointed by the beginning of 1973, but there was a delay in appointing members because of disagreements over the composition

557

Table 6.4
National Health Service Scotland, Health Boards and Districts, 1974

Health Board	Population 1975 (thousands)	Districts	Population (thousands)
1. Highland	182.0	Northern Southern	41.5 140.6
2. Orkney	17.7		
3. Shetland	18.5		
4. Western Isles	29.6		
5. Grampian	448.8	West North South	80.6 123.3 244.9
6. Tayside	402.0	Angus Dundee Perth and Kinross	88.1 194.7 119.2
7. Fife	336.3	East West	212.8 123.5
8. Lothian	754.0	West South North	121.2 321.9 310.9
9. Borders	99.4		
10. Forth Valley	269.3	Stirling Falkirk	126.5 142.8
11. Argyll and Clyde	459.4	Argyll and Bute Dumbarton Renfrew Inverclyde	64.6 80.1 208.9 105.8
12. Greater Glasgow	1105.6	Western Northern Eastern South Eastern South Western	256.9 203.1 243.8 230.5 171.4
13. Lanarkshire	565.5	Monklands/Cumbernauld Motherwell/Lanark Hamilton/ East Kilbride	162.8 214.7 188.1
14. Ayrshire and Arran	374.4	North Ayrshire and Arran South Ayrshire	214.5 159.9
15. Dumfries and Galloway	143.7		
Total Scotland	5206.2		

Source: The Registrar General, Scotland, *Annual Estimate of the Population of Scotland* (HMSO, Edinburgh, 1976) Table 3.

Notes: Because of rounding of totals, the population totals in the Health Board and Health District columns differ by three thousand.

See Maps 3 and 4.

and size of the boards. It was eventually agreed that where geographical circumstances created difficulties in representing essential district and sectional interests, the Health Boards could be increased from the desired size of 14 to as many as 22. The boards were appointed in the autumn of 1973. The average membership of the Health Boards was about 18. Delay in establishing the Health Boards set back the timetable for the Local Health Councils. Consultation with the Health Boards over the district arrangements for Local Health Councils were not completed until after the appointed day.[382] The Health Boards were not ready with draft schemes until late in 1974 and the full Local Health Council structure was not in place until the autumn of 1975. The Local Health Councils were less free from Health Board control than their English and Welsh counterparts. The local authorities nominated only one-third of the members; the Health Board appointed the remaining membership, another one-third after consultation with voluntary bodies, the rest being drawn from health administrative bodies and trade unions.

Staff Appointments

One of the first of the reorganisation circulars dealt with the delicate issue of the administrative structure of the Health Boards.[383] This determined the pattern of officer appointments at the area and district level. This problem was the occasion for prolonged and agitated exchanges between SHHD, DHSS, CSD and the Treasury. As already noted in the context of management arrangements in England, the Scottish health department formulated its ideas at an early stage, and without recourse to the elaborate management study undertaken in England. SHHD soon came to the conclusion that management by chief executive was unacceptable because of the expectation in the medical profession that this post would fall to the administrative medical officer.[384] The alternative idea of a duuvirate between the senior administrator and senior administrative medical officer of the kind operating since 1948 was rejected by the Treasury because it was assumed that the medical officer would be the dominant party.[385] It was also necessary to respond to the increasing aspirations of nurses and finance officers. Therefore, by a process of elimination, SHHD concluded that the only viable basis for local administration was adoption of an 'executive group' of senior officers operating at both the area and district levels. It was proposed that the work of these groups would be co-ordinated by the senior administrative officer.[386] As already noted, SHHD was obliged to slow down its deliberations until the English and Welsh management studies had reached essentially the same conclusions by an entirely different and more laborious route. However, the Scottish Ministers were unwilling to disguise the trend of their thinking, which they insisted on disclosing during the Second Reading Debate in the House of Commons. SHHD accepted that its conclusions were based on pragmatic considerations, and represented a compromise agreed by all the professions involved, but the executive group was also claimed as a minor victory for management thinking on account of acceptance by the medical profession that co-ordination would be undertaken by a lay officer.[387]

The Scottish management arrangements contained some important differences from the English pattern. The most important difference was that the district executive group (comprising the District Medical Officer, Nursing Officer, Finance Officer and Administrator) was accountable as a whole to its counterpart at the Health Board level, whereas in England the DMT was accountable to the area authority.[388] Also the district executive group in Scotland comprised only the appointed officers, excluding the two representatives of the medical advisory committees included in the England and Wales.

DHSS remained convinced that the Scottish proposals were fundamentally flawed. As a parting shot, DHSS reiterated its earlier verdict:

> In general our criticism - as we explained when we saw your discussion papers - is that a team to team managerial relationship is not workable. Our view is that it would neither ensure effective co-ordination within, nor uniform delegation to District teams. We also thought that it would probably in practice soon deteriorate into a form of accountability from individual officer to officer in the various disciplines at the different levels.[389]

There was some reason to believe that the proposed structure in Scotland would fragment; indeed the circular accepted that 'on matters of concern to only one of the professions in the district executive group, the district officer of the profession would consult the superior officer at the area level'.[390] Such sentiments were alien to the English management philosophy, which exercised much ingenuity in avoiding the impression that area officers were the superiors of the district team.

As in England, arrangements for recruitment and the transfer of staff were overseen by a staff commission. In April 1972 agreement was reached with CSD and the Treasury concerning the Scottish NHS Staff Commission, and it was agreed that this body of four members should be chaired by Mr A P Robertson, formerly Joint General Manager of the Royal Bank of Scotland.[391] On 15 June the staff commission was set up in a shadow capacity as the Scottish NHS

Staff Advisory Committee; the Commission itself came into formal existence on 21 August 1972. The Commission was assisted by a specially-formed Scottish Health Services Appointments Unit in Edinburgh.

Owing to the disappearance of the 5 RHBs, 76 Boards of Management, 25 Executive Councils and 56 local health authorities, and their replacement by fifteen Health Boards and the Common Services Agency, reorganisation involved major redeployment of staff. SHHD hoped to advertise its chief officer appointments in the autumn of 1972 and make appointments early in 1973, almost a year in advance of the parallel programme in England and Wales.[392] However, it was also necessary to work out a consistent approach to recruitment, which exposed disagreements between the health departments, and caused a delay in the Scottish timetable. Partly because of the more radical nature of the changes in Scotland, staff groups were more apprehensive about redundancy and therefore more opposed to open competition for posts. The Scottish Ministers sympathised with this concern and proposed to limit senior appointments to existing health service personnel.[393] Both Jellicoe and Joseph argued for open competition, especially for top appointments, but as the plans were confirmed, outside entrants were virtually disqualified.[394] Complex consultations over the terms and conditions of senior appointments eroded the Scottish lead, with the result that the chief officers of the Health Boards were not appointed until late in 1973, only slightly in advance of their English and Welsh counterparts. Subsequent appointments followed the pattern already described for England.[395]

Central Structure
The entirely new and experimental central organisation necessitated careful preparation, in the course of which the end-product became considerably more complicated than was originally intended. The Treasury generally accepted the safeguards offered by SHHD at the White Paper stage, but CSD continued to express misgivings, fearing that the health department was effectively transferring the control of the health service to the Planning Council and the Common Services Agency.[396]

As already noted, the Planning Council was symbolic of the new spirit of partnership which it was intended to forge between the central department and the Health Boards in the reorganised health service. The first chairman of the Scottish Health Service Planning Council was Professor Sir Hugh N Robson, the Principal and Vice-Chancellor of Edinburgh University. The important post of Secretary of the SHSPC went to Mr T D Hunter, former Group Secretary and Treasurer of the Royal Edinburgh and Associated Hospitals. Since the SHSPC was

561

mainly concerned with long-term strategic planning, its main work was inevitably conducted through specialised committees, a bewildering variety of which were soon in existence. The SHSPC itself met for the first time on 21 June 1974. In response to the insistence of CSD, it was decided that secretarial support and services for the SHSPC would be provided by a separate Planning Unit associated with SHHD, rather than by a Planning Unit attached to SHSPC, or by CSA, as proposed in previous discussion documents.[397] Although the Planning Unit contained both civil servants and staff from NHS authorities, it was envisaged that the revised arrangement would ensure that SHHD would exercise firm control over the SHSPC's activities.

Under the reorganisation legislation SHHD was committed to establishing a complex central and local consultative structure. At the central level, seven National Consultative Committees were set up by the main professional groups by the end of 1974, leaving only the committee representing paramedical staff still to be formed.

With respect to the Common Services Agency, the original conception proposed in the White Paper was preserved.[398] New criteria were evolved to establish the line of division between the central department and the CSA. It was agreed that the health department would devise policy, assess demand, establish priorities, supervise the execution of policies, and determine that the health service was effectively managed. The CSA would provide SHHD and the health boards with executive and advisory services most efficiently provided centrally, and give expert professional and technical advice to SHHD and health boards based on the most advanced information systems.[399] As noted in chapters V and VII, this reassortment of central responsibilities necessitated the formation of complex web of committee structures designed to preserve harmony and prevent fragmentation of the central administrative structure.

The Common Services Agency drew together a broad range of disparate organisations, having many kinds of relationship with SHHD. These services included: the Scottish Ambulance Service and the Blood Transfusion Service; medical records; work study; information services; health education; management and training; planning, and some building and supply functions; prescription pricing and dental estimates. In services such as supplies, reorganisation was taken as an opportunity to greatly extend the central supplies function.[400] It is therefore not surprising that the CSA emerged as a formidable organisation employing some 4,000 staff.

The Scottish Ambulance Service and the Blood Transfusion Service were representative of long-standing services absorbed by the CSA. Both had been in existence since the beginning of the NHS. The Ambulance Service was established on the basis of a contract between the Secretary of State and a voluntary body, the St Andrew's Ambulance Association. The service was managed by a central committee and offshoots committees representing the various health service and voluntary interests. Since there was general satisfaction with this arrangement, it was decided to continue with a similar organisation, placed under the wing of CSA, rather than transfer the ambulance service to Health Boards.[401] It was similarly decided to maintain the separate existence under the CSA of the Blood Transfusion Service.[402] This had been reviewed as recently as 1966, when it was decided that the service would continue to be administered by the Scottish National Blood Transfusion Association and its five regional centres. The only significant innovation was the creation of a Central Consultative Committee to advise the Secretary of State on policy and development questions. At the other end of the age spectrum was the Scottish Health Education Unit, which was established only in 1968 and it was administered directly by SHHD. The Health Education Unit was regarded as one of the few outstanding successes in the relatively barren field of health education in Britain.[403]

The CSA was supervised by a management committee responsible to the Secretary of State. The membership of this committee comprised an equal balance between representatives of SHHD and NHS authorities. The original proposal for the CSA to be headed by a chief executive was abandoned on account of the danger of giving too much authority and independence to the head of CSA. Instead, it was decided to appoint a more neutral secretary, who would play a primarily co-ordinating role, supported by a strongly-placed finance officer, who would oversee the economical running of services.[404] The first chairman of the Management Committee was the influential Simpson Stevenson, the Chairman of the Greater Glasgow Health Board, and former Chairman of the Western Regional Hospital Board. Inevitably the main responsibility for management rested on the supervisory arrangements adopted for the individual units and divisions operating under the broad umbrella of the main management committee of the CSA.

(ix) REORGANISATION IN WALES

As noted above, the Welsh Office was the last of the three government departments responsible for the health services to indicate its intentions concerning reorganisation. Responses to the Welsh Green Paper issued in March 1970 were therefore not fully evident until after the General Election. The Conservative administration found that the Green Paper scheme had met with general approval. The proposal for seven area health authorities coextensive with local government areas, but independent of local

563

government, was generally accepted, although there was some doubt concerning the viability of Powys, and also suggestion that East Glamorgan might be split into two in order to retain the integrity of the Cardiff teaching hospital district. Many organisations pressed for greater representation on the area boards, often arguing that the boards should not contain as many as one-third nominated by the Secretary of State. There was much complaint about lack of definition concerning the role of district committees, and pressure for district committees to take on a representative character. The greatest concern related to the important and radical proposal to dispense with any regional or national body apart from the Welsh Office. This was attacked as an encroachment of central government influence into the health services, and further erosion of democratic involvement, without parallels in either England or Scotland. Naturally, the critics were led by the Welsh Hospital Board, which was threatened with extinction, but support for some kind of independent body to represent local interests at the centre was also forthcoming from a wide range of other bodies, including the Welsh Council, the BMA, the Society of Medical Officers of Health, the Royal College of Nursing, and the Association of Municipal Corporations. The critics demanded some kind of non-civil service, all-Wales body, but they varied in their attitudes to this arrangement. At one extreme, the Welsh Hospital Board advocated its own elevation into a regional health authority consistent with the English pattern, whereas at the other extreme, some organisations would have been satisfied with a modest advisory structure.[405] In expressing his initial views on the all-Wales question, Gibson-Watt advised the Secretary of State that he supported the case for a regional authority, and believed that the Welsh Hospital Board acted as a valuable buffer between the Welsh Office and the areas.[406]

The Green Paper had pronounced firmly against the region, but it conceded some consultative role for the Welsh Council. The latter was primarily involved in economic affairs, but its newly-constituted Health Panel was already taking on some of the functions of a national consultative body. The Welsh Council regarded itself as well-placed to assume a more ambitious consultative role, but recognised that its legitimacy was weakened by its status as a nominated body and by poor representation of health interests. The Royal Commission on the Constitution seemed likely to make proposals for upgrading the Health Panel of the Welsh Council into a Welsh Health Council, which could then assume more extensive and ambitious tasks, including a major role in health service administration.[407]

Within the Welsh Office there was a sharp difference of outlook on the way forward. The majority view favoured retaining the Green

Paper proposals, placing emphasis on strong areas and their direct accountability to the Welsh Office. This approach also envisaged retreat from Crossman's intention to introduce a prominent representative element in the appointment of area authorities. Consistent with the conclusion reached in Scotland, it was suggested that the Welsh areas were analogous to English regions; therefore all members should be nominated by the Secretary of State. The opposing point of view advocated greater continuity with the existing system, implying retention of a regional tier and a greater representative element in the health authorities at each level, as well as some form of consultative machinery at the national level. The first recorded exchanges between the two sides date from September 1970, and the argument smouldered on in the Welsh Office without remission until the Consultative Document was issued in June 1971.[408]

Apologists for the region pointed to the risk that without the interposition of the region, Ministers would be drawn into time-wasting inter-area disputes and parochial quarrels of all kinds. Secondly, it was urged that the equitable allocation of resources required a separate all-Wales body enjoying a degree of authority and independence of outlook inevitably missing within a government department. Thirdly, much disruption would be caused by dispensing with the region, which would adversely affect efficiency and undermine confidence in the central health department. Fourthly, critics were sceptical about the prospects for promised economies in staff; the Welsh Office would require much expansion in order to take on functions currently performed by the region and DHSS. Fifthly, this new, untried system, involving specially-created central administrative structures was likely to incorporate inefficiencies, and involve expansion in the civil service, against the express intentions of the Government. Sixthly, by maintaining the region, the Secretary of State would no longer need to appoint all area board members, an activity likely to provoke local resentment and therefore embarrassment to Ministers. Finally, responses to the Green Paper indicated that the public in Wales were resistant to the further centralisation of power. The region, albeit not particularly democratic, at least provided an additional protection of local interests. In view of the strength of opposition to complete abolition of the region and failure to substitute any effective, independent all-Wales machinery, advocates of the region were not convinced that the public would tolerate the plan advocated by the majority within the health department. The argument that in abolishing the region, Wales was merely following an appropriate Scottish precedent, was not accepted because the elaborate, central 'partnership' arrangements proposed in Scotland were not to be replicated in

Wales. There was also some scepticism concerning the capacity of the partnership structure to provide an effective substitute for regions in Scotland.[409] Even the opponents of the region realised that renewed emphasis on the region in English planning would increase pressure on the Welsh Office to introduce a regional health authority.[410]

The dominant party within the health department in Wales was undeterred by these criticisms; it stood by the original Green Paper plan based on strong area authorities coterminous with local government areas. Sceptics were assured that the Welsh Office was adequate to control seven areas, whereas regions were unavoidable in England on account of the much larger number of areas. There was confidence that many regional functions could be devolved to the area, leaving a minority of services requiring centralisation. For this purpose unwelcome expansion of the central health department could be avoided by following the Scottish precedent and constituting a common services agency. The Treasury and CSD abided by their traditional preference for the single tier, and agreed to tolerate about one hundred additional civil servants in the Welsh Office in return for this gain in simplification of health service administration.[411]

Consultative Document
Much of the detailed work in preparing the Consultative Document was taken up in considering alternative means of handling services beyond the capacity of single areas, and ultimately in preparing a convincing case for the common services agency. Before reaching a final decision on the Consultative Document, on 16 April 1971 the Secretary of State convened a private conference of about twenty experts to discuss outstanding issues.[412] The meeting generally supported the scheme for seven areas. Although it was arguable that Powys might not be viable and that East Glamorgan merited division into two areas, the conference exerted no firm pressure for action on these points. The conference was also conciliatory on the question of membership of boards; providing some members represented the interests of local government and the medical profession, the meeting accepted that a majority should be appointed by the Secretary of State.

Welsh planners were mainly absorbed with discussing various schemes for all-Wales organisation. There was little support for retaining the Welsh Hospital Board with expanded powers; the many suggestions included: a small central body exercising executive powers; a large, exclusively advisory committee similar to the Central Health Services Council, and like the latter operating through specialist advisory committees; or a large central watch-dog authority, acting as the all-Wales equivalent of the local community

566

health councils. However, after much discussion the meeting expressed preference for some kind of all-Wales organisation modelled on the existing Welsh Council - either a reconstituted Welsh Council, a parallel Welsh Health Council, or a Health and Personal Social Services Council.

The experts also found themselves divided over the status and functions of the common services organisation. Some members favoured the Scottish solution, which envisaged granting this organisation a wide range of functions and a high degree of independence. Welsh Office representatives argued for a much more limited range of functions and limited independence. It was finally agreed that research and intelligence functions should be located in the Welsh Office, but in the interests of commanding support from the areas, the common services agency should not be controlled by an chief executive accountable to the Secretary of State, but by a small management board, containing some representation from the areas. Much difficulty was experienced in arriving at a settled name for the common services organisation. There was clearly an instinct to avoid the title applied in Scotland. 'Common Services Unit' was used in the papers prepared for discussions on 16 April, but the meeting suggested 'Welsh Health Management Services Organisation', or 'Welsh Building and Technical Services Organisation', while the Minister of State proposed 'Welsh Health Technical Services Organisation', which became the settled title in subsequent planning documents.[413]

In briefing Ministers on preparation of the Consultative Document, the Permanent Secretary was dismayed by the confusion of thinking within the health department. He insisted on firm adherence to the single tier principle and a dominant role for the Welsh Office. The Consultative Document should therefore include proposals for: seven area health authorities directly responsible to the Secretary of State; all possible executive responsibilities vested in the area authorities; selection of all members of the area authorities by the Secretary of State on the criterion of management ability; community health councils of a representative character coterminous with area authorities; a management services organisation responsible to the Secretary of State, and headed by either a chief executive or management board; and finally, a specially-constituted national advisory council, rather than the any of the proposed variants of the Welsh Council. Any arrangement involving the Welsh Council was regarded as unwelcome in view of the possibility that the Commission on the Constitution might recommend greatly extended powers for this body, a prospect which was viewed as a threat to its authority by the Welsh Office. Elimination of the Welsh Council from formal participation in the reorganised NHS was therefore an important pre-emptive strike to protect the authority of the Welsh Office.[414]

The debate among officials was not quite over. The above heavily-centralised model was slightly watered down. In line with Cabinet recommendations about the composition of area authorities, acceptance that England and Wales should adopt a common policy with respect to composition of health authorities, and rejection of the idea that areas in Wales should be treated like regions in England, it was conceded that local authorities and universities should be allotted representation on area authorities.[415] With respect to all-Wales arrangements, the idea of a formally-constituted advisory council dealing with both health and social services was dropped in order to avoid a demand for local government representation. Although some officials were sympathetic to the idea of a Welsh Health Council associated in some way with the Welsh Council, this idea was not recommended on account of the Permanent Secretary's view that such a body would constitute a 'Frankenstein's monster'.[416]

On 13 May 1971 Ministers accepted the above proposals for the Consultative Document, but with two significant changes. The Secretary of State insisted that the common services agency should be controlled by a small board having links with the area authorities, and after a lengthy discussion it was agreed to adopt the Ministers' proposal to reinstate a Welsh Health Council as the most appropriate agency for all-Wales consultation.

The final draft of the Consultative Document was agreed by Ministers on 18 May and it was published on 8 June 1971.[417] Ministers were reticent about participation in the launch of this document, but eventually the Minister of State was persuaded to hold a press conference in London.[418] The Consultative Document was no better received than the original Green Paper, and it was greeted with suspicion by some of the main organisations involved in health affairs. Labour and local authority associations demanded a fifty per cent local government representation on area health authorities. Local government associations argued that community health councils would not be necessary if there was proper democratic control of health authorities. Betraying its increasing drift away from its original enthusiasm for the Porritt approach, the BMA showed signs of scepticism about the entire reorganisation enterprise, doubting whether it would lead to an improvement in patient care. In reaction to local authority demands, the BMA asked for fifty per cent medical representation on health authorities and no local authority membership. The BMA was split over the region issue, its general practitioners opposing the region unanimously, whereas the hospital interest was in favour.[419] The Welsh Council of the BMA

568

supported the idea of an all-Wales consultative body only by a small majority, and the Welsh GMSC supported it only on the condition that area authorities would dominate its membership. Many of the hospital administrative bodies continued to favour the all-Wales consultative body, but there was some erosion in support among other organisations. The specific proposal for a Welsh Health Council received only lukewarm support.[420] Ministers therefore firmly rejected demands by the Health and Social Services Panel of the Welsh Council for an executive role in the reorganised health service.[421]

Given the relatively passive attitude towards many aspects of the scheme proposed in the Consultative Document, and the tendency of criticisms to cancel one another out, in drafting the White Paper, the Welsh Office saw no reason to depart from its stated plan. The only significant adjustments introduced were dictated by the agreement to preserve uniformity with English arrangements concerning such matters as coterminosity with local government, the composition of area health authorities, the setting up of community health councils, and the professional advisory machinery.

The only major point of uncertainty remained the all-Wales arrangements, where officials persisted with their bad-tempered arguments concerning the merits of the regional tier. The anti-region faction remained dominant, but it was not satisfied with Ministers' insistence on retaining some kind of statutory central consultative body.

Although senior officials insisted that there was no clear role for the Welsh Health Council described in the Consultative Document, for political reasons Ministers remained wedded to this proposal, and plans for the White Paper were made on this basis.[422] However, at the eleventh hour, Ministers were persuaded to abandon this idea in favour of relying on the existing Health and Social Services Panel, which in 1971 was formed from the Health Panel of the Welsh Council, making the possibility of further strengthening of this central consultative machinery dependent on the recommendations of the Royal Commission on the Constitution, and future government responses to the report of this Commission.

White Paper and Legislation
The first draft of the White Paper on reorganisation in Wales was circulated in May 1972 and the White Paper was published on 3 August, two days after the English White Paper.[423] As already mentioned, the only point in the English and Welsh White Papers causing difficulty within the Cabinet was the proposal concerning composition of the area health authorities, upon which it was agreed to await responses to the White Papers.[424]

Reform of local government in Wales was determined by the Local Government Act 1972, which embraced both England and Wales. On the contentious issue of local government in South Wales, the Government finally decided to separate off the Cardiff area as South Glamorgan, creating a total of eight county areas. As already indicated, this arrangement had already been considered in the context of health service reform. In order to preserve congruity between local government and health administration, the White Paper on health service reorganisation duly increased from seven to eight the number of proposed area health authorities. The arrangements for area authorities, professional advisory machinery, and community health councils followed the lines of the English White Paper. Because of the absence of the regional tier, it was proposed to establish the Welsh Health Technical Services Organisation to provide services required on an all-Wales basis. The scope proposed for the WHTSO was more modest than its counterpart in Scotland, and it was made clear that it was under greater direct control of the Secretary of State.

The pattern of reorganisation for the English and Welsh health services was close enough for the original plan for separate Welsh legislation to be dropped. This followed the precedent set in local government reorganisation, where it was also originally intended to introduce separate Welsh legislation. Such amalgamation was necessary in order to complete the tight timetable dictated by the adoption of 1 April 1974 as the date for reorganisation of the health services and local government. This joint action was not altogether welcome; Welsh officials were afraid that their interests would be neglected, while their English counterparts suspected that Welsh Labour MPs would be a disruptive force during parliamentary proceedings, and that complications and delay would be caused by the need to brief Welsh Ministers.[425]

A foretaste of the difficulties ahead was provided when Labour requested a debate in the Welsh Grand Committee on health service reorganisation, and there was no choice but to offer 21 November 1972 as the date, which was discomforting for the Government because it necessitated bringing forward publication of the health service reorganisation Bill, and exposing this measure to parliamentary scrutiny ahead of the formal introduction of the Bill in the House of Lords.[426] This initial exposure to debate was to some extent useful in providing advance warning about points on which the Government was vulnerable to criticism. The debate indicated demands for separate legislation for Wales, retention of the regional tier, and especially for greater local authority and professional participation on health authorities and the strengthening of community health councils.[427] In general it was felt that the proposed changes involved an erosion of local democratic accountability and a strengthening of central bureaucracy. As caricatured by one Welsh Office observer, the parliamentarians complained that 'overmuch power was being centred on faceless and unresponsive Civil Servants'.[428]

The parliamentary stages of the NHS Reorganisation Bill have been described in the earlier part of this chapter. Welsh aspects of the Bill were fully debated; Welsh sensitivities were especially observed by devotion to Wales of the second half of the Second Reading debate in the House of Commons on 27 March 1973. Although the discussion of Welsh issues caused no change in the Government's plans, it indicated that there was a greater degree of opposition to the reorganisation plan in Wales than in England. On the contentious question of all-Wales arrangements, the Government claimed considerable support for eliminating the regional authority, but it was not able to argue that opponents of the region were in favour of extended powers for the Welsh Office. Indeed, most of them advocated some form of all-Wales authority; in some cases they favoured such an authority possessing greater powers than the current Welsh Hospital Board.[429] At the Second Reading Debate, George Thomas stated that Labour would establish an elected Welsh Council, which would be granted the powers enjoyed by RHAs in England.[430] The contributions of Lord Watkins and Lady White in the House of Lords provided a particularly good insight into the degree of dissension existing in Wales.[431] They were annoyed that there was no separate Welsh legislation and no arrangements for an entirely separate and Welsh-speaking Health Service Commissioner. They invoked the strength of opinion in favour of local authority administration of the unified health service, and attacked the centralisation of control by the Welsh Office. They complained that the Welsh Council was an inappropriate body for giving central advice. They argued that the proposed area arrangements gave too little opportunity for representation of local interests and that the new system was particularly inappropriate for the rural parts of Wales. They suggested modification of district arrangements, and also considerable alteration of the Community Health Councils, including arrangements for links with the community councils of local government.

The peers were particularly vitriolic in their criticism of the Welsh Management Study, which they dismissed as a minor variant of its English equivalent, rather than a genuinely independent management exercise. They pointed out that the authors of the Welsh Management Study had failed to consult the Welsh Hospital Board, and that the chairman of this body had resigned from the steering committee in protest about the direction of its thinking.

Like George Thomas, Lord Watkins argued for an elected Welsh Council to take over the functions of the Welsh Hospital Board.

Logistics of Reorganisation

All relevant health authorities in Wales were informed about the Royal Assent in a circular issued in July 1973, which marked the formal beginning of the reorganisation timetable.[432] In view of the imminence of the appointed day, as in England and Scotland, preparations for reorganisation were already well advanced by this date. NHS staff were kept informed about progress through a bilingual news-sheet entitled *Welsh Health Reorganisation News: Newyddion*, issued between January 1973 and March 1974.

Detailed technical guidance on the management structure of the reorganised health service was evolved along the lines adopted in England. This management study involved the same outside consultants, and it was supervised by a parallel steering committee. The result was the substantial Welsh management study, published in September 1972, shortly after its English equivalent.[433] This report was generally known as the 'Red Book' on account of the colour of its cover.[434] The management schemes for areas in England and Wales were almost identical. The main differences in the Welsh management report arose from the need to take account of the absence of a regional tier, and the substitution of the WHTSO. The management report contained hints of disagreements within the steering committee. The Foreword indicated that 'not all members would subscribe to every idea in the Report'. On the all-Wales problem, it was admitted that 'we have not had views from the Welsh Hospital Board itself', an omission which helps to explain the resignation from the steering committee of Gwilym Prys-Davies, Chairman of the Welsh Hospital Board.[435] In his public statement associated with this resignation, Mr Prys-Davies complained that the steering committee was being asked to 'support proposals which will reduce public participation in the planning and management of the Health Service'. He concluded that the 'Management consultants' goals do not include certain fundamental concerns for democracy and the consumer to the same extent that they include management matters'.[436]

The scheme for health service reorganisation is summarised in Table 6.5, and the geographical layout in relation to local government reorganisation is indicated in Maps 5 and 6. As shown by Table 6.5, by English standards, the eight Welsh Area Health Authorities were small in population. The only AHA (Teaching) was South Glamorgan, which absorbed the facilities previously controlled by the Cardiff Board of Governors. Of the eight AHAs, only Mid Glamorgan possessed a population of more than 500,000, while at the

Table 6.5
National Health Service Wales,
Area Health Authorities and Districts, 1974

	Area Health Authority	Population 1973 (thousands)	Districts	Population 1973 (thousands)
1.	Clwyd	368.8	North South	159.0 209.9
2.	Dyfed	317.0	Ceredigion Carmarthen - Dinefwr Preseli - S. Pembrokeshire Llanelli - Dinefwr	55.4 70.6 98.8 92.1
3.	Gwent	441.1	North South	118.0 323.1
4.	Gwynedd	222.1		
5.	Mid Glamorgan	536.1	Ogwr Rhymney Valley East Glamorgan Merthyr-Cynon Valley	126.6 103.8 174.6 131.1
6.	Powys	99.4		
7.	South Glamorgan	392.2		
8.	West Glamorgan	372.6	Neath Swansea	124.7 247.8
	Total Wales	2749.3		

Source: *Health and Personal Social Statistics for Wales*, No. 1, 1974, Table 1.01.

Note: See Maps 5 and 6.

other extreme, the population of Powys was only 99,000. As shown by Maps 5 and 6, the areas with smallest population were geographically large and diverse in character. On account of such small populations, the Welsh Office initially inclined to dispense with district arrangements in rural Wales. However, in response to demands for a more systematic approach to district organisation, in 1973 proposals were made to introduce districts in all areas except Gwynedd, Powys and South Glamorgan. The most elaborate district structure was introduced in South Wales, where 8 of the 14 districts were concentrated. The geography of this administrative pattern and its relationship with local government reorganisation are shown on Maps 5 and 6.

Early in 1973 Joint Liaison Committees were established in each of the eight AHA areas. These committees operated very much like their English counterparts. In July 1973 the Secretary of State announced the names of the Chairmen of the 8 new Area Health

573

Authorities. The members of these authorities were appointed over the summer and they held their first national conference at Llandrindod Wells on 25 and 26 October 1973. By this date most of the senior officers of the AHAs had also been appointed. By the end of the year, the AHAs had established Family Practitioner Committees, and appointments of their chief officers were made in January 1974.

The final elements in the statutory structure were the local professional advisory committees, and the joint consultative committees linking health authorities with local authorities. On account of the need for elaborate consultation with the interests involved, these were set in place only shortly before the appointed day.

Since the NHS Reorganisation Act 1973 was unspecific about arrangements for establishing Community Health Councils, and in response to parliamentary and public anxieties expressed on this issue, the Secretary of State trod warily, and undertook extensive consultations before deciding that CHCs should be established for every health district. In the absence of a regional authority in Wales, the Secretary of State supervised the constitution of CHCs. The guide-lines for membership of CHCs followed the English pattern.

The new arrangements necessitated important alterations in the central department. As already noted, the Welsh Office assumed health service responsibilities in 1969, in the course of which the Welsh Board of Health was eliminated. The abolition of the Welsh Hospital Board in 1974 brought a further increment to the authority of the Welsh Office. Consideration was given to hiving-off some functions to the WHTSO, but after careful consideration, research and intelligence, and also legal services, were retained within the Welsh Office.

The planning of all-Wales functions was assisted by the Welsh NHS Joint Liaison Committee, which brought together representatives of the local liaison committees, the Welsh Hospital Board and the Welsh Office. This national liaison committee established six specialist working groups to consider each aspect of all-Wales operations, including the scope and organisation of the WHTSO.

In October 1973, Mr S Lloyd Jones, the Town Clerk and Chief Executive of Cardiff City Council was appointed Chairman of the WHTSO. At the same time a Board of six members, three nominated by the AHAs and three from the Welsh Office, was appointed to manage the WHTSO. This represented a minor attempt to imitate the more elaborate partnership arrangements which were applied more fully in the Scottish central organisation.

The Chairman and Board of the WHTSO was guided by the Welsh Joint Liaison Committee in organising the transfer of responsibility and staff to the new organisation. After appointment of four chief officers, the WHTSO made preparations to take responsibility for the design and execution of major capital works, certain supplies functions, the provision of computer services, and work formerly undertaken by the Welsh Joint Pricing Committee. For this latter purpose it was necessary to set up a new Statutory Committee of the WHTSO, which was similar in composition to the Welsh Joint Pricing Committee and was served by an independent chief officer. In the absence of an all-Wales consultative body, the WHTSO was also expected to advise the Welsh Office and area authorities on matters within its range of competence.

Controversy concerning the all-Wales level of organisation gradually subsided. The Welsh Board of Health and the Welsh Hospital Board were abolished without disastrous consequences. Central functions were performed by the Welsh Office and the WHTSO without the appearance of excessive centralisation. Establishment of a central consultative mechanism was deferred pending the report of the Royal Commission on the Constitution. However, this long-awaited report gave little directly-applicable guidance and it failed to fulfil the expectations of advocates of devolution. The possibility of granting legislative and executive powers to regional councils was discussed by the Commission, but only moderate support was given for granting such powers to a Welsh Council. The report included a proposal supported by three members for a Welsh Advisory Council, involving an elaborate structure, but only the most limited influence, the remit of which was expected to include the organisation and administration of public services. No specific reference was made to the health services.[437] None of these recommendations caused undue discomfort to the Government. Pending more general measures of devolution, in 1974 the Welsh Council and its Health and Social Services Panel were reconstituted. Officials were pessimistic whether the Panel would find a constructive role among the multitude of alternative advisory bodies. In the event, the sceptics proved wrong; even at the inception of its activities it became evident that the Panel was well-placed to make a constructive contribution with respect to important policy issues affecting many of the most vulnerable client groups served by the NHS.[438]

To deal with the delicate process of appointments to the new authorities and procedures for transfer of staff, in March 1972, the NHS Staff Advisory Committee for Wales was established under the chairmanship of Mr D G Badham. This committee was transmuted into the Staff Commission for Wales, also under the chairmanship of Badham, immediately after the NHS Reorganisation Act received the Royal Assent. By this stage the Advisory Committee was already well advanced with its task. Circulars had been issued concerning the filling of top posts. Indeed advertisements for many of these posts had already been issued and the closing dates were past before the NHS Bill had reached its final stages.

(x) IDES OF MARCH

As a logistic exercise, reorganisation was a success. Although disadvantaged by a late start and by much greater complexity of the mechanism than was originally envisaged, by the end of March 1974, the health departments and NHS authorities had efficiently set in place most elements in new system of administration. This formidable logistic exercise was a great test of the NHS, and its success demonstrated that the health service had matured into an impressive corporate force.

The tranquillity of this operation reflected the tradition of loyalty and sense of dedication among the staff, which the NHS was able to draw upon for exceptional effort at times of need. The strain taken up by the administrative staff was aptly described by Brown:

> The activists in the joint liaison committees were carrying a double workload, punctuated by absences on training courses, until they secured posts in the new structure. Others then had to act up to keep the old authorities functioning after their seniors had left. The most crushing load of all was probably due to the procedures adopted by the Staff Commission, since assessors had to be found, mainly among existing senior staff, to sit on many hundreds of interview panels.[439]

Even this effective vignette overlooks the degree of trauma associated with big administrative changes. Accumulated uncertainties, breaks in continuity of career, transfer to unexpected and perhaps uncongenial appointments, tensions associated with reorientation, the strains of new responsibilities, all generated anxiety and often led to the premature end of a promising career. Reorganisation was the civilian equivalent to war, and as in the postwar situation, even victorious combatants were liable to sustain permanent damage.

For minorities, such as staff taken over from the local health authorities, the changes were dramatic. The culture shock was particularly great for the former public health doctors, whose office now vanished and they faced enforced rehabilitation as the new specialty of community medicine. This group experienced the greatest amount of disorientation; many of the former Medical Officers of Health and their staffs never became accommodated to the new situation; some drifted on in a state of shell-shock until they availed themselves of early retirement.[440]

For the majority of health service personnel, once grading was settled and new contracts were introduced, reorganisation made little difference to their lives. The changes introduced new challenges and brighter prospects in the field of middle management. District and area management offered exciting challenges to younger professionals, and expansion of the administrative structure generated many opportunities for promotion and new types of appointment. Nurse managers in particular experienced a spectacular rise in status and opportunities; but also other groups such as hospital administrators, finance officers, supplies officers and senior scientists experienced a rise in status and authority. On the other hand, the rushed timetable for reorganisation precluded establishment of agreed salary structures for these top personnel. Imposition of salaries represented an unfortunate precedent, while the differentials inherent in these salary scales caused resentment and reinforced some of the existing inequalities. This resulted in senior nurses in particular being disadvantaged compared with other members of the consensus management teams.

With respect to prospects for success of the new system, there was a division of opinion. Initially, the health management experts were optimistic. Professor Chester, one of the most experienced observers, who had been responsible for the Acton Trust reports fifteen years earlier, reviewed the problems thrown up by reorganisation, but believed that these were not insuperable. He concluded that 'within its terms of reference the integration of the former tripartite system was justified and timely. Whether it was carried out as efficiently as possible only history will tell'.[441]

Others were more sceptical about the success of reorganisation. At a time of escalating demand for public participation, growing effectiveness of single-issue interest groups representing deprived sections of the community, and of greater assertiveness and radicalisation within the health professions, the transformation of the health service into a vast hierarchical and managerial structure seemed out of touch with the times. It was also inconsistent with changes occurring in other public services, where the local community was demanding and receiving a greater voice in the management of its schools, or more participation in the planning of its local environment. By contrast, the health service seemed to be drifting further away from public surveillance and control. The NHS was seen as a battle ground between the values of corporatism and democracy; reorganisation seemed to have brought about the extinction of a particular tradition of public service and had substituted a corporate edifice in its place. There was little confidence that defences of the public interest provided by such

577

bodies as the new Community Health Councils, even in their strengthened form, would effectively represent community aspirations or even prevent erosion of the Cinderella services. The reorganised NHS was portrayed as a rigid power structure, evolving into a monolithic corporation which would not be sufficiently sensitive to the real needs of the sick.[442] Similar views were expressed to the Sub-Committee of the Expenditure Committee investigating the state of the preventive services. The committee commented with some surprise on the 'great many hard things said about the reorganisation of the health services'. Even at this early stage the Sub-Committee recommended that serious consideration should be given to eliminating one of the tiers of the management structure.[443]

Criticisms also emanated from experts engaged in monitoring specific services. The Health Advisory Service believed that morale in the services for which it was responsible had declined on account of reorganisation. The 'heavy and cumbersome' bureaucracy of the new service and its multiplicity of committees absorbed the energies of consultants to a disproportionate extent and deflected them away from patient care. The new decision-making mechanism was slow, inefficient, and subject to frustrating delays. The complex web of horizontal and vertical management relations provided ample opportunity for conflict and confusion, and evasion of responsibility concerning decision-making. Reorganisation reduced still further the place of the mental sector in the health service hierarchy, with the result that multi-disciplinary teams responsible for these services at unit level felt powerless and isolated, or sometimes subjugated to inexperienced and junior officials at group level. This sector also experienced disadvantages associated with the administrative separation of health and social services. AHAs and local authorities were coterminous, but at an operational level, social services and health services were organised on a district basis, where coterminosity was often absent. The frustrating problems of co-ordination between hospital and community services were therefore left unresolved by reorganisation.[444] Consequently, with respect to services required by vulnerable groups such as the mentally handicapped, the mentally sick, the elderly, and the disabled, it was by no means certain that the benefits of reorganisation outweighed the disadvantages. Looking back on events in 1974, even management specialists were struck by the high degree of dissatisfaction, which it was acknowledged was 'strongest among, but by no means confined to doctors'. The criticisms were aimed at many aspects of the management arrangements, but most commonly related to the 'remoteness of the new authorities, delays in decision-making, the excessive amount of time spent on consultations, the administration of hospitals being left to young and inexperienced administrators without adequate authority'.[445] Coincidentally, this general summary precisely echoed the criticisms made with respect to the long-stay sector. In view of this powerful undercurrent of scepticism, it was from the outset doubtful whether the vast reorganisation exercise would survive long enough to command general assent.

579

CHAPTER VII

Crisis of Confidence

The General Election on 28 February 1974 was conducted in an atmosphere of crisis reminiscent of 1931. The immediate precipitating factor was the Government's confrontation with the miners, but this was just one aspect of the wider economic and social malaise facing the nation. Edward Heath took a gamble by calling an early General Election, calculating that he would gain a decisive mandate for his administration's policies. The Conservatives hoped that a short and aggressive election campaign conducted during the State of Emergency would result in decisive defeat for Labour and its trade unionist allies.

Heath's prospects for a working majority faded during the final days of the campaign. Labour increased its number of MPs from 287 to 301; the Conservatives decreased from 323 to 297. However, Labour was 33 short of an overall majority owing to gains made by the Liberals, nationalists, and other minority parties. After an abortive attempt by Heath to frame a pact with the Liberals, Harold Wilson was invited to form his third administration, the first minority Government since 1931. The instability of this situation prompted Wilson to seek a more definitive mandate by calling a further General Election on 10 October 1974. This campaign was an echo of its predecessor, with a similarly indecisive outcome. By contrast with his experience in 1966, Wilson's gamble failed to pay off. Early predictions of a comfortable majority were not confirmed. Labour increased its seats to 319, while the Conservatives fell back to 277, but Labour was left three short of an overall majority owing to continuing strong showing of the nationalists and other minority parties. Despite this stalemate, Labour was able to continue in office until 1979, albeit latterly dependent on alliance with the Liberals. Two General Election defeats undermined the authority of Edward Heath, who faced growing calls for his resignation. He hung on until February 1975, when he failed to obtain a vote of confidence from his colleagues and was replaced by Margaret Thatcher.[1]

(i) MINISTERS AND DEPARTMENTS

Wilson's Cabinet was illustrative of his characteristic balancing acts between left and right. As Chancellor of the Exchequer, Denis Healey and his subordinates represented stout financial orthodoxy.

The left were concentrated in the fields of industry and employment. There was no obvious candidate to take over the health and social services portfolio. In opposition between 1970 and 1974, Labour made an indifferent showing with respect to health and the personal social services. Its record in detecting points of weakness and harassing the Government was less convincing than in the previous comparable period of opposition, when Robinson showed himself to be well-informed on NHS affairs and energetic in pursuing points of weakness in the Government's record.

Part of the explanation for Labour's poor showing was absence of continuity at a senior level. The first shadow health and social security spokesperson, appointed in July 1970, was Mrs Shirley Williams. However, her political fortunes were on the ascendant, and she was appointed shadow Home Secretary in December 1971. At this date Barbara Castle lost her place in the shadow cabinet elections, thereby allowing Callaghan to supplant her as employment spokesperson. Recognising her ability and seniority, Wilson appointed Castle as the chief health and social security spokesperson. However, in November 1972, Castle once again failed to secure a place in the elected front-bench team. Wilson invited her to continue as the health and social security spokesperson, but she declined, and spent the rest of the opposition period without front-bench responsibilities. The health and social security post was then offered to John Silkin, who had tied with Peter Shore for the last place in the shadow cabinet, but had stood down in favour of Shore. Silkin continued with his health and social security duties until the February 1974 General Election, despite the fact that in November 1973, he also failed to obtain an elected place in the shadow cabinet. Throughout the period in opposition Shirley Summerskill provided continuity as the junior health spokesperson. Like her mother, the formidable Edith Summerskill (Baroness Summerskill), Shirley Summerskill was medically trained. Shirley Summerskill to some extent replicated the functions of Robinson ten years earlier, but without making the same impact.

Wilson's decision to appoint Barbara Castle rather than Silkin as Secretary of State for Social Services was a logical and appropriate position for a politician of her standing. After an uncomfortable spell on the back-benches, and no doubt aware that age was not on her side, Castle was naturally apprehensive about her chances of appointment to a senior position within the Government. With some anxiety she telephoned Wilson immediately after it became evident that he would become Prime Minister, and was relieved to be told that she was to be offered Health and Social Security, with the option of taking over Silkin's shadow team.[2] This appointment and the warm welcome it received among Labour MPs was regarded with

581

relief by Castle; it was 'as if they wanted to make good for all the humiliations I have suffered in being thrown off the Shadow Cabinet'.[3] Her return to the Cabinet seemed like final confirmation of reconciliation after the bitterness generated by her association with *In Place of Strife*.

Castle in some respects represented a return to the ethos associated with her recently-deceased ally, Richard Crossman. However, she was less experienced in the field of the social services, without his wider social service co-ordination functions, and generally a less powerful figure in the Cabinet. Under Wilson, the Social Services Committee was chaired by the Education Secretary, Edward Short, and the Home Affairs Committee by Home Secretary, Roy Jenkins, neither of them especially friendly to Castle. Also, she was in a slightly vulnerable position on account of age. Approaching 63, she was one of the older members of the Cabinet, indeed the oldest Minister to hold responsibility for the health and personal social services since World War II.[4] However, she was still a formidable and impressive political force. As the Chief Secretary of the day recalls, she was not one of the Ministers who could be easily persuaded to accept cuts in the course of bilateral discussions. As in the case of Bevan, she was well-prepared for confrontation with the Treasury, and Treasury Ministers needed to plan carefully for their meetings with her, since she tended 'to go down fighting in Cabinet' rather than volunteer concessions.[5] The following sections of this chapter provide many examples of Castle's pugnacious defence of the interests of her department.

Barbara Castle selected an able team of junior Ministers. On the social security side of her department, Brian O'Malley was an obvious choice. She rejected Shirley Summerskill for health in favour of David Owen, who was also medically qualified. He had previously held a junior ministerial post in the Ministry of Defence, and had served in the front bench shadow team for the first two years of the Heath administration. At the instigation of Owen, Castle pressed Wilson to appoint him from the outset at the level of Minister of State, which was at first rejected, but then conceded in July 1974.[6] As compensation for Owen's initial lower rank, Castle was allowed to enlarge her team of junior Ministers. On the health side, Castle's team was strengthened by inclusion of outside advisers. The experienced Professor Brian Abel-Smith represented continuity with the Crossman regime; the young barrister and former National Union of Students leader, Jack Straw, was imported at the suggestion of Castle's husband to become a general adviser; the industrial relations expert, Dr W E J McCarthy, was appointed as adviser to undertake a review of the Whitley machinery; and naturally, other advisers were employed on the social security front.[7] A further bold action was appointment of Jack Ashley as her Parliamentary Private Secretary. On account of his deafness, Ashley knew the problems of the handicapped at firsthand, and he fought hard and effectively for their rights. Castle also periodically drew upon the experience of veterans in health affairs such as Laurie Pavitt, who occupied a minor place in the administration as Assistant Whip and was Chairman of the Labour parliamentary Health Group.[8]

The Castle ministerial team was not particularly liked by their civil servants, who found some of their policy priorities inconvenient and alien. However, the Ministers were pursuing the declared policy objectives of the Labour Party and more generally they tried to be constructive, despite the inclement economic climate in which they were operating. Owen spoke warmly of Castle's approach to her duties: 'she knew the need to be able to dominate civil servants - who by the limitations of the job can't be bold or innovatory'.[9] Equally, although Castle appreciated that her officials found Owen 'irritating', she was pleased that he came up with 'endless policy initiatives'.[10]

Barbara Castle inherited responsibility for the health and personal social services at a particularly inauspicious moment. She inherited Joseph's scheme for reorganisation, which had been attacked consistently by Labour, and which was subject to growing criticism both from within the health service and from outside. The economic crisis had inevitable continuing adverse consequences for the funding of the health and personal social services. Controversies over the remuneration of many important groups soon erupted more fiercely than before. Finally, Labour's manifesto commitment to phase out pay-beds from NHS hospitals exacerbated already bad relations with hospital doctors and with the medical profession in general.

Castle became the object of much adverse press comment, both on account of problems in the NHS and other issues such as the European community. She was soon subjected to press rumours about her imminent replacement, for instance in May 1975, when it was suggested that her post would be offered to Anthony Wedgwood Benn.[11] In January 1976 Joel Barnett detected a hint from Wilson that he would like to 'shuffle Barbara Castle out' of the Cabinet, and promote Brian O'Malley and David Owen, presumably to Cabinet posts.[12] At precisely this time, Wilson directed a scarcely veiled threat to Castle that if he resigned, then also 'you'd go'.[13]

In March 1976, Castle incautiously spoke to Wilson about her wish to resign after the safe completion of the pay-beds legislation. At this point she discovered that the Prime Minister had also decided to retire in the near future.[14] This interview perhaps had a more decisive influence than she expected. On 16 March Wilson notified his Cabinet colleagues about his retirement.[15] Callaghan was selected to replace Wilson by MPs on 5 April.[16] On 8 April the new Prime Minister called in Barbara Castle and asked for her resignation, giving the need to reduce the average age of the Cabinet as his reason. He refused to name her substitute.[17] The other Ministers removed by Callaghan on this occasion were Mellish, Ross and Short. These changes achieved a modest reduction in the average age of the Cabinet from 56.6 to 54.3 years.

Castle was replaced by David Ennals, a appointment which met with her shock and evident disapproval. As on a previous occasion, she expressed willingness to stand down in favour of Judith Hart, but she found it a humiliation to be turned out in favour of Ennals. Castle also expressed surprise that Callaghan should have used this opportunity to reduce the number of women in the Cabinet.[18] As noted in chapter III, Ennals had served under Crossman, indeed had briefly been the Minister of State responsible for health. But his main experience lay in the field of social security. Crossman generally, but not invariably, reported favourably on his abilities.[19] In 1970 Ennals lost his seat at Dover. From 1970-1973 he was Campaign Director for the National Association of Mental Health. In 1974 he returned to Parliament as MP for Norwich North. Castle asked for his services in her department, but perhaps on account of his strong international relations interests, Wilson wanted him as Minister of State at the Foreign and Commonwealth Office, where he served until his big promotion as Secretary of State for Social Services under Callaghan.[20] Ennals had at an earlier stage worked for Callaghan, and he actively supported his campaign for the leadership.[21] Ennals undoubtedly possessed much of the experience relevant to his health and social security post. Although a person of ambition and energy, he was dogged by ill-health during his term of office, and even at his best was nothing like the political stature of his two Labour predecessors.[22] His disadvantages were a handicap at a time when the health and personal social services were experiencing their worst period of sustained crisis since the beginning of the postwar welfare state. Although Callaghan had promoted Ennals to the Cabinet, he was not entirely satisfied with his performance. The following sections indicate many points of irritation, especially during the health service industrial relations disputes that dominated NHS affairs during the last few months of the administration.[23]

After the departure of Short from the Government, Callaghan combined the Home Affairs and Social Services Committees of the Cabinet to form the Home and Social Affairs Committee, an arrangement more favoured previously under Conservative rather than Labour administrations. The Home and Social Affairs Committee was chaired by Merlyn Rees, a former school teacher, trusted associate of Callaghan, and Home Secretary. David Owen stayed on briefly in his post after the departure of Barbara Castle, until in September 1976 he moved to become a Minister of State in the Foreign and Commonwealth Office.[24] His place as a Minister of State responsible for health in DHSS was taken by Roland Moyle, who had previously been a Minister of State in the Northern Ireland Office with responsibility for education, health and social services. With the appointment of Ennals, Ashley and Straw left their posts, but Abel-Smith stayed on as an adviser.

At the Scottish Office, the veteran William Ross picked up in 1974 where he had left off in 1970. This appointment installed an opponent of devolution as Secretary of State for Scotland at a time of a new zenith of Scottish nationalism, which inevitably called for a more conciliatory attitude from Labour towards Scottish and Welsh aspirations. On account of age and his traditionalism, Ross was vulnerable to criticism. Indeed Crossman recorded that Ross was fortunate to survive in office during the reshuffles undertaken by Wilson before 1970. Ross was finally removed by Callaghan and replaced by his experienced Minister of State, Bruce Millan, who had been involved with health as a junior Minister under Ross between 1966 and 1970. Whereas Ross was said to have 'never identified himself with any positive response to the rise of nationalist feeling', Millan had at least been cautious about antagonising the advocates of devolution.[25] The main responsibility for health at SHHD devolved to one of the Under-Secretaries of State, Robert Hughes until July 1975, and thereafter Harry Ewing.

John Morris, who was appointed as Secretary of State for Wales in 1974, was much more favourable to devolution than his colleague Ross. Also, twenty years younger than Ross, he was not at risk in the Callaghan round of compulsory retirements.

Health Departments
At DHSS, Sir Philip Rogers was due to retire in the summer of 1974, but he was willing to stay on, and Sir William Armstrong was supportive of this course of action. Barbara Castle was not so enthusiastic. She naturally inclined to favour a head of department not associated with the previous regime. She found Rogers 'deeply conventional, instinctively out of line with the far-reaching reforms we want to make, but not obstructive'.[26] In the absence of a more acceptable candidate, and in view of some positive estimates of Rogers, she allowed him to continue. However, in October 1974 she reasserted the need for a change, but once again found it difficult to arrive at an acceptable alternative.[27] Despite his perceived disadvantages, Rogers turned out to be a completely reliable short-term appointee, and upon retirement he earned applause from his

Ministers and colleagues alike.[28] Lancelot Errington, the Second Permanent Secretary, responsible for the social security side of the department, followed Rogers into retirement in 1976.

In July 1975 the name of Sir Patrick Nairne was proposed as a possible successor to Rogers. This candidate enjoyed warm support from various quarters, including Denis Healey and David Owen, who had worked with him at the Ministry of Defence. Castle also formed a good opinion; she found him 'far less conventional' than Rogers. Like Rogers, Nairne was a newcomer to DHSS, but whereas Rogers had spent a brief period in a senior position at the CSD, Nairne's rise to seniority had taken place in the Ministry of Defence, and then the Cabinet Office, where he was Second Permanent Secretary from 1973 to 1975. Nairne's name had been canvassed for the headship of the new Civil Service College established in 1970.[29]

Nairne took up his appointment as Permanent Secretary at DHSS at the end of October 1975 and continued until his retirement in 1981. Nairne's lack of Treasury experience was compensated for by the presence on the health side of his department of two Deputy Secretaries recruited from the Treasury, and another with some Treasury experience. Most of the senior personnel had extensive experience in other departments, which was an enormous contrast with the Ministry of Health up to 1960. Even with its more cosmopolitan leadership, DHSS was difficult to manage, and its problems were compounded by the times of unparalleled stress. Nairne frankly admitted that the department was 'elephantine' in its nature, and in risk of the fate of the dinosaurs.[30] It was of course the complaint levelled at the old Ministry of Health. Not only were the HPSS and Social Security sides of the department largely separate and completely different administrative entities, but also the NHS and Personal Social Services sides of HPSS represented completely different administrative traditions, yet under NHS and local government reorganisation they were supposed to operate in complete harmony.

The Government's drive for greater economy in administration combined with dissatisfaction with NHS reorganisation brought the DHSS central organisation under renewed scrutiny. At a discussion with RHA Chairmen in December 1975 on the need to reduce the costs of administration and achieve greater devolution, it was agreed that a small team of Chairmen would examine the functions of DHSS in its relation with the RHAs. The report of this group, published in July 1976, included some twenty recommendations affecting the organisation of the central department.[31] This enquiry, generally known as the Three Chairmen's Report, was relevant to the management review of the central department, which began in December 1976. This review was a high-level exercise, directed by an impressive steering committee chaired by Nairne. The committee included one of the RHA Chairmen involved in the Three Chairmen's Report. This review was completed in 1978.[32] It concentrated on the organisation of the top management of the department. Having experienced the traumas of reorganisation, the review emphatically insisted that it was important to avoid change for its own sake. The report concluded that 'there was both insufficient evidence to show that the gains from structural change would justify the cost and sufficient evidence to show that there was more which could be effectively done to improve the organisation as it is'.[33] The main recommendations were confined to vague proposals for encouraging better co-ordination and planning within the department. Among the more specific suggestions were the encouragement of a more positive administrative role for the Chief Scientist, the consolidation of the role of the Principal Finance Officer, and removal of certain functions from the divisions controlled by the Principal Establishment Officer.[34] The main positive outcome of this review was establishment in 1978 of an HPSS Strategy Committee, supported by a Policy Planning Unit. The management review therefore sanctioned continuation of the slow process of adaptation which was already occurring within the department.[35]

As in the case of DHSS, the process of incremental change in divisional arrangements within SHHD continued after the major departmental reorganisation of 1974.[36] The main outstanding problems related to achieving a smooth working relationship between SHHD and the extraordinarily elaborate associated central machinery established in response to NHS reorganisation, the main elements of which were the Common Services Agency and the Scottish Health Service Planning Council. The CSA acted as an umbrella organisation for a variety of functions which had formerly been largely autonomous. The directors of divisions of the CSA and their steering committees soon found the CSA secretary and management committee an unwelcome imposition, and steps were taken to ensure that such functions as the ambulance service, the blood transfusion service and the Health Education Unit could operate with reasonable autonomy. The larger problem related to the SHSPC, which was designed to be a more powerful organisation than the CHSC and its Standing Advisory Committees in London. The SHSPC spawned an elaborate infrastructure, two main elements of which were its programme planning groups and its specialist advisory groups. In order to monitor the operations of these committees, and also such agencies as the statutory National Consultative Committees, SHHD established a high-level Policy Group, and the Planning Unit, already mentioned in chapter VI. The Planning Unit

587

was an important new element in SHHD, and it was closely connected with the secretariat of the SHSPC.

A draft background paper announced that the SHSPC would ensure that strategic policy would be determined in a 'spirit of basic concord and consensus'.[37] The difficulty of achieving this utopian objective was soon exposed by the row which broke out over the drafting of the 'memorandum' *The Health Service in Scotland. The Way Ahead*.[38] As noted below, SHHD was under pressure to produce this document in concert with its English counterpart in view of the need to provide firm guidance to health authorities on priorities at a time of sharp reductions of funding. The problem was explained by senior officials at a meeting of the SHSPC in November 1975, but the Planning Council heard little more until they were presented with the completed document in March 1976, shortly before its publication. This produced a furious response, especially from medical representatives from the hospital service and universities, who complained about lack of meaningful consultation on policies which they believed were against the interests of their sectors of the health service.[39] The economic crisis and pressures for retrenchment produced continuing strains within the SHHD-SHSPC mechanism, which was well-designed to exploit opportunities for expansion, but was less well suited for a regime of retrenchment. Whereas in England, the combined efforts of the Treasury and DHSS stifled opportunities for production of reports containing additional expenditure commitments, in Scotland the SHSPC could not be contained in the same manner; it proved to be a fertile source of such reports. SHHD experienced the greatest difficulty in establishing that these reports were not more than consultative in their status.[40] The efforts by SHHD to contain SHSPC generated complaints from the latter that it was being marginalised and prevented from fulfilling the functions intended at its inception.[41]

(ii) ARK OF OUR COVENANT

During its period of opposition, the health service occupied only a minor place in the policy deliberations of the Labour Party.[42] It was not until August 1973 that Labour issued a policy document of any substance relating to health care. This was the eighth in a series sponsored by the National Executive Committee of the Party; it possessed little importance and understandably attracted virtually no media attention. This 'Green Paper', although presented as a radical discussion document, was largely a restatement of policies already adopted within the health service. It avoided expenditure commitments, not even calling for the abolition of health service charges. The Government's proposals for health service reorganisation were attacked, but no substantial alteration of the

Conservative scheme for reorganisation was proposed. Although the tone of comment on private medicine within the health service was unfavourable, only minor limitations were suggested, designed to prevent private practice being 'parasitic' on the NHS. The most noteworthy feature of the Green Paper was the proposal for a National Service for the Mentally Handicapped, which was seen as the only realistic way to achieve a break with the existing system of institutional care.[43]

The preoccupations of the rank and file within the Labour Party were better indicated by Barbara Castle's speech on the social services at the October 1973 conference, when she promised that 'we will eliminate private practice from our NHS' and thereby end the two nations service, in which the 'cheque book carves a priority path of consultant services and a private bed'. She admitted that eliminating health service charges would be beyond Labour's competence, but promised that removing the prescription charge would be an urgent priority.[44]

Given the importance of the National Health Service as an electoral asset to Labour, it is perhaps surprising that this weapon was not employed with more effect in its February 1974 General Election manifesto. This omission was all the more evident on account of the much more elaborate treatment of health in the Conservative manifesto. The Labour prospectus on health amounted to no more than one-tenth of the Conservative equivalent. The few words devoted to health were confined to predictable generalities. Labour promised to: 'Revise and expand the NATIONAL HEALTH SERVICE; abolish prescription charges; introduce free family planning; phase out private practice from the hospital service, and transform the area health authorities into democratic bodies'.[45]

In the October 1974 manifesto the NHS received considerably greater attention. The Government drew attention to its on-going efforts to increase resources available for health care, improve pay, reduce the impact of health service charges, introduce greater democracy into the administration, and it promised continuing efforts to phase out pay-beds. Labour also promised to 'reduce regional inequality of standards; put the emphasis on prevention and primary care and give a clear priority to spending on services for the mentally ill and mentally handicapped'.[46] Even with this improvement, the Labour manifesto was in certain respects less adequate than its Conservative equivalent, especially with respect to the latter's specific reference to the Briggs and Halsbury Reports relating to nursing, and the need for a review into the workings of the Whitley pay machinery.[47]

In the Debate on the Address, immediately after her appointment, Barbara Castle described the National Health Service as the 'ark of our covenant'.[48] Despite her dramatic promises to strengthen and protect the health service from erosion, this speech was uninformative about the Government's intentions, largely owing to Treasury insistence on avoidance of expenditure commitments. Castle was furious at being made to recount 'a lot of turgid banalities' on this important parliamentary occasion.[49]

Since some specific commitments, especially relating to the improvement of pensions, were possible, social security was allocated the dominant place in her speech. Consistent with the limitations imposed, the HPSS part of the speech concentrated on complaints about NHS reorganisation, explaining that in the short term it was impracticable for the Government to interfere with Joseph's scheme, but action to democratise the administration was promised. The main additional pledge related to the renegotiation of senior hospital medical staff contracts, continuing negotiations begun by Joseph, but Castle proposed to link this with Labour's contentious proposal for phasing out pay-beds. She also announced that, in the interim, charges for pay-beds would be increased.

Castle admitted that the priority given to pension increases ruled out the elimination of prescription charges in the short term. Despite the manifesto pledge, and in contrast with Labour's interventions in 1964, the best that Castle could promise was correction of anomalies in the current charges arrangements. With respect to other policy intentions of Labour, Castle confined herself to vague promises to strengthen community services, and services relating to mental health and mental 'subnormality', rehabilitation, and dentistry; also she promised action to reduce waiting lists.[50]

Despite its fears about Castle's expansionist proclivities, the Treasury was heartened by the new administration's avoidance of specific expenditure commitments. Especially important, promises concerning reduction in health service charges were considerably more limited than in 1964. In reviewing prospects for the future, the Treasury anticipated that Castle would attach high priority to abolition of the prescription charge, but all further costly items were expected from the social security side of her department rather than HPSS. An increase in pensions was the first priority, which was estimated to add £100m to the social security budget. It was hoped that immediate developments on the HPSS side could be limited to removing charges for family planning services.[51]

As during all earlier Labour administrations, stark economic realities prevented the Wilson and Callaghan teams from embarking on an expansionist programme in the social services. Nevertheless, despite the unpropitious economic circumstances, taking the period 1973/74 to 1978/79 as a whole, the share of national resources devoted to the NHS climbed slowly, from 3.78 to 5.27 as a percentage of GDP.[52] During the 1970s, expenditure on the NHS averaged at about 4.8 per cent of GDP. The yield from the NHS Contribution and direct charges remained constant at about 8 per cent and 2 per cent of health service spending respectively.[53] The small yield from local taxation ended with NHS reorganisation. At 1970 prices, over the period 1974 to 1979, NHS expenditure increased by 9.8 per cent in cost terms, and by 11.5 per cent in volume terms. The pattern for cost and volume follow roughly the same tend, with a peak at the beginning of the period occasioned in the volume estimate by a small expansion in services, and in the cost estimate by big wage rises, of which the Halsbury award to nurses was the largest. After the first year there was a virtual cessation of growth for the greater part of the Labour administration, but a very small recovery at the end of our period in the cost estimate, which was occasioned by wage factors. Thus, in cost terms, 4.6 per cent of the increase took place in the first year, and only 5.2 per cent over the succeeding four years. The volume estimate indicates a 7.2 per cent increase during the first year, and 4.3 per cent over the succeeding four years. With respect to current expenditure, of the 12.4 per cent increase in the cost estimate, 5.3 per cent occurred during the first year; while of the 13.5 per cent increase in the volume estimate, 7.2 per cent occurred during the first year. It is evident that after the dramatic escalation of costs occasioned by wage inflation at the beginning of the period, in conditions of acute economic crisis, the Labour administration imposed a regime of rigid containment, which effectively brought an end to a long phase of incremental growth in spending on the health service.[54]

Whereas HPSS expenditure remained fairly constant as a share of GDP during the Labour administration, education declined from about 6.3 to 5.3 per cent. Education, like housing, also fell back in their share of the social services budget, whereas the HPSS sector held its own. The only slight rise occurred in social security, reflecting higher benefits and the growth of unemployment.[55] The next section of this chapter will describe the above changes in HPSS expenditure in the appropriate political context.[56]

(iii) FINANCING THE HEALTH SERVICE
The initial decisions concerning resources for the health service occurred in the context of Healey's first budget, which took a broadly relaxed view of public expenditure, allowing modest increases on many fronts; social security was a main beneficiary, but only minor increases were incurred by the HPSS sector.

Castle versus the Treasury
Barbara Castle began her tenure as it was to continue, on

argumentative terms with the Treasury. She proposed to increase the age of prescription charge exemption for children from 15 to 16, and to reduce the age of exemption for women from 65 to 60. Although these were only minor concessions, the Treasury reminded DHSS of the necessity for prior consultation on all proposals with expenditure implications. Consequently, as already noted, her intention to announce these concessions during the Debate on the Address was vetoed by the Treasury, supported by the Prime Minister. Castle immediately stepped out of line for a second time, by instructing Owen, Ashley and Straw to produce a Cabinet paper proposing the abolition of charges for family planning services. Although the cost was small, and found from her existing budget, the Treasury was concerned about longer term implications and precedents. However, Treasury Ministers were not advised to intervene destructively, although it was agreed to take steps to prevent repetition of Castle's errant practices.[57]

After this shaky start, Ministers ratified both Castle's proposals for removal of family planning charges and her other suggestion for minor relaxation of prescription charges. The Prime Minister reminded her that no further reduction of prescription charges would be possible in the foreseeable future.[58] The total cost of these concessions was only £3.7m in England for 1974/75.

Castle made her announcement on charges in the Budget debate. Even this was not free from controversy because the Treasury refused to allow her to give an assurance that the Government would not increase eye service and dental charges.[59] Despite the disappointingly small scale of her package of health service concessions, Castle was pleased with the response in Parliament, and by the television interest in her announcement on family planning.[60] It is worth noting that yet another source of tension in relations between DHSS and the Treasury during the early months of the Castle tenure related to publication of the Sharp Report on the mobility of the physically disabled, which came under the social security aspect of Castle's responsibilities. After these initial perturbations, the Treasury hoped for a 'spell of quieter relations'.[61]

In considering longer-term expenditure plans, the base-line for HPSS was depressed by £111m as a consequence of the cuts in public expenditure for 1974/75 announced under the previous administration in December 1973. Initial estimates from DHSS relating to HPSS spending from 1975/76 onwards suggested an average 3.2 per cent rate of growth. This involved scaling down the rate of increase assumed under the previous administration, especially respecting capital programmes and personal social services current spending. Despite mounting demands for a radical increase in spending on the NHS, Castle was forced to adopt a policy of restraint. In response, not long after the February General Election, the newspapers began to focus on evidence concerning crisis within the health service.[62] In July 1974, the BMA, BDA, RCN and RCM made a joint approach to the Prime Minister, warning about the imminent collapse of the health service, seeking a substantial injection of additional resources, and also calling for establishment of an independent enquiry into the NHS.[63] As noted below, this initiative was the prelude to the establishment of the Royal Commission on the NHS.

Although not immediately productive from the point of view of the professions, their agitation caused the Treasury to moderate its attitude in the course of negotiations with health Ministers. Healey met Castle on 9 July for a preliminary review of her spending plans. This meeting was dominated by bad-tempered disagreements over social security spending.[64] Healey's hand was strengthened by the Cabinet decision on 26 July to limit public expenditure to a growth rate of 2.75 per cent. Castle was among the Ministers most unsympathetic to this decision, which she regarded as impossible from the point of view of her department.[65] In the course of bilateral discussions, Castle was regarded as the Minister most likely to breach the 2.75 per cent limit, largely on account of her plans for social security spending.

Healey was warned that the Secretary of State's plans for social security spending were even likely to threaten confidence in sterling. Bilateral discussions also exhibited differences of opinion concerning the HPSS programme. Echoing the rhetoric of the professions, Castle claimed that the health service was facing a 'catastrophic situation'. Every section of the service was in revolt against the neglect suffered over the years. The Permanent Secretary confirmed that in his experience the situation was the gravest he had ever known. Another senior official believed that health service staff were so demoralised that was a danger that the quality of their work would deteriorate.[66]

Castle was successful in her first minor skirmish, when she persuaded colleagues to introduce a freeze on dental charges, which under the previous administration had been regularly adjusted to yield 50 per cent of the cost of the service.[67] The more important test came with the bilateral discussions held after the October 1974 General Election. These were dominated by haggling over social security, but there were lesser disagreements over HPSS spending. Here, the Chancellor's first priority was to obtain a reduction in the growth rate for the personal social services. Healey argued that the NHS was already being granted a protected status by being excluded from cuts. By way of compromise he offered a £14m a year increase for the health service, and full supplementation for the Halsbury pay awards to doctors, dentists and nurses, on condition that a reduction for the personal social services of about £14m each year was imposed. He also offered amounts rising to £15m by 1978/79 for the new invalid mobility scheme. Discussions were dominated by social security issues. Castle broadly accepted this compromise, but insisted on the addition of a £35m non-recurrent grant for the capital programme for 1975/76 to cover urgent maintenance of hospital buildings.[68]

The two parties were near enough to agreement to avoid a major confrontation. However, relations between the Treasury and DHSS once again deteriorated owing to Castle's failure to consult the Treasury over her statement in the Debate on the Address concerning the phasing out of pay-beds. The Treasury pointed out that this would entail lost revenue amounting to at least £20m a year, while the total expenditure implications of this change of policy were considerably greater. It was claimed that this change had not been taken into account during previous discussions concerning HPSS spending plans.[69]

After a general review of PESC recommendations in November 1974, further discussions with Ministers took place on remaining points of disagreement. Castle offered no offsetting savings with respect to phasing out pay-beds, and also proposed additional capital spending for both the health service and personal social services, as well as further expansion in social security. According to her department's estimate, these suggestions went only part way to restoring the cuts made by the previous administration. On account of the need to implement community care policies to which the Government was committed, she refused to confirm the provisionally agreed reductions in personal social services spending. Treasury officials were alarmed that she was using each agreement as a springboard for the next demand. Healey therefore refused to contemplate restoration of levels of spending of the previous administration, or to offer further concessions. Castle reluctantly accepted that with respect to HPSS spending, Healey had done what he could 'to spare the programme from the full rigour of the cuts made by our predecessors'. Her residual disagreements were reserved for outstanding issues relating to social security.[70]

In early 1975, Castle communicated to health authorities that their expenditure plans could be conducted on the assumption of a 2 per cent growth rate for hospital and community services, which was disappointing, but in the economic circumstances the most that could be expected. A similar level of increase was adopted for the personal social services, and just above 3 per cent for the family practitioner services. In preparing for a further attempt to increase resources available to the health and personal social services, Castle considered all the alternatives available to her predecessors, without any startling new insights. Her opposition to direct charges remained steadfast. She was more sympathetic to increasing the contribution from the National Insurance Fund, especially in lieu of patients spending more than eight weeks in hospital, for whom benefits were reduced. She also devoted some attention to the possibility that local authorities and health authorities might operate lotteries to raise funds for their services.[71] However, none of these alternatives offered substantial yield, and these plans proved to be an academic exercise, since they were overtaken by the Treasury's decision that substantial cuts in public expenditure were unavoidable.

The entire world economy continued to feel the shocks associated with the oil price rise, but United Kingdom experienced higher inflation and a larger external deficit than its competitors. These problems showed every sign of accelerating out of control. No sooner had departments accustomed themselves to the discipline imposed by the January 1975 Public Expenditure White Paper than the Treasury proposed a reduction of £1bn in public expenditure for 1976/77. This was to be reinforced by the regime of cash limits, which were due to take effect in the same year.[72] These emergency measures were directly precipitated by the large scale of the winter pay increases, but they were also designed as a first step towards containing the Public Sector Borrowing Requirement, which was forecast to reach £7.5bn in 1975 and rise even higher in the following year. Haunted by the ghost of the devaluation crisis of 1966/67, the recommendation for £1bn cuts in public expenditure was reluctantly accepted by Ministers on 25 March 1975. Castle was among the Ministers who regarded the proposal as a piece of blackmail, sprung on spending departments, without the opportunity for a reasoned assessment of the case on account of the proximity of the budget. Castle described the conduct of the Treasury as little short of an outrage.[73]

Castle greeted this decision as a 'traumatic blow'.[74] Not only were reductions of £62m for 1976/77 in prospect for HPSS, but there were also adverse implications for 1975/76, especially with respect to the capital programme. DHSS was unable to release to NHS authorities the agreed figures relating to their capital spending for the year beginning April 1975. The Treasury now proposed to reduce the growth rate for the hospital and community services from 2 to 1 per cent, and in the personal social services from 2 per cent to nil. It was also suggested that the HPSS budget should absorb the loss of revenue associated with the phasing out of pay-beds. The effect of the cuts was also exacerbated by the freeze on dental charges. Taking into account such additional factors, the total cut envisaged amounted to £100m rather than £62m. Although the proposed reductions related to 1976/77, Treasury officials warned that there would be no return to higher rates of growth in the foreseeable future. Castle pointed out that proposed growth rate was less than the 1.5 per cent dictated by demographic factors. She suggested that the effects of the cuts might be reduced if the NHS was given the benefit of the subsidy to the National Insurance Fund provided by the NHS with respect to patients hospitalised for longer than eight weeks, and if the National Insurance Contribution ceiling were to raised. A small saving was offered through suspension of the mid-term Census.[75]

The Treasury stood by its £62m target for cuts, plus the cost of phasing out pay-beds, bringing the total to £75m. It decided to resist allowing DHSS to have an additional supplementation from the National Insurance Fund, or resources from the contingency fund.[76] On 10 April 1975 the Cabinet agreed to a package of cuts amounting to about £900m, including the £75m assigned to HPSS. The Prime Minster asked for the pay-beds issue to be further discussed by the Social Services Committee. This was an unhappy outcome for Castle, who protested about the arbitrary nature of the economies and their incompatibility with manifesto commitments. She also claimed that for the first time since the inception of the NHS, cuts in services would be unavoidable. She even contested the correctness of the minutes relating to her comments relating to health service charges.[77] In the aftermath of this decision, DHSS proposed, and the Treasury agreed that the major part of the cuts would fall on the capital programme.[78]

Given the new atmosphere of retrenchment, Castle was forced to review her attitude to dental and eye service charges. The progressive fall in the contribution from these charges was creating strains on other parts of the hard-pressed NHS budget. She was also under pressure from the Treasury to increase the yield from these charges. Ministers were unenthusiastic; they first rejected the suggestion for increased charges and instructed the health departments to consider whether the required savings of about £18m a year could be found through economies in NHS administration. When it was clear that this saving was impossible in the short term, Wilson proposed to sanction the dental and eye service charges without further discussion, but at Foot's insistence, this matter was again referred to Ministers. The Cabinet was uneasy, but Ministers reluctantly concluded that higher charges were unavoidable. It was agreed to replace the cost-related system in operation since 1971 with a flat-rate payment of £3.50 for a course of dental treatment, up to a maximum of £12. Charges for spectacle frames and lenses were also converted to an approximation to a flat-rate charge. The aim of these changes was to generate 18 per cent of the cost of the dental service and 54 per cent of the cost of the eye service from direct charges; it was also proposed to maintain these proportions thereafter.[79]

In the course of 1975 the Treasury pursued a course which necessitated further cuts in public expenditure. In the second half of the year, the value of sterling against the dollar steadily declined; foreign currency borrowing increased, and the PSBR continued to increase. The terms for a further IMF loan included a fresh reduction of £3bn in public expenditure, which Healey aimed to reach in 1978/79. A smaller cut of £1.6bn was adopted as the most that was realistic for 1977/78. According the Barnett, Healey intended to resign unless he achieved agreement to public expenditure reductions on this scale.[80] At the Cabinet meeting on 13 November 1975 Healey made the case for cuts amounting to £3.75bn, which was narrowly agreed by his colleagues. Castle accused him of betraying the labour movement by embarking on measures calculated to make the poor poorer.[81]

Castle aligned herself with Benn in preparing to mount an 'attack on the new philosophy which is now spreading...to the effect that cuts in public expenditure are positively socially desirable'.[82] At the bilateral talks on the proposed reductions Castle and her team stuck stubbornly to their line that a minimum growth rate of 1.5 per cent for the health service and 2 per cent for the personal social services was the lowest level of funding they were willing to accept. They also refused to accept an increase in the prescription charge as means of attaining this objective.[83] The Treasury suggested HPSS cuts of £252m in 1977/78 and £462m in 1978/79; Castle initially offered £130m and £166m. After further bilateral talks, which extended into the dates fixed for the relevant Cabinet meetings, they agreed on reductions of £145m and £204m.[84] The total reductions agreed for 1977/78 and 1978/79 were £1.5bn and £3bn respectively, compared with expenditure levels announced in the previous public expenditure White Paper.[85]

Ennals and the Treasury
The Treasury embarked on a third round of major public expenditure economies shortly after the departure of Castle. Sterling continued its decline; a further big standby credit arrangement was reached with the Central Banks. Healey decided that a further round of cuts, amounting to £1bn in public expenditure for 1977/78, was required in order to reduce the public sector's claims on resources, lower the PSBR to £10bn or less, and stimulate the regeneration of industry. These proposals were agreed by the Cabinet on 6 July 1976 in the face of vigorous opposition from some Ministers, but not from Ennals.[86]

The Chief Secretary faced some awkward negotiations in working out the distribution of the cuts with the spending departments. The Treasury proposed that Ennals should absorb £20m cuts in social security, and £100m in HPSS. Ennals complained that the HPSS share was disproportionate. The health Ministers vetoed the Treasury proposal to raise the prescription charge, but they were less averse to increasing dental and eye service charges. A package comprising £20m reductions in capital expenditure, £20m from increased dental and ophthalmic charges, and £10m through economies in prescribing and overheads was agreed. This left a substantial residue, which Ennals offered to raise through recovery from insurance companies of the full cost of treating road accident victims. This required legislation, but was likely to amount to £40m in a full year. The Treasury was suspicious about resurrection of an old idea that had failed on previous occasions. However, Ennals gave assurances that the relevant legislation could be attached to the forthcoming drink and driving Bill.[87] Agreement was therefore reached on a package of £90m in economies for HPSS. After further anguished discussion in the Cabinet, this third round of cuts was announced on 22 July 1976.[88]

The economic situation failed to improve. Sterling continued to depreciate against the dollar. Foreign currency borrowing and the PSBR remained high. In this atmosphere of crisis, Healey approached IMF for a big loan, which necessitated a fourth round of £1bn and £1.5bn cuts in public expenditure for 1977/78 and 1978/79 respectively.

Before the IMF storm finally broke, in discussion of long term expenditure plans, Ennals introduced additional bids with a view to restoring current health expenditure to a 1 per cent growth rate, and personal social services to 3 per cent. These requests were rejected by the Treasury. To the surprise of the Treasury, DHSS officials indicated that Ennals was prepared to drop all of his extra bids if the Treasury would concede increments relating to demography and changing demand within the Family Practitioner Services from 1980/81 onwards. This unexpected pliability on the part of Ennals was well-received within the Treasury. Having succeeded better than expected, Barnett was inclined to concede much less than DHSS wanted for the demographic factor.[89]

Having offered these sacrifices in response to the grave economic situation, Ennals warned Barnett that anything less would 'shatter morale in the NHS' and be 'indefensible politically'.[90] Notwithstanding this plea, on Barnett's advice, the Cabinet reduced the allowance for demographic change to the entered in the Public Expenditure White Paper.[91] Ennals complained to the Prime Minister about the severe treatment of HPSS spending plans.[92] Given

598

the harsh handling of Ennals in the public expenditure round, he was let off lightly in the fourth round of cuts. The HPSS share was £15m in 1977/78, and £25m in 1978/79.[93] On 15 December 1976, Healey announced the economy measures imposed as a condition for the IMF loan.

Relations between Ennals and the Treasury were not improved by the failure of DHSS to implement its agreed economies. With respect to social security, substantial losses were incurred by defeats of the Government on the Social Security (Miscellaneous Provisions) Bill. As Treasury sceptics anticipated, Ennals decided to abandon the road traffic casualties legislation and he offered virtually no offsetting savings. Desultory discussion were held about increasing the prescription charge or the NHS Contribution, but these were not pursued.[94]

During 1977 Ennals began his campaign to restore NHS spending to a growth rate of 3 per cent, which he urged should be attainable from 1979 onwards. The Treasury regarded 2 per cent as the most that should be conceded when the economy returned to a more stable condition, which was ratified by the Cabinet on 7 July 1977.[95] In the face of an unyielding response from the Treasury, Ennals stepped up the pressure for additional resources for 1978/79. He was spurred on by mounting adverse publicity concerning closure of NHS facilities, and the likely need to mothball new hospitals. This had made him the victim of a great 'volume of bitterness and adverse comment'.[96] Ennals made similar representations to the Prime Minister, appealing for an immediate injection of £30m to compensate for the squeeze on current spending. He urged that small gestures of this kind, or parallel concessions in the field of social security such as an increase in the mobility allowance, would be politically advantageous to the Government.[97] The Treasury was alarmed when Callaghan expressed sympathy for Ennals' propositions. It seemed as if Ennals was attempting to circumvent the PESC system by reaching ad hoc agreements on additional expenditure through direct negotiations with senior Ministers.[98]

The first relaxation from the regime of cuts in public expenditure occurred in October 1977, with the announcement of a package of measures to stimulate output and employment, involving a total cost of £1bn in 1977/78, and £2bn in 1978/79. Few of the proposed changes brought relief to the health and personal social services. A £1bn increase in public expenditure was introduced for 1978/79, but this included virtually no compensation for the previous cuts relating to health and social services, with the exception of the £500m allocated to stimulate central and local government spending on construction. The HPSS sector in England received £37m for 1978/79 and £18m for the following year.[99] Since capital programmes had borne the brunt of previous rounds of cuts, this small contribution was a step towards preventing a continuing downwards slide.

Ennals opted to pursue his case for additional resources through the Home and Social Affairs Committee. He argued the case for a £50m increment in 1978/79, £112m in 1979/80, and a growth rate of 3 per cent thereafter. Once again the Treasury believed that Ennals was selecting the Home and Social Affairs Committee as an avenue for pressing his claims because this was likely to yield more positive results than the PESC negotiations. Treasury officials concentrated on detecting potential sources of economies, which would enable Ennals to achieve his objectives without further increase in resources made available to the NHS. Their first target was administration, where a one-third increase in administrative and clerical staff had occurred over the last five years. Other possibilities for economies were the drug bill and reductions in the cost of hospital services consequent on the growth of community care.[100] The Treasury case was strengthened by evidence from experts in the field suggesting practical means to economise on the drug bill, and from sources such as the Salmon Report on supplies, which reached damning conclusions about the inefficiency of the fragmented supplies organisation within the NHS.[101]

Ennals took his case to the Home and Social Affairs Committee on 22 February 1978. He drew attention to the detrimental effects of the lower rate of growth of expenditure on the NHS under Labour compared with levels planned by the Conservative administration, and argued that it was essential for Labour to offer some token of its commitment to higher expenditure to coincide with the thirtieth anniversary of the health service. Barnett retorted that in the context of a stagnant economy, the NHS had been treated favourably. He drew attention to the scope for efficiency savings. Ministers were satisfied that Ennals had produced some alarming evidence concerning the fragility of the NHS; they were satisfied that something was needed to restore public confidence in Labour's stewardship, but it was agreed that release of additional resources for the NHS would depend on further Ministerial discussions on public expenditure.[102]

At this stage Ennals appealed to the Prime Minister for support. He expressed disquiet about Labour's continuing reassurances about the adequacy of funding of the health and social services, when in reality the health service was 'near crisis situation', as proven by such widely-publicised problems as ward and hospital closures, unemployed nurses, record waiting lists, patients dying through lack of renal dialysis machines, and new hospitals standing idle for want of resources to support their facilities. Ennals concluded that 'unless more money is found, services to patients will suffer and we will be increasingly vulnerable to political attack'.[103] On behalf of the Health Services Advisory Committee of the TUC, Albert Spanswick made similar representations to the Prime Minister, and he expressed disappointment that the Government's revised expenditure plans were bringing little benefit to the health service.[104] Callaghan was more impressed by the case made by Spanswick than by the arguments of Ennals. As already noted Callaghan had already formed the view that some gesture was required to bring relief to the health service. However, before aligning himself with Ennals and the unions, he took further advice from the Treasury and from Bernard Donoughue, the Head of the Prime Minister's Policy Unit and Sir Kenneth Berrill, the Head of CPRS. The Treasury was predictably negative, but the two economists concluded that 'on an impressionistic basis there seems to be a good case for allocating an extra £50m for the health service this year in view of public discontent with the service and the level of morale in the NHS. But the Secretary of State's paper does not provide all the information on which a judgement of that kind can be made. Nor does it describe the methods by which the £50m would be directed to the priority areas'.[105]

Callaghan was therefore subjected to discordant advice. According to the Treasury, the Prime Minister was dissatisfied with Ennals' presentation, 'which merely catalogued a series of problems and did not begin to analyse the underlying causes seriously'.[106] Accordingly, the health Ministers were asked to specify more exactly how they would utilise £50m of additional funds. Their main suggestions related to acceleration of the opening dates of new hospitals, provision of hospital facilities such as operating-theatres and four-hundred new renal dialysis machines, improvement of staffing levels in long-stay hospitals, and projects connected with inner cities.[107] This information confirmed the suspicions of sceptics within the Treasury that the £50m was being swallowed up by the acute hospital services, rather being directed to proposed priority fields. While it was appreciated that political factors argued for some concession, £25m was regarded as sufficient for the purpose. In the light of additional assurances extracted from Ennals about attention to the priorities policy, and the increasing level of public agitation on this issue, the Cabinet agreed that it was not realistic to allocate less than the extra £50m for 1978/79 requested by Ennals.[108]

This concession by the Cabinet left open the question of the continuation of the £50m increment in future years, and the much bigger issue of Ennals' claim for an overall growth rate of 3 per cent. The Prime Minister was reminded of the futility of token concessions when he met a delegation of from the TUC on 5 April 1978. The delegation argued that £150m represented the least acceptable increase for 1978/79, and it pressed for considerably greater sums for following years.[109] Following his small, but encouraging success at the Cabinet, Ennals tried to drive home his advantage by seeking support of the Home and Social Affairs Committee for his broader expenditure objectives. The approach of the thirtieth anniversary of the NHS suggested that it was the ideal moment for this initiative. In view of the positive response from the Home and Social Affairs Committee at the previous discussion in February 1978, Ennals was encouraged to make a second bolder application.

Ennals' hopeful mission was dogged by misfortune. DHSS hoped to add to the authority of the health departments' case by drawing CPRS into the preparation of the memorandum for Ministers. The Treasury was able to block this attempt to co-opt CPRS as a collaborative partner, thereby throwing the health departments back on their own resources.[110] The Treasury was quietly satisfied that DHSS followed its habit of listing 'alleged ailments', with 'no serious analysis of the causes or of relative priorities', 'nor did they tackle the question of waste and better use of existing resources'.[111]

The Treasury case was strengthened by fresh evidence from Ennals' own department concerning the prevalence of waste, particularly with respect to the drug bill, supplies procurement, and hospital building. On 19 April 1978 Ennals initiated a campaign to save £30m a year on the pharmaceutical service by encouraging economies in prescribing and greater responsibility among the public about the consumption of medicines. Ennals himself suggested that savings of 10 per cent, or £75m a year were feasible.[112] Even more embarrassing to Ennals was the draft report of the Supply Working Group, which called for 'urgent action' to correct a 'most unsatisfactory situation'. The chairman, Brian Salmon, judged the NHS to be ten years behind other departments or private industry in the use of its resources to the best advantage.[113] The Treasury also co-opted the former Chief Architect of DHSS, who provided evidence concerning extravagance and lack of cost-effectiveness in hospital building, a problem highlighted in a recent investigation into the excessive costs incurred in the rebuilding of St Thomas's Hospital.[114]

Suitably primed with evidence concerning the scope for economies in the health service, the Prime Minister asked the Home and Social Affairs Committee to avoid conclusions about the level of spending on the NHS, instead directing Ministers to 'sorting out the priorities' and the scope for better use of resources. By this stage, the ground was taken from under Ennals, whose circulated paper was primarily an argument a growth rate of 3 per cent. At the meeting of the Home and Social Affairs Committee Ennals' pleas for a higher growth rate were cancelled out by the Chief Secretary's telling arguments concerning the scope for economies. Ministers representing Scotland

and Wales were more faithful to the Prime Minister's instruction by concentrating on the question of priorities. Ministers drifted into unfocussed exchanges concerning the crisis in the health service. The Home Secretary concluded that further progress would not be made without more detailed guidance on priorities and improvements possible under growth rates lower than 3 per cent.[115] Ennals responded with a further short paper for the Home and Social Affairs Committee, which went some way towards representing his priorities, but it still assumed a 3 per cent growth rate, and ignored the problem of economies. At this stage Ennals' leg thrombosis intervened and he was prevented from participating in the ministerial discussion. Moyle attended, but left early for another engagement. Other Ministers decided that the difficult issues raised by Ennals were best further considered in full Cabinet in the context of PESC deliberations.[116]

With respect to its main purpose of establishing a case for a 3 per cent rate of growth in the HPSS sector, Ennals' campaign had if anything been counterproductive. It had stiffened Treasury resolve concerning the existence of extensive opportunities for efficiency savings. Accordingly, in preparing his expenditure plans for the period 1979-1983, the Chief Secretary was discouraged from directing special concessions towards the health departments. Pessimistic forecasts about prospects for economic growth reinforced the inclination to maintain tight controls on public expenditure. The Chief Secretary proposed spending limits for the HPSS sector assuming discontinuation of the recent £50m increase, and elimination of estimating changes usually allowed for the family practitioner services. Not only was there no allowance for return to a 3 per cent growth rate, but the maximum level of 2 per cent was not envisaged before 1981/82. The planned growth levels for 1979/80 and 1980/81 were 0.8 per cent and 1.6 per cent respectively.[117]

Given the likelihood of a September 1978 General Election, it was not envisaged that the current administration would be responsible for completing work on the Public Expenditure White Paper. This inclined Ministers from main spending departments to advocate less stringent limits. Ennals was naturally among the main petitioners for higher expenditure. Writing from his bed in Westminster Hospital, Ennals expressed alarm about restrictions proposed by the Chief Secretary.[118] Ennals not only made the obvious demand for retention of his recent £50m increase, but also reiterated his plea for immediate reinstatement of a 3 per cent rate of growth. Political factors were cited as crucial support for his argument.

We must also have regard to the confidence of our supporters and the approaching election: we will need to put before the electorate

603

some socially desirable and attractive developments; and we ought to plan now to make at least some progress towards fulfilling our likely manifesto commitments in the first two years of the next Parliament. Some selected additions to programmes for 1979/80 and 1980/81 are therefore politically essential if we are to carry conviction as a reforming and socially committed - as well a responsible - Government. They might include items in the fields of education and help for the inner cities as well as meeting pressing needs in my own programmes.

This supplication by Ennals was reinforced by a brief but forceful letter to the Prime Minister signed by five trade union leaders, and the Presidents of the RCN and RCM. On the occasion of the thirtieth anniversary of the health service, they urged that dedicated staff were prevented from achieving the objectives of the NHS for want of resources.[119] The effect of this submission was reduced by evidence that it was produced in collusion with DHSS.[120] Barnett warned the Prime Minister that 'we stand to lose much more from any appearance of slackening control of expenditure, and disturbing the still fragile balance of the gilt-edged and foreign exchange markets, than we could stand to gain from promising more spending on individual programmes'. He hoped that Labour would not launch into another cycle of over-commitments followed by subsequent cuts. The Chief Secretary insisted that the NHS was being treated as generously as possible in the circumstances. Barnett insisted that efficiency savings should be required to fund any expansion beyond the 2 per cent level projected by the Treasury.[121] At the Cabinet discussion on public expenditure, Orme argued his own and Ennals' case for higher spending. Although this expansionist view was widely supported, the Prime Minister summed up in favour of the Treasury proposals.[122]

The Cabinet set HPSS spending at a level that precluded continuation of the £50m for 1978/79 into 1979/80. DHSS argued that the £50m had been awarded on the understanding that it was a continuing commitment, and this impression had been conveyed to NHS authorities. The health departments now faced the embarrassment of imposing a further 'cut' in NHS expenditure if the decision was not reversed. The Treasury was disinclined to compromise on this front, but offered instead to reinstate the small allowance usually given for estimating changes in the family practitioner services.[123] Uncertainty about the date of the General Election delayed further Ministerial discussion on these issues until the autumn. Ennals demanded his £50m, and also warned the Treasury that he was not abandoning 3 per cent as his target for growth in the longer term. At first Barnett rejected this request, suggesting that since HPSS spending was running about £50m below its limit, absence of a further £50m supplementation need not cause embarrassment.[124] The Treasury then softened its line, conceding £45m for 1979/80, providing that Ennals was willing to accept a 2 per cent growth rate after that date. Ennals insisted that 2.5 per cent was his minimum.[125] In the absence of agreement, the fate of Ennals' £50m rested on a verdict by the Cabinet. Ministers decided that of the £100m left over for distribution between departments, £57m should be divided between education and health.[126] A meeting between relevant Ministers failed to reach agreement, with the result that the matter was once again referred to the Cabinet, where a slight increase in this sum was conceded in order to allow Ennals to secure continuation of his £50m increase into 1979/80.[127]

During the final months of the Labour administration controversy over HPSS expenditure subsided, but it was by no means at an end. Arguments immediately broke out about the continuation of the £50m increment beyond 1979/80. Recent increases collectively had the effect of raising the growth rate of HPSS expenditure for 1979/80 to 2 per cent. This assisted with the positive presentation of Labour's expenditure plans for the HPSS sector, especially in that 2 per cent had already been adopted for the final years of the planning period.[128] However, 1980/81 fell between the stools, and remained at 1.4 per cent. Ennals appealed for totals to be raised to produce a consistent 2 per cent growth picture, a suggestion that was resolutely rejected by Barnett.[129] As the Labour administration faded into the background, officials busied themselves with their contingency planning, taking stock of their extensive behind-the-scenes discussions about the scope for 'economies' in health service expenditure, which were expected to assume greater relevance with a change of Government. Following a well-worn path, they reviewed the prospects for increases in health service charges. With respect to actual economies, the Treasury was frustrated by its continuing failures in two major areas, the Family Practitioner Services and the health capital programme, both of which were subjected to investigation by joint working parties during the last months of the Labour administration.[130]

Throughout the long phase of active hospital rebuilding, the Treasury remained sceptical about the value for money given by these developments, and it believed that decisions involving commitment to huge capital schemes were made without scientific examination of the balance of costs and benefits. After a long period of exchanges between DHSS and the Treasury concerning the revenue consequences of capital schemes, in 1978 a working group with representatives of DHSS, the Treasury, and CPRS conducted a review of NHS capital spending. The report was not completed by the date of the General Election, but the working group had provisionally concluded that there was considerable opportunity to improve performance in this field. It believed that future schemes should be justified on the basis of investment appraisal and monitoring techniques. It was expected that the application of these analytical methods would produce a big change in the capital programme, and generate far more economical, but productive developments at the expensive of grandiose but wasteful schemes.

Cash limits had produced a satisfactory degree of control over much current expenditure, and this method offered the prospects of allowing allocations to be directed according to stated priorities. However, the effectiveness of this system was undermined by exemption of the Family Practitioner Services, which automatically exercised the first call on extra resources. In practice this mechanism operated to deflect resources into what the Treasury regarded as an already inflated bill for pharmaceutical products, which accounted for approximately half of FPS spending. A joint working party between the Treasury and DHSS examined the feasibility of adopting a cash limit embracing hospital and family practitioner services. Opinion within DHSS was divided on the merits of this scheme, especially on account of the predictably hostile reception it was likely to meet from the BMA. In view of the explosive nature of this issue, DHSS was not sorry for the completion of the working party report to be deferred until after the General Election.

(iv) PLANNING, PRIORITIES AND INEQUALITIES

The first concerted attempts at long term planning in the NHS related to capital development, where the reconstruction of the hospital system obviously required attention to planning conducted over a considerable period. The concept of comprehensive planning of services only came to fruition in the context of the 1974 reorganisation and through the work of the Devolution Working Party.

In the context of planning for the reorganised health service, the health departments became committed to adoption of a broad national strategy for the entire range of services relating to all client groups. This strategy aimed to take account of human and physical resource availability, as well as the constraints imposed by levels of funding. This framework would enable the health departments to make annual strategic assessment of their health and personal social service policies, ensure that the pursuance of these policies would be consistent with the levels of spending permitted under the PESC mechanism, and enable informed, rational decisions to be made about the relative priority to be assigned to particular policies. At the level of the field authorities, the central planning mechanism was to be matched by strategic and annual plans produced according to a predetermined cycle.

The first pilot run with a departmental planning submission was made in 1974. A more detailed document entitled 'Departmental Planning system: 1974/75 cycle: planning submission' was completed in February 1975. DHSS aimed to issue this guidance on strategy and priorities in a consultative form in the spring of 1975, and revise this in time to provide definitive guidance enabling the new NHS planning system to become operative in 1976/77. The Labour Government added a further important reinforcement to this system, when in 1976, as part of its efforts to control public expenditure, it extended the application of cash limits to the greater part of NHS expenditure.

The adoption of an integrated planning system brought DHSS into line with other departments, and it satisfied the long-standing complaints directed from the Treasury about absence of attention to planning and priorities within DHSS. However, the Treasury was not entirely satisfied. Before reorganisation, the Treasury had attempted to draw DHSS into a PAR investigation into health service priorities. This had been side-tracked, with the result that the planning system had taken precedence. Despite continuing attempts by the Treasury to press the advantages of a separate PAR study, this proposal was not welcomed by DHSS.

With support of Ministers, DHSS aimed to publish its strategy consultative document in April 1975, with a view to completing the consultation exercise by the end of the year and the issue of definitive instructions for 1976/77. Given the instability of public expenditure plans, the Treasury refused to sanction this timetable. DHSS continued to exert pressure. Unless the department produced its planning document, a senior official warned that the 'credibility of the department's planning work will be destroyed'.[131] In an attempt to purchase compliance from the Treasury, DHSS recast its planning totals to allow for either nil or 2 per cent growth. However, when DHSS Ministers refused to contemplate nil growth, DHSS indicated that the minimum acceptable growth level was 1.5 per cent, and they also produced projections for a 3 per cent maximum growth rate. Debate over these norms caused further delay in the timetable for publication of the consultative document, until in late February 1976 the two sides settled on 1 per cent and 3 per cent as alternative norms.[132] This cleared the way for publication of the *Priorities* consultative document, which appeared on 24 March 1976.[133]

Priorities for Health and Personal Social Services experienced a difficult gestation, but despite indifferent prospects for growth in services, the document was recognised as an important milestone in planning

607

within the NHS. For the first time since the beginning of the health service, the health department set out a comprehensive statement of the objectives for the health service, costed according to realistic expenditure forecasts. This exercise gave an opportunity for the department to draw together data from disparate planning documents relating to particular client groups or services, and assess how these various commitments could be accommodated within more stringent expenditure limits than had been anticipated in the past. These expenditure projections for the period to 1979/80 were consistent with the Public Expenditure White Paper (Cmnd.6393), published in February 1976, which allowed for an overall growth rate of about 2 per cent. Since family practitioner services were demand led, and were expected to increase at a rate of 3.7 per cent, it was inevitable that other services would be restricted to growth rates below 2 per cent. The *Priorities* document advocated holding down spending on acute, general and maternity hospital services to allow a growth rate of about 3 per cent for such groups as the elderly and the mentally handicapped. Although adopting modest targets for growth, *Priorities for Health and Personal Social Services* also contained much detail about more distant targets, and it included a comprehensive set of norms and guide-lines from which it would be evident that much greater increase in expenditure would be required in order to meet expectations within a reasonable length of time.

The *Priorities* document appeared at a particularly inopportune time. As noted above, the national economic emergency suspended opportunities for expansion in public expenditure. The health services, although not as badly squeezed as some public services, were deprived of any certainty about future prospects for expansion. Even if financial constraints and the disciplines imposed by cash limits had been less severe, experience had demonstrated that changes of the kind envisaged in the *Priorities* document - a shift towards community care, assumption of new responsibilities within general practice, the run-down of long-stay hospitals, or slow-down in the rate of the incremental advance in cost of acute hospital services - were likely to be implemented only slowly, even if their realisation was not completely undermined by unsympathetic vested interests. Also, the recently-introduced NHS management structures were not designed to speed up decision-making, while the new, untried arrangements for joint planning and funding were unlikely to bear the weight anticipated in the *Priorities* document. In the face of such hazards, the sequel to the *Priorities* document, published in September 1977, was much more circumspect in its expectations.[134] *The Way Forward* was much shorter than its predecessor; perhaps best described as a set of amplified notes or short commentary, subtitled a 'further discussion of the Government's national strategy'.

The priorities exercise threw into relief the problem of disparities in health provision in different parts of the country. The arrangements for rational distribution of resources between programmes outlined in the *Priorities* document necessitated closer attention to the equitable geographical distribution of resources determined by reference to objective demographic and epidemiological factors. Without this basic condition being fulfilled, the effectiveness of the priorities exercise would be largely undermined. As noted in chapter I, only moderate success was achieved during the first decade of the NHS in equalising the distribution of resources and services, with the result that big geographical disparities persisted. The continuing allocation of funds on the basis of the cost of maintaining existing service plus an addition to compensate for inflation caused ossification of the existing pattern of expenditure. Continuing attempts at greater equalisation occurred with respect to planning of the growth of consultant establishments, or in the distribution of hospital capital expenditure. The hospital plan also improved the situation on account of relating new hospital provision to population and including an amount in the annual allocation for the revenue consequences of capital schemes. In order to speed up redistribution, beginning in the year 1971/72, a plan originating during Crossman's time was adopted for equalising revenue spending in the English regions over a period of ten years. Under this formula, half of the allocation was based on population served, one-quarter on the number of beds provided, and one-quarter with respect to the number of cases treated. This method was extended to community services after the 1974 reorganisation, but it had the disadvantage of not taking account of teaching hospitals, and its effect was also reduced by the phasing out of the funds available for the revenue consequences of capital schemes.

By the date of reorganisation it was evident that the methods adopted for resource redistribution were too limited in their effect, and insufficiently comprehensive in their framework. It was necessary to evolve a more scientific basis for redistribution, preferably not excluding any branch of the health service, and taking account of both revenue and capital expenditure. Also, in the light of the new situation created by planning for devolution and NHS reorganisation, it was unavoidable to consider more scientifically the problem of distribution of resources between the parts of the United Kingdom and between the regions. In May 1975 Barbara Castle set up the Resource Allocation Working Party, which produced an interim report in November 1975 and its final report in September 1976.[135]

Priorities for Health and Social Services alluded only briefly to inequalities in resource distribution, but it acknowledged big differences between the highest and lowest spending regions with respect to per capita expenditure on hospital services, family practitioner services, and personal social services. These divergences were taken as a sign a problem of 'major inequities in the distribution of services which must be corrected'.[136] *The Way Forward* embraced the findings of the RAWP report to adopt the geographical redistribution of resources as one of its major objectives.[137] Furthermore it included a tabulation which demonstrated the disparity of regional distribution of resources for the main health service programmes. The ranking order of regions had changed little since 1958, and the least-favoured regions tended to be at a disadvantage for primary care, as well as most of their hospital services.[138]

RAWP was primarily concerned to arrive at a method for distribution of the capital and revenue allocation with respect to the objective needs of the population. The size of the population, its age and sex composition provided the basic data. It was then necessary to introduce a weighting reflecting the pattern of morbidity within the population, for which purpose standard mortality ratios were used as a proxy.[139] Revenue targets determined by the RAWP formula were therefore at best an approximation. Although the authors of the RAWP appreciated the limitations of their methodology, once established, there was every likelihood that more burden would be placed on the RAWP formula than it was capable of bearing. At the worst, the RAWP formula was capable of directing resources away from deprived areas, such as the inner cities, where the objective need for services was greatest, and where services were likely to be expensive to provide. Moreover, the RAWP formula ignored expenditure on the family practitioner services, which were also likely to be less-well developed in inner-city areas than elsewhere. The RAWP formula for capital distribution was similarly capable of yielding some perverse results. Even if the RAWP formula was not vulnerable to criticism, the Government was presented with considerable difficulties in evolving a method for redistribution, since at a time of financial constraint, the better-off regions were likely to suffer a net loss in resources, which might then be deflected to regions that were incapable of using their new funds efficiency owing to such factors as cuts in capital investment.

Despite the problems raised by the RAWP approach, on 21 December 1976 Ennals signified his intention of adopting its principles for the revenue allocation from 1977/78 onwards. After taking account of experience in the first year, it was proposed to apply the method to both revenue and capital allocations in subsequent years.[140]

The limitations of the RAWP formula were discussed by the Ministerial Group on Urban Priorities, which was given assurances that DHSS was aware of the disadvantages and would not regard the formula as the sole factor for determining resource distribution at the district level. Moyle admitted that in some cases such as Hackney, there was an overprovision of hospital facilities, but this reflected the poor quality of family practitioner services. He conceded that the department possessed no method for measuring the need for family practitioner services, and if measured, there was no clear way of bringing about improvement in these services.[141]

The Treasury was naturally suspicious that the RAWP exercise would be used as a vehicle for demanding additional resources, to enable distribution to take place without causing hardship among the 'loser' authorities. In view of this risk, it was beneficial from the Treasury perspective to slow down the application of RAWP. It therefore applied much effort into destructive criticism of the RAWP approach, the first results of which were communicated to DHSS in December 1976. A reply was not forthcoming until April 1977, when DHSS indicated that it was fully aware of the pitfalls inherent in RAWP and that it was never envisaged that allocations 'should be determined mechanically by arithmetical calculation without the interposition of informed judgement'.[142]

In order to soften the effect of RAWP, it was agreed that no region would be expected to tolerate a growth rate of less than 1 per cent in its revenue allocation, and none would be granted an increase above 5 per cent. This considerably slowed down the convergence between the better-off and less well-favoured regions. Consequently, in 1979, the worst-off region was about 9 per cent below its target allocation, while the best-off was 13 per cent above.

RAWP created the paradox that the attempt to redistribute resources to the advantage of the least-favoured regions risked disfavouring some of the most disadvantaged communities. This danger was emphasised in the comments made by the TUC in its response to the *Priorities* document. The TUC drew attention to data suggesting that, according to a variety of health indicators, there remained substantial and persistent differences in health standards between the social classes. The TUC called for more attention to correcting such inequalities.

Especially since the 1967 devaluation crisis, and consequent cuts in social support, the problem of persisting inequality in the welfare state became an increasing object of disquiet. Richard Titmuss, whose *Poverty and Population: A Factual Study of Contemporary Social Waste* (1937), was a classic study of class and regional distribution of health inequalities, expressed concern that the resources of the health service were being distributed unequally between the social classes, with the result that the more affluent social classes were gaining disproportionate advantages.[143] The conclusion reached by Titmuss were not universally shared, but the majority of the evidence was supportive.[144]

Enhanced attention was attracted to the problem of maldistribution of resources by Julian Tudor Hart, a general practitioner from the Glyncorrwg Health Centre, Port Talbot, South Wales, who postulated his 'inverse care law' which stated that the 'availability of good medical care tends to vary inversely with the need of the population served'.[145] There was ample support for conclusions regarding occupational, class, and income differentials in health, from OPCS data. Increasingly, experts linked these health inequalities with defects in the system of resource distribution.[146]

RAWP confirmed that deprived regions were indeed receiving less than their fair share of resources. Concern over this problem was expressed by Sir John Brotherston, the Scottish CMO in his Galton Lecture, also in a speech to the Socialist Medical Association by Ennals on 27 March 1977, where it was announced that he had invited the Chief Scientist, Sir Douglas Black, to head an investigation into this problem.[147] The objectives of the Working Group on Inequalities in Health were: '(i) to assemble available information about the differences in health status among the social classes and about factors which might contribute to these, including relevant data from other industrial countries; (ii) to analyse this material in order to identify possible causal relationships, to examine the hypotheses that have been formulated and the testing of them, and to assess the implications for policy; and (iii) to suggest what further research should be initiated'.

This small Working Group was chaired by the Chief Scientist, and it also contained Professor J N Morris, Professor of Community Health at the London School of Hygiene and Tropical Medicine, Dr Cyril Smith, Secretary of SSRC, and Professor Peter Townsend, Professor of Sociology at Essex University. Both Morris and Townsend had been associates of Titmuss, and their investigation was to a large extent an application of the methods applied in *Poverty and Population*. Papers published by Morris and Townsend before the establishment of the Black Committee contained much that reappeared in the recommendations of the Black Report.

Establishment of the Black Committee was briefly mentioned in *The Way Forward*, but its activities were not much noted during the rest of the term of the Callaghan administration.[148] As suggested by its remit, the Black enquiry was regarded essentially as a research exercise, which many within the health department regarded as primarily for the purpose of departmental guidance. However, the scope of this review was more ambitious than originally envisaged.

The opportunities for the group to engage in independent initiative was increased when Sir Douglas Black retired as Chief Scientist at the end of 1977, to become President of the Royal College of Physicians. Given their freedom, Black's highly-motivated team took an expansive view of their remit. Their report, the product of much debate and redrafting, was not submitted to Ministers until April 1980. The Black Report was issued without ceremony on 29 August 1980, but in view of its energetic exposition of the problem of inequality and its wide-ranging and controversial recommendations, it became installed along side *Poverty and Population* as one of the social science classics of the century.[149] In its original form, the Black Report was almost twice the weight of the Report of the Royal Commission on the NHS. In some respects it was an alternative to the Royal Commission Report, composed from a more radical perspective. Although the Royal Commission expressed its commitment to 'equality' within the NHS, on this issue its report contained little analysis of the kind found in the Black Report.

(v) STATE OF THE HEALTH SERVICE
Immediately after the February 1974 General Election, leading medical organisations embarked on a campaign to reverse the recently-imposed reductions in resources. As during previous times of crisis, they also demanded an independent enquiry into the health service. The adverse circumstances facing the Labour administration precluded immediate resolution of the problems agitating the medical profession. The call for an injection of additional resources, and for an independent investigation rapidly gained in momentum. The credibility of this demand was increased by support from nursing associations. Soon after the February 1974 General Election, the RCN demanded to discuss their grievances with the Secretary of State, declaring that 'radical action is required on fundamental issues; palliatives are now both totally inadequate to deal with the situation and totally unacceptable to the Profession'.[150]

As already noted, on 8 July 1974, the Secretary of the BMA, on behalf of the BMA, BDA, RCN and RCM, requested an urgent meeting with the Prime Minister to consider the state of the National Health Service. Stevenson pronounced ominously that he was writing out of 'obligation to the nation'. He claimed that the recently imposed cuts had reduced an already under-funded service to a state of imminent collapse.[151] It was clear that anxieties expressed by the professions originated from a range of factors, some common to the entire national workforce, others unique to the NHS. Health groups were understandably anxious about their economic position at a time of spiralling wage demands. For reasons already given, they were disaffected about NHS reorganisation, while the Government's democracy in the NHS initiative offered no particular relief to these groups. Indeed, the Government was suspected of favouring unionised workers in the NHS at the expense of the professions. This clash of class interests was also fuelled the hostility of doctors to the Government's plan to phase out pay-beds from the NHS. All of these factors generated fear among the professions that under Labour the NHS would spiral into an uncontrollable decline. These fears were echoed and cultivated by the Tory press.

At first the Prime Minister was advised by his own officials and by the Treasury to reject the request for a meeting, on the grounds that the professional groups were merely one of the client groups pleading their case for special treatment in the competition over public expenditure.[152] Press speculation that Wilson would 'cold shoulder' the caring professions, as well as evidence of sympathy among MPs, caused a change of heart. It was agreed that no useful purpose would be served by rejecting a meeting with a delegation. This was seen as a useful opportunity to communicate the Government's case and clarify any misunderstandings.[153]

In preparation, the Treasury and DHSS concentrated on defensive briefings, pointing out that the professions' demand for £500m a year in additional resources was completely impracticable in current economic conditions. The Treasury's primary objective was to prevent an enquiry into the NHS. A whole string of instances from the past, ranging from Guillebaud to Halsbury, were invoked to demonstrate that independent enquiries resulted in inescapable demands for additional resources. It was contested that 'any plea for a special inquiry therefore strikes at the heart of the Government's machinery for taking resource decisions, and would be intended to take the third biggest spending programme (after social security and education) outside the system'.[154]

The Treasury was confident that the impressive evidence assembled by the Prime Minister's advisers would overawe the delegation. Unwelcome repercussions were therefore not anticipated from this meeting with the caring professions. In view of this optimism, it was decided that the Chief Secretary would attend in place of the Chancellor of the Exchequer. The Chief Medical Officer warned against this complacency. He pointed out that the arguments presented by the officials would 'not wash with the people who have to operate the service'. The CMO was not satisfied that the Government side had disposed of the main contention of the delegation that since the Government was unable to provide a comprehensive health service, or suggest alternative methods of financing, only a public enquiry could make further progress over the financing of health care, or the identification of services that might be abandoned.[155] Barbara Castle was responsive to this argument. She warned the Prime Minister that 'I, my CMO, and my other officials are convinced that the Service is presently seriously under-funded, and that this is a major cause of the present industrial unrest in the Service'. She therefore advocated a constructive approach to the representations of the delegation.[156]

On 31 July 1974, the Prime Minister and other Ministers received the delegation.[157] The professions argued their case for additional resources. The Prime Minister expressed sympathy with the 'sombre picture' presented by the delegation, and agreed that the 'under-financing of the Health Service was well understood'. He assured the professions that within the limitations of economic constraints, the Government was committed to according high priority to the health service. He outlined the steps already being taken, which he contended constituted a substantial step towards meeting their demands. On Treasury advice, Wilson firmly resisted the professions' demands for an independent enquiry into the health service on the grounds that it was unlikely to reveal new information, or influence the course of policy. Wilson also rejected the suggestion that higher direct charges should contribute to increasing resources for the health service. He further insisted that there was little opportunity for departing from the current system of financing the health services. The Prime Minister agreed to remain in contact with the professions over detailed aspects of their demands.[158]

Anxieties within the professions were not satisfied by their meeting with Ministers. In October 1974 they returned with a call for even more substantial additional resources rising to £900m at 1974/75 prices over a four-year period. They also reiterated their demand for an independent enquiry to investigate the future financing of the health service.[159]

Evasion on the part of the Government failed to quell the agitation of the professions. On 2 July 1975 Castle once again met a delegation, on this occasion strengthened by attendance of representatives from the Joint Consultants Committee. The likelihood that an enquiry would be used by the BMA to push for alternative ways of financing the NHS, including much higher direct charges, exacerbated the negative feelings of Castle and Owen about this course of action.[160] Once again Castle assured the professions about the Government's high priority for spending on the NHS. With respect to the renewed demand for an enquiry, she concluded that it would be 'irresponsible at this present moment of great national economic difficulty to believe that we can escape our financial difficulties in the NHS by establishing an inquiry with the implicit belief that there are extra financial resources waiting to be tapped if only we knew how to do it'.[161]

Such negative responses were no deterrent to the BMA, which mobilised any available platform to remind the Government of this issue. The dispute over junior doctors' pay and conditions proved to be an ideal vehicle for pressing the case for an enquiry and this demand was duly added to their list of grievances. The intractable nature of this dispute meant that the call for an enquiry was constantly brought to the administration's attention; indeed it became the object of almost hysterical attachment within the BMA leadership. This may seem somewhat perverse, since the enquiry was adventitious to the junior doctors' problems, but it was fundamental to the BMA's wider aim of preventing erosion of the system of private practice operating within the NHS.

In October 1975 Ministers finally capitulated. The lead seems to have been taken by the Prime Minister who, on the advice of his officials, concluded that the offer of an enquiry might improve relations with the medical profession and take the NHS out of the headlines.[162] Castle was less decided. Having been unsympathetic to an enquiry, reversal of attitude would seem like a 'snub to me' and she feared that it might be used to frustrate her efforts to eliminate pay-beds.[163] However, the Secretary of State also recognised that an enquiry might offer a means to unlock greater resources for the NHS. She therefore accepted the advice of her officials that the balance of advantage lay in acceptance of the enquiry, and it was anticipated that this would ease relations with junior hospital doctors. At this stage Owen also was convinced that an enquiry was desirable. On the other hand the Treasury remained unconvinced and its Ministers were advised to oppose this proposal as forcefully as possible. The enquiry was 'at best useless, and at worst a major nuisance'.[164]

In response to a request from Wilson for a neutral paper on the question of an enquiry, Castle informally circulated to the Cabinet her memorandum on 'The State of the NHS'. This expressed alarm that in recent weeks the demand for an enquiry had reached a crescendo:

it is now clear that the profession are attaching enormous symbolic importance to such an enquiry, despite the fact that it is no solution to our immediate problems, and in any event I cannot believe it is likely to tell us anything new about the way the service should be run or financed. The case for acceding to the call for an enquiry is therefore a political one, as to whether it will help resolve the present impasse between the Government and the doctors. Part of the profession's interest in an enquiry lies in their hope that this might recommend greater reliance on private insurance schemes and increased patient charges; partly it lies in their concern about future demands on the service, and as to how these demands may be met. I told the profession that I have not closed my mind to an enquiry but I am still not satisfied that it would serve a useful purpose. I am still considering whether the advantages would outweigh the disadvantages.[165]

These reservations were abandoned in favour of a more positive oral presentation, with the aim of obtaining sanction for an enquiry in time for an announcement at a crucial meeting with the junior doctors scheduled for later in the day of the Cabinet meeting. Relevance to the junior doctors' dispute therefore figured prominently in Castle's statement of the case for an independent enquiry. She also believed that the Government's consent to an enquiry would finally suppress the unfounded hysteria about crisis within the NHS, and bring to an end the campaign of unprecedented violence against her personally. She proposed that the enquiry should 'examine the financial and manpower resources available to the NHS, their use and management'. Pay-beds and private practice were to be excluded since they were matters needing attention without delay. Ministers were divided over Castle's proposal. She was supported on various grounds by Wilson, Foot, Jenkins, Morris, Silkin and Mellish, but the enquiry was not favoured by Healey, Callaghan, Crosland and Ross. Williams and Lever were also unsympathetic, regarding trouble with the medical profession as a product of Castle's rash action over pay-beds and private medicine, issues which would be difficult to exclude from the enquiry. Notwithstanding this divergence of opinion, Wilson called for massive support for Castle from the Cabinet, both in her dealings with junior doctors and on the setting up of an enquiry. In an attempt to meet the views of critics, he referred the question of terms of reference to a group of relevant Ministers, who would also decide between the merits of a Royal Commission and departmental enquiry.[166]

The Treasury was naturally distressed about this outcome. It was also disconcerted by the obligation to reach an immediate decision on the revised terms of reference. Modifications to the original formula were demanded, but the revised terms were much less restrictive than the Treasury wanted:

'To consider in the interest both of the patients and of those who work in the National Health Service the best use and management of the financial and manpower resources of the National Health Service'.[167]

News about the enquiry was conveyed in a muddled manner to the doctors later in the day. The BMA leaders immediately fastened on the question of private medicine, clearly intent on using the enquiry as a Trojan horse in their bid to undermine the Government's objectives concerning pay-beds. Castle gave them no grounds for believing that the Government would be swayed from its course. The doctors responded with threats about confrontation.[168] The BMA protested that the Government was adding to the crisis within the NHS by excluding an important and controversial issue from the remit of the Royal Commission.[169]

The announcement concerning establishment of the Royal Commission was made by the Prime Minister on 20 October 1975.[170] Wilson used this occasion to briefly defend the Government's record, and he insisted that they would not be deterred from phasing out pay-beds and imposing licensing on private practice. However, he conceded that the Royal Commission would be permitted to investigate boundary questions concerning the relationship between the NHS and private practice. Unusual for committees discussed in this book, but not so unusual among Royal Commissions, it was agreed that the enquiry into the NHS should relate to all parts of the United Kingdom.

In the light of the Government's failure to capitulate on the question of private practice, BMA leaders requested a further meeting with the Prime Minister. In the presence of his colleagues, Wilson confirmed that the Royal Commission would be permitted to consider issues relating to private practice. The doctors' main purpose was to persuade Wilson that this issue could not be investigated without attention to pay-beds and licensing of private medical facilities. In that case, any interference from the Government on these fronts would be taken by the profession as a breach of faith. Wilson robustly defended the right of the elected Government to make policy and implement legislation according to its electoral mandate. This uncompromising retort was greeted warmly by Castle.[171]

Appointment of the Chairman of the Royal Commission was accomplished with unusual smoothness. After brief period during which legal names were canvassed for the chairmanship, the name of Sir Alec Merrison FRS, a distinguished physical scientist and Vice-Chancellor of Bristol University came into discussions.[172] He was sufficiently experienced on account of having recently chaired the committee investigating regulation of the medical profession. His success in this sensitive assignment had impressed supporters of both the Government and the BMA. In January 1976 Merrison was offered the chairmanship. After clarification on four points, including the issue of pay-beds, Merrison accepted the appointment.[173] Merrison was fully consulted on the selection of members of his Commission. The choice of members presented the usual questions regarding balance between constituencies. The main aim was to prevent the Commission becoming a representative body

618

for the numerous powerful professional groups who were likely to demand a place. This objective was achieved by selection of professional members from the academic world rather than the professional associations. The exclusion of elite hospital specialties was carried to an extreme. Among the fifteen members, the only representative of hospital medicine was a professor of psychiatry. Academic dentistry was more conventionally represented by a professor from a dental school. The two other representatives of medicine were general practitioners, both from northern industrial towns.[174] Nursing was represented by a professor of nursing, also from a northern industrial town, and medical social work by a senior lecturer from the National Institute for Social Work Training. The health authorities were represented by two senior chairmen of health boards from Northern Ireland and Glasgow. Two of the English members were members of health authorities, although they were not selected for this reason. The other members were: a lawyer, an academic economist and management expert, a journalist and MEP, an officer of the TUC, an officer of the Whitley Council, and a banker. Scotland had two representatives, and one other had held a senior social work position in Scotland. Wales and Northern Ireland each had one representative. Five of the members were women. Five members had obvious links with the labour and trade union movement. Two of the members of the Commission, Clothier and Prime, had served with Merrison on the Committee on the Regulation of the Medical Profession. With respect to service on Government committees, Batchelor was arguably the most experienced member of the Commission. The Commission enjoyed an unusual degree of stability of its membership. For reasons discussed below, the economist, Professor Alan Williams resigned in 1978, while in January 1979, Cecil Clothier resigned to become Parliamentary Commissioner for Administration and Health Service Commissioner.[175] Information distributed about the Royal Commission was somewhat reticent about the age of the Commissioners, perhaps reflecting a wish to avoid drawing attention to the high age of some of its members, although the average age worked out at about 57.

The Royal Commission successfully included a diversity of interests, but few of its members were in a position to make an outstanding contribution; they were equipped to bring real strength to only limited areas of their remit. Their undertaking was of course onerous, and would have constituted a big test for any group, but it was unlikely that their contribution would match up to the proficiency of the previous Royal Commissions on mental health or medical education, or the work of the more effective independent Committees, such as the recent Briggs, Lane, or Davies committees, or even the Jay Committee, or the National Development Group for Mental Handicap, which were contemporaneous with the Royal Commission. Despite its limitations, the work and conclusions of the Merrison Commission merit further brief consideration in the final part of this chapter.

Establishment of the Royal Commission was received as a helpful concession on the part of the Government, but it made no immediate contribution to easing the many problems confronting the NHS. The leaders of the medical profession continued to make direct representations to the Government about the need for urgent moves to improve morale within the NHS. Their main aims related to resources, or pay and conditions of work, but they also advanced ideas for more symbolic gestures. Sir Rodney Smith, President of the Royal College of Surgeons and Chairman of the Conference of Presidents of Royal Colleges and Deans of Faculties, wrote to the Prime Minister giving his own view of the crisis affecting the health service, and proposing that the various staff groups should subscribe to some kind of declaration of support for the basic principles of the NHS. This proposition was discussed by the Prime Minister and other Ministers, and although rejected, it was later revived by Ennals in the context of the thirtieth anniversary of the health service. Smith continued to press his idea for a symbolic gesture to indicate identity of purpose between the Government and the professions.[176]

(vi) PHASING OUT PAY-BEDS

As already noted, the Royal Commission on the NHS to some extent originated as a device invented by the medical profession to obstruct the Government's declared objectives concerning private medicine. Both the February and October 1974 Labour Party manifestos contained an unambiguous commitment to phase out private beds from NHS hospitals. This objective was widely although not universally supported within the Labour movement, and it was particularly tenaciously promoted by the health service unions.[177] Barbara Castle was in no doubt that the separation of private practice from the NHS was an inescapable commitment. However, this policy was disliked by her officials and was violently opposed by the leaders of organisations representing hospital medical staff, who regarded this intention as a breach of faith with respect to understandings reached at the outset of the NHS. The Secretary of State was therefore subjected to conflicting pressures; any backsliding over phasing out pay-beds would alienate the unions, while any move towards this objective promised confrontation with the doctors, handing the Tory press the excuse they needed to further demonise one of their favourite targets for abuse. The 4,500 pay-beds in the NHS (the largest concentration of which were in London, with fewer than 400 in Scotland) therefore assumed a high degree of political significance contrasting with their minuscule importance in the health care of the nation, and the pay-beds dispute proved to be an enervating experience for all concerned, absorbing huge amounts of time and energy which might have been devoted to other and more obviously productive purposes.

Barbara Castle cannot be faulted for rushing forward into confrontation with the medical profession over private medicine. The issue was not raised in the Queen's Speech, although during the Debate on the Address, Castle announced that the joint working party considering the consultants' contract would also discuss arrangements for private practice.[178] The possibility of agreement over pay-bed policy through quiet negotiation was shattered by a dispute at the new Charing Cross Hospital, where NUPE threatened industrial action if the private patients wing was not diverted to NHS uses, while the consultants threatened action if private accommodation was cut back. Although an uneasy truce was negotiated, this dispute adversely affected Castle's relations with the consultants.[179]

The above confrontation was indicative of escalation of union activism over pay-beds. Accordingly, after the October 1974 General Election, some response from the Government was unavoidable. Wilson once again excluded the matter from the Queen's Speech, but he agreed that Castle should in the Debate on the Address declare her intention to phase out private beds during that session of Parliament.[180] This announcement attracted some publicity, excited the doctors, and evinced expressions of discomfort from Castle's officials.[181] Only slow progress was made in framing policy on pay-beds. Castle called for adoption of common waiting lists for NHS and private patients, and for a reduction in the number of under-utilized pay-beds, but the medical profession refused to co-operate.[182] The joint working party on the consultant contract also ground to a halt.[183]

Faced with animosity from the consultants, Owen was noticeably more reticent than Castle to force the pace over pay-beds, and he favoured a more conciliatory policy. The trade unions kept up the pressure; COHSE threatened to join the industrial action unless some declaration of Government policy was made before 8 May 1975.[184] During March Castle prepared to take her proposals to the Cabinet, but Healey warned her that unless she was willing to stand the cost from her existing budget, it would be necessary to hold prior discussions with the Treasury. The Cabinet memorandum was therefore withdrawn for further consultation.[185] At this stage a dispute over pay-beds broke out at Westminster Hospital. After brief consideration by the Cabinet on 25 March, the issue was referred to the Social Services Committee.[186] Castle appealed for early legislation to take powers to abolish pay-beds from 1 November 1976, perhaps followed by later legislation to control the private sector. Ministers agreed to allow Castle to make a policy statement. Castle took this as an 'enthusiastic endorsement'.[187] Short told the Prime Minister that the Ministers regretted being forced into action by the trade unions, but they agreed with Castle that early legislation was desirable, although they expressed reservations about taking wider powers to control private practice.[188] Wilson (who was attending a meeting of Commonwealth Prime Ministers in Jamaica) and his Ministers commented actively on the draft statement. Castle made her statement during a short debate on pay-beds on 5 May 1975. She confirmed that pay-beds would be eliminated from NHS hospitals without delay. Consultations were promised about the details of phasing out and about licensing arrangements for existing and substitute facilities in the private sector. Pending agreement on the logistics of phasing-out, Castle announced that the number of pay-beds would be reduced from 4,500 to 4,000 to divert under-used facilities to NHS purposes. Consultants were once again encouraged to introduce common waiting lists. The Government promised to compensate NHS authorities for any loss of income occasioned by the elimination of private facilities.[189]

Castle's statement pacified the unions, whose leaders speculated that their members were likely to hold back from further militant action for some eighteen months on condition that the administration pursued its policy vigorously.[190] Barbara Castle satisfied the trade unions that she was determined to achieve the undiluted implementation of Labour Party policy on pay-beds, regardless of any inconvenience occasioned by opposition from the medical profession. Castle's colleagues were unenthusiastic conscripts. Even Owen, who in public loyally supported the Secretary of State, in private urged compromise with the doctors. Ministerial colleagues were even more lukewarm about extending their battles with the doctors to this further front. At the Cabinet meeting on 3 July 1975, Castle had difficulty in establishing a place for the pay-beds Bill, even on the reserve legislative programme.[191] Divisions of opinion were evident at the Social Services Committee. Some Ministers were favourable to preserving reciprocal links between the private sector and the NHS, while others wanted the severing of all links, and the limitation of the private sector to its 1974 level. Castle's consultation document was agreed only 'on balance' by Ministers.[192] The consultation document on private beds was published on 11 August 1975, a date calculated to avoid publicity, and while the Secretary of State was enjoying a break in Corfu.[193] Two significant alterations resulted from deliberations in the Social

Services Committee. First, additions were made to relate the document to conditions in Scotland and Wales. Secondly, whereas the draft indicated that the short-stay private sector would be kept 'broadly in line with the present scale of provision for private patients', the consultation document stated that the private sector would not 'substantially exceed the level of NHS pay beds and beds in private nursing homes and hospitals at March 1974'.

Castle faced opposition on two fronts. First, a fifth column within the Cabinet, led by Harold Lever, embarked on a passionate defence of the private sector, leading Castle to conclude that 'Some people in the Cabinet began to get cold feet. Harold Wilson schemed with his old friend, Arnold Goodman, to frame a compromise'.[194] More seriously, the medical profession embarked on a vitriolic campaign against Castle's policy, backed up by a threat of industrial action, including mass resignation from the NHS. Attacks on Castle from the Tory press reached a new level of vehemence. It was even rumoured that Castle's Permanent Secretary and top officials were threatening resignation over this issue.[195] In the face of this onslaught, the Parliamentary Labour Party and trade union leaders insisted that a pledge concerning legislation should be inserted in the Queen's Speech scheduled for November 1975. To Castle's relief, this was approved.[196]

In view of the ferocity of the response from the medical profession to the consultation document, the Prime Minister agreed to meet their representatives. The leading medical negotiators were Mr A H Grabham and Mr Walpole Lewin, Chairmen respectively of the Central Committee for Hospital Medical Services and the Council of the BMA. The medical delegation was unimpressed by Wilson's guarantee that the Government was not attempting to undermine private medical practice outside the NHS, and the doctors were incensed by the Government's unwillingness to refer the issue of private beds to the recently-announced Royal Commission. The profession attacked the proposals of the consultation document as a threat against the traditional independence and freedom of the medical profession. If the Government proceeded with its policy, it would be a breach of the understanding reached with Bevan in 1948, which had been a condition for the profession's entry into the NHS. If this understanding was revoked, the profession would never again be willing to trust the Government.[197] The representatives of the Royal Colleges issued a press statement condemning the consultation document, which was represented as a 'serious threat to the care and safety of patients and to the standards of medical practice in this country now and in the future'. The Royal Colleges expressed 'feelings of deep sorrow that a noble profession has been brought to a point of open conflict with the Government'.[198]

Castle forged ahead with preparations for her pay-bed legislation. On 20 November 1975, in the face of much dissent from colleagues, she obtained provisional sanction for a Bill to provide for: phasing out of pay-beds; a timetable of one year, unless there were exceptional circumstances; a licensing system operating for private hospitals with more than 75 beds; and guarantees of the right to private practice outside the NHS.[199] She concluded that the doctors were alienating the responsible press and the public by their premature threats of industrial action. The Secretary of State furthermore believed that militancy within the medical profession was waning. Ministers did not share this confidence and they were by no means united in their support for Castle's scheme. Members of the Social Services Committee were lukewarm about the proposals for licensing and they were not confident that legislative time could be found for a Bill containing licensing provisions. These doubts were shared by Lord Shepherd, the Labour Leader in the House of Lords.[200] William Rodgers expressed even stronger reservations, aligning himself with the position taken by Harold Lever, in opposing regulation of the private sector.[201] The Prime Minister concluded that Castle had embarked on a needlessly reckless course. He therefore insisted on slowing down the pace, pending further meaningful negotiations with the doctors, and delaying legislation until agreement was reached.[202] The Cabinet exposed Castle to much criticism, especially from Lever, Williams, Elwyn-Jones and Mellish, and she received virtually no support, but Wilson persuaded Ministers to entrust further 'thorough consultations' with the doctors to a 'small Ministerial group' under his supervision.[203] Both sides of the debate attached great importance to the outcome. Lever believed that the future of the health service was threatened by the policies of Castle, whereas Benn thought that the path of compromise would 'in a way herald the end of the Health Service'.[204]

The ministerial group comprised only Wilson and Castle, with one appointed adjutant, who was Wilson's appointed agent of compromise, the ebullient and emollient lawyer, Arnold Goodman. At Wilson's behest, Castle, not unwillingly, took on Goodman as a go-between.[205] However, the expectations of Wilson and Castle were at variance; the former expected Goodman to work out an accommodation with the doctors, whereas Castle expected Goodman to persuade the doctors to return to negotiations with her. Castle's initial meetings with Goodman were friendly, and the latter was confident that a settlement could be reached without undue difficulty.[206]

Castle soon complained that Goodman was assuming too much authority, that he possessed little understanding of the issues, was naive in his understanding of the commitments of the Labour Party, and was conveying the impression that Castle's hands were being tied and that she was being over-ruled by Wilson. She insisted that Wilson should recognise unambiguously that the authority for negotiations rested in her hands.[207] Amid confusion about their relative roles in representing government policy, with evident ill-feeling between Wilson and Castle, and without having reached an understanding about their negotiating position, Wilson, Castle and Goodman met the doctors' delegation on 3 December. The animosities and disagreements were so pronounced that Wilson considered excluding Castle from the meeting. Wilson was supplied with numerous briefs for the meeting, but he must have found it impossible to remember the intricacies of the argument.[208] The main features of this meeting were long and confused interventions by Wilson, which conveyed to the doctors the impression that the Government would offer major concessions, a statement of a new set of policy proposals by Goodman issued without reference to Castle, and tangential remarks from Castle indicative of her lack of faith in Wilson and Goodman.[209]

Goodman retained the initiative. After the meeting, he redrafted his proposals. These rather than Castle's policy documents became the basis for subsequent negotiations. Goodman proposed:

1) That in the event of the Government proceeding with the legislation referred to in the Queen's Speech for the phasing out of pay beds, the Consultants etc. would cease their present resistance - whilst of course retaining their individual right of democratic objection. It would therefore be accepted that the phasing out of pay beds on the basis set out below would be an agreed item of national policy being enacted by Parliament.

2) The phasing out of pay beds would as to timing be the subject of consultation between the Government and the professions.

3) The phasing out of pay beds would be subject to a solitary safeguard that an independent commission composed say of three persons appointed by the Government - after consultations with the professions - would be required in any particular district to certify that the beds could from time to time be dispensed with because there were available sufficient accommodation and facilities for the reasonable operation of private medicine in that particular district.[210]

Castle was left 'in despair' and turmoil about this outcome. The public assumption of authority by Goodman she found deeply humiliating. Between them, Wilson and Goodman had reversed many of Castle's declared policies, and opened the way to further compromise.[211] Coincidentally this reverse took place on the day upon which Castle delivered the Aneurin Bevan memorial lecture, an event which reminded her of the similarity in the predicaments faced by the two leftist Ministers. Wilson also harboured a sense a grievance following press reports of Castle's speech, which prompted him to complain that she was attempting to wreck negotiations with the doctors.[212] Once tempers subsided, Castle and Goodman worked together reasonably harmoniously in time-consuming and exhausting discussions; by slow degrees the profession was steered towards agreement.[213] Castle described the final week of discussions as 'one of the most intensive weeks of my ministerial life', after which she was 'completely drained'.[214] At the end of negotiations, all sides claimed to have rescued honour. Castle was satisfied that she had 'safeguarded the major principles of our policy'.[215] Wilson believed that his Prime Ministerial intervention had rescued the health service from anarchy. Goodman was pleased to have brought about an accommodation that was beyond the capacity of the politicians to negotiate. The medical politicians contended that their strong-arm tactics had forced an unreasonable Labour administration to make painful concessions. The dissatisfied parties were the outsiders, particularly the Labour Party and the trade unions, which suspected that the compromises would slow down, and possibly undermine the phasing out of private medicine from the NHS.

Castle announced provisional agreement with the medical profession on 15 December 1975.[216] After the long delays occasioned by negotiations with the doctors, she was keen to set the legislation in motion without delay.[217] Wilson insisted on further delay, in the first place until after the BMA ballot.[218] When this produced inconclusive results, Wilson insisted that the issue should be reconsidered by the Cabinet, which held two further long discussions, in which Castle faced some rear-guard sniping from her traditional critics, but Wilson finally railroaded through the proposal to embark on legislation, on the understanding that further consultations would be held about licensing. Also a significant concession was agreed against Castle's wishes, the effect of which was to exclude from licensing hospitals with fewer than 100 beds in London, and 75 elsewhere. This represented a compromise between the uniform level of 75 proposed by Castle and the 150 demanded by the private hospitals.[219]

In January 1976 Castle's officials began work on the NHS (Miscellaneous Provisions) Bill, later known as the Health Services Bill. The text was finalised at the end of March, and the first print was considered by the Legislation Committee a few days before Castle's dismissal from office.[220]

After the departure of Wilson and Castle, Callaghan was petitioned by the BMA to abandon the Health Services Bill and the Prime Minister's advisers saw the advantage of this course of action. However, Callaghan rejected this advice.[221] The arrival of Ennals made no essential difference to the Health Services Bill, but there was a much better atmosphere of co-operation with the medical profession. The Health Services Act received the Royal Assent in November 1976. Under this Act, one thousand pay-beds were subject to revocation after a period of six months, which reduced the number of pay-beds in Great Britain to about 3,500. The Act also established the Health Services Board and separate Scottish and Welsh Committees, to supervise the phasing out of the remaining pay-beds and control the authorisation of new developments in the private sector.[222] It was envisaged that the Board would make recommendations at six-monthly intervals for the withdrawal of further pay-beds. Progress with the implementation of this policy was painfully slow. The Health Service Board agreed that in return for abandoning the idea of a terminal date for the phasing out of pay-beds, the profession would accept common waiting lists for pay-beds remaining in the NHS. In May 1977, the Health Services Board made suggestions for common waiting lists, but the professional organisations continued to be obstructive. Accordingly, in July 1978 the Health Service Board released further proposals for waiting lists, but this produced renewed complaints about lack of consultation from the JCC. In the interests of retaining better relations with the profession, Ennals refrained from pressing the issue.[223] On account of ambiguities in the procedures for phasing out private beds, and the need to ensure that satisfactory alternative arrangements were in place, very few pay-beds were phased out. By the end of the Callaghan administration, about 2,800 pay beds remained in the NHS. The major functions of the Health Services Board related to regulation of the expansion of the private sector, but this power was limited in its effectiveness owing to the exclusion of smaller hospitals.[224] The original intention of using the Health Service Board to restrict the expansion of the private sector was not observed. If anything the policy of phasing out pay-beds operated to stimulate growth in the private sector, and the Health Services Board found itself presiding over this expansion.[225] Labour therefore failed in its objective to eliminate pay-beds from the NHS, and it succeeded in stimulating rather repressing the private sector of health care.

(vii) DEMOCRACY IN THE NHS
Whereas Labour was united in its criticism of the Joseph scheme for reorganisation, the Party was divided over the way forward. For the long term it was recognised that further change was needed, but

there was little agreement on the nature of the changes required. At one extreme, Crossman and the local authority associations preferred transferring the health service to local government. The unions favoured some modification of the existing system. All agreed that greater democracy needed to be introduced into the health service. As mentioned above, one of the few specific pledges in the February 1974 General Election manifesto was to 'transform the area health authorities into democratic bodies'.

The new administration appreciated that it was unrealistic to contemplate more than marginal changes within the health service administration and management structure that were only just in process of being set in place. However, under the flag of 'democratisation' it seemed possible to make significant adjustments without causing undue disruption. Although the possibilities for action were limited in the short term, Castle was committed to building up the functions of the AHAs at the expense of the RHAs, which she expected to be limited to strategic planning functions, 'little more than the regional arm of the DHSS'.[226] Owen aspired to introduce changes 'in an evolutionary way, aimed at making the health service more responsive to patient needs and somewhat less bureaucratic in structure'.[227]

The new Secretary of State reaffirmed her commitment to democracy at the first opportunity, which was the Debate on the Address, when she gave prominence to an undertaking to make the AHAs more representative.[228] The Treasury was unenthusiastic about this initiative. Castle was warned that you 'must guard against the risk that any changes in membership of the NHS authorities to give greater weight to local authority nominees (or the professional staff) might weaken the ability of Health Ministers to shape and guide the health services so as to secure the most effective service to patients within the resources available'.[229]

In warning the new RHA Chairmen about her intentions, the Secretary of State received a polite but frosty reception. The Chairmen were clearly disturbed that their own authority would be undermined by the proposed changes.[230] Despite evident lack of enthusiasm from NHS authorities, preparations to extend democracy within the NHS were given high priority. Production of the draft English White Paper was supervised by Owen. The agreed text was circulated on 10 April 1974, initially with the assumption that one White Paper would be issued for England, Scotland and Wales.[231] However, it quickly became apparent that insufficient common ground existed to merit a single policy presentation. Ministers in Wales were insistent on a radical shift in the direction of representation, but were undecided about the approach to be adopted at the national level, which would need to be reconciled with devolution proposals. Officials in the Welsh Office were reluctant to produce their own White Paper, but this course of action was insisted upon by Ministers. Scottish Ministers inclined to take no account of devolution, and restrict themselves a separate White Paper introducing minimum concessions to the demand for changes in existing arrangements.[232]

Castle presented her initial thoughts to colleagues on 17 May 1974. Her first aim was to establish the level of representation of local authority members at one-third of the membership of RHAs and AHAs, as envisaged in Crossman's Green Paper. She intended to give health service staff other than doctors and nurses a place on health authorities, and also strengthen CHCs. Ministers were generally supportive and pointed out that the proposals would harmonise well with the Devolution Commission's Report, which also was concerned with extending democratisation in regional government. Significantly, the only negative view came from Millan, who pointed out that in Scotland there had been little demand for local authority representation on health authorities and only lukewarm support for the Local Health Council proposal.[233]

The short English, bilingual Welsh, and Scottish White Papers on democracy in the NHS were published on 30 May, 24 June, and 22 July 1974 respectively.[234] In content and general tone, the English and Welsh documents were similar. If anything the Welsh version was the more evangelical in its advocacy of greater democracy. On the other hand, the Scottish White Paper avoided using 'democracy' in the title, and the word seems not to have been used in the text. These differences support the impression that SHHD was a reluctant participant in this exercise. Given the past determined resistance of Scottish Ministers to relinquishing control over their Health Boards, the whole democracy exercise must have seemed alien and disruptive.

The Scottish White Paper communicated satisfaction with administrative and management arrangements in Scotland. However, it was acknowledged that there was an argument for making the 'system more responsive to the views of those it serves and to take greater account of the contribution which those who work in the service can make to its management'.[235] As noted in the previous chapter, Scotland was relatively late to set up its Local Health Councils. The White Paper was therefore used to confirm arrangements for these bodies. Unlike the position in England and Wales, there was no statutory barrier to inclusion of Local Health Council members on Health Boards, but the White Paper discouraged this practice. With respect to the crucial question of local authority nominees on Health Boards, upon which SHHD had been traditionally unenthusiastic, minor alterations to the ground rules were suggested, having the effect of increasing the total number of local authority nominees from 60 to 68 (between three and seven on each Health Board according to its size, producing an average of about 25 per cent). Apparently more radical was the proposal to assign two or three places on each Health Board to the Scottish TUC, but this represented a formalisation and minor extension of arrangements already in place. Paralleling the proposals in the English and Welsh White Papers, was the suggestion to allow other groups among health service personnel to join doctors and nurses on the Health Boards, giving a total of five health care personnel on each board.

The English and Welsh White Papers were antagonistic to the arrangements introduced by Joseph, which they condemned as undemocratic, and they rejected any attempt to draw a clear-cut distinction between management and representation. Accordingly, it was proposed to alter the balance of AHAs (and RHAs in England) to recruit one-third of the members from local government. In constituting AHAs, it was proposed to take two (four in single-district areas) members from Community Health Councils, and two from other NHS staff to join the existing doctor and nurse members. It was also proposed to include two staff representatives on RHAs. As well as recommending CHC representation on AHAs, the English and Welsh White Papers promised further extension of the authority of these new bodies, which it was hoped to develop into a 'powerful forum where consumer views can influence the NHS'.[236] All three White Papers were favourable to establishing a national body to advise and assist CHCs or LHCs.

Consultations on the democracy documents were largely completed by the date of the October 1974 General Election. Progress towards implementation slowed down. According to Castle, Owen was 'conducting a running war with officials' on this issue. She believed that officials were unsympathetic with the proposed changes and were therefore attempting to obstruct implementation.[237] Eventually Owen achieved agreement on general lines of policy, which were then ratified by the Secretary of State in April 1975.[238]

In general the democracy proposals were warmly received by local government and CHCs, but not by NHS authorities and the medical profession. NHS authorities were particularly concerned that the alterations would have a further unsettling effect, and add to uncertainties and low morale within the health service. The proposal to introduce CHC members on to AHAs received a particularly hostile reception from NHS bodies, which insisted that this would result in a confusion of roles. CHCs were not adamant about representation, but they wanted to send a delegate to meetings, with opportunity to speak but not vote. This compromise, which obviated the need for legislation, was accepted by Ministers. The CHCs were also reticent about the Government's plan for a National Council to assist their work. Accordingly this idea was abandoned in favour of the counter-proposal from the CHCs for establishment of a National Association, which was seen as better protection of their independence.

Infiltration of local government influence into NHS authorities had been one of the most hotly debated issues during preparations for reorganisation. In many respects, Castle and her colleagues were reverting to the intentions of Crossman's Green Paper. Much of the old debate was repeated in the context of the democracy White Papers. However, some of the friends of democracy were not sympathetic to the White Paper proposals on account of their preference for direct election or other alternatives for greater community participation. Despite absence of consensus, Ministers agreed to retain their one-third local representation principle for both RHAs and AHAs. This cleared the way for difficult discussions on the precise manner of achieving the intended representation from the many contenders in the local government field, without causing a big increase in the size of NHS authorities.

Proposals for additional staff representation on NHS authorities were welcomed in principle by the staff interests, but at first they demanded three rather than two members. When this was rejected, they found it difficult to arrive at an acceptable method for appointing staff representatives. At the last moment, the staff groups proposed a system of election organised by health authorities. Ministers agreed to this proposal, and also suggested that it should extend to medical and nursing members.

Castle and Morris circulated their proposals to Edward Short and other members of the Social Services Committee, with a request to make a statement on implementation of the democracy package. The only provisional element in their proposals related to the form of selection to be used by the staff groups.[239] Ministers agreed to these proposals without further discussion. The only substantial issue raised by Ministers related to the possible impact of these arrangement on consultations over industrial democracy. However, it was decided that the NHS represented a special case, not likely to be cited as a precedent within industry.[240]

Castle announced her intentions on 11 July 1975 in a written statement in Parliament and in an address to the first annual meeting of the National Association of Area Health authorities.[241] The increase in local government representation on health authorities, and the modest strengthening of the role of CHCs was introduced without delay, but staff organisations failed to agree on a method of selection for their representatives. Consequently, although health trade unionists found their way on to health authorities, this occurred by other means than the allocated places described in the democracy White Papers.

Decisions on the *NHS and the Community* White Paper in Scotland took place in May 1975. The various parties reacted very much as in England and Wales. Scottish officials complained that the response was 'disappointingly low and does no provide a reliable basis on which to base our decisions'. In the light of this limited response and lack of consensus, officials advised Ministers to follow departmental thinking, which inclined to less radical changes than were contemplated in England and Wales. Ministers agreed to establish a national association of Local Health Councils, but they rejected LHC nominees on Health Boards, or their right of attendance at board meetings. It was also agreed that the Secretary of State would hold on to the right to appoint the chairperson and all members of Health Boards. However, it was conceded that the pattern of membership proposed in the consultative paper should be adopted. This in fact involved little change from the existing pattern. As in England and Wales, no final decision was made on the proposal to include NHS staff members of Health Boards.[242] In Scotland this omission was to some extent compensated for with respect to trade unionists among the health workers by the generous provision of places on Health Boards for nominees of the Scottish TUC.

Community Health Councils

The democracy exercise constituted an early boost to the morale of the newly-formed Community Health Councils, and a propitious beginning for the Local Health Councils in Scotland. David Owen declared that he was a 'tremendous supporter' of the CHCs; he regarded them as 'one of the most successful aspects of the health service reorganisation'. In particular, he looked forward to CHCs becoming a leading advocate of the Government's new prevention and health promotion policies.[243]

This affirmation of support was helpful in view of the troubled progress of the clauses relating to these bodies in the health service legislation. The CHCs had emerged with considerably greater independence and authority than was intended by the Heath administration, or was wanted by NHS authorities or officials within DHSS. CHCs and LHCs differed in their composition in significant respects, reflecting the attitudes of DHSS and SHHD evident in the above discussion concerning the democracy exercise. Whereas the CHCs drew half of their members from local government, this group comprised only one-third of the membership of LHCs. On the other hand, whereas in Scotland, the Scottish TUC nominated two or three members of each LHC, in England, trade unionists only found their way on to CHCs at the discretion of the RHA, which controlled only one-sixth of the total membership, and was under no obligation to appoint trade unionists within this constituency. The CHCs and LHCs were given only vaguely drawn guide-lines for making representations to the authorities managing the health service.[244]

Apart from their general responsibilites to represent consumers, CHCs possessed the right to receive information, to visit hospitals, and to be consulted about plans for development. In the context of its democracy exercise, the Labour Government further strengthened the position of CHCs, especially, by allowing attendance at AHA meetings, and also by giving the CHCs greater powers with respect to consultation over the closure of hospitals. A further product of this process was establishment of the Association of Community Health Councils for England and Wales, and the Association of Scottish Local Health Councils.

Given their novelty, it is not surprising that CHCs were the subject of many conferences and seminars during their formative months, and they were kept under surveillance from the moment of their inception. Sir Keith Joseph appointed Councillor Kenneth Collis and Mrs Mary Marre (Lady Marre) as his Advisers on CHCs. They completed their short final report in March 1975. They had observed the process of establishment of the CHCs and held discussions with the first cohort of CHC chairpersons and members. The Advisers completed their work before the CHCs had done more than familiarise themselves with the nature of their responsibilities. The main worries of the Advisers at the initial stage related to the reticence of AHAs and FPCs to supply the CHCs with essential information, even about the open parts of AHA meetings. Their special concern was absence of a mechanism for making the findings of the Hospital Advisory Service available to CHCs. The Advisers discovered that 'the fear that CHCs would release a flood of individual complaints has been proved completely unfounded. On the contrary CHCs have yet to make sufficient contact with the public to enable them to come forward with confidence'. The establishment of meaningful contact between CHCs and their local communities was recognised as one of the main challenges for the CHCs. If this contact was not made, the CHCs risked being viewed as co-optees of local health service managements.[245] Progress in reaching their public was slow. In 1977, Cartwright and Anderson estimated that only 2 per cent of patients were aware of the existence of CHCs.[246] The impressive investigation into the membership and early operations of CHCs by Klein and Lewis confirmed the findings of Councillor Collis and Lady Marre. On the important question of the relationship between CHCs and NHS management, they concluded: 'the themes were very much the same everywhere: lack of information and failure to consult'.[247]

CHCs and LHCs were as diverse as their local communities, and they reflected the character of the local political and social environment. Their identity was also greatly affected by the preoccupations of their officers and dominant members. The most radical CHCs were found in inner London, where the Wandsworth and East Merton CHC headed its first Annual Report, *Patient Power - The First Year*. Although few other CHCs conducted themselves like confraternities of the French Revolution, CHCs were the least stereotyped entities within the new health service. Although consigned to the peripheries of influence, the better CHCs succeeded in making an impact, and their diversity of character, unpredictability, spontaneity, and eccentricity, protected them from the fate of institutional sclerosis which befell many advisory bodies in the health service. The economic crisis afflicting the NHS, cuts in services, threatened closure of hospitals, continuing evidence of malaise within long-stay institutions, created ready-made issues for the CHCs to bond with their communities, and for them to capture media attention, and establish a degree of public esteem necessary to ensure their survival.

District Management Teams and health service trade unions discovered that CHCs were useful allies in struggles with higher authority. Regional authorities found that CHCs operated as useful checks with respect to the more questionable decisions of AHAs. Relations between CHCs and FPCs were rarely particularly close or cordial. In 1977 the FPCs successfully resisted Ennals' proposal to allow CHC observers to attend their meetings.

Regardless of their youth, inexperience and other limitations imposed on them, the CHCs made their mark. Even in 1975, the Hospital Advisory Service discovered that CHCs had begun 'to emerge as a potentially powerful force' in local health affairs. These positive impressions were confirmed in the following year, when the CHCs provided the HAS with useful background information about the state of services in their districts.[248] In similar vein, a short report produced in 1977 concluded that 'for all their failures and frustrations, and puny resources', the CHCs continued to thrive and were capable of taking on even more ambitious functions.[249] The value of an effective CHC was demonstrated with respect to scandals at the Normansfield Hospital and this was acknowledged in the Inquiry Report published in 1978.[250] More scientific analysis of the CHCs drew attention to their strengths and weaknesses.[251]

CHCs and LHCs fulfilled many of the expectations of their advocates. Nevertheless, within the NHS administration CHCs were not entirely accepted. It was argued that the energies and resources absorbed by CHCs could be put to better use, that AHAs and local government bodies could fulfil all the main functions of CHCs, and that they exceeded their remit by turning themselves into campaigning bodies on national issues and political matters.[252] Although the health departments were often irritated by the actions of CHCs, in evidence to the Royal Commission they were presented as a 'net benefit to the NHS'.[253] The Royal Commission evaded the issue and pronounced that five years was not long enough for an assessment to be made. Nevertheless, it was conceded that they had made an important contribution in representing public opinion to NHS management; it was recommended that they should be given further support and greater resources.[254]

(viii) PROTECTING THE VULNERABLE
This section resumes the discussion of many items on the agenda for improvement in services to vulnerable groups, and for general reform of the mechanism for handling complaints and grievances about the health services. As already noted, this process was initiated by Crossman and pursued by Joseph in very much the same spirit. However, most of the tasks remained unfinished by the date of return of the Labour administration. In addition to topics already considered in earlier chapters, this section will deal with the initiative to produce a policy document relating to services for the elderly.

Hospital (Health) Advisory Service
The appointment in 1973 of the geriatrician, Dr Eluned Woodford-Williams as Director of the HAS rendered the inspectorate less threatening and thereby created conditions for consolidation of the work of the visiting teams. Woodford-Willams remained in this post until her retirement in 1978. On account of the interests of the Director, constraints on staffing created by the economic crisis and reorganisation, and the fact that mental handicap had dominated the first phase of the visitations, the HAS narrowed down its work and concentrated on geriatric and psychiatric services. This cut-back occasioned adverse comment from the Davies Committee, which saw any retrenchment within the HAS as an attack on the machinery for facilitating complaints. It called for the HAS to be reflated as soon as possible to enable it to 'review standards of care of all hospital patients who come within its existing terms of reference, whether or not the Service is given wider responsibilities that may be appropriate in an integrated health service'.[255] The reservations made by the Davies Committee were not applicable to Scotland, where the Scottish HAS remained on its previous course, with Dr J K Hunter remaining as Director, and without any significant change in

functions.[256] In this case, the HAS was exposed to the rather different limitation that its closer identification with SHHD and NHS authorities reduced to some extent its scope for independent criticism. This increased the onus on the Scottish Mental Welfare Commission to protect the interests of the vulnerable.

Contrary to the trend to limit the scope of the HAS, incoming Labour Ministers, supported by their advisers and outside expert opinion, were in favour of a wider function. This was consistent with the promise of improvements in quality control in the health service promised in the Democracy White Paper.[257] One possibility was extending the advisory service to cover the entire hospital service; another entailed amalgamation of the HAS and the Social Work Service to create a unified advisory body for services involving contributions from both health and local authorities. The former was rejected on account of known hostility of the medical profession. Conveniently, the latter option was favoured as a first priority on account of the need to maintain vigilance over the most vulnerable groups. Owen suggested the title 'Health Advisory Service' for the extended HAS. An announcement regarding this facet of the democracy programme was made on 31 July 1974.[258] The Secretary of State announced that she would embark on a consultative exercise, to consider adopting the new title for the HAS and achieving linkage of function between the HAS and SWS, including with respect to children undergoing long-term care in hospital, other than the mentally handicapped.

It soon became apparent that amalgamation of the two bodies raised serious problems. Inheriting the functions of the Children's Service of the Home Office, the SWS was a statutory inspectorate for some of the services administered by local authorities, whereas the HAS possessed no remit in the local authority area. It was soon concluded that the better course was to increase the liaison between the two systems of visitation, and in August 1974 a trial was conducted in Cheshire.[259]

In January 1975 a short consultative document was circulated to test opinion on the possibilities for extension in the work of the HAS.[260] This exposed marked differences of outlook. NHS administrators complained that there were already too many sources of advice; they therefore favoured maximum amalgamation of inspecting agencies. Local authorities suspected health authorities of trespassing into their field. Accordingly, they objected to formal links between the HAS and SWS.[261] Following this inconclusive response, the Ministers decided to implement their original plan, with minor modifications. From 1 April 1976, the title of the English and Welsh Hospital Advisory Service was changed to Health Advisory Service. Its function was extended to all cover the hospital, community health

636

and local authority social service department services relating to psychiatric and geriatric client groups. The HAS also established a team to monitor services for children receiving long-term care in hospital.[262] In view of this extended remit, the first annual report of the Health Advisory Service for the year 1976 was a more substantial document than its predecessors.[263] To some bewilderment among expert observers, the practice of publishing this important report was then discontinued.[264] While there was no convincing reason for terminating these reports, continuity was made slightly more difficult by the retirement of Dr Woodford-Williams in mid-1978, followed by appointment of an interim Director for a short period, during which it was decided to appoint the psychiatrist, Dr D H Dick as Director. He took up this appointment in April 1979.[265]

The published reports of the HAS were modest about the scale of its achievements and pessimistic about the state of the long-stay services. Any complacency would have been misplaced, as witnessed by the sequence of hospital scandals that punctuated the period of the Labour administration. The worst of these resulted in full-scale hospital enquiries, as at Warlington Park (1976), Darlington Memorial (1976), St Augustine's(1976), Mary Dendy (1977), Normansfield (1978), Winterton (1979), and Church Hill House (1979).[266] Many of the worst examples of malpractice took place on institutions visited by the HAS, often on more than one occasion. Although the HAS worked hard to cultivate better practice, it is evident that it exerted only limited impact. Given limitations of resources and attitudes, it was perhaps unrealistic to expect the limited interventions made by the HAS to have exerted more than a marginal influence on the system as a whole.

Complaints Procedures
With the appointment of the Health Commissioners for England, Scotland and Wales, those with complaints about their handling by the health service were supplied with a long-stop, but in England and Wales they were without a credible in-field.[267] This problem was addressed by the Davies Committee, the exemplary report of which was published on 17 December 1973.[268] This 163-page document was issued in the economical A4 format usually reserved for papers of lesser importance.[269]

The Davies Committee conducted a comprehensive review of the evidence relating to complaints and the various arrangements for dealing with them, including assessments of the role of the Health Service Commissioner, the Hospital Advisory Service, and the likely role of the CHC. As noted above, in an interim representation, the Davies Committee recommended for CHCs a more active role in the handling of complaints than the Government was willing to concede.

These additional mechanisms for facilitating complaints were regarded as especially important because they would assist with expression of legitimate concerns on behalf of those who were not in a position to make direct complaints. Intermediaries active in such cases were likely to require protection against victimisation. The Davies Committee hoped that independent and vigorous CHCs and the HAS would together fulfil this protective role.

The Davies Committee laid down guiding principles governing complaints procedures, which refined the guide-lines contained in HM(66)15. The Committee was dissatisfied with the convention adopted by DHSS that NHS authorities should be allowed discretion to evolve their own methods for implementing these principles. The Committee insisted that patients should be protected by a readily intelligible, accessible and mandatory code of practice designed to secure uniformity in procedures from one place to another. The Report contained a model code of practice, which set out operational procedures in great detail, including variants appropriate to Wales.[270] The Davies Report also provided guide-lines for the conduct of independent professional investigations or formal inquiries for cases where complex or serious problems required adjudication. The Davies Report was the first official document in the lifetime of the NHS to recognise the great importance of the complaints system. It constituted an embryonic Bill of Rights for patients. Naturally, such idealistic constructs are likely to stumble across obstructions in the path to implementation, and Davies was no exception.

Initially, it was hoped that consultations on the Davies Report would be completed by March 1974, and that the code of practice would be in place for use by the new NHS authorities appointed in connection with reorganisation. This timetable was disrupted by the February 1974 General Election and subsequent preoccupation of Ministers with other priorities. There was little unanimity in response to the Davies Report. Consumer organisations such as the Patients' Association, the National Council of Social Service and the National Association for Mental Health were supportive. However, the latter was suspicious that establishment of the complaints procedure relied too much on good will. NAMH therefore insisted on machinery for enforcing the complaints procedure and for regular review and evaluation. If these conditions were not met, NAMH hinted that it would oppose the Davies recommendations. Among the professional bodies, although nursing organisations complained about their under-representation on the Davies Committee, they were generally supportive. On the other hand, medical organisations were generally antagonistic and annoyed that they had not been consulted more fully in the course of the Committee's deliberations. They insisted on full consultation before a final decision on implementation was reached.

The JCC, representing consultant opinion, conducted a belligerent attack on the Davies Committee, which it believed was slanted against the medical profession. NHS authorities were also unenthusiastic; they assented to the Davies proposals in general terms, but insisted on their imposition in a greatly simplified and more flexible form, and urged that further action should be delayed until greater stability existed within the NHS.

The main point of contentiousness was the proposal for independent regional panels headed by a senior lawyer, to provide for the independent investigation of complaints where litigation might be involved. The Davies Committee argued that in most cases the complainants were not committed to litigation, but saw this as their only recourse to obtain satisfaction. The Committee believed that if complainants were presented with an alternative means of answering their complaint fully and fairly, they would prefer to take this option. The Committee pointed out that independent review could not be undertaken in these cases by the Health Service Commissioner, either because they often involved the exercise of clinical judgement, or because the complainant was considering recourse to the courts.[271]

Medical bodies expressed intransigent opposition to these investigating panels. They were alarmed about the recent multiplication of bodies subjecting their work to scrutiny. They regarded the investigating panels as an intolerable threat, especially because they were to be directly concerned with clinical matters. At the opposite pole, consumer organisations were suspicious that the Davies regional investigating panels appointed by RHAs would lack independence. Sympathisers recognised the practical difficulties in establishing fourteen such panels and they appreciated that designation of litigious complaints unlikely to reach the courts was likely to present a major problem.

The Davies recommendations relating to investigating panels also ran contrary to the Government's opposition to allowing the Health Service Commissioner or the Davies procedures to provide a substitute for the courts. The Davies proposal was also received badly by the Health Service Commissioner, who already possessed limited discretion to investigate potentially litigious cases, but only when clinical judgement was not the sole factor in the complaint. He argued that any steps in the direction proposed by Davies would be better undertaken under the aegis of the Health Service Commissioner. Otherwise there was risk of duplication and confusion of responsibility.[272]

Officials within DHSS were supportive of the general aims of the Davies Report, but were swayed in their response by the widespread criticism and lack of positive support within the NHS. They inclined to the view that no further progress was possible without the sanction of the main staff interests, in the course of which major concessions were likely to be required:

> It is clear that it would be extremely unwise to try to introduce the Code of Practice, particularly on a mandatory basis, without further consultation on the details with both the health service authorities and staff interests. And it is by no means clear that staff co-operation could be assumed following consultation on the Code in its present form if mandatory implementation were envisaged.[273]

In the light of objections mentioned above, officials also adopted an unsympathetic attitude to investigating panels. The outlook for the main recommendations of the Davies Report was therefore bleak. Support derived from relatively powerless consumer groups, whereas within the NHS it possessed few friends and many powerful enemies.

On this occasion the politicians were insufficiently engaged with this problem to provide a counterweight to forces within the NHS. Indeed, for Ministers, the Davies Report was an inconvenient complication at a time of already difficult relations with the medical profession. Owen hoped initially that an improved mechanism for dealing with complaints might feature as part of the Democracy exercise, but this idea was abandoned in favour of a more modest reform. The Minister of State gave his first attention to the Davies Report in April 1975, when he instructed officials to seek advice from relevant advisers and suggested that this problem might be suitable for reference to the Select Committee on the Heath Service Commissioner.[274]

Health Ministers agreed to issue a statement indicating: acceptance for the principle of a uniform code of practice for the handling of complaints, that this code would extend to the entire health service except the family practitioner services, and that further consultations would be held to establish the detail of this code. On the proposal for investigating panels, health Ministers recommended referral to the Select Committee on the Parliamentary Commissioner, which also covered the Health Service Commissioner.[275] This course of action was sanctioned by the Social Services Committee in July 1975.[276]

At first, the Select Committee believed that issues raised by the Davies Report lay outside its remit, but given that the proposal for investigating panels raised important questions about the functions of the Health Service Commissioner, it was decided to take on this enquiry. However, the Select Committee indicated that further delay would ensue, since its investigation was likely to take between eighteen months and two years.[277] DHSS was relieved about this delay, since deferment of the contentious issue of investigating panels would assist in relations with the medical profession. According to Owen, the 'overwhelming need now is a period of peace in the health service'. Although general practitioners were relatively subdued, Owen believed that their leaders were in a mood to make trouble in order to demonstrate their solidarity with the consultants. They were therefore 'searching for an issue of confrontation with the Government'. Deferring action on the Davies proposals seemed like a suitable conciliatory gesture in the quest for reducing the opportunities for confrontation with the doctors. Castle concurred with this analysis.[278] Castle's announcement concerning consultations on a uniform code of practice and reference to the Select Committee was finally made in February 1976. She indicated that the Select Committee would be asked to 'undertake a review of the present jurisdiction of the Health Service Commissioners for England, Wales and Scotland affecting the hospital services having regard to the recommendations of the Davies Committee about Investigating Panels'.[279]

Given the known lack of sympathy of the Health Service Commissioner to some of the main proposals of the Davies Report, as well as a strong link of sentiment between the Select Committee and the Health Service Commissioner, it was unlikely that this investigative mechanism would a throw a life-line to the hard-pressed Davies Committee. The retirement of Sir Alan Marre in 1976, and his replacement by Sir Idwal Pugh made no difference in the response of the Health Service Commissioner on questions raised by the Davies Report.[280]

The Select Committee launched into a full-scale investigation of the health service complaints machinery, retracing the steps of the Davies Committee, but with little explicit reference to the Davies report.[281] The Select Committee report was published on 1 December 1977.[282] Davies himself submitted a brief memorandum to the Committee, written in a combative style, but on the crucial question of investigating panels, conceding that these might be replaced by investigations conducted under the aegis of the Health Service Commissioner.

The work of the Select Committee contained the characteristic strengths and weaknesses of its genre. The evidence constitutes an important documentary source, but the conclusions of the report are not defended by measured argument of the kind found in the Davies Report. The Select Committee matched the Davies Committee in its expressions of disquiet concerning the existing system for handling complaints. It also agreed with Davies on the need for a radically different system, but it proposed a much simpler approach than favoured by Davies, advocating the model adopted in Scotland as a more suitable starting point. Another main departure from the Davies Report was over the question of investigating panels. The Select Committee rejected this suggestion, and instead proposed that all such cases should be handled by the Health Service Commissioner; in order to perform this task, it was suggested that the powers of the Health Service Commissioner should be extended to cases involving clinical judgement. In addition to reiterating the objections to independent regional panels received from NHS authorities, the committee concluded that it was better to build on the mechanism that had established 'a capital of confidence and trust among Health Authorities', reflecting the 'wide acceptance and respect since his office was established in 1973'.[283] Members of the Davies Committee would undoubtedly argue that the Health Service Commissioner was more palatable to the health authorities because it was likely to be less threatening to their interests, and thereby less effective in giving satisfaction to complainants.[284]

Ennals promised early consultations on the Report of the Select Committee.[285] The main effect of the Report of the Select Committee was to cancel out the Davies Report, but without generating viable alternative options. Widening the scope for investigations by the Health Service Commissioner was more palatable to the health authorities, but it was not acceptable to the medical profession. Since co-operation of the medical profession was indispensible for evolving the code of practice for handling complaints, Ministers were unwilling to invite further confrontation with the doctors by raising the question of the Health Service Commissioner's remit in the sphere of clinical activity. Although NHS authorities regarded this extension of the Health Service Commissioner's powers as a reasonable compromise, they also wanted to avoid confrontation with the doctors.[286]

The doctors closed ranks in their opposition to extending the powers of the Health Service Commissioner. They expressed collective outrage over the prospect of being submitted to the injustice of 'double jeopardy'. Any doubt concerning their intentions was dispelled by a strongly worded resolution on this issue featuring at the BMA annual meeting in July 1978, where the proposer of the motion described the intrusion of the Health Service Commissioner into the field of clinical judgement as 'the greatest danger to the NHS since its inception'.[287] A similar view was communicated by a BMA delegation.[288] The mood of hostility was no less among the negotiators representing the consultants at meetings with the JCC held on 2 February, 24 August, and 11 October 1978.[289] Officials reluctantly concluded that 'no involvement of any kind by the Commissioner in clinical judgement complaints would be acceptable to the professions'.[290] Indeed, the JCC warned that no mechanism involving laypeople would be accepted. The most they were willing to contemplate was adoption of some form of medical audit, which might in some way take into account complaints made by patients.

Given the antagonism of the medical profession to the proposals of the Davies Committee and the Select Committee over lay intrusion into the investigation of complaints relating to clinical judgement, further tangible improvement in the complaints mechanism rested on consultations relating to the Davies code of practice, which was circulated for comment to the NHS authorities and a wide range of other bodies in June 1976.[291] Perhaps indicative of the bad relations between consultants and Ministers, the JCC castigated the code as an 'open invitation to patients to complain and it could jeopardise a consultant's position in any ensuing legal action'. Their 'aversion to the code was so profound that only a radical revision would be acceptable to the profession'. This dictum was backed up with a threat of non-co-operation. The JCC insisted that this issue was sufficiently grave to merit a meeting with the Secretary of State.[292] Again perhaps reflecting the bad relations between the Government and hospital doctors, this meeting proved difficult to convene. On some fifteen occasions, dates were rejected or meetings cancelled at the last moment.[293] The Secretary of State finally met the JCC on 21 March 1977. The Chief Medical Officer held a further meeting on 15 July 1977, which instituted detailed discussions on the code of practice and procedures for formal inquires. By the end of the year general agreement had been reached on the mechanism for the initial handling of complaints and on formal inquires.[294] Further progress was delayed by the unproductive discussions over the extension of the Health Service Commissioner's powers. Agreements concerning revision of the code of practice revealed that Ministers had offered major concessions. It was accepted that the code of practice should be greatly simplified, that it would make a point of deterring unnecessary complaints, and that it wold also be employed as a vehicle for encouraging constructive suggestions for improvements in services. It was agreed that the new emphasis would be on better communications rather than on complaints.[295]

Ennals hoped for publication of the code by the end of 1977. However, the degree of departure from the original conception for the code of practice proved so great that the timetable was greatly slowed down. DHSS signified to the Royal Commission on the NHS that the revised code would be issued in 1979. This target also proved unattainable. The change of Government caused further delay. The new procedures for handling complaints were embodied in circular HC(81)5, issued in April 1981, and in a version suitable for consumers, *Comments, suggestions and complaints about your stay in hospital*, published in May 1982, a title which hints how little from the Davies Committee survived the onslaught of the doctors.[296]

Bettering Services for the Mentally Ill

As observed in chapter V, the draft policy document on services for the mentally ill had reached an advanced stage under the Heath administration. Sir Keith Joseph's personal interest in this project was undiminished with the approach of the General Election. His last comments on the draft date from 17 February 1974.[297] By this stage the skeleton document had reached its fourth draft. Joseph was satisfied that it was a sufficiently firm statement of policy to merit being issued as a White Paper. With some reservation, this view was shared by the Permanent Secretary. Officials made preparations for discussions with other departments and selected outside bodies immediately after the General Election.

The incoming Labour Ministers approved this course of action. Barbara Castle notified the Labour MP, Christopher Mayhew, that she intended to publish the policy document as a White Paper, without delay, and without undertaking a further round of general consultation.[298] The first full draft of the White Paper was available on 5 July 1974. This was examined by Ministers and their advisers, without evoking much demand for changes.[299]

David Owen was anxious to bring out the White Paper with the minimum delay. He therefore decreed that there should be no attempt to work out detailed resource implications either nationally or locally. The White Paper would therefore be exclusively concerned with 'the overall philosophy for the development of services'. Barbara Castle also conceived the White Paper as a 'broad social document'. In the existing circumstances, neither saw any prospect for a realising the definite five-year plan, probable ten-year plan, or tentative 20-25 year plan, envisaged at an earlier stage of this policy exercise. Given this limitation, the policy document would be simpler to produce. On this assumption, Owen adopted a provisional target for publication in the New Year. He asked for revision to indicate: (a) that the Government, although unable to state specific local planning targets, was firmly committed to shifting resources to this neglected sector, and details should be given of the timetable for this operation; (b) that Ministers regarded the White Paper as a major policy statement, which implied a 'bolder and more challenging approach by acknowledging and discussing some of the more difficult and controversial aspects of mental illness in present day society'.[300] In less tentative terms than Joseph, Owen produced lists of specific subjects which he wished to see covered in the redrafting. He also asked for the White Paper to set out the historical context in greater detail, and for comparisons to be made with services in other countries.[301]

Owen soon developed reservations about issuing a generalised statement of policy. He decided that a document lacking guidance on resources would seem like a repetition of conventional wisdom. He therefore concluded that Ministers were obliged to include a significant statement about priorities and resources to be allocated. This decision implied delaying publication until May 1975. Owen envisaged that the White Paper would provide information to field authorities, enabling them to draw up detailed plans for the development of their services. While allowing that some flexibility among localities was necessary, he favoured exerting maximum pressure for movement towards the objectives defined by Ministers.[302]

The text of the White Paper was accepted by Owen in January 1975. He was enthusiastic for this document to be adopted by Wales and Scotland. SHHD pointed out that the SHSPC was the appropriate vehicle for generating policy in Scotland; the Welsh Office hesitated, but decided against subscription to the English document.[303]

The need for consultation with Ministers, as well as arguments with the Treasury about specification of norms for services resulted in the May deadline for publication being missed. The resultant discussions largely eliminated specific expenditure commitments of the kind which Owen believed were essential for the credibility of this exercise. The draft White Paper was considered by Ministers on 10 June 1975. Castle argued that the White Paper was an inescapable commitment in view of promises already made to honour the previous administration's decision to issue a strategy document for mental health. Castle claimed that the draft White Paper fulfilled this promise without containing commitments for additional expenditure. Nevertheless, Barnett opposed publication on account of the likelihood that it would complicate negotiations with local authorities and lead to the expectation of increased resources in the future.[304] Castle described this response as 'another example of the philistinism of the Treasury'. She regarded herself as fortunate to escape with reference back to the new Consultative Council on Local Government Finance.[305] Further minor modifications of the White Paper resulted from discussions in the Consultative Council, finally clearing the way for publication of the White Paper.[306] *Better Services for the Mentally Ill* was issued on 16 October 1975.[307]

After the splash into red adopted for the mental handicap White Paper, the department reverted to the customary blue covers and conventional design. This reversion possessed unintentional symbolic significance. The White Paper reflected the compromises demanded when the optimistic philosophy of the Better Services initiative came into contact with the cold economic realism of the oil crisis. From the perspective Ministers, the slow-down of implementation of improvements in services was embarrassing and regrettable, but it

645

saved them from the prospect of controversies over the future direction of services that had complicated the drafting of the mental handicap White Paper. Similar disagreements plagued the mental health field. While there was general agreement with a shift towards community care, experts in the field were at odds about the likely pace of change, the rate of run-down of the old mental hospitals, and the form of organisation to be adopted for the new integrated mental health services. The prospect of slowing the vast engine of the psychiatric services to a snail's pace presented the mechanics with a welcome excuse to escape premature commitment to a particular course and an opportunity to change direction according to the exigencies of situation. Whatever the verdict of history on *Better Services for the Mentally Ill*, Ministers were determined to escape embarrassment stemming from failure to honour grandiose promises of the kind made by Enoch Powell in 1961.[308] Ministers were therefore perhaps relieved in this contentious arena of policy to admit that 'the scope for making progress during the next few years will be very limited', or 'very little material progress in the shape of new physical development is to be expected in the next few years'.[309] Unlike the earlier mental handicap White Paper, *Better Services for the Mentally Ill* was therefore presented as a 'long-term strategic document', or a 'statement of objectives' against which to set whatever short-term improvements were possible in the prevailing conditions of economic constraint.

On the basis of its diffuse remit, the White Paper was a rambling document, considerable in length, commendable for its pious expressions, but deficient in practical content. The document also contained digressions into policy concerning such subjects as secure units, or alcohol and drug abuse, and the development of research, which arguably deserved consideration in separate policy documents. Much of the content of more immediate relevance was confined to generalities. The patient reader could piece together the essential elements of policy, which were generally a restatement of long-established principles: the mentally ill should be treated locally, as outpatients to the maximum extent, with residential facilities and hospitals being available for cases of special need. The immediate priorities were to build up community services, complemented by psychiatric services based on district general hospitals, and to progressively reduce reliance on the old mental hospitals. The White Paper gave firm reassurances that closure of existing mental hospitals would not occur until alternative services were fully in place. It was expected that progress towards this goal would take place slowly over a twenty-five year period. It recommended, as in previous planning documents produced in connection with reorganisation, that the various groups of personnel

646

working with mental patients should be combined into teams operating on a district basis. In fact, this represented only a limited step towards integration, since the primary care team, the therapeutic team, and the social work team under this model maintained a separate existence and worked in parallel rather than in harmony, and were not even sure to be organised in compatible geographical units. The White Paper promised that when resources permitted, staffing levels would be improved to allow for multi-disciplinary assessment of patients' needs, as well as greater emphasis on early intervention and prevention. In order to improve co-ordination, the White Paper briefly alluded to the importance of joint planning, including the great expectations from the Joint Consultative Committees to be set up as a consequence of reorganisation. Statistical information and guide-lines and were scattered through the White Paper, but were difficult to evaluate, containing little indication about the progress expected towards meeting these targets in the short term. This latter deficiency was to some extent corrected in chapter VII of *Priorities for Health and Personal Social Services in England*, which in the course of six pages condensed all the meaningful content of the 91-page White Paper. The *Priorities* consultative document described what was likely to be achieved by 1979/80 in the provision of new and substitute services. It was hoped that the population of mental hospitals would fall from 90,000 in 1974 to 75,000 in 1979.[310] However, the positive commitments of 1976 were largely eliminated from *The Way Forward* in the following year. While such sectors as mental health, mental handicap and the elderly, were still accepted as priorities, *The Way Forward* appreciated that the *Priorities* document was too optimistic in its forecasts; it therefore reverted to vaguer statements concerning progress towards the goals adopted for these services.[311]

Befitting its modest pretensions, *Better Services for the Mentally Ill* received a subdued reception. It excited no expectations of radical improvements in care. As already noted, the steady flow of hospital scandals and enquiries reminded the public of the slow pace of improvement in the mental health services. The mental hospital lobby blamed this problem on demoralisation of staff stemming from the Government's policy of running down these institutions. The Royal Commission on the NHS was receptive to this argument. It complained that mental hospitals had been undermined by the policy of diverting resources into psychiatric units of district general hospitals. It called for the Government to admit a 'continuing need for most of the mental illness hospitals, and we recommend that the health departments should now state categorically that they no longer expect health authorities to close them unless they are very isolated, in very bad repair or obviously redundant due to major

647

shifts of population'.[312] Such sentiments indicate the high degree of frustration generated by the slowness of improvement within the mental health services. The Better Services initiative had brought about the crumbling of the old services without creating a sufficiency of superior replacements. In this worst of all worlds situation, it was understandable that laypersons became suspicious of change and reverted to the security of the old system.

As already noted, one of the most consistent reasons given for the terrible flaws in the performance of mental hospitals was the inadequacy of management arrangements. Romantics believed that things were better in the days of the Medical Superintendents, and they inclined to lay the blame for the scandals at the door of NHS reorganisation management arrangements. Throughout the 1970s, concern was expressed about the seriousness weaknesses in management within mental hospitals.[313] This problem was specifically addressed by a working group set up in 1977 under the chairmanship of Mr T E Nodder, a Deputy Secretary in DHSS; as an official in the Long Term Policy Division, Nodder had been closely involved with planning for reorganisation. He was therefore well-informed about the history of NHS management arrangements. The Nodder Report was not published until September 1980, and then in a form suitable for limited circulation.[314] In order to correct the vacuum in authority left by the lapse of the Medical Superintendent, and on account of the tendency for mental health administration to fall into the hands of relatively junior staff, the Report proposed the establishment of District Psychiatric Teams to oversee strategic policy and general management issues at the health district level. This team would not have authority over personal social services, but the Report proposed that it should contain social services representatives and make its decisions in the light of an overview of the entire local service. At the unit level, the Report suggested appointment of small Hospital Management Teams, comprising three members.

The Nodder Report contained a lucid analysis of the general problem of management, and laid down a model framework for management by objectives. The report described in detail specific standards relevant to mental hospitals and even provided practical check-lists for the evaluation of services. The latter had been evolved for use in Wales and were derived from the Welsh Office. Although largely concerned with the technical question of management, the Nodder Report argued that the procedures it laid down were a necessary condition to improving care in mental hospitals and setting in place a system in which staff were more highly motivated to achieve a more adequate level degree of satisfaction and rehabilitation of patients under their care.

Although peripheral to this study, it is important to note that the Labour Government capitulated to the growing demand for a review of the Mental Health Act 1959. This campaign was spearheaded by the National Council for Civil Liberties, and especially the National Association for Mental Health (usually known as MIND by this date), and particularly by Larry Gostin, its Legal and Welfare Rights Officer. The thinking of MIND was particularly influenced by a succession of complaints relating to the special hospitals, Broadmoor, Moss Side, and Rampton.[315] Other proposals for review emanated from the Royal College of Psychiatrists.[316]

In January 1975 David Owen announced that the Government would review the Mental Health Act.[317] This project was trusted to an interdepartmental committee of officials chaired by a member of DHSS, which also provided the secretariat. On 5 August 1976 a substantial consultative document was issued.[318] The rival parties expressed their attitude to the consultative document at a conference held on 25 October 1976, when MIND indicated its dissatisfaction with the timidity of the Government's approach. Subsequently, Ennals was frequently asked about progress with the White Paper, which he had promised for 1977.[319]

In preparing the White Paper, officials took account of publications produced by such groups as MIND and the British Association of Social Workers, more than three hundred comments received on the consultative document, and reports emanating from Lord Butler's Committee on Mentally Abnormal Offenders. By the end of August 1977, agreement had been reached on all sections of the White Paper, except the part dealing with protection of the public, where the Home Office took the lead. At this point the timetable slowed down, jeopardising the possibility of amending legislation in the 1978/79 session. This was a disappointment to Ennals, who complained to Rees that the delay had caused him embarrassment and led to accusation that the Government was intentionally delaying action to amend the mental health legislation.[320]

The draft White Paper restricted itself to modest proposals which in the main were thought to be uncontroversial. DHSS attempted to steer an intermediate course, responding to such organisations as MIND, which urged a radical review of the law with a view to attaining greater protection for the patient and rights of access to enlightened services, but also noting the more conservative demands from NHS interests, who wanted clarification of the rights of staff. The draft White Paper sought to establish a new balance between treatment and detention. The proposals aimed to clarify the rights of voluntary patients, set out a clear legal framework regarding compulsory treatment, remove uncertainties among professional staff about their position regarding these matters, and introduce new safeguards for patients. The Government acquiesced to the widespread call for automatic reviews by Mental Health Tribunals. The draft White Paper also raised possibilities for a new compulsory power in the community to avoid unnecessary admission to hospital, introduction of a power for courts to remand offenders to hospital instead of to prison, and the sponsorship of experimental schemes for patients' advisers. The draft White Paper also suggested the updating of terminology, for instance at long last eliminating the term 'subnormality', and replacing it by the less rebarbative 'mental handicap'.

The draft White Paper was discussed by Ministers in July 1978. The Home Office and DHSS had failed to agree over the circumstances in which restriction orders of unlimited duration could be imposed. DHSS wanted the order to relate to the length of the sentence which the crime would attract. An order without limit would only be made for cases where the maximum penalty was life imprisonment. DHSS believed that unlimited orders at the discretion of a judge would be criticised on civil liberties grounds. The Home Office was concerned about such examples as persistent delusions or sexual compulsions, which raised the possibility that the person might commit a serious crime. It argued that it was absurd for the crime to be committed before making an order. The Home Office was particularly concerned to avoid public outcry of the kind associated with sex attacks. The Home Office believed that sufficient protection was provided by the proposal for biennial review of such cases. Ministers decided by a majority to adopt the Home Office alternative.[321]

The White Paper was published on 12 September 1978.[322] Although there was general agreement that the White Paper represented was an improvement on the existing situation, its concessions were insufficient to satisfy such organisations as MENCAP or MIND. From the libertarian stand-point adopted by the latter, the White Paper was an 'unforgivable betrayal of the rights and liberties of psychiatric patients'.[323] For MENCAP, the White Paper was equally unsatisfactory because it failed to emancipate the handicapped from a legal framework designed for entirely different purposes. Other groups such as the Royal College of Psychiatrists were disappointed that the White Paper contained no provision for a body serving the purposes of the Scottish Mental Welfare Commission. The *Times* pronounced that there was still insufficient agreement to justify legislation on the basis of the White Paper.[324] Heated discussions once again broke out, the results of which were not again considered by Ministers until 1981.[325] These deliberations formed the prelude to the further White Paper of 1981, and the

Mental Health Act 1983, which embodied further concessions to the demands of the critics of the 1978 White Paper.

Policy for Mental Handicap
Deflection of the HAS away from the mental handicap services created a gap in the visitation mechanism relating to the vulnerable groups most in need of improvement of services. Soon after his appointment, Owen expressed pessimism about existing arrangements, which he believed would lead to:

> more scandals, more circulars from the Department, but very little of the executive drive which *Better Services for the Mentally Handicapped* certainly demanded if it was to have any effect. Good intentions are not enough. I just do not believe that the AHAs are capable of making the necessary process towards local community care.

Owen instructed officials to give serious consideration to the proposal in the Labour Party Green Paper for a separate National Service for the Mentally Handicapped, supervised by an Executive directly responsible to Ministers, with the longer term intention of placing this service in the hands of local authorities.[326] Officials were less than enthusiastic about Owen's ideas. However, some action was clearly needed. Reacting to expressions of concern from the pressure groups, in February 1975, the Secretary of State announced that she would establish a non-statutory Development Group for this sector to act as a national advisory body concerned with the formulation of policy, and also one or more interdisciplinary Development Teams to supervise implementation of policy at the field level.[327] The National Development Group for the Mentally Handicapped was established without delay.[328] It was chaired by Professor Peter Mittler, Professor of Special Education and Director of the Hester Adrian Research Centre at Manchester University, who was recognised as an outspoken and enlightened leader of opinion within his field.[329] Dr G B Simon, the Vice-Chairman of the Development Group, was appointed Director of the Development Team.

The short consultative paper concerning proposals for establishing the Development Team was not issued until November 1975. Subsequent discussions exposed important differences of opinion. The Development Group was apprehensive that the Development Team was evolving into a separate and distinct entity, undermining the Group's view that the two bodies should be inseparable and that teams should be constituted from a large panel, according to the needs of the situation. There was also difficulty in overcoming the suspicion of the interest groups about the professional complexion of the team hierarchy. Since Dr Simon came from a medical background, Owen agreed to appoint three Associate Directors, one representing nursing, and two from local government. This top-heavy structure was not popular with officials or the Development Group.[330]

The National Development Group took the care of children as its first priority. It was energetic in the pursuit of its remit, producing a Bulletin, five informative and sometimes substantial pamphlets, and an important report on the mentally handicapped in hospital.[331]

The Development Team was a less threatening operation than the HAS. Its visitations occurred by invitation, and reports were made direct to the field authority. After the Normansfield scandal, the Secretary of State reserved the right to request intervention by the Team, although this power was not used. The Development Team was an exclusively advisory body. The teams were more ephemeral than their HAS counterparts. In the period under consideration, the work of the Development Team was described in two general reports, shorter in length and more restrained in character than the published HAS reports.[332]

Following the completion of its report on the mentally handicapped in hospital, the future of the National Development Group was in doubt. Already in 1978, officials were in favour of disbanding the group in order to free its members for participating of the department's review of the mental handicap services. The Development Group was not immediately suppressed, but its activity was confined to the review.[333] By the date of the General Election it was clear that the Development Group was unlikely to survive. The decision was finally made by the new administration, which also suspended the preparation of circulars based on its work.[334] The Development Team was allowed to continue, as the counterpart to the HAS, which was also not under threat.

In the short time of their operation before the change of Government, the Development Group and Team exerted a positive influence on services and they succeeded in creating an enlightened atmosphere surrounding the conduct of policy. As in the case of the reports of the HAS, the Development Team reports realistically described a 'sombre landscape', with only limited points of illumination.[335] As the succession of reports of hospital enquires indicated, mental handicap hospitals were not immune from the worst excesses of failure resulting from flaws in the system. The report on Normansfield, published in November 1978 was among the most disturbing of these reports.[336] The Prime Minister was shaken by the gruesome evidence concerning maltreatment of patients. He accused DHSS of complacency in dealing with this problem, and he insisted that Ennals should make a much less defensive admission than was originally intended of the health department's responsibility for these failures.[337]

The extent of shortcomings in care was also exposed by research exercises conducted into specific client groups such as children in long-stay hospitals. It has already been noted that representations by the Council for Children's Welfare to Barbara Castle resulted in more active monitoring of conditions faced by children in long-stay hospitals. This organisation continued to draw attention to this problem, for instance in a widely-publicised pamphlet produced by a working party chaired by Peggy Jay, and also containing Virginia Bottomley, who was at the time an ILEA social worker.[338] A further member of this group was Maureen Oswin who, under the auspices of the Spastics Society, conducted an important investigation into the wards housing children with multiple handicaps in eight mental handicap hospitals. Her study was published on 4 April 1978 .[339] The Oswin study caused a stir on a smaller scale, but reminiscent of the *Sans Everything* affair a decade earlier. One of the results of this new wave of concern was initiation of a new campaign which became known as 'Exodus', which demanded removal of all handicapped children from hospitals by a target date of 1 January 1982.[340] On this occasion the Secretary of State contributed to the public discussion, not disputing Oswin's conclusions, but pointing out that his department had reached the same conclusions about the need to improve services, and confirming that the necessary alterations were taking place.[341] Indeed, a review of developments in the mental handicap services undertaken by officials in association with the National Development Group, in parallel with the Jay enquiry, reached pessimistic conclusions about the state of the mental handicap services. Officials frankly admitted the existence of 'severe shortcomings within the services, which have been made worse by poor leadership, weak managerial capacity and interest in this field, related to the persistent low attraction of the work for professionals. Lack of money is also a major factor'.[342] This review of mental handicap was not completed until after the end of the Labour administration.[343]

A parallel review of the mental handicap services was conducted in Scotland under the aegis of the SHSPC and the Advisory Council for Social Work, by a committee chaired by Mr D A Peters, District Administrator, Renfrew Health District. This committee was established in 1975 and it reported in 1978.[344] In presenting his draft report to the SHSPC, Peters admitted that steps towards implementation had been 'inadequate and almost without exception have had little effect on the transfer of patients from hospital to community care'.[345] As with the parallel planning documents dealing with the elderly and the elderly with mental disability mentioned

653

below, the Peters Report acknowledged the substantial resource implications of its proposals. In view of the immediate constraints on expansion, it anticipated a short delay before the development of community care could be resumed. The Peters Report rejected establishment of a separately administered service for the mentally handicapped, and it stressed the continuing role of hospital services for the severely mentally handicapped.[346] A similar conclusion was reached by the Royal Commission on the NHS.[347]

Jay Report

There was persistent concern about the low levels of training and inferior status of the staff employed in the field of mental handicap. This had also been noted by the Briggs Committee, which recommended separate investigation of this problem. Soon after his appointment, Owen outlined a proposal for a Mental Handicap Executive, which he envisaged would oversee the establishment of a new caring profession for the mentally handicapped, which would be part of the local authority social services. It was appreciated that transfer from the nursing-orientated ethos of the large mental handicap institutions to the rehabilitation-based work of social service departments would be a politically sensitive, complex and expensive operation.[348]

In her speech at the National Society for Mental Handicapped Children's Conference in February 1975, Barbara Castle listed this problem as one of the issues upon which she would institute an investigation. In July 1975 she announced establishment of this enquiry, including the terms of reference and identification of the members.[349] This committee was chaired by Mrs Peggy Jay JP, an obvious choice on account of her record of commitment in this field, but also because of her Labour connections. Mrs Jay was chair of the North Camden CHC, and also a leading figure in the National Association for the Welfare of Children in Hospital, and the Council for Children's Welfare. This role as an activist on mental handicap was laudable, but not viewed in all quarters as a benefit, since she was a known advocate of community care, and therefore it was believed by the consultant and hospital union interests that she was insufficiently appreciative of the role of hospital services. These fears were exacerbated by the pamphlet, *No Childhood*. Although the published version played down Jay's role, it added to distrust in hospital circles about her partisanship.

In its rather lengthy and convoluted remit, the Jay Committee was asked to:

consider recommendation 74 of the Report of the Committee on Nursing (Briggs Committee), in particular to inquire into the nursing and care of the mentally handicapped in the light of developing policies, to examine the roles and aims of nurses and residential care staff required by the health and personal social services for the care of mentally handicapped adults and children; the interrelationships between them and other health and personal social services staff; how existing staff can best fulfil these roles and aims; in the interest of making the best use of available skills and experience, the possibilities of the career movement of staff from one sector or category to another; the implications for recruitment and training; and to make recommendations.

This Committee was a large body comprising 18 members in addition to Mrs Jay.[350] This large size reflected the attempt to achieve balance between health authority and local authority interests, to give representation to the professional specialisms engaged in the field of mental handicap, and to ensure representation for Scotland and Wales. The committee contained two medically-qualified members and four nurses. These together with the GNC member, the health service trade unionist, and the clinical psychologist, represented the hospital interest. These nine members were the counterbalance to the eight members and the chairperson, who broadly represented local government, social work and the social sciences. In addition to Mrs Jay, there were four women on the committee.

The Jay Committee started work on 17 July 1975. In the expectation that Briggs legislation would feature in the parliamentary timetable for the following year, the committee was under pressure to report quickly. Repeated delays in the Briggs timetable permitted a more relaxed timetable. The committee finally completed its deliberations in November 1978. The two-volume Jay Report was published on 8 March 1979.[351] Since the main report was 184 pages in length, the Jay Committee also produced a short summary for the benefit of staff working in the service.

The Jay Committee was guided by a 'Philosophy' outlining a 'Model of Care', which constituted one of the boldest features of the report. This statement of principles was broadly consistent with advanced thinking in the field of mental handicap. It proposed that all mentally handicapped people should be treated no differently than other members of the community and have access to the same services as others. Care should therefore approximate as much as possible to the circumstances of normal family life. It was outside the remit of the committee to pronounce on the pattern of services, but their thinking implied a radical shift away from institutional care and towards the community, precisely the aim adopted in the early drafts of *Better Services for the Mentally Handicapped*. To the extent that residential care was needed, it was proposed that this should be provided in small units, as an integral part of the local community. The description of the model for care envisaged that even the most severe cases of handicap would be housed in 'home' type of accommodation. Terminology associated with medical treatment and hospitals was avoided almost entirely.

In order to realise these aspirations, it was calculated that residential care staff needed to be doubled in numbers to reach a target of 60,000 for Great Britain. Initially, the Jay Committee hoped that this build-up of numbers would occur in 12 years, but the report abandoned this target as unrealistic in view of the likely restrictions on public expenditure.

Following the Briggs recommendation that 'a new caring profession for the mentally handicapped should emerge gradually', it was proposed that a common training should be developed for NHS and local authority staff. The Jay Committee went further than Briggs by proposing abandonment of the nursing model for training in favour of the social services alternative. The committee was divided about the organisation of this new training. Consistent with the social services option, a majority favoured giving this responsibility to the existing Central Council for Education and Training in Social Work, providing a specialist advisory council was established within CCETSW to oversee the changes. The basic qualification proposed was the Certificate in Social Service, a three-year course, suitably adapted for those specialising in the care of the mentally handicapped, or mentally handicapped children. However it was recognised that assimilating mental handicap into the social work profession possessed certain disadvantages: it would involve abandonment of registration and the associated status provided by the nursing qualification, whereas the Certificate in Social Service was a relatively new and not entirely satisfactory qualification. Consequently, there was some feeling on the Jay Committee that the CCETSW was not a suitable body to be trusted with the mental handicap qualification. However, on the basis of past experience, the nursing training bodies also possessed severe disadvantages, and the Briggs reforms, as well as developing EEC requirements, were likely to exacerbate these disadvantages. Accordingly, two members of the Committee recommended creation of a new independent training council entrusted with the development of the new mental handicap training. Once this was established, consideration would be given to assimilation with the CCETSW.[352] A minority report by Mr D O Williams, Assistant General Secretary of COHSE and Chairman of the Staff Side of the Nurses and Midwives Whitley Council, recommended that there should be a unified residential care service administered by the NHS and staffed by mental handicap nurses, equipped for the task by further modification to their training.[353]

In his initial statement on the Jay Report, Ennals was primarily concerned to prevent the collapse of morale among hospital nursing staff. While he expressed general support for the integration of the mentally handicapped into the community, he emphasised that the existing mental handicap nursing staff would continue to occupy a key role and that the proposal for major changes in patterns of training would be subjected to the fullest consultation and were likely to take many years to bring to fruition. Ennals indicated the way in which consultation would be handled in England, Scotland and Wales. He announced that his own department would publish a series of discussion documents on the various aspects of mental handicap policy.[354]

Divisions within the Jay Committee were indicative of the lack of consensus concerning future policy for mental handicap. On account of the serious implications for their status, staff groups were preoccupied with the proposals for alterations in training arrangements. A fierce and emotional debate on these issues was in full sway, even before the publication of the report. The nursing and social work interests were entirely at odds. Adoption of the social services model for training was presented as betrayal of responsibilities to patients by the nurses, while perpetuation of the nursing model was regarded by social workers as a refutation of the hard-won gains in the mental handicap services made during the 1970s. This impasse was in fact a blessing to hard-pressed politicians, who regarded the Jay Report as unrealistic and even utopian in its expectations. They detected no way of releasing resources on anything like the scale required to finance the new model of care, or even the more expensive form of training for the new unified care profession. As the consultation process was launched, there was little ground for optimism. Even within DHSS it was admitted that 'many will no doubt see mental handicap as remaining a Cinderella service and may suggest that the winding up of the National Development Group and the failure to provide additional resources means that the mentally handicapped are being abandoned to their fate. This last view is likely to be emphasised by the pressure groups and their voice is likely to be the loudest and most publicised'.[355]

Policy for the Elderly

The elderly constituted the obvious omission in Crossman's programme for formal policy commitments relating to groups likely to find themselves incarcerated in long-stay hospitals. Of all the groups under consideration, the elderly were the largest, and the client group for whom the most obvious argument existed for maximisation of community care. Although the established policy of community care was expected to bring benefits to the elderly, the health departments were slow to draw together the various strands of their thinking to produce a comprehensive policy document to guide the promotion of better services for this large and expanding sector of the community.

Prospects of escalating costs, and the chance that community services would bring about economies, attracted the Heath administration to refer the question of the elderly to the Central Policy Review Staff, for one of the first Programme Analysis and Review exercises.[356] The elderly was the first and only offer put forward by DHSS in the first batch of about a dozen topics for PAR investigation. A brief interim statement on the problems of the elderly was presented to Ministers in January 1972, but at Joseph's suggestion it was withdrawn pending further discussions between departments.[357] The Treasury was apprehensive that the continuation of this PAR exercise would yield few economies and spark off demand for additional resources across a broad front. At the next discussion among Ministers, further short-term and long-term studies were sanctioned, with priority being given to housing questions, on the understanding that the exercise was primarily designed to reallocate resources within existing expenditure totals.[358] In April 1973 CPRS provided Ministers with a digest of data relating to health services for the elderly. Ministers were alarmed by the expenditure implications of meeting even modest guide-lines for community services. For instance, it was pointed out that the home nursing service would need to be expanded at least five-fold. It was also evident that no offsetting savings were possible on the hospital front, where considerable expansion of geriatric provision was envisaged. In view of limitations in resources, as well as cut-backs in local authority expenditure, it was decided to scale down planning to concentrate on pilot projects and the needs of the severely handicapped.[359]

Bettering services for the elderly was not picked up with alacrity by the Labour administration. The elderly were missed out in the deliberations of the Expenditure Sub-Committee on preventive medicine, and in the *Prevention and Health: Everybody's Business* consultative document, both of which are further considered in the next section of this chapter. The White Paper, *Prevention and Health* confined itself to homely advice, rather like a parish magazine, telling the elderly that they would benefit by wearing 'well-fitting shoes, a rubber ferule at the end of a walking stick, the avoidance of slippery polished floors and loose mats or carpet edges'. With respect to more systematic planning of their services, the elderly were told to expect a White Paper in 1979.[360]

More specific was the consultative document produced for the priorities exercise, which contained six pages of basic data about services for the elderly, including the first comprehensive set of provisional guide-lines for these services ever issued in an official publication. It was accepted that services fell seriously short, even with respect to these provisional guide-lines.[361] Ennals committed himself to issue revised guide-lines on services for the elderly in the autumn of 1977. However, this pledge was instantly regretted. The successor consultative document, issued in September 1977, eliminated the section on services for the elderly, erased information about specific guide-lines, and reverted to the technique of vagueness about desirable objectives.[362]

In view of the expectation of decisive leadership from the Government aroused at the conference on the elderly convened by Ennals in July 1977, when he promised a Green Paper or White Paper on the needs of the very old, Ministers accepted that they were obliged to offer further clarification of policy. It was agreed to produce a discussion document dealing with both health and social security matters, followed by a White Paper in the spring of 1979.[363]

In the spring of 1978 Ennals submitted his draft discussion document to Ministers, with a view to publication in June. The document was slight in its content and mainly concerned with social security. The main issues of concern to Ministers were the proposals relating to the age of retirement and the equalisation of pensions. They also expressed disquiet about the proposed title: 'A Happier Old Age'.[364] After dilution of commitments on the sensitive social security issues at the request of the Cabinet, *A Happier Old Age* was published on 27 June 1978 under the signatures of Ennals, Morris and Orme.[365] Commenting on the use of much larger type than was usual in official reports, it was suggested that this was a thoughtful concession to elderly readers, but also the document 'would look too short with normal type'. The discussion document was criticised for being vacuous and patronising.[366] Notwithstanding its limitations, the discussion document attracted a huge volume of comment, creating pressure for production of a more substantial policy statement.

As with other policy initiatives, expectation of a General Election in the autumn of 1978 caused the proposal for a White Paper on the elderly to be deferred.[367] In view of the likelihood that the Government would not be able to issue more than a tentative 'progress report', Ennals was not averse to this delay. He regarded July 1979 as the next feasible date for the definitive policy statement.[368] This document was not completed before the end of the Callaghan administration. The new Conservative administration wrestled further with this policy document, which was eventually reincarnated in 1981 as a White Paper. With respect to its modest content on the health and social services, this document was free from specific targets and therefore without the implied expenditure commitments of the kind found in *Priorities for Health and Personal Social Services in England*.[369]

By contrast with the laborious evolution of the policy document relating to the care of the elderly in England, the Scottish planning system offered a much easier and more painless route to a similar end. A multi-disciplinary working party was set up in 1975 under the aegis of the SHSPC and the Advisory Council for Social Work, chaired by Mrs E M M Macdonald. This was asked to 'advise on national policies relating to the provision of health, social work and related services for the elderly'. A progress report was issued in 1976, and the main report was published in March 1979.[370] To the irritation of the Treasury, this report contained expenditure implications on many fronts, particularly with respect to its recommendations concerning meeting targets for community care. Any satisfaction within the Treasury concerning elimination of commitments of this kind from the English draft White Paper was tempered by anguish at retention of the spirit of the *Priorities for Health and Personal Social Services* in the parallel Scottish document.[371]

(ix) PREVENTION AND HEALTH

It was by no means evident that the unified and reorganised health service would improve on the inadequate performance of the earlier fragmented service in the field of prevention and promotion. Much depended on leadership from the central health departments. The following paragraphs will complete the case studies of fluoridation, tobacco, and family limitation, each of which constituted a dominant element in the Government's strategy for prevention. It will then consider some other aspects of preventive medicine which impinged on the consciousness of Ministers, and especially the efforts made under the Labour administration to evolve a more rational framework for preventive medicine. This initiative was by no means the result of a spontaneous flash of inspiration from Ministers or the health departments. The pressure to give greater attention to prevention by the mid-seventies became impossible to resist, partly because of the growing effectiveness of pressure groups concerned with such issues as smoking, alcohol, and diet. Many of these groups had either been founded or resuscitated in the mid-sixties, and were reaching their maturity as political forces in the mid-seventies. Their influence was reinforced as a result of revitalisation in the field of preventive medicine, involving reaffirmation of the dominance of preventive measures in past improvements in health. There was widespread demand for restoration of these values, and ample evidence to support the proposition that prevention and promotion would yield major benefits in health, and potentially contribute to ironing out embarrassing inequalities in health status between the regions, occupational groups and social classes.

Both fluoridation and smoking continued to attract attention among MPs, and both were the subject of cross-party alliances. Although fluoridation was the lesser issue with respect to the loss of human life, it attracted a much greater volume of attention from MPs. Also, whereas opinion in Parliament gradually drifted towards acceptance of the need for action on smoking and health, anti-fluoridation feeling showed no sign of diminution. The Royal Commission on the NHS also showed more concern with fluoridation than with smoking. It was of course favourable to action on both fronts, and recognised that only limited success had been achieved in combating smoking, but it paid only scant regard to this problem, which is a noticeable contrast with its detailed commentary and strong recommendations on fluoridation.[372]

Fluoridation.
The case history of fluoridation demonstrates that squaring the circle was not rendered easier by 1974 reorganisation of the health service and water undertakings. Under the Water Act 1973 and the Local Government (Scotland) Act 1973, there was a massive simplification in the water supply administration. The numerous undertakings operative before 1974 were consolidated into nine Regional Water Authorities in England, and in Wales, the Welsh National Water Development Authority. In Scotland, water supply was placed under the Regional Councils. Since the Area Health Authorities were not coterminous with the regional water authorities, action over fluoridation required concerted action by a number of AHAs operating in conjunction with one or more water undertakings. In reality, the administrative confusion was little different from before 1974. Also, during their settling-in period, the new health and water authorities were reticent to court unpopularity by plunging into contentious initiatives like fluoridation.

Ever the optimist, Dr Owen was determined not to abdicate authority over fluoridation.[373] In April 1975 Owen offered unambiguous support for fluoridation, basing his confidence on the impressive body of authoritative support for this measure. He concluded that 'over 20 years of careful and intensive epidemiological studies have demonstrated the safety of controlled-water fluoridation as consistently as its effectiveness in the prevention of dental decay'. The Minister confirmed that fluoridation would count as one of the measures constituting a part of the duties of AHAs to provide facilities for the prevention of illness. He expressed confidence that the 'more democratic health authorities' introduced by Labour would press forward with fluoridation.[374] The new health authorities were advised that it would be unreasonable for one health authority to obstruct another in the pursuit of fluoridation. Also, while there was no legal requirement on water authorities to obey requests from AHAs for fluoridation, Ministers suggested that the Government expected them to co-operate and introduce fluoride into their water supplies as soon as reasonably practicable.

Owen's horse fell at the first jump. In Cornwall the County Council had long favoured fluoridation and had taken the first steps towards this objective before reorganisation. Fluoridation was taken up promptly by the new Cornwall and Isles of Scilly Area Health Authority. This policy was quickly activated, consistently maintained, and the AHA gained an important ally when it was supported by its Community Health Councils. Also the Devon AHA gave support for fluoridation in principle. As the MP for Plymouth Devonport, Owen no doubt looked on these events with satisfaction.[375] In the face of Government policy, the South West Water Authority refused to comply with the request of the Cornwall AHA; it also expressed a negative attitude towards fluoridation, which attracted widespread publicity; and finally it made preparations for terminating the supply of fluoridated water in parts of Cornwall already participating the fluoridation scheme.

In order to escape humiliation at the hand of the South West Water Authority, Owen turned for support to Denis Howell at the Department of the Environment.[376] Howell refused to comply. The Department of the Environment took the line that the water authorities were responsible to provide a wholesome supply of water. Whereas fluoridated water was wholesome, it was clear that preventive medicine was not a function of water authorities. Since there was no statutory means of control over the water authorities in this respect, the Department of the Environment was not in a position to require them to comply with a request to fluoridate. It was therefore proposed to allow the decision whether to fluoridate to rest with the water authorities. Despite this defensive attitude, the Department of the Environment agreed to consider updating its earlier guidance on the question of fluoridation.[377]

In March 1976 the South West Water Authority formally rejected the application from the Cornwall AHA to introduce fluoridation, and it decided to suspend the existing supply of fluoridated water to part of Cornwall. The authority claimed that it was responding to expressions of concern from the public. Owen once again complained to Howell and asked either for more supportive action from the Department of the Environment, or discussion concerning the taking of powers to compel water authorities to fluoridate their water supplies.[378] After some delay Howell merely repeated his offer to consider issuing updated guide-lines relating to fluoridation.[379] Further unproductive correspondence between Owen and Howell evoked the customary defence that the water industry was not convinced that it could withstand a challenge in the courts against fluoridation. This conclusion seemed perverse and disappointing to DHSS, especially in the light of authoritative support for fluoridation in 1975 from the World Health Organisation, and in the following year from the Royal College of Physicians.[380] The health departments had consistently encouraged fluoridation, and in 1975 they provided resources to offset the costs of any authority undertaking this measure.

In Scotland, fluoridation was consistently advocated by the Scottish Health Services Planning Council on the advice of the National Dental Consultative Committee. It was agreed to take action in advance of the Royal College of Physicians Report and recommend the Secretary of State to encourage the fluoridation of all water supplies in Scotland. It was also agreed that Health Board members should be encouraged to proselytise in favour of fluoridation in their areas.[381] The SHSPC obtained support from Ministers and persuaded the Scottish Office to send out supportive circulars to health and water authorities. However, Millan was unwilling to take further action on account of the danger of provoking a counter-offensive from the anti-fluoridation lobby.[382]

Although the health departments were satisfied that the accumulation of medical evidence was steadily strengthening the case for fluoridation, the anti-fluoridation lobby was resourceful in attracting publicity concerning threats to health from fluoridation. Consequently, legal advice sought by the Thames Water Authority and Lord Douglas of Barloch suggested that the anti-fluoridation organisations might be in a position to mount a challenge to water authorities which introduced fluoride into their water. Following this legal advice the regional water authorities, supported by the National Water Council, took the line that no further action should be taken to fluoridate water until the legal position was clarified.

This conclusion was embarrassing to health Ministers, who had instructed the NHS authorities to take up the option of fluoridation. Prompted by their dental officers and in many cases supported by CHCs and LHCs, the NHS authorities had demonstrated widespread enthusiasm.[383] There was now a risk that the fluoridation initiative might completely collapse owing to reticence on the part of the water authorities and ambiguities in the law.

The embarrassment of the health departments was increased by the prominence given to fluoridation in major planning documents. The Court Report on the Child Health Services (1976) called for fluoridation. The DHSS consultative document, *Priorities for Health and Personal Social Services* (1976) announced setting aside funds to help AHAs with the capital cost of fluoridation. Its sister consultative document, *Prevention and Health: Everybody's Business*, also published in March 1976, similarly identified fluoridation as one of the key aspects of preventive medicine. Fluoridation was also highlighted in the Scottish planning document, *The Health Service in Scotland: the Way Forward*. Fluoridation also featured in meetings on preventive medicine encouraged by DHSS, at which Ministers promised that the first of the follow-up papers to *Prevention and Health: Everybody's Business* would relate to fluoridation. This paper was duly drafted by the relevant advisory committees in the three parts of Great Britain. However, the consolidation of opposition to fluoridation among water authorities forced the health departments to reconsider their plans and in some confusion suspend preparations for the proposed policy document on fluoridation. This effort was further undermined by the deliberations of the Social Services and Employment Sub-Committee of the Expenditure Committee, which considered fluoridation fully in the course of its investigation of preventive medicine. Although the bulk of technical evidence reaching this committee favoured fluoridation, some of the members were clearly hostile and unreceptive; their report concluded that further research was needed in this field before fluoridation was adopted as policy by the Government.[384] Although in their subsequent White Paper, *Prevention and Health*, the health departments rejected this view, fluoridation was accorded less prominence than in the preceding consultative document.[385]

After a delay occasioned by Owen's promotion, the fluoridation problem was handled by Roland Moyle, but the latter discovered no opportunity to advance on the position arrived at by Owen. Moyle found himself constantly under pressure to reduce the backing given to AHAs over fluoridation, as for instance, when the large Hampshire AHA recommended fluoridation against the wishes of its county council and 10 out of 12 of its district councils.[386] In Scotland, Ministers were persistently criticised for failing to implement a settled policy decision, but without effect.[387]

The Callaghan administration ended without resolution of the impasse over fluoridation. By 1979, there was virtual unanimity among health authorities about the desirability of fluoridation, but less than 10 per cent of the English and Welsh population had access to fluoridated water supplies, while the extent of fluoridation was negligible in Scotland and Northern Ireland.[388] This result was ascribed to the 'fanatical advocacy of pure,(supposedly pure) water by a small group believing every bit of ill-founded, scientific comment on the risks of fluoride, but none of the carefully documented evidence that fluoridation is not dangerous'.[389]

Evidence in favour of fluoridation continued to accumulate, and strenuous support was forthcoming from the Royal Commission on the NHS.[390] However, despite their continuing supportive attitude towards fluoridation, the Callaghan administration was reticent to commit itself to legislation, and it confirmed its support for the traditional reliance on consent.[391]

The vulnerability of the position adopted by the health departments was exposed by events in Scotland, where in 1977 the massive Strathclyde Regional Council and its four Health Boards reached agreement to implement fluoridation.[392] However this plan was suspended on account of a legal challenge, which began in 1978. This became the first case in the UK courts to result in a definitive judgement. In the Court of Session in Edinburgh, Lord Jauncey found in 1983 that while the proposed levels of fluoride were likely to be beneficial and seemed to pose no threat to health, the water authorities were not justified under the concept of 'wholesome water' embodied in the Water (Scotland) Acts of 1946 and 1980, to add fluoride to their water supplies. This brought an end to the equivocation of successive administrations about legislation.[393] Legal sanction for fluoridation was finally provided by the Water (Fluoridation) Act 1985.

Smoking and Health

Despite energetic entreaties by Joseph, he achieved little more than the warning notice on cigarette packets.[394] Castle was a smoker, but Owen was among the converted and he grasped the opportunity to challenge his colleagues to take further action against the tobacco interests.[395] Castle referred to this as Owen's 'pet campaign against smoking'.[396]

In July 1974 Owen presented the tobacco industry with a list of demands: first, a levy on their profits to finance education campaigns against smoking at a more realistic level; secondly, restrictions on sponsorship of sports events, especially motor racing; thirdly, abandonment of the use of coupons; fourthly, abolition of advertisements in cinemas; fifthly, inclusion of information about tar yields on cigarette packets; sixthly, strengthening the health warning on cigarette packets and its insertion in a more prominent position; seventhly, transfer of control of the code of advertising practice to the Advertising Standards Authority. The industry replied in February 1975. The first three of these objectives were rejected out of hand. Most of the other parts of Owen's package were also unacceptable, but at least they were subjected to negotiation. In April 1975 Owen reported that the industry had agreed for the code of advertising to be taken over by the Advertising Standards Authority, for withdrawal of advertising at 'U' films, for further negotiation over signifying tar yields on cigarette packets, and about the rewording of the health warning.[397]

In reporting to their colleagues, the health Ministers outlined the above desirable objectives, as well mentioning encouragement of tobacco substitutes, and increasing the relative price of cigarettes. In discussion, Owen stressed as his immediate objective the termination of sports sponsorship by the tobacco industry. Coincidentally, as in the case of fluoridation, progress on this front was dependent on co-operation from Howell. The latter expressed little sympathy, but was willing to discuss a voluntary code of practice with the tobacco industry. As in previous meetings of Ministers of both persuasions, the tobacco industry was not short of apologists. One Minister was afraid of adverse reaction from the Government's own supporters; another was worried about the negative economic impact on the newspaper industry and small shops; a third made the bizarre speculation that savings in one area of health expenditure would be offset by the increased demands on mental health services. However, it was reported that the overwhelming majority of the committee supported the approach advocated by Owen.[398]

In the light of legal advice, Owen decided that legislation would be needed to control the sale, advertisement and labelling of tobacco products. Legislative controls took on a new level of importance in view of the prospect of widespread experimentation and possible massive consumption of tobacco substitutes and additives. Like their Conservative predecessors, Labour Ministers were unsympathetic to legislation and insisted on further negotiations with the tobacco industry. In view of the opposition of the Chairman of the Advertising Standards Authority, it was decided that legislation to introduce further controls on advertising was undesirable. On this point also, Ministers recommended further negotiation.[399]

Further exchanges with the tobacco industry dragged on inconsequentially. Owen came under further pressure to introduce statutory controls of tobacco labelling and consumption from MPs who shared his view that controls were best handled by an independent scientific body operating under the terms of the Medicines Act. The Independent Scientific Committee on Smoking and Health, which was already investigating procedures for dealing with tobacco substitutes and additives, was regarded as a suitable body to take on more extended statutory responsibilities. In order to dissuade private members from pressing ahead with an Order under the Medicines Act, Owen was obliged to offer similar action on the part of the Government.[400]

After Owen's departure from DHSS, further negotiations were handled by Ennals and Moyle. They faced increasing demands for greater Government initiative from the Social Services and

Employment Sub-Committee, the Royal College of Physicians, as well as ASH and other pressure groups.[401] In addition, the administration's own new consultative document on prevention drew attention to the importance of combating smoking, although it was careful not to arouse expectations concerning specific measures.[402]

In view of these escalating demands for combating smoking, health Ministers were anxious to conclude their negotiations with the tobacco industry. At first it seemed likely that the industry would comply with regulation of tobacco substitutes and additives under the Medicines Act. This involved placing an Order under section 105(1) of the Act, which would require licences for all products containing tobacco substitutes and additives. Control of this operation would have been vested in the Independent Scientific Committee. This agreement collapsed as a result of opposition from one of the major tobacco interests, which threatened to contest in court the applicability of the Medicines Act to such products. Ennals urged his colleagues to introduce a short Bill to clear up ambiguity in the law over Medicines Act. Once again Ministers refused to countenance legislation, with the result that advanced preparations for statutory regulation were abandoned.[403] Ennals complained to the Prime Minister that 'the whole of our strategy on smoking would collapse without some sign of decisive action', and he warned that this retreat on legislation would undermine his negotiating position.[404] However, Ministers were unwilling to sanction any measures other than agreed by negotiation. Ennals was left to scramble for the best deal he could scrape together from this position of weakness in which he had been placed by his colleagues.

An agreement was announced by Ennals on 8 March 1977. In the place of statutory control, the industry conceded a voluntary monitoring role to the Independent Scientific Committee with respect to substitutes and additives. In view of the great expectations aroused by tobacco substitutes and additives, this agreement could be presented as a major step forward. However, neither consumers nor anti-smoking groups accepted these substitutes. Ministers were lukewarm in their pronouncements, while the Health Education Council was positively hostile. Substitutes and additives were therefore soon recognised as a futile digression.

Ennals' sole further tangible gain from negotiations was alteration of the warning on cigarette packets. Owen wanted this to read 'DANGER. CIGARETTES CAUSE LUNG CANCER, BRONCHITIS, HEART DISEASE', and for this to be located in a more prominent position. Ennals settled for 'H.M. Government Health Departments' WARNING: CIGARETTES CAN SERIOUSLY DAMAGE YOUR HEALTH'. This minor variant of the existing warning was to remain on the sides of the packet. The industry avoided indicating tar levels on cigarette packets, but agreed to voluntary curbs on advertising high-tar groups, and also reduction in the production of high-tar cigarettes. In return for these minor concessions, the Government agreed to a moratorium on further controls for the space of at least three years.[405] Separate from the agreement, the industry offered to withdraw cigarette advertising from 'A' and 'AA' films.

The concord with Ennals represented a coup for the industry. At a time of heightened public concern over smoking and expectation of strong moves against the tobacco interests, backed by legislation, the industry completely escaped action over limitation of smoking in public places, control over the siting of cigarette machines, imposition of a levy to support health education, sponsorship of sports, limitation of coupons, or indication of tar yields on tobacco packets. It escaped with minor concessions relating to advertising in the cinema, and a slight modification of the health warning on cigarette packets. In return it obtained an invaluable moratorium on further action for three years. Most of the concessions had been wrung out of the industry by Owen; virtually nothing was added by Ennals and Moyle.

Indicative of the Government's climb-down was the unresponsive attitude expressed in the White Paper, *Prevention and Health* towards the Social Services and Employment Sub-Committee's recommendations on smoking and health. This is all the more surprising considering that Ennals had promised a separate White Paper on this subject. However, after the chastening experience of negotiating with the tobacco interests, he thought better of this idea. The *Prevention and Health* White Paper accepted only two of the Sub-Committee's ten recommendations: first, the proposal to limit sponsorship of sporting events; secondly, the provision of non-smoking areas in public places. Ironically, neither of these issues was accorded special priority in negotiations conducted by Ministers. The White Paper accepted with reservation some less important recommendations from the Social Services and Employment Sub-Committee relating to further research into physiological aspects of smoking and into psychological problems of smokers, and about directing anti-smoking education to specific target groups. The White Paper also offered to give further consideration to the important proposal to impose annual increases in the price of cigarettes designed to reduce consumption, but it rejected the recommendations respecting abolition of cigarette coupons, limitations on cigarette machines, and further strengthening of warnings on cigarette packets.[406] The White Paper on *Prevention and Health* in effect signified that the Government had advanced on the smoking front as far as it was willing to go. In view of this prudential calculation, unsurprisingly, the prospective policy document on smoking and health announced in *Prevention and Health: Everybody's Business*, was discreetly shelved.[407]

After the Ennals concordat with the tobacco interests, only limited additional interventions were sanctioned by Ministers. In both England and Scotland, Ministers invited voluntary restraints on smoking in public places.[408] Faced with apparent abdication on the part of the Government, the campaigning organisations redoubled their efforts and they succeeded in attracting media attention, the most ingenious expression of which was the work of Granada TV, which prompted 600,000 applications for its anti-smoking kit.[409] Ingenuity on the part of the campaigners was no match for the power of the tobacco industry, which in 1975 was spending £70m a year on promotion, whereas health education campaigns absorbed about £330,000. By 1979, smoking relating illness was costing the NHS about £100m a year. By this stage it was evident that the public was supportive of more decisive action than the Government was willing to contemplate. A *Sunday Times* poll suggested that 73 per cent of the public were in favour of a ban on advertising of cigarettes.[410] In the debate on smoking preceding the agreement with the tobacco industry reached by the Thatcher administration, Ennals admitted that he had been too lenient in his negotiations. He called for a much tougher approach, especially with respect to advertising. Even then, his suggestions were still far short of the controls on tobacco envisaged by Owen in 1974.[411]

Family Limitation
As noted above, one of the first additional expenditure commitments made by Barbara Castle was implementation of Labour's pledge to a policy of free family planning facilities, so resolving the issue which had caused discomfort to the previous administration. The free service was available from clinics from the date of reorganisation of the health service, and from many general practitioners and hospitals from July 1975. The Government's leading policy statements on preventive medicine gave prominence to maternal and infant health. Promotion of sex education, optimising maternal health, immunization for rubella, screening for congenital abnormalities, reduction of perinatal mortality, and the care of the newborn were included as key aspects of prevention policy in the *Prevention and Health* White Paper published in December 1977. Here, family planning was described as 'potentially one of the most effective measures in preventive medicine'. This emphasis was intended to reduce utilisation of the less desirable alternative of abortion.[412] Family planning was a relatively uncontentious area of policy, although the Family Planning Association complained that the

new health authorities failed to give sufficient priority to these services, which therefore remained insufficient, and less accessible to those in need than was promised by the Labour administration. For some reason the Royal Commission on the NHS failed to comment on this important facet of the preventive services.

Labour's main difficulties over family limitation issues related to policy over abortion. The Abortion Act 1967 was an uneasy compromise. As noted in chapter V, Joseph conceded to pressure from the anti-abortionists by establishing the Lane Committee to examine the workings of the Abortion Act. This committee took much longer to produce its report than was originally anticipated, but this secured for the Heath administration some welcome relief from the bitterly-contested abortion controversy.

This lull in the abortion warfare ended with the publication of the Lane Report in April 1974.[413] As already noted, the Lane Committee was restricted in its remit to investigation of the way in which the Abortion Act was working, not the principles underlying the Act itself. In practice, it was impossible for the Committee to keep strictly within this limitation. The Lane Report declared conclusively in support of the Abortion Act, which it believed had brought about great humanitarian gains. It discovered that abortion was being undertaken on social grounds, and that there was evidence of some commercial malpractice. However, notwithstanding such departures from the terms of the legislation, it recommended that 'solutions should be sought by administrative and professional action, and by better education of the public. They are not, we believe, indications that the grounds set out in the Act should be amended in a restrictive way'.[414] The committee believed that the high rate of demand for abortion was a transient phase. It was confident that the promised development of comprehensive family planning services under the NHS would bring about a reduction in demand for abortion. Nevertheless, in the short term it called on the NHS to iron out gross discrepancies in access to abortion services in line with the Government's declared policies for family limitation.[415]

The three-volume Lane Report constituted an exhaustive investigation of this issue, by means of which the Committee hoped to satisfy all parties to accept its recommendations as an impartial and definitive adjudication. Any confidence that this unanimous and impressive report would carry decisive weight was soon disappointed. On account of the mutually incompatible expectations concerning the outcome of this enquiry, any hope of consensus was of course likely to be frustrated. Neither extreme in the debate was satisfied by the Lane recommendations, but the greater disappointment rested with the anti-abortionists, who expected that the Lane investigation would be impressed by the extent of evidence concerning violation of the 1967 Act, and thereby would contribute to the case for strengthening the law on abortion.[416]

Although, the Lane Report retains its value as a repository of evidence concerning the workings of the Abortion Act, it exercised little direct influence, largely because the anti-abortionists rejected its conclusions and immediately renewed their campaign for amendment of the law. Their lobbying in Parliament soon ensured that a Select Committee of the House of Commons went over the entire ground afresh and effectively exercised greater direct impact on policy.

Although not acquiescing to a policy of abortion on demand, the line adopted by the Lane Committee was interpreted by critics of abortion as connivance with further trends in that direction. The opponents of abortion made common ground with some supporters of the 1967 legislation, who were unhappy about the latitude given to abortion on demand under the existing system. To the discomfort of the Wilson administration, the initiative to amend the Abortion Act emanated from its own side, in the form of the private member's Bill introduced by James White, the Labour MP for the predominantly Roman Catholic constituency of Glasgow (Pollock). Furthermore, White was supported by Leo Abse, Labour MP for Pontypool, another supporter of the 1967 Act, and a well-known liberal on social matters. Known support from Labour ranks, together with the broad coalition in favour of the White Abortion (Amendment) Bill, presented Wilson with a serious problem. Whereas a majority of his Ministers were supportive of the existing legislation, Labour had traditionally allowed a free vote on matters connected with family limitation, and the Labour administration maintained a position of impartiality. There was accordingly a real risk that the Abortion Act would be amended in a direction contrary to the wishes of the dominant element in the administration.

Notwithstanding the pleas of White and Abse that they were returning to spirit of the 1967 reform, the Amendment Bill was more restrictive than any of the previous abortion Bills. White intended that abortion should be restricted to cases where the risk to the woman's life was 'grave', or where 'serious' injury to health was incurred. For this purpose, the testimony of two doctors was required, which was consistent with the 1967 Act, but now it was proposed that the two doctors should have been in practice for five years, and not be members of the same practice. It was furthermore intended to prevent abortion after twenty weeks, except in limited instances, where twenty-four weeks would be permissible. In order to eliminate the private abortion market for foreigners, it was proposed to introduce a twenty-week residence requirement, but the White Bill also proposed substantial limitations on the provision of advice concerning abortion facilities.[417]

671

Ministers adopted a cautious line to the White Bill. They agreed to try to persuade White to withdraw the Bill on the promise of a Select Committee to advise on further legislation. If this failed, it was agreed that Ministers should argue in debate for the merits of a Select Committee. In order to pacify the critics, it was also agreed that the Government should announce its rejection of the Lane recommendation for mandatory sex education in schools.[418]

Supporters of the Abortion Amendment Bill were divided over compliance with the Government's suggestions. The Bill was given a large majority at its Second Reading, after which the House of Commons voted to refer the Bill to a Select Committee.[419] Naturally, appointment of the Select Committee was surrounded by much tension.[420] The ALRA and its supporters claimed that the committee, as constituted, was unreasonably biassed against their interests. By contrast with the woman-dominated Lane Committee, the Select Committee was dominated by men, the four women members being outnumbered by eleven men. The committee contained eight known supporters of the White Bill, among whom only one was a woman. Each side campaigned energetically to influence the Select Committee. Unsurprisingly the committee failed to complete its work by the end of the session. In view of this delay, it issued three brief interim reports containing proposals for modifications in regulations applying under the Abortion Act. On grounds of their general consistency with the Lane Report, the nine recommendations contained in the third of these interim reports were adopted by the Government.[421] They had the effect of curtailing some of the abuses, but the increased bureaucracy was detrimental to NHS services.

The Abortion Amendment Bill and the Select Committee came to an end with the conclusion of the parliamentary session. With this prospect in mind, Ministers were faced with a delicate decision about re-convening the Select Committee to enable its final report to be completed. Castle argued that there was no further use for the Select Committee and that its existence was standing in the way of full implementation of the Lane recommendations. It was hoped that a conciliatory response from Castle concerning the interim recommendations of the Select Committee would cause its supporters of leave further initiative to the Government.[422] It soon became apparent that the Select Committee was determined to continue its operations, raising the possibility of a majority report in favour of the White proposals. The English health Ministers tried unsuccessfully to persuade their colleagues to oppose re-establishment of the Select Committee. This idea was decisively rejected. Ministers decided that the Government was obliged to facilitate reappointment of the Select Committee with the same membership and identical terms of reference. In the relevant debate, health Ministers were instructed to present both sides of the argument, but like other members, they were also allowed to indicate their own opinion and act accordingly in a free vote. Ministers were unable to agree on further concessions likely to persuade anti-abortionists to abandon their campaign.[423]

Indicative of the tension within the Parliamentary Labour Party over the abortion issue, the Prime Minister summoned Barbara Castle for an interview and reminded her of the obligations on health Ministers to preserve impartiality, and warning that if she was seen to favour the abortionists, other Ministers would need to state the opposing argument. Castle described this a ' major row'.[424] She was forced to alter the speech prepared for the debate on this issue at the PLP. In the event, this meeting showed less support for the White proposals than had been anticipated.[425]

Contrary to the advice of Owen in the debate, MPs voted by a large majority to reconvene the Select Committee.[426] In protest at imbalance within the Select Committee, the six members with the greatest pro-abortion leanings resigned.[427] Pressure groups with similar views were virtually unanimous in refusing to testify to the Committee. The rump of nine members of the Select Committee produced their report on 28 July 1976.[428] Unsurprisingly, this reflected the bias of the White Amendment Bill.

The Government maintained its view that it was premature to consider amending the Abortion Act 1967, especially in view of the findings of the Lane Committee and the gathering consensus among medical organisations in support of the Abortion Act. The anti-abortionists were left to promote their cause from the back-benches. With decreasing effect and more limited objectives, William Benyon in 1977, Sir Bernard Braine in 1978, and William Corrie in 1979, promoted abortion amendment Bills, but none of these came near to success.[429] Abortion therefore became established as a last-resort measure in the field of family limitation. The abortion campaigners were therefore satisfied on the point of principle, but they remained concerned about the overall deficiency and gross regional differences in the provision of abortion facilities under the NHS. The Labour administration failed to act on the recommendations of the Lane Committee concerning the development of services or the elimination in disparities of access. Official publications were somewhat coy in their attention to abortion. Although abortion was recognised as integral to the family planning service, and therefore a key feature of the prevention campaign, the White Paper, *Prevention and Health*, contained only passing reference to abortion, while its relevant amplification, *Reducing the Risk*, although purporting to deal with all aspects of family planning, and devoting much space to screening, failed to describe the abortion facilities available under the NHS.[430]

The Royal Commission on the NHS reflected the disquiet about the provision of facilities for abortion. It pointed out that the proportion of women obtaining abortion in the NHS ranged from 90 per cent in the Northern RHA to about 22 per cent in the West Midlands RHA. It concluded that 'equality of access to health services was one of the objectives we set out in Chapter 2 and abortion is a conspicuous example of lack of such equality'.[431] The degree to which abortion services were neglected by the NHS is suggested by the relegation of assessment of this subject to the chapter in the Merrison Report devoted to relations between the NHS and private medicine.

Prevention and Health

The Labour administration confronted important questions relating to preventive medicine and prevention policy on many fronts. Issues which had been dormant for a long period had begun to fulminate. Inaction was no longer a realistic option. One of the most important and overdue problems related to modernisation of the haphazard agglomeration of services relating to health and safety at work. These had been developing since the establishment of the first factory inspectorate at the beginning of nineteenth century. The relevant inspectorates were left untouched by the formation of the NHS, but they were caught up in the tide of reorganisation. Much to the disappointment of the BMA, at no stage was integration with the NHS seriously contemplated. Progress towards rationalisation was slow. The Health and Safety at Work Committee chaired by Lord Robens was set up in 1970 by the Wilson administration. This reported in 1972.[432] After much interdepartmental wrangling lasting from the summer of 1972 to November 1973, the Heath administration introduced its Health and Safety at Work legislation, but its consideration by Parliament was cut short by the change of government. Labour generally supported the objectives of this Bill and its own Health and Safety at Work Bill was a minor variant. However, before this was introduced, Labour faced some difficult decisions and delicate problems of reconciling conflicting interests both among government departments and among its own supporters concerning the amalgamation under the proposed Health and Safety Commission of such bodies as the Agricultural Safety Inspectorate, the Alkali and Clean Air Inspectorate, the Mines and Quarries Inspectorate, and the Nuclear Installations Inspectorate.[433] The process of interdepartmental wrangling was repeated, but on a lesser scale. The Health and Safety Commission and its operational agency, the Health and Safety Executive were set up under the 1974 health and safety legislation, preserving the traditional separation between the occupational health services and the NHS. Demands for this separation to be ended continued and they were undiminished, but were resisted by the Government. This issue caused evident difficulties for the Royal Commission on the NHS, but it also concluded that separation was justified.[434]

A further piece of unfinished business of the Heath administration picked up by Labour was the uncontroversial Protection of the Environment Bill, which was mainly concerned with the more efficient disposal and recycling of waste. The aspect of this Bill with the most immediate bearing on health was the provision for the control of lead in petrol emissions. This was the first preventive health measure to be considered as a response to an EEC draft directive. The Heath administration made preparations to move in line with its European partners, but adoption of targets was deferred as a consequence of the oil crisis. Discussions of the Wilson administration exposed disagreements between departments. The Department of Energy suggested less stringent targets than were being applied in West Germany, whereas the Department of the Environment favoured adoption of EEC norms. Much embarrassment was being caused by evidence of high levels of lead in the atmosphere near motorways, and over possible effects of lead on the health of schoolchildren. Ministers agreed that lower targets were unavoidable, but favoured postponement of any price-rise repercussions until after the October 1974 General Election.[435] In the event, the Government decided to defer action to reduce the level below that advocated by the Department of Energy on the pretext that further medical and economic investigations were required.[436] The issue was not taken up again until 1976, when reduction of the limit in compliance with the EEC directive was reconsidered. The Department of the Environment again pressed for the lower limit, but this was vigorously opposed by both the Treasury and the Department of Energy. It was suggested that the cost of this project would be better spent on improving the quality of drinking water, where Britain again risked failure to comply with the EEC standard. DHSS argued that the resources would be better spent on other aspects of public health, such as fluoridation, cervical cancer screening, foetal screening, or campaigns against smoking and alcohol abuse. Ministers also believed that the evidence about the health risks from lead pollution were not conclusive. They therefore opted to accept in principle, but defer adoption of the EEC target of 0.40gm per litre. The latter was introduced in 1981, when it was also decided that the 0.15gm limit already in place in West Germany at the outset of the Labour administration would not be introduced in Britain until 1985 at the earliest.[437]

675

Given the expanding range of interconnected issues relating to prevention, it was opportune for the health departments to draw the threads of its policies together and signify the Government's intention to keep the public fully informed about the practicalities across the entire field of prevention. As noted above, the theorists of preventive medicine, the pressure groups and public opinion also demanded a more positive response from the Government. These influences inevitably impinged upon MPs, and contributed towards the decision of the Social Services and Employment Sub-Committee of the Expenditure Committee to undertake its pioneer investigation into preventive medicine. This Sub-Committee was chaired by the Labour MP, Renée Short. Its enquiries were conducted between November 1975 and July 1976. The 86-page report and two substantial volumes of evidence were published in April 1977.[438] The conclusions of the Sub-Committee relating to smoking and fluoridation, two of the dominating issues in its proceedings, have already been noted. The report made 58 recommendations covering many aspects of preventive medicine. It called for more leadership from the health departments on the control of alcohol and tobacco abuse, family planning, diet, encouragement of sport, and screening for cancer. It also called for more support for government-related health education agencies, and for more sophisticated utilisation of the opportunities for health campaigning in the mass media.

As usual with the reports of select committees, the quality of the coverage was uneven. The main utility of this exercise was its platform for experts in the field, and for campaigning organisations. Ministers and officials were subjected to some searching questioning, but they were not unduly discomforted. Perhaps the most interesting comment emanated from Dr Owen, who acknowledged that the health service needed to redirect its energies towards promotion, 'which I think it has moved away from progressively'.[439] The most colourful interview with an official was with the Director of the Health Education Council, who made vitriolic attacks on his colleagues in both DHSS and DES, whom he accused of neglecting health education and undermining the work of the HEC.[440] His views received general backing from the Chairman of the HEC.[441]

The intervention by the Select Committee necessitated urgent action of the part of the health departments to regain the initiative and preclude policy in the field of prevention from being dictated by outsiders. The immediate result was a hastily compiled and impressionistic consultative document, *Prevention and Health: Everybody's Business*, issued under the names of the four Secretaries of State representing the parts of the United Kingdom, and published on 16 March 1976.[442] Ennals and Morris admitted that this document was a significant albeit belated innovation: 'this radical new approach to the delivery of health services is long overdue'.[443] Owen saw the object of this exercise as the 'changing public attitudes so that the National Health Service is not seen as the sole provider of health in this country, but that each of us should develop a responsibility for our own health'.[444] This conclusion was welcomed by the Treasury, which saw *Prevention and Health: Everybody's Business* as a sign of greater sensitivity to the need for expenditure restraint within DHSS.

Prevention and Health: Everybody's Business briefly reviewed the achievements of the golden age of public health, especially drawing attention to the success of vaccination and immunization. It then identified such major strategic targets as tobacco, alcohol, and narcotics, and it used this opportunity to point to the more obvious dangers stemming from unwise dietary practices, and the advantages to dental health that would derive from fluoridation of water supplies.

Prevention and Health: Everybody's Business was careful to avoid forays into sensitive policy issues, or cases which raised expenditure implications. Sceptics could therefore point to the lack of genuine commitment of the Government to an interventionist strategy in the field of preventive medicine on the many fronts where personal initiative was incapable of achieving the preventive objective. Even on smoking and health, where the document was most forthcoming about Government intentions, it was proposed to operate controls in the context of the Medicines Act, but only 'after consultation with interests likely to be substantially affected'. Introduction of such limitations effectively precluded the prospects for dramatic advance.[445] Even in cases such as fluoridation or compulsion over the wearing of seat-belts, where the arguments in favour were formidable, and which raised few expenditure issues, no indication was given that the Government was prepared to assume more active leadership. In cases such as screening for cancer or reduction in lead emissions in petrol, where expenditure was involved, the *Prevention and Health: Everybody's Business* consultative document was reticent to the point of being positively discouraging. Finally, the formal agencies involved in health education were scarcely mentioned.[446] Perhaps to protect itself from criticism on account of excessive equivocation, the Government promised to 'follow up this paper over the next two or three years by publishing a series of more detailed papers on specific aspects of prevention. The momentum will be maintained'.[447]

Prevention and Health: Everybody's Business attracted little press attention owing to preoccupation with the announcement of the resignation of Harold Wilson on the date of its publication. In health service circles it was greeted as a constructive beginning to policy

677

formulation. Perhaps indicative of the thirst for leadership in this field, little attention was paid to the evident shortcomings of this document. In subsequent exchanges, this document became known as the 'Red Book' or 'Red Booklet' on prevention, on account of the background colour of its cover. This consultative document also struck out into more original design than adopted previously for publications of this type, by displaying a stylized map of the United Kingdom (ingeniously deleting the Irish Republic), densely populated with cartoon figures. This map became the unifying design feature of further booklets in the prevention series.[448]

Prevention and Health: Everybody's Business was a helpful pre-emptive move against the Expenditure Sub-Committee, which was part way through its deliberations on preventive medicine at the time of publication. *Prevention and Health: Everybody's Business* was a more convincing substitute for the few inadequate paragraphs on preventive and promotive medicine in the *Priorities* consultative document, also published in March 1976.[449]

The prevention consultative document became the English health department's basis for the defence of its position. In the subsequent White Paper, the consultative document was said to have 'represented an unequivocal change of policy within the Health Departments towards prevention'. It was promised that the new unified strategy for health care would entail greater emphasis prevention.[450]

This rapid rise in the profile of preventive medicine was a necessary response to the probings of the Expenditure Sub-Committee. Consequently, in *The Way Forward* sequel to the *Priorities* document, published in September 1977, prevention was projected forward in the order of priorities. Instead of occupying a few paragraphs at the end of the third chapter on primary care, community health and prevention, it occupied the first place in the order of discussion of services.[451] Also notable was the affirmation of support for the Health Education Council, which instead of being largely ignored, was now promised an enhanced role and a substantial increment to its budget, as recommended by the Expenditure Sub-Committee.

The main sign of the Governments conversion to prevention was the substantial White Paper, *Prevention and Health*, published on 15 December 1977.[452] Indicative of the importance attached to the Expenditure Sub-Committee's intervention, the White Paper was not issued as the sequel to *Prevention and Health: Everybody's Business*, but rather as a response to the Sub-Committee's recommendations. Accordingly, the points of emphasis of the White Paper were dictated by the Sub-Committee's report, not by the contents of *Prevention and Health: Everybody's Business*.[453]

As in the case of *The Way Forward, Prevention and Health* placed health education first, and offered an extended discussion of the role for health education agencies in promoting the new prevention policy. The White Paper briefly reviewed the health departments' policies with respect to the broad range of issues raised by the Expenditure Sub-Committee, its most detailed comments being reserved for smoking, and child health including preventive dentistry, the topics which were dominant concerns of experts testifying to the Sub-Committee.

The investigation by the Expenditure Sub-Committee into prevention was therefore instrumental in focussing attention within the health departments on the entire field of its preventive and promotive policies. Secondary beneficiaries of this trend were the agencies directly concerned with health education. As noted in earlier chapters, the administration of health education was not uniform throughout the United Kingdom. In Scotland, the main organisation was the Health Education Unit, which was part of the Common Services Agency, and thereby closely attached to SHHD. This arrangement was subject to the criticism that the Unit lacked independence and was therefore likely to become a creature of the health department. In practice, the Health Education Unit was innovative and generally thought to have made a greater impact than the nominally more independent Health Education Council in London, which was concerned with the rest of the United Kingdom. Before the Prevention and Health initiative, the Health Education Council conducted low-level campaigning relating to such problems as smoking, family planning, venereal disease, dental health, and accidents in the home. The Health Education Council complained that its work was made more difficult by reorganisation of the health service and by the economic constraints of the time. The Prevention and Health initiative produced a change of fortunes; the Health Education Council was given an injection of resources and greater freedom to conduct its campaigns. In early 1978 it launched a 'Better Health: Look After Yourself Campaign', which was a minor success story, and showed that at its best the Health Education Council was capable of matching the work of the Scottish Health Education Unit. The HEC also proved its political usefulness when it was co-opted by Ennals to lend support for his campaign for savings in the massive NHS drug bill. The HEC 'Treat Medicines with Respect' campaign launched in 1978 was not particularly effective, but it eased Ennals' relations with the BMA and the Treasury, both of which demanded that more aggressive anti-medication publicity should be directed at patients.

Regardless of its higher profile, the Health Education Council remained poorly resourced; its relationship with Ministers and DHSS was not always tranquil. Also HEC was impeded by the difficulty in establishing a harmonious working relationship between those holding the appointment of Chairman and Director General. Stabilising the Health Education Council was not assisted by the rapid rotation of Chairmen: no fewer than six individuals held this position between 1968 and 1979.[454]

Vaccination and Immunization

The unanticipated potential for disaster in the field of prevention was exhibited by the few paragraphs devoted to vaccination and immunization in the *Prevention and Health* White Paper.[455] By contrast with the triumphalist tone of the treatment of these subjects in the prevention and health consultative document, the White Paper acknowledged that serious harm had been done to the reputation of vaccination and immunization by evidence of damage to the health of infants caused by whooping cough vaccine. The publicity surrounding this problem undermined confidence in these prophylactic measures and prompted a general decline in the uptake of vaccination and immunization. The White Paper pointed out that one consequence was higher incidence of poliomyelitis in 1976 and 1977. As a direct consequence of the whooping cough scare, the uptake of poliomyelitis vaccination had fallen by one-third, and similar trends were evident in all other vaccinations and immunizations administered to infants.

In fact, even before the whooping cough vaccine problem, the success of the newer immunization programmes against measles and rubella was not particularly outstanding, with acceptance rates as low as 50 per cent in the case of measles. In the 1960s, whooping cough vaccination was usually administered as part of a triple antigen, giving protection against diphtheria and tetanus as well as whooping cough. Vaccination levels for whooping cough rose in England to 79 per cent in 1973, which was a success, although below the level required to eradicate the disease. The safety of the whooping cough vaccine was suspect from the outset. In 1976 arguments broke out in the *Lancet* among experts about the efficacy and safety of this vaccine. This attracted further adverse media comment, with the result that the uptake of whooping cough vaccination fell in England to 31 per cent in 1978. Similar trends occurred elsewhere in the United Kingdom, but there were local differences. For instance, in Wales, the vaccination level fell to 16 per cent in 1978. This problem was investigated as a matter of urgency by the Joint Committee on Vaccination and Immunization, which confirmed existing policies, but this was insufficient to restore confidence of the public, with the result that the acceptance rate for whooping cough vaccination failed to recover. Given the low level of protection, the incidence of whooping cough increased, the epidemic lasting from 1977 to 1979 being the worst since the 1956-57 outbreak.[456] The Parliamentary Commissioner for Administration reached the embarrassing conclusion that the health departments had in general neglected their obligation to keep the public well-informed about vaccination and immunization. He also supported the view of the Association of Parents of Vaccine Damaged Children that the Government had failed in its duty to inform parents about the dangers of whooping cough vaccine.[457]

The Government faced further embarrassment connected with vaccine damage over the question of compensation. The Association of Parents of Vaccine Damaged Children waged a high-profile campaign in which they were supported by Barbara Castle's erstwhile Parliamentary Private Secretary, the popular Jack Ashley MP. The parents threatened to picket clinics and therefore risked undermining the entire vaccination programme. The Prime Minister's office urged Ennals to make a statement giving assurances of the Government's sympathetic attitude towards families affected by this problem. Callaghan expressed sympathy for the campaign both behind the scenes and in a television interview; he used his influence to back the case for compensation.[458] Ennals proposed that Ministers should give agreement in principle for compensation in advance of the Report of Lord Pearson's Royal Commission on Civil Liability and Compensation for Personal Injury. It was argued by Ennals that in view of the evidence incriminating the vaccine, and the official backing for the vaccination campaign, the Government had a moral responsibility to offer compensation. He estimated that compensation would cost about £10-15m. On behalf of the Scottish Office, Ewing opposed this suggestion, arguing that it was not proved that vaccination was responsible for the damage to health, that conceding the principle of compensation would imply acceptance of guilt, and he pointed out that compensation might not restore confidence in the vaccination programme. Elwyn-Jones, the Lord Chancellor, on legal grounds urged that it was inadvisable to make commitments ahead of the Pearson Report. The Chief Secretary supported these objections and expressed concern that this would set a precedent for many other cases of injury owing to health care interventions, and also in the field of industrial injuries.[459]

Ministers failed to agree, and resumed their discussions after consultation with Lord Pearson, who broadly supported the proposal made by Ennals. Ministers were alarmed at the effects of the 'continuous pressure and odium' stirred up against the Government by Ashley's campaign. Substantial support was shown for Ennals, but in the light of vehement opposition by a minority to early concession to the principle compensation, this issue was referred to the

Cabinet.[460] In presenting the case to Ministers, the Home Secretary concentrated on negative aspects of the case, warning of the dangers of premature acknowledgement of liability in this case. Ennals repeated his arguments in favour of acceptance in principle of the need for compensation. Unless this concession was offered, he warned that the Government's entire vaccination and immunization programme would continue to be eroded on account of adverse publicity. Ministers were divided, but the majority were not opposed to making a commitment in principle to a scheme of compensation in advance of the Pearson Report. The Prime Minister therefore proposed a compromise whereby he would arrange for discussions with Lord Pearson, with a view to arriving at an exchange of letters, which might give some satisfaction to the parents of vaccine-damaged children, and help to restore confidence in the vaccination and immunization programmes, but without finally conceding the right to compensation.[461] Some complicated exchanges ensued, which led to Lord Pearson's agreement to participate in an exchange of letters signifying his provisional support for the principle of compensation.[462] In the light of Lord Pearson's support, Ministers agreed to allow Ennals to make a statement expressing sympathy in principle for a scheme of payments for those suffering from vaccine damage, but indicating that it would not be possible to work out the provisions of a scheme until after publication of the Pearson Report.[463]

Ennals' statement temporarily stemmed the volume of protest. Further progress awaited publication of the Pearson Report, which was expected in the autumn of 1977. In the event there was a minor delay, with the result that it was not published until 16 March 1978. The Prime Minister used this occasion to make conciliatory remarks about compensation for vaccine damage.[464] By this stage the vaccine protesters were again running out of patience. Ministers returned to the task of devising a scheme for compensation. Once again, Ennals failed to gain acceptance for his proposals. When Ministers proved unable to agree about the guide-lines for a compensation scheme, the matter was referred for further consideration by a group of Ministers chaired by the Lord President.[465] Following their agreement, Ennals made his statement outlining the scheme for compensation on 9 May 1978.[466]

As already noted, relatively low levels of acceptance exposed the population to risk from epidemics of common infectious diseases. After vacillation occasioned by disagreements between expert committees, in February 1978 Ennals launched a campaign designed to regain confidence in vaccination and immunization.[467] This limited exercise underestimated the degree to which confidence had been undermined. Infectious diseases therefore risked becoming a more serious health hazard. Rubella constituted one of the most serious dangers since it resulted in congenital abnormalities among babies born to women who had contracted the disease. The Government was criticised in the press for not giving a public warning concerning the likely high incidence of rubella predicted for the summer of 1978. Ministers were censured for not bringing the dangers of this situation to the attention of the public, and they were also criticised for their unhelpful attitude towards the campaign mounted by the Spastics Society. The *Guardian* pointed out that this episode undermined the credibility of the Government's contentions about commitment to prevention.[468] The failure of Ministers to inform the public about the dangers of rubella was all the more surprising in the light of the insistence by the Parliamentary Commissioner for Administration that the Government possessed a duty to keep the public fully informed about issues relating to vaccination and immunization.[469] As predicted by epidemiologists, the epidemic of rubella was worse than in previous years, and it was five times the level experienced in the previous two summers.[470] The Ministers' reputation was not much helped when after much delay, in November 1978, it was announced that the Health Education Council would issue a leaflet on rubella, but this was available only after the end of epidemic.

Alcohol Abuse

During the Labour administration there was an increasing call for a comprehensive review of the problem of alcohol abuse. This contrasted with narcotic abuse, which although long under review by official committees, was not yet perceived by Ministers as a major problem.[471] A more pessimistic construction of the narcotics problem dates only from the final months of the Labour administration.[472]

The Labour administration was under pressure to take action on liquor licensing following the Erroll (England and Wales) and Clayson (Scotland) Reports dating from 1972 and 1973 respectively, and for the introduction of breath tests and changes in sentencing policy to combat drink and driving, following the Blennerhassett Report of 1976. However, alcohol policy was difficult to handle owing the many and often conflicting departmental interests. The Home Office was for instance suspicious that DHSS was trespassing into its territory with its increasing intervention in the alcohol field, especially when DHSS unilaterally established its departmental advisory committee on this problem.

The health departments were slow to appreciate the importance of alcohol abuse. As with narcotics, this problem came under more active review during the 1960s.[473] A modest programme for development of treatment facilities was initiated in 1970; grants for hostels were available from 1973 onwards; and a beginning was made with regional detoxification centres.[474] DHSS policy was summarised in *Better Services for the Mentally Ill* published in 1975.[475] In the same year, Castle and Morris set up an Advisory Committee on Alcoholism chaired by Professor W I N Kessel. This committee was tolerably active. Its first report, dealing with prevention, was published in November 1977.[476] This advocated higher tax on alcoholic drinks, no relaxation of licensing hours, and more intensive health education.

The problems associated with alcohol abuse were forcefully presented to the Expenditure Sub-Committee. The hesitant recommendations made by the Sub-Committee reflected the lack of consensus among their expert witnesses.[477] The health departments' reticence over this problem is indicated by their acceptance of only one of the seven recommendations of the Expenditure Sub-Committee's report.[478] However, the *Prevention and Health* documents drew attention to the estimate that there were as many as 500,000 persons with a serious drink problem in England and Wales (or 1 per cent of the population), and proportionately more in Scotland, where the problem was acknowledged to be of even more serious dimensions. Prudence and uncertainty prevented commitment to a figure for Scotland.[479] DHSS conceded to the Expenditure Sub-Committee's wishes by allowing the Health Education Council at last to begin active campaigning on this front.[480]

Influences from the direction of the Expenditure Sub-Committee were reinforced by prompting from the EEC that member states should examine alcohol problems associated with rising consumption. Paradoxically, the EEC was simultaneously preparing for harmonisation of liquor taxation, which threatened to reduce the relative price of wine and thereby stimulate alcohol consumption.[481] On account of the many departmental interests involved, the alcohol issue was delegated to CPRS. In the absence of leadership from the health departments, CPRS was keen to give prominence to the health dimension of this problem. A short initial review was completed in December 1977.[482] This soon evolved into one of the CPRS draft Social Topic Notes, which it was agreed by interested Ministers should be referred to the Home and Social Affairs Committee.[483] It was also accepted that Ennals should submit his draft consultative document on alcoholism for discussion at the same meeting. CPRS was disconcerted when, on the eve of this meeting, Ennals withdrew his document on the grounds that further discussion within his department was needed.[484]

CPRS presented alarming figures on the rise of consumption, increased consumer spending, the decline in the real price of alcoholic drinks. It pointed to huge increase in admissions to hospital connected with alcohol misuse, and a big increase in deaths caused by cirrhosis of the liver. Ministers were impressed by the findings of CPRS, and they agreed that the Government could not duck the issue, but they insisted that the proximity of a General Election reduced opportunities for intervention. The Government therefore abandoned its consideration of changes in the licensing laws. Ministers even believed that it would be unwise to proceed with the promised consultative document on alcohol promised in the *Prevention and Health* White Paper. Ennals supported this view, but his colleagues nevertheless insisted on commenting on his outlines for a consultative document.[485] Although many of the Ministers expressed opposition to the production of a draft consultative document, the Home Secretary concluded that the draft should be produced with a view to publication at the end of 1978. It was also agreed that the CPRS review should be completed.[486] The Advisory Committee on Alcoholism was allowed to run on until 1978, but it was then disbanded after production of its reports on services for problem drinkers, and education and training.[487] Like the Select Committee and CPRS, the Advisory Committee was inclined to make recommendations unacceptable to Ministers. Its elimination therefore removed a potential source of embarrassment.

Owing to the expectation of a General Election in the autumn of 1978, further consideration of the alcohol issue lapsed and it was not resumed until the autumn of 1979 under the new administration. The CPRS review was suppressed, but the promised consultation document was issued in December 1981 as the little pamphlet, *Drinking Sensibly*, published as part of the Prevention and Health series. By this stage the alcohol problem was attracting much greater public attention. Britain's leading epidemiologist suggested that the nation was facing a 'new epidemic of alcoholism'. He called for more determined government action and complained that it was insufficient for the DHSS to limit its preventive efforts to issuing booklets. He also called for the formation of a national campaigning body to take up this issue. With the support of the medical profession, steps were taken to build a more effective organisation to confront the alcohol problem.[488]

The vacillations associated with whooping cough and alcohol contributed towards a subdued ending to Labour's programme for prevention. This unsatisfactory conclusion was reflected in the findings of the Royal Commission on the NHS. In line with the Government's aspirations, preventive medicine was ranked third in the items upon which the Royal Commission was asked to comment and its report accorded prominence to the consideration of this subject. Its analysis was not particularly incisive, but it expressed a generalised concern that opportunities in this field were not being grasped. It called for a 'much tougher attitude' on the part of the

Government towards the major preventive problems, as well as greater expenditure on, and more sophisticated use of health education. It advocated specific action to extend proven screening programmes, and compulsion over the wearing of seat belts.[489] The damage to the credibility of the immunization and vaccination campaigns was noted with regret, but the Royal Commission tactfully avoided elaboration on this problem. Indeed this key aspect of preventive medicine occupied only two sentences of the report.[490]

(x) NURSING AND MIDWIFERY PROFESSION

The Wilson administration was under an obligation to declare its position concerning the Briggs Report, which had awaited an official response since its publication in October 1972. Further vacillation was rendered more difficult by the agreement to use consent powers under the Counter-Inflation Act to make selective increases in nurses pay, primarily designed to give better reward to nurse tutors. This award was subject to a statement by Michael Foot on 6 May 1974. Since the grounds for this award related to the Briggs recommendations, it was imperative to make a simultaneous announcement about the Briggs Report. Owen took up this issue immediately after his appointment. He complained about the lack of sense of urgency over the Briggs Report. Officials invoked lack of resources as the primary reason for delay.[491] Ministers concluded that it was essential to make an early statement on Briggs.[492] Castle communicated this suggestion to Edward Short in his capacity as Chairman of the Social Services Committee.[493]The Treasury agreed to this suggestion on the understanding that any additions to public expenditure implied by the policy statement would be absorbed in the existing budget of DHSS.[494]

Castle praised the Briggs Report as an 'important milestone in the development of nursing and midwifery in this country'. The Government accepted the main recommendations, particularly relating to the need for a new pattern of education and training, and also a new structure of statutory bodies for the nursing and midwifery professions. The new pattern of education would comprise an eighteen-month basic course leading to a certificate of nursing practice, followed by a further eighteen-month course leading to registration, with provision thereafter for specialised training leading to a higher certificate. The details of this scheme would be the responsibility of the new statutory bodies. The Government accepted in principle that the age of entry to nurse training should be reduced first to 17½ and then to 17.

The new statutory bodies would comprise a Central Council for Great Britain, which would be the registration body, associated with a Standing Midwifery Committee, and supported by Education Boards for England, Scotland and Wales. This structure would replace the existing General Nursing Councils, Central Midwives Boards, and the Council for the Education and Training of Health Visitors. In order to settle anxieties among health visitors, it was agreed that the title should be preserved, and included in the name of the new Central Council, parity with midwives was promised through a Standing Health Visiting Committee.

Castle promised further consultations on future developments. She was unable to provide specific assurances concerning the timetable for change, or the date of legislation. In the meantime the Secretary of State promised improvements in the career structure and numbers of nursing staff involved in teaching. She pointed out that the announcement made by the Secretary of State for Employment would add £18m, or 3 per cent to the total pay bill for nurses.[495]

Ministers hoped that the specific nature of their policy statement and minor investment in nurse tutors would reduce anxieties within the nursing profession, and purchase breathing space for further consideration of resource implications and the timetable for legislation. By the end of May 1974, two short consultation documents amplifying Castle's parliamentary statement were prepared for circulation.[496] Castle was hoping to introduce comprehensive legislation in January 1975, paving the way for establishment of the new nursing bodies, and the introduction of changes in nursing education in 1977.[497] This timetable proved to be hopelessly over-optimistic.

Although Castle promised that the total legislation would be only modest in length and uncontroversial, her colleagues were pessimistic about the chances of inclusion in the legislative timetable for 1974/75.[498] Preparation of the legislation was also delayed by lack of agreement between the nursing organisations concerning the constitution of the new statutory bodies. It was also unclear what proportions of members should be allocated to the parts of Great Britain or the UK. This issue was complicated by the need to be consistent with other UK bodies constituted under the new general devolution arrangements currently under discussion.[499] In December 1974, SHHD announced that Scottish Ministers would need to completely reconsider their views about the new statutory bodies. SHHD concluded that the Briggs proposal for a strong central council established on a Great Britain or UK basis was unlikely to be acceptable to Scottish opinion, even with arrangements for largely autonomous national education boards. Since Scotland had possessed its own statutory bodies for nursing and midwifery for over fifty years, it would seem perverse if, at a time of renewed pressure for

687

devolution, these arrangements were scrapped in favour of a UK organisation. SHHD concluded that it would be necessary to transfer the main powers to national education boards, and restrict the new central council to a minimum role in co-ordination.[500] DHSS appreciated the difficulties faced in Scotland, but insisted that the central council could not be reduced to the status of a co-ordinating body. SHHD insisted that on account of the dramatic changes in public opinion over recent months associated with continuing rise of nationalist sentiment, it was essential for Ministers to respond constructively.[501] This disagreement risked derailing the legislative timetable, but to the surprise of Scottish officials, their Ministers agreed to proceed along lines suggested by DHSS. They accepted the need for a body to speak for the entire nursing profession, and to safeguard professional standards on a GB or UK basis.[502] Although expressing reservations of the kind emanating from Scotland, Northern Ireland Ministers also signified their willingness to join in with the Briggs arrangements.[503]

The first draft of instructions to Parliamentary Counsel for the nursing legislation was completed in December 1974. DHSS officials concluded that comprehensive legislation was not feasible until the 1975/76 session. In response to prompting from Owen, they produced a revised timetable envisaging the Royal Assent by March 1976, establishment of the new statutory bodies in April 1977, and introduction of the new training courses in October 1978.[504] In transmitting the draft legislation to the Treasury, DHSS admitted that it was 'rather obscure' when the Bill could be introduced.[505] This caution was well-advised, since at its meeting on 3 July 1975, the Cabinet consigned the Briggs Bill to a low order of priority on the reserve list for the 1975/76 session. This set-back was not unwelcome to the Treasury on account of expenditure considerations. It also provided the occasion for SHHD to renew its concerns about devolution. SHHD suggested that on grounds of the economic climate and the 'emerging situation on devolution' the Briggs legislation might profitably be shelved.[506]

The economic crisis forced DHSS to consider the expenditure implications of its Briggs legislation more carefully than before. It was estimated that the cost of full implementation would rise to about £27m in the course of seven years. It was envisaged that the initial cost could be absorbed from efficiency savings, but after three years there would need to be relevant adjustments to the PESC estimates.[507]

Rumours concerning delays in the Briggs legislation added to anxiety within the nursing profession. The Chief Nursing Officer frankly expressed 'gloom' concerning this outcome. She feared that it would add to suspicion that the 'Briggs Report has been quietly shelved and that there is no real intention to implement its recommendations'. She warned that this was likely to undermine morale still further, and add to already alarming rates of wastage among nurse tutors and senior staff.[508]

In desperation to introduce the Briggs Bill in 1975/76, Owen instructed officials to investigate whether it was possible to introduce a 'rag-bag Health Bill' including about five clauses relating to Briggs, rather than a Bill specifically devoted to nursing, which was expected to need between 40 and 60 clauses. Officials were initially resistant to this suggestion, believing that it would be regarded as an affront within the nursing profession.[509] However, the idea continued to be canvassed; in the face of increasing obstacles to legislation, it was suggested that the minimum feasible legislative package was a Bill containing a few clauses facilitating establishment of a new UK advisory/consultative body, which would perform some of the functions of the proposed UK council and national education boards.[510]

The Social Services Committee allowed Castle to issue a consultative documents on the Government's policy on the relationship between the health service and the nurse training system, and on the statutory framework for the implementation of the Briggs Report, but the Cabinet, as in the previous year, consigned Briggs legislation to the reserve list for the 1976/77 session.[511] This further delay carried the prospect of continuing erosion of morale within nursing. The blow to the image of nursing was made worse by the prospect that the Government would sanction legislation on the regulation of the medical profession, based on the Merrison Report published as recently as 1975.[512] In view of the expectation among nurses that a commitment to nursing legislation would be contained in the Queen's Speech, at the instance of the Chief Nursing Officer, the Secretary of State met leaders of nursing organisations to explain the continuing delay in introducing the nursing legislation. Ennals reaffirmed the Government's firm commitment to legislate on Briggs as soon as parliamentary time permitted. This meeting agreed to establishment of a co-ordinating committee to advise on arrangements for nursing education. DHSS promised to re-examine the feasibility of producing a Nursing Bill providing for the setting up of a UK central council and national education boards, but leave the administrative infrastructure and detailed arrangements for education to be dealt with by regulations.[513] The arrangements for establishing the Co-ordinating Committee were agreed at a meeting with Moyle on 20 January 1977.[514] A wide range of activities were proposed for this Co-ordinating Committee, which was expected to act as a shadow advisory organisation or non-statutory council, preparing the way for the statutory bodies to be established when the opportunity was presented.[515]

In considering whether a place could be found in the 1977/78 legislative programme, DHSS came upon a further obstacle in the form of objections from the Treasury. Hitherto, the Treasury had taken little interest in Briggs. The immediate financial implications were insignificant, and sizeable expenditure was not likely to be incurred for some years. However, revised estimates suggested that the cost of the educational changes would rise from £6m in the first year to £40m in the seventh. The Treasury regarded this as a minimum, likely to be exceeded in practice. It therefore insisted on full consultation before further efforts were made to secure a place for the nursing Bill in the legislative programme.[516] Ennals made a weak attempt to introduce Briggs expenditure into his additional bids in the 1976 PESC exercise. In 1977 Ennals decided that he would improve his chances of achieving a place for the Merrison legislation by willingness to sacrifice Briggs.[517] Officials therefore approached the preparation of a draft memorandum for the Home and Social Affairs Committee in a defeatist manner, regarding the Briggs Bill as a 'weak runner'.[518] However, partly on account of increasing outside agitation, and the emergence of greater consensus among nursing bodies, DHSS found itself in a position of fighting for Briggs more strenuously than was originally intended. DHSS officials were angered by Treasury obstruction of this established policy commitment of the Government. The increased costs of implementation were merely a reflection of generally increasing costs. The Treasury was reminded that 'we are buying nurses, not the Retail Price Index; the various increases in nurses' pay during the intervening years fully account for the difference'.[519] The position of DHSS was strengthened on account of the decision to narrow down the scope of its legislation to clauses relating to the new statutory bodies, which was expected entail only minimal additional costs. However, Treasury objections were not withdrawn on the ground that formation of the new statutory bodies would arouse the expectation of further educational reforms. Treasury Ministers were therefore advised once again to oppose inclusion of the Briggs legislation in the legislative programme and object to its mention in the Queen's Speech.[520]

Ennals took his plea to the Home and Social Affairs Committee, which sanctioned support for legislation to establish the new statutory bodies on condition that no commitment to reform of nursing education was given. However, it was left for the Cabinet to decide about the timing of legislation.[521] On this occasion, the Cabinet agreed to inclusion of the Briggs legislation in the 1977/78 timetable, according to the conditions specified by the Home and Social Affairs Committee.

Against continuing Treasury resistance, DHSS pressed on with its limited Bill.[522] However, the timetable once again fell behind, partly because of disagreements among the professional organisations and training bodies, and especially continuing distrust from midwives and health visitors, who feared that their special interests would be sacrificed under the new unified structure. The need for consistency with the devolution principles embodied in the Scotland and Wales devolution Bills constituted a further cause for delay. The large amount of parliamentary time occupied by devolution also reduced the opportunities in the timetable for any non-essential legislation.[523] Yet another delaying factor was the requirement for the legislation to be consistent with the EEC directives for general nursing, which were mandatory from June 1979. DHSS officials recognised that these further delays would 'drop a bombshell on an already nervous profession' and would exercise a 'shattering effect on nursing opinion'.[524] Moyle publicly admitted defeat, announcing that there would be no time for the nursing legislation in the 1977/78 session. He combined this with the ritual assurance that the Bill would be introduced at the first opportunity.[525]

The Nurses, Midwives and Health Visitors Bill was not presented to the Legislation Committee until November 1978. The Treasury maintained its opposition, but on this occasion Treasury Ministers were overruled. On account of the widespread support for the nursing Bill and its generally uncontroversial character, Ministers considered introducing the Bill in the House of Lords. However, the continuing vocal opposition from some professional groups persuaded Ministers that it would be more prudent to introduce the Bill in the House of Commons. It was hoped to adopt the Second Reading Committee procedure, but this was not accepted by the opposition.[526]

The Nurses, Midwives and Health Visitors Bill received its Second Reading on 13 November 1978. The Bill was much longer than originally envisaged, comprising twenty-three clauses and seven schedules. The Bill provided for a new governing body, the UK Central Council for Nursing, Midwifery and Health Visiting, with main executive functions being exercised by four National Boards. Arrangements were included for establishment of standing committees of both the Council and the Boards. It was proposed to protect the interests of midwifery through a Midwifery Standing Committee of the Council, and health visiting though a Health Visiting Joint Committee. The Bill described the detailed arrangements for membership of these bodies. It provided for a single, centralised registration system for all qualified nurses, midwives and health visitors, and for a unified disciplinary process involving both the Central Council and the National Boards. Finally,

691

the Bill included provisions relating to the Scotland and Wales Acts and EEC nursing directives.

The Government was relieved by the general welcome for the Bill, which included active support from Lord Briggs. The Bill enjoyed a relatively untroubled passage through Parliament, but some of its provisions continued to be unacceptable to some powerful professional groups, especially the Central Midwives Board and the Council for the Education and Training of Health Visitors.[527] These two organisations had earlier united in proposing a rival organisational framework, a voluntary federation of the existing statutory bodies. It was difficult for the Government to offer further concessions to the midwives and health visitors on account of the risk of alienating nursing organisations. The General Nursing Council for Scotland was particularly opposed to strengthening the position of midwives or health visitors.

In view of the continuing anxieties expressed by midwives and health visitors, immediately after the Second Reading, DHSS Ministers decided that further concessions were needed to satisfy these groups that substantial and genuine delegation would be made to the committees representing their interests. The need to conciliate the midwives was increased by vocal support on their behalf from the Royal College of Obstetricians and Gynaecologists and the Joint Consultants Committee.[528] The midwives were satisfied with the offer of a new clause 1, significantly increasing the authority of the Central Council's Standing Midwifery Committee. DHSS was more reticent to make substantial concessions to the health visitors, not only on account of opposition from nursing groups, but also because of the precedent, likely to spark off demands for similar treatment from groups such as district nurses and mental nurses. DHSS abandoned its intention to insert a new clause relating to health visitors, and it introduced only minor changes to clause 7, which related to health visitors. These concessions proved sufficient to satisfy Parliament, although clause 7 remained the most contentious clause in the Bill, and the health visitors remained dissatisfied with the outcome.[529] The Nurses, Midwives and Health Visitors Act received the Royal Assent on 4 April 1979. Crossman's initiative for a review of nursing education thus took more than a decade to yield its first significant fruits. The new United Kingdom Central Council took over from antecedent bodies in November 1980, but there were further long delays before the Government responded to the Briggs recommendations relating to the content of education and training, and associated human resources implications.

(xi) INDUSTRIAL RELATIONS

The period between 1974 and 1979 represented the worst phase of industrial unrest in the health service since its inception.[530] Disputes left no sector of the workforce untouched. The tone for this disharmony was set by the doctors, whose traditional aggressive defence of their economic interests became infused with a new peak of venom. Although the Tory press fastened their adverse reporting on disputes involving such groups as ambulance drivers or ancillary workers, the most dramatic and exhausting confrontations were waged by the doctors, for whom the Wilson administration, and Barbara Castle in particular, came to epitomise the embodiment of evil. The normally friendly *Financial Times* criticised the doctors for behaving like dockers, and it accused them of attacking the health service at its roots.[531] The equally friendly *Daily Telegraph* likewise confronted the doctors, and urged discontinuation of their industrial action on the grounds that there was 'no justification whatever for inflicting further suffering on sick people'.[532]

This plunge into industrial unrest was not entirely predictable. The Wilson administration initially adopted a relaxed approach to incomes policy. The atmosphere of the first few months is well-encapsulated by Coates:

> As the Labour Government returned to power it was in no position to build on the statutory incomes policy inherited from the Heath Government. Nor was there any political will to do so. On the contrary, for at least a number of leading Cabinet members such a retreat from statutory wage control was near to being a defining element of their political faith. So the Pay Board was abolished, as promised, and there was no Stage 4 to replace the Stage 3 of the Conservatives' incomes policy when that expired in July 1974. Instead the miners were given a generous pay settlement, and this set the pace for the wage agreements to follow...by November 1974 the average level of wage settlements stood 25 per cent higher than it had twelve months before.[533]

Among the beneficiaries of these big increases were local government white-collar staff, one of the groups important for comparability purposes within the NHS. Consequently, expectations were aroused of increases in the region of 25 per cent, and anything less implied that NHS personnel were being subjected to perpetuation of their traditional position of disadvantage with respect to the rest of the national workforce.

Barbara Castle was plagued by industrial troubles from the moment of her appointment. She explained to the Prime Minister that the NHS was being overtaken by an 'unprecedented series of

693

industrial disputes now threatening services to patients'. She concluded that 'all of these troubles can be attributed wholly or party to the harmful effect which the previous Government's Statutory Incomes Policy had on salaries and wages in the National Health Service, and to the effects of reorganisation on morale within the National Health Service, particularly at a time of financial stringency'.[534]

The first dispute facing Castle related to the small but important group of *medical physics and physiological measurement technicians*. In 1972, the Industrial Arbitration Board recommended that their salaries should be revalued after the ending of statutory controls. By the end of the Heath administration these technicians had run out of patience. During May and June 1974 they undertook damaging industrial action. Their dispute was settled in July 1974, when as a consequence of Whitley Council negotiations, they accepted a 20 per cent increase backdated to November 1973.

Many groups of staff were dissatisfied with the salary arrangements adopted for the reorganised health service. The most important staff affected, was the small, but highly important group of *senior nurse managers*, whose salaries were imposed, and set at a level well below their colleagues in the consensus management teams. As noted below, this anomaly was not corrected until 1979.

Other groups were not so patient. *NHS works officers* at area and district level claimed that their work load had been increased as a consequence of reorganisation. They therefore claimed an increase in pay in addition to the Stage 3 increase awarded from April 1974. Refusal to grant the increase prompted industrial action, which had a particularly severe effect on laundry output. This dispute was settled at the end of July 1974, entailing a further increase of 18 per cent for relevant grades of works staff.

Nurses' Pay 1974-1975

The biggest problem facing Castle on the pay front related to nurses, midwives and professions supplementary to medicine. It has already been noted in chapter V that nurses were frustrated by the Government's avoidance of their revaluation claim, originally made in 1972, and they were dissatisfied by the failure of the Pay Board to undertake a definitive study of relativities relating to nursing. Although the nurses agreed in early 1974 to a standard Stage 3 award, they were not willing to regard this as more than an interim award. Soon after the change of Government, Castle made a bid for a 10 per cent general increase for nurses on top of the Stage 3 settlement, which would have cost £70m. Although the Treasury was 'struck by the moderation of the nurses' pay settlements for several years', it opposed this concession on grounds of appearing to reopen

Stage 3 settlements.[535] The Treasury also objected to an alternative concession proposed by Castle, which was for a small increase for career grades of nurses at the cost of £18m. Castle proposed this increase as a candidate for the application of statutory pay control consent powers. Once again, the Treasury was opposed to both this concession and similar cases from outside the health service. The shortlist was reviewed by the Economic Policy Committee Subcommittee on Pay, eliminating all except the nursing increase, which was referrred to the Cabinet. On the recommendation of Foot and Castle, the Cabinet approved the £18m increase for nurses as a special case, on grounds of social justice and the need to respond to the Briggs Report, which would not carry the risk of sparking off further claims from the trade unions. Ministers hoped that this modest concession would relieve anxieties over the Briggs Report and reduce pressures for immediate general revaluation of pay.[536]

Any idea that nurses would be satisfied by this small concession and the associated promise to implement the Briggs Report was soon disappointed. The deeper anxieties of this group were apparent when a delegation from the nursing and midwifery Staff Side met the new Secretary of State to express their demoralisation and frustration over the pay situation. This meeting was held against a backdrop of a noisy demonstration by a thousand nurses. Castle expressed sympathy and agreed to consider the Staff Side request for an independent review of their pay and conditions of work.[537] A similar demand was made by a large deputation from the Royal College of Nursing on 8 May. On 14 May the Staff Side of the Whitley Council refused to discusss implementation of the £18m increase on the grounds that it would create anomalies and exacerbate the crisis over pay. Various of the nursing organisations threatened industrial action to back up their claims. Given the support for the nurses among Labour MPs and in the press, as well as signs that various other groups were succeeding in reopening their Stage 3 settlements, the Prime Minister agreed to meet their delegation to hear their plea for a general interim increase and an independent review of their pay problem.[538] Ministers offered to give prompt and sympathetic consideration to the request for an independent enquiry.[539]

The Government hoped that by conceding the request for an enquiry, nurses would drop their demand for an interim pay increase. Although Treasury Ministers raised objections, Foot and Castle believed that an enquiry was unavoidable. On 23 May 1974 Castle announced that a committee under Lord Halsbury would enquire into the pay and conditions of service of nurses and midwives.[540] In response to approaches from the Professional and Technical Whitley Council 'A', Ministers agreed that the Halsbury enquiry should also consider the pay of professions supplementary to medicine. On 3 July

695

1974 Castle announced that Lord Halsbury's team would also examine the pay and conditions of chiropodists, dietitians, occupational therapists, orthoptists, physiotherapists, radiographers, remedial gymnasts and speech therapists.[541] It was accepted that any pay increases resulting from the Halsbury enquiries would be backdated to 23 May 1974.

Although the Halsbury enquiries were conducted with maximum speed, with the aim of reporting in mid-September, some nurses and radiographers, especially members of COHSE and ASTMS, undertook industrial action in support of their demand for an interim pay increase. COHSE warned that it would instigate general industrial action if the Halsbury report was not completed by the end of August. In response to entreaties by Castle to COHSE and ASTMS, the unions agreed reluctantly to call off industrial action, on condition that interim payments were announced when the Halsbury Report was received.[542]

In the event the Halsbury Report was published on 17 September 1974.[543] As promised, an interim award was immediately announced. The report was immediately accepted by the Government. It envisaged increases of 30 per cent for nurses and midwives, and 22 per cent for professions supplementary to medicine. The report also proposed reforms in the grading structures, various specific changes in pay and allowances, and alterations in conditions of service. It also reinforced many of the recommendations of the Briggs Committee. Application of the Halsbury recommendations was remitted to the Nurses and Midwives Whitley Council.

The Halsbury award represented a substantial gain for nurses, and it temporarily relieved their sense of injustice. The new scale for staff nurses was £1,692 to £2,202. Notwithstanding these gains, further dispute soon broke out in the context of the pay claim due to take effect in April 1975. Given the success of the Halsbury intervention, this should have been a routine matter. The nurses were offered a modest cost of living increase of about 11 per cent, but they objected that this increase left first-year students short of the TUC low-pay target of £30 a week. After agitated negotiation during March 1975, this concession was granted. The revised scale for the staff nurse was £2,121 to £2,646.[544]

The decision to establish the Halsbury enquiry drew attention to the limitations of the Whitley Council system. Indeed, the widespread industrial troubles of 1974 generated a fresh crisis of confidence in the Whitley negotiating machinery. Although there were complaints from all sides, there was no consensus over policy for the future. Even the unions differed among themselves about the changes required.[545] It was also difficult to decide on the method to be adopted for reviewing the Whitley system.

Investigation by an independent committee or ACAS was rejected on the grounds that conclusions unacceptable to major interests or Ministers might be forthcoming. Barbara Castle therefore employed Dr W E J McCarthy of Nuffield College Oxford for this task. It was agreed that his investigation should proceed by negotiation with the parties involved, with the idea of reaching a commonly agreed solution.[546] Lord McCarthy's brief report was submitted in October 1976, and published shortly afterwards.[547] By this date, incomes policy reduced opportunities for friction within the Whitley system, thereby relieving the instinct for reform. Apart from alteration in arrangements for representation of NHS authorities on the Management Sides, by 1979 only slow progress had been made in implementing other recommendations of the McCarthy Report.[548]

Doctors' and Dentists' Pay 1974-1975

During the first months of the Wilson administration the medical staff of the NHS were a slumbering leviathan. Paradoxically, as already noted, they were prodded into threats of industrial action, not by their usual militancy concerning remuneration, but by union action over pay-beds. This perturbation proved to be the prelude to more sustained industrial action over pay-beds, which lasted until the eve of Castle's departure from office. This underlying grievance inevitably heightened anxieties and added to the inclination to militancy on the pay front or indeed with respect to any other cause of tension. All major groups of medical personnel were soon locked in dispute with the Government, consultants over pay-beds and their contract, junior hospital doctors over their contract, and general practitioners on account of fear that the Labour Government would not implement the Review Body recommendations. All of these groups backed up their demands with preparations for industrial action. These threats were soon translated into unofficial and official action by both senior and junior hospital medical staff, so producing the biggest direct interference with clinical services since the beginning of the NHS.

Establishment of the review body procedure was designed to reduce the likelihood of conflict over remuneration. As observed in chapter III, this expectation had only been incompletely realised during the 1964-1970 Labour administration. Experience of the Review Body during the 1970s was not altogether free from tension, but the twin operation of the Review Body and incomes policy temporarily reduced opportunities for major confrontation between the doctors and the Government over pay, albeit generating a build up of frustrations, which threatened explosive consequences once incomes policy was relaxed.

The Halsbury Review Body Report completed in May 1974 was consistent with the Stage 3 Pay Code of the Heath administration. It recommended an average increase of 7.4 per cent, to apply for one year, with effect from April 1974. Ministers were satisfied that the award was not out of line with the Pay Code. Accordingly, they sanctioned the award, with only minor reservations about small details in the recommendations. Ministers were divided over the merits of paying threshold payments to doctors.[549] Castle argued that the doctors would react with outrage if they were denied these payments, and that this would lead to even greater non-co-operation over their contracts and pay-beds. Other Ministers vigorously opposed threshold payments to the well-paid. A compromise was reached whereby threshold payments were paid only to those doctors and dentists earning below £8,500.[550]

Although scrupulous in maintaining consistency with pay policy, the Halsbury Report expressed concern that doctors and dentists had fallen 7 and 11 per cent respectively behind comparable groups.[551] Professional bodies were not slow to exploit this anomaly. The Secretary of the BMA warned the Prime Minister that the doctors' patience with unjust treatment over pay was not inexhaustible; he demanded that Wilson should meet a BMA delegation. After some hesitation, Wilson referred the doctors to Castle.[552] Rumours concerning the likelihood of interim pay awards to professions supplementary to medicine resulted in an outburst of similar demands from other groups, including the doctors.

Castle reminded an aggressive BMA delegation that although statutory controls over pay settlements were abolished on 25 July 1974, the Government and the TUC expected pay agreements to last for twelve months. However, it was agreed that the professions were at liberty to submit papers to the Review Body making the case for an interim adjustment of remuneration.[553]

The scene was set for a classic confrontation with the Government over the claim for a interim pay adjustment. However, on this occasion the venom of the profession was deflected away from Castle, and towards the unlikely Halsbury. It seems that Halsbury and perhaps the majority of the DDRB were sympathetic to an interim payment. However, Halsbury was sensitive to pressure from the Government to abide by the twelve-month rule. In a momentary lapse, Halsbury told a reporter from the magazine, *Pulse*, that he would 'feel it ill-advised if doctors were to breach that social contract before it has been breached by anyone else'. This comment was leaked to the *Guardian* and reported on 20 September. The BMA responded with predictable outrage, as a result of which Halsbury reluctantly resigned from the chair of the DDRB.[554] Most of the remaining members of the DDRB remained at their post. In

February 1975, Sir Ernest Woodroofe was appointed to replace Halsbury.[555]

The DDRB reaffirmed the need to stand by the twelve-month rule. Nevertheless, the BMA continued its agitation for an interim increase, which returned the spotlight to Castle. In anticipation of a supportive response from the DDRB, Castle conceded that there was a 'strong obligation on the Government not to interfere with the timing and implementation of the recommendations in the next report of the DDRB'. In reply to this constructive response, the BMA withdrew its threat of industrial action, but in view of the uncertainty, asked GPs to submit undated resignations, for use if the next set of recommendations of the DDRB were not accepted by the Government.[556] Castle's assurance slightly eased troubled relations with the doctors, but it earned a stiff rebuke from Edmund Dell, the Paymaster General in the Treasury, who complained that Castle had, by unilateral action, gone well beyond the assurances traditionally given concerning the Government's commitment to honour recommendations of review bodies.[557]

The doctors and dentists awaited the Fifth Report of the DDRB with optimism, anticipating that freedom from statutory controls would permit the righting of past wrongs. Their expectations were also heightened by the big settlement for nurses recommended by the Halsbury enquiry, supplemented by the additonal increase taking effect from April 1975. The professions were not disappointed. The DDRB report, completed and published in April 1975, recommended increases averaging at 30 per cent (or 35 per cent including consolidation of threshold payments), the cost of which amounted to about £134m.[558] The most generous increases were directed to general practitioners, who were judged to have fallen behind their colleagues during the last few years. Castle made the case for acceptance of the award in its entirety. She warned that any shortfall would provoke further industrial action from junior hospital doctors and consultants, and would provoke the GPs into activating their letters of resignation. Ministers agreed that there was little choice but to endorse the DDRB recommendations without modification.[559]

Consultant Contract

The consultant contract was an intermittent source of confrontation between Ministers and senior hospital medical staff throughout the life of the 1974/79 Labour administration. As already noted, Barbara Castle hoped that prompt action to establish a joint working party chaired by David Owen would enable a new contract to be worked out, which would satisfy consultants, but also become a vehicle for two major and related policy aims of Labour: first, the phasing out of pay-beds; secondly, consolidation of the advantage of whole-time service. On pay-beds, the two sides soon became embroiled in bitter dispute, which soured relations, created a mood of suspicion and animosity on the part of the consultants, so reducing the likelihood of agreement on the consultant contract. Without the irritant of the pay-beds dispute, it is unlikely that disagreements over the contract would have blown up into a full-scale dispute.

There was a small area of common agreement. Both parties were willing in principle to transfer to a closed contract, with extra allowances for additional duties. However, the two sides on the Owen working party pursued incompatible objectives. The health departments aimed to increase the advantages of the whole-time contract by such inducements as a complete commitment allowance and Career Structure Supplements, and by eliminating merit awards. By contrast, the doctors sought a common contract, with all consultants being permitted to undertake private practice, and there was also advocacy of a contract based on fee for item of service. In August 1974 the BMA conducted a survey of consultants, which revealed a division of opinon. A small majority of consultants were broadly satisfied with existing arrangements and were unwilling to consider militant action to change their contract. However, a substantial minority were in favour of change, and most of these were willing to impose sanctions, ranging from working to contract to signing letters of resignation.[560]

The Government's position was weakened by its acquiescence to an unrealistic target date of the end of November 1974 for the drafting of the new contract. The doctors' negotiators took their survey as a mandate for change. In early November the consultants presented their proposals for the contract, and insisted on a prompt reply from the Government. The menacing stance of the medical negotiators was reinforced by outbreak of unofficial industrial action.

The need for further ministerial discussions concerning top salaries pay reviews and the health departments' draft contract forced Castle to play for time. The Cabinet received her proposals on the new contract on 19 December 1974. Castle found her colleagues irritable and impatient. They neither understood nor sympathised with her proposals. According to Castle's *Diaries*, she was 'viciously, unfairly and unscrupulously' attacked by Dell. Foot gave the official line of his department, which was also unsympathetic, but he concluded by recommending that Castle should be left with the discretion to handle negotiations, providing that the pricing of the new contract by the Review Body was subjected to further meaningful discussion by the Cabinet. To the evident annoyance of Dell, Foot's generous compromise was supported by the Prime Minister.[561] Castle's proposals made significant concessions to the consultants, but they introduced certain significant innovations dictated by Labour aspirations. Consultants currently in employment were to be allowed to retain their existing contracts. For new appointees, there would be a standard five-day contract, with two variants: Option A, an eight-plus-two session contract carrying the entitlement to private practice; Option B, a contract for ten sessions for those favouring whole-time service. Arrangements were included for additional payment for certain types of work not covered in basic sessions. Additional sessional payments were also available, but mainly for those with Option B contracts. The latter would also be advantaged by Career Structure Supplements. Consultants taking Option A were not to be excluded from these supplements, but deductions would be made with respect to their earnings from private practice. Introduction of the Career Structure Supplements entailed abolition of distinction awards.

The draft contract was distributed shortly before the meeting on 20 December 1974, when Castle and her colleagues faced a large and predictably hostile medical delegation.[562] Castle noted that the doctors were 'lined up for war', and their mood was not improved by Castle's refusal to give further consideration to a fee for item of service contract, which represented a reversal of a concession to the doctors mentioned at an earlier stage by Owen.[563] The medical negotiators claimed that the new contract represented a sinister attempt to drive consultants into whole-time contracts, thereby reneging on the agreements of 1948, threatening the independence of doctors, and in the words of one of the leading negotiators, 'totally alien to medical tradition in the country'.[564] As a consequence of this confrontation, industrial action, known euphemistically as 'sanctions', became intensified, mainly spearheaded by the break-away Hospital Consultants and Specialists Association, but imitated out of fear of loss of face by the BMA.

After this stormy beginning, the medical negotiators gave formal consideration to the new contract, which they decided was not a viable basis for further negotiation. They therefore switched their ground and concentrated on securing more advantageous terms for the existing contract. Castle made patient attempts to keep negotiations on the rails. Responsibility for the next stage of discussions was largely entrusted to the Chief Medical Officer.[565] The issues under consideration were relatively trivial, but negotiators for the profession sustained an atmosphere of relentlessness, culminating in a marathon meeting with Castle and her colleagues on 16 April 1975, which lasted from about 4.00pm to 7.00am the next day. The meeting agreed to a number of modifications to the current consultant contract, including shortening of the incremental scale, introduction of London weighting, and a scheme for remunerating family planning work in hospitals. It was also agreed to institute further negotiations to work out schemes for recompense of such items as emergency recalls, administrative work, voluntary extra sessions, and on possibilities for replacement of distinction awards by Career Structure Supplements.[566] On 18 February 1975, called 'climax day' by Castle, after a long meeting, the medical representatives voted by a big majority to accept the agreement and to recommend the ending of sanctions.[567] The first steps were made towards implementation of this agreement, but progress was then delayed by the counter-inflation policy announced on 11 July 1975, which precluded introduction of further improvements in remuneration. As described below, further active discussion of the consultants' contract recommenced in 1977.

Junior Hospital Doctors Dispute
Labour inherited a long-running problem concerning the excessive hours and unsatisfactory contract affecting some 20,000 junior doctors and dentists.[568] Some small ameliorative changes had been made to pacify the increasingly disgruntled junior hospital doctors. In 1970 a new system of Extra Duty Allowances was introduced. In November 1973 the Joint Negotiating Committee of the medical profession presented proposals for a new contact. The junior doctors pressed for their standard working week to be defined as 40 hours, with supplementary payments for additional hours of work, or on call. After exploratory meetings during the last months of the Heath administration, the first substantive discussion of the new contract occurred in April 1974. In July 1974, 80 hours replaced 102 hours as the threshold for eligibility for EDAs.

Ministers met junior doctors representatives on 8 January 1975, when they successfully cleared up misunderstandings and agreed on the principles of a new contract. The main features of the new system were: payment of a basic salary for a 40-hour week; salary supplements for additional hours, paid at two levels, Class A for standby work in hospital, and Class B, a lower rate for on call time.[569] The parties agreed that the new system would be introduced in October 1975. It was expected that the costs would be largely covered by the scrapping of the EDA scheme, which was estimated to cost about £12m a year, equivalent to about 12 per cent of the junior doctors' pay bill. Castle was 'jubilant at our success' in reaching a compromise on this long-standing problem and potentially treacherous issue.[570]The next stage was the pricing of the contract by the DDRB. In June 1975, Castle approached Michael Foot in his capacity of Secretary of State for Employment to seek permission to submit joint evidence to the Review Body. Since January, the Government's attitude towards pay had changed sharply, and Ministers were preparing to announce the first stage of their new pay policy. Foot therefore insisted that in view of the substantial pay increase received by junior doctors in April 1975, application of a 12 month rule entailed that the total cost of new payment must fall within the cost of the EDA scheme. He also suggested that supplementary payments should begin at 48 hours or even higher.[571] Castle complained that the restrictions suggested by Foot were likely to provoke a confrontation with the junior doctors, and asked for them to be recognised as an anomaly, meriting an increase in their pay bill of 5 per cent. Foot refused, but agreed to 40 hours as the threshold for new supplementary payments.[572] After further protest Castle agreed to proceed on the basis proposed by Foot. Her position was weakened by lack of support from Ross, who believed that the junior doctors were being treated with unnecessary leniency. He favoured delaying the pricing of the contract until April 1976.[573]

On 5 September 1975 the DDRB issued its report on pricing of the new contract.[574] The report followed the lines of agreement between health departments and the doctors, except that it proposed 44 hours as the threshold for salary supplements.[575] Class A and Class B salary supplements were to be paid at 30 per cent and 10 per cent of plain-time rates respectively. The Review Body estimated that one-half of junior doctors would gain by these arrangements, but one-third would be worse off. On account of the difficulty of providing worthwhile levels of the new salary supplements within the limitations of the Government's anti-inflation policy, it was decided to devote the whole of the EDA fund to supplements, thereby removing protection of earnings from the one-third who likely to be adversely affected by the new contract. This lack of no detriment provision was the most controversial aspect of the Review Body report.

Despite some disappointment, on 2 October 1975, the recently-formed Hospital Junior Staff Committee of the BMA voted to accept the Review Body report. The main reservation expressed by the HJSC related to qualifying hours, where it favoured 40 rather than 44 hours. It also asked for delay of the starting date for the new contract until 6 October. This outcome was regarded with some relief in Government circles, and NHS authorities were instructed to make arrangements to introduce the new contract. The authors of the new contract completely misjudged the degree of opposition to the new arrangements at the grass roots level. The strength of this backlash forced the HJSC and the Joint Negotiating Committee to revise their position and rescind support for the new contract. They insisted on inclusion of a no detriment clause, as well as a 40-hour threshold for supplementary payments. These demands were communicated to DHSS on 9 October, forcing the health departments to abort implementation of the new contract.

Scepticism about the Government's intentions and doubts about the effectiveness of the junior doctors' leadership, prompted outbreaks of unofficial industrial action. Once this commenced, it spread like a bush fire, until within a few weeks about half the regions were badly affected; in the North-West the majority of hospitals were limiting services to accident and emergencies. The junior doctors changed their leadership and became radicalised; the BMA allowed itself to be swept along by the tide and made little attempt to exert a conciliating influence.

Castle pleaded with her colleagues to make some concession to the junior doctors' demands, but on grounds of the need to maintain rigid consistency with pay policy she was rebutted. Foot and Treasury Ministers favoured delaying implementation of the new contract until April 1976, when they suggested that no detriment provision could be offset against the £6 a week limit envisaged as Stage 2 of incomes policy.[576] Ross warned that this device was unlikely to reduce hostility, since it would provoke further resentment among the large number of junior doctors who stood to gain from the new contact.[577] Castle was placed in difficult situation; Ministers insisted on strict adherence to pay policy, the medical profession demanded terms which inevitably raised the cost of the settlement and thereby breached pay policy.

Castle and her team embarked on frenetic negotiations with the junior doctors and their seniors. The first gain by Ministers came at the end of October, with the agreement of the doctors to suppress a hostile ballot. This was replaced by a substitute ballot taking account of small concessions announced on 31 October 1975. The revised proposals allowed for all junior doctors to stay on their old contact with EDAs paid at existing rates, starting at 80 hours until they changed job. The new contract according to the terms previously described would be introduced gradually as juniors changed their posts. In April 1976, subject to the Review Body's agreement, the new contract would be introduced for everyone, with a no detriment clause financed out of the £6 per head per week which would be available for all junior doctors for their next pay settlement under the counter-inflation policy. The agreement also proposed to the Review Body certain alternative methods of achieving the no detriment provision in April 1976. The health departments also offered tacit support for reducing the threshold for supplementary payments from 44 hours to 40 hours. Finally, the health departments offered certain other reassurances protective of the interests of junior medical and dental staff. The medical side offered to put the new offer to a ballot, and the BMA advised that the proposals represented a 'significant change'. Castle reported these developments in the Debate on the Address.[578] Notwithstanding this positive development, various competing factions came forward with other demands, including a claim for a 40-hour week, with all additional work being charged at premium overtime rates of the kind paid in industry. Industrial action continued as before, while the ballot failed to settle the issue; a majority favoured the revised settlement, but a large minority were in favour of continuing industrial action in order to extract improved terms. Although on 20 November 1975, Foot and Castle made renewed attempts to explain pay-policy constraints to the HJSC, the BMA Council endorsed the extended claims of the junior doctors and instituted official industrial action.

The basis for a compromise emerged from an unexpected direction. The Junior Hospital Doctors' Association, which contained about 5,000 members, claimed that the hitherto accepted total of £12m for the cost of the EDA scheme was an underestimate, since it was based on out-of-date information. On 11 December 1974, an agreement was hammered out between the health departments and the HJSC, under which the most recent EDA payments would be subject to independent audit. The parties confirmed their earlier agreement over a 40-hour threshold for supplementary payments; they proposed to frame joint evidence to the Review Body on the standard working week, and it was agreed to undertake a joint investigation into the problem excessive working hours.[579]

At its meeting on 16 December, the HJSC experienced difficulty in confirming the agreement reached by its negotiators, and it refused to call off industrial action. The HJSC stopped short of making demands for further concessions; instead it called for clarification of various points, offering to reconsider calling off industrial action if a satisfactory response was received from the Government.[580] These minor points were quickly cleared up, allowing a letter to NHS administrators to be dispatched at the end of the year, setting out arrangements for introduction of the new contract.[581] In February 1976, the Review Body issued its report, taking account of the independent audit on the EDA payments.[582] On the basis of this estimate, the Review Body was able to increase from £11.9m to £14.2m the amount available for payments under the new contract. The Review Body recommended that the whole of this extra amount should be used to reduce the threshold for the new salary supplements to 40 hours. The main missing element in the recommendations was lack of a no detriment provision, but in view of the lapse of time this issue was becoming less important. The Review Body's recommendations were accepted without reservation by the Government.

This brought the junior doctors dispute to a temporary conclusion, but the major problem of excessive hours remained to be settled.

705

Also, more embarrassment was caused for the Government when it was discovered that the cost of implementation of the new contract was much higher than the £14.2m allowable under pay policy. Already in April 1974, according to one estimate the cost would be £31.8m.[583] DHSS discovered that part of the explanation was longer hours of work than anticipated, but the main cause was the predominance of Class A supplementary payments. Whereas it had been assumed that there would be an equal balance between A and B units, in practice the ratio was 9 to 1.[584] The Government's conscientious effort to prevent the new contract from breaching pay policy was therefore a failure. Expectations that the new contract would reduce complaints from junior doctors also proved to be misfounded. Already in July 1976, the doctors representatives were back on the doorstep of the Prime Minister, demanding no detriment provision with respect to reduced payments to junior doctors during annual and study leave, a dispute which sparked off a new round of unofficial industrial action.[585] Following further negotiations and clarification of ambiguities in the new contract, a further agreement was reached in September 1976, when Ennals expressed the hope that industrial action would end, so heralding 'a new era of improved relations between the Government and the medical profession'.[586]

Merrison

A further small but necessary gesture towards pacifying the medical profession was response by the Government to the long-running grievance about the General Medical Council. Little had changed since 1858; the GMC was tolerated but little respected. The Todd Commission on medical education was scarcely a vote of confidence in the GMC. There was a general feeling that the GMC was a self-perpetuating gerontocracy, out of touch with current medical thinking. As a manifestation of their wave of militancy at the time of Crossman, the doctors demanded action to reform the GMC. In 1970 a Special Representative Meeting of the BMA demanded that a majority of the GMC should be elected by the profession, and this view was backed up by a threat of withholding the annual retention fee for the Medical Register. In response to continuing threats from the doctors, the Heath administration established an enquiry into the regulation of the medical profession, headed by Dr A W Merrison of Bristol University. This committee reported on 16 April 1975.[587] The Merrison Report made wide-ranging proposals concerning the regulation of medical training. It suggested that the supervisory powers of the GMC should be extended from the undergraduate period to cover the all stages of medical training. Merrison went further than the Todd Report in its suggestions for reorganisation of graduate clinical training. The Merrison recommendations

706

concerning graduate clinical training raised questions about the length of medical training, and therefore possessed substantial expenditure and manpower implications. Under the Merrison proposals, the GMC would be able to control standards of training through its maintenance of an indicative specialist register. The Merrison Report also made suggestions for overhauling the arrangements for registration of doctors holding overseas qualifications. Among the various recommendations relating to fitness to practise, the most attention was attracted by the proposal to establish a committee of the GMC with powers either to suspend or subject to conditions the registration of a doctor whose fitness to practice was in doubt on grounds of mental or physical ill-health. In order to equip the GMC for its extended role, the Merrison Report made suggestions for substantial changes in its composition. The recommendations concerning constitution of the GMC represented a delicate balancing act with respect to the many classes of claimants. The Merrison proposals anticipated an increase in members from 46 to 98, of which 54 would be elected. Ten of the nominated members would be laypersons. It was suggested that the Republic of Ireland would cease to be represented.

Formal consultation on the Merrison Report began in September 1975. Given the wide range of recommendations by the Merrison Committee, and the likelihood of disagreement over many of the proposals concerning medical training, it was evident that comprehensive legislation would be long-delayed. The disagreements following the Todd Report, and slow progress over implementation of Briggs recommendations confirmed that progress was likely to be slow. Since the BMA attached more importance to reform of the GMC than any other matter, it sought an undertaking from the Government that it would adopt a piecemeal approach to Merrison legislation, beginning as a matter of urgency with reconstitution of the GMC. In return, the BMA agreed to co-operate over increase in the annual retention free from 1 May 1976 and to allow the GMC to be allocated new powers in connection with EEC Medical Directives needing implementation by December 1976, but only on condition that legislation on the composition of GMC was introduced without delay.

The health departments were reluctant to embark on split legislation on Merrison, but in view of insistence from the BMA there was little choice. In October 1976, Ministers agreed to signify acceptance in principle of the major recommendations of the Merrison Report, and to the introduction of early legislation to reconstitute the GMC and grant new powers of control over the registration of doctors who were unfit to practise.[588] This cleared the way for preparation of the Medical Bill, which in March 1977

Ministers agreed to introduce during the current session, providing that the opposition agreed to Second Reading Committee procedure. This agreement was obtained, but the health departments were unable to complete work on the Bill in time for its inclusion in the 1976/77 legislative programme. However, medico-political factors necessitated some strong indication of progress, otherwise Merrison was likely to figure in the list of grievances aired at the Annual Representative Meeting scheduled for July 1977. Ennals therefore proposed to announce introduction of the Medical Bill during the last few weeks of the 1976/77 session, and reintroduction at an early stage during the next session. By this means he hoped to avoid withholding of retention fees. The nature of the Bill was unchanged, except for the addition of provision for separate Branch Councils of the GMC for England and Wales.

The Treasury held up this proposal on account of its associations with Briggs legislation. Since the health departments had at one stage evolved a proposal for a short Bill containing the minimum essential elements of Briggs and Merrison, the Treasury assumed that both analagous elements in the Bill entailed longer term expenditure commitments. Accordingly, Treasury officials, supported by the Chief Secretary, assumed that separate Bills relating to Briggs and Merrison would also possess expenditure implications, and were therefore open to the same objections as the joint Bill. With some difficulty DHSS managed to satisfy the Treasury that the Merrison Bill was free from hidden expenditure consequences, leaving Ennals free to make his conciliatory gesture in advance of the BMA Annual Representative Meeting.[589] The Merrison Bill was accorded first place in the DHSS legislative programme for 1977/78. Although Ennals was initially unenthusiastic about introducing the Merrison Bill in the House of Lords, owing to the likelihood of criticism concerning its narrow remit, this course was followed, and the anticipated problems failed to materialise. The Merrison legislation, known as the Medical Bill, received its Second Reading on 29 November 1977, and the Medical Act obtained the Royal Assent on 5 May 1978, coincidentally, exactly one hundred and twenty years after the first Medical Act to which the GMC owed its origins.

Incomes Policy
Optimism within the Wilson administration about the ending of statutory pay restraint was shortlived. Foot assured Parliament that 'people throughout the country should not believe that we have any intention of reinstating a freeze or statutory control...we shall not return to the statutory system'.[590] Dismal economic indicators, including inflationary wage settlements, many of them in the region of 30 per cent, negotiated between October 1974 and April 1975,

elicited a change of heart among Wilson's colleagues. At first, the trade unions, while not enthusiastic participants, went along passively with the new incomes policy. On 11 July 1975 the Government announced its aim to reduce inflation to less than 10 per cent by the summer of 1976, which necessitated restricting pay settlements to a limit of £6 a week during the following twelve-month period. This was Stage 1 of an incomes restraint policy expected to last for several years. Stage 2, introduced in July 1976, adopted a limit of 4.5 per cent. Stage 3, introduced in the summer of 1977, was only supported to a limited extent by the trade unions. This envisaged holding public sector pay increases to 10 per cent. In July 1978, in the face of growing trade union antagonism, the Government toughened its incomes policy, to adopt a norm of 5 per cent for Stage 4.[591] During the autumn of 1978, it became apparent that the Government was unlikely to obtain adherence to its target. Following substantial breaches on 5 per cent within the private sector, in January 1979 industrial militancy in the public sector was on the increase. The number of working days lost in January 1979 was the greatest since February 1974, at the height of the three-day week. Thus, the ghost of Heath's pay confrontations returned to haunt Callaghan during the dying months of his administration.[592]

As in other public services, all groups of personnel within the health services were submitted to the discipline of incomes policy, and in common with other groups, it became increasingly difficult to hold the line, until during the last months of 1978 there was a slide into a free-for-all as Stage 4 of Healey's incomes policy disintegrated.

In common with other public sector groups, health service personnel observed the Labour Government's pay code, but each successive stage was marked by increasing signs of distress within the Whitley Councils and the DDRB. Barbara Castle quickly appreciated that the DDRB would find it difficult to function under the new incomes policy and might well become a source of embarrassment to the Government. She therefore considered closing down the DDRB completely for next pay round after completion of its work on pricing of the junior hospital doctors contract.[593] In the event the DDRB scrupulously followed the Government's guide-lines, but it expressed concern about the anomalies generated by the pay code and drew attention to what it regarded as mounting injustice faced by its clients. The carefully constructed pyramid of relativities was immediately undermined by incomes policy. Whereas the highest paid were penalised by the cut-off point of £8,500 for the £6 a week increase and threshold payments, the junior doctors substantially improved their position through their new contract, which ran counter to the intentions of pay policy.

709

In presenting his seventh report to the Prime Minister, Woodroofe expressed 'profound misgivings about the rigidity that has characterised the measures of the last two years', made worse by the Government's interpretation of its pay policy. As a consequence, in the area of doctors' and dentists' pay 'injustice and nonsense abound'. He urged that the credibility of the Review Body was being undermined, which constituted a grave threat to the NHS. Woodroofe therefore called for progress towards 'restoring order to the pay structure of these professions'.[594] Notwithstanding these strictures, the seventh report completed in May 1977 also followed the pay code, but it conceded that the professions had fallen 10 per cent behind counterparts in their level of remuneration. The seventh report evoked the complaint from the BMA and BDA about their members' 'quite disproportionate sacrifices in the national interest' made under Stages 1 and 2 of incomes policy.[595] These representations were sufficiently serious to merit the Prime Minister receiving a delegation from the doctors and dentists.[596]

Armed with supportive comments from the sixth and seventh reports of the DDRB and resolutions from the Annual Representative Meeting of the BMA, the professions claimed an interim pay increase. This proposal was rejected by the DDRB in its interim report, but Woodroofe warned the Prime Minister that his sympathies were with the professions. The DDRB was impressed by the 'growing feeling of hopelessness and disillusionment at the ever-increasing deterioration' in the position of the professions. Woodroofe therefore announced that the Review Body would be making recommendations to 'start on restoration of order to the pay structure' of their clients.[597] The DDRB concluded that the professions had fallen 15 per cent behind comparable groups in their pay, a conclusion which the Treasury regarded as a 'piece of pretty fair nonsense'.[598] After discussions among experts, the Treasury concluded that the professions had not fallen behind by more than 8 per cent.[599] Treasury officials were indignant that the health departments had not been more effective in correcting the erroneous judgements of the DDRB.

The eighth report of the DDRB, completed in April 1978, predictably contained proposals for rectifying the anomalies described by Woodroofe. The latter again complained that incomes policy had left the professions at 'levels far short of that which is needed to bring doctors and dentists into a proper relationship with the community as a whole'. The DDRB therefore proposed an immediate increase averaging 10 per cent from April 1978, but also a further adjustment of 18 per cent, to be implemented in two stages, ending at the latest in April 1980, to bring the professions up to the

710

desired level. Woodroofe and his colleagues issued a veiled threat of resignation if these recommendations were not sanctioned.[600]

The eighth report of the DDRB placed the Government in a difficult position. The Treasury was desperate to hold down pay settlements in preparation for a low target for Stage 4 of incomes policy. Trade union leaders told Callaghan that they were unwilling to hold back their members if the professions were granted an award of more than the 10 per cent permitted under Stage 3, with no promises concerning prospective adjustments.[601] Ministers were at odds over their response to the eight report. Their problem was compounded by simultaneous emergence of similar claims relating to the universities, the non-industrial civil service, and higher ranks in the armed forces. A big prospective increase for the latter was recommended by the Armed Forces Review Body. When the Subcommittee on Pay Negotiations of the Ministerial Committee on Economic Strategy accepted the armed forces increases, but proposed to defer the parallel recommendations from the DDRB, Ennals predicted that Woodroofe and his colleagues would resign and that the professions would embark on a damaging campaign of disruption. He therefore argued for parity with the armed forces and insisted on the implementation of the eighth report in full. Ennals argued that the agreement for an exception with respect to the 'law and order' group should be extended to his field on grounds that 'life and death' deserved parity of treatment.[602] The Pay Subcomittee was 'split down the middle' over giving a forward commitment to the doctors and dentists. Ennals assured them that acceptance of the DDRB recommendations would not damage future policy because it was rectifying past anomalies.[603] The debate continued at the Cabinet, where Foot and Booth made the case for conceding no more than a 10 per cent increase. Callaghan argued the case for full implementation of the award. He was supported by Owen and Williams, who cited the recent history of relations with the doctors, which suggested that they would be tough and totally unscrupulous opponents if given the opportunity to confront the Government. Ministers agreed by a majority to support full implementation of the eighth report of the DDRB.[604]

This endorsement of the DDRB recommendations was a satisfying conclusion for the professions, and it guaranteed peace on their wage front for a further two years, placing them in the unusual position of being disinterested observers during the winter of discontent. While others wrestled to gain increases of more than 5 per cent, the professions within the remit of the DDRB were recommended for an increase of nearly 26 per cent in the ninth report, which was issued on the eve of the 1979 General Election. Sanction for this increase was given by the Thatcher administration.

For most groups of NHS personnel, the dissolution of the Labour Government's pay policy entailed spiralling conflict and an unsatisfactory outcome. In line with Stage 3 limits, during the early months of 1978, such groups as ancillary workers, ambulance staff and nurses settled for about 10 per cent. The awards produced only temporary respite. Each group sought ways of improving its pay position. The nurses immediately pressed for shorter working hours, and also a 'compensatory award'. Shorter hours had been recommended by the Halsbury enquiry, but no action had been taken owing to pay policy. The nurses also hoped for compensation on account of their ineligibility for rewards from productivity schemes. Ennals made representations on behalf of the nurses, but he was rebuffed by the Treasury and he was not supported by Millan.[605] Disappointment among nurses concerning this outcome was exacerbated by tactless remarks made in a speech by Ennals to the Royal College of Nursing conference in Harrogate in June 1978.[606] After this episode, Ennals wrote again to Healey urging steps to improve the pay position of nurses. Healey once again refused, and the Prime Minister commented that 'this is the kind of thing that will set off the wage spiral chase once again'.[607] In October 1978 Callaghan again discussed nurses wages with Ennals, and was similarly negative in his response.[608]

In the autumn of 1978 most groups of health workers were preparing claims above the 5 per cent limit announced by the Government. The unions representing ancillary workers drew up a claim for a basic rate of £60 for a 35 hour week, which amounted to an increase of about 40 per cent. Ambulance workers made a similar, but slightly higher claim. In the light of such claims, Alan Fisher of NUPE predicted that there would be a 'serious winter of discontent' over the Cabinet's pay policy.[609] The *Daily Express* headline declared that a 'New Health Pay War Looms'.[610] In October the nurses representatives held two meetings with Ennals to make the case for an interim 15 per cent 'special case' or 'exceptional treatment' award. Ennals sympathised with the nurses to some extent, but some badly chosen remarks earned him a bad press.[611]

Given absence of progress in addressing their grievances, on 18 January 1979, the nurses held a protest meeting at Central Hall, Westminster, followed by a mass lobby of MPs. Unions representing health workers participated in a national 'day of action' on 22 January, which was the start of a wider campaign of selective industrial action against Government's pay policy. From then until mid-March, the NHS was seriously disrupted by strikes. Industrial action by ambulance staff and ancillary workers attracted particularly wide publicity.[612]

Ennals appealed for some concession to nurses above the pay limit of 5 per cent, in anticipation of a later award from a comparability study. Ennals warned of 'the most serious disruption of the health services we have yet seen. Feeling among the nurses is running very high indeed. This is a new phenomenon, since the unions concerned have traditionally been very moderate'.[613] Healey bluntly refused on the grounds of the danger of creating a precedent, or a 'loophole through which any group with public sympathy or industrial muscle could sail'.[614] In an effort to contain the political damage, the Prime Minister met the Staff Side of the Nurses and Midwives Whitley Council. Callaghan read the nurses a lecture on the economic situation, once again emphasising the 'vicious circle of spiralling inflation'. Although no direct concessions were offered, he encouraged further discussions about the possibility of a comparability review.[615]

On 13 February 1979 Ennals met the two sides of the Nurses and Midwives Whitley Council separately to encourage acceptance of a modest pay award from April 1979, with any subsequent increase being dependent on a comparability study.[616] In response the full Whitley Council expressed dissatisfaction with their treatment over recent years compared with other groups inside and outside the NHS. They complained that nurses' pay was treated as a minor adjunct to the pay settlements of manual and ancillary workers. Furthermore, the nurses had been denied many of the advantages in conditions of work enjoyed by other groups. The Whitley Council insisted on the separate determination of nurses' pay on the merits of the case.

The Nurses and Midwives Staff Stide pointed out that nurses had borne the burden of outbreaks of industrial unrest within the NHS, but in return they had been cynically treated by the Government owing to their conscientiousness and unwillingness to take industrial action. As an addition to any settlement negotiated for April 1979, they demanded a substantial payment on account with respect to the comparability award. They also insisted that the comparability study should be completed no later than August 1979, and that its recommendations should be implemented in no more than two parts, the first being dated April 1979.[617] The pay-claim submitted by the Staff Side for April 1979 envisaged a minimum basic salary of £60 a week, with proportionate increases for higher grades, and also the restoration of differentials eroded during the period of incomes policy. This claim would have entailed a 70 per cent increase in the pay bill.[618]

Ennals urged that some substantial concession needed to be made to the claim by the nurses. Ministers agreed to offer the nurses 9 per cent, plus £1 a week on account for the comparability exercise, which was precisely the same as the settlement agreed by unions representing most of the ancillary workers, but rejected by NUPE members. On 5 March 1979, after extensive preparatory discussions, the nurses and midwives were offered a 9 per cent increase from April 1979, a comparability study, to be implemented in two stages (August 1979 and April 1980), and an advance payment of £1 a week from April 1979.[619] The Staff Side expressed disappointment, especially regarding the date for implementation of the first stage of the comparability award, and the low level of the payment on account. Although, from a later vantage-point, the differences between the Government and the nurses may seem trivial, at the time the Government's offer was fiercely attacked in the media as 'miserly', or 'insulting' to the nurses. The nurses' cause attracted much media, public and parliamentary sympathy. Treasury Ministers were warned that the nurses were 'winning the publicity battle hands down'.[620] The issue was referred to the Cabinet, where opinion was divided. Ennals called for concessions to the nurses, but others advocated a firm line in the interests of incomes policy. The majority followed the Prime Minister in favouring a modest compromise. It was agreed to make a small adjustment in the payment on account to £2 for the most junior staff and £2.50 for career grades.[621] This concession was accepted by the Nurses and Midwives Whitley Council and it was announced on 3 April 1979.[622] In opting to abandon their campaign, the nurses were no doubt influenced by the settlements made by unions representing the ancillary workers. Between 26 and 29 March all the unions called off their industrial action. For the Labour administration, this marked the end of the health service industrial disputes. However, this situation ought to be regarded as an intermission rather than a solution. Already, at the time of the General Election it was evident that the comparability study could not be completed by the promised date of August 1979.[623] The new administration was therefore faced with the sensitive task of determining the level of a further interim award payable from August 1979. Also the appearance of the long-awaited Speakman Report on the pay of top officers in NHS authorities had profound implications for nursing pay, and provided them with a new platform upon which to base their future claims.

Consultant Contract Resumed

As described above, the counter-inflation policy of 1975 interfered with the implementation of the hard-fought agreement reached on the consultant contract in April 1975. On reflection, both sides were not dissatisfied with a suspension in negotiations. Both the profession and the health departments came to the conclusion that their interests were not best served by reliance on war of attrition. By the end of 1976 there was a consensus that a renewed attempt should be made to obtain agreement on a new contract. The pace was set by the Negotiating Subcommittee of the CCHMS, which in the autumn of 1976 prepared a draft outline consultant contract.[624] Following informal exchanges, in January 1977 Ennals suggested that negotiations should begin with the aim of developing a 'more rational basis for contracts in the future'.[625] The profession was quite frank about its motives for favouring a new contract: providing the improvements agreed in 1975 were incorporated, they believed that a contract in which the main items of work were separately remunerated offered the only realistic means to obtain 'justice', which broadly meant a much higher financial return for the work currently undertaken for the NHS, without sacrificing opportunities for additional remuneration from private practice.[626] The consultants were also guided by the experience of the new contract for junior hospital doctors introduced in 1975, where transfer to an industrial-type contract had led to big financial gains for overtime work. The health departments were also influenced by experience with the junior doctors contract, and accordingly set about minimising opportunities for additional payments occasioned by a closed contract. Ennals and his staff adopted as their main aims: a basic commitment of 10 sessions, with one extra session to cover on call, and emergency call fees, but with no additional payment for continuing clinical responsibility; a lower maximum number of sessions for those undertaking private practice; reforms to the distinction awards system to give greater weight to shortage specialties and unpopular regions; and transfer of the contract to the area level of administration.[627] This agenda represented a major retreat from the 'new deal' designed by Castle, and it was a major concession to the demands of the profession. Officials persuaded Ministers to accept as a negotiating objective, 'the development of a contract for salaried service which encourages whole-time commitment while not discriminating unnecessarily against private practice'.[628]

The joint working group formed to discuss the new contract began work on 23 February 1977. By contrast with the situation in 1974, the negotiations were conducted amid little publicity, on a pragmatic basis, and without acrimony. The atmosphere was improved by retreat into the background of the pay-bed issue, and the greater amount of common ground between the two parties. The joint working party was shadowed by a steering committee representing the health departments, which began its work in June 1977. Agreement was largely reached by the end of 1977, but discussions on a few outstanding points of disagreement and drafting details extended until the end of April 1978.

The main point of controversy was private practice, where the medical negotiators refused to accept that consultants prepared to renounce the right to private practice should be allowed to take on a greater number of additional sessions than those opting for a contract permitting private work. Gaining concessions on this point was symbolically important for the medical side, while resistance to such changes was essential for the political credibility of the Labour Ministers. Ennals tested the compromise arrangement on Ministers, proposing that whole-time consultants might be permitted to contract for 15 notional half-days, whereas those undertaking private work would be limited to 13 notional half-days. He pointed to other aspects of the contract that were likely to benefit whole-time consultants, and suggested tentatively that those with whole-time contracts should be allowed to undertake small amounts of private work. Ministers reluctantly accepted Ennals' proposals, but refused to consider allowing private practice for all consultants, and they were convinced that Ennals had already made too many concessions to the BMA.[629] The two sides eventually agreed on a vague formula under which employing authorities, when considering the number of notional half-days above the basic ten for which a consultant was contracted, would take 'full account of the extent to which his time can be committed to the NHS, in the light of his other commitments including private practice' in deciding whether to offer a contract for 13 or 15 notional half-days.

Also potentially explosive was the Government's suggestion that the contracts of consultants should be held by AHAs rather than RHAs, but Ministers decided not to press this point on account of uncertainly over the future of AHAs. The final exchanges related to distinction awards, where it was agreed to leave the system basically unchanged, but with small modifications to attain more even spread with respect to geography and specialties.[630] By the spring of 1978, the consultant leaders were satisfied that they had gained the best compromise attainable under the circumstances. On the NHS side there was less satisfaction. When the RHA Chairmen raised their reservations about transfer to an 'industrial' contract, and especially about opportunities for fraud offered by emergency recall fees, the doctors vehemently denied that the spirit of their contract had been altered, and they expressed confidence that new contractual arrangements would not increase the amount of dishonesty among consultants.[631]

The next hurdle was a ballot of consultants on the new contract, but their leaders were sufficiently confident to push forward with preparations for implementation in advance of the verdict of their colleagues. The two sides agreed to establish a joint working group on implementation of the contract, which commenced work on 14 June 1978. The result of the ballot, announced on 22 June, revealed that seventy per cent of those responding were in favour of the new contract.

The two sides in negotiations now reversed their traditional roles. The health departments became the more reluctant partner; with memories of the fiasco over the junior doctors contract, officials were suspicious that the contract would lead to a further escalation in the cost of consultant services. The doctors' leaders pressed for early implementation, urging the Labour administration not to dissipate the opportunity to purchase goodwill among the consultants.[632] The doctors aimed to have their contract in place by April 1979. By dragging their heels slightly, the health departments were able to make this timetable unattainable. The departments insisted on allowing RHAs to conduct a survey of consultants' workload; it was then necessary to prepare evidence for the DDRB, which priced the contract in conjunction with its 1979 review of doctors' and dentists' remuneration, which was published in June 1979. The consultants were disappointed by the pricing, which led to a further outburst of hostility against the health departments. The CCHMS even refused to submit the priced contract to a ballot. It was also necessary to consider further alterations to the contract in line with the views of the Conservative administration.[633] Final agreement on the new contract therefore eluded the Labour administration, notwithstanding negotiations which had lasted with intermittent breaks for the whole of its tenure.

The Royal Commission monitored progress of discussions on the new consultant contract with some alarm. While it was not in principle opposed to changes which made the contract more 'workload sensitive', it judged the contract negotiated by Ennals 'of most benefit to the surgical specialties and to be injurious to those shortage specialties and clinical areas which the health departments have identified as priorities'. The Commission also believed that the inducements to whole-time practice and academic employment were insufficient. The Commission warned that the new contract had repeated the errors of the junior doctors' contract, by sacrificing the concept of the 'traditional role of a doctor in assuming the total care of his patients regardless of times of duty or other commitments'.[634]

(xii) ROYAL COMMISSION ON THE NHS

The Royal Commission on the NHS received its Royal Warrant in May 1976. Given the huge task with which the Commission was faced, it is not surprising that its report was not completed until the end of June 1979, after which it was published promptly in July 1979, shortly after the change of administration.[635] This sequence of events coincided with the timetable adopted at an early stage in the project.[636] The main departure from the Chairman's original intentions was the failure to produce an interim report on matters of immediate importance. Merrison originally intended to produce such a report after 6 months.[637]

As already mentioned, the Royal Commission had an unusual genesis. Normally, the decision to establish a Royal Commission emerges after much antecedent discussion, in the course of which a consensus is reached that a particularly grave problem requires an investigation carrying the kind of authority that only a Royal Commission is able to provide. A Royal Commission is often the only means of satisfying the public that the caring professions and the agencies of Government are amenable to an impartial solution to a problem a great national importance.

The Royal Commission on the NHS fulfils hardly any of these criteria. Perhaps a Royal Commission ten years earlier would have fulfilled these conditions, since there was an argument for such an investigation in advance of a decision about NHS reorganisation. Crossman later regretted that this course had not been followed. There was much less point in establishing a Commission just after reorganisation, and before the new system was given an opportunity to prove itself. As indicated in this volume, many enquiries of a specialist nature, ranging in status from the Royal Commission on Medical Education to humble departmental working parties, reviewed the many problems afflicting the NHS. It would be difficult to claim that the Merrison review stemmed from public concern, or that it was necessary for some objective reason only intelligible to the expert. As already indicated, the Ministers and health departments saw no need for a general review of the NHS, and they were only reluctantly persuaded to change their mind, and then without conviction. The Royal Commission owes its origin to a perverse cause. It was conceived by the medical politicians, especially by the BMA, as an apt device to undermine the Wilson administration's policy of phasing out private beds from the NHS. Having appreciated that the Royal Commission would first delay, and then perhaps contest Labour's policies regarding private medicine, other justifications for a review were then invented and grafted adventitiously on to the argument. Once the conflict over private beds had broken out, then the medical politicians pronounced that the 'NHS is chronically, seriously sick', and they drew up an agenda of problems sufficient to justify a general review, appreciating that the Government would reject any proposal for remitting the problem of pay-beds or private medicine to an independent enquiry.[638] On the basis of this wider platform, the BMA was able to attract a certain amount of support from other organisations such as the Royal medical and nursing colleges, and the demand for a Commission was even smuggled into the junior hospital doctors' negotiations for a new contract.

When it became clear that the Royal Commission would be unable to interfere with the Government's plans for phasing out pay-beds, the BMA largely lost interest in this exercise. The Government was left with the unwanted child. The Royal Commission was dutifully established, shunted on to a branch line, and allowed to pursue its enquiries without any sense that it possessed immediate relevance to any of the pressing problems of health care confronting the Labour administration. There is little evidence that outside pressure groups expected the Royal Commission to influence events, while in Government circles the Commission was rarely mentioned. It was treated more as an gesture of piety than as a determinant of policy.

The broad remit given to the Commission constituted an invitation to diffuse and superficial comment. Even for the most expert and experienced group of Commissioners, a comprehensive investigation into the NHS would have constituted a formidable challenge. For the group actually appointed, it is arguable that the task was beyond their competence. From their partisan standpoint, the medical politicians commented adversely on the membership of the Royal Commission. Dr Davies of the BMA complained that there was no member with specialist acute hospital medicine or surgery credentials, but five representatives of NHS administration.[639] In replying to a similar complaint from a delegation from the Royal Colleges, Ennals argued that the members of the Royal Commission were not delegates or representatives, but a small group selected for their 'experience, expertise and wisdom'.[640]

The Royal Commission held 35 meetings, and established subcommittees which held 83 meetings.[641] The Commission also travelled widely, including outside the United Kingdom. It reviewed about 2,500 pieces of written evidence, while oral interviews were conducted with 70 organisations. In line with the increasing research-orientation of Commissions, the Merrison group sponsored a variety of research reports, of which one was included in the Commission's Report, while six others were published separately.[642] The reports were predominantly based on surveys; for this reason they retain permanent interest as sources of information. Despite these forays into research, as a sponsor of reports, one investigator places the Merrison Commission 'somewhere at the bottom end of the league', and with respect to its utilisation of current research, 'the Report failed to capitalise on existing and on-going work'.[643] The role of researchers in the work of the Commission was the source of early disagreements between the secretariat and Professor Alan Williams. The latter argued that the subcommittees established by the Commission required guidance from experts from the outset, whereas the secretariat favoured grafting on researchers at a later stage according to the needs of the occasion.[644] Professor Williams continued to espouse the cause of research, and he made suggestions for in-depth investigations, even if this was likely to add to the cost of

719

the project and delay the report.[645] The secretariat contested William's methodology, and insisted that his suggestions were inappropriate to an investigation undertaken by a group of 'gifted amateurs'. Williams remained dissatisfied and this disagreement contributed to his resignation from the Commission.[646]

In March 1977, after a seminar held by the Commission, Merrison summarised their tentative conclusion in the form a list of draft recommendations. This list provides a useful insight of the ideas uppermost in the thinking of the Commission at this relatively early stage in their work: (1) People should be prevented from becoming patients; (2) Efficiency needed to improve, and the deficiencies of care in the community should be corrected; (3) Hospitals need to be integrated more closely with community services; (4) The morale of NHS personnel needs to be improved; (5) Districts should be established as statutory health authorities; (6) Area Health Authorities should be abolished; (7) Regions should be retained as planning authorities; (8) The health departments' top management function should be transferred to a NHS Board; (9) Encouragement should be given to private practice outside the NHS.[647]

Merrison appreciated that some of these draft recommendations would be difficult to translate into practice, while others were far from commanding a consensus within the Commission. However, most of these ideas survived in a recognisable form into the final report.

Reactions from members of the Commission to the draft recommendations varied. Most were supportive. Bramley liked the opening sentiment because it indicated sensitivity to the idea of positive health, and therefore promised to give a leading role to prevention. This priority offered a chance to strike a blow for preventive dentistry. In Bramley's view, the 'biggest disgrace is the failure of the Health Service and Government to do anything about fluoridation'.[648] Some members were unsympathetic with Merrison's approach. Richards complained about lack of attention to continuity of care and failure to treat the patient as a whole. This was reflected in Merrison's acceptance of the fragmented administration of the health and personal social services, including the damaging division between hospital and community services.[649] Richards continued to voice similar complaints. With respect to the draft report she commented that 'despite our statement in the Task of the Commission, the patient does seem to have got a bit lost, and when not lost, has been divided'.[650] In response to this criticism, chapters were rearranged, especially to give more focused attention to the patient in Part II of the Report.[651] However, this device overlooked Richards' insistence that continuity of care should be reflected in the organisation of services.

720

Reorganisation was the issue which caused the greatest amount of worry to the Commission. Members were united in favouring simplification of the administrative structure of the NHS, but there was little consensus concerning preferences for change.[652] The members from Scotland, Wales and Northern Ireland were broadly satisfied with their current arrangements. The most favoured view was represented by Merrison's provisional recommendations (5) to (8). These proposals were supported by a paper from the secretariat, which concluded that the weight of opinion in the evidence 'is that there is a need for a regional organisation below which there should be one operational level of management (the single district area pattern), but that whatever the general pattern there should be room for local variations (particularly in London)'. Although abolition of the area emerged as favoured alternative, the secretariat was not entirely convinced that it was necessary to introduce wholesale reorganisation. It was also recognised that the evidence submitted was dominated by NHS authorities, and therefore might have represented expressions of self-interest on the part of administrators. The secretariat also appreciated that 'another prior question is whether or not the NHS should be handed over to local government', but this alternative was not considered significant enough to merit discussion in the memorandum.[653]

Although not an issue covered by Merrison's initial recommendations, much evidence was received supporting the integration of Family Practitioner Committees with AHAs, which approximated to the position in Scotland. However, this suggestion was vigorously contested by the BMA and its allies, which favoured strengthening the autonomy of the FPCs. In discussion on this point within the Commission, Richards and Batchelor argued for abolition, and Merrison was persuaded that this was the right course.[654] Despite its contentiousness, the final Report of the Commission included abolition of FPCs as one of its major recommendations relating to reorganisation.[655]

The most radical idea relating to reorganisation emanating from the Commission constituted draft recommendation 8. Merrison insisted on including this 'non-runner' in order to encourage further discussion, and on account of his own uneasiness 'about the modern myths of the Secretary of State and his accountability to Parliament'.[656] Despite the small amount of evidence in its favour, and absence of information from the health departments concerning earlier discussions of this idea, Merrison continued to press his enthusiasm for the NHS Board.[657] In August 1978, at the request of the Commission following their discussions at a conference at Runnymede, where renewed support was given to the Board idea, the secretariat produced a memorandum providing possible models for a

721

NHS Board, and also on alternatives such as strengthening the powers of RHAs, or a inspectoral commission to take over and extend the HAS and to manage CHCs. A link with the past was provided by evidence from Lord Taylor, a veteran supporter of this idea. It was suggested that the NHS Board would control: pay and conditions of NHS staff, manpower planning and training, allocation of capital and revenue to top tier authorities, operation of the planning system, management of the NHS research programme, guidance on hospital building, equipment and supplies, policy development for specific services, liaison with local authority services, and provision of advice to professional groups.[658] The NHS Board or 'health commission' alternative was given sympathetic consideration in the final Report, but it was not adopted as a recommendation, although Ministers were asked to keep the idea under review.[659]

The question of transferring the administration of the health service to local government was widely mentioned in the evidence, but this issue was little considered by the Commission. Richards was favourable to this idea, while Batchelor regarded it as a most important and difficult issue requiring expanded discussion.[660] DHSS monitored discussions within the Commission and it confirmed that the local authority alternative was not supported by 'any strong tide of thinking' within the Commission.[661] The Treasury was satisfied that medical members of the Commission would use their influence to suppress this proposal. However, the Treasury was sufficiently concerned about the possibility of the Commission recommending local government control of the health service to merit preparation of defensive briefs on this subject.[662] The final Report of the Commission decisively rejected the local government alternative.[663]

The Commission owed its origins to the pay-bed dispute. In view of the contrasting expectations of the Government and the medical profession, this topic presented the Commission with an awkward problem of balance. Enthusiastic endorsement of private medicine would have been an embarrassment to Labour Ministers, while a negative assessment would have generated an onslaught from the medical profession, which would have cited this conclusion as definitive proof that the Commission lacked impartiality. Members of the Commission were therefore sensitive to likely criticism from the medical profession. One expressed concern that despite much redrafting, their treatment of private practice was 'still negative, crabby and rather slanted'.[664] The Commission feared that its credibility would be undermined if private medicine was not accorded a prominent and judicious assessment. The treatment of private medicine in the final Report generally succeeded in satisfying the medical profession and it was also broadly in line with the thinking of the incoming Conservative administration.[665]

722

Table 7.1
Concordance between the chapter content of the First Draft
and Final Report of the Royal Commission on the NHS

June 1978 Draft	July 1979 Report
Part I INTRODUCTION	
Ch. 1 Introduction	Ch. 1 Introduction
	Part I A PERSPECTIVE OF THE NATION'S HEALTH AND HEALTH CARE (Chapters 2-4)
Ch. 2 Definitions and Objectives	Ch. 2 Objectives of the NHS
Ch. 3 How Good the Service is Now	Ch. 3 How Good the Service is Now
Ch. 4 and Ch. 5 Failures and Cures	Ch. 4 What Others Say
Part II SERVICES TO PATIENTS	Part II SERVICES TO PATIENTS (Chapters 5-11)
	Ch. 6 Priorities
Ch. 6 Introduction	
Ch. 7 Preventive Medicine	Ch. 5 Good Health
Ch. 8 General Medical Practice	Ch. 7 Primary Care Services
Ch. 9 Dentistry	Ch. 9 Dentistry
Ch. 10 Pharmacists, Opticians and Chiropodists	Ch. 8 Pharmaceutical, Ophthalmic and Chiropody Services
Ch. 11 Hospital Services	Ch. 10 Hospital Services
PART III NHS AND OTHER SERVICES	PART IV THE NHS AND OTHER INSTITUTIONS (Chapters 16-18)
Ch. 12 Local Authority Services	Ch. 16 The NHS and Local Authorities
Ch. 13 Occupational Health	(Part of Chapter 5)
(Part of Chapter 11)	Ch. 17 The NHS, the Universities, and Research
Ch. 14 Private Medicine	Ch. 18 The NHS and Private Practice
Part IV NHS AND THE CONSUMER	
Ch. 15 CHCs	Ch. 11 The NHS and the Public

Part V MANPOWER	Part III THE NHS AND ITS WORKERS (Chapters 12-15)
Ch.16 Introduction	Ch. 12 General Manpower Questions
Ch. 17 Nurses	Ch. 13 Nurses, Midwives and Health Visitors
Ch. 18 Doctors	Ch. 14 Doctors
Ch. 19 Other Staff Groups	Ch. 15 Ambulance, Ancillary, Professionals, Scientific and Technical, Works and Maintenance Staff
PART VI MANAGEMENT AND FINANCE	PART V MANAGEMENT AND FINANCE (Chapters 19-21)
Ch. 20 Central Management	Ch. 19 Parliament, Health Ministers and their Departments
Ch. 21 Local Management	Ch. 20 Health Authorities and their Organisation
Ch. 22 Finance	Ch. 21 Finance
	Ch. 22 Conclusions and Recommendations

The first full draft of the final report of the Commission was circulated in June 1978.[666] It is instructive to note the structural similarities and differences between this first draft and the final Report. The two are generally very similar. The differences may be summed up as follows: the first two parts and the final part are broadly similar; in the central sections, the order of the parts dealing with manpower and relations with other services are reversed; finally the single chapter part IV in the draft is eliminated and absorbed into chapter 11 of the final Report. Either orderings of the parts was justifiable. The main additions in the final Report were the chapters on priorities and on universities and research. These constituted significant additions. The chapter on priorities allowed greater prominence to be accorded to community care and services to vulnerable groups such as the elderly, the mentally handicapped, and the mentally ill. The main losses from the draft were the separate chapters on CHCs and occupational health, but these were assimilated into other chapters of the final Report. Naturally, there was much room for redrafting within the chapters, but even here the main lines of the recommendations changed little after June 1978.

To its frustration, little indication of the conclusions of the Commission reached the the Treasury. However, some impressions were picked up at a meeting with the Commission on 19 March 1979, when the Commissioners concentrated on the prospects for raising more resources for the health service, examining such long-standing issues as hypothecation, or little-considered options such as lotteries.[667] It was estimated that some £40m a year might be raised from lotteries, but the Treasury warned that such initiatives were counterproductive since they would prompt a proportionate reduction in Exchequer funding. The Treasury complained about the Commission's preoccupation with 'ingenious ways of raising funds for the NHS'.[668]

Despite its likely electoral advantage to Labour, Ennals made no attempt to extract the report from the Royal Commission in advance of the General Election, even though such a target could have been met without difficulty. There is every indication that the Merrison team trod water to avoid their report appearing during the election period, presumably to avoid any suspicions of partisanship, and in order to allow their work to be assessed in a calmer political atmosphere.

In course of his congratulatory letter to the new Secretary of State, Merrison mentioned that the report had reached its fourth draft and that publication was likely in July. The Chairman estimated that the text would amount to between 200 and 250pp.[669] The report was published on 11 July 1979.[670]

The emerald green-covered Report emerged as 491-page volume. The conclusions of the Commission were summarised in 117 recommendations. The last part of the Report included about ninety pages of appendices, which were miscellaneous in character, the most unusual of which is Appendix J, a 26-inch-wide diagram of the medical advisory structure in Trent RHA. Unlike some previous Royal Commissions, the oral evidence was not published.

The Report was an unpretentious and accessible review of the health service - the first such report produced since the beginning of the NHS, and indeed the first comprehensive, independent, but officially-instigated report on health care in Britain ever undertaken. The nearest approximate antecedent was the Report of the Royal Sanitary Commission of 1871, but that was much more specialised in its remit. The only real analogue was the Cathcart Report of 1936, but that was confined to Scotland.[671] For reasons already given, the Royal Commission was a less formidable investigation than suggested by its elevated status. At the time, the Report was welcomed as a constructive contribution, but it turned out to exercise negligible influence and has made little permanent impression. This was indeed the logical consequence of the circumstances of the genesis of the Royal Commission. The Treasury was exactly right in its predictions: 'it is probable that, after the build-up, the report will come as something of a damp squib, and Mr.Jenkin's rather cautious statement will do nothing to set it alight'.

Many of the detailed reflections and recommendations of the Commission have already been cited in preceding pages. The main thrust of the report was adequately expressed in a brief prepared for the Prime Minister:

> The report attempts to dispel the notion of crisis, whilst admitting that demand will always exceed supply and that their recommendations for substantial additional expenditure could only be afforded as the nation got wealthier; it offers strong support for the Government's proposals on simplification of the administrative structure of the NHS and devolved responsibility; it dismisses the consultants contracts negotiated by the previous Government, as indeed have the professions themselves since the Election and it provides some support for the Government's proposals on private practice. It rejects alternative methods of financing the NHS by insurance.[672]

This summary indicates that, fortuitously, the Report of the Royal Commission proved to be helpful in smoothing the transition from Labour to the new Conservative administration. One of the few recommendations discomforting for the incoming administration was the proposal for the gradual but complete extinction of direct charges.

(xiii) LABOUR AND REORGANISATION

As noted in the previous chapter, the 1974 reorganisation was from the outset widely criticised from many perspectives. The Labour Party was among the critics, but the Wilson administration regarded it as unrealistic to embark on further disruption by introducing additonal major administrative changes until firm conclusions had been reached about a superior, viable alternative form of organisation. Schemes for further reorganisation proliferated, many of them envisaging radical departure from the existing structure. For instance, as early as 1975, Professor M D Warren suggested that the health service in England should be organised along the lines adopted in Scotland and Wales, on the basis of 28 area health boards, subdivided into districts.[673] This conclusion was also reached by David Owen. Already in 1975, Castle recorded consideration of his paper on the reorganisation of the NHS, where Owen 'argued extremely effectively for the elimination of the regional tier'.[674] Such ideas percolated through to the Chairmen of the new RHAs, who pressed Castle to give assurances that the Government was not intending to eliminate one of the existing tiers of the health service.[675] Responding to these anxieties, Castle assured her colleagues that the Government was 'not proposing to drop the

Regional tier or to make any sudden drastic changes in any of the tiers'.[676] Within these limitations Labour was able to introduce some significant changes in line with its policy aspirations. Alterations in the composition of health authorities and the extension of powers of CHCs, undertaken in the context of the 'democracy in the NHS' exercise have already been described in detail. The health departments also made suggestions for closer co-operation of health and local authorities, although it is not altogether clear whether the changes improved the situation, or merely contributed to the profusion of committees and administrative confusion. Commentary on these collaborative arrangements and joint planning initiatives emphasised the slow pace of change and the paltry scale of the resultant projects.[677]

Despite efforts to shore up the existing system, even within NHS there was general support for simplification of the administration. As calls for economies in management costs increased, NHS administrators were persuaded that these objectives could not be attained without reorganisation. Their favoured option was evolution towards a system modelled on the existing single-district areas. In the course of 1977 and 1978 about a dozen proposals for amalgamating districts were considered, and many of these adjustments were adopted.[678] As a consequence, the number of districts was reduced from 205 in 1974 to 199 in 1979.[679]

A further aspect of the reorganised health service requiring consideration by the Labour administration was the future status of the 14 postgraduate teaching hospitals in London. Owing to failure to work out a place for these institutions in the reorganised structure, section 15 of the NHS Reorganisation Act 1973 allowed for these hospitals to continue under their Boards of Governors, initially for a period of five years. This issue was considered by the Royal Commission, but the Secretary of State also worked separately to achieve a solution. Discussions began in April 1976, with the circulation of an 'Aide Memoire' by DHSS. This was followed by a discussion paper in March 1977, and the establishment of a study group in September 1977. In November 1977 Ennals convened a small conference, which authorised the production of a consultative document, which was discussed at a second conference in June 1978. This conference expressed preference for establishment of a Postgraduate Health Authority, occupying a position analogous to a RHA, with direct links to DHSS. Consultations on this proposal were still under consideration at the date of the 1979 General Election.[680] As an interim measure, in March 1979, the Boards of Governors of the London Postgraduate Hospitals were accorded an extension for a further three years.[681]

The most radical organisational change anticipated at this time related to the devolution White Paper, which envisaged transfer of major responsibilities for the administration of health services to elected Scottish and Welsh Assemblies, but these policies were abandoned with the collapse of the devolution initiative.[682]

Labour came under increasing pressure to declare its position on NHS reorganisation in advance of the report of the Royal Commission. The Government was keen to gain full electoral advantage by being seen to improve on the unpopular system introduced in 1974. Vague proposals by the Government for applying the principle of devolution to the 'English Dimension' produced few tangible results. However, these discussions revived earlier disagreements over local government reform, which inevitably raised questions about the health and personal social services. Much speculation was aroused by statements issued by Peter Shore in January and August 1978, in which he declared that the Government would sponsor 'organic' reform of local government, meaning limited, pragmatic changes, designed to correct the worst anomalies stemming from the Local Government Act 1972. Shore gave an undertaking to pay regard to the recommendations of the Merrison Commission before embarking on this programme.[683] The Queen's Speech in November 1978 contained an announcement that the Government would amend the Local Government Act 1972 'to secure the better functioning of local democracy in a number of large towns and cities in England'.[684] These intentions were amplified in the Organic Change White Paper published in January 1979.[685] This included proposals to transfer social service departments from some county councils to the more populous non-metropolitan districts. In view of the relevance of these proposals to health care, the Royal Commission on the NHS complained, and argued that the Government should not commit itself to a firm decision until after the Commission had reported.[686] Shore's proposals were put out for consultation, where they ran into widespread opposition among experts on local government. This consultation process was not completed by the date of the General Election.

The health service was prominently mentioned in the Cabinet 'Forward Look' discussion held in September 1978, occasioned by Callaghan's decision not to opt for an autumn General Election. The meeting identified themes suitable for Labour to exploit in the run-up to the postponed election. On the social services front, Ministers were of course concerned about resource constraints, but also they were sensitive to a great deal of public dissatisfaction with the growth of apparently unfeeling and incompetent bureaucracies. They feared that the NHS gave the impression of being designed for the people who administered it rather than for the needs of the sick.

728

It was therefore necessary to give assurances that the service would be responsible to, and careful of the needs of, those it existed to serve. The Prime Minister emphasised that the health service was ideally suited to illustrate Labour's commitment to democracy and participation. Other Ministers favoured immediate steps to reform the NHS and make further changes in local government. Ennals subscribed in general terms to the Prime Minister's aspirations, but on the whole he believed that the health service was not in a position to bring electoral assets to Labour, since it was plagued by too much controversy. In the field of pay, cuts in services, and hospital closures, further unpopular decisions were inevitable and could not be delayed. Ennals favoured campaigning on such issues as human rights, women's rights, the elderly, value for money in public expenditure, preventive medicine, and community care.[687]

Some members of the Cabinet favoured issuing a general indication of policy regarding health service reorganisation at the Labour Party Conference in October 1978. Ennals strongly disapproved and told the Prime Minister that this would only serve to alienate the Royal Commission and open the Government to attack from the opposition, especially since Labour was not within sight of a settled policy on reorganisation. He argued that the central problem needing attention was the level of resources not organisation, which he believed was reflected in the limited interest in reorganisation revealed by motions to the Annual Conference.[688] However, Callaghan's speech at the Conference included a firm statement of the Government's intention to 'repair the damage done by the Tory reorganisation' and make the service more responsive to patients and its workforce. Out of deference to the strictures of Ennals, Callaghan added that legislation might not be possible during the following session of Parliament and that it would take account of the Report of the Royal Commission.[689]

This speech and rumours circulating at the Conference prompted press speculation that Labour was intending to reorganise the NHS in advance of the report of the Royal Commission, and place the service 'under worker control'. The press ascertained from Ministers that the area tier of administration was likely to be abolished, while officials hinted that the Royal Commission might be asked for an interim report to give guidance on reorganisation. The *Times* speculated that Labour might have been driven to declare its hand on reorganisation by press reports that the Conservatives were committed to abolishing the area tier.[690] Ennals was evidently embarrassed by these reports and attempted to dampen down rumours of an imminent policy initiative. The press then pilloried him for being either ignorant of, or out of step with policy deliberations in the Cabinet.

Press rumours quickly subsided, but the Royal Commission expressed anxiety and suspicion.[691] The Prime Minister only slowly abandoned the reorganisation initiative. He suggested that relations with the Royal Commission would not be damaged if the Commission were persuaded to produce an interim report, after which the Government would be free to introduce reorganisation legislation.[692] Ennals insisted that the Royal Commission was unlikely to come up with simple and radical formula for large-scale reorganisation that was sought by Labour. He suspected that the Commission would favour flexibility, which the department also preferred. Since within the health service and the Labour Party opinion was divided about the future direction of policy, Ennals suggested that they were best-advised to progress by 'organic change', especially by encouraging amalgamation of districts to increase the number of single-district areas. This simplification would greatly improve management arrangements and thereby improve efficiency.[693] Before abandoning the idea of proceeding with reorganisation, Callaghan insisted on holding a discussion with Merrison. The Prime Minister no longer favoured an interim report. Merrison confirmed that the Royal Commission had not come to any straightforward conclusions concerning reorganisation. Indeed, at that stage the Commissioners were not entirely united over the path to follow. Merrison, like Ennals, was not in favour of imposing a uniform system.[694] Immediately after his meeting with Merrison Callaghan confirmed in Parliament that since the Report of the Royal Commission would not be available for several months, there was no possibility of legislation on NHS reorganisation during the current session.[695] As with many other instances discussed in this chapter, this major policy challenge facing the Labour administration ended without resolution, and in this case with complete indecisiveness.

CONCLUSIONS

(i) ANNIVERSARIES

In the opening chapter of this study it was observed that the tenth anniversary of the NHS was marked by a spontaneous wave of applause for the principle of the National Health Service. The new health service had been unable to realise its full potential, mainly owing to resource constraints, but its achievements were sufficiently momentous for the youthful NHS to merit recognition as an addition to our permanent national institutions. The next two decades constituted further convenient landmarks, providing fresh opportunities for testimony about the standing of the NHS. At no stage was there any significant erosion of the popular estimate of the health service, and politicians of all persuasions were consistently reassuring about protecting the integrity of the service. Despite many incremental modifications and the major reorganisation of 1974, the health service of 1979 was the recognisable descendant of the service established by Aneurin Bevan in 1948. The NHS was predominantly funded by direct taxation and most of the services were free at the point of delivery. Direct charges had impinged on the family practitioner services, but this erosion of the free health service had occurred so early in the life of the NHS that charges for prescriptions, glasses and dental care, although never popular, became grudgingly accepted as a part of life. Reorganisation had hardly affected the family practitioner services, which were the patients' main contact with the health service. The big administrative and management changes in hospital and community services below the level of the region were important for the NHS workforce, but they hardly impinged on the patient. Despite the importation of industrial models of management into the health service, what some were attempting to designate as its consumers or customers, were still predominantly known and treated as 'patients'. This linked them with old traditions of care, in some ways protective of their status, in other respects demeaning to their rights.

Despite the apparent stability of the NHS, the preceding chapters have drawn attention to continuous undercurrents of anxiety. Already in 1958 there was widespread alarm about the failure to modernise hospitals, make a beginning with a system of primary care based on health centres, or develop services for care in the community. These concerns prompted leading medical organisations to sanction a comprehensive review of the health service under the chairmanship of Sir Arthur Porritt. The Porritt Report of 1962 was the first major planning document to conclude that the problems of health care in Britain were unlikely to be solved without total reorganisation of the health service.

Although the regime of retrenchment was relaxed to a modest extent, allowing for launch of the hospital plan, revival of the health centre programme, and renewed hopes for community care following the Seebohm report, the twentieth anniversary was a dull and restrained affair. This was partly a reflection of uncertainties associated with the impending amalgamation of the Ministries of Health and Social Security, also insecurity about the direction of policy concerning health service reorganisation and indeed the whole future structure of the welfare state, and finally renewed fears about the return of resource restrictions in the wake of the devaluation crisis. Robinson convened a big conference to mark the twentieth anniversary, which was held at Church House Westminster. This was an austere and uninspiring event, which attracted little outside attention. The publication derived from the conference was suitably funereal in appearance.[1] This episode indicated how little the Ministry of Health had learned about the important art of public relations. Symptomatic of the crisis of leadership existing at this time, Robinson was careful to restrict the more charismatic Crossman to the margins of the celebrations.[2]

During the 1970s, especially after the oil crisis, the storm clouds closed around the health and personal social services. Barbara Castle complained that during her first twenty months of office she had been 'inundated with talk of "crisis" or "breakdown" and of abysmally low morale in the NHS'.[3] Castle blamed the Conservatives for the damage inflicted by their reorganisation scheme and for then stirring up the idea that Labour was responsible for the crisis existing in the NHS.[4]

At the thirtieth anniversary the Labour Government was preparing for a General Election. Although the health service had been spared from the worst of the cuts in public expenditure, the mood was even more sombre than at the twentieth anniversary. The economic situation from 1974 onwards had turned out to be even worse than after the 1967 devaluation. The Joseph scheme for health service reorganisation was confirmed as a failure. Both media and academic commentary was dominated by analysis of 'crisis' and 'conflict' in the health service.[5] This pessimism was increased by the generalised loss of confidence in high-technology medicine within Western society. The mood of discontent was illustrated by the general air of dissatisfaction emanating from the annual congress of the Royal College of Nursing held just before the thirtieth anniversary. The rebuke by Ennals that the pessimism of the nurses was unfounded and his claims that the health service was enjoying an 'upturn' added to the rage of the nurses, and earned him a poor press.[6] Ennals frankly admitted to the Prime Minister that the Government's message of well-being was unacceptable to a disbelieving NHS workforce and the general public.[7] By an unhappy coincidence Ennals issued his celebratory message to mark the thirtieth anniversary from his hospital bed.[8] The general bleak economic and industrial relations scene, uncertainties specific to the NHS, as well as the Secretary of State's illness, contributed to the low-key approach to the thirtieth anniversary. Pleasantly designed booklets were produced to underline the achievements of the health and personal social services.[9] In Ennals' absence, the Prime Minister hosted a reception at Lancaster House to mark the anniversary. This modest event attracted virtually no press attention. Contrasting with the large supplement published by the *Times* to mark the tenth anniversary, on this occasion, both the *Times* and the *Sunday Times* ran series on the crisis in the NHS.[10] Not improving the tone of the celebrations, adverse publicity was attracted by Ennals' revival of the old idea emanating from a leading surgeon that all groups working within the health service should bury their differences and sign a declaration of loyalty to the NHS. With difficulty, some of the unions were persuaded to comply, but they only agreed to subscribe to a vacuous statement. The BMA denounced this proposal as a political gimmick neither required nor justified by the situation of 1978.[11]

(ii) MINISTERS, POLITICS AND POLICY

Neither the present volume nor its predecessor offer straightforward generalisations about party political lines of division in the conduct of policy in the field of health care. Continuities in policy are sufficiently pronounced for some commentators to conclude that health care was depoliticised as far as party politics was concerned.[12] However, as indicated by the content of these volumes, disagreements between the parties were not limited to inessentials, but often equally striking are the differences of outlook exhibited within the parties, with the result that even successive Ministerial teams from the same party were likely to display substantial differences of bias on important policy issues. Because Britain's health care system was unified, placed largely under central government control, and funded largely from general taxation, Ministers were inevitably projected into the front-line of policy-making. Since health care made strenuous demands on resources, necessitated attention to a succession of awkward policy questions, and was subject to many unforeseen crises, it was rarely out of the political limelight. It is entirely erroneous to regard policy-making as the province of bureaucrats and pressure groups. As this volume indicates, health Ministers and their colleagues were much more than onlookers in the process of policy formulation.[13]

The health portfolio offered few opportunities for easy successes and many invitations to disaster. It was therefore in many respects an unattractive assignment and was scarcely ever the passport to political stardom. Of the fourteen persons appointed as Ministers of Health/Secretaries of State for Social Services from 1948 to 1979, only three, all Conservative, went on to hold a further Cabinet appointment.[14] Of these, Barber served as Minister of Health for only the briefest time. Macleod made solid advances, reaching the post of Chancellor of the Exchequer, but only for one month before his premature death. Joseph was the principal long-term political survivor, although this was not especially on account of his record at the DHSS. After this last episode of 'statism' in his career, he became politically rehabilitated, and enjoyed the transition from the status of Mrs Thatcher's mentor to being her epigone. For Walker-Smith, Powell, Robinson, Crossman, Castle, and Ennals, who are considered in this volume, responsibility for the health service effectively marked the summit, and effectively the end, of their ministerial careers. Of course, the reasons were different in each case. The approach of the age of retirement or illness provide the most obvious, but not invariably applicable explanations for the fading of these senior politicians.

At the other end of the seniority scale, the health departments were often a stepping-stone for the aspiring politician. The most conspicuous example of meteoric rise was David Owen, who reluctantly accepted a junior ministerial appointment under Barbara Castle, but was soon granted the status of Minister of State(Health). After a high-profile performance in this capacity, in September 1976 he was appointed Minister of State at the Foreign and Commonwealth Office; then after a few months, upon the premature death of Anthony Crosland, he became Foreign Secretary. No other junior Minister in the English health department was destined for such rapid promotion. The nearest comparisons among Scottish junior Ministers with health responsibilities during the period under consideration were Bruce Millan and Judith Hart, who were promoted to important ministerial posts, although only the former retained Cabinet rank for more than a short time.

Although Derek Walker-Smith is not usually counted as one of the more significant figures among the Ministers of Health, his contribution was far from negligible. This success occurred without the support of a strong team at the top of his department. Both the Permanent Secretary and Chief Medical Officer were reaching the end of their careers. Walker-Smith was also disadvantaged by being outside the Cabinet, which was not the case with the education Minister his main competitor for resources.

Walker-Smith not only brought much-needed stability to his office, but as a barrister with relevant interests, he was ideally placed for overseeing the smooth translation of the Report of the Royal Commission on Mental Illness into law in the form of the Mental Health Act 1959. Not the least important aspect of the mental health legislation was its proposals for expanding community care. Walker-Smith conscientiously attempted to obtain resources for this objective. This constituted one of the elements in his five-year plan for the further development of the health and welfare services. A second element was the proposal for a long-term plan for hospital building, which was near to fruition by the date of his departure from office. In seeking additional resources for the health and welfare services, Walker-Smith was unamenable to making countervailing savings. He was not swept along by the fashion within the Cabinet for higher direct charges and funding health care on the basis of compulsory insurance. He joined forces with Boyd-Carpenter in resisting increases in the NHS Contribution. Not only did he object to expanding health service charges, but he also subscribed to the Guillebaud Committee's conclusion that these charges should be phased out.

Walker-Smith was responsible for overseeing implementation of the findings of the Royal Commission on Doctors' and Dentists' Remuneration, which entailed settling long-standing grievances over pay, and then taking the first steps to establish the Doctors' and Dentists' Review Body. A less effective intervention was the Hinchliffe Committee on prescribing practice, but this also created a helpful intermission, protecting his successor from having to deal with a problem that no administration found capable of resolution.

Largely on the basis of his association with the hospital plan Powell is conventionally regarded as the first Minister of Health since Bevan to have exercised a major constructive influence. Although Powell himself attached little importance to Cabinet rank, it was hardly a disadvantage to be promoted to the Cabinet for the last year of his term of office. Powell was fortunate to take up his appointment at a time of a more relaxed attitude to public expenditure, as a result of which, for the first time, the health service was no longer regarded as the delinquent among the social services. He also enjoyed the benefit of fresh and outstanding appointments as Permanent Secretary and Chief Medical Officer. Sir Bruce Fraser introduced a new era of improved relations with the Treasury, which enabled Fraser to consolidate Walker-Smith's proposals for hospital development into the ten-year hospital plan. Acquiescence to such planning initiatives was less controversial owing to filtration of long-term planning into fields such as school building, and the general adoption of Plowden philosophy, the most tangible expression of which was the PESC system. Powell was therefore more the beneficiary than the originator of this trend towards long-term capital investment. His contribution was nevertheless significant in providing leadership at the time of preparatory discussions with health authorities and at the launch. His most noteworthy contribution was the speech to the NAMH in which he pronounced, with dramatic clarity, albeit prematurely, a death sentence on the discredited mental hospital system.

The famously expensive hospital plan seems an incongruous legacy for a Minister of Health who conducted the affairs of his department as if it were a suzerainty of the Chief Secretary to the Treasury. The anomaly is less pronounced when it is appreciated that the hospital plan was costed at an unrealistically low level, and accompanied by a 'contract' with the Treasury, making virtually no allowance for the current expenditure consequences of hospital capital development. Since it was a necessary condition for economy in the use of hospital facilities, Powell aspired to give precedence to community care, but in practice resources were not made available for this objective, while the Community Care Plan of 1963 was an even more inadequate planning document than the Hospital Plan of 1962.

Powell's retrenchment-minded approach to his responsibilities is evident in most other areas of policy. 'Astringent' constituted one of his favoured catch-words. This astringency was applied regardless of the political cost. This is best illustrated by his attempt to maximise the yield from health service charges and the NHS Contribution. Either objective represented a political risk, but pursuit of both simultaneously exposed the Macmillan administration to damaging criticism. Another incautious application of Powell's astringency lay in the field of nursing remuneration. His negotiating tactics over nurses' pay courted much adverse publicity and yielded no positive economies. The nurses were vindicated at two adjudications by the Industrial Court. Powell's attempts to strike a hard bargain with the nurses was in obvious contrast to his attitude to the pay of doctors and dentists, where he attempted no such intervention.

A further example of inconsistency in the application of Powell astringency is provided by his bid for medicines to be provided for private patients on NHS terms. Although this was a vague policy commitment of the Conservatives, all previous Ministers had evaded its implementation on account of the risk of adverse consequences of a kind that should have been apparent to a former Financial Secretary. When fresh to his post, Powell reversed this line, thus precipitating a clash with senior Ministers, ending with rejection for Powell. This incident arguably highlighted the disadvantageousness of Powell's lack of Cabinet experience, which rendered him insufficiently familiar with the outlook prevailing among senior Ministers more experienced in dealing with political calculations of this kind.

After the brief tenure of Barber, Robinson held responsibility for health service for the first four years of the Wilson administration. Once again the Minister of Health was relegated to the status of middle-ranking departmental Ministers and excluded from the Cabinet. Robinson lost Fraser to DES, but his replacement, Sir Arnold France, continued the Treasury links of the health department. Robinson's already difficult assignment was made more onerous by the ambiguities created during the final months of his appointment by preparations for amalgamation of the Ministries of Health and Social Security. At this stage Robinson's position was also adversely affected by Crossman's overlordship of the social services.

Robinson was outstandingly well-qualified for his post. He was familiar with the NHS regional administration and had served a successful apprenticeship as opposition health spokesman. However, he was disadvantaged by his limited political influence and by his lack of an active advisory team. Robinson's identification with his departmental duties earned the rebuke from Crossman that he was 'the most rigid departmental Minister in Whitehall'.[15]

Robinson was not particularly successful in attracting greater resources for the NHS. He was unlucky in inheriting a commitment to abolish the prescription charge, which immediately used up his credit with the Treasury and therefore stiffened resistance to any pleas for extra resources for such purposes as community care or hospital building. Although he was unable to revalue the hospital plan on anything like the scale desired, Robinson was reasonably successful in keeping up the momentum of hospital building. The weakness of his position became evident at the devaluation crisis, where major decisions about cuts and changes of policy were made by senior Ministers, the effect of which was to place Robinson in an humiliating position with respect to the reintroduction of prescription charge.

Robinson's positive qualities were demonstrated to advantage in the pay dispute with the family doctors. By his conciliatory efforts, Robinson steered out of a potentially disastrous situation and enhanced his own reputation through association with the Family Doctors' Charter. However, this episode does not rank as one of the epic confrontations with the medical profession. The political parties were not at odds over the issues raised by this dispute; no major conflicts of principle intervened; the leadership of the doctors was basically moderate and they were pushed somewhat unwillingly into a confrontation; joint working parties had already worked out the lines of agreement on some of the main issues under discussion; and

737

finally, since the pricing of the contract was in the hands of the Review Body, this removed a further big potential source of friction. Given these advantageous circumstances, although the medical leaders opened their campaign in a traditionally belligerent manner, in practice they worked hard to secure an agreement. Although the issues involved in the new contract were complex, agreement was reached with remarkable speed. Robinson mainly acted as a facilitator for the contract devised by the profession. While the new arrangements were generally not objectionable to the Minister, his department played only a minor part in their formulation. Robinson's handling of this problem at the Ministerial level was shrewd, but it alienated the Treasury on account of the much higher costs than admitted in the course of ministerial discussions. This lapse further stiffened resistance on the part of the Treasury to granting additional resources for such purposes as community care, which under normal circumstances would have been treated as a priority.

Some other policy areas show Robinson in a favourable light. In opposition he advocated expansion of the medical schools and a Royal Commission into medical education, both of which came to fruition when he was Minister. The controversial Abortion Act 1967 originated as a private member's Bill, introduced by David Steel, but Robinson's department assisted from the sidelines. Robinson was also an advocate of extension of family planning services. Only modest progress on this front was recorded, and then by virtue of another private member's Bill, but Robinson was supportive. Robinson was also engaged constructively in the intricate manoeuvring which resulted in the independent enquiry into the personal social services.

Two important issues show Robinson in a less favourable light: first, the state of the long-stay hospitals, and secondly, health service reorganisation. On account of budgetary limitations, Robinson was understandably unable to attract resources for the expansion of community care on a scale envisaged by the hospital and community care plans. The run-down of the big mental hospitals or mental handicap institutions therefore proceeded at snail's pace. Although the Ministry of Health issued circulars laying down guide-lines for better practice, little positive effort was made to guarantee implementation of improvements and generally raise standards to an appropriate level. As an expert on the mental health services, Robinson was well-placed to appreciate this problem. However, his department's response to the initial wave of media revelations about scandalous conditions in long-stay hospitals was over-defensive; the six enquiries sanctioned by him failed to command respect; soon, their credibility was completely undermined by the Ely enquiry, which remained unpublished when Robinson was transferred to another post.

When Labour was returned in 1964, neither political party expected that reorganisation of the health service would emerge as a major policy issue. This was perhaps short-sighted, given the enthusiasm with which the Porritt Report was taken up among medical politicians in Scotland and Wales. It must also have been evident that the major policy reviews relating to local government, the personal social services, and medical education, as well as many other more specific instances cited in chapter IV, consistently raised doubts about the continuing viability of the current organisation of the health service. Reorganisation was quickly embraced by Judith Hart in Scotland, although this enthusiasm was not shared by her successor. The case for reorganisation was conceded only with reluctance by Robinson. No doubt his scepticism was increased by the prospect that this issue would open up further controversy with the medical profession over the proposal for local government control of the health services, and by the emergence of other unwelcome suggestions, such as the hiving-off of the health service to an independent corporation.

It was not until November 1967 that Robinson and Ross sanctioned limited investigation into reorganisation, and their Green Papers were not published until July 1968, by which time the Seebohm Report was already completed. The opportunity for an early and comprehensive study of the case for reorganising the health service was therefore lost, and no serious consideration was given to a scientific evaluation of the issue. Deliberations in London on this difficult and controversial subject were limited to a small group within the health department, whereas in Scotland, the Green Paper proposals had at least the advantage of prior discussion and support in principle from the main relevant interest groups. Unsurprisingly the Robinson Green Paper was attacked from almost every side. The whole process of reorganisation was impaired by these weak foundations provided by Robinson's lack of early attention to this problem.

With the appointment of Crossman the NHS was back in the hands of a major politician, who was in control of a large department, combined with overlordship of the social services, and of course a seat in the Cabinet. Crossman was able to play a big role, akin to the Ministers of Health before the break up of the department in 1951. This lofty political position endowed Crossman with the support of departmental Ministers and other valuable sources of liaison and advice. It may seem somewhat perverse that he relocated Ennals from health to social security, rejected Shirley Williams and Roy Hattersley, and installed Beatrice Serota as his Minister of State

(Health). Despite the disadvantage of her location in the House of Lords, it is likely that she was as successful in this office as any of the alternatives among the political rising stars. In view of her LCC Children's Department background, she was seen as a particular asset in the complex political struggle over the Seebohm changes.

With the departure of Sir Arnold France to the Inland Revenue, Sir Clifford Jarrett became Permanent Secretary, strengthening the dominance of the social security culture within the new department. In order to compensate for this bias, and on account of his limited faith in his officials, Crossman consulted widely outside the department and placed much confidence in his appointed advisers. These came into their own in such situations as the Post-Ely Policy Working Party, or in the preparation of *Better Services for the Mentally Handicapped* and the second Green Paper on health service reorganisation. With respect to Professor Abel-Smith, Crossman commented unusually warmly about their personal and professional association.[16] Crossman more than compensated for lack of colour among some of his predecessors. Although egotistical and erratic, Crossman was stirred by genuine compassion when confronted by some of the great problems confronting him. He responded without the over-defensiveness or narrow regard for departmental interests which characterised Robinson and most other ministerial colleagues.

Crossman's personal responsibility for the health service extended for only eighteen months, but it was an eventful time, which saw active consideration of the reports of the Royal Commission on Medical Education, the Royal Commission on Local Government, and the Seebohm Committee, as well as establishment of the Briggs Committee on Nursing. All of these issues engaged Crossman personally, but his energies were most concentrated on health service reorganisation and the aftermath of the Ely Report. Initially, there was not much opportunity for his imaginative intervention on the question of funding. In view of the devaluation crisis and his obligations as social services co-ordinator, his room for manoeuvre was limited. Nevertheless, in the last few months of his term in office, Crossman's patience wore thin. He made known his distaste for health service charges, and levies of all kinds, including the motor accident levy. Controversially, he began exploring means of increasing the role of graduated insurance in the funding of health care. Crossman's most audacious action was saved until the eleventh hour, when he attempted to breach the PESC limits, instructing his officials to prepare for a 7 per cent rate of growth in health service expenditure by 1973/74. The Wilson administration ended before the strength of Crossman's resolve on this issue was tested.

With respect to the perilous area of pay Crossman adopted a relaxed attitude. A potential conflict with nurses was avoided, but at the cost of a one-year 20 per cent settlement. He also faced a difficult decision over doctors' and dentists' pay, where the Review Body proposed an increase of 30 per cent. Ministers failed to make their decision on this award until the eve of the 1970 General Election. Crossman overlooked the pitfalls associated with doctors' pay, with the result that the BMA was presented with the opportunity to engage in an hysterical campaign against the Government at the time of a General Election. This episode compares with Crossman's most celebrated oversight, when in May 1969 he ratified an increase in health service charges only two days before the local elections.

Crossman's positive qualities were best demonstrated in his response to the Ely scandal. Immediately the matter was brought to his attention, he insisted that the full report should be published and that the department should give high priority to reforming the long-stay hospital sector. In order to prevent back-sliding, the main lines of action were determined by a hand-picked committee of officials and outside experts under his own chairmanship. This Post-Ely Policy Working Party functioned for only a few months, but it proved to be one of the most fertile agencies of change in the entire history of the British health service. The immediate remit of PEP related to the long-stay hospitals, but its impact was much wider. Among the policy advances significantly affected by PEP were: introduction of the Hospital Advisory Service; a programme for immediate imposition of minimum standards; initiation of work on long-term policy, which eventually materialised as the Better Services documents for mental handicap and mental health; preparations for an independent committee to review complaints procedures in hospitals; and facilitating moves towards establishing a health Ombudsman. The scandalous condition of the long-stay hospitals was not capable of resolution by any crash programme, but the interventions of Crossman helped to facilitate a secular change in attitudes. Administrative inertia was broken; the morale of the advocates of mentally handicapped and other priority groups was enhanced, and it was no longer realistic for NHS authorities to hide away from their obligations. From the date of Crossman's appointment, pressure groups representing the vulnerable attended their mission with a new sense of determination and with greater expectation of success.

In the case of the long-stay hospitals, services were so defective that many of the remedies were self-evident. The situation was entirely different with the problem of health service reorganisation, which soon took on the appearance of insolubility. Robinson's plan, although unrealistic, at least had the virtue, albeit unwittingly, of adoption of the fundamental principle, deriving from the 1871 Sanitary Commission, of a 'unified administration of the medical and related services in an area by one authority, in place of the

741

multiplicity of authorities concerned in the present arrangements'.[17] From the 1944 White Paper to the Robinson Green Paper, advocates of unification subscribed to the vague objective of consolidating the administration of health and even personal social services in England and Wales under about 40 area boards. The local authorities insisted that these area boards should be coterminous with reformed local government areas, and preferably absorbed into local government, a view that was supported by the Royal Commission on Local Government. By contrast, the powerful hospital interests regarded areas as artificial constructs, unrelated to the needs of medical services. They favoured an administrative system based on regions and districts, administered separately from local government.

In the context of a plethora of conflicting advice Crossman anguished over the riddle of reorganisation. His frequent changes of mind and impetuous grasping at panaceas, generated frustration among the planners. Between May 1969 and January 1970 he presented the Social Services Committee with three entirely different proposals for reorganisation. The last of these was issued as the second Green Paper published in February 1970. This plan came nearest to his personal inclinations, but it was further modified in his draft White Paper, never published on account of the change of Government, and then completely disowned by Crossman, who regretted that the Wilson administration had not opted to unify the health services under local government. Crossman therefore succeeded no better than Robinson in locating a policy for health service reorganisation that was likely to command universal support, or be recognised as a viable solution. It is a dismal epitaph for both Robinson and Crossman that their handling of the problem of health service reorganisation must be counted as one of the major policy failures of the Wilson administration.

Crossman regarded Joseph as a worthy successor. With Joseph's appointment, the health service, and now the unified personal social services, remained the responsibility of one the most senior members of the Cabinet, although not quite with the degree of power wielded by Crossman. Coincidentally consistent with the precedent set by Crossman with respect to Serota, appointment of Lord Aberdare as Minister of State(Health) resulted in the Secretary of State's health adjutant being located in the House of Lords. This was put to good effect when the health service reorganisation legislation was remitted to the House of Lords. Sir Philip Rogers, the new Permanent Secretary, possessed wide civil service experience. The centre of gravity of DHSS therefore again shifted away from social security into neutral hands sensitive to the need to balance and integrate health and social security. Although Joseph was receptive to intellectual interaction and superior to Crossman in his studious attention to policy detail, he was not temperamentally suited to surrounding himself with officially-appointed advisers.

In the light of future developments, it might be expected that this study would throw light on the genesis of Joseph's reaction against statism. Responsibility for one of the largest spending departments containing in microcosm most of the types of social service provision, meant that he had an ideal opportunity to witness the limitations of the welfare state, as well as the remorseless pressure for additional resources. Although he pursued the quest for additional resources with moderation, and with conscientious regard for Government policy, he was nevertheless a conventional spending Minister, genuinely supportive of the expansionist policies for the health and personal social services bequeathed by his Labour predecessor. It was indeed anticipated that Joseph would adopt a liberal approach to the health and personal social services. Early predictions concerning Joseph's altruistic and liberal interpretation of his brief were fulfilled in almost every respect.[18] National Health Service reorganisation provided him with a opportunity for importation of commercial concepts of management efficiency into the field of the social services. Exposure of neglect in services for the mentally handicapped and other vulnerable groups gave him ample opportunity for expression of social concern. In both spheres, Joseph exhibited exemplary conscientiousness, arguably more than any Minister before or since, examining his briefs with meticulous care, commenting profusely on their content, instigating time-consuming quests for supplementary information, and even undertaking as much reading in the subject area as was possible for a busy Minister. This seriousness of commitment leaves behind a great deal of evidence, demonstrating that Joseph was an undogmatic student, using each policy exercise as a genuine quest for intellectual enlightenment. As Secretary of State for Social Services, he displayed none of the instinct for simplistic formulae, or doctrinaire campaigns associated with the groups with which he later aligned

This nervous, scholarly, monastic approach to his responsibilities was associated with a degree of modesty rare among successful politicians. As John Biffen pointed out, 'Joseph worked loyally with the team, was straight forward and wholly devoid of vanity'.[19] Michael Alison reported that Joseph 'courted no commendation or publicity for his campaign of improvement' in services for vulnerable groups'.[20] The evidence cited in chapters V and VI confirms these impressions.

There was of course a negative dimension to Joseph's instinct for analysis and self-examination; he was demanding on the time and energies of his colleagues and staff, irritatingly lacking in self-confidence, and therefore inclined to be pedantic and indecisive, as illustrated by the handling of NHS reorganisation. By contrast with

743

Crossman, who was an ardent self-publicist, who never missed on opportunity to grab the limelight, Joseph's natural modesty expressed itself in self-effacement. His major speeches were mundane and lacking sense of occasion. This instinct for the shadows was satisfied by the decision to remit the health service reorganisation legislation to the House of Lords, and furthermore to attach controversial family planning clauses to this legislation. This enabled Joseph to evade some of the fire from the opposition, but caused difficulties for the Government, and extended still further the already long-drawn out timetable for the NHS reorganisation legislation. Also, despite his ostensible independence over policy-making, he was in practice rarely able to withstand the entreaties of his officials. Although Joseph earned respect from friends and enemies alike, and even though he was one of the few politicians regarded as an equal by Crossman, Joseph left office with little sense of achievement or satisfaction. Soon his mood of self-examination turned to self-immolation. The whole of his earlier ministerial career, and especially the four years at Health and Social Security were regarded with misgiving on account of his failure to escape from 'my chrysalis of statism'. He admitted that he 'never lifted my head and protested' during the entire period of the Heath administration.[21]

The Joseph tenure was dominated by the question of reorganisation. Fortunately he was not troubled by many other controversial issues. At the inception of the Heath administration, under pressure from outside groups, it seemed that there might be a shift to financing the health service through graduated insurance. This idea was rapidly shelved, and its only legacy was a graduated prescription charge, which was also dropped. Pay was a potential problem area, but once the ruffled sensitivities of the doctors and dentists had been settled and the new Review Body installed, no further problems occurred on this front. The Government's incomes policy, introduced in November 1972 temporarily suspended opportunities for confrontation, although it stored up trouble for Joseph's successor.

Joseph made some small gains in the course of the PESC negotiations, especially with respect to supporting the reconstruction of the personal social services. Joseph remained faithful to Crossman's programme for improving services for vulnerable groups. The *Better Services* policy document for the mentally handicapped was published in 1971, while the equivalent document for the mentally ill was drafted. Joseph and Campbell pressed forward with proposals for a Health Service Commissioner and relevant clauses were included in the health service reorganisation legislation. The Davies Committee on hospital complaints completed its report in 1973, but as in the case of the Briggs Committee on nursing which reported in October 1972, no policy commitment was made before the end of the Heath administration.

Controversies over family limitation proved difficult to handle. The 1967 legislation failed to settle the dispute over abortion. The Heath administration faced immediate pressure to amend this legislation. This invitation to further controversy was side-stepped by appointment of the Lane Committee, the diligence of which saved Joseph from further preoccupation with this issue. However, he was unable to avoid decision on the related question of family planning, where he was faced with a demand for provision of a comprehensive and free service. The excuse of a departmental review enabled Joseph to buy time, but he was unable to avoid clarifying the Government's position with respect to the relevant clauses of the NHS reorganisation legislation. Failure to commit the Government to a free service precipitated a controversy over clause 4 of the NHS Reorganisation Bill lasting from December 1972 to July 1973. Although only minor concessions were made, this issue attracted unwelcome adverse publicity for the Government, which added to anxieties about prospects for the reorganised health service.

Joseph's biggest test was NHS reorganisation. He approached this question with his customary caution, scepticism and intellectual fascination. It was not until November 1971 that he declared the Government's intention to resume preparations for reorganisation; his characteristically low-key Consultative Document was not issued until May 1971. Whereas Crossman had been primarily concerned with maximising local accountability, Joseph's own first priority was management. The two philosophies were in direct conflict at many points. Consequently, the preparation of Joseph's Consultative Document necessitated major departures from Crossman's plan.

To assist with his management objectives, Joseph took on management consultants from the Government's Business Team, from Brunel University, and from McKinsey & Co. Inc. As noted in chapter VI, these experts disagreed among themselves; Joseph's scheme for management by chief executives was a primary casualty of this disarray. Professional realities at the top of NHS authorities led to adoption of management by consensus between the main professional groups, which represented a major retreat from Joseph's position. Despite this concession, the Consultative Document promised a robust approach to management, to be mainly achieved by changing the character of NHS authorities. In compensation, 'consumers' were awarded a small voice at the periphery of the service through the agency of newly-invented Community Health Councils. On account of demands from other Ministers, the consumers were also granted a substantial voice on health authorities, so creating ambiguities concerning their management role. Further complication was caused by the need to construct an elaborate advisory structure for the benefit of the medical profession. The most serious complication arose out of Joseph's attempt to appease all the rival interest groups by adoption of three tiers of local administration. Although statutory health authorities were established at only the region and area levels, in practice there was also a district tier administered by the consensus management team.

Converting the above complications into a viable management structure represented a formidable challenge to the management consultants. The final management plan was not completed by the date of the reorganisation White Paper in August 1972. The Management Report was available by the date of publication of the NHS Reorganisation Bill in November 1972, but the parallel exercise on collaboration with local government was not completed by this date. The legislative process was not completed until July 1973, which left perilously little time to complete preparations for reorganisation by 1 April 1974, the appointed day for both local government and health service reorganisation. Joseph's conscientious attempt to build a strong management structure had been thwarted; his final plan entailed such a large element of compromise that his cherished designs for an effective management structure were largely obscured. The concessions offered to satisfy demands from all quarters generated a scheme of vast complexity which failed to inspire confidence, even among its promoters.

As indicated in chapters VI and VII, the negative response to the long-gestated 1974 reorganisation contrasts with the widespread satisfaction with Bevan's hastily contrived plan for the new health service. Even not particularly friendly voices such as the *Economist* and the *Times* welcomed Bevan's scheme as a 'valiant attempt' to solve an intractable problem that had defeated his predecessors. The *Economist* was satisfied that Bevan's plan was 'more successful than any previous proposals', while the *Times* believed that the new plan would permit the 'rapid development of a well-knit yet flexible' system of health care.[22] It was difficult to make any of these claims for the Joseph plan. Indeed, it was even difficult to argue that it was superior to the much-criticised schemes produced by Joseph's predecessors.

During the first Wilson administration, the appointment of Crossman had blocked Castle's promotion to head the joint health and social security department. Delay until 1974 removed some of the lustre of Castle's eventual success. Wilson was nearing the end of his career, which determined that Castle's chance of ministerial survival was remote. Callaghan immediately dispensed with her services. He nevertheless conceded that she had 'fought with fierce determination and tenacity for the elderly, the sick and the disabled'.[23] Even the normally unfriendly *Times* paid tribute to Castle's 'brilliant and spirited political career'.[24]

For the first time since the formation of DHSS, the whole ministerial team was located in the House of Commons. From the outset, the Minister of State (Health) David Owen was recognised as a more formidable presence than his predecessors in this office. The Treasury was fearful about 'Dr Owen's general inclination ... to press for announcements of rapid advance'.[25] In practice Owen was an economic realist, and he recognised that the onset of retrenchment might provide an opportunity to extract efficiency savings reliant on confrontation with vested interests which might have been difficult to realise in other circumstances. During his brief period at DHSS Owen prompted initiatives across a broad front. Apart from his role in the time-consuming negotiations with the doctors over contracts and pay, he was engaged in working out a plan for democratising and reorganising the health service, further steps towards improving services for the mentally handicapped, increasing the efficiency of prescribing by general practitioners, introducing an initiative on prevention, inspiring action on fluoridation, and attempting to introduce tough measures against smoking. These instances are illustrative of Owen's high level of initiative. Such qualities are of course the hallmarks of a competent Minister, but are rarely evident, particularly in fields such as health, where technicalities and labyrinthine complexities are wont to deter all but the most determined and able politician. High motivation was not a guarantee of success. Unlike the officials who were his sparring partners, Owen was at a disadvantage on account of being a generalist operating in a field of entrenched specialist administrators. As the case studies described in chapter VII demonstrate, Owen was rarely able to devote sufficient time to any one issue to overcome inertia within the system and see his ideas through to fruition.

The troubled atmosphere in which they worked inevitably exposed strains in the relations between Castle and Owen. For instance, during the pay-bed dispute, Castle complained that, although Owen was 'inventive', he trimmed at the first sign of opposition.[26] She made similar observations with respect to the consultants contract; Owen allowed himself to be 'brainwashed' by the consultants, and then attempted to 'railroad' Castle away from key Labour objectives.[27] However, even in the pay-bed context, Castle acknowledged that they made 'a good pair' or complemented each other extremely well.[28]

Both Castle and Owen followed Crossman's example by making active use of formally-appointed and informal outside advisers, the leading figure among whom was Brian Abel-Smith. In Jack Straw, Castle possessed an outstanding political adviser, who came into his own in the many troubled moments during Castle's brief tenure. During the row over the junior hospital doctors' contract, Castle praised Straw as an 'invaluable informal channel of communication'; the junior doctors 'discussed with him, all hours of day and night'. Also in this context, she believed that 'the value of the Special Advisers has been well demonstrated over the past week or so'.[29] Castle was slightly disadvantaged by the continuation of her predecessor's Permanent Secretary, something which had not occurred since Walker-Smith became Minister.[30] Sir Patrick Nairne, the capable replacement for Rogers, was scarcely settled into his post by the date of Castle's removal.

Restrictive economic circumstances in the aftermath of the oil crisis, especially the Government's decisions in April and November 1975 to make big cuts in public spending, precluded an expansionist programme in the HPSS sector. Castle was able to record only marginal gains, such as extending exemptions from prescription charges and introducing free family planning services. For the rest, her position was essentially defensive. As Barnett recorded, she 'was determined not to allow the Chancellor and me to win any easy victories' and she subjected them to 'long harangues about the need for her programmes to have a bigger allocation'.[31]

Castle suffered the distraction of persistent and enervating industrial disputes, especially with the doctors. On her arrival in office, the main problem related to the nurses, but this crisis was resolved by the Halsbury enquiry. The doctors and dentists shaped up for a major confrontation over pay, but their anxieties were relieved by the large award recommended by the DDRB in April 1975. The Government's incomes policy then temporarily limited opportunities for dispute on other fronts. The main arguments and damaging industrial action broke out in unanticipated areas. The consultants insisted on tight timetable for their new contract; after much hard bargaining, provisional agreement was reached early in 1975, but further progress was precluded by the new pay policy. No such easy agreement proved possible over junior doctors' contracts. This group came under increasing militant leadership, but even in their case provisional agreement was reached in February 1976.

Despite conciliatory gestures towards the doctors, such as prompt implementation of the Merrison Report, and even the establishment of a Royal Commission on the NHS, troubled relations persisted. The main irritant was the Government's policy to phase out private practice from the NHS, which was demanded by the trade unions and the Labour Party, but which was repugnant to most within the medical profession and was condemned by the leading medical organisations. The doctors were unused to an administration persisting with policies alien to the medico-political leadership. In this case, all the belligerent noises emanating from Tavistock House were ignored by Castle, who had no real choice but to press ahead with Labour's manifesto pledge. The confrontation with medical leadership over this issue lasted only for a few months, and agreement was reached in December 1975, but the dispute was fatal for Castle's reputation. More than anything else it contributed to her political demise.

Both the pay-bed dispute and other tangles with the doctors represented absorption of energies that might have been applied more effectively elsewhere. Nevertheless, the Castle team recorded progress on many fronts. The democracy exercise strengthened CHCs and reduced criticism concerning lack of local accountability in the NHS. The work of Crossman and Joseph was continued in the fields relating to vulnerable groups. A real effort was made to give greater attention to prevention. The priorities documents for the first time laid down planned and costed guide-lines for the long-term development of services to all client groups within the context of a comprehensive planning system. In recognition of the defects in resource distribution arrangements and failure to correct inequalities in health, the Resource Allocation Working Party was established, which represented the most serious attempt yet made to address these problems. Consequently, notwithstanding the economic crisis, limitations imposed by the unsatisfactory results of NHS reorganisation, and the incubus of controversy with the doctors, within the short duration of its operation, the Castle team proved itself to be a constructive force, indeed one of the best-balanced and most effective ministerial groups ever to be responsible for the health service.

At the date of writing, Ennals was the last Labour Minister ever to hold the health portfolio. Ennals and his team were faced with formidable problems. Granted, constraints on public expenditure were slightly relaxed towards the end of his term of office, but the health departments were confronted with awesome demands for additional expenditure for such purposes as reversing cuts in capital investment, applying recent advances in high technology medicine, speeding up the provision of health centres, implementing the Briggs reforms of nursing training or the Better Services initiatives in mental health and mental handicap, including restoring the cuts made in the personal social services and community care budget. It was clear that Ennals would not be able to meet more than a small fraction of these demands with the meagre extra funds made available to the HPSS sector. The appearance of generosity was also difficult owing to the new disciplines associated with imposition of cash limits and RAWP redistribution arrangements. The many sectors of the health service unable to fulfil their obligations

749

inevitably tended to apportion some of the blame to reorganisation, so adding to the unpopularity of the Joseph scheme, and causing restlessness over Labour's failure to come forward with a superior alternative. The existing sense of grievance within the health service over pay was compounded by the instabilities associated with collapse of the administration's incomes policy.

The regime of hospital and ward closures, staff cuts, delays in opening new facilities, postponement of much-needed capital projects, cutbacks in the development of community care, continuing embarrassments about conditions in long-stay hospitals, even loss of public confidence in vaccination and immunization, were all highly visible signs which rendered it difficult for Ennals to dispel the notion that the health and personal social services were in a state of crisis. Although many of the limitations in the performance of the health and personal social services were clearly the responsibility of the administration as a whole, the blame for this situation was inevitably attached to Ennals himself.

In wrestling with the mounting problems of the health and personal social services, Ennals was disadvantaged by the promotion of Owen and his replacement by Moyle. Ennals retained Abel-Smith, but lacked the kind of rapport with a sizeable group of formal and informal advisers of the kind that had existed under Crossman and Castle. On the other hand, Ennals possessed a particularly competent team of top officials on the health side of his department, headed by Sir Patrick Nairne, who was inherited from Castle.

Although the appointment of Ennals was not unreasonable, his gifts lay in the field of commonwealth and foreign affairs. He shared with his two brothers, John and Martin, identification with the cause of the dispossessed, the persecuted and the immigrant. To the advocate of Tibet and the Dalai Llama, the miserable rounds of economies, or the vortex of industrial disputes into which he was swept during the final months of his tenure were not well-suited to his political skills. These wars of attrition must have seemed enervating and irksome. They demanded qualities of patience and shrewdness which were alien to his nature. His amiable and genial gifts were better suited to less troubled times, when more opportunities would have existed for launching initiatives connected with vulnerable groups.

In tense situations Ennals was prone to misjudgement, as illustrated by his notorious attack on a respected woman district nursing officer at the Royal College of Nursing congress in June 1968.[32] This was followed by further lapses of judgement in his dealings with the nurses. His poor relations with the nurses were not helped by a succession of delays in introducing the legislation required to give effect to the recommendations of the Briggs

Committee. Ennals paid dearly for his public relations errors and other failings in his dealings with the nurses. Although not entirely justified, the press overwhelmingly characterised Ennals as inept and complacent, and calls for his resignation were more common than for any of his predecessors.[33]

The adverse comparison with respect to the Castle and Owen team is evident in the preceding narrative on matters large and small. For instance, Ennals' first experience of PESC negotiations produced no more than token resistance to the demands of the Treasury. At the first hurdle Ennals threw away all of his bids for additional resources on the understanding that his core demand for increases relating to demographic factors would be protected; but he was then manoeuvered into adopting lower figures for demographic change than either DHSS or the Treasury regarded as defensible. It is hardly likely that Castle, or Ennals' more effective colleagues among the spending Ministers, would have contemplated any of these concessions.

With the advent of a slightly more relaxed approach to public expenditure, Ennals embarked on a campaign to reverse the cuts affecting his department. This effort was not entirely unsuccessful. On account of the adverse media attention attracted by the NHS, Callaghan decided that a single injection of £50m in additional funds might be psychologically helpful in restoring confidence among health service personnel and the public. Ennals grasped this opportunity and the imminence of the thirtieth anniversary of the health service to mount a further effort to attain consent to a higher growth rate for the HPSS sector. However, his position was undermined by compelling counter-evidence gathered by the Treasury regarding wasteful expenditure and the scope for economies in the NHS. From this point onward, the Treasury increasingly insisted on financing growth through economies.

With respect to lesser specific policy issues, it is difficult to establish examples of successful initiatives attributable to Ennals. Not unreasonably, in the light of Ennals' experience at MIND, Unsworth suggested that he was 'determined to further the process of achieving reform of the Mental Health Act'.[34] However, the review was sanctioned by Owen, long before Ennals' appointment; under Ennals the review lost momentum, while the White Paper eventually produced failed to satisfy the liberal aspirations of campaigning groups with which Ennals had formerly been associated.

Ennals' negotiations with the tobacco industry provide a further example of weakness in the face of determined negotiators. Notwithstanding the high degree of public support for strong action, the powerful scientific case assembled by expert bodies, and the determined start made by Owen, Ennals failed to persuade his

751

colleagues to back a more decisive policy. Therefore he negotiated from a position of weakness. In return for only derisory concessions from the industry, he granted them a concordat, which placed a moratorium on further action for three years. Even Ennals in retrospect admitted that he had been over-indulgent with the industry, which was not a trivial matter in view of the great loss of life involved. Britain, although first in the field with research in this area, and with a long history of agitation on this issue, had by 1979 fallen behind many of its neighbours in addressing itself to the control of the tobacco smoking hazard.

Even the attempt made by Ennals to mobilise the thirtieth anniversary of the health service to his advantage yielded few returns. The direct plea to Ministers for additional resources was not effectively handled. As already noted, the idea of a declaration of loyalty turned into a demonstration of discord. Then, his attempt to orchestrate collective action on the part of leading organisations representing health workers fell flat owing to evidence of collusion between the DHSS and the supposedly independent outside petitioners.

In the cases cited above, it is reasonable to have expected more effective leadership and sounder judgement than was displayed by Ennals. However, it would be unrealistic to hold Ennals accountable for all the failures to bring long-standing policy problems to a satisfactory conclusion. In the case of the failure to make headway in the improvement of health service complaints procedures, an issue that had been under continuous consideration for more than a decade by 1979, already Castle and Owen had decided that the rights of patients should be sacrificed in order to avoid a further major confrontation with the medical profession. Ennals merely followed the drift of existing policy. In the case of the failure to produce a definitive policy statement concerning services for the elderly, or to turn policy into reality with respect to other vulnerable groups, limitations were imposed by resource restrictions or difficulties in overcoming obstruction by the Treasury. Despite some mitigating factors, it is difficult to regard Ennals as a major asset to the NHS at a time when the service was facing the worst crisis of confidence in its history. Effective leadership in these circumstances was of course a daunting task for any politician. Undoubtedly, alternative appointees would displayed their own disadvantages, but the reservations expressed at the time by contemporaries about the performance of Ennals seem to be largely justified by the documentary evidence.

(iii) DETERMINANTS OF CHANGE

As we are reminded from the instances cited in the case of Ennals, Ministers were faced with demands for resources far outstretching the political will of either Labour or Conservative administrations. The tendency of health services to absorb an expanding share of national resources constituted a phenomenon general to the Western health care system. Much of this increased cost of health care can be objectively justified and was in many respects unavoidable.

The pressures for expansion and modernisation came from many directions. The least tangible of these forces was the tide of rising expectation. Working people were proverbially stoical and had too long tolerated demeaning standards of health care. With the creation of the NHS, the middle classes became for the first time active users of these public services, which were to some extent adjusted in accordance with their higher expectations. Their more assiduous attention to health, active exploitation of services, as well as their general social activism, added to the incentive for improved and more humane standards of care. The impact of vague aspirations among the more articulate classes was greatly intensified by the formation of new pressure groups and the regeneration of old ones. By the 1970s, the combined forces of national and local pressure groups relating to consumers or patients in general, or particular client groups, such as mothers and infants, children, the elderly, the mentally ill, the mentally handicapped, those suffering from specific diseases, or vaccine-damaged children, determined that any shortcomings of the NHS were widely publicised. After 1974 Community Health Councils became the focus for the agitation of many of the above organisations. These voluntary organisations were often associated with experts in their field, professional associations, and research-orientated charities. The combined impact of lay pressure groups, charities, and professional organisations was sometimes decisive in influencing policy decisions and therefore in determining the distribution of resources. Naturally, in some cases, notably in issues relating to fertility or childbirth, not all of the organisations pulled in the same direction.

The spectrum of pressure groups and professional lobbies to a large extent reflected the changing pattern of need, as indicated by epidemiological or demographic indices. The biggest demand on the health and personal social services stemmed from the growing population of the elderly. As indicated in chapter I, this trend was already evident in 1958; by 1979, of the total population of the UK, about 12 per cent of men and 17.5 per cent of women were above the age of 65; 5.5 per cent of the population was above 75, and 1 per cent above 85. Since an over-65 was estimated to cost the health service six times the amount spent on a younger adult, by 1979 the elderly population were established as the dominant users of many of the services provided by the NHS. In order to meet their needs, the new specialty of geriatrics struggled forward to compete with the more

753

established specialties. At the other end of the age spectrum, 1958 marked the beginning of a peak in fertility, which lasted until the mid-sixties, after which there was a steady decline until by 1979 the level of births was back to its interwar level. This decline produced little reduction in costs to the health service since it was associated with a rise of deliveries in hospital, which stood at about 60 per cent in 1958, but had risen to about 97 per cent in 1979. As a consequence of the high level of fertility, the child population greatly expanded, and since this constituted another active user of health services, it was a further source and demand for expenditure. As indicated in previous chapters, this was another area where there was need for radical overhaul of services in order to improve conditions for the practice of the expanding specialty of paediatrics.

Further increases in costs of health care were attributable to advances in medical science. In principle some of the advances represented economies. Vaccination and immunization were cheap interventions which permitted economies in expensive hospital accommodation. The NHS derived a bonus from the large sector of hospital accommodation freed for other purposes as a result of the retreat of tuberculosis. By 1979, the more effective application of drug therapy for the relief of mental illness had permitted a substantial reduction in beds provided in the mental sector. However, any economies were dwarfed by rise of demand and the higher costs of most new medical interventions; it was even doubtful whether community care when fully developed, represented a saving for most of the client groups involved. Many of advances, such as automated analysis in pathology laboratories, recently-evolved scanning devices used in diagnosis, the most advanced radiotherapy equipment, or fully-equipped intensive care wards, were hugely more expensive than the facilities they supplanted. For instance the 10 Megavolt Linear Accelerator used in the treatment of cancer was thirteen times the cost of the 300 Kilovolt Deep Therapy Unit previously established for this purpose.

The early stages of the therapeutic revolution affecting the modern health services were outlined in chapter I. Advances in drug therapy continued, and the pace increased as the pharmaceutical companies expanded to become one of the most successful and powerful elements in the Western industrial complex. Compared with the one antibiotic available in 1948, 33 were in use in 1968; compared with one corticosteroid in 1948, there were 11 in 1968; whereas the diuretic of choice in 1948 required injection, 24 were available in 1968, most of which were effective orally; in 1948 there was no effective drug therapy for hypertension or mental depression, but in 1968 there were 15 antihypertensives and 18 antidepressants.[35] Trends evident in 1968 continued in the course of the next decade. Previous progress had been most notable with respect to the control of infectious diseases. During the 1970s relief for many debilitating chronic conditions became available, for instance by the use of beta-adrenoceptor agonists for asthma, selective beta-adrenoceptor agonists (beta-blockers) for the relief of angina or hypertension, and further developments in non-steroidal anti-inflammatory drugs for relief in arthritis. Advances in drug therapy were also important in such fields as anaesthesia, which witnessed important developments in the use of inhaled and injected anaesthetics, local anaesthetics, and muscle relaxants. The development of a greater range of anticoagulants was important in facilitating advanced surgery, for example in the treatment of cardiovascular disease. On the eve of the thirtieth anniversary of the NHS, after a period of intensive research, cyclosporin A had emerged as a promising immunosuppressant, which soon proved invaluable in the further exploitation of organ transplant surgery.

The advantage of vaccination and immunization, or drug therapy continued to be offset by tragedies such as thalidomide, vaccine damage in the case of whooping cough, or the less measurable but nevertheless serious consequences of the irresponsible use of addictive drugs. Attention to regulation of drugs and monitoring for safety described in this volume made some contribution to reducing these problems, but they were by no means eliminated, as indicated by the problems associated with benoxaprofen (Opren), which in 1979 was a hopeful new discovery, but the licence for which was suspended in 1982, after evidence of implication in the deaths of elderly patients.

Since 1958, advances in technology transformed the capacities of acute medical services. By 1979, mechanised and computerised techniques were dominant in the measuring of physiological functions or in visualisation methods used for diagnosis. Endoscopy, ultrasound, isotope scanning, and X-ray transmission computed tomography had become established for diagnostic visualisation, while nuclear magnetic resonance imaging and emission computed tomography had reached the advanced testing stage. A variety of advanced technologies were brought together in intensive care units or special baby care units.

Symbolic of the strides made by medical science was the birth of Louise Brown on 25 July 1978, almost exactly coinciding with the thirtieth anniversary of the NHS. This was the first baby to be born as a result of in vitro fertilization. This achievement opened up a vast new area of medical intervention offering new hope to the many couples experiencing problems in reaching parenthood. Parallel with this development, in the late-70s, major improvements in pre-natal screening, especially amniocentesis, greatly increased the chances of early detection of congenital abnormalities.

By 1979, replacement and transplantation surgery had become routine. In that year some 20,000 hip replacements were performed. Bone marrow transplantation was available for certain forms of anaemia, leukaemia, immunodeficiency, metabolic disorders, and thalassaemia. In 1979, some 12,000 cases were treated in cardiac units, about one third each of valvular, ischaemic and congenital cases, the biggest increases being recorded in coronary artery bypass graft operations. Heart transplantation was banned in 1969 after some adverse results, but it was regarded as sufficiently safe in 1979 to be reintroduced, and units for this purpose were established at Papworth and Harefield, both former tuberculosis hospitals. The best-established and largest programme of transplant surgery existed in response to end stage renal failure. Britain was especially active in this field of transplantation. By 1979 there were about 3,000 patients with functioning transplants. This programme, together with complementary dialysis services had been built up entirely since 1958, and the most rapid advances had been made since 1975. By 1979 the rate of intake of new patients had reached a level of about 22 per million population, which was less than half the level adopted as the target during the 1980s. Since end stage renal failure services were well-developed, they were early to establish a European-wide system of registration. Such comparative data showed Britain succeeding well by some criteria but not others. Comparative statistics and performance league tables constituted a fresh and compelling source of evidence demonstrating the need for a higher level of services in Britain.

As a result of this closer integration of the Western medical system, it was no longer realistic for Britain to ignore trends elsewhere, and in most cases harmonisation carried cost implications. Such factors in the formulation of policy had been hardly relevant previously. It has been noted that in some important areas relevant to prevention, EEC directives began to exercise their influence, albeit not always to positive effect. EEC proposals for tax harmonisation with respect to alcohol, the control of lead emissions in petrol, or regulation of tobacco smoking, caused the UK administration to alter policy, or at least adopt a convincing defensive posture, and in some cases speed up its reaction in some fields where response had been lamentably slow. The NHS was also affected by EEC supplies directives, which obliged the health service to open up its major contracts to European suppliers. The largest impact of the EEC related to the medical and nursing professions, where directives necessitated mutual recognition of qualifications and the co-ordination of provision for free movement of personnel. Such directives were a new experience and they inevitably gave rise to teething troubles. For instance the Medical Qualifications (EEC

Recognition) Order 1977 ran into complaints from the parliamentary Joint Committee on Delegated Legislation, which criticised the health departments for implementation by means of the negative resolution procedure. The EEC nursing directives complicated preparations for the already long-delayed Nurses, Midwives and Health Visitors Bill. Both the medical qualifications and nursing qualifications Orders ran into trouble with the European Commission owing to stipulations about imposing a knowledge of English as a precondition for registration.

Although the momentum of the devolution process was largely dissipated in the course of the 1970s, this problem absorbed substantial amounts of labour within the health departments, and it left some lasting legacy. The most important effect was to cause reassessment of the rationale for the distribution of resources between the parts of Great Britain, which inevitably drew attention to the idiosyncratic nature of existing arrangements, and led to the formulation of more scientific methods, of which RAWP and its analogues were the descendants. It has also been noted how the politics of devolution caused complication of the already much-delayed attempts to implement the Briggs recommendations concerning establishment of UK arrangements for regulation of the nursing, midwifery and health visiting professions.

With the growth in expectations, the rise of technology, and changing pattern of need, Ministers were forced to sponsor policy initiatives to ensure that treatment was adapted in line with scientific advance and social expectations, and that the nation was supplied with a sufficient quantity of the right types of trained personnel. Only by this means was the NHS supplied with the larger and more intensively-trained workforce capable of exploiting safely and effectively diagnostic and treatment facilities of a kind that scarcely existed at the beginning of the health service.

The above paragraphs have conveyed the impression that changing circumstances conspired to escalate the costs of health care. The population became better educated and more health conscious, but there was little evidence of invasion of the doctors' surgery with trivial complaints. The elderly were particularly slow to avail themselves of services, even when it was evident that they were in distress. Of course not all innovations were expensive and many of them contributed to economy by obviating the need for more expensive forms of treatment. Also, advancing knowledge demonstrated that many forms of therapy and surgical intervention were virtually useless and should therefore be abandoned. Nevertheless, demographic change, rising expectations, policy changes and therapeutic innovation collectively created formidable demand for expanding the resources devoted to health care, but not, as demonstrated below, to the excessive extent suggested by some alarmists.

(iv) COSTS OF HEALTH CARE

The above paragraphs have drawn attention to the multiplicity of factors operating in the period covered by this volume conspiring to drive up the costs of health care. However, the British National Health Service demonstrated more successfully than most of its Western counterparts that the most pressing obligations of health care could be met within a system admitting only limited increases in resources.

Unlike most other Western health care systems, which are funded on some kind of contributory basis, the British health service is funded largely from general taxation. This principle represents one of the few constants in the NHS. This mode of financing health care was adopted by Bevan on account of its simplicity, and consistency with the principles of redistribution and progressive taxation. However, as Bevan himself discovered, his solution rendered the funding of the NHS entirely dependent on the vagaries of central Government policy. Resources for health care were therefore affected by the political weight of the health Ministers and their departments. In this competitive situation, the health service was in rivalry in the first place with other social services, but also it was dependent on levels fixed for public expenditure, and therefore subject to the vicissitudes of the economy, or fiscal and monetary policy. Volume 1 of this study described tensions in the Attlee Cabinet over the respective demands of the Korean War and the NHS. This volume has drawn attention to the impact of the Suez invasion, which was less momentous, but it illustrates to degree to which even minor policy or economic perturbations were capable of sending shock waves into the health care system.

As indicated by Appendix 3.2, the NHS occupied a middling position in the social services sector of public expenditure. Whereas competing votes, such as education, housing or social security experienced larger fluctuations in line with policy changes or demand, the NHS accounted for a fairly constant share, usually about 20 per cent of the social services budget. The local authority welfare services fell back during the 1950s, but then enjoyed a small increase as a consequence of the Seebohm reorganisation and community care policy.[36] Other presentations of the data tend to reach a similar conclusion. Representative samples collected by Lowe suggest that the health and personal social services taken together, account for a constant proportion of public expenditure, social expenditure, or social expenditure relative to the growth of GDP in the period from 1948 to the mid-seventies.[37] In the five years following the Seebohm reforms and NHS reorganisation, the combined HPSS sector steadily strengthened is position in the hierarchy of social service spending.[38]

Notwithstanding this remarkable degree of uniformity in the role of the HPSS sector in the overall pattern of the national economy, some minor, but significant shifts in spending on the health services have taken place. With respect to its share of national resources, after a momentary peak at the beginning of the service, expenditure on the NHS fell back to reach a low-point of about 3.5 per cent of GPD in the mid-1950s, after which there was a slow recovery. During the 1970s the level stabilised at an average of about 4.8 per cent, rising to just above 5 per cent in the last year covered by this study.[39]

In constant price terms, whether using cost or volume estimates, during the first five years of the new service there was an irregular pattern of spending, but on aggregate producing virtually no growth before 1954. From the mid-1950s until the mid-seventies a modest rate of growth in NHS expenditure was maintained. Then the economic instability associated with the Barber boom and oil crisis generated the impression of a sudden sharp rise, but only for a single year, after which there was a return to a stagnant situation, with a lower rate of growth than previously, and only a slight recovery at the end of the Labour administration. Part of this trend is explained by the initial low level of capital investment and then its steady increase until the mid-seventies, at which point there was a check and then noticeable decline.[40] The index of current expenditure shows a more modest, but regular increase. As already noted, such factors as the ageing population, the higher costs associated with medical advance, and policy innovations implied that a steady increase in resources was required to provide a constant level of service.

The trends in expenditure under each administration have been examined in earlier chapters. For summary purposes it is perhaps most useful to concentrate on the trend in current expenditure expressed in volume terms.[41] With a slight degree of simplification it is possible to derive a pattern which relates to the rotation of administrations, at least after the unsettled position between 1948 and 1953, which can be attributed to the not inconsiderable birth pangs discussed in detail in the previous volume. From 1954 until 1958 growth took place at a modest level, averaging at about 2.4 per cent. Gradually a consensus emerged between the Treasury and the health departments that this represented a fair rate of increase; 2.5 per cent (which was also a favoured estimate for the rate of growth of the economy) became enshrined as a principle having some objective merit, although in practice it evolved accidentally. From 1959 to 1964 there was a sudden jump to about 3.5 per cent and then a steady decline to 1.9 per cent coinciding with the tenure of Powell, but ending with restoration to a level above 3 per cent under Barber. The average annual increase for these years was about 3.3 per cent, indicating that the PESC system, although introducing greater discipline and rationality into the control of public expenditure, in practice allowed an increase by a percentage point in the rate of growth of health service current expenditure. The general trend in the rate of growth of current expenditure in volume terms under the Conservatives was clearly upwards, starting from an aggregate nil baseline before 1954 and ending with about 3.3 per cent. Under Labour the growth rate inched up by a further percentage point and this was maintained for three years, but this effort completely collapsed after the devaluation crisis, and Labour ended in 1969 with a 1 per cent reduction by comparison with the previous year, the first occasion an actual cut in expenditure had occurred since 1952. The position was quickly restored, and a level of growth averaging at about 3.4 per cent was sustained until 1974. Then as already mentioned, during the transition from the Heath to Wilson administration, the rate of increase in 1975 shot up to 7.2 per cent, which should be seen as an artefact symptomatic of the instability of this period rather than a planned exercise bringing real advantages to the NHS. The Wilson administration was exposed to the full gale of economic catastrophe from the outset. There was no room for laxity with expenditure on the social services. The rate of growth in expenditure on the health service was consistently held down to a level averaging at about 1.4 per cent, which marked a return almost to the pre-1954 situation. The wheel of change with respect to growth in current expenditure measured in volume terms had thus come full circle.

Opinion within the health departments has been uncertain concerning the size of the increment needed to take account of demographic change and medical advance. Indeed, such adjustment must be variable on account of such factors as demographic fluctuation and the variable cost of implementation of medical innovations. Most often, the estimate of increased costs of services related to the hospital sector, or hospitals and community services, but on other occasions Ministers made bids relating to a broader range of services. As their estimated rate of growth for preserving a constant level of services, or taking account of minimum demands for innovation, as already noted, in the mid-fifties Ministers generally adopted 2.5 per cent; Castle also cited 2.5 per cent as her minimum; but Vosper in 1957, Robinson in 1966, and Ennals in 1977 and 1978 adopted 3 per cent; by contrast, under pressure from the Treasury at the time of Ennals, DHSS adopted 1.5 per cent. Lower estimates tend to relate to the hospital and community sector, while higher levels of increase implied inclusion of the family practitioner services, as well as medical and policy innovations. In view of the large number of variables and choice of different methods of correcting for inflation, it is notoriously difficult to reach firm conclusions about adequacy of the rate of growth in health service expenditure. If it is assumed that a consistent 2.5 per cent rate of increase was required to maintain a constant level of the entire service, taking account of innovations in medicine and policy, as well as demographic change, with reference to the index of current expenditure in volume terms, taking 1950 as the base-line, the NHS failed to meet this target for most of the period under consideration. If 2 per cent is taken as the target rate of growth, this was attained only during the second half of our period.

As evident from the above summary, contrary to the fears of alarmists that expenditure on the NHS would prove impossible to contain,[42] the health service was not in practice any more difficult to control than other sectors of public expenditure. Indeed, it represented one of the most stable and containable elements among the services dependent on central government funding. This study has demonstrated the ease with which the bids for additional resources emanating from the health departments were dispatched using the established mechanisms of control exercised by the Treasury. As relatively weak political forces, the health Ministers and their departments were never at risk of gaining the upper hand. Owing to the introduction of cash limits, only isolated examples, such as pharmaceutical costs, persistently resisted effective regulation. Many other examples were uncovered where greater scope for economy of existed, but this was true of every area of public expenditure. By 1979 the problems of waste and efficiency savings were being seriously addressed and health authorities were becoming accustomed to being expected to finance expansion on the basis of efficiency savings. As the Treasury conceded, if the health service had been placed under local government administration, as was the case of education, it would have been more difficult to control. Also, compared with other social services, the health service offered greater scope for direct contributions from its recipients, in the form of direct charges, or the NHS Contribution, the exploitation of which presented political problems, but which represented a substantial relief to the Consolidated Fund. The British health service therefore demonstrated that it was possible for the state to fund and provide a modern comprehensive health service without incurring the much higher costs characteristic of rival systems of health care elsewhere in the Western economies.

On account of the dominance of general taxation, other sources of funding for the NHS attract little notice. However, for the period ending in 1974, local authority rates accounted for about half the cost of services provided by local health and welfare authorities. This source of funding for health services was eliminated with NHS reorganisation, but it retained its importance in the personal social services, which constituted one of the most rapidly expanding areas of social services expenditure.[43]

At the outset of the NHS, direct charges were not expected to feature in its funding and there was ambiguity about the role of the National Insurance Fund.[44] Attlee's administration allowed the share from the NHS Contribution to drift downwards and this trend persisted under the Conservatives until the mid-fifties. Those favouring maximising the NHS Contribution were apt to claim that Beveridge intended the 'health stamp' to be set at a rate enabling the Insurance Fund to support the NHS to the extent of 20 per of its total cost. However, there is little support for this assertion, while in 1961 Beveridge himself stated that his report 'left entirely open the question of whether or not payment towards the cost of the Health Service should be included in the social insurance contribution'.[45] The lower yield from this source was therefore entirely consistent with Beveridge's intentions. Until the mid-fifties, the Treasury tended to regard the NHS Contribution as an inconvenient historical anomaly. It constituted a drain on the hard-pressed National Insurance Fund, and was misleading to contributors because they thought that the entire cost of the health service was borne by their 'stamp'.

Contrary to the natural flow of events, the Macmillan ministerial team made a determined attempt to radically increase the role played by direct charges and the NHS Contribution in the funding of the NHS. From the outset of their introduction, every increase of charges proved to be complicated and politically disadvantageous. The benefits to the Exchequer scarcely outweighed the political opprobrium incurred. With difficulty the Macmillan administration wrenched up charges to the point where they contributed about 5 per cent of the cost of the health service. After Powell, no other Minister, in either Labour or Conservative administrations was willing to contemplate radically higher charges for prescriptions, dental care, and the eye service. Anything more than minor adjustment in direct charges was also rendered more untenable by the prices and incomes polices adopted during the 1970s. By 1979, the yield from direct charges had fallen to less than 2 per cent of the cost of the health service.

Under Macmillan the NHS Contribution replaced direct charges as the tax of choice for relieving the Consolidated Fund. Indeed, Macmillan and some of his senior Ministers were attracted by the notion of extending this principle in order to transfer a substantial part of the funding of the NHS to some form of compulsory insurance. This important shift of policy was consistent with the campaign being waged by some outside experts from the political right, although it is unclear how far Macmillan was directly influenced by these advocates. The first fruits of this new policy, the NHS Contribution increases of September 1957 and July 1958, were easily-won victories against a supine opposition. The high point of deliberations on this issue occurred between 1959 and 1960, with discussions at the Ministerial Committee on NHS Finance, the Social Services Committee, and finally the Figgures Working Party on NHS Finance. By this stage the insurance idea no longer commanded ready compliance among Ministers, and no enthusiasm for this course of action was shown by the Figgures Report. Powell insisted on ploughing on in the face of expert advice and less favourable political circumstances. Powell was formally vindicated by the NHS Contribution increase imposed in July 1961. After the increases in charges and the health stamp introduced by Powell, the combined yield from these sources amounted to about 20 per cent of the cost of the health service. This marked the end of a steady climb from the low point of about 11 per cent in the mid-fifties. This trend represented a significant alteration in the funding mechanism for the health service, and if continued it would have brought the British system nearer to its continental counterparts. However, the Powell exercise was politically damaging to the Macmillan administration, and it offered a much-needed boost to the morale of Labour. Powell's intervention therefore effectively killed off any idea that the NHS Contribution could be developed into an hypothecated tax to support the NHS, or that it was a viable basis for some other kind of graduated health insurance charge.

The NHS Contribution was again adjusted by a small amount in response to the devaluation crisis, and transfer to a graduated contribution was used to increase the employer's share. However, such adjustments were made to prevent the value of the NHS Contribution from falling below the level of 8 per cent of the cost of the NHS, the level preserved for most of the 1970s. Health insurance was periodically fleetingly revived, especially by the incoming Heath administration, but the idea was not pursued with the conviction displayed at the time of Macmillan, which was disappointing to ideologues of the right, who had succeeded in co-opting substantial support within the BMA for this idea. Despite the enthusiasm for insurance funding of the NHS among members of the Heath Cabinet while in opposition, once they entered Government their interest rapidly waned. During the 1970s, largely because of prices and incomes policy, both political parties for reasons of policy and prudence displayed an aversion to increasing direct charges and the health contribution; consequently the combined yield from these sources was allowed to drift down, rarely exceeding 12 per cent of the cost of the health service.

The NHS Contribution and direct charges provide a leading example of a policy area where Labour and Conservative were in disagreement. Labour was committed to elimination of direct charges and it opposed attempts by the Conservatives to expand the NHS Contribution. However, neither Party acted with resolution or consistency over these levies. Expanding the NHS Contribution and transition to compulsory insurance arrangements for health care were not direct policy commitments of the Conservatives, and were pursued with vigour only under Macmillan and for a brief time at the beginning of the Heath administration. On both occasions there was no consensus among Ministers about this policy. Leading Ministers regarded the NHS Contribution as a fundamentally unsound tax on the grounds that it was regressive, and therefore was open to objections to poll taxes of all kinds. Direct charges raised no particular objections among Conservatives, but such factors as prices and incomes policy, as well as political calculation, determined that in the period covered by this volume the yield from these charges was of insignificant importance as a contribution to the cost of the health service.

Labour was formally unsympathetic to experimenting with insurance funding of the NHS, but influential figures such as Houghton and Crossman had no objections to moving in this direction, and this idea was taken up with determination by Crossman just before the 1970 General Election. It was little source of pride in Labour circles that the Attlee administration had introduced direct charges. Subsequently, abolition of these charges became a main policy commitment, indeed one of the few features of health policy followed with unswerving commitment by the Labour Party for the whole of the period covered by this volume. However, little success was experienced in achieving this objective. Granted, the prescription charge was abolished in 1965, but it was reimposed in 1968. In view of this humiliating reversal, Labour was more circumspect in its promises in 1974, and introduced only minor exemptions from the prescription charge. In practice, in the 1970s Labour followed the same course as the Conservatives, introducing small upward adjustments in some charges, but further rises were precluded by prices and incomes policies, or risks of further offence to the rank and file of the Labour Party.

Although, as indicated above, the record of health service spending can be divided into phases approximately coinciding with the succession of administrations, it is difficult to argue that levels of commitment of resources to the health service or personal social services were determined by party-political considerations. Each party complained that the health service was neglected by its rival, and they offered conveniently ambiguous pledges about higher spending. In practice, the rise of expenditure on the health service closely follows the general trend of public expenditure; the fate of the NHS was therefore most determined by the general economic context, and only to a lesser degree by party political commitments. With respect to the overall level of resources, opportunity for influence of party or individual Ministers was therefore limited to the margins. Walker-Smith experienced only minor success in securing a larger share of resources for the health service, whereas his successor, Powell, exercised only a limited influence in reining back expenditure. Equally, in their brief spell in office, neither Crossman nor Castle discovered a way of breaking out of the regime of containment imposed on account of economic crisis, whereas Ennals was not successful in exploiting the minor opportunity for relaxation of the regime of retrenchment. The small advances in the resources available to health and personal social services occurred mainly by a slow process of accretion, with the result that the campaigns begun under one Minister were likely to see their completion at a much later date, quite possibly under a rival administration. The bigger accelerations of spending occasioned by such factors as pay awards containing large retrospective elements, the hospital plan, health service reorganisation, or transfer of the personal social services to local government, were likely to have been incurred at similar costs under Governments of either persuasion.

(v) IDEALS AND REALITIES

Persisting Inequalities. Benefits deriving from increased resources were only imperfectly realised without attention to priorities between services and equitable distribution with respect to social and population factors. Egalitarian objectives had been uppermost in the objectives of the architects of the NHS, but as the experience of the first decade indicated, this goal was not achievable without a more conscious act of policy than was forthcoming at the time. The continuing disparities in provision of services have been outlined in chapter I, while chapter VII indicated that this problem was not fully confronted until the 1970s, by which date a formidable body of research had confirmed the irrational nature of disparities in service provision and resource distribution. The leading vehicle for redressing the balance was RAWP and its counterparts for Scotland and Wales. Owing to the economic crisis, opposition from the better-provided NHS regions, and awareness of the fallibility of this method of redistribution, RAWP was applied in a slow incremental manner, with the expectation that no region would be unduly penalised. Even with its faults, RAWP confirmed the extent of maldistribution of resources. At the outset of the RAWP exercise the distances of regions from target revenue allocation ranged from 11 per cent below to 15 per cent above. Alternative estimates suggested even bigger disparities. An examination of per capita revenue expenditure at the eve of reorganisation indicated a range extending from the SW Metropolitan RHB, which was 41 per cent above the mean, to Sheffield RHB, which was 23 per cent below the mean.[46]

Within the regions disparities were even greater; it was not uncommon for areas to be 20 per cent below target or 30 per cent above target. With respect to per capita current spending, in the Trent region, the Sheffield teaching area was 34 per cent above the national average, but the other seven areas, including the two new teaching areas of Nottinghamshire and Leicestershire, were on average 34 per cent below the national average.[47] In April 1979, with respect to regions at the top and bottom of the league, the gap had reduced to 9 per cent below target and 13 per cent above. With minor variations, the same regions were in the top and bottom parts of the resources league-table as in 1958.[48] The amount of variation within regions remained greater than the variation between regions. When it is considered that there was no guarantee that the advantaged health authorities would divert their additional resources to the benefit of the most-disadvantaged client groups, while regions experiencing cuts were at liberty to impose economies on the same disadvantaged groups, it is far from evident that the RAWP mechanism would achieve the egalitarian objectives assumed to be its primary purpose. In their circumstances of increasing hardship, health authorities which were RAWP beneficiaries were likely to use additional resources to reduce pressure on their hard-pressed acute services, while the victims of the formula followed customary practice by locating their economies in community services in order not to sacrifice their core acute services.[49] RAWP therefore had the perverse effect of contributing to the sense of crisis surrounding resource distribution. Among the paradoxes exposed by the RAWP debate was the sensitive issue of resource distribution within the UK. This problem had been under discussion since the beginning of preparations for devolution, but it was not publicly confronted by the Government. Although not much debated on account of political sensitivities, it was pointed out that application of the RAWP formula to the UK as a whole placed England 4 per cent below target, and Scotland 23 per cent above target.[50]

One of the major disadvantages of the RAWP system was its failure to take account of the primary care and personal social services. Naturally, these might have compensated for the maldistribution of resources in the hospital and community health sector. However this was not the case. General practitioner services

766

in particular tended to reinforce the pattern of distribution exposed by RAWP. In 1979, for every 100,000 population, Scotland had 62, Wales 52, and England 46 general practitioners. With respect to expenditure on the family practitioner services and the distribution of general practitioners between regions in England, the differences evident at the beginning of the health service were very slow to change.[51] For most of the time, the West Midlands was at the bottom of the league-table, and the South West was at the top. In 1979 Trent was at the bottom and NW Thames at the top. The percentage disadvantage of the worst-provided regions reduced from about 20 per cent at the beginning of the health service to 15 per cent in 1979. In practical terms this meant that on average practitioners in the northern regions were likely to have list sizes containing between 100 and 200 more patients than their southern colleagues.[52] The precise importance of this difference depended on the quality of the general practitioners, upon which the evidence provides less guidance concerning a north/south divide.[53]

The regional disparities evident for resources inevitably showed up in services. For instance consultant numbers showed a substantial increase, but the unevenness of their distribution was not entirely corrected. In England in 1958 there were 15 consultants per 100,000 population, while in Scotland in 1956 there were 17. In England the figure climbed to 22 in 1979 and in Scotland there was an even greater increase to 33. The extent of the increase is greater than these figures suggest since the totals for the earlier date relate to individuals, whereas for the later date whole-time equivalents. In England, the regional disparities evident in 1948 and 1958 survived into 1965 and 1979. At the latter date there were 18 consultants per 100,000 population in Trent, but 26.5 in NE Thames.[54] Naturally, these differences were reflected in disparities in regional services. The first systematic study of this problem demonstrated wide disparities in thirty-one different services, with the Sheffield region being the most usual candidate for the bottom place in the league-table.[55] This proved to be an on-going problem affecting services of all types, including the most recent additions. A review of renal transplantation exposed 'manifest inequitable distribution of renal resources', with the regions having the lowest level of service, mainly in the north, having rates less than half the level in NE Thames, which headed the league table. The author also commented that the 'inequalities appear to be widening'.[56] Similarly, a survey drawing attention to the rapid growth of coronary artery bypass grafting discovered that there was a ten-fold difference between the most and least active regions, with the greatest development of this service being found in the London metropolitan area.[57]

Limitation in access to services was of course not merely a matter of geographical location. On account of resource limitations, principles of selection were evolved, which discriminated against certain groups. For instance, access to end stage renal failure services was reduced for those over the age of 45, or even those who were single rather than married.[58] Inevitably, the client groups who suffered most from the failures to realise the ambitious goals of the priorities and planning system were the most vulnerable sections of the community. The inadequacies of their services, noted in chapter I, became the object of active analysis and policy initiative only in the 1970s. By 1979 the first steps towards run-down of the Victorian system of institutions had been taken, and community care was more than a theory. But organisations representing the relevant client groups were depressed by the slow pace of change. In their award-winning book, Ryan and Thomas complained that 'only for a small minority of the mentally handicapped people has life changed significantly', while their colleague suggested that improvements had been superficial and the most wretched problems remained unresolved.[59] This failure to respect the rights of patients hitherto incarcerated in long-stay institutions was largely but not entirely connected with shortages in human and material resources. This problem also exposed limitations of will and genuine humanitarian commitment. As the reports relating to hospital scandals confirmed, for the large numbers remaining in long-stay institutions, conditions were sometimes as bad as ever they had been in the real or fictional world of Dickensian social horrors. As the Normansfield investigators discovered: 'the wards were bare and, as one witness put it, reminiscent of scenes from a workhouse of old. We saw patients who were dressed, apparently habitually, in a manner which was degrading and slovenly by any standard'.[60] Such evidence reminds us that just as the National Health Service embodied and improved on many of the finest traditions in the practice of medicine and health care, it also imported some elements from the darker and disreputable penumbra, which grew into abuses that were insufficiently observed and therefore not effectively counteracted.
Positive Health. The ideal of 'optimum' or 'positive health' had been elevated into a necessary objective for the health services since the days of the League of Nations Health Commission. Such aspirations had been at the forefront of the work of the Pioneer Health Centre at Peckham, dating from the same period. While the National Health Service claimed from the outset to give high priority to the promotion of health, symbolised by the intention to incorporate 'health centres' as a key feature of the new service, in reality this aspect of the service was never more than weakly developed, notwithstanding claims to the contrary habitually made in

768

ministerial speeches. The health centre programme was immediately abandoned, and when reintroduced after 1965, the ambitious expectations of 1948 were not revived. This neglect of promotive health provoked the jibe that the NHS was in reality a sickness service rather than a genuine service for health. Of the case studies investigated in detail in this volume, health Ministers and their colleagues displayed lack of resolution in addressing themselves to such issues as tobacco and alcohol abuse, or the fluoridation of water. With respect to the tobacco issue, one review understandably complained that after thirty years of confronting this problem, the Departments appeared to possess no coherent policy on smoking, and had made only paltry efforts to deal with this problem.[61] On the question of fluoridation, the distinguished epidemiologist, Sir Richard Doll, remarked caustically that why prophylactic medicine had 'not been extended to prevent dental caries, by the simple expedient of adding fluoride to water supply, is a mystery that should provide a good topic for historical inquiry'.[62]

Even in the field of vaccination and immunization, health Ministers periodically ran into controversy, and were criticised both for delay over introduction of new vaccines, and for permitting use of vaccines causing damage to health. Despite set-backs such as the whooping-cough episode, and other cases of maladroit handling by the Government, vaccination and immunization continued to yield great benefits at low cost, and with major savings to other parts of the health service.

Notable extension took place in services connected with family limitation, but only after long delays, with the consequence that in 1979 family planning services were poorly co-ordinated, badly distributed with respect to need, and defective, especially in provision of essential services in the fields of gynaecology and abortion. Nevertheless, these services were a major source of relief to women, and they undoubtedly brought about savings in many parts of the welfare programme.

It is difficult to argue that NHS reorganisation greatly assisted the cause of promotion and prevention. By the 1960s, public health medicine had struggled to its feet after the set-backs of 1948. The elimination of the Medical Officer of Health and public health departments in 1974 created a vacuum that was only incompletely filled by the more fragmented arrangements established after health service and local government reorganisation. Promotion and prevention were a much lesser priority with respect to the new specialty of community medicine, which was inevitably increasingly preoccupied with the general management of resources and therefore concerned with the hospital sector rather than residual functions associated with public health.[63] It was supposed that

769

general medical practitioners would assume further responsibility for much of the preventive work previously undertaken by local authorities. A start had already occurred before reorganisation with attachment schemes, whereby local authority personnel such as health visitors and district nurses had become part of the general practitioner team. Reorganisation accelerated this tend. As with many aspects of general practice, attention to prevention and promotion lay at the discretion of the individual practitioner, with no particular incentive for the less energetic doctors to raise their standards to the level of the best.

Area Health Authorities possessed responsibilities for integrated planning of the health services and were therefore in a position to take strategic initiatives connected with prevention and promotion. Community Health Councils were supportive, but the new AHAs were preoccupied with other more pressing problems and were for most of the time operating in an atmosphere of crisis. These other priorities inevitably detracted from the effort and resources that might have been directed into prevention and promotion. Many areas established health education units, but these exercised little influence, even within schools, where health education activity had traditionally been concentrated.

During the 1970s medical organisations paid more active attention to prevention. The Royal College of Physicians was prominent in its opposition to smoking, and advocacy of seat belts, fluoridation, and sound diet. Lack of sufficient Government leadership on these issues attracted the notice of the Social Services and Employment Sub-Committee of the Expenditure Sub-Committee, and this stimulated the health departments to pay more attention to prevention and promotion. A further side-effect of the work of the Select Committee was for fresh life to be breathed into the Health Education Council, which also entailed some extra resources. Funding of health education more than doubled between 1977 and 1979. Even after this increase, the health education agencies disposed of only £4.7m, about 0.05 per cent of the NHS budget in 1979, which was minuscule when compared with the promotional spending of the giant interests whose products undermined health. The failure of the Government to give health education agencies the capacity to exercise influence in the mass media such as television prompted adverse comment from the Royal Commission on the NHS.[64] Despite periodic reviews of health education policy, in 1979 this issue still failed to attract the attention it deserved, and the Government had reached no settled conclusion about the manner in which it should exercise its responsibilities in this vitally important field. The areas of failure were obvious and earned reproach from the Royal Commission on the NHS, which pointed out that there were 'major areas where government action could produce rapid and certain results: a much tougher attitude towards smoking, towards preventing road accidents and mitigating their results, a clear commitment to fluoridation and a programme to combat alcoholism, are among the more obvious examples'.[65] The Royal Commission also advocated a much more aggressive attack on obesity and unsound nutritional habits.[66] As indicated in previous chapters, the reasons for these evident shortcomings were complex and different in each case, but they warn that Britain's health service and the cumbersome central Government decision-making structures were poorly-equipped to respond appropriately and with sufficient urgency to such massive threats to health as alcohol and narcotic abuse, AIDS, environmental pollution, and food safety, most of which were more than incipient dangers in 1979, but were to prove of ever rising importance in the near future.

Accountability. Despite the general trend in public services for increased participation and accountability, the health services failed to reflect this development and indeed showed signs of moving in the opposite direction as a consequence of reorganisation. As already noted, the 1974 reorganisation intentionally adopted a managerial emphasis, with the aim of increasing efficiency in the use of resources. It is doubtful whether the structure evolved was suitable for this purpose, but despite concessions offered in the interests of preserving some element of local accountability, the system operated to increase the authority of the bureaucrat and the manager. At its inception, the NHS was the only personal social service not administered by local government. The hospital system adopted as the model for its administration the regional structure found among utilities such as gas or electricity. In view of the remoteness of the regional and local hospital management structure, individuals or communities wishing to intervene about local problems were driven to the unsatisfactory alternative of making representations through their MP and Parliament. The changes of 1974 took the health service one step further away from meaningful accountability to its local community, setting a trend that was to continue without interruption thereafter.

Lacking mechanisms of local accountability, the patient's last resort was the complaints procedure. But this also was defective. The weaknesses of the system were described with some exasperation by the Davies Committee and by the Select Committee on the Parliamentary Commissioner for Administration. The latter described the complaints system as 'complicated, fragmented and slow'. It agreed with the Community Health Councils that patients and relatives were 'totally bewildered by the maze of avenues through which complaints had to be pursued'.[67]

771

Such descriptions are reminiscent of frustrations experienced in much earlier days, when Chancery possessed 'the means abundantly for wearing out the right; which so exhausts finances, patience, courage, hope'.[68] To its complainants, the system evolved by the NHS for handling their representations must have seemed like the reincarnation of Dickens' High Court of Chancery. Sir Michael Davies wrote with some exasperation about lack of progress in developing a code of practice for the handling of complaints, a situation in which the convenience of health authorities colluded with the defensiveness of the medical profession. He found it 'incredible they would really wish to sabotage the introduction of a meaningful Code of Principles and Practice'.[69]

One measure of the health bureaucracy's retreat from transparency concerning its activities was the discontinuation of some of its mechanisms for regular reporting on important activities, the net effect of which was to reduce the availability of essential information about the health services. As Dr Owen pointed out, 'in a democracy, access to information is power'; yet despite the promise of greater transparency, the supply of information was in some respects eroded in the last years covered by this review. The publications associated with a department of state or a major public service should not merely be a formal requirement undertaken mechanically without any real operational function. They provide an opportunity for a convincing demonstration of the wisdom of big policy and expenditure decisions. Reports and other means of communication are also an important vehicle for maintaining contact with the public and preventing the impression that the health service was evolving into an alien and unfeeling bureaucracy. Also it as been pointed out that regular reports have contributed 'to an impression of intellectual and moral leadership which cannot be sustained by the occasional circular and proliferation of handouts of ministerial speeches'.[70]

Abolition of the post of Medical Officer of Health in 1974 was used as an opportunity to terminate the production of statutory annual reports about the health services in each locality. These reports had been produced continuously for over a century, and they constitute a fundamental repository of statistical information for purposes of comparison and evaluation. That record ceased in 1974. Although after reorganisation, RHAs and AHAs had the discretion to produce reports, few of them produced regular reports of any kind, and some of the regional authorities which had issued reports since 1948 discontinued this practice. The public was therefore deprived of access to basic, standardised information about health care in their district, and there was usually not even accessible information regarding the identity of members and senior officers of local health authorities.

The other key elements in the reporting system were the annual reports of the health departments and the Chief Medical Officers. Elimination of a separate School Health Service in 1974 brought an end to the famous series of reports, *Health of the Schoolchild*, produced under the aegis of the Chief Medical Officer in his capacity as Chief Medical Officer to the education department. This series of reports constituted a record extending back to the first decade of the century. The annual reports of DHSS, SHHD and the associated Chief Medical Officers' reports continued after 1974. However, these noticeably declined in length and quality. The DHSS report ended after 1977.[71] The other standardised sources of information which made their appearance in the late 1950s were the annual health statistical publications. These took over some of the functions of the annual reports and they continued after reorganisation. However, the English series was interrupted after 1978.[72]

The only element in the reorganised health service required to produce an annual report was the Community Health Council. Since CHCs were peripheral bodies, having limited access to information, and with slender resources, they were unable to take on the burden of systematic reporting laid down by the powerful NHS management bodies at regional, area, and district levels.

Not all the innovations of the 1970s constituted permanent gains. This is well-illustrated by the reports of the Hospital Advisory Service, one of the most-heralded innovations of the Crossman era. This report helped to satisfy the public that the horrifying problems exposed by the Ely enquiry were being confronted systematically and realistically. For the first few years informative annual reports were produced; these were not much liked by NHS authorities, but they were welcomed by the public and they attracted media attention. In 1976 the HAS was transmuted into the Health Advisory Service with promises of wider remit for its work. The report for 1976 turned out to be the last ever produced, which elicited the rebuke that it was 'inconsistent for the government on the one hand repeatedly to stress the need to inform and change public attitudes to the mentally ill and handicapped, while at the same time undermining the process by eliminating the highest calibre source of information'.[73] With respect to the mentally handicapped, the deficit was to some extent compensated for by the publications of the National Development Group for the Mentally Handicapped, established in 1976, but this was wound up in 1979, as part of the purge, which also eliminated the Central Health Services Council, the Personal Social Services Council, and many other bodies, entailing a further erosion in reports and investigative activities. Some of these extinguished bodies went back to the early years of the NHS; others were products of NHS reorganisation. In merit, they varied, but they were usually potentially constructive to the purposes of the welfare state, and their extinction tended to reduce still further the sources of independent commentary on the work of the health and personal social services.

Exeunt. The success of the National Health Service in translating the advances of modern medical science into benefits for those in need was expressed in simple non-technical terms by the group of leaders from main NHS occupational groups who made representations to the Prime Minister on the occasion of the thirtieth anniversary of the health service:

> Advances in medicine and science have revolutionised the treatment of often crippling and disabling diseases, while diseases which used to kill thousands of our people have been practically eradicated. Every day health care is given in our homes, in the community, and in hospitals, and its availability is not dependent on the ability to pay. These very real achievements are a tribute to the largely unsung dedication of all those in numerous professions, occupations and skilled groups who work in the NHS, often in poor and unrewarding conditions.

Notwithstanding these successes, it was frankly admitted that the NHS had failed to meet many of the high expectations of its founders. Many of the shortcomings evident in 1978 have been considered in detail in this volume. From the vantage point of 1978, the outstanding challenges were:

> variations in the health of people in different geographical locations, social groups, and occupations. Too many elderly, mentally ill and mentally handicapped people are still looked after in unsuitable hospitals and homes. Too many of our hospitals are old. There are shortages of staff. Too often the needs of patients cannot be met without long delay. The solution to these problems is largely one of allocating more money, although there are other faults in the National Health Service, and with medical science constantly advancing at great speed, resources will never be sufficient to meet all needs.[74]

With little amendment, this catalogue of desiderata might have emanated from 1968, 1958, or even 1948. The only new feature was the greater concern with problems of inequality, which in earlier decades it was anticipated would have been cleared up more painlessly than proved to be the case. The authority of the Black Report, published just after the thirtieth anniversary of the NHS was required before the problem of inequality was accorded the public attention it merited. Services connected with such vulnerable groups as the elderly, the disabled, the mentally sick, and the mentally disordered were traditionally the weakest elements in the NHS, and this remained the case in 1978. The old, inappropriate, institutional services had persisted longer than was defensible in a nation esteemed for its advanced welfare system and humane social values, while their replacement community services had developed on nothing like the scale promised or required. From the outset, the energies, resources and priorities of the NHS were dominated by the manifold demands stemming from the imperatives imposed by advances in medical science. In this latter sphere, the National Health Service with difficulty matched the pace set by its counterparts in other Western economies, where expenditure on health care was generally much higher, but this effort entailed neglecting much-needed improvement on other fronts. Despite some well-intentioned but largely abortive planning exercises in the 1970s, the NHS failed to maximise its opportunities for the development of comprehensive planning and priorities systems, which was potentially easier under Britain's more unified health care administration than in the more decentralised systems existing elsewhere.

At the thirtieth anniversary of the service, as in previous decades, the most general demand for improving the performance of the health service and resolving the crisis which was becoming one of its main identifying features, was the correction of under-resourcing. Data to support this argument was mobilised on many fronts: expenditure in the UK was lower than elsewhere in the Western economies; England was at a disadvantage to Scotland over resources, but Scotland fared badly according to most health indices; the traditionally depressed regions and districts remained at a disadvantage to the more prosperous areas; the Cinderella services were neglected, but also the acute sector was unable to keep up with the pace of modernisation; the health service both in capital and current spending had never enjoyed the priority it deserved in the allocation of public expenditure, etc.etc. The argument for additional resources never attained the credibility it deserved on account of damaging instances of inefficiency in the utilisation of resources, and the many institutionalised arrangements which seemed not to give value for money. Also, the 1974 reorganisation of the health service promised more than it proved able to deliver with respect to improved management and efficiency gains.

Notwithstanding the soundly-based nature of many of the claims regarding resources and the many areas where services fell short of equivalents in the health services elsewhere, there was no sign of erosion of the traditional high level of satisfaction with the service,

775

or public esteem for the principle of the NHS. Surveys undertaken in the context of the Royal Commission on the NHS indicated that 80 per cent of hospital in-patients were satisfied or very satisfied, while studies ranging over such diverse areas as primary care, services for children and old people, or localities as diverse as London, Cumbria, or the Western Isles, suggested general appreciation among users.[75] The elaborate studies of doctor-patient relations undertaken by Ann Cartwright over many years also demonstrated a high degree of patient satisfaction. Investigations by Cartwright and Anderson in 1977 discovered widespread satisfaction with general practice, especially among working-class people. Among the working classes, 64 per cent described themselves as very satisfied.[76] With respect to the National Health Service as an institution, 75 per cent of middle classes, and 81 per cent of the working classes expressed support for the principle, which is high, but perhaps indicated the beginnings of erosion of the almost universal confidence about the service expressed at earlier dates.[77] A review of the evidence concluded that support for the principle of the NHS remained firm, but dissatisfaction was addressed to more specific shortcomings: 'the combination of general support for the NHS and specific criticisms would seem to indicate that the public make a sort of implicit cost-benefit analysis of the Service and have decided that the costs, in terms of waiting lists and unsatisfactory ward conditions, are less than the benefits of a comprehensive service of the kind available'.[78]

As already demonstrated, expressions of confidence in the NHS were often indicative of tolerance of services that were unacceptably low in their standards. Low levels of expectation were partly an expression of a tradition of stoical acceptance of illness and primitive forms of treatment, but it was also suggestive of a touching respect for the NHS as an institution, which like an errant member of a family would be best improved by encouraging support rather than carping criticism. A worrying but not altogether unexpected result was that Community Health Councils were also over-tolerant of low standards. The Hospital Advisory Service was alarmed to hear favourable comments from the CHCs about services for the elderly that were in the view of the HAS visiting teams 'far from satisfactory. Clearly the representatives were expressing their impressions of public satisfaction and, in the teams' view, low expectations of the service'.[79]

Fortunately for the politicians, whatever their shortcomings in the trusteeship of the health service, the attachment to the ideal of the NHS was strong enough for their public to be indulgent. Despite its faults, and notwithstanding the expansion of the NHS into a huge bureaucratic organisation, those attending the millions of appointments as ambulatory patients, or experiencing in-patient treatment, predominantly recorded positive recollections of services delivered with compassion and sensitivity. The NHS therefore confounded the scepticism of the great Lord Dawson, who had concluded that it was impossible to combine socialism in the administration of health care with individualism in its practice.[80] The terminal date adopted for this study was of course not the end of Bevan's socialised National Health Service, but it constituted an important staging post, albeit now seeming increasingly remote. The presuppositions adopted by a wide spectrum of opinion, within the health service and among political groups of all persuasions during the period 1958-1979, were soon questioned and many of them were discarded in the course of the process of continuous reassessment that has taken place since that date.

Appendix 1.1
Ministers of Health/Secretaries of State for Social Services, 1919-1979

First Names	Surname (b.-d.)	Inclusive dates in office
Christopher	ADDISON (1869-1951) Viscount Addison (1945)	25.6.19 - 31.3.21
Sir Alfred Moritz	MOND (1868-1930) Lord Melchett (1928)	1.4.21 - 23.10.22
Sir Arthur Sackville Trevor	GRIFFITH-BOSCAWEN	24.10.22 - 6.3.23
Arthur Neville	CHAMBERLAIN (1869-1940)	7.3.23 - 26.8.23
Sir William	JOYNSON-HICKS (1865-1932) Viscount Brentford (1929)	27.8.23 - 21.1.24
John	WHEATLEY (1869-1930)	22.1.24 - 5.11.24
Arthur Neville	CHAMBERLAIN (1869-1940)	6.11.24 - 6.6.29
Arthur	GREENWOOD (1880-1954)	7.6.29 - 24.8.31
Arthur Neville	CHAMBERLAIN (1869-1940)	25.8.31 - 4.11.31
Sir Edward Hilton	YOUNG (1879-1960) Lord Kennet (1935)	5.11.31 - 6.6.35
Sir Howard Kingsley	WOOD (1881-1943)	7.6.35 - 15.5.38
Walter Elliot	ELLIOT (1888-1958)	16.5.38 - 12.5.40
Malcolm John	MACDONALD (1901-1981)	13.5.40 - 7.2.41
Alfred Ernest	BROWN (1881-1962)	8.2.41 - 10.11.43
Henry Urmston	WILLINK (1894-1973)	11.11.43 - 2.8.45
Aneurin	BEVAN (1897-1960)	3.8.45 - 16.1.51
Hilary Adair	MARQUAND (1901-1972)	17.1.51 - 29.10.51
Harry Frederick Comfort	CROOKSHANK (1893-1961)	30.10.51 - 6.5.52
Iain Norman	MACLEOD (1913-1970)	7.5.52 - 19.12.55
Robert Hugh	TURTON (1903-1994) Lord Tranmire (1974)	20.12.55 - 16.1.57
Dennis Forwood	VOSPER (1916-1968) Lord Runcorn (1964)	17.1.57 - 16.9.57
Derek Colclough	WALKER-SMITH (1910-1992) Lord Broxbourne (1983)	17.9.57 - 26.7.60
John Enoch	POWELL (1912-)	27.7.60 - 19.10. 63
Anthony Perrinott Lysberg	BARBER (1920-) Lord Barber of Wentbridge (1974)	20.10.63 - 17. 10. 64

Richard Howard Stafford	CROSSMAN (1907-1974)	1.11.68 - 19.6.70
Sir Keith Sinjohn	JOSEPH (1918-1994) Lord Joseph of Portsoken (1987)	20. 6.70 - 4.3.74
Barbara Anne	CASTLE (1910-) Baroness Castle of Blackburn (1990)	5.3.74 - 7.4.76
David Hedley	ENNALS (1922-1995) Lord Ennals (1983)	8.4.76 - 4.5.79

Notes:

The Ministry of Health was established in June 1919 upon the dissolution of the Local Government Board.

The Ministry of Health and Ministry of Social Security were combined into the Department of Health and Social Security on 1 November 1968, when Crossman assumed the title of Secretary of State for Social Services.

The problems involved in arriving at consistency with respect to the inclusive dates in office for Ministers is discussed in D. Butler and G. Butler, eds, *British Political Facts 1900-1985*, 6th edition (Macmillan, 1986), pp xvi-xvii. The present tabulation follows the same methodology, but the details have been checked independently and therefore differ in minor respects from *British Political Facts*.

Appendix 1.2
Secretaries of State for Scotland, 1926-1979

First Names	Surname (b.-d.)	Inclusive dates in office
Sir John	GILMOUR (1876-1940)	15.7.26 - 6.6.29
William	ADAMSON (1863-1936)	7.6.29 - 24.8.31
Sir Archibald Henry Macdonald	SINCLAIR (1890-1970) Viscount Thurso (1952)	25.8.31 - 27.9.32
Sir Godfrey Pattison	COLLINS (1875-1936)	28.9.32 - 28.10.36
Walter Elliot	ELLIOT (1880-1958)	29.10.36 - 15.5.38
David John	COLVILLE (1894-1954) Lord Clydesmuir (1948)	16.5.38 - 13.5.40
Alfred Ernest	BROWN (1881-1962)	14.5.40 - 7.2.41
Thomas	JOHNSTON (1881-1965)	8.2.41 - 24.5.45
Albert Edward Henry Mayer Archibald	PRIMROSE (1882-1974) Earl of Rosebery (1929)	25.5.45 - 2.8.45
Joseph	WESTWOOD (1884-1948)	3.8.45 - 6.10.47
Arthur	WOODBURN (1890-1978)	7.10.47 - 27.2.50
Hector	McNEIL (1907-1955)	28.2.50 - 29.10.51
James Grey	STUART (1897-1971) Viscount Stuart of Findhorn (1959)	30.10.51 - 12.1.57
John Scott	MACLAY (1905-1992) Viscount Muirshiel (1964)	13.1.57 - 12.7.62
Michael Antony Cristobal	NOBLE (1913-1984) Lord Glenkinglas (1974)	13.7.62 - 17.10.64
William	ROSS (1911-1988) Lord Ross of Marnock (1978)	18.10.64 - 19.6.70
Gordon Thomas Calthrop	CAMPBELL (1921-) Lord Campbell of Croy (1974)	20.6.70 - 4.3.74
William	ROSS (1911-1988) Lord Ross of Marnock (1978)	5.3.74 - 7.4.76
Bruce	MILLAN (1927-)	8.4.76 - 4.5.79

Notes:
See also Appendix 1.1.

The title Secretary for Scotland dates from August 1885; the post was upgraded to Secretary of State for Scotland in July 1926.

The Scottish Board of Health, founded in 1919, was reorganised into the Department of Health in 1929. The Home Department and the Department of Health were combined into the Scottish Home and Health Department in 1962. Housing responsibilities were at this date transferred from the Department of Health to the Scottish Development Department.

Appendix 1.3
Secretaries of State for Wales, 1964-1979

First Names	Surname (b.-d.)	Inclusive dates in office
James	GRIFFITHS (1890-1975)	18.10.64 - 5.4.66
Cledwyn	HUGHES (1916-) Lord Cledwyn of Penrhos (1979)	6.4.66 - 5.4.68
Thomas George	THOMAS (1920) Viscount Tonypandy (1983)	5.4.68 - 19.6.70
Peter John Mitchell	THOMAS (1920-) Lord Thomas of Gwydir (1987)	20.6.70 - 4.3.74
John	MORRIS (1931-)	5.3.74 - 4.5.79

Notes:
See also Appendix 1.1.

Minor delegation of health responsibilities had existed since the formation of the Board of Health for Wales in 1919; further ministerial responsibility followed establishment of the post of Secretary of State for Wales in 1964.

Appendix 1.4
Permanent Secretaries, Ministry of Health/Department of Health and Social Security, 1919-1979

First Names	Surname, Honours (b.-d.)	Inclusive dates in office
Robert Laurie	MORANT KCB (1863-1920)	1919-1920
William Arthur	ROBINSON GCB, GBE (1874-1950)	1920-1935
George William	CHRYSTAL KCB (1880-1944)	1935-1940
Evelyn John	MAUDE KCB (1883-1963)	1940-1945
William Scott	DOUGLAS GCB, KBE (1890-1953)	1945-1951
John Malcolm Kenneth	HAWTON KCB (1904-1981)	1951-1960
Bruce Donald	FRASER KCB (1901-1993)	1960-1964
Arnold William	FRANCE GCB (1911-)	1964-1968
Clifford George	JARRETT KBE, CB (1909-1995)	1968-1970
Philip	ROGERS GCB, CMG (1914-1990)	1970-1975
Patrick Dalmahoy	NAIRNE GCB (1921-)	1975-1981

Notes:
See also Appendix 1.1.

With respect to honours, the usual conventions of precedence have been followed, giving only the two most senior distinctions in the civil orders.

Sir Clifford Jarrett, Permanent Secretary of the Ministry of Social Security, became the Permanent Secretary of DHSS on the amalgamation of the Ministry of Health and the Ministry of Social Security in November 1968.

Appendix 1.5
Secretaries, Department of Health for
Scotland/Scottish Home and Health Department, 1929-1979

First Names	Surname, Honours (b.-d.)	Inclusive dates in office
John	JEFFREY GBE, KCB (1971-1947)	1929-1933
John Elborn	HIGHTON CB (1884-1937)	1933-1937
William Scott	DOUGLAS GCB, KBE (1890-1953)	1937-1939
William Robert	FRASER KCB, KBE (1891-1985)	1939-1943
George Henry	HENDERSON KBE, CB (1889-1958)	1943-1953
Harold Ross	SMITH CB (1906-1956)	1953-1956
John	ANDERSON KBE, CB (1908-1965)	1956-1959
Thomas Douglas	HADDOW KCB (1913-1986)	1959-1962
Ronald Ernest Charles	JOHNSON Kt, CB (1913-1996)	1963-1972
Ronald Petrie	FRASER CB (1917-)	1972-1977
Archibald Louden	RENNIE CB (1924-)	1977-1984

Notes:
See also Appendices 1.2 and 1.4.

John Jeffrey was joint Secretary with J. T. Maxwell of the Board of Health since its establishment in 1919, and sole Secretary between 1927 and 1929.

John Anderson (Secretary of Scottish Home Department) served as Secretary during the transition from DHS to SHHD in the latter half of 1962.

Appendix 1.6
Chief Medical Officers, Ministry of Health/Department of Health and Social Security, 1919-1979

First Names	Surname, Honours (b.-d.)	Inclusive dates in office
George	NEWMAN GBE, KCB (1870-1948)	1919-1935
Arthur Salisbury	MACNALTY KCB (1936) (1880-1969)	1935-1940
William Wilson	JAMESON GBE, KCB (1885-1962)	1940-1950
John Alexander	CHARLES GCB, Kt (1893-1971)	1950-1960
George Edward	GODBER GCB (1908-)	1960-1973
Henry	YELLOWLEES KCB (1919-)	1973-1983

Notes:
See also Appendices 1.1 and 1.4.

Sir George Godber was Chief Medical Officer to the Ministry of Health until November 1968, and the DHSS from that date until 1973.

Appendix 1.7
Chief Medical Officers, Department of Health for Scotland/Scottish Home and Health Department, 1929-1979

First Names	Surname, Honours (b.-d.)	Inclusive dates in office
John Parlane	KINLOCK (1886-1932)	1929-1932
James Law	BROWNLIE (1890-1946)	1932-1937
James Macalister	MACKINTOSH (1891-1966)	1937-1940
Andrew	DAVIDSON Kt (1892-1962)	1940-1954
Henry Kenneth	COWAN Kt (1900-1971)	1954-1964
John Howie Flint	BROTHERSTON Kt (1915-1985)	1964-1977
John James Andrew	REID KCMG (1925-1994)	1977-1985

Notes:
See also Appendices 1.2, 1.4 and 1.5.

There was no position of Chief Medical Officer of the Scottish Board of Health. Sir Kenneth Cowan was CMO of the Department of Health until 1962, and SHHD thereafter until 1964.

785

Appendix 2.1
The Health Services in England and Wales, 1939

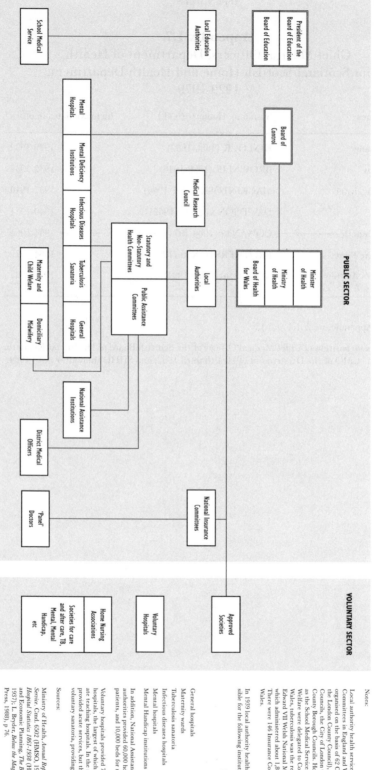

Notes:

Local authority health services and Insurance Committees in England and Wales were mainly organised on the basis of 62 County Councils (including the London County Council), 28 Metropolitan Borough Councils, the City of London Corporation, and 82 County Borough Councils. However, some services, such as the School Medical Service, and Maternity and Child Welfare were delegated to County District Councils. In Wales, tuberculosis was the responsibility of King Edward VII Welsh National Memorial Association, which administered about 1,800 beds in 18 sanatoria. There were 146 Insurance Committees in England and Wales.

In 1939 local authority health committees were responsible for the following institutional services:

	number of hospitals	number of beds (thousands)
General hospitals	110	70
Maternity wards	-	5
Tuberculosis sanatoria	179	23
Infectious diseases hospitals	900	38
Mental hospitals	100	130
Mental Handicap institutions	200	37

In addition, National Assistance (former Poor Law) authorities provided 60,000 hospital beds for chronic patients, and 10,000 beds for mental handicap.

Voluntary hospitals provided 77,000 beds in about 1,000 hospitals, the largest of which were the 24 undergraduate teaching hospitals. In the main, voluntary hospitals provided acute services, but there were also about 100 voluntary sanatoria, providing about 8,000 beds.

Sources:

Ministry of Health, *Annual Reports*; *A National Health Service*, Cmd. 6502 (HMSO, 1944); R. Pinker, *English Hospital Statistics 1861-1938* (Heinemann, 1966); Political and Economic Planning, *The British Health Service* (PEP, 1937); L. Bryder, *Below the Magic Mountain* (Clarendon Press, 1988), p 76.

Appendix 2.2
The Health Services in Scotland, 1939

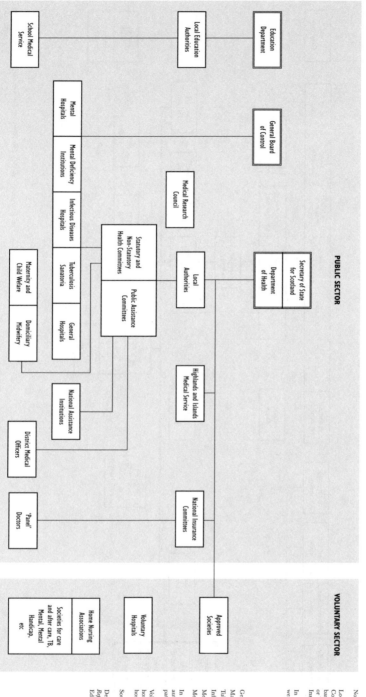

PUBLIC SECTOR

VOLUNTARY SECTOR

Notes:

Local authority health services and Insurance Committees in Scotland were mainly organised on the basis of 33 County Councils, 24 Councils of large Burghs, or Town Councils of four large Cities. There were 54 Insurance Committees in Scotland.

In 1939 local authority health committees in Scotland were responsible for the following institutional services:

	number of hospitals	number of beds (thousands)
General hospitals	9	5.0
Maternity wards	-	0.7
Tuberculosis sanatoria	115	5.5
Infectious diseases hospitals	107	7.6
Mental hospitals	23	13.0
Mental Handicap institutions	13	3.9

In addition, Public Assistance (former Poor Law) authorities provided 1,700 hospital beds for chronic patients.

Voluntary hospitals provided 14,000 beds in about 220 hospitals, including four undergraduate teaching hospitals.

Sources:

Department of Health for Scotland, *Annual Reports*; DHS, *Report on the Hospital Survey of Scotland* (HMSO, Edinburgh, 1946). See also sources cited in Appendix 2.1.

Appendix 2.3
The National Health Service in England and Wales, 1948

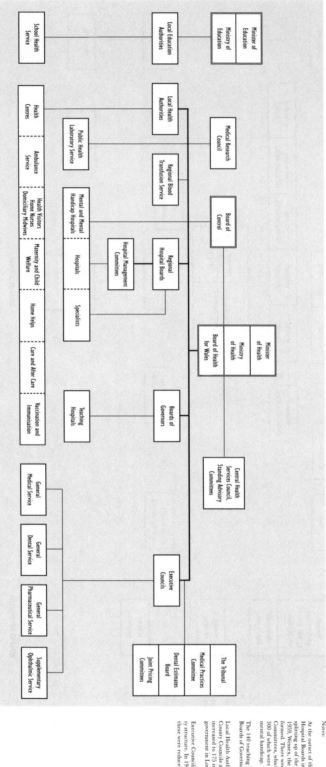

Notes:

At the outset of the NHS there were thirteen Regional Hospital Boards in England and one in Wales. With the splitting up of the South West Metropolitan RHB in 1959, Wessex, the fourteenth **RHB** in England was formed. There were 377 Hospital Management Committees, which administered about 2,800 hospitals, 300 of which were concerned with mental illness and mental handicap.

The 140 teaching hospitals were administered by 36 Boards of Governors.

Local Health Authorities were constituted from 146 County Councils and County Borough Councils. These increased to 175 in 1965 with the reorganisation of local government in London.

Executive Councils in general followed the local authority structure. In 1948 there were 140 Executive Councils; these were reduced to 134 by 1974.

Appendix 2.4
The National Health Service in Scotland, 1948

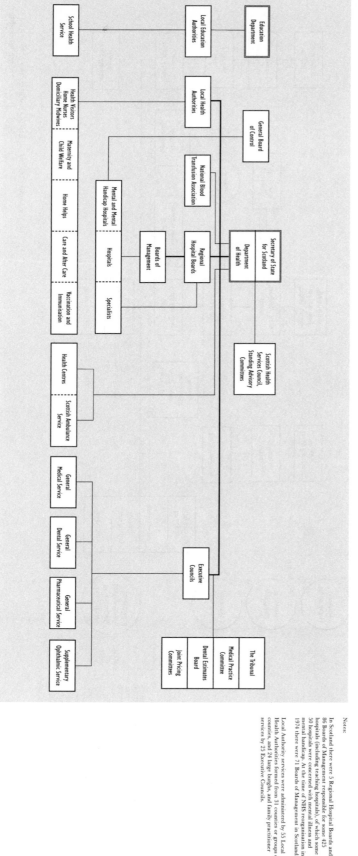

Notes:

In Scotland there were 5 Regional Hospital Boards and 86 Boards of Management responsible for some 425 hospitals (including teaching hospitals), of which some 50 hospitals were concerned with mental illness and mental handicap. At the time of NHS reorganisation in 1974 there were 71 Boards of Management in Scotland.

Local Authority services were administered by 55 Local Health Authorities formed from 31 counties or groups of counties, and 24 large burghs, and family practitioner services by 25 Executive Councils.

Appendix 2.5
The Reorganised National Health Service in England, 1974

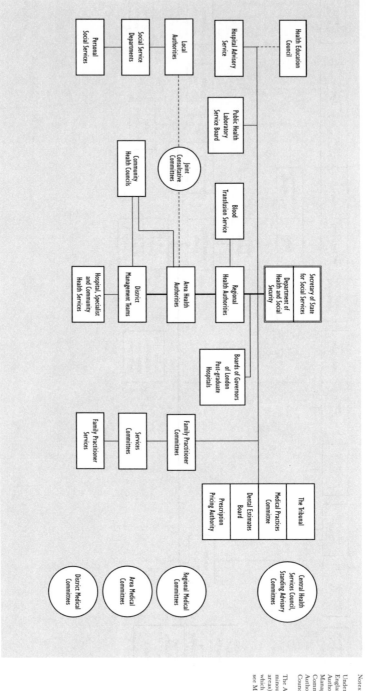

Notes:

Under the 1974 reorganisation, health services in England were administered by 14 Regional Health Authorities, 90 Area Health Authorities, and 205 District Management Teams. The Family Practitioner Committees followed the Boundaries of the Area Health Authorities. At district level 207 Community Health Councils were established.

The Area Health Authorities were approximately coterminous with 32 London Boroughs (grouped into 16 areas), 36 Metropolitan Districts outside London (two of which were paired), and 39 non-metropolitan Counties; see Maps 1 and 2.

Appendix 2.6
The Reorganised National Health Service in Wales, 1974

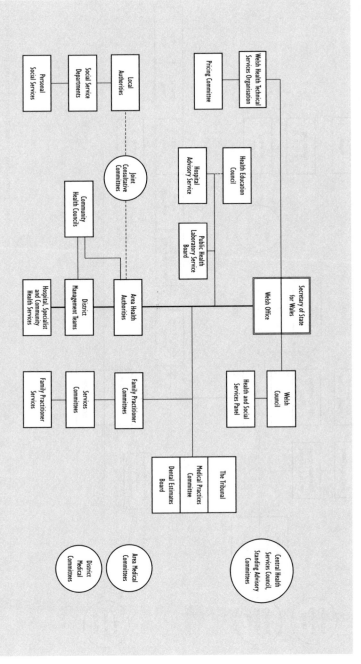

Notes:

Under the 1974 reorganisation, health services in Wales were administered by 8 Area Health Authorities and 17 District Management Teams. The Family Practitioner Committees followed the boundaries of the Area Health Authorities. One Community Health Council was established for each District. The Area Health Authorities were coterminous with the Welsh County Councils, see Maps 5 and 6.

Blood transfusion services were provided by the South Glamorgan Area Health Authority for South and Mid-Wales, and from the Mersey Regional Health Authority for North Wales.

Appendix 2.7
The Reorganised National Health Service in Scotland, 1974

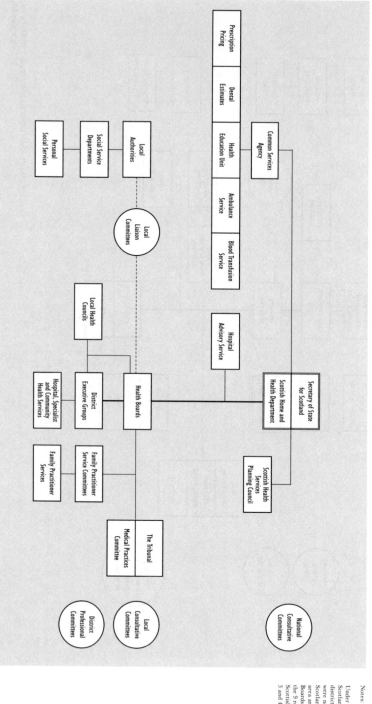

Notes:

Under the 1974 reorganisation, health services in
Scotland were administered by 15 Health Boards and at
district level by 34 District Executive Groups. There
were no separate Family Practitioner Committees in
Scotland. 48 Local Health Councils were established at
area and district level. The boundaries of the Health
Boards and District Executive Groups related to two of
the 9 regions and combinations of the 53 districts of
Scottish local government established in 1975; see Maps
3 and 4.

Appendix 2.8
Headquarters Organisation of the Ministry of Health, 1952

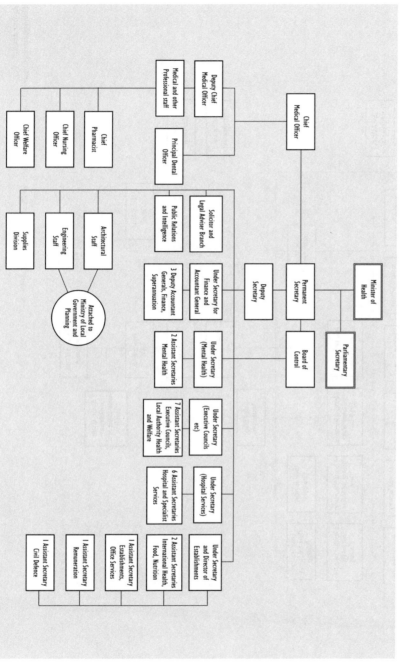

Notes:

1952 has been selected as the date for this diagram to reflect changes in organisation taking place after the establishment in the NHS in 1948, and the separation of housing and local government functions from the Ministry of Health in 1951.

Appendix 2.9
Headquarters Organisation of the Department of Health for Scotland, 1952

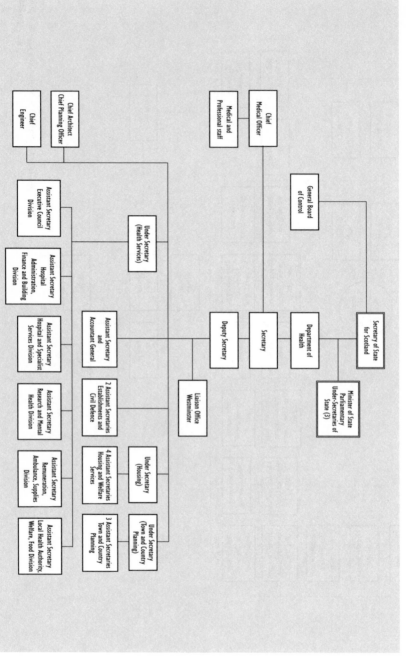

Notes:

1952 has been selected as the date for this diagram to reflect changes in organisation taking place after the establishment of the NHS in 1948, and to facilitate comparison with the Ministry of Health, where it was not practicable to adopt a date before 1952 (see Appendix 2.8).

Appendix 2.10
Headquarters Organisation of the Scottish Home and Health Department, 1963

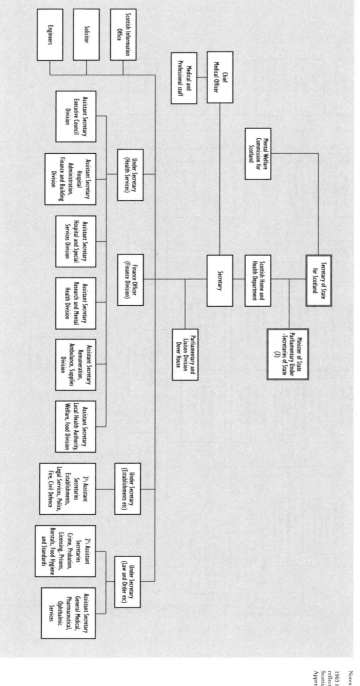

Notes:

1963 has been selected as the date for this diagram to reflect changes in organisation upon the formation of the Scottish Home and Health Department in 1962 (see Appendix 1.2).

Appendix 2.11
Headquarters Organisation of the Ministry of Health, 1968

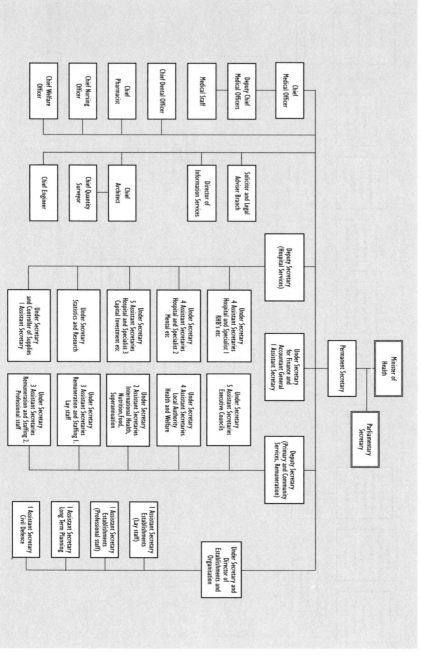

Notes:

1968 has been selected as the date for this diagram to reflect the final stages of organisation in the Ministry of Health before the formation of the Department of Health and Social Security in 1968 (see Appendix 1.1).

Appendix 2.14
Medical Representative Machinery following NHS Reorganisation, England, 1974

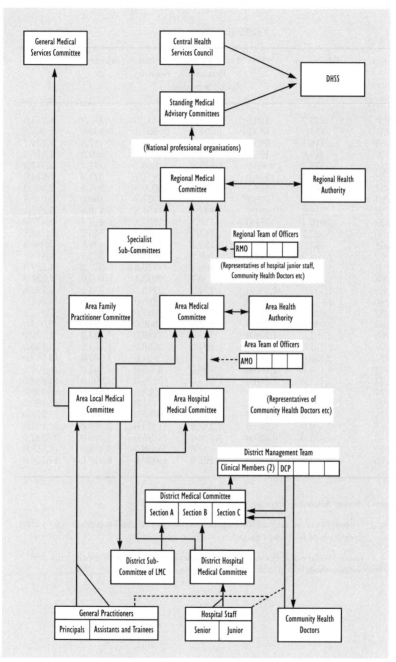

Source: Adapted from R. G. S. Brown, *Reorganising the National Health Service. A Case Study of Administrative Change* (Blackwell and Martin Robertson, 1979), Figure 2, p 35

Appendix 3.1
Public Expenditure on National Health Service and Other Social Services, UK, 1949-1980

£ million (actual prices)

Financial Year	Education	NHS	Local Welfare/ Personal Social Services	Social Security	Housing	Total
1949/50	328.7	459.9	96.2	653.8	346.9	1,885.5
1950/51	354.9	483.9	94.6	665.4	364.8	1,963.6
1951/52	416.1	493.9	105.7	701.7	417.3	2,134.7
1952/53	449.0	497.7	119.8	844.8	504.8	2,416.1
1953/54	472.3	508.9	118.6	888.7	544.0	2,532.5
1954/55	517.7	537.0	120.1	914.1	525.9	2,614.8
1955/56	567.4	583.1	129.4	1020.3	501.6	2,801.8
1956/57	671.3	639.2	142.7	1067.7	490.0	3,010.9
1957/58	756.8	684.7	132.6	1151.4	446.6	3,172.1
1958/59	810.4	731.6	136.1	1387.1	412.7	3,477.9
1959/60	882.3	787.7	144.9	1458.2	445.2	3,718.1
1960/61	953.9	888.7	154.7	1498.9	494.6	3,990.8
1961/62	1,087.9	912.8	169.9	1674.4	569.1	4,414.1
1962/63	1,233.0	951.7	186.1	1776.3	512.2	4,659.3
1963/64	1,345.4	1,047.3	200.7	2032.4	607.0	5,232.8
1964/65	1,437.8	1,158.0	224.2	2119.1	853.5	5,792.6
1965/66	1,636.0	1,319.0	240.0	2499.0	953.0	6,647.0
1966/67	1,824.0	1,447.0	272.0	2647.0	1,052.0	7,242.0
1967/68	2,046.0	1,588.0	312.0	3006.0	1,101.0	8,053.0
1968/69	2,207.0	1,709.0	312.0	3410.0	1,134.0	8,772.0
1969/70	2,397.0	1,797.0	404.0	3656.0	1,184.0	9,438.0
1970/71	2,750.0	2,111.0	474.0	3927.0	1,307.0	10,569.0
1971/72	3,154.0	2,405.0	499.0	4578.0	1,265.0	11,901.0
1972/73	3,717.0	2,746.0	615.0	5175.0	1,606.0	13,859.0
1973/74	4,228.0	3,101.0	835.0	5725.0	2,610.0	16,499.0
1974/75	5,403.0	4,152.0	1,173.0	7171.0	4,299.0	22,198.0
1975/76	7,002.0	5,471.0	1,551.0	9755.0	4,500.0	28,279.0
1976/77	7,408.0	6,249.0	1,732.0	11575.0	5,199.0	32,163.0
1977/78	7,881.0	6,896.0	1,826.0	13844.0	5,095.0	35,542.0
1978/79	8,697.0	7,835.0	2,053.0	16458.0	5,416.0	40,459.0
1979/80	9,963.0	9,362.0	2,492.0	19530.0	6,419.0	47,766.0

Source: *Annual Abstract of Statistics 1964, 1971, 1976, 1981*

Notes: Includes current and capital expenditure of central and local government after deduction of fees and charges.

Local Welfare and Personal Social Services includes school meals, milk and welfare foods.

Appendix 3.2
Proportions of Public Expenditure on National Health Service and Other Social Services, UK, 1949-1980

Financial Year	Education (%)	NHS (%)	Local Welfare/ Personal Social Services (%)	Social Security (%)	Housing (%)
1949/50	17.4	24.4	5.1	34.7	18.4
1950/51	18.1	24.6	4.8	33.9	18.6
1951/52	19.5	23.1	5.0	32.9	19.5
1952/53	18.6	20.6	4.9	35.0	20.9
1953/54	18.6	20.1	4.7	35.1	21.5
1954/55	19.8	20.5	4.6	35.0	20.1
1955/56	20.3	20.8	4.6	36.4	17.9
1956/57	22.3	21.2	4.7	35.5	16.3
1957/58	23.8	21.6	4.2	36.3	14.1
1958/59	23.3	21.0	3.9	39.9	11.9
1959/60	23.7	21.2	3.9	39.2	12.0
1960/61	23.9	22.3	3.9	37.5	12.4
1961/62	24.7	20.7	3.8	37.9	12.9
1962/63	26.5	20.4	4.0	38.1	11.0
1963/64	25.7	20.0	3.8	38.9	11.6
1964/65	24.8	20.0	3.9	36.6	14.7
1965/66	24.6	19.9	3.6	37.6	14.3
1966/67	25.2	20.1	3.8	36.7	14.2
1967/68	25.4	19.7	3.9	37.3	13.7
1968/69	25.1	19.5	3.6	38.9	12.9
1969/70	25.4	19.1	4.3	38.7	12.5
1970/71	26.0	20.0	4.5	37.1	12.4
1971/72	26.5	20.2	4.2	38.5	10.6
1972/73	26.8	19.8	4.4	37.3	11.7
1973/74	25.6	18.8	5.1	34.7	15.8
1974/75	24.3	18.7	5.3	32.3	19.4
1975/76	24.8	19.3	5.5	34.5	15.9
1976/77	23.0	19.4	5.4	36.0	16.2
1977/78	22.2	19.4	5.1	39.0	14.3
1978/79	21.5	19.4	5.1	40.7	13.3
1979/80	20.9	19.6	5.2	40.9	13.4

Source: See Appendix 3.1

Notes: See Appendix 3.1

Appendix 3.3
Public Expenditure on the National Health Service, UK, 1948-1980

£ million (actual prices)

Financial Year	NHS Current	NHS Capital	NHS Total	GDP at Factor Cost	NHS Total as % of GDP at Factor Cost
1948/49	272.3	10.2	282.4	10,421.8	2.71
1949/50	443.5	16.4	459.9	11,086.5	4.15
1950/51	460.1	17.0	477.1	11,697.5	4.08
1951/52	475.6	18.3	493.9	12,902.8	3.83
1952/53	508.9	16.8	525.7	13,978.3	3.76
1953/54	516.8	16.0	532.8	14,980.8	3.56
1954/55	526.6	22.0	548.6	15,872.0	3.46
1955/56	573.1	22.5	595.6	17,032.0	3.50
1956/57	626.7	24.5	651.2	18,366.5	3.55
1957/58	663.1	29.4	692.5	19,370.5	3.58
1958/59	710.0	34.1	744.1	20.740.8	3.59
1959/60	768.5	35.5	804.0	21,346.0	3.77
1960/61	855.7	42.4	898.1	22,787.3	3.94
1961/62	880.1	52.2	932.3	24,171.3	3.86
1962/63	930.0	58.2	988.2	25,202.0	3.92
1963/64	1,039.0	82.0	1,121.3	27,340.0	4.10
1964/65	1,122.0	94.0	1,216.0	29,481.0	4.12
1965/66	1,347.0	104.0	1,451.0	31,692.0	4.58
1966/67	1,353.0	114.0	1,467.0	33,560.3	4.37
1967/68	1,484.0	135.0	1,619.0	35,558.8	4.55
1968/69	1,611.0	144.0	1,755.0	37,963.5	4.62
1969/70	1,676.0	144.0	1,820.0	40,484.5	4.50
1970/71	1,962.0	170.0	2,132.0	44,884.5	4.75
1971/72	2,230.0	210.0	2,440.0	50,545.3	4.83
1972/73	2,531.0	255.0	2,786.0	65,963.0	4.22
1973/74	2,671.0	296.0	2,967.0	78,419.8	3.78
1974/75	3,905.0	302.0	4,207.0	98,276.8	4.28
1975/76	5,175.0	405.0	5,580.0	114,961.5	4.85
1976/77	5,958.0	423.0	6,381.0	130,693.8	4.88
1977/78	6,634.0	410.0	7,044.0	149,243.3	4,72
1978/79	7,526.0	466.0	7,992.0	151,543.5	5.27
1979/80	9,028.0	529.0	9,557.0	174,587.3	5.47

Source: *Annual Abstract of Statistics, 1962, 1964, 1971, 1976* and *1981*

Notes: Includes current and capital expenditure of central and local government after deduction of fees and charges.

Appendix 3.4
National Health Service Expenditure in Cost Terms, UK,
1949-1979

Calendar Year	NHS Expenditure at 1970 Prices £ million			Indices of Expenditure at Constant Prices 1950=100		
	Current	Capital	Total	Current	Capital	Total
1949	916	33	949	91.0	94.3	91.1
1950	1,007	35	1,042	100.0	100.0	100.0
1951	975	35	1,010	96.8	100.0	96.9
1952	895	28	921	88.7	80.0	88.4
1953	911	29	940	90.5	82.9	90.2
1954	920	32	952	91.4	91.4	91.4
1955	957	34	991	95.0	97.1	95.1
1956	989	32	1,021	98.2	91.4	98.0
1957	1,022	40	1,062	101.5	114.3	101.9
1958	1,036	43	1,079	102.9	122.9	103.6
1959	1,101	50	1,151	109.3	142.9	110.5
1960	1,182	53	1,235	117.4	151.4	118.5
1961	1,228	61	1,289	121.9	174.3	123.7
1962	1,228	74	1,302	121.9	211.4	125.0
1963	1,279	79	1,358	127.0	225.7	130.3
1964	1,349	98	1,447	134.0	280.0	138.9
1965	1,454	112	1,566	144.4	320.0	150.3
1966	1,534	121	1,655	152.3	345.7	158.8
1967	1,645	145	1,790	163.4	414.3	171.8
1968	1,721	160	1,881	170.9	457.1	180.5
1969	1,752	147	1,899	174.0	420.0	182.2
1970	1,860	151	2,011	184.7	431.4	193.0
1971	1,907	164	2,071	189.4	468.6	198.8
1972	1,984	183	2,167	197.0	522.9	208.0
1973	2,054	210	2,264	204.0	600.0	217.3
1974	2,357	193	2,550	234.1	551.4	244.7
1975	2,481	185	2,666	246.4	528.6	255.9
1976	2,568	189	2,757	255.0	540.0	264.6
1977	2,584	157	2,741	256.6	448.6	263.1
1978	2,621	154	2,775	260.3	438.7	266.3
1979	2,649	150	2,799	263.1	427.4	268.6

Source: Royal Commission NHS, Table E8; Health Departments' statistics

Notes: Cost Terms involves actual NHS expenditure deflated by a general price index and hence includes the relative price effect.

Appendix 3.5
National Health Service Expenditure in Volume Terms, UK, 1949-1979

Calendar Year	NHS Expenditure at 1970 Prices £ million			Indices of Expenditure at Constant Prices 1950=100		
	Current	Capital	Total	Current	Capital	Total
1949	1,065	24	1.089	90.7	96.0	90.8
1950	1,174	25	1,199	100.0	100.0	100.0
1951	1,183	23	1,206	100.8	92.0	100.6
1952	1,157	24	1,181	98.6	96.0	98.5
1953	1,177	25	1,202	100.3	100.0	100.3
1954	1,200	27	1,227	102.2	108.0	102.3
1955	1,235	28	1,263	105.2	112.0	105.3
1956	1,264	28	1,292	107.7	112.0	107.8
1957	1,293	33	1,326	110.1	132.0	110.6
1958	1,324	35	1,359	112.8	140.0	113.3
1959	1,371	41	1,412	116.8	164.0	117.8
1960	1,416	44	1,460	120.6	176.0	121.8
1961	1,424	56	1,480	121.3	224.0	123.4
1962	1,451	66	1,517	123.6	264.0	126.5
1963	1,485	76	1,561	126.5	304.0	130.2
1964	1,533	98	1,631	130.6	392.0	136.0
1965	1,602	104	1,706	136.5	416.0	142.3
1966	1,672	113	1,785	142.4	452.0	148.9
1967	1,748	119	1,867	148.9	476.0	155.7
1968	1,800	153	1,953	153.3	612.0	162.9
1969	1,781	140	1,921	151.7	560.0	160.2
1970	1,860	151	2,011	158.4	604.0	167.7
1971	1,900	165	2,065	161.8	660.0	172.2
1972	1,960	185	2,145	167.0	740.0	178.9
1973	2,041	190	2,231	173.9	760.0	186.1
1974	2,114	162	2,276	180.1	648.0	189.8
1975	2,267	175	2,442	193.1	700.0	203.7
1976	2,310	173	2,483	196.8	692.0	207.1
1977	2,360	144	2,504	201.0	576.0	208.8
1978	2,387	144	2,529	203.3	574.5	210.9
1979	2,401	140	2,539	204.5	556.7	211.7

Source: Royal Commission NHS, Table E7; Health Departments' statistics

Notes: Volume Terms involve actual NHS expenditure deflated by an NHS price index and hence excludes the relative price effect.

Appendix 3.6
Sources of National Health Service Finance, UK, 1948-1980

£ million (actual prices)

Financial Year	Consolidated Fund & Local Taxation	NHS Contribution	Charges	Total
1948/49	251.7	28.3	2.4	282.4
1949/50	416.0	40.9	3.0	459.9
1950/51	432.3	41.4	3.4	477.1
1951/52	443.9	42.1	7.9	493.9
1952/53	464.8	40.9	20.0	525.7
1953/54	467.2	41.3	24.3	532.8
1954/55	482.4	41.2	25.0	548.6
1955/56	527.6	41.3	26.7	595.6
1956/57	580.9	41.7	28.6	651.2
1957/58	595.1	64.7	32.7	692.5
1958/59	606.3	104.8	33.0	744.1
1959/60	656.4	112.6	35.0	804.0
1960/61	745.5	115.9	36.7	898.1
1961/62	735.7	148.3	48.3	932.3
1962/63	776.4	162.1	49.7	988.2
1963/64	902.7	166.6	52.0	1,121.3
1964/65	996.8	166.2	53.0	1,216.0
1965/66	1,259.1	163.9	28.0	1,451.0
1966/67	1,270.3	166.7	30.0	1,467.0
1967/68	1,427.3	160.7	31.0	1,619.0
1968/69	1,523.6	185.4	46.0	1,755.0
1969/70	1,582.5	179.5	58.0	1,820.0
1970/71	1,855.4	215.6	61.0	2,132.0
1971/72	2,129.0	233.0	78.0	2,440.0
1972/73	2,159.2	236.8	90.0	2,486.0
1973/74	2,629.0	238.0	100.0	2,967.0
1974/75	3,797.0	289.0	112.0	4,207.0
1975/76	4,980.5	489.5	110.0	5,580.0
1976/77	5,590.5	658.5	132.0	6,381.0
1977/78	6,198.7	697.3	148.0	7,044.0
1978/79	7,043.7	791.3	157.0	7,992.0
1979/80	8,440.0	922.0	195.0	9,557.0

Source: *Annual Abstract of Statistics, 1964, 1971, 1976, 1981*
Health Department's statistics

Appendix 3.7
Proportional Sources of National Health Service Finance, UK, 1948-1980

Financial Year	Consolidated Fund & Local Taxation %	NHS Contribution %	Charges %
1948/49	89.1	10.0	0.9
1949/50	90.5	8.9	0.6
1950/51	90.6	8.7	0.7
1951/52	89.9	8.5	1.6
1952/53	88.4	7.8	3.8
1953/54	87.7	7.7	4.6
1954/55	87.9	7.5	4.6
1955/56	88.6	6.9	4.5
1956/57	89.2	6.4	4.4
1957/58	85.9	9.4	4.7
1958/59	81.5	14.1	4.4
1959/60	81.6	14.0	4.4
1960/61	83.0	12.9	4.1
1961/62	78.9	15.9	5.2
1962/63	78.6	16.4	5.0
1963/64	80.5	14.9	4.6
1964/65	82.0	13.7	4.3
1965/66	86.8	11.3	1.9
1966/67	86.6	11.4	2.0
1967/68	88.2	9.9	1.9
1968/69	86.8	10.6	2.6
1969/70	87.0	9.8	3.2
1970/71	87.0	10.1	2.9
1971/72	87.3	9.5	3.2
1972/73	86.9	9.5	3.6
1973/74	88.6	8.0	3.4
1974/75	90.3	7.0	2.7
1975/76	89.3	8.8	1.9
1976/77	87.6	10.3	2.1
1977/78	88.0	9.9	2.1
1978/79	88.1	9.9	2.0
1979/80	88.3	9.7	2.0

Source: See Appendix 3.6

Appendix 3.8
Distribution of National Health Service Current Expenditure between Services, UK, 1948-1980

£ million (actual prices)

Financial Year	Hospital	Family Practitioner Services	Local Health Authorities	Miscellaneous
1948/49	146.6	85.2	10.2	30.2
1949/50	235.9	158.7	31.7	17.2
1950/51	254.0	158.4	36.2	15.5
1951/52	272.1	147.2	38.7	17.6
1952/53	273.4	169.0	43.2	23.3
1953/54	286.4	138.4	43.4	28.6
1954/55	306.7	145.9	45.5	28.7
1955/56	337.4	156.9	49.7	29.1
1956/57	368.1	173.9	54.7	30.0
1957/58	389.6	183.4	58.5	31.6
1958/59	417.2	196.2	62.2	34.4
1959/60	452.9	209.8	68.5	37.3
1960/61	494.6	248.4	72.8	39.9
1961/62	527.8	227.2	81.0	44.2
1962/63	562.0	231.1	86.9	50.1
1963/64	626.0	298.0	96.3	19.0
1964/65	675.0	322.0	104.0	21.0
1965/66	743.0	463.0	118.0	23.0
1966/67	809.0	387.0	132.0	25.0
1967/68	886.0	424.0	147.0	27.0
1968/69	973.0	444.0	162.0	32.0
1969/70	1,046.0	483.0	112.0	35.0
1970/71	1,238.0	557.0	127.0	40.0
1971/72	1,424.0	609.0	146.0	51.0
1972/73	1,621.0	678.0	167.0	65.0
1973/74	1,840.0	743.0	-	88.0
1974/75	2,819.0	960.0	-	126.0
1975/76	3,898.0	1,141.0	-	136.0
1976/77	4,427.0	1,346.0	-	185.0
1977/78	4,928.0	1,504.0	-	202.0
1978/79	5,538.0	1,763.0	-	225.0
1979/80	6,665.0	2,082.0	-	281.0

Source: *Annual Abstract of Statistics, 1962, 1971, 1976, 1981*

Notes: Local Health Authority and Hospital Services were assimilated together in 1974.

Miscellaneous is mainly the cost of departmental administration and centrally administered services.

Appendix 3.9
Proportional Distribution of National Health Service Current
Expenditure between Services, UK, 1948-1980

Financial Year	Hospital (%)	Family Practitioner Services (%)	Local Health Authorities (%)	Miscellaneous (%)
1948/49	53.9	31.3	3.7	11.1
1949/50	53.2	35.8	7.1	3.9
1950/51	55.2	33.6	7.9	3.3
1951/52	57.2	31.0	8.1	3.7
1952/53	53.7	33.2	8.5	4.6
1953/54	55.4	30.7	8.4	5.5
1954/55	58.2	27.7	8.6	5.5
1955/56	58.9	27.4	8.7	5.0
1956/57	58.9	27.7	8.7	4.7
1957/58	58.8	27.7	8.8	4.7
1958/59	58.8	27.6	8.8	4.8
1959/60	58.9	27.3	8.9	4.9
1960/61	57.8	29.0	8.5	4.7
1961/62	60.0	25.8	9.2	5.0
1962/63	60.4	24.8	9.3	5.4
1963/64	60.2	28.7	9.3	1.8
1964/65	60.2	38.7	9.3	1.8
1965/66	55.1	34.4	8.8	1.7
1966/67	59.8	28.6	9.8	1.8
1967/68	59.7	28.6	9.9	1.8
1968/69	60.4	27.6	10.0	2.0
1969/70	62.4	28.8	6.7	2.1
1970/71	63.1	28.4	6.5	2.0
1971/72	63.9	27.3	6.5	2.3
1972/73	64.0	26.8	6.6	2.6
1973/74	68.9	27.8	-	3.3
1974/75	72.2	24.6	-	3.2
1975/76	75.3	22.1	-	2.6
1976/77	74.3	22.6	-	3.1
1977/78	74.3	22.7	-	3.0
1978/79	73.6	23.4	-	3.0
1979/80	73.8	23.1	-	3.1

Source: See Appendix 3.8

Notes: See Appendix 3.8

Appendix 3.10
Current Expenditure on Family Practitioner Services, UK, 1948-1980

£ million

Financial Year	General Medical Service	Pharmaceutical Service	General Dental Service	Ophthalmic Service
1948/49	33.8	17.9	20.7	12.8
1949/50	48.2	36.6	49.3	24.6
1950/51	48.9	40.5	46.6	22.4
1951/52	48.8	52.5	36.3	9.6
1952/53	87.3	49.7	25.2	6.8
1953/54	59.9	46.4	24.5	7.6
1954/55	61.0	49.7	26.9	8.3
1955/56	63.7	51.6	32.8	9.0
1956/57	67.8	60.6	36.0	9.6
1957/58	72.6	61.7	39.0	10.1
1958/59	76.5	67.2	42.4	10.1
1959/60	76.7	74.9	46.9	11.3
1960/61	103.5	83.5	49.8	11.6
1961/62	87.7	77.4	52.0	10.1
1962/63	88.6	79.8	52.9	9.8
1963/64	93.0	114.0	66.0	19.0
1964/65	95.0	133.0	68.0	20.0
1965/66	104.0	155.0	70.0	22.0
1966/67	112.0	163.0	80.0	23.0
1967/68	130.0	179.0	82.0	24.0
1968/69	138.0	186.0	85.0	25.0
1969/70	148.0	204.0	92.0	28.0
1970/71	181.0	222.0	110.0	31.0
1971/72	196.0	249.0	122.0	28.0
1972/73	212.0	285.0	132.0	31.0
1973/74	228.0	313.0	147.0	35.0
1974/75	265.0	440.0	204.0	51.0
1975/76	341.0	485.0	239.0	76.0
1976/77	384.0	618.0	265.0	79.0
1977/78	406.0	745.0	273.0	80.0
1978/79	463.0	880.0	330.0	90.0
1979/80	574.0	1,004.0	395.0	109.0

Source: *Annual Abstract of Statistics, 1964, 1972, 1980*

Notes: For dates before 1963/64 no separate information is supplied in the AAS tabulation about capital expenditure, but the amount of capital investment before this date was negligible.

Appendix 3.11
Proportions of Current Expenditure on Family Practitioner
Services, UK, 1948-1980

Financial Year	General Medical Service (%)	Pharmaceutical Service (%)	General Dental Service (%)	Ophthalmic Service (%)
1948/49	39.7	21.0	24.3	15.0
1949/50	30.4	23.1	31.0	15.5
1950/51	30.9	25.6	29.4	14.1
1951/52	33.2	35.7	24.6	6.5
1952/53	51.7	29.4	14.9	4.0
1953/54	43.3	33.5	17.7	5.5
1954/55	41.8	34.1	18.4	5.7
1955/56	40.6	32.8	20.9	5.7
1956/57	39.0	34.8	20.7	5.5
1957/58	39.6	33.6	21.3	5.5
1958/59	39.0	34.3	21.6	5.1
1959/60	36.6	35.7	22.4	5.3
1960/61	41.7	33.6	20.0	4.7
1961/62	38.6	34.1	22.9	4.4
1962/63	38.3	34.5	22.9	4.3
1963/64	31.9	39.0	22.6	6.5
1964/65	30.1	42.1	21.5	6.3
1965/66	29.6	44.2	19.9	6.3
1966/67	29.6	43.1	21.2	6.1
1967/68	31.3	43.1	19.8	5.8
1968/69	31.8	42.8	19.6	5.8
1969/70	31.4	43.2	19.5	5.9
1970/71	33.3	40.8	20.2	5.7
1971/72	32.9	41.9	20.5	4.7
1972/73	32.1	43.2	20.0	4.7
1973/74	31.5	43.3	20.3	4.9
1974/75	27.6	45.8	21.3	5.3
1975/76	29.9	42.5	20.9	6.7
1976/77	28.5	45.9	19.7	5.9
1977/78	27.0	49.5	18.2	5.3
1978/79	26.3	49.9	18.7	5.1
1979/80	27.6	48.2	19.0	5.2

Source: See Appendix 3.10

Notes: See Appendix 3.10

Appendix 3.12
Distribution of National Health Service Expenditure within the UK, 1949-1979

£ million (actual prices)

Calendar Year	England and Wales		Scotland		Northern Ireland	
	Hospital	FPS	Hospital	FPS	Hospital	FPS
1949	203.6	124.8	27.0	15.1	5.5	4.2
1950	225.2	138.1	29.9	16.7	6.1	4.6
1951	240.8	129.6	32.1	16.1	6.9	4.1
1952	253.1	152.3	32.8	18.2	7.4	4.8
1953	260.7	132.9	33.9	15.6	8.1	4.5
1954	274.1	138.5	36.6	16.9	8.9	4.5
1955	297.9	150.2	40.1	17.9	9.6	4.8
1956	326.5	164.5	43.6	19.2	10.6	5.3
1957	351.1	176.4	45.6	20.9	11.9	5.7
1958	378.4	177.1	48.1	22.0	12.9	6.1
1959	406.6	200.5	53.1	23.5	14.1	6.7
1960	445.1	223.0	57.1	25.5	14.6	7.3
1961	483.8	235.2	63.0	26.9	15.4	7.7
1962	521.1	229.7	66.0	26.6	18.0	7.8
1963	565.2	244.3	72.3	27.7	18.9	8.4
1964	617.9	261.7	77.8	29.2	22.2	9.0
1965	679.1	292.6	84.8	32.6	25.0	10.0
1966	747.8	317.9	95.0	35.0	27.6	11.6
1967	818.3	346.5	105.4	38.0	29.9	12.3
1968	894.7	366.3	113.4	41.4	32.9	13.6
1969	987.7	393.1	131.0	44.8	36.1	14.4
1970	1,137.6	448.0	153.4	50.1	42.8	15.6
1971	1,320.6	498.7	179.7	54.3	48.9	17.9
1972	1,534.7	553.4	208.0	62.1	54.5	19.2
1973	1,645.1	602.5	238.8	66.8	63.4	21.2
1974	2,020.1	696.6	308.1	77.5	75.6	24.7
1975	2,852.0	926.1	396.9	103.2	103.3	32.2
1976	3,298.5	1,090.5	456.8	125.1	125.5	39.1
1977	3,654.8	1,277.7	518.5	136.0	141.5	45.0
1978	4,102.3	1,461.0	628.7	160.8	158.5	51.8
1979	4,844.5	1,698.2	754.2	185.4	192.3	59.1

Source: *Annual Abstract of Statistics, 1955, 1962, 1964, 1971, 1981*

Appendix 3.13
National Health Service Expenditure per Head of Population in the UK, 1949-1979

£ (actual prices)
Population million

Calendar Year	England and Wales			Scotland			Northern Ireland		
	Pop. m	Hospital £	FPS £	Pop. m	Hospital £	FPS £	Pop. m	Hospital £	FPS £
1949	43.79	4.65	2.85	5.16	5.24	2.93	1.37	4.01	3.07
1950	44.02	5.12	3.14	5.17	5.79	3.23	1.38	4.42	3.33
1951	43.82	5.14	3.15	5.10	6.29	3.16	1.37	5.04	2.99
1952	43.96	5.76	3.46	5.10	6.43	3.57	1.38	5.36	3.48
1953	44.11	5.91	3.01	5.10	6.65	3.06	1.38	5.87	3.26
1954	44.27	6.19	3.13	5.10	7.17	3.31	1.39	6.40	3.24
1955	44.44	6.70	3.38	5.11	7.84	3.50	1.39	6.91	3.45
1956	44.67	7.31	3.68	5.12	8.52	3.75	1.40	7.57	3.79
1957	44.91	7.82	3.93	5.13	8.90	4.08	1.40	8.50	4.07
1958	45.11	8.39	3.93	5.14	9.36	4.28	1.40	9.21	4.36
1959	45.39	8.96	4.42	5.16	10.28	4.55	1.41	10.00	4.75
1960	45.76	9.73	4.87	5.18	11.03	4.92	1.42	10.28	5.14
1961	46.20	10.47	5.07	5.18	12.15	5.19	1.43	10.77	5.38
1962	46.64	11.17	4.92	5.20	12.70	5.12	1.44	12.50	5.42
1963	46.90	12.05	5.21	5.21	13.89	5.32	1.45	13.03	5.79
1964	47.22	13.09	5.54	5.21	14.94	5.61	1.46	15.21	6.16
1965	47.54	14.28	6.15	5.21	16.28	6.26	1.47	17.01	6.80
1966	47.82	15.64	6.65	5.20	18.27	6.73	1.48	18.65	7.84
1967	48.11	17.01	7.20	5.20	20.27	7.31	1.49	20.07	8.26
1968	48.35	18.51	7.58	5.20	21.81	7.96	1.50	21.93	9.07
1969	48.54	20.35	8.10	5.21	25.15	8.60	1.51	23.90	9.54
1970	48.68	23.37	9.20	5.21	29.42	9.61	1.53	27.97	10.20
1971	48.85	27.03	10.21	5.22	34.45	10.40	1.54	31.75	11.62
1972	49.03	31.30	11.29	5.21	39.92	11.92	1.55	35.16	12.42
1973	49.15	33.47	12.26	5.21	45.82	12.82	1.55	40.90	13.68
1974	49.16	41.09	14.17	5.22	59.06	14.86	1.55	48.77	15.96
1975	49.16	58.01	18.84	5.21	76.24	19.82	1.54	67.08	20.98
1976	49.14	67.12	22.19	5.21	87.76	24.03	1.54	81.49	25.41
1977	49.12	74.41	26.01	5.20	99.79	26.17	1.54	91.88	29.30
1978	49.12	83.52	29.75	5.18	121.39	31.05	1.54	102.92	33.64
1979	49.17	98.53	34.54	5.17	146.96	35.88	1.55	124.06	38.28

Source: See Appendix 3.12

Appendix 3.14
Regional Allocation of Expenditure and Beds, Great Britain, 1948-1951

Region	Population (million) 1948	% Population	% Initial Revenue Allocation	% Capital Expenditure 1950/51	Number of Beds		Beds per 1000 Population		% Beds	
					General & Special 1948	Mental & Mental Deficiency 1948	General & Special 1948	Mental & Mental Deficiency 1948	General & Special 1948	Mental & Mental Deficiency 1948
Newcastle	2.862	7.09	5.56	12.64	17,407	9,505	6.08	3.32	6.44	5.23
Leeds	3.030	7.50	7.05	7.37	20,801	14,093	6.87	4.65	7.69	7.75
Sheffield	4.058	10.05	7.48	7.19	23,087	13,524	5.69	3.33	8.54	7.44
E. Anglian	1.391	3.44	2.92	2.53	8,867	5,522	6.37	3.97	3.28	3.04
N. W. Metropolitan	3.821	9.46	10.35	8.75	21,763	14,616	5.70	3.83	8.05	8.04
N. E. Metropolitan	2.955	7.32	9.00	7.81	23,554	11,631	7.97	3.94	8.71	6.40
S. E. Metropolitan	3.107	7.69	9.67	8.76	27,732	13,599	8.93	4.38	10.26	7.48
S. W. Metropolitan	4.402	10.90	15.07	12.75	29,675	35,668	6.74	8.10	10.98	19.62
Oxford	1.357	3.36	3.12	3.77	8,055	5,635	5.94	4.15	2.98	3.10
S. Western	2.650	6.56	7.19	9.09	18,369	16,052	6.93	6.06	6.79	8.83
Birmingham	4.335	10.73	8.79	8.47	25,629	17,079	5.91	3.94	9.48	9.39
Manchester	4.360	10.80	8.84	6.31	29,535	17,248	6.77	3.96	10.92	9.48
Liverpool	2.061	5.10	4.96	4.56	15,887	7,645	7.71	3.71	5.88	4.20
England	40.389	83.98	84.74	78.22	270,361	181,817	6.69	4.50	83.67	83.49
Wales	2.552	5.31	5.35	4.94	14,960	9,793	5.86	3.84	4.63	4.50
Scotland	5.150	10.71	9.91	16.84	37,816	26,164	7.34	5.08	11.70	12.01

Sources:

Acton Society Trust, *Hospitals and the State*, Part 6 (1959); RHB Chairmen mtg, 21 February 1950; Department of Health for Scotland

Notes:

Current expenditure is taken from the initial revenue allocation.

1950/51 has been selected as an early date for current and capital expenditure because of the escalating current expenditure at the beginning of the NHS, and the negligible level of capital expenditure.

Bed numbers are total allocations for the stated groups of specialities.

Bed allocations for December 1948 represent the situation at the beginning of the NHS.

Appendix 3.15

Regional Allocation of Expenditure and Beds, Great Britain, 1958

Region	Population (million) 1948	% Population	% Initial Revenue Allocation 1957/58	% Capital Expenditure 1957/58	Number of Beds General & Special 1958	Number of Beds Mental & Mental Deficiency 1958	Beds per 1000 Population General & Special 1958	Beds per 1000 Population Mental & Mental Deficiency 1958	% Beds General & Special 1958	% Beds Mental & Mental Deficiency 1958
Newcastle	2.961	6.97	6.39	10.27	8,998	11,269	3.04	3.81	6.36	5.89
Leeds	3.080	7.25	7.13	5.43	10,764	15,412	3.49	5.00	7.60	8.05
Sheffield	4.271	10.06	8.08	11.41	11,604	14,745	2.72	3.45	8.20	7.71
E. Anglian	1.505	3.54	2.89	2.98	5,092	6,303	3.38	4.19	3.60	3.29
N. W. Metropolitan	4.027	9.49	9.44	7.41	12,565	16,883	3.12	4.19	8.88	8.82
N. E. Metropolitan	3.182	7.49	8.71	6.54	12,221	12,007	3.84	3.77	8.63	6.27
S. E. Metropolitan	3.229	7.61	8.93	7.50	12,053	14,323	3.73	4.44	8.52	7.48
S. W. Metropolitan	4.750	11.19	13.83	11.42	15,879	36,400	3.34	7.66	11.22	19.02
Oxford	1.532	3.61	3.36	6.25	4,663	6,002	3.04	3.92	3.29	3.14
S. Western	2.797	6.59	7.33	7.10	9,770	11,166	3.49	3.99	6.90	5.83
Birmingham	4.589	10.81	9.29	8.73	14,323	18,948	3.12	4.13	10.12	9.90
Manchester	4.398	10.36	9.43	8.67	14,410	19,360	3.28	4.40	10.18	10.12
Liverpool	2.136	5.03	5.19	6.18	9,197	8,569	4.31	4.01	6.50	4.48
England	42.457	84.55	93.67	81.77	141,539	191,387	3.33	4.51	75.18	81.52
Wales	2.615	5.21	2.12	6.83	9,390	16,631	3.59	6.36	4.99	7.08
Scotland	5.141	10.24	4.21	11.40	37,326	26,770	7.26	5.21	19.83	11.40

Sources: MH48/49; Department of Health for Scotland, *Scottish Health Statistics* Notes: Bed numbers are total allocations for the stated groups of specialities.

814

Appendix 3.16
Regional Allocation of Expenditure and Beds, Great Britain, 1971

Region	Population (million) 1971	% Population 1971	% Initial Revenue Allocation 1970/71	% Capital Expenditure 1970/71	Number of Beds 1971	Beds per 1000 Population 1971	% Beds 1971
Newcastle	3.047	6.61	6.59	5.98	28,400	9.32	6.71
Leeds	3.232	7.01	7.40	6.16	32,400	10.02	7.65
Sheffield	4.654	10.10	8.38	9.71	34,700	7.46	8.20
E. Anglian	1.763	3.83	3.21	5.06	14,200	8.05	3.35
N. W. Metropolitan	4.136	8.97	8.89	7.94	39,700	9.59	9.38
N. E. Metropolitan	3.369	7.31	8.03	5.48	30,200	8.96	7.13
S. E. Metropolitan	3.534	7.67	7.96	6.83	31,800	9.00	7.51
S. W. Met. & Wessex	5.267	11.43	13.15	11.57	59,400	11.30	14.00
Oxford	1.999	4.34	3.84	7.10	15,400	7.70	3.64
S. Western	3.177	6.89	7.23	7.76	32,500	10.23	7.68
Birmingham	5.118	11.10	10.19	10.13	41,600	8.13	9.82
Manchester	4.572	9.92	9.77	9.87	40,300	8.81	9.52
Liverpool	2.222	4.82	5.36	6.41	22,900	10.31	5.41
England	46.090	85.28	83.02	81.92	423,500	9.19	82.73
Wales	2.725	5.04	5.03	6.89	25,900	9.50	5.06
Scotland	5.229	9.68	11.95	11.19	62,487	11.95	12.21

Sources:

DHSS, *Health and Personal Social Services Statistics for England and Wales*;

SHHD, *Scottish Health Statistics*

Appendix 3.17

Regional Allocation of Expenditure and Beds, Great Britain, 1979

Region	Population (million) 1979	% Population 1979	% Initial Revenue Allocation 1978/79	% Capital Expenditure 1978/79	Number of Beds 1979	Beds per 1000 Population 1979	% Beds 1979
Northern	3.087	6.65	6.36	6.60	25,000	8.10	6.96
Yorkshire	3.577	7.71	7.27	7.69	30,000	8.39	8.36
Trent	4.544	9.79	8.46	14.02	32,000	7.04	8.91
E. Anglian	1.863	4.01	3.53	4.67	13,000	6.98	3.62
N. W. Thames	3.433	7.40	8.89	6.86	28,000	8.16	7.80
N. E. Thames	3.691	7.95	9.68	7.14	30,000	8.13	8.36
S. E. Thames	3.542	7.63	9.19	6.32	28,000	7.91	7.80
S. W. Thames & Wessex	5.539	11.93	12.08	10.99	45,000	8.12	12.53
Oxford	2.283	4.92	4.13	3.85	14,000	6.13	3.90
S. Western	3.208	6.91	6.23	6.60	25,000	7.79	6.96
W. Midlands	5.152	11.10	9.96	7.69	36,000	6.99	10.03
N. Western	4.018	8.65	8.69	10.43	31,000	7.72	8.64
Mersey	2.485	5.35	5.53	7.14	22,000	8.85	6.13
England	46.422	85.39	82.65	85.03	359,000	7.73	81.22
Wales	2.775	5.11	5.11	5.10	24,000	8.65	5.43
Scotland	5.167	9.50	12.24	9.87	59,000	11.42	13.35

Sources:

DHSS, *Health and Personal Social Services Statistics for England;*

Welsh Office, *Health and Personal Social Services Statistics for Wales;*

SHHD, *Scottish Health Statistics*

816

Appendix 3.18
Regional Distribution of Maternity Beds, Great Britain, 1949

Region	Live and Still Births 1950	Live and Still Births in NHS Hospitals 1950	Maternity Beds 1949	Maternity Beds per 1000 Live and Still Births 1949/1950	Maternity Beds per 1000 Live and Still Births in NHS Hospitals 1949	Live and Still Births in NHS Hospitals per Maternity Bed 1949
Newcastle	52,273	19,494	852	16.30	43.71	22.88
Leeds	50,618	21,660	1,136	22.44	52.45	19.07
Sheffield	68,905	28,622	1,615	23.44	56.43	17.72
E. Anglian	26,173	6,515	413	15.78	63.39	15.77
N. W. Metropolitan	58,914	29,019	1,468	24.92	50.59	19.77
N. E. Metropolitan	52,878	30,201	1,456	27.54	48.21	20.74
S. E. Metropolitan	43,510	23,275	1,417	32.57	60.88	16.43
S. W. Metropolitan	70,511	33,486	1,615	22.90	48.23	20.73
Oxford	22,689	7,971	457	20.14	57.33	17.44
S. Western	43,236	18,623	1,089	25.19	58.48	17.10
Birmingham	73,060	28,580	1,516	20.75	53.04	18.85
Manchester	76,663	37,422	1,956	25.51	52.27	19.13
Liverpool	36,273	20,230	985	27.16	48.69	20.54
England	675,703	305,098	15,975	23.64	52.36	19.10
Wales	43,776	21,107	1,097	25.06	51.97	19.24
Scotland	92,530	51,661	2,698	26.12	52.23	19.15

Sources:

Ministry of Health, *Annual Report 1949*, Appendix II (Maternity Services in Hospitals and Homes); *Report of the Maternity Services Committee* (HMSO, 1959) (Cranbrook Report); Department of Health for Scotland, *Annual Report 1949*

Notes:

Figures for maternity beds relate to 31 December 1949; figures for live and still births are calculated from the information supplied about local health authorities for 1950, included in the Cranbrook Report, Appendix III, pp 106-9.

The tabulation excludes 891 beds in provincial teaching hospitals and 823 beds in London teaching hospitals.

Bed figures relate to available beds, which equate with "staffed beds" or "available staffed beds" for later years.

817

Appendix 3.19
Regional Distribution of Maternity Beds, Great Britain, 1963

Region	Live and Still Births 1963	Live and Still Births in NHS Hospitals 1963	Maternity Beds 1963	Maternity Beds per 1000 Live and Still Births 1963	Maternity Beds per 1000 Live and Still Births in NHS Hospitals 1963	Live and Still Births in NHS Hospitals per Maternity Bed 1963
Newcastle	57,472	37,357	1,439	25.04	38.52	25.96
Leeds	57,344	38,363	1,460	25.46	38.06	26.28
Sheffield	84,102	50,041	1,825	21.70	36.47	27.42
E. Anglian	27,336	14,269	575	21.03	40.30	24.82
N. W. Metropolitan	80,230	53,915	1,940	24.18	35.98	27.79
N. E. Metropolitan	60,104	38,947	1,724	28.68	44.27	22.59
S. E. Metropolitan	59,299	38,307	1,458	24.59	38.06	26.27
S. W. Metropolitan	88,076	56,633	1,885	21.40	33.28	30.04
Oxford	34,282	22,763	753	21.96	33.08	30.23
S. Western	50,583	34,093	1,368	27.04	40.13	24.92
Birmingham	94,776	58,382	1,999	21.09	34.24	29.21
Manchester	82,242	54,773	2,134	25.95	38.96	25.67
Liverpool	45,209	31,692	1,121	24.80	35.37	28.27
England	821,055	529,535	19,681	23.97	37.17	26.91
Wales	47,992	35,322	1,343	27.98	38.02	26.30
Scotland	104,688	82,848	3,044	29.08	36.74	27.22

Sources:

Department of Health; Registrar General, *Statistical Review 1963*; *Scottish Health Statistics 1963*

Notes:

Wessex was split off from the South West Metropolitan RHB in 1959. To facilitate comparisons with 1949, Wessex and S.W. Metropolitan RHB are included together.

The tabulation includes beds in teaching hospitals. Bed figures relate to "staffed beds" and "available staffed beds".

Appendix 3.20

Regional Distribution of Maternity Beds, Great Britain, 1968

Region	Live and Still Births 1968	Live and Still Births in NHS Hospitals 1968	Maternity Beds 1968	Maternity Beds per 1000 Live and Still Births 1968	Maternity Beds per 1000 Live and Still Births in NHS Hospitals 1968	Live and Still Births in NHS Hospitals per Maternity Bed 1968
Newcastle	51,065	40,903	1,524	29.84	37.26	26.84
Leeds	55,632	44,895	1,541	27.70	34.32	29.13
Sheffield	82,404	59,413	1,919	23.29	32.30	30.96
E. Anglian	28,154	17,878	644	22.87	36.02	27.76
N. W. Metropolitan	72,005	58,108	2,046	28.41	35.21	28.40
N. E. Metropolitan	56,916	43,996	1,800	31.63	40.91	24.44
S. E. Metropolitan	54,726	42,194	1,595	29.15	37.80	26.45
S. W. Metropolitan & Wessex	99,639	78,366	2,512	25.21	32.05	31.20
Oxford	35,565	28,701	915	25.73	31.88	31.37
S. Western	49,196	40,341	1,505	30.59	37.31	26.80
Birmingham	94,491	71,057	2,193	23.21	30.86	32.40
Manchester	79,491	63,672	2,280	28.68	35.81	27.93
Liverpool	40,973	34,253	1,144	27.92	33.40	29.94
England	787,465	623,777	21,618	27.45	34.66	28.85
Wales	44,951	39,602	1,417	31.52	35.78	27.95
Scotland	96,211	88,229	3,235	33.62	36.67	27.27

Sources:

Digest of Health Statistics for England and Wales 1969, 1970, 1972;

Scottish Health Statistics 1972; Domiciliary Midwifery and Maternity Bed Needs (HMSO, 1970) (Peel Report)

Notes:

The tabulation includes beds in teaching hospitals. Bed figures relate to "staffed beds".

Appendix 3.21
Regional Distribution of Maternity Beds, Great Britain, 1980

Region	Live and Still Births 1980	Live and Still Births in NHS Hospitals 1980	Maternity Beds 1980	Maternity Beds per 1000 Live and Still Births 1980	Maternity Beds per 1000 Live and Still Births in NHS Hospitals 1980	Live and Still Births in NHS Hospitals per Maternity Bed 1980
Northern	41,536	41,403	1,455	35.03	35.14	28.46
Yorkshire	48,140	47,112	1,733	36.00	36.78	27.19
Trent	60,783	55,922	2,051	33.74	36.68	27.27
E. Anglia	24,933	24,372	839	33.65	34.42	29.05
N. W. Thames	47,817	40,443	1,470	30.74	36.35	27.51
N. E. Thames	52,009	52,874	1,818	35.96	34.38	29.08
S. E. Thames	46,012	45,342	1,552	33.73	34.23	29.22
S.W. Thames & Wessex	69,895	66,582	2,406	34.42	36.14	27.67
Oxford	33,225	32,551	988	29.74	30.35	32.95
S. Western	39,423	36,488	1,241	31.48	34.01	29.40
West Midlands	71,778	72,510	2,309	32.17	31.84	31.40
North Western	54,840	56,162	1,925	35.10	34.28	29.18
Mersey	32,503	31,644	1,084	33.35	34.26	29.19
England	622,894	603,405	20,871	33.51	34.59	28.91
Wales	37,602	35,741	1,149	30.56	32.15	31.11
Scotland	69,355	67,700	2,689	38.77	39.72	25.18

Sources:

Health and Personal Social Services Statistics for England 1982;

Health and Personal Social Services Statistics for Wales 1981;

Scottish Health Statistics 1980

Notes:

The tabulation includes beds in teaching hospitals.

Bed figures relate to "staffed beds".

Appendix 3.22
International Comparison of Patient Flow
in the Hospital Acute Sector,[1] 1949-1979

	Beds per 1000 Population	Cases Treated[2]		Percentage of Available Beds Occupied	Length of Stay (days)
		per 1000 Population	per Available Bed		
England & Wales (1949)	3.5	49.1	14.2	79.2	18.8
England & Wales (1958)	3.5	63.8	18.5	78.1	15.4
England & Wales (1960)	3.4	68.4	19.1	76.2	14.5
Saskatchewan (1961)	6.2	170.3	27.5	78.3	10.4
Sweden (1960)	4.9	96.3	19.5	76.7	14.3
Norway (1960)	5.6	102.7	18.4	75.0	14.9
England (1979)	2.8	93.5	30.0	75.5	8.8
Wales (1979)	3.8	116.8	30.7	71.0	9.0
Scotland (1979)	3.1	100.7	28.1	74.5	10.0
Canada (1979)	5.4	151.0	27.8	79.9	9.9
Denmark (1979)	5.8	182.0	31.6	77.6	9.3
Norway (1979)	5.4	143.0	26.6	79.3	10.9
Sweden (1979)	4.9	154.0	31.6	76.0	8.9

Sources:

Ministry of Health, Annual Reports; D. Paige and K. Jones, Health and Welfare Services in Britain in 1975 (Cambridge University Press, 1966), Table 11; Health and Personal Social Services Statistics for England 1982; Scottish Health Statistics 1979; Health and Personal Social Services Statistics for Wales 1980; OECD, OECD Health Systems (OECD, 1993).

Notes:

[1] The acute sector excludes psychiatric, mental handicap, geriatrics, tuberculosis, and "chronic" cases.

[2] Cases treated are estimated on the basis of data on discharge and deaths.

Appendix 3.23
Regional Distribution of Consultants, England 1948-1979

Region	Population (million) 31.12.48	Number of Consultants 1948	Consultants per 100,000 Population	Population (million) July 1956	Number of Consultants 31.12.58	Consultants per 100,000 Population	Population (million) 1965	Number of (whole-time equivalent) Consultants 1965	w.t.e. Consultants Per 100,000 Population	Population (million) 1979	Number of (whole-time equivalent) Consultants 1979	w.t.e Consultants Per 100,000 Population
Newcastle (Northern 1979)	2.862	280	9.8	2.912	457	15.7	3.076	532	17.3	3.087	729	23.6
Leeds (Yorkshire 1979)	3.030	295	9.7	3.058	369	12.1	3.221	461	14.3	3.577	749	20.9
Sheffield (Trent 1979)	4.058	332	8.2	4.189	453	10.8	4.641	549	11.8	4.544	823	18.1
East Anglian (E. Anglia 1979)	1.391	168	12.1	1.476	209	14.3	1.735	250	14.4	1.863	429	23.0
N.W. Metropolitan (N.W. Thames 1979)	3.821	675	17.7	3.890	740	19.0	4.186	955	22.8	3.433	910	26.5
N.E. Metropolitan (N.E. Thames 1979)	2.955	467	15.8	3.063	576	18.8	3.400	569	16.7	3.691	959	26.0
S.E. Metropolitan (S.E. Thames 1979)	3.107	461	14.8	3.197	610	19.1	3.555	638	17.9	3.542	890	25.1
S.W. Metropolitan (including Wessex 1965) S.W. Thames & Wessex 1979)	4.402	679	15.4	4.616	822	17.8	5.244	944	18.0	5.339	1242	22.4
Oxford	1.357	179	13.2	1.471	256	17.4	1.937	314	16.2	2.283	473	20.7
S. Western	2.650	301	11.4	2.752	381	13.8	3.116	459	14.7	3.208	616	19.2
Birmingham (W. Midlands 1979)	4.335	433	10.0	4.490	610	13.6	5.145	744	14.5	5.152	1056	20.5
Manchester (N. Western 1979)	4.360	326	7.5	4.380	498	11.4	4.561	623	13.7	4.018	916	22.8
Liverpool (Mersey 1979)	2.061	255	12.4	2.601	347	13.3	2.263	396	17.5	2.438	524	21.3
Total England	40.389	4851	12.0	42.095	6328	15.0	46.080	7434	16.1	46.395	10816	22.2

Sources:
Department of Health, 94112/4/65 (1958); MDH/1/4 (1965); Hospital, 94112/4/102/1 (1948); Medical Staff England and Wales, Regional Tables, 30 September 1979 (DHSS, 1980).

Notes:
Consultant totals include SHMOs with allowance.
Totals of whole-time and part-time consultants are given for 1948 and 1958; whole-time equivalents for 1965 and 1979.
For 1958 consultants serving in more than one area have been counted more than once.
1948, 1958, 1965 and 1979 includes consultants in teaching hospitals, except for exclusion in 1979 of 595 consultants in London postgraduate teaching hospitals.

Appendix 3.24
Regional Distribution of Consultants, Scotland, 1956-1979

Region	Population 1956	Number of Consultants 31. 12. 56	Number of Consultants per 100,000 Population 1956	Population 1979	Number of (whole-time equivalent) Consultants 30. 9. 79.	Number of (whole-time equivalent) Consultants per 100,000 Population 1979
Northern	190,000	26	13.7	260,510	66.7	25.6
N. Eastern	496,000	84	16.9	469,168	142.3	30.3
Eastern	411,000	98	23.8	672,838	215.7	32.1
S. Eastern	1,139,000	230	20.2	1,190,836	401.5	33.7
Western	2,909,000	459	15.8	2,573,648	875.7	34.0
Total Scotland	5,145,000	897	17.4	5,167,000	1701.9	32.9

Notes:

Total of whole-time and part-time consultants are given for 1956, and whole-time equivalent for 1979.
Regional administration in Scotland was ended in 1974. The following Health Boards are taken as the equivalents for the earlier regions:

Northern:	**N. Eastern:**	**Eastern:**	**S. Eastern:**	**Western:**
Highland	Grampian	Forth Valley	Borders	Argyll and Clyde
Orkney		Tayside	Fife	Ayrshire and Arran
Shetland			Lothian	Dumfries and Galloway
Western Isles				Greater Glasgow
				Lanarkshire

Sources:

Royal Commission DD; *Scottish Health Statistics 1979*

Appendix 3.25
National Health Service Workforce, England and Wales, 1949, 1958, 1968

	1949	1958	thousand[1] 1968
Part II Hospital Service			
Medical & Dental	12.1	16.0	21.9
Nursing & Midwifery	137.3	173.1	230.2
Administrative & Clerical[2]	25.7	29.9	41.4
Professional & Technical	14.5	20.6	31.7
Works, Maintenance & Ancillary	140.1	171.3	193.4
Others[3]	3.7	5.6	9.0
Part III Local Health Authority			
Medical and Dental[4]	2.9	3.2	2.6
Domiciliary Midwives	7.8	7.5	5.2
Home Nurses	5.8	7.7	8.7
Health Visitors	3.8	4.2	4.6
Home Helps	10.6	22.8	35.5
Ambulance staff	6.0	10.0	14.0
Part IV Executive Council			
General Practitioners	17.2	19.6	19.9
Dentists	9.5	10.3	10.6
Pharmacists	14.3	15.8	13.4
Eye Service	7.8	8.6	7.0
Administrative[5]	6.4	6.0	6.7
Total	**425.5**	**532.2**	**655.8**

Sources:

Ministry of Health, *Annual Reports;* NHS Notes; *Digest of Health Statistics for England and Wales 1969;* DH, 94501/9/2A, 94501/9/6 (Guillebaud Committee); Select Committee on Estimates, *6th Report, 1956-57*

Notes:

1. Expressed in whole-time equivalents.
2. Includes HMC and BG administration and clerical staff.
3. Others include RHB staff, blood transfusion, mass radiography, PHLS.
4. Includes School Medical Service.
5. Includes Executive Councils, Dental Estimates Board, Joint Pricing Committees.

Appendix 3.26
National Health Service Workforce, Scotland, 1949, 1958, 1968

	1949	1958	thousand [1] 1968
Part II Hospital Service			
Medical & Dental	1.9	2.8	3.6
Nursing & Midwifery	19.4	23.2	33.5
Administrative & Clerical	2.7	3.1	5.2
Professional & Technical	2.7	3.3	4.9
Works, Maintenance & Ancillary	20.0	23.0	28.4
Others[2]	0.6	0.8	1.0
Part III Local Health Authority			
Medical and Dental[3]	0.4	0.5	0.5
Domiciliary Midwives	0.8	0.8	0.6
Home Nurses	0.9	1.0	0.9
Health Visitors	1.0	1.2	1.2
Home Helps	1.4	3.4	5.0
Scottish Ambulance Service			
Ambulance staff	0.9	1.0	1.1
Part IV Executive Council			
General Practitioners	2.8	2.6	2.7
Dentists	1.0	1.0	1.1
Pharmacists	1.5	1.6	1.4
Eye Service	0.9	0.9	0.7
Administrative[4]	1.0	0.9	1.1
Total	**59.9**	**71.1**	**92.9**

Sources:

Scottish Department of Health, *Annual Reports;* Department of Health, *Annual Reports;* SHHD, *Annual Reports; Scottish Health Statistics. DH 94501/9/2A* (Guillebaud Committee). Royal Commission DD, p620

Notes:

1. Expressed in whole-time equivalents.
2. Includes RHB staff, blood transfusion, mass radiography.
3. Includes School Health Service.
4. Includes Executive Councils, Dental Estimates Board, Joint Pricing Committees.

Appendix 3.27
Health and Personal Social Services Workforce, Great Britain, 1979

	England	Wales	Scotland
			thousand[1]
Hospital and Community Services			
Medical & Dental	37.8	2.2	5.9
Nursing & Midwifery[2]	354.4	22.3	56.0
Administrative & Clerical	103.0	5.6	13.1
Professional & Technical[3]	65.7	3.5	8.3
Works, Maintenance & Ancillary	192.0	13.2	30.3
Ambulance	17.1	1.3	1.6
Family Practitioner Committees[4]			
General Medical Practitioners	22.7	1.4	3.2
General Dental Practitioners	12.8	0.6	1.2
Pharmacists[5]	4.6	0.7	1.4
Eye Service	7.0	0.4	0.6
Local Authority Social Services			
Social Work Staff	110.4	3.3	7.5
Home Helps	44.9	2.9	6.6
Residential Accommodation Staff	78.1	5.0	12.5

Sources:

Department of Health; Scottish Home and Health Department; *Health and Personal Social Services Statistics for Wales 1980; Scottish Health Statistics 1979*

Notes:

Headquarters, Blood Transfusion Centre, Mass Radiography Unit, and for Scotland the staff of the Common Services Agency, are included in the groups of staff to which they relate.

Excluded from this tabulation are the headquarters staff of DHSS, the Dental Estimates staff (1,600), and the Prescriptions Pricing staff (2,500).

1. Expressed in whole-time equivalents.

2. Includes:

	England	Wales	Scotland
Health Visitors	8.0	0.5	1.3
Home Nurses	10.5	0.9	1.6

3. Includes Works (Professional).

4. Administrative and Clerical FPC staff are included in Health Authority Administrative and Clerical.

5. Relates to the number of chemists' establishments.

Appendix 3.28
Doctors and Population in Great Britain, 1783-1979

Year	Population (million)	Number of Doctors[1] (thousand)	Doctors per 10,000 Population	Population per Doctor
1783[2]	9.347	5.3	5.7	1,764
1841[3]	18.551	16.8	9.0	1,107
1851[3]	20.879	17.3	8.3	1,205
1861[4]	23.129	20.5	8.9	1,128
1901[4]	37.000	23.5	6.4	1,574
1911[4]	40.831	26.7	6.5	1,529
1921[4]	42.769	27.8	6.5	1,538
1931[4]	44.795	33.4	7.5	1,341
1951[1]	48.854	48.2	9.9	1,014
1961[1]	51.284	59.2	11.5	866
1974[5]	54.376	60.2	11.1	903
1978[5]	54.296	66.5	12.2	816
1979[5]	54.338	67.3	12.4	807

Sources:

J. Lane, 'The Medical Practitioners of Provincial England', *Medical History,* 1984, **28**:353-71; I. Loudon, *Medical Care and the General Practitioner 1750-1850,* Tables 1, 19, 20, Appendix VII; *The Lancet,* 1905, i, p503; Willink Report; Royal Commission ME, Table 1; Royal Commission NHS, Table 14.1; DH 94256/6/117/1A; *Health and Personal Social Services Statistics for England 1978, 1982; Health and Personal Social Services Statistics for Wales 1980; Scottish Health Statistics 1979*

Notes:

1. For the period 1951-1979 number of doctors are limited "economically active" doctors. The numbers for 1974-1979 are given in whole-time equivalents. The totals for 1951 and 1961 are numbers of individuals employed, and are therefore higher than the whole-time equivalent totals given in Appendix 3.29.

2. The totals of doctors for London, Scotland and Wales in 1783 are speculative estimates, based on the assumption that the ratio between these areas and provincial England in 1783 was the same as in 1841.

3. The totals for 1841 and 1851 follow Loudon, except that they eliminate medical students. Accordingly, this tables gives fewer doctors for population and is nearer in its assumptions to the "economically active" concept.

4. Figures for 1861-1931 are derived from the *Medical Register.*

5. For further details, see Appendix 3.29.

Appendix 3.29
Doctors in Great Britain,
1949-1979

						thousand[1]
	1949	1958	1968	1974	1978	1979
Hospital Doctors[2]						
England	11.7	15.7	21.4	25.6	29.3	30.4
Wales				1.5	1.7	1.8
Scotland	2.0	2.8	3.6	4.4	4.8	4.9
General Medical Practice[3]						
England	19.2	19.6	20.1	21.5	22.7	22.1
Wales				1.4	1.4	1.4
Scotland	2.8	3.0	2.7	3.0	3.1	3.2
Community and School Health Services						
England	2.1	2.2	2.1	2.3	2.8	2.8
Wales				0.2	0.2	0.2
Scotland	0.3	0.3	0.3	0.3	0.5	0.5
Total	**38.1**	**43.6**	**50.2**	**60.2**	**66.5**	**67.3**

Sources:

Health and Personal Social Services Statistics for England 1982; Health and Personal Social Services Statistics for Wales 1980; Scottish Health Statistics 1979; DHS (SHHD) Annual Reports; MH Annual Reports; NHS Notes; Royal Commission NHS, Table 14.1

Notes:

1. Figures are given in whole-time equivalents.

2. Hospital Doctors includes regional board/authority doctors, and doctors in blood transfusion and mass radiography services.

3. General Medical Practice includes assistants and trainees.

Appendix 3.30
Regional Distribution of General Practitioners, Great Britain, 1952-1963

Region	1 Population (million) 1952	2 Calculated Population (million) 1952	3 Number of GPs 1952	4 Number of GPs per 100,000 Population (cols. 2 & 3) 1952	5 Average List size 1952	6 Calculated Population (million) 1963	7 Population (million) 1965	8 Number of GPs 1963	9 Number of GPs per 100,000 Population (cols. 6 & 8) 1963	10 Average List size 1963
Northern	3.118	3.101	1,135	36.60	2,732	3.242	3.309	1,344	41.46	2,412
Yorkshire & Humberside	4.476	4.064	1,551	38.16	2,620	4.690	4.712	1,964	41.88	2,388
E. Midlands	2.917	3.172	1,196	37.70	2,652	3.278	3.272	1,319	40.24	2,485
E. Anglia	1.408	1.366	565	41.36	2,417	1.443	1.559	650	45.05	2,220
S. Eastern	15.238	14.719	6,350	43.14	2,318	16.893	16.954	7,409	43.86	2,280
S. Western	3.269	3.334	1,512	45.35	2,205	3.551	3.585	1,703	47.96	2,085
W. Midlands	4.426	4.362	1,568	35.95	2,782	4.889	4.975	1,955	39.99	2,501
N. Western	6.437	6.228	2,347	37.68	2,654	6.604	6.704	2,721	41.20	2,427
England	41.289	40.346	17,298	42.87	2,548	44.590	45.070	19,065	42.76	2,343
Wales	2.565	2.447	1,074	43.89	2,278	2.658	2.693	1,270	47.78	2,093
Scotland	5.079	5.096	2,310	45.33	2,206	5.205	5.210	2,735	52.55	1,903

Sources: **Registrar General**, *Annual Statistical Review*; Ministry of Health, *Annual Reports 1953, 1964*; *Scottish Health Statistics*

Notes: It will be noted that the " Calculated Population" derived from data on numbers of general practitioners and list size is slightly different from the population recorded in the **Registrar General's** *Annual Statistical Review*. The regional populations for 1952 have been recalculated in accordance with the **Registrar General's** revised regions adopted in the 1965 Annual Statistical Review.

The estimates for numbers of general practitioners relate to principals providing unrestricted service.

Appendix 3.31
Regional Distribution of General Practitioners, Great Britain, 1968-1972

Region	Population (million) 1968	Number of GPs 1968	Number of GPs per 100,000 Population 1968	Average List size 1968	Population (million) 1972	Number of GPs 1972	Number of GPs per 100,000 Population 1972	Average List size 1972
Northern	3.341	1,307	39.12	2,522	3.296	1,348	40.90	2,474
Yorkshire and Humberside	4.804	1,881	39.15	2,587	4.825	1,959	40.60	2,510
E. Midlands	3.322	1,304	39.25	2,636	3.416	1,386	40.57	2,580
E. Anglia	1.637	690	42.15	2,312	1.711	731	42.72	2,321
S. Eastern	17.230	7,309	42.42	2,442	17.318	7,713	44.54	2,367
S. Western	3.700	1,699	45.92	2,217	3.833	1,783	46.52	2,224
W. Midlands	5.084	1,938	38.12	2,660	5.152	2,117	41.09	2,493
N. Western	6.755	2,604	38.55	2,595	6.753	2,738	40.54	2,502
England	45.873	18,732	40.83	2,494	46.304	19,775	42.71	2,421
Wales	2.725	1,225	44.95	2,231	2.735	1,323	48.37	2,067
Scotland	5.200	2,604	50.08	1,997	5.210	2,625	50.38	1,985

Source: *Health and Personal Social Services Statistics for England and Wales; Scottish Health Statistics; Domiciliary Midwifery and Maternity Bed Needs* (HMSO, 1970) (Peel report)

Notes: The estimates for general practitioners relate to principals providing unrestricted service.

Appendix 3.32
Regional Distribution of General Practitioners, Great Britain, 1979

Region	Population (million) 1979	Number of GPs	Number of GPs per 100,000 Population	Average List Size
Northern	3.087	1,376	44.57	2,342
Yorkshire	3.577	1,620	45.29	2,285
Trent	4.544	1,973	43.42	2,385
E. Anglian	1.863	858	46.05	2,175
N. W. Thames	3.433	1,739	50.66	2,263
N. E. Thames	3.691	1,741	47.17	2,299
S. E. Thames	3.542	1,685	47.57	2,256
S. W. Thames & Wessex	5.539	2,610	47.12	2,243
Oxford	2.283	1,027	44.98	2,316
S. Western	3.208	1,552	48.38	2,128
W. Midlands	5.152	2,300	44.64	2,325
N. Western	4.018	1,760	43.80	2,347
Mersey	2.485	1,116	44.91	2,301
England	46.396	21,357	46.03	2,286
Wales	2.775	1,448	52.18	1,916
Scotland	5.153	3,190	61.91	1,615

Sources:

Health and Personal Social Services Statistics for England 1982; *Health and Personal Social Services Statistics for Wales 1980*; *Scottish Health Statistics 1979*

Notes:

The estimates for numbers of general practitioners relate to principals providing unrestricted service.

NOTES

Chapter I
THE NATIONAL HEALTH SERVICE IN 1958

1.   See Appendices 3.3, 3.25, 3.26, 3.27. In 1948 the personal social services existed
     on a negligible scale; by 1979 they accounted for about 1 per cent of GDP.

2.   For a survey of opinion poll findings among doctors and the public, see P F
     Gemmill, *Britain's Search for Health. The First Decade of the NHS* (University of
     Pennsylvania Press, 1960); see also A Lindsey, *Socialized Medicine in England and
     Wales. The National Health Service, 1948-1961* (University of North Carolina Press,
     1962), pp 473-4.

3.   HC Debates, vol 592, cols 1382-506, 30 July 1958.

4.   *Times,* 'NHS Supplement', 7 July 1958.

5.   *Observer,* 29 June 1958.

6.   H Guy Dain, 'The NHS after Ten Years', *British Medical Journal,* 1958, ii,
     Supplement, 1-3, 5 July 1958.

7.   See John Fry from the College of General Practitioners, *Observer,* 6 July 1958;
     Bruce Cardew from the Medical Practitioners' Union, *Manchester Guardian,* 2
     October 1958.

8.   H Eckstein, *The English Health Service: its origins, structure and achievements* (Harvard
     University Press, 1958); O L Peterson, 'A Study of the National Health Service'
     (typescript, Rockefeller Foundation, 1951); Lindsey, *Socialized Medicine in England
     and Wales.*

9.   *Report of the Committee of Enquiry into the Cost of the National Health Service,* Cmd.9663
     (HMSO, 1956); B Abel-Smith and R M Titmuss, *The Cost of the National Health
     Service in England and Wales* (Cambridge University Press, 1956).

10. Speech to the Executive Councils Association, 7 October 1947, quoted from C
     Webster, ed, *Aneurin Bevan on the National Health Service* (Oxford Wellcome Unit for
     the History of Medicine, 1991), p 140.

11. Lindsey, *Socialized Medicine in England and Wales,* p 472; Don Cook, *Harper's
     Magazine,* May 1959, p 37.

12. *Report on the Grading Structure of Administrative and Clerical Staff in the Hospital Service*
     (HMSO, 1957), pp 41-2.

13. *Select Committee on Estimates, Session 1956/57, Sixth Report* (HC 222), paras 6,37.

14. Poll findings are summarised in Gemmill, *Britain's Search for Health.*

15. In 1951 the staff of the Ministry of Health was reduced from 5,300 to 2,700. In
     1958 the staff was about 2,000. See Appendix 2.8 for the headquarters
     organisation of the Ministry of Health in 1952.

16. Acton, 6, p 3 expresses this point in a curious way, suggesting that civil servants
     lacking in confidence were hesitant to take initiatives, concentrating on 'avoiding
     mistakes rather than on bold constructive action. The admirable sentiment "He

who makes no mistakes makes nothing" hardly gets a fair chance; and the native hue of resolution may often be sicklied o'er by the pale cast of thoughts about the P.A.C.'.

17. Bevan, HC Debates, vol 592, cols 1382-98, 30 July 1958. This conclusion is supported by Acton, 6, p 3, and with respect to Kenneth Robinson by Richard Crossman, *Diaries*, i, p 200, and more generally in Crossman's Godkin lectures at Harvard in 1970, published as *Inside View* (Cape, 1972). For further evidence, chapter III below. Enoch Powell argues that in his own case, absence of Cabinet rank for part of his time in office was not an impediment to his influence as Minister of Health, *A New Look at Medicine and Politics* (Pitman, 1966), pp 2-3. Chapter II below suggests otherwise.

18. For the headquarters organisation of the Department of Health for Scotland, see Appendix 2.9.

19. See Appendices 3.4, 3.5. OHE Compendium, Table 2.1 gives a 14 per cent increase for the period 1949-1958 at 1949 prices.

20. See Appendices, 3.3, 3.6. Between 1949/50 and 1957/58 the share of GDP absorbed by education increased from 2.96 to 3.91 per cent.

21. See Appendices 3.6, 3.7.

22. Calculated on the basis of data in Appendix 3.6.

23. See Appendix 3.2.

24. M Penelope Hall, *The Social Services of Modern England*, 4th edn (Routledge, 1959); D Marsh, ed, *An Introduction to the Study of Social Administration* (Routledge, 1965); J Parker, *Local Health and Welfare Services* (Allen and Unwin, 1965); N Timms, *Psychiatric Social Work in Great Britain (1939-1962)* (Routledge, 1962), especially chapter VI; J Tizzard, *Community Services for the Mentally Handicapped* (Oxford University Press, 1964); C Webster, 'The Elderly and the early National Health Service', in M Pelling and R M Smith, eds, *Life, death and the elderly. Historical Perspectives* (Routledge, 1991), pp 165-93.

25. See Appendix 3.9.

26. See Appendix 3.25. For similar trends in Scotland, see Appendix 3.26.

27. Evidence provided by Professor Anne Digby suggests that in England this ratio applied from about the time of the Medical Act, 1858. She also draws attention to big regional variations, *Making a Medical Living. Doctors and Patients in the English Market for Medicine, 1720-1911* (Cambridge University Press, 1994), p 15, Table 11. In 1911 the ratio in the least-favoured group of counties was 1:2,128; for the most-favoured counties it was 1:1,149. In 1951 the ranking order for the five groups of counties was unaltered, with the least-favoured group being 1:1,388 and the most-favoured 1:833, recalculated from J and S Jewkes, *The Genesis of the British NHS*, p 58, Table XVIII. The above ratios relate to doctors as a whole; naturally, the ratios for general practitioners give fewer doctors for the relevant population.

28. DH, 94256/6/117/1A (Willink Committee). See also Appendix 3.28.

29. Royal Commission ME, p 141.

30. See Appendices 3.25, 3.26; *MH Report 1958*, pp 147, 157, 161, 165; for details with respect to full-time and part-time staff, C Webster, 'The Elderly and the early NHS', pp 182-4.

31. *An Inquiry into Health Visiting. Report of a Working Party* (HMSO, 1956), Jameson Report, para 397.

32. Ministry of Health to Treasury, 22 September 1960, DH, 94402/7/42, data for 1959; *Health and Welfare. The Development of Community Care*, Cmnd. 1973 (HMSO, 1963), pp 53, 275, 367.

33. J Hogarth, 'General Practice', in G.McLachlan, ed, *Improving the Common Weal. Aspects of the Scottish Health Service 1900-1984* (Edinburgh University Press and NPHT, 1987), pp 153-212; R Stevens, *Medical Practice in Modern England* (Yale University Press, 1966), pp 153-68; S Taylor, *Good General Practice* (Oxford University Press, 1954).

34. *MH Report 1958*, p 93; Royal Commission DD, Evidence, p 700; DH, 94256/6/117/1A (Willink Committee).

35. *MH Report 1958*, p 92.

36. See Appendix 3.30.

37. *MH Report 1958*, pp 95-7.

38. DH, 94256/6/117/1A (Willink Committee).

39. DH, 94256/6/117/1A (Willink Committee).

40. Comparing the first six months of 1956 and 1957, there was about a 20 per cent fall in the average number of prescriptions dispensed, *MH Report 1958*, p 129. The 1956 total was not again reached until 1964, shortly before the abolition of the prescription charge, *MH Report 1965*, p 120.

41. For a summary of these objections against the charges in the debate on the Government's social policies, HC Debates, vol 565, cols 1219-343, 19 March 1957.

42. Webster I, p 227.

43. *Final Report of the Committee on the Cost of Prescribing* (HMSO, 1959), para 92.

44. W Sneader, *Drug Discovery* (Wiley, 1985), pp 175-6.

45. SCPC(57)21, and Dunlop Committee, 6th mtg, 15 January 1958, MH 133/86. *DHS Report 1956*, p 43.

46. DH, 94256/6/117/1A (Willink Committee).

47. Stevens, *Medical Practice in Modern England*, pp 153-7; J Fry, J Hunt, and R J F H Pinsent, eds, *A History of the Royal College of General Practitioners* (MTP Press, 1983); RCGP, *Forty Years On* (Atalink, 1995).

48. T Osborne, 'Mobilizing Psychoanalysis: Michael Balint and the General Practitioners', *Social Studies of Science*, 1993, **23**, 175-200.

49. *MH Report 1958*, p 342.

50. Royal Commission DD, Evidence, pp 12-13, 582, 640-1. Webster I, p 365.

51. *MH Report 1958*, p 123. This compared with about 18 per cent for the general dental service, and 15 per cent for the pharmaceutical service.

52. Reflecting the introduction of charges, the number of pairs of glasses supplied fell from a peak of 8.3m in 1950 to reach 3.4m in 1952. There was a only a slight subsequent increase above this level, *MH Report 1958*, pp 119-21.

53. *MH Report 1958*, p 324. P Cook and R O Walker, 'The Geographical Distribution of Dental Care in the United Kingdom', *British Dental Journal*, 1967, **122**, 441-7, 494-9, 551-8.

54. *MH Report 1959*, p 91.

55. Sir G Godber, *The Health Service: Past, Present and Future* (Athlone Press, 1975), pp 27-8.

56. *MH Report 1958*, pp 56-7, 268, 278. For England, on the basis of a summation of regional consultant numbers, for the same period, an increase from 4,851 to 6,328 is recorded, which is 30 per cent, see Appendix 3.23.

57. NHS Notes, Table 5. For 1949, an a similar alternative estimate of 3,773 whole-time equivalent consultants, or 4,983 including other senior grades, is given by Abel-Smith and Titmuss, *The Cost of the National Health Service*, p 118.

58. *MH Report 1958*, p 268. See also Appendix 3.25. For this group, Scotland experienced a 47 per cent increase, see Appendix 3.26.

59. *MH Report 1958*, pp 56-7, 278.

60. *MH Report 1958*, pp 36-7; *DHS Report 1958*, pp 68-9.

61. See Appendix 3.25.

62. Webster I, p 325.

63. DH, 94256/6/117/1A (Willink Committee).

64. Evidence of Sheffield RHB to Willink Committee, DH, 94256/6/117/1A; Webster I, p 309.

65. G Joseph, *Women at Work: the British Experience* (Philip Allan, 1983).

66. 'Westminster Commentary', *Spectator*, 21 November 1958, p 670. See also Webster I, pp 336-7; Webster, 'Nursing and the Crisis of the Early NHS', *History of Nursing Group Bulletin*, 1986, **7**, 4-12; M.Carpenter, *Working for Health. The History of COHSE* (Lawrence and Wishart, 1988), pp 281-304.

67. See Appendices 3.25, 3.26.

68. *NW Metropolitan RHB Survey* 1954-1958 (NW Metropolitan RHB, 1958), pp 70-1, 85-6. *NW 20* (NW Metropolitan RHB, 1968), p 39 reports that more than a thousand German women had been recruited under this scheme since its inception in 1951. The same source reported that in 1968 the region was training nurses and midwifery students from 71 countries, including 400 from Jamaica.

69. See Appendices 3.25, 3.26.

70. Between 1949 and 1958, in England and Wales there was an increase of 16 per cent in administrative and clerical staff, and in Scotland a rise of 15 per cent, see Appendices 3.25, 3.26.

71. *Report on the Grading Structure of Administrative and Clerical Staff in the Hospital Service* (HMSO, 1957). For a review of limitations of administrative staff structures, Treasury minute, 27 November 1959, T 227/1225.

72. *MH Report 1958*, pp 8, 17-18, 23.

73. For instance, of the 14 large schemes in progress in Scotland in 1958, six related to mental health and mental handicap, three to general hospital provision, two to maternity hospitals, two to radiotherapy, and one to neurosurgery, *DHS Report 1958*, p 19.

74. See Appendix 3.22.

75. See Appendices 3.18, 3.19. See also, A Macfarlane and M Mugford, *Birth Counts* (HMSO, 1984), vol 1, pp 156-7 and Table A7.27.

76. L Bryder, *Below the Magic Mountain: a History of Tuberculosis in Twentieth-Century Britain* (Oxford University Press, 1989); F B Smith, *The Retreat of Tuberculosis 1850-1950* (Croom Helm, 1988); C Webster, 'Tuberculosis', in C Seale and S Pattinson, *Medical Knowledge. Doubt and Certainty* (Open University Press, 1994), pp 36-59.

77. *MH Report 1958*, pp 29-31; *DHS Report 1958*, pp 27-8, 124; C Clayson, 'Tuberculosis', in McLachlan, ed, *Improving the Common Weal. Aspects of the Scottish Health Services 1900-1984*, pp 383-410.

78. Acton, 6, Appendix I.

79. Editorial, 'Financial Allocations', *Hospital Service Finance*, 1962, 7-11.

80. See Appendix 3.23.

81. Macleod to Butler, 26 April 1954, T, SS 267/02A. It was also pointed out that capital spending of the NHS was less than the London County Council prewar, and that the prewar capital spending of the Middlesex County Council exceeded the entire NW Metropolitan RHB in any year up to 1956, *NW 20* (NW Metropolitan RHB, 1968), p 7.

82. Abel-Smith and Titmuss, *Cost of the NHS*, Appendix G, pp 137-8.

83. The Scottish hospital was at Vale of Leven, south of Loch Lomond, opened in 1955, *DHS Report 1956*, p 58. The most advanced equivalents in England and Wales were the Princess Margaret Hospital at Swindon, and the West Wales General Hospital at Glangwili near Carmarthen, where the first phases were completed in 1959.

84. *Report of Committee of Enquiry on the Cost of the National Health Service*, paras 67-8, 319; Walker-Smith, C(58)158, 18 July 1958, CAB 129/94.

85. Ministry of Health, 'Hospital Capital Expenditure', April 1959, T, SS 267/491/01D.

86. From 1949/50 to 1958/59, total capital expenditure in England and Wales was about £122m, and in Scotland £25m, *MH Reports; DHS Reports; Scottish Health Statistics*.

87. Not taking account of the teaching hospitals, Leeds contained 7.70 per cent of the population and received 6.5 per cent of capital resources, Birmingham 10.73 per cent population, 9.3 per cent capital resources, and Manchester 10.80 per cent population, 8.9 per cent capital resources. The four metropolitan regions contained about 35 per cent of the population and received a similar percentage of resources.

88. Acton, 6, Appendix I, Tables 3 and 4, which cover the period 1948/49 to 1956/57. The figures for 1957/58 are supplied from *MH Report 1958*, p 20. See also Appendices 3.14, 3.15 for capital allocations for the beginning and end of the decade, but these are of limited value because of big annual fluctuations.

89. See Appendix 3.14. Mental hospital beds are not a useful basis for comparison because of the heavy concentration of these beds in the South West Metropolitan region. It is also not helpful to compare capital allocations for single years because the very small scale of capital expenditure, which resulted in big fluctuations from year to year with respect to any region.

90. See Appendix 3.15.

91. Editorial, 'Financial Allocations', *Hospital Service Finance*, 1962, 7-11. This weighting exercise was conducted on the basis of estimating the costs of maintaining the various categories of beds, rather than with respect to demographic and epidemiological factors.

92. Webster I, pp 385-7.

93. Townsend, *Last Refuge. A survey of residential institutions and homes for the aged in England and Wales* (Routledge, 1962).

94. For example, D Armstrong, *Political Anatomy of the Body: Medical Knowledge in Britain in the Twentieth Century* (Cambridge University Press, 1983); M Foucault, *The Birth of the Clinic: an Archaeology of Medical Perception* (Tavistock, 1973); I Illich, *Medical Nemesis: the Expropriation of Health* (Marion Boyars, 1975); B Ehrenreich and D English, *Complaints and Disorders: the Sexual Politics of Sickness* (Writers and Readers Publishing Cooperative, 1976); J Mitchell and A Oakley, eds, *The Rights and Wrongs of Women* (Harmondsworth, 1976); T S Szasz, *The Myth of Mental Illness: Foundations of a Theory of Personal Conduct* (Macmillan, 1963).

95. D Crossley, 'The introduction of leucotomy: a British case history', *History of Psychiatry*, 1993, **4**, 553-64; *MH Report 1958*, p 23; Webster, 'Tuberculosis'.

96. H Bakwin, 'Pseudoxia Paediatrica', *New England Journal of Medicine*, 1945, **232**, 691-7; J F Woodward, 'The changing practice of otolaryngology', *Archives of Otolaryngology*, 1956, **64**, 486-513.

97. NW Metropolitan RHB, *Survey 1954-1958*, pp 65-6. P Taylor, *Smoke Ring. The Politics of Tobacco* (Bodley Head, 1984), pp 5-6; C Webster, 'Tobacco smoking addiction: a challenge to the NHS', *British Journal of Addiction*, 1984, **79**, 7-16.

98. See Appendices 2.3, 2.4.

99. Most notably, *Co-operation between Hospitals, Local Authority and General Practitioner Services* (HMSO, 1952).

100. D Macmillan, 'Community Health Services and the Mental Hospital', in H Freeman and J Farndale, eds, *Trends in the Mental Health Services* (Pergamon, 1963), pp 226-37; H L Freeman, 'Oldham and District Psychiatric Service', *Lancet*, 1960, i, 218-21, 23 January 1960.

101. Treasury minutes, 27 November 1959 and 2 February 1960, T 227/1225.

Chapter II
CONSERVATIVES AND CONSOLIDATION

1. For the Conservative Party context, see J Ramsden, *The Age of Churchill and Eden, 1940-1957* (Longman, 1995), chapter 7. For the politics of welfare, see N Timmins, *The Five Giants. A Biography of the Welfare State* (Harper Collins, 1995), chapter 2.

2. In May 1963 this responsibility passed to Henry Brooke, who was Butler's successor as Home Secretary.

3. See Appendix 1.1.

4. Macmillan diary, quoted in Alistair Horne, *Macmillan 1957-1968* (Macmillan, 1989), p 402.

5. *Economist*, 19 January 1957, pp 186-7.

6. The Parliamentary and Joint Parliamentary Secretaries for this period were J K Vaughan-Morgan (January-September 1957); R H M Thompson (September 1957-October 1959); Edith M Pitt (October 1959-July 1962); B Braine (July 1962-October 1964); Lord Newton (September 1962-April 1964); the Marquess of Lothian (April-October 1964).

7. Walker-Smith represented the Board of Trade views on this issue at HA(57) 7th mtg, 22 March 1957, CAB 134/1968.

8. See Appendix 1.2.

9. For the Conservative Party context, J Ramsden, *The Winds of Change: Macmillan to Heath, 1957-1975* (Longman, 1996), chapter 1.

10. Horne, *Macmillan 1957-1968*, pp 137-71.

11. Horne, *Macmillan 1957-1968*, pp 240-2.

12. By coincidence, one of Walker-Smith's main anti-European allies was Robert Turton, a former Minister of Health.

13. Enoch Powell, *Reflections: Selected Writings and Speeches* (Bellew, 1992); Patrick Cosgrave, *The Lives of Enoch Powell* (Bodley Head, 1989); Robert Shepherd, *Iain Macleod A Biography* (Hutchinson, 1994), pp 42-5. Largely concerned with Powell on immigration, Paul Foot, *The Rise of Enoch Powell* (Cornmarket Press, 1969).

14. Shepherd, *Macleod*, pp 67-9; Cosgrave, *Lives of Enoch Powell*, p 119.

15. Cosgrave, *Lives of Enoch Powell*, pp 170-88.

16. Horne, *Macmillan 1957-1968*, p 541. Macmillan believed that the Treasury team resignation was their plot to unseat him, Horne, *Macmillan 1957-1968*, p 78. For other uncomplimentary remarks about Powell by Macmillan, Horne, p 72.

17. Macmillan to Powell, 1 August 1960, PREM 11/3438.

18. Ramsden, *The Winds of Change*, pp 164-71. For a convenient summary, K Alderman, *Contemporary Record*, 1992, **6**, 243-65.

19. Horne, *Macmillan 1957-1968*, pp 331-59.

20. Horne, *Macmillan 1957-1968*, pp 342-4; Shepherd, *Macleod*, pp 279-80.

21. Crookshank was a Cabinet Minister by virtue of his office of Leader of the House. In 1962 the number of Parliamentary Secretaries in the Ministry of Health was increased from one to two, see above n.6.

22. Cosgrave, *Lives of Powell*, p 179.

23. In July 1962 Maclay faced attacks from Labour MPs on account of closure of Scottish coal mines. It is suggested that Maclay had in advance of the July purge signified his wish to retire (Maclay's Obituary, *Times*, 21 August 1992), but others suggest that he was surprised by the dismissal (Maclay's Obituary, *Independent*, 21 August 1992).

24. Randolph Churchill, *The Fight for the Tory Leadership* (Heinemann, 1964), pp 65-9; Cosgrave, *Lives of Powell*, pp 182-4.

25. PREM 11/5008. For a positive view of Macmillan's intervention, Churchill, *Fight for the Leadership*; Horne, *Macmillan 1957-1968*, pp 342-4. For Macmillan's critics, Iain Macleod, 'The Tory Leadership', *Spectator*, 17 January 1964; Shepherd, *Macleod*, pp 321-7. See also Anthony Howard and Richard West, *The Making of the*

Prime Minister (Cape, 1965), chapters 3-5; Ramsden, *The Winds of Change*, pp 196-213.

26. For Macmillan's six-page memorandum on the Conservative Leadership, 15 October 1963, PREM 11/5008.

27. Shepherd, *Macleod*, p 316.

28. Shepherd, *Macleod*, pp 327-32; Cosgrave, *Lives of Powell*, p 187.

29. Ramsden, *The Winds of Change*, pp 206-21.

30. See Appendices 1.1, 1.4.

31. The most notable example was D A V Allen (later Lord Croham), who was from 1958 to 1960 an Under Secretary in the Ministry of Health; he then returned to the Treasury, became Permanent Secretary at the Department of Economic Affairs, then in 1968 Permanent Secretary at the Treasury. The usefulness of such transfers was immediately demonstrated by the insight provided by Allen about the Ministry of Health in evidence to the Plowden Committee, T 227/1225.

32. See Appendix 1.6.

33. Sir George Godber, *The Health Service: Past, Present and Future* (Athlone Press, 1975); *The British National Health Service. Conversations with Sir George Godber* (US Department of Health, Education, and Welfare, 1976).

34. See Appendix 2.9.

35. Treasury minute, 27 November 1959, T 227/1225.

36. Treasury minute, 8 October 1957, T 227/957.

37. Treasury minute, 2 February 1960, T 227/1225.

38. *MH Report 1958*, pp 41-3.

39. Report to CHSC, 9 November 1965, DH, G/C 15/5.

40. L Gunn and R Mair, *New Society*, 20 July 1967, p 82.

41. Macleod to Macmillan, 14 October 1957, BN 72/131,

42. BN 72/131.

43. Boyd-Carpenter to Macmillan, 25 June 1962, BN 72/131.

44. For continuing Conservative advocacy of a department of health and social security, by its social services spokesman, Maurice Macmillan, *Daily Telegraph*, 20 June 1968.

45. See Appendix 1.5.

46. *SHHD Report 1962*, p 2.

47. Tam Dalyell, Johnson's Obituary, *Independent*, 13 March 1996.

48. See Appendix 1.7.

49. See Appendix 2.9. Acton,5; Sir D Milne, *The Scottish Office* (Allen and Unwin, 1957); SHHD, Memorandum to the Fulton Committee, 1967, HH 101/3520; J W Sinclair and I J MacKenzie, *Future Central Organisation of the Scottish Health Services* (Scottish Office Management Services, Edinburgh, 1972).

50. See Appendix 2.10.

51. Operation Vigilant, draft report, May 1964, T, 2SS 1086/01B.

52. Walker-Smith, HA(61)68, 6 June 1961, CAB 134/1986; HA(61) 10th mtg, 16 June 1961, CAB 134/1984.

53. See Appendix 3.3.

54. See Appendices 3.4, 3.6, and 3.7, taking 4 per cent as the share of gross expenditure derived from local taxation.

55. See Appendices 3.4, 3.5.

56. SEP(68)47, 25 June 1968, T, 2EAS 9/285/03B.

57. See Appendix 3.2.

58. Vosper, 'The Future of the NHS', January 1957, T 227/1116.

59. For the economic context to the following sections, F T Blackaby, ed, *British Economic Policy 1960-74: Demand Managmement* (Cambridge University Press, 1978); J C R Dow, *The Management of the British Economy 1945-60* (Cambridge University Press, 1970); N F R Crafts and N Woodward, eds, *The British Economy since 1945* (Clarendon Press, 1991).

60. PREM 11/1602; T 227/413-5.

61. Webster I, pp 211-16.

62. Treasury minute, 9 January 1959, T 227/744.

63. See Appendix 3.7.

64. Treasury minute, 28 December 1956, T 227/425.

65. Brooke to Macmillan, 31 December 1956, T 227/425.

66. Macmillan to Brooke, 31 December 1956, T 227/425.

67. Treasury minute, 1 January 1957, T 227/425.

68. CM(57) 2nd mtg, 8 January 1957, CAB 128/30; Cabinet Secretary's Notebook (Brook). Eden announced his resignation at the Cabinet meeting on 9 January. Macmillan was backed by the Governor of the Bank of England, who on 20 December 1956 called for 'radical measures', or a 'radical attack on the fundamentals' on account of over-extended social service, military and political commitments, T, Bound budget papers 1957, vol 3(xi).

69. Thorneycroft minute, 14 January 1957, T 230/408.

70. Thorneycroft, 'Skeleton For Policy', 16 January 1957, T 230/408.

71. Thorneycroft minute, 18 January 1957, T 230/408.

72. Powell, Vosper and officials mtg, 15 January 1957, T 227/1116. Treasury minute, 18 January 1957, T 227/485.

73. Vosper, draft Cabinet memorandum, c.11 January 1957, T 227/1116.

74. Treasury minutes, 20 to 30 January 1957, T 227/485, 1116.

75. Ministers mtg, 24 January 1957, T 227/1116.

76. CC(57) 2nd mtg, 21 January 1957, CAB 128/31.

77. Exchanges between Ministers, and related briefs, January to February 1957, PREM 11/2758; T 227/425.

78. Thorneycroft, C(57)16, 30 January 1957, CAB 129/85.

79. Vosper, C(57)17, 30 January 1957, Hailsham, C(57)19, 30 January 1957, Boyd-Carpenter, C(57)20, 30 January 1957, CAB 129/85; Cabinet Secretary's Notebook (Brook).

80. CC(57) 5th mtg, 31 January 1957, CC(57) 7th mtg, 5 February 1957, CAB 128/31.

81. Cabinet Secretary's Notebook (Brook). One-fifth rather than one-third was the maximum for the insurance contributory element assumed by Beveridge.

82. Treasury minutes, 31 January and 1 February 1957, T 227/425.

83. Ministers mtg, 3 February 1957, T 227/425.

84. GEN 573/ 1st mtg, 10 February 1957, CAB 130/122.

85. Thorneycroft, C(57)31, 13 February 1957, Boyd-Carpenter, C(57)36, 14 February 1957, CAB 129/85.

86. CC(57) 11th mtg, 15 February 1957, CAB 128/31. Welfare milk had stood at $1\frac{1}{2}$d a pint since 1946; school meals charges had been increased in stages from a level of 5d in 1949.

87. Thorneycroft, HC Debates, vol 565, cols 209-16, 19 February 1957, Vosper, vol 566, cols 9-30, 4 March 1957. For discussions of the practicalities of the increased NHS Contribution, GEN 573, CAB 130/122; T 227/425-426; HA(57) 6th mtg, 8 March 1957, CAB 134/1968.

88. HC Debates, vol 569, cols 205-42, 1 May 1957, vol 569, cols 990-1106, 8 May 1957. T 227/427.

89. Treasury minute, 23 April 1957, T 227/485.

90. Treasury minute, 23 April 1957, T 227/485.

91. Lennox-Boyd, HA(57)99, J Vaughan-Morgan, HA(57)60, CAB 134/1970; HA(57) 19th mtg, 31 July 1957, CAB 134/1968.

92. Treasury minute, 24 July 1957, T, 2SS 292/494/01D.

93. Macmillan to Thorneycroft, 30 July 1957, Thorneycroft to Macmillan, 1 August 1957, T, 2SS 292/494/01D.

94. CC(57) 63rd mtg, 27 August 1957, CAB 128/31.

95. Thorneycroft to Macmillan, 27 May 1957, T 233/1369.

96. Macmillan to Thorneycroft, 28 May 1957, T 233/1369.

97. CC(57) 55th mtg, 19 July 1957, CAB 128/31; Thorneycroft to Macmillan, 30 July 1957, T 233/1369. Thorneycroft repeated a previous appeal to the Prime Minister made on 24 July 1957.

98. Macmillan to Ministers, 10 August 1957, PREM 11/2306.

99. Macmillan, C(57)194, 1 September 1957, paras VII-IX, CAB 129/88.

100. CC(57) 66th mtg, 10 September 1957, CC(57) 67th mtg, 12 September 1957, CC(57) 68th mtg, 17 September 1957, CAB 128/31. For Thorneycroft's statement and its reception, *Times*, 20 September 1957.

101. Thorneycroft statement, cited in *Times*, 20 September 1957.

102. Powell to Thorneycroft, 6 December 1957, T 233/1459.

103. Powell to Thorneycroft, 16 December 1957, T 233/1459.

104. Two Treasury minutes, 6 December 1957, T 233/1459.

105. Thorneycroft minute, 9 December 1957, T 233/1459.

106. Thorneycroft to Macmillan, 8 December 1957, T 172/ 2137.

107. GEN 625/ 1st mtg, 11 December 1957, CAB 130/139.

108. Treasury minute, 10 January 1958, T 233/1459.

109. Draft Cabinet papers for Chancellor of Exchequer, c.10 December 1957, 17 December 1957, T 233/1459.

110. Thorneycroft, C(57)295, 27 December 1957, CAB 129/90.

111. Macmillan's biography leaves no doubt that he believed Powell's 'fanaticism' exercised a decisive influence on Thorneycroft, *Riding the Storm 1956-1959* (Macmillan 1971), pp 368, 372. Other authorities differ in their treatment of this point. Relevant sources include: Horne, *Macmillan 1957-1968*, pp 71-8; Shepherd, *Macleod*, pp 131-3; J Boyd-Carpenter, *Way of Life* (Sidgwick and Jackson, 1980), 137-9; S Brittan, *Steering the Economy* (Penguin, 1971), pp 207-19; R Lowe, 'Resignation at the Treasury: the Social Services Committee and the Failure to Reform the Welfare State', *Journal of Social Policy*', 1989, **18**, 505-26.

112. Macmillan Diary, 22 and 23 December 1957, quoted in Horne, *Macmillan 1957-1968*, p 71. GEN 625/ 2nd mtg, 23 December 1957, CAB 130/139.

113. CC(57) 86th mtg, 31 December 1957, CAB 128/31; Cabinet Secretary's Notebook (Brook). The following paragraphs identify the day upon which meetings were held; this detail is often given incorrectly in the sources cited in note 111.

114. Macmillan to Ministers, 1 January 1958, Macmillan to Walker-Smith, 1 January 1958, PREM 11/2306.

115. GEN 625/ 3rd and 4th mtgs, 1 and 2 January 1958, CAB 130/139; Powell minute, 2 January 1958, T 233/1459.

116. CC(58) 1st mtg, 3 January 1958, CAB 128/32; Cabinet Secretary's Notebook (Brook).

117. CC(58) 2nd mtg, 3 January 1958, CAB 128/32; Cabinet Secretary's Notebook (Brook).

118. Macmillan Diary, 5 January 1958, quoted in Horne, *Macmillan 1957-1968*, p 71.

119. Macleod to Macmillan, 5 January 1958, PREM 11/2306.

120. CC(58) 3rd mtg, 5 January 1958, CAB 128/32; Cabinet Secretary's Notebook (Brook).

121. CC(58) 4th mtg, 6 January 1958, CAB 128/32; Cabinet Secretary's Notebook (Brook).

122. Simon, 'Central Control of Public Expenditure', 12 February 1958, CAB 21/3194.

123. CAB 21/3194; T 233/1459.

124. Powell, HC Debates, vol 569, col 210, 1 May 1957: 'It was fair to take into account those charges on the users in connection with these contributions derived from the contribution made by insured persons'.

125. Treasury minutes, January 1958, T 227/746. A letter from Ministry of Health to Treasury, 10 January 1958, indicated that Walker-Smith objected to the combined yield rising above 20 per cent, cited in Treasury minutes, 30 and 31 December 1959, T 227/748.

126. GEN 625/ 5th mtg, 9 January 1958, CAB 130/139.

127. Treasury minutes, January to February 1958, T 227/746.

128. CC(58) 29th mtg, 3 February 1958, CAB 128/32. HC Debates, vol 583, cols 221-74, 25 February 1958, vol 583, cols 1185-298, 5 March 1958, vol 585, cols 35-160, 24 March 1958.

129. Ministry of Health to Treasury, 19 November 1957, cited in Treasury minute, 4 September 1958, T 227/1117.

130. Heathcoat Amory, Simon and Walker-Smith mtg, 2 September 1958, T 227/1117.

131. It was reported by Conservative Central Office that an undertaking was given to opticians by Walter Elliot on behalf of the Health Committee of the Conservative Party in 1950, and by Macleod as Minister of Health in 1953, who said that 'in no circumstances then foreseen would the supplementary ophthalmic service be amalgamated with the hospital service', Treasury minute, 27 August 1958, T 227/1117. See also similar pledge given by Macleod in 1955, Webster I, p 372.

132. Walker-Smith, cited in Ministry of Health to Treasury, 15 October 1958, T, SS 292/494/02C.

133. Amory to Macmillan, 12 September 1958, and associated memorandum, T 227/744. Amory was not much involved with the drafting of the letter and associated memorandum because he was preparing for a visit to India.

134. T 227/1117.

135. Treasury minute, 13 October 1958, makes it clear that this apportionment scheme originated in the Treasury SS Division, T 227/1118.

136. Briefs for Macmillan, September 1958, CAB 21/3194.

137. Macmillan to Simon, 5 October 1958, T 227/1118.

138. Treasury minutes, October to November 1958, T 227/1118.

139. Amory to Macmillan, 20 November 1958, T 227/744.

140. Briefs for Prime Minister, 16 December 1958, 19 January 1959, Butler to Macmillan, 5 January 1959, PREM 11/2758. Macmillan to Butler, 31 December 1958, brief for Macmillan containing terms for the NHS committee, 19 January 1958, GEN 677.

141. Treasury brief for meeting of 20 January 1959, T 227/744.

142. Prime Minister and Ministers mtg, 20 January 1959, T 227/744.

143. Permanent Secretaries mtg, 2 February 1959, T 227/744.

144. Treasury minute, 17 February 1959, T 227/744.

145. Treasury minute, 25 February 1959, T 227/744.

146. Amory, GEN 677/2, 9 March 1959, CAB 130/160.

147. Walker-Smith, GEN 677/1, 5 February 1959, CAB 130/160.

148. Walker-Smith, GEN 677/3, 10 March 1959, CAB 130/160.

149. Walker-Smith, GEN 677/4, 10 July 1959, CAB 130/160.

150. GEN 677/ 1st mtg, 14 July 1959, CAB 130/160.

151. Brief for Macmillan, 20 July 1959 on Butler, C(59)125, CAB 130/160.

152. CC(59) 44th mtg, 21 July 1959, CAB 128/33.

153. Maclay and Walker-Smith, HA(59)14, 20 February 1959, CAB 134/1977.

154. HA(59) 4th mtg, 20 February 1959, CAB 134/1976.

155. GEN 677/ 1st mtg, 14 July 1959, CAB 130/160.

156. Briefs for Macmillan, 4 and 16 March 1960, PREM 11/3438.

157. Treasury minute, 1 January 1960, T 227/745.

158. CC(60) 15th mtg, 8 March 1960, CAB 128/34; Cabinet Secretary's Notebook (Brook).

159. Redmayne to Macmillan, 18 March 1960, PREM 11/3438.

160. GEN/713 1st mtg, 9 May 1960, CAB 130/173.

161. Drafts of statement on private medicine, March to April 1960, PREM 11/3438.

162. Powell to Macmillan, 20 August 1960, PREM 11/3438.

163. Powell, HA(60)125, 19 September 1960, Boyle, HA(60)129, 20 September 1960, CAB 134/1983; HA(60) 19th mtg, 22 September 1960, CAB 134/1980.

164. Briefs for Prime Minister, c.5 October, 17 October 1960, PREM 11/3438, 26 October 1960, CAB 21/3370.

165. Butler, C(60)137, 3 October 1960, CAB 129/102; CC(60) 53rd mtg, 6 October 1960, CAB 128/34; Cabinet Secretary's Notebook (Brook).

166. CC(60) 54th mtg, 18 October 1960, CAB 128/34; Cabinet Secretary's Notebook (Brook).

167. PREM 11/3438.

168. CC(60) 56th mtg, 27 October 1960, CAB 128/34; Cabinet Secretary's Notebook (Brook).

169. Brief for Prime Minister, 28 October 1960, Powell to Butler, 31 October 1960, PREM 11/3438.

170. Briefs for Macmillan on C(59)108, 6 July 1959, CAB 21/3194, and on C(59)165, 9 November 1959, PREM 11/3290.

171. Treasury minute, 10 November 1959, T, SS 5/333/01G.

172. Treasury minutes, 6 November to 10 November 1959, T 227/1119.

173. See Appendix 3.7.

174. Treasury minutes, 30 and 31 December 1959, T 227/748.

175. Treasury minute, 26 January 1960, T, 2SS 21/419/01A.

176. Treasury minute, 29 January 1960, T, 2SS 21/419/01A.

177. Brief for Macmillan, 15 January 1960, PREM 11/3438.

178. Amory to Butler, 11 January 1960, T 227/748.

179. Amory, SS(60)6, 13 January 1960, Boyd-Carpenter, SS(60)8, 15 January 1960, Walker-Smith, SS(60)9, 19 January 1960, CAB 134/2533; SS(60) 2nd mtg, 25 January 1960, SS(60) 3rd mtg, 29 January 1960, CAB 134/2533.

180. Butler to Macmillan, 2 February 1960, PREM 11/3438.

181. Kilmuir, C(60)13, 1 February 1960, CAB 129/100.

182. CC(60) 5th mtg, 3 February 1960, CAB 128/34.

183. Butler to Macmillan, 3 and 4 February 1960, PREM 11/3438.

184. CC(60) 6th mtg, 9 February 1960, CAB 128/34.

185. Amory, SS(60)5, 9 January 1960, CAB 134/2533.

186. SS(60) 4th mtg, 8 February 1960, CAB 134/2533.

187. Walker-Smith, SS(60)11, 5 February 1960, CAB 134/2533.

188. CAB, 16/8/14/1; T 227/745.

189. Treasury minute, 5 February 1960, T 227/745.

190. Treasury minute, 8 February 1960, T, 2SS 21/419/01A.

191. Treasury minute, 18 May 1960, T, 2SS 21/419/01A.

192. Second Treasury minute, 18 May 1960, T, 2SS 21/419/01A.

193. CAB, 16/8/14/1.

194. Treasury minute, 24 June 1960, and brief for Amory, June 1960, T, 2SS 21/419/01A.

195. Cabinet Office to Lord Chancellor, 11 July 1960, CAB, 16/8/14/1.

196. Treasury minute, 8 July 1960, T, 2SS 21/419/01A.

197. Amory minute, 16 July 1960, Treasury minute, 20 July 1960, T, 2SS 21/419/01A; Treasury minute, 17 August 1960, T, 2SS 444/01A.

198. Lloyd to Kilmuir, 11 October 1960, Kilmuir to Lloyd, 13 October 1960, CAB, 16/8/14/1. For the Figgures draft report and its circulation on 16 August 1960, T, 2SS 21/419/01A.

199. Two Treasury minutes, 28 October 1960, T, 2SS 444/01A.

200. Briefs for Lloyd, 21 September to 10 October 1960, T, 2SS 21/419/01B; brief for Macmillan, 17 October 1960, PREM 11/3438.

201. Treasury minute, c.17 August 1960, T, 2SS 444/01A.

202. Lloyd, C(60)148, 12 October 1960, CAB 129/102.

203. Powell, C(60)150, 14 October 1960, CAB 129/102.

204. Boyd-Carpenter, C(60)151, 17 October 1960, CAB 129/103; Treasury minutes, 13 and 14 October, 1960, T, 2SS 21/419/01B.

205. Macleod to Macmillan, 18 October 1960; brief on C(60)148, 150, 151, 17 October 1960, PREM 11/3438.

206. CC(60) 54th mtg, 18 October 1960, CAB 128/34; Cabinet Secretary's Notebook (Brook).

207. Boyd-Carpenter to Macmillan, 19 October 1960, T, 2SS 21/419/01B. For the attack on the Government's insurance scheme, Richard Crossman, speech to Labour Women's Sections, 18 October 1960, *Guardian*, 19 October 1960.

208. Treasury minute, 20 October 1960, T, 2SS 21/419/01B.

209. Treasury minute, 19 October 1960, T, 2SS 21/419/01B.

210. Lloyd, C(60)153, 21 October 1960, CAB 129/103.

211. Boyd-Carpenter, C(60)156, 22 October 1960, Boyd-Carpenter, C(60)157, 24 October 1960, CAB 129/103.

212. Briefs for Macmillan on C(60)153, 156, 24 and 26 October 1960, PREM 11/3438.

213. CC(60) 55th mtg, 25 October 1960, CC(60) 56th mtg, 27 October 1960, CAB 128/34.

214. Lloyd to Macmillan, 4 November 1960, Boyd-Carpenter to Macmillan, 9 November 1960, accepted by Macmillan as an 'inescapable' conclusion, PREM 11/3438.

215. Powell to Lloyd, 3 November 1960, T, 2SS 21/419/01C.

216. Lloyd to Powell, 7 November 1960, T, 2SS 21/419/01C.

217. Treasury minute, 9 November 1960, T, 2SS 21/419/01C.

218. Treasury minute, 13 November 1960, T, 2SS 21/419/01C.

219. Lloyd, Maclay and Powell mtg, 17 November 1960, T, 2SS 444/01A.

220. Powell, HA(60)177, 13 December 1960, CAB 134/1983; HA(60) 25th mtg, 16 December 1960, CAB 134/1980. Brief for Macmillan, 16 December 1960, PREM 11/3438.

221. Treasury minute, 20 December 1960, T, 2SS 444/01A.

222. Briefs on C(60)193, c.20 December 1960, (for Macmillan) PREM 11/3438,(for Lloyd) T, 2SS 21/419/01C.

223. Brief for Macmillan, 20 December 1960, PREM 11/3438.

224. Butler, C(60)193, 19 December 1960, CAB 129/103; CC(60) 65th mtg, 21 December 1960, CAB 128/34. Cabinet Secretary's Notebook (Brook), Treasury minute, 30 December 1960, T, 2SS 444/01A.

225. Macmillan to Lloyd, 31 December 1960, Lloyd to Macmillan, c. 2 January 1961, T, 2SS 444/01A.

226. Lloyd, Maclay, Powell, and Soames, C(61)1, 16 January 1961, CAB 129/104.

227. Boyd-Carpenter, C(61)6, 16 January 1961, CAB 129/104.

228. Lloyd, C(61)8, 20 January 1961, CAB 129/104.

229. Brief on C(61)1 and 6, 16 January 1961, PREM 11/3438.

230. CC(61) 1st mtg, 17 January 1961, CC(61) 2nd mtg, 24 January 1961, CAB 128/35.

231. CC(61) 3rd mtg, 31 January 1961, CAB 128/35.

232. Powell, HC Debates, vol 633, cols 987-94, 1 February 1961.

233. Powell minute, 21 February 1961, T, 2SS 444/01C. The motion was signed by 26 Conservative MPs; it called for relief to low wage earners.

234. For Labour's gains in morale and effectiveness, *The Backbench Diaries of Richard Crossman*, ed, J Morgan (Cape, 1981), pp 925, 929, 932-3.

235. For the NHS(Contributions) Bill, HC Debates vol 634, cols 1412-636, 15 February 1961, vol 635, cols 805-1052, 23 February 1961, vol 636, cols 696-842, 9 March 1961, vol 636, cols 983-1150, 13 March 1961. For the NHS Bill, vol 636, cols 37-194, 6 March 1961, vol 637, cols 1351-422, 29 March 1961; for the NHS (Charges for drugs and appliances) Regulations 1961, HC Debates, vol 634, cols 1841-918, 3 February 1961.

236. HC Debates, vol 643, cols 406-532, 8 February 1961.

237. D M Johnson, *The British National Health Service. Friend or Frankenstein?* (C Johnson, 1962), p 9.

238. Lloyd to Powell, 14 July 1961, Powell to Lloyd, 17 July 1961, T, 2SS 21/786/01A.

239. Treasury minute, 26 October 1961, T, 2SS 21/786/01A.

240. Lloyd, HC Debates, vol 645, cols 433-40, 26 July 1961.

241. Submission to Powell, 25 June 1963, T, 2SS 21/786/01A.

242. Treasury minute, 1 July 1963, T, 2SS 21/786/01A.

243. SHHD to Treasury, 10 July 1963, T, 2SS 21/786/01A.

244. Treasury minute, 27 June, 1963, T, 2SS 21/786/01A.

245. Maudling, Powell and officials mtg, 2 July 1963, T, 2SS 21/786/01A.

246. Boyd-Carpenter to Powell, 30 July 1963, Powell to Boyd-Carpenter, c.4 August 1963, T, 2SS 21/786/01A.

247. Treasury and Ministry of Health mtg, 26 May 1964, T, 2SS 21/786/01B.

248. T, 2SS 21/786/01B.

249. D E Allen, *Hospital Planning. The Development of the 1962 Hospital Plan. A Case Study in Decision Making* (Pitman Medical, 1979), mostly decision-making theory.

250. In February 1955, Churchill reported that the Queen had expressed concern about the 'arrest of hospital building in England compared with Australia', and asked to be kept informed about developments, Prime Minister's notes, February 1955, Capital Expenditure on Hospitals, 1954-1962, PREM 11.

251. Treasury minute, 17 February 1959, T 227/744.

252. Major schemes were those costing more than £250,000. These were selected by the health departments and they required prior approval from the Treasury.

253. Vosper, 'The Future of the National Health Service', January 1957, T 227/1116.

254. Walker-Smith to Thorneycroft, 3 October 1957, T, SS 267/291/01B.

255. Thorneycroft and Walker-Smith mtg, 9 October 1957, T, SS 267/291/01B.

256. *Report of the Committee of Enquiry into the Cost of the National Health Service*, paras 67-8, 319.

257. Walker-Smith, 'Five-Year Plan in the Health Field', February 1958, T, SS 267/491/01D.

258. Ministry of Health and Scottish Department of Health minutes, April to May 1958, MH 137/138.

259. Ministry of Health minute, 28 June 1958, MH 137/138.

260. CC(58) 64th mtg, 24 July 1958, CC(58) 66th mtg, 31 July 1958, CAB 128/32.

261. GEN 657/ 1st mtg, 28 July 1958, CAB 130/153.

262. GEN 657/ 2nd mtg, 24 September 1958, CAB 130/153.

263. Simon, C(58)196, 26 September 1958, CAB 129/94.

264. Lloyd, C(58)148, 14 July 1958, CAB 129/93; Maclay, C(58)153, 15 July 1958, Lloyd, C(58)197, 26 September 1958, CAB 129/94.

265. Walker-Smith, C(58)158, 18 July 1958, CAB 129/94.

266. CC(58) 73rd mtg, 29 September 1958, CAB 128/32.

267. *Times*, 10 October 1958.

268. Treasury to Ministry of Health, 6 October 1958 and 24 November 1958, MH 137/138.

269. Ministry of Health to Treasury, 7 August 1958, T, SS 267/491/01C.

270. Treasury minute, 6 November 1958, T, SS 267/491/01C.

271. Amory to Macmillan, 12 September 1958, T 227/1117.

272. Treasury to Ministry of Health, 18 November 1958, T, SS 267/491/01C.

273. Ministry of Health to Treasury, 24 November 1958, T, SS 267/491/01C.

274. DHS, 'Hospital Building Programme 1958-60', February 1958, T, HOP 223/443/01; Ministry of Health, 'Hospital Capital Expenditure', April 1959, T, SS 267/491/01D.

275. Walker-Smith, 'Five Year Plan for the Health Services', 4 June 1959, T, SS 267/491/01D.

276. Treasury minute, 1 July 1959, T, SS 267/491/01D.

277. CC(59) 47th mtg, 28 July 1959, CAB 128/33.

278. Craig, *Election Manifestos*, pp 219, 225.

279. A L Abel and W Lewin, Report on hospital building sponsored by the CCSC of the BMA, *British Medical Journal*, 1959, i, Supplement, 109-14, 4 April 1959, and additional papers by G E Godber, L Farrer-Brown, T McKeown, and J Fry, pp 115-26. This report complemented work on hospital planning sponsored by the Nuffield Provincial Hospitals Trust, especially, *Studies in the Functions and Design of Hospitals* (1955), and *The Demand for Hospital Beds* (1960). HL Debates, vol 219, cols 783-868, 19 November 1959.

280. Treasury minute, 26 September 1958, T 227/957.

281. The level for delegation to regions was raised from £30,000 to £60,000, and to the health departments from £60,000 to £250,000, T, 2SS 471/185/01A.

282. Ministry of Health to Treasury, 4 December 1959, T, SS 267/491/01F.

283. CPE (SC 3) 2nd mtg, 26 November 1959, T 227/1225.

284. This arrangement was firm enough to be mentioned in the *DHS Report 1961*, p 39.

285. Treasury and health departments mtg, 4 April 1960, T, 2SS 1/21/01A.

286. Fraser, 'Hospital Capital Programme', c.June 1960, MH 137/41.

287. Treasury minute, 22 July 1960, T, 2SS 1/21/01A.

288. Treasury minute, 29 June 1960, T, 2SS 1/21/01A.

289. Brief for Powell, 6 December 1960, MH 137/41.

290. Treasury and Ministry of Health mtg, 25 July 1960, T, 2SS 1/21/01A.

291. For drafts, September 1960, MH 137/41.

292. 'Hospital Building', draft circular, 19 October 1960, T, 2SS 1/21/01A.

293. Treasury and Ministry of Health mtg, 8 November 1960, Ministry of Health to Treasury, 17 November 1960, Treasury minutes, 25 November and 1 December 1960, T, 2SS 1/21/01A. Treasury brief for Chancellor, c.5 December 1960, MH 137/41.

294. Brief for Powell, 6 December 1960, MH 137/41.

295. Powell and officials mtg, 9 December 1960, Ministry of Health minute, 14 December 1960, DH, 94202/5/1A.

296. Powell and RHB Chairmen mtg, 20 December 1960, MH 90/83.

297. Powell to Butler, 20 December 1960, T, 2SS 1/21/01A. For Butler's short but positive acknowledgement, Butler to Powell, 28 December 1960, T, 2SS 1/21/01B. Butler commented 'we all felt the Minister of Health had done an excellent job' and prompted the Prime Minister to thank Powell, which he did on 27 December 1960, Capital Expenditure on Hospitals, 1954-1962, PREM 11.

298. Treasury minute, 9 January 1961, T, 2SS 1/21/01B.

299. Treasury minutes, 30 December 1960, 4 and 9 January 1961, T, 2SS 1/21/01B.

300. Treasury minute, 5 July 1961, T, 2SS 1/21/01B.

301. HM(61)4, 17 January 1961.

302. Powell, HC Debates, vol 633, cols 33-5, 25 January 1961(WA).

303. *Times*, 18 January 1961.

304. Powell, 'Mental Hospitals of the Future', National Association of Mental Health, 9 March 1961, *Times*, 10 March 1961. See below, note 388.

305. Treasury and DHS mtg, 6 March 1961, T, 2SS 1/21/01B. DHS submission to Ministers, 23 March 1961, SHHD, HOS 5/W 201/2.

306. Notes on Visits to Newcastle, Manchester and Liverpool regions, March 1961, MH 137/42.

307. MH 137/41, 42.

308. Powell to Butler, 26 September 1961, and a co-operative reply from Butler, 29 September 1961, T, 2SS 1/21/01B.

309. Treasury minute, 2 October 1961, T, 2SS 1/21/01B.

310. Powell to Brooke, 26 October 1961, T, 2SS 1/21/01B.

311. Brooke to Powell, 16 November 1961, T, 2SS 1/21/01C.

312. Powell and RHB Chairmen mtg, 21 November 1961, MH 90/83.

313. Exchanges between Brooke and Powell, December 1961, T, 2SS 1/21/01C, MH 137/42.

314. Ministry of Health, *A Hospital Plan for England and Wales*, Cmnd.1604 (HMSO, 1962).

315. *Times*, 24 January 1962.

316. DHS, *Hospital Plan for Scotland*, Cmnd.1602 (HMSO, Edinburgh, 1962).

317. Editorial, *Times*, 24 January 1962; *British Medical Journal*, 1962, i, 307, 3 February 1962.

318. Robinson, HC Debates, vol 661, cols 43-56, 4 June 1962.

319. The Atomic Energy Authority received about £35m a year for capital investment at this time, *Public Expenditure in Great Britain October 1962*, Cmnd.1849 (HMSO, 1962).

320. See for example, letters from: Central Middlesex Hospital, *Times*, 15 February 1962, Great Ormond Street Hospital, *Times*, 19 June 1964.

321. Letter from Royal Free Hospital, *Times*, 17 June 1964.

322. Powell to Macmillan, 1 October 1962, Macmillan to Powell, 25 November 1962, CAB, 16/8/14/6-7.

323. GEN 829, CAB 130/95.

324. Ministry of Health, *A Hospital Plan for England and Wales (Revision to 1972-73)* (HMSO, 1963).

325. Ministry of Health, *A Hospital Plan for England and Wales (Revision to 1973-74)* (HMSO, 1964).

326. Treasury and Ministry of Health mtg, 26 May 1964, T, 2SS 21/786/01B.

327. SHHD, *Revision of Hospital Plan for Scotland* (Edinburgh, HMSO, 1964).

328. T, 2SS 1/21/01G.

329. *Guardian*, 20 December 1963; *Observer*, 1 March 1964; *Times*, 1 May 1964 and 12 June 1964; *Financial Times*, 8 July 1964.

330. Robinson, HC Debates, vol 698, col 28, 4 June 1964.

331. Barber, HC Debates, vol 698, cols 24-9, 4 June 1964.

332. Ministry of Health to Treasury, 10 June 1964, T, 2SS 21/786/01B.

333. Editorial, *Lancet*, 1964, ii, 129, 18 July 1964.

334. Paige and Jones, *Health and Welfare Services in 1975*, p 124.

335. DHS submission to Ministers, 23 March 1961, SHHD, HOS 5/W 201/2.

336. K Jones, *Mental Health and Social Policy 1845-1959* (Routledge, 1960), chapter 5, 'The Growth of Community Care', referring to the period between 1914 and 1939.

337. Treasury minute, 16 May 1955, T 227/509.

338. Vosper, 'The Future of the National Health Service', T 227/1116.

339. Walker-Smith, 'Proposals in the Health Sphere', February 1958, T, SS 267/491/01D.

340. G Godber, 'Health Services Past, Present and Future', *Lancet*, 1958, ii, 1-6, 5 July 1958.

341. Walker-Smith, 'Five-Year Plan in the Health Field', T, SS 267/491/01D.

342. Craig, *Election Manifestos*, p 219. The National Council for Social Work Training proposal derives from the *Report of the Working Party on Social Workers in the Local Health and Welfare Service* (HMSO, 1959) Younghusband Report.

343. For the various strands of community care, A Walker, ed, *Community Care. The Family, the State and Social Policy* (Blackwell and Robertson, 1982); C Unsworth, *The Politics of Mental Health Legislation* (Clarendon Press, 1987), pp 261-4; J Busfield, *Managing Madness. Changing ideas and practice* (Hutchinson, 1986), pp 326-57.

344. For the Royal Commission and the Mental Health Act 1959, Jones, *Mental Health and Social Policy*, chapter 12 and Appendix III; Unsworth, *Politics of Mental Health Legislation*, chapter 9.

345. *Royal Commission on the Law Relating to Mental Illness and Mental Deficiency, 1954-1957, Report*, Cmnd.169 (HMSO, 1957).

346. *Royal Commission on Mental Illness*, para 7.

347. *Royal Commission on Mental Illness*, paras 595-716.

348. *Royal Commission on Mental Illness*, para 702.

349. Kilmuir and Walker-Smith, HA(58)11, 5 February 1958, CAB 134/1973; HA(58) 2nd mtg, 7 February 1958, CAB 134/1972.

350. Unsworth, *Politics of Mental Health Legislation*, p 301.

351. DHS, *First Report by a Committee on Mental Health Legislation* (HMSO, Edinburgh, 1958); DHS, *Second Report by a Committee on Mental Health Legislation* (HMSO, Edinburgh, 1959).

352. Maclay, HA(59)68, 1 July 1959, CAB 134/1978; HA(59) 11th mtg, 3 July 1959, CAB 134/1976. Maclay, HA(59)85, 15 July 1959, CAB 134/1978; HA(59) 13th mtg, 17 July 1959, CAB 134/1976.

353. B Wootton, *Social Science and Social Pathology* (Allen and Unwin, 1959).

354. *Special Hospitals, Report of a Working Party* (HMSO, 1961). For details of enquiry, MH 140/58, 59.

355. Royal Commission on Mental Illness, 'Provisional Conclusions', Paper No.38/2, 24 November 1954, MH 121/42.

356. Association of Psychiatric Social Workers, Numbered Paper 81, National Corporation for the Care of Old People, Numbered Paper 83, MH 121/41.

357. Consultations with medical organisations on Royal Commission Report, 1957, MH 137/395.

358. Ministry of Health to Treasury, 23 May 1957, MH 137/400.

359. Treasury, Ministry of Health and DHS mtgs, 14 June and 11 July 1957, MH 137/400.

360. *Report of the Committee of Enquiry into the Cost of the National Health Service*, Cmd.9663 (HMSO, 1956), paras 580, 586, 612.

361. *Report of the Committee of Inquiry on the Rehabilitation and Resettlement of Disabled Persons*, Cmd.9883 (HMSO, 1956), Chairman, William Piercy, Baron Piercy(1886-1966).

362. Vaughan-Morgan, HA(57)95, 25 July 1957, CAB 134/1970; HA(57) 19th mtg, 31 July 1957, CAB 134/1968.

363. Powell, HA(57)138, 14 November 1957, Walker-Smith, HA(57)146, 26 November 1957, CAB 134/1971; HA(57) 27th mtg, 6 December 1957, CAB 134/1968. Treasury minute, 28 November 1957, T 227/505.

364. Thorneycroft to Walker-Smith, 23 December 1957, Walker-Smith to Amory, 13 January 1958, Amory to Walker-Smith, 27 January 1958, Maclay to Amory, 11 February 1958, MH 137/400. Treasury minutes, December 1957 to January 1958, T 227/505. Maclay was relaxed about this problem because in Scotland it had not been decided what response should be made to the Percy Report.

365. Ministry of Health minute, 15 January 1965, MH 137/400.

366. Ministry of Health minute, 30 June 1958, MH 137/398.

367. Circular 9/59, 4 May 1959, and HM(59)46, May 1959.

368. See for instance, conference of Hospital Management Committees, 12 June 1959, and especially the National Association of Mental Health Conference, 'Mental Health at Home and Abroad', 24 March 1960. The NAMH also issued a pamphlet for popular use, *Mental Health is Everybody's Business*.

369. Listed in T 227/666.

370. Walker-Smith and senior Ministers mtg, 20 January 1959, T 227/744.

371. Exchanges between health departments and Treasury, December 1958, T 227/666.

372. Treasury minute, 25 February 1959, T 227/744.

373. Walker-Smith, HC Debates, vol 601, cols 1-4, 2 March 1959; Circular 15/59, 21 April 1959.

374. HA(57) 28th mtg, 13 December 1957, CAB 134/1968.

375. Walker-Smith, HA(59)124, 28 October 1959, CAB 134/1979; HA(59) 18th mtg, 30 October 1959, CAB 134/1976; Maclay and Walker-Smith, HA(59)147, 9 December 1959, CAB 134/1979; Boyd-Carpenter, HA(59)158, 10 December 1959, CAB 134/1979; HA(59) 19th mtg, 6 November 1959, CAB 134/1976; Maclay and Walker-Smith, HA(60)67, 17 May 1960, CAB 134/1982; Boyd-Carpenter, HA(60)76, 18 May 1960, CAB 134/1982; HA(60) 12th mtg, 20 May 1960, CAB 134/1980; Butler, HA(60)87, 27 June 1960, CAB 134/1982; HA(60) 14th mtg, 1 July 1960, CAB 134/1980.

376. T, 2SS 358/122/01B; DH, E/H 27/01. HC Debates, vol 657, cols 821-48, 6 April 1962. Circular 12/62, 3 July 1962.

377. Robinson, HC Debates, vol 623, cols 1-3, 9 May 1960, vol 627, cols 11-12, 18 July 1960. Editorial, *Guardian*, 23 June 1960; editorial, *Times*, 12 July 1960.

378. Pitt, HC Debates, vol 627, col 166, 27 July 1960(WA).

379. T, 2SS 551/117/05, 2SS 322/117/01A-B.

380. Titmuss, 'Community Care-Fact or Fiction?', in National Association for Mental Health, *Emerging Patterns for the Mental Health Services and the Public*, NAMH Conference, 9-10 March 1961 (NAMH, 1961), pp 66-70, reprinted in H Freeman and J Farndale, eds, *Trends in the Mental Health Services* (Pergamon, 1963); P Townsend, *Last Refuge*, p 399.

381. Fowl pest, HA(62) 11th mtg, 6 July 1962, CAB 134/1989. Missiles, CAB 129/91.

382. Treasury minutes, December 1959 to January 1960, T, SS 267/549/01A, C.

383. Ministry of Health to Treasury, 29 March 1960, T, SS 267/549/01C.

384. Walker-Smith to Amory, 11 July 1960, T, 2SS 1/1128/01A.

385. T, 2SS 1/1128/01A-C

386. Ministry of Health to Treasury, 22 September 1960, T, 2SS 1/1128/01A.

387. T, 2SS 1/1128/01B.

388. Powell, 'Mental Hospitals of the Future', opening address to National Association of Mental Health Conference, 9 March 1961, in *Emerging Patterns for the Mental Health Services and the Public* (NAMH, 1961), pp 5-10. 'End of Mental Hospitals is Forecast', *Times*, 10 March 1961.

389. Powell to Macmillan, 20 December 1961, Capital Expenditure on hospitals, 1954-1962, PREM 11.

390. Macmillan, speech to East Midlands Conservative Organisation, 5 March 1962, T, SS 109/324//01A.

391. Powell to Lloyd, 17 July 1961, T, 2SS 21/786/01A.

392. Ministry of Health minutes, January 1961 to April 1961, DH, 94202/5/1A.

393. Ministry of Health minute, 12 April 1961, DH, 94202/5/1A. *Hospital Plan*, pp 9-12.

394. Submission to Powell, 12 April 1961, DH, 94202/5/1A.

395. Circular 2/62, 'Development of Local Authority Health and Welfare Services', 23 January 1962.

396. *Health & Welfare. The Development of Community Care. Plans for the Health and Welfare Services of the Local Authorities in England and Wales*, Cmnd.1973 (HMSO, 1963). DH, 94202/5/1B-D. T, 2SS 630/278/01A.

397. *Health & Welfare. The Development of Community Care*, para 4.

398. Ministry of Health to Treasury, 8 June 1961, Treasury to Ministry of Health, 15 June 1961, T, 2SS 630/278/01A. The literature tends to regard the Gillie Report(1963) as the ten-year plan for general practice. Indeed, the committee was set up partly to consider implications of the hospital and local authority plans. However, it was a Standing Medical Advisory Committee initiative, and

was not designed as an adjunct to the two long-term plans. Powell acknowledged the helpfulness of the Gillie Report for planning purposes, but he argued that 'in reality, the development of general practice is not a process which lends itself to expression in terms of a phased and quantified programme', *Address to Executive Councils Association, 3 October 1963* (ECs Association, 1963).

399. Powell to Lloyd, 29 June 1961, T, 2SS 630/278/01A.

400. Powell to Brooke, 7 February 1962, T, 2SS 1/1128/01C.

401. Treasury minute, 6 March 1962, T, 2SS 1/1128/01C.

402. Treasury minute, 16 February 1962, T, 2SS 109/110/05A.

403. T, 2SS 21/28/07, 2SS 21/786/01A.

404. Ministry of Health to Treasury, 8 May 1963, T, 2SS 1/1128/01C.

405. CM(64) 27th mtg, 13 May 1964, CAB 128/38.

406. Barber to Boyd-Carpenter, 23 June 1964, T, 2SS 1/1128/01D.

407. For a lively review, T Gould, *A Summer Plague. Polio and its Survivors* (Yale University Press, 1995).

408. Vosper, HC Debates, vol 570, cols 408-10, 15 May 1957.

409. Polio Vaccine, 1957, PREM 11/2426.

410. Vaughan-Morgan, HA(57)79, 3 July 1957, CAB 134/1970; HA(57) 16th mtg, 8 July 1957, 17th mtg, 19 July 1957, CAB 134/1968.

411. Circular 6/57, May 1957, Circular 16/57, November 1957.

412. CC(58) 13th mtg, 30 January 1958, CAB 128/32; Walker-Smith, HA(58)11, 5 February 1958, CAB 134/1973; HA(58) 2nd mtg, 7 February 1958, CAB 134/1972.

413. Walker-Smith, HA(58)42, 16 April 1958, CAB 134/1974; CC(58) 34th mtg, 24 April 1958, 35th mtg, 29 April 1958, CAB 128/32.

414. Maclay and Walker-Smith, HA(58)64, 13 June 1958, CAB 134/1974; HA(58) 11th mtg, 20 June 1958, CAB 134/1972.

415. See for instance, Maclay and Walker-Smith, HA(59)102, 23 July 1959, CAB 134/1978; HA(59) 15th mtg, 29 July 1959, CAB 134/1976.

416. *MH Report 1958*, pp 177, 185-6.

417. Walker-Smith, HA(59)156, 9 December 1959, CAB 134/1979; HA(59) 23rd mtg, 11 December 1959, CAB 134/1976. Walker-Smith, HA(60)7, 27 January 1960, CAB 134/1981; HA(60) 2nd mtg, 29 January 1960, CAB 134/1980.

418. Maclay and Walker-Smith, HA(61)126, 18 October 1961, CAB 134/1988; HA(61) 18th mtg, 20 October 1961, CAB 134/1984.

419. Ministry of Health, *Report on the Outbreak of Poliomyelitis during 1961 in Kingston-upon-Hull and the East Riding of Yorkshire* (HMSO, 1963).

420. T, 2SS 21/160/01A-B.

421. DH, 95005/7/1A, 34. United Kingdom Mission, *The Fluoridation of Domestic Water Supplies in North America as a means of controlling Dental Caries* (HMSO, 1953).

422. Exchanges between Macleod and Churchill, September to November 1954, Fluoridation, 1954-1962, PREM 11.

423. DH, 95005/7/1B.

424. DH, 95005/7/22A.

425. DH, 95005/7/14.

426. World Health Organisation, *Fluoridation*, Technical Report Series No. 146 (WHO, 1958).

427. Maclay and Walker-Smith, HA(58)61, 17 June 1958, CAB 134/1974; HA(58) 11th mtg, 20 June 1958, CAB 134/1972.

428. Maclay and Walker-Smith, HA(58)87, 16 July 1958, CAB 134/1974; HA(58) 15th mtg, 18 July 1958, CAB 134/1972.

429. Maclay and Walker-Smith, HA(58)104, 23 September 1958, CAB 134/1975; HA(58) 18th mtg, 23 September 1958, CAB 134/1972. Maclay and Walker-Smith, HA(59)127, 3 November 1959, CAB 134/1979; HA(59) 19th mtg, 6 November 1959, CAB 134/1976.

430. Ministry of Health, *The Conduct of the Fluoridation Studies in the United Kingdom and the Results Achieved after Five Years* (HMSO, 1962).

431. Maclay, Joseph, and Powell, HA(62)66, 21 June 1962, CAB 134/1991; HA(62) 10th mtg, 29 June 1962, CAB 134/1989.

432. Brief for Macmillan, June 1962, Fluoridation, 1954-1962, PREM 11.

433. Powell, HC Debates, vol 699, cols 25-6, 10 December 1962, cols 871-4, 17 December 1962. Circular 28/62, 14 December 1962.

434. Circular 12/63, 25 June 1963.

435. Webster I, pp 233-7.

436. GEN 456, February 1954, CAB 130/100; GEN 524, April 1956, CAB 130/115; GEN 588, April to May 1957, CAB 130/127; Butler, C(57)135, 4 June 1957, CAB 129/87; CC(57) 45th mtg, 6 June 1957, CAB 128/31. Vaughan-Morgan, HC Debates, vol 572, cols 428-34, 27 June 1957.

437. Circular 8/58, August 1958.

438. Walker-Smith, HA(59)18, 11 March 1959, CAB 134/1977; HA(59) 5th mtg, 20 March 1959, CAB 134/1976.

439. Walker-Smith, HA(60)60, 27 April 1960, CAB 134/1982; HA(60) 10th mtg, 29 April 1960, CAB 134/1980.

440. Himsworth to Hailsham, 1 March 1962, CAB, 16/2/3 Part 2.

441. Powell, HC Debates, vol 655, cols 885-9, 12 March 1962.

442. GEN 762, February 1962, CAB 130/185; GEN 763, 1962-1964, CAB 130/185.

443. Hailsham to Macmillan, 12 July 1962, CAB, 16/2/3 Part 3. Smoking and Health, 1954-1964, PREM 11. Macmillan, HC Debates, vol 674, cols 570-2, 21 March 1963.

444. Ministerial Committee on Smoking and Health, HS(64), February to June 1964, CAB 134/2518; Smoking and Lung Cancer 1964, PREM 11.

445. Ministry of Health, *Health Education. Report of a Joint Committee of the Central and Scottish Health Services Councils* (HMSO, 1964).

446. Sir Kenneth Cowan, 'Retrospect', *Health Bulletin*, January 1964, No.1. See also, Sir George Godber, 'Health versus Greed', *New York State Journal of Medicine*, December 1963, pp 1248-9; Taylor, *Smoke Ring*, p 7.

447. DH, 94151/21/1.

448. Ministry of Health minute, 19 October 1960, DH, 94151/21/1.

449. Ministry of Health, *Health Education. Report of a Joint Committee of the Central and Scottish Health Services Councils* (HMSO, 1964).

450. MH 151/5; T, 2SS 1076/469/01.

451. *Health Education*, p 58.

452. T, 2SS 1076/469/01.

453. Robinson to Diamond, 15 December 1965, T, 2SS 1076/469/01.

454. Robinson, HC Debates, vol 724, col 432, 9 February 1966.

455. See Appendix 3.10.

456. *CMO Report 1965*, p 142.

457. See Appendices 3.10, 3.11.

458. Treasury minutes, 1 and 10 October 1957, T, SS 5/333/01D.

459. See for example, exchanges between Treasury and Ministry of Health over the limited list, following persistent advocacy of this idea by Dr Charles Hill, Chancellor of the Duchy of Lancaster, T, SS 5/333/01D.

460. Ministry of Health minute, 10 January 1956, MH 133/83.

461. MH 133/83.

462. Sir Geoffrey Vickers to Turton, 20 November 1956, MH 133/83.

463. MH 133/83; SHHD, HPS 11/41.

464. Vosper, HC Debates, vol 571, col 159, 7 June 1957(WA); Maclay, HC Debates, vol 572, col 16, 25 June 1957(WA).

465. *Final Report of the Committee on the Cost of Prescribing* (HMSO, 1959). MH 133/89.

466. *Report of the Scottish Committee on Prescribing Costs* (HMSO, Edinburgh, 1959).

467. CCP(57) 1st mtg, 19 June 1957, MH 133/85.

468. MH 133/88. *Interim Report of the Committee on Cost of Prescribing* (HMSO, 1958).

469. Editorial, *Times*, 23 June 1958.

470. Letter from Professor D M Dunlop to Douglas Committee, 10 January 1958, SCPC(58)8, MH 133/86.

471. *Report of the Scottish Committee on Prescribing Costs*, para 127.

472. *Report of the Scottish Committee on Prescribing Costs*, para 59.

473. *Report of the Scottish Committee on Prescribing Costs*, para 64.

474. *Final Report of the Committee on the Cost of Prescribing*, para 12.

475. *Final Report of the Committee on the Cost of Prescribing*, paras 298-9.

476. *Final Report of the Committee on the Cost of Prescribing*, paras 274-91.

477. Douglas and Hinchliffe mtg, 20 August 1958, MH 133/86.

478. *Final Report of the Committee on the Cost of Prescribing*, para 288.

479. *Final Report of the Committee on the Cost of Prescribing*, paras 289-93.

480. Treasury minutes, 14 May, 27 May, 10 June 1959, T, SS 5/333/01G.

481. Treasury minute, 27 May 1959, T, SS 5/333/01G.

482. Walker-Smith, HC Debates, vol 609, col 440, 15 July 1959.

483. Treasury minute, 14 July 1959, T, SS 5/333/01G.

484. Powell, HC Debates, vol 655, col 27, 5 March 1962.

485. Webster I, pp 226-7.

486. Treasury minutes, 13 December 1957, 14 October 1958, T, SS 5/333/02D-E.

487. Ministry of Health to Treasury, 21 January 1959, T, SS 5/333/01F.

488. H Miller and M Smith, 'The Cost of Drug Treatment', *Lancet*, 1960, i, 45-7, 2 January 1960.

489. Treasury minute on Comptroller and Auditor General's Report, April 1958, T, SS 5/333/01F.

490. Report of Working Party on Drug Price Regulation, October 1959, T, SS 5/333/02F.

491. T, 2SS 188/197/01A.

492. Treasury minute, 1 July 1960, T, 2SS 188/197/01A.

493. T, 2SS 188/197/01A.

494. Powell, HC Debates, vol 632, cols 84-5, 15 December 1960(WA).

495. *Administered Prices: Drugs* (US Senate Sub-Committee on Anti-Trust, 1961).

496. For a popular survey, B Inglis, *Drugs, Doctors and Disease* (Mayflower, 1962). From the industry perspective, F H Happold, *Medicine at Risk* (Queen Anne Press, 1967).

487. *Times*, 28 February 1961.

498. T, 2SS 188/197/01B.

499. T, 2SS 188/197/01F.

500. H Steele, 'Patents, Restrictions and Price Competition in the Ethical Drug Industry', *Journal of Industrial Economics*, 1964, **12**,198-223.

501. *Special Report and First and Second Reports from the Committee of Public Accounts, Session 1959-60* (HMSO, 1960).

502. *First, Second and Third Reports from the Committee of Public Accounts, Session 1961-62* (HMSO, 1962). HC Debates, vol 668, cols 1511-946, 6 December 1962.

503. H A Clegg and T E Chester, *Wage Policy and the Health Service* (Blackwell, 1957). For general assessment, see F T Blackaby, 'Incomes Policy', in Blackaby, ed, *British Economic Policy 1960-74: Demand Management*, pp 360-401; G A Dorfman, *Wages Politics in Britain, 1945-1967* (Iowa State University Press, 1973); R Taylor, *The Trade Union Question in British Politics: Goverment and the Unions since 1945* (Blackwell, 1993).

504. DH, 94259/3/27B.

505. WP(58) 8th mtg, 25 November 1958, CAB 134/2572; Walker-Smith, WP(59)2, 13 January 1959, WP(59) 2nd mtg, 19 January 1959, CAB 134/2573.

506. Ministry of Health to Treasury, 8 April 1960, T, 2SS 21/162/01A.

507. Powell, HA(61)121, 6 October 1961, CAB 134/1988; HA(61) 18th mtg, 20 October 1961, CAB 134/1984. ECL 97/61, 20 October 1961.

508. Treasury minute, 29 September 1961, T, 2SS 21/162/01B. The full title of this committee: Central NHS (Chemists Contractors) Committee of the National Pharmaceutical Union.

509. T, 2SS 21/162/01B.

510. T, 2SS 21/162/01C.

511. Treasury minute, 25 May 1964, T, 2SS 21/162/01D.

512. T, 2SS 21/162/01C-D. Barber, HC Debates, vol 696, cols 224-5, 18 June 1964(WA).

513. The 4 per cent increase was only conceded after much debate in the Wages Policy Committee. For the final agreement, CC(58) 80th mtg, CAB 128/32. For interdepartmental discussions, T 227/768.

514. Webster I, pp 230-3. Macmillan, HC Debates, vol 566, cols 979-84, 12 March 1957 (establishment of the Royal Commission). Macmillan, HC Debates, vol 568, cols 1753-7, 16 April 1957 (first interim increase in remuneration).

515. *Royal Commission on Doctors' and Dentists' Remuneration 1957-1960, Report*, Cmnd. 939 (HMSO, 1960).

516. Treasury minute, 10 May 1957, T, SS 5/150/01D.

517. Treasury minutes, 24 June to 2 July 1957, T, SS 5/150/01J, 23 January 1958, T 227/765.

518. Treasury minute, 6 March 1958, T 227/766.

519. Treasury and Health departments mtg, 3 July 1957, T, SS 5/150/01J.

520. DH, 94256/20/3.

521. Treasury minute, 23 January 1958, T 227/765.

522. CSO minute, 17 February 1958, T 227/765.

523. Treasury minute, c.December 1957, T, SS 5/150/01J.

524. Treasury minute, 17 December 1957, T 227/765.

525. Treasury minute, 21 January 1958, T 227/765.

526. T 227/768.

527. Treasury minutes, 25 February 1958, T 227/765, 6 March 1958, T 227/766.

528. Royal Commission DD, para 179. This working party was chaired by Sir Robert Platt, President of the Royal College of Physicians. Its report, *Report of the Joint Working Party on the Medical Staffing Structure in the Hospital Service* (HMSO, 1961) suggested establishment of a new sub-consultant grade of Medical Assistant. For discussion, see Stevens, *Medical Practice in Modern England*, pp 150-2.

529. Royal Commission DD, paras 399, 437.

530. Royal Commission DD, para 428.

531. Royal Commission DD, para 13.

532. Royal Commission DD, para 430.

533. Royal Commission DD, para 432.

534. Royal Commission DD, para 429.

535. Royal Commission DD, pp 159-84.

536. Treasury minute, 1 February 1960, T 227/770.

537. Royal Commission DD, paras 12, 166.

538. Treasury and health departments mtg, 17 February 1960, T 227/770.

539. Maclay and Walker-Smith, W(60)16, 17 March 1960, Amory, W(60)17, 16 March 1960, Amory, W(60)19, 19 March 1960, CAB 134/2560; W(60) 21st mtg, 3 March 1960, W(60) 24th mtg, 21 March 1960, CAB 134/2559. Amory, C(60)54, 22 March 1960, Maclay and Walker-Smith, C(60)55, 18 March 1960, CAB 129/101; CC(60) 20th mtg, 24 March 1960, CAB 128/34.

540. Walker-Smith, HC Debates, vol 621, cols 813-4, 11 April 1960.

541. Health Ministers and profession mtg, 29 March 1960, Ministry of Health to BMA, 5 April 1960, DH, 94603/3/79/22.

542. T, SS 5/150/01S.

543. T, SS 5/83/01B; T, SS 5/150/01S.

544. Royal Commission DD, rec. 43.

545. DD(63) 1st mtg, 4 January 1963, CAB 134/1599.

546. DD(63) 4th mtg, 24 January 1963, DD(63) 6th mtg, 24 June 1963, CAB 134/1599.

547. DD(63)23, Kindersley to Wilson, 18 February 1963, DD(66)27, Wilson to Kindersley, 27 February 1963, CAB 134/1599. Doctors Pay Review Body, 1963-64, PREM 11.

548. Ministry of Health, ES(I)(63)5, 1 March 1963, Treasury, ES(I)(63)6, 1 March 1963, Ministry of Health, ES(I)(63)7, 4 March 1963, ES(I)(63) 2nd mtg, 4 March 1963, CAB 134/1902. Powell, WN(63)18, 8 March 1963, Maudling, WN(63)19, 8 March 1963, WN(63) 4th mtg, 12 March 1963, CAB 134/2571. Maudling, C(63)48, 13 March 1963, CAB 129/112; CC(63) 16th mtg, 14 March 1963, CAB 128/37. Macmillan, HC Debates, vol 674, cols 125-31, 25 March 1963(WA).

549. MH 149/141.

550. Review Body minute, 18 December 1963, T, 2SS 1289/01A.

551. *Review Body on Doctors' and Dentists' Remuneration. Fifth Report*, Cmnd.2585 (HMSO, 1965), paras 22-4. The complex negotiations within the profession are described by Stevens, *Medical Practice in Modern England*, pp 290-300.

552. *Review Body on Doctors' and Dentists' Remuneration. Fifth Report*, para 25.

553. *Times*, 9 November 1963.

554. DD(64) 1st mtg, 2 January 1964, DD(64) 3rd mtg, 17 June 1964, CAB 134/1601.

555. As noted above, Kindersley's assertion is not supported by the evidence of the Review Body's initial proceedings. By 1963, Kindersley must have been more aware of the pitfalls of three-year reviews of the kind adopted by his committee.

556. Permanent Secretary and Kindersley mtg, 3 May 1963, MH 149/141.

557. Barber, WA(64)11, 3 February 1964, WA(64) 5th mtg, 5 February 1964, CAB 134/2562; Barber, WA(64)16, 10 February 1964, WA(64) 7th mtg, 19 February 1964, CAB 134/2562.

558. Industrial Court, Award No. 2632.

559. MH 78/208.

560. Thorneycroft, C(57)231, 15 October 1957, CAB 129/89.

561. CC(57) 73rd mtg, 15 October 1957, CAB 128/31.

562. Maclay and Walker-Smith, C(57)238, 18 October 1957, CAB 129/89.

563. CC(57) 74th mtg, 21 October 1957, CAB 128/31.

564. TUC to Macmillan, 14 November 1957, Whitley Council Staff Side to Macmillan, 17 November 1957, PREM 11/4947.

565. CC(57) 81st mtg, 21 November 1957, CAB 128/31. GEN 623/ 1st mtg, 2 December 1957, CAB 130/139.

566. Whitley delegation and health Ministers mtg, 2 December 1957, Whitley General Council Staff Side to Macmillan, 4 December 1957, PREM 11/4947.

567. Whitley Council delegation and Macmillan mtg, 23 December 1957, PREM 11/4947.

568. W(58) 1st mtg, 27 January 1958, CAB 134/2558; Maclay and Walker-Smith, C(58)23, 28 January 1958, CAB 129/91; CC(58) 13th mtg, 30 January 1958, CAB 128/32.

569. Walker-Smith, C(57)280, 21 November 1957, CAB 129/90.

570. W(58) 1st mtg, 27 January 1958, CAB 134/2558; Walker-Smith, C(58)25, 28 January 1958, CAB 129/91; CC(58) 13th mtg, 30 January 1958, CAB 128/32.

571. AC 347, 31 March 1958, MH 78/208.

572. W(58) 2nd mtg, 25 March 1958, CAB 134/2558; Walker-Smith, C(58)62, 24 March 1958, CAB 129/92; CC(58) 26th mtg, 27 March 1958, CAB 128/32.

573. W(58) 3rd mtg, 23 April 1958, W(58) 4th mtg, 9 May 1958, CAB 134/2558; Walker-Smith, C(58)82, 21 April 1958, Walker-Smith, C(58)101, 10 May 1958, CAB 129/92; CC(58) 41st mtg, 13 May 1958, CAB 128/32.

574. WP(59) 6th mtg, 12 May 1959, CAB 134/2573.

575. Industrial Court, Award No.2732, July 1959.

576. Walker-Smith to Macmillan, 24 June 1959, Lloyd to Macmillan, 26 June 1960, PREM 11/4947.

577. Nurses and Midwives Whitley Council, Staff Side to Management Side, 27 November 1958, DH, M/N 57/06A. Ministry of Health to Treasury, 17 December 1958, T 214/995.

578. WP(59) 1st mtg, 13 January 1959, WP(59) 2nd mtg, 19 January 1959, CAB 134/2573. Treasury and Ministry of Health mtg, 22 January 1959, T 214/995.

579. Treasury minute, 16 February 1959, T 214/995.

580. Treasury minute, 18 March 1959, T 214/995.

581. Nurses and Midwives Whitley Council, 1959, MH 78/417.

582. Maclay and Walker-Smith, WN(60)2, 5 December 1960, WN(60) 1st mtg, 8 December 1960, CAB 134/2567. Maclay and Walker-Smith, WN(60)3, 20 December 1960, WN(61) 1st mtg, 5 January 1961, CAB 134/2567.

583. Nurses and Midwives Whitley Council, 1960, MH 78/418-419. T 214/1293.

584. Nurses and Midwives Whitley Council, Staff Side to Management Side, 11 August 1961, DH, M/N 57/02.

585. Fraser to H A Goddard, 10 August 1961, DH, M/N 57/02.

586. Nurses and Midwives Whitley Council, 26 September 1961, MH 78/420.

587. Ministry of Health minutes, and draft submission to Minister, October 1961, DH, M/N 57/02.

588. Ministry of Health minutes, 2 and 9 November 1961, DH, M/N 57/02.

589. Powell minute, 11 November 1961, DH, M/N 57/02.

590. Ministry of Health minutes, 20 and 22 December 1961, DH, M/N 57/02.

591. Ministry of Health to Treasury, 2 January 1962, T 214/1295.

592. WN(62) 1st mtg, 8 January 1962, Powell, WN(62)1, 2 February 1962, Powell, WN(62)4, 2 February 1962, WN(62) 3rd mtg, 6 February 1962, WN(62) 5th mtg, 21 February 1962, CAB 134/2568.

593. Nurses and Midwives Whitley Council, 13 March 1962, MH 78/420.

594. HC Debates, vol 655, cols 873-9, 12 March 1962, vol 656, cols 1031-152, 27 March 1962, vol 657, cols 1153-320, 13 April 1962. Cosgrave, *Lives of Powell*, pp 174-6.

595. Powell to Macmillan, draft, 13 March 1962, DH, M/N 57/02.

596. Brief for Prime Minister, 2 May 1962, PREM 11/3745.

597. *Times*, 8 May 1962.

598. Powell, WN(62)31, 7 May 1962, WN(62) 18th mtg, 9 May 1962, CAB 134/2569. CC(62) 32nd mtg, 10 May 1962, CAB 128/36.

599. Robinson, HC Debates, vol 659, cols 933-45, 14 May 1962.

600. Powell, HC Debates, vol 659, cols 945-52, 14 May 1962.

601. Walker-Smith, HC Debates, vol 659, cols 959-67, 14 May 1962.

602. Editorial, *Daily Telegraph*, 15 May 1962; see also editorial, *Times*, 15 May 1962.

603. Exchanges between Ward and Lloyd, May 1962, T 214/1297.

604. WN(62) 21st mtg, 4 June 1962, CAB 134/2568.

605. Nurses and Midwives Whitley Council, NC(M & SC) 144, 12 June 1962, MH 78/421.

606. WN(62)44, 9 June 1962, CAB 134/2569; WN(62) 23rd mtg, 25 June 1962, CAB 134/2568.

607. WN(62)49, 31 July 1962, CAB 134/2569; WN(62) 26th mtg, 1 August 1962, CAB 134/2568.

608. DH, M/N 57/06A.

609. Industrial Court, Award No.2931, 3 September 1962. Powell, WN(62)54, 10 September 1962, CAB 134/2569.

610. Editorial, *Times*, 7 September 1962.

611. Powell, WN(62)81, 10 December 1962, Powell, WN(62)82, 17 December 1962, CAB 134/2570; WN(62) 37th mtg, 19 December 1962, CAB 134/2568. Nurses and Midwives Whitley Council, 11 December 1962, MH 78/421.

612. Industrial Court. Award No. 2962, 19 April 1963.

613. WA(63) 3rd mtg, 6 November 1963, CAB 134/2561. T, 2SS 116/78/02.

614. CAB, 16/8/14/6-7.

Chapter III
LABOUR RESTORED

1. *Members One of Another* (Labour Party, 1959).

2. Craig, *Election Manifestos*, p 266.

3. L Pavitt, *The Health of the Nation. The Second Stage of the NHS* (Fabian Society, 1965), p 2. This pamphlet was originally issued in 1963.

4. Crossman, *Diaries*, iii, pp 752, 801, 937.

5. See Appendix 1.1. For obituaries and personal appreciations of Robinson, *Times*, 20 February 1996; *Guardian*, 21, 23, and 28 February 1996; *Independent*, 21 February 1996; *Daily Telegraph*, 22 February 1996. Robinson was knighted in 1983. The office of Parliamentary Secretary in the Ministry of Health went to the veteran Sir Barnett Stross, a doctor and an expert on industrial disease, who represented a potteries constituency. In February 1965 Stross was replaced by Charles W Loughlin; in January 1967 this post passed to Julian W Snow.

6. Robinson, HC Debates, vol 706, col 1206, 17 February 1965.

7. *Select Committee on Estimates, Sixth Report (1956-57)*.

8. Robinson was excluded from an important Cabinet discussion on long-term targets for public expenditure (CC(65) 5th mtg, 28 January 1965), about which he complained vociferously, Robinson to Callaghan, 1 February 1965, T, 2SS 21/786/01C. Crossman, *Diaries*, ii, pp 645-6, 772.

9. Amalgamation of Ministries, 1965-1966, PREM 11.

10. Robinson to Wilson, March 1966, BN 72/116.

11. Balniel, HC Debates, vol 753, cols 644-5, 6 November 1967.

12. Douglas Houghton (1898-1996), described in an Obituary as 'prominent trade union leader, trusted broadcaster, a birth control campaigner and a devoted advocate of animal rights', *Times*, 3 May 1996.

13. T, 2SS 100/519/02.

14. Amalgamation of Ministry of Health and Ministry of Social Security, 1968, PREM 11.

15. Crossman, *Diaries*, ii, pp 769, 772, iii, pp 17, 83-4, 165, 194. DH, J/N 179/14B.

16. Crossman, *Diaries*, iii, p 17.

17. Crossman, *Diaries*, ii, p 772.

18. CC(65) 13th mtg, 2 March 1965, CAB 128/39.

19. Wilson and Kindersley mtg, 3 May 1966, Doctors' and Dentists' Pay, 1966, PREM 11.

20. Crossman, *Diaries*, iii, pp 665, 667, 677.

21. CAB 134/3031, 3118, 3119.

22. A Howard, *Crossman. The Pursuit of Power* (Cape, 1990).

23. Crossman, *Diaries*, ii, p 682, 14 February 1968.

24. Crossman, *Diaries*, ii, pp 721-2, 19 March 1968.

25. See Appendix 1.1. Crossman, *Diaries*, iii, pp 237, 396, 738, 758. Reservations concerning Crossman's personality are aptly summarised by Hennessy, *Whitehall*, pp 495-6. See also Robinson's Obituaries, note 5 above.

26. Wilson first suggested Shirley Williams, and Roy Hattersley was also under consideration for promotion to Minister of State in DHSS. Both were rejected by Crossman. Serota was a further suggestion by Wilson. On the basis of warm support from officials, Crossman agreed, and Serota was appointed on 24 October 1969, Crossman, *Diaries*, iii, pp 375, 378, 380. Serota's appointment precluded the promotion of Julian Snow, formerly Parliamentary Secretary to the Ministry of Health, later Parliamentary Under-Secretary of State at DHSS. Snow suffered a stroke in February 1969, and was replaced by Dr John Dunwoody in October 1969. For Crossman's satisfaction at Dunwoody's appointment, *Diaries*, iii, pp 680-3.

27. Crossman, *Diaries*, iii, pp 496, 673, 732, 776.

28. Crossman, *Diaries*, iii, pp 380, 496.

29. Crossman, *Diaries*, iii, pp 378, 732.

30. See Appendix 1.2. For an uninformative valedictory essay by Ross, 'Approaching the Archangelic', in H M Drucker and M G Clarke, eds, *The Scottish Yearbook* 1978 (Paul Harris, 1978), pp 1-20.

31. See Appendix 1.5.

32. See Appendix 1.7.

33. See Appendix 1.3.

34. CAB, 2MS 25/56/01B-G. At Gordon Walker, Robinson and officials mtg, 7 June 1967, Robinson and his Permanent Secretary rehearsed objections to devolution

of health responsibilities to Wales, CAB, 2MS 25/56/01E. Robinson to Wilson, c.16 October 1967, confirmed that he was 'strongly opposed to it and I need not perhaps again rehearse the arguments', CAB, 35/10 Part 1.

35. Crossman, P(68)8, 18 June 1968, CAB 134/3031.

36. T, 2SS 100/519/02.

37. See Appendix 1.4. For Fraser's Obituary, *Independent*, 26 August 1993.

38. K Theakston, 'Evelyn Sharp (1903-85)', *Contemporary Record*, 1993, **7**, 132-48.

39. See Appendix 1.4. Crossman, *Diaries*, iii, pp 83, 165, 194.

40. Crossman, *Diaries*, iii, pp 736-7.

41. Jarrett's Obituaries, *Daily Telegraph*, 14 July 1995, *Times*, 19 July 1995.

42. See Appendix 1.6.

43. Crossman, *Diaries*, iii, pp 413-4.

44. T, 2SS 21/01A.

45. T, 2SS 21/01A.

46. Treasury minute, 10 October 1967, T, 2SS 21/01A.

47. Operation Vigilant, draft report, May 1966, 2SS 1086/01B.

48. DH, J/N 179/32. For Robinson's announcements about this committee, HC Debates, vol 716, cols 8-9, 12 July 1965 (WA), vol 733, col 1172, 8 August 1966. The members listed in the first announcement were B Abel-Smith, Professor W J H Butterfield, Sir Edward Collingwood, G E Godber, R Huws Jones, Sir Peter Medawar, Professor M Roth, and Miss M Scott Wright. This committee was also called by Robinson 'advisory group' or 'study group'.

49. Crossman, *Diaries*, iii, p 35.

50. SS(64)1, 6 November 1964, CAB 134/2534.

51. Houghton, SS(64)3, 12 November 1964, CAB 134/2534.

52. SS(64) 4th mtg, 21 December 1964, CAB 134/2534.

53. See Appendix 3.3.

54. See Appendices 3.3, 3.6.

55. See Appendices 3.4, 3.5.

56. See Appendix 3.2.

57. For the economic context to the following section, F T Blackaby, ed, *British Economic Policy 1960-74: Demand Management*; W Beckerman, ed, *The Labour Government's Economic Record 1964-1970* (Duckworth, 1972); Crafts and Woodward, eds, *The British Economy since 1945*. For the politics of welfare, see N Timmins, *Five Giants*, chapter 12.

58. Craig, *Election Manifestos*, pp 255, 266.

59. There was of course a small contribution from local taxation, amounting to about 4 per cent of the gross cost of the NHS; this contributed to the support of local authority administered services. See Appendix 3.6.

60. Treasury minutes, October to November 1964, T, 2SS 550/282/01A. Treasury minute, 22 December 1964, T, 2SS 214/324/03A.

61. Queen's Speech, HC Debates, vol 701, col 40, 3 November 1964.

62. Robinson to Callaghan, 19 October 1964, T, 2SS 550/282/01A. Robinson to Callaghan, 22 October 1964, Ross to Callaghan, 22 October 1964, T, 2SS 21/786/01C.

63. SS(64) 1st mtg, 19 November 1964, CAB 134/2534; Callaghan, C(64)7, 28 October 1964, CAB 129/119; CC(64) 3rd mtg, 28 October 1964, CAB 128/39; Cabinet Secretary's Notebook (Burke Trend). Crossman, *Diaries*, i, pp 34-5, 28 October 1964.

64. Brown to Wilson, 12 November 1964, Callaghan to Robinson, 13 November 1964, Robinson to Callaghan, 16 November 1964, Callaghan to Robinson, 17 November 1964, T, 2SS 550/282/01A. Robinson, HC Debates, vol 704, cols 581-4, 17 December 1964.

65. *Daily Telegraph*, 20 November 1964; *Financial Times*, 18 December 1964. On 1 January 1965 Robinson wrote to general medical practitioners individually to ask for their co-operation over abolition of the prescription charge, T, 2SS 550/282/01A.

66. Robinson to Callaghan, 22 October 1964, T, 2SS 21/786/01C.

67. Callaghan, annotation on Treasury minute, December 1965, T, 2SS 550/282/01A.

68. Crossman, *Diaries*, i, pp 316, 607, 645-6.

69. Treasury minute, 29 January 1965, T, 2SS 21/786/01C.

70. Treasury minute, 13 January 1965, T, 2SS 21/786/01C.

71. Treasury minute, 29 January 1965, Robinson to Callaghan, 1 February 1965, Treasury and Ministry of Health confidential mtg, 1 February 1965, Treasury minutes accepting error, 8 and 24 February 1965, T, 2SS 21/786/01C. CC(65) 5th mtg, 28 January 1965, CAB 128/39; Cabinet Secretary's Notebook (Burke Trend).

72. CC(65) 5th mtg, 28 January 1965, CAB 128/39.

73. A 3.5 per cent rate of increase was conceded for Scotland for 1966/67, but for one year only, Treasury minute, c.5 July 1965, T, 2SS 21/786/01C.

74. Treasury minute, 13 January 1965, T, 2SS 21/786/01C.

75. Callaghan to Robinson, 9 February 1965, T, 2SS 21/786/01C.

76. Robinson to Callaghan, 18 February 1965, T, 2SS 21/786/01C.

77. Robinson to T Balogh, 1 June 1965, T, 2SS 21/1287/01E.

78. Robinson to Callaghan, 6 December 1964, Diamond to Robinson, 11 December 1964, T, 2SS 1/21/01G. Robinson to Callaghan, 14 December 1964 and associated minutes, T, 2SS 1/21/01H.

79. Robinson, C(65)6, 18 January 1965, CAB 129/120; CC(65) 3rd mtg, 21 January 1965, CAB 128/39; Cabinet Secretary's Notebook (Burke Trend).

80. Treasury minute, 29 January 1965, T, 2SS 1/21/01H.

81. Treasury minute, 21 January 1965, T, 2SS 1/21/01H.

82. *The Hospital Building Programme. A revision of the Hospital Plan for England and Wales*, Cmnd.3000 (HMSO, 1966). Treasury and Ministry of Health mtg, 4 August 1964, T, 2SS 21/786/01B. In fact, the agreed figures for hospital spending for England and Wales added up to c.£800m for the ten-year period.

83. Robinson to Wilson, 11 May 1966, Hospital Capital Expenditure, 1965-1968, PREM 11.

84. W A Shee, 'Getting Value in New Hospitals', *Times*, 23 February 1965. Shee was former Secretary of the Leeds RHB. T, 2SS 1/21/01H. In 1974, Poulson was imprisoned for five years on charges of corruption and conspiracy. Hospital building figured prominently in the charges against Poulson, see 'Seven men John Poulson used to build his hospital empire', *Times*, 31 March 1974.

85. SHHD, *Revision of the Hospital Plan for Scotland* (HMSO, Edinburgh, 1966). SHHD to DEA, 13 July 1965, T, 2SS 21/786/01C.

86. T, 2SS 1/21/01K-L. See also, HM(68)76, *Management of Capital Investment (RHB) Forward Planning*.

87. *Hospital Plan*, para 20; *Hospital Building Programme*, para 13.

88. CHSC(66) 1st mtg, 11 January 1966, DH, G/C 15/7.

89. CHSC(66) 2nd mtg, 19 April 1966, DH, G/C 15/7. Bonham-Carter was knighted in 1969.

90. *The Functions of the District General Hospital* (HMSO, 1969).

91. CHSC(69) 2nd mtg, 15 April 1969, DH, G/C15/14.

92. *Functions of the District General Hospital*, rec. 4 and paras 14-16.

93. PEP(69) 10th mtg, 16 July 1969, DH, F/P 239/06B.

94. *Functions of the District General Hospital*, pp iv-v.

95. See for instance, *People*, 22 May 1966.

96. Treasury and Ministry of Health mtg, 12 January 1966, T, 2SS 550/282/01A.

97. Treasury minute, 9 May 1966, T, 2SS 93/36/01A.

98. T, 2SS 93/36/01A-C.

99. Robinson to Callaghan, 22 June 1966, T, 2SS 21/786/01D.

100. Robinson, PE(66)7, 12 July 1966, Robinson, PE(66)16, 21 October 1966, PE(66) 6th mtg, 1 November 1966, PE(66) 7th mtg, 7 November 1966, CAB 134/2395.

101. T, 2EAS 9/285/02A.

102. Houghton suggested that the NHS should be financed to a greater degree by contributory insurance, and that the NHS stamp might be used as the vehicle for this insurance when the National Insurance system was reshaped, CC(65) 13th mtg, 2 March 1965, CAB 128. Cabinet Secretary's Notebook (Burke Trend). At a later dates, both Robinson and Crossman unsuccessfully proposed expanding the role of the NHS Contribution.

103. Treasury minute, 23 May 1967, T, 2SS 21/786/01D.

104. CC(67) 66th mtg, 16 November 1967, CAB 128.

105. A Cairncross and B Eichengreen, *Sterling in Decline: the Devaluations of 1931, 1949 and 1967* (Blackwell, 1983).

106. T, 2SS 300/301/07A.

107. Treasury minute, 13 December 1967, T, 2SS 550/282/02A.

108. Wilson in his TV statement on 18 November 1967, promised that 'housing, school and hospital building would be safeguarded', T, 2SS 300/301/07C.

109. Treasury minute, 13 December 1967, T, 2SS 550/282/02A.

110. Treasury minute, 13 December 1967, T, 2SS 550/282/02A.

111. Callaghan and Robinson mtg, 15 December 1967, 2SS 300/301/07A. Robinson to Jenkins, 18 December 1967 and 2 January 1968, T, 2SS 550/282/02A.

112. Treasury minute, 13 December 1967, T, 2SS 300/301/07A.

113. Jenkins and officials mtg, 1 January 1968, T, 2SS 550/282/02A.

114. Callaghan, HC Debates, vol 754, col 952, 20 November 1967.

115. Crossman, *Diaries*, iii, pp 619-21, 27 December 1967. Jenkins was repeating a point made by the editor of the *Financial Times* to a Treasury official on 12 December, T, 2SS 300/301/07A.

116. Jenkins, C(68)5, 3 January 1968, Robinson, C(68)14, 11 January 1968, CAB 129. CC(68) 3rd mtg, 5 January 1968, CC(68) 4th mtg, 11 January 1968, CAB 128. Crossman, *Diaries*, iii, pp 637-8, 643-5.

117. Callaghan and Robinson mtg, 15 December 1967, T, 2SS 300/301/07A. Robinson to Jenkins, 18 December 1967, T, 2SS 550/282/02A.

118. When implemented, for purposes of rounding, the employer's contribution was increased by 1/2d and the employee's by 51/2d.

119. CC(67) 49th mtg, 19 July 1967, CAB 128.

120. Wilson, HC Debates, vol 756, cols 1577-618, 16 January 1968. *Public Expenditure in 1968-1970*, 16 January 1968, Cmnd.3515 (HMSO, 1968).

121. *Financial Times*, 17 January 1968; *Economist*, 20 January 1968, headlined the changes: 'Rake's Regress'.

122. Crossman, *Diaries*, ii, pp 707-8, describes embarrassing criticism at a meeting of the Parliamentary Labour Party on 13 March 1968. On 30 May 1968, the Prayer to annul the proposed Order reintroducing the prescription charge attracted 49 votes from Labour MPs.

123. Stewart, C(68)38, 22 February 1968, CAB 129; CC(68) 14th mtg, 22 February 1968, CAB 128; Robinson, SS(68)4, 16 February 1968, SS(68) 3rd mtg, 19 February 1968, CAB 134/3282. T, 2SS 550/282/02A-B. Crossman, *Diaries*, ii, pp 747, 775.

124. Crossman and Ross, SS(68)47, 1 November 1968, CAB 134/3284; SS(68) 18th mtg, 18 November 1968, CAB 134/3282; Crossman and Ross, SS(69)33, 1 July 1969, CAB 134/3287; SS(69) 7th mtg, 3rd July 1969, CAB 134/3285. T, 2SS 550/282/02C.

125. Crossman, *Diaries*, iii, p 262, 18 November 1968.

126. CC(68) 33rd mtg, 27 June 1968, CAB 128.

127. Treasury minute, T, 2EAS 9/285/03A.

128. Treasury minute, 19 June 1968, T, 2EAS 9/285/03C.

129. Treasury minute, 15 December 1967, T, 2SS 301/96/011A.

130. Treasury minute, 22 January 1968, T, 2SS 301/96/011A.

131. Robinson to Stewart, 20 February 1968, T, 2SS 301/96/011A.

132. Treasury minute, 4 March 1968, T, 2SS 301/96/011B.

133. SS(68) 2nd mtg, 7 February 1968, SS(68) 8th mtg, 14 May 1968, CAB 134/3282.

134. SS(69) 1st mtg, 19 February 1969, CAB 134/3285.

135. Treasury minute, 24 May 1968, T, 2SS 300/1128/04A.

136. SS(68) 11th mtg, 20 June 1968, 12th mtg, 4 July 1968, 13th mtg, 9 July 1968, CAB 134/3282. T, 2SS 300/1128/04A-B.

137. Treasury minute, 6 January 1969, T, 2SS 300/1128/04B.

138. Crossman to Jenkins, 1 January 1969, T, 2SS 64/020.

139. The Public Expenditure Review Committee was established in the summer of 1968 to 'review the arrangements for the planning and control of public expenditure'.

140. T, 2GE 16/42/06A.

141. T, 2SS 21/282/01A.

142. Treasury minute, 28 October 1969, T, 2SS 21/282/01A.

143. T, 2SS 21/786/01E.

144. Treasury minute, 16 July 1969, T, 2SS 21/786/01E.

145. Crossman first indicated that he valued the role of the NHS Contribution in a memorandum dated 18 July 1968, T, 2SS 64/012G.

146. Crossman, HC Debates, vol 783, cols 42-50, 5 May 1969.

147. Crossman, *Diaries*, iii, pp 475-82.

148. Crossman, *Diaries*, iii, pp 489, 500, 533-4, 537-9, 541-3.

149. Crossman, *Diaries*, iii, pp 538-9, 26 June 1969. On this date Crossman discovered that the Conservatives were planning a censure motion on his handling of health service charges. The Morrison Lecture was published in December 1969, *Paying for the Social Services* (Fabian Tract 399, 1969), quotation from pp 18-19.

150. Crossman, *Diaries*, iii, pp 542-3, 1 July 1969.

151. Crossman, HC Debates, vol 786, cols 253-66, 1 July 1969 (col 262 for comment on charges). Crossman was also criticised for giving £19m as the total capacity of the charges system; this was corrected in Hansard to £90m, Treasury minute, 7 July 1969, T, 2SS 21/786/01E.

152. Crossman, HC Debates, vol 786, cols 1077-84, 7 July 1969.

153. Crossman, *Diaries*, iii, pp 550-1, 7 July 1969.

154. Treasury minute, 7 July 1969, T, 2SS 21/786/01E.

155. Jenkins and Crossman mtg, 9 July 1969, T, 2SS 115/553/01B.

156. CC(69) 32nd mtg, 10 July 1969, CAB 128. Crossman, C(69)83, 15 July 1969, Jenkins, C(69)84, 15 July 1969, CAB 129; CC(69) 34th mtg, 17 July 1969, CAB 128. Crossman, *Diaries*, iii, pp 556-7, 577-8, 10 and 17 July 1969. Pavitt's motion was debated on 21 July, without misadventure for the Government, but with expression of further bad feeling among Labour MPs, HC Debates, vol 786, cols 1369-402. Wilson's letter to Pavitt was cited at length by Crossman, col 1377.

157. T, 2SS 21/786/01E, 2GE 16/42/06C.

158. CC(69) 34th mtg, 17 July 1969, CC(69) 37th mtg, 24 July 1969, CC(69) 38th mtg, 29 July 1969, CAB 128; Cabinet Secretary's Notebook (Burke Trend). Crossman, *Diaries*, iii, pp 574, 593-4, 599-600.

159. T, 2SS 109/324/01B.

160. The motor accident levy was a contribution exacted from insurance companies towards the treatment of motor accident casualties in hospital. It was assumed that any increase in the levy would be passed on to motorists in increased premiums. It was estimated that only one-tenth of the full cost of treatment was currently being recovered on the basis of the existing rate of £1 per vehicle a year. The full cost therefore implied a levy of £10, Treasury and DHSS mtg, 23 July 1969, T, 2SS 115/553/01B.

161. Treasury minute, 30 October 1969, T, 2SS 115/553/01C.

162. T, 2SS 64/01G.

163. *National Superannuation and Social Insurance*, Cmnd.3883, January 1969 (HMSO, 1969). The 1 per cent relating to the NHS was subsumed under the 4 per cent deduction for 'Social insurance benefits, industrial injuries and a contribution to the National Health Service'.

164. Jenkins, Crossman and officials mtg, 10 November 1969, T, 2SS 21/212/01A.

165. Treasury minute, 3 November 1969, T, 2SS 21/786/01E.

166. Treasury minute, 10 November 1969, T, 2SS 115/553/01C.

167. Treasury minutes, February 1970. T, 2SS 300/1128/06A.

168. Crossman, *Diaries*, iii, pp 826-7, 19 February 1970.

169. DHSS to Treasury, 20 February 1970, T, 2SS 300/1128/06A.

170. Treasury minute, 25 February 1970, T, 2SS 300/1128/06A.

171. Crossman to Jenkins, 17 March 1970, T, 2SS 300/1128/06A.

172. Jenkins, Diamond and officials mtg, 19 March 1970, T, 2SS 300/1128/06C.

173. Jenkins to Crossman, 20 March 1970, Crossman to Jenkins, 25 March 1970, T, 2SS 300/1128/06C.

174. T, 2SS 300/1128/06C-D.

175. Most noticeably, the *Special Report and First and Second Reports from the Committee of Public Accounts, Session 1959-60* (HMSO, 1960); *First, Second and Third Reports from the Committee of Public Accounts, Session 1961-62* (HMSO, 1962). Harold Wilson was chairman of the PAC at this time. These reports gained additional publicity when in 1962 the practice began of debating them in Parliament.

176. For the cost of the Pharmaceutical Services as a whole, see Appendix 3.10.

177. T, 2SS 188/197/01F.

178. Diamond to Robinson, 21 December 1964, Robinson to Diamond, 30 December 1964, T, 2SS 21/786/01C.

179. George Woodcock, TUC, to Robinson, 25 November 1964, MH 140/1.

180. Ministry of Health minute, December 1964, MH 140/1.

181. Treasury minute, 1 July 1964, T, 2SS 188/197/01F.

182. Cyanamid, the manufacturer of tetracylines, claimed a profit of 37 per cent on capital employed. The Ministry of Health calculated that the profit was 45 per cent, the Treasury believed that it was at least 55 per cent, while the Board of Trade calculated 80 per cent. Tetracyclines were available from Poland at almost one-tenth of the price paid under VPRS. Treasury minutes, July to August 1965, T, 2SS 188/197/01F-G. For publicity concerning criticisms of the pharmaceutical industry by M A Philips, *People*, 2 January 1966. Editorial, *Times*, 3 March 1966, concluded 'in general the drug companies make huge profits through charging exorbitant prices'.

183. The Pharmacy and Poisons Act 1933 was supplemented by the Therapeutic Substances Act 1956, which introduced controls relating to the purity of therapeutic substances. Following the United Nations Single Convention on Narcotic Drugs 1961, the United Kingdom introduced the Dangerous Drugs Acts of 1964 and 1965 to control the manufacture, import and export of addiction-producing substances and related raw materials. The problem of non-narcotic but habit-forming drugs was addressed by the Drugs (Prevention of Misuse) Act 1964. See, J Braithwaite, *Corporate Crime in the Pharmaceutical Industry* (Routledge, 1984); R Blum, A Herxheimer, C Stenzl, J Woodcock, eds, *Pharmaceuticals and Health Policy* (Croom Helm, 1981); A Chetley, *A Healthy Business? World Health and the Pharmaceutical Industry* (Zed Books, 1990).

184. Robinson, HC Debates, vol 708, cols 30-3, 8 March 1965.

185. Ministry of Health minute, December 1964, Sainsbury to Robinson, 26 and 31 March 1965, MH 140/1.

186. Ministry of Health minute, 30 April 1965, MH 140/1.

187. Robinson, HC Debates, vol 713, col 145, 31 May 1965 (WA).

188. For Sainsbury Committee meetings and evidence, MH 104/2-95.

189. Sir D Dunlop, *Practitioner*, January 1965. For the Subcommittee on Adverse Reactions, W H W Inman, 'The United Kingdom', in W H W Inman, ed, *Monitoring for Drug Safety* (MTP Press, 1980), pp 9-48.

190. Committee on Safety of Drugs, *Report for the year ended 31 December 1965* (HMSO, 1967).

191. *Classification of Proprietary Preparations. Report of the Standing Joint Committee* (HMSO, 1965).

192. A G Macgregor, 'The work of the Standing Joint Committee on the Classification of Proprietary Preparations', *Prescribers' Journal*, February 1967, pp 106-7.

193. *Report of the Committee of Enquiry into the Relationship of the Pharmaceutical Industry with the National Health Service, 1965-1967*, Cmnd.3410 (HMSO, 1967).

870

194. *Forthcoming Legislation on the Safety, Quality, and Description of Drugs and Medicines*, Cmnd.3395 (HMSO, 1967).

195. *Sainsbury Report*, paras 84-94, 287-97.

196. *Sainsbury Report*, paras 329-31.

197. *Sainsbury Report*, chapter 10.

198. *Sainsbury Report*, para 319.

199. *Sainsbury Report*, para 151.

200. *Sainsbury Report*, para 329.

201. *Sainsbury Report*, paras 344-81.

202. *Sainsbury Report*, pp 63-4.

203. *Sainsbury Report*, pp 70-1.

204. *Sainsbury Report*, para 348.

205. *Sainsbury Report*, para 99.

206. *Sainsbury Report*, chapter 5.

207. Philip Colebrook, Chairman of Pfizer, *Financial Times*, 28 September 1967.

208. ABPI press statement, 29 September 1967.

209. Ministry of Health and ICI mtg, 14 December 1967, MH 104/97.

210. Editorial, *Times*, 29 September 1967.

211. Robinson, HC Debates, vol 751, cols 1326-30, 23 October 1967.

212. Treasury minutes, 18 and 28 September 1967, T, 2SS 250/1137/01C.

213. Submission to Diamond, 19 February 1968, T, 2SS 250/1137/01D.

214. T, 2SS 250/1137/01D-E.

215. Merrett Cyriax Associates, 'Profitability in the Pharmaceutical Industry', January 1968, T, 2SS 250/1137/01D; M H Cooper, *Prices and Profits in the Pharmaceutical Industry* (Pergamon, 1966); Runnymede Research, *Competition, Risk and Profit in the Pharmaceutical Industry* (Runnymede, 1975); W D Reekie, 'Some Problems associated with the Marketing of Ethical Pharmaceutical Products', *Journal of Industrial Economics*, 1970, **19**, 33-49.

216. W D Reekie and M H Weber, *Profits, Politics and Drugs* (Macmillan, 1979), pp 120-7.

217. M Silverman and P R Lee, *Pills, Profits and Politics* (University of California Press, 1974).

218. Ministry of Health and ICI mtg, 14 December 1967, MH 104/97.

219. Ministry of Health and ICI mtg, 14 December 1967, MH 104/97.

220. Editorial, *British Medical Journal*, 7 October 1967.

221. The new clause had a chequered history. It was introduced as new clause 5 at the Commons' Report Stage, then translated into clause 25 at the Lords' Report Stage, deleted owing to defeat of the relevant amendment, but later reinserted

by the House of Commons in a redrafted form as clause 59. HC Debates, vol 762, cols 78-108, 1 April 1968. HL Debates, vol 292, cols 960-95, 27 May 1968. HC Debates, vol 786, cols 651-60, 10 July 1968. The Banks Report gave backing to this provision, *The British Patent System*, Cmnd.4407 (HMSO, 1970).

222. Robinson, HC Debates, vol 767, cols 43-6, 24 June 1968.

223. *British Patent System: Report of the Committee to Examine the Patent System and Patent Law*, Cmnd.4407 (HMSO, 1970), paras 399, 424.

224. Treasury minute, 18 November 1968, T, 2SS 250/1137/01F.

225. T, 2SS 250/1137/01F.

226. Treasury minute, 13 March 1969, T, 2SS 250/1137/01H.

227. Crossman to Diamond, 9 April 1969, Diamond to Crossman, 16 April 1969, T, 2SS 250/1137/01J. Crossman and ABPI mtg, 13 October 1969, T, 2SS 250/1137/01K. Crossman, HC Debates, vol 788, cols 272-4 (WA).

228. Treasury minute, 2 July 1970, T, 2SS 300/1128/07A. See Appendix 3.10 for expenditure on the pharmaceutical service. In the event, the cost of pharmaceutical products for 1974/75 was about £410m.

229. T, 2SS 300/1128/06, 2SS 300/1128/07A.

230. Chief Secretary and officials mtg, 25 March 1970, T, 2SS 188/522/01C.

231. T, 2SS 250/1137/01H-M.

232. For an excellent review of hospital enquiries, and the wider problems of long-stay hospitals, J P Martin, *Hospitals in Trouble* (Blackwell, 1984).

233. AEGIS was first publicised by a letter signed by Lord Strabolgi, Baroness Beaumont, Lord Heytesbury, Professor Brian Abel-Smith, Edward Ardizzone, Audrey Harvey, Dr John Hewetson, the Rev Bill Sargent, the V Rev Daniel Woolgar, and Mrs Barbara Robb, *Times*, 10 November 1965. Mrs Robb was a trained psychotherapist and wife of the artist, Brian Robb, who was head of the Illustration Department, Royal School of Art. Mrs Robb's concern was alerted by a visit to an elderly woman artist in a north London mental hospital.

234. *Sunday Times*, 4 June 1967. For a similar alarming report of conditions at the Warwick Mental Hospital, emanating from the Medical Superintendent, *Sunday Times*, 19 March 1967.

235. *Sans Everything. A Case to Answer. Presented by Barbara Robb on behalf of AEGIS* (Nelson, 1967). In *Sans Everything*, like Young, Abel-Smith argued the case for appointment of a Hospital Commissioner.

236. 'Twenty-Four Hours', BBC Television, 30 June 1967.

237. Robinson and officials mtg, 21 February 1967, DH, F/C 121/3.

238. Robinson, HC Debates, vol 751, cols 175-6, 26 July 1967.

239. *Findings and Recommendations Following Enquiries into Allegations Concerning the Care of Elderly Patients in Certain Hospitals*, Cmnd.3687 (HMSO, 1968).

240. Robinson, HC Debates, vol 768, cols 213-6, 9 July 1968.

241. See especially, *Sunday Telegraph*, 14 July 1968, 'Man Alive', BBC television, 16 July 1968.

242. *Report of the Council on Tribunals for 1968* (HMSO, 1969), pp 10-14.

243. Burton to Robinson, 25 July 1968, Robinson to Burton, 30 July 1968, and subsequent exchanges; Burton to Crossman, 26 March 1969, DH, J/N 179/23B. Baroness Burton had a link with Crossman because she had been MP for Coventry South, whereas he was MP for Coventry East. She was appointed to head the Council on Tribunals in 1967.

244. DH, F/P 239/01C, 02.

245. 'Hospital Psychiatric Services', brief for Robinson for meeting with RHB Chairmen, 16 July 1968. The statement was in fact delivered by the Permanent Secretary, DH, F/P 239/02.

246. SAMOs mtg, 29 October 1968, DH, F/P 239/02.

247. For the Welsh Board of Health's dealings with Howe's Committee, WO, HS 234/10/36J Parts 1-4.

248. Ministry of Health minute, 9 September 1968, DH, G/C 188/12A.

249. *Report of the Committee of Inquiry into Allegations of Ill-Treatment of Patients and other irregularities at the Ely Hospital, Cardiff*, Cmnd.3975 (HMSO, 1969), pp 1-5.

250. Thomas had opened a Children's Adventure Playground at Ely Hospital on 8 August 1966. His brief for this occasion contain a glowing account of progress at the hospital. However, a report by nursing officers, dating from 1967, condemns standards of care and levels of staff training, WO, HS 234/10A Part 1. According to Crossman, this report was known in London, but ignored, *Diaries*, iii, p 411.

251. Crossman blamed Ennals for the delay, and praised Serota for diligence, Crossman, *Diaries*, iii, p 410, 12 March 1969.

252. Crossman, *Diaries*, iii, pp 408-9, 10-11 March 1969.

253. Crossman, *Diaries*, iii, p 409, 11 March 1969.

254. Crossman, *Diaries*, iii, pp 408-13, 418-20, 425-30, 485.

255. Wilson and Crossman, telephone discussion, 12 March 1969, Response to Sans Everything, 1969, PREM 11.

256. Crossman, SS(69)12, 20 March 1969, CAB 134/3287; SS(69) 2nd mtg, 24 March 1969, CAB 134/3285; CC(69) 14th mtg, 25 March 1969, CAB 128.

257. Crossman, HC Debates, vol 780, cols 1808-19, 27 March 1969.

258. Martin, *Hospitals in Trouble*, pp 9-27.

259. Crossman, HC Debates, vol 782, cols 123-4, 24 April 1969 (WA). Initially PEP was known as a group, or working group, but Crossman also called it his 'post-Ely policy advisory council', *Diaries*, iii, p 489.

260. For an oblique reference to the initial decision to set up this committee, Crossman, *Diaries*, iii, p 420, 19 March 1969.

261. Crossman, HC Debates, vol 780, cols 1808-18, 27 March 1969; Crossman, HC Debates, vol 782, cols 723-4, 24 April 1969(WA).

262. For efforts by officials to curb PEP, beginning May 1969, DH, G/H 207/1B. See also Secretary of State's weekly meetings, 27 October and 3 November 1969, BN 72/91.

263. The Mental Health SAC was informed about the PEP initiative in June 1969, SAC(MH)(69) 3rd mtg, 25 June 1969, DH, F/C 53/33. This meeting discussed the HAS and was divided over its merits; some members thought that it would repeat the faults of the Board of Control.

264. RHB Chairmen mtgs, 30 April, 16 July, and 3 December 1969, DH, F/P 239/06C. Crossman attributes the idea of a 1 1/2 per cent switch to Abel-Smith, *Diaries*, iii, p 466 (Crossman gives 1 1/4 as the figure).

265. *Report of the Committee of Inquiry into Allegations of Ill-Treatment of Patients and other irregularities at the Ely Hospital*, para 561.

266. Crossman, Serota and officials mtg, 12 March 1969, DH, G/H 207/1A.

267. RHB Chairmen mtg, 30 April 1969, DH, F/P 239/06C.

268. Crossman and Joint Consultants Committee mtg, 29 April 1969, DH, G/H 207/1A.

269. PEP(69) 2nd mtg, 14 May 1969, DH, G/H 207/1A. Howe to DHSS, 11 September 1969, DH, F/P 239/06C.

270. Crossman, *Diaries*, iii, pp 599, 619, 627, 649-50, 655, 665.

271. HM(70)17, March 1970. The HAS was based in Sunderland House, Sutton, Surrey. For drafts of the Plan of Operation, DH, G/H 207/1B.

272. HAS(70)(MH2)(51), 12 October 1970, DH, F/P 239/86.

273. Welsh Office minute, c.25 April 1969, WO, HS 234/10/36J Part 1.

274. Exchanges between DHSS and Welsh Office, August to September 1969, DH, G/H 207/1B.

275. Thomas to Crossman, 14 May 1969, DH, G/H 207/1A.

276. SHHD to DHSS, 5 June 1969, DH, G/H 207/1B. The scheme had not by this stage been sanctioned by Scottish Ministers.

277. SHHD, Proposed Scottish Hospital Advisory Service, August 1969, DH, G/H 207/1B.

278. SHM 13/1970, 11 March 1970, SHHD, HOS/76/4 Part B.

279. Select Committee on the Parliamentary Commissioner for Administration, *Second Report Session 1967/68*, para 37.

280. PEP(69) 14th mtg, 9 October 1969, DH, J/N 179/23A.

281. *Proposals for a Health Commissioner in the Reorganised National Health Service* (DHSS, 1970).

282. Summary of responses to the consultation document on a Health Commissioner, June 1970, DH, J/N 179/23D.

283. Report of Working Group on Complaints Procedure, PEP(69)42, 29 July 1969, DH, F/P 239/06C.

284. PEP(69) 12th mtg, 29 July 1969, DH, F/P 239/06C.

285. DH, G/C 369/1.

286. DH, F/M 271/01A. The plan adopted for this 16 page report was: I, Persons to be served; II, The Services required for children, adolescents, and adults; III,

Services available for these groups under existing policy; IV, Recommendations.

287. Ministry of Health minute, August 1969, MH 150/167.

288. Secretary of State's weekly meeting, 17 December 1969, MH 150/168.

289. Conference on services for the mentally handicapped, 3 and 4 October 1969, DH, F/P 239/30.

290. For the views of the Mental Health SAC, which largely reiterated points made at the October conference, SAC(MH)(69) 5th mtg, 22 October 1969, DH, F/C 53/33.

291. For instance, on 22 December 1969 experts met to discuss the latest findings on the level of mental handicap within the population, MH 150/168.

292. PEP(69)62, December 1969, MH 150/168.

293. *Guardian*, 20 December 1969.

294. Secretary of State and officials mtg, 5 May 1970, MH 150/169.

295. Crossman, *Diaries*, iii, pp 916, 921, 943, 950.

296. See, Robinson's address to the London Boroughs committee, 1 January 1965, MH 148/153; Robinson, HC Debates, vol 716, cols 1092-4, 19 July 1965.

297. MH 148/162.

298. Circular 15/65, 3 August 1965. *Fluoridation* (Ministry of Health, 1965), 14 pp. CCHE Conference on fluoridation, 8 December 1965, MH 148/153.

299. MH 148/155, 158, 177, 178.

300. Fluoridation, 1966, PREM 11.

301. *The Fluoridation Studies in the United Kingdom and the Results Achieved after Eleven Years* (HMSO, 1969). MH 148/155.

302. *Fluoridation Studies*, p iv.

303. Secretary of State, weekly mtg, 20 January 1970, BN 72/92. Fluoridation, 1969, PREM 11.

304. Crossman and Thomas, H(69)20, 15 April 1969, H(69) 8th mtg, 18 April 1969, CAB 134. For the single sheet popular exposition, DHSS, Scottish Office, Welsh Office, MHLG, *Fluoridation in the United Kingdom. The Results After Eleven Years* (HMSO, 1969).

305. Crossman, HC Debates, vol 788, cols 752-3, 20 October 1969, vol 797, cols 885-6, 9 March 1970. For Crossman's reactions on fluoridation, *Diaries*, iii, pp 421, 552, 555, 588, 852.

306. HC Debates, vol 694, cols 1620-97, 8 May 1964, (Robinson, cols 1691-2).

307. 'This Week', BBC TV, 16 January 1964.

308. Taylor, *Smoke Ring*, p 81.

309. Robinson to Wilson, 31 December 1964 and 4 January 1965, Banning Cigarette Advertisements, 1964-1968, PREM 11.

310. Robinson, C(65)9, 26 January 1965, CAB 129/120; CC(65) 6th mtg, 1 February 1965, CAB 128/39. Cabinet Secretary's Notebook (Burke Trend). Brief for Prime

Minister, 27 January 1965, Banning Cigarette Advertisements, 1964-1968, PREM 11.

311. Robinson, HC Debates, vol 706, cols 10-14, 8 February 1965. For Robinson's reminiscences, Taylor, *Smoke Ring*, p 82.

312. Robinson, H(65)16, 10 February 1965, CAB 134/1998; H(65) 5th mtg, 12 February 1965, CAB 134/1997.

313. Ministers mtg, 12 May 1965, Banning Cigarette Advertisements, 1964-1968, PREM 11.

314. Robinson, H(66)7, 25 January 1966, H(66) 3rd mtg, 3 February 1966, CAB 134.

315. Robinson, H(66)75, 10 October 1966, H(66) 22nd mtg, 21 October 1966, Ross and Robinson, H(67)5, 17 January 1967, H(67) 2nd mtg, 20 January 1967, CAB 134.

316. Ross and Robinson, H(67)62, 29 June 1967, H(67) 20th mtg, 29 June 1967, Ross and Robinson, H(67)111, 10 October 1967, H(67) 28th mtg, 13 October 1967, H(67) 29th mtg, 19 October 1967, CAB 134.

317. Robinson, HC Debates, vol 751, cols 1328-9, 23 October 1967. Taylor, *Smoke Ring*, pp 82-3.

318. Robinson, H(68)83, 16 July 1968, H(68) 18th mtg, 19 July 1968, CAB 134. Taylor, *Smoke Ring*, p 84.

319. Crossman, *Diaries*, ii, pp 532, 556, iii, 70, 147, 202, 365. Taylor, *Smoke Ring*, pp 84-5.

320. See for instance, Crossman in reply to a question from Dr John Dunwoody, HC Debates, vol 722, cols 462-3, 4 November 1968.

321. Crossman, HC Debates, vol 790, col 647, 3 November 1969. This statement also hinted that the promised legislation against tobacco advertising might not be pursued.

322. See especially, *CMO Report 1968*, pp 226-31, where smoking is equated with 'evil'.

323. Secretary of State, weekly mtg, 16 September 1969, BN 72/91.

324. Secretary of State, weekly mtg, 22 September 1969, BN 72/91.

325. Crossman, HC Debates, vol 791, cols 321-2, 19 November 1969 (WA).

326. Dunwoody, HC Debates, vol 792, col 334, 10 February 1970. Dunwoody became Honorary Director of Action on Smoking and Health 1971-73.

327. DH, 94300/1/113. For an informative general review, A Leathard, *The Development of Family Planning Services in Britain 1921-74* (Macmillan, 1980).

328. The CMO was a Roman Catholic and brother-in-law of the future Cardinal Hume.

329. Ministry of Health to Treasury, 9 March 1964, DH, V/G 16/010.

330. Robinson, HC Debates, vol 694, col 881, 4 May 1964. Robinson attacked the Government for its 'hole-and-corner' attitude to the Family Planning Association.

331. Leathard, *Family Planning*, p 134.

332. Ministry of Health to Treasury, 19 August 1965, T, 2SS 659/01A.

333. Hart minute, 15 December 1965, HH 61/1005. Sir Dugald Baird, 'A Fifth Freedom?', *British Medical Journal*, 1965, ii, 1141-8, 25 May 1965 (Mandos Foundation Lecture, University College London). Baird's fifth freedom was 'freedom from the tyranny of excessive fertility'. Baird was especially well-known for his pioneering work on maternity services in Aberdeen. For an interview with Baird, *Times*, 18 June 1969.

334. Treasury minute, 21 December 1965, T, 2SS 659/01A.

335. Robinson, SS(65)43, 16 December 1965, CAB 134/2536; SS(65) 21st mtg, 22 December 1965, CAB 134/2535.

336. Houghton to Wilson, 23 December 1965, Wilson to Houghton, 24 December 1965, Family Planning, 1965-1966, PREM 11.

337. Ministry of Health, 'Family Planning', Circular 5/66, 17 February 1966; SHHD, H & WS Circular 10/1966, 1 June 1966.

338. Brooks held his first discussions with health department officials on 26 May 1966. He explained that he would have introduced the abortion Bill if Steel had declined, MH 156/61.

339. Robinson to Wilson, 24 June 1966, Wilson to Ministers, 10 June 1966, Family Planning, 1965-1966, PREM 11.

340. Diamond to Robinson, 3 June 1966, Loughlin to Diamond, 7 June 1966, T, 2SS 659/01A.

341. SHHD exchanges, June 1966, HH 61/1005.

342. Ross to Robinson, 28 June 1966, T, 2SS 659/01A.

343. For papers relating to the Family Planning Bill, MH 156/61-2. For abortion, V Greenwood and J Young, *Abortion in Demand* (Pluto Press, 1976); K Hindell and M Simms, *Abortion Law Reformed* (Peter Owen, 1971); A Hordern, *Legal Abortion: the English Experience* (Pergamon, 1971); J Keown, *Abortion, doctors and the law. Some aspects of the legal regulation of abortion in England from 1803 to 1982* (Cambridge University Press, 1988).

344. Family Planning, Circular 15/67, 31 July 1967.

345. Leathard, *Fight for Family Planning*, pp 158-9.

346. H(69) 5th mtg, 28 February 1969, CAB 134/1969. Circular 11/1970, 10 August 1970.

347. Crossman, address to Family Planning Association conference, *Times*, 26 June 1969; Crossman, HC Debates, vol 788, cols 749-50, 20 October 1969.

348. Crossman, *Select Committee on Science and Technology: Sub-Committee C, Minutes of Evidence*, 11 March 1970, cols 110-27. Crossman, *Diaries*, iii, p 749, 7 December 1969. Family Planning, Circular H9, 11 December 1969. For a later speech by Crossman advocating free family planning services, *Times*, 9 December 1970.

349. Crossman, *Diaries*, iii, p 693, 22 October 1969.

350. For labour relations during the Wilson administration, F T Blackaby, 'Incomes Policy', in Blackaby, ed, *British Economic Policy 1960-74: Demand Management*, pp 360-401; R Richardson, 'Trade Unions and Industrial Relations', in Crafts and Woodward, eds, *The British Economy since 1945*, pp 417-42; D Robinson, 'Labour Market Policies', in W Beckerman, ed, *The Labour Government's Economic Record*,

pp 300-34; Dorfman, *Wages Politics in Britain, 1945-67*; Dorfman, *Government versus Trade Unions in British Politics since 1968* (Macmillan, 1979), chapter 2; W H Fishbein, *Wage Restraint by Consensus: Britain's Search for an incomes policy agreement 1965-79* (Routledge, 1987); R Taylor, *The Trade Union Question in British Politics*.

351. Powell minute, 9 June 1961, DH, G/S 143/1A.

352. Ministry of Health minute, 21 July 1961, DH, G/S 143/1A.

353. DHS to Ministry of Health, 22 September 1961, DH, G/S 143/1A.

354. Treasury to Ministry of Health, 12 October 1961, T, 2ED 65/179/013.

355. For establishment of the Salmon Committee, MH 159/58-59.

356. For the papers of the Salmon Committee, MH 159/61-75. *Report of the Committee on Senior Nursing Staff Structure* (HMSO, 1966). See also, the popular, twelve-page booklet, *The Senior Nursing Organisation in Hospitals. An Introduction to the report of the Salmon Committee* (HMSO, 1966).

357. Ministry of Health minute, 6 May 1966, DH, M/S 145/01A.

358. *Report on Senior Nursing Staff Structure*, para 1.10.

359. Summary of comments received from Regional Hospital Boards, November 1966, summary of comments from professional organisations, December 1966, DH, M/S 145/4.

360. Editorial, *Nursing Mirror*, 13 May 1966.

361. See for instance, 'Tutors in Post', *Nursing Times*, 1 July 1966, 'Minority Report', *Hospital World*, September 1966.

362. Report on Institute of Hospital Administrators' response to the Salmon Report, *Nursing Times*, 30 December 1966.

363. Robinson, HC Debates, vol 742, cols 186-7, 6 March 1967(WA).

364. SHHD and Ministry of Health meeting, 2 May 1966, DH, M/S 145/25B, M/S 145/01A-B.

365. *Progress on Salmon* (DHSS and Welsh Office, 1972), p 8.

366. Mary K Chisholm, 'A public health look at the Salmon Report', *Nursing Mirror*, 15 December 1967.

367. *Report of Working Party on Management Structure in the Local Authority Nursing Services* (DHSS, 1969). DH, E/L 89/14, M/L 102/02.

368. Nurses and Midwives Whitley Council 1963-64, MH 78/422.

369. Nurses and Midwives Whitley Council 1965-66, MH 78/425-6.

370. Robinson, PI(67)41, 27 May 1967, CAB 134/3060; PI(67) 13th mtg, 24 May 1967, CAB 134/3058. NC (M & SC) 199, 13 June 1967, MH 78/428.

371. National Board for Prices and Incomes, *Report No.60. Pay of Nurses and Midwives in the National Health Service*, Cmnd.3585 (HMSO, 1968).

372. The top of this scale was modified to £985 at implementation.

373. *Pay of Nurses and Midwives*, para 143.

374. T, 2SS 116/78/02A. DH, M/N 59/039A. NMC Circular, No. 139, 1968, NMC Circular, No. 146, 1969.

375. *Pay of Nurses and Midwives*, para 143.

376. Non-resident students received a £66 living-out allowance to compensate for their loss of free meals.

377. In reply to much criticism by MPs, pay-as-you-eat was defended by Ennals, HC Debates, vol 782, cols 803-10, 24 April 1969.

378. NC (M & SC) 218, 13 May 1969, MH 78/429.

379. Crossman to Jenkins and Castle, 9 May 1969, Jenkins to Crossman, 16 May 1969, Castle to Crossman, 12 May 1969, DH, M/N 57/036A.

380. Serota, PI(69)29, 16 May 1969, CAB 134/3065; PI(69) 12th mtg, 21 May 1969, CAB 134/3064. T, 2SS 116/78/02A. MH 78/429. Crossman, *Diaries*, iii, pp 450, 500.

381. NC (M & SC) 219, 30 May 1969, MH 78/429.

382. Crossman, *Diaries*, iii, pp 692-3, 695.

383. DH, M/N 57/039A.

384. Ministry of Health minute, 5 December 1969, CAB, 16/1 Part 6. Serota to Wilson, 16 December 1969, Inquiry into Nursing Profession, 1969-1970, PREM 11. For discussions in DHSS on increasing the NHS Contribution to pay for the nurses' increase, BN 72/94.

385. Treasury minute, 30 December 1969, T, 2SS 116/78/02B.

386. Crossman, PI(69)86, 29 December 1969, CAB 134/3066; PI(69) 28th mtg, 31 December 1969, CAB 134/3064. Crossman, *Diaries*, iii, pp 768-70, 31 December 1969 (the PI meeting in some detail). Brief for Prime Minister, 31 December 1969, Inquiry into Nursing Profession, 1969-1970, PREM 11.

387. NC (M & SC) 226, 13 January 1970, NC (M & SC) 227, 27 January 1970, MH 78/418.

388. Jenkins to Wilson, 15 January 1970, Inquiry into Nursing Profession, 1969-1970, PREM 11.

389. Jenkins, Castle and Crossman mtg, 2 February 1970, T, 2SS 116/78/02B. Jenkins, Castle and Crossman exchanges, 4-5 February 1970, DH, M/N 57/039A.

390. Brief for Prime Minister, 11 February 1970, Inquiry into Nursing Profession, 1969-1970, PREM 11.

391. Brief for Prime Minister, 16 December 1969, Inquiry into Nursing Profession, 1969-1970, PREM 11.

392. Crossman, PI(70)12, 10 February 1970, PI(70) 4th mtg, 11 February 1970, CAB 134/3067. Crossman, C(70)29, 11 February 1970, CAB 129; CC(70) 7th mtg, 12 February 1970, CAB 128. Crossman, *Diaries*, iii, pp 814-6, 12 February 1970.

393. Jenkins, Castle and Crossman exchanges, 13-16 February 1970, T, 2SS 116/78/02B.

394. *Daily Mail* and *Daily Sketch*, 14 February 1970.

395. Drafts of letters from Crossman to Secretary of Nurses and Midwives Whitley Council, c.17 March 1970, DH, M/N 57/039A. Crossman, *Diaries*, iii, pp 820-1, 822-4, 16-17 February 1970.

396. NC (M) 1622, 17 February 1970, MH 78/430.

397. CC(70) 8th mtg, 17 February 1970, CAB 128. Crossman, *Diaries*, iii, pp 820-1, 822-4, 16-17 February 1970. NC (M & SC) 229, 17 February 1970, MH 78/418.

398. Crossman, HC Debates, vol 797, cols 36-43, 2 March 1970. MH 78/418. NC (M & SC) 230, 10 March 1970, MH 78/418. NC (M & SC) 231, 24 March 1970, MH 78/418. NMC Circular, No.152, April 1970.

399. *A Reform of Nursing Education* (RCN, 1964), chairman, Sir Harry Platt.

400. Robinson, HC Debates, vol 732, cols 108-10, 20 July 1966; HM(67)57, 14 September 1967.

401. DHSS, Welsh Office and General Nursing Council mtg, 21 January 1970, DH, M/N 45/116G.

402. Ministry of Health minute, 25 October 1968, DH, M/N 45/116G.

403. *Report of the Nurse Tutor Working Party* (DHSS, 1970).

404. One senior official suggested that an enquiry would 'put the whole thing to bed for a year or two, relieve Ministers inexperienced in nursing politics of some possible trouble, and indeed give them some credit with an awkward profession', Ministry of Health minute, 25 October 1968, DH, M/N 45/116G.

405. DH, M/N 45/116G.

406. Ministry of Health minute, 24 June 1969, DH, M/N 45/116G.

407. 'An Inquiry into Nurse Training', October 1968, DH, M/N 45/116G.

408. DHSS, SHHD, DES mtg, 20 December 1968, DH, M/N 45/110.

409. DHSS weekly policy mtg, 4 August 1969, BN 72/91. SHHD brief for Ministers, 23 July 1969, DH, M/N 45/116A.

410. Exchanges between Treasury and DHSS, August to October 1969, T, 2SS 116/117/04.

411. Report on discussion between Wilson and Crossman, 23 October 1969, DH, M/N 45/116A.

412. Crossman to Wilson, 5 November 1969, Wilson to Crossman, 5 November 1969, Crossman to Wilson, 17 November 1969, Inquiry into Nursing Profession, 1969-1970, PREM 11. Crossman, Serota and officials mtg, 10 November 1969, exchanges over the choice of chairman, October to December 1969, DH, M/N 45/116A.

413. Crossman to Briggs, 9 December 1969, DH, M/N 45/116A. Asa Briggs was a leading historian, authority on Victorian Britain, and the first Vice-Chancellor of Sussex University.

414. Crossman, HC Debates, vol 797, cols 36-43, 2 March 1970.

415. Crossman to Briggs, 3 March 1970, DH, M/N 45/116G.

416. DH, G/H 124/03.

417. Editorial, *Lancet*, 1965, i, 533, 6 March 1965. For an excellent brief review of the subject-matter of the following paragraphs, Stevens, *Medical Practice in Modern England*, pp 306-17.

418. DD(64) 3rd mtg, 17 June 1964, CAB 134/1601.

419. DD(65) 1st mtg, 5 January 1965, CAB 134/1605.

420. *Review Body on Doctors' and Dentists' Remuneration. Third, Fourth and Fifth Reports*, Cmnd. 2585 (HMSO, 1965). The third and fourth reports were concerned with remuneration of senior hospital staff below the rank of consultants, and with minor upward revision in the number of B and C distinction awards.

421. DD(64)98, 30 November 1964, CAB 134/1603.

422. CC(65) 7th mtg, 5 February 1965, CAB 128/39.

423. Editorial, *British Medical Journal*, 1965, i, 203, Supplement, 18, 23 January 1965.

424. *British Medical Journal*, 1965, i, Supplement, 31, 13 February 1965.

425. *Sunday Telegraph*, 21 February 1965.

426. Editorial, *Lancet*, 1965, i, 419-20, 20 February 1965.

427. *British Medical Journal*, i, 1965, Supplement, 51, 20 February 1965.

428. *Daily Telegraph*, 4 October 1963.

429. *Financial Times*, 18 February 1965. Because the BMA press conference was held in the evening of 17 February, it was little noticed in the newspapers the following day.

430. Robinson, HC Debates, vol 706, cols 1203-18, 17 February 1965.

431. Ministry of Health to Review Body, 19 February 1965, in DD(65)18, 22 February 1965, CAB 134/1606.

432. DD(65) 2nd mtg, 25 February 1965, CAB 134/1605.

433. Wilson, HC Debates, vol 707, cols 230-1, 2 March 1965(WA), includes letter from Kindersley to Wilson, 26 February 1965. The source of this letter is DD(65)20, 26 February 1965, CAB 134/1606.

434. Robinson to Wilson, 24 February 1965, Doctors' and Dentists' Remuneration, 1965, PREM 11.

435. Robinson, C(65)37, 26 February 1965, CAB 129/120; CC(65) 13th mtg, 2 March 1965, CAB 128/39; Cabinet Secretary's Notebook (Burke Trend). Brief for Prime Minister on C(65)37, Doctors' and Dentists' Remuneration, 1965, PREM 11.

436. *Times* and *Guardian*, 9 March 1965; *Times, Guardian* and *Daily Telegraph*, 11 March 1965.

437. *British Medical Journal*, 1965, i, 548, Supplement, 51, 20 February 1965. For restatements of the four principles of the charter, Supplement, 63-4, *British Medical Journal*, 1965, i, 603, Supplement, 83, 6 March 1965.

438. *British Medical Journal*, 1965, i, Supplement, 84, 6 March 1965. The six members were J C Cameron, I M Jones, E V Kuenssberg, A M Maiden, D P Stevenson, and W Hedgcock.

439. Editorial, *British Medical Journal*, 1965, i, 669-70, Supplement, 89-96, 13 March 1965.

440. *Financial Times, Times* and *Guardian*, 9 March 1965; *Times, Guardian* and *Daily Telegraph*, 11 March 1965; *Spectator*, 12 March 1965.

441. *Times*, 1 March 1965; *Lancet*, 1965, i, 548, 6 March 1965.

442. Robinson, C(65)43, 15 March 1965, CAB 129/120; CC(65) 16th mtg, 16 March 1965, CAB 128/39.

443. Editorial, *British Medical Journal*, 1965, i, 875-6, Supplement, 113-27, 3 April 1965.

444. SS(65) 6th mtg, 31 March 1965, CAB 134/2535.

445. Robinson, SS(GP)(65)2, 1 April 1965, SS(GP)(65) 1st mtg, 5 April 1965, CAB 134/2538.

446. MH 153/247, 271-277.

447. 'Practice Expenses. Interim Report of informal joint study group of the health departments and the GMSC', 1 April 1964, T, 2SS 1289/01B.

448. Editorial, *British Medical Journal*, 1965, i, 264, 30 January 1965. For a report to the Fraser working party, summarising the views expressed at 28 regional meetings convened by the BMA, Supplement, 27-33.

449. T, 2SS 1288/78/01D.

450. DD(65) 3rd mtg, 25 April 1965, 4th mtg, 12 May 1965, CAB 134/1605.

451. MH 153/298; T, 2SS 1288/78/01D. DD(65) 5th mtg, 27 May 1965, CAB 134/1605; Robinson, SS(GP)(65)5, 21 May 1965, CAB 134/2538. *Remuneration and Terms of Conditions of Service of General Practitioners in the National Health Service. Joint Report of Discussions between General Practitioner Representatives and the Minister of Health* (BMA, 2 June 1965).

452. Diamond and Robinson mtg, 14 May 1965, T, 2SS 1288/78/01D.

453. The General Practice Finance Corporation was introduced under section 8(3) of the National Health Service Act 1966. The first chairman of the Corporation, appointed on 21 March 1966, was Sir Frederick A Hoare Bt, formerly Lord Mayor of London. T, 2SS 1288/1294/01A-B. For the first report of the Corporation published in October 1967, *Report of the General Practice Finance Corporation for the period 21 November 1966-31 March 1967* (HMSO, 1967). Loans and applications for loans amounted to about £2m by the beginning of 1968.

454. Robinson to Wilson, 28 May 1965, Doctors' and Dentists' Remuneration, 1965-66, Part 2, PREM 11.

455. Treasury minute, 18 June 1965, T, 2SS 1288/78/01D.

456. Report of GMSC to BMA Council, 27 May 1965, MH 153/298.

457. Report of BMA Council, 28 May 1965, MH 153/298.

458. For the after-effects of the Swansea resolution, Stevens, *Medical Practice in Modern England*, pp 314-5.

459. Robinson, SS(GP)(65)6, 9 July 1965, SS(GP)(65) 3rd mtg, 13 July 1965, CAB 134/2538.

460. Robinson, SS(GP)(65)6, 9 July 1965, CAB 134/2538.

461. T, 2SS 1288/78/01E.

462. Robinson, SS(GP)(65)7, 23 September 1965, CAB 134/2538.

463. *Family Doctor Service. Second Report of Joint Discussions between General Practitioner Representatives and the Minister of Health* (BMA, 6 October 1965); reprinted in *British Medical Journal*, 1965, ii, Supplement, 153-9, 16 October 1965. A third report, largely consolidating the previous reports, was published on 4 May 1966, and reprinted in *British Medical Journal*, 1966, i, Supplement, 135-43, 7 May 1966.

464. *British Medical Journal*, 1965, ii, Supplement, 149-51, 9 October 1965.

465. Treasury minutes, 24 September 1965 and 29 October 1965, T, 2SS 1288/78/01E.

466. Treasury and DEA mtg, 29 October 1965, T, 2SS 1288/78/01E.

467. T, 2SS 1288/78/01E.

468. Robinson, C(65)147, 9 November 1965, CAB 129/122.

469. CC(65) 62nd mtg, 18 November 1965, CAB 128/39.

470. Kindersley to Wilson, 25 March 1966, Wilson to Kindersley, 29 March 1966, Doctors' and Dentists' Remuneration, 1965-66, Part 2, PREM 11.

471. *Review Body on Doctors' and Dentists' Remuneration. Seventh Report*, Cmnd. 2992 (HMSO, 1966)

472. Treasury minute, 29 March 1966, T, 2SS 1288/78/01F.

473. Treasury minute, 30 March 1966, T, 2SS 1288/78/01F.

474. Brown to Robinson, 5 April 1966, T, 2SS 1288/78/01F.

475. Ross and Robinson, C(66)62, 25 April 1966, CAB 129.

476. Brown and Callaghan, C(66)64, 26 April 1966, CAB 129.

477. CC(66) 21st mtg, 28 April 1966, CAB 128.

478. Robinson to Wilson, 29 April 1966, Doctors' and Dentists' Pay, 1966, PREM 11.

479. Wilson and Kindersley mtg, 3 May 1966, Doctors' and Dentists' Pay, 1966, PREM 11.

480. Wilson, Robinson and medical delegation mtg, 4 May 1966, Doctors' and Dentists' Pay, 1966, PREM 11; MH 149/151.

481. Robinson to Cameron, 4 May 1966, T, 2SS 1288/78/01F. Wilson, HC Debates, vol 727, cols 1629-35, 4 May 1966.

482. Robinson to Callaghan and Brown, 6 May 1966, T, 2SS 1288/78/01F.

483. *Prices and Incomes Standstill*, Cmnd.3073 (HMSO, 1966).

484. Wilson and medical delegation mtg, 1 August 1966, Doctors' and Dentists' Pay 1966-1969, PREM 11. According to Crossman, Robinson once again considered resigning over this issue, *Diaries*, iii, p 587, 26 July 1966. Robinson to Stevenson (2 letters), 1 August 1966, *British Medical Journal*, 1968, ii, Supplement, 93, 6 August 1966.

485. Robinson to Wilson, 4 August 1966, Doctors' and Dentists' Pay, 1966-1969, PREM 11. For acceptance of the duty of doctors to be supportive of the Government's decision, editorial, *British Medical Journal*, 1966, ii, 315, 6 August 1966.

486. Kindersley to Wilson, 3 April 1968, T, 2SS 1288/78/01G. *Review Body on Doctors' and Dentists' Remuneration. Ninth Report*, Cmnd.3600 (HMSO, 1968).

487. *British Medical Journal*, 1968, i, Supplement, 143, 25 May 1968.

488. Editorial, *Times*, 21 July 1968.

489. *Review Body on Doctors' and Dentists' Remuneration. Tenth Report*, Cmnd.3884 (HMSO, 1969). The *Eleventh Report* submitted in May 1969 proposed an increase in the number of distinction awards.

490. DD(68)135, 27 November 1968, CAB 134/2683.

491. Treasury minute, 13 January 1969, T, 2SS 1288/78/01H. Jenkins, C(69)8, 20 January 1969, Short, C(69)13, 21 January 1969, CAB 129. CC(69) 5th mtg, 23 January 1969, CAB 128; Cabinet Secretary's Notebook (Burke Trend). Crossman, *Diaries*, iii, pp 320-1, 325, 329-30, 333-4.

492. Editorial, *British Medical Journal*, 1969, i, 395-6, 15 February 1969.

493. Treasury minute, 19 March 1970, T, 2SS 1288/78/01J.

494. Kindersley to Wilson, 2 April 1970, Doctors' and Dentists' Pay, 1969-1970, PREM 11. DD(70)95, CAB 134/2690.

495. Crossman, *Diaries*, iii, pp 879, 906-7, 935-7.

496. Wilson to Kindersley, 25 April 1970, T, 2SS 1288/78/01J.

497. PM(70) 9th mtg, 16 April 1970, PM(70) 10th mtg, 20 April 1970, CAB 134/3119.

498. Crossman MISC 267(70)1, 1 May 1970, MISC 267(70) 1st mtg, 6 May 1970, CAB 130. Jenkins to Wilson, 8 May 1970, T, 2SS 1288/78/01J.

499. DD(70)100, 102, 106, CAB 134/2690.

500. Stevenson to Wilson, 11 and 18 May 1970, Doctors' and Dentists' Pay, 1969-1970, PREM 11.

501. Wilson to Stevenson, 14 May 1970, T, 2SS 1288/78/01J.

502. PM(70) 14th mtg, 15 May 1970, CAB 134/3119. Wilson to Crossman, 22 May 1970, Wilson to Stevenson, 22 May 1970, Doctors' and Dentists' Pay, 1969-1970, PREM 11.

503. Stevenson to Wilson, 26 May 1970, Doctors' and Dentists' Pay, 1969-1970, PREM 11.

504. Crossman, MISC 267(70)2, 11 May 1970, CAB 130.

505. PM(70) 15th mtg, 26 May 1970, CAB 134/3119. Crossman, *Diaries*, iii, pp 925-7, 26 May 1970.

506. Kindersley was informed on 22 May about Wilson's letter to the professions of the same date, and shown Crossman's imminent statement on the morning of 27 May, DD(7) 14th mtg, 27 May 1970, CAB 134/2687.

507. Crossman, HC Debates, vol 801, cols 2037-42, 28 May 1970.

508. Wilson, Government representatives and delegation from the professions mtg, 28 May 1970, Doctors' and Dentists' Pay, 1969-1970, PREM 11. Crossman, *Diaries*, iii, pp 928-30, 28 May 1970.

509. Kindersley to Wilson, 27 May 1970, Doctors' and Dentists' Pay, 1969-1970, PREM 11.

510. *Review Body on Doctors' and Dentists' Remuneration. Twelfth Report*, Cmnd.4352 (HMSO, 1970).

511. Crossman, MISC 267(70)3, 1 June 1970, MISC(70) 2nd mtg, 2 June 1970, CAB 130. DD(70)117, 4 June 1970, CAB 134/2687. *Times*, 5 June 1970.

512. DD(70) 15th mtg, 4 June 1970, CAB 134/2687. Review Body to Wilson, 4 June 1970, Wilson to Kindersley, 5 June 1970, Doctors' and Dentists' Pay, 1969-1970, PREM 11. For Crossman's interpretation of the resignation, Crossman, *Diaries*, iii, pp 935-70, 4 and 5 June 1970.

513. Editorial, *Times*, 5 June 1970. For Ministers' final deliberations on the action taken by general practitioners, Crossman, MISC 267(70)4, 8 June 1970, MISC(70) 3rd mtg, 9 June 1970, CAB 130.

514. Crossman, *Diaries*, iii, pp 939, 942-3, 946.

515. Webster I, pp 355-6.

516. *Report of the Committee to Consider the Future Numbers of Medical Practitioners and the Appropriate Intake of Medical Students* (HMSO, 1957), para 113; mid-1950s intake total from Walker-Smith, HC Debates, vol 627, cols 18-19, 18 July 1960.

517. Professor Jewkes amplified his doubts in the context of the Robbins Report, *Times*, 8 November 1963.

518. For circulation of the draft paper by Squire, T, 2SS 21/1287/01A; F.Lafitte and J.R.Squire, 'Second Thoughts on the Willink Report', *Lancet*, 1960, ii, 538-42, 3 September 1960.

519. Interdepartmental mtg, 13 September 1960, T, 2SS 21/1287/01A.

520. Treasury minute, 30 December 1960, T, 2SS 21/1287/01A.

521. Powell, HC Debates, vol 650, cols 923-5, 29 November 1961.

522. Treasury to UGC, 20 July 1964, MH 149/344. See also T, 2SS 21/1287/01D.

523. Braine, HC Debates, vol 686, cols 1495-6, 19 December 1963.

524. MH 149/344; DH, 94106/8/11; T, 2SS 21/1287/01D.

525. Barber, HC Debates, vol 699, col 1090, 27 July 1964. The Advisory Committee for the Nottingham Medical School, chaired by Sir George Pickering, Regius Professor of Medicine at Oxford, was established in October 1964; for its ambitious thinking, *Report of the Medical School Advisory Committee* (Nottingham University, June 1965).

526. UGC to Treasury, 28 May 1964, MH 149/344.

527. T, 2SS 21/1287/01D; MH 149/344.

528. Treasury minute, 29 April 1966, T, 2SS 941/867/02B.

529. Robinson, HC Debates, vol 636, cols 26-7, 6 March 1961; Robinson, HC Debates, vol 695, col 96, 14 May 1964.

530. *Report of the Interdepartmental Committee on Medical Schools* (HMSO, 1944).

531. MH 133/83

532. UGC Medical Subcommittee, 13 February 1962, UGC 8/97.

533. UGC Medical Subcommittee, 9 October 1962, 12 December 1963, UGC 8/97. Janet Vaughan had been a member of the Goodenough Committee.

534. Letter to the Chairman of the University Grants Committee, December 1963, signed W Melville Arnott, F W Rogers Brambell, J R Ellis, R J Kellar, Aubrey Lewis, R Milnes Walker, H J Seddon, and Janet Vaughan, Paper 19/M/63, UGC Medical Subcommittee, 9 October 1962, 12 December 1963, UGC 8/97. An annotation to a copy of this document (ED 188/299), as well as a note by Sir George Godber (minute 8 May 1965) suggested that the initiative for this letter came from Arnott, MH 149/336. Arnott was a colleague of Squire at Birmingham.

535. Meeting of senior officials from relevant departments, 16 January 1964, MH 149/335.

536. Ministry of Health minutes, 28 January and 7 February 1964, MH 149/335.

537. ED 188/299-300; MH 149/335; T, 2SS 941/867/01A. These files suggest that the prospective chairman declined on account of known opposition to an enquiry by the GMC.

538. Exchanges between Boyle and Cohen, July to September 1964, ED 188/299-300.

539. Boyle, HC Debates, vol 695, col 96, 14 May 1964.

540. DES brief, 4 November 1964, ED 188/300. Stewart to Robinson, 6 November 1964, Robinson to Stewart, 18 November 1964, T, 2SS 941/867/01A.

541. Stewart, SS(64)8, 4 December 1964, SS(64) 3rd mtg, 9 December 1964, CAB 134/2534; Crosland, C(65)25, 18 February 1965, CAB 129/120; CC(65) 11th mtg, 22 February 1965, CAB 128/39.

542. Ministry of Health minutes, 26 November and 3 December 1964, MH 149/336.

543. Interdepartmental mtg, 30 June 1964, Boyle and Cohen mtg, 21 July 1964, MH 149/335.

544. MH 149/335-6; T, 2SS 941/867/01A.

545. Wilson, HC Debates, vol 715, cols 315-9, 29 July 1965.

546. T, 2SS 941/867/02A.

547. Ministry of Health to DES, 2 December 1964, MH 149/344; interdepartmental mtg, 19 March 1965, MH 149/345.

548. Interdepartmental mtg, 21 May 1965, MH 149/345.

549. Exchanges between Crosland and Robinson, July to August 1965, MH 149/345.

550. Ministry of Health minute, 22 December 1965, MH 149/345.

551. RCME/ 1st mtg, 10 September 1965, ED 129/11.

552. RCME/ 7th mtg, 2 June 1966, ED 129/11; 'Interim Memorandum on Medical Education', 15 June 1966, Todd to Crosland, 17 June 1966, T, 2SS 941/867/01A. This memorandum is reproduced in Appendix 12 of the Royal Commission Report.

553. Treasury minute, 25 May 1965, T, 2SS 941/867/01A.

554. Royal Commission ME, pp 280-1.

555. For trends in doctors and population, see Appendix 3.28.

556. Todd to Wilson, 1 February 1968, T, 2SS 22/02A.

557. Treasury minute, 19 February 1968, 'Royal Commission on Medical Education - Report. Main Recommendations', T, 2SS 22/02A.

558. *Royal Commission on Medical Education 1965-1968. Report.* Cmnd.3569 (HMSO, 1968).

559. Wilson, HC Debates, vol 762, cols 142-3, 4 April 1968 (WA).

560. Royal Commission ME, paras 246-60.

561. Royal Commission ME, para 114.

562. Royal Commission ME, paras 114-32.

563. Royal Commission ME, paras 133-44.

564. Royal Commission ME, para 328.

565. Royal Commission ME, para 364.

566. Royal Commission ME, paras 412-39.

567. Royal Commission ME, para 447.

568. Royal Commission ME, para 453.

569. Royal Commission ME, para 500.

570. Todd to Wilson, 1 February 1968, T, 2SS 22/02A.

571. Royal Commission ME, para 479.

572. Treasury minute, 19 February 1968, T, 2SS 22/02A.

573. Crosland to Callaghan, 10 July 1967, T, 2SS 21/1287/01E.

574. Williams, HC Debates, vol 774, col 530, 8 December 1968 (WA).

575. Treasury minute, 21 August 1968, T, 2SS 22/02B.

576. Treasury minutes and correspondence with DHSS, December 1968, T, 2SS 22/02B.

577. Treasury minute, 18 December 1968, T, 2SS 22/02B.

578. Crossman to Diamond, 10 January 1969, T, 2SS 22/02C.

579. Jenkins and Crossman mtg, 4 March 1969, T, 2SS 22/02D.

580. Diamond to Crossman, 7 March 1969, T, 2SS 22/02D.

581. Crossman to Diamond, 14 March 1969, Jenkins, Diamond, Crossman and officials mtg, 18 March 1969, T, 2SS 22/02D.

582. Crossman, *Diaries*, iii, p 419, 18 March 1969.

583. Crossman, HC Debates, vol 781, cols 806-10, 14 April 1969.

584. For a brief survey, Joan Cooper, *The Creation of the British Personal Social Services 1962-1974* (Heinemann, 1983). For more detailed studies, see below, especially monographs by Hall and Murphy.

585. *Children and Young Persons, Scotland,* Cmnd.2306 (HMSO, Edinburgh, 1964). For excellent discussion of Ingleby and Kilbrandon, J Murphy, *British Social Services. The Scottish Dimension* (Scottish Academic Press, 1992), pp 118-37.

586. Younghusband, *Times,* 11 March 1965. For a similar view, S Hastings and P Jay, *The Family and the Social Services* (Fabian Tract, 359, Fabian Society, February 1965).

887

587. *Times*, 28 April 1965; *Lancet*, 1965, i, 1009; R Titmuss, *Journal of the Royal Society of Health*, 1966, **186**, 19. The lecture was given at Eastbourne on 27 April 1965. This policy was backed by Ann Lapping, 'Is Family Service Enough?', *New Society*, 5 August 1965.

588. Queen's Speech, HC Debates, vol 701, col 40, 3 November 1964.

589. Houghton, SS(64)3, 12 November 1964, CAB 134/2534; Robinson, SS(65)4, 20 January 1965, CAB 134/2536.

590. Alice Bacon, SS(65)5, 2 March 1965, Ross, SS(65)6, 5 March 1965, Robinson, SS(65)8, 5 March 1965, CAB 134/2536; SS(65) 1st mtg, 13 January 1965, SS(65) 4th mtg, 17 March 1965, CAB 134/2535.

591. The links between Titmuss and Judith Hart at the Scottish Office are noted by Cooper, *British Personal Social Services*, and Murphy, *British Social Services: the Scottish Dimension*, pp 138-9. Alice Bacon had served on the Longford Committee and was closely associated with the family service lobby.

592. Houghton, SS(65)9, 22 March 1965, CAB 134/2536; SS(65) 5th mtg, 24 March 1965, CAB 134/2535.

593. CAB, 12/7. MH 156/63; T, 2SS 301/96/04A-B. The family service was supported especially by the Council for Children's Welfare, and the unified social service by a group associated with the Standing Conference of Organisations of Social Workers and the National Institute for Social Work Training.

594. Houghton, Bacon and Robinson mtg, 2 June 1965, T, 2SS 301/96/04A.

595. Houghton, SS(65)24, 29 June 1965, CAB 134/2536; SS(65) 13th mtg, 7 July 1965, CAB 134/2535.

596. Interdepartmental mtg, 9 July 1965, MH 156/63.

597. *The Child, the Family and the Young Offender*, Cmnd. 2742 (HMSO, 1965).

598. Jenkins, H(65)55, 20 June 1965, Houghton, H(65)57, 28 June 1965, CAB 134/1999; HA(65) 13th mtg, 2 July 1965, CAB 134/1997.

599. Interdepartmental officials mtg, 10 May 1965, T, 2SS 301/96/04A.

600. Robinson to Houghton, c.10 July 1965, MH 156/63.

601. For exchanges over establishing the Seebohm Committee, MH 156/63-64; T, 2SS 301/96/04B.

602. Seebohm was knighted in 1970, and obtained a life peerage in 1972.

603. See Standing Conference of Organisations of Social Workers, Discussion Paper No.1, *The Reorganisation of Social Work Services*, 1965.

604. In March 1965, on the basis of her experience as Chairman of the LCC Children's Committee, Mrs Serota passed on to Houghton a detailed plan for a new Family Service, T, 2SS 301/96/04A.

605. Of the nine members of the committee apart from the Chairman, R Huws Jones of the National Institute for Social Work Training, Dr R A Parker of the Department of Social Administration, LSE, and Professor J N Morris of the London School of Hygiene and Tropical Medicine, had particularly close associations with Titmuss. The other members of the Seebohm Committee, apart from those already named, were P Leonard of NISWT, Sir Charles Barratt and W

E Lane representing local government organisations, and M R F Simson of the National Corporation for the Care of Old People.

606. See Titmuss, see note 171 above.

607. Soskice, HC Debates, vol 722, col 373, 20 December 1965.

608. For a useful short study of the Seebohm Committee, P Hall, *Reforming the Welfare. The politics of change in the Personal Social Services* (Heinemann, 1976).

609. HLG 120/762.

610. Robinson to Houghton, 17 June 1966, and following exchanges, CAB 253/2.

611. Seebohm, Ministers and officials mtg, c.July 1966, CAB 253/2.

612. The Seebohm Report was passed to the Prime Minister on 23 April 1968, CAB 253/2. For full discussion of the work of the Seebohm Committee, Hall, *Reforming the Welfare*, pp 36-80.

613. *Report of the Committee on the Local Authority and Allied Personal Social Services*, Cmnd.3707 (HMSO, 1968). For initial tension between Seebohm and Robinson over the Seebohm Report, Crossman, *Diaries*, iii, pp 22, 86.

614. HLG 120/761-2, 935-48.

615. With the exception of junior training centres which should transfer to Local Education Departments.

616. Editorial, *Times*, 24 July 1968.

617. Editorial, *Guardian*, 24 July 1968.

618. Editorial, *Times*, 24 July 1968.

619. Editorial, *Lancet*, 1968, ii, 201-2, 27 July 1968.

620. Editorial, *British Medical Journal*, 1968, ii, 197-8, 27 July 1968.

621. Peter Townsend, 'Family Welfare and Seebohm', *New Society*, 1 August 1968, pp 159-60.

622. Kilbrandon Report, paras 90-7.

623. Ross, SS(66)22, 15 July 1966, CAB 134/3280.

624. SS(66) 7th mtg, 21 July 1966, CAB 134/3280.

625. *Social Work and the Community*, Cmnd. 3065 (HMSO, Edinburgh, 1966).

626. Murphy, *British Social Services. The Scottish Dimension*, pp 138-84, for a full discussion of these events.

627. DH, E/S190/7C-F, H/S 19/1A-D.

628. T, 2SS 301/469/01A.

629. Crossman, *Diaries*, iii, pp 147, 150-1, 160, 553-5.

630. Cabinet Office minute, 17 July 1968, CAB 253/2.

631. Treasury minute, 12 July 1968, T, 2SS 301/469/01A.

632. Callaghan, Short, Greenwood and Robinson, C(68)88, 16 July 1968, CAB 129; CC(68) 36th mtg, 18 July 1968, CAB 128.

633. Crossman and Seebohm mtg, 4 November 1968, CAB, 18/4 Part 2.

634. Ministry of Health to Treasury, 4 July 1968, Home Office to Treasury, 4 July 1968, T, 2SS 301/469/01A.

635. LGRP(68) 1st mtg, 22 July 1968, 2nd mtg, 18 September 1968, T, 2SS 301/469/01A.

636. Treasury minute, 19 August 1968, T, 2SS 301/469/01B.

637. Crossman, SS(69)4, 14 February 1969, CAB 134/3286. For a review of responses to Seebohm, Hall, *Reforming the Welfare*, pp 81-97.

638. SS(69) 1st mtg, 19 February 1969, CAB 134/3285.

639. SS(O)(69), 2nd mtg, 3 March 1969, CAB 134/3295. The agreed recommendations of officials concerning draft legislation were embodied in SS(O)(69)9, 14 May 1969, CAB 134/3295.

640. Treasury minute, 8 May 1969, T, 2SS 301/469/01D.

641. SS(69) 4th mtg, 20 May 1969, SS(69) 8th mtg, 9 July 1969, CAB 134/3285; Robinson, SS(69)36, 8 July 1969, Callaghan and Crossman, SS(69)37, 8 July 1969, CAB 134/3287. Crossman, C(69)81, 14 July 1969, CAB 129; CC(69) 33rd mtg, 16 July 1969, CAB 128; Cabinet Secretary's Notebook (Burke Trend). Treasury minute, 2 July 1969, T, 2SS 301/469/01D. For Crossman's perspective, *Diaries*, iii, pp 498-9, 554-5, 571-2. Thomson's argument related to Government's difficulties over the House of Commons (Redistribution of Seats)(No.2) Bill.

642. Crossman, HC Debates, vol 787, cols 435-6, 24 July 1969 (WA).

643. Hall, *Reforming the Welfare*, pp 92-3, 96-7, 140-7; B Lapping, 'Go-Slow on Seebohm', *New Society*, 6 February 1969, pp 208-9; C Smart, 'Parliament and Seebohm', *British Hospital Journal and Social Service Review*, 5 September 1969, pp 1664-5. Cooper, *British Personal Social Services*, pp 105-8.

644. HC Debates, vol 790, cols 631-2, 28 October 1969.

645. Treasury minute, 13 November 1969, T, 2SS 301/469/01D.

646. Sir M. Stevenson, SS(69)59, 27 October 1969, Crossman, Callaghan and Thomas, SS(69)63, 12 November 1969, CAB 134/3288; SS(69) 16th mtg, 14 November 1969, CAB 134/3285. Crossman, SS(69)60, 27 November 1969, Association of Municipal Corporations to DHSS, SS(69)69, 18 December 1969, CAB 134/3288; SS(69) 17th mtg, 18 December 1969, CAB 134/3285.

647. Crossman, C(70)3, 8 January 1970, Crosland, C(70)4, 8 January 1970, CAB 129; CC(70) 1st mtg, 13 January 1970, CAB 128; Cabinet Secretary's Notebook (Burke Trend). Crossman, *Diaries*, iii, p 780.

648. Crossman, HC Debates, vol 796, cols 1406-22, 26 February 1970.

649. Callaghan, SS(70)26, 19 March 1970, CAB 134/3290; SS(70) 7th mtg, 24 March 1970, CAB 134/3289. Callaghan, HC Debates, vol 801, cols 309-10, 14 May 1970 (WA).

650. Cooper, *British Personal Social Services*, pp 112-22.

651. Chief Medical Officer to Permanent Secretary, 3 May 1965, MH 150/64.

652. Exchanges between Robinson and JCC, July to September 1965, MH 150/64. SHHD submission to Ministers, 22 November 1965, MH 150/64.

653. *Administrative Practice of Hospital Boards in Scotland. Report of a Committee of the Health Services Council* (HMSO, Edinburgh, 1966), paras 212, 231-2. William Marshall Farquharson-Lang was Chairman of the North Eastern RHB, and Vice-Chairman of ths SHSC. This committee contained eight members, only two of whom were medical.

654. For incomplete papers relating to the English working party, MH 150/65-67.

655. *Organisation of Medical Work in the Hospital Service in Scotland* (HMSO, Edinburgh, 1967); *First Report on the Organisation of Medical Work in Hospitals* (HMSO, 1967).

656. *Organisation of Medical Work in Hospitals*, p 7.

657. Editorial, *Hospital and Social Services Review*, November 1967.

658. Ministry of Health and SMOH mtg, 16 October 1967, MH 150/68.

659. Chief Medical Officer minute, 8 September 1970, DH, G/C 367/01A.

660. *Second Report of the Joint Working Party on the Organisation of Medical Work in Hospitals* (HMSO, 1972). The Scottish Working Party was reconstituted in December 1969; it elaborated detailed schemes for medical advisory structures relevant to all groups of doctors working a unified health service, *Doctors in an Integrated Health Service* (HMSO, Edinburgh, 1971).

661. See Appendices 3.25, 3.26.

662. DH, K/P 311/03E.

663. DH minute, 11 August 1966, DH, K/P 311/03E.

664. SAMOs mtg, 27 October 1966, RHB Chairmen mtg, 21 February 1967, DH, K/P 311/03E.

665. Zuckerman to Ministers, 29 August 1968, Robinson to Zuckerman, 3 October 1968, MH 195/6. Zuckerman was former Professor of Zoology at Birmingham University, Deputy Chairman of the Advisory Council on Scientific Policy, and Chief Scientific Adviser, 1964-1971. He received a peerage in 1971. The Zuckerman Committee was a joint Ministry of Health-SHHD venture. Out of the seven members, Professor A R Currie, Regius Professor of Pathology at Aberdeen, represented Scotland.

666. Ministry of Health minute, 2 August 1968, MH 195/6.

667. *Hospital Scientific and Technical Services. Report of the Committee 1967-1968. Chairman: Sir Solly Zuckerman* (HMSO, 1968).

668. *Hospital Scientific and Technical Services*, para 8.2.

669. Ennals, HC Debates, vol 774, cols 1961-5, 6 December 1968.

670. Webster I, pp 255-6; G Larkin, *Occupational Monopoly and Modern Medicine* (Tavistock, 1983).

671. General Whitley Council to DHSS, 11 November 1969, DH, K/P 311/02A

672. Crossman, HC Debates, vol 795, cols 252-3, 9 February 1970.

673. DH, K/P 311/4A.

674. For authoritative discussion, see J Lewis, *What Price Community Medicine? The philosophy, practice and politics of public health since 1919* (Wheatsheaf, 1919). See also Webster I, pp 373-80; Lindsey, *Socialized Medicine in England and Wales*, pp 364-96.

675. Royal Commission ME, para 51.

676. Royal Commission ME, paras 133-44.

677. *Report of the Committee on Personal Social Services*, paras 381-6.

678. Crossman, Serota, officials and SMOH mtg, 15 October 1969, DH, J/N 179/44A.

679. Dr Hunter was knighted in 1977, and he became a life peer in 1978.

680. DH, J/N 179/01A.

Chapter IV
LABOUR AND REORGANISATION

1. Klein, *Politics of the NHS*, pp 31-61; Lindsey, *Socialized Medicine in England and Wales*, pp 94-8, 146-9, 450-4; Webster I, pp 396-7.

2. SHHD, 'Structure of the National Health Service in Scotland', HH 101/2283.

3. HH 101/1187.

4. Medical Services Review Committee, *A Review of the Medical Services in Great Britain* (Social Assay, 1962). For background to the Porritt Committee, Lindsey, *Socialized Medicine in England and Wales*, pp 146-9.

5. *Review of the Medical Services*, para 77.

6. The report pronounced in favour of giving tax relief for private health insurance, and for providing medicines at prescription cost to private patients, paras 129, 132.

7. Stevens, *Medical Practice in Modern England*, pp 248, 263.

8. HH 102/492. G Murray Jones, 'An Area Health Board for Wales', *British Hospital. Journal*, 6 January 1967.

9. MH 153/345.

10. 'Area Health Boards in Wales', *British Medical Journal*, 1968, i, Supplement, 19-21, 27 January 1968. See also *British Medical Journal*, 1967, ii, Supplement, 65-66, 9 December 1967, for divisions of opinion within the BMA over the Porritt Report and Welsh BMA proposals. For the full report, Welsh Committee of BMA, 'Second Report of Subcommittee on Area Health Boards', HH 101/3605.

11. HH 101/2031.

12. HH 101/492, 2282, 3225.

13. HH 101/492, 2031.

14. Porritt to Robinson, 23 November 1964, MH 153/345.

15. MH 150/64; HH 101/3226.

16. MH 150/64.

17. Ministry of Health minute, 26 November 1964, MH 153/345.

18. Porritt to Robinson, 11 February 1965, Robinson to Porritt, 1 March 1965, MH 153/345.

19. MH 153/345.

20. MH 150/64; HH 101/3226.

21. MH 150/64.

22. *The British National Health Service. Conversations with Sir George Godber*, p 18.

23. DH, J/N 179/32.

24. Robinson, HC Debates, vol 733, cols 1151-72, 9 August 1966. The reference in the Foreword to the 1968 Green Paper (pp 5-6) was added at the Minister's instigation.

25. Robinson, SS(65)16, 14 May 1965, CAB 134/2536; SS(65) 10th mtg, 26 May 1965, CAB 134/2535. For inconsequential negotiations with the Treasury on this plan, T, 2SS 21/98/05.

26. Crossman, *Diaries*, ii, p 331, 21 September 1965; Alexander, *The Politics of Local Government*, pp 17-19.

27. *Report of the Committee on the Staffing of Local Government* (HMSO, 1967), p 71.

28. Royal Commission ME, paras 472-82, 489-501.

29. T, 2SS 301/96/04A.

30. *Revision of the Hospital Plan for Scotland* (HMSO, Edinburgh, 1966), chapter 1.

31. *Organisation of Medical Work in the Hospital Service in Scotland* (HMSO, Edinburgh, 1967), p 11.

32. National Board for Prices and Incomes, *Report No. 60. Pay of Nurses and Midwives in the National Health Service*, Cmnd.3585 (HMSO, 1968), para 90; this enquiry began in June 1967 and the report was published in March 1968. See also *Report No.29. The Pay and Conditions of Manual Workers in Local Authorities, the National Health Service, Gas and Water Supply*, Cmnd.3230 (HMSO, 1967), paras 71-2.

33. See for instance, *Public Employees Journal*, November 1965, which records support for reorganisation from NUPE and MPU, as well as the TUC General Council.

34. L Pavitt, *The Health of the Nation. The Second Stage of the NHS* (Fabian Society, 1965).

35. D Paige and K Jones, *Health and Welfare Services in Britain in 1975* (Cambridge University Press, 1966), pp 27, 35-6, 130.

36. See, for instance, King's Fund, *Working Together. The Shape of Hospital Management in 1980* (King's Fund, 1967); F Prochaska, *Philanthropy and the Hospitals*, pp 215-21; G McLachlan, *History of the NPHT*, pp 107-35.

37. *Report of the Royal Commission on Medical Education*, Cmnd. 3569 (HMSO, 1968), para 56.

38. Braine, HC Debates, vol 773, cols 1155-60, 9 August 1966.

39. Owen, HC Debates, vol 773, cols 1151-55, 9 August 1966.

40. Robinson, HC Debates, vol 773, cols 1160-72, 9 August 1966.

41. HH 101/3226.

42. Treasury to Ministry of Health, September 1965, T, 2SS 21/98/04.

43. HH 101/2282, 3226.

44. SHHD, 'Report of Working Group Study, Amalgamation of NHS Bodies', 16 September 1965, HH 101/2030.

45. HH 101/3225.

46. SHHD minute, 26 January 1966, HH 101/3225.

47. HH 102/492.

48. SHHD minutes, 10 January and 8 February 1966, HH 101/3225, 29 June 1966, HH 101/2282.

49. For Robinson's continuing defence of co-ordination within the existing structure and experiment, HC Debates, vol 733, col 1172, 9 August 1966, and in an interview with the medical press, *Lancet*, 1966, ii, 957-9, 29 October 1966.

50. SHHD minute, 5 September 1966, HH 101/2282.

51. T, 2SS 21/98/04.

52. SHHD minute, 27 April 1966, HH 101/3225.

53. HH 101/2282.

54. Ross minute, 4 August 1966, and Ross, Millan and officials mtg, 9 August 1966, HH 101/2282.

55. Hennessey, *Whitehall*, pp 190-202.

56. T, 2SS 21/01A.

57. *Report into the Cost of the NHS*, paras 142-6; Powell, *Medicine and Politics*, pp 10-11; Acton, 6, pp 61-3; J Wiseman, 'A Health Corporation', *British Medical Journal*, 1967, ii, 102-3, 8 April 1967. For background, Lindsey, *Socialized Medicine in England and Wales*, pp 97-8. The Select Committee on Estimates questioned Sir John Hawton about the possibility of placing the NHS under a quasi-independent corporation, *Select Committee on Estimates, Sixth Report 1956/57*, Q.2866-70.

58. *The Civil Service. Volume 1. Report of the Committee 1966-68. Chairman: Lord Fulton*, Cmnd. 2638 (HMSO, 1968), paras 188-90. For evidence of Sir A France opposing hiving-off, 18 July 1967, BA 1/9.

59. *The Civil Service, Volume 5*, pp 584-604.

60. T, 2SS 21/01A.

61. SHHD minute, 7 November 1966, reports that R Huws Jones and Professor J N Morris had been exerting influence in favour of reorganisation in 'the highest possible quarters', HH 101/2282.

62. Ministry of Health memorandum, 'NHS Integration', 22 June 1966, HH 101/2282.

63. SHHD minute, 28 September 1966, HH 101/2282.

64. SHHD minutes, 21 December 1966 and 11 January 1967, HH 101/2282.

65. DH, J/N 179/14A.

66. HLG 69/4, 902.

67. SHHD minute, 23 January 1967, HH 101/2282.

68. SHHD minute, 7 February 1967, HH 101/2282.

69. MH and Scottish Office Ministers and officials mtg, 10 April 1967, HH 101/2282.

70. Stevenson to Robinson, 21 December 1966, DH, J/N 179/11.

71. Robinson, HC Debates, vol 746, col 250, 2 May 1967 (WA).

72. Treasury minute, 27 June 1967, T, 2SS 21/01A.

73. LP(67)9, 2 July 1967, DH, J/N 179/14A.

74. HH 101/2282. Treasury minute, 19 September 1967, T, 2SS 21/01A.

75. DH, J/N 179/14A.

76. Treasury minute, 19 September 1967, T, 2SS 21/01A.

77. DH, J/N 179/14A. Exchange of letters between Robinson and Ross, October 1967, HH 101/2282.

78. Robinson, SS(67)19, 13 October 1967, Ross, SS(67)22, 13 October 1967, CAB 134/3281; SS(67) 3rd mtg, 18 October 1967, CAB 134/3281.

79. Robinson, HC Debates, vol 753, cols 643-4, 6 November 1967. Ross, HC Debates, vol 753, col 102, 7 November 1968 (WA).

80. CAB 134/3196, 3198 HC Debates, vol 744, cols 244-51, for explanation of Green Paper procedure by Michael Stewart.

81. 'First Draft Green Paper', 8 November 1967, DH, J/N 179/14A. An untitled draft was circulated on 5 October 1967, HH 101/2283.

82. T, AT 1159/02A-B; DH, J/N 179/12B.

83. Ministry of Health minute, 30 October 1967, DH, J/N 179/14A.

84. Report of meeting with the Royal Commission on Local Government, 30 April 1968, DH, J/N 179/11.

85. Treasury minute, 15 February 1968, T, 2SS 21/01B.

86. On rival ideas on reorganisation within the Treasury, see for instance, minute of 28 February 1968, T, 2SS 21/01B.

87. T, 2SS 21/01A; DH, J/N 179/12B.

88. T, 2SS 21/01C; DH, J/N 179/12B.

89. *British Medical Journal*, 1968, i, Supplement, 86, 23 March 1968.

90. DH, J/N 179/11.

91. DH, J/N 179/11.

92. CAB, 16/1 Part I.

93. T, 2SS 21/01C; DH, J/N 179/12B, including Treasury and Ministry of Health mtg about their differences over the Green Paper, 7 May 1968. For a further meeting, 5 July 1968 and correspondence between Taverne and Robinson, DH, J/N 179/12C.

94. Ministry of Health minute, 22 March 1968, DH, J/N 179/12B.

95. SS(68) 9th mtg, 28 May 1968, CAB 134/3282; Robinson, C(68)82, 1 July 1968, CAB 129; CC(68) 35th mtg, 9 July 1968, CAB 128. Cabinet Secretary's Notebook (Burke Trend). Crossman, *Diaries*, iii, pp 86, 128.

96. Wilson to Robinson, 27 May 1968, DH, J/N 179/12C.

97. DH, J/N 179/12C. Robinson's public relations coup was also undermined by a leak in the *Daily Telegraph*, 20 May 1968.

98. DH, J/N 179/12C.

99. Crossman, *Diaries*, iii, p 154.

100. *National Health Service. The Administrative Structure of the Medical and Related Services in England and Wales* (HMSO, 1968), paras 54-6.

101. *National Health Service. Administrative Structure in England and Wales*, para 18.

102. *National Health Service. Administrative Structure in England and Wales*, paras 63-5.

103. *National Health Service. Administrative Structure in England and Wales*, paras 57-9.

104. *National Health Service. Administrative Structure in England and Wales*, paras 43-7.

105. *National Health Service. Administrative Structure in England and Wales*, paras 78-82.

106. *National Health Service. Administrative Structure in England and Wales*, paras 69-71.

107. SHHD, 'Structure of the National Health Service in Scotland', HH 101/2283.

108. HH 101/2031; SHHD, HOS 2/170.

109. Ross, SS(68)46, 13 November 1968, CAB 134/3284; SS(68) 19th mtg, 27 November 1968, CAB 134/3282.

110. SHHD, *Administrative Reorganisation of the Scottish Health Services* (HMSO, Edinburgh, 1968).

111. *Administrative Reorganisation of the Scottish Health Services*, para 72.

112. Ministry of Health minute, December 1968, DH, J/N 179/14C.

113. Crossman, *Diaries*, iii, pp 86, 753.

114. *The Scotsman*, 13 December 1968. For other advocates of the local government option, McLachlan, *Improving the Common Weal*, pp 130-1.

115. *Royal Commission on Local Government in Scotland, Report*, Cmnd. 4150 (HMSO, Edinburgh, 1969), paras 540-9.

116. Reports on reception of the Scottish Green Paper, T, 2SS 21/01G; HH 101/2030, 2284, 3606; CAB 152/91.

117. DH, J/N 179/11.

118. Editorial, *Lancet*, 1969, i, 31-2, 4 January 1969.

119. DH, J/N 179/14C.

120. DH, J/N 179/50-56.

121. The Royal Medico-Psychological Association was one of the few major medical bodies not to comment adversely on the abolition of regions, DH, E/S 190/7C.

122. Editorial, *Times*, 30 January 1969.

123. Crossman and Stevenson mtg, 18 November 1968, DH, J/N 179/11.

124. Muriel Bowen, *Sunday Times*, 5 October 1969.

125. Crossman, *Diaries*, iii, pp 328-9.

896

126. Crossman, *Diaries*, iii, pp 329, 613, 804-5.

127. Crossman, *Diaries*, iii, p 456.

128. Crossman, *Diaries*, iii, pp 456, 499, 737-8, 745-6 for the sympathies of Crossman with the local authority lobby.

129. Crossman, *Diaries*, iii, p 673.

130. DHSS minutes, December 1968, DH, J/N 179/14C.

131. RHB Chairmen and Minister of State mtg, 17 December 1968, DH, J/N 179/14C.

132. DHSS mtgs, 10 and 17 January 1969, DH, J/N 179/14C.

133. *Times*, 29 February 1969.

134. DH, E/S 190/7F.

135. CAB, 16/1 Part III.

136. CAB, 16/1 Part VI.

137. Crossman and officials mtg, 2 May 1969, DH, J/N 179/14C.

138. CAB, 16/1 Part III.

139. Serota, SS(69)20, 15 May 1969, CAB 134/3287; SS(69) 4th mtg, 20 May 1969, CAB 134/3285.

140. Crossman, *Diaries*, iii, p 499.

141. Crossman, SS(69)28, 19 June 1969, CAB 134/3287; SS(69) 6th mtg, 23 June 1969, CAB 134/3285. This outcome was not mentioned in Crossman's *Diaries*.

142. See especially, Treasury minute, 24 June 1969, T, 2SS 21/01G.

143. Treasury minute, 25 June 1969, T, 2SS 21/01G.

144. Crossman, SS(69)31, 27 June 1969, Taverne, SS(69)35, 2 July 1969, CAB 134/3287; SS(69) 7th mtg, 3 July 1969, CAB 134/3285. This episode was also not mentioned in Crossman's *Diaries*.

145. See below, n.152.

146. Treasury minute, 9 July 1969, T, 2SS 21/01H.

147. T, 2SS 21/01H.

148. T, 2SS 21/01J.

149. CAB, 16/1 Part III. DHSS, LP Division minute, October 1969, DH, J/N 179/14D.

150. CAB, 16/1 Part III; DH, J/N 179/14D. Crossman, *Diaries*, iii, p 605.

151. CAB, 16/4 Part I.

152. *Royal Commission on Local Government in England Report*, vol 1, Cmnd. 4040 (HMSO, 1969), paras 359-67, 574, vol 2, D Senior, *Memorandum of Dissent*, paras 283-308.

153. For instance, the Treasury made a high-level approach to DHSS demanding that regional bodies should contain no representatives, and suggesting that they were best constituted as branches of the central department, Treasury to DHSS, 26 August 1969, CAB, 16/1 Part III.

154. For a summary of departmental positions on reorganisation, see Treasury and CSD mtg, 11 September 1969, T, 2SS 21/01J. See also Treasury to DHSS, 16 September 1969, and Treasury and DHSS mtg, 18 September 1969, DH, J/N 179/14D. For Judith Hart's views on participation, see her speech reported in *Times*, 20 September 1969.

155. Crossman, *Diaries*, iii, p 605, 4 August 1969.

156. Crossman, *Diaries*, iii, pp 605, 606, 613, 621, 752-3.

157. Serota, SS(69)54, 2 October 1969. Taverne, SS(69)56, 6 October 1969, CAB 134/3288; SS(69) 12th mtg, 9 October 1969, CAB 134/3285. Crossman, *Diaries*, iii, p 673.

158. Treasury minute, 'Management Structure of Future NHS', October 1969, T, 2SS 21/01K.

159. PM(69) 14th mtg, 21 October 1969, CAB 134/3118 The brief prepared for the Prime Minister for this meeting by CSD, 15 October 1969, was generally favourable to the Treasury position, NHS Reorganisation, 1969-1970, PREM 11. Crossman, *Diaries*, iii, p 692, for his own more positive perspective on this meeting.

160. DH, J/N 179/12F, 14E.

161. Crossman, *Diaries*, iii, p 712.

162. Taverne to Crossman, 5 November 1969, T, 2SS 21/01K; Crossman to Taverne, 6 November 1969, T, 2SS 21/01L.

163. CAB, 16/1 Part VII. For Crossman's preliminary meetings with the local authority associations on 6 February and 17 July 1969, CAB 151/91.

164. Crossman, weekly mtg, 10 November 1969, BN 72/91.

165. Crossman, *Diaries*, iii, pp 737-8.

166. DH, J/N 179/14E. Crossman, *Diaries*, iii, pp 745-6.

167. Serota, weekly mtg, 8 December 1969, BN 72/91.

168. Crossman and officials mtgs, 4 and 9 December 1969, CAB 16/1 Part VI.

169. CAB, 16/1 Part VI; DH, J/N 179/12E; Crossman, *Diaries*, iii, pp 752-3.

170. CAB, 16/1 Part VI.

171. On the inspiration of Crossman, the scheme evolved in December 1969 reduced the areas to 64, and envisaged still further reduction, CAB, 16/1 Part VI; *Reform of Local Government in England*, Cmnd. 4276, (HMSO, 1970).

172. CAB, 16/1 Part VII.

173. Treasury minute, 31 December 1969, T, 2SS 21/01M.

174. Jenkins, minute on SS(69)73, T, 2SS 21/01M.

175. DH, J/N 179/12F.

176. Crossman, *Diaries*, iii, pp 773-4, 778.

177. Crossman, SS(69)73, 29 December 1969, CAB 134/3288; SS(70) 1st mtg, 2 January 1970, CAB 134/3289. Crossman, SS(70)3, 8 January 1970, CAB 134/3289; SS(70) 2nd mtg, 12 January 1970, CAB 134/3289.

178. For initial exchanges between Crossman and Ross on this issue, HH 101/3606.

179. T, 2SS 21/01N.

180. CC(70) 2nd mtg, 15 January 1970, CAB 128. Cabinet Secretary's Notebook (Burke Trend). Crossman, *Diaries*, iii, pp 781-2.

181. CC(70) 3rd mtg, 20 January 1970, CAB 128. Cabinet Secretary's Notebook (Burke Trend). Crossman, *Diaries*, iii, pp 784-5. Burke Trend's briefs on the relevant memoranda, 14 and 19 January 1970, are not as favourable to Crossman as the latter believed, NHS Reorganisation, 1969-1970, PREM 11.

182. Crossman, SS(70)10, 23 January 1970, SS(70) 3rd mtg, 28 January 1970, CAB 134/3289; CC(70) 5th mtg, 3 February 1970, CAB 128.

183. Report of Subcommittee of the Welsh Committee on Area Health Boards, May 1966, HH 102/492.

184. Second Report of Subcommittee on Area Health Boards, February 1968, HH 101/3605.

185. *Royal Commission on the Constitution 1969-1973. Volume 1. Report*, Cmnd. 5460 (HMSO, 1973), para 354.

186. WO, NHSR 1/1.

187. Thomas, SS(69)27, 18 June 1969, Thomas, SS(69)30, 30 June 1969, CAB 134/3287.

188. Treasury minute, 20 June 1969, T, 2SS 21/02A. Thomas, SS(69)55, 6 October 1969, CAB 134/3288; SS(69) 12th mtg, 9 October 1969, CAB 134/3285; Thomas, SS(70)15, 10 February 1970, Thomas SS(70)16, 12 February 1970, CAB 134/3290; SS(70) 5th mtg, 16 February 1970, CAB 134/3289.

189. WO, NHSR 1/1; DH, J/N 179/12E. An early hint of this thinking was given at a meeting in London of Welsh Ministers with the BMA, where it was mentioned that the upper tier in Wales was likely to 'be linked with a Welsh elected council', 5 March 1969, DH, E/S 190/7F.

190. WO, HL 34/92/1 Part 1.

191. Welsh Office to DHSS, 10 November 1969, DH, J/N 179/12F; Welsh Office to Treasury, 17 November 1969, T, 2SS 21/02A.

192. DH, J/N 179/12E.

193. WO, NHSR 1/2 Part 1; Welsh Office to Treasury, 9 December 1969, T, 2SS 21/02A; Welsh Office to DHSS, 9 December 1969, DH, J/N 179/12F.

194. Welsh Office to Treasury, 16 January 1970, T, 2SS 21/02A.

195. *The Reorganisation of the Health Service in Wales* (HMSO, 1970).

196. Welsh Office, *Local Government Reorganisation in Glamorgan and Monmouthshire*, Cmnd.4310 (HMSO, 1970). Pearce, *The Machinery of Change in Local Government*, pp 81-2, 122, 128.

197. WO, NHSR 1/2 Part 2.

198. CAB, 16/1 Part VIII.

199. Opening the title with 'National Health Service' was consistent with the first Green Paper, but was more understandable in 1968 because NHS was not

subsequently repeated. The first Green Paper specifically mentioned 'England and Wales'; after brief discussion 'England' was omitted from the title of the second Green Paper. In announcing the imminent publication of this document, Crossman referred to it as the 'Green Paper with white edges', HC Debates, vol 795, col 904, 9 February 1970.

200. *Lancet*, 1970, i, 341-2, 14 February, 1970.

201. *British Medical Journal*, 1970, i, 379-80, 14 February 1970.

202. DH, J/N 179/23E, 110. *Times*, 7 May 1970.

203. *Lancet*, 1970, i, 705-6, 4 April 1970.

204. DH, J/N 179/110. Fabian Society, *The National Health Service. Three Views* (Fabian Society, 1970).

205. Crossman, *Diaries*, iii, p 814. HC Debates, vol 315, cols 1255-61, 11 February 1970.

206. Crossman, *Diaries*, iii, pp 834-5, 25 February 1970.

207. Ministers and RHB Chairmen mtg, 22 April 1970, WO, NHSR 1/68/3.

208. Crossman, *Diaries*, iii, p 900, 23 April 1970.

209. For Crossman's Advisory Group on Regional Health Councils, which met in March and April 1970, WO, NHSR 1/68/1. For a report on Crossman's concessions to the RHBs, weekly mtg, 1 April 1970, BN 72/92.

210. Crossman, *Diaries*, iii, pp 876-7, 895-6, 1 and 22 April 1970.

211. Discussion Paper on Regional Health Councils, 7 May 1970, CAB, 16/4 Part I.

212. Ministers and CHSC mtg, 2 June 1970, WO, NHSR 1/68/3.

213. DHSS minute, 4 May 1970, SHHD, HOS 2/170.

214. DH, J/N 179/111A; CAB, 16/4 Part I.

215. CAB, 16/4 Part I; T, 2SS 21/01P.

216. Treasury to DHSS, 5 June 1970, CAB, 16/4 Part I; T, 2SS 21/286/01.

217. MHLG to DHSS, 9 June 1970, CAB, 16/4 Part I; DoE, LG 7/505/18.

218. Crossman, *Diaries*, iii, p 943.

Chapter V
VALUE FOR MONEY

1. *Times*, 5, 6, and 8 June 1970. Crossman, *Diaries*, iii, p 941.

2. Webster, 'The elderly and the Early NHS', in Pelling and Smith, eds, *Life and Death of the Elderly*, pp 169-70; Acton, 5, p 67; HLG 120/1103.

3. See Appendix 1.1. *Times*, 22 June 1970.

4. Morrison Halcrow, *A Single Mind - Keith Joseph* (Macmillan, 1987); Joseph interview with A Seldon, *Contemporary Record*, 1987, **1**, 26-31; Profile by Ronald Butt, *Times*, 6 May 1971; Obituaries, *Independent on Sunday, Observer, Sunday Telegraph,* and *Sunday Times*, 11 December 1994, *Guardian, Independent, Daily Telegraph,* and *Times*, 12 December 1994. *All Souls College. Keith Joseph. Addresses delivered at the Commemorative Gathering. 3 June 1995* (All Souls College, Oxford, 1995). For general political context, Ramsden, *The Winds of Change: Macmillan to*

Heath, 1957-1975, chapter 6; J Campbell, *Edward Heath* (Cape, 1993). For the politics of welfare, see Timmins, *Five Giants*, chapter 14.

5.   There was also Enoch Powell, who kept up some interest in health; see his *A New Look at Medicine and Politics* (Pitman, 1966), but this was not his main political avocation, see Paul Foot, *The Rise of Enoch Powell* (Penguin, 1969).

6.   Howe, 'Reform of the Social Services. Conservatism in the post-Welfare State', in Bow Group, *Principles in Practice* (Conservative Political Centre, 1961), pp 58-73.

7.   Crossman, *Diaries*, iii, pp 426-7, on Crossman's good opinion of Howe.

8.   Howe, 'Key to a healthier Health Service', *Daily Telegraph*, 12 August, 1969.

9.   Joseph and Macmillan were of similar age, both from a successful business background, and with a almost the same length of parliamentary experience; but Joseph had the advantage of more continuity and marginally greater ministerial seniority. In 1955 Balniel became Chairman of the Conservative parliamentary Health and Social Security Committee. He became a member of the NW Metropolitan RHB in 1957. In 1965 Balniel was consulted by the Labour Government in connection with its plans for reorganisation of the personal social services (T, 2SS 301/96/24A). Balniel was Chairman of the National Association for Mental Health (Lord Butler was its President). For the interventions of Balniel and Macmillan as opposition spokesmen on the question of NHS reorganisation, see Chapter IV. Miss Mervyn Pike had also briefly spoken for the opposition on social security, but in 1970 she was near to retirement.

10. Crossman, *Diaries*, iii, p 810, 9 February 1970.

11. Aberdare served for a few months in 1974 as Minister without Portfolio.

12. See Appendix 1.2.

13. See Appendix 1.3.

14. See Appendix 1.4. Crossman, *Diaries*, iii, pp 755-7, 895. Rogers' Obituaries, *Times*, 31 May and 2 June 1990.

15. Marre's Obituary, *Daily Telegraph*, 24 March 1990.

16. See Appendix 1.6.

17. See Appendix 1.5.

18. See Appendix 1.7.

19. See Appendix 2.9.

20. J W Sinclair and I J MacKenzie, *Future Central Organisation of the Scottish Health Services* (Scottish Office Management Services Unit, 1972). For the following paragraphs, see Appendices 2.12 and 2.13.

21. While recognising the difficulties of this arrangement, a leading authority concluded that 'the nature of the impediments to collaboration listed above indicates that bringing together SWSG and SHHD within one department of the Scottish Office would not be the panacea that many seem to believe', C Wiseman, 'Policy making in the Scottish health services at national level', in *The Scottish Government Yearbook 1980* (Paul Harris, 1979), p 145. See also Murphy, *British Social Services. The Scottish Dimension*, pp 166-77.

22. See Appendix 2.13.

23. DHSS, Circulars 20/70, 22/71.

24. Jarrett to Crossman, 13 February 1970, CAB 152/107.

25. CAB 152/107.

26. For papers relating to this review, CAB 152/107; DH, S/E 025. The final report, *The DHSS in Relation to the Health and Personal Social Services* (DHSS, 1972).

27. Appendix 2.12 shows the headquarters organisation in 1979, which is similar in most respects to the situation during the Heath administration.

28. As indicated by Appendix 2.12, outside this main structure was the Works Group under the Chief Works Officer, which reported directly to the Permanent Secretary.

29. Craig, *Election Manifestos*, pp 338-9.

30. Craig, *Election Manifestos*, pp 339-40.

31. Joseph to Heath, c.29 October 1970, Heath and Joseph mtg, 9 November 1970, Abortion and Family Planning, 1970-1974, PREM 11.

32. Heath and Joseph mtg, 31 December 1970, Abortion and Family Planning, 1970-1974, PREM 11.

33. For the economic and political context to the following sections, see Blackaby, ed, *British Economic Policy 1960-74: Demand Management*; Crafts and Woodward, eds, *The British Economy since 1945*; R Dornbusch and R Layard, eds, *The Performance of the British Economy* (Clarendon Press, 1987); M Holmes, *Political Pressure and Economic Policy: British Government 1970-74* (Butterworth, 1982).

34. See Appendix 3.7.

35. See Appendices 3.4, 3.5.

36. See Appendix 3.2.

37. 'Health Service Financing', *British Medical Journal*, 1970, i, Supplement, 86-92, 25 April 1970.

38. Conservative Central Office supplied the Treasury with about half-dozen of these documents, T, 2SS 21/338/01A.

39. *Times*, 16 July 1970; Treasury minute, 17 July 1970, T, 2SS 21/282/01A.

40. Report of NHS organisation study group, 21 April 1971, T, 2SS 21/338/01E.

41. Treasury minute, 26 June 1970, T, 2SS 21/786/01E.

42. Treasury minutes, June to July 1970, T, 2SS 21/786/01E.

43. Joseph, Ministers and officials mtg, 28 July 1970, T, 2SS 21/786/01E.

44. Howe, address to Fellowship of Freedom in Medicine, 9 May 1970, T, 2SS 21/338/02.

45. Joseph to Barber, 1 September 1970, T, 2SS 21/786/01F.

46. Treasury minute, c.1 September 1970, T, 2SS 21/786/01F.

47. Jenkin minute, 14 September 1970, Macmillan minute, 15 September 1970, Barber to Joseph, 16 September 1970, T, 2SS 21/786/01F. See also Treasury Ministers' comments, August to September 1970, T, 2SS 21/338/01A.

48. Macmillan and Joseph mtg, 19 August 1970, T, 2SS 21/338/01A.

49. For papers of the Working Party on NHS Finance, T, 2SS 21/338/01A-F, 2SS 21/338/02.

50. Treasury minutes, October 1970, T, 2SS 21/338/01A.

51. Inland Revenue memorandum, January 1971, T, 2SS 21/338/01B.

52. Treasury minute, 27 November 1970, T, 2SS 21/338/01A.

53. Treasury minute, 12 January 1971, T, 2SS 21/338/01C.

54. Treasury minute, 2 December 1970, T, 2SS 21/338/01A.

55. *Times*, 21 December 1970.

56. Joseph, HC Debates, vol 809, cols 1177-8, 16 January 1971.

57. T, 2SS 21/338/01B-C. Institute of Economic Affairs, *Choice in Welfare* (IEA, January 1970). The Treasury concurred with the criticism of the pamphlet by J V Donnison, *New Society*, 14 January 1971. Representative Treasury verdicts: 'price is its most impressive feature', 'strange', '99 per cent rubbish'.

58. Working Party on NHS Finance, May to June 1971, T, 2SS 21/338/01C. Working Party on NHS Finance-Report, June 1971, 40pp and appendices, T, 2SS 21/338/01F.

59. Treasury minute, 7 May 1971, T, 2SS 21/338/01E.

60. Macmillan and officials mtg, 8 June 1971, T, 2SS 21/786/01F.

61. CM(70) 8th mtg, 23 July 1970, CAB 128.

62. Treasury minute, 23 June 1970, T, 2SS 300/1128/07A.

63. Treasury minutes, 2 July 1970, T, 2SS 300/1128/01A; 13 July 1970, T, 2SS 550/282/03A; and 16 July 1970, 2SS 214/324/03D, reporting on the findings of the Chief Secretary's Group on Public Expenditure. School milk and school meals were of course savings in the education sector, but they had strong health associations and were usually considered in tandem with health service economies.

64. Treasury minute, 29 July 1970, T, 2SS 300/1128/07A.

65. Macmillan to Joseph, 31 July and 4 August 1970, T, 2SS 550/282/03A.

66. DHSS to Treasury, 13 August 1970, T, 2SS 300/1128/07B. Treasury minute, 13 August 1970, T, 2SS 21/282/01A.

67. For ophthalmic services it was intended to retain a free eye test, and to continue to exempt priority classes from charges. For the dental service it was agreed also to introduce legislation to reduce the age of exemption from 21 to 18. With respect to the welfare milk subsidy, it was agreed to retain this temporarily for the poor and large families.

68. DHSS memorandum on hospital boarding charges, 3 July 1970, and subsequent Treasury version following the same lines, T, 2SS 300/1128/07A. Treasury minutes, 13 and 14 July 1970, T, 2SS 21/282/01A.

69. Macmillan and Joseph mtg, 19 August 1970, T, 2SS 21/338/01A. See also T, 2SS 300/1128/07B for associated briefs.

70. Macmillan, CP(70)39, 10 September 1970, CAB 129; CM(70) 17th mtg, 15 September 1970, CAB 128.

71. Joseph, CP(70)54, 24 September 1970, CAB 129.

72. Joseph to Macmillan, 25 September 1970, T, 2SS 300/1128/07C (refusal to withdraw prescription charge exemptions); CM(70) 24th mtg, 29 September 1970, 26th mtg, 5 October 1970, CAB 128. T, 2SS 550/282/03A. The public announcement on the increased expenditure was made by Joseph, HC Debates, vol 806, cols 391-8, 11 November 1970.

73. Barber, HC Debates, vol 805, cols 37-51, 27 October 1970.

74. The subsidiary changes were intended to maintain dental charges at half the cost of the service, and ophthalmic charges at the full cost of the service, subject to a maximum of £3.50p, from April 1971.

75. 'Treasury Historical Memorandum, No.17, Decisions on Public Expenditure for 1971-72 and 1974-75', (unpublished, November 1971), T, 2GE 7/224/04.

76. Joseph, Campbell and Thomas, SL(71)27, 13 April 1971, SL(71) 8th mtg, 21 April 1971, CAB 134.

77. Joseph, CP(71)55, 26 April 1971, CAB 129; CM(71) 23rd mtg, 19 April 1971, CAB 128

78. Exchanges between Treasury and DHSS, May to July 1971, T, 2SS 550/282/03C.

79. Joseph, CP(71)83, 12 July 1971, CAB 129; CM(71) 38th mtg, 15 July 1971, CAB 128. The political sensitivity of the prescription charges was indicated by the rumours circulating in the media and Parliament in early August 1971 that a 50p prescription charge was about to be introduced.

80. Treasury minute, 21 June 1972, T, 2SS 21/786/01F.

81. Joseph, CP(71)69, 21 June 1971, CAB 129. Macmillan and Joseph mtg, 13 July 1971, T, 2SS 21/786/01F. Macmillan, CP(71)87, 19 July 1971, CAB 129; CM(71) 40th mtg, 22 July 1971, CAB 128.

82. Joseph, HC Debates, vol 826, cols 957-64, 22 November 1971.

83. CM(71) 50th mtg, 19 October 1971, CAB 128.

84. Joseph, Campbell and Thomas, CP(71)124, 1 November 1971, CAB 129; CM(71) 53rd mtg, 4 November 1971, CAB 128. Joseph, HC Debates, vol 826, col 72, 15 November 1971 (WA).

85. *Financial Times*, 16 November 1971.

86. For instance, headlined by *News of the World*, 'Shock Threat to Britain's Health', 21 November 1971.

87. Joseph, and Thomas, CP(72)56, 19 May 1972, CAB 129; CM(72) 28th mtg, 25 May 1972, CAB 128.

88. Treasury minute, 28 July 1972, T, 2SS 109/110/05K.

89. Jenkin and Joseph mtg, 15 May 1972, T, 2SS 1128/96/02.

90. Treasury minute, 16 May 1972, T, 2SS 1128/96/02.

91. Treasury minute , 10 July 1972, T, 2SS 1128/96/02.

92. Treasury minute, 28 June 1972, T, 2SS 1128/96/02.

93. Treasury minute, 9 February 1973, T, 2SS 300/1128/015A.

94. Joseph to Barber, 28 August 1973, T, 2SS 300/1128/015A.

95. Barber to Joseph, 8 September 1973, T, 2SS 300/1128/015A.

96. Jenkin and Joseph mtg, 25 September 1973, T, 2SS 300/1128/015F.

97. Barber, HC Debates, vol 866, cols 952-80, 17 December 1973.

98. For details relating to England, Joseph, HC Debates, vol 868, col 247, 21 January 1974 (WA).

99. HC Debates, vol 868, cols 107-72, 28 January 1974, cols 252-378, 29 January 1974.

100. 'Scottish Hospital Advisory Service', SHHD, *Report 1970*, pp 67-9. SHHD to DHSS, 1 January 1971, reporting on general satisfaction with the Scottish HAS, DH, G/H 207/5B.

101. Joseph and Baker mtg, 13 November 1970, DH, MS(H) 2/3A.

102. Joseph and officials mtgs, 17 December 1970, 8 March 1971, DH, MS(H) 2/3B.

103. DHSS minute, 17 December 1970, DH, G/H 207/5B.

104. Brief for Ministers, and RHB Chairmen's mtg, 2 June 1971, DH, G/R 39/23. *Annual Report of NHS Hospital Advisory Service* (HMSO, 1971). For a public expression of complaints by Dr J L Crammer, and Sir Desmond Bonham-Carter, Chairman of the South West Metropolitan RHB, *British Medical Journal*, 1971, iv, 359, 746-7, 487 (robust reply by Baker), November to December 1971.

105. Joseph and officials mtg, 22 February 1972, DH, MS(H) 2/3C.

106. 'Report on the Hospital Advisory Service', February 1972, DH, MS(H) 2/3D. For Baker's commentaries on the report, 7 March and 6 April 1972, DH, MS(H) 2/3D. He complained that the effectiveness his teams was undermined by failure of the department to act on their recommendations.

107. DHSS minutes on the Hospital Advisory Service, July 1972, DH, MS(H) 2/3D.

108. Chief Medical Officer to Permanent Secretary, 13 July 1972, DH, MS(H) 2/3D. For discussion of reform of HAS, RHB Chairmen mtg, 14 June 1972, DH, G/R 39/24.

109. RHB Chairmen mtg, 10 October 1973, DH, G/R 39/25.

110. For Sir George Godber's reservations about the Hospital Advisory Service, *The British National Health Service*, p 78.

111. DH, G/H 207/14.

112. DHSS, Changes in the Operation of the HAS, 13 November 1973, office mtg, 4 January 1974, DH, G/H 207/17A.

113. See R Klein and P Hall, *Caring for Quality in the Caring Services* (Centre for Studies in Social Policy, 1973).

114. *All Souls College. Keith Joseph.*

115. Joseph minutes, 22 July and 18 September 1970, Aberdare to Joseph, c.25 July 1970, MH 150/170.

116. Joseph minute, 11 July 1970, MH 150/170.

117. Joseph minutes, July to September 1970, DH, MS(H) 2/3A.

118. Joseph and officials mtg, 29 September 1970, DH, MS(H) 2/3A.

119. DHSS minute, 15 September 1970, DH, D/M 107/01B.

120. For instance, Ann Shearer, *Guardian*, 30 January 1971.

121. Joseph minute, 10 April 1971, DH, D/M 107/01C.

122. Joseph, notes on draft White Paper on mental handicap, c.2 March 1971, MH 150/171.

123. Brief for Joseph, 12 May 1971, DH, D/M 107/01C.

124. *Better Services for the Mentally Handicapped*, Cmnd.4683 (HMSO, 1971). For papers associated with the launch of *Better Services*, DH, F/P 239/85A. Joseph, HC Debates, vol 819, cols 305-7, 23 June 1971 (WA).

125. *Services for the Mentally Handicapped* (SHHD, SED, 1972).

126. Peter Townsend, *Sunday Times*, 27 June 1971.

127. Mary Applebey, communication to Alf Morris, cited by him, HC Debates, vol 821, col 87, 12 July 1971.

128. RHB Chairmen mtg, 12 July 1972, DH, G/R 39/24.

129. DHSS minute, 8 October 1970, MH 150/171. RHB Chairmen mtgs, 2 June, 7 July, 6 October, 1 December 1971, DH, G/R 39/23.

130. Scottish Health Services Council, *Services for the Elderly with Mental Disorder* (HMSO, Edinburgh, 1970). The chairman of the subcommittee producing this report was Professor W Malcolm Millar, Professor of Mental Health, University of Aberdeen. This report reinforces Royal Medico-Psychological Association (Scottish Division), *Psychiatric Services for Old People in Scotland* (RMPA Scotland, 1969). These reports are also echoed by DHSS, HM(72)71, 11 October 1972.

131. *Services for the Elderly*, para 191.

132. HM(71)97, *Hospital Services for the Mentally Ill*, 7 December 1971.

133. *Hospital Services for the Mentally Ill*, para 16. Joseph, HC Debates, vol 827, col 281 (WA), 7 December 1971.

134. J J Bradley, *British Medical Journal*, 1971, iv, p 811, 25 December 1971.

135. Editorial, *British Medical Journal*, 1971, iv, 700, 18 December 1971.

136. *Times*, 27 February 1971; *Lancet*, 1973, ii, 527-8, 10 March 1973. Joseph was no doubt aware that reneging on his promise would be exploited by Labour. David Ennals was Campaign Director for NAMH. In this capacity he was responsible for launching a 'Minds Matter' campaign in February 1971. Christopher Mayhew, Labour MP for Woolwich East, was active in the Campaign for the Mentally Handicapped, founded in 1971, with the aim of eliminating mental handicap hospitals within 15 years.

137. DHSS minute, 26 March 1973, DH, F/P 239/85A.

138. DH, F/P 239/85A-B.

139. Brian Abel-Smith, 'A hospital Ombudsman?', *New Society*, 22 April 1971, which draws attention to recent recommendations of the Farleigh enquiry, which urged the appointment of a health service commissioner. See also Barbara Robb, *Daily Telegraph*, 26 May 1971.

140. 'Reading List for the Secretary of State', 25 June 1970, DH, J/N 179/23E.

141. Joseph, Ministers and officials mtg, 29 July 1970, DH, J/N 179/23F.

142. Joseph, speech at 88th General Meeting and Conference of the Association of Hospital Matrons, 31 October 1970, DH, J/N 179/23G.

143. Draft report on health service commissioner, 25 November 1970, DH, J/N 179/23G.

144. DHSS minute, 27 November 1970, SHHD to DHSS, 10 December 1970, DHSS and SHHD mtgs, 13 and 23 December 1970, DH, J/N 179/23G.

145. DHSS minute, 9 December 1970, DH, J/N 179/23G.

146. Office of Parliamentary Commissioner to DHSS, 23 December 1970, DH, J/N 179/23G.

147. Interdepartmental mtg of senior officials, 9 February 1971, DH, J/N 179/23G.

148. Joseph, BMA and JCC mtg, 15 June 1971, DH, J/N 179/23I.

149. Joseph, Ministers and officials mtg, 21 September 1971, DH, J/N 179/23J.

150. *Times*, 5 August and 4 November 1971; *Lancet*, 1971, ii, 365, 14 August 1971.

151. DHSS to SHHD, 10 August 1971, SHHD to DHSS, 13 August 1971, DH, J/N 179/23J.

152. Office of Parliamentary Commissioner for Administration to DHSS, 25 August and 10 September 1971, senior officials of DHSS and PCA mtg, 30 September 1971, DH, J/N 179/23J.

153. Report on discussions between DHSS, Scottish Office and Welsh Office, 3 December 1971, DH, J/N 179/23K. Correspondence between Joseph, Scottish and Welsh Secretaries of State, December 1971 to January 1972, DH, J/N 179/23L.

154. Joseph, HC Debates, vol 831, cols 1104-14, 22 February 1971, Aberdare, HL Debates, vol 328, cols 419-25, 22 February 1972. For interdepartmental exchanges over the announcements, DH, J/N 179/23M.

155. Editorial, *Times*, 23 February 1972.

156. *Administrative Practice of Hospital Boards in Scotland*, paras 146-7.

157. *Suggestions and Complaints in Hospitals. Report of a Working Party* (HMSO, Edinburgh, 1969).

158. DH, G/C 369/1.

159. Exchanges between Prime Minister's office and DHSS, November 1970, DH, G/C 369/1.

160. DH, G/C 369/1. Michael Davies was knighted and appointed a High Court judge during the course of his committee.

161. Joseph, HC Debates, vol 810, col 408, 3 February 1971.

162. For the papers of the Davies Committee, DH, G/C 369/10-15.

163. Joseph, HC Debates, vol 866, col 272, 17 December 1973 (WA).

164. Davies Committee, Memorandum on Community Health Councils, February 1972, DH, G/C 369/4A.

165. DHSS minutes on Davies memorandum on Community Health Councils, March 1972, DH, G/C 369/4A.

166. Leathard, *Fight for Family Planning*, chapter 20.

167. *A Birth Control Plan for Britain* (Birth Control Campaign, 1971).

168. *Times*, 20 July 1970.

169. Joseph and St John-Stevas delegation mtg, 30 July 1960, DH, MS(H) 2/3A.

170. Joseph and Royal College of Obstetricians and Gynaecologists mtg, 30 September 1970, Joseph and medical delegation led by Harold Gurden MP mtg, 14 October 1970, DH, MS(H) 2/3A.

171. Joseph and Abortion Law Reform Association mtg, 26 October 1970, DH, MS(H) 2/3A.

172. Secretary of State and officials mtgs, 14 and 22 October 1970, DH, MS(H) 2/3A.

173. Joseph to Heath, c.29 October 1970, Heath and Joseph mtg, 9 November 1970, Abortion and Family Planning, 1970-1974, PREM 11.

174. DH, MS(H) 2/3A.

175. Joseph, SL(70)25, 23 December 1970, SL(70) 1st mtg, 6 January 1971, CAB 134.

176. DHSS minute, c.12 November 1970, DH, E/A 223/31.

177. Joseph, HC Debates, vol 812, cols 313-8, 23 February 1971.

178. CHSC/SMMAC, *Domiciliary Midwifery and Maternity Bed Needs* (HMSO, 1970), published 28 July 1970, para 273.

179. Joseph and Royal College of Obstetricians and Gynaecologists mtg, 30 September 1970, DH, MS(H) 2/3A.

180. Joseph and officials mtgs, 15 and 16 July 1970, DH, MS(H) 2/3A.

181. Secretary of State and officials mtgs, 14 September and 22 October 1970, DH, MS(H) 2/3A.

182. Joseph to Heath, 29 October 1970, Abortion and Family Planning, 1970-1974, PREM 11.

183. SL(71) 1st mtg, 6 January 1971, CAB 134.

184. Family Planning, Circular 36/71, July 1971.

185. Leathard, *Fight for Family Planning*, pp 162-3.

186. Joseph and officials mtgs, 14 July and 23 September 1971, to plan the experimental schemes, DH, MS(H) 2/3B.

187. Joseph and officials mtg, 2 May 1972, DH, MS(H) 2/3C.

188. DH, E/F 1/36A-E, 38.

189. Joseph, HS(72)70, 4 July 1972, HS(72) 18th mtg, 14 July 1972, CAB 134.

190. Joseph, HS(72)125, 30 November 1972, HS(72) 29th mtg, 4 December 1972, CAB 134.

191. Joseph, HC Debates, vol 848, cols 234-40, 12 December 1972. For criticisms by the Prime Minister and Lord President of Joseph's draft speech, Family Planning, 1972-1973, PREM 11.

192. HL Debates, vol 337, cols 8-316, 4 December 1972.

193. HL Debates, vol 337, cols 950-69, 987-1014, 19 December 1972.

194. Editorial, *Times*, 21 December 1972; editorial, *Guardian*, 5 February 1973.

195. Joseph, HC Debates, vol 849, cols 194-5, 24 January 1973 (WA), vol 850, col 53, 6 February 1973.

196. HS(73) 3rd mtg, 2 February 1973, CAB 134. The population report was published on 22 March 1973: *Report of the Population Panel*, Cmnd.5258 (HMSO, 1973). For Prior's announcement, HC Debates, vol 853, cols 176-7, 22 March 1973.

197. Prior, HS(73)39, 1 March 1973, HS(73) 7th mtg, 5 March 1973, CAB 134.

198. CM(73) 15th mtg, 8 March 1973, CAB 128.

199. Jenkin to Barber, c.14 March 1973, T, 2SS 550/282/03D.

200. Joseph to Carr, 14 March 1973, Family Planning, 1972-1973, PREM 11.

201. *Times*, 23 March 1973, headlined the family planning proposal as the most significant aspect of the report .

202. Joseph, HC Debates, vol 853, cols 934-9, 26 March 1973.

203. HC Debates, vol 853, cols 923-1052, 26 March 1973.

204. For a detailed account of the NHS Reorganisation Bill, see chapter VI. For DHSS papers on clause 4, DH, C/F 1/04.

205. DH, C/F 1/01A, E/F 60D-G. M Simms, 'Payments for Pills', *Eugenics Society Bulletin*, 1978, **10**, 49-56.

206. Joseph and officials mtgs, 29 July and 16 November 1970, 4 January 1971, DH, M/S(H) 2/3A-B.

207. Abortion and family planning, 1970-1974, PREM 11.

208. Joseph to Heath, 13 January 1971, Heath to Joseph, 25 January 1971, Joseph to Heath, 9 February 1971, Fluoridation, 1970-1971, PREM 11.

209. DH, A/F 6/7C, 52.

210. Michael Alison, in *All Souls College, Keith Joseph*. Taylor, *Smoke Ring*, pp 87-8, for a less positive view of Joseph on tobacco.

211. Joseph and officials mtg, 30 July 1970, DH, MS(H) 2/3A.

212. Joseph, HA(70)63, 26 November 1970, CAB 134.

213. HA(70) 9th mtg, 9 December 1970, CAB 134. For the Royal College of Physicians report, *Smoking and Health Now* (Pitman, 1971).

214. Joseph, officials and Tobacco Advisory Committee mtg, 31 December 1970, DH, MS(H) 2/3B.

215. DH, MS(H) 2/3B. Joseph, HA(71)23, 1 March 1971, HA(71) 5th mtg, 9 March 1971, CAB 134. Joseph, HC Debates, vol 812, cols 1190-8, 16 March 1971 (agreement with tobacco interests). Joseph, HC Debates, vol 819, cols 340-4, 24 June 1971 (WA) (details of health warning).

216. Officials, HS(71)61, 'Cigarette Smoking and Health', October 1971, 71pp; Joseph, HS(71)68, 9 December 1971, HS(71) 15th mtg, 22 December 1971, CAB 134. For the interdepartmental exercise to produce 'Cigarette Smoking and Health', CAB 152/25-8.

217. Joseph, HS(72)134, 7 December 1972, HS(72) 31st mtg, 18 December 1972, CAB 134. Dr Hunter served as chairman from 1973 until 1980.

218. Heath to Nixon, 1 March 1971, President Nixon and Cancer Research, 1971-1973, PREM 11.

219. President Nixon and Cancer Research, 1971-1973, PREM 11. Lord Zuckerman, *Cancer Research* (HMSO, 1972).

220. Zuckerman, 'A Possible UK initiative in the socio-economic field in the context of the EEC', 12 September 1972, CAB 467/12.

221. Heath, drafts of speech to EEC summit, 19 October 1972, CAB 467/12.

222. For the context to the following section, F T Blackaby, 'Incomes Policy', in Blackaby, ed, *British Economic Policy 1960-74: Demand Management*, pp 360-401; R Richardson, 'Trade Unions and Industrial Relations', in Crafts and Woodward, eds, *The British Economy since 1945*, pp 417-42; G A Dorfman, *Government versus Trade Unionism in British Politics since 1968*, chapter 3; W H Fishbein, *Wage Restraint by Consensus: Britain's Search for an Incomes Policy Agreement 1965-79*; R Taylor, *The Trade Union Question in British Politics: Government and the Unions since 1954*.

223. Macleod and senior Ministers mtg, 23 June 1970, Doctors' and Dentists' Remuneration, 1970-1971, PREM 11.

224. Joseph, doctors' and dentists' representatives mtg, 26 June 1970, DH, MS(H) 2/3A. Joseph to Dr Ronald Gibson, Chairman of the BMA Council, 26 June 1970, *British Medical Journal*, 1970, iii, Supplement, 39, 4 July 1970; for Gibson's report and recommendations for removal of sanctions at Special Representative Meeting, Supplement, 37-40, 29 June 1970.

225. Editorial, *British Medical Journal*, 1970, iii, 1-2, 4 July 1970.

226. EPC(70) 1st mtg, 3 July 1970. CAB 134.

227. Joseph, doctors' and dentists' representatives mtg, 15 July 1970, DH, MS(H) 2/3A. Three further meetings failed to produce an improvement on the initial offer. For the formal offer, Joseph to Gibson, [usually cited as 6 August 1970], *British Medical Journal*, 1970, iii, Supplement, 73, 5 August 1970.

228. Editorial, *British Medical Journal*, 1970, iii, 359, Supplement, 76, 13 August 1970. *British Medical Journal*, 1970, iii, Supplement, 77-80, 29 August 1970.

229. Joseph, Ministers and officials, BMA and BDA mtgs, 21 October and 19 November 1970, DH, MS(H) 2/3A, 14 January 1971, MS(H) 2/3B.

230. P(70) 5th mtg, 22 December 1970, CAB 134. Maudling, CP(70)125, 31 December 1970, CAB 129; CM(71) 1st mtg, 5 January 1971, CAB 128. Joseph to Gibson, 19 January 1971, T, 2SS 27/78/05A.

231. Stevenson to Joseph, 22 April 1971, Joseph, Ministers, officials, BMA and BDA mtg, 12 May 1971, DH, MS(H) 2/3B. Treasury minute, 30 April 1971, T, 2SS 27/78/05A.

232. John Anthony Hardinge Giffard, the 3rd Earl of Halsbury, was born in 1908. He held industrial directorships, but was also a prominent member of various medical and scientific bodies.

233. *Report of the Review Body on Doctors' and Dentists' Remuneration. 1971*, Cmnd.4825 (HMSO, 1971).

234. Treasury minute, 8 November 1971, T, 2SS 27/78/05A. Joseph, P(71)77, 12 November 1971, CAB 134.

235. *Report of the Review Body on Doctors' and Dentists' Remuneration. 1972*, Cmnd.5010 (HMSO, 1972). DH, B/D 112/097C, T, 2SS 27/78/05B-C.

236. Joseph, P(72)25, 15 June 1972, CAB 134.

237. DHSS minutes, November to December 1970, DH, M/N 57/040; Treasury minutes, December 1970, T, 2SS 116/78/02B. Carr, P(70)7, 23 December 1970, CAB 134. CM(71) 2nd mtg, 14 January 1971, CAB 128.

238. Macmillan minute, 19 January 1971, T, 2SS 116/78/02B.

239. Joseph, P(71)4, 15 January 1971, P(71) 3rd mtg, 19 January 1971, CAB 134.

240. NC(M & SC)241, 23 February 1971, DH, M/N 57/040. For the announcement, Joseph, HC Debates, vol 813, cols 1166-8, 16 March 1971. NMC Circular, No.158, May 1971 (pay), NMC Circular No.159, September 1971 (hours).

241. DH, M/N 57/041; T, 2SS 116/78/02C. NC(M & SC)250, 22 February 1972, DH, M/N 57/041. NMC Circular, No.163, April 1972.

242. Maudling, CP(71)89, 22 July 1971, CAB 129; CM(71) 41st mtg, 27 July 1971, CM(71) 42nd mtg, 28 July 1971, CAB 128.

243. CM(73) 12th mtg, 1 March 1973, 14th mtg, 6 March 1973, CAB 128.

244. Joseph, HC Debates, vol 852, cols 1176-83. 15 March 1973.

245. CM(73) 15th mtg, 8 March 1973, CM(73) 16th mtg, 15 March 1973, CM(73) 17th mtg, 20 March 1973, CAB 128.

246. CM(73) 18th mtg, 22 March 1973, CM(73) 19th mtg, 29 March 1973, CAB 128.

247. CM(73) 22nd mtg, 5 April 1973, CAB 128. *Times*, 11, 13 and 16 April 1973.

248. Editorial, *Times*, 16 April 1973.

249. DH, M/N 57/042; T, 2SS 116/78/02C. NC(M & SC)268, 3 April 1973, DH, M/N 57/042. NMC Circular, No.170, May 1973.

250. Heath and Administrative and Clerical Staff Side mtg, 18 June 1973, Heath and Nurses and Midwives Staff Side mtg, 20 June 1973, NHS Administrators and Nurses, 1973, PREM 11.

251. Heath and Joseph mtg, 20 June 1973, NHS Administrators and Nurses, 1973, PREM 11.

252. DHSS progress report on Pay Board enquiry, 5 November 1973, DH, M/N 57/042.

253. *Review Body on Doctors' and Dentists' Remuneration. Third Report. 1973*, Cmnd.5353 (HMSO, 1973). T, 2SS 27/78/05D.

254. DH, M/N 57/046. NC(M & SC)279, 22 January 1974, DH, M/N 57/046. NMC Circular No.174, April 1974.

255. Heath and Halsbury mtg, 17 January 1974, Doctors' and Dentists' Pay, 1974, PREM 11.

256. Serota to Briggs, 3 March 1970, DH, M/N 45/116G.

257. Two members subsequently left the committee and were replaced by substitutes from the same constituencies.

258. CN(70) 1st mtg, 12 June 1970, DH, M/N 45/136A.

259. For the papers of the Briggs Committee, DH, M/N 45/136A-R.

260. Treasury view reported in DHSS minute, 22 September 1972, and Treasury to DHSS, 22 September 1972, T, 2SS 116/117/04B.

261. DH, M/N 45/193. Joseph, Campbell and Thomas, HS(72)108, 26 September 1972, CAB 134. *Report of the Committee on Nursing*, Cmnd.5115 (HMSO, 1972). Joseph, HC Debates, vol 843, col 37, 17 October 1972 (WA), the briefest statement expressing gratitude to the Briggs Committee for its 'comprehensive and penetrating study'.

262. For initial written responses to the Briggs Report, DH, M/N 45/194A-E; for meetings with leading organisations, April to June 1973, M/N 45/194B.

263. Briggs Report Steering Group, BRSG(72)1, December 1972, DH, M/N 45/194A.

264. DHSS to Treasury, 14 May 1973, DH, M/N 45/193.

265. Treasury minutes, May to July 1973, T, 2SS 116/117/04B

266. Prior to Joseph, 30 April 1973, Joseph to Prior, 14 May 1973, Prior to Joseph, 21 May 1973, Joseph to Prior, 29 May 1973, Prior to Joseph, 31 May 1973, Campbell to Prior, 11 June 1973, Joseph to Prior, 13 June 1973, Prior to Joseph, 18 June 1973, DH, M/N 45/193.

267. Joseph, HS(73)178, 10 December 1973, HS(73) 39th mtg, 14 December 1973, CAB 134.

268. DHSS minute, 17 December 1973, DH, M/N 45/193. For the revised statement, Joseph, Campbell, and Thomas, HA(74)14, 6 February 1974, CAB 134. The Home and Social Affairs Committee of the Heath administration met for the last time on 1 February 1974, and therefore was never able to sanction the statement on Briggs.

269. 'Briggs: When is the DHSS going to Act?', *SNAP*, 7 December 1973.

270. Conference on Scottish Hospitals Scientific Council, 15 January 1971, DH, K/P 311/4A.

271. HM(71)47, May 1971, HSC(IS)16, April 1974.

272. Aberdare and Whitley Professional and Technical Staffs Side mtg, 15 October 1970, DH, K/P 311/4A.

273. DH, K/P 311/03E,15A.

274. Seventh mtg of Regional Scientific Officers, 28 February 1974, DH, K/P 311/15A.

275. DHSS and British Psychological Society mtg, 10 October 1969, DH, K/P 311/13.

276. SAC(MH)(69) 3rd and 4th mtgs, 25 June and 25 September 1969, DH, F/C 53/33.

277. DHSS and British Psychological Society mtg, 7 March 1972, DHSS minutes, 1 and 14 June 1972, DH, F/C 53/38A.

278. SAC(MH)(72) 2nd mtg, 17 May 1972, DH, F/C 53/33.

279. For the papers of the Trethowan Committee, DH, B/C 53/1, F/C 53/38A-B, 57A, K/P 311/13,

280. Excellently reviewed by Lewis, *What Price Community Medicine?*, pp 82-116.

281. Hunter to Joseph, 14 July 1970; this alteration of remit was agreed by Joseph on 14 July 1970, DH, B/N 179/04.

282. MA 11th mtg, 27 November 1970, DH, B/N 179/01A.

283. DHSS minute, 7 January 1971, Chief Medical Officer minute, 8 January 1971, DH, B/N 179/04.

284. Joseph, speech to Institute of Hospital Administrators, 6 May 1971, DH, B/N 179/01A.

285. MA 19th mtg, 18 May 1971, B/N 179/01A.

286. MA 20th mtg, 15 September 1971, B/N 179/01B.

287. Hunter to Joseph, 19 April 1972, Joseph to Hunter, 25 April 1972, DH, B/N 179/04. *Report of the Working Party on Medical Administrators* (DHSS, 1972).

288. Editorial, *Community Medicine*, 2 June 1972.

289. Chief Medical Officer minute, 20 September 1972, DH, B/N 179/013. P Draper and T Smart, 'Social Science and Health Policy in the United Kingdom', *International Journal of Health Sciences*, 1974, **4**, 453-70, pp 455-7.

Chapter VI
CONSERVATIVES AND REORGANISATION

1. HLG 120/1103, 9-10 March 1967.

2. Balniel, HC Debates, vol 753, cols 644-5, 6 November 1967.

3. *Daily Telegraph*, 20 June 1968.

4. G Howe, 'Key to a healthier Health Service', *Daily Telegraph*, 12 August, 1969. For an alternative Conservative view, more sympathetic to local government control, T Raison, *Evening Standard*, 25 February 1970.

5. Balniel, HC Debates, vol 790, cols 521-32, 31 October 1969.

6. Balniel, HC Debates, vol 790, cols 529-30, 31 October 1969.

7. Crossman, weekly mtg, 1 April 1970, BN 72/92. However, the Conservative Research Department memorandum, 'Administration of the NHS', 21 May 1970, prepared for Joseph, followed the lines of Balniel's speech, CAB, 16/4 Part 2.

8. Craig, *Election Manifestos*, p 339.

9. See briefing mtgs for the debate on the Queen's Speech, CAB, 16/4 Part 2.

10. Joseph, HC Debates, vol 803, cols 1176-7, 13 July 1970; Aberdare, HL Debates, vol 311, col 332, 9 July 1970; Campbell, HC Debates, vol 804, col 276, 24 July 1970 (WA).

11. Report of House of Lords Health Group, June 1970, and commentary by Chief Medical Officer, DH, J/N 179/120B.

12. Joseph, minute on NHS reorganisation, 8 August 1970, DH, J/N 179/120A.

13. 'National Health Service Reorganisation', 3 July 1970, CAB, 16/4 Part 2.

14. Comment by Joseph at office mtg, 8 July 1970, CAB, 16/4 Part 2.

15. Acton, 6, pp 53-4; *MH Report 1958*, pp 41-3.

16. Webster I, p 256.

17. Joseph, minute on NHS reorganisation, 8 August 1970, DH, J/N 179/120A.

18. Treasury minutes, 27 October 1970, 22 and 23 December 1970, T, 2SS 21/04A.

19. Joseph, Ministers and officials mtgs, 8 and 10 September 1970, DH, J/N 179/120A. Memorandum on the National Corporation, 4 September 1970, DH, J/N 179/120A.

20. Joseph and officials mtgs, 8 and 10 September 1970, DH, J/N 179/120A.

21. Joseph, SL(70)12, 25 October 1970, SL(70) 4th mtg, 28 October 1970, CAB 134/3249.

22. Joseph, HC Debates, vol 805, cols 437-9, 5 November 1970 (WA); Campbell, HC Debates, vol 805, cols 453-4, 5 November 1970 (WA).

23. Treasury brief on SL(70)12, 27 October 1970, T, 2SS 21/04A.

24. Treasury minute, 18 September 1970, T, 2SS 21/04A.

25. Treasury minute, 23 October 1970, T, 2SS 21/04A.

26. DHSS to Treasury, 22 October 1970, T, 2SS 21/04A.

27. Treasury minute, c.15 November 1970, T, 2SS 21/04A.

28. Treasury minutes, 19 and 23 November 1970, T, 2SS 21/04A. The Business Team was also criticised for attempting to impose unrealistic conditions on DHSS, Treasury minute, 2 December 1970, T, 2SS 21/04A.

29. Joseph and RHB Chairmen mtg, 7 October 1970, DH, J/N 179/120A.

30. DH, J/N 179/127A, J/N 179/130.

31. Regional Chairmen, 'Health Service Reorganisation', October 1970, and mtg with Joseph, 7 October 1970, DH, J/N 179/120A.

32. Joseph, mtg with Sir Thomas Holmes Sellars (representing Royal College of Surgeons) and Sir John Richardson (Chairman of the JCC), 22 September 1970, DH, J/N 179/127A.

33. Treasury minute, 7 October 1970, T, 2SS 21/04A; Joseph, Ministers and officials mtg, 12 October 1970, DH, J/N 179/120A.

34. Joseph minute, 26 September 1970, DH, MS(H) 3/2A.

35. Joseph, Ministers and officials mtg, 12 October 1970, DH, J/N 179/120A. For discordant views from the AG division and the Treasury, Treasury minutes, 2 and 16 December 1970, T, 2SS 21/04A.

36. Nursing Division minute, 17 November 1970, Joseph, Ministers and officials mtg, 28 November 1970, DH, J/N 179/120B.

37. Joseph, Ministers and officials mtg, 28 November 1970, DH, J/N 179/120B.

38. Joseph, Ministers and officials mtg, 28 October 1970, DH, J/N 179/120B.

39. DHSS minutes, 8 and 16 December 1970, DH, J/N 179/120C.

40. Joseph, Ministers and officials mtg, 15 December 1970, DH, J/N 179/120C.

41. King's Fund, *The Shape of Hospital Management in 1980* (King's Fund, 1967). K F Prochaska, *Philanthropy and the Hospitals of London. The King's Fund 1897-1990* (Clarendon Press, 1992), pp 202-3.

42. DHSS minute, 26 October 1970, DH, J/N 179/120A. This minute also pointed out that Jacques' findings were contrary to the conclusions adopted by McKinsey's in their work for the Oxford Board of Governors. Treasury minute, 18 September 1970, T, 2SS 21/04A.

43. DHSS minute, 19 October 1970, DH, J/N 179/120B.

44. Joseph, Ministers and officials mtg, 28 October 1970, DH, J/N 179/120A.

45. LP(70)11, 'Chief Officers of Regional and Area Health Authorities', December 1970, DH, J/N 179/120C.

46. DHSS minute, 21 October 1970, DH, J/N 179/120A. For Scotland, Treasury minute, 9 December 1970, T, 2SS 21/04A.

47. Meyjes wanted both a chief executive and full-time chairman of health authorities, Treasury minute, 19 December 1970, T, 2SS 21/04B.

48. Joseph, Meyjes and officials mtg, 10 February 1971, DH, J/N 179/120C.

49. 'National Health Service Reorganisation: Consultative Document', 23 December 1970, DH, J/N 179/120C.

50. DHSS to Treasury, 23 December 1970, T, 2SS 21/04B.

51. 'NHS Reorganisation: Consultative Document', DH, J/N 179/120C.

52. 'NHS Reorganisation: Consultative Document', paras 14-15, DH, J/N 179/120C.

53. Treasury and SHHD mtg, 4 March 1971, T, 2SS 21/85/01A.

54. Treasury minute, 26 January 1971, T, 2SS 21/04A.

55. Treasury brief on SL(71)18, 22 March 1971, T, 2SS 21/04B.

56. Treasury minutes and exchanges with CSD, January-March 1971, T, 2SS 21/04B-C.

57. Treasury minutes, 14, 19 and 21 January 1971, T, 2SS 21/04B.

58. Joseph, SL(71)18, 19 March 1971, Campbell, SL(71)22, 20 March 1971, Thomas, SL(71)23, 20 March 1971, CAB 134. Neither the Scottish nor Welsh draft mentioned the mechanism for appointment of area board members, but by implication it was assumed that they would follow the English pattern. As indicated by the discussion in the Social Services Committee, the Secretaries of

State for Scotland and Wales interpreted this silence in diametrically opposite ways.

59. SL(71) 7th mtg, 23 March 1971, CAB 134; brief for PM on CP(71)42, 31 March 1971, NHS Reorganisation, 1971, PREM 11; Treasury minute, c.30 March 1971, T, 2SS 21/04C.

60. Treasury minute, c.30 March 1971, T, 2SS 21/04C.

61. CSD brief on CP(71)42, 31 March 1971, T, 2SS 21/04C.

62. Short, CP(71)42, 29 March 1971, CAB 129; CM(71) 19th mtg, 1 April 1971, CAB 128; Cabinet Secretary's Notebook (Burke Trend).

63. SHHD submission, 21 April 1971, T, 2SS 21/85/01A.

64. Treasury briefs on SL(71)28, 27 April 1971, T, 2SS 21/04C.

65. Joseph wanted to avoid direct medical representation because he believed that medical organisations would nominate unsatisfactory appointees.

66. Joseph, SL(71)28, 22 April 1971, CAB 134; SL(71) 9th mtg, 28 April 1971, CAB 134; brief for Heath on SL(71)28, 23 April 1971, NHS Reorganisation, 1971, PREM 11. Thomas was unable to attend this meeting, but he wrote to the Home Secretary reporting that his soundings of opinion in Wales had revealed support for local authorities to appoint members, but he was surprised that the professional representatives made no similar demand, Thomas to Maudling, 28 April 1971, T, 2SS 21/04C.

67. Treasury brief on CP(71)56, 5 May 1971, T, 2SS 21/04C.

68. Joseph, CP((71)56, 4 May 1971, CAB 129; CM(71) 24th mtg, 6 May 1971, CAB 128; Cabinet Secretary's Notebook (Burke Trend). Brief for PM on SL(71)56, 5 May 1971, NHS Reorganisation 1971,PREM 11.

69. For relevant announcements on the consultative documents, Joseph, HC Debates, vol 817, cols 239-40, 17 May 1971 (WA); Thomas, HC Debates, vol 818, col 332, 8 June 1971 (WA).

70. *National Health Service Reorganisation. Consultative Document* (DHSS, May 1971).

71. The Consultative Document was also not very fastidious about such elementary points as providing complete references to official documents cited in the text.

72. *National Health Service Reorganisation*, Foreword, p 2.

73. *National Health Service Reorganisation*, para 10.

74. *National Health Service Reorganisation*, para 8.

75. *National Health Service Reorganisation*, para 25.

76. *National Health Service Reorganisation*, paras 21-2.

77. *National Health Service Reorganisation*, para 23, Appendix I and II.

78. DHSS minute, 26 February 1971, DH, J/N 179/127A.

79. *British Medical Journal*, 1971, ii, Supplement, 2, 3 July 1971.

80. *National Health Service Reorganisation*, para 6.

81. 'NHS Reorganisation. Consultative Document', para 5, DH, J/N 179/120C.

82. *National Health Service Reorganisation*, para 7; 'NHS Reorganisation: Consultative Document', para 8, DH, J/N 179/120C.

83. *National Health Service Reorganisation*, para 17.a. This change is evident to the keen eye because 'some' is not perfectly aligned with the adjacent text.

84. *National Health Service Reorganisation*, para 17.c.

85. *National Health Service Reorganisation*, para 20.

86. DH, J/N 179/127A.

87. *General Practitioner*, 8 October 1971. For further details on responses, DH, J/N 179/146A-B.

88. *Times*, 18 May 1971; for a similar view, *Economist*, 22 May 1971.

89. *New Society*, 29 July 1971; *British Medical Journal*, 1971, ii, 1971, Supplement, 1-4, 3 July 1971.

90. *British Medical Journal*, 1971, ii, Supplement, 2, 3 July 1971; *Lancet*, 1971, ii, 538-9, 4 September 1971.

91. *New Statesman*, 13 August 1971.

92. G McLachlan, ed, *Challenges for Change* (NPHT, 1971); J A D Anderson, *Lancet*, 1971, ii, 538-9, 4 September 1971; G Smith, *Times*, 17 November 1971.

93. Secretary of State and RHB Chairmen mtg, 21 June 1971, DH, J/N 179/14E.

94. *British Medical Journal*, 1971, ii, Supplement, 6, 3 July 1971. *Lancet*, 1972, i, 1006-7, 6 May 1972; see also *Economist*, 22 May 1971; *New Society*, 29 July 1971; *General Practitioner*, 8 October 1971.

95. Aberdare to Joseph, 14 June 1971, DH, MS(H) 3/2B.

96. Joseph, HC Debates, vol 820, cols 601-9, 1 July 1971.

97. Williams, HC Debates, vol 820, cols 592-601, 1 July 1971.

98. Crossman, HC Debates, vol 820, cols 609-17, 1 July 1971. Crossman mounted a similar attack at a meeting of the Fabian Society on 2 August 1971, where Mrs Williams disagreed with him about local authority control of the health service, DH, J/N 179/146B.

99. Joseph minute, 2 July 1971, DH, MS(H) 2/3B.

100. Joseph meeting with delegation of Conservative MPs, headed by Timothy Raison, from the House of Commons Health and Social Services Committee, 26 May 1971, DH, MS(H) 3/2B.

101. Exchanges between Joseph and Whitelaw, July 1971 and March 1972, DH, MS(H) 3/2B, MS(H) 3/2D.

102. Joseph, Ministers and officials mtg, 14 April 1972, DH, MS(H) 2/3B.

103. Joseph, Ministers and officials mtg, 14 October 1971, DH, MS(H) 2/3C.

104. DH, J/N 179/138A, MS(H) 3/2B-C.

105. DH, MS(H) 3/2B.

106. Joseph and BMA-JCC delegation mtg, 1 November 1971, DH, MS(H) 2/3B.

107. Joseph minute, 5 December 1970, DH, J/N 179/120C.

108. Webster I, p 269.

109. LP(71)1, January 1971, Ministers and officials mtg, 7 January 1971, DH, J/N 179/120C.

110. For the following paragraph, see Maps 1 and 2.

111. *National Health Service Reorganisation*, para 10.

112. HSO(71)12, 12 September 1971, DH, MS(H) 3/2B; see also MS(H) 3/2C, report on correspondence with East Midlands, December 1971.

113. HSO(71)12, 12 September 1971, DH, MS(H) 3/2B; see also MS(H) 3/2C, Joseph and officials mtg, 7 September 1971.

114. DHSS minute, 2 September 1972, DH, MS(H) 2/3F.

115. LP(71)5, c.February 1971, DH, MS(H) 2/3C.

116. For a general review of the London hospital problem at this date, see G.Rivett, *The Development of the London Hospital System 1823-1982*, chapter 13.

117. *National Health Service. The Administrative Structure of the Medical and Related Services in England and Wales*, paras 38-42, 103.

118. *National Health Service. The Future Structure of the National Health Service*, Appendix 1.

119. LP(70)10, 16 December 1970, DH, J/N 179/120C.

120. Aberdare, comments on LP(70)10, DH, J/N 179/120C.

121. Joseph minute, 25 January 1971, DH, J/N 179/120C.

122. See Rivett, *Development of the London Hospital System*, chapter 13 for further discussion of the doughnut (an inner-London region comprising the undergraduate teaching hospitals, extracted from the Greater London area) and the starfish (an integrated structure involving five regions, in which the populations of the home counties and greater London would be served by integrated services, including the undergraduate teaching hospitals in central London).

123. LP(71)2, 4 January 1971, DH, J/N 179/120C.

124. LP(71)4, c.27 January 1971, and supporting minute, 28 January 1971, DH, J/N 179/120C.

125. DHSS minute, 22 February 1971, DH, J/N 179/120C.

126. *National Health Service Reorganisation*, para 25.

127. *National Health Service Reorganisation*, Appendix 1.

128. Lord Cobbold to Joseph, 8 July 1971, DH, MS(H) 3/2B. Lord Cobbold was a former Governor of the Bank of England; he was Chairman of the Middlesex Hospital Board of Governors and Medical School Council, also Chairman of the London Undergraduate Teaching Hospitals Committee. Lord Cottesloe had formerly been Chairman of the NW Metropolitan RHB; he was Chairman of the Hammmersmith Hospital Board of Governors, and Chairman of the British Postgraduate Medical Federation.

129. Briefs for meeting of Secretary of State with London undergraduate teaching hospitals representatives, 26 July 1971, DH, MS(H) 3/2B.

130. DHSS minute, 15 October 1971, reports of both conciliatory comments and threats by Cobbold; see also H R Moore (London Hospital) to Joseph, 29 October 1971, DH, MS(H) 3/2B.

131. Joseph and London undergraduate teaching hospitals delegation mtg, 24 January 1972, DH, MS(H) 3/2B.

132. Exchanges between Joseph and Cobbold, 25 January 1972 to 30 March 1972, DH, MS(H) 3/2D.

133. Joseph and RHB Chairmen mtg, 2 February 1972, DH, B/N 1/27.

134. London Consultation Document, 29 March 1972, DH, MS(H) 3/2D.

135. Joseph and Teaching Hospitals Association mtg, 16 May 1972, and reports of informal exchanges associated with that meeting, DH, MS(H) 3/2E.

136. Joseph minute of conversation with Lord Reigate, 3 August 1972, DH, MS(H) 2/3F.

137. DHSS minute, 17 October 1972, DH, J/N 179/31N.

138. DHSS minute, 5 October 1972, DH, J/N 179/31N. A similar scheme was proposed by Professor Walter Holland, 7 March 1972, DH, MS(H) 3/2D.

139. Aberdare to Joseph, 9 October 1972, DH, J/N 179/31N.

140. Joseph, Ministers and officials mtg, 10 October 1972, DH, J/N 179/31N.

141. Ministers favoured five or even one London FPC, but were persuaded by officials to accept one-to-one relationship between FPCs and AHAs, DHSS minute, 27 July 1972, DH, MS(H) 2/3F.

142. London Working Party mtg, 26 October 1972, DH, J/N 179/31N.

143. DHSS minutes, November 1972, DH, J/N 179/31N.

144. *Future Structure of the NHS*, paras 54-5.

145. *National Health Service Reorganisation*, para 20.

146. J N Morris, 'Tomorrow's Community Physician', Delamar Lecture, 1969, *Lancet*, 1969, ii, 811-16, 18 October 1969.

147. Ministers and deputation of National Association of Leagues of Hospital Friends mtg, 14 December 1971, DH, J/N 179/56B.

148. Mrs Mary Applebey, General Secretary of NAMH, to Joseph, 28 July 1971, DH, J/N 179/56A.

149. DHSS minute, 11 October 1971, DH, J/N 179/56A.

150. DHSS minutes, November 1971 to January 1972, DH, J/N 179/56B.

151. *The Brighton and East Sussex Project. Advisory Group Report* (September, 1972).

152. P Draper and T Smart, *The Future of Our Health Care. NHS Reorganisation Project* (Department of Community Medicine, Guy's Hospital Medical School, 1972).

153. DHSS brief on draft White Paper, 14 July 1972, DH, MS(H) 3/10.

154. Joseph to Permanent Secretary, 11 October 1972, DH, J/N 179/156C.

155. R Klein and J Lewis, *The Politics of Consumer Representation* (Centre for Studies in Social Policy, 1976), p 15.

156. For an excellent review, B Harris, *The Health of the Schoolchild. A History of the School Medical Service in England and Wales* (Open University Press, 1995).

157. Harris, *Health of the Schoolchild*, p 209.

158. Central Health Services Council-Standing Medical Advisory Committee, *Report of a Sub-Committee on Child Welfare Centres* (HMSO, June 1967) Chairman Sir Wilfrid Sheldon, para 35. DH, J/N 179/10A.

159. DES and MH exchanges, October to December 1967, DH, J/N 179/10A. This development followed an initiative from Douglas Houghton, in his capacity as Cabinet coordinator of policy in the social services field.

160. MH minute, 8 September 1967, DH, J/N 179/10A.

161. MH minute, 28 November 1968, DH, J/N 179/10A.

162. DHSS minute, 19 March 1969, DH, J/N 179/10A.

163. DHSS minute, 14 July 1969, DH, J/N 179/10A; DES to MH, 22 August and 19 September 1969, DES, M26/1/368.

164. DES-DHSS exchanges, October 1969, DH, J/N 179/10A.

165. *The Future Structure of the National Health Service*, para 32.

166. *The Future Structure of the National Health Service*, para 33.

167. *National Health Service Reorganisation. Consultative Document*, para 3.

168. DHSS brief on HS(71)14, October 1971, DH, MS(H) 3/2B.

169. 'First Report of the Sub-Committee on the School Health Service - July 1972', in *A Report from the Working Party on Collaboration between the NHS and Local Government on its activities to the end of 1972* (HMSO, 1973), pp 60-75.

170. *National Health Service Reorganisation. England*, para 20.

171. *National Health Service Reorganisation. England*, para 22. *Report from the Working Party on Collaboration between the NHS and Local Government to the end of 1972*, para 6.45, where it was also recommended that current local education authority powers in the field of child guidance should not be 'in any way limited as a consequence of legislative changes' connected with proposals for health service unification.

172. *The Future Structure of the National Health Service*, para 40.

173. *National Health Service Reorganisation. England*, para 25.

174. *National Health Service Reorganisation. England*, para 31.

175. *National Health Service Reorganisation. England*, para 35.

176. *National Health Service Reorganisation. England*, para 24.

177. *National Health Service Reorganisation. England*, para 82.

178. *National Health Service Reorganisation. England*, para 186(e).

179. The Chairman was Mr A R W Bavin from DHSS. The local authority

associations were represented by 19 members, 4 of whom were Medical Officers
of Health. 8 members came from NHS authorities; most of these were
clinicians. There were two general practitioners among the 17 departmental
nominees, most of whom came from DHSS, but also the Department of
Education and Science, the Department of the Environment and the Welsh
Office were represented.

180. *A Report from the Working Party on Collaboration between the NHS and Local Government
on its activities to the end of 1972* (HMSO, 1973).

181. *A Report from the Working Party on Collaboration between the NHS and Local Government
on its activities from January to July 1973* (HMSO, 1973); *A Report from the Working
Party on Collaboration between the NHS and Local Government on its activities from July
1973 to April 1974* (HMSO, 1974).

182. For the initial problem, R Rowbottom and A Hey, 'Collaboration between
Health and Social Services', in E Jacques, ed, *Health Services. Their nature and
organization, and the role of patients, doctors, nurses, and the complementary professions*
(Heinemann, 1979), pp 179-203. See also chapter VII, and for a summary of the
later position, G Wistow, 'Joint Finance and Community Care', *Health Care UK
1984*, pp 69-74; Wistow, 'Community Care for the Mentally Handicapped:
disappointing progress', *Health Care UK 1985*, pp 69-78.

183. *Report from the Working Party on Collaboration to the end of 1972*, para 2.6.

184. *Report from the Working Party on Collaboration to the end of 1972*, paras 2.7-14.

185. *Report from the Working Party on Collaboration to the end of 1972*, paras 2.24.1-8.

186. DHSS minutes, March to May 1971, and correspondence between CSD and
DHSS, May to June 1971, CAB 157.

187. SCM(71) 1st meeting, 5 August 1971, DH, G/N 185/8A.

188. DHSS, *Reorganisation Management Study. First Tentative Hypotheses* (DHSS, May
1972); DHSS, *Management Arrangements for the Reorganised NHS* (HMSO,
September 1972).

189. Joseph, HC Debates, vol 851, col 240, 23 February 1973 (WA).

190. Management Steering Committee mtgs, February to May 1972, DH, G/N
185/8B-C

191. Joseph and NHS Chief Officers mtg, 7 May 1971, DH, MS(H) 3/2B.

192. Treasury minute, 1 September 1971, T, 2SS 21/278/01A.

193. CSD to SHHD, 18 January 1972, T, 2SS 21/85/01A.

194. Treasury, CSD, and SHHD mtg, 3 February 1972, T, 2SS 21/85/01A.

195. Management Steering Committee mtg, 27 April 1972, DH, G/N 185/8C.

196. DHSS to Treasury, 6 March 1972, T, 2SS 21/01E.

197. Discussion of SCM(72)12, Management Steering Committee mtg, 27 April
1972, DH, G/N 185/8C.

198. Management Steering Committee mtg, 7 January 1972, DH, G/N 185/8B.

199. Discussion of SCM(72)12, Management Steering Committee mtg, 27 April
1972, DH, G/N 185/8C.

200. 'National Organisational Model for a Unified Service', c.February 1972, CAB 157.

201. Joseph, Ministers, officials, NHS representatives, and management experts mtg, 1 March 1972, DH, MS(H) 3/2C.

202. Joseph, Ministers, officials, NHS representatives, and management experts mtg, 6 March 1972, DH, MS(H) 3/2C.

203. Meyjes to Joseph, 9 March 1972, and related exchanges, March 1973, CAB, 157.

204. Joseph minute on 29 July 1971 summary of White Paper, 12 August 1971, DH, MS(H) 3/2B. Capitals as in the original.

205. Treasury minutes, 23 August, 1 September, and 12 November 1971, T, 2SS 21/278/01B.

206. The final draft dated 7 June 1972, DH, MS(H) 3/10. For summaries and drafts, DH, J/N 179/138B-D.

207. Treasury brief on HS(72)66, 5 May 1972, T, 2SS 21/01E.

208. Joseph, HS(72)66, 23 June 1972, HS(72) 18th meeting, 30 June 1972, CAB 134. For a report by the Home Secretary, 3 July 1972 and letter from Rippon to Heath in support of Walker, 7 July 1972, NHS Reorganisation, 1972, PREM 11.

209. Joseph, CP(72)79, 12 July 1972, Thomas, CP(72)80, 14 July 1972, CAB 129; CM(72) 37th meeting, 20 July 1972, CAB 128. At this meeting the Home Secretary was Robert Carr, who had replaced Reginald Maudling. The latter resigned on 18 July on account of his involvement with the bankrupt architect, John Poulson. It was improper for Maudling to remain as Home Secretary in view of police investigations into the affairs of Poulson. For Treasury brief on CP(72)79, 18 July 1972, demanding no concession to Walker, T, 2SS 21/04E.

210. Joseph, HC Debates, vol 842, col 87, 1 August 1972 (WA). *National Health Service Reorganisation: England*, Cmnd.5055 (HMSO, 1972); *National Health Service Reorganisation: Wales*, Cmnd.5057 (HMSO, 1972).

211. DHSS minute, 19 July 1972, DH, J/N 179/138D.

212. *NHS Reorganisation: England*, Appendix III, pp 57-62.

213. *NHS Reorganisation: England*, para 40.

214. *NHS Reorganisation: England*, Foreword, p v.

215. *NHS Reorganisation: England*, Conclusions, para 207.

216. *NHS Reorganisation: England*, para 20.

217. *NHS Reorganisation: England*, para 25.

218. *NHS Reorganisation: England*, Section VIII.

219. *NHS Reorganisation: England*, para 53. See Maps 1 and 2.

220. *NHS Reorganisation: England*, Section XXII.

221. *NHS Reorganisation: England*, p 13, footnote.

222. *NHS Reorganisation: England*, Section XIII.

223. Webster I, p 348.

224. *NHS Reorganisation: England*, Section VII.

225. *NHS Reorganisation: England*, Section X.

226. *NHS Reorganisation: England*, Section XI.

227. *NHS Reorganisation: England*, para 101.

228. For a diagrammatic representation of the medical advisory structure in England, see Appendix 2.14.

229. *NHS Reorganisation: England*, Section XIII.

230. See article by Peter Draper, and associated correspondence, *Lancet*, 1972, ii, 967, 4 November 1972. See also P Draper and T Smart, *The Future of our Health Care. NHS Reorganisation Project* (Department of Community Medicine, Guy's Hospital, 1972).

231. *Daily Telegraph*, 2 August 1972.

232. *Times*, 9 August 1972. Crossman expanded on this view in his Bloch lecture, *A Politicians View of Health Service Planning* (Glasgow University, December 1972).

233. *Guardian*, 2 August 1972.

234. *Tribune*, 8 December 1972.

235. *Economist*, 5 August 1972; *New Statesman*, 4 August 1972.

236. *General Practitioner*, 15 September 1972.

237. *Observer*, 6 August 1972; *Guardian*, 2 August 1972.

238. *Times*, 2 August 1972; *Guardian*, 2 August 1972; *Sunday Times*, 6 August 1972.

239. *Times*, 16 September 1972.

240. RHB Chairmen, 'NHS Reorganisation: Management Arrangements', DH, G/R 39/24.

241. For the drafting of the Bill, DH, 'NHS Reorganisation Bill 1973', 4 vols, mainly vols 2 and 4.

242. For fuller consideration of the Scottish legislation, see below, section (viii). For discussions in the Legislation Committee, Joseph, L(72)85, 10 November 1972; L(72) 24th meeting, 14 November 1972, CAB 134. Treasury briefs on the Legislation Committee discussions, November 1972, T, 2SS 21/98/07B.

243. Aberdare, HL Debates, vol 339, cols 526-7, 27 February 1973.

244. *NHS Reorganisation Bill*, clause 2.

245. HL Debates, vol 337, cols 8-138, 4 December 1972.

246. HL Debates, vol 337, cols 8-18, 4 December 1972.

247. HL Debates, vol 337, 132-6, 4 December 1972.

248. HL Debates, vol 337, cols 32-7, 82-9, 4 December 1972.

249. HL Debates, vol 337, cols 32-7, 101-7, 4 December 1972.

250. See HL Debates, vol 337, 4 December 1972, Serota (col 19), Amulree (col 30), Cobbold (cols 36-7), Watkins (cols 73-4), Cottesloe (col 85).

251. This issue was emphasised by Baroness Serota, Lady Ruthven, the Bishop of Lichfield, Lord Burntwood, Lord Grenfell, Baroness Masham, Lord Watkins, Lord Beaumont, Lord Milverton, Lord Hayter, and Baroness White.

252. HL Debates, vol 337, col 121, 4 December 1972.

253. HL Debates, vol 337, cols 821-919, 18 December 1972, cols 950-69, 987-1072, 19 December 1972, vol 338, cols 10-85, 96-149, 23 January 1973, cols 255-67, 279-376, 25 January 1973, cols 430-84, 29 January 1973, cols 1243-59, 1262-390, 12 February 1973, cols 1402-17, 13 February 1973.

254. Secretary of State and officials mtg, 13 November 1972, DH, J/N 179/156C.

255. Joseph minute, 19 October 1972, DH, J/N 179/156D.

256. Alison minute, 30 October 1972, Conservative Central Office minute, 27 October 1972, DH, J/N 179/156D.

257. Aberdare, HL Debates, vol 338, cols 107-26, 23 January 1973.

258. Howe to Alison, 9 February 1973, DH, J/N 179/156D. J Rogarty, *Financial Times*, 23 January 1973.

259. HL Debates, vol 338, cols 1454-80, 13 February 1973.

260. 'Community Health Councils', editorial, *Lancet*, 1973, i, 357-8, 17 February 1973.

261. CM(73) 16th mtg, 15 March 1973, CAB 128.

262. HC Debates, vol 857, cols 1223-333, 12 June 1972.

263. HL Debates, vol 337, cols 840-53, 18 December 1972, vol 338, cols 1262-70, 12 February 1973.

264. HC Debates, vol 857, cols 1334-42, 12 June 1972.

265. *Report from the Working Party on Collaboration to the end of 1972*, para 5.8-40.

266. Notes on amendments to clause 18, T, 2SS 21/04A, Annexe.

267. Joseph, HC Debates, vol 853, cols 363-4, 28 March 1973 (WA).

268. *NHS Reorganisation News*, No.9, June 1973, was given over entirely to this subject.

269. L(72) 24th mtg, 14 November 1972, CAB 134.

270. Joseph, Minister and officials mtgs on House of Lords amendments on local authority representation, 24 and 30 January 1973, DH, MS(H) 2/3D.

271. DHSS minute, 27 December 1972, DH, MS(H) 2/3F.

272. Drafting of Joint Liaison Committee circulars, BN 30/42. HRC(72)3, 'Joint Liaison Committees', June 1972; *NHS Reorganisation News*, No.1, September 1972. B Edwards and P R Walker, *Si vis pacem: Preparation for Change in the National Health Service* (NPHT, 1973); I G Yule, 'Prelude to Reorganisation: a commentary on the preparatory work of Joint Liaison Committees', *Health Trends*, November 1974, pp 63-5.

273. Office mtg, 25 August 1972, BN 30/5.

274. Office mtg, 15 November 1972, BN 30/38.

275. Brown, *Reorganising the National Health Service*, pp 85-6.

924

276. Yule, p 65.

277. For a description of the work of the Joint Liaison Committee of the Humberside area, see Brown, *Reorganising the National Health Service*, pp 50-2, 86-91. This committee produced the newsletter, *Humberside Health*.

278. HRC(73)23, 'Transitional Arrangements: Staff Support for Regional and Area Health Authorities', September 1973.

279. F Barnes et.al., *Community Medicine*, 1972, **128**, 550-8.

280. For an indication of the staff groups involved and their numbers, see Appendix 3.25.

281. *Future Structure of the National Health Service*, para 100.

282. National Health Service Reorganisation Act 1973, section 20.

283. For establishment of National Staff Commissions, October 1971-November 1972, BN 30/1, 2, 5; T, 2SS 21/04D.

284. For a full review of the work of the Commission, see DHSS, *National Health Service Staff Commission Report (1972-5)* (HMSO, 1975).

285. In connection with reorganisation the number of National Staff Committees was eventually increased to five, covering the main functional groups of non-medical staff.

286. The other members of the Staff Advisory Committee and Staff Commission were D G Hoffenden, a barrister and ICI executive, Mrs R W Kelly, a member of Sheffield RHB, A Milner Smith, barrister and Town Clerk of Lewisham, and Lord Wright of Ashton-under-Lyne, former General Secretary of the Amalgamated Weavers Association, and Chairman of Ashton and Glossop HMC.

287. Top NHS Salaries, memoranda and briefs for Prime Minister, July 1972 to July 1973, PREM 11.

288. Some 150 assessors were used in this operation, BN 30/2.

289. DHSS minute, 16 May 1974, BN 30/40.

290. DHSS minute, 20 February 1974, BN 30/2.

291. DHSS and Regional Personnel Officers mtg, 16 May 1974, BN 30/40.

292. BN 30/40.

293. BN 30/40.

294. BN 30/2.

295. The Works Officer was the other member of the regional team. This was a new office without a direct parallel in the RHB. This post tended to be occupied by former regional architects or engineers. For the following paragraphs, see Maps 1 and 2.

296. A greater impression of change is given if the comparison is made with 1971, since many retirements took place in the run up to reorganisation. Even in these cases, replacements tended to made by internal promotion.

297. DHSS minute, 13 March 1973, DH, J/N 179/037.

298. Joseph minute, 22 March 1973, DH, J/N 179/037.

299. DHSS to BMA, 5 October 1973, DH, J/N 179/037.

300. In the cases of Sheffield, Oxford and Manchester the SAMOs were recent appointees. The Oxford SAMO was a woman; she became the only woman among the RMOs.

301. *National Health Service Reorganisation: England*, Appendix 1, p 54. The Management Report, published two months later than the White Paper, used the existing names for the regions, *Management Arrangements*, p 19.

302. National Health Service (Determination of Regions) Order 1973 (SI 1973, No.1191); National Health Service (Constitution of Regional Health Authorities) Order 1973 (SI 1973, No.1192).

303. A similar anomaly was created when part of north Lincolnshire was transferred to the Yorkshire region.

304. DH, J/N 179/21A, MS(H) 2/3D.

305. DH, MS(H) 2/3D.

306. In 1948 there were three Chairmen with labour affiliations, Webster I, p 274.

307. Crossman, *Diaries*, iii, p 466.

308. *Local Government in England: Government Proposals for Reorganisation*, Cmnd.4584 (HMSO, 1971).

309. *National Health Service Reorganisation. Consultative Document*, para 8.

310. Separate metropolitan district status for St Helens and Knowsley was a late decision in passage of the local government Bill. The mid-Lancashire boroughs hoped that this decision would assist their own claim to area status. However, despite having a joint population of nearly 400,000, St Helens and Knowsley were not regarded as meriting AHA status separately, BN 30/5.

311. DHSS minute, 2 March 1973, DH, MS(H) 2/3D. At the Legislation Committee, Aberdare suggested there would be 80 AHAs, L(72) 24th meeting, 14 November 1972, CAB 134.

312. Joseph and mid-Lancashire delegation mtgs, 13 and 28 March 1973, DH, MS(H) 2/3D.

313. *Management Arrangements,* Appendix 1, pp 112-5.

314. This problem is well illustrated by the case-history of Hull, where the Secretary of State overturned the JLC proposal for a single north bank Humberside district, Brown, *Reorganising the NHS*, pp 91-6.

315. National Health Service (Determination of Areas) Order 1973 (SI 1973, No.1275); National Health Service (Constitution of Area Health Authorities) Order 1973 (SI 1973, No.1305).

316. Occupational analysis of AHA chairmen, 31 March 1976, DH, G/H 223/37C.

317. Secretary of State and officials mtg, 6 July 1973, DH, MS(H) 2/3D.

318. Labour figures such as David Ennals, Kenneth Robinson, Peggy Jay and Baroness Serota were considered but rejected as London teaching group chairmen, Joseph and officials mtg, 14 June 1973, DH, MS(H) 2/3D, also G/H 223/1A.

319. Joseph and GMSC delegation mtg, 2 May 1973, DH, MS(H) 2/3D.

320. HRC(73)32, 'Establishing Family Practitioner Committees', October 1973.

321. BN 30/34.

322. *National Health Service Reorganisation, Consultative Document*, para 18.

323. *National Health Service Reorganisation: England*, paras 100-104.

324. BN 30/35.

325. HRC(74)9, 'Local Advisory Committees', February 1974.

326. *National Health Service Reorganisation: England*, para 103. DH, J/N 179/80A; Aberdare to Joseph, 13 July 1971, DH, MS(H) 3/2B.

327. DH, F/C 53/58A-B.

328. Report for Ministers on Proposed PSSC, October 1970, DH, LA/P 337/01A.

329. Joseph, HC Debates, vol 827, cols 334-5, 8 December 1971(WA).

330. DH, LA/P 337/01B-G.

331. Joseph, HC Debates, vol 860, col 298, 23 July 1973(WA).

332. Waddilove had served on the MacKenzie working party, set up in 1968 following the Social Work(Scotland) Act 1968 to advise on the functions of the new social service departments in Scotland.

333. Heading to article by Elizabeth Dunn, *Daily Telegraph*, 11 November 1973.

334. CHCs, submission to Ministers, 19 October 1973, DH, J/N 179/156J.

335. HRC(74)4, 'Community Health Councils', January 1974.

336. DHSS minute, November 1974, DH, J/N 179/156N.

337. DHSS minute, 3 April 1974, DH, J/N 179/156L.

338. J Hallas and B Fallon, *Mounting the Health Guard. A Handbook for CHC Members* (NPHT, 1974).

339. Campbell signified his approval on 3 July 1970, HH 101/3606. Other departments were not consulted at this stage. In December 1970, the Treasury was informed that Ministers had not yet formed firm views, but were unlikely to depart from the thinking of their officials, Treasury minute, T, 2SS 21/04A.

340. Campbell, HC Debates, vol 804, col 276, 24 July 1970 (WA).

341. SHHD, 'Central Arrangements. Discussion Paper', March 1971, T, 2SS 21/85/01A.

342. CMO minute, 1 May 1969, HH 101/2030.

343. CMO minute, 29 June 1969, HH 101/2284.

344. SHHD minute, 9 October 1970, HH 101/3606.

345. Treasury minute, 9 December 1970, T, 2SS 21/04A.

346. Campbell, HC Debates, vol 805, cols 453-4, 5 November 1970 (WA).

347. SHHD minute, 23 February 1971, HH 101/3607.

348. SHHD, 'Area Health Boards, Discussion Paper', May 1970, HH 101/3606. For drafts, see HH 101/2429.

349. Scottish Office, *Reform of Local Government in Scotland*, Cmnd.4583 (HMSO, Edinburgh, 1971).

350. SHHD to Treasury, 23 February 1971, HH 101/3607; also SHHD to Treasury, 2 March 1971, T, 2SS 21/85/01A. In December 1970, the Treasury was informed that 13 Area Health Boards were favoured, SHHD to Treasury, 9 December 1970, T, 2SS 21/04A. In SL(71)22, 20 March 1971, CAB 134, 13-15 area boards were mentioned.

351. SHHD and Scottish Council of BMA mtg, April 1970, HH 101/2429; at this stage the Scottish BMA was expecting the medical profession to be granted one-third of the membership of area boards, SHHD to Treasury, 23 February 1971, HH 101/3607.

352. SHHD to Treasury, 23 February 1971, HH 101/3607.

353. SHHD to Treasury, 13 April 1971, T, 2SS 21/85/01A.

354. Revised discussion paper on central arrangements, 27 April 1971, T, 2SS 21/85/01A.

355. Exchanges between the Treasury, DHSS and SHHD, March to July 1972, T, 2SS 21/85/01A.

356. T, 2SS 21/298/02.

357. SHHD to Treasury, 30 June 1971, T, 2SS 21/298/02.

358. Campbell, SL(71)14, 1 July 1971, SL(71) 4th meeting, 9 July 1971, CAB 134.

359. SHHD, *Reorganisation of the Scottish Health Services*, Cmnd.4734 (HMSO, Edinburgh, 1971).

360. *Reorganisation of the Scottish Health Services*, paras 4, 10, 19.

361. *Reorganisation of the Scottish Health Services*, paras 29-43.

362. See for instance, *Reorganisation of the Scottish Health Services*, para 43.

363. *Reorganisation of the Scottish Health Services*, para 29.

364. *Reform of Local Government in Scotland*, Cmnd.4583 (HMSO, Edinburgh, 1971).

365. *Reorganisation of the Scottish Health Services*, paras 14-18.

366. *Reorganisation of the Scottish Health Services*, para 45.

367. *Reorganisation of the Scottish Health Services*, paras 11, 24-7.

368. SHHD, Summary of comments on White Paper, 22 November 1971, T, 2SS 21/298/02.

369. Early drafts of Scottish reorganisation Bill, October-November 1972, T, 2SS 21/298/08A.

370. Campbell, L(72)9, L(72) 3rd meeting, 18 January 1972, CAB 134.

371. It will be recalled that the England and Wales Bill was introduced almost a year later than the Scottish Bill. This should be borne in mind with reference to any comparisons between the two Bills.

372. HL Debates, vol 327, cols 1072-121, 8 February 1972, vol 328, cols 677-755, 24 February 1972, vol 329, cols 34-57, 7 March 1972, vol 329, cols 836-9, 23 March 1972.

373. SL(72) 5th meeting, 15 February 1972, CAB 134.

374. HC, Scottish Grand Committee, NHS Reorganisation (Scotland) Bill, cols 1-58, 2 May 1972, cols 59-108, 4 May 1972.

375. HC, First Scottish Standing Committee, NHS Reorganisation (Scotland) Bill, cols 1-432, 16 May to 22 June 1972.

376. Millan, First Scottish Standing Committee, NHS Reorganisation (Scotland) Bill, cols 112-5, 23 May 1972.

377. SL(72) 19th mtg, 14 July 1972, CAB 134. For exchanges between Treasury and SHHD, T, 2SS 21/298/08E.

378. T, 2SS 21/85/01B.

379. 'Proposed Health Board Areas', October 1972, T, 2SS 21/85/01E.

380. NHS (Determination of Areas of Health Boards) (Scotland) Order 1971 (SI 1973, No.266).

381. HSR(73)C6, 'Advance Studies in Areas', March 1973; HSR(73)C7, Health Board Districts, March 1973.

382. NHS Circulars 1974(GEN)38 and 90.

383. HSR(72)C3, 'The Administrative Structure of the Health Boards', November 1972.

384. SHHD and BMA mtg, 8 April 1970, HH 101/2429.

385. Treasury minute, 9 December 1970, T, 2SS 21/04A.

386. SHHD, Discussion Paper on Area Health Board Management Structure, 13 December 1971, revised 6 January 1972, T, 2SS 21/85/01A.

387. SHHD, CSD, and Treasury mtg, 3 February 1972, T, 2SS 21/85/01A.

388. As noted below, the Welsh line of accountability was nearer to the Scottish model.

389. DHSS to SHHD, 24 October 1972, T, 2SS 21/85/01E.

390. HSR(72)C3, para 19.

391. SHHD to Treasury, April 1972, T, 2SS 21/85/01B.

392. SHHD to Treasury, 5 April 1972, T, 2SS 21/85/01C.

393. Campbell to Joseph, 7 July 1972, T, 2SS 21/85/01D.

394. Exchanges between SHHD, CSD and DHSS, July to September 1972, T, 2SS 21/85/01D.

395. HSR(73)C6; T, 2SS 21/85/01F.

396. CSD to Treasury, 15 March 1972, T, 2SS 21/85/01B; exchanges between CSD and SHHD, April to June 1972, T, 2SS 21/85/01C,D.

397. SHHD to Treasury, 11 August 1972, SHHD, H/RHS/1/18; SHHD, 'Common Services Agency', 24 August 1972, T, 2SS 21/85/01D.

398. HSR(72)C2, 'Common Services Agency', November 1972, For exchanges between the Treasury, CSD and SHHD on the CSA, 1972, T, 2SS 21/85/01B,E.

399. Scottish Office Management Services, *Future Central Organisation of the Scottish Health Services* (SOMS, March 1972).

400. SHHD, 'Supplies Function of CSA', 13 June 1972, T, 2SS 21/85/01D. HSR(73)C21, 'Supplies Functions', June 1973.

401. SHHD, 'Scottish Ambulance Service', 17 April 1972, T, 2SS 21/85/01C. HSR(73)C26, 'Ambulance Service', July 1973.

402. SHHD, 'Scottish Blood Transfusion Service', 2 May 1972, T, 2SS 21/85/01C,D; SHHD, HOS 26/1/3.

403. After some hesitation, the Scottish Council for Health Education, dating from 1943, was allowed to drift on as an independent body, but with considerably reduced functions following reorganisation.

404. SHHD to Treasury, 16 October 1972, and draft circular on CSA, 18 October 1972, T, 2SS 21/85/01E. At this stage CSD altered its line and decided that a strong chief executive would be best to secure the efficiency of the CSA, CSD to SHHD, 19 October 1972, T, 2SS 21/85/01E.

405. WO, NHSR 1/2 Part 3.

406. Gibson-Watt to Thomas, December 1970, WO, NHSR 1/2 Part 8.

407. Welsh Council, Provisional Statement on the Welsh Green Paper, November 1970, WO, NHSR 1/2 Part 3. Proposals for a Welsh Health Council, October 1970, WO, HL 34/92/3 Part 1.

408. Welsh Office minute, 14 September 1970, WO, NHSR 1/2 Part 4.

409. Welsh Office minute, 26 February 1971, WO, NHSR 1/2 Part 6.

410. Welsh Office minute, 14 January 1971, WO, NHSR 1/2 Part 6.

411. Treasury minute, 19 March 1971, DH, J/N 179/91A.

412. WO, NHSR 12/2/1.

413. Ministers and officials mtg, 13 May 1971, WO, NHSR 8/92/1. For Welsh Office discussions with the Treasury concerning the WHSTO, T, 2SS 21/102/01D.

414. Welsh Office minute, 6 May 1971, WO, NHSR 1/2 Part 9.

415. At this stage the Welsh changed from the Scottish to the English terminology for area authorities.

416. Welsh Office minute, c.10 May 1971, WO, NHSR 1/2 Part 9.

417. DH, J/N 179/91A.

418. WO, NHSR 8/76/1. Welsh Office, *National Health Service Reorganisation in Wales* (HMSO, Cardiff, 1971).

419. DH, J/N 179/91A.

420. WO, NHSR 8/61/1-8.

421. WO, EP 303/1/71 Part A.

422. WO, HL 34/92/1 Part 1.

423. *National Health Service Reorganisation in Wales*, Cmnd.5057 (HMSO, 1972). For drafts, dated May and June 1972, DH, J/N 179/91B.

424. CM(72) 37th mtg, 20 July 1972, CAB 128.

425. Exchanges between English and Welsh Ministers, December 1970-January 1971, and office discussions, WO, NHSR 1/2 Part 6.

426. DH, J/N 179/91D.

427. HC, Welsh Grand Committee, National Health Service Reorganisation in Wales, cols 2-104, 21 Nov 1972. Notes for Secretary of State for Wales, 11 November 1972, DH, MS(H) 3/2C.

428. Welsh Office to DHSS, 24 November 1972, DH, J/N 179/91D.

429. DHSS, notes on amendments to clause 5, T, 2SS 21/04 Annexe.

430. Thomas, HC Debates, vol 853, col 1113, 27 March 1973.

431. HL Debates, vol 337, cols 72-7, 106-26, 4 December 1972.

432. Welsh Office, Circular WHRC(73)16.

433. WO, NHSR 1/2 Part 6, NHSR 10/69/2; DH, J/N 179/91C.

434. Welsh Office, *Management Arrangements for the Reorganised National Health Service in Wales* (HMSO, Cardiff, 1972).

435. *Management Arrangements in Wales*, p 36. Mr Prys-Davies (later Lord Prys-Davies) was a solicitor from the firm of Morgan, Bruce and Nicholas, of Cardiff and elsewhere in South Wales. He was originally from Merioneth, and was educated at Aberystwyth University College.

436. Resignation of Prys-Davies, July 1972, WO, NHSR 1/2 Part 6.

437. *Royal Commission on the Constitution 1969-1973, volume 1, Report*, Cmnd.5460 (HMSO, 1973), paras 949, 1174-8.

438. WO, HL 34/73/1.

439. Brown, *Reorganising the National Health Service*, p 60.

440. For an expression of concern about the 'anxiety and insecurity' faced by public health medical staff, Serota, HL Debates, vol 337, col 27, 4 December 1972.

441. T E Chester, 'NHS reorganisation after one year', *Hospital and Health Services Review*, April 1975, pp 117-21.

442. John Cunningham, report on conference held by radical health workers, *Guardian*, 22 November 1973; Draper and Smart, *The Future of Our Health Service*.

443. *First Report from the Expenditure Committee. Session 1976-77. Preventive medicine. volume 1 Report* (HMSO, 1977), paras 51-66. This committee began work in November 1975.

444. *Annual Report of the Health Advisory Service 1976*, paras 12, 306-20. For a similar view, letter by Sir Godfrey Nicholson, *Times*, 9 April 1976.

445. N W Chaplin, ed, *Health Care in the United Kingdom* (Kluwer, 1982), p 29.

Chapter VII
CRISIS OF CONFIDENCE

1.   For general context, see M J Artis and D Cobham, eds, *The Labour Government 1974-79* (Oxford University Press, 1991); N Gardner, *The Decade of Discontent* (Blackwell, 1987); M Holmes, *The Labour Government 1974-79: political aims and economic reality* (Macmillan, 1985); D Coates, *Labour in Power? A Study of the Labour Government 1974-1979* (Longman, 1980); Ramsden, *The Winds of Change: Macmillan to Heath, 1957-1975*, pp 427-57. See also notes 42 and 56 below.

2.   Barbara Castle, *The Castle Diaries 1974-76* (Weidenfeld and Nicolson, 1980), pp 33-4, 4 March 1974.

3.   Castle, *Diaries*, p 37.

4.   See Appendix 1.1.

5.   Joel Barnett, *Inside the Treasury* (Andre Deutsch, 1982), pp 65-6.

6.   Castle, *Diaries*, pp 38-9, 78, 143, 156.

7.   For Abel-Smith and Straw, Castle, *Diaries*, pp 34, 38. For Castle's difficulties in securing the appointment of McCarthy, *Diaries*, pp 271, 290, 315.

8.   Castle, *Diaries*, pp 74, 92 and passim.

9.   Owen, *Personally Speaking*, p 54.

10. Castle, *Diaries*, p 143. See also p 242: 'David is a curious mixture. He has excellent ideas but less good on follow through'.

11. Castle, *Diaries*, p 385, 7 May 1975. Benn, *Against the Tide. Diaries 1973-76* (Hutchinson, 1989), p 375. Benn blames the rumour on Wilson.

12. Barnett, *Inside the Treasury*, p 83.

13. Castle, *Diaries*, p 629, 21 January 1976.

14. Castle, *Diaries*, pp 671-2, 4 March 1976. Benn, *Against the Tide*, sporadically mentions rumours of Wilson's resignation, but the first serious reference relates to 7 March 1976 (p 527).

15. Pimlott, *Wilson*, pp 678-80 for the context of this announcement.

16. Callaghan is said to have taken special interest in the health service owing to the association of his wife with Great Ormond Street Hospital, while one of his daughters was married to a general practitioner, Donoughue, *Prime Minister*, pp 113-5.

17. Castle, *Diaries*, pp 623-5, 8 April 1976.

18. Castle, *Diaries*, pp 727, 730, 8 April 1976. At the outset of his parliamentary career, Ennals had been Parliamentary Private Secretary to Castle at the Ministry of Overseas Development.

19. For the relationship between Crossman and Ennals, Tam Dalyell, Ennals' Obituary, *Independent*, 19 June 1995. At the point of Ennals' transfer to social services responsibilities in DHSS, Crossman remarked that he was 'doing extremely well' as Minister of State (Health), Crossman, *Diaries*, iii, p 380, 24 October 1969.

20. Castle, *Diaries*, p 37, 5 March 1974.

21. Ennals had worked with Callaghan at the Home Office from 1967 to 1968.

22. It is reported that in 1989 Ennals admitted to an addiction to valium for 17 years, beginning in the early 1970s, Obituary, *Guardian*, 19 June 1995.

23. Donoughue, *Prime Minister*, pp 113-5; Barnett, *Inside the Treasury*, pp 175, 177, 181.

24. Owen spoke to both Castle and Barnett in January 1976 about his wish to become Chief Secretary, It seems that Wilson had him in mind for this position, Castle, *Diaries*, p 713; Barnett, *Inside the Treasury*, p 83.

25. *Times*, 9 April 1976.

26. Castle, *Diaries*, pp 40, 52, 59.

27. Castle, *Diaries*, p 198.

28. Castle, *Diaries*, p 534, 23 October 1974. Rogers' Obituaries, *Times*, 31 May and 2 June 1990.

29. Hennessy, *Whitehall*, p 525.

30. Nairne, cited by Andrew Marr, *Independent*, 12 November 1987.

31. *Regional Chairmen's Enquiry into the Working of the DHSS in Relation to Regional Health Authorities* (DHSS, 1976).

32. 'Management Review of Department of Health and Social Security. Report by the Steering Committee', February 1978, DH, ROM/41B.

33. 'Management Review of DHSS', para 145.

34. At the end of 1977, the Chief Scientist, Sir Douglas Black retired to become President of the Royal College of Physicians. He was succeeded in January 1978 by Professor A J Buller, Professor of Physiology and Dean of the Medical Faculty at Bristol University, who initially held this post on a part-time basis.

35. See Appendix 3.12.

36. See Appendix 3.13.

37. Background paper on SHSPC, 15 March 1974, HH 99/45.

38. *The Health Service in Scotland. The Way Ahead* (HMSO, Edinburgh, 1976).

39. HH 99/32-4.

40. SHHD memorandum, 'Problem of the SHSPC', July 1978, and related discussion of Policy Group, HH 99/73.

41. For the SHSPC Secretary's view, T D Hunter, 'Close Encounters of a Bureaucratic Kind', *Political Quarterly*, 1987, **58**, 180-90.

42. For the welfare state and the NHS 1974-79, see A Atkinson, J Hills, and J Le Grand, 'The Welfare State', in Dornbusch and Layard, *The Performance of the British Economy*, pp 211-52; J Hills, ed, *The State of Welfare. The Welfare State in Britain since 1974* (Clarendon Press, 1990); Klein, *Politics of the NHS*, chapter 4; Timmins, *Five Giants*, chapter 15.

43. Labour Party, *Opposition Green Paper. Health Care. Report of a Working Party* (Labour Party, August 1973). This committee was established in October 1972; it comprised: Dr John Dunwoody (Chairman), Nicholas Bosanquet, Barbara Castle MP, Frank Honigsbaum, Laurie Pavitt MP, Aubrey Sheiham, Dr Shirley Summerskill MP, and Sue Lancaster(Secretary).

933

44. *Times*, 4 October 1973.

45. Graig, *Election Manifestos*, p 404. Capitals as in the original.

46. Graig, *Election Manifestos*, p 458.

47. Graig, *Election Manifestos*, p 440.

48. Castle, HC Debates, vol 870, col 530, 15 March 1974.

49. Castle, *Diaries*, p 44, 15 March 1974. For the interventions by Barnett and Wilson to curtail Castle's commitments, Treasury minutes, 14-15 March 1974, T, 2SS 550/282/03E.

50. The latter list largely repeats the main recommendations of the 1973 Labour Green Paper.

51. Treasury minute, 5 March 1974, T, 2SS 300/1128/016A.

52. See Appendix 3.3.

53. See Appendix 3.7.

54. See Appendices 3.4., 3.5. For a parallel analysis, J Le Grand, D Winter and F Woolley, 'The National Health Service: Safe in Whose Hands?', in J Hills, ed, *The State of Welfare*, pp 88-134.

55. See Appendix 3.2.

56. For the economic and political context to the following sections, see A J Britton, *Macroeconomic Policy in Britain 1974-87* (NIESR, 1991); Crafts and Woodward, eds, *The British Economy since 1945*; R Dornbusch and R Layard, eds, *The Performance of the British Economy* (Clarendon Press, 1987); M Wright, ed, *Public Spending Decisions. Growth and Restraint in the 1970s* (Allen and Unwin, 1980); T A Booth, ed, *Planning for Welfare. Social Policy and the Expenditure Process* (Blackwell, 1979). See also note 1 above.

57. Treasury minutes, March 1974, T, 2SS 300/1128/016A.

58. Castle, C(74)9, 19 March 1974, CAB 129; CC(74) 5th mtg, 21 March 1974, CAB 128. Castle noted that her colleagues accepted these proposals without demur, *Diaries*, p 47, 21 March 1974. See also Benn, *Against the Tide*, p 125.

59. Castle, HC Debates, vol 889, cols 650-2, 28 March 1974.

60. Castle, *Diaries*, p 58, 28 March 1974.

61. Treasury minute, 27 March 1974, T, 2SS 300/1128/016B.

62. For instance, *Daily Mail*, 15 June 1974, article by John Stevenson and editorial, arguing the health service 'is *already* on the point of collapse'.

63. Dr D Stevenson to Wilson, 8 July 1974, T, 2SS 21/786/02.

64. Castle, *Diaries*, p 140, 9 July 1974.

65. CC(74) 29th mtg, 26 July 1974, CAB 128. Cabinet Secretary's Notebook (Hunt). Castle, *Diaries*, pp 155-6, 26 July 1974. See also Benn, *Against the Tide*, p 207, and Barnett, *Inside the Treasury*, p 47.

66. Healey, Castle and officials mtg, 3 September 1974, T, 2SS 300/1128/016F. Castle, *Diaries*, pp 171-2, 3 September 1974, reports being satisfied with the meeting, but on social security matters deferring disagreements to a 'fight in Cabinet'.

67. CC(74) 35th mtg, 12 September 1974, CAB 128.

68. Healey, Castle and officials mtg, 22 October 1974, T, 2SS 300/1128/016H. Castle, *Diaries*, pp 199-201, 22 October 1974, again reports a positive outcome after an inauspicious start.

69. Treasury minute, 4 November 1974, T, 2SS 300/1128/016H.

70. Castle to Healey, 14 November 1974, Healey to Castle, 19 November 1974, Castle to Healey, 22 November 1974, T, 2SS 300/1128/016H-J.

71. T, 2SS 21/786/01G.

72. Extension of cash limits was formally announced in *The Attack on Inflation*, Cmnd.6151 (HMSO, July 1975), paras 43-5.

73. CC(75) 16th mtg, 25 March 1975, CAB 128. Cabinet Secretary's Notebook (Hunt). Castle, *Diaries*, pp 351-4. Benn, *Against the Tide*, pp 356-7. Barnett, *Inside the Treasury*, pp 64-5.

74. Castle, *Diaries*, p 352.

75. Barnett, Castle, O'Malley, Owen and officials mtg, 27 March 1975, 2SS, 21/786/01G.

76. Barnett minute, 8 April 1975, T, 2SS 300/1128/018B. Barnett, *Inside the Treasury*, pp 65-6.

77. CC(75) 19th mtg, 10 April 1975, CAB 128. Cabinet Secretary's Notebook (Hunt). Castle, *Diaries*, p 360.

78. Treasury minute, 11 April 1975, T, 2SS 300/1128/018B.

79. CC(75) 41st mtg, 25 September 1975, CC(75) 45th mtg, 30 October 1975, CAB 128. Increased dental and optical charges, 1974-1975, PREM 11.

80. Barnett, *Inside the Treasury*, p 80.

81. CC(75) 48th mtg, 13 November 1975, CAB 128. Cabinet Secretary's Notebook (Hunt). Castle, *Diaries*, pp 548-9. Benn, *Against the Tide*, p 461.

82. Castle, *Diaries*, p 559, 24 November 1975.

83. Barnett, Castle, O'Malley, Owen, and officials mtg, 24 November 1975, T, SS 23/24/01B.

84. T, SS 23/24/01B. CC(75) 54th mtg, 9 December 1975, 55th mtg, 11 December 1975, CAB 128. Benn, *Against the Tide*, pp 475-9. Not recorded in Castle, *Diaries*. Barnett, *Inside the Treasury*, pp 80-1.

85. *Public Expenditure to 1979/80*, Cmnd.6393 (HMSO, 1976) published 19 February 1976.

86. CM(76) 13th mtg, 6 July 1976, CAB 128. Cabinet Secretary's Notebook (Hunt). Benn, *Against the Tide*, pp 590-2. Barnett, *Inside the Treasury*, pp 89-91.

87. T, SS 23/24/02B-C. The details of these negotiations were reported in the *Lancet* on 17 July (pp 157-8) from an anonymous correspondent, whom the Treasury identified as a health Minister, Treasury minute, 19 July 1976, T, SS 23/24/02C. Details about the cuts as a whole were leaked to *New Society*, Benn, *Against the Tide*, p 587.

88. CM(76) 17th mtg, 19 July 1976, 19th mtg, 21 July 1976, CAB 128. Benn, *Against the Tide*, pp 598-600. Barnett, *Inside the Treasury*, pp 91-6.

89. Treasury minutes, 30 September 1976 to 20 October 1976, T, SS 23/24/02D.

90. Ennals to Barnett, 25 October 1976, T, SS 23/24/02D.

91. CM(76) 25th mtg, 26 October 1976, CAB 128. Cabinet Secretary's Notebook (Hunt).

92. Ennals to Callaghan, 8 November 1976, T, SS 23/24/02D.

93. CM(76) 31st mtg, 11 November 1976, CAB 128.

94. CM(77) 5th mtg, 10 February 1977, CAB 128. T, SS 23/24/02F.

95. T, SS 23/24/02D-E. Barnett, Ennals and officials mtg, 17 July 1977, T, SS 23/24/02J.

96. Ennals to Healey, 30 September 1977, T, SS 23/24/02L.

97. Ennals to Callaghan, 17 October 1977, T, SS 23/24/02L.

98. Callaghan to Healey, 16 October 1977, and related Treasury minutes, T, SS 23/24/02L.

99. T, SS 23/24/02M.

100. Treasury minute, 2 February 1978, T, SS 23/24/04A.

101. *Report of the Supply Board Working Group* (HMSO, May 1978) (Chairman, Brian Salmon). This investigation was instigated by the Three Chairmen's Report. The group was established in 1976. This was the last and most important of a sequence of reports on hospital supplies, comprising the Messer Report (1958), the Hunt Report (1966), the Collier Report (1976). See also parallel SHHD initiative, *Report of the Working Party on Hospital Supplies Organisation in Scotland* (HMSO, Edinburgh, 1969). The Salmon Report led in 1980 to the establishment of the NHS Supply Council.

102. Ennals, HS(78)11, 16 February 1978, HS(78) 5th mtg, 22 February 1978, CAB 134. This paper was revised to become HS(78)22.

103. Ennals to Callaghan, 24 February 1978, Future of the NHS, 1976-1978, PREM 11.

104. Spanswick to Callaghan, 2 February and 17 March 1978, draft reply c.20 March containing the usual reassurances, Future of the NHS, 1976-1979, PREM 11.

105. Donoughue and Berrill to Callaghan, 17 March 1978, Future of the NHS, 1976-1979, PREM 11.

106. Treasury minute, 22 March 1978, T, SS 23/24/04C.

107. Ennals to Healey, 22 March 1978, T, SS 23/24/04C.

108. Ennals to Callaghan, 31 March 1978, T, SS 23/24/04C. Rees, CP(78)28, 2 March 1978, CAB 129; CM(78) 11th mtg, 4 April 1978, CAB 128. Editorial, *Guardian*, 4 April 1978, encouraging Ministers to support additional resources for the NHS, is well-informed about the relevant Cabinet papers.

109. Callaghan, Ministers and TUC delegation mtg, 5 April 1978, Future of the NHS, 1976-1979, PREM 11.

110. T, SS 23/24/04E,G.

111. Treasury minute, 6 June 1978, T, SS 23/24/04H.

112. This was the tail end of an initiative begun by Owen in the summer of 1976, when a scheme was evolved for limitation in quantities prescribed, and the complete exclusion of certain drugs, Treasury minute, 10 January 1978, T, 2SS 74/77/01A.

113. Brian Salmon to Ennals, 17 May 1978, introducing his report, T, SS 23/24/04J.

114. Treasury minute, 20 June 1978, T, SS 23/24/04J.

115. Ennals, HS(78)53, 9 June 1978, HS(78) 17th mtg, 14 June 1978, CAB 134.

116. Ennals, HS(78)60, 19 June 1978, HS(78) 20th mtg, 6 July 1978, CAB 134. For interpretation of these events, Treasury minute, 21 June 1978, T, SS 23/24/04J.

117. Barnett, CP(78)69, 27 June 1978, CAB 129.

118. Ennals to Callaghan, 4 July 1978, Future of the NHS, 1976-1979, PREM 11.

119. Reg Birch, Geoffrey Drain, Alan Fisher, Catherine Hall, Brenda Maddocks, Brenda Mee, and Albert Spanswick to Callaghan, 3 July 1978, Future of the NHS, 1976-1979, PREM 11.

120. With respect to the trade unionists' letter, a Treasury official noted: 'I understand that the letter was in fact co-ordinated and put together at DHSS itself. It was in fact typed on the same machine as Mr. Ennals' own minute of 4 July to the Prime Minister', T, SS 23/24/04K.

121. Barnett to Callaghan, 5 July 1978, T, SS 23/24/04K.

122. CM(78) 25th mtg, 6 July 1978, CAB 128. Barnett, *Inside the Treasury*, pp 153-4. Benn, *Conflicts of Interest. Diaries 1977-80* (Hutchinson, 1990), pp 320-2. From September 1976, Stanley Orme was a member of the Cabinet as Minister for Social Security.

123. T, SS 23/24/04K.

124. Barnett and Ennals mtg, 7 September 1978, T, SS 23/24/04L.

125. Barnett and Ennals mtg, 25 September 1978, T, SS 23/24/04L.

126. CM(78) 35th mtg, 17 October 1978, CAB 128.

127. Ministers mtg, 18 October 1978, T, SS 23/24/04P. CM(78) 36th mtg, 26 October 1978, CAB 128. Barnett, *Inside the Treasury*, pp 154-6.

128. Ennals, HC Debates, vol 960, cols 774-5, 17 January 1979. Ennals claimed a '£173m boost to HPSS spending' in his DHSS Press Release.

129. Ennals to Barnett, 15 November 1978, Barnett to Ennals, 28 November 1978, and subsequent exchanges, T, 2SS 23/24/04S.

130. For a summary of these developments, Treasury minutes, January 1979, T, 2SS 23/24/04S.

131. DHSS to Treasury, 15 July 1975, T, 2SS 1128/1894/01.

132. T, SS 92/24/01A.

133. Castle, HC Debates, vol 908, col 194, 24 March 1976 (WA). *Priorities for the Health and Personal Social Services in England: A Consultative Document* (HMSO, 1976). For Wales, *Proposed All-Wales Policies and Priorities for the Planning and Provision of Health and Personal Social Services from 1976-77 to 1979-80* (HMSO, Cardiff, 1976).

134. *Priorities in the Health and Social Services. The Way Forward* (HMSO, 1977). For Scotland, *The Health Services in Scotland. The Way Ahead* (HMSO Edinburgh, 1976).

135. *Sharing Resources for England. Report of the Resource Allocation Working Party* (HMSO, 1976). For the Scottish equivalent, using a slightly different methodology, *Scottish Health Authorities Revenue Equalisation. Report of the Working Party on Revenue Resource Allocation* (HMSO, Edinburgh, 1977). For Wales, *Report of the Steering Committee on Resource Allocation in Wales* (HMSO, Cardiff, 1977).

136. *Priorities for Health and Personal Social Services*, para 1.5.

137. *The Way Forward*, para 1.1.

138. *The Way Forward*, Figure 7, p 7.

139. In a further elaboration, the service increment for teaching (SIFT), was applied for the benefit of hospitals teaching medicine and dentistry.

140. Ennals, HC Debates, vol 932, cols 91-3, 21 December 1976 (WA). NHS authorities were first circulated with instructions concerning RAWP on 21 February 1977.

141. GEN 38(76) 3rd mtg, 11 November 1976, GEN 38(77) 2nd mtg, 20 January 1977, CAB 130.

142. Treasury to DHSS, 9 December 1976, DHSS to Treasury, 6 April 1977, T, SS 5/21/01A.

143. This point was first developed in an appendix to Titmuss, *Essays on the 'Welfare State'*, 2nd edn (Allen and Unwin, 1963) pp 208-10. It was repeated in an essay dating from 1965, included in his *Commitment to Welfare* (Allen and Unwin, 1968), p 196.

144. For a thorough review, A Cartwright and M O'Brien, 'Social Class Variations in Health Care and in the Nature of General Practitioner Consultations', in M Stacey, ed, *The Sociology of the National Health Service*, Sociological Review Monograph, 22 (University of Keele, 1976), pp 77-98.

145. J Tudor Hart, 'The inverse care law', *Lancet*, 1971, i, 405-12, 27 February 1971.

146. See for instance, J Noyce, A H Snaith, and A J Trickey, 'Regional variations in the allocation of financial resources to the community health services', *Lancet*, 1974, i, 554-7, 30 March 1974; P Townsend, 'Inequality and the Health Service', *Lancet*, 1974, i, 1179-90, 15 June 1974.

147. J Brotherston, 'Inequality: Is it Inevitable?', in C O Carter and J Peel, eds, *Equalities and Inequalities in Health* (Academic Press, 1976). For Ennals' statement, *Times*, 28 March 1977. For Black's report to the Chief Scientist's Research Committee, Chief Scientist's Research Committee mtg, 30 March 1977, DH, J/C 397/13.

148. *The Way Forward*, p 29.

149. *Inequalities in Health. Report of a Research Working Group* (DHSS, 1980). The Black Report was issued by Penguin Books in 1982, and reprinted often, latterly in conjunction with Margaret Whitehead's *The Health Divide* (1987). See Timmins, *Five Giants*, pp 379-80.

150. RCN, telegram to Castle, 27 March 1974, and 'The State of Nursing', May 1974, DH, M/B 72/2.

151. Stevenson to Wilson, 8 July 1974, T, 2SS 21/786/02.

152. Treasury minutes and briefs for the Prime Minister, c.10 July 1974, BMA and NHS Reorganisation, 1974-1975, PREM 11, 2SS 21/786/02.

153. Brief for the Prime Minister, 15 July 1974, BMA and NHS Reorganisation, 1974-1975, PREM 11.

154. Brief for Chief Secretary, 26 July 1974, T, 2SS 21/786/02.

155. Chief Medical Officer minute, 29 July 1974, T, 2SS 21/786/02.

156. Castle to Wilson, 30 July 1974, BMA and NHS Reorganisation, 1974-1975, PREM 11.

157. The Royal Colleges were represented by Sir Rodney Smith, President of the Royal College of Surgeons, and Chairman of the Conference of Presidents of Royal Colleges and Deans of Faculties.

158. Wilson, Ministers and health professions mtg, 31 July 1974, T, 2SS 21/786/02. For Castle's perspective on this meeting, *Diaries*, pp 162-3.

159. 'The Financing of the National Health Service', 28 October 1974, T, 2SS 21/786/02.

160. Castle, *Diaries*, pp 443-4, 2 July 1975.

161. Castle to Lewin, 5 July 1975, *British Medical Journal*, 1975, iii, Supplement, p 118, 12 July 1975.

162. Wilson to Castle, 14 October 1975, CAB 109/26.

163. Castle to Wilson, c.15 October 1975, BMA and NHS Reorganisation, 1974-1975, PREM 11.

164. Treasury minute, 15 October 1975, T, SS 10/01A.

165. Castle, 'The State of the National Health Service', 10 October 1975, and related exchanges with Wilson, CAB 109/26.

166. CC(75) 43rd mtg, 16 October 1975, CAB 128. Cabinet Secretary's Notebook (Hunt). Castle, *Diaries*, pp 524-5.

167. Treasury minutes, 16 October 1975, T, SS 10/01A. Castle, *Diaries*, p 525, 16 October 1975.

168. Castle, *Diaries*, pp 526-7, 16 October 1975.

169. Stevenson to Wilson, 17 October 1975, T, SS 10/01A.

170. Wilson, HC Debates, vol 898, cols 35-45, 20 October 1975. For Castle's priming of Wilson, *Diaries*, p 528, 20 October 1975.

171. Wilson, Ministers and BMA mtg, 21 October 1975, Future of the NHS, 1975-1976, PREM 11. Castle, *Diaries*, p 530, 21 October 1975.

172. Castle, *Diaries*, pp 541, 551.

173. Castle, *Diaries*, pp 541, 621-2, 626.

174. One of these had held offices in the BMA, the other was associated with the Royal College of General Practitioners, but neither was a dominant medical politician.

175. The members of the Royal Commission were: Sir Alexander Walter Merrison (Chairman), Vice-Chancellor of Bristol University; Sir Thomas Brown (Vice-Chairman), Chairman of Eastern Health and Social Services Board, Northern

Ireland; Professor Ivor R C Batchelor, Professor of Psychiatry, Dundee University; Professor Paul A Bramley, Professor of Dental Surgery, Sheffield University; Cecil M Clothier QC, Recorder and Judge of Appeal, Isle of Man; Ann Clwyd, journalist, broadcaster, and MEP, previously member of the Welsh Hospital Board; Peter R A Jacques, Secretary of the Social Insurance and Industrial Welfare Department of the TUC; Professor Jean K McFarlane, Professor of Nursing, Manchester University; Audrey M Prime, Chairman, Enfield and Haringey AHA (until 1976 Staff Side Secretary of the NHS General Whitley Council); Kay B Richards, Assistant Director of Social Services, Hertfordshire County Council (until 1977 Senior Lecturer in Social Planning, NISWT); Lady Sherman, Borough Alderman, Hackney, Member of NE Thames RHA; Sir Simpson Stevenson, Chairman of the Greater Glasgow Health Board (formerly Chairman of the Western RHB); Councillor Dr Cyril Taylor, general medical practitioner, Liverpool; Dr Christopher J Wells, general medical practitioner, Sheffield; Frank R Welsh, Chairman of Dunford and Elliott, and Director, Grindley's Bank; Professor Alan H Williams, Professor of Economics, York University.

176. Sir Rodney Smith to Wilson, 3 August 1973, Wilson, Ennals, Ministers and officials mtg, c.10 September 1976, Wilson to Smith, 25 October 1976, Smith to Wilson, 27 October 1976, Smith to Wilson, 24 July 1977, Future of the NHS, 1976-1978, PREM 11.

177. Labour MPs expressed their reservations about private medicine in the NHS in a lengthy amendment to the House of Commons Expenditure Committee Report, *NHS Facilities for Private Patients*, March 1972. However, neither this nor the Labour Party Green Paper, *Health Care*, August 1973, recommended phasing out of pay-beds.

178. Castle to Healey, 13 March 1974, Barnett to Castle, 14 March 1974, T, 2SS 300/1128/016B. Castle, HC Debates, vol 870, col 532, 15 March 1974.

179. Castle, *Diaries*, pp 126-7, 130-8, 170-1.

180. Castle, HC Debates, vol 880, cols 544-51, 1 November 1974.

181. Castle, *Diaries*, pp 208-9; see also pp 170-1.

182. The occupancy rate for pay-beds in England was 52 per cent, compared with 81 per cent for NHS beds, while in Scotland the occupancy rate was 37 per cent, compared with 83 per cent for NHS beds.

183. The joint working party established a private practice panel, which on 20 September 1974 discussed the DHSS background paper, 'The phasing out of private practice from NHS hospitals'.

184. Castle, *Diaries*, pp 286-7, 293, 303, 313, 321-2, 380-1. Alan Fisher to Wilson 10 March 1975, Wilson to Fisher, 10 April 1975, Phasing out Pay Beds, 1975, PREM 11.

185. Healey to Castle, 11 March 1975, Castle to Healey, 11 March 1975, Phasing out Pay Beds, 1975, PREM 11.

186. Castle, C(75)27, 10 March 1975, CAB 129; CC(75) 17th mtg, 25 March 1975, CAB 128. Castle, SS(75)18, 17 April 1975, SS(75) 8th mtg, 22 April 1975, CAB 134.

187. Castle, *Diaries*, p 374.

188. Short to Wilson, 24 April 1975, Phasing out Pay Beds, 1975, PREM 11.

189. Castle, HC Debates, vol 891, cols 1092-103, 5 May 1975. Castle, *Diaries*, p 384.

190. Castle, *Diaries*, pp 380-1, 384, 388-9.

191. CC(75) 32nd mtg, 3 July 1975, CAB 128. Castle, *Diaries*, pp 445-7.

192. Castle, SS(75)28, 21 July 1975, SS(75) 13th mtg, 31 July 1975, CAB 134. Castle, *Diaries*, p 475.

193. *The Separation of Private Practice from NHS Hospitals* (DHSS, SHHD, Welsh Office, 1975); the full text is included in Castle, *Diaries*, Appendix V.

194. Castle, *Diaries*, p 516. Agitated correspondence between Lever and Castle, July to October 1975, Phasing out of Pay Beds, 1975, PREM 11.

195. *Daily Mail*, 27 October 1975.

196. For PLP, Castle, *Diaries*, p 535, 27 October 1975. Len Murray to Wilson, 15 October 1975, Wilson to Murray, 21 October 1975, Phasing out of Pay Beds, 1975, PREM 11.

197. Wilson, Ministers, and medical delegation mtg, 21 October 1975, Phasing out of Pay Beds, 1975, PREM 11. For similar exchanges, Castle and medical delegation mtg, 13 November 1975, Castle, *Diaries*, pp 549-50. Castle and other Government observers regarded Grabham as the most effective professional negotiator. Goodman is reported as describing him as a 'tiresome man with terrifying influence - a Napoleon of the medical profession', brief for Prime Minister, 2 December 1975, Phasing out of Pay Beds, 1975, PREM 11.

198. Presidents and Deans of Royal Colleges and Faculties, press statement, 26 November 1975, *Times*, 27 November 1975. Sir Rodney Smith asked for a private interview with Wilson to discuss these problems, an action which was greeted with suspicion by other medical groups, Smith to Wilson, 27 November 1975, Phasing out of Pay Beds, 1975, PREM 11.

199. Castle, SS(75))45, 17 November 1975, SS(75) 19th mtg, 20 November 1975, CAB 134.

200. Lord Shepherd to Wilson, 25 November 1975, Phasing out of Pay Beds, 1975, PREM 11.

201. Rodgers to Wilson, 26 November 1975, Phasing out of Pay Beds, 1975, PREM 11.

202. Wilson minutes, 14 and 21 November 1975, Phasing out of Pay Beds, 1975, PREM 11.

203. Short, C(75)132, 24 November 1975, CAB 129; CC(75) 51st mtg, 27 November 1975, CAB 128. Cabinet Secretary's Notebook (Hunt). Castle, *Diaries*, pp 567-8.

204. Benn, *Against the Tide*, pp 470-1.

205. Castle, *Diaries*, p 556, 20 November 1975.

206. Castle. *Diaries*, pp 560-1, 24 November 1975, pp 571-3, 1 December 1975.

207. Castle to Wilson, 2 December 1975, Phasing out of Pay Beds, 1975, PREM 11.

208. At least nine briefs and additional notes for the Prime Minister, dated 2 December 1975, Phasing out of Pay Beds, 1975, PREM 11.

209. Wilson, Castle, Goodman and medical delegation mtg, 3 December 1975, Phasing out of Pay Beds, 1975, PREM 11. The medical delegation was similar to

the one on 21 October, but the Government delegation was different. Other Ministers were not present; they were replaced by members of Wilson's own staff, Joe Haines and Bernard Donoughue. See Timmins *Five Giants*, pp 339-40.

210. Goodman, 'Memorandum of proposals submitted at Downing Street meeting. 3 December 1975', Phasing out of Pay Beds, 1975, PREM 11.

211. Castle, *Diaries*, pp 575-8, 3 December 1975.

212. Castle, *Diaries*, pp 578, 580. 582.

213. Castle, *Diaries*, pp 582, 583, 585-90, 593, 594, 602, 604, 606-9. Pay Bed Dispute, 1975-1976, PREM 11.

214. Castle, *Diaries*, pp 590, 608.

215. Castle, *Diaries*, p 606.

216. Castle, HC Debates, vol 902, cols 971-9, 15 December 1975.

217. Castle to Wilson, 5 January 1976, Wilson to Castle, 27 January 1976, Pay Bed Dispute, 1975-1976, PREM 11.

218. The results of this ballot were announced on 12 February 1976. Only 40 per cent of consultants replied. There remained strong opposition to phasing out of pay-beds and licensing of private facilities, but an equal degree of support for the Goodman compromise. Only a small minority were in favour of resignation from the NHS.

219. Wilson to Castle, 16 February 1976, Castle, C(76)19, 17 February 1976, CAB 129; CC(76) 6th mtg, 19 February 1976, CAB 128. Cabinet Secretary's Notebook (Hunt). Castle, *Diaries*, pp 655-6. Castle, C(76)40, 23 March 1976, CAB 129; CC(76) 12th mtg, 25 March 1976, CAB 128. Castle, *Diaries*, pp 703-4.

220. Castle, *Diaries*, pp 711-4, 31 March to 1 April 1976.

221. Dr E Grey-Turner, BMA to Callaghan, 6 April 1976, brief for the Prime Minister, 8 April 1976, Phasing out of Private Beds, 1976, PREM 11.

222. The Chairman of the Health Services Board was Basil Wigoder Q.C, Lord Wigoder, who was a prominent figure in the Liberal Party. The Health Services Board also contained two doctors and two senior trade union officials.

223. Dr J Cameron, BMA to Callaghan, 31 July 1978, Ennals to Callaghan, c.10 August 1978, Phasing out of Private Beds, 1978, PREM 11.

224. Royal Commission NHS, paras **18**.32-9.

225. Health Services Board, *Developments in the basis of revocation proposals to be made by the Health Services Board in 1979 and beyond* (HMSO, 1978).

226. Castle, *Diaries*, p 242.

227. Owen, *In Sickness and Health*, p 18.

228. Castle, HC Debates, vol 870, cols 531-2, 15 March 1974.

229. Barnett to Castle, 14 March 1974, WO, HL 44/82/1 Part 1.

230. Castle, *Diaries*, pp 41, 142-3, 13 March and 10 July 1974. RHA Chairmen mtgs, 13 March and 10 July 1974, DH, G/R 39/25.

231. DHSS to Welsh Office, 10 April 1974, WO, HL 44/82/1 Part 1.

232. Welsh Office minutes, April 1974, WO, HL 44/82/1 Part 1. SHHD, draft White Paper, 22 May 1974, HH 99/72.

233. Castle, SS(74)19, 14 May 1974, SS(74) 6th mtg, 17 May 1974, CAB 134.

234. *Democracy in the National Health Service. Membership of Health Authorities* (HMSO, 1974). *Cynrychiolaeth fwy Democrataidd ar Awdurdodau iechyd Cymru. Making Welsh Health Authorities more Democratic* (Cardiff, HMSO, 1974). *The National Health Service and the Community in Scotland* (Edinburgh, HMSO, 1974). On the title-pages, a red typeface was used for the English and Welsh documents, while the Scottish kept to the conventional black type.

235. *National Health Service and the Community in Scotland*, para 1.

236. *Democracy in the National Health Service, para 9, Cynrychiolaeth fwy Democrataidd ar Awdurdodau iechyd Cymru*, para 14.

237. Castle, *Diaries*, p 242, 2 December 1974.

238. Owen and officials mtg, 26 February 1975, submission to Castle, c.26 March 1975, Castle, Owen and officials mtg, 21 April 1975, DH, G/H 223/45A.

239. Castle to Short, 28 May 1975, DH, G/H 223/45A.

240. Foot to Castle, 20 June 1975, DH, G/H 223/45B.

241. Castle, HC Debates, vol 895, cols 299-300, 11 July 1975 (WA). Morris, HC Debates, vol 895, cols 389-90, 11 July 1975 (WA).

242. SHHD, submission to Ministers, 13 May 1975, DH, G/H 223/43.

243. Interview with Owen, *Times*, 9 and 14 February 1976.

244. DHSS, HRC(74)4; WO, WHRC(74)3; SHHD, NHS Circular 1974(GEN)90.

245. 'Final Report of Advisers on Community Health Councils', 26 March 1975, G/H 207/24B. Lady Marre, was wife of the Health Service Commissioner and she was selected to chair the new National Association of CHCs.

246. A Cartwright and R Anderson, *General Practice Revisited. A Second Study of patients and their Doctors* (Tavistock, 1981), p 187.

247. R Klein and J Lewis, *The Politics of Consumer Representation. A Study of Community Health Councils* (Centre for Studies in Social Policy, 1976), p 128.

248. *Annual Report of the Hospital Advisory Service 1975,* paras 309-15; *Annual Report of the Hospital Advisory Service 1975*, paras 250-8.

249. M Baily, *Times*, 16 February 1977.

250. Martin, *Hospitals in Trouble*, pp 168-9.

251. R G S Brown, *New Bottles, Old Wine?* (Institute for Health Studies, Hull, 1975); Klein and Lewis, *The Politics of Consumer Representation*; R Levitt, *The People's Voice in the NHS* (King's Fund, 1980). See also series of six short articles by Neville Hodgkinson, *Times*, 9-14 February 1976.

252. Role and Scope of CHCs, 1975-1979, DH, G/C 388/25A.

253. DH, G/C 388/57A.

254. Royal Commission NHS, paras **11**.1-11, 35, **20**.5, **22**.36.

255. *Report of the Committee on Hospital Complaints Procedure* (HMSO, 1973), para **10**.47.

256. Scottish Hospital Advisory Service, *Quinquennial Report* (Edinburgh, 1976). SHHD to DHSS, 31 July 1974, DH, G/H 207/17A.

257. *Democracy in the National Health Service*, paras 6-7.

258. Castle, HC Debates, vol 878, cols 414-6, 31 July 1974.

259. DH, G/H 207/17A.

260. *Consultation Paper on proposals for the future activities of the Health Advisory Service* (DHSS, 1975).

261. DH, G/H 207/17C.

262. Circulars HC(76)21, WHC(76)37, Health Advisory Service.

263. *Annual Report of the Health Advisory Service 1976* (HMSO, 1977).

264. In fact a report for 1977 and the first half of 1978, up to the retirement of Dr Woodford-Williams, was drafted, but its completion was delayed for so long that it seems that in late 1979 it was thought to be too late to undertake publication. This created a discontinuity which became perpetuated, DH, D/M 310/13D.

265. DH, D/M 310/13D.

266. Discussed with meticulous care by Martin, *Hospitals in Trouble*, chapter 2. These enquires related to both mental illness and mental handicap hospitals.

267. As noted in chapter V, the Scottish system for handling hospital complaints, introduced in 1970, was regarded as a success. In 1976 it was extended to other services, except FPC services. For evidence relating to the operation of the Scottish system, *First Report from the Select Committee on the Parliamentary Commissioner for Administration. Session 1977-78. Independent Review of Hospital Complaints in the NHS*, pp 168-221.

268. Davies to Joseph, 12 October 1973, Joseph to Davies, 19 October 1973, DH, G/C 369/15A. For the papers of the Davies Committee, DH, G/C 369/4-12.

269. *Report of the Committee on Hospital Complaints Procedure* (HMSO, 1973).

270. *Report of the Committee on Hospital Complaints Procedure*, pp 121-63.

271. *Report of the Committee on Hospital Complaints Procedure*, paras **8**.13-34.

272. DH, G/C 369/15A-B, 17A, 18A-B.

273. DHSS minute, December 1974, DH, G/C 369/17B.

274. Owen minute, 21 April 1975, DH, G/C 369/17B.

275. Owen and officials mtg, 18 June 1975, DH, G/C 369/17C.

276. Castle, SS(75)27, 17 July 1975, SS(75) 12th mtg, 24 July 1975, CAB 134.

277. DH, G/C 369/17D-E.

278. Owen to Castle, and Castle to Owen, 17 January 1976, DH, G/C 369/17E.

279. Castle, HC Debates, vol 905, cols 85-6, 9 February 1976 (WA).

280. Pugh remained Health Service Commissioner until January 1979, when he was replaced by Cecil M Clothier QC. At the end of 1976, J L Scarlett was replaced by G H Weston as Deputy Health Service Commissioner.

281. For DHSS evidence to the Select Committee, DH, G/H 236/10B-C.

282. *First Report from the Select Committee on the Parliamentary Commissioner for Administration. Session 1977-78. Independent Review of Hospital Complaints in the NHS* (HMSO, 1977).

283. *First Report from the Select Committee on the Parliamentary Commissioner for Administration. Session 1977-78. Independent Review of Hospital Complaints in the NHS*, paras 42-3.

284. Martin, *Hospitals in Trouble*, pp 150-62.

285. Ennals, HC Debates, vol 940, col 437, 2 December 1977 (WA).

286. RHA Chairmen mtg, 17/18 February 1978, DH, G/H 236/21B.

287. *Guardian*, 13 July 1978.

288. Chief Medical Officer and BMA delegation mtg, 23 June 1978, DH, G/H 236/21C.

289. DH, G/H 236/21B,D.

290. DHSS minute, 1 November 1978, DH, G/H 236/21D.

291. Circular HM(76)107, 14 June 1976.

292. JCC mtg, DH, G/C 369/A.

293. DH, G/C 369/C-D.

294. DH, G/H 236/21A.

295. Ennals and JCC mtg, 21 March 1977, DH, G/C 369/D.

296. For further comment, Martin, *Hospitals in Trouble*, pp 152-4.

297. Joseph minute, 17 February 1974, DH, F/P 239/85B.

298. Castle to Mayhew, 7 May 1974, DH, F/P 239/85B.

299. Owen and officials mtg, 22 October 1974, DH, F/P 239/85B.

300. Owen was thinking of issues such as stress, juvenile delinquency, and industrial strife associated with boredom at work.

301. Owen and officials mtg, 22 October 1974, DHSS minute, 23 October 1974, DH, F/P 239/85B.

302. Owen and officials mtg, 18 November 1974, DH, F/P 239/85B.

303. DHSS minutes, December 1974 to January 1975, DH, F/P 239/85B.

304. SS(75) 9th mtg, 10 June 1975, CAB 134. Castle tried to obtain agreement as a formality by circulating the draft White Paper for ratification in advance of the meeting, and not producing a SS memorandum.

305. Castle, *Diaries*, p 411, 10 June 1975.

306. Castle, C(75)85, 23 July 1975, CAB 129.

307. *Better Services for the Mentally Ill*, Cmnd.6233 (HMSO, 1975).

308. Owen minute, 30 September 1974, DH, F/P 239/85B.

309. *Better Services for the Mentally Ill*, Foreword, paras 9-10.

310. *Priorities for Health and Personal Social Services in England. A Consultative Document* (HMSO, 1976).

311. *Priorities for Health and Personal Social Services. The Way Forward* (HMSO, 1977).

312. Royal Commission NHS, para **10**.60.

313. Royal Commission NHS, para **20**.32.

314. *Organisational and Management Problems of Mental Illness Hospitals* (DHSS, 1980). For appreciation of the importance of the Nodder Report, Martin, *Hospitals in Trouble*, pp 205-9, 214-6.

315. L Gostin, *A Human Condition. The Mental Health Act from 1959 to 1975*, 2 vols, (MIND, 1975-1977), and the widely known popularisation, *Is it Fair? - The Mental Health Act 1959* (MIND, 1977). Conditions in the Special Hospitals caused increasing alarm, for instance as expressed by the *Second Report from the Estimates Committee, Session 19767-68* (HMSO, 1968). This prompted establishment in 1972 of the Committee on Mentally Abnormal Offenders, chaired by Lord Butler. This produced an interim report in July 1974 recommending as a matter of urgency the establishment of regional secure units, *Interim Report of the Committee on Abnormal Offenders*, Cmnd.5698 (HMSO, 1974). This proposal was elaborated in the final report, *Report of the Committee on Mentally Abnormal Offenders*, Cmnd.6244 (HMSO, 1975). By 1979 very little progress had been made towards establishing these units.

316. Royal College of Psychiatrists, *Report of the Working Party to Review the Mental Health Act, 1959* (R.Coll.Psych., 1974).

317. DH, D/M 107/24A. Owen, HC Debates, vol 884, cols 1272-3, 24 January 1975.

318. *A Review of the Mental Health Act 1959* (HMSO, 1976).

319. For comments on the consultative document, DH, D/M 107/31A-F.

320. 'Delay on law for mentally ill', *Guardian*, 30 July 1977. For reassurances from Ennals, address at Mental Health Foundation, 24 September 1977, *Times*, 26 September 1977. Ennals to Rees, 12 October 1977, Rees to Ennals, 31 October 1977, DH, D/M 107/38A. For drafting of the White Paper, DH, D/M 107/32A-G.

321. Ennals, HS(78)61, 20 June 1978, HS(78) 20th mtg, 6 July 1978, CAB 134.

322. *A Review of the Mental Health Act 1959*, Cmnd.7320 (HMSO, 1978).

323. *Times*, 13 September 1978.

324. Editorial, *Times*, 13 September 1978.

325. For responses to the White Paper, DH, D/M 107/24H-J.

326. Owen minute, 25 March 1974, DH, M/B 80/6A.

327. Castle, HC Debates, vol 887, cols 158-61, 26 February 1975. This statement was amplified in a speech to the National Society for Mentally Handicapped Children's Conference, also on 26 February 1975, *Times*, 27 February 1975.

328. DH, D/M 310/3A.

329. For her view of Mittler, Castle, *Diaries*, pp 469, 592.

330. DH, D/M 310/3A-B.

331. National Development Group for the Mentally Handicapped, *Helping Mentally Handicapped People in Hospital* (DHSS, 1978). For Mittler's explanation of the work of the Development Group to the Jay Committee, 24 May 1976, DH, D/C 446/7.

332. Development Team for the Mentally Handicapped, *First Report: 1976-1977* (HMSO, 1978), *Second Report: 1978-1979* (HMSO, 1980).

333. DHSS, Review of Mental Handicap Policy, 15 December 1978, DH, D/C 446/23.

334. DH, D/M 310/13D, OEA 57/3/7.

335. Martin, *Hospitals in Trouble*, p 212.

336. *Report of the Committee of Inquiry into Normansfield Hospital*, Cmnd.7357 (HMSO, 1978).

337. Normansfield Inquiry, 1978, PREM 11. Ennals, HC Debates, vol 958, cols 1093-104, 21 November 1978,

338. Council for Children's Welfare, *No Childhood. The Handicapped Child at Home and in Hospital in the 1970's* (CCW, 1975).

339. M Oswin, *Children Living in Long-Stay Hospitals* (Heinemann, 1978).

340. Letter from four organisations including the Spastics Society, *Times*, 10 April 1978; the campaign was launched by five organisations on 22 June 1978, *Times*, 23 June 1978.

341. Ennals, *Times*, 13 April 1978.

342. DHSS, Review of Mental Handicap Policy, 15 December 1978, DH, D/C 446/23.

343. DH, OEA 57/3/7. This review evolved into *Mental handicap: Progress, Problems and Priorities* (DHSS, 1980).

344. As noted in chapter V, in Scotland, policy was guided by *Services for the Mentally Handicapped* (SHHD-SED, 1972). The Peters Committee was a sub-committee of the Mental Disorder Programme Planning Group set up by the SHSPC and the Advisory Council for Social Work.

345. SHSPC, 10th mtg, 10 June 1977, HH 99/47.

346. *A Better Life. Report on Services for the Mentally Handicapped in Scotland* (HMSO, 1979), 119 pages.

347. Royal Commission NHS, para **10**.66.

348. Castle, Owen and officials mtg, 5 April 1974, DH, M/B 80/3.

349. Castle, HC Debates, vol 895, cols 568-9, 17 July 1975 (WA). For appointment of the Jay Committee, DH, D/C 446/1B.

350. One member retired in 1977.

351. *Report of the Committee of Enquiry into Mental Handicap Nursing and Care*, Cmnd.7468 (HMSO, 1979). *Summary of the Jay Report. A brief outline of their Report by Members of the Committee of Enquiry into Mental Handicap Nursing and Care* (HMSO, 1979). The second volume was a survey of staff commissioned from OPCS. For papers of the Jay Committee, DH, D/C 446/7-26.

352. *Report of the Committee of Enquiry into Mental Handicap Nursing and Care*, pp 150-6.

353. *Report of the Committee of Enquiry into Mental Handicap Nursing and Care*, pp 157-60.

354. Ennals, HC Debates, vol 963, cols 814-7, 8 March 1979 (WA). For the initial submission to Ennals on the Jay Report, 15 December 1978, DH, D/C 446/23.

355. DHSS minute, 11 June 1980, DH, D/C 446/24C. For consultations on Jay, DH, D/C 446/24A-C.

356. For the background to the PAR exercise, October 1970 to June 1971, CAB, Q 31/1 Part 1.

357. Joseph, Campbell and Thomas, HS(72)12, 28 January 1972, HS(72) 4th mtg, 1 February 1972, CAB 134.

358. Joseph, HS(72)31, 20 March 1972, HS(72) 10th mtg, 28 April 1972, CAB 134.

359. CPRS, 'Services for the Elderly', 72pp + Appendix, April 1973, HS(73)88, 22 May 1973, HS(73) 20th mtg, 12 June 1973, CAB 134.

360. *Prevention and Health*, Cmnd.7047, paras 223-7.

361. *Priorities for Health and Personal Social Services in England. A Consultative Document*, pp 38-44.

362. *Priorities for Health and Personal Social Services. The Way Forward*, paras **2**.18,21.

363. Ennals, HS(77)68, 11 November 1977, HS(77) 19th mtg, 16 November 1977, CAB 134. For relevant Treasury minutes, T, SS 132/401/01A. For the conference held on 26 July 1977 at Imperial College, 'Review of policies to meet needs of the aged', *Times*, 27 July 1977.

364. Ennals and Orme, HS(78)46, 3 May 1978, HS(78) 14th mtg, 17 May 1978, CAB 134.

365. *A Happier Old Age: A discussion document on elderly people in our society* (HMSO, 1978).

366. Editorial, *Hospital and Health Services Review*, August 1978.

367. Ennals, HC Debates, vol 957, cols 36-7, 6 November 1978 (WA).

368. Official Steering Group on the Elderly mtg, 21 December 1978, SS 132/401/01C.

369. *Growing Older. White Paper on the Elderly*, Cmnd.8173 (HMSO, 1981).

370. *Changing Patterns of Care: Report on services for the elderly in Scotland* (HMSO, Edinburgh, 1980). See also HH 99/48.

371. Treasury unease was compounded by the related report, *Services for the Elderly with Mental Disability in Scotland* (HMSO, Edinburgh, 1979), which also called for big expansion in support services. See also HH 99/47-48.

372. Royal Commission NHS, paras **5**.5,6,14,23,31.

373. Unless indicated otherwise, documents cited in the following section derive from DHSS, 'Fluoridation of Water Supplies. Submission to Minister of State for Health', 1977, MH 61/1011.

374. Owen, HC Debates, vol 889, cols 1700-6, 11 April 1975.

375. Owen, *In Sickness and Health*, pp 118-9, encourages CHCs to participate in the fluoridation debate.

376. Owen to Howell, 24 February 1976, DoE, WS 111/12 Part 1. Howell was Minister of State (Sport, Recreation and Water Resources). In the record dry summer of 1976, Howell was given the added title of Drought Minister.

377. Howell to Owen, 27 February 1976, DoE, WS 111/12 Part 1.

378. Owen to Howell, 31 March 1976, DoE, WS 111/12 Part 1.

379. Howell to Owen, 7 July 1976, DoE, WS 111/12 Part 1.

380. Royal College of Physicians of London, *Fluoride, Teeth and Health* (Pitman, 1976).

381. SHSPC, 3rd mtg, 12 February 1975, HH 99/46.

382. SHSPC, 4th mtg, 11 June 1975, HH 99/46; 6th mtg, 10 March 1976, 8th mtg, 10 November 1976, HH 99/47.

383. For details concerning the high degree of support for fluoridation among health authorities in the UK, Royal Commission NHS, para **9**.58. In Scotland, it was reported in 1977 that all Health Boards had approved fluoridation, SHSPC, 9th mtg, 9 March 1977, HH 99/47.

384. *First Report from the Expenditure Committee. Session 1976-77. Preventive Medicine. vol 1, Report* (HMSO, 1977), recommendation 40.

385. *Prevention and Health*, Cmnd.7047 (HMSO, 1977), paras 128-30.

386. Moyle, HC Debates, vol 953, cols 1232-5, 11 July 1978.

387. See for instance, SHSPC, 9th mtg, 9 March 1977, HH 99/47, and Child Health Group, 'Health Services for Children at School. I. Dental Services', March 1978, Recommendation 1, advised Ministers to undertake 'close and sympathetic examination of the apparent lack of harmony between Health Boards and Regional Councils with the aim of achieving fluoridation in Scotland', HH 99/48.

388. Royal Commission NHS, para **9**.58. For a list of English AHAs supporting fluoridation, Moyle, HC Debates, vol 960, cols 627-8, 15 January 1979 (WA).

389. Godber, *The British National Health Service*, pp 87-8.

390. Royal Commission NHS, paras **9**.58-64.

391. DH, B/F6, 138G, 182D, F Ennals was reported to have told the General Dental Council in 1977 that he would introduce legislation, SHSPC, 11th mtg, 9 November 1977, HH 99/47.

392. HH 61/1011. According to the SHSPC, delay was then caused by inundation of the Strathclyde Regional Council with anti-fluoridation propaganda, 13th mtg, 14 June 1978, HH 99/49.

393. SHSPC, 11th mtg, 9 November 1977, HH 99/47. *Times*, 30 June 1983. See also M Winstanley, 'Fluoridation: Scotland Bites Back', *Times*, 13 July 1983.

394. For the Labour administration's record on smoking and health, Taylor, *Smoke Ring*, pp 87-92; M Daube, 'The politics of Smoking: Thoughts on the Labour Record', *Community Medicine*, 1979, **1**, 306-14.

395. Owen, *In Sickness and Health*, pp 114, 115, 118.

396. Castle, *Diaries*, p 487.

397. Owen, HC Debates, vol 889, cols 453-5, 10 April 1975.

398. Castle, Ross and Morris, SS(75)21, 30 June 1975, Howell, SS(75)26, 14 July 1975, SS(75) 11th mtg, 17 July 1975, CAB 134.

399. Owen, SS(75)31, 31 July 1975, SS(75) 14th mtg, 5 August 1975, CAB 134.

400. Owen, HC Debates, vol 896, cols 246-7, 23 July 1975 (WA), vol 897, cols 253-4, 6 August 1975 (WA), vol 786, cols 802-14, 16 January 1976.

401. Royal College of Physicians of London, *Smoking and Health: Third Report* (Pitman, 1977). *First Report from the Expenditure Committee. Session 1976-77. Preventive Medicine. vol 1, Report* (HMSO, 1977), paras 143-61, recommendations 23-32.

402. *Prevention and Health: Everybody's Business*, pp 38, 59-61, 92.

403. GEN 25(76), CAB 130; CAB 280/3 Part 1.

404. Ennals to Callaghan, 16 July 1976, CAB 280/3 Part 1.

405. Ennals, HC Debates, vol 927, cols 463-5, 8 March 1977 (WA).

406. *Prevention and Health*, Cmnd. 7047, p 78.

407. *Prevention and Health: Everybody's Business*, p 10.

408. Health Services Planning Group, 90th mtg, 8 March 1979, HH 99/58.

409. *Times*, 25 October 1977.

410. *Sunday Times*, 2 March 1980.

411. Ennals, HC Debates, vol 984, cols 706-14, 9 May 1980. In 1979 the EEC Commission called for harmonization of policy on smoking. This was first discussed by health Ministers on 16 November 1979.

412. *Prevention and Health*, Cmnd.7047, para 172.

413. *Report of the Committee on the Working of the Abortion Act*, Cmnd.5579 (HMSO, 1974).

414. *Report of the Committee on the Working of the Abortion Act*, para 605.

415. For analysis of the work of the Lane Committee, Ashley E Wivel, 'Gynaecologists and the Lane Committee, 1971-1974', (unpublished Oxford University M.Sc. dissertation, 1994).

416. For controversy following the Lane Report, Keown, *Abortion, Doctors and the Law*, chapters 5 and 6; Greenwood and Young, *Abortion in Demand*, chapters 2, 3 and postscript.

417. Greenwood and Young, *Abortion in Demand*, pp 46-56; Keown, *Abortion, Doctors and the Law*, pp 141-6.

418. SS(75) 3rd mtg, 5 February 1975, CAB 134.

419. HC Debates, vol 885, cols 1758-868, 7 February 1975.

420. For papers relating to the White Bill, DH, E/A 223/101A-B.

421. Castle, HC Debates, vol 898, col 244, 21 October 1975 (WA).

422. Castle, SS(75)35, 2 October 1975, SS(75) 16th mtg, 7 October 1975, CAB 134.

423. Castle, SS(75)46, 19 November 1975, SS(75) 20th mtg, 24 November 1975, CAB 134.

424. Castle, *Diaries*, pp 628-9, 21 January 1976.

425. Castle, *Diaries*, p 629, 22 January 1976. For the earlier parallel debate within the National Executive Committee of the Labour Party, Benn, *Against the Tide*, p 422, 22 July 1975.

426. HC Debates, vol 905, cols 100-70, 9 February 1976. The vote in favour of establishing the Select Committee was 313 to 172.

427. Those resigning on 16 February were: **Labour**: Betty Boothroyd, Joyce Butler, Helene Hayman, Maurice Miller, **Conservative**: Sir George Sinclair, **Liberal**: David Steel.

950

428. *First Report of the Select Committee on Abortion. Session 1975-76*, 28 July 1976. For Abse's defence of this report, *Times*, 29 July 1976.

429. Keown, *Abortion, Doctors and the Law*, pp 146-58. For papers relating to these Bills, DH, E/A 223/152A-B, CPO 9/16.

430. *Prevention and Health*, Cmnd.7047, paras 212-3. *Reducing the Risk. Safer Pregnancy and Childbirth* (HMSO, 1977).

431. Royal Commission NHS, para **18**.12.

432. *Safety and Health at Work*, Cmnd.5034 (HMSO, 1972).

433. H(74) 1st mtg, 19 March 1974, 7th mtg, 3 May 1974, CAB 134. The eventual result of these deliberations was the Health and Safety Act 1974.

434. Royal Commission NHS, paras **5**.25-9, and Appendix F.

435. H(74) 3rd mtg, 29 March 1974, 9th mtg, 21 June 1974, CAB 134.

436. Howell, HC Debates, vol 889, col 257, 27 March 1975 (WA) announced that 0.5gm per litre had been adopted from 1 November 1974.

437. H(76) 3rd mtg, 30 January 1976, CAB 134; Howell, HC Debates, vol 906, col, 1671, 4 March 1976. For the debate on lead in petrol, HC Debates, vol 906, cols 1671-702, 4 March 1976, vol 909, cols 165-93, 5 April 1976. For announcement of reduction in the permitted level to 0.45gm per litre, Howell, HC Debates, vol 918, 28 October 1976, cols 307-8 (WA).

438. *First Report from the Expenditure Committee. Session 1976-77. Preventive Medicine.* vol 1, *Report*, vols 2 and 3, *Evidence* (HMSO, 1977)

439. Q.1602.

440. *Expenditure Committee, Evidence*, pp 100-119.

441. *Expenditure Committee, Evidence*, pp 94-9.

442. Castle, HC Debates, vol 907, cols 514-6, 16 March 1976 (WA).

443. Ennals and Morris, Foreword to *Annual Report of the Hospital Advisory Service 1975*, p iv.

444. Owen, *In Sickness and Health*, p 114. For a virtually identical sentiment, interview with Owen on CHCs, *Times*, 9 February 1976.

445. *Prevention and Health: Everybody's Business*, p 61.

446. Health education was allocated one paragraph in *Prevention and Health: Everybody's Business*, pp 87-8.

447. *Prevention and Health: Everybody's Business*, pp 10, 96.

448. The first of these accessible but informative discussion papers were, *Reducing the Risk. Safer Pregnancy and Childbirth* (HMSO, September 1977), *Occupational Health Services. The Way Ahead* (HMSO, December 1977), *Eating for Health* (HMSO, 1978). A further paper on alcoholism was promised for 1978, and thereafter papers on heart disease, health education, care of the elderly, and mental health, *Prevention and Health* Cmnd.7047, para 14.

449. *Priorities for Health and Personal Social Services in England. A Consultative Document* (DHSS, 1976), paras **3**.19-25.

450. *Prevention and Health*, Cmnd.7047, pp 4-5.

451. *Priorities for Health and Personal Social Services. The Way Forward* (HMSO, 1977), paras **2**.1-6.

452. *Prevention and Health*, Cmnd.7047 (HMSO, 1977), 85 pp. This was issued by the Secretaries of State for Social Services, Education and Science, Scotland and Wales. HC Debates, vol 941, cols 407-8, 15 December 1977 (WA).

453. For the drafting of the White Paper, *Prevention and Health*, DH, V/H 184/28A.

454. Review of Health Education Council, DH, V/H 184/29.

455. *Prevention and Health*, Cmnd.7047, paras 102-3.

456. For a general survey, Committee on Safety of Medicines and the Joint Committee on Vaccination and Immunization, *Whooping Cough* (HMSO, 1981).

457. Parliamentary Commissioner for Administration, *Sixth Report. Session 1976-77. Whooping Cough Vaccination* (HMSO, 1977). This matter was referred to the Commissioner by Jack Ashley MP.

458. Briefs for Prime Minister, January 1977, correspondence between Ashley and Callaghan, March 1977, Compensation for Vaccine Damage, 1977, PREM 11.

459. Ennals, HS(77)14, 1 April 1977, HS(77) 5th mtg, 6 April 1977, CAB 134.

460. Officials, HS(77)17, 22 April 1977, Ennals, HS(77)18, 22 April 1977, HS(77) 6th mtg, 27 April 1977, CAB 134.

461. Rees, CP(77)39, 29 April 1977, Ennals CP(77)41, 2 May 1977, CAB 129. CM(77) 18th mtg, 5 May 1977, CAB 128.

462. Background papers and exchanges between Callaghan and Lord Pearson, May to June 1977, also letter from Callaghan to Pearson, 6 June 1977, and Pearson to Callaghan, 9 June 1977, Compensation for Vaccine Damage, 1977, PREM 11; CAB 189/30 Part 1.

463. Ennals, HC Debates, vol 933, cols 240-8, 14 June 1977, includes an extract from the letter of Lord Pearson.

464. Callaghan, HC Debates, vol 946, cols 636-45, 16 March 1978.

465. Ennals, HS(78)25, 10 March 1978, HS(78) 8th mtg, 15 March 1978, CAB 134. GEN 128(78), April to May 1978, chaired by Michael Foot, CAB 130.

466. Ennals, HC Debates, vol 949, cols 973-85, 9 May 1985.

467. *Times*, 22 November 1977, 8 February 1978; *Sunday Times*, 27 November 1977.

468. Editorial, *Guardian*, 3 November 1978. See also *Sunday Times*, 1 October 1978. For the Prime Minister's concern, Rubella, 1978, PREM 11.

469. *Parliamentary Commissioner for Administration, Sixth Report. Session 1976-77* (HMSO, 1977), para 60.

470. Macfarlane and Mugford, *Birth Counts*, pp 185-6.

471. For the earlier steps in dealing with the narcotics problem, see chapter III. The narcotic problem was kept under review by the Interdepartmental Committee on Drug Addiction (Chairman Sir Russell Brain, later Lord Brain), established in 1958. This committee reported in 1961 and 1965. Consistent with its recommendations was the Dangerous Drugs Act of 1967. The Brain Committee

also led to the Advisory Committee on Drug Dependence, established in 1967, chaired by Sir Edward Wayne. The legislation was consolidated and extended in the Misuse of Drugs Act 1971. Under this Act, a statutory Advisory Council on the Misuse of Drugs was established. The Advisory Council issued its first interim report on rehabilitation and treatment in 1977. During the 1970s, the reports of the Advisory Committee and Chief Medical Officer were generally optimistic about the drug problem. In Scotland a specialist subcommittee reported in 1970, 1972 and 1975. The last of these reports expressed 'guarded optimism that the problem was diminishing', SHHD, *Misuse of Drugs in Scotland* (HMSO, Edinburgh, 1975). The only reference to this problem in the Report of the Merrison Commission was a passing comment in the section dealing with the work of accident and emergency departments.

472. J G Edwards and C Busch, eds, *Drug Problems in Britain: a ten year survey* (Academic Press, 1981).

473. The first concerted attention to this problem in official circles was the Scottish SMAC Subcommittee on Alcoholism established in 1963 (Chairman Professor A K M Macrae). This published helpful reports in 1965 and 1970. The first south of the border equivalent was the slight English and Welsh SMAC report *Alcoholism: Medical Memorandum on Alcoholism* (DHSS, November 1973).

474. DHSS and SHHD mtg on services for alcoholics, 22 July 1974, HH 99/4. To indicate the small scale of facilities for treating alcohol problems, in 1973 there were in England and Wales: 24 hostels, 18 treatment units and a further 15 were planned, SMAC, *Alcoholism*, pp 10-13.

475. *Better Services for the Mentally Ill*, chapter 8.

476. Advisory Committee on Alcoholism, *Report on Prevention* (DHSS and Welsh Office, 1977).

477. *First Report from the Expenditure Committee. Session 1976-77. Preventive Medicine. vol 1, Report*, paras 122-42.

478. *Prevention and Health*, Cmnd.7047, pp 77-8.

479. *Prevention and Health: Everybody's Business,* p 39; *Prevention and Health*, Cmnd.7047, para 153. *Improving the Common Weal*, the 630-page review of health care in Scotland, does not feature alcohol in the index. CPRS estimated that there were 100,000 with a serious drink problem in Scotland, or 2 per cent of the population, see below, HS(78)9. In 1980 the Government conceded that the figure for those with a serious drink problem in England should be revised to 740,000, *CMO Report 1980*, p 104.

480. In his evidence to the Subcommittee, the HEC Director complained that DHSS had hitherto prevented work in this field, *First Report from the Expenditure Committee. Session 1976-77. Preventive Medicine*, Q.438. Ennals launched the HEC alcohol campaign directed to the North East of England on 7 November 1977. This was modelled on a rather more ambitious campaign conducted in Scotland by the Scottish Health Education Unit.

481. CPRS minutes, November 1977, CAB, Q 6/49 Part 1.

482. This document was discussed at a seminar on 15 December 1977, CAB, Q 6/49 Part 1.

483. Correspondence between Ministers, January 1978, CAB, Q 6/49 Part 1.

484. CPRS minute, 22 March 1978, CAB, Q 6/49 Part 1.

485. CPRS, HS(78)9, 14 February 1978, HS(78) 6th mtg, 1 March 1978, CAB 134.

486. Ennals, HS(78) 38, 14 April 1978, HS(78) 11th mtg, 19 April 1978, CAB 134. For the completed CPRS document, *Social Trends Note No.4. Alcohol. June 1978* (CPRS, 1978), 11 pp, CAB, Q 6/49 Part 1.

487. Advisory Committee on Alcoholism, *The Pattern and Range of Services for Problem Drinkers* (DHSS and Welsh Office, 1978). For a critique, *British Journal of Addiction*, 1979, **74**, 113-32, 1980, **75**, 3-8.

488. Sir Richard Doll, 'Prospects for Prevention', *British Medical Journal*, 1983, **286**, 445-53, 5 February 1983. Doll was reinforcing R E Kendell, 'Alcoholism: a medical or social problem?', *British Medical Journal*, 1979, i, 367-71, 10 February 1979, who wrote of the alarming growth of medical and social problems associated with drink.

489. Royal Commission NHS, paras **5**.31-4.

490. Royal Commission NHS, para **5**.12.

491. Owen minute, 25 March 1974, DH, M/B 80/5. DHSS minute, 27 March 1974, DH, M/B 80/3.

492. Castle, Owen and officials mtg, 5 April 1974, DH, M/B 80/3.

493. Castle to Short, 1 May 1974, T, 2SS 116/117/04C.

494. Barnett to Castle, 6 May 1974, T, 2SS 116/117/04C.

495. Castle, HC Debates, vol 873, cols 55-7, 6 May 1974 (WA).

496. 'Briggs Committee on Nursing - The Government's Proposals', 8 May 1974, DH, M/B 80/3. 'Government Proposals for legislation to implement the Briggs Committee's Recommendations', May 1974, DH, M/B 80/2.

497. Timetable for Briggs legislation, 11 April 1974, DH, M/B 80/3. Castle to Short, 29 July 1974, T, 2SS 116/117/04C.

498. Short to Castle, 31 July 1974, DH, M/B 80/3.

499. DH, M/B 80/2, 6A-B.

500. SHHD to DHSS, 5 December 1974, DH, M/B 80/6B.

501. DHSS to SHHD, 11 December 1974, SHHD to DHSS, 20 December 1974, DH, M/B 80/6B.

502. SHHD to DHSS, 13 January 1975, DH, M/B 80/6B.

503. Department of Health and Social Services, Belfast to DHSS, January to March 1975, DH, M/B 80/6B.

504. DHSS minute, 21 May 1975, DH, M/B 80/6B.

505. DHSS to Treasury, 4 July 1975, T, SS 350/351/01A.

506. SHHD to DHSS, 7 July 1975, DH, M/B 80/6B.

507. Owen and officials mtg, 21 July 1975, DH, M/B 80/6B.

508. Chief Nursing Officer minute, 7 July 1975, DH, M/B 80/6B.

509. DHSS minutes, October 1975, DH, M/B 80/6C.

510. DHSS minute, 18 May 1976, DH, M/B 80/6C.

511. Castle, SS(76)4, 24 January 1976, CAB 134, agreed without discussion, Short to Castle, 6 February 1976, DH, M/B 80/3. This cleared the way for distribution of the two consultative documents 'Relationship between Services and Education' and 'The Statutory Framework' issued with Circular HC(76)22 in May 1976.

512. DHSS minute, 21 January 1977, listing prospective Bills, attached the first priority to the Merrison Bill on account of its non-contentious nature, its brevity, and the need to conciliate the doctors, DH, M/B 80/6B.

513. Chief Nursing Officer minute, 19 October 1976, DH, M/B 80/6B. Ennals and nursing delegation mtg, 30 November 1976, DH, M/B 80/12A.

514. Moyle and nursing delegation mtg, 20 January 1977, DH, M/B 80/12A. The Briggs Co-ordinating Committee contained about 20 members, representing a wide range of organisations with nursing interests. It began work in March 1977.

515. With establishment of the Co-ordinating Committee, the Briggs Joint Liaison Committee, composed of the UK nursing statutory and non-statutory educational and training bodies, which had been in existence since 1975, was disbanded. The Co-ordinating Committee established three working groups, concerned with: preparation for legislation, funding and handover; the status of nurse learners; and the funding of further nurse training.

516. Treasury to DHSS, 13 April 1977, T, SS 350/351/01A. Objections repeated in Barnett to Callaghan, 20 May 1977, DH, M/B 80/6D.

517. DHSS minute, 9 March 1977, DH, M/B 80/6D.

518. DHSS minute, 28 April 1977, DH, M/B 80/6D.

519. DHSS to Treasury, 31 May 1977, T, SS 350/351/01A.

520. Treasury minutes, July 1977, T, SS 350/351/01A.

521. Ennals, HS(77)37, 27 June 1977, HS(77) 14th mtg, 27 July 1977, CAB 134.

522. DHSS to Treasury, 18 October 1977, T, SS 350/351/01A.

523. DHSS minute, 23 February 1978, DH, M/B 80/6F.

524. DHSS minutes, 8 March 1978, DH, M/B 80/6F.

525. Moyle, HC Debates, vol 946, col 232, 15 March 1978 (WA).

526. Ennals, LE(78)85, 25 October 1978, LE(78) 17th mtg, 1 November 1978, CAB 134.

527. DH, M/B 80/24A-D.

528. DHSS exchanges with RCOG and JCC, October 1978 to March 1979, DH, NTU/45A.

529. DHSS minute, 14 November 1978, Moyle, officials and midwives delegation mtg, 24 November 1978, Moyle, officials and health visitors delegation mtg, 30 November 1978, DH, M/B 80/6J. DH, M/B 80/6K.

530. For the context to the following section, R Richardson, 'Trade Unions and Industrial Relations', in Crafts and Woodward, eds, *The British Economy since 1945*, pp 417-42; G A Dorfman, *Government versus Trade Unionism in British Politics since 1968*, chapter 4; W H Fishbein, *Wage Restraint by Consensus: Britain's Search for an*

Incomes Policy Agreement 1965-79; R Taylor, *The Trade Union Question in British Politics: Government and the Unions since 1954*; D Coates, *Labour in Power?*; M Carpenter, *Working for Health*, pp 365-80.

531. 'When doctors behave like dockers', *Financial Times*, 2 December 1975.

532. Editorial, *Daily Telegraph*, 2 December 1975.

533. D Coates, *Labour in Power?*, pp 59-60.

534. Castle to Wilson, c.30 July 1974, T, 2SS 21/786/02. Since the following section is inevitably a synoptic account of very complex developments, file references will be kept to a minimum.

535. Treasury minutes, April 1974, T, 2SS 116/78/02D.

536. Foot, C(74)33, 29 April 1974, CAB 129; CC(74) 14th mtg, 2 May 1974, CAB 128. Castle, *Diaries*, pp 98-9. For the announcement of this increase, Castle, HC Debates, vol 873, cols 55-7, 6 May 1975 (WA).

537. Castle, Owen, officials and nursing Staff Side delegation mtg, 30 April 1974, DH, M/N 57/046. For the demonstration, Castle, *Diaries*, p 94.

538. See editorial, 'Nurses and Special Cases', *Times*, 14 May 1974; 'The Scandal of Nurses' Pay', *Daily Mail*, 14 May 1974; editorial, 'Tomorrow's Militants', *Sunday Times*, 19 May 1974.

539. Wilson, Foot, Castle, Hughes, officials, and Staff Side delegation mtg, 29 May 1974, T, 2SS 116/78/02D.

540. Castle, HC Debates, vol 874, cols 686-97, 23 May 1974. The membership of the Halsbury Committee was announced on 7 June 1974. Apart from Lord Halsbury, chairman of the DDRB, the members of the enquiry were: Mr H W Atcherley, a personnel director and member of the DDRB, Professor R H Graveson, an academic lawyer and also member of the DDRB, Dame Mary Green, a former headmistress, who was soon to become a member of the DDRB, Mr. I W Macdonald, an industrialist and member of the DDRB, Mrs Dorothy Wedderburn, an academic sociologist, and Mrs Norah Willis, a director of the London Co-operative Society.

541. Castle, HC Debates, vol 876 , col 212, 3 July 1974 (WA).

542. DH, M/N 57/047. Castle, *Diaries*, p 165, 1 August 1974.

543. *Report of the Committee of Inquiry into the Pay and Related Considerations of Service of Nurses and Midwives* (HMSO, 1974)

544. DH, M/N 57/050A; T, 2SS 116/78/02D.

545. For representations of the unions on reform of NHS pay machinery, Jack Straw and unions delegation mtg, 14 January 1975, DH, N/W 42/36A.

546. DH, N/W 42/36A.

547. *Making Whitley Work: a Review of the Operation of the National Health Service Whitley Council System* (HMSO, 1976).

548. DH, N/W 42/56A-D.

549. Castle, HC Debates, vol 874, col 392 4 June 1974 (WA). *Review Body on Doctors' and Dentists' Remuneration. Fourth Report 1974*, Cmnd.5644 (HMSO, 1974). T, 2SS 22/78/05E; D/H, B/D 112/0131A,C.

550. Castle to Wilson, 28 May 1974, and subsequent ministerial exchanges, Doctors' and Dentists' Review Body, 1974-1975, PREM 11.

551. Halsbury also complained about the use of Review Bodies as 'blind instruments of economic policy' at a meeting of the Top Salaries Review Bodies Chairmen with Wilson, 21 June 1974, Doctors' and Dentists' Review Body, 1974-1975, PREM 11.

552. Stevenson to Wilson, 27 June 1974, Wilson to Stevenson, 10 July 1974, Doctors' and Dentists' Review Body, 1974-1975, PREM 11.

553. Castle, Owen, Hughes, officials and BMA delegation mtg, 1 August 1974, DH, B/D 112/0138. Castle, *Diaries*, pp 166-7, 1 August 1974.

554. Halsbury to Wilson, 6 November 1974, Wilson to Halsbury, 12 November 1974, DH, B/D 112/0141.

555. Wilson to Woodroofe, 19 February 1975, Woodroofe to Wilson, 20 February 1975, DH, B/D 112/0141. Woodroofe had been Chairman of Unilever, and was a Director of Schroders.

556. Castle, Owen, Hughes, officials and GMSC delegation mtg, T, 2SS 22/78/05G. Castle, *Diaries*, p 271, 8 January 1975.

557. Dell to Castle, 14 January 1975, T, 2SS 22/78/05G.

558. *Review Body on Doctors' and Dentists' Remuneration. Fifth Report 1975*, Cmnd.6032 (HMSO, 1975).

559. Wilson, HC Debates, vol 890, cols 171-2, 18 April 1975 (WA). DH, B/D 112/049A; T, 2SS 22/78/05H.

560. DH, MDH 32B.

561. Castle. C(74)143, 4 December 1974, Healey, C(74)144, 4 December 1974, Foot, C(74)145, 10 December 1974, Castle, C(74)147, 17 December 1974, CAB 129; CC(74) 52nd mtg, 19 December 1974, CAB 128. Castle, *Diaries*, pp 256-7.

562. The text of the new contract is given in Castle, *Diaries*, Appendix 1, pp 741-7.

563. Castle, *Diaries*, pp 257-61, 20 December 1974.

564. Dr D E Bolt, BMA, letter, *Economist*, 25 January 1975, p 6.

565. Castle, HC Debates, vol 884, cols 33-42, 13 January 1975, vol 886, cols 906-16, 17 February 1975, Castle to Stevenson, 28 January 1975, *Times*, 31 January 1975. Castle *Diaries*, pp 275, 277, 287, 294, 295, 300, 311. DH, MDH 32B.

566. Castle to Dr C Astley, Chairman, CCHMS, 17 April 1975, DH, MDH 32B. Castle, *Diaries*, pp 364-5, 16 April 1975.

567. Castle, *Diaries*, pp 367-70, 18 April 1975.

568. The following section relates to the small number of junior hospital dentists as well as doctors.

569. Castle, Owen and junior hospital staff mtg, 8 January 1975, DH, B/D 112/053A.

570. Castle, *Diaries*, pp 269-70, 8 January 1975.

571. Castle to Foot, 12 June 1975, Foot to Castle, 16 June 1975, Dell (Paymaster General) to Castle, 19 June 1975, supporting Foot, T, SS 196/68/01.

572. Castle to Foot, 4 July 1975, Foot to Castle, 8 July 1975, T, SS 196/68/01.

573. Ross to Castle, 23 June and 11 July 1975, T, SS 196/68/01.

574. *Review Body on Doctors' and Dentists' Remuneration. Supplement to Fifth Report, 1975*, Cmnd.6243 (HMSO, 1975).

575. Adoption of 44 hours rather than 40 hours helped to maximise the value of the salary supplements; it was also justified by reference to a survey suggesting that 43 hours was the average basic working week for junior doctors.

576. Castle to Foot, 13 October 1975, Foot to Castle, 15 October 1975, and comment by other Ministers, T, SS 196/68/01.

577. Ross to Foot, 15 October 1975, T, SS 196/68/01.

578. Castle, HC Debates, vol 901, cols 347-53, 21 November 1975. Castle, *Diaries*, pp 536-9, 29 October to 4 November 1975.

579. Castle, HC Debates, vol 902, cols 828-39, 12 December 1975. Castle, *Diaries*, pp 597-9, 602-4.

580. Stevenson to Castle, 17 December 1975, DH, B/D 112/053F.

581. Letter to NHS Administrators, 30 December 1975.

582. *Review Body on Doctors' and Dentists' Remuneration. Third Supplement to Fifth Report, 1975*, Cmnd.6406 (HMSO, 1975).

583. Treasury minute, 7 April 1974, T, SS 196/68/01.

584. DHSS minute, 9 April 1976, T, SS 196/68/01.

585. Callaghan, Ennals, and BMA delegation mtg, 16 July 1976, Junior Doctors' Contract, 1975-1976, PREM 11. Exchanges between Ministers, July 1976, T, SS 196/68/01. DH, B/D 112/053G.

586. Ennals, Press Statement, 3 September 1976. For detail on the summer 1976 dispute and investigation into the unanticipated high cost of the new contract, DH, MDH 51.

587. *Report of the Committee of Inquiry into the Regulation of the Medical Profession*, Cmnd.6018 (HMSO, 1975). Castle, HC Debates, vol 890, cols 128-30, 16 April 1975 (WA).

588. Castle, HS(76)25, 4 October 1976, HS(76) 1st mtg, 14 October 1976, CAB 134.

589. Barnett to Callaghan, 20 May 1977, exchanges between DHSS and Treasury, May 1977, T, SS 350/351/01A. Ennals, HC Debates, vol 935, cols 347-9, 18 July 1977.

590. Foot, HC Debates, vol 880, col 910, 5 November 1974.

591. The Cabinet was far from united over the wisdom of imposing a 5 per cent limit, but the critics were in a small minority, CM(78) 26th mtg, 13 July 1978, CM(78) 27th mtg, 20 July 1978, CAB 128. Benn, *Conflicts of Interest*, p 326.

592. For reviews of Labour incomes policy, Coates, *Labour in Power?*, chapter 2,

593. Castle to Foot, 4 July 1975, Junior Hospital Doctors' Contract, 1975-1976, PREM 11.

594. Woodroofe to Callaghan, 1 April 1977, T, SS 238/01B.

595. Secretaries of BMA and BDA to Callaghan, 6 July 1977, Doctors' and Dentists' Pay, 1977-1978, PREM 11.

596. Callaghan and representatives of BMA and BDA mtg, 13 July 1977, Doctors' and Dentists' Pay, 1977-1978, PREM 11.

597. Woodroofe to Callaghan, 7 December 1977, Doctors' and Dentists' Pay, 1977-1978, PREM 11.

598. Treasury minute, 15 December 1977, T, SS 238/01C.

599. Treasury minute, 10 April 1978, T, SS 238/01C.

600. Woodroofe to Callaghan, 4 April 1978, Doctors' and Dentists' Pay, 1977-1978, PREM 11.

601. Callaghan, Drain, Fisher, and Spanswick mtg, 5 April 1978, T, SS 238/01C.

602. Ennals to Callaghan, 19 April 1978, Doctors' and Dentists' Pay, 1977-1978, PREM 11.

603. Brief for Prime Minister, 28 April 1978, Doctors' and Dentists' Pay, 1977-1978, PREM 11.

604. Hattersley, CP(78)50, 2 May 1978, CAB 129; CM(78) 17th mtg, 4 May 1978, CAB 128. Cabinet Secretary's Notebook (Hunt). Callaghan, HC Debates, vol 749, cols 500-1, 10 May 1978. *Review Body on Doctors' and Dentists' Remuneration. Eighth Report 1978*, Cmnd.7176 (HMSO, 1978).

605. Ennals to Healey, 21 April 1978, and associated correspondence, T, SS 350/680/01A.

606. *Times*, 8 June 1978.

607. Ennals to Healey, 14 June 1978, Callaghan minute, 16 June 1978, Nurses' Pay, 1978-1979, PREM 11.

608. Callaghan, Ennals and officials mtg, 16 October 1978, Nurses' Pay, 1978-1979, PREM 11.

609. *Times*, 18 September 1978.

610. *Daily Express*, 30 October 1978.

611. For instance, editorial, *Guardian*, 31 October 1978, which attacked Ennals for complacency and exploitation of NHS staff. See also, *Daily Telegraph*, 31 October 1978.

612. Ennals himself became a focus for industrial action by NUPE, when he spent a few days in Westminster hospital in early March 1979, *Times*, 7 and 8 March 1979.

613. Ennals to Healey, 17 January 1979, T, SS 350/68/01A.

614. Healey to Ennals, 22 January 1979, T, SS 350/68/01A.

615. Callaghan and Nurses and Midwives Staff Side mtg, 24 January 1979, Nurses' Pay, 1978-1979, PREM 11.

616. Ennals and Nurses and Midwives Staff Side mtg, 13 February 1979, DH, M/N 57/058A.

617. Nurses and Midwives Whitley Council to Ennals, 13 February 1979, DH, M/N 57/058A.

618. Ennals to Healey, 19 February 1979, T, SS 350/68/01A.

619. Ennals to Healey, 7 March 1979, T, SS 350/68/01A.

620. Treasury minute, 8 March 1979, T, SS 350/68/01A.

621. Hattersley, CP(79)20, 13 March 1979, CAB 129; CM(79) 12th mtg, 15 March 1979, CAB 128.

622. N.C.(M&SC) 345, 27 March 1979, DH, M/N 57/058B. Ennals, HC Debates, vol 965 col 1154, 3 April 1979.

623. Standing Commission on Pay Comparability, Report No.3, *Nurses and Midwives*, Cmnd.7795 (HMSO, 1980). Also at this date, the Commission produced comparability reports relating to ancillary staffs, ambulance workers, and professions supplementary to medicine.

624. This evolved into Joint Negotiating Committee, 'New Contract for NHS Consultants', January 1977, DH, MDH 32C.

625. Ennals to Dr J Cameron, BMA, 4 January 1977, DH, MDH 32C.

626. DHSS, report of comments by Dr D E Bolt at joint meeting, 23 February 1977, DH, G/C 313/5A.

627. Ennals, Moyle, and officials mtg, 17 March 1977, DH, MDH 32C.

628. DHSS submission to Ministers, February 1977, DH, DMH 32C.

629. Ennals, HS(77)85, 9 December 1977, HS(77) 22nd mtg, 14 December 1977, CAB 134.

630. DH, DMH 32D.

631. Ennals, RHA Chairmen and BMA representatives mtg, 3 May 1978, DH, G/C 313/5B.

632. Moyle, Grabham, Bolt and Grey-Turner mtg, 19 July 1978, DH, G/C 313/5B.

633. DH, DMH 32E, B/D 112/075; T, SS 238/01D. The Treasury estimated that transfer to the new contract would entail an average increase in income of 14 per cent.

634. Royal Commission NHS, para **14**.71.

635. *Royal Commission on the National Health Service. Chairman: Sir Alec Merrison. Report*, Cmnd.7615 (HMSO, 1979).

636. Royal Commission minutes, 8 November 1976, BS 6/2539 and 3087.

637. Merrison and DHSS mtg, 24 April 1976, BS 6/3086.

638. Editorial, *British Medical Journal*, 1975, ii, 185-6, 25 October 1975.

639. T F Davies, *British Medical Journal*, 1976, ii, 1376-8, 4 December 1976.

640. Ennals, letter, *British Medical Journal*, 1975, ii, 130, 10 July 1976.

641. The first four subcommittees established in the autumn of 1976 were: SC1, Quality of Service; SC2, Management and Finance; SC3, Manpower; SC4, Primary Care, BS 6/2524.

642. Maurice Kogan and Nancy Korman, *The working of the NHS*, Research Paper No.1 (HMSO, June 1978); John Perrin, *Management of Financial Resources in the NHS*, Research Paper No.2 (HMSO, July 1978); Martin Buxton and Rudolf Klein, *Allocating Health Resources: a Commentary on the Report of the Resource Allocation Working Party*, Research Paper No.3 (HMSO, August 1978); Alan Maynard and Arthur

Walker, *Doctor Manpower 1975-2000: alternative forecasts and their resource implications*, Research Paper No.4 (HMSO, September 1978); Janet Gregory, *Patients' Attitudes to the Hospital Service*, Research Paper No.5 (HMSO, January 1979); National Consumer Council, *Access to Primary Care*, Research Paper No.6 (HMSO, February 1979). Not all of these research papers were well-received by the health departments, see BS 6/2668 and 3176 for comment on No.4.

643. R.Taylor, 'The Contribution of Social Science Research to Health Policy: the Royal Commission on the National Health Service', *Journal of Social Policy*, 1981, **10**, 531-48, p 547. See also, R.Klien, 'Royal Commissions', *British Medical Journal*, 1975, 297-8, 1 November 1975.

644. Secretariat to Merrison, 16 July 1976, BS 6/3086.

645. For Williams' proposals on research, BS 6/2509.

646. Exchanges between Merrison and Williams, December 1977 to August 1978, letter of resignation, Williams to Callaghan, 9 August 1978, BS 6/3140.

647. Merrison, 'The Future Work of the Commission', March 1977, BS 6/2578.

648. Bramley to Merrison, 31 March 1977, BS 6/2578.

649. Richards to Merrison, 6 April 1977, BS 6/2578.

650. Royal Commission mtg, 18/19 December 1978, BS 6/2687.

651. BS 6/2702.

652. Royal Commission minutes, November 1978, BS 6/2675.

653. Secretariat, 'One tier too many?', BS 6/2586.

654. Royal Commission minutes, November 1978, BS 6/2675.

655. Royal Commission NHS, paras **20**.53-7, 69, **22**.70.

656. Merrison, 'The Future Work of the Commission', March 1977, BS 6/2578.

657. Support for an NHS Board emanated from four individuals, and also the Association of Anaesthetists of GB and Ireland, the British Orthopaedic Association, the Royal College of Surgeons, whereas ten organisations made representations against such a Board, BS 6/2660.

658. Secretariat, 'A NHS Board and other Options', 11 August 1978, BS 6/2660. Note on discussions at Runnymede, July 1978, BS 6/2651.

659. Royal Commission NHS, paras **19**.28-32.

660. Royal Commission minutes, November 1978, BS 6/2675.

661. DHSS to Treasury, 26 March 1979, T, SS 10/01E.

662. Treasury minutes, March 1979, T, SS 10/01E.

663. Royal Commission NHS, paras **16**.16-22.

664. Royal Commission minute, 3 January 1979, BS 6/2687.

665. Royal Commission NHS, chapter 18.

666. BS 6/2648.

667. Royal Commission and Treasury mtg, 19 March 1979, T, SS 10/01E.

668. Treasury minute, 21 March 1978, T, SS 10/01E.

669. Merrison to Jenkin, 8 May 1979, T, SS 10/01E.

670. Jenkin, HC Debates, vol 970, cols 1790-1, 18 July 1979.

671. *Committee on Scottish Health Services. Report*, Cmd.5204 (HMSO, Edinburgh 1936).

672. Brief for Prime Minister, 13 July 1979, SS 10/01E.

673. M D Warren, *British Medical Journal*, 1975, **4**, 183-4,

674. Castle, *Diaries*, p 447, 4 July 1975.

675. RHA Chairmen (75) 2nd mtg, 21 October 1975, DH (RHA Chairmen, Minutes 1974-1981), Castle, *Diaries*, p 529, 21 October 1975.

676. Castle, HC Debates, vol 898, col 1054, 27 October 1975.

677. Circular HC(77)17, 'Joint Care Planning: Health and Local Authorities'. R Rowbottom and A Hey, 'Collaboration between Health and Social Services', in Jacques, *Health Services*, pp 179-203. For a summary of the later position, G Wistow, 'Joint Finance and Community Care', *Health Care UK 1984*, pp 69-74; Wistow, 'Community Care for the Mentally Handicapped: disappointing progress', *Health Care UK 1985*, pp 69-78.

678. For a summary, BS 6/2581.

679. See Table 6.2.

680. BS 6/2646.

681. DH, ROS12; BS 6/2646. Ennals, HC Debates, vol 961, col 370 (WA), 30 January 1979.

682. *Our Changing Democracy: Devolution to Scotland and Wales*, Cmnd.6348 (HMSO 1976).

683. Shore, speech to Labour Local Government Conference, *Times*, 28 January 1978. Shore, HC Debates, vol 955, cols 752-4, 3 August 1978 (WA).

684. Shore, HC Debates, vol 957, col 5, 1 November 78.

685. *Organic Change in Local Government* (HMSO, 1979). Shore, HC Debates, vol 961, cols 231-3, 25 January 1979 (WA).

686. For complaints of the Royal Commission and reassurances by Ennals to Merrison, 24 January 1979, BS 6/2677.

687. CM(78) 31st mtg, 14 September 1978, CAB 128. Cabinet Secretary's Notebook (Hunt).

688. Ennals to Callaghan, 21 September 1978, Future of the National Health Service, 1978-1979, PREM 11.

689. Exchanges between Callaghan and Ennals, September to October 1978, CAB 109/26.

690. *Times*, 4 October 1978. For the statement by Patrick Jenkin on abolition of area authorities, *Times*, 16 May 1978. See also, 'Party Political Bidding over the NHS', *Times*, 9 October 1978.

691. Brief for Prime Minister, 11 October 1978, Future of the National Health Service, 1978-1979, PREM 11.

692. No.10 Downing Street to DHSS, 12 October 1978, Future of the National Health Service, 1978-1979, PREM 11.

693. Callaghan, Ennals and Nairne mtg, 16 October 1978, Future of the National Health Service, 1978-1979, PREM 11.

694. Callaghan and Merrison mtg, 3 November 1978, Future of the National Health Service, 1978-1979, PREM 11.

695. Callaghan, HC Debates, vol 957, cols 218, 3 November 1978.

CONCLUSIONS

1. DHSS, *National Health Service. Twentieth Anniversary Conference Report* (HMSO, 1968).

2. Crossman, *Diaries*, iii, p 118, 4 July 1968.

3. Castle, *NHS Revisited*, p 1.

4. Castle, *Diaries*, pp 528-9, 19-21 October 1975.

5. For instance, D Widgery, *Health in Danger. The Crisis in the National Health Service* (Archon, 1979); S Haywood and A Alaszewski, eds, *Crisis in the Health Service. The Politics of Management* (Croom Helm, 1980); K Barnard and K Lee, eds, *Conflict in the National Health Service* (Croom Helm, 1977).

6. *Times*, 6 and 7 June 1978.

7. Ennals to Callaghan, 24 February 1978, Future of the NHS, 1976-1978, PREM 11

8. *Times*, 6 July 1978.

9. DHSS, WO, and COI, *NHS and Social Services. Thirtieth Anniversary*. NHS Leaflet 7, (DHSS, July 1978); SHHD, *The National Health Service in Scotland* (SHHD, 1978).

10. *Times*, 6 July 1978, devoted only a few sentences on p 4 to the Lancaster House event. This compares with a six-part series on 'NHS in crisis' which ran between 9 and 15 August 1978, and a parallel 'Crisis' series in the *Sunday Times* on 16, 23 and 30 July 1978.

11. *Times*, 5 July 1978; editorial, *British Medical Journal*, 1978, ii, 1-2, July 1978 .

12. Klein, *The Politics of the NHS*, pp 32-3.

13. The following section briefly characterises the work of successive Ministers of Health/Secretaries of State for Social Services. As indicated in the text, in Scotland and Wales, on account of their diverse responsibilities, the Secretaries of State were less directly concerned with the health service than their counterparts in England. In the case of Scotland, health service duties tended to be divided between junior Ministers, who were rotated more often than their seniors. In view of these factors it is difficult to draw Scotland and Wales into this short survey.

14. See Appendix 1.1.

15. Crossman, *Diaries*, iii, pp 555-6.

16. Crossman, *Diaries*, iii, p 921.

17. *National Health Service. The administrative structure of the medical and related services in England and Wales*, p 6.

18. R Butt, Profile of Sir Keith Joseph, *Times*, 6 May 1971, which predicted that Joseph would strive for a 'balance of efficiency and social concern'.

19. *Daily Telegraph*, 9 October 1989.

20. *All Souls College. Keith Joseph.*

21. A Seldon, Interview with Sir Keith Joseph, *Contemporary Record*, 1987, **1**, 26-31, pp 27-8.

22. *Times*, 22 March 1946; *Economist*, 30 March 1946.

23. *Times*, 9 April 1976.

24. Editorial, *Times*, 9 April 1976.

25. Treasury minute, 3 May 1974, T, 2SS 116/98/22D.

26. Castle, *Diaries*, p 589.

27. Castle, *Diaries*, pp 257-61, 269-70.

28. Castle, *Diaries*, p 591.

29. Castle to Wilson, 4 November 1975, Junior Hospital Doctors' Contract, 1975-1976, PREM 11.

30. Except for the short interlude occupied by Barber.

31. Barnett, *Inside the Treasury*, p 47.

32. Ennals criticised Miss Hope Trenchard for 'prejudice or political' bias when she expressed pessimism about the future of the NHS, *Times*, 6 June 1978.

33. Other cases of asserted ineptitude in 1978 relate to such varied issues as his handling of the closure of the Elizabeth Garrett Anderson Hospital, the dispute concerning senior hospital engineers and works supervisors, and his apparent ignorance about the Prime Minister's intentions regarding NHS reorganisation.

34. Unsworth, *The Politics of Mental Health Legislation*, p 336.

35. Professor W J H Butterfield, 'Changing Medical Needs', *Twentieth Anniversary Conference*, p 16. See also, *CMO Report 1975*, pp 103-7.

36. Appendix 3.2.

37. Lowe, *The Welfare State in Britain*, pp 339-41.

38. Hill, ed, *The State of Welfare*, Table 8A.2.

39. Appendix 3.3.

40. Appendices 3.4, 3.5.

41. See Appendix 3.5.

42. This fear was first elaborated by Frangcon Roberts, *The Cost of Health* (Turnstile, 1952).

43. For the level of personal social services and local health authority expenditure, see Appendices 3.1, 3.8 and 3.9.

44. For data relating to the following paragraphs, see Appendices 3.6 and 3.7.

45. Beveridge, HL Debates, vol 228, col 613, 13 February 1961.

46. J Noyce, A H Snaith, and A J Trickey, 'Regional variations in the allocation of financial resources to the community health services', *Lancet*, 1974, i, 554-7, 30 March 1974. See also Appendix 3.17.

47. M J Buxton and R E Klein, 'Distribution of hospital provision: policy themes and resource variations', *British Medical Journal*, 1975, i, 345-9, 8 February 1975.

48. *Hospital and Health Services Review*, March 1979. In Scotland, under SHARE, by April 1979, the disadvantage of Tayside, the most underfunded Health Board was reduced from 15 to 13 per cent below target, while the best-placed Health Board, Ayr and Arran saw its allocation reduced from 35 to 27 per cent above target. In Wales redistribution was only just beginning in 1979.

49. M Buxton and R E Klein, *Allocating Health Resources*, Royal Commission on the NHS, Research Paper No.3 (HMSO, 1978); H Elcock and S Haywood, *The Buck Stops Where? Accountability and Control in the NHS* (Institute for Health Studies, Hull University, 1980); N Mays and G Bevan, *Resource Allocation in the Health Service: A Review of the Methods of the Resource Allocation Working Party* (Bedford Square Press, 1987). R Beech, G Bevan and N Mays, 'Spatial Equity in the NHS: the Death and Rebirth of RAWP', *Health Care UK 1990*, 44-61.

50. B Birch and A Maynard, *The RAWP Review* (Centre for Health Economics, York University, 1986).

51. For 1971/72 it was shown that expenditure on the family practitioner services was between 6 and 10 per cent above the per capita national average in three Metropolitan regions and the South Western region, but between 7 and 11 per cent below the average in the Sheffield, Birmingham, and NE Metropolitan regions, J Noyce, A H.Snaith, and A J.Trickey, 'Regional variations in the allocation of financial resources to the community health services'.

52. In practice the differences were rather greater owing to the larger extent of differences within regions.

53. See Appendices 3.30, 3.31 and 3.32.

54. See Appendices 3.23 and 3.24.

55. M H Cooper and A J Culyer, 'Equality in the National Health Service: Intentions, performance and problems in evaluation', in M M Hauser, *The Economics of Medical Care* (Allen and Unwin, 1972). See also M Buxton and R E Klein, 'Distribution of hospital provision: policy themes and resource variations'.

56. R Dowie, 'Deployment of resources in treatment of end stage renal failure in England and Wales', *British Medical Journal*, 1984, **288**, 988-91, 31 March 1984. This survey cites data from 1981.

57. T A H English, A R Bailey, J F Dark and W G W Williams, 'The UK cardiac surgical register, 1977-1982', *British Medical Journal*, 1984, **289**, 1205-8, 3 November 1984.

58. Editorial, *British Medical Journal*, 1978, ii, 1449-50, 25 November 1978. This problem was not resolved and attracted widespread attention as a result of the Yorkshire Television programme, 'A Lottery for Life', 31 March 1984.

59. J Ryan and F Thomas, *The Politics of Mental Handicap* (Penguin, 1980), p 118; A Tyne, *Looking at Life in a Hospital, Hostel, Home or Unit* (Campaign for Mental Health, 1978).

60. *Report of the Committee of Inquiry into Normansfield Hospital*, Cmnd.7357 (HMSO, 1978), Section II, A First Impression of Normansfield.

61. J Henderson and D Cohen, 'No Strategy for Prevention', *Health Care UK 1984*, pp 63-8, p 65.

62. Sir Richard Doll, 'The Prospects for Prevention', *British Medical Journal*, 1983, **283**, 445-53, 5 February 1983, p 451.

63. Fully discussed in J.Lewis, *What Price Community Medicine?*

64. Royal Commission NHS, para **5**.21.

65. Royal Commission NHS, para **5**.31.

66. Royal Commission NHS, para **5**.5.

67. *First Report from the Select Committee on the Parliamentary Commissioner for Administration. Session 1977-78*, para 16.

68. Dickens, *Bleak House*, chap 1.

69. *First Report from the Select Committee on the Parliamentary Commissioner for Administration. Session 1977-78*, p 234, para 8.

70. Martin, *Hospitals in Trouble*, p 145.

71. The final DHSS Report issued for 1977, was only 62pp compared with more than 350pp in 1958. A Health Service Report was issued by DHSS between 1984 and 1987, but this was more akin to a public relations brochure. The CMO Report was 276pp in 1968; by 1982 it had shrunken to half that size.

72. The publication of *Health and Personal Social Service Statistics* was resumed again in 1982.

73. Martin, *Hospitals in Trouble*, p 144.

74. Whitley leaders to Prime Minister, 3 July 1978, T, SS 23/24/04K

75. Royal Commission NHS, paras **3**.3-5.

76. Cartwright and Anderson, *General Practice Revisited*, p 177.

77. Cartwright and Anderson, *General Practice Revisited*, pp 178-80.

78. R Klein, 'Public opinion and the National Health Service', *British Medical Journal*, 1979, i, 1296-7, 12 May 1979.

79. *Annual Report of the Hospital Advisory Service 1975*, para 313.

80. *Economist*, 30 March 1946.

Abbreviations

A *General Abbreviations*

ACAS	Advisory, Conciliation and Arbitration Service
AEGIS	Aid for the Elderly in Government Institutions
AHA	Area Health Authority
AHA(T)	Area Heath Authority (Teaching)
AIC	Associated Industrial Consultants
ALRA	Abortion Law Reform Association
AMC	Association of Municipal (*later* Metropolitan) Corporations
AMO	Area Medical Officer
ANO	Area Nursing Officer
ABPI	Association of the British Pharmaceutical Industry
ASH	Action on Smoking and Health
ASTMS	Association of Scientific, Technical and Managerial Staffs
BDA	British Dental Association
BG	Board of Governors
BMA	British Medical Association
CCA	County Councils Association
CCETSW	Central Council for Education and Training in Social Work
CCHE	Central Council for Health Education
CCHMS	Central Committee for Hospital Medical Services of the BMA
CCSC	Central Consultants and Specialists Committee of the BMA
CHC	Community Health Council
CHSC	Central Health Services Council
CMO	Chief Medical Officer
COHSE	Confederation of Health Service Employees
CPRS	Central Policy Review Staff
CSA	Common Services Agency
CSD	Civil Service Department
DDRB	Doctors' and Dentists' Review Body
DEA	Department of Economic Affairs

967

DES	Department of Education and Science
DGH	District General Hospital
DHS	Department of Health for Scotland
DHSS	Department of Health and Social Security
DMT	District Management Team
EDA	Extra Duty Allowance
EEC	European Economic Community
EFTA	European Free Trade Association
FPC	Family Practitioner Committee
FPS	Family Practitioner Services
GLC	Greater London Council
GMC	General Medical Council
GMSC	General Medical Services Committee
GNC	General Nursing Council
GP	General Medical Practitioner
HAS	Hospital (*later* Health) Advisory Service
HCSA	Hospital Consultants and Specialists Association
HEC	Health Education Council
HJSC	Hospital Junior Staff Committee of the BMA
HMC	Hospital Management Committee
HPSS	Health and Personal Social Services
ICI	Imperial Chemical Industries
ILEA	Inner London Education Authority
IMF	International Monetary Fund
JCC	Joint Consultants Committee
JHDA	Junior Hospital Doctors' Association
JLC	Joint Liaison Committee
LHA	Local Health Authority
LMC	Local Medical Committee
MEP	Member of European Parliament
MENCAP	National Association of Parents of Backward Children
MH	Ministry of Health
MHLG	Ministry of Housing and Local Government
MIND	See NAMH
MOH	Medical Officer of Health
MP	Member of Parliament
MPU	Medical Practitioners' Union
MRC	Medical Research Council
NALGO	National and Local Government Officers Association
NAMH	National Association for Mental Health

968

NBPI	National Board for Prices and Incomes
NHS Notes	National Health Service Notes 1-13 and Appendices (DHSS, 1969)
NISWT	National Institute for Social Work Training
NUPE	National Union of Public Employees
OHE Compendium	Office of Health Economics, *Compendium of Health Statistics*, 5th edition (OHE, 1984)
OPCS	Office of Population Censuses and Surveys
PAC	Public Accounts Committee
PAR	Programme Analysis and Review
PEP	Post-Ely Policy Working Party
PERC	Public Expenditure Review Committee
PESC	Public Expenditure Survey Committee
PLP	Parliamentary Labour Party
PSBR	Public Sector Borrowing Requirement
PSSC	Personal Social Services Council
PWG	Working Group on the Future Pattern of Mental Subnormality Services
RAWP	Resource Allocation Working Party
RCM	Royal College of Midwives
RCN	Royal College of Nursing
RCOG	Royal College of Obstetricians and Gynaecologists
Royal Commission DD	*Royal Commission on Doctors' and Dentists' Remuneration 1957-1960. Report*, Cmnd.939 (HMSO, 1960)
Royal Commission ME	*Royal Commission on Medical Education 1965-68. Report*, Cmnd.3569 (HMSO, 1968).
Royal Commission NHS	*Royal Commission on the National Health Service. Chairman Sir Alec Merrison. Report*, Cmnd.7615 (HMSO, 1979)
Sainsbury Report	*Report of the Committee of Enquiry into the Relationship of the Pharmaceutical Industry with the National Health Service, 1965-67*, Cmnd.3410 (HMSO, 1967)
SCOPE	Steering Committee on Public Expenditure
SEP	Steering Committee on Economic Policy
SHHD	Scottish Home and Health Department
SHSC	Scottish Health Services Council
SHSPC	Scottish Health Services Planning Council
SMAC	Standing Medical Advisory Committee
SMHAC	Standing Mental Health Advisory Committee
SMMAC	Standing Maternity and Midwifery Advisory Committee

SNAC	Standing Nursing Advisory Committee
SMOH	Society of Medical Officers of Health
SPUC	Society for the Protection of the Unborn Child
SSRC	Social Science Research Council
SWS	Social Work Service
THA	Teaching Hospitals Association
TUC	Trades Union Congress
UGC	University Grants Committee
VPRS	Voluntary Price Regulation Scheme
Webster I	*The Health Services since the War. Volume I. Problems of Health Care. The National Health Service before 1957* (HMSO, 1988)
WHTSO	Welsh Health Technical Services Organisation
WO	Welsh Office

B *Abbreviations Relating to Official Records*

(a) Departmental Records in the Public Record Office
Following the general form:
CAB 128/34; CAB 129/1342; CAB 134/1986;
BA 1/9
                Cabinet Office
ED 55/262; ED 188/299; UGC 8/97
                DES/ Department for Education and Employment
BD 18/3520; BN 37/636;
BS 10/76; MH 145/277;
PIN 23/196
                DHSS/ Department of Health
HLG 69/902; HLG 120/762
                Department of the Environment
T 172/2137; T 227/425; T 233/1369
                Treasury
PREM 11/1602
                Prime Minister's Office

(b) Departmental Records in the Scottish Record Office

HH 98/151; HH 101/3520
                DHS/SHHD

(c) Records in Government Departments
Following the general form:
CAB followed by PRO class number, but no assigned piece number (e.g. CAB 128; CAB 134)
CAB, followed by registered file numbers (e.g. 16/4 Part 1; 2MS 25/56/01B; Q 31/1 Part 1)
Cabinet Secretary's Notebook, followed by Cabinet Secretary's name in brackets (constituting Cabinet Secretary's record of Cabinet meetings)
                    Cabinet Office
DES, followed by prefix and registered file numbers (e.g. M 26/1/368)

                    Department of Education and Science/
                    Department for Education and
                    Employment
DH, followed by prefix and registered file numbers (e.g. B/D 112/0138; J/N 179/12B; LA/P 337/01B; M/B 80/3; MDH 23C; ROS/12)
                    Department of Health
DoE, followed by prefix and registered file numbers (e.g. LG 7/505/18; WS 112/12)
                    Department of the Environment
SHHD, followed by HOS, H/RHS and registered file numbers (e.g. HOS 2/170; HOS 76/4 Part B)
                    SHHD
T, followed by prefixes such as AT, EAS, ED, GE, SS, (or 2AT, 2EAS etc) followed by registered file numbers
                    Treasury
PREM 11, followed by heading of file, inclusive dates, with no assigned piece number
                    Prime Minister's Office
WO, followed by EP, HL, HS, LG, or NHSR, and registered file numbers(e.g. HS 234/10/36J; NHSR 1/2 Part 3)
                    Welsh Office

INDEX

Council for Children's Welfare 654, 888, 947
Council for the Education and Training of
Health Visitors 122, 687, 692
County Councils, see local authorities
Cowan, (Sir) H K 41, 135, 785
Crammer, Dr J L 905
Cranbrook, Earl of 330
Cranbrook Committee/Report on maternity
services 330
Crookshank, H F C (Viscount Crookshank)
31, 778
Minister of Health 838
Crosland, C Anthony R 202
and NHS reorganisation 359, 364
and pay negotiations 287, 290, 295
and personal social services 300, 308, 309
Crossman, R H S
ministerial career 181
Secretary of State for Social Services 179,
181-5, 187, 188, 376, 779, 833, 863, 932
and health service finance 81, 84, 203-13,
391, 392, 740, 764, 765, 846, 866
and hospital services 227, 229, 231-7, 317,
399, 740, 741
and mental health 229, 231, 232, 241, 405,
740, 741
and NHS reorganisation 329, 348, 350-64,
366, 370-3, 473, 475, 476, 511, 534, 740, 742
and pay negotiations 255-9, 263, 279-83,
317, 384, 741
and personal social services 300, 303, 305,
319
and pharmaceutical services 226
and preventive and promotive services 242,
244, 245, 249
Cumberland, reorganisation in 476
Cumbria, reorganisation in 476, 545
Currie, Professor A R 891

D

Dain, Dr H Guy 2, 832
Dalyell, Tam 345
Danckwerts award 156, 159
Darlington Memorial Hospital 637
Davidson, Sir Andrew 785
Davies, Dr A B 164
Davies, (Sir) Michael 413, 772, 907
Davies, Dr T F 719, 960
Dawson of Penn, Lord 777
de Gaulle, General 426
Dell, Edmund 699
Democracy in the National Health Service 629
Demographic change 1-4, 397, 414, 419, 420,
598, 610, 611, 753, 754, 760, 761
Dental hospitals and schools 117
Dental service/dentists
charges 387, 592, 595, 596, 598, 762, 834
costs during first decade of NHS 15, 16
inequalities 15-16, 835
see also BDA; Doctors and Dentists, Royal
Commission on Remuneration of; McNair
Committee/Report; NHS finance, direct
charges
Department of Economic Affairs 277, 278,
839
Department of Education and Science 289,
290, 291, 295, 380, 489, 490
see also Ministry of Education

Department of Energy 675
Department of the Environment 468, 495,
662, 675
Department of Health and Social Security
appointments to 377, 378, 585, 586
and complaints procedures 410, 639, 643
and democracy in NHS 632
formation 181
HPSS sector 376, 378-81, 395-8, 586, 587,
592, 593, 595, 596, 598
and health service finance 208, 210, 211,
213, 387, 389, 394-6, 592-6, 598, 601, 605,
606, 869
management review 586
and medical education 261
and mental health 446, 649, 650, 652
and NHS reorganisation 351, 355-8, 368,
372, 452, 455, 456, 458, 459, 461, 464-9,
479, 495, 500, 503, 505, 511, 515, 522-5,
537, 560
Nursing Division 687, 688, 692
O and M unit 454
organisation and staffing 586
and pay negotiations 434, 445, 703, 706,
708
and pharmaceutical services 226
and planning and priorities 607, 608
and preventive and promotive services 664,
675, 679
and school health service 380, 773
and services for the elderly 658
structure 380, 381
Three Chairmen's Report 586, 587, 936
Department of Trade (and Industry) 518
Derby, reorganisation in 477
Development Team for the Mentally
Handicapped 651, 652
Devon AHA 662
Diamond, John 214, 224, 226, 271, 274, 296,
364
Dick, Dr D H 637
Diphtheria immunisation 128
Distinction awards 157-9, 276, 716
District administration and NHS
Reorganisation 459, 460, 468, 473, 481,
485, 508, 537, 573
see also district management teams
District general hospitals
future of 311, 352
and the hospital plans 105, 107, 196, 197
and mental health 230, 403, 405, 646, 647
District management teams 500, 501, 509,
542, 560, 634
District nurses 110, 692, 770
Doctors and Dentists
pay and conditions 155-65, 264-83, 384,
422, 428-31, 436, 437, 527, 616, 693, 697-
706, 710, 714-17
Remuneration, Royal Commission on 69,
70, 155, 162, 269, 859
Doll, Sir Richard 769
Donoughue, Bernard 601, 941
Douglas Committee on the Cost of
Prescribing (Scotland) 14, 141-7
Douglas of Barloch, Lord 242, 663
Douglas, (Sir) James Boyd 141
Douglas, Sir William Scott 782, 783
Douglas-Home, Sir Alexander F (14th Earl of
Home) 36, 37